THE ANNALS OF
LONDON

THE ANNALS OF
LONDON

A Year-by-Year Record of a Thousand Years of History

JOHN RICHARDSON

CASSELLPAPERBACKS

First published in the United Kingdom in 2000 by Cassell & Co

This paperback edition first published in 2001 by
Cassell Paperbacks, Cassell & Co
Wellington House, 125 Strand
London, WC2R 0BB

A CIP catalogue record for this book is available
from the British Library

ISBN 184188135X

Designed by Peter Butler
Edited by Bob Davenport
Printed and bound in Italy

ACKNOWLEDGEMENTS

The author would like to thank particularly Roger Cline and Richard
Knight for help in resolving some of the queries he had in completing
the *Annals*, and also Bob Davenport, the copy-editor, for his
constructive contributions to the manuscript.

Most illustrations were reproduced by permission of Historical
Publications Ltd. The exceptions are listed below, and the author and
publisher thank the following for their permission to use pictures as
detailed: Donald Cooper (page 390); London Borough of Camden
(pages 278 and 356); The London Eye (page 393); London Metropolitan
Archives (pages 333 and 339 (bottom)); The Metropolitan Police
(page 253); Peter Jackson Collection (pages 2–3); Rothmans
International (page 339 (top)); Sainsbury plc (page 293).

INTRODUCTION

London is nearly two thousand years old, and there will no doubt be extravagant parties in 2043 to mark its birthday. Since the Romans set up their first dwellings near the Thames at the beginning of their 360 years of rule, London has grown from a settlement behind walls to a city whose boundaries would be difficult to recognize were it not for the occasional local-authority road sign. It blends into 'home county' land without much impediment. Today, a city that could once be walked in under an hour is one that on a good day needs two hours to drive across.

London since 1065 – the area covered by these *Annals* – has encompassed not only the old parishes which came to form inner London, but also large tracts of Kent, Essex, Hertfordshire and Surrey which have been wrenched from their ancient county loyalties to be members of the metropolis. Poor Middlesex, a county over which the City of London at one time had jurisdiction, has disappeared altogether except for the convenience of the Post Office.

These *Annals* record the waves of change that have occurred in London and also the surprising resilience and longevity of many of its institutions and buildings. The City of London itself, which began within the old Roman walls, still survives, seemingly impervious to attempts to lessen its autonomy or to incorporate it into the overall structure of London government. By the mid 19th century it was the only central London area to have adequate governance, yet it managed to evade inclusion in the Act which established the Metropolitan Board of Works in 1855 and it similarly avoided the authority of the London County Council in 1889 and the Greater London Council in 1965. It will, in 2000, remain outside the Greater London Assembly.

Despite so many changes, and for better or for worse, numerous institutions have survived and evolved for hundreds of years – the Inns of Court and various schools, colleges, livery companies and societies, to name but some – as have their ceremonies and customs. Often these bodies reflect and reinforce a conservative side to London's nature, and superficially they may be contrasted with the appetite to transform the capital during the last 20 years or so. But often people have a foot in both camps – in the past and in the present – so that the city is a melting pot rather than a background to a hostile battle between generations.

London, for all its mellow ancient structures and its retention of historic features, is not preserved in aspic, as the Covent Garden area demonstrates. The planners were defeated in their attempt to demolish most of Covent Garden, but the old buildings have since found new functions with a rapidity that only commercial nimbleness can make possible. In areas of London once stripped of residents, such as Clerkenwell, Finsbury and Southwark, there has been an influx of population, there to settle in converted warehouses, offices and factories. Modern art is being produced not in old artistic haunts such as Fitzrovia and Chelsea but in the unusual ambience of Hoxton and Hackney, where studio space is much cheaper. In high streets, restaurants and specialist retailers have filled the vacuum left as many shops lost out to warehouse shopping. Major developments are bringing new areas to life – no more so than in the previously derelict docklands. Ambitious architecture everywhere is gradually superseding the dreary post-war slab blocks.

Most importantly, there is rejuvenation along the river – happily on both sides of it – so that the Thames is once again a cherished and spectacular highway through one of the great cities of the world. It is without question an invigorating time to be in London. As the 20th century closed, the city took on new energy from a wave of fresh ideas and technologies reminiscent of the upheavals that occurred in the last half of the 19th century.

Historians of London are confronted by an excess of material. No other city has such marvellous archives, or so many books written about it, its institutions and its people; hardly a detail of its past has lain ignored. The compilation of these *Annals* – the first to cover the whole of the area of modern London – has been almost as much about what to leave out as about what to include. But I hope that the result will give perspective to the development of London and an insight into the activities of any given period.

JOHN RICHARDSON

THE EARLY YEARS OF LONDON

The Romans invaded Britain for the second time in AD 43. They landed at Richborough, near Sandwich in Kent, under the command of Aulus Plautius; after a major battle, probably near Rochester, they pursued the Britons towards the Thames, where the native armies forded the river to regroup on the northern bank. It is not known for certain where they and the invaders crossed the Thames – a description by Cassius Dio, 150 years later, is imprecise and could indicate Westminster, Brentford, Battersea or Fulham – but the old Watling Street ran from the Kent coast (where the Romans continued to offload armies and supplies in subsequent years) to the point where Westminster Bridge now stands, which strongly suggests Westminster as the most likely place.

Westminster, however, was marshy and badly drained, inundated often by arms of the river Tyburn, which enclosed Thorney Island, now roughly the area of Parliament Square. It may well have been a useful first crossing point in the rush to pursue and subdue the British tribes, but it was not an area in which to establish a settlement, either civil or military. Yet a port on the Thames was needed so that the invasion, complete with elephants, could be consolidated and trade begun. One can imagine the Romans scouring the unpeopled river banks for a suitable site. They would need, first, a place where a bridge could be

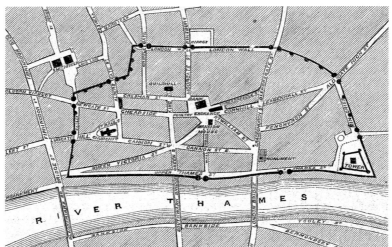

The Roman City wall superimposed on modern-day highways.

erected across the Thames. Second, it had to be accessible to ships coming in on the tides of the estuary, but sufficiently to the west so that the tide's force was weak enough to allow the building and maintenance of a bridge.

They found, at least on the northern bank, the perfect situation, where terraces of gravel and clay dropped down to the river, interspersed by the fresh water of the rivers later named the Fleet and the Walbrook. The opposite, southern, bank was less promising. It was low-lying, frequently flooded, interlaced with streams and marshes, and difficult to garrison. Did it have sufficient standing for a bridgehead? Evidently so, for we know that the Romans built a wooden bridge here (though we do not know how soon after the invasion), very near the line of today's London Bridge, and some time between AD 43 and AD 60 they founded the first Londinium – a name whose derivation is still not known. And on the opposite shore were the beginnings of Southwark – the 'southern defensive work'.

Whatever progress was made in the way of buildings was ended in AD 60. In a bloody rebellion that year the Iceni and Trinovantes of East Anglia and Middlesex, under the fabled Queen Boudicca, swept aside a depleted and surprised Roman army at Colchester. London was, at that time, also ill-protected. Although the Roman governor, Gaius Suetonius

Paulinus, arrived from Wales before the rebels reached London, he had few troops to provide resistance. According to Tacitus, he

decided to sacrifice the single town in the interest of the province as a whole. Neither the tears nor the entreaties of the stricken citizens bent him from his purpose. He gave the order for the departure, taking those who would follow as part of his column; and those who from the weakness of sex, frailty of age, or reluctance to leave their homes remained within the town were overwhelmed by the enemy.

The Britons were uncompromising when they arrived. 'The enemy neither took nor sold prisoners nor indulged in any of the traffic incidental to ordinary warfare, but massacred, hanged, burnt and crucified with a headlong fury that was stimulated by the knowledge of forthcoming retribution,' said Tacitus. That retribution did indeed follow, at an unknown place, probably north of St Albans, where the outnumbered Roman army massacred the Britons, whose leader committed suicide by poison.

We do not know the extent of the loss of life in the fledgling Londinium, but we do know that the settlement was destroyed by fire – the evidence for this has been discovered in excavations 13 ft below the present surface, east and west of the river Walbrook, on the slope up from the riverside and the bridge.

The initial function and status of London have still not been determined. Was it a military base that became a civilian settlement, or was it planned as a town from the beginning? The virtual absence of military artefacts in excavations suggests the latter. But there is no doubting London's developing role as a port and as the hub of a road system along which the Romans went deeper into the country. The erection of London Bridge ensured London's pre-eminence, and during the years of Roman protection, which lasted until AD 410, it became the trading place of the British province, its citizens familiar with and dealing in the manufactures of Europe and the Middle East. A planned grid of streets at the heart of the city is evident, as well as a gravelled market place at the junction of Gracechurch Street and Fenchurch Street.

The rebuilt London enjoyed sustained peace, and grew in size and prosperity. This is indicated by the locations of burial places, which by Roman law had to be a certain distance from the settlement: 1st-century burials have been discovered not far west from the Walbrook, and to the east at the corner of Fenchurch Street and Billiter Street, but burial places of the 2nd century are much further afield, in the areas of St Paul's, the Minories and Bishopsgate. It seems also that Londinium became the headquarters of the Provincial Council by AD 100. About the year 200 the province of Britain was divided into two, York being the capital of Lower Britain and London the capital of Upper Britain, and when, a century later, the province was divided into four, London was still recognized as the principal capital.

A late-1st-century basilica and forum astride the line of Gracechurch Street on the site of the old gravelled market place indicate by their size, if by nothing else, that London was a force to be reckoned with in this peripheral Roman province. The basilica served as a law court and an administrative centre – whatever body governed London would have held its meetings there.

We also know of a large building that was almost certainly the governor's palace and two public baths by the end of the 1st century. The palace was built on the site of today's Cannon Street station and its grounds went down in terraces to the waterside. Incorporated in the entrance facing a road roughly on a line with Cannon Street was what is now called the 'London Stone'; this is now housed in a niche in a bank building in the street. There were also two bathhouses – one in Huggin Hill, just above Upper Thames Street, and the other off Cheapside, opposite St Mary-le-Bow. Bathhouses were an important facility for the Romans – they were not only hygienic but also acted as social centres.

Up to this time London appears to have been without significant military buildings. It was probably about the year 122 – the year that the emperor Hadrian visited Britain and, presumably, London – that a fort was erected at Cripplegate. It was located away from the civilian population, and so it seems likely that it served the purpose of a barracks rather than a defensive stronghold.

It had long been assumed that Roman London had an amphitheatre, but until 1988 no trace of it had been found. And then, when an area of Guildhall Yard, previously the site of the medieval Guildhall chapel, and more lately the Guildhall Art Gallery, was being excavated, a portion of the amphitheatre was discovered. It was probably built at the end of the 2nd century, on the outskirts of the city, very near to the barracks at the fort and a potential audience.

The most spectacular archaeological find in modern years was the discovery of the Temple of Mithras in September 1954 on the east bank of the Walbrook river. The Walbrook was thought to have had sacred powers and to have been the recipient of votive offerings. The first substantial find in the temple was that of the head of the god Mithras himself, and the diggers subsequently found heads of Minerva (goddess of learning) and Serapis (god of harvest), a figure of Mercury, and other classical figures.

The discovery of the Mithraeum was a first substantial insight into the religious life of Roman London. Although it had the form of an early Christian church, it had nothing but pagan deities within it. The Indo-European Mithras, renowned for his courage and strength, was one of several gods 'imported' into Rome from its domains, just as the Egyptian Isis became a cult. Admission to the sect required an initiation rite, and a newcomer would then progress through grades of learning under the guidance of a pater. The temple and its contents appear to have been deliberately desecrated, probably by Christians, whose religion received the authority of Rome with the conversion of the emperor Constantine in 312. In 314 the first bishop of London, named Restitutus, was appointed, but nothing of great substance is known of the early Christian influence in Londinium.

For London to be protected it needed a wall, and the enormous project to build one was begun between 190 and 200. The wall encompassed a considerably enlarged city, stretching in an arc some 2 miles from the sites of the Tower of London in the east to Blackfriars in the west. At its north-west corner it included the Cripplegate fort, a feature which accounts for the odd angled shape of the city in that area. The wall was about 20 ft high, topped by a parapet wall, and the thickness varied from 8 to 9 ft; in addition, a wide U-shaped ditch, 6 ft deep, was built outside the wall to form a first obstacle to attackers. It has been calculated that at least 1,300 barge journeys would have been needed to bring the 85,000 tons of ragstone used to build the wall from the Maidstone district of Kent. There were also internal towers which carried staircases to the the parapet walks, and there were initially four gates – Aldgate leading out to the Colchester road, Bishopsgate for the road to York, Newgate for Silchester, and Ludgate to the south-west – though west and north gates of the enclosed Cripplegate fort were also constructed. A riverside wall seems not to have been built at first – perhaps because it was thought that the river itself was a sufficient defence, but most likely because it would have hindered the activities of the wharves along the waterside. However, at some time in the 4th century a river wall was built; remnants have been found beneath Upper and Lower Thames Street, but very little is known about it.

The Roman occupation lasted over 360 years – now an almost unimaginable span of stable administration. This is not to imply that Britain was remote from the political upheavals of the later Roman empire. In 259 Postumus, governor of a German province, rebelled against Emperor Gallienus and established his own empire in western Europe, which included Britain and Gaul – a short-lived affair which was suppressed in 274. But then in 286 Marcus Carausis, in charge of the Roman Channel fleet, declared himself emperor of Britain; after his murder in 293, the emperor regained control of Britain in 295, though bedevilled by mercenaries of the losing army who occupied and plundered London. A contemporary writer, Eumenius, wrote that when the emperor's forces reached Londinium they 'found survivors of the barbarian mercenaries plundering the city, and, when these began to seek flight, landed and slew them in the streets. And not only did they bring safety to your subjects, but, in addition, induced a sentiment of gratitude and pleasure at the sight.'

The 4th century was marked by escalating raids by Picts and Scots. In 367–8 a combined attack by them, and by Saxons from the North Sea coast, overran Britain and they were able to ransack London. Another army was sent from Rome to recapture the province, and at the same time Londinium was renamed Augusta – after the emperor, and therefore an indication of the prestige of Britain's capital.

In 410 the emperor Honorius, hard-pressed in a declining empire, abandoned the military support of, among others, his British province. The 5th and 6th centuries are, archaeologically, dark periods in London's history, and written records provide few clues to what happened within the walls. It is hard to imagine that the city was abandoned completely once the Roman legions had returned home. There would perhaps have been retired soldiers who preferred life in London; there would have been an indigenous population which had served the garrison and the administrative sections of the Roman community that would have remained when the soldiers left. But, whatever we surmise, remarkably little evidence so far illuminates that time, which remains an enigma. Why, for example, did the Roman road system within the walls virtually disappear? Roads and tracks are long-lasting and quite often delineate property boundaries, but even the important conjunction of roads at the Mansion House and the Bank of England is of Saxon origin. And why have no Anglo-Saxon burials of that period been found within 8 miles of London?

Germanic tribes were the new masters of Britain and of London. Angles from north-west Germany settled in the North, the Midlands and East Anglia; their neighbours, the Saxons, controlled Wessex, Sussex and Essex. Jutes, from Jutland, took Kent.

It was the kingdom of Kent which, at the end of the 6th century, was to be instrumental in the reintroduction of Christianity into Britain and into London. Ethelbert of Kent, who seems to have been overlord also of the kings of the Saxon kingdoms to the north, married the Christian daughter of the king of the Franks. He was persuaded to allow a mission by St Augustine into Kent, and in 597 Ethelbert was himself converted. Augustine founded a church at Canterbury, and in 601 he was appointed archbishop of southern England. It had been the pope's intention to have two archbishops in Britain – one based in York, the other in London – but the influence of Ethelbert led to the southern archbishopric remaining at his own power base of Canterbury. From this arose the apparently odd circumstance that London, for all its later power and myriad religious institutions, was not the seat of the principal see of England.

London at this time was governed by Saeberht, nephew of Ethelbert. Saeberht was persuaded to appoint Mellitus as bishop of London in 601, and three years later the first St Paul's Cathedral was established. The new religion was hardly established in London when both Ethelbert and Saeberht died, and the city and its rulers returned to paganism until the mid 7th century, when the East Saxon kingdom, of which London was nominally a part, was converted to Christianity.

A succession of modern finds point conclusively to a Saxon settlement along the Strand – probably the one described c. 730 by Bede as 'a metropolis … a mart of many peoples coming by land and sea'. On the evidence we have, this description could not fit the walled city, and it had puzzled historians until the archaeologists began to piece together this settlement, called Lundenwic (the Old English ending 'wic' means 'port' or 'trading town'). Additionally, roughly on the line of Drury Lane, connecting the Strand with the Roman highway that is today's High Holborn, there was a road called Aldewic, which means 'old port', probably taking its name from an area of land at its southern end. Aldewic was presumably so named after the Saxons had once again taken up residence within the walls of London, apparently from necessity when the raids of the Vikings in the 9th century became too predatory.

It seems likely that the administration of London in the 7th and 8th centuries was based in the fort of Cripplegate. This would imply that Saeberht lived there, but archaeologists have not discounted the suggestion that somewhere in Lundenwic, outside the walls, a palace may yet be discovered.

The Vikings began attacking England at the end of the 8th century, and a great slaughter in London is recorded for the years 842 and 851. In 865 Danes massed in East Anglia and gradually took control of eastern and northern England. They spent the winter of 871–2 in London, and in 877 they attacked the kingdom of Wessex, the last Saxon kingdom outside their control. Here they met their match in Alfred, king of Wessex, who retaliated so far as to recapture old Saxon territory and refortify London in 886. He was made king of all England not then under Danish control soon after. A temporary halt to the conflict was effected when a treaty between the two sides divided England into two, with the Danes taking the north and east and Alfred the south and west, their areas demarcated by a diagonal line running roughly from the Wirral to east of London.

London was still then officially part of the kingdom of the East Saxons and in the see of Essex, usually then under the control of the Danes; but politically London was part of Mercia and under the control

first of Alfred and then, in 886, of Ethelred, his son-in-law. Ethelred died in 911 and Edward, Alfred's son, took control of London; in 925 Edward was succeeded by his eldest son, Athelstan, who was crowned at a ceremony at Kingston upon Thames. Athelstan went on to complete the rout of the Danish and, according to his coins, became 'king of all Britain'.

However, towards the end of the 10th century there were more attacks from Scandinavia as the Danes sought to regain their lost territory. In 994 Sweyn Forkbeard, son of the king of Denmark, and the Norwegian Olaf Tryggvason attacked London for the first time. They were paid off by Ethelred II (the Unready – which meant 'without counsel'), but they returned on several occasions and in 1013 finally took control of London. Ethelred (968?–1016) now fled the country, and on the death of Sweyn in 1014 Sweyn's son Cnut (Canute) inherited London. An alliance was then forged between the exiled Ethelred and another Olaf (later to become king of Norway and St Olaf, with a number of London churches dedicated to his memory). These allies returned to London in 1014 and pulled down London Bridge, and Ethelred re-established himself in the capital while Cnut went back to Denmark to enlist more forces.

Cnut returned in 1015–16 and Ethelred had difficulty in amassing a sufficiently loyal force under the command of his son Edmund Ironside (981?–1016). In 1016 Cnut turned his attention to London, where Ethelred was in control, but Ethelred died before Cnut's forces got there. His kingdom was then rent by divisions: some supported Cnut, others Edmund, though London remained in support of the latter. A battle was fought in October at Ashingdon, Essex, which Cnut won, and England was divided once more between Saxon and Dane – Edmund taking Wessex, and Cnut taking Mercia and its appendage, London. This was a very temporary arrangement, because Edmund died a month later in 1017 and Cnut became king of Wessex as well.

Cnut married Emma, widow of Ethelred, and in so doing did much to unite the factions in the country. The sons of Edmund were exiled and the succession of Cnut's son by Emma, Hardacnut, to the kingdom of all England seemed assured at Cnut's death in 1035. However, a witan resolved that Hardacnut should rule only over Wessex, while his half-brother Harold Harefoot, the son of Cnut and a former wife, was to take Mercia. In effect, government of Wessex was carried out by Emma and Godwin, earl of Wessex (c. 990–1053), as Hardacnut spent much of his time in Denmark and Norway. Eventually, Wessex too was taken by Harefoot. When Harefoot died in 1040, Hardacnut became king of both Mercia and Wessex. One of his first acts after his coronation was to have Harefoot's body disinterred from Winchester, beheaded, and thrown into the Thames. The body was rescued by fishermen and reinterred in St Clement Danes in the Strand, but was once again dug up and thrown for a second time into the Thames.

The unpopular Hardacnut died suddenly in 1042, at a wedding feast at Lambeth. He was childless, and by popular consent the crown was offered to Edward, the exiled 7th son of Ethelred, who became known as Edward the Confessor (meaning 'the priest').

The Confessor's reign was not entirely harmonious. It was marred by a dispute with his father-in-law, Godwin, whom in 1051 he summoned to a witan at London. Godwin and his sons set up camp at Southwark from which to conduct negotiations, but were later exiled. Godwin returned the following year, regained his old Wessex possessions, and remained in England. It was his son Harold who was to be vanquished by William of Normandy at the Battle of Hastings in 1066.

Edward the Confessor appears to have issued no clear intention as to who should succeed him. He was still indecisive as 1065 began, and the consecration of his new abbey of St Peter, Westminster, was imminent.

1065

THE BUILDING OF WESTMINSTER ABBEY

These annals begin outside the London city walls, on an island – a low-lying triangle of land to the west. On two sides ran arms of the river Tyburn, one of which turned an abbot's watermill; the third side faced the river Thames. This bramble-infested land, measuring some 470 by 370 yards and liable to flooding, was Thorney Island, largely taken up today by Parliament Square and the buildings around. Here the monastic church of St Peter had been built at an unknown date. With an eye to upstaging St Paul's in the City, legends and chronicles insisted that the original wooden structure had been consecrated by St Peter himself.

Why erect an important building so early in this vicinity, given the precarious and desolate existence of its land at the mercy of the Thames? The answer is surely that when the Romans arrived they found a wider and shallower river than we have today: it was possible at times to ford the stream roughly on the route of Westminster Bridge. Also, the flow of the sea into the river was less forceful all those years ago when the land mass of south-east England was higher. Many years after the Roman era, as will be noted in subsequent pages, it was occasionally possible to walk across the river bed.

From this crossing two Roman roads led north and south – Watling Street (the present Edgware Road) and, on the other side, a main road to Kent.

Whatever the reason, about the year AD 785 King Offa of Mercia established a community of Benedictine monks here. Later kings Edgar (d. 975) and Cnut were both patrons, and the

The Bayeux Tapestry's depiction of the funeral of Edward the Confessor at Westminster Abbey.

latter may well have been the first king to establish his court at Westminster and may have built its first palace. (Legend intrudes once again in asserting that the famous occasion of Cnut unsuccessfully commanding back the waves took place here by the Thames.)

Edward the Confessor, stepson of Cnut, was crowned king of England at Winchester in 1043. He had spent much of his life in exile in Normandy, and his later tastes derived more from that region than from the Saxon kingdom of England he inherited. This showed particularly in his chosen style for the new church and monastic buildings he began on Thorney Island in 1051. The new abbey was the first substantial Romanesque church in England, and it is generally thought that its form and architecture were based on those of the church of Jumièges in Normandy. The abbey was not, nor has it been since, except briefly in the 16th century, a cathedral. But the original and continued patronage of the kings of England has ensured that it has had privileges of status and autonomy.

The Confessor, who spent a pious later life, was too ill to appear at the abbey's consecration on 28 December 1065 (his wife, Edith, attended in his stead), but nine days later he was the first to be buried there.

The abbey precincts covered the whole island apart from the land taken by the king's buildings on the site of part of the present Houses of Parliament by the river. When Westminster Hall was built in 1099 the older part was said to be in Old Palace Yard, and the new premises, in the area of today's Big Ben, became New Palace Yard.

1066

THE NORMAN CONQUEST AND LONDON

Edward the Confessor died on 5 January in his palace at Westminster; next day he was buried in his own church of St Peter – the Westminster Abbey he had created. The funeral procession is depicted in the Bayeux Tapestry, as also is the steeplejack who had, not long before the consecration, put the finishing touch to the tower.

The Confessor, it seems, had left ambiguous wishes as to the kingdom's succession. Earlier he had promised the crown to his kinsman William of Normandy. Later, the earl Godwin's son, Harold Godwin, had appeared to be the chosen candidate having had an alleged deathbed blessing. Whatever the merits of the claims, they led in the short run to Harold taking the throne with the declared support of nobles and the City of London, and his coronation took place, probably at Westminster Abbey, within days. In the longer run the Confessor's ambiguity led to the Battle of Hastings and Harold's death.

Once victory at Hastings was behind him, William had to consolidate. With London having declared Edgar Atheling, a Saxon, as the new king, he advanced on the City with circumspection. Kent, or those parts of it which did not submit, were overcome first, and then it was the turn of Southwark: what was then a nondescript, poor settlement, strung out along the river, was destroyed by fire. The City forces crossed London Bridge in a show of opposition, but William had the better of the fight; the City withdrew, while William decided not to risk a possibly bloody advance across the bridge and invaded the north bank via Wallingford instead.

A battle for London was never fought. Terms were agreed at Berkhamsted, and the City submitted to the Conqueror, abandoning Atheling and the Saxon inheritance for ever. London's reward was the continuance of its status and privileges.

It was almost a smooth transition, and the crown of Arabian gold and Egyptian gems was placed on William's head on Christmas Day in Westminster Abbey almost without incident. Unfortunately, one part of the ceremony required those present to acclaim the new king (as it still does), and the enthusiastic shouts inside were misjudged by the Norman soldiers guarding the outside as insurrection, and it is said they fired houses in the Westminster area in the immediate panic.

The choice of the abbey for the coronation is significant since, after all, the most important church was St Paul's, in the City. But William was underpinning the legitimacy of his claim to be Edward's successor: he took the crown in Edward's church, near Edward's tomb and, by inference, with Edward's approval. The kings and queens of England and Great Britain have done so ever since.

1067

FORTIFYING LONDON

The Battle of Hastings was decisive only in retrospect. For some time William I's hold over his new kingdom was uncertain, and if a strong rival had come forward the Norman might well have been dislodged. From this year William set about fortifying his new domain.

It is probable that a start was now made on what became the Tower of London. It is possible that two other fortifications to the west, by Blackfriars – Baynard and Montfichet castles – were also begun.

The original Tower fortress was a wooden structure, thrown up as temporary protection. Its site displayed William's usual tactical wisdom. The building was tucked into the far south-east corner of London, the Roman wall to the east and the river to the south protecting two of its sides. To the west, in an arc, were a ditch, a rampart and a palisade. Thus the Tower not only impressed Londoners but also overlooked the Thames, where invasion might come especially from the Danes. It has been suggested recently that there was already a Roman lighthouse here and that it was this structure that gave the fortress the sobriquet of 'Tower' instead of 'castle'.

After his coronation William moved out of London to the fishing village of Barking to the east. Here he briefly held court in the guest houses of the Benedictine Barking Abbey. He received the submission of leading Saxons, including Atheling, and prudently took them all with him to Normandy when he returned there in February.

Barking Abbey had been founded on the bank of the River Roding c. 666 by Erkenwald, bishop of London, who later became a cult figure in the City. He died c. 673, probably at Barking, and there was considerable competition to bury him – a contest won by St Paul's. Barking, however, managed to retain his bell, and this was carried in yearly processions on his commemorative day.

Barking Abbey was built on marshy land near the Thames, and was extremely desolate. Yet by the time of the Conquest it was the most prominent nunnery in the kingdom, and one of the richest: its remoteness, then fashionable, was an advantage in attracting endowments.

The 15th-century curfew tower at Barking Abbey.

FIRST MENTION OF CHEAPSIDE

The most important road in Roman and medieval London was Cheapside. It was the widest street, the principal market, and strategically placed near St Paul's, the dock at Queenhithe and London Bridge. In a 1067 record it was called Westceape – the Old English word 'ceap' meant 'market' or 'barter' – to distinguish it from Eastcheap, east of London Bridge, which dealt mostly with meat and merchandise offloaded at Billingsgate. The name 'Cheapside' is not found in records until about 1510.

Cheapside was lined with stalls which were projections from buildings; some of these became permanent structures, with small warehouses behind called selds. A market was in the middle of the road. Over the centuries trades congregated as specialists in streets to north and south. Bread Street, Wood Street, Milk Street and Ironmonger Lane denote the merchants, and Friday Street indicates the sale of fish in Catholic London on that day of the week. Saddlers and loriners (who made metal harness fittings) functioned in Foster Lane, goldsmiths by Friday Street, mercers in the area of their hall today, cordwainers by St Mary-le-Bow, poulterers, of course, in Poultry. The butchers tended to be to the west, spilling over from the Shambles in Newgate Street.

FIRST MENTION OF ST MAGNUS THE MARTYR

This church, by London Bridge, overlooks Billingsgate, one of the earliest docks in London. The church is mentioned in a document recording a grant this year as being, unusually, made of stone – clearly a building of significance. Though the document is dated 1067, it is a 12th-century forgery. However, it may still be accurate as to the church's date and composition. The parish included the buildings on London Bridge, and the church later received compensation from the chapel built on the stone bridge for loss of alms from travellers.

1068

THE QUEEN IS CROWNED

Throughout his reign William I spent much of his time in France. Having put in place in England a feudal administration governed by grateful Normans and Saxons, he felt free to be peripatetic. For some of this year he was back in London, and on Whit Sunday Matilda, his queen, was crowned at Westminster Abbey, a short while before the birth of her fourth son, the future Henry I.

A CHARTER FOR ST MARTIN'S LE GRAND

It is probable that William at this period confirmed by charter the status of a number of institutions in London, since he was anxious to retain the City's loyalty. We know, for example, that the charter of St Martin's le Grand, a collegiate church or royal free chapel, was ratified this year. This establishment, on the later site of the General Post Office, had been founded c. 1056 by Ingelric, earl of Essex, and Eirard, his brother. The former, who possessed land in the Aldersgate area, had served as an adviser to the Confessor and held the same post under William. The king's charter exempted the church and its precincts from the interference of bishops and archdeacons and, as the City was to find, its status as a liberty placed it outside the jurisdiction of the civic authorities as well. From its rights and privileges also developed its role as a place of sanctuary in which those fleeing from authority could live for a time.

1069

HARMONDSWORTH GRANTED TO ROUEN

Increasingly the country's estates and positions of wealth and responsibility were being taken by Normans. Already much of the land had been parcelled out to William's supporters – not to mention the vast tracts taken by the king himself. William also imposed the concept that the possession of land depended on the grant of the king.

Some estates were taken by establishments or people in Normandy. The manor of Harmondsworth, in Middlesex, for example, was granted this year to the abbey of Rouen. By 1391 it was owned by the newly established Winchester College.

1070

THE BUILDING OF ST MARY-LE-BOW

Precise building dates are rarely available for this period, but it is thought that between 1070 and 1090 the crypt of St Mary-le-Bow, Cheapside, was built. In its construction some Roman bricks were used.

The early name of this church was St Mary de Arcubus, denoting that it was built upon the arches of the crypt – the only part of the original church still to survive. The appeal court of the archbishop of Canterbury, the Court of Arches, met in this crypt. The more modern name of the church, St Mary-le-Bow (again referring to the shape of the arches), was being used by c. 1270.

1077

A GREAT FIRE IN LONDON

London was seriously damaged by fire several times before the most famous conflagration of 1666. An extensive blaze, causing unspecified damage, was recorded for 1077, but there had been other large fires before that.

The frequency was hardly surprising. London by this time had at least 10,000 inhabitants, and the houses, packed in narrow streets, were made of wood and thatch. Firefighting equipment consisted of water buckets and hooks to pull down the burning thatch so that it might be dealt with on the ground. No doubt there were also some grappling irons and chains to demolish houses in the path of the flames to create a firebreak.

Many outbreaks arose from the temptation to keep fires alight all night, since it was difficult to kindle them in the morning. So serious was this problem that the king courted unpopularity by ordering that all fires and lights should be covered or extinguished at the ringing of a bell in the evening. This order of 'cuevrefeu' is the origin of the word 'curfew'.

FIRST MENTION OF ST LUKE'S CHARLTON

The parish church of Charlton first occurs in records this year, though it was no doubt a Saxon foundation. It was made of chalk and flint, and was a possession of Bermondsey Abbey. This tiny building sufficed until 1630 when the lord of the manor, Sir Adam Newbold, left money to rebuild it – a rare example of a church built in the reign of Charles I.

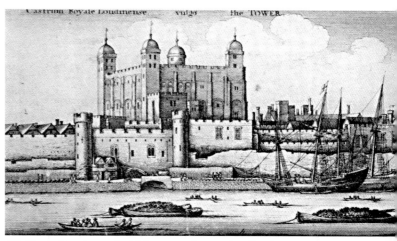

The Tower of London in the 17th century, showing the White Tower.

1078

BUILDING THE WHITE TOWER

The time had come to build the Tower of London in stone. Gundulf, bishop of Rochester, supervised the construction of what is now the White Tower, at that time by far the largest secular building in the country. (Gundulf was also responsible for building Rochester Castle and Cathedral.) The squarish keep, 90 ft high with walls 11 ft thick, was made of Caen stone; it was built on a basement the walls of which were 15 ft wide at their base. It was to serve as a residence, treasury, prison and stronghold.

The single entrance, on the south side, led up removable steps to a hall and chamber used by guards and menials for eating and resting. Further upstairs were the grander rooms, including a great hall for entertaining and royal chambers. Here too was St John's Chapel, which has been altered little since the Conqueror's time. Around its interior runs an arcade of cylindrical pillars, and above them is a gallery. South of the keep was the bailey containing ancillary buildings; at first it was defended towards the City by a ditch.

1080

THE BUILDING OF BAYNARD'S CASTLE

The first Baynard's Castle, erected during the reign of William I, was just inside the old line of the western City wall, on the site of the later Blackfriars friary. It appears to have been completed about this year by Ralph Bainard, a Norman who had been granted considerable estates in eastern England, including Little Dunmow, Essex, which was his seat: several manors under his jurisdiction in that area had to pay or serve 'castle-guard' for the castle in London.

1082

BERMONDSEY ABBEY FOUNDED

A priory, later to be transformed into Bermondsey Abbey, was founded this year on Bermondsey Marsh, between the present Grange Walk and

Long Walk. The founder was Aylwin Child, citizen of London (the Aylwin housing estate today commemorates him), and the original dedication was to St Saviour. It was later occupied by Cluniac monks (see 1089).

1084

ST NICHOLAS ACON BUILT

In this year the first mention occurs, in a grant to Malmesbury Abbey, of the church of St Nicholas Acon in Nicholas Lane, off Lombard Street. Probably newly built, its dedication was to the obscure archbishop Nicholas of Myra in Asia Minor, and the 'Acon' is a corruption of 'Hacun', probably a benefactor of the church in the 12th century. Destroyed in the Great Fire and not replaced, its churchyard still exists.

1085

FIRST ST ALFEGE CHURCH

By about this date the church of St Alfege in Greenwich was built. Alfege, archbishop of Canterbury, had been murdered in 1012 by the Danes after he had refused to sanction a ransom for his release from them. It was a popular belief that the church was built on the site of the killing.

1086

DOMESDAY SURVEY COMPLETED

The Domesday Book was a survey of land ownership which formed the basis of taxation. Consisting of two volumes – one dealing with Essex, Norfolk and Suffolk, and the other with the remainder of England – it was based upon the administrative areas of 'hundreds', each one of which was broken down into 'vills'. Unfortunately, the City of London was not included.

The abbey of Westminster was a major landowner – it had the seventh largest income of all the monasteries surveyed. By 1100 the abbey estates exceeded 60,000 acres, with land in Hampshire, the west Midlands, Battersea and Wandsworth. In the immediate vicinity of his abbey the abbot had a meadow, pasture for livestock, woodland for 100 swine, 4 vineyards recently planted, and 25 houses.

1087

AN EARLY GREAT FIRE OF LONDON

This year, marked by the death of William I, was disastrous for London in a number of ways. An epidemic, probably enteric fever, was prevalent. There was civil strife, and there was yet another great fire. In this conflagration, the *Anglo-Saxon Chronicle* related, 'the holy church of St Paul, the [cathedral] of London, was burnt down, as well as many other churches and the largest and fairest part of the whole city'. The first, wooden, St Paul's, built by Ethelbert in 604, had also burnt down. Its successor, built in stone by Erkenwald *c.* 680, had been destroyed by the Vikings in 962. The replacement – the last Saxon St Paul's – was the building lost this year.

Bermondsey Abbey, from a print published in 1805.

CORONATION OF THE NEW KING

William Rufus, second son of the Conqueror, grasped the throne despite the better claim of his elder brother, Robert. He was crowned at Westminster Abbey on 26 September, and held court at Westminster at Christmas. Described variously as avaricious, irreligious, unchaste and intemperate, he was a strong and ruthless person who made himself unpopular with the clergy during his reign.

1088

LONDON EMBROILED IN REVOLT

William's seizure of the throne of England was resented by Bishop Odo, the late king's one-time closest adviser and half-brother. Odo, bishop of Bayeux and responsible for the manufacture of the famous tapestry, was a formidable man. Despite his ecclesiastical position he had fought in full armour at Hastings, albeit with the permitted mace rather than the sword, and was prominent in the battle. He received the castle of Dover and the earldom of Kent as a reward, and in the ensuing years, when the king was in Normandy, acted as his deputy. He was an unpopular choice, for he rode roughshod over the English and, like his master, over the clerics.

But Odo's self-aggrandizement, including an ambition to be pope, led eventually to dispute with the Conqueror and imprisonment in Rouen – he was initially exempted from William I's deathbed pardon. Back in England he was at first part of William II's court, but soon was the centre of a Norman plot to depose the new king in favour of his brother Robert. With civil strife already begun, William made London his headquarters, but, while he was besieging Pevensey Castle, Odo's forces attacked both London and Canterbury. In fact there was a strong pro-Odo party in London which seems to have led to a minor rebellion in the city.

1089

THE CLUNIACS COME TO BERMONDSEY

The priory at Bermondsey, founded in 1082, was endowed with the manor of Bermondsey by William II. With the completion of the building this year and William's endowment, four monks of the Cluniac order, an ascetic branch of the Benedictines, were invited over from La Charité on the Loire, to establish a settlement. It was to grow into the principal Cluniac centre in the country.

1091

VIOLENT STORM OVER LONDON

Various chronicles agree that a violent storm hit London on 16 November, but the extent of the damage is not reported consistently. One improbable version relates that the rafters of the church of St Mary-le-Bow were found embedded in the ground outside to a depth of 22 ft. However, there is no doubt that the roof of the church was lifted clean off and that considerable damage was done to houses throughout the City. As a consequence of the wind, the force of the tide in the Thames was whipped up, causing flooding and severe damage to the wooden London Bridge.

1094

A DISPUTED CONSECRATION

St Mary, the parish church of Harrow, was consecrated this year.

Opinion differs as to the antiquity of the name 'Harrow'. The generally accepted version is that it derives from the Old English word 'hearg', meaning 'heathen temple', usually on a hilltop. It is not surprising that the highest hill in central Middlesex should have attracted some kind of primitive monument, nor that in Christian times it should have been the site of an early church.

The manor was owned from Saxon times by the archbishop of Canterbury, and, although it was within the see of the bishop of London, it remained a 'peculiar' – that is, outside the jurisdiction of the bishop. This anomaly led to some embarrassment at the consecration – at least if we are to believe legend. The bishop of London felt that it was his responsibility to officiate, whereas the powerful archbishop Anselm of Canterbury decided that it was his. On the day Anselm found that the holy oil was missing, and it was suggested that it had been stolen by an agent of the bishop. Miraculously, we are assured, the oil was replaced.

1096

A CHURCH BY THE WALBROOK

The first mention of the church of St Stephen Walbrook occurs this year: its name refers to one of the 'lost' rivers of London. The Walbrook rose in the boggy area of Moorfields north of the city wall; in the 14th century the land was still waterlogged enough to float a boat with six passengers. Possibly this condition was due to the wall inhibiting the natural flow of water down to the Thames. The Walbrook was shallow, about 10 ft wide, and described in 1739 as 'a great and rapid stream'; it is now about 32 ft below modern road level. It ran beneath the churches of St Margaret, Lothbury, and St Mildred, Poultry, under part of the Bank of England, past the western side of St Stephen's and, south of the church, by the site of the ancient Temple of Mithras, and then joined the Thames at Dowgate.

At this time the church was situated on the west side of Walbrook Street, but it was rebuilt in 1429 on the other side of the road.

1097

A BUILDING TAX

Three substantial building projects were in progress in London this year: the construction of a new wall and moat on the western side of the Tower of London, the repair of London Bridge (possibly rectifying damage caused in the storm of 1091) and the construction of Westminster Hall.

The cost of this work was met by national taxation and by enforced direct labour. The *Anglo-Saxon Chronicle* records that 'Many districts which with their work belonged to London were grievously oppressed, through the wall that they were building around the tower, and through the bridge, which was almost carried away by flood, and through the work on the king's hall which was being built at Westminster.'

1098

EARLY CANTERBURY POSSESSIONS

A document of about this date lists some possessions of the see of Canterbury in London and at the same time gives us the first reference to a number of buildings. These include the church of St Dionis Backchurch (now demolished), in Fenchurch Street, which was the only church in the City dedicated to the French St Denis; 'Backchurch' derived from a person called Bac and not, as has often been said, to its standing back slightly from the road. Also mentioned is All Hallows, Barking, a church still standing near the Tower of London, which was owned by Barking Abbey.

FIRST MENTION OF ST MARY ALDERMARY

This church in Bow Lane received its first definite mention this year, but it was undoubtedly a much older building and it is suggested that the name means 'older Mary' – older, that is, than St Mary-le-Bow in Cheapside, itself sometimes called St Mary Newchurch. The jurisdiction of the archbishop of Canterbury rather than the bishop of London over Aldermary also points to an ancient foundation.

1099

WESTMINSTER HALL FINISHED

In this, the last full year of his reign, William II held his first banquet and court in the newly completed Westminster Hall. This building, an extension of Edward the Confessor's palace, is now the only surviving part of the old Palace of Westminster. William had wanted something more impressive. He pronounced it 'too big for a chamber and not big enough for a hall', but even so it was the largest hall in the country. It measured 240 ft long and 68 ft wide, and it was 20 ft high. At that time it had two rows of wooden pillars down its length holding up the roof, with a gallery around it: effectively, it was a room divided into three sections. This layout was changed in the late 14th century, when the present magnificent hammerbeam span was inserted.

1100

A NEW KING IS CROWNED

The unexpected death of William II in the New Forest found his younger brother Henry nearby and the already frustrated elder brother, Robert, on the high seas. It was Henry who seized the nation's treasure and declared himself king, and Robert was left once more to make unavailing attempts to claim the inheritance of England.

Henry I's coronation was at Westminster Abbey on 5 August – a ceremony performed by the bishop of London in the absence of both the archbishop of Canterbury, who was in exile, and the archbishop of York, for whom Henry was too impatient to wait. On 11 November his queen, Matilda, was crowned in the same abbey.

NUNNERY AT CLERKENWELL FOUNDED

Another Benedictine establishment was founded, this time on the site of the present-day St James, Clerkenwell. This was the nunnery of St Mary, endowed by Jordan de Bricett, a Suffolk landholder, with land sloping down to the river Fleet. Eventually the nunnery's estate was to include large parts of Muswell Hill and Holloway.

FIRST MENTION OF CORNHILL

A cornhill, a place where a corn market was held, is first noted this year. By c. 1125 it gave its name to a street extending from today's Bank to St Mary Axe. In the built-up city it is difficult to appreciate the gradients of land beneath, but Cornhill was one of the two hills within the walls, the other being Ludgate Hill, upon which St Paul's stands.

EARLY ST MARTIN VINTRY

The church of St Martin Vintry, which appears in a grant to the monastery of St Peter, Gloucester, about this year, was on the east side of College Hill, fronting Upper Thames Street. In a forged document dated 1067, the name of the church is St Martin Baremannecherche, thought to mean 'carrier' or 'porter' and perhaps intended to refer to the carriers of wine imported into the area from the docks.

1101

BUILDING WORKS AT BOW

About this time two significant developments occurred in Bow, in east London. It is likely, since they were adjacent, that they were connected.

One was the building across the river Lea of Bow Bridge, said to be the first stone bridge in England. Legend asserts that it was built at the instigation of Queen Matilda, either because she had heard how difficult the Lea crossing was or else because she herself had had some experience of it. Previously the way east had crossed the Lea at Old Ford, the lowest point where the river could be forded, but the Lea was tidal this far, and no doubt there were many occasions when it was dangerous to cross in this way. The shape of the new bridge, an arch, inspired the place name of Stratford-atte-Bowe, first recorded in 1279.

Perhaps the reason for the building of the bridge was the foundation in this period of the convent of St Leonard, Bow – its existence is recalled today in the names of St Leonard Street and Priory Street. The lady chapel of the convent became a parish church after the Reformation, but it was swept away by the approach roads to the Blackwall Tunnel and only part of the churchyard is left as a reminder.

ESCAPE FROM THE TOWER

The first recorded prisoner in the Tower of London was also the first to escape, and the nature of his flight suggests that the building was not erected as a prison in the first place.

The agent of William II's voracious appetite for money had been the unpopular and unscrupulous bishop of Durham, Rannulf de Flambard, and on the unexpected death of the king he was arrested by Henry I and put in the Tower. Treatment there was not harsh – he had his own servants, and he occupied rooms in the White Keep well above river level. His method of escape on 2 February illuminates the state of his imprisonment – at a feast, he intoxicated his warders with wine from a butt which also contained a rope down which he climbed to freedom.

1102

ST MARY ABBOTS BUILT

About this year was built the first church of St Mary Abbots, Kensington High Street. It was built on land owned by the abbot of Abingdon – local street names recall this connection. This church was replaced in the 14th century.

1106

ST THOMAS'S HOSPITAL FOUNDED

The famous hospital of St Thomas sprang from a priory in Borough High Street, one of the oldest thoroughfares of London; Southwark Cathedral now stands on the site. Previously there had been a nunnery, begun perhaps in the 7th century and re-endowed by St Swithin, bishop of Winchester, c. 852. In 1106 two Normans, William Pont de l'Arche and William Dauncy, built a priory here, and the hospital began within its precincts. Medical care was in the charge of secular Augustinian canons, an order chosen also to administer St Bartholomew's Hospital in 1123.

The building was within the see of Winchester, and it is believed that the bishop, William Giffard, designed the nave of the church, which was called St Mary Overie (Overy). The origin of this name is thought to be 'over the water', and there is a legend that the first nunnery was paid for by a ferryman made rich by his trade across the Thames.

The hospital, which provided a practical way to express Christianity, was named after St Thomas à Becket after his canonization in 1173.

1107

EARLY MENTION OF ST MARY ALDERMANBURY

First mention is made this year of this church, one of the few to possess a cloister; it was undoubtedly of a much earlier foundation. The old churchyard, now a public garden, contains the remains of the actors John Heming and Henry Condell, who published the first folio of the plays of their friend Shakespeare. The building's successor, erected after the Great Fire, was devastated in the last war and has now been reconstructed in Missouri, in the United States.

1108

HOLY TRINITY FOUNDED

The founding of Holy Trinity Priory near Aldgate this year illustrates the growing ascendancy of the Augustinian order over the Benedictines. It was endowed by Queen Matilda, and was the largest religious house within the City walls until the advent of the various friaries. Once again, as in the case of St Mary Overie (see 1106), the canons were 'secular' rather than 'regular' – that is, they were not removed from the ordinary world as many monks were.

The site of the endowment was at present-day Mitre Street and Dukes Place, north of the junction of Fenchurch Street and Leadenhall Street. It was just inside Aldgate, a structure which Matilda also owned and gave to the canons.

The priory was also called Christchurch, spelt in early records 'Crichurch', which explains the name of the present St Katharine Cree church, built as a parish church within the priory grounds.

The original monastic buildings were short-lived – they were destroyed in the fire of 1133 (q.v.).

1111

FIRST MENTION OF ST BENET'S ON THE THAMES

The church of St Benet Paul's Wharf is first mentioned in records for this year, as St Benet on the Thames. It still exists, as the Welsh church on Upper Thames Street, opposite what used to be Paul's Wharf, an inlet and loading quay belonging to St Paul's Cathedral. The old church, which contained the tomb of the architect Inigo Jones, was destroyed in the Great Fire and was replaced by the present building designed by Wren.

1114

THE THAMES RUNS DRY

According to the *Anglo-Saxon Chronicle*, 'there was an ebb-tide which was everywhere lower than any man remembered before; so people went riding and walking across the Thames to the east of London Bridge'.

MERTON PRIORY AND PARISH CHURCH FOUNDED

Gilbert, sheriff of Surrey, founded the Augustinian Merton Priory this year and work began on building St Mary, the parish church of the village. Three years later the priory was moved to its later site; the old doorway from this newer building was re-erected (and still exists) in the parish churchyard.

1117

LEPER HOSPITAL FOUNDED

Leprosy was a difficult problem for urban areas. While it was imperative that those affected should be isolated, it was also useful to have them situated in a place where they might gather alms for their own upkeep.

The hospital of St Giles-in-the-Fields was on such a site. As the name implies, it was in the fields and away from both Westminster and the City, but it was near enough to busy highways to attract attention.

The buildings, which can be seen on the Elizabethan map drawn by Ralph Agas, were in the triangle of land between today's Charing Cross Road, St Giles High Street and Shaftesbury Avenue. The hospital was founded by Queen Matilda about this year (not 1101, which is the usual date given) for 14 lepers, and until 1299 it seems to have been administered by the City, but was then granted to a lazar house in Leicestershire.

1118

THOMAS À BECKET BORN IN CHEAPSIDE

Thomas à Becket, the future archbishop of Canterbury and saint, was born in December in his father's house at the corner of Cheapside and Ironmonger Lane; both his parents were of Norman stock. After his death his sister gave the house to the hospital of St Thomas of Acon, and when this was dissolved at the Reformation the Mercers' Company, which already rented part of the site for its hall, took over the whole premises. The company still occupies the site.

Thomas's early schooling was at the newly founded Merton Priory (see 1114). From there, he attended school in London and studied further in Paris where he remained until he was 21. By 1143 he had obtained a post in the household of the archbishop of Canterbury.

At the time of Becket's childhood, and for long afterwards, Cheapside was the principal shopping street of London, and one through which all important processions passed and in which tournaments were held.

KNIGHTS TEMPLAR ESTABLISHED IN HOLBORN

The Knights Templar were established after 1099 to protect pilgrims on their way to the Holy Land. They were awarded land near the Dome of the Rock on Mount Solomon in Jerusalem, and became known as the Knights of the Temple of Solomon of Jerusalem, and later as Knights Templar. In the 14th century their popularity, influence and wealth were to be their undoing, for they were persecuted by the Church and by envious kings. In 1118, however, they were granted some land in Holborn, opposite present-day Gray's Inn Road and east of Chancery Lane. Here they built a round church – a shape they often used to imitate the circular church of the Holy Sepulchre in Jerusalem. The site is now occupied by Southampton Buildings.

When they moved to what became known as the Temple area, south of Fleet Street, their old house in Holborn was bought by the bishop of Lincoln for his town house.

1119

FIRST MENTION OF ST ANTHOLIN'S CHURCH

The church of St Antholin stood in Watling Street by Budge Row until 1875. The first mention of a building here occurs this year, when a dispute took place between two men, one of them a priest, as to their right to the church. They made a compact not to injure each other in the matter and resolved instead to donate the building to the canons of St Paul's.

1122

AN EARLY GUILDHALL BUILT

It is not known when the first guildhall was built, but about this year the City possessed a piece of land, for which it paid two shillings rent per annum to St Paul's, which is referred to in a document of c. 1127 as 'terra Gialle'. The location is unknown. In 1260 a testament was proved in 'Gildhall Lond'.

1123

FOUNDATION OF ST BARTHOLOMEW'S PRIORY AND HOSPITAL

The ascendancy of the Augustinian priors continued with the founding of what were to be two of the most enduring establishments in London. Rahere, a courtier of William II and a protégé of the bishop of London, founded both a priory and a hospital this year at West Smithfield. Both faced out on to a field which by the end of the 13th century included some gallows. The choir of the priory church, which became a parish church at the Reformation (while the rest of the buildings were gradually demolished), still remains as St Bartholomew the Great – its entrance from Smithfield is a doorway of the original west front. St Bartholomew's, excepting the chapel in the Tower of London, is the oldest church in London, and certainly the most splendid from that period. The hospital is now the mass of buildings called St Bartholomew's or Bart's Hospital.

1125

ST BOTOLPH, ALDGATE

Included in a grant to the Holy Trinity Priory, Aldgate, this year was the church of St Botolph without Aldgate. This is the first record of this building, though it was most likely established in Saxon times. As its name implies, it is outside Aldgate, and therefore beyond the City wall.

There were three other 'Botolph' churches in London, all of them by gates: at Aldersgate, at Bishopsgate and at Billingsgate, where the river wall had an entrance and a loading quay. St Botolph is sometimes known as the patron saint of travellers, and this is presumably the reason for the dedication of churches in his name at gates.

THE RIVER FLEET

The river Fleet features frequently in London history. It was associated with a prison, with Fleet Street itself, and with much pollution. In its earlier days it was navigable from the Thames up to Holborn Bridge, and in its upper reaches it was a clear stream meandering through the fields of Kentish Town.

The stream had its beginnings in Hampstead, near today's Vale of Health, and at Kenwood in Highgate; these tributaries joined at Kentish Town and, via King's Cross, Farringdon and Holborn, went down to today's Blackfriars in a deep valley.

Unfortunately, it was also used as a sewer and by the butchers at Newgate, who deposited in it whatever bits of carcasses they couldn't sell, in the hope they would flow into the Thames. Gradually the stream became silted up, and in rainy seasons this created serious problems further north, especially around St Pancras, where the low-lying land was flooded, leaving the old parish church marooned sometimes.

At its southern end the Fleet was spanned by two bridges – Holborn Bridge (where Holborn Viaduct now crosses) and Fleet Bridge (at today's Ludgate Circus). Between these, on the east side, it ran past the Fleet Prison, where the inmates suffered the stench from the water, and beyond the Holborn bridge it was called Turnmill Brook – the derivation of today's Turnmill Street in Clerkenwell. On this stretch were located numerous mills to take advantage of the river's swift current. These were a feature well into the 18th century.

The river is mentioned in a land deed of c. 1125–30.

1128

THE CHAPEL FOR PRISONERS

The chapel called St Peter ad Vincula on Tower Hill was begun about this year. By the end of the 13th century it was within the walls of the Tower, but at this stage it was outside the fortifications and may possibly have been a parish church before it was absorbed into the Tower precincts as a royal chapel. The church's dedication means 'St Peter in chains', and this has led to speculation that the chapel was intended for prisoners in the Tower. However, the dedication predates the general use of the Tower as a prison, and in any case St Peter overthrew his chains and such cause for optimism is unlikely to have commended the name. Possibly the church was dedicated on the first day of an August, the feast day of St Peter in chains.

In the 16th century the rebuilt chapel received the bodies of many famous people executed at the Tower. They included two of Henry VIII's wives, Anne Boleyn and Catherine Howard, others who crossed the king, such as Sir Thomas More and Thomas Cromwell, and the unfortunate Lady Jane Grey.

1130

A CHARTER FOR THE CITY

Between 1130 and the year of his death, 1135, it is probable that Henry I granted London a charter which was a considerable advance on any it had received before. The original does not exist, but most scholars are inclined to regard an early-13th-century copy as genuine, although its generosity – uncharacteristic of the king – casts doubts on its authenticity.

The City, if the document is genuine, was granted the administration (the shrievalty) and the king's revenues of the county of Middlesex as well as the right to elect its own sheriff. Citizens were not required to provide hospitality to the royal household, and the various estates were confirmed. There were other clauses relating to taxation, all advantageous to Londoners.

THE PORTSOKEN DISPUTE

The rector of St Peter ad Vincula set in motion about this year a series of legal moves to claim rights over the Portsoken area outside the eastern wall of the City, beyond Aldgate, in which stood the church of St Botolph. He was opposed by the prior of Holy Trinity, Aldgate, who eventually won control instead. From that time the parish of St Botolph without Aldgate included the Portsoken area and came under the jurisdiction of the priory.

1133

LARGE FIRE IN LONDON

There is confusion as to the date of this, another major fire in London, which damaged St Paul's, St Bride's and London Bridge, and appears to have destroyed property as far east as Aldgate. This seems to be a remarkable spread for the fire, to be compared only with that of the Great Fire of 1666. Perhaps there were two distinct fires affecting different ends of the City in different years, which might explain the fact that various chronicles give other years, such as 1132, 1135 and 1136, for this major event. Accounts also vary as to the extent of the damage to St Paul's and to London Bridge. The bridge was not rebuilt until 1163–9, and this suggests that the old structure was only damaged in 1133, for Londoners would probably not have relied only on ferries for over 30 years.

ORIGINS OF BARTHOLOMEW FAIR

What became a famous London event had its origins this year, when the king granted the priory of St Bartholomew in West Smithfield the right to hold an annual fair. It may already have been in existence since the founding of the priory ten years earlier.

Originally the fair was situated within the grounds of the priory and consisted mainly of stalls set up by mercers and drapers. The local street today called Cloth Fair is a reminder of that early specialization. As the fair developed it was administered by a 'Court of Pie Poudre' – a name thought to derive from 'pieds poudreux', meaning 'dusty-footed', as many of the traders and visitors must have been.

1134

KILBURN PRIORY FOUNDED

The Kilburn stream – its name probably means 'cold water' – was a tributary of the river Westbourne. At about the point where several streams joined, just east of today's Kilburn High Road, before flowing south in one river to Hyde Park and the Thames, the abbot of Westminster founded a small Benedictine priory this year. This was a development from an existing hermitage, and the hermit Godwin was appointed priest of the new establishment, which at first consisted of three nuns who had been maids of honour to Matilda, queen of Henry I.

Dispute soon arose as to whether the house was under the jurisdiction of the abbot of Westminster or the bishop of London. It was

The remains of Kilburn Priory in 1722, a print published in 1814.

resolved eventually that the abbot had the right to appoint the priest and the bishop to approve him. Kilburn Priory remained for the rest of its existence a small establishment.

MENTION OF ST BRIDE'S

Archaeological excavations have shown that St Bride's, Fleet Street, is on an ancient sacred site. The date of the original church is uncertain, but most probably it was built in the 11th century, and it is mentioned in 1134 in a grant of forges to the Templars. The combination of the dedication ('Bride' is a corruption of Bridget, the 6th-century Irish saint) and 6th-century archaeological remains has led to speculation that a Christian church existed here very much earlier, but it is more likely to have acquired its name and its building during the Viking period of the 10th and 11th centuries.

1135

POLITICAL UPHEAVAL

The death of Henry I in December brought turmoil to the country and London. The late king had only one surviving child from his marriage to Matilda (although an acknowledged 20 outside of it) and, despite the fact that he himself had ignored the primogeniture principle in seizing the throne of England, he insisted that his daughter, also called Matilda (or Maud), widow of the emperor Henry V, was his heir and successor.

As before, however, the person with the opportunity took it. Matilda was out of the country, and Stephen, Henry's favourite nephew, claimed the throne and held his coronation at Westminster Abbey on 22 December – St Stephen's Day. He was aided in this by his brother, the bishop of Winchester, and by the citizens of London, who seem to have been quite united in his cause. The reason for their preference for him can only be guessed at, but they were able to bargain for even more privileges, including the acknowledged rather than the tacit right to choose the king. Henceforth, in the tangled struggle with the empress Matilda, London was to remain loyal to Stephen.

STRATFORD LANGTHORNE ABBEY FOUNDED

This Cistercian house was founded about this year by William de Montfichet, lord of Ham. It stood by the Channelsea River at Stratford; the modern Abbey Road and Abbey Lane mark the route of the old road from West Ham village through the abbey grounds, by the abbey mill and across Stratford Marsh to the London Road. The abbey owned much of what is now East Ham and West Ham, as well as woodland in Buckhurst.

The present coat-of-arms for the London Borough of Newham includes a crozier – a reminder of the abbey's existence.

1137

FOUNDATION OF THE CHURCH OF THE HOLY SEPULCHRE

This church in Newgate Street, originally dedicated to St Edmund, was bestowed on Rahere, the prior of St Bartholomew's, who promptly appointed its first-known priest. It is suggested that its later name of the Church of the Holy Sepulchre derived from its location just outside the north-west gate of the City – like the Church of the Holy Sepulchre in Jerusalem. It became the custom for men going to the crusades to assemble here for prayer before departure. It should be noted also that the headquarters of the Knights Templar, protectors of pilgrims to Jerusalem, was then a short distance away in Holborn, and that the Saracen's Head inn was just to the west of the church until its demolition for the construction of the Holborn Viaduct.

1138

ST MARTIN WITHIN LUDGATE
This church on Ludgate Hill is first recorded about this year. Subsequently it was quite often called St Martin the Less, to differentiate it from nearby St Martin's le Grand. Unlike the other churches at the City gates, it stood within the City wall and not outside it.

FIRST MENTION OF ST MICHAEL LE QUERNE
This church stood at the western end of Cheapside, near today's underground station, and is recorded first about this year. A quern was a stone on which corn was milled, and at this location corn was sold. In front of the church, facing Cheapside, was one of the Cheapside crosses.

1140

CLERKENWELL PRIORY FOUNDED
Jordan de Bricett, who had already founded on his Clerkenwell lands the nunnery of St Mary (see 1100), about this year established a priory nearby, administered by the Knights of the Order of St John. The Knights, whose original function was the care of the sick, were closely involved in the crusades, and their work was supported by those Christian states which sent forces to the Holy Land. The order, driven out of Palestine, set up a kingdom in Rhodes, and when this fell to the Turks they retreated to Malta: Valetta, its present capital, was founded by them and was named after their Grand Master. The St John's Ambulance Brigade, which has its headquarters at St John's Gate, Clerkenwell, stems from these origins.

A document of 1338 shows that the establishment then included a cook, chamber servants, dispensers, a janitor, two millers, a slaughterer, a brewer, a pig-keeper, a laundress, an attorney, clerks and a procurator-general.

ENFIELD CHASE EMPARKED
About this year Enfield Chase was emparked – that is, fenced and reserved for the use of the lord of the manor of Enfield. As the name implies, this land, to the west of the village green, was used for hunting. It comprised 8,349 acres – more than half the parish.

THE HARROW TOWER
The tower of the church of St Mary, Harrow, was finished about this year. It now forms the lower part of the present tower and spire which today are still a landmark. The west door of the church is also of this date.

LEPER HOSPITAL FOUNDED AT ILFORD
A hospital for lepers was founded by the abbess Adeliza in what is now Ilford Broadway.

1141

LONDON UNDER SIEGE
Political events since Stephen's disputed accession to the throne impinged heavily on London this year. In 1140 Stephen had sheltered in the Tower relatively safe from the forces of the empress Matilda. But in February 1141 the king unwisely left the fortress and was captured at Lincoln. Powerful friends, including his own brother, the bishop of Winchester, deserted him and the empress was declared 'Lady of England' – in effect, queen. At Winchester, an ecclesiastical synod laid claim to the right of the Church not only to consecrate a sovereign but also to elect one – a clear breach of the right that Londoners thought was theirs.

The City sent a delegation to Winchester to plead for Stephen's release. This was hardly likely to meet with success, and instead a month of negotiation ensued between the empress and City leaders so that she might be received into London preparatory to a coronation. She arrived in London in June, but then managed to alienate the citizens by her imperious behaviour, wrought of long years of having her own way; she extorted large sums of money and refused to honour previous charters. Within days she was driven out of the City and the citizens proceeded to attack the Tower, which was under the custodianship of her ally Geoffrey de Mandeville.

De Mandeville was an unpopular figure. He had, by political acumen, achieved great wealth, including the grant of the earldom of Essex from Stephen, who had hoped to buy his support. Once the king had been captured, he sided instead with the empress, who made him sheriff of London, Middlesex and Hertfordshire – an enormously powerful and lucrative concentration of posts, and one much resented. Even worse, he was appointed constable of the Tower. It was no way to appease London. A spontaneous uprising of Londoners – what was then called in documents 'the commune' – forced the empress out of the City, leaving the way clear for the appearance in London of Stephen's queen and champion, yet another Matilda. De Mandeville switched allegiance back to the king, and more rewards followed once Stephen had been rescued. The treacherous de Mandeville was subsequently killed at the siege of Burwell in 1144.

1144

WINCHESTER HOUSE BEGUN
The bishop of Winchester, William Giffard, had already helped to establish the priory of St Mary Overie at the southern end of London Bridge (see 1106). He is also credited with establishing the town house of his see, just to the west of the priory. However, it appears that it was really founded at the instigation of King Stephen's brother, Henry of Blois, a later bishop of Winchester, who about this year bought the site.

1146

CHANGE OF NAME IN THE STRAND
The building date of the first church of St Mary le Strand is unknown. Until 1146 the church was known as Holy Innocents, but from this year it is generally known as St Mary and gradually its location is appended.

The old church was not on its present site, which was then occupied by an ancient, possibly Danish, cross. Instead it was built on the site of today's Somerset House, and remained there until the duke of Somerset demolished it in 1549.

1147

ALDGATE REBUILT

Aldgate, the east gate in the Roman wall, was rebuilt between 1108 and 1147. This structure, in the middle of Aldgate High Street, separated the City from the Portsoken outside the wall. The spelling in 1052 was 'Aestgate', and from then usually 'Alegate'; the spelling 'Aldgate', which has led people to assume it is a corruption of 'old gate', does not appear until the late 15th century.

1148

ST KATHARINE'S HOSPITAL FOUNDED

East of the Tower of London was established this year a hospital for the poor; more recently its site was that of St Katharine's Dock. It was founded at the instigation of Matilda, Stephen's queen, on 13 acres bought by her from the priory of Holy Trinity, Aldgate; on its completion the building was handed over to the priory to administer, although it continued to enjoy the patronage of the queens consort of England. Later, this area of the Portsoken acquired autonomy from the City authorities, probably because it had been settled by employees of the royal household who worked in the Tower.

1154

A PLANTAGENET CHARTER

For once the royal succession was peaceful. On the death of Stephen, Henry II, the first of the Plantagenet line, was enthroned at Westminster Abbey on 19 December.

With a proven record of making or breaking kings, the City was in a good position to bargain for privileges, but the details of a charter granted this year by the new king do not indicate much generosity on his part. Being the only legitimate successor now available, he was in a strong position, and he appears to have dampened the aspirations of those Londoners seeking autonomy within the kingdom. On the other hand it was confirmed that citizens of the City could not be tried beyond the walls, and were free from tolls outside them.

1155

WEAVERS INCORPORATED

The oldest of the City livery companies, the Weavers' Company, which had existed since at least 1130, was granted a charter of incorporation this year – the first royal charter to any craft organization known to exist. On the seal of this charter is the stamp of Thomas à Becket, archbishop of Canterbury.

1156

TOWER OF LONDON STRENGTHENED

The new king took care to strengthen fortified garrisons around the country. Among these was the Tower of London, which was restored where damaged, and enforced where weak. The work was supervised by the new chancellor, Thomas à Becket.

1157

TRADING PLACES

Foreign merchants, however unpopular with the indigenous traders, gradually established permanent quarters in the City. The wine merchants of France were here in numbers even before the Conquest; the Danes were trading with London in the 11th century, using premises by Dowgate wharf in Upper Thames Street, on a site now covered by Cannon Street station. In the 12th century, however, the most energetic foreign merchants were those from Germany. William of Malmesbury, writing in 1125, mentioned the London wharves as packed with goods of merchants coming from all countries, and especially from Germany, adding that in bad harvest years the deficiency was made up with grain from that country.

In the earlier part of the century the merchants from Cologne were predominant, and to them in 1157 the Danes sold their hall by Dowgate wharf. It is probable that both nationalities continued to use it despite the change of ownership, and equally possible that the Cologne merchants had been part users before. At this time the building was called the Haus zu Colner and later, when other German merchants began to use it, the House of Teutons.

1158

THE THAMES RUNS DRY

On an occasion this year the Thames was virtually dry at London. According to Henry Chamberlain, writing in 1770, 'there happened so remarkable a deficiency of water in the river Thames, that the citizens passed through the bed of the river on foot, without being wet'.

1159

THE TEMPLARS' WATERMILL

The Knights Templar, still established in Holborn, were granted a site this year on the east bank of the Fleet, near to its Thames outlet, on which to erect a watermill. Most probably they were permitted only to make use of the running stream, but they appear to have erected two gates on either side of the Fleet, reclaiming land on both sides in the process and otherwise encroaching on neighbouring holdings. In subsequent lawsuits the plaintiffs urged that the Fleet had always been open for navigation and that the Templars' installations prevented this. The gates were removed by the mayor himself. This was not the end of the matter, however, for as late as 1306, the earl of Lincoln was still petitioning against Templar interference with the course of the Fleet.

1161

DEVELOPMENTS IN FLEET STREET

This year the Knights Templar moved their headquarters from Holborn (see 1118) to what is now the area of the Middle and Inner Temple by the Thames. The names of the modern inns of court are derived from the circular Temple church built in this period by the Templars, part of which still remains. The architectural style is a blend of Gothic and Romanesque. At the same time a 'New Street' was constructed, now called Chancery Lane, that led from the Templars' old premises to the new. The fact that a road came into existence suggests that the transitional period between one headquarters and the other extended over quite a few years – indeed, the Temple church was not consecrated for another 24 years (see 1185).

It is likely, too, that what became Temple Bar was first established this year. Many prints exist of its last form, the splendid arch and gate built by Wren, but originally it was a simple bar of posts and chain.

Temple Bar marked the boundary of the City and Westminster, and even today the sovereign, on state occasions, is welcomed into the City at this point. This line between commercial city and royal liberty appears to have been fixed about the year 1000.

1163

PROHIBITION ON THE CLERGY

This year the Council of Tours prohibited clergy from participating in surgery, or at least in operations which were bloody. As a result, surgery became partly the province of barbers and, sometimes, smiths. This function of barbers had probably derived from Roman times, when slaves – called tonsures – dressed hair, shaved their masters, cut nails and drew teeth. They were familiar with the use of sharp instruments for such delicate operations, as were the later Christian monks. The long-established barber's pole, of red and white (one of the few surviving trade signs), represents blood drawn in venesection: older versions included a blood-letting cup beneath.

In London, members of the Barber-Surgeons' Company were responsible for surgery until the surgeons broke away in the 18th century.

A SHRINE TO EDWARD THE CONFESSOR

The supposedly monk-like and pious life of Edward the Confessor attracted many admirers, including a later prior of Westminster Abbey, Osbert of Clare, who promoted the cause of the canonization of the Confessor to the pope. The matter was delayed by the pontiff for some years while proof of miracles or other evidence which would warrant canonization was sought.

A favourable response would be financially advantageous to the abbey – a shrine, with all the revenue and donations that it would attract, was much to be desired. The Confessor was canonized in 1161, and a shrine was erected in the abbey. Henry II, who must have been just as anxious to have Edward canonized, since it enhanced his own descent from the king, was present at the service of translation administered by Thomas à Becket on 13 October 1163.

FIRST MENTION OF ST DUNSTAN IN THE WEST

Although the first record of this church in Fleet Street appears this year, its dedication to the 9th-century abbot of Glastonbury implies that it

was a Saxon foundation, since the Norman archbishop of Canterbury, Lanfranc, forbade new churches from being named after Saxon saints. There were, at this time, two churches dedicated to St Dunstan in the City – this one, in the far west, and the other near the Tower, which is now a ruin from the last war.

William Tyndale, the translator of a controversial version of the New Testament, was curate here in the 16th century, and Pepys occasionally worshipped in the old building before it was destroyed in the Great Fire; it was here during divine service that he 'stood by a pretty, modest maid, whom I did labour to take by the hand and body' until he 'could perceive her to take pins out of her pocket to prick me if I should touch her again'.

1169

A NEW WOODEN BRIDGE

It is not clear if London Bridge was destroyed or merely damaged in the fire of 1133. However, a complete rebuilding in elmwood began in about 1163 and was completed this year. Its architect was Peter of Colechurch, a chaplain of St Mary Colechurch.

Archaeological evidence shows that the Roman bridge ran from the site of Hay's Wharf, where two important roads converged, to roughly that of St Magnus church. The next reference to a bridge here comes in the time of King Edgar (957–75), when it is noted that a woman accused of witchcraft was thrown from the bridge to her death. In 1010–14 the bridge is described as so broad that two wagons could pass each other; it had towers and parapets, and was supported by piles driven into the bed of the river.

1170

PRISONERS FOR THE FLEET

Although the first mention by name of the infamous Fleet Prison is not until 1197, a document from this year relates to prisoners evidently intended for incarceration there. In fact there is strong evidence for the prison's existence by 1130, and certainly by 1155. It stood on the east bank of the Fleet, between Seacoal Lane and Ludgate Hill, surrounded by a moat.

ST MARY AXE

The derivation of the name of this church, a building first mentioned about this year, is an unusual one. An earlier dedication was to St Mary the Virgin, St Ursula and the Eleven Thousand Virgins – a reference to an unlikely legend of a large number of maidens setting sail from England in the 5th century only to die at the hands of three axe-wielding executioners under the command of Attila the Hun. One of the relics held by the church was one of the supposed axes. This church disappeared in the 16th century, but its title survives in the street name.

1174

THE FITZSTEPHEN ACCOUNT

The first general account of London was written about this year, although it was not generally known until John Stow published it in the

16th century in his *Survey of London*. It was extracted from the preface to a biography of Thomas à Becket written by the secretary and admirer of the archbishop, William Fitzstephen (d. 1190?).

Fitzstephen's work helps to reconstruct the atmosphere of London at the time, even if it is sometimes vague on specifics. He tells us, for example, about an early restaurant centre: 'Besides, there is in London upon the River's Bank a public Place of Cookery, among the Wines to be sold in the shops, and in the Wine Cellars. There every day you may call for any dish of Meat, roast, fryed or sodden … ' And those who have nothing in the cookpot when unexpected guests call he advises to 'let the servants give them water to wash, and Bread to stay their Stomach, and, in the mean time, they run to the water side, where all things that can be desired are at hand'.

His account lists the sports and entertainments available, the jousting, archery, boar-fighting and bull-baiting. He describes the excitement of Moorfields when that waterlogged area is frozen over; here there is a description of an early skateboard: 'Men go to sport upon the Ice: then fetching a Run, and setting their feet at a distance, and placing their Bodies sideways, they slide a great Way.'

He also touches upon the water supplies of London, including the famous Clerks' Well (from which the name 'Clerkenwell' is derived). This well, by the south-west wall of the nunnery of St Mary, was an occasional venue of the parish clerks, who performed plays around it. It was still used early in the 19th century, but by 1857 it was covered over and its site, off Farringdon Road, was forgotten until workmen came upon it in the 1920s.

Fitzstephen informs us that there were 126 churches and 13 conventual churches in the City and the wards outside the wall. Some of the churches were Saxon foundations, but most likely the rest were the product of an affluent Norman era in which leading citizens felt bound to leave their mark.

Smithfield Market is described:

Without one of the Gates is a certain Field smooth both in Name and Situation. Every Friday, except some greater Festival come in the way, there is a brave sight of gallant Horses to be sold. Many come out of the City to buy or look on, to wit, Earls, Barons, and Knights, Citizens, all resorting thither. It is a pleasant Sight there to behold the Nags well fleshed sleik and shining, delightfully walking, and their Feet on either Side up and down together by turns. In another part stand the Country People with Cattle and Commodities of the Field, large Swine and Kine with their Udders strutting out, fair-bodied Oxen, and the woolly flock. There are also Cart-Horses, fit for the Dray, the Plough, or the Chariot.

1176

NEW LONDON BRIDGE BEGUN

Work began on building a stone bridge across the Thames. This structure, designed and supervised by the priest, Peter of Colechurch, was to last into the 19th century, one of the most picturesque sights of the city. Some notable bridges were begun in this era. The 23-arch bridge across the Rhône at Avignon is contemporaneous, as is Elvet Bridge at Durham, and Bow Bridge had been built some years earlier. Even so, the priest's enterprise, a bridge across 900 ft of tidal water, was a considerable innovation which took 33 years to complete.

The line of the bridge was slightly east of the present structure, seemingly the same as that of the wooden bridge it replaced. There were 19 arches and an opening of about 28 ft in the southern half

spanned by a drawbridge; the carriageway was 20 ft wide, and it rose slightly in the centre to a height of just over 30 ft above low-water level. The placing of the foundations must have presented considerable problems. Coffer dams were unknown, and the foundations would have had to be secured at low tide from floating barges; throughout the centuries the openings between the piers were gradually reduced as more and more strengthening was added to the bases.

Towards the centre of the bridge was built a chapel dedicated to St Thomas à Becket – not only had he recently been canonized, but Becket had been baptized at the architect's own church, St Mary Colechurch.

Peter of Colechurch did not live to see the completion of the bridge, although most of it was finished when he died in 1205. He was buried in the crypt of the chapel on the bridge: his bones were discovered by workmen demolishing the structure in 1832 and, it seems, were disposed of in the river.

1177

JEWISH BURIAL GROUND OPENED

A Jewish burial ground was opened in what became Jewin Street just outside the London Wall, an area now covered by the Barbican development. It was to be in use for only 100 years. The increasing hostility of the London population to Jews resulted in their expulsion in 1290, and the burial ground was built over in the 16th century.

1181

FIRST MENTION OF LOTHBURY

This street appears about this year as 'Lodebury'. The derivation of its name is not certain, but the most satisfactory suggestions are that the street was home to a man called Loda, or else that that the name came from a 'lode', i.e. a channel or drain, leading into the river Walbrook.

THE JEWS' QUARTER

Earliest mention is made of 'The Jewry' this year, in a document relating to the church of St Olave in what is now Old Jewry. The Jews, who settled in numbers after the Conquest, mainly occupied the area stretching from Lothbury to Wood Street and Milk Street, north of Cheapside.

ST PETER-LE-POER

The last manifestation of this church in Broad Street was not demolished until 1907. It first appears in records of 1181 as St Peter in Bradstrete, and it was not until the 16th century that it acquired the appendage of le Poer or Poor.

1183

THE HOLBORN BARS

In this year first mention is made of the Holborn Bars, which marked the western boundary of the City. Initially a simple contraption of posts and rails, they were positioned just east of the junction with Gray's Inn Road, opposite Staple Inn. The 18th-century bars appear in Hogarth's *Seven Stages of Cruelty*. Two granite obelisks now replace them.

The road is quite wide here, by old London standards. Middle Row, a group of low-standard houses, used to occupy the centre of the roadway just west of the bars, causing congestion both sides of it. This impediment to traffic was cleared away in the 19th century.

ST LAWRENCE JEWRY

First mention is made about this year of the church of St Lawrence Jewry near the Guildhall, although it was probably a Saxon foundation. By the end of the 13th century the patronage was in the hands of Balliol College, Oxford. The present building is the guild church of the Corporation of London.

1184

A VISIT FROM NOTABLES

Ostensibly on a pilgrimage, but actually on business for the German emperor, Philip, archbishop of Cologne, and Philip, count of Flanders, visited London this year. This was an early occasion when the visit of foreign luminaries prompted the City authorities to clean the streets and decorate houses.

1185

THE PATRIARCH IN LONDON

London received a visit from Heraclius, the patriarch of Jerusalem, this year. He consecrated two churches: that of the Knights Templar off Fleet Street, and that of the Knights Hospitaller (Knights of St John) in Clerkenwell. These two organizations were of importance to him since their work revolved around the success or support of crusaders.

1188

NEWGATE PRISON FOUNDED

A document of about this year records the purchase of land adjacent to Newgate for the purpose of building a jail, and there is evidence that by the following century the gatehouse over the actual gate was also being used for prisoners. The land bought was on the south side of the gate, and gradually, with successive rebuildings, it was extended southward on the area called the old bailey – land between fortifications outside the City Wall.

1189

RICHARD I CROWNED

The people of England were unfortunate enough to have Richard I, or 'the Lionheart', as he is romantically called, for their next king. He was the third son of Henry II, the other two having predeceased him. He had been so unpopular with his father that the king had threatened to disinherit him three years previously for his disorderly conduct. Of the ten years of his reign, Richard spent about six months in England. The rest were spent abroad participating in the crusades, for which he

exacted heavy taxation from the luckless English. In his absence the bishop of Ely, William Longchamp – a man loathed by the population for his extortion – ruled as chancellor.

The coronation of Richard at Westminster Abbey on 3 September was an extravagant but not an auspicious occasion. Apart from the reported incident of a bat flying around the head of the new king as he sat on his throne, the occasion ended disastrously in the killing of Jews. Despite a proclamation that no Jews should be present at the ceremony, some had come with conciliatory gifts for the new king, and the mob set upon them. Some were murdered, and anti-Jewish riots continued elsewhere, particularly in Lincoln and York. The Jews, made wealthy by the only occupation they were permitted – usury – were an easy target, and in the prevailing religious fever, which had the capture of Jerusalem as its goal, they were the nearest infidels to hand in the country.

THE FIRST MAYOR OF LONDON

Debate continues to this day about the first appointment of a mayor for London, but the Corporation celebrated the 800th anniversary in November 1989, with some degree of confidence in its own research.

It is thought that before this year the City was administered by groups of leading citizens. From about 1190 a pattern emerges of sheriffs elected in pairs with, above them, a head citizen called a mayor. The first mayor of whom we have record is Henry FitzAilwin, appointed this year and still mayor in 1212, the year of his death. His name is English, and that is about as much as we know about him for certain. He presided over a tumultuous period.

1190

THE TOWER EXPANDED

Work began this year on the westward expansion of the Tower of London, under the supervision of William Longchamp. No doubt the chancellor had an eye to the possibility of armed revolt by the king's brother, John, and in this judgement he was correct, for in the following year London and the kingdom entered into one of their unhappier periods.

Longchamp, to the dismay of the City, doubled the size of the Tower precincts. He also constructed a moat west and north of the building, and by breaching the Roman wall in the north-east corner he carried the water round to another ditch constructed on the east side of the wall. In this he encroached upon land belonging to the hospital of St Katharine.

1191

LONDON UNDER SIEGE

With the king away, there developed an inevitable clash between the unpopular Longchamp and John, the king's brother, the latter posing as the people's saviour. John arrived from France early in the year, and Longchamp, fearing a disadvantageous meeting, repaired to London. On 7 October he addressed a gathering of leading citizens, urging the City to support the king against John, whom he denounced as about to usurp the Crown. Longchamp was not the best advocate for the king, and the citizens were divided in their loyalty. With rebellion in the wind, the chancellor fled to the Tower, leaving the people of London to admit John or not. They did so on 7 October, but at a price.

Longchamp fell, and John, acting as head of the kingdom rather than king, granted the City 'commune' status and confirmed London's corporate rights. The City, for its part, swore fealty to the king and to John as his successor. Oddly, the City has no charter of incorporation, although the privileges extracted in this period were the basis for the charters of numerous other English towns and cities in the future.

St Mary Woolnoth

Earliest mention is made of this church in Lombard Street this year. The usually accepted derivation of its name is that it comes from a Saxon with the family name of Wulfnoth: in 12th-century records a Wulfnoth de Walebroc (the river Walbrook is nearby) appears. The old building was rebuilt *c.* 1438.

1193

First Kingston Bridge

The first bridge upstream from the City was built of wood by this year at Kingston upon Thames. The town was an important one, built on a site where the river could be forded – the earliest name of the settlement was Moreford, 'the Great Ford'. Several Saxon kings were crowned or 'hallowed' here, and the coronation stone is still in the market place. A charter of AD 946 mentions Kingston as a 'royal town where consecration is accustomed to be performed'. It was important enough to warrant a charter from King John in 1200.

1194

Cologne Privileges

German traders who operated from the guildhall of the Cologne merchants, or the Steelyard as it was later known, on the site of Cannon Street station, were this year granted a charter by Richard I which freed them of rent for their hall (the freehold belonged to the Crown) and enabled them to trade throughout the kingdom. Unusually, they had the obligation – inherited it seems from the Danes, the previous owners of the hall – to contribute in large measure to the upkeep of Bishopsgate.

A King's Ransom

The king's adventures in the crusades were of storybook material: famous battles, massacres by both sides, great bravery and then ignominy – when returning home, he was shipwrecked and had to make his way through Austria disguised as a menial. There he was captured and put up for ransom by the emperor for 150,000 marks, which English taxpayers (particularly Londoners) paid. On his release this year the king made one of his rare visits to England, attended a service at St Paul's to give thanks for his release, had himself crowned again – this time at Winchester – and promptly went back abroad, leaving behind him a country ravaged by his taxation.

1196

Uproar in the City

The extortionate ransom paid to free the king in 1194 had consequences this year. The money had been raised by taxation – unfair taxation, if we

are to believe the allegations of William FitzOsbert, a demagogue who led a popular revolt against the method of gathering it. His accusation was that the elite who ran the City had shifted the burden to the poorer taxpayers, leaving themselves relatively unchastened.

The small shopkeepers, the craftsmen, flocked to hear FitzOsbert denounce the civic fathers. The movement inevitably led to skirmishes with the authorities, and in one of these FitzOsbert killed one of the king's men and, instead of seizing the moment to enlist popular support, withdrew to the church of St Mary-le-Bow in Cheapside, where he and his friends claimed the right of sanctuary. In this instance, ecclesiastical niceties were ignored and the justiciar of London promptly smoked the dissidents out. FitzOsbert was dragged in agony from a horse's tail all the way through the City to the Tower. He and his fellow agitators were executed at Smithfield on 6 April.

First Mention of St James Garlickhythe

This church in Garlick Hill is first noted this year as being near the vintners' part of London – the association with garlic does not begin until the late 13th century. It is a reminder that garlic was a conspicuous ingredient in English cooking then – used, like spices, to flavour or disguise the taste of old meat. Garlic and wine probably arrived on the same ships, which explains the topographical relationship between the two products in this part of London.

1197

The Beginnings of Lambeth Palace

Lambeth Palace, the London home of the archbishop of Canterbury, had its origins this year in the acquisition by the archbishop of the manor of Lambeth. He had already, in 1190, bought some adjacent land on which to found a college of secular canons – a project which did not materialize. The site included the manor house by the river Thames, and it was here after a few years that construction of the original palace began. Nothing of this first building now survives.

Hospital Founded

St Mary's Spital was founded this year on the east side of Bishopsgate. Recent excavations have shown that it was north of today's Spital Square and south of Folgate Street. Its extensive grounds stretched a little further north, and east to today's Commercial Street to include the site of Spitalfields Market, and south beyond today's Bishopsgate Institute. 'Spital' was the old word for 'hospital', and it is remembered in the place names Spitalfields and Spital Square.

1199

King John's Coronation

The nation was rescued from the taxation necessary to fuel Richard's military fervour only to be plunged into years of disorder caused by a war against the French and internal rebellion by the barons under the despotic monarchy of his brother, John. Already assured of the throne when Richard died on 6 April, he arrived from France in London on 26 May; his coronation took place at Westminster Abbey the following day. During his brief reign John was to be crowned on four different occasions.

1200

THE FIRST CHURCH OF ST MARYLEBONE

The earlier name of the parish of St Marylebone was 'Tyburn', from the river which ran through it (though not, incidentally, beneath or particularly near the site of the famous gallows). Another manor, Lileston (Lisson), to the west, made up the rest of the parish. The parish church, opened about this year, was on what is now Oxford Street, between Stratford Place and Marylebone Lane, and was then dedicated to St John. Only in 1400, when its replacement, dedicated to St Mary, was opened further north on Marylebone High Street, was the parish called Marybourne.

1201

THE BEGINNINGS OF ST KATHARINE CREE

This church originated in a chapel built about this year in the church-yard of the Holy Trinity Priory in what is now Leadenhall Street. The church itself was built c. 1280.

1209

LONDON BRIDGE COMPLETED

Four years after the death of its architect, Peter of Colechurch, the first stone London Bridge was completed. Picturesque though it may have been, it was also a fortification on the Southwark side. Here there were a solid stone bastion, massive doors and a portcullis, and another gate beyond the considerable deterrent of the drawbridge.

The building of the bridge was a considerable feat of skill and tenacity. It has been suggested that an alternative course of the river was first cut on the southern side of the river where the area was marshy anyway, so that men could work on the river bed. But Sir Christopher Wren was positive that this did not happen, and that the piles were driven in at low tide.

The piers of the bridge effectively reduced the width of the river from 900 to about 500 feet – the resulting rapids were a hazard to shipping from then on, so dangerous at times that people being ferried along the river had to disembark at the bridge, walk round it, and then take another boat. William Fitzstephen, writing c. 1173 while the bridge was being built, describes the sport, of those daring enough to attempt it, of standing in a boat and hitting a target near the bridge as the current took the boat swiftly along.

It is extraordinary that the City authorities permitted the building of 'stately houses on both sides', whose bulk, several storeys high, overhung the bridge, propped up by diagonal beams. King John's grants in 1201 of 'rents and profits of the several houses which shall be erected upon the bridge' indicate that the buildings were there from an early date. By 1460 the number of tenements built on the structure numbered 129, housing cutlers, bowyers, haberdashers, jewellers and the like. The bridge became a community of its own. The chapel dedicated to St Thomas à Becket was on the ninth pier, and later, in Elizabeth's reign, Nonesuch House was built on the seventh. The Becket chapel, in which Peter of Colechurch himself was buried, was sufficiently important to have two priests and four clerks attached to it.

1210

ST HELEN'S PRIORY FOUNDED

The Benedictine priory of St Helen was founded about this year in Bishopsgate; the founder was William Fitzwilliam, son of a goldsmith. The original parish church there was added to by the construction of a parallel nave on the northern side for the nuns, and the two congregations were separated by a screen. Regulations which exist from 1460 stipulate that the nuns should not be seen during divine service. The church escaped the Great Fire, and this layout still exists. It is thought that Mincing Lane, where the nuns held property, is named from the Anglo-Saxon word for nuns, 'mynchens'.

1211

THE CITY DITCH REDUG

A protective ditch outside the City wall existed in Roman times. It is likely that it was in poor condition when work began on its reconstruction about this year; it was recut to a width of 80–90 ft, and at its most south-western point, east of Blackfriars, it was open to the Thames. Some parts of it may still be seen on a 16th-century map of London, but generally by then it had been built upon – the street Houndsditch is a reminder of one part of its route.

1212

DISASTROUS FIRE ON THE SOUTH BANK

Within three years of the completion of London Bridge a fire broke out at its Southwark end. Accounts vary as to how many people died and, indeed, sometimes the year is put at 1213, although there is agreement on 11 July. There is no doubt, however, that it was a major blaze, which also destroyed much of Borough High Street, including the church of St Mary Overie.

John Stow's account, published at the end of the 16th century, records that the fire began in Southwark, razed the church, and then spread to the bridge, on which huge crowds gathered to watch it consume the houses. Unfortunately, the fire jumped beyond them, burning houses on the bridge behind them so that people were trapped between the two blazes. Many vessels came to their aid as people clambered down the piers to the river, but there they were caught by the treacherous rapids and many boats were sunk and people drowned.

Stow suggested that about 3,000 people died. The bridge lost much of its chapel as well as many houses.

FIRST MENTION OF ST BOTOLPH WITHOUT BISHOPSGATE

The church of St Botolph just outside the old Bishopsgate is first noted in records this year. Nowadays its church and burial ground are dwarfed by Liverpool Street station and the Broadgate development.

The first church survived the Great Fire but was rebuilt in the 18th century. Buried in the original building was Sir Paul Pindar, merchant, whose house front still graces the Victoria & Albert Museum bookshop (see 1890), and christened here was Edward Alleyn, founder of Dulwich College.

1213

ST THOMAS'S REFOUNDED

Among the buildings destroyed in the Southwark fire of 1212 was the hospital of St Thomas attached to the priory by London Bridge. This year it was refounded on the east side of Borough High Street, on land of the bishop of Winchester.

No records exist of treatment of hospital patients in those early days, though the doctor of physic in Chaucer's *Canterbury Tales,* with his reliance on astronomy and astrology, may not have held sway in St Thomas's, since it was a monastic institution. We must assume that the sick lay on rushes on the floor – beds were not common until the end of the 13th century, when patients would have shared them where practicable.

1215

THE TAKING OF LONDON

A conflict between barons and king had been simmering for years and now neared its conclusion. With the king housed at the Tower of London, the citizens welcomed the barons' army through Aldgate on 24 May. The houses of royalists and Jews were attacked – the latter because they had lent money to the king. Even the Jewish burial ground in the Barbican area was desecrated. The Tower of London was besieged, and the king was forced to make concessions.

Negotiations and the signing of the famous Magna Carta took place at Runnymede, west of Staines, in June. The barons celebrated with a jousting tournament at Hounslow shortly after. This was a premature relaxation, for the king reneged on the charter and, with the pope's blessing, took on foreign mercenaries and prepared for war again.

CITY GATES REBUILT

John Stow records that two of the City gates, Ludgate and Aldgate, were rebuilt this year. Ludgate, in the west, was reconstructed using stones taken from Jewish houses. There is a myth, which survives in the mouths of some London tourist guides to this day, that Ludgate was first built by King Lud in 66 BC – a belief perpetuated by statues of this imaginary king and his two sons placed here in Elizabethan times. However, the City wall at this point (just east of Old Bailey on Ludgate Hill) dates from the Roman building of AD 200, and this is the likely construction date for Ludgate too.

1216

THE DAUPHIN RECEIVED IN LONDON

It is a measure of the high feeling of the time that the high taxation, broken promises, resentment by the nobles and outrage felt by Londoners and others at their treatment by the king all led the barons, supported by London, at this point to offer the crown of England to Louis, dauphin of France, if he could defeat John. The dauphin, with such a prize in sight, swiftly arrived in England with a large army and was received in London in June. If this desperate step had succeeded in uniting the thrones of England and France it would have had quite unpredictable results. As it happened, John conveniently died in October, and the barons and Londoners lost their enthusiasm for the

French connection. To the chagrin of Louis, the English barons championed instead the legal claim of John's nine-year-old son, Henry.

FIRST MENTION OF ST BENET FINK

This church in Threadneedle Street, first mentioned in records this year, derived its odd name, Stow thought, from Robert Fink or Finch, who paid for its erection. Certainly there was a family of that name in the parish in this period – nearby Finch Lane was originally called Fynkeslane.

1217

THE NEW REIGN'S TROUBLES

While the barons deserted the expectant dauphin and swore allegiance to the young Henry, Londoners remained loyal to the Frenchman – a reason, perhaps, why Henry III had been crowned at Gloucester the previous year and not at Westminster.

The impasse was resolved by a major battle at Lincoln, in which the dauphin received a heavy defeat. Two prisoners taken by the king's forces were prominent London barons – Robert Fitzwalter, whose Baynard's Castle had been destroyed on the orders of King John in 1213, and Richard de Montfichet, who owned the fortified tower adjoining the castle. Louis retired to London to await reinforcements, virtually a prisoner in his new country, but in vain. The French fleet was intercepted in the Channel, and London was invested and threatened with starvation.

On 11 September a meeting between the warring parties was held at either Staines or Kingston. The dauphin withdrew his claims to the throne and escaped excommunication from the pope, and Henry, who had little choice at his age, swore to restore to barons and people the liberties that had been neglected during the reign of his father. London was pardoned for choosing the wrong side, although a pro-Louis faction survived and made its presence felt occasionally in later years.

ST MARTIN OUTWICH

This church, which stood in Threadneedle Street at the junction with Bishopsgate, is first mentioned in a record of about this date. The appendage to the dedication appears to be related to a family – particularly to Martin de Ottewich, whose widow had land in the parish about this date – but it is unclear if the family name derived from the church or vice versa.

The church escaped the Great Fire but, damaged in the Cornhill blaze of 1765, was taken down in 1796; it was rebuilt, but was demolished in 1874. Among the medieval bones moved to Ilford Cemetery at this time were those of Abigail Vaughan, who had left four shillings to the parish to buy faggots to burn heretics.

1219

ST MICHAEL PATERNOSTER ROYAL

The earliest clear mention of this church in College Hill occurs this year.

The name contains references to two trades in the area: the selling of paternosters or rosaries, in Paternoster Lane, and the importing and trading in wine from the Gascony town of La Reole. The church was occasionally called Tower Royal – a reference to a nearby house, Tower

Medieval London

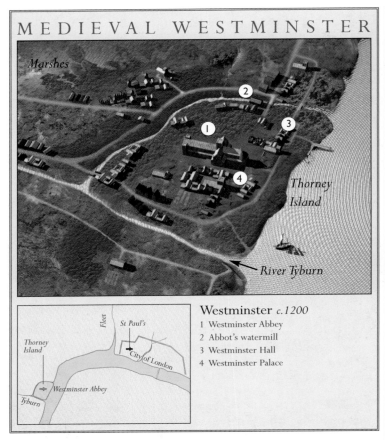

Marshes

Thorney Island

River Tyburn

Westminster c.1200

1 Westminster Abbey
2 Abbot's watermill
3 Westminster Hall
4 Westminster Palace

Fleet
St Paul's
Thorney Island
City of London
Westminster Abbey
Tyburn

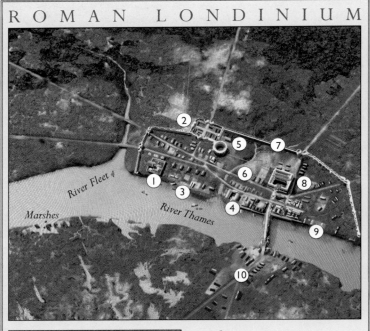

River Fleet

Marshes

River Thames

Londinium c. AD 250

1 Religious precinct
2 Fort
3 Huggin Hill bathhouses
4 Governor's palace
5 Amphitheatre
6 Temple of Mithras
7 Fortified wall
8 Basilica and forum
9 Billingsgate bathhouses
10 Southwark

LONDON 2000

LONDINIUM 250

River Fleet

St Paul's Wharf

marshes and mudflats

MEDIEVAL CITY OF LONDON

The reconstruction above shows the growth of London inside the original Roman walls.

By 1210 St Paul's spire had risen 450 ft above a city with a population of 10,000 and 100 churches, convents, priories and monasteries, as well as 5 hospitals.

1 St Giles-in-the-Fields Hospital
2 House of the Knights Templar
3 St Bride's, Fleet Street
4 Fleet prison
5 Ludgate
6 Baynard's Castle
7 Montfichet Tower
8 St Martin within Ludgate
9 St Mary's nunnery
10 Church of the Holy Sepulchre
11 Newgate

Riole, built in the 14th century with a tower on the site of premises occupied by the merchants.

THE EARLY BARKING MARKET
The village of Barking, in Essex, was an important one, with the most prominent nunnery in the kingdom and a flourishing fishing trade. This year the first mention occurs of a market, owned by the abbess of Barking.

1220

THE TOWER EXPANDS
The stability of the new reign was uncertain. There were still rebellious barons, the king was a minor, and the regent had just died. This situation probably inspired a decade of refortification and expansion at the Tower of London. Most importantly, the eastern boundary, the old Roman wall, was demolished and land was taken so that a new curtain wall could be constructed. The present Wardrobe Tower to the east of the White Tower marks the old eastern boundary. The precincts were also expanded by the introduction of a new wall to the north and north-west. The Wakefield (then called Blundeville) Tower was built, and probably the Lanthorn Tower was begun; the line marked today by the Devereux, Flint, Bowyer, Martin, Constable, Broad Arrow and Salt towers delineates the expansion of this period. Also, at this stage the church of St Peter ad Vincula was brought within the walls of the Tower.

DEVELOPMENTS AT THE ABBEY
The new king laid the foundation stone of the new Lady Chapel at Westminster Abbey – a project begun by the monks, and in particular Abbot Richard of Barking.

1221

THE BLACK FRIARS COME TO LONDON
Thirteen Dominican Black Friars arrived in England on 6 August, to a welcome at Canterbury and then at London and Oxford. It is not clear which year they settled in London, but their residence was confirmed in 1224. They occupied ground on the east side of Shoe Lane, at the top end, virtually opposite St Andrew's Holborn, granted them by chief justiciar Hubert de Burgh. Here they remained until 1278.

STEEPLE FINISHED AT ST PAUL'S
Since the fire of 1087 work had continued on the rebuilding of St Paul's, and this year, about 130 years later, the steeple was completed. The church was not completed or rededicated for another 20 years.

1222

RIOT IN LONDON
Two different accounts exist of a serious civil disturbance occurring in London this year. The first attributes it to a wrestling match between citizens of Westminster and the City, held on 25 July near the leper hospital of St Giles-in-the-Fields. The Londoners won easily and a return match

was fixed for 1 August, when armed Westminster supporters beat up those from London. After licking their wounds the Londoners sallied forth again, under the leadership of one Constantine, and wrecked the premises of the convent of St Peter at Westminster Abbey. For this, Constantine was executed by the City justiciar.

Another chronicler gives a different version – this time a political one. The arguments which had raged at the time of the succession of Henry III were still not over. The City, champions of the dauphin of France, had reluctantly settled for Henry, but there was still a party in the dauphin's favour. One of its leaders, Constantine FitzAthulf, caused a riot at a tournament by proclaiming his allegiance to Louis and, despite a large offer of money to save him, was executed by the City authorities.

It is impossible now to arrive at the truth, but both versions imply hostility between the people of the City and those of Westminster and the court.

WESTMINSTER TRUNCATED
A decretal this year resolved a dispute between the abbot of Westminster and the bishop of London. The boundaries of Westminster were more exactly defined; as a result, St Clement Danes was made a separate parish and the area of Farringdon Without was officially made part of the City. The judgement also provides the first record of a chapel which grew into the church of St Martin-in-the-Fields; this was excluded from the parish of St Margaret, Westminster, and remained under the jurisdiction of the abbey.

ST FAITH'S CHURCH
This small church in St Paul's churchyard served quite a large parish, stretching from the north of St Paul's to Newgate Street. It continued to do so even after 1256, when, because of the extension of the cathedral, the church was demolished and put underground into the eastern crypt of St Paul's. In 1551 it was moved once again, this time to a chapel elsewhere in the crypt, but this was lost during the Great Fire. The location of the earlier underground church is shown by a brass strip in the present crypt.

The earliest record of it this year describes it in its original site as 'St Faith's by St Paul's'.

1223

THE BEGINNINGS OF WHITEHALL
Whitehall is now a wide, monumental road leading from Trafalgar Square to Parliament Square. In medieval times it consisted of an upper stretch called Charing Cross leading down to King Street, which itself ended at the Palace of Westminster and the abbey. This year, in the area now taken by Whitehall Place and Horse Guards Avenue on the eastern side, the chief justiciar, Hubert de Burgh, acquired some buildings which were later to be transformed into a palace for the archbishop of York and, in the time of Henry VIII, into Whitehall Palace.

1225

GREY FRIARS ESTABLISHED IN LONDON
Nine Franciscan friars, sent by St Francis of Assisi, reached England in 1224; five remained at Canterbury and four came on to London, where

they lodged for 15 days in Holborn, then at a house in Cornhill. In 1225 they were granted some land in Newgate Street on which to establish a priory. Their extensive grounds eventually bordered on Newgate Street to the south, St Bartholomew's Hospital to the north, St Martin's le Grand on the east, and the City wall on the west; the present Christchurch is on the site of the choir of the priory church.

In front of the priory, in the middle of Newgate Street, was a meat market called The Shambles, renowned for its smells and grisly sights. Facing the street, too, was St Nicholas Shambles, a church which excavations show to have been an 11th-century foundation.

Law Courts Fixed in London

The king's law courts often travelled with him, and although the tendency was for them to be based in London, it was by no means the custom. This year it was agreed that they should be fixed in Westminster, and they have remained in that city ever since, though the present law courts in the Strand are as near as it is possible to be to the City boundary.

1226

Chichester Inn

About this year the bishop of Chichester, Ralph Nevill, acquired land on both sides of the New Street (Chancery Lane) on which to build his London residence. The site of the inn and its grounds on the west are now taken up by part of Lincoln's Inn, Bishop's Court and Chichester Rents, while the bishop's garden on the east is the land bounded on the south by Cursitor Street.

1227

Fleet Street

The road leading from the City to Westminster is undoubtedly one of the oldest in London. Beginning at Ludgate on the west of the old Roman wall, it crossed the river Fleet by a stone bridge and later joined the Strand at a point where the City and Westminster eventually shared their boundaries. The name 'Strand' reminds us that the Thames shoreline was much nearer that road than it is today. The road then turned south, following the bend of the river, at today's Charing Cross, a name deriving from the Old English word 'cierring', meaning 'bend' or 'turning', and the cross erected by Edward I after 1290 in memory of his queen, Eleanor.

Fleet Street was known in 1227 as 'In vico de Fletebrigge'. By 1274 it had its present name.

The First Jewish Synagogue

A grant of land this year mentions the first recorded Jewish synagogue. It stood in Ironmonger Lane, off Cheapside, very near Thomas à Becket's house.

Seacoal Lane

Seacoal Lane (in recent years renamed Limeburner Lane) was once a slightly mysterious road off Ludgate Hill. Its name, first mentioned this year, and that of nearby Old Seacoal Lane, suggest that coal for London was landed hereabouts on the banks of the Fleet.

1230

Shelter at Charing Cross

An Augustinian priory situated at Rouncevalles, in Navarre, about this year established an English house at the eastern corner of the Strand and Whitehall. One purpose of St Mary Rouncevale's Hospital, as it was called, was to give shelter to pilgrims on their way to the shrine of Edward the Confessor, but it was also there to gather alms for the parent priory, frequently by the outrageous sale of indulgences – Chaucer dwells at length on the 'gentil pardoner of Rouncival'. The establishment was closed during the reign of Richard II.

1231

Isleworth Market Established

A market was granted to the lord of the manor of Isleworth this year, although it seems to have functioned for only a short while. The grant is probably related to the king's gift of this manor to his brother Richard, earl of Cornwall, four years earlier. The Domesday Book calls the manor Gristlesworde, and it included Heston and Twickenham. During Richard's time a new manor house was built, close to the present Duke of Northumberland pub, and a new chapel. In 1264, during yet another phase of conflict between Crown and barons, a force of men led by the latter went to Isleworth and here wrecked the manor house and its watermills.

1232

A House for Jewish Converts

Anti-Jewish feeling was rife in London. Not only did the indigenous population resent them for religious reasons, but additionally there was a fever of antagonism against foreigners generally. This was exacerbated in the case of the Jews because they were able to lend money for profit – an occupation forbidden to Christians. Although there were few Jews in London before the Conquest, their presence was common from the time of William I, particularly in an area south of the Guildhall. As a source of money to be borrowed at critical periods, they were under the protection of the king, but they were taxed heavily for their privileges.

This year a house was established on the site of the present Public Record Office to accommodate Jews who had converted to Christianity. This establishment, called the Domus Conversorum, was run by Carthusians.

The Chief Justice on the Run

The career of the chief justiciar, Hubert de Burgh, had spanned turbulent times. He had supported King John and then the succession of his young son, Henry III. With the regent dead, de Burgh became the chief man in the land and enriched himself and his relations without stint. He was resented by Londoners for his brutal treatment of the ringleaders of the riots of 1222, and he was detested by barons, who felt that he was not of sufficient social class, and by foreigners whose influence he worked hard to eradicate.

While he retained the king's loyalty all was well, but Henry III was becoming increasingly his own man, however inadequate that was.

A turning point in de Burgh's fortunes came in 1229, when the fleet which was to take the king on a foolhardy attack on France was found to be badly organized and for this de Burgh was blamed. He continued in office but increasingly without the support of the king – so much so that this year Henry invited complaints to be heard about him. De Burgh fled to Merton Priory, where he claimed sanctuary, and the king urged London to send men to go and get him out, dead or alive. A force of 20,000 men, if we are to believe the chronicles, set out from London, but the king had second thoughts and allowed de Burgh to surrender of his own accord and answer the charges.

De Burgh's subsequent life was full of incident until, surprisingly, he died a natural death. He was buried in Blackfriars Convent, a house he had generously endowed. His own house in Whitehall was eventually the home of the archbishop of York and, later, the king's palace in Westminster.

1233

PARISH CLERKS LICENSED
It is an established tradition that the Fraternity of Clerks (which became the Company of Parish Clerks) was licensed this year, though no evidence supports this other than a reference in the 1633 edition of Stow's *Survey of London* to this effect. More certainly the company was in existence in 1274 and received a charter in 1442. Membership was restricted to the parish clerks of London, and today it is still confined to the 150 parishes that qualify.

1235

BEGINNINGS OF THE TOWER MENAGERIE
One of the sights of London for hundreds of years was the Tower menagerie. Its genesis has been usually thought to have been the gift to the king this year of three leopards, from the emperor Frederick II. However, recent research suggests that King John brought exotic animals to London in 1204 and possibly housed them in the Tower.

1236

FRESH WATER TO THE CITY
As London grew, its water requirements exceeded the capacity of the more local wells and springs. This year the City obtained permission to tap the Tyburn springs at what is now Stratford Place, off Oxford Street, 'for the profit of the City and good of the whole realm thither repairing, to wit for the poor to drink, and the rich to dress their meat'. For some distance the lead pipes followed the Tyburn and then cut across by Piccadilly to Charing Cross and then along Fleet Street to Cheapside. The main obstacle on this route, never satisfactorily overcome, was the deep depression of the Fleet valley at Ludgate. At this point the pipe crossed the Fleet bridge on the site of today's Ludgate Circus – mention is made of a repair here in 1350.

A SNUB TO THE MAYOR
Henry III, with his new queen, Eleanor of Provence, was crowned again at Westminster Abbey. This time the City celebrated, but the day was not without its problems, for the king declined to allow the mayor, Andrew Bukerel, to perform the traditional duties of the mayor of London at the coronation ceremony.

JEWS TAKE REFUGE IN THE TOWER
Anti-Jewish feeling vented itself once more. The Jewish community took shelter in the Tower of London.

ST LEONARD'S, FOSTER LANE, BUILT
St Leonard's was built or rebuilt on the west side of Foster Lane about this year. It was a small building and parish, and may well have been founded by the nearby conventual house of St Martin's le Grand to serve as a parish church for that precinct as well. It was one of the churches burnt in the Great Fire, and was not replaced.

1237

FIRST PUBLIC LAVATORY REPAIRED
Near Queenhithe, which from the time of Henry I was a possession of the queen, a public lavatory had been erected at the expense of Matilda for the 'common use of citizens'. In 1237 it was repaired, and there is a record in 1314 of one Alice Wade appearing in court for connecting her own privy via a wooden pipe with the drain which took rain water to clean the Queenhithe latrines.

1240

ST PAUL'S REDEDICATED
Still incomplete, the new St Paul's was at last rededicated by the bishop of London, in the presence of the archbishop of Canterbury and six bishops.

Sir William Dugdale, writing eight years before it was destroyed in the Great Fire of 1666, said, 'I have thought fit in the first place to begin with the church of St. Paul, as one of the most eminent structures of that kind in the Christian World.' It was a most remarkable building, said to be able to hold the whole of the population of London at the time. Larger and much higher than the present cathedral, it was 596 ft long and 104 ft wide (excluding transepts) and stood on over 3 acres; the top of the spire was 489 ft from the ground.

The spire, damaged by lightning in 1444 and destroyed in a fire of 1561, was by far the tallest which existed and, had it survived, would have been the tallest building in England well into the 20th century. It attracted exhibitionists and suicides alike. At the coronation of Queen Mary in 1553, one man climbed to the top of the weathervane to wave a flag.

The central tower was open to the base of the spire, and there were two bell towers on the west side. The nave had twelve bays, and a Lady chapel was at the east end. In the crypt below the choir was the parish church of St Faith, whose site the new cathedral had taken. The rose window in St Katharine Cree church is said to be a copy of that in old St Paul's.

MORE CHURCH COMPLETIONS
The year was notable also for the culmination of the building of three other outstanding churches. The nave of St Bartholomew the Great in

Smithfield was completed, and the Early English choir of the Temple church off Fleet Street was finished. In Southwark, the rebuilt St Mary Overie was complete.

TOWER WALL COLLAPSES

The extensions to the Tower of London ordered by the king were not popular with the City. Apart from the taxation to fund the work, the precinct had devoured land previously held by others, and the building remained an unspoken threat of royal power. It must have given some pleasure to Londoners, then, that this year the new western wall to the Tower collapsed during building operations.

DEVELOPMENTS IN WHITEHALL

This year some houses in what is now Whitehall were acquired by the archbishop of York. 'Our houses in the street of Westminster' were bought from Hubert de Burgh, chief justiciar of England. Five years later, when it became the official London residence of the see, a large house was on the site, grand enough to have a chamber for the king's use, and so extensive that it served as a meeting place for Parliament in 1360. The last archbishop to occupy it was Cardinal Wolsey, in the 16th century. He made it such a desirable residence that upon his fall from grace the covetous Henry VIII took it for his own residence under the new name of 'Whitehall'.

A WHALE IN THE THAMES

Much excitement was caused when a whale, 'a monster of prodigious size', swam beneath London Bridge, pursued by sailors armed with ropes, slings and bows. After a long fight they killed it at Mortlake.

1241

TOWER OF LONDON WHITEWASHED

The central keep building of the Tower of London was whitewashed this year. It became known, and is still, as the White Tower. This was part of a general improvement of the building, especially of the inner ward, so that it was more comfortable. In this period the Great Hall was rebuilt, and new kitchens and staff lodgings were provided. The king's own apartments were in the Wakefield Tower, and in the upper storey an oratory was included.

The orderliness of today's buildings makes it difficult to imagine what life there was like in the 13th century. Animals would have been kept and the gardens would have been intensively farmed, so that food was available in the event of siege. But during normal times traders would have come in great numbers into the inner ward to sell food, clothes and provisions. All sorts of traders – such as washerwomen, armourers, knife and sword sharpeners, physicians and barbers – would have found some living here when the king and his court were lodging.

WHITE FRIARS SETTLE IN LONDON

The Carmelites, or White Friars as they were known from their white aprons, are believed to have arrived in England on Christmas Day 1240 and to have founded their priory south of Fleet Street the following year. This colony of hermit friars had been driven out of Mount Carmel by the Saracens and were then encouraged to settle in London by the earl of Cornwall. In 1247 they obtained permission from the pope to become mendicant friars and live and work in the community.

The site of their precinct is today bounded by the Temple,

Whitefriars Street and Tudor Street; in the 18th century it became a notoriously violent area called Alsatia, and in the 20th century it was one of the main centres of newspaper production.

A cemetery was at the northern end, the priory was on an east–west axis, and the gardens went down to the Thames, with stairs to the water; there was also a mill house on the south-east side by Water Lane, an alley which led up from, and was open to, the Thames.

PAUL'S CROSS

The first clear reference to Paul's Cross occurs this year, when citizens gathered by it, in the north-east part of St Paul's churchyard, to assent to the king's departure for Gascony. The cross was a traditional site for folkmoots or general assemblies, but later it became a place of ecclesiastical importance where preachers could be sure of an audience and where papal announcements could be read.

1242

THAMES FLOODS LAMBETH

There were few defences against the Thames, and floods occurred frequently until the building of the Embankment in the 19th century. We know that extra defences were put in place at important riverside places such as Billingsgate, and terracing has been discovered (and is still apparent) at the Temple, as some sort of barrier. But Westminster Hall was frequently flooded well into the 18th century, and if such an important building was a victim then it must be assumed that the lesser landlords had neither the finance nor the expertise to repel the river.

Things were much worse on the southern side, where the land was low-lying for some distance from the shoreline; this only added to the general undesirability of the south bank. This year the Thames is reported to have broken through the banks at Lambeth and to have flooded to a distance of 6 miles.

1243

ST MARY-AT-LAMBETH TOWER COMPLETED

Despite the floods of the previous year, the completion of the wooden tower of St Mary, the parish church of Lambeth, was achieved. Today

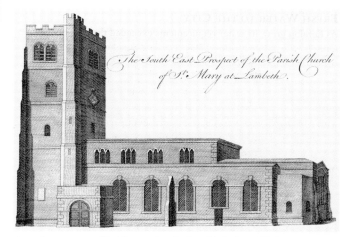

A south-east view of St Mary-at-Lambeth, published in 1756.

the church is tucked into the environs of Lambeth Palace, but in 1243 it stood virtually by itself facing the horse-ferry route across the river; most probably the local inhabitants owed much of their income to the traffic going to and from Westminster.

Despite the generally unpromising situation of low-lying Lambeth, the archbishop of Canterbury was not the only illustrious landlord. The manors of Vauxhall and Kennington, where the Black Prince once had a palace, were both owned by the king, and today much of the latter is owned by the Duchy of Cornwall.

1245

REBUILDING OF WESTMINSTER ABBEY BEGINS

Increasingly, the pious Henry III took an interest in Westminster Abbey. By 1242 goldsmiths were working on a new shrine for Edward the Confessor, the man invoked to give legitimacy to the king's occupation of the throne. But, ironically, Henry's greatest tribute to his idol was to replace the building Edward had spent so long in building. In about 1245 work began on rebuilding the abbey, overseen by Edward of Westminster and the master mason Henry of Reynes, and it is calculated that some £50,000 was spent from 1245 to 1272. Materials by the boatload arrived at Westminster from Kent and Normandy, and tin came from Cornwall, lead from Derbyshire, and Purbeck marble from Dorset. In one week of 1253 a total of 391 workers were employed in the work.

It was a huge task, and not to be finished even in the long reign of Henry III: the nave was still incomplete 11 kings later, when Henry VII was building his own chapel.

ERECTION OF THE GREAT CONDUIT

Work had begun soon after 1236 to construct water pipes to bring water to the City from the springs at today's Stratford Place, Oxford Street. About 1245 work began on building what became known as the Great Conduit in Cheapside. This stood in the middle of the road at the far east of the street, opposite Mercers' Hall, just before Poultry begins. There must have been some problem in raising the money to build it, or else the system for conveying water was slow in completion, for it appears that the conduit was not finished for 50 years. After that certain classes of trades – brewers, cooks and fishmongers, who used more water than most – were often to be found subscribing to its maintenance.

1246

THE BEGINNINGS OF THE SAVOY

Today's Savoy Hotel derives its name from the occupation of a house on its site by Peter, earl of Richmond, uncle of Henry III's queen, Eleanor. On its site by the Thames by 1189 there had existed a mansion built by Robert de Breteuil, earl of Leicester; on 12 February 1246 this was granted to Peter by the king. In 1263, when Peter had built a substantial palace in its stead, he was made count of Savoy and henceforth lived in his new principality. The house, meanwhile, retained his title.

On Savoy's death in 1263 he left his Strand property to the hospice of Great St Bernard at Montjoux in Savoie, but about seven years later the queen bought it back, so as to give it to her son, the earl of Lancaster, brother of the future Edward I.

The Savoy, as depicted by George Vertue in 1736. At that time the large rear building housed soldiers, and the building on the far left was a prison.

QUEENHITHE LEASED BY THE CITY

There were two principal harbours for the City of London in medieval times – Queenhithe, upstream from London Bridge, and Billingsgate, downstream. In time, as trading boats grew larger and the arches beneath London Bridge became smaller with the buttressing of the piers, Billingsgate took more and more of the traffic, especially the fish and coal trade.

Saxon records indicate that Queenhithe was owned by Ethelred, and this royal ownership continued with the grant of the harbour by King John to his mother, Queen Eleanor. In about this year the City leased it for a rent of £50 per annum.

1247

THE BEGINNINGS OF BEDLAM

The notorious lunatic hospital popularly called 'Bedlam' began as the priory of St Mary Bethlehem, founded this year on the later site of Liverpool Street station; the bishop-elect of Bethlehem, Godfrey de Vico, made the journey for the dedication ceremony on 23 October.

It was then a straightforward priory, founded by a sheriff of London, Simon FitzMary; a hospital there is not recorded until 1329, and the specialization in insane people is not apparent until 1403.

ROMFORD MARKET ESTABLISHED

Henry III granted a market to Romford this year, although it may well have existed before. It was open each Tuesday for hogs and calves, and on Wednesdays for corn and leather. Its descendant, the cattle market in the main street on Wednesdays, was a familiar sight until fairly recent years.

Romford sat astride the Roman road to Colchester. In medieval times it was an adjunct of the royal palace at Havering-atte-Bower, and its earlier town centre was at Oldchurch.

EARTHQUAKE IN LONDON

On 13 February 'there happened a dreadful earthquake, which threw down many of the houses in the city of London, and occasioned other considerable damage' (Henry Chamberlain in his *History of London*, 1770).

1248

WESTMINSTER FAIR ESTABLISHED

London and the king were still at loggerheads. He incensed the population even further by suspending trade in London for 15 days and obliging everyone to come to a fair he had established at Westminster.

It is likely that an annual fair was held at Westminster from Saxon times, but it was not until 1245 that the monks at Westminster Abbey obtained their first charter to hold two annual fairs, each of three days, in January and October. However, in 1248 the October fair was extended by royal command to a two-week event, and it was ordered that all other fairs held in England at this time of the year were to be suspended and all the shops in the City of London were to be closed during this fortnight. The chronicler Matthew of Paris records that this new development had two purposes: to fund the rebuilding of the abbey and to discipline the king's rebellious subjects in the City.

1250

THE DEVELOPMENT OF RUISLIP

The parish church of St Martin, Ruislip, was built about this year – the nave of that date still exists, as do a number of the older cottages at the end of the high street. The new building may well have replaced an earlier one, for the Domesday survey records a priest among the inhabitants.

The remote village had a moated manor house of Norman date, owned by the Benedictine abbey of Bec in France. Many of William I's followers donated some of their newly acquired lands to this abbey, and there was a cell of Benedictine monks in Ruislip by the 12th century.

1251

POLAR BEARS AT THE TOWER

As noted in 1235, three leopards were housed in the Tower of London. This year the king of Norway sent Henry the gift of a polar bear, together with a keeper. These too went to the Tower. The citizens of London were ordered to pay for a chain and a muzzle, and for their money they had the spectacle of watching the bear fish in the river.

1253

FOUNDATION OF AUSTIN FRIARS

Humphrey de Bohun, earl of Hereford and Essex, founded a priory of Augustinian friars this year, on the west side of Old Broad Street. Its site, now bounded by Copthall Avenue at the west, was just inside the London wall, and the church, which was rebuilt in the 14th century, was later used by Dutch settlers in London. Its successor, the Dutch Church, remains today. The passageway, Austin Friars, led from Broad Street into the conventual buildings.

The friars were of the order called Friars Hermits of St Augustine of Hippo, which sprang from a number of hermit communities in Italy. They probably arrived in England from Gascony.

ESSEX MARKETS ESTABLISHED

Two markets were established in Essex this year. One, granted to Waltham Abbey, was at Epping Heath. It was to be held every Monday, with an annual fair. The other was granted to Richard de Montfichet at West Ham, to be held each Tuesday, with an annual fair in July.

The Montfichet family's connection with the area called Ham went back to the 12th century when it was acquired by William de Montfichet. It was he who built the abbey of Stratford Langthorne c.1130.

1254

AN ELEPHANT AT THE TOWER MENAGERIE

Another exotic animal presented to the king this year was also housed at the Tower of London. This time it was an elephant – an astonishing sight for Londoners. It was the gift of Louis IX of France, and the City sheriffs were to provide a house 40 ft by 20 ft at a cost of over £22.

1257

CONFRONTATION WITH THE KING

Relations between the City and the king had worsened with each additional taxation. This year the king ordered a folkmoot at St Paul's to hear some allegations against the City magistrate. The aldermen refused to attend, and the dispute continued throughout the year. On command of the king, the citizens were obliged to spend large amounts to repair the City walls – indignation was increased the following year when those appointed to collect the money were found to have embezzled some of it. As a further exasperation, a half-brother of the king was denounced as having wounded several citizens of the City, and in retaliation he was stoned to death.

1258

A HARD YEAR IN LONDON

Famine and disease, possibly related, were abroad in London. One dramatic report relates that poor people were fighting over carrion and dead dogs, and that they drank the wash that was normally given to pigs. Another gives a death toll of 20,000 people, including Fulk Basset, the bishop of London.

THE KING UNDER PRESSURE

The king was obliged by the barons to delegate his power to a council of 24 people, of whom 12 were chosen by him. Custody of the Tower of London was transferred to the barons, now strongly under the influence of the king's brother-in-law, Simon de Montfort, earl of Leicester, and they also assumed the responsibility for appointing the justiciar. Neither of these two developments was to the satisfaction of the City, since it felt that its own privileges were being encroached upon. Hugh Bigod, appointed justiciar by the barons, offended the citizens by insisting on sitting at the Guildhall in a role normally taken by the sheriffs, and, in the distress caused by a shortage of bread, he summoned bakers there and dealt savagely with those selling below weight.

1259

GENERAL ASSEMBLY AT PAUL'S CROSS

London was caught in the crossfire between barons and king. This year Henry III commanded a general assembly at Paul's Cross, in St Paul's churchyard, at which every youth above the age of 12 was to swear before an alderman to be true to the king.

1260

GERMAN MERCHANTS THRIVE IN LONDON

The recent famines had resulted in increased imports of grain and other foodstuffs from Germany. It was probably no coincidence that this year the privileges of the German traders at their guildhall in Cannon Street were confirmed. In the years following they bought properties adjoining. The whole complex of buildings in which the merchants lived became known as the Steelyard. A number of suggested derivations for this name have been advanced. The two most plausible are that it comes from the steelyard or beam used for measuring the weight of imported goods, or from the Middle German Stalhof, meaning a sample in a courtyard, applied in this instance to a place where samples were displayed on stalls.

1262

THE JEWRY RANSACKED

The war between the barons and the king, their taxation and intervention in the government of London, the advantageous trading position of foreign merchants in the recurrent famines of the period, and the increased influence in financial affairs of the Jewish community all made London an uneasy and contentious city. Some sort of riot was likely, and it was sparked off by a quarrel about interest between a Christian and a Jew by the church of St Mary Colechurch in the Jewry. The Jew wounded the Londoner, and, trying to escape, was set upon by the mob and stabbed. In the tumult which followed, the Jewry was ransacked and many Jews were injured.

REBELLION IN THE CITY

The insurgence of the barons against the autocratic rule of the king was mirrored by the increasing resentment of the common people of the City at the rule of the autocratic elite of guilds. They found their champion in Thomas FitzThomas, mayor from 1261 to 1265, who encouraged the citizens of London to have a voice in decisions made. It was in this atmosphere that the populace felt free to attack Jews and foreigners, and to reopen rights of way which had been stopped up by those with power.

1263

CITY TREASURY SEIZED

An impasse in the negotiations between king and barons occurred. The king shut himself up in the Tower and, although not attacked, was effectually in a state of siege. His son, the future Edward I, arrived in London with forces, and in a surprise move on 29 June ransacked the City's treasury housed in the headquarters of the Templars, in Fleet Street – £10,000 was stolen. In retaliation the citizens spat at and pelted the queen as she travelled by barge beneath London Bridge on her way from the Tower to Windsor and attacked the homes of a number of the king's allies.

When asked to declare their loyalty, Londoners sided with Simon de Montfort, leader of the barons. In October the king took arms against de Montfort, who was lodged at Southwark; had not Londoners rescued him, the earl would have been captured. The dispute continued until the beginning of 1264, when the matter was referred for arbitration to the king of France.

A GATHERING OF BLACK FRIARS

A general chapter of Dominican friars took place at the premises of the London contingent, on the east side of Shoe Lane, this year. It is reported that 700 friars attended.

1264

THE BARONS IN THE ASCENDANCY

London was now firmly in the hands of the rebels headed by Simon de Montfort. Forces under the command of the City ventured to Isleworth, where they sacked the property of one of the king's allies. A major battle took place at Norbury, at what was subsequently called Battle Green, but the dispute came to a head at the Battle of Lewes this year, with de Montfort victorious and the king and his son, Edward, taken. For about 15 months de Montfort acted as governor of the kingdom, with Henry as his puppet.

With the king out of the way the mob turned against his supporters. In the front line were the London Jews, who were once again attacked.

1265

FIRST PARLIAMENT AT WESTMINSTER HALL

On 20 January, what is regarded as the first genuine Parliament convened at Westminster Hall. To this, two knights from each county, two citizens from each city, two burgesses from each borough, 120 churchmen and 23 barons were summoned. They met to discuss the release of the king's son and heir, Edward, and the general reconciliation of the dispute between barons and king. De Montfort's regime lasted for only a short while after. He fell out with the earl of Gloucester, who, with the aid of Edward, defeated and slew him at the Battle of Evesham in August.

Retribution was in store for London. Its support for the anti-royalist camp provoked a heavy punishment. For the next five years the king took the City into his own custody, governing it by a warden. The City had some difficulty in presenting its submission to Henry, but was eventually allowed to at the church of All Hallows, Barking, by the Tower, to a representative of the king. The mayor, the implacable FitzThomas, was commanded to Windsor with a guarantee of safe conduct, but he and his colleagues were imprisoned; some regained their liberty, but of the mayor no more is known. The property of 60 citizens was confiscated and the City as a whole was fined 20,000 marks. The queen, who had been insulted by Londoners as she travelled beneath London Bridge in 1263, was given the income from it.

For the time being the City was cowed.

1267

REBELLION IN THE CITY AGAIN

The twists and turns of the long reign of Henry III continued. The earl of Gloucester, who, by defeating his erstwhile ally, de Montfort, had brought about the renewed rule of the king, now sought to inspire rebellion in the City. With the support of those who had been disinherited by the king, Gloucester obtained entry to the City and, with the populace behind him, leading citizens were placed under arrest. In subsequent negotiations between Gloucester and the king Londoners received a partial pardon for their previous behaviour.

1268

GOLDSMITHS AND MERCHANT TAYLORS IN CONFLICT

A violent affray occurred in the streets of the City between members of the Goldsmiths' and Merchant Taylors' companies; other guild members joined in, until about 500 men were involved. Many were killed, and the battle was not put down until the sheriffs had raised an armed force to cope with it. Thirteen of the ringleaders were executed.

1269

WESTMINSTER ABBEY CONSECRATED

It is surprising that work on the reconstruction of Westminster Abbey had continued during the instability of the past years. It was still unfinished in 1269, but a consecration took place in the presence of its benefactor, Henry III, together with the translation of the relics of Edward the Confessor into a new shrine.

The king did not stint on expenditure at the abbey. The magnificent shrine – which alone took 20 years to make – was the work of Italian craftsmen. Bejewelled and enamelled, it stood on a platform approached by four steps, and it was covered with a canopy that could be raised and lowered by ropes.

Henry III reinvigorated the prestige of Edward the Confessor. It is difficult now to know if this was a political ploy to underline his own antecedents, or from a genuine admiration for Edward. At any rate, he named his first-born son Edward.

THE CITY UNDER NEW MANAGEMENT

This year the City was placed under the authority of the heir to the throne, Edward, but was effectively ruled by Sir Hugh FitzOtes, who was appointed constable of the Tower and warden of the City.

THE THAMES FROZEN

A severe frost began in November and lasted until February. Ships were unable to navigate the frozen Thames, and merchandise for London had to be brought by land from the sea ports.

1270

RECOVERY OF RIGHTS

After five years the City recovered some of its rights. It was allowed to elect its own mayor and sheriffs, for an annual fee of £400. The restoration of the City's various charters cost the citizens another 600 marks.

FLOODS AND FAMINE

Heavy rains this year ruined crops and also caused the Thames to flood, doing much damage to property and land. Famine once again was present in London.

1271

FALL OF STEEPLE

The wooden steeple of St Mary-le-Bow church in Cheapside collapsed, killing a number of people. It was not replaced for over 200 years.

ST OLAVE BROAD STREET DEMOLISHED

The building of the Austin Friars buildings in Broad Street necessitated the demolition about this year of one of London's many parish churches. Little is known of this building except that its dedication to St Olaf of Norway would make it no older than the mid 11th century. Five churches in the City and one in Southwark were dedicated to him.

1272

FIRST CHARTER FOR THE FISHMONGERS

The first of many charters was this year granted to the Fishmongers' Company. It regulated (to the benefit of its own members, of course) the sale of fish, and could arbitrate in disputes between vendors and the public. Fishmeters still examine fish coming into London today, to 'Survey whether the same be wholesome for Man's body and fit to be sold or not'.

A MAYORALTY DISPUTE

In 1271 Walter Hervy had been elected mayor – the popular choice of ordinary citizens and the non-elite guilds, but not that of the old-guard aldermen. When he was re-elected in 1272 the aldermen took the matter to the king, even persisting when Henry was in seriously bad health and fading fast. After the king's death in November this year it was decided that Hervy should continue in office.

1273

REFOUNDING OF ST KATHARINE'S HOSPITAL

During the upheavals of the reign of Henry III, St Katharine's Hospital by the Tower, under the patronage of the queen of England, fell on hard times. It was refounded on 5 July this year by Henry III's widow, Queen Eleanor. The new establishment consisted of a master, three brothers and three sisters. Each day of the year excepting one, alms to the value of 12 pence were to be distributed to 24 poor people (including six scholars); the excepted day was one dedicated to chanting an obituary to the late king, and 1,000 recipients then received a halfpenny each.

1274

EDWARD I CROWNED
Nearly two years after his accession, King Edward arrived back in the country from the Continent, receiving an enthusiastic welcome in London on 18 August: he was crowned next day at Westminster Abbey.

THE FIRST TOWN CLERK
The first town clerk of the City of London was appointed this year. He was, and still is, the most important paid official of the Corporation, responsible for administrative and ceremonial affairs. His appointment coincides with the beginning, in 1275, of the Corporation's records – the most complete of any city in the world. They survived even the Great Fire, having been lodged beneath the paved floor of the Guildhall.

1275

BAYNARD'S CASTLE BOUGHT
Baynard's Castle had apparently lain derelict since it had been destroyed on the orders of King John in 1213. This year, together with the Montfichet tower adjoining, it was conveyed to the archbishop of Canterbury so that he might provide a home for the Dominican friars already established in Shoe Lane. At about the same time permission was given to demolish the City wall in this vicinity, so that the buildings of the Black Friars could be extended westward (see 1278 and 1283).

FIRST CUSTOM HOUSE BUILT
There appear to have been two custom houses on the Thames: one belonging to the City and the other to the Crown. The latter – the most important – is first recorded to the east of the present site in Lower Thames Street this year, at the Old Wool Quay.

JEWS BANNED FROM USURY
Edward I bowed to public hostility towards the Jews and prevented them from practising usury in future. Effectively, this meant that Jews had no good means of making a living, since they were precluded from joining the guilds of London.

EARTHQUAKE IN LONDON
An earthquake this year damaged many houses and churches in London.

1276

LONDON BRIDGE MARKET SUPPRESSED
A market which had sprung up on London Bridge irritated the City fathers, since it infringed the City's monopoly. This year it was proclaimed that no market should be held there without licence of the Common Council, and also that no person should go to Southwark to buy wares which might be bought in the City.

1277

A CARTWHEEL BAN
A wry old London observation was that the streets had been built for wheelbarrows before carts were invented. Certainly they were narrow: even such an important road as Poultry was approached at both ends by remarkably restricted passageways. The streets off Cheapside were worse in this respect, and the narrowness was compounded at first-floor level, where the 'solars' of the houses extended beyond the street line of the ground floor; this was permissible as long as there was 10 ft of space beneath – enough for a man on horseback. It was possible for occupants on opposite sides of a road like Wood Street to shake hands across the road at solar level.

The best that could be hoped for in road surfaces was gravel, and even this would be confined to the principal highways. Elsewhere the streets were of mud, in summer offensive from the garbage and detritus thrown into them, in winter difficult to negotiate because of the poor drainage. The situation was made worse with the introduction in the 13th century of cartwheels cased with metal. If the carts were carrying heavy loads the ruts made by the wheels caused havoc for later traffic. This year a City by-law was announced which prohibited carts serving the City with water, wood, stones etc. if they had wheels 'shod with iron'.

1278

THE BUILDING OF BLACKFRIARS
The site allocated to the Dominicans, otherwise known as the Black Friars, south of Ludgate Hill, was a large one. Facing the Thames on the south, on the west it was bounded by the Fleet (now beneath New Bridge Street) and on the east by St Andrew's Hill. To the north stood their cemetery, adjacent to Ludgate, and their buildings below were grouped around a central cloister.

A grant this year confirms the Black Friars' occupation of the site, and it is likely that their church, at the west end of Carter Lane, was begun the next year.

FIRST MENTION OF ST ETHELBURGA, BISHOPSGATE
Situated on the east side of Bishopsgate today is the ruin of St Ethelburga-the-Virgin, the smallest of the remaining City churches. The church, which escaped the Great Fire, had 14th-century features and probably replaced the Norman church mentioned in a grant this year. It is not clear if the Ethelburga in the dedication is the abbess of Barking in the 7th century or the daughter of Offa, the king of Mercia, in the 8th century.

VARIOUS DEATHS
At a hearing before London sheriffs, it was alleged that one Matthew was set upon by three Jews in Ironmonger Lane and stabbed; from his wounds he later died.

Another man, Gilbert, who was drunk at midday, fell over London Bridge and was drowned.

Henry le Lanfare, one of those guarding St Mary Staining church, in which a robber had taken sanctuary, was killed by the priest of the church as Henry sought to prevent the robber escaping.

IMPRISONMENT OF THE JEWS

Edward I launched a purge against the clipping of the coinage. It was the general opinion that Jews were primarily responsible for this offence, and in London hundreds were rounded up and imprisoned in the Tower. The persecution of the Jewish community was soon to reach its peak and they no longer had the protection of the king. With public support, Edward was instead encouraging Lombardy merchants to come to London to take over the financial role of the Jews.

Eventually, 600 Jews were imprisoned in the Tower, of whom 293 were hanged.

1279

MINT ESTABLISHED IN THE TOWER

It is thought that the principal mint of the kingdom, that of London, was moved to the security of the Tower this year from Old Change near Cheapside. At the same time its keeper was appointed master moneyer for the whole kingdom.

The manufacture of coinage was a laborious process. The Saxons had engraved their coins freehand, but by the 9th century dies were available for punching each item of the design. The actual blanks were formed from silver ore melted in a crucible, allowed to cool, and then beaten into sheets of the right thickness before being cut to shape with shears. Also in 1279, new punches which incorporated larger sections of the design came into use.

1280

KINGSLAND LEPER HOSPITAL FOUNDED

The Kingsland Leper Hospital and Chapel in Kingsland Road, Hackney, were founded near the junction with Balls Pond Road. The chapel was later dedicated to St Bartholomew once the hospital of that name had taken responsibility for the administration of the premises.

LONDON BRIDGE IN BAD REPAIR

Since 1265 toll revenues from London Bridge had belonged to Henry III's queen. These moneys, previously used to maintain the structure, went into the royal coffers instead, and it was no wonder that Edward I, in 1280, granted permission to the City to solicit donations for the bridge's repair. This was ineffective, since the main remedy was in his own hands, and the following year he yielded the customs of the bridge to the City to be used for repairs.

THE BEGINNINGS OF ELY PALACE

About this year Sir John de Kirkby, chancellor of England in 1272, began buying property in Holborn opposite St Andrew's church. He appears to have been a permanent civil servant who took over the chancellorship whenever the incumbent was abroad, and it fell to him to raise money for Edward I. The grateful king heaped benefices upon him, to the scandal of Church dignitaries. Though only a deacon by merit, he was appointed in various places dean, archdeacon and bishop. In 1285, acting on behalf of the king in a dispute with the City, he took over the

administration of London and was instrumental in depriving the City of a mayor until 1298. In 1286 he was appointed bishop of Ely. He died in 1290, and in his will he left his Holborn property to the see of Ely. This became, in time, Ely Palace.

Today, St Etheldreda's, the chapel of the palace, and Ely Place are reminders of Kirkby's landholdings.

BANGOR INN ESTABLISHED

Another ecclesiastical residence was being established nearby. The bishop of Bangor purchased land on the west side of Shoe Lane, south of St Andrew's church, so that he might have a London home.

FIRST MENTION OF ST MARY WHITECHAPEL

The district of Whitechapel does not appear in records until 1340. It then clearly takes its name from the chapel of ease there, presumably built of white stone, of St Mary Matfelon, first noticed in 1280 as St Mary Mantefelune. The reason for this odd name is not clear. The most satisfactory suggestion is that it was founded by someone of that name – the French surname 'Matefelune' ('kill-felon') is that of a wine merchant with business interests in London in 1230.

1281

WORKS AT THE TOWER

More fortification was proceeding at the Tower of London. From about 1275 until this year a western wall was built – this now stands between the present outer wall and the White Tower. One of its features is the Beauchamp Tower, which replaced a gatehouse. It derived its name from the imprisonment of Thomas, earl of Warwick, of the Beauchamp family, during the reign of Richard II.

1282

DISASTER ON THE THAMES

The winter had been one of the most severe that people could remember. From Christmas Day the previous year, well into 1282, frost and snow covered London. The Thames was frozen, and it was possible to walk on it from Westminster to Lambeth.

The ice brought down five arches of London Bridge, which already was badly in need of repair.

SAFEKEEPING OF THE CITY

Provisions enacted by the mayor and aldermen this year illustrate the dangers of the City at this period. The gates were to be open during the day, but each was to be manned by two serjeants who were to be 'skilful men, and fluent of speech, who are to keep a good watch upon persons coming in and going out; so that no evil may befall the City'. Also, a curfew bell was to be rung at each parish church, taking time from the traditional curfew bell of St Martin's le Grand; at this time the gates were to be shut as well as all taverns. In each ward six people were to patrol the streets and arrest anyone abroad without good excuse. The Thames was to be guarded, and no one was to cross the river at night.

It is not certain what provoked this order. Possibly it had to do with the war on the Welsh being pursued by the king at this time, but the measures of 1283 and 1285 relating to the Tun and to St Paul's indicate a general instability in the City.

1283

STOCKS MARKET COMPLETED

The locations of markets were already well established in London. Cheapside was the principal retail street. Butchers were to the west in the Newgate area and to the east in Eastcheap. Fishmongers congregated in Old Fish Street, south of St Paul's, and, as Billingsgate specialized more, in Fish Street Hill. Grain came into Queenhithe and Billingsgate, and to a market at Newgate. Cornhill had a general market, and West Smithfield, outside the walls, sold livestock.

The visit of Edward I to London in 1274 prompted the City authorities to clean up Cheapside. The stalls of the fishmongers and butchers were moved to a new location by the City's fixed stocks, on the site of today's Mansion House, by St Mary Woolchurch and the Walbrook river. The rents from the stalls of this new 'Stocks' Market went to the upkeep of London Bridge.

CITY WALL EXTENDED

The building of the Black Friars' monastery on the site of the old Baynard Castle had necessitated the demolition of the City wall in this vicinity – the precincts extended further to the west than the grounds of the castle. To accommodate them, the king ordered this year that the rebuilt wall should be diverted from the former line south of Ludgate down to the Thames; instead it was begun along the bank of the river Fleet, now beneath New Bridge Street.

THE CORNHILL TUN ERECTED

A measure of the uncertainties of the time is contained within an ordinance of Edward I that 'persons wandering at night' unless they be 'a great lord, or other substantial person of good reputation', or one of such a person's household having a warranty from them, shall be placed in 'the Tun, which for such misdoers is assigned'. The Tun prison in Cornhill, between Change Alley and Birchin Lane, was erected this year, apparently next to an old well which later was incorporated into a conduit. The night walkers described above also encompassed prostitutes and men 'taken in fornication'. Even more specifically, 'If any priest be found with a woman he shall be taken unto the Tun on Cornhulle, with minstrels' playing before him.

The prison's name derived from its round shape, like an upended tun (wine cask).

TALLOW MELTERS EXCLUDED

More evidence of the cleaning up of Cheapside is provided by an order of the City this year that those occupied in melting tallow to make candles were to be removed from that street. They were, however, 'at liberty to provide themselves elsewhere, if they see fit'. This measure at once removed a fairly malodorous occupation and also relocated one of the more obvious fire risks.

THE FIRST LORD MAYOR

The first recorded mayor of London was in 1189, but the first description of a 'lord' mayor occurs this year. It does not appear that the title has ever officially been bestowed, but it has been in common use since the end of the 13th century.

1284

GUILDHALL BUILT

By about this year, a guildhall for the City of London existed on its present site. Recent excavations show that it was partly on the area of a Roman amphitheatre, and that its 13th-century gatehouse is directly over the amphitheatre's southern entrance. This suggests that remains of the older building were still extant when the Guildhall was built.

ST SAVIOUR'S ROBBED

Burglars forced their way into the abbey of St Saviour, Southwark, in April, and stole from chests and coffers £68 and gold and silver. It is not recorded if the culprits were caught.

1285

MAYORALTY ABOLISHED

A dispute between the king and the City this year caused the abolition of the mayoralty. Ostensibly the affair revolved around a summons of the mayor, sheriffs and aldermen to the Tower, where the king's justices were in session. Because of a technicality in the timing of the summons, the mayor declined to attend as mayor. Instead he handed over the seal of his office to an alderman and then went to the Tower to act unofficially, but informed those present that the 'mayor' had not received sufficient notice to attend. The affront to the justices was considerable.

John de Kirkby, the king's agent, declared that the City was now under the custody of the king, since it had no mayor. For the next 13 years a nominee of the Crown governed the City.

ENCLOSURE OF ST PAUL'S

It was ordered this year that a wall should be built around the churchyard and precincts of St Paul's. It ran from Cheapside along Paternoster Row to Ave Maria Lane, then south to Carter Lane, where it turned east, and then went north at Old Change. Six gates were introduced, the main one being on Ludgate Hill, and these were to be open from dawn to sunset.

It has been suggested that the three lanes on the line of the wall – Paternoster Row, Ave Maria Lane and Creed Lane – derive their names from the regular processioning of the bounds by the clergy. At Paternoster Lane the Lord's Prayer would be said, at Ave Maria Lane the 'Hail Mary', and at Creed Lane the credo was chanted. This neat explanation is now stock-in-trade for tourist guides, but is unlikely to be true. Ave Maria Lane and Creed Lane did not acquire their names until the 16th century, just at the time when it was most unlikely that a Catholic ritual would be commemorated. Creed Lane derives its name from the text writers who lived there. Paternosterers were rosary-bead makers – their occupation is commemorated in the street name by 1312.

SYNAGOGUE CLOSED

Edward I now felt confident enough to pursue the Jews still further, and the synagogue in Ironmonger Lane was closed. This was a popular move, and there were no doubt many citizens owing money to Jews who were happy to see their creditors in a parlous state. They were not so pleased, however, that Edward allowed increasing numbers of foreigners into London, able to trade at will.

1287

St Peter ad Vincula Rebuilt

The garrison church of the Tower of London, now within the precinct wall, was entirely rebuilt.

1288

Walbrook to be Cleansed

Like the Fleet, the river Walbrook was used as a sewer. It was ordered this year that the stream should be cleared of dung and other nuisances. The cost was to be charged to each house along its course.

A Lion at the Menagerie

The king, who was in Gascony, sent back a lion and an 'ounce' (a lynx) to the Tower, to join the other animals there. He allowed tenpence a day for their keep and threepence each to a man and his three sons, their keepers. It is still not clear where the lion was housed – the Lion Tower received its name rather later and initially, it is thought, this denoted nearness to the lion's enclosure. The same year a small sum of money was spent on the 'house of the elephant and the white bear'.

1290

Expulsion of the Jews

The events of previous years led inexorably to the expulsion of the Jews this year. It is estimated that about 15,000 Jews were obliged to quit the country, leaving their houses and their debtors behind them. The order was given in July and had to be obeyed by 1 November. Most went to France, many at a cheap rate of fourpence. It was a short-sighted policy on Edward's part, since he now had no means of raising money at short notice on such advantageous (because repressive) terms. The Jews' successors, the Lombards and the goldsmiths, were more difficult to exploit.

The records of the House for Converted Jews in Chancery Lane suggest that not all the Jews left. In 1290 the Domus Conversorum, as it was called, held 80 converts who, because of their former religion and inability now to obtain work with either gentile or Jew, were wholly dependent on the charity of the king. The royal bounty consisted of 1½d a day for a man, and 1d for a woman – a sum of money which had been obtained by the levy of a tax on Jews. Once the Jews had been expelled the tax was not replaced and the converts were in a parlous state. The House continued to receive baptized Jews almost without a break until the days of James I.

Complaint about the Fleet

The pollution of the river Fleet, at least in its lower reaches, was heavy. This year the White Friars at Newgate, who were about 200 yards away, complained to the king about the stench from the river, which, they said, was powerful enough to overwhelm the smell of the incense in their church.

St James's Fair Established

A leper hospital dedicated to St James the Less had existed on the site of today's St James's Palace, Westminster, since Norman times – the date of foundation is not known. It appears to have been for women only, for in 1290 the 'leprous maidens' were granted the right to hold a seven-day fair by their premises each July.

Death of the Queen

Eleanor of Castille, queen of Edward I, died this year in Nottinghamshire. Her body was embalmed, and her husband accompanied it on its journey from Lincoln to London; she was buried at Westminster Abbey, although her heart was interred at Blackfriars. At each stopping place the king ordered that a cross be erected to her memory. In London, two such crosses were built: one in Cheapside, the other at Charing – a settlement at the bend of the Thames between the Strand and Westminster which ever since has been called Charing Cross.

The Cheapside Cross, originally built by about 1296, stood in the centre of the road between Gutter Lane and Wood Street – it is not certain if the monument which appears in the earliest prints is the first cross on the site. The Charing Cross, probably the most elaborate of those built, was on the site of the present statue of Charles I, south of Trafalgar Square, until 1647. Today there is a fanciful reincarnation in the forecourt of Charing Cross station.

1292

St Stephen's Chapel Begun

St Stephen's Chapel in Westminster was the king's private chapel – his courtiers worshipped in its crypt, known as St Mary Undercroft. It was begun this year by Edward I in an attempt to emulate the Sainte Chapelle in Paris, but it was badly damaged by fire in 1298 and rebuilt in 1347. St Stephen's was later used as the chamber of the House of Commons.

Hunting in Stepney

The bishop of London this year attempted to enclose two woods of his in the village of Stepney. He was opposed by citizens of London who stated that 'time out of mind' they had been used to chase hares, foxes, rabbits and other beasts without hindrance in these woods, and were opposed to the enclosure.

Appointment of Pig Impounders

The City appointed four men to take any pigs found wandering in the streets and kill them, unless the owner paid a fine of fourpence.

1293

The Beginnings of the Minories

The area south of Aldgate High Street now called the Minories derives its name from the convent of St Clare, founded here this year by Edmund, earl of Lancaster (brother of the king), and Blanche, his wife: the nuns belonged to an order of Sorores Minores – Little Sisters. The abbey occupied a site on which St Clare Street and Haydon Walk now stand; the street called the Minories runs on the old ditch which encircled the City wall.

Strengthening the Savoy

Lancaster was also busy elsewhere. He had received as a gift from his mother, the queen mother, the mansion on the Strand called the Savoy.

This year on 21 June he obtained permission from the king to strengthen the house with a wall of stone and mortar and to 'castellate' the building.

BEGINNINGS OF BAKEWELL HALL
When the Jewry was ransacked in 1262–3 a number of houses were destroyed. By 1275 there had been erected on the site of some of them a mansion which on 4 December 1293 was granted to an alderman of the City named John de Bauquell – a name to be spelt in various ways in future documents. The house, at the corner of Basinghall Street and Gresham Street, was then a private residence, but in 1396 it was to be a market for woollen cloths.

A SAVAGE RETRIBUTION
The City was still under the rule of the king's agent. Some idea of the underlying resentment and turbulence in London this year may be deduced from the successful attempt by a group of men to seize a prisoner being carried to jail by the sheriff. Three of the ringleaders later had their hands amputated by the common hangman in Cheapside.

1294

ST PAUL'S RANSACKED
The king continued his repressive ways of obtaining money. He ordered the ransacking of churches and monasteries throughout England, including the seizure of £2,000 from St Paul's – which caused a dean to die of a fit.

CHESTER INN ESTABLISHED
The bishop of Chester established a London house to the south of the Strand, on part of the site of today's Somerset House. It was later, under the name of Strand Inn, to be one of the Inns of Chancery.

1296

BEGINNINGS OF ELTHAM PALACE
By 1295 the manor of Eltham was owned by the bishop of Durham, Anthony Bec. It is thought that between 1296 and 1311 he erected the moated medieval mansion before presenting it to Edward, the prince of Wales, son of Edward. It then became a royal palace. An Elizabethan plan for the house suggests that Bec's building had octagonal towers at its corners, with a gatehouse also flanked by towers.

1297

ST ETHELDREDA'S BUILT
Ely Palace, occupied by the king's detested tax gatherer and bishop of Ely, John de Kirkby, until his death in 1290, was now the official London residence of the see of Ely. A private chapel attached to the house was finished about this year. It became and still is St Etheldreda's (in Ely Place), and, by virtue of its being sold back to the Roman Catholic Church in 1874, it is the oldest building in London used by Catholics.

CURFEW CONFIRMED
A curfew had existed for some years in London. The prohibitions were detailed again in an order this year. No one was to be found walking the streets after the bell at St Martin's le Grand had sounded, no taverns were to have their doors open after that time, and when summoned each citizen was liable to act as a watchman. The same order enjoined that each citizen should keep the street before his house clean, that no pigs should roam the streets, and that projections from houses which did not clear the height of a man on a horse should be demolished.

IMPRISONMENT OF THE CLERGY
In March the king issued an order forbidding the City, through its watchmen, from arresting clergy. He alleged that, out of spite, 'clerks' had been taken as felons and imprisoned in the Tun prison in Cornhill.

MAKING OF THE CORONATION CHAIR
In 1296 Edward I had seized the Stone of Scone from Scotland and brought it in triumph to Westminster Abbey. The stone is supposed to have been the one on which Jacob rested his head at Bethel. More significantly, it was the stone in Scone Palace on which the kings of Scotland were crowned and its theft remained a matter of resentment among Scots until modern times. In 1297 Edward had a magnificent oak coronation chair made at the abbey, with the stone symbolically housed beneath it. The chair has remained in the abbey ever since, except when it was carried across to Westminster Hall for the installation of Oliver Cromwell as Protector, and during the Second World War when it was prudently stored in Gloucester cathedral. The stone was returned to Scotland in 1999.

1298

MAYORALTY RESTORED
With the king increasingly desperate for money and reliant on London for its supply, the City was able to negotiate the re-establishment of its mayoralty this year. Each inhabitant was taxed sixpence in the pound for the privilege.

CRUTCHED FRIARS FOUNDED
The house of the Crossed Friars was founded this year at the south-east end of Hart Street; their garden looked out at the gallows of Tower Hill on the south, and the City wall on the east. By Stow's time, in the late 16th century, much of the site was taken by carpenter's yards and tennis courts, and the friars' hall was used for glassmaking until in 1575 it was destroyed by fire.

The friars were also called 'Crouched' Friars – 'crouch' being another word for cross, a spelling represented again in the north-London district of Crouch End. In time, 'Crouched' became 'Crutched'.

1299

ATTACK ON THE TUN
A number of citizens attacked the Tun prison this year, in an attempt either to demolish it or to release prisoners. The cause and precise nature of this affair are not known.

1300

MISCELLANEOUS REPAIRS

It was agreed that the bishop of London, since he derived considerable income from the toll at Bishopsgate, should be responsible for replacing the gate's hinges. It was also agreed that the parishioners of St Stephen Walbrook were responsible for repairing the 'covering' over the river Walbrook next to their church.

1302

ROLLING OUT THE BARREL

In June some young men were arrested for filling an empty cask with stones one evening about midnight and rolling it along Gracechurch Street to London Bridge, to the 'great terror' of citizens. The men were imprisoned in the Tun.

1303

ENFIELD MARKET AND FAIR ESTABLISHED

Remnants of the village greens around London may still be seen; in Enfield only the shape may be recognized. The green was to the west of the main London road, with the parish church of St Andrew to its north and the medieval manor house to the south. The lords of the manor were the earls of Hereford, and this year the king granted them a weekly market and two annual fairs of three days – one in August, the other in November.

ROBBERY AT THE TREASURY

Part of the king's treasure was kept at Westminster Abbey in the Chapel of the Pyx. It was discovered that this had been robbed, and the abbot, Walter de Wenlock, and at least 48 of the monastic community were suspected of involvement in the crime. Ten were put in the Tower of London, and all were eventually released without trial after serving two to five years' imprisonment; however, six laymen were executed.

1305

WILLIAM WALLACE EXECUTED

For some years the king had been fighting to subdue the Scots, whose leader was William Wallace. By 1304 the Scots nobles had capitulated, and Wallace was taken the following year. He was brought to London, met by the London mob, and lodged in a house near or in Fenchurch Street. His trial began with a parody. He was placed on a scaffold in Westminster Hall with a laurel wreath on his head and charged with treason against the king. He replied that, since he and other nobles had never accepted the English king as ruling over the Scots, the charge was invalid.

The verdict was inevitable. The sentence was that he be taken from the Tower, through the City to the Elms at Smithfield (the usual execution place, outside St Bartholomew's), there to be hanged and drawn, then beheaded and his various parts burnt.

1306

FIRST MENTION OF THE TABARD

The Tabard inn in Southwark was made famous by Chaucer in his *Canterbury Tales:* it was the starting place of many pilgrimages to Canterbury. It is first mentioned this year as adjoining the lodgings of the abbot of Hyde. When Chaucer was writing, some 70 years later, its host was the member of Parliament for Southwark, Henry Baillie, but the building which attained such immortality was probably taken down in about 1629.

VIGIL AT THE TEMPLE

The Scots rebelled again, this time under the leadership of Robert Bruce, who was crowned king of the Scots. The Bruce family owned land in Tottenham, and it is thought that Bruce Castle stands on the site of their moated house.

Before his journey to Scotland to engage in battle, King Edward held a ceremony at the Temple church, off Fleet Street, in which he knighted many young men who were to accompany him. Before the ceremony they camped out in the gardens of the Temple and kept vigil.

COMPLAINT ABOUT THE FLEET

The earl of Lincoln had, in 1285, bought the first house of the Black Friars, in Shoe Lane, west of the river Fleet. In 1306 the earl complained to Parliament that the river was silted and polluted and asserted that the Fleet had once been wide enough to contain ten or twelve ships abreast as far up as today's Ludgate Circus. Aside from the tanners using the stream to dispose of obnoxious material, the Knights Templar had diverted water to their mill near the river outlet by the Thames.

1307

ROBBERY AT WHITEFRIARS

Monastic houses were used as secure places to store treasure. This year Whitefriars, the Carmelite priory in Newgate Street, was burgled and 40 pounds weight of silver was taken. The robbers, helped by someone later called Friar Judas, 'bound in an atrocious way the hands of the prior and several of the friars and one they killed and then took their departure'. The traitorous friar went with them, but was later found and hanged.

A BAN ON BRICK KILNS

While the queen was lodging at the Tower, the king ordered a prohibition on the brick kilns in the vicinity: 'so long as Queen Margaret shall stay at the Tower, whereby the air may be in any way infected or corrupted as the Queen is going to the Tower shortly to stay there for some time and the King wishes to avoid the danger that may arise to her and other magnates who are coming to be there from the infection and corruption of the air by such burning of kilns'.

MARKET AT BRENTFORD

Brentford was one of the more important small towns ringing London, standing astride the principal road west. It became, in effect, an entrepôt for London, where grain and cattle were left and traded between country and city. This year it received a charter for a weekly market and a six-day annual fair.

1308

CORONATION OF EDWARD II

Edward I had died the previous year on his journey to fight Robert Bruce in Scotland. His son, Edward II, then aged 23, was crowned at Westminster Abbey on 25 February. It was the beginning of another reign of conflict.

The coronation, however, was a sumptuous affair, attended in full regalia by the mayor and aldermen of London.

SUPPRESSION OF THE TEMPLARS

The Knights Templar had for long been the envy of kings and the target of the pope. In 1306 the French king captured their leader and, in a sudden and surprise move, arrested every Templar in his country; many were tortured and burnt as heretics. In London, the French king's son-in-law, the new king of England, Edward II, declined to do the same until ordered by the pope. Throughout England, on 8 January, members of the order were arrested and its dissolution began. Imprisonment and torture began in earnest, and the jails of London were filled with knights.

The Templars' watermill on the bank of the Fleet (see 1306) was demolished to give access to boats up to Holborn Bridge once more.

WHALE TAKEN AT GREENWICH

A whale, 70 ft long, was captured at Greenwich.

1309

NEW ORDERS FOR CLEANING THE STREETS

One of a succession of orders from the City authorities to keep the streets clean was issued this year. It complained of 'ordure' in the streets and lanes, and ordered that it should always be disposed of in the Thames or outside the City.

THE INQUISITION OF THE TEMPLARS

The inquisition of the Knights Templar continued for much of the year. It was generally held in the Holy Trinity Priory, Aldgate, or else at All Hallows Barking by the Tower.

REBUILDING OF ST ANTHONY'S HOSPITAL

St Anthony's Hospital, which had been given a chapel in Threadneedle Street in 1343, rebuilt it this year. The building was so splendid that it drew people (and revenue) from the nearby St Benet Fink church.

1310

BAN ON SCOURING FURS

In a rather desperate-sounding order, the City acknowledged that, although on numerous occasions the tailors had been forbidden to scour furs during the daytime, the law was still being disobeyed, especially in Cheapside. As a compromise, a new order stated that any tailor with such business to perform during the day must do it in some 'dead lane, such as behind St Martins le Grand or near the London Wall, where no great lords are passing, either going or coming'.

1311

ST MARY STRATFORD BUILT

The church of St Mary Stratford-atte-Bow, in east London, was begun this year. At this time Stratford was part of Stepney parish, and the new church was a chapel of ease for residents disinclined to make the long journey to St Dunstan's in Stepney High Street. Some of the old Stratford building survives in the present church in the middle of the road, although heavily disguised by successive restorations.

1312

GUARDING THE CITY

Strife between king and barons, principally related to the activities of the king's favourite, Piers Gaveston, once more impinged on London life. With an attack by the barons feared, it was ordered that the City be put on intensive guard and that no armed strangers should enter. The gates and walls were to be put in full repair, and each gate was to be posted with six men; between 100 and 200 men were to patrol the city each night.

A SHORT-SIGHTED OFFICIAL

City merchants complained that the tronager, the keeper of the City weighing platform, or tron, had defective sight and was measuring inaccurately.

1313

A VISIT TO ST BARTHOLOMEW'S

A record of a visitation of the hospital of St Bartholomew in Smithfield about this year notes that there were seven brothers and four sisters looking after the inmates. It was ordered that the brethren should wear cloaks of frieze, the sisters tunics and overtunics of grey, not longer than to their ankles, and the lay brethren short tunics or tabards.

1314

REPLACING THE BALL AND CROSS OF ST PAUL'S

This year the cross and ball of the belfry of St Paul's were taken down because they were dangerous. A 'new cross with a ball well gilded was set up, and many relics of saints for the protection of the belfry and of the whole edifice attached to it were with a great and solemn procession replaced in the cross by the bishop'. At the same time various measurements were noted: the belfry tower measured 260 ft from the ground and the wooden spire 274 ft; the ball of the steeple could contain 10 bushels of wheat, and the length of the cross above the ball was 15 ft and its width was 6 ft.

LOOKING AFTER THE LION

The king ordered that his lion, housed at the Tower of London menagerie, should be fed a quarter of mutton each day and that his keeper should be paid 3½d.

1315

CITY WALL STILL UNFINISHED

The rebuilding of the City wall around the precincts of the Black Friars (see 1283) was still incomplete, and the king granted the City customs revenues to finance the building work. A new turret was built at the furthest corner overlooking the Thames.

ATTACK ON THE TOWER

Further strengthening of the Tower of London had been proceeding, in which the king had built a new wall to the south-west of the Lion Gate, which aroused the hostility of the City – probably it encroached on its land. On a summer's night this year 'an earthen wall … was thrown down … by malefactors of the City of London with a body of armed men on horseback and on foot'.

FINSBURY LEASED TO THE CITY

The manor of Holywell, which included the marshy area of Moorfields, was leased to the City this year by the owner, St Paul's Cathedral. This arrangement survived until 1867.

COMPLAINT ABOUT THE STRAND

The inhabitants of Westminster complained that the footway from Temple Bar to the King's Palace at Westminster (the Strand) was so bad that the feet of horses and rich and poor men received constant damage, and that it was interrupted by thickets and bushes.

1316

RULES FOR THE PEPPERERS

The Pepperers, based in Soper Lane, were the forerunners of the Grocers' Company, in which the Spicers of Cheapside and the Apothecaries also played a part. They had strong connections with the Italian merchants who came in with the Lombard bankers, and were, as their name implies, specialists in spices; but they also dealt in drugs – a cause of dispute with those who called themselves apothecaries and who later, in the 17th century, managed to obtain a charter and monopoly for themselves.

This year ordinances were published which governed the activities of the Pepperers. They were prohibited from mixing old and new produce, or mixing inferior goods with better goods in the same package. Also, they were not to 'moisten … such as saffron, alum, ginger, cloves by steeping the ginger, or turning the saffron out of the sack and then anointing it, or bathing it in water' in an attempt to increase its weight.

1317

DROUGHT AND FAMINE

A serious drought and famine had been evident in the country since the previous year. In 1317 it reached its peak in London, where hundreds died of heat and starvation. A 'phenomenal' thunderstorm is recorded which caused the Fleet to rise dramatically, causing much damage to the Holborn and Fleet bridges.

1319

A FELLING OF OAK TREES

The abbess of Barking Abbey was granted permission to fell 300 oaks in her wood at Hainault (Hainault Forest), so that she could repair the abbey and other buildings nearby. The earliest known spelling of the name (1221) was 'Henehout', meaning 'the community wood'.

PILLORY PUNISHMENT

The use of the pillory was a common punishment in medieval times. It inflicted not only discomfort (and sometimes death) on the recipient but also, more importantly, disgrace.

A butcher, William Sperling of West Ham, was this year convicted of selling two beef carcasses 'putrid and poisonous' at the Stocks Market. Sperling denied that the meat was bad, but a jury found otherwise. He was put in the pillory here and the carcasses were burnt beneath him.

1320

PAVING THE COURT OF LEADENHALL

An indication that the City was paving principal areas of London occurs this year, when the garden attached to the mansion called Leadenhall, opposite the church of St Peter upon Cornhill, was taken by the mayor 'for completion of the pavement'. The house itself, which later became a market, seems to have been used as a court of justice during this period.

1321

PINNER PARISH CHURCH REBUILT

St John the Baptist, the parish church of Pinner, stands on a knoll at the end of the High Street. It is of some antiquity, since it was rebuilt about this year, although the lancet windows of the transepts and south aisle appear to be part of an earlier building. The windows are unaltered except for the 15th-century east window, and the font is early 14th century.

Pinner at this time was part of the parish of Harrow, which itself came under the jurisdiction of the archbishop of Canterbury. A house in Pinner – Headstone – was a manor house of the see and appears to have been occupied by its representative from the middle of the 14th century.

A CITY INVESTIGATION

A grand inquiry, called an iter, was begun this year at the Tower. Instituted by the king, it dealt with the management and behaviour of the City, and required the availability for six months of past and present holders of office. Feelings ran high during the long inquiry, and the City was placed in the hands of the king's commissioner. Though the king's attitude softened during the proceedings (it is thought because of an insurrection in Wales which might have obliged the king to seek the City's support), it did not prevent the aldermen retaliating with an indictment against the king's constable of the Tower for encroachment and corruption.

The iter was brought to a sudden end in July. The king capitulated to political necessity, restored the mayoralty to London, and asked for the City's support against the forces led by his brother-in-law, the earl of Hereford. The City, however, declined to commit itself so positively, and even went so far as to agree to meet the earl. Hereford's aim, he said, was the overthrow of the king's favourites, the Despensers – those behind the holding of the iter. The City retired into a position of neutrality, offering neither help nor hindrance to either party.

1322

DISASTER AT BLACKFRIARS
At daybreak on 3 July a great many people assembled at the gate of the Black Friars' priory seeking alms; 52 men and women were crushed to death.

LANCASTER TABLET REMOVED
The king had reneged on his agreement with the barons made the previous year and restored the Despensers to power. The earl of Lancaster, a favourite with Londoners and an old enemy of the king, was taken at the Battle of Boroughbridge and executed. The tablet he had erected in St Paul's commemorating the king's submission to ordinances in 1311 which reduced Edward's powers, and around which Londoners gathered to remember Lancaster, was taken down, although it was restored once the king himself had fled London (see 1326).

1324

TEMPLARS' PROPERTY TO THE HOSPITALLERS
The Knights Templar, who had about 16,000 lordships in the country, had been suppressed in 1308. Generally their assets had been appropriated by the Crown. In 1324 the king transferred their headquarters, the Temple, off Fleet Street, to his favourite, Hugh le Despenser the younger, though Parliament had decreed that it should go to the Knights Hospitaller.

1325

DEATH IN SANCTUARY
A quarrel between two Flemings, Nicholas Crane and John Daling, ended in Crane's death from stabbing. Daling fled to All Hallows Barking by the Tower, claiming sanctuary. He died there two weeks later from his wounds.

FOREIGNERS DEPRIVED OF FREEDOM
It was ordered this year that most of the foreigners who had already received the freedom of the City now had this honour cancelled. Exceptions included the merchants of Amiens, importers mainly of onions and garlic, who had been granted privileges in 1237 and had contributed to the expense of bringing water from the Tyburn springs to the City. Furthermore, no aliens were in future to be admitted to the freedom without the express permission of the Court of Husting.

1326

MOB RULE IN LONDON
In September the estranged wife of the king, Queen Isabella, returned from France with her lover, Roger Mortimer, and armed forces, prepared to depose the king in favour of the prince of Wales. Edward fled west, leaving the City to be wooed by the queen. London's leaders remained neutral, but the queen's popular support was more active. An alleged spy of the Despensers was beheaded in Cheapside, and the mob then moved on to the king's treasurer, the bishop of Exeter, at his house in the Strand. As it happened, the bishop was already on his way to the City to investigate the tumult; he was intercepted before he could reach sanctuary in St Paul's and was dragged from his horse. With two aides he was taken to Cheapside and he too was beheaded. The corpses were left in the road and his head was sent to the queen.

Such was the terror that it was not until dark that the canons of St Paul's came out in procession to retrieve the bishop's body. They decided it was impolitic to keep it in the precincts; instead, it was transported secretly to St Clement Danes, the bishop's nearest parish church, for burial, but the incumbent there refused it. It was eventually buried in unconsecrated ground, but was later exhumed and reburied in Exeter Cathedral.

Still on the rampage and with that hatred of foreigners for which Londoners were renowned, the mob attacked the houses of Lombard merchants in the City, and then went on to the Tower, where they released all the prisoners, including the bishop of Lincoln and the children of Roger Mortimer. In a few days the tablet commemorating the ordinances agreed by the king to the barons (see 1322) was replaced. Not until November was order restored in the City, and then only on the queen's intervention.

1327

DEATH OF THE KING
The disastrous reign of Edward II came to an end in January 1326 at Kenilworth, when he was deposed. On 21 September he was murdered at Berkeley Castle, in the horrendous manner described by Marlowe, and his son, Edward III, was crowned at Westminster Abbey on 29 January this year. The new king was under 14, and was immediately under the sway and command of the former queen and her lover, Roger Mortimer.

CITY COMPANIES CONSOLIDATE
A number of guilds took advantage of the support London had given the former queen to consolidate their positions. Charters were obtained by the Girdlers, the Pellipers or Skinners, and the Goldsmiths. The girdle, a common article of clothing at the time, now had its metallic content strictly defined: 'no man … should cause any girdle of silk, of wool, of leather, or of linen thread, to be garnished with any inferior metal than with latten, copper, iron and steel'. The Pellipers, responsible for producing fur skins, were also granted ordinances stipulating quality.

A CITY AFFRAY
The loriners – makers of bits, spurs and bridles – are mentioned in a description of a dispute in May. In Cheapside and Cripplegate battle

took place between saddlers, on the one hand, and painters, joiners and loriners, on the other. Several were killed and others wounded in a confrontation caused by a trade-demarcation dispute. The City authority acted as arbitrators and peacemakers, and leaders of the two factions were brought together to reach an amicable solution.

RIVAL MARKETS PROHIBITED

The City obtained further privileges while the time was ripe. It was ordered that there should be no other markets within seven miles of the City, except for that which existed in Southwark, and the small market at Westminster.

1328

GREAT WARDROBE MOVES

The building called the Great Wardrobe contained the king's ceremonial robes, clothes, bedhangings, furniture, tapestries and other effects. It was called 'Great' because of the quantity of clothes stored there, but it was in fact a part of the King's Wardrobe, itself a department of the Exchequer, which handled the king's disbursements and revenues. The Great Wardrobe was located in a house in Bassishaw at the end of Edward II's reign, but in 1328 the new king bought a house in Lombard Street, formerly owned by Lombardy merchants and no doubt empty after the eruption of the London mob in 1326.

THE CITY IN THE MIDDLE

Disputes between king and barons continued into the reign of Edward III, now fuelled by resentment of the power of the former queen and her lover, Roger Mortimer, over the young king. The earl of Lancaster, nominal guardian of the king, found himself without much power and appealed to the City for help in resolving the situation. The mayor and aldermen attempted to negotiate between the factions, without success.

1329

TRIAL OF THE EX-MAYOR

A conference of bishops and barons was convened at St Paul's, but they came to no conclusion as to how to proceed in the political situation. The earl of Lancaster found himself in an increasingly weak position, and the king was strong enough to order the mayor and aldermen to meet him at St Albans on 22 January, where they were commanded to punish all those who had supported Lancaster against Edward II.

In February the trials of Lancaster's supporters began. Among those arraigned was a former mayor of London, Hamo de Chigwell, who escaped death by claiming benefit of clergy and was taken to an episcopal prison. Mortimer's hand was seen behind the persecutions, and his excesses enraged the population.

PROTECTING THE FISH

Laws to protect the smaller fish in the Thames and prevent overfishing were already in place. This year fishermen from Erith, Rainham and Dagenham were arraigned before the mayor and aldermen charged with fishing in the Thames with nets whose holes were only ½ inch wide instead of the stipulated 1½ inches, from which the small fish, called fry, were unable to escape. The offending nets were burnt in

Cheapside, although the fines their owners paid were remitted to them since they were so poor.

ELSING SPITAL FOUNDED

The hospital of St Mary within Cripplegate, usually called Elsing Spital, was founded this year by William Elsyng, a mercer, to care for 100 blind people, with priority given to afflicted priests. It stood to the east of Wood Street, facing London Wall.

1330

EXECUTION OF MORTIMER

The king finally threw off the influence of his mother and Mortimer this year. The latter was arrested at Nottingham castle and hustled down to London to stand trial for numerous offences, including the murder of the king's father. On 29 November he was hanged, drawn and quartered at either Smithfield or Tyburn.

1331

ROYAL TOURNAMENT IN CHEAPSIDE

John Stow describes a tournament held in the presence of Edward III in September this year, in Cheapside:

the stone pavement being covered with sand, that the horses might not slide when they strongly set their feet to the ground, the King held a tournament three days together, with the nobility, valiant men of the realm, and other strange knights. And to the end the beholders might with the better ease see the same, there was a wooden scaffold erected across the street, like unto a tower, wherein the Queen Philippa and many other ladies, richly attired, and assembled from all parts of the realm, did stand to behold the jousts.

ESTABLISHMENT OF LINCOLN'S INN

The origins of one of today's four Inns of Court were in the lodgings owned by Thomas of Lincoln, himself a lawyer, on the south side of Holborn: from about this year he was letting them out to 'apprentices' in law. Eight years later two chancery clerks were killed by four apprentices from the 'rent of Thomas de Lyncoln'.

1333

SLAUGHTERING BAN

A ban was imposed on slaughtering animals in main streets. This was directed principally at the butchers of Eastcheap and Newgate. Shops which sold the bowels and tripe were also restricted to side streets.

1334

ST LAWRENCE POUNTNEY COLLEGE FOUNDED

About this year Sir John de Pulteney, mayor of London, founded a College of Corpus Christi for a master and seven chaplains. This establishment – a college in the old ecclesiastical sense of the word – adjoined the church of St Lawrence in today's Laurence Pountney Lane.

Pulteney, a draper, had a mansion and a business in a place called the Manor of the Rose, on the west side of Suffolk Lane: it was also called Pountney's Inn. On his death it was left to the college.

1335

FLEET PRISON REBUILT
About this year the Fleet prison, in today's Farringdon Street just north of Ludgate Circus, was rebuilt.

The keeper of the Fleet was appointed by the Crown – it was a post of much profit. The prisoners here were not necessarily criminals but quite often those who in some way had offended the king. This latter category often had the money to make their lives comfortable in captivity, and the keeper was entitled to any payments made by them.

1337

DUCHY OF CORNWALL LANDS ESTABLISHED
The king this year granted his son, Edward the Black Prince, duke of Cornwall and earl of Chester, the royal manors of Kennington and Vauxhall. These lands were henceforth vested in the heir to the throne; in the absence of an heir, the estates reverted to the Crown until one was born.

The place name 'Kennington' is a corruption of the Old English 'cyne-tun', meaning 'royal manor', while 'Vauxhall' is derived from Falkes de Breaute, who married the heiress of the manor c. 1220.

Much of the estate around the Oval Cricket Ground still remains in the hands of the present prince of Wales and duke of Cornwall.

SHORTAGE OF WATER IN CHEAPSIDE
It was reported that there was a shortage of water at the Cheapside conduit because of the excessive use made of it by local brewers. They send 'day after day, and night after night, their brewers to the said

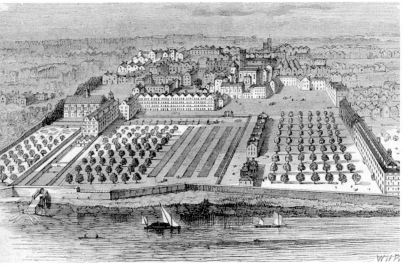
A bird's-eye view of The Temple and gardens to the Thames in 1671.

Conduit with their vessels, called "tynes", and make the ale which they sell with the water thereof'.

LAWYERS IN THEIR CHAMBERS
About this year lawyers began to occupy the old premises of the Knights Templar off Fleet Street. Today the barristers are divided into Middle Temple and Inner Temple, but it is not clear if in 1337 they arrived as two already separate bodies. The premises they took over then contained two halls – separate refectories of Templar priests and knights – and this factor may have determined the establishment of the two Inns of Court.

1338

HOLBORN CROSS BUILT
Holborn Cross, later to be the location of a conduit, was erected by this year. Its site has now been obliterated by the building of Holborn Viaduct and Farringdon Street, but it was approximately by the south-west end of Cock Lane.

LONDON SENDS SHIPS
London appears to have sent three ships to aid the king's war on France. They were called *La Jonette* of London, *La Cogge* of All Hallows, and *La Sainte Marie Cogge*, owned by William Haunsard, an ex-sheriff of London.

ROBBER DROWNED IN THE FLEET
John le Brewere was one of five robbers who assaulted two Florentine merchants on their way from Romford to Brentwood. He was recognized by them near Newgate Street when they came to London, and he fled to St Paul's Quay on the Thames, where he plunged in at low tide with the intention of excaping beneath the wharves up to Fleet Bridge. Unluckily for him the tide turned and he was drowned; his body was later washed up on the banks of the Fleet, complete with 140 florins and a seal belonging to the merchants.

1339

A WATCH ON THE THAMES
The threat of a French invasion up the Thames caused a watch to be kept – the mayor and aldermen took it in turns to keep guard at the river.

BATTLE BETWEEN FISHMONGERS AND SKINNERS
An affray between members of the Fishmongers' and Skinners' companies resulted in deaths. Prisoners were taken by the mayor and aldermen, but they were set free by two of the mob. These two in their turn were taken and, after a trial, were beheaded in Cheapside.

1340

GEOFFREY CHAUCER BORN
Geoffrey Chaucer was born this year. It is thought that the event took place in his parents' house in Upper Thames Street, backing on to the

river Walbrook, in the area of the City called the Vintry – his father was a wine merchant. He would almost certainly have been baptized at St Martin Vintry, his nearest church.

1343

A Place for Butchers
In a misguided act to encourage public hygiene, the City provided the butchers of Newgate Street Shambles with a place by the river Fleet in which to clean out entrails. This merely moved the nuisance and the stench away from the main highway down to the already polluted river by Seacoal Lane. Particularly affected were the inmates of the Fleet prison next door, already at the mercy of the smells of the tanneries nearby and the use of the Fleet as a sewer. The butchers paid an annual rent of a boar's head to the City.

1344

Clifford's Inn Begins
About this year a house immediately behind St Dunstan's in the West, in Fleet Street, was let by Robert de Clifford's widow to law students for a rent of £10 per annum. The house, Clifford's Inn, became an Inn of Chancery, a term thought to originate in the specialization in the tuition of Chancery clerks, responsible for writs in the king's courts. Eventually there were to be eight Chancery Inns, none of which had the power to call students to the Bar; each became affiliated to one of the Inns of Court – in the case of Clifford's Inn, to the Inner Temple.

An alley, Clifford's Inn Passage, still runs from Fleet Street to the site of the old Inn's gatehouse.

1345

Poultry Market Established at Leadenhall
The selling of poultry at Leadenhall began this year. A proclamation at Leaden Hall to men of the poultry trade from outside the City said that those who had previously 'sold their poultry in lanes, in the hostels of their hosts, and elsewhere in secret, to the great loss and grievance of the citizens and at extortionate prices' should now bring 'the same to the Leaden Hall and there sell it, and nowhere else, on pain of forfeiting the poultry, and going bodily to prison'.

Dowgate Silted up
One of the principal docks of the City, rivalling Billingsgate and Queenhithe, was Dowgate: the inlet is now filled in, but it was to the west of Cousin Lane. It was reported this year that it was so corrupted by dung and other filth thrown into it that the carters who carried water from the Thames to different places in the City were unable to use it. A toll was inaugurated on goods coming through the dock, to help pay for its cleansing.

The Drunken Spurriers
Spurriers – the men who made spurs – came in for criticism this year. It was alleged, in drawing up new regulations for their occupation,

that 'many of their trade are wandering about all day, without working at all at their trade; and then, when they have come drunk and frantic, they take to their work, to the annoyance of the sick and of all their neighbourhood, as well as by reason of the broils that arise between them and the strange folks who are dwelling among them'.

1346

Lepers Removed from City
The king ordered this year that all lepers should be removed from the City. The spread of their disease was helped, it was said, 'by the contagion of their polluted breath, and by carnal intercourse with women in stews'. Fourteen residents were moved to the St Giles Leper Hospital.

1347

St Stephen's Chapel Completed
St Stephen's, the king's private chapel at Westminster, begun after a destructive fire in 1298, was structurally complete about this year, although the decoration took a further 15 years. The building, sumptuously gilded, was tall, with two storeys and four turrets at the corners. From the 16th century it was used by the House of Commons as a debating chamber, with members sitting in the choir stalls, facing each other (the format of today's building). The Speaker sat where the altar had once been. It is thought that the practice of bowing to the Speaker on entry or exit originates from genuflecting to the altar.

The crypt of the old chapel (St Mary Undercroft) survived the fire of 1834 and now, carefully restored, is used for worship by members and for their marriages and their children's baptisms.

1348

The Black Death Reaches London
The most destructive plague ever to visit the country was reported in the port of London in September – by then the epidemic was over its worst in Italy. The bubonic Black Death, which began in central Asia, wiped out about a third of the population of western Europe. Spread by rats carrying infected fleas, it travelled from country to country via caravans, ships and carts. Though bubonic plague usually killed within days, there are numerous records of people succumbing within hours.

It was generally thought that the disease was carried on the wind, and that flight was the only worthwhile precaution. If this was impossible then the air was to be purified by the constant burning of aromatic woods or powders, or else windows were to be sealed with waxed cloth. The symptoms were inflammatory swellings, agonizing thirst and high fever. There was no cure, and treatments such as excessive bleeding were if anything detrimental to the patient's health.

The disease caused xenophobia everywhere. The English blamed it on the French. The Swiss voted to eject the Jews, and in Basle they burnt them alive; thousands of Jews were murdered in Germany and France, for they were thought to have brought in the plague.

The full effects of the disease in London were to be felt in the following year.

1349

ROOM FOR THE VICTIMS

The London churchyards could not cope with the numbers of Black Death victims. The bishop of London, shocked at the many who were buried 'unhousel'd, unanointed, unannealed', bought 3 acres near Clerkenwell for a new burial ground, but even this was not enough. Sir Walter Manny bought from St Bartholomew's Priory a further 13 acres, called Spital Croft, the site of today's Charterhouse Square. On this burial ground a chapel was built and dedicated. Another cemetery was opened in Southwark. It is surprising that men could be found to do the burying.

The plague raged for most of the year. Whole households were wiped out, all but one of the inmates of St James's Hospital in Westminster died, and the abbot and 27 monks of Westminster succumbed. No contemporary account of the scenes in London survives, but we must imagine that the nightmare was worse than in the well-documented Great Plague of 1665. In 1349 the death toll was higher, the terror was greater, and resources and organization were more inadequate. Boccaccio's graphic description in *The Decameron* of the epidemic's consequences in Florence was no doubt appropriate to London as well.

THAVIE'S INN

A first mention occurs of Thavie's Inn, an Inn of Chancery, this year. It is contained in the will of John Tavy, armourer of Holborn – perhaps he too was a plague victim. He left a house (roughly on the site of today's New Fetter Lane) 'wherein the apprentices [law students] used to dwell'. Evidently the students had moved out of Tavy's Inn before his death and moved next door (to the east), to the house belonging to John de Besvile, which retained the name of their original premises.

1350

ST MARY GRACES ABBEY FOUNDED

The last great abbey to be established in London was that of the St Mary Graces in East Smithfield – its site was later used by the Royal Mint. It was the last Cistercian abbey in the country; unusually, for this order, the East Minster, as it was also called, was adjacent to a city rather than in remote countryside.

1353

WESTMINSTER WOOL STAPLE ESTABLISHED

The Statute of the Staples established a wool staple or market at Westminster, which served for London. A hall and chambers were erected, together with a landing-stage and a weigh-house.

WORKMEN DESERT WESTMINSTER

A royal mandate to the City complained that workmen engaged on works at the Palace of Westminster had, of late, deserted their jobs and gone to work in the City instead where, presumably, the pay was better. It threatened that anyone employing such men would be imprisoned in the Tower.

1354

AUSTIN FRIARS REBUILT

A hundred years after it began, the priory of the Austin Friars off the west side of Old Broad Street was refounded and rebuilt by Humphrey de Bohun, grandson of the original founder. The nave and aisles of the new building survived the Reformation and a 19th-century fire only to be destroyed in the Second World War.

Architecturally it was one of the first churches in London to be 'decorated Gothic', with a great deal of rich tracery. It had a large nave, since the churches of the Austin Friars were used for sermons rather than ceremonies around the altar. It was also a wide building – wider, for example, than Ely Cathedral.

In a century when the Church, as portrayed by Chaucer, waxed fat on tithe revenue, the mendicants of Austin Friars distinguished themselves in 1371 by presenting a petition to the king urging that the clergy should contribute to the country's needs.

1355

THE SMELLS OF THE FLEET

Once again the condition of the Fleet river was brought to the City's notice. A writ from the king says that the stream, which also formed a moat around the Fleet prison, was choked up by filth from latrines built upon it, and other refuse, and that the stench and foul air posed a threat to the lives of those inside the jail.

1357

CELEBRATING POITIERS

The victory of Edward, the Black Prince, over the French at Poitiers was described in a letter from him to the City in October 1356. The French lost 6,000 men, of whom 800 were of the nobility, and their king and his son were taken prisoner.

On May 24 this year the prince entered the City in triumph, parading the French king at his side. They were first met by the civic leaders in all their finery at Southwark, and were then escorted over a river bedecked by boats to the City. The captured king was dressed in purple and rode a magnificent white horse, while his conqueror rode a diminutive black horse. The roads were decorated with tapestries, and the churches, leading citizens and guilds brought out their plate, furniture and silks. On the balconies, bows, arrows, shields and spears were shown as testament to London's appetite and ability for battle.

CLEANING UP THE CITY

Once again a proclamation on the sanitary state of the City was issued, although this time it might well have had some connection with the celebrations in the City mentioned above. It complains of dung and other filth and nuisances, boxes, empty tuns, and other articles 'lying and placed in the streets and lanes, before the doors of divers folks'. It was ordered that no man should carry

any manner of rubbish, earth, gravel, or dung, from out of his stable or else-where, to throw and put the same into the rivers of Thames and Flete, or into the Fosses around the walls of the city; and as to the dung that is found in the streets and lanes, the same shall be carried and taken elsewhere out of the City by carts, as heretofore; or else by the rakers to certain spots, that the same may be put into the dungboats without throwing anything into the Thames.

1359

VAGRANTS EXPELLED FROM CITY

A proclamation criticized the number of beggars in the City who made their livelihood to the detriment of those people, such as the lepers or the blind, in real need of alms. Henceforth these able-bodied beggars were to quit the City; those found remaining would be put in the stocks in Cornhill for half a day for a first offence, a day for the second; a third offence would bring 40 days in prison.

1360

TEMPLE ACCESS TO THE THAMES

At an inquiry, the City sought to have it resolved that from 'time out of mind' the City had had free access to the Thames through 'the great gate of the Templars' – a reference to those buildings, south of Fleet Street, formerly occupied by the Knights Templar, and which were increasingly the premises of practitioners in law. It is also noted that the occupiers of the Temple were obliged to maintain a jetty there, and also the latrines adjoining.

1361

THE WARDROBE MOVES

The mansion of Sir John Beauchamp on the south side of Carter Lane was purchased this year to house the Great Wardrobe. The move from the old house in Lombard Street (see 1328) took place on 1 October.

The house was on the corner of today's Blackfriars Lane, a street which runs along the course of a tidal inlet from the Thames. There was space enough in the house to manufacture many of the items, and to house the official keeper and his staff. Facilities included workrooms, a great hall, royal halls, a chapel, a treasury, a kitchen and chambers.

The Wardrobe was a growing concern, and by 1660, just before the house was destroyed in the Great Fire, it employed 800 people, some of whom lived in the Great Wardrobe precincts, spinning, weaving, embroidering and lacemaking.

SLAUGHTERING OUTSIDE THE CITY

One of the many, but futile, injunctions against butchers slaughtering large animals within the City was made this year. Parliament decreed that large beasts should be killed at Knightsbridge or Stratford and the entrails 'secured' before being brought to the City. It is likely that this was not enforced.

PLAGUE RETURNS TO LONDON

The bubonic plague which had terrorized London in 1348–9 returned, but to a lesser extent. It is usually recorded that about 1,200 people died in the space of two days, but this might well be an exaggeration.

1362

A HURRICANE IN LONDON

In January London was visited by a severe gale. It levelled 'high houses, lofty edifices, towers, and belfreys, trees, and other things, both hardy and durable, with the greatest violence'. We know that the steeple of the newly built Austin Friars blew down this year, presumably as a result of the hurricane.

The extent of the damage may be imagined from the text of a royal ordinance which said:

we have been given to understand that under pretext of the tempest of wind which has of late unhappily occurred in divers parts of our realm by reason whereof many buildings have been levelled with the ground, and many dilapidated, broke, and damaged, and great multitudes of tiles and other coverings have been wholly or for the greater part torn from the roofs thereof; those who have tiles to sell, and other things suitable for roofing such houses, do sell the same, entirely at their own pleasure, at a much higher price than they were wont to do; and that the tilers and the roofers of buildings, seeing so great an urgency for persons of their calling, hesitate to follow their trade, or to do any work, unless they receive excessive wages.

1363

THE MAYOR AND FIVE KINGS

An enduring legend is that this year, in a rare period of peace, a former mayor of London entertained at a sumptuous dinner the kings of England, France, Scotland, Denmark and Cyprus. Modern historians have objected that all five kings were never in London together, but facts have never stood in the way of a good myth. Certainly the Vintners' Company still celebrates the occasion, when the company is toasted with five cheers.

1365

ARCHERY PRACTICE

This year the king commanded the sheriffs of London to proclaim that

every one of the said City, strong in body, at leisure times, on holydays, should use in their recreations bows and arrows, or pellets, or bolts, and learn and exercise the art of shooting, forbidding all and singular in our behalf, that they do not after any manner apply themselves to the throwing of stones, hand-ball, football, bandy-ball, lambuck, or cock fighting, nor such other like vain plays which have no profit in them.

1366

MORE WORK AT THE PALACE OF WESTMINSTER

We have seen (1353) that building works were in progress at the Palace of Westminster. Two buildings, one of which survives, were erected by the end of this year. One was the Clock Tower, a medieval version of Big Ben, on the north side of New Palace Yard. Built by Henry Yevele, the principal architect of his time (he later also built Westminster Hall), it had a pyramidal roof and a bell, weighing over 4 tons, known as 'Edward of Westminster'.

On the south-west corner of Old Palace Yard, by Westminster Abbey, was built the Jewel Tower. This surviving three-storeyed building was surrounded by a moat; like the Clock Tower, it was built of ragstone, probably by Yevele. It was on Westminster Abbey land but part of the Palace of Westminster, and originally housed the king's valuables.

1369

NEW PLAGUE IN LONDON
A recurrence of bubonic plague, which had always hovered since the disastrous Black Death of 1349, dismayed Londoners again. To add to their troubles it was a very wet year, which devastated the harvest and forced up the price of wheat.

CHEAPSIDE EVENING MARKET BANNED
It was reported that of an evening a market dealing in old clothes opened on Cheapside. However, the old clothes often turned out to be stolen and passed off as new, to the detriment of those buying them. In future, no clothes were to be sold in the street after the bell had been rung at sunset at the Tun prison.

BUTCHERS' JETTY BANNED
After the complaints of many people, including the Black Friars, the butchers of Newgate Shambles were forbidden to carry entrails and offal through the streets from Newgate to the Thames (at the mouth of the Fleet) to dump them in the water there. The residents complain of blood running in the streets on the butchers' route to the river, and of the stench and filth from the water.

1370

GATEHOUSE PRISON BUILT
More building work at Westminster. The new gatehouse to the conventual buildings of Westminster Abbey at Broad Sanctuary was finished. It contained then, or later, two jails: one used by the bishop of London for prisoners to be judged by clerical law, and the other for lay offenders. Both were administered by the abbot of Westminster.

The prison's most famous occupants were Sir Walter Ralegh, who spent his last night here before being executed in Old Palace Yard in 1618, and the poet Richard Lovelace, whose oft-quoted lines 'Stone walls do not a prison make / Nor iron bars a cage' were written here in 1642.

The approximate site of the prison is that of today's war memorial to former scholars of Westminster School, outside the abbey.

FRENCH INVASION THREAT
The mayor and aldermen warned citizens that galleys containing armed men were anchored off the Isle of Thanet preparing to attack London. The king's ships were lying at Ratcliff in Wapping to engage them if necessary, but the City was to be on guard, and watch was to be kept between the Tower and Billingsgate with 40 men-at-arms and 60 archers continually there.

A HOSPITAL FOR LUNATICS FOUNDED
A hospital was established at All Hallows Barking for poor priests and others sick of 'the phrenzie'. This is the first known hospital for people suffering from mental illness. Although the priory of St Mary Bethlehem, later known as Bedlam, had been founded in 1247, the first sure date of its treating lunatics is in the early 15th century.

ST MARY ABBOTS REBUILT
The church of St Mary Abbots, Kensington, was rebuilt this year. There was a further rebuilding in 1696, which retained the old tower, when it became necessary to demolish this 14th-century building to accommodate William III and his court once they had moved into Kensington Palace.

1371

CHARTERHOUSE FOUNDED
The Carthusian monastery of Charterhouse was founded on 28 March on land at Smithfield adjoining the Black Death burial ground. Its benefactor was either Sir Walter Manny, who had bought the original ground and was buried in the chapel in 1372, or else the bishop of London, Michael de Northburgh. Seven years later, 4 acres belonging to the Order of St John, Clerkenwell, were added to the grounds. The word 'Charterhouse' derives from Chartreuse in France, where a monastery was founded in about 1084. The first English establishment was founded by Henry II after the murder of Thomas à Becket in 1170, near the Selwood Forest.

The early buildings were erected by Henry Yevele. They consisted of cells around a quadrangle – two-storey buildings with their own gardens, workroom, wood store and living room – and a chapel and a refectory. Progress was slow, and there were still five cells unfinished when the first prior died in 1398.

The monks lived alone, but had a communal meal once a week, after which they were allowed to talk with each other while on a walk out-side the monastery. They had no personal possessions and, alone among the monastic orders in London, were not allowed to eat meat. Once a week the meal consisted of bread and water, but on other days there were eggs, vegetables, cheese, fruit, wine and beer. An arduous routine was imposed. Having retired at seven, they were woken for matins at midnight, which lasted until about two o'clock, and then returned to bed until five, when they were up again. It was a rigorous and lonely life – combined sometimes with self-flagellation – which at one time attracted Sir Thomas More, who spent some years here.

BOWYERS AND FLETCHERS SEPARATE
It was agreed that the bowyers, who made bows, and the fletchers, who made arrows, should become two separate guilds. The bowyers also agreed not to work at night, as it was acknowledged that work of sufficient standard could not be achieved after daylight.

COMPLAINT ABOUT PLUMBERS
A complaint was lodged that plumbers (workers in lead) smelted metal by St Clement's Lane 'to the great damage and peril of death of all who shall smell the smoke'. It was agreed that, as the place had been used for smelting for many years, operations might continue provided that the plumbers erected a taller ventilation shaft, so that the smoke went higher up.

1372

EFFECTS OF THE HUNDRED YEARS WAR

War against the French had begun in 1338 with Edward III attempting to enforce his claims to the kingdom of France; with short intervals of truce, it lasted until 1453, by which time England had lost all its Continental possessions except Calais. There were notable victories, such as those of Poitiers and Crécy, which persuaded the English citizens that the increasing tax demands on them were worthwhile, but as the years went by the cause of the English Crown was increasingly perceived to be lost.

This year Edward III set out with many nobles and a large army containing a band of London archers and crossbow men. His object was the relief of La Rochelle, but the expensive expedition was disastrous.

1374

CHAUCER MOVES TO ALDGATE

Geoffrey Chaucer was granted a life occupancy of the dwelling above the Aldgate; this was rent-free so long as he kept the structure in good repair. He was here from May this year until 1386. Previously a diplomat, doing much work in Italy for John of Gaunt, he was appointed in 1374 as comptroller of the customs and the subsidy of wools, leathers and skins for the Port of London.

GRACECHURCH MARKET

A proclamation this year confirms that a regular market for the sale of hay and corn was held at Gracechurch, although it is not clear when it began. Its site was probably at the junction of Gracechurch Street and Fenchurch Street. It is suggested that the antiquity of a market here selling hay is probably the derivation of the names Gracechurch Street (from 'grass') and Fenchurch Street (from the Latin *faenum*, meaning 'hay').

DISPUTES IN CHANCERY LANE

The bishop of Chichester complained that one Roger Leget, owner of property in Chancery Lane next to his own, had dug a ditch so close to the bishop's building that the walls were breaking and the bakehouse and brewhouse were in danger of collapsing into the ditch. Leget retorted that the buildings were in such a bad state of repair that the wind and rain were blowing them over. Leget was also not popular with law students who used his fields for sport – he set mantraps there, and was imprisoned in the Fleet for this.

1375

A BEQUEST TO ST PAUL'S

The value and rarity of books at this period is illustrated in a bequest by John de Kenyngton, rector of St Dunstan in the East, who left a religious book called *Catholicon* to St Paul's, with instructions that it should be kept in a case and that whoever used it should pray for his soul.

RESTRICTIONS ON ALESTAKES

It was the custom to fix a horizontal pole to the outside of inn premises, on which to hang a sign. It was reported this year that a number

Gates in the City wall. The oldest were Aldgate, Bishopsgate, Newgate and Ludgate.

of these poles in Cheapside were so long as to be a danger to those riding along the road, and that some were too heavy and thus a danger to the safety of the houses themselves. It was ordered that the maximum length of an alestake should be 7 ft.

1376

ELECTION BY THE GUILDS

There had been sufficient turbulence between political factions in the City for the king to threaten that he would intervene. The old battle between the oligarchy and the less well-to-do reappeared, but now the latter were dressed up as guild members. By this year there were about 50 guilds in London, and their strength brought about a new system of government in the City. Under the leadership of John of Northampton, a draper, it was agreed that henceforth the Common Council should be made up of people nominated by the guilds instead of by the wards, and should have the right to meet with the mayor and sheriffs eight times a year. It was also agreed that no member of the council should officiate in the collection of the king's revenues – a decision no doubt brought about by the indictment in April, by Parliament, of three City aldermen for embezzlement of the king's income. This system of election was to be short-lived: the old one was reinstated in ten years.

HOSTILITY TO LANCASTER

Ecclesiastical reform was in the air, led by the theologian John Wyclif and his champion the duke of Lancaster, John of Gaunt. However, Lancaster was at odds with London because he proposed this year the abolition of the mayoralties and a reduction of the City's privileges.

1377

WYCLIF ARRAIGNED

The teachings of Wyclif caused widespread controversy and his opinions, even though championed by the duke of Lancaster, could not be left to rest unchallenged. He opposed the Church's intervention in temporal affairs — an opinion likely to irritate many an ambitious bishop. He criticized the vast property ownership of the Church, infuriating his ecclesiastical colleagues but delighting lay people keen to add to their estates. He believed, too, in predestination.

On 19 February he was arraigned at St Paul's before the bishop of London on a charge of heresy, but his support from Lancaster (some suggest that the trial of Wyclif was in effect an attack on Lancaster by his enemies) ensured that the result was indecisive.

ATTACK ON THE SAVOY

While Londoners might have sympathized with some of the teachings of Wyclif, they were quite opposed to the arrogant ways of John of Gaunt, duke of Lancaster. At the arraignment of Wyclif he abused the bishop of London, and this so aroused sections of the population that the following day a mob besieged Lancaster's house, the Savoy Palace in the Strand. The duke, however, had been forewarned and had retreated to his sister's house at Kennington. There he was surrounded by the mob, while back in the City his coat of arms was hung back to front (a sign of treason) on the doors of St Paul's and Westminster Hall.

Lancaster did not do the sensible thing and placate London. Instead, he insisted that its leaders should appear before the dying king at Shene. For their acquiescence in these events, the mayor was replaced, and a fresh election of aldermen took place.

OLD AND NEW KINGS

Edward III died at his manor house at Shene in June. Later, this house was to be transformed into Richmond Palace. London sent a deputation to Shene urging the new king, Richard II, to intervene in the City's dispute with Lancaster and bring about a reconciliation.

The new king, Edward's ten-year-old grandson, was crowned at Westminster Abbey on 16 July. It was an elaborate occasion. The young boy was escorted from the Tower to the abbey by the duke of Lancaster, as steward of the realm, together with numerous knights who had washed, with ceremony, in a bath before putting on their robes. The day was marred by the boy collapsing — he had fasted and spent the previous night in prayer. For the time being he was guided by a council of administrators which excluded Lancaster.

FLOODING AT BARKING AND DAGENHAM

The abbess of Barking Abbey petitioned the new king to be relieved of the tax being imposed to raise money for the war with the French, as her lands in Barking and Dagenham had been inundated by the Thames. Three years later there was more flooding and the abbess stated that her income had decreased considerably because of it.

1378

FACTIONS IN THE CITY

Despite the apparent reconciliation with Lancaster, London was still in turmoil. Two principal factions existed. One supported the mayor, John Philipot, and Nicholas Brembre, his predecessor; the other was led by John de Northampton and William Walworth, who themselves were supporters of the duke of Lancaster. In the new reign, with the continuation of war against France, Lancaster needed the wealth of the capitalists of London, and it mattered greatly to him which faction won.

Tempers ran high, and in three years' time hostility to Lancaster was to bubble over during the Peasants' Revolt. Meanwhile the parish clerk

of one of the London churches was arrested for speaking disrespectfully of the duke. This may have been a result of Lancaster's support for Wyclif, which in many people's eyes only compounded his political arrogance. Indeed, the controversy over Wyclif exploded in a fight between members of the Goldsmiths' and the Pepperers' companies.

RIGHT OF WAY THROUGH A CHURCH

The church of St Michael le Querne stood roughly on the site of today's St Paul's underground station. Through it ran a right of way, and this year the rector and others were arraigned for blocking up this path by building a wall whose gate was not always open, thereby preventing people using the door of the church and therefore the right of way.

1380

ORDINANCES FOR CUTLERS

Rules for trade practices were published for cutlers. The trade was divided into four parts — the bladesmiths, the hafters, the sheathers and the cutlers themselves, who put all the components together and sold the result to the public.

CHAPEL ON STEPNEY MARSH

Stepney Marsh, now called the Isle of Dogs (a name not yet satisfactorily explained), was quite often flooded by the Thames. However, since the reign of Edward II, channels had been cut so as to preserve much of the land for agriculture — sufficient in any case to establish a chapel here by 1380.

1381

THE PEASANTS' REVOLT IN LONDON

This famous revolt against a poll tax followed a bloody course and had a violent end in London. The peasants, from Essex and Kent, armed only with primitive weapons, were able to storm and ransack the capital at will and oblige the king to negotiate face to face.

The trouble stemmed from the young king's shortage of money and the unpopularity of the de facto head of government, John of Gaunt, duke of Lancaster. A poll tax was imposed — by no means the first. It was ungraduated: regardless of income, each man paid the same. This imposition was felt badly by peasants, who were still precluded from negotiating higher wages even when labour was short in the years following the Black Death.

Ferment began first in Essex, where resistance to the tax in three villages led to a general uprising in the county. A similar revolt occurred in Kent, and the groups of rebels from the two counties marched on an unprepared and undefended London.

The Kent rebels, headed by an obscure figure called Wat Tyler, set out from Canterbury on 11 June and in less than two days had covered the 70 miles to Blackheath; simultaneously the Essex men laid siege to east London, camping at Mile End.

On 13 June the situation was thought serious enough for the king to offer concessions, and he and his advisers set off from the Tower by barge, down to Greenwich to negotiate with Tyler. The sight of the massed forces on the other bank decided the royal party on retreat instead — a withdrawal interpreted as both an insult and a provocation.

The rebels then went west to Southwark, opened up Marshalsea prison, and proceeded to Lambeth Palace in a vain attempt to seize the hated archbishop of Canterbury, Simon Sudbury. London Bridge fell with sufficient ease to suggest that they were allowed on to the bridge by an accommodating populace, and once on the north bank they pressed on to the Fleet prison, where more men were released. The Temple was ransacked and legal records were burnt.

The mob, augmented by Londoners, then turned to the Savoy Palace, the house of the duke of Lancaster. A number of his servants were executed, but some of the rebels also lost their lives when, in a drunken state, they were trapped in the wine cellars as the house above was burnt down.

By now Tyler's men were an undisciplined and uncoordinated mob; in Cheapside, some lawyers, Flemings and others were summarily executed. A particular enemy was the prior of the order of St John of Jerusalem, the king's treasurer, who was beheaded; the order's premises in Clerkenwell were destroyed, as was the prior's house in Highbury. A man was dragged out of the church of St Martin's le Grand and beheaded; Newgate jail was emptied of prisoners. And, to the mob's delight, the archbishop of Canterbury was found at the Tower of London and was beheaded on Tower Hill. There was a massacre in the Vintry area of the City and, according to the *Anonimalle Chronicle,* trouble spread across a large area of London:

A 15th-century miniature of the slaying of Wat Tyler by William Walworth.

Then a party of them went to Westminster and set afire a place belonging to John de Butterwyk, sub-sheriff of Middlesex, and houses of various other people and took away all prisoners condemned by the law and returned to London by way of Holborn. Before the church of St Sepulchre they set afire the houses of Symond Hosteler and several other houses, and they broke into Newgate and took out all the prisoners regardless of the cause for which they had been imprisoned.

The end of the revolt and the blood-letting came quickly. On 15 June the king, accompanied by the mayor of London, William Walworth, rode to Smithfield to discuss terms with Tyler. It is not certain what happened there, but Walworth appears to have mistaken an action of the rebel leader as threatening to the king and promptly struck Tyler down with a dagger — accounts vary as to whether Tyler died immediately or else later in the nearby hospital of St Bartholomew. Surprisingly, the royal party escaped from this incident and the rebels appear to have lost heart at the death of their leader.

One prominent leader, Jack Straw, was executed after confessing to an intention to kill the king and to put peasants in control of the country. It was also revealed that the rebels wanted to overthrow the bishops and implement the teachings of Wyclif.

1382

BACKLASH TO THE REVOLT

The ruling class took advantage of the outrage at the Peasants' Revolt to press home opposition against the teachings of Wyclif. A council of bishops was convened on 17 January by the new archbishop of Canterbury at Blackfriars monastery to condemn Wyclif — an event underlined by a minor earthquake in London, a sign taken as support both for and against the bishops. However, it seems that a large majority of Londoners were still supporters of the preacher. London elected a mayor, John de Northampton, who was sympathetic to Wyclif, and under his administration the fees of city parsons were reduced.

The burning of St John's Priory, Clerkenwell, during the Peasants' Revolt.

AN EXPENSIVE LINING

At a time of great poverty in the land, the mayor and aldermen concerned themselves with the case of the alderman of Walbrook who, contrary to tradition, had appeared at the procession on the Feast of Pentecost in a green cloak but without the prescribed green taffeta lining. His punishment was unusual. Not only was he to make good the omission in future but he was to entertain the mayor and alderman to a dinner at his house.

1383

ESTABLISHMENT OF FURNIVAL'S INN

Furnival's Inn was an Inn of Chancery, later to be annexed by Lincoln's Inn, on the north side of Holborn – on the site of today's Prudential Building. It is uncertain when it was first used to house law students, but when William, Lord Furnival, died in 1383 his property consisted of two houses and 13 shops. Two years later there is a reference to a manciple, a college bursar, living in 'the rent of Sir Furnevall, knight', and by 1407 there is a record of a principal for the Inn.

WALBROOK STOPPED UP

The river Walbrook was a subject of frequent complaint. Once again this year it was reported that people threw dung and filth into the stream so that it was silted up. Adjacent parishes were required to scour it, but it was still allowed that houses along its course could have latrines over the water, for the sum of two shillings a year.

1384

LONDON BRIDGE CHAPEL REBUILT

The City made a start this year on the rebuilding of the chapel of St Thomas on London Bridge. This time it was designed in the Perpendicular style by Henry Yevele. The new building retained the entrance at river level which had been a feature of the previous building – at low tide a mariner or fisherman could alight at the starling on which the pier stood and go up a stairway to the chapel.

RIOTING IN THE CITY

Factions still spilled blood in the City – this time the basis of the dispute seems to have been the exclusion of victuallers, such as fishmongers and vintners, from government of the City. Also at stake was the protection of trade interests by monopolies. John de Northampton had been ousted from the mayoralty in October 1383 by his old rival Nicholas Brembre, but there must have been conflict afterwards, because Northampton was bound over to keep the peace in January against a fine of £5,000. The following month he was arrested and imprisoned in Corfe Castle, Dorset, and one of his supporters, a cordwainer named John Constantyn, was executed for inciting riot.

AN INVASION THREAT

With the threat of an invasion from France, the City urged that those able and willing to defend the sea coast should go there – the City would pay them at the rate of 12 pence a day for a man fully armed, and 6 pence for archers. Those able men who declined to go were to be arrested as traitors.

The chapel of St Thomas on London Bridge, rebuilt between 1384 and 1396. It had special access from the river, used by fishermen and mariners.

NEW CUSTOM HOUSE OPENED

About this year a new custom house was established in the house of John Churchman at Woolwharf, just slightly east of the present building in Lower Thames Street. Here there were a weighing machine for wool and facilities to keep accounts. In charge of this building was the poet Geoffrey Chaucer, who in 1374 had been appointed comptroller of the customs and the subsidy of wools, skins and hides in the Port of London.

Remains of this building were excavated in 1973. Uncovered was a small extension, thought to have been built in 1383, which housed a latrine – possibly used by Chaucer himself.

PILLORY FOR A PROCURESS

The City court heard the story of a woman, an embroiderer called Elizabeth, who accommodated young apprentice women whom she used as prostitutes. One such young woman, Johanna, was hired out to a chaplain for the night but returned home without having asked for any money. She was sent again the following night, and once more had not the heart to ask for money but instead stole a breviary, which Elizabeth later pawned.

Elizabeth, for acting as a procuress, was sentenced to be put in the pillory in Cornhill as often as it pleased the mayor and aldermen, and then to be expelled from the City.

1387

BURNING OF THE 'JUBILEE'

Discontent at the ousting of John de Northampton from the mayoralty in 1384 still simmered. A book, purporting to be the true regulations for the administration of the City, called the 'Jubilee', and which Northampton is supposed to have compiled, was seized by the authorities and publicly burnt in Guildhall Yard. This infuriated the cordwainers, supporters of Northampton – it was a cordwainer who had been summarily executed in the riots of 1384.

Northampton was released from confinement in April, but the king declined to restore him and his confederates into their estates. At this time the king was in a difficult position. Not only was he prosecuting an expensive and ineffective war against the French, but he was trying to oust his uncle, the duke of Lancaster (whom Northampton supported), from influence. The king in fact needed the support of Londoners in this battle, but their sympathy could be bought only by the release of Northampton. A commission of regency, under the duke of Gloucester, another of the king's uncles, had been appointed to curb the excesses of the king's actions, and in November it accused the king's counsellors, including Nicholas Brembre, of treason.

In this new dispute between king and barons Londoners sided with the barons, led by the duke of Gloucester. With the king holed up in the Tower, the City let hostile soldiers camp around the building until, at last, the king succumbed to the barons' demands. Some of his favourites were executed, including Sir Simon Burley, who was beheaded on Tower Hill.

1388

THE TYBURN GALLOWS SET UP
By this year the gallows belonging to the manor of Tyburn (St Marylebone) were set up at the corner of today's Oxford Street and Edgware Road. It is not clear why this site, well outside the City, should have become the most notorious place of execution for London. It could not have been that Londoners were too squeamish to have the hangings within the walls – public executions continued at places like Smithfield, Tower Hill and Newgate.

This year, Nicholas Brembre, four times mayor of London and one of the king's detested advisers, was hanged at Tyburn, having been drawn from the City. If we are to believe Thomas Walsingham, Brembre was a turbulent influence in the land. Not only had he conspired in a plot to kill Gloucester, but he intended to place himself at the head of the City, which he would rename 'Little Troy'. An associate, Justice Tressilian, was dragged from Westminster Abbey and hanged.

PRISON FOR AN INSULT
Richard Bole, a butcher at Newgate, was charged with uttering offensive words to an alderman of the City. Being found guilty, he was sentenced to six months in Newgate prison and on his release he was to walk barefoot, carrying a lighted taper, from Newgate to the Guildhall as a sign of his atonement. The prison term was later remitted.

1389

GUILD WARFARE SIMMERS
The long-standing hostility broke out again between the old manufacturing guilds such as the Goldsmiths, Drapers and Mercers and the upstarts such as the Fishmongers and Vintners. Voted into office as mayor was a Grocer – an appointment strongly opposed by the old guard.

Geoffrey Chaucer – an oil painting by an unknown artist. The poet worked as a civil servant, and was appointed as clerk of the king's works in 1389.

CHAUCER MADE CLERK OF THE KING'S WORKS
Geoffrey Chaucer, civil servant and poet, was this year made clerk of the king's works, succeeding the mason and architect Henry Yevele. Fortunately for Chaucer he was allowed to appoint a deputy, for his responsibilities included the maintenance and development of, among other places, the Tower of London, the Palace of Westminster, the king's manors at Eltham, Kennington and Shene, and the mews at Charing Cross where the king kept his falcons. Chaucer appears to have held the post for only two years.

1390

CHURCHES REBUILT
The rebuilding of three churches was completed this year. St John Zachary, at the junction of Noble Street and Gresham Street, owed its name to its gift by the canons of St Paul's to a man called Zacharie in 1180. It was rebuilt in 1390 at the expense of a former mayor, Nicholas Twiford, who was buried here. The church was destroyed in the Great Fire, but its churchyard remains as a public garden.

St Mary Overie in Southwark was rebuilt after being damaged by fire in 1385, and a new St Giles Cripplegate, by the London wall, was completed.

JOUSTING ON THE BRIDGE
As a result of an argument between Lord Welles, ambassador of England to Scotland, and Sir David de Lindsay, a Scot, as to the valour of their two nations, a joust was held between the two men in the carriageway of London Bridge on 23 April. As a state of hostility

existed between the two countries, Lindsay and his supporters were granted safe custody in England for the occasion. The king and his court were present, and no doubt half of London was watching from the shore. Two runs produced no result, but on the third Welles was unseated and Lindsay went to his aid; it is reported that the Scot attended the Englishman at his bedside for days afterwards. The unlikely end to this chivalrous occasion was that Lindsay was later appointed Scots ambassador to England, where his reputation among Londoners stood him in good stead.

CHAUCER ROBBED

On a journey to see the king at Eltham Palace in his new capacity as clerk of the king's works, Chaucer was twice robbed on one day: once at Westminster, where he was 'feloniously despoiled' of £10, and again at the 'fowle oak' at Hatcham, near New Cross, where he lost £9 3s 6d. In fact the cash he was carrying was Crown money, and in 1391 a writ was issued discharging Chaucer of the liability of repaying it.

1391

FAMINE IN LONDON

There was famine in London at a time when it was alleged that the king employed 300 domestics in his kitchen alone and at times entertained 6,000 people. The mayor and aldermen subscribed £20 each to buy corn from abroad to feed the poor.

1392

TROUBLE WITH THE KING

Pleading poverty, the City declined to advance a loan to the extravagant Richard II. Having then borrowed the sum he needed from a Lombard, the king found that the money had been raised by the moneylender from the City. Incensed by this, the king waited for a suitable occasion to take revenge. It came in the form of a civil disturbance in Fleet Street. At the root of this lay a theft from a baker by a servant of the bishop of Salisbury. The mob attacked the thief, but were prevailed upon to disperse peacefully. However, the bishop complained to the king.

Summoned to meet the king at Nottingham, the mayor, sheriffs and aldermen were accused of governing the City badly and of insulting the king: the mayor and sheriffs were imprisoned. On 1 July, Sir Edward Dalyngrigge appeared at the Guildhall armed with the king's writ to govern the City. London was fined £100,000, but peace between the two parties was restored by the end of the year, with liberties restored and the fine unpaid.

1393

FARRINGDON DIVIDED

By now, a large population lived outside the City walls. The largest ward by far was that of Farringdon, stretching nearly as far west as Chancery Lane, and beyond Smithfield to the east, down to the Thames in the south and beyond Smithfield to the north. Its governance was therefore declared 'too laborious and grievous for one person to occupy and duly govern the same' and it was divided into two parts: that within the wall and that without. The name 'Farringdon' derives from Walter Farendon, goldsmith, who was alderman of the whole ward in 1281.

Another change in government applied to aldermen – they were in future to be elected for life and not for just a year.

1394

SHENE PALACE PARTIALLY DESTROYED

The manor house of Shene, situated in what is now called Richmond, had come into the hands of Henry I. By the time of Richard II the house was a palace, large enough in which to entertain thousands for dinner. Edward III had a household there which included chaplains, a physician, an apothecary, several butlers, tailors, numerous artisans such as carpenters and smiths, hundreds of soldiers, and, of course, the great officers of court.

Richard II held elaborate events there. His queen, Anne of Bohemia, who had introduced the horned cap into the fashions of the country, helped him make Shene Palace a spectacular and extravagant place. She had not only her own apartments, but also her own gardens. Stow asserts (one suspects with much exaggeration) that 10,000 people sat down to dine at times.

This year, plague raged in London. One of its victims was Queen Anne. The king, who appears to have genuinely loved her, was distraught, and in his frenzy he ordered that Shene Palace be destroyed. To an extent it was, but much remained to house soldiers.

1395

THE CHEAPSIDE STANDARD

What was known as the Cheapside Standard is first mentioned this year: Stow says it was here by 1293, but gives no evidence. Made of wood and housing a conduit supplying water from the river Tyburn at Oxford Street, it was also used as a place for executions and other punishments. It was situated at the end of Honey Lane, nearly opposite St Mary-le-Bow.

SADDLERS OBTAIN CHARTER

The Company of Saddlers was incorporated this year. The Saddlers were one of the older guilds, with great control within their trade, though in 1327 they had been unsuccessful in forcing those tradesmen making the smaller parts of the saddle, such as the metal fittings (made by loriners), to work exclusively for them. Another group of workers, the fusters (hence Foster Lane, where saddlery was centred), made the wooden part of the saddle.

1396

DISASTER AT A ROYAL PROCESSION

The king's new bride-to-be, Isabella of France, seven years old, entered London. The mayor and aldermen went to Blackheath to receive her and the king, and then escorted them to the Tower. It was while crossing London Bridge that disaster happened. So many people had gathered to catch a glance of the child queen that at least seven were crushed to death.

BAKEWELL HALL ACQUIRED BY THE CITY

Bakewell (or Blackwell) Hall, at the junction of Basinghall Street and Gresham Street, was acquired by the City for use as a wool market. The site of this large mansion was taken in the 19th century by the City of London law courts.

1397

FIRST MAYORALTY OF DICK WHITTINGTON

The beginning of the Whittington legend was not auspicious. When the elected mayor of London, Adam Bamme, died this year the king insisted on appointing his successor – Whittington. This was the final period of the king's unpopularity with his citizens. Many, indeed, thought that he was unhinged since the death of his first wife. To support himself and his extravagances, the king was raising money by forced loans – perhaps Whittington was one of those to whom he owed money.

Whittington was subsequently elected to the mayoralty three times – at the next proper election in 1397 and in 1406 and 1419. Being elected three times in the 14th century was not uncommon, and the passage of time between the elections does not indicate that Whittington was more than usually popular.

Very little of the Whittington legend, apart from the number of his elections, appears to be true. He was certainly no poor boy from the country making good in London: he came from a well-to-do West Country family and, as a prominent mercer in the City, appears on a list as a contributor towards a City loan nearly 20 years before his appointment as mayor. He was also a merchant adventurer, chartering or owning ships, importing and exporting. By the end of the 14th century he was a very wealthy man whose generosity was courted by both Richard II and Henry IV. It is most unlikely that he would have set off for home as a young man, only to turn back on Highgate Hill at the sound of Bow Bells, if only because that wouldn't have been on the way back to Gloucestershire. He did not marry the daughter of his London master – his wife was the daughter of a West Country knight. There is also no evidence that he was ever knighted, or that at a banquet for the king he tore up the bonds to cancel the king's debts to him.

Whittington did, however, leave much of his fortune to the City, and it is probably from these bequests that his legend was engendered.

EARLY DAYS OF GRAY'S INN

When lawyers first resided in Gray's Inn is not known. The manor of Purtpool in Holborn was in the possession of the Gray family by 1307, and during the course of the following century it was occupied by lawyers.

1399

CITY HELPS TO OVERTHROW THE KING

In February the death of John of Gaunt, duke of Lancaster, at Ely Palace in Holborn, sparked off the overthrow of Richard II. Eager for loot, the king seized the Lancaster estates; those counties which had

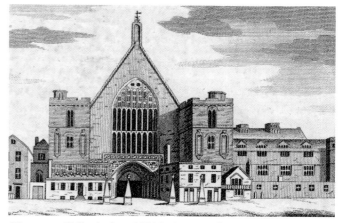

Westminster Hall, rebuilt in 1399 by Henry Yevele.

supported the factious duke of Gloucester (whom the king had had murdered in 1397) were charged with treason and obliged to purchase their pardons. The earl of Northumberland was declared a traitor and his estates were confiscated; the earl of Arundel had already been executed for treason. In Ireland there was rebellion, and in a battle there Roger Mortimer, royal ward and heir presumptive to the throne, was killed. His two sons eventually died without issue, but their sister married the second son of the duke of York. In these events lay the beginnings of that squalid contest romanticized under the name 'the Wars of the Roses': the seemingly endless battle between the houses of Lancaster and York.

In 1399, with Richard away in Ireland in a vain attempt to stamp out revolt, John of Gaunt's son, Henry, claimed the throne of England. His title was not particularly authentic, but his popularity was. Informed of Henry's return from prudent exile in France, the mayor and 500 citizens went to meet him and accompanied him back to the City – the day was kept as a holiday. London supplied 1,200 men of the force which subsequently deterred the king from continuing his reign and, with his position hopeless, Richard resigned the crown. The king, who, when a boy, had captured London's heart by his confrontation of the Peasants' Revolt in 1381, ended an extravagant and brutal career ignominiously.

WESTMINSTER HALL COMPLETED

It is ironic that the first Parliament to be held in the rebuilt Westminster Hall, upon which Richard II had lavished so much public wealth, was that in which the throne stood empty. Here the Commons heard the resignation of Richard, and the claim to the throne by Henry, son of the duke of Lancaster, on the grounds of right of descent from Henry III and of the misgovernment of Richard: wisely, the throne was not claimed through conquest. A week later Parliament met again, and this time Henry was king. The coronation took place at the abbey across the road on 13 October. The banquet in the hall was a lavish affair. Guests enjoyed boar's head, pheasant, peacock, stuffed pigs, cranes, herons and venison, and nine fountains spouted wine.

The hall that Richard rebuilt is still with us. The old roof, built during the reign of William II, had gone. This had rested on two lines of pillars so that, in effect, the chamber was divided into three, much like a church. Under the supervision of Henry Yevele and his master carpenter, Hugh Herland, the walls were raised and buttressed, and a magnificent hammerbeam roof, which spanned the hall, was erected; it weighed 660 tons.

1400

CHAUCER AND YEVELE DIE

The two most important English artists of the last part of the 14th century both died this year. Geoffrey Chaucer, poet and civil servant, reduced to living on a pension, died in October, with his great work, *The Canterbury Tales,* still unfinished. By then a widower, he had taken a house in the garden of the Lady Chapel, Westminster – the site is now covered by the Henry VII Chapel of the abbey. He was buried in that part of the abbey which is now called Poets' Corner.

The architect, Henry Yevele, also died. He was born *c.* 1320 and by 1356 was regarded as one of the most important masons in London. In 1358 he was engaged in rebuilding Kennington Palace for the Black Prince, and then became architect for any works on the Tower of London. In 1393–4 he began work on his most famous building, the reconstructon of Westminster Hall, and it was he who installed the hall's famous hammerbeam roof (see 1399).

GREEK EMPEROR AT ELTHAM

The Greek emperor, Manuel Palaiologos, visited King Henry in the hope of securing aid in his war with the Turks. He was met by the king at Blackheath on 21 December, and stayed two months at Eltham Palace.

NEW CHURCH AT ST MARYLEBONE

The parish church of what is now St Marylebone, and was then called Tyburn, was in Oxford Street, between today's Stratford Place and Marylebone Lane. This was then a fairly uninhabited and desolate area, the influential part of the parish having established itself further up Marylebone High Street. The residents complained that the old church was 'in too lonely a place' and that 'on account of the snares and plunderings of robbers, the books, vestments, images, bells, and other ornaments cannot be preserved as they should be'.

Permission was granted this year to demolish the old church dedicated to St John and build a new one, this time to the west of the High Street. It was this time dedicated to St Mary, and its nearness to the river Tyburn brought about the gradual change of name of the parish – in 1453 it was Maryburne, and by 1626 Marylebone.

ST ETHELBURGA'S, BISHOPSGATE, REBUILT

It is probable that the small church of St Ethelburga-the-Virgin, Bishopsgate, was rebuilt between 1390 and 1400. It just escaped the Great Fire, and was therefore of great interest to historians. Until 1933 it had a late-medieval entrance, with shops of the same date at either side, but when these were taken down to widen the road the original late-14th-century doorway was revealed. A south gallery in the church was added in 1629, 'only for the Daughters and Maidservants of the Parish to sit in'.

1401

THE LOLLARD SUPPRESSION

The so-called Lollards, followers of the teachings of John Wyclif, were now being persecuted in earnest. One of the earliest to die for heresy was William Chatris, priest of the church of St Benet Sherehog in St Pancras Lane. He was burnt at Smithfield, a venue which was to see a depressing number of such executions.

TUN PRISON COVERTED TO CONDUIT

The Tun prison in Cornhill, mainly used to incarcerate 'lewd women', was demolished and a conduit was erected in its place, fed by water from the Tyburn springs. Adjacent were built a cage (a prison), stocks for the punishment of night-walkers, and a pillory in 'which dishonest millers and bakers were exposed to the scorn of the public'.

1403

LUNATICS AT ST MARY BETHLEHEM

By 1346, when the City of London took over its supervision, the hospital of St Mary Bethlehem in Bishopsgate was referred to as Bethleem. By 1403 it specialized in the treatment, if such it could be called, of mentally disturbed people, and the word 'bedlam', meaning a scene of uproar, had come into the English language.

STATIONERS' COMPANY BEGINS

A brotherhood began this year of writers of text-letters, limners, bookbinders and booksellers, to become in later years the Company of Stationers and Newspaper Makers. Before Caxton's introduction of printing, the emphasis of their business was the preparation of manuscripts, but they were soon to be responsible for the trade of book production. It was not until 1911 that the company relinquished its right to register each book published.

1404

NEW ALMSHOUSES FOR THE MERCHANT TAYLORS

The Merchant Taylors' Company this year acquired a site in Threadneedle Street, next to the church of St Martin Outwich, to build some almshouses. They eventually consisted of seven dwellings.

1405

BAN ON ASSEMBLY IN SOUTHWARK

Trouble in Southwark led to the bailiffs there being ordered 'to make unlawful assemblies within the town and suburbs of Suthewerk'; only lords, great men, knights and esquires were permitted to wear armour and weapons.

HORN TAVERN GIVEN TO GOLDSMITHS' COMPANY

The Horn Tavern, on the site of 164 Fleet Street, was given to the Goldsmiths' Company by one of its members, 'for the better support and sustentation of the infirm members of the Company'. In 1879 it was replaced by Anderton's Hotel.

1406

RIOT AT BARKING

Numerous references are found in the City records referring to the fishing regulations on the Thames. Even as early as this period there was considerable danger of overfishing, so that it was found necessary to ban nets whose holes were small enough to catch younger fish and hinder the natural restocking of the river. Many of the fishermen hauled before the City courts came from Barking and Dagenham. This year tempers boiled over. When an inspector of nets was spotted, the parish bell of Barking was sounded and a mob, armed with bows and arrows, gathered to meet him. The ringleaders of this uprising were eventually tried, but were allowed to resume their occupations under certain restrictions.

New Site for Romford Church

The village of Romford, Essex, was frequently affected by the flooding of the river Rom. The parish church, in what is known as the district of Oldchurch, was increasingly at risk, and permission was obtained this year to demolish it and move it to its present site, where a small wood had first to be cleared. The new church lasted for about 400 years.

1407

Plague in London

Plague rarely left London, but in some years it surfaced with great severity. This year was particularly bad, and it is reported that about 30,000 people died.

1409

The Parish Clerk Thespians

There were no theatres in London at this time. When the Company of Parish Clerks performed a play this year, they did so near the Skinners' Well in Clerkenwell. The play in question, called *The Creation of the World,* which took eight days to perform, was written by an Ironmonger mayor of London.

St Michael Paternoster Royal Rebuilt

One of the earliest benefactions of Richard Whittington was the rebuilding this year of his local church, St Michael Paternoster Royal. He himself lived in a house adjoining, at which, after his death, was formed a College of Priests.

The ecclesiastical historian John Strype (1643–1737) described the new church as 'a curious Free-stone building with Battlements and a lofty towered steeple'. Whittington's tomb here was lost when the church was destroyed in the Great Fire. According to John Stow (writing in the later 16th century), Whittington was buried here three times: first by his executors, then again in the reign of Edward VI, after the parson had had him dug up in the belief that great riches were buried with him, and once again, for an unspecified reason, in the reign of Queen Mary.

1410

The Thames Frozen

It was a severe winter. A contemporary chronicle records that 'Thys yere was the grete frost and ise and the most sharpest winter that ever man sawe, and it duryd fourteen wekes so that man myght in dyvers places both goo and ryde over the Temse.'

Another Lollard Burning

John Bradley, a tailor, having been found guilty of heresy because of his support for the views of John Wyclif, was carried in a cask to be burnt at Smithfield. Prince Henry (the future Henry V) was present on this gruesome occasion, and, according to Henry Chamberlain in his 1770 *History of London,* offered a free pardon if Bradley should recant, but he refused to do so.

… the fire being lighted, the flames soon reached his body, which occasioned his crying out in the most piteous manner. The young prince was so affected by this circumstance, that he gave orders to take him instantly out of the fire, renewed the offer of a pardon and even promised to allow him a pension of threepence per day in consideration of the injury he had already sustained by the fire. This offer likewise the resolute martyr rejected, upon which he was reconducted to the flames, which soon put a period to his life.

Stamford Bridge Built

The eastern limit of the parish of Fulham, separating it from Chelsea, was Counters Creek, a watercourse now covered by a railway. Across this at Fulham Road was built this year Stamford Bridge — it was maintained by the bishop of London, whose country house in Fulham became Fulham Palace, and it was possibly erected at his expense. The name of the bridge is today that of Chelsea football ground.

1411

Rebuilding the Guildhall

Work began this year on the rebuilding of the Guildhall, under the direction of master mason John Croxton. It took about 20 years, and this magnificent hall mostly survived the flames of the Great Fire and the bombing of the Second World War. We can surmise that the earlier building, of unknown age, had been found to be wanting or in bad repair, for it was described by a contemporary observer as 'an olde and lytell Cotage'.

The origins of the Guildhall are still unresolved, connected as they are with the early medieval development of London which is still shrouded in speculation. Did a building on this site always have a significant role in the government of post-Roman London? Several factors suggest that it had. First, the name of the adjacent street, Aldermanbury: down to the reign of Cnut, the alderman was the head of the shire. Second, the Guildhall stands at the junction of three of the most ancient of the wards. Third, remains of a Roman amphitheatre have been discovered adjoining: the suggestion that a site of such significance would have continued in 'government' use is irresistible, but it is not proved.

Part of the stone undercroft of the 'lytell Cotage' was retained in the Croxton building. His original porch survives, though its façade was rebuilt in the 18th century. The floor was paved with Purbeck marble at the expense of the executors of Richard Whittington, who also, with others, paid for various stained windows and statues. There is still debate as to whether the roof was of stone or of wood — it went, in any case, in the Great Fire. The hall was then the second largest in the kingdom, exceeded only by Westminster Hall; it measured 152 ft long and about 48 ft wide.

Leadenhall Market Taken by City

This year seems to mark a new administrative purpose on the part of the City. Not only did it begin rebuilding the Guildhall, it also acquired Leadenhall, a mansion which had been used as a market, principally for poultry, cheese and butter. Croxton, though busy on the new Guildhall, was engaged here on additional works. Leadenhall Market, still specializing in poultry, is owned by the City today.

1412

A False Collector

It is recorded this year that one William Derman, a labourer, walked the streets of the City with a 'box bound with iron' collecting money for the inhabitants of the hospital of St Mary Bethlehem. He was not, however, connected with that establishment, and used the money for his own benefit. He received the surprisingly light punishment of an hour in the pillory with the box tied round his neck.

1413

Coronation of Henry V

The troubled reign of Henry IV came to an end when he died of a fit in the Jerusalem Chamber at Westminster Abbey on 20 March. His son, Henry V, was crowned at the abbey on 9 April, amid a violent storm.

Sir John Oldcastle Arrested

The Lollard persecution continued. The sect's acknowledged leader, Sir John Oldcastle, was brought before an ecclesiastical court held first in St Paul's, but then at the Black Friars' monastery. He was adamant at his hearing: he believed that bread remained bread after consecration, and that confession was unnecessary to procure salvation. The verdict was inevitable, despite his previous friendship with the new king. He was imprisoned for forty days in the Tower of London as a temporary measure, but from there he escaped on the night of 19 October, and for the next two months he plotted the downfall of the king.

1414

Lollard Uprising Crushed

The day of 9 January was meant to be one in which the Lollards, supported by the citizens of London, would rise against the king's regime. Those Lollards who dared gathered at St Giles's Fields, by today's Charing Cross Road, and waited for Londoners to join them. However, the City gates remained closed and instead the leaders, about 60 in number, were arrested and hanged at Newgate. Oldcastle escaped but remained at large in the capital, hiding at houses in Aldersgate and Smithfield.

West Sheen Monastery Founded

In what is now Richmond, Henry V founded a Carthusian monastery, with an estate of 32 acres, to the north of the royal manor house there. It consisted of 30 sets of chambers around a courtyard; the monks lived and fed apart from each other.

Poems by Charles, duke of Orleans, (see 1415) were later illustrated. Here he is seen in the White Tower, with Billingsgate and London Bridge behind.

1415

Agincourt Celebrated

After the famous victory at Agincourt, Henry V returned, happy no doubt to justify his loans from London. On first reports of his victory the newly elected mayor and his colleagues had walked from the City to Westminster to give thanks at the abbey, although it was carefully stated that such a pilgrimage should not in any way set a precedent. The king was met by the mayor, aldermen and 300 citizens at the traditional Blackheath venue on his return; clergy joined the throng at Deptford, dressed in 'magnificent copes, and preceded with rich crosses, and censers smoking with frankincense'. Tapestries were hung in the streets of the City, the conduits ran with wine, and children were dressed as angels.

One of the prisoners brought back by the king and kept in London for some years was Charles, duke of Orleans, whose poems, composed in captivity, were later illustrated by the first known views of London Bridge and Billingsgate.

Moorgate Built

The exit through the wall into the Moorfields area was a postern gate. This year it was enlarged into a proper gate. It was reported at the time that the moor contained a common latrine which so overflowed that the nearby residences were affected by 'many sicknesses, and other intolerable maladies, arising from the horrible, corrupt, and infected atmosphere'. It was ordered that the moor should be divided into gardens and cultivated, and the latrine was to be taken away.

Twickenham Convent Formed

A precise date, 3 March, is known for the foundation of a convent at Twickenham this year. This establishment was the only house in

England of the Bridgettine Order, named after a daughter of the Swedish royal house who had founded a monastery in Vadstenna in 1344. Philippa, daughter of Henry IV, married Eric XIII of Sweden, and one of the English diplomats with her at the Swedish wedding, Sir Henry Fitzhugh, donated his manor house in Cambridgeshire to found an English house of the order. However, in 1408 Parliament forbade the establishment of alien priories, and Henry V, needing to ingratiate himself with the pope, had to find a way around this by founding Syon as the first house of a new English order — indeed, he went further, by endowing it with lands taken from suppressed alien priories.

The foundation charter provided that the monastery should be composed of an abbess and 59 nuns, with 25 religious men, of whom 13 were to be priests. The brothers and sisters lived in separate courts but shared a common church, in which the sexes were strictly segregated.

It was not long, however, before the buildings proved inadequate and the site unhealthy. The convent moved to Isleworth in 1431.

1416

THE VISIT OF EMPEROR SIGISMUND

Sigismund, the Holy Roman Emperor, arrived in England on 1 May in an attempt to mediate between Henry V and the French. He was met, as usual, at Blackheath, and then installed in the Palace of Westminster, the king himself moving out to the archbishop of Canterbury's house in Lambeth.

Attended by 1,000 of his own nobles, Sigismund was invested as a Knight of the Garter at Windsor. Officiating at this ceremony was the first Garter King of Arms, Sir William Bruges, who later entertained the emperor at his house in Kentish Town. We do not know how many attended this banquet halfway up today's St Pancras Way, but we do have some indication of the quality: in procession the guests came from the bishop of Ely's palace in Holborn, headed by the 'Craftys of London, standyng in theyr Lyveries in places accustomed'. Then came soldiers, the mayor and his brethren, the king's trumpets, the officers of arms,

The 'cruell Martyrdome' of Sir John Oldcastle in 1417.

gentlemen and esquires in blue and gold, the bishop himself on a 'Palfreye in whyte and golde', the duke of Briga, the prince of Hungary and the emperor, the duke of Holland, and so on. It was a remarkable occasion for a relatively small house in a village outside London.

Sir William met the procession, knelt bare-headed before its members, then led them to his house, where they were entertained by minstrels and sackbuts. The meal included 9 pigs, 7 sheep, 100 pullets, 100 pigeons, 30 capons and 20 hens, plus hares, rabbits, kids, salmon, eels, crabs, oysters, and pies of boar, lamprey and deer. It cost the then enormous sum of £193 without the wine.

1417

OLDCASTLE EXECUTED

Sir John Oldcastle, Lollard leader and inveterate schemer against the king, was at last caught and brought to trial. He was heard before Parliament in December 1416 and was convicted of treason and heresy. Early in January, he was taken from the Tower to the new Lollard gallows at St Giles-in-the-Fields and there, according to one account, was burnt while he hung.

BROTHELS PROHIBITED

An ordinance was issued which prohibited brothels ('stews') in the City and Southwark. It was to be as ineffectual as the other such regulations which succeeded it.

SHIPS ON THE FLEET

The width of the Fleet may be judged in a report this year of two ships of 20 tons each bringing stones up to Holborn Bridge (now replaced by Holborn Viaduct). An unsubstantiated record, also from this year, reports an order of the king to repair and pave the miry roads of Holborn, and it may well be that the stones were for that purpose.

1418

PLAYS BANNED AT CHRISTMAS

Enlarging on an order of the previous year, the City prohibited mumming, plays and interludes during the Christmas period, and the wearing of false beards and other disguises.

LUDGATE PRISON CLOSED

The City alleged in an ordinance that Ludgate prison was now peopled by prisoners who went there to live on alms and avoid paying their debts, whereas originally it had been set aside for the incarceration of freemen of the City and clergy when found guilty of trespass or defaulting on debts. It was ordered that the prison be closed and all prisoners be moved to Newgate, which was presumably less desirable.

It was an unfortunate decision, for a few months later, during the last mayoralty of Whittington, it was admitted that several ex-prisoners of Ludgate who had been moved to Newgate were now dead of the conditions there. Ludgate was therefore reopened for approved prisoners.

A NEW TOWN CLERK

John Carpenter, who had worked in the town clerk's department for some years, was appointed town clerk of London in 1416. He is of particular importance because he set about compiling a volume known as the *Liber Albus*. Completed this year, it detailed London's laws, customs, privileges and usages, extracted from the archives.

1420

LYON'S INN ESTABLISHED
This Inn of Chancery is first mentioned this year in connection with housing law students. It derived its name from the tavern it took over, owned by James Lyon, and was located in one of the many lanes swept away by the building of the Aldwych half-circle early in the 20th century.

A COUNT OF BREWERIES
It was calculated that there were 290 breweries within the City and liberties this year. Ale was then made from malt, yeast and water, and did not keep; it was therefore drunk new, often in front of the brewery.

BARNET CHURCH REBUILT
One of the best-known landmarks north of London is Barnet church, St John the Baptist, standing at the top of a long hill, at the junction of two ancient streets. This year it was enlarged and rebuilt at the expense of John Beauchamp, a local brewer.

1421

GREY FRIARS' LIBRARY FOUNDED
Richard Whittington provided £400 with which to build and furnish the library of the Grey Friars in Newgate Street, and laid the foundation stone on 21 October.

TOWER OF ST MICHAEL'S, CORNHILL, REBUILT
The parishioners of St Michael's rebuilt its steeple in three tiers. The lower one, from which the porch opened, was tiled; in the second was a large glass window; and in the third tier two smaller windows were inserted.

THE WHITTINGTON LONGHOUSE
It is not known when Whittington first provided a public lavatory in Vintry ward, on top of which he built almshouses, but, if it was erected during his lifetime, 1421 is probably near the correct year. The privy, called Whittington's Longhouse, contained two long rows each of 64 seats – one side for men, the other for women – the seats overhanging a gully flushed by the Thames twice a day. There were five or six rooms above this building which served as almshouses, but by the 17th century these were being let in the usual way to any who wanted this as an address. The location of Whittington's privy was approximately that of Bell Wharf Lane.

1422

A DIVIDED PROTECTORSHIP
Henry V died in France in August, leaving as his heir a nine-month-old son, whose misfortunes in quantity were to surpass the successes of his father. In the regency which followed, the kingdom was once again entwined in the schemes of important men, particularly the late king's brothers, the dukes of Bedford and Gloucester. London, on the whole, backed the wrong protector by favouring Gloucester.

Henry V was buried at Westminster Abbey on 7 November. The mayor and his colleagues, clad in white gowns and hoods, met the coffin at Southwark in the midst of hundreds of flaming torches. They then accompanied it to St Paul's, where obsequies were performed, and the following day the procession went to Westminster, each livery company headed by a torchbearer.

LINCOLN'S INN MOVES
The law students who occupied Thomas of Lincoln's Inn on the south side of Holborn were by 1422 lodged in the bishop of Chichester's London house on the west side of Chancery Lane; they are still there today. The first of the famous 'Black Books' of Lincoln's Inn reveals that by this date there was a fully fledged society of lawyers in existence. Despite the fact that the bishop retained the freehold (he sold it to the society in 1580 for £820), substantial buildings were added over the next century.

THE REBUILDING OF ST MARY WOOLCHURCH
The old church of St Mary Woolchurch, on the site of the Mansion House, had become so 'old and feble' by this year that instructions were issued for its rebuilding. Particular care was to be taken that the light within the Stocks Market should not be impaired. The revenues of London Bridge were used to help with the rebuilding.

1423

DEATH OF WHITTINGTON
Richard Whittington, legendary mayor of London, died early in March. He had no children, and his will, drawn up in 1421, was one of unmatched benefactions to the City in which he had become so wealthy. The first Guildhall Library, a collection of mainly theological books chained in their cases, was established by 1425. Run by the City and open to scholars, it can claim to have been the first local-authority library. Sadly, it was plundered in 1549 by the duke of Somerset, who wanted to furnish his new mansion in the Strand. The present Guildhall Library derives from a foundation of 1828.

Some projects had been begun before Whittington's death. The paving of the new Guildhall's floor, the foundation of the Grey Friars' library, the rebuilding of St Michael Paternoster have all been referred to.

Ordinary Londoners had good reason to be grateful to him as well – water bosses were constructed at Billingsgate and Queenhithe, and at his house in what is now College Hill an almshouse for 12 poor people was built in 1424. Administered by his own livery company, the Mercers', this moved out to Highgate *c.* 1824, to be superseded by the Mercers' School. His house also contained a College of Priests attached to St Michael's, an institution which was wound up at the Reformation. The regime of the almspeople was disciplined. Daily they prayed for the souls of Whittington, his wife and their respective parents, and they had to recite frequent paternosters; they were not allowed to leave the building without permission. The establishment of the almshouse was part of a new fashion of the livery companies of the period: the Skinners had opened almshouses in Wood Street in 1416, and the Brewers built some next to their hall in Addle Street in 1423.

Richard Whittington, mayor of London, left much of his fortune to the City.

The City was also able to undertake the rebuilding of Newgate prison, which had long been housed partly in the gate itself and partly in some old and fetid extensions. From the Whittington bequest came a five-storey prison, 85 ft by 50 ft.

1424

MARRIAGE OF THE SCOTTISH KING

In the convoluted politics of the time it was counted an advantage by the duke of Bedford's party, which included the bishop of Winchester, that James I of Scotland should marry the bishop's niece, the young Jane Beaufort. James had been imprisoned, or at least restricted in his movements, by Henry V for some years, and in the regency that followed the death of Henry his release was contingent on his marriage.

The ceremony took place on 12 February at St Mary Overie, Southwark, and the banquet was at Winchester House nearby. The bride's dowry consisted of paper money – a remission of 10,000 marks of the ransom demanded for James's release and resumption of his throne.

1425

ANTI-ALIEN RIOTS

There was particular hostility in London to the Fleming merchants. A mob nailed a threat to them on the door of the bishop of Winchester, who was thought to favour alien merchants, and threatened to throw him into the river.

A THREAT FROM WINCHESTER

Enmity existed between the duke of Gloucester, one of the regents of the kingdom, and the bishop of Winchester, Henry Beaufort. In October Gloucester persuaded the City authorities that Beaufort threatened an insurrection, and London Bridge was barred at its southern end. The bishop's men broke the chains, and news of an impending fight spread like wildfire on the north bank. Forces soon confronted each other at opposite ends of the bridge, but the situation was defused by the mayor and aldermen.

1426

NEW DRAWBRIDGE FOR THE BRIDGE

Work began this year on the construction of a new drawbridge on London Bridge – the mayor, John Reynwell, laid a foundation stone. The skulls and other human trophies on the old structure were removed for the time being, but were replaced when the new drawbridge was complete.

1428

BAYNARD'S CASTLE DESTROYED BY FIRE

Baynard's Castle, which had been rebuilt on the Thames front after its old site had been taken by the Black Friars, was this year so damaged by fire that it had again to be rebuilt. Its new owner and occupier was Humphrey, duke of Gloucester.

GROCERS' HALL OPENED

The Grocers' Company obtained a charter this year and also opened its first hall on the present site in Princes Street, opposite the Bank of England.

1429

HENRY VI CROWNED

Despite his age (not yet eight years), it became necessary to crown Henry VI king of England so that he could also be proclaimed king of France. The coronation at Westminster Abbey on 6 November was a splendid affair – the last cause for rejoicing for the young boy, since he was then taken off to France, where Joan of Arc was rallying a dispirited nation. He did not return to London until 1432.

CARPENTERS' HALL BUILT

At a time when most houses were built of wood the Carpenters' Company had much affluence. Its first hall, opened this year, was located, as it is today, in the Throgmorton Avenue area. Its extensive garden saved the building during the Great Fire, and the hall was used by several lord mayors during the rebuilding of their own mansions. The custom now is for newly elected lord mayors to dine first at the Carpenters' Hall.

1430

GUILDHALL CHAPEL BEGUN

The Guildhall chapel was already 150 years old and looked decidedly inadequate and ruinous set against the rebuilt Guildhall buildings. This year the City received a royal licence to rebuild it; however, because its funding generally relied upon public alms and bequests, it took twenty years to build. The architect was John Croxton. Late in the 18th century the chapel was converted to a court room, and it was subsequently demolished to make way for the Guildhall Art Gallery.

1431

SYON CONVENT ESTABLISHED

The Bridgettine community established at Syon, Twickenham (see 1415), soon found its premises inadequate and badly drained. Having received the manor of Isleworth as part of its endowment, the community moved to a new monastery built in Isleworth and originally intended for a Celestine order. The duke of Bedford had laid the foundation stone in 1426, and the Bridgettines moved in on 11 November 1431, after a ceremony attended by the archbishop of Canterbury, the duke of Gloucester and others of the nobility.

The house became one of the richest in the country, with land in almost all the southern counties. Syon House, which incorporates much of the old structure, is on the site today.

FLEET BRIDGE REBUILT

The Fleet Bridge, which connected Ludgate Hill with Fleet Street, was rebuilt at the expense of John Welles, mayor of London, this year. Stow describes it as 'fair coped on either side with iron pikes; on which, towards the south, be also certain lanthorns of stone for lights to be placed in the winter evenings for commodity of travellers'.

WATER TO CHARTERHOUSE

By a royal licence of 2 December, the monks at Charterhouse were permitted to draw water by pipes from a spring at the southern end of today's Barnsbury Road in Islington. A conduit was erected on the site, and in the 17th century a public house called the White Conduit, a famous Islington tea garden, was added, although by then the water supply had diminished and it was regarded more as a medicinal facility than anything else. It was not, it seems, ever a plentiful source of water, and as soon as the New River established its works nearby the conduit became redundant for Charterhouse.

1433

GREENWICH PALACE BUILT

This year saw the development of an estate at Greenwich which was to develop into the great Tudor palace of Placentia. The abbey on the site passed to Humphrey, duke of Gloucester, who set about developing the old building and constructing a new one. The abbey became Bella Court – 'a faire building in the towne' – and it was joined by a fortress-like tower. At the same time Gloucester annexed 200 acres of Blackheath which much later became Greenwich Park. Bella Court was built of rose-pink brick and contained the duke's magnificent library, which he was to leave to the Bodleian, Oxford. The house was just to the west of the present Royal Naval College. The tower, sometimes called Greenwich Castle, was intended as a lookout for invasion up the Thames.

1434

SEVERE COLD IN LONDON

A severe frost began on 24 November and continued until 10 February the following year. Stow records that the Thames froze once more, and

A 17th-century view by Wenceslaus Hollar of Duke Humphrey's Tower at Greenwich (see 1433).

foreign ships were obliged to unload as far downstream as Gravesend, with goods being brought in by cart.

LOLLARDS' TOWER BUILT AT LAMBETH
A tower on the west side of the chapel at Lambeth Palace was begun this year, under the supervision of Archbishop Chichele. It is known nowadays as the Lollards' Tower, in the belief that it housed followers of Wyclif at this time of religious persecution. No evidence has been found for this.

FISHMONGERS BUILD NEW HALL
The Fishmongers' Company, one of the more affluent and aggressive of the City companies, was this year bequeathed the land and premises by London Bridge which is now the site of the company's present hall. The company appears to have occupied houses on the site since 1310.

1436

EPIDEMIC AT THE TOWER MENAGERIE
An epidemic in the king's menagerie at the Tower of London carried off most of the animals there.

FLEMINGS SEEK ROYAL PROTECTION
As the interminable war against the French went badly, thereby severely taxing the resources and temper of Londoners, aliens were once again the target of hostility. The Flemings, particular enemies of City merchants, were so harassed that they sought and obtained royal protection.

1437

COLLAPSE ON LONDON BRIDGE
The Great Stone Gate collapsed on 14 January – or rather the pier on which it stood fell, bringing with it the arches on either side, the gate above and some houses. There is no record of a temporary structure while new stone arches were built, but presumably, as the bridge was so important to London, something must have been put up to take light traffic.

1438

MORE WATER FOR THE CITY
More conduits in the City were opened in or about this year. Sir William Eastfield, mayor this year, brought water from springs at Highbury down to St Giles Cripplegate; Fleet Street conduit was rebuilt this year, and another conduit was opened in Aldermanbury.

1439

ST STEPHEN WALBROOK REBUILT
This year saw the completion of the rebuilding of the church of St Stephen in Walbrook. Work had begun ten years earlier, and this

time the church was built on the east side of the street, on a larger site bought from the Grocers' Company with room for a churchyard.

The work was paid for by Sir Robert Chicheley, grocer and alderman of London, and brother of the archbishop of Canterbury.

ESTABLISHMENT OF BARNARD'S INN
Barnard's Inn, an Inn of Chancery eventually attached to Gray's Inn, was located between Fetter Lane and today's Dyer's Buildings, on the south side of Holborn. In 1358 the property consisted of two houses owned by Roger Leget (see 1374), who fell foul of the peasants in the revolt of 1381 and was executed at Cheapside. By 1385 the property was in the hands of Sir Robert de Plesyngton, and by 1439, when his house was described as 'new built', it was leased to one Lionel Bernard or Barnard, principal of what was known as Barnard's Inn and sometimes Mackworth Inn. Mackworth, dean of Lincoln, was freeholder of the property, and in 1454 it was bequeathed by him to the dean and chapter of Lincoln for the maintenance of a chantry in the cathedral. It is likely that Mackworth built the hall which later was incorporated in the Mercers' School on the site, and which still survives – the oldest of any of the legal halls.

1440

LONDON AFFRAYS
Two serious riots took place this year. One was in Holborn, where the law students confronted the butchers who cleansed carcasses in the Fleet and thereby caused much annoyance to those who lived near. Armed men were found in Thavie's and Barnard's Inns, and the Master of the Rolls and the Lord Chancellor were obliged to enter into a bond that in future the students would keep the peace towards the butchers.

There was also a violent fight between apprentices of the Merchant Taylors' and the Drapers' companies, over the election of the mayor.

THE EXECUTION OF RICHARD WICK
The burning on Tower Hill this year of Lollard sympathizer Richard Wick, vicar of Deptford, attracted a crowd hostile to the authorities. The vicar of nearby All Hallows Barking took advantage of the situation. He mixed spices with the ashes of the fire and persuaded the gullible that the scent indicated the poor man had been a martyr; he then sold them candles and relics of the ashes at considerable profit.

CHURCH BUILDINGS
A familiar feature of today's riverscape, the tower of Fulham church, was built about this year – at that time it had a wooden spire. It is mentioned in a petition from the inhabitants of Fulham complaining that stones intended for the church, and the workmen employed on it, were being taken away for the 'king's own project' (Eton College).

St Margaret Lothbury was rebuilt, partly over the course of the Walbrook river.

1441

THE PENANCE OF THE DUCHESS OF GLOUCESTER
The duchess of Gloucester, the former Eleanor Cobham, was found to have committed witchcraft in an attempt to ascertain the date of the

death of the frail and half-witted king — it was her hope that her husband would then assume the crown. For three days in November she was obliged to do penance in the streets of London by walking barefoot with lighted taper in hand, shrouded in a white sheet. On the first day she walked from Temple Bar to St Paul's, on the second along Thames Street, and on the third from Queenhithe to Cornhill.

The disgrace of his wife spelt the political demise of the duke of Gloucester.

1443

A NEW WESTMINSTER CONDUIT

A water conduit existed in New Palace Yard, Westminster, from the 14th century — we know that it was specially decorated for the coronation of Henry IV in 1399. It was replaced about this year by a larger structure, shown in a drawing by Hollar in the 17th century.

1444

ST PAUL'S STRUCK BY LIGHTNING

The steeple of St Paul's was much damaged by lightning this year. Stow describes the accident thus:

The 1st of February, in the year 1444, about two of the clock in the afternoon, the steeple of Paules was fired by lightning, in the midst of the shaft or spire, both on the west side and on the south; but by labour of many well-disposed people the same to appearance was quenched by vinegar, so that all men withdrew themselves to their houses, praising God; but between eight and nine of the clock in the same night the fire burst out again more fervently than before, and did much hurt to the lead and timber, till by the great labour of the mayor and people that came thither, it was thoroughly quenched.

LEATHERSELLERS OBTAIN CHARTER

The Company of Leathersellers obtained a charter this year. Traditionally, until tanning was exiled to Bermondsey, the trade in leather and hides had taken place on the north side of the City, within the wall, in the Moorgate area. There were two advantages to this location: the easy access to water, which the tanners had in plenty on the marshy Moor Fields, and the short distance from the main cattle market at Smithfield.

1445

A GRANARY AT LEADENHALL

A mark of the growing scope of government in London was the construction about this year of a granary at Leadenhall, the mansion-cum-market that the City had bought in 1411. It was a wise provision, for there were extremely harsh years in which the crops failed and there was a panic to buy corn from abroad. The new building was paid for by the mayor, Simon Eyre.

The Leadenhall mansion had an enclosed courtyard, several storeys high, and in this, until 1455, when they moved inside, the market traders in poultry and dairy products did their daily business.

1446

A BAN ON WOODEN CHIMNEYS

By the 14th century it was common to place the fire against a wall rather than in the centre of the room. The smoke escaped through a hole in the roof, and the back of the fire, called the reredos, was of brick. Although such an arrangement was considered dangerous, the smoke was thought to be healthy. A wistful writer remarked:

Now have we manie chimneys and yet our tenderlings complain of rheums, catarhs, and poses. Then had we none but reredosses and our heads did never ache. For as the smoke in those days was supposed to be a sufficient hardning for the timber of the house, so it was reputed a far better medecine to keepe the good man and his familie from the quacks.

However, the early chimneys, made of wood as they were, were also dangerous. In 1446 the mayor ordered that any one lighting a fire beneath a wooden chimney would be fined, and anyone repairing such a chimney would commit an offence.

VINTNERS BUILD ALMSHOUSES

Already noted has been a trend for the City companies to build almshouses for their members. The Vintners this year were bequeathed funds for this purpose; 13 almshouses were later built next to their hall in Thames Street.

The Vintners were by now a wealthy class of merchants, their trade based on the previously close relationship between England and France, which made trade in wine a commonplace. They were previously called Wine-tunners, referring to the barrels, or tuns, used for transportation. It is interesting to note that the word 'tonnage' refers originally not to weight but to the number of tuns on board.

BRENTFORD BRIDGE REBUILT

As the place name Brentford implies, a ford across the river Brent was originally here (there was also an ancient ford across the Thames here at times — it is thought that Julius Caesar used it to cross the Thames in 54 BC). In the 13th century the Brent ford was superseded by a bridge — a wooden structure which carried the important road to the west of England. It was replaced about this year by a stone bridge.

CHISWICK CHURCH TOWER BUILT

Chiswick (deriving from 'cheese-farm') was a fishing village, and its church's dedication to St Nicholas, patron saint of mariners and fishermen, reflects this. The older part of the parish, by the river to the east, contains the church. Today's building of 1882 includes a tower completed about 1446, at a time when a ford here across the Thames was occasionally available.

1447

CAMPAIGN FOR GRAMMAR SCHOOLS

A petition to establish grammar schools in their parishes was presented to the king by the rectors of All Hallows the Great, St Andrew Holborn, St Peter upon Cornhill and St Mary Colechurch. It was stressed that in London there was not a 'sufficeant number of Scholes, and good Enfourmers in Gramer'. The king agreed, and a number of parish schools were founded in the ensuing years.

1448

ST JAMES'S LEPER HOSPITAL TO ETON COLLEGE
The king was busy endowing his new project, Eton College (see 1440). This year the St James's Hospital for 14 leprous maidens and its right to hold a fair, on the site of St James's Palace, was granted to the college.

PAUL'S CROSS REBUILT
Paul's Cross, at the east end of St Paul's churchyard, was rebuilt this year, this time with a roofed pulpit for public preaching. The Cross was also used for the pronouncement of papal bulls and public cursing.

STEPNEY MARSH SUBMERGED
Stepney Marsh, today's Isle of Dogs, was submerged when the embankment was breached.

1449

IMPROVEMENTS AT WESTMINSTER
A fire in 1447 had seriously damaged the monks' quarters at Westminster. This year work began on installing a hammerbeam roof in the monks' dormitory – this is now part of the Westminster School buildings.

BILLINGSGATE EXTENDED
One of the earliest depictions of London is that included in a volume of poetry compiled by Charles, duke of Orleans, during his imprisonment in London (see 1415). It shows London Bridge, the Tower and Billingsgate. The last, even allowing for errors in perspective, seems to be a substantial affair of two storeys, above arcades which probably provided shelter for unloaded goods. The building date is unknown, but in 1449 the City paid the executors of Sir Thomas Haseley £1,000 for land for the extension of Billingsgate.

1450

THE CADE REBELLION
For some years past the king, Henry VI, had been heavily under the influence of William de la Pole, earl of Suffolk, an adviser unpopular with the Commons, who in 1447 impeached him as being in collusion with the French with the intent of putting his son on the throne. The loss of the French provinces in 1450 settled his fate, but his life was temporarily spared by the king, who banished him to France instead. On the flight across the Channel he was taken by his enemies and executed on the high seas.

Violence against his supporters then ensued. But a larger insurrection was forming, known as the Cade Rebellion. This was primarily a protest by taxpayers against the maladministration and corruption of the regime, and in particular of the sheriff of Kent, William Crowmer, and his father-in-law, Lord Saye and Sele, the king's treasurer.

The new Paul's Cross in St Paul's churchyard (see 1448).

The revolt began in Kent, apparently aided by respectable citizens. It is not clear who led them, but when on 1 June they assembled at Blackheath the opportunist Jack Cade, about whom very little is known, was the leading spirit. A delegation from the king, led by Sir John Fastolf, went to ascertain their demands. The rebels retreated to Sevenoaks, where they were engaged in battle, and then, victorious, they returned to Blackheath. On 1 July they entered Southwark, using the White Hart inn as their headquarters, and by the 3rd they were in the City.

Lord Saye and Sele was taken from the Tower and executed at the standard in Cheapside, and the sheriff of Kent was captured at Mile End and beheaded there. But Cade lost the support of the City through the indiscriminate plundering of his forces. London Bridge was closed to them one morning before Cade could re-enter it from his Southwark base, and in the ensuing battle the rebels pushed the Londoners back to the drawbridge section. One account relates that the rebels then set fire to the drawbridge, another that the houses on the bridge were fired, with loss of life. Hour after hour the struggle went on 'ande many a man was slayne and caste in Temys, harnys, body and alle'.

The dispute ended in mutual exhaustion. The rebels were bought off by a general pardon; Cade received a particular pardon made out in his assumed name of Mortimer and, foolishly, he stayed on at leisure in Southwark for a few days after his men had dispersed, to arrange for the transportation of his booty. The pardons were not honoured. Many rebels were later rounded up and executed, and Cade was taken and wounded at Heathfield in Sussex. He died in the cart conveying him to London and his body was taken to the King's Bench prison in Southwark. There it was beheaded and quartered and the remains were trundled on a hurdle through the streets of London. Though his head was erected on London Bridge, his parts were sent to other cities as grim warnings to others.

CHURCH REBUILDING

It was a period of much church rebuilding, when a number of the Saxon churches were found to be inadequate or in decay and were replaced with new structures, many of which were lost in the Great Fire of 1666.

St Sepulchre in Newgate Street was rebuilt, as was St Dionis Backchurch in Lime Street. The present church of St Olave, Hart Street – the one used by Pepys – was constructed about this time at the expense of Robert and Richard Cely; this building, much restored, survives today.

LORD MAYOR BY BARGE

It was the custom for the newly elected mayor to travel by horseback to Westminster, there to be received by the king. This was the forerunner of the Lord Mayor's Show. At some stage this journey was made by barge instead, but it is not until 1450 that a clear record of going by water occurs, for the mayoralty of Sir John Norman. He was allegedly rowed by silver oars, but certainly the prestige to the watermen must have been considerable.

1451

RUISLIP GIVEN TO KING'S COLLEGE

As well as founding Eton College, Henry VI established King's College, Cambridge. Part of its endowment this year were the manors of Ruislip and Northwood. The college is, in fact, still the titular lord of the manor of Ruislip. The existing Manor Farmhouse was built by the college in 1500 as was the Little Barn, rebuilt in the 16th century and now used as a public library.

1452

THE CITY BACKS THE KING

The growing mental incapacity of the king encouraged the resurgence of factions around him. The current favourite, though in disgrace because of the loss of the French possessions during his time as lieutenant of France, was Edmund Beaufort, duke of Somerset, but the duke of York decided to strike against him. In January he appeared at the gates of the City, confidently expecting a welcome, only to find that the City was backing the king. York withdrew to Dartford, and the king's forces encamped at Blackheath. An untidy truce ensued.

1453

MORE WATER FOR LONDON

London's thirst for water was growing. This year springs at Paddington were harnessed by permission of the bishop of London and the supply was fed into the system in Oxford Street, by the site of Stratford Place, which took water from the river Tyburn.

AN HEIR TO THE THRONE

The king's mind gave way entirely at the same time as his queen presented him with a son. The ambitious duke of York could hardly let these events go by without interference. The City wished to remain neutral in any conflict, and all citizens were urged to provide themselves with armour for emergencies; they were also enjoined to refrain from partisan statements which might provoke a riot.

1454

THE DUKE OF YORK TAKES POWER

With the king indisposed and his heir an infant, a power vacuum existed at a time when the retention of Calais vexed the Exchequer and the country. The duke of York with a force behind him marched to London; he was accompanied by his son, the future Edward IV. The City, anxious not to offend either party, remained neutral and paid court to both the duke and the queen until April, when the duke became regent during the illness of the king. With Somerset in prison, York held the power he wanted.

SALTERS BUILD A HALL

The Salters had a trade monopoly not only in salt – an important ingredient in food preservation – but also in other chemicals such as potash. To this day the Company of Salters is involved in the chemical industry. It built this year a hall in Bread Street, together with some almshouses at the rear.

1455

KING CAPTURED BY YORK

The king briefly regained sanity, released Somerset from the Tower, and ended York's regency. Deprived of his temporary power, York took to force and at the Battle of St Albans in May routed the king's forces in a conflict in which a number of lords, including Somerset, were killed. The king was taken and placed under house detention with York in the bishop of London's house in St Paul's churchyard.

1456

VIOLENCE IN LONDON

At the end of April a prominent Lucchese merchant was assaulted by three English servants. Complaint was made to the mayor, and one of the assailants, a mercer, was imprisoned. A mob of workers in the mercery trade gathered, forced the sheriffs to hand back their colleague, and then proceeded to riot against other Italian merchants. It was, given the uncertain political situation of both London and the country, a dangerous situation – serious enough for the mayor to summon the master of the Mercers' Company and for the latter to warrant the good behaviour of his members. On 4 May the mayor with a force of men rode out into the City to restore order.

A COMET APPEARS

What has subsequently been identified as Halley's Comet appeared in the sky in June. Coming so soon after the anti-alien riots of the previous month, this served only to confirm a general air of unease and foreboding.

1457

More Violence

In early February two Italian ships carrying wool were seized by soldiers at Tilbury, supposedly on the orders of the Wool Staple in London. In June a group of young men planned to murder foreign merchants and gathered for that purpose at Hoxton; there they pledged to live and die with each other in the attack. The City authorities, however, got wind of the plan and summoned up forces to prevent it, but a riot of some sort, involving mercers again, did take place.

There was conflict between the law students of Barnard's Inn and men of Bridge ward. The principal of Barnard's Inn deposed to the mayor that any future troublemakers would be expelled.

Prisoners in Newgate rioted and took over the building – their reason was the appalling conditions they were expected to endure. The mutineers were 'sore ponysshed' with irons and fetters.

St Mildred Poultry Rebuilt

The church of St Mildred in Poultry was rebuilt this year, partly over the course of the Walbrook. In 1739, when the post-Fire church had taken its place, the river was described as 'a great and rapid stream … running under St Mildred's church steeple at a depth of 16 feet'.

Ironmongers Acquire Hall Site

The Ironmongers, or ferroners, who made such things as horseshoes and cartwheel rims, bought some houses on the north side of Fenchurch Street this year. Later, these were to be the site of the company's hall. The company obtained its charter in 1463.

1458

Reconciliation at St Paul's

Civil war still threatened. On the one hand was the party of the queen, supported by the young duke of Somerset, and on the other the duke of York, supported by the earl of Warwick. A general reconciliation was called by the ineffective king Henry VI on 25 March at St Paul's, but, although on the surface the quarrel was patched, it was a temporary measure. In this tense situation the City authorities put a force of 3,000 men on the streets to preserve the peace between the factions.

1459

Affray in Fleet Street

On 13 April there was a pitched battle between men of the Fleet Street area and those from the court at Westminster. In the affray the premises of Clifford's Inn were damaged.

1460

A City Dilemma

The turbulent reign of Henry VI was nearing its end, ushering in yet more conflict. In this an important element was the support of London's populace for the York faction, despite the more neutral approach of the City administration. Yorkist forces landed from Calais in June, in a bid to win the succession; the City guardedly admitted them, but Lord Scales, the keeper of the Tower, remained loyal to the king, and his garrison had to be starved into submission. It surrendered in July, and Scales, attempting to flee to Westminster, was murdered by boatmen.

The king was captured at the Battle of Northampton, and was brought to London. In October he was obliged to assent to the duke of York's claim to be heir apparent – one which had much legitimacy. But a last twist of fate intervened: in December, York's forces met those of the queen at Wakefield, and here he was killed in battle. It was left to his son, Edward, to take the prize the following year. The London contingent, fighting on York's side, was heavily routed and its leader was beheaded. The queen then turned her attention to the City.

Barking Abbey Curfew Tower Built

The curfew tower attached to the influential Barking Abbey was erected this year. It is one of the few parts of the building which still survive.

1461

Bargaining with the Queen

For a time the queen's forces were in the ascendancy. Rumours of wholesale executions of her enemies justifiably alarmed the City, caught, as it had been, on York's side. In February panic spread at the news of her defeat of Warwick and the duke of Norfolk at St Albans and the recapture of her husband. But the war was still not ended, and the queen needed provisions. For these she turned to London, and made a deal which permitted the City, at least for the time being, to be exempt from the predations of her soldiers in exchange for supplies. But, just as the carts were about to set out, news came of a victory by York's son, Edward, who had rallied Warwick's army and was now bearing down on London; the populace refused to allow the provisions to move.

The die was indelibly cast now for London. Although many of the citizens were probably Lancastrian sympathizers, London had now irrevocably opted for York. The walls were manned to prevent incursion, and, accepting that the danger of storming the City was too great, the queen and her army fell back northward and were roundly defeated by the reformed Yorkists. Edward took up residence at Baynard's Castle, and in March the chancellor called a meeting of nobles and populace in the open fields of Clerkenwell, there to explain Edward's claim to the throne and obtain approval for the deposition of Henry. Both were approved by Londoners and, in effect, the reign of Edward IV began thereafter. On 4 March he was declared king in Westminster Hall, and on 29 June he was crowned at the abbey.

1462

Southwark Fair Chartered

Southwark Fair was second only to Bartholomew Fair in London, and it was already established by the time the City obtained a charter (dated 9 November this year) which confirmed its jurisdiction over Southwark and its fair. Stalls were located in the middle of Borough High Street,

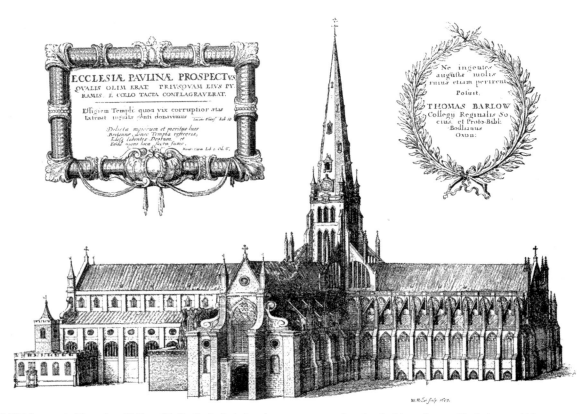

A 1657 drawing by Wenceslaus Hollar of St Paul's Cathedral with its spire intact, though it had been destroyed by lightning 100 years earlier.

right outside the famous Southwark inns such as the Tabard and the George, and spread into the streets and alleyways alongside.

Originally the fair lasted from 7 to 9 September, but gradually it grew to two weeks' duration. John Strype, writing in 1720, said that it was famous for 'shows, as drolls, puppet-shows, rope-dancing, music booths and tippling houses'. There is a well-known drawing by Hogarth of the fair as it was in the 18th century.

FLOODING AT BARKING AND DAGENHAM
Severe flooding of the Thames occurred at Barking and Dagenham. Once again, the lands belonging to the abbess of Barking were rendered worthless – flooding was a problem for landowners and residents until the 20th century.

NEW SPIRE FOR ST PAUL'S
The completion of a new spire for St Paul's Cathedral was attended by disaster. Stow describes the final positioning of the weather-cock: 'Robert Godwin, winding it up, the rope brake, and he was destroyed on the pinnacles, and the cock was sore bruised.'

CHARTERS FOR THE BARBERS AND TALLOW CHANDLERS
Two important City companies obtained charters this year. The Barbers, by virtue of their handling of relatively sharp and delicate instruments, used to assist monks in medical operations until the clergy were forbidden in 1163 to participate in such things. Barbers then took on the work of surgery and were senior even to surgeons, with whom in 1540 they were joined as a company.

The Tallow Chandlers' trade was mostly in candles, made of tallow, for everyday use; best-quality candles made from wax, used mainly by the rich and by ecclesiastical bodies, were made by the Wax Chandlers.

1463

THE ENLARGEMENT OF LUDGATE PRISON
Ludgate jail was principally for freemen imprisoned for debt. This year it was considerably enlarged with the provision of a chapel, a tower and an exercise area at the expense of Dame Agnes Forster, in memory of her husband, Stephen, fishmonger and mayor of London in 1454. (A romantic legend asserts that Dame Agnes met her husband when he himself was in prison here for debt.) She also bequeathed money to ensure that future inmates had free lodging and water. Stow describes the exercise area as about 38 ft long and the walls containing it as 6 ft thick.

1466

CROSBY PLACE BUILT
One of London's finest medieval houses, Crosby Place, was begun this year in Bishopsgate. By an odd quirk, its hall still survives, but it has been transplanted to Danvers Street in Chelsea.

In 1466 (Sir) John Crosby, by trade a woolman but a member of the Company of Grocers, obtained a 99-year lease of some ground on the east side of Bishopsgate, the property of St Helen's Priory. Just north of the junction with Threadneedle Street, some of its site today is covered by Crosby Square. He built what Stow describes as the highest building in London at the time – here Richard of Gloucester was staying in 1483 when he was told of the murder of the princes in the Tower. As a domestic building, it demonstrates the rise of the merchant class in this period.

1469

COLLAPSE AT ST MARY OVERIE

The stone-vaulted roof of the nave of St Mary Overie fell in this year and was rebuilt in wood.

1470

HENRY REGAINS THE THRONE

The convolutions of royal politics caught up with the City again this year. In 1465 the old king, Henry VI, had been captured and placed in the Tower. The following years were to be ones in which his queen, conspiring with the French and the Scots, sought his restoration. Edward IV, wasting his earlier popularity, alienated both his own brother, the duke of Clarence, and his ally the earl of Warwick, who then both joined forces with the former queen. In the various skirmishes that followed, Edward himself was captured and imprisoned in York, so that, briefly, both the kings of England were in prison at the same time. Eventually, Warwick and his supporters retreated to France, and from there in September 1470 they launched a counter-attack. By the end of September Warwick was at the City gates. Meanwhile, Edward fled to Holland, and his queen and children went into sanctuary at Westminster Abbey, where, in the next few months, the future Edward V was born.

Warwick, in effect, was now master of the kingdom. Henry VI was released from the Tower and could resume his reign. London, for the time being, cooperated with the new regime.

1471

THE BATTLE OF BARNET

The decisive battle of this part of the prolonged struggle between the Yorkist and Lancastrian factions – the Wars of the Roses – took place on 14 April at Barnet in north London.

After landing in the Humber estuary, Edward IV had managed to avoid two Lancastrian armies and he slipped into London about 10 April. By the 13th, Warwick and his forces were on the Great North Road, camped at Monken Hadley, a mile north of Barnet, and that night Edward moved out of London to confront them. The armies faced each other overnight, and in the morning there was dense fog. The balance of the early battle went against Edward, but a mistake by some of Warwick's forces, in which they attacked their own army in the mist, led to a Lancastrian rout. Warwick himself was killed. 'This battayle duryd, fightynge and skirmishing, ryght doubtefully, because of the myste, by the space of three hours, ere it was fully achivyd,' related a chronicler.

Two days later, news arrived of the landing of Henry's queen and her son at Weymouth. Edward went off west to battle again, and on 4 May he was victorious at Tewkesbury. The son was either killed or murdered, and the queen was taken. Lured northward by a reported insurrection, Edward was at Coventry when he heard of a much more serious uprising in the south, led by a naval captain called Thomas Falconbridge, who was encamped at Kingston upon Thames. His forces tried to gain an entry to the City – on 12 May there was an attempt to cross London Bridge and to set fire to beerhouses near the Tower, and on other days attacks were made on the gates of Aldgate and Bishopsgate.

Edward, at the head of 30,000 men, arrived in London on 21 May – the day in which the unhappy Henry VI died in the Tower. Chased to Kent, Falconbridge eventually surrendered at Sandwich. It was, for the time being, the end of the Lancastrian insurgence.

1472

MORE LONDON STOCKS

It was ordered that each London ward should provide its own set of stocks.

1473

HIGHGATE LEPER HOSPITAL FOUNDED

William Pole, a leper and a follower of Edward IV, was granted a piece of land on Highgate Hill on which to found the hospital of St Anthony for the treatment of leprosy – or rather, since there was little that could be done, for the containment of its unfortunate victims. The land measured 60 ft by 34 ft and was part of the site of today's St Mary's wing of the Whittington Hospital.

1474

PEWTERERS OBTAIN CHARTER

Pewter, an alloy of tin, lead and copper, was until the 17th century the principal material for tableware and, in many churches, for ecclesiastical use. The first pewterer we know of had premises in or near Ludgate Hill at the end of the 12th century, and by the 14th century the pewterer fraternity had ordinances for the governance of its trade in London; this year, 1474, it obtained its coveted royal charter. It was a flourishing trade, helped along by the mayor and aldermen specifying that every brewer, hosteller, cook, piebaker and huckster selling ale should use pewter pots.

1475

YORK HOUSE, BATTERSEA, BUILT

About the year 1475 the bishop of Durham, Lawrence Booth, built himself a house on the curve of the river Thames at Battersea Creek. He was later translated to the archbishopric of York but he continued in this house, which was named York House. York Place and York Road nowadays signify its existence, and the large Price's Candle Factory is on the actual site.

KNIGHTSBRIDGE LEPER HOSPITAL ESTABLISHED

Hard on the heels of the foundation of the Highgate leper hospital (see 1473), another one was established well outside the City walls, this time at Knightsbridge.

GERMAN MERCHANTS CONSOLIDATE

The German merchants of the Hanseatic ports who inhabited the Steelyard in Upper Thames Street (now covered by Cannon Street station) were permitted this year to buy the freehold of their building. The traders led almost a collegiate life here. No member was allowed to visit a woman or to marry; they had to be in the premises by a fixed hour of the night, and they dined communally.

1476

CAXTON SETS UP AT WESTMINSTER

William Caxton, formerly a mercer, but enthused by the new practice of printing he had studied in Cologne, set up shop in the precincts of Westminster Abbey. He was the first printer in the country, and his contribution to the cultural history of the English language was immense. He had already printed two of his own translations on the Continent, probably in Bruges – these were the first English-language books to be typeset and published. The first known document from his Westminster press was an indulgence granted by the abbot of Abingdon, and on 18 November 1477 a book, *The Dictes and Sayings of the Philosophers,* appeared – it introduced a colophon and a place and date of publication. This was undoubtedly the first book to be printed in England. During the next 15 years Caxton printed 96 books or editions. His signboard was that of a 'reed pale', a shield with a red band running vertically.

Caxton was a prominent parishioner at St Margaret's, Westminster, regularly witnessing or auditing the church accounts.

1477

RESTORATION OF THE WALL

Recent events had shown that the City wall was far from redundant. However, the northern section was in need of a major renovation. The City authorities decided that it should be repaired with bricks made from Moorfields clay at the expense of parishioners, who were to pay sixpence each Sunday.

FIRST CLERK OF THE WORKS APPOINTED

On 21 April the City appointed Edward Stone as its first 'clerk of the City's works', a position that continued right down to the time of the famous James Bunning in 1843; after then the title was changed to that of 'city architect'.

1478

A SITE FOR THE HABERDASHERS

The haberdashers were originally part of the Mercers Company and were themselves divided into two parts – the hurrers or cappers, who made hats, and the milliners, who derived their name and income from importing goods from Milan.

This year the Company of Haberdashers, which had received a charter in 1448, was bequeathed a site in Staining Lane, on which its hall has remained ever since.

TANNERS EXPELLED TO BERMONDSEY

One of the more obnoxious trades in London was that of the tanners. This year they were expelled to Bermondsey – an area which became the centre of London's leather trade and where the Leather Exchange was opened in 1879.

1479

THE EXPANSION OF ELTHAM PALACE

Eltham Palace had been growing since the beginning of the 14th century, when the manor house came into royal ownership. Despite, or because of, its popularity as a retreat with successive monarchs, it went into serious decline at the time of the Commonwealth and was rescued in recent times only by the wealth and persistence of Stephen Courtauld.

A new Great Hall, completed about 1479, was approached by a 15th-century bridge across the moat. This set piece of the palace was and is (for it still survives) 101 ft long and 36 ft wide; the roof – one of the building's main features nowadays – is 55 ft high and in hammerbeam style. It is thought that it was the work of the king's carpenter, Edmund Graveley, and that the overall design of the building was by Thomas Jordan, the king's mason, who may well have been responsible for Crosby Place (see 1466) too.

BISHOPSGATE REBUILT

Bishopsgate, which straddled one of the Roman roads, Ermine Street, leading north out of the City, was rebuilt this year at the expense of the Hanse merchants located in the Steelyard: indeed, this event may well be linked with the permission those merchants obtained to buy the freehold of their building in 1475.

The derivation of the gate's name is elusive, though it is thought that in early times the gate was kept in repair by the bishop of London, for in *c*. 1181 a document of the bishop refers to 'his gate

Part of London Wall remaining at All Hallows Barking, depicted in 1818. Further remnants may be seen today near the Museum of London.

called Bissupsegate'. The involvement of the Hanse merchants in its maintenance was not new, for they were certainly responsible in the 13th century, and no doubt this odd arrangement had been the result of a bargain which allowed them trading privileges in the City.

1480

CLEMENT'S INN ESTABLISHED
This Inn of Chancery, which derived its name from its location near St Clement Danes church, was established about this year.

CHURCH ROBBING
Fugitives from the law could, as a last resort, take refuge in churches, where the right to sanctuary prevailed for 40 days. During this period the felon was fed by church officers and could at any time send for the coroner and swear his intention to quit the kingdom, in which event he was deprived of all possessions and given a strict journey timetable to a specified port of embarkation.

Sanctuary was a privilege granted by the Church, and one that it guarded jealously. No one – not even the mayor – was permitted to drag a criminal out of a church, and it was one of the trials of local administration that if someone had taken refuge in this way the church had to be watched night and day to ensure that he didn't leave it surreptitiously. The exception to this procedure was if a church declined to grant safety. This could happen if the church itself was the victim of the crime, as happened this year at St Martin's le Grand, the most famous of the sanctuary churches, where five thieves were caught robbing the building. All were taken out, and three were hanged on Tower Hill and the other two pressed to death.

1481

A WEAKENED BRIDGE
London Bridge was showing signs of strain. Not only was there a continuous street of houses along it, but recent improvement in the manufacture of cart wheels was resulting in much damage. The iron rims now common on wheels were causing vibrations which affected the safety of the structure. In future, it was ordered this year, no 'shod' carts should go over. By 1497 it was decided that the ageing drawbridge should not be raised unless absolutely necessary, such as for defensive purposes. Billingsgate, downstream of the bridge, profited from this regulation, reaping the trade of the larger ships which otherwise would have gone on to Queenhithe. The drawbridge fell into disuse, and when in 1500 Henry VII decided to sail his royal barques beneath the bridge, carpenters had to work day and night to ensure that the ruinous drawbridge functioned on the day.

1483

DRAMATIC EVENTS
Edward IV died 'of a surfeit' at Westminster on 9 April, leaving as his heir Edward, an 11-year-old boy. Two parties sought power. One was the old nobility, personified by the late king's brother, Richard, duke of Gloucester; the other was headed by the queen's Woodville family,

Nicholas John Visscher's view of London Bridge, made before 1632.

which depended heavily on the accession of Edward V. The story of ensuing events is familiar from Shakespeare's *Richard III,* though much has been written since to clear Richard's name, especially of the charge of having Edward V and his brother murdered in the Tower. But, as far as London was concerned, normality existed on the death of Edward IV. The City authorities rode out to Hornsey Wood (now Finsbury Park) on 4 May to welcome the young Edward and his uncle Richard on their arrival in London. Gloucester, armed with the title of Protector, moved into Crosby Place in Bishopsgate; the former queen, already alarmed, sought sanctuary in Westminster Abbey; and the king and his brother were lodged at the Tower.

But the coronation which the City had prepared for did not take place. Richard decided to reach for the throne himself. He claimed that Edward IV had not been legally married to Elizabeth Woodville and therefore Edward V was not legitimate. On 22 June at Paul's Cross a political sermon was given, attended by Gloucester, which explained how the late king had, in contract at least, been married to another woman before Elizabeth Woodville became his wife. Elsewhere in the City it was also preached that Edward IV himself had been illegitimate.

At Baynard's Castle on 26 June the City authorities waited on Gloucester and invited him to accept the crown. The next day he did, seating himself on the throne at Westminster without more ado. The coronation at the abbey was on 2 July.

THE PENANCE OF JANE SHORE
An early victim of Richard's coup was Lord Hastings, accused by Gloucester of complicity in a plot against him. He was summarily beheaded, and Jane Shore, previously the mistress of Edward IV and later of Hastings, was put in imminent danger. After a spell of imprisonment in the Tower she was sentenced, as a harlot, to do penance in the streets of London by walking with taper in hand to Paul's Cross.

A Matter of Precedence

By 1515 the City had 'sette, ordeyned and agreed' an order of precedence among the City companies, which had some relationship to their foundation dates as known at that time. But in 1483, before this settlement, the Merchant Taylors and Skinners were constantly at odds as to which of them should be sixth or seventh in the annual procession by barge from the City to Westminster. This year the dispute led to bloodshed, and the mayor was called upon to arbitrate. His decision, still acted upon today, is that they should each be sixth in alternate years. They were also to lash their boats together when nearing Westminster and drink a mutual toast.

New Church for Islington

The present church of St Mary in Upper Street, Islington, is at least the fourth on the site. A stone from a building of the 12th century was later found in the present crypt, and in 1751, when the medieval church, which contained a monument dated 1454, was being demolished, the date 1483 was found carved on the steeple. Often churches took many years to complete, and the steeple might follow years after the main body of the structure was in use.

1484

The College of Arms Founded

By the time of the Wars of the Roses the practice of displaying armorial bearings was one of much sophistication. Each man's device had to be, like fingerprints, unique to him and, furthermore, accurately reflect his family and his position within it. The inspectors of arms were called 'heralds'. They had other functions, too: they were used as emissaries during disputes and battles, and they were messengers who could not, or should not, be shot. A grimmer task was to comb the field of battle after the fighting had finished, to note those killed and the arms they bore. In happier times their status rose with their ability and practice in arranging jousting tournaments.

This year Richard III granted them a charter and a house in Upper Thames Street. From this developed the College of Arms.

The City Barge at Strand-on-the-Green

It is claimed that the City Barge public house on the riverside at Strand-on-the-Green was built in 1484 and then called the Navigator's Arms.

1485

End of an Age

With the death this year of Richard III on Bosworth Field came the end of the Wars of the Roses and, as most historians see it in retrospect, the medieval period. The coronation of the Tudor Henry VII took place on 30 October at Westminster Abbey.

The Sweating Sickness

A new epidemic was rampant in the City, called 'sweating sickness'. Victims were carried off in the space of 24 hours, and within a week it took two mayors and six aldermen, plus thousands of others. Sir Thomas Hille was the first mayor to die, and within four days his successor was dead too; a third man was nominated for the final month of the mayoralty, but he was rarely to be seen in the City and because of this he was not chosen at the next election.

Caxton Output

This year at his Westminster press William Caxton published Sir Thomas Malory's *Le Morte D'Arthur*. He had already printed a large folio edition of Chaucer's *Canterbury Tales*.

1486

Rebuilding of St Margaret's

Nothing is left now of the medieval St Margaret's, Westminster. Rebuilding of this parish church in the shadow of the abbey began about this year, at a time when Caxton lived a few yards away. He would have seen before his death the beginnings of the south aisle arise under the supervision of Robert Stowell, master mason of the abbey. The nave and its aisles were finished about 1504.

First Consecration in Lambeth Palace

The chapel at Lambeth Palace had been built during the term of Boniface as archbishop of Canterbury in the 13th century, but the first archbishop to be consecrated here was Archbishop Morton this year.

1490

Hall at Lincoln's Inn Begun

The lawyers of Lincoln's Inn, who had taken over the old premises of the bishop of Chichester in Chancery Lane, this year began rebuilding. The celebrated Old Hall, which survives still, was begun this year.

1491

Cripplegate Rebuilt

According to Stow, this gate was rebuilt this year at the expense of former mayor Edmund Shaw, goldsmith. It had previously been the responsibility of the Brewers' Company, whose members, with their breweries clustered near the gate, were its main users.

Henry VIII Born at Greenwich Palace

By this time the palace at Greenwich (see 1433) had been rebuilt out of recognition by Henry VII. Dominated by a tower that extended over the water, it stretched for 100 yards. Here Henry VIII was born this year, and the building remained his favourite palace outside London.

1492

Jousting at Shene

Shene Palace (at today's Richmond-upon-Thames), a building which had developed from a manor house over the years, was the favourite retreat of Henry VII. According to Stow, he held a month-long jousting tournament here in May this year.

1493

RIOT AT THE STEELYARD

The regulation of foreign trade was a sensitive issue in London. As part of a protectionist plan, the king had in 1492 banned the Flemings from trading in the City. However, the main beneficiaries of this had been the Hanseatic League merchants based in the Steelyard in Upper Thames Street, who were able to obtain the privilege of importing Flemish cloth. London merchants who had previously traded with the Flemings were out of pocket, and feelings ran high enough for a riot in which the Steelyard was attacked and damaged this year.

1496

THE BUILDING OF BELSIZE HOUSE

The use of bricks in building was becoming more common, but only in buildings of distinction, such as Shene Palace and Crosby Place.

Westminster Abbey this year contracted to make the vast number of 400,000 bricks on its estate in Hampstead. It is possible that they were intended for Westminster, though no building work of that period is known to have demanded such a number and, of course, the carriage of such bulk on carts along primitive roads would not have been sensible. More likely they were intended for the construction of the first Belsize House, Hampstead, a large mansion which was certainly in existence by 1550.

FIRST MENTION OF DOCTORS' COMMONS

This year first mention is made of a body usually known as Doctors' Commons but properly as the College of Advocates and Doctors of Law. It housed the practitioners of the ecclesiastical and Admiralty courts – a body of lawyers separate from ordinary barristers, and which was to remain in existence until the mid 19th century. Their premises were in Paternoster Row, but by 1570 they were off Knightrider Street, near St Paul's churchyard.

1497

SHENE PALACE DESTROYED BY FIRE

On the evening of 21 December Shene Palace, where the royal family were settled for Christmas, was mostly destroyed by fire. The blaze must have spread quickly, with little time for removal of possessions, for the Privy Purse accounts show £20 expended 'for rewardes yeven to them that founde the King's juels at Shene'.

WARBECK PARADED

The crown of Henry VII was relatively secure, but for the past few years the activities of one Perkin Warbeck had been troublesome. Warbeck claimed to be Richard, duke of York, one of the princes thought to have been murdered in the Tower. (It must be remembered that what are thought to be their skeletons were not found until 1674, and claims that one or more of them were still alive could attract some credence.) Warbeck, supported by the Woodvilles and the Scots, proclaimed himself Richard IV and raised some sort of force, but he was captured in September 1497. Henry VII treated him leniently. He

was paraded through London on 28 November as an object of derision, before being lodged initially in the Tower.

CORNISH REBELLION PUT DOWN

A force of men from Cornwall, driven to arms by the frequent taxation to meet Henry's military ambitions, marched to London. The rebels were defeated on 22 June at Blackheath; chronicles report that the number of deaths was high, and local legend has it that some of the various hillocks on Blackheath are burial mounds. The leader of the rebels, a disaffected nobleman, Lord Audley, was led from Newgate to Tower Hill in a paper coat of armour and there beheaded.

1498

HOLBORN CONDUIT BUILT

A cross and a conduit were established at what is today the junction of Snow Hill, Cock Lane and Smithfield – the cross by 1338 and the conduit in 1498. The conduit was fed from either a spring or a tributary of the Fleet, at the top of today's Lamb's Conduit Street. That street got its name from William Lambe, who rebuilt the system in 1577.

WARBECK ESCAPES

The pretender to the throne, Perkin Warbeck, in seemingly relaxed captivity in the king's court, escaped but was soon recaptured, at Syon House. In June he was placed in stocks at Westminster Hall and for five hours at Cheapside, and was then again lodged in the Tower.

PRINCE HENRY IN THE CITY

The seven-year-old Prince Henry, the future Henry VIII but not, at that time, the heir to the throne, paid a visit to the City on 30 October, when he was presented with a pair of gilt goblets. In anticipation of the visit there was a considerable clean-up of the streets and a proclamation that all vagbonds and people affected by the 'great pockes' should leave the city.

1499

PLAGUE IN LONDON

Plague was endemic in London, though some years were more remarkable than others. An epidemic which raged through to 1500 is said to have taken 20,000 lives and been severe enough to cause Henry VII to flee to Calais.

WARBECK AND WARWICK EXECUTED

Perkin Warbeck pressed the king's leniency too often this year. An ill-conceived plot to corrupt his keepers in the Tower and blow up the building in alliance with the earl of Warwick led to the execution of both of them. In fact Warwick's involvement in this matter has never been proved; some historians believe that his implication was a fraud and that his death was judicial murder by a king anxious to be rid of him. Warwick's influence could also prevent the marriage which Henry planned between the king's eldest son, Arthur, and Catherine of Aragon.

With Warwick's death on Tower Hill the male line of the Plantagenets ended.

1500

ERASMUS AT ELTHAM

The noted Dutch scholar Erasmus had been in England since 1498. In 1500 he met (Sir) Thomas More at Greenwich while staying there with his friend Lord Mountjoy. More took him for a walk to Eltham to see the king's palace there, and they were shown into the presence of the royal children, including the future Henry VIII. Erasmus described the incident thus: 'When we came to the great hall there were assembled together not only those of the royal household, but Mountjoy's train also. In the midst stood Henry, then only nine years old, but of right royal bearing, foreshewing a nobility of mind, in addition to a person of singular beauty.'

HAMMERSMITH LEPER HOSPITAL

First mention is made this year of a hospital for lepers at Hammersmith. The location is not known, nor the foundation date, though the formation of the leper hospitals in Highgate and Knightsbridge in the 1470s suggests that there was a concerted effort to establish such places outside the City at this period.

1501

FROM SHENE TO RICHMOND

It is rare to be able to date a town name in London. Richmond-upon-Thames is an example, for about this year Shene Palace was rebuilt after the disastrous fire of 1497 and renamed by the king Richmond Palace, after his earldom in Yorkshire. Gradually, the hamlet attached to the house became known by the same name.

The palace occupied 10 acres. The master mason was Henry Smyth, and the carpenter Thomas Mauncy. We know also that the king employed foreign joiners and decorators.

Baynard's Castle, from a view published in 1790.

Its completion this year was timely, for it coincided with the arrival of Catherine of Aragon for her marriage to the king's eldest son, Arthur, both of them 15 years old. She arrived in November, and they married at St Paul's on the 14th. Arriving by barge at the Tower, she was greeted with a particularly lavish welcome in the City. Soon after, the royal party went to Richmond Palace. They disembarked from barges at Mortlake – an indication that the watergate at Richmond was not yet built – and, in a procession illuminated by torches, went to the royal home, described by one witness as 'this ertheley and secunde Paradise'. He also observed that the building was quadrangular, enclosed by a brick wall studded with towers, with strong oak gates. Local streams fed a fountain and conduits. The Great Hall was 100 ft long and 40 ft wide, with a screen and minstrels' gallery; the floor was paved with tiles.

Shortly afterwards, the young couple – who, it seems, were judged too young to cohabit – were sent off to Wales, where, six months later, the heir to the throne died of fever. The prince described a year earlier by Erasmus as 'of singular beauty', and having 'right royal bearing' was to be king – and to change the history of England in the most significant manner.

BAYNARD'S CASTLE REBUILT

Not content with lavish expenditure at Richmond, the king was busy at Blackfriars. About this year he rebuilt Baynard's Castle. This building, burnt down in 1428 and re-erected by Humphrey, duke of Gloucester, during his ownership of the site in 1415–47, was reconstructed as a house rather than a castle, and was to be his main London home.

Recent excavations have shown that the old stone wharf was converted into a walled garden, and on the river front two octagonal towers were at the corners of a long wall, probably matched by similar towers at the northern end of the grounds.

LAMBETH PALACE GATEHOUSE BUILT

The gatehouse to Lambeth Palace was completed about this year; this red-brick building with black-brick diapering still survives, on the river side of the palace. Five-storey towers are on either side of the double-gate entrance – one gate for carriages, the other for pedestrians. At the time it was built there was no embankment by the river and the gatehouse was much nearer to the shoreline. Building was initiated by Archbishop Morton, who combined his ecclesiastical role with ministerial duties, in the manner of the time, and it was in his household here that the young Thomas More received his training. In the same palace in 1534 More was to be examined by Thomas Cromwell on his refusal to sign the Oath of Supremacy.

FIRST LORD MAYOR'S BANQUET AT THE GUILDHALL

Sir John Shaw or Shaa, mayor this year, held the traditional mayoral banquet at the Guildhall, which had been newly installed with kitchens. This was the first occasion the banquet was held there, and began a tradition which still survives.

1503

FUNERAL OF THE QUEEN

Henry VII's queen, Elizabeth, died. Elaborate mourning arrangements were made in the City, which required each ward to line the streets with men holding lighted tapers.

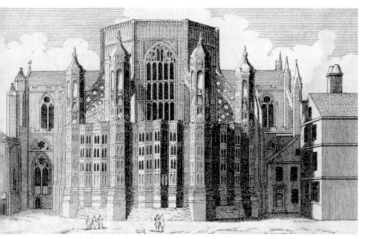

Henry VII's Chapel at Westminster Abbey, from an engraving of 1770. The foundation stone was laid in 1503 and the building was completed in 1519.

The king, being pressed by the Spanish for the return of Catherine of Aragon's dowry now that Prince Arthur was dead (and, indeed, they were anxious to retrieve Catherine herself), now proposed a match between himself and the widow. This so shocked the Spanish that they were precipitated into an agreement that Catherine would marry Prince Henry instead – a marriage which finally took place in 1509.

HENRY VII'S CHAPEL BEGUN
Henry VII's Chapel, in Westminster Abbey, was begun in January. The original plan was that it should hold the tomb of his uncle, the deposed, and possibly murdered, Henry VI, which at that time was at Windsor. Henry's intention was that the former king should be canonized at the same time, but the pope wanted so much money to agree to this that the chapel was devoted to the Virgin Mary instead.

The work was under the supervision of master mason Robert Vertue. Washington Irving (1783–1859) writing about it said, 'Stone seems, by the winning labour of the chisel, to have been robbed of its weight and density, suspended aloft, as if by magic and the fretted roof achieved with the wonderful minuteness and airy security of a cobweb.'

HOUNDSDITCH PAVED
On the authority of John Stow it is recorded that Houndsditch, a track following the line of the ditch outside the City wall from Aldgate to Bishopsgate, was paved this year. Stow also suggests that the name derived from the practice of dumping dead dogs in the ditch, but this seems rather unlikely.

1504

ST JOHN'S GATEWAY COMPLETED
The gatehouse of the priory of St John Clerkenwell, the headquarters of the Knights Hospitaller, was finished in 1504. It still stands, and is the only gateway in London straddling a highway. This new building, consisting of two 47-ft towers connected by a room above the arch, was part of a general refurbishment by the prior, Thomas Docwra – his arms may be seen on the north and south of the gateway and beneath the arch. Because the street level outside has risen by about 6 ft since 1504, the original ground floors of the towers are now below ground.

1505

SAVOY CHAPEL HOSPITAL FOUNDED
The old Savoy Palace, destroyed in 1381 in the Peasants' Revolt, appears to have lain derelict, or hardly used, since that time. One of the last public benefactions of Henry VII was to begin this year the building on this site in the Strand of a hospital (an almshouse) dedicated to St John the Baptist. Also included was a chapel to replace that in which Chaucer had been married to John of Gaunt's sister-in-law.

Though heavily restored, much of this building remained until 1864, when a fire destroyed virtually everything except the walls.

LINCOLN'S INN LIBRARY ESTABLISHED
A library at Lincoln's Inn is first mentioned in 1474, but it was not until 1505 that one John Nethersale bequeathed 40 marks to 'build or newly erect the Library within the Inn'. This building, probably adjoining the Old Hall in Old Square, was completed in 1508.

1506

BROTHELS SUPPRESSED
A royal ordinance this year suppressed the 'stews', or brothels, of Southwark, but 12 of the 18 were allowed to reopen shortly afterwards.

1509

THE KING IS DEAD, LONG LIVE THE KING
Henry VII died at Richmond Palace on 22 April. On 9 May his corpse was conveyed to St Paul's, being met on its way at St George's in the Fields by the mayor, aldermen and 104 commoners, all dressed in black and on horseback. Streets in the City were lined with livery-company members, bearing torches; their numbers were swollen by merchants of nationalities which traded in London – Genoese, Venetians,

The gatehouse to St John's Priory, Clerkenwell, which survives today.

Florentines, Spaniards and Germans. The next day the procession went to Westminster, where the late king was buried in his own chapel.

On 20 June the new king, Henry VIII, and his bride, Catherine of Aragon, whom he had married on 11 June, rode through the streets of the City from the Tower to Westminster. The City put on what observers thought was its most sumptuous display yet. The stalls of the Goldsmiths, at the west end of Cheapside, were occupied by girls dressed in white and holding tapers of white wax, while priests stood by with censers of silver and wafted incense over the king and queen as they passed.

1510

ST PAUL'S SCHOOL FOUNDED

Several dates are given for the establishment of this school in today's New Change, opposite the east end of St Paul's. The immensely wealthy dean of St Paul's, John Colet, set about founding the school in 1509, and buildings were completed by 1512, in which year he had already bought land within the churchyard to enlarge the school. However, the inscription 'MDX' on a stone of the building, and the fact that the school celebrated its 300th birthday in 1810, suggests that the school actually opened in 1510.

The building, which supplanted a number of bookbinders' shops, consisted of a school room, a chapel and dwellings for two masters. The largest school in the country at that time, it was intended for 153 boys who could already read and write, without restriction as to their nationality. (This odd number is supposed to relate to the number of draught fishes in the Gospel parable – a fish is in the school emblem.) Colet placed the administration of the school in the hands of his own livery company, the Mercers'.

THE REBUILDING OF FULHAM PALACE

Richard Fitzjames had been appointed bishop of London in 1506. In 1510 he set about rebuilding the manor house belonging to the see in Fulham. He demolished the old range of buildings and erected what is now known as the Fitzjames Quadrangle, two storeys of red brick with a diamond design of grey brick within it, containing a Great Hall. A moat still surrounded the building, and a well (thought to be of the same era as Fitzjames's rebuilding) was sunk in the quadrangle to a depth of 320 ft. These old buildings still exist. It was in the hall that the notorious Bishop Bonner tortured the luckless Thomas Tomkins in the 1540s, holding his hand in the flame of a candle as a foretaste of the pain of burning at a stake.

1511

THE HERMIT OF ISLINGTON

Hermits were not uncommon in London, and their status was rather different to the modern interpretation of the word. They did, indeed, live alone, and for the most part kept to their own company, but they had, in return for an ecclesiastical income, to perform certain tasks. At Highgate, for example, the hermitage at the top of Highgate Hill (where Highgate School now stands) was a place of worship at which the occupier seems to have officiated; he was also responsible for the upkeep of the main road in the village.

In 1511 the Knights Hospitaller founded a hermitage near Islington, at the top end of St John Street, in the apex with today's Goswell Road. It served as a chapel, and was of sufficient standing for Richard Cloudesley, a local landowner, to bequeath money in his will for the hermit to say a regular prayer for his soul.

A CELEBRATORY JOUST

The birth of a son to the king and Catherine of Aragon inspired considerable celebration. A sumptuous jousting tournament, in which the king himself took part, was held in the Whitehall area. In Westminster a temporary theatre was erected and a pageant was enacted in which a forest scene was fashioned out of silk, satin, velvet and damask. Joy was premature, however, as the prince died later in the year.

MOORFIELDS IMPROVED

The open expanse called Moorfields, which stretched westward from Bishopsgate to Finsbury, was virtually unusable except for recreation. For much of the year it was covered by water from streams and tributaries of the Walbrook; in winter it was covered with ice and was a favourite place for skating; in summer it was used with official encouragement for archery. Ralph Agas's map of about 50 years later shows women using it for airing laundry or else stretching cloth; a few men are practising with bows and arrows, and elsewhere cattle graze; the only significant building is one called the 'Dogge hous'.

This year the mayor ordered the construction of dykes and the levelling of ground so that the fields should be 'made more commodious for passage'.

1512

FIRE AT THE PALACE OF WESTMINSTER

Fire severely damaged much of the king's quarters at the Palace of Westminster, although the Hall, St Stephen's Chapel and the Exchequer were unscathed. From this year the old palace ceased to be a royal home and became, once the Commons were installed in St Stephen's, the home of government. The king, who had ample living space at Eltham, Richmond, Greenwich and Baynard's Castle, was also about to build himself a palace at Blackfriars, but within 18 years was back at Westminster, where he acquired Wolsey's sumptuous house in Whitehall.

1513

DOCKYARDS ESTABLISHED

The great Tudor navies have their origins about this year with the establishment of dockyards at Woolwich and Deptford.

At Woolwich the first commission was to build what was then the largest ship afloat, the *Harry-Grace-à-Dieu*, popularly known as the *Great Harry*. Deptford, situated on a ford across the river Ravensbourne, was to be the larger establishment. In time it was to cover 30 acres, containing two wet docks, three slips for naval vessels, workshops, mast houses, rope manufactures and quarters for officers.

FIRST MENTION OF LAMBETH HORSE FERRY

Undoubtedly of much older establishment, the horse ferry which provided a crossing of the Thames from outside Lambeth Palace to the north bank where Horseferry Road is today is first mentioned this year. Inns on both sides of the river gave shelter if the weather was bad or sustenance if the boat was awaited. The ferry disappeared after the erection of Westminster Bridge in the 18th century.

1514

WOLSEY BUYS HAMPTON COURT

The rise of Thomas Wolsey was speedy – just like his fall. He was appointed chaplain to Henry VII in 1507, became a fully occupied diplomat with a few minor benefices, and then, just before the king's death, was made dean of Lincoln. In 1509 he leased land to the south of St Bride's, Fleet Street, as well as the parsonage itself, from the Knights Hospitaller. Honours and titles were rained on him by a grateful, if unpredictable, young king, Henry VIII, but Wolsey was unwise enough to flaunt his personal and ecclesiastical wealth.

In 1514 he was made both bishop of Lincoln and, later, archbishop of York. Immense riches were his, and in the same year he made another arrangement with the Hospitallers, this time to buy a site on the banks of the river at Hampton. From 1515 he was a cardinal and lord chancellor of England, and the residence at Hampton grew into a palace with hundreds of rooms and a staff of over 500. It is the earliest surviving example of such a large domestic building, although a few defensive features, such as a moat, were included. It is, perhaps, the last great medieval house to have been built in this country.

BRUCE CASTLE REBUILT

Bruce Castle in Lordship Lane, Tottenham, now houses the local-history collection of the London Borough of Haringey. It is on the site of the manor house of Tottenham – in early records it is called Lordship House. Its name derives from the possession of the manor and its house in the 13th century by the Scottish royal family, but when Robert Bruce claimed the Scottish throne in 1306 he forfeited his English lands. 'Bruce Castle' appears as a name only in the late 17th century.

In 1514 Tottenham Manor was bought by Sir William Compton. It is not clear when he rebuilt the house. It is described by some architectural historians as late Elizabethan, but John Norden, writing at the end of Elizabeth's reign, described it as a 'proper ancient house'.

1515

THE BEGINNINGS OF BRIDEWELL

The area south of St Bride's church in Fleet Street, bounded by the river Fleet to the east (now beneath New Bridge Street), was described in 1422 as a 'vacant waste'. The land, consisting of an orchard and 12 gardens, was low-lying and at the mercy of the Fleet and the Thames – the former by now notorious for its stench.

The choice of this site for the new royal palace of Bridewell is therefore surprising, although the king, with his Westminster palace substantially damaged by fire in 1512 and Baynard's Castle made over to his queen, Catherine of Aragon, was in need of a new building to play with.

The site had to be drained and the buildings raised to escape the inundations of the rivers. Two courtyards, side by side, were south of

Bride Lane, and a gallery ran down towards the Thames. As was the fashion of the time, the building was mainly of brick, although the gallery, of which no trace remained after the Great Fire, was probably largely made of wood.

1516

ROYAL EVENTS

Greenwich Palace was the retreat most favoured by Henry VIII. It had grown a great deal over the last 90 years. The grounds extended to the top of the hill, where a watchtower was built, and the palace itself was around a series of courtyards entered from a large gatehouse by the river. Even a Franciscan monastery had been added in 1480. There was good hunting, and the king was near to his dockyard, where he could keep an eye on the progress of shipbuilding.

His daughter by Catherine of Aragon, the future Mary I, was born here in February. On 31 December the first masquerade known in this country was performed here, with a mock castle, weapons, dungeons and (with a special eye to the king) six ladies dressed in russet satin embroidered with gold. Among the audience was his sister, Margaret, the exiled queen of Scotland, whom Henry had gone to meet in May at Bruce Castle, Tottenham, after her flight from the north.

LAWLESS LONDON

London took its turn in engaging the favour of Wolsey, who by now was the predominant power behind the throne. A sycophantic delegation from the City went to see the cardinal on 6 March, with no expense spared in its apparel and presentation, but in June Wolsey sternly informed the mayor of a list of abuses in the City. Sedition, he thought, was rife there, the government was disobedient, vagabonds and 'masterless folk' roamed the streets, and unlawful gambling was allowed. He was vindicated when a long-standing grievance over Moorfields exploded. For years, it seems, residents of outlying places such as Hoxton, Islington and Shoreditch had been encroaching on the fields, traditionally assumed to be the recreation space of young men and 'auncient persones' of London. One morning, a force of London men assembled with shovels and proceeded to knock down any fences and to fill in any ditches which had been dug by the outsiders. The King's Council assembled at the Grey Friars' monastery and commanded the mayor to recall the citizens. Peace was restored, but Wolsey was to have much to complain about in the following year.

1517

EVIL MAY DAY

Hostility towards foreigners, and in particular foreign merchants, had long been a feature of London life; with trade precarious, jealousy was bound to arise between denizen and alien over rights and privileges. By this year foreign traders were back in favour at court and able to monopolize areas of business. A merchant called John Lincoln took the first step towards the events known later as Evil May Day. He persuaded a canon, Dr Bell, who was giving the Easter Tuesday sermon at the open-air pulpit attached to St Mary Spital in Bishopsgate, to use the occasion to vindicate the rights of Londoners and spell out the wrongs they were suffering at the hands of foreign merchants.

The sermon was an inflammatory one, and Lincoln had already whipped the audience into a mood of expectancy. Feelings ran high in the City and trouble was anticipated, especially on the May Day holiday, always one of high spirits. On 28 April a number of assaults involving foreigners took place, and several Londoners were imprisoned, probably in Bread Street Compter.

Edward Hall, a contemporary chronicler, reports that the king sent for the mayor on 30 April and urged him to take care there should be no trouble. A curfew was ordered, but there was hardly time to announce it let alone enforce it. An alderman helped to spark off the riot by trying to stop a friendly sword fight in the streets, and within an hour an eruption of apprentices took place. Hall says that people arose from every quarter, including servants, watermen and courtiers, and by 11 at night there were 700 assembled in Cheapside and 300 in St Paul's churchyard. They broke open the prisons in which their colleagues of two days previously had been put, and then proceeded on their trail of havoc. At St Martin's le Grand, Thomas More, then an undersheriff for London, tried reasoning with them, to no avail. Houses were broken into and ransacked – in particular that of John Meautys, a merchant from Picardy, in Leadenhall. The riot seems to have petered out by three in the morning.

The ordnance at the Tower had sounded its guns, the earls of Shrewsbury and Surrey had arrived with forces, but on the whole the event appears to have been bloodless and quite mild compared with previous occasions. However, it was taken very seriously indeed by the king, who probably used the occasion to clip the wings of London. Surprisingly, those captured – there were several hundred prisoners – were charged with high treason rather than riot. Ten pairs of mobile gallows were constructed, and a number of prisoners were hanged in different parts of the City. Lincoln, as leader, was hanged, drawn and quartered; and then the executions stopped. Many of the prisoners were quite young people, some of them women. The queen is said to have interceded on behalf of the women, and, in a cynical attempt to curry favour with Londoners, Wolsey pleaded for the rest to be spared.

1518

FEVER HITS LONDON
What was called the 'Sweating Sickness' had hung around London for several years, but in 1518 it broke out with ferocity, accompanied by epidemics of smallpox and measles. The king ordered that inhabitants of infected houses should keep indoors, marking their houses with wisps of straw. When absolutely necessary they were allowed out, but only if they carried a white wand. Beggars, vagabonds and slaughterhouses were expelled outside the City walls.

The worst effects of the disease must have lessened by the end of the year, because the French ambassador stayed in the City in October, lodged at the Merchant Taylors' hall. He was here to negotiate a marriage treaty between Henry's daughter, Mary, then two years old, and the even younger dauphin of France. On 3 October the king in procession rode out to St Paul's for a pre-marriage ceremony, and on the 5th the marriage was solemnized at Greenwich – a gold ring was placed on Mary's young finger.

COLLEGE OF PHYSICIANS FOUNDED
It was appropriate that in the year of such a fever the Royal College of Physicians, today the oldest medical society in this country, was

founded. Its inspiration was Thomas Linacre, whose students had included More, Erasmus and Prince Arthur, and whose patients included Henry VIII and Wolsey.

By 1518 Linacre had given up the practice of physic and was living on a number of ecclesiastical sinecures. The college was granted a charter by the king on 23 September; this granted sole power to license physicians in London and for 7 miles around. Early meetings were held in Linacre's house in Knightrider Street – premises which he bequeathed to the college on his death.

LINCOLN'S INN GATEHOUSE BUILT
Three large gatehouses of this period survive still in London – those at Lambeth Palace and St John's Gate, Clerkenwell, have already been noted. At Lincoln's Inn, the development of the old bishop of Chichester's property on the west side of Chancery Lane into accommodation for lawyers was still proceeding. The Great Hall was not yet complete, but this year the gatehouse, which carries the arms of Sir Thomas Lovell, Henry VIII and the earl of Lincoln, was begun.

Nearly a third of the cost of construction was donated by Lovell, who might well have had a hand in its design. He was also a beneficent force in the building of Gonville and Caius College in Cambridge and Holywell convent in Shoreditch, near to his own town house.

1519

THE THROWSTONE BEQUEST
Two buildings were to benefit by the will of John Throwstone, who died this year. One was the church of St Vedast in Foster Lane, which was rebuilt; unhappily, this was almost entirely lost in the Great Fire. It has been demonstrated that 'Foster' is a corruption of 'Vedast', the name of a French saint who was at one time emperor of the Franks. This explains the full title of the church: St Vedast-alias-Foster.

Nearby, in Gutter Lane, Throwstone's money was used to acquire a site for a hall for the Embroiderers' Company – a name which itself has become corrupted to the Broderers' Company. A hall existed on the site until it was destroyed in the last war.

1520

PROSPECT OF WHITBY BUILT
It is claimed that the first Prospect of Whitby tavern, in Wapping Wall, was built this year. It was then known as the Devil's Tavern, from its association with thieves and smugglers; it received its new name in 1777, when a ship called the *Prospect*, registered in Whitby, moored there for a considerable time.

ST PETER AD VINCULA REBUILT
The little church within the north-west wall of the Tower of London was rebuilt after a fire had destroyed most of the medieval building. The historian Macaulay (1800–1859) said about it, 'In truth, there is no sadder spot on earth.' He was here referring to the succession of notable people executed on Tower Hill for treason and interred in this simple church: Anne Boleyn and Catherine Howard for cuckolding Henry VIII, and John Fisher and Sir Thomas More for opposing him; Lady Jane Grey and her husband for temporarily occupying the

throne; the duke of Monmouth and a number of Jacobites for rebellion; and many others who in some way displeased a monarch.

1521

THE MIDSUMMER SHOW

The origin of the Lord Mayor's Show was the custom, on election, of the mayor travelling by horseback to Westminster to be accepted by the king. This became known as a 'riding', and by the 15th century was an elaborate affair made by barge along the Thames with the full paraphernalia of the City decorations; on that day the mayor was accompanied by barges of each City company.

But there was another show, which gradually declined as the Lord Mayor's Show in November became more elaborate. This was the Midsummer Show, which was simply an annual pageant paid for by the livery company whose member was mayor that year. The Venetian ambassador left a description of the event for 1521. He relates how one tableau featured

naked boys dyed black like devils, with the dart and buckler in their hands, goading the followers of Pluto, who was on a pulpit under a canopy seated on a serpent that spat fire; he himself being naked, with a drawn sword in his hand so contrived that, when he brandished it it made the serpent vomit fetid sulphuric fire-balls; and on the pulpit in front of Pluto were figures of an ox, a lion, and some serpents.

1523

THE EMPEROR IN LONDON

The Holy Roman Emperor, Charles V of Spain, visited London in the hope of persuading Henry VIII to support him in his quarrel with the king of France. The emperor was to be accommodated at the Black Friars' monastery, while the king was to take up residence across the river Fleet at his new Bridewell Palace. For the occasion, a bridge was built from one building to the other.

On 6 June the two kings progressed from Greenwich Palace to Blackfriars by way of Southwark, London Bridge and Cheapside, the crimson velvets of the emperor's retinue mingling with the purples of the king's and the scarlets of the mayor and aldermen. It was a day of pageants, depicting King Arthur, John of Gaunt, Charlemagne and the like. The next day was primarily devoted to tennis, and on the 8th the assembly, all in white, went to Whit Sunday mass at St Paul's and later in the day, after feasting, to Westminster.

ST MARGARET'S, WESTMINSTER, CONSECRATED

The rebuilt church of St Margaret's, Westminster, was consecrated on 9 April. It was virtually the building we see today in Parliament Square, but was almost very short-lived, for 17 years later Edward Seymour, the duke of Somerset, Protector during the reign of Edward VI, needed building materials for his new palace on the Strand and his plan to demolish St Margaret's for ready materials had to be resisted by force.

The building appears to have been the last church in London decorated in the Catholic tradition before the Reformation. On either side of a great rood were figures of St Mary and St John, richly painted. Numerous chapels adorned the building, all embellished.

FINE FOR REFUSING THE MAYORALTY

George Monoux, alderman and draper, who had been mayor in 1514–15, was fined £1,000 for refusing to become mayor again on grounds of expense. It was also decided that this fine should automatically apply on any similar occasion in future. The punishment on Monoux was later remitted, and instead he donated to the City his brewhouse in Southwark.

FEAR OF THE DELUGE

Almanac compilers and soothsayers provoked alarm in London by predictions of great rains and inundations in the City. Many withdrew to the neighbouring hills for safety, among them Bolton, prior of St Bartholomew's, who retired to Harrow-on-the-Hill with two months' supply of provisions.

1524

THE MERCERS BUILD THEIR HALL

The Mercers of London, whose livery company is first in precedence amongst the City companies, were centred on Cheapside near Friday Street, and since 1347 they had met in part of the hospital of St Thomas Acon at the junction with Ironmonger Lane. By 1524 they had bought the Cheapside frontage and completed their new hall and chapel. During the Reformation, when the hospital was suppressed, they took over the rest of the building.

1525

BONFIRES IN LONDON

The country was now at war with France, and in February Francis I, the French king, was captured. On 11 March this event was celebrated in London. Bonfires were lit around the City, and the chamberlain provided a hogshead of wine at each. Minstrels played in the streets, and the children of the parish clerks sang ballads and 'other delectable and joyfull songs'.

LESNES ABBEY SUPPRESSED

Wolsey, twice disappointed of being elected pope, was compensated with the bishopric of Durham and the papal authority to suppress some minor monasteries, whose income was to be devoted to founding and maintaining colleges. His particular project was to transform the monastery of St Frideswide in Oxford into a college. To this end some small establishments were suppressed (not without opposition), including the Augustinian monastery of Lesnes Abbey, in New Road, Bexley.

1526

TROUBLE AT GRAY'S INN

An allegorical play produced this year at Gray's Inn suggested that insurrection was the result of misgovernment. This displeased Wolsey considerably, and in the king's name the author, John Roo, serjeant-at-law, was kept in the Fleet prison for some time, along with one of the players.

1500s

1527

MONOUX ALMSHOUSES ESTABLISHED

Sir George Monoux, who had been fined for refusing to accept the mayoralty (see 1523), established 13 almshouses in Walthamstow, together with a school. The almshouses, rebuilt in the 18th century, are claimed to be the oldest on their original site in London. Monoux himself lived at a house called Moons on the site of Monoux Grove.

1528

GREAT HALL AT YORK PLACE ERECTED

Wolsey's career was now in jeopardy. Already, in 1526, he had made a propitiatory 'gift' of Hampton Court Palace to the king, who in exchange had given him Richmond Palace, which hardly compared.

Wolsey's ecclesiastical residence in London, York Place, was still being developed, however. It was located east of Whitehall, between today's Great Scotland Yard and Richmond Terrace, its principal buildings overlooking the Thames. Completed this year was the great hall. This had a deep-pitched roof supporting a lantern; it was 70 ft long and 40 ft wide, comprising six bays.

MORE'S CHAPEL AT CHELSEA

The rising star of the reign was now Sir Thomas More, who later succeeded Wolsey as chancellor (the first layman to hold the post). Born in Milk Street to a barrister and his wife, and educated at St Anthony's School, he was trained at Lambeth Palace and Lincoln's Inn. By 1523, More, now knighted, a fully fledged diplomat and a protégé of Wolsey, was living either in Bucklersbury or in Crosby Place, Bishopsgate. He had also bought land at Chelsea, on which he was to build a mansion which he and his numerous family occupied from the 1520s until his execution. No trace remains of the house, but his chapel in Old Chelsea Church – a 1528 rebuilding of a previous chapel – survives, and is an interesting example of transitional Renaissance architecture.

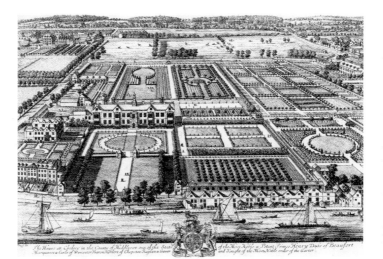

'The House at Chelsey', Sir Thomas More's house by the Thames.

1529

THE KING TAKES YORK PLACE

Wolsey's fall from grace this year was complete. Fortunate to escape with his life, he withdrew from public affairs, but was comforted by being restored to the archbishopric of York in 1530 (the year of his death). In the meantime the king, tired of Bridewell and envious of York Place, engineered the transfer of the latter from the see of York

to his own possession on 2 November. For the next 170 years Whitehall Palace, as it was soon called (though no conclusive reason has been found for the name 'Whitehall'), was to be the royal home.

Henry also developed west of today's Whitehall, mainly with buildings devoted to recreation. These included the Great Close Tennis Court, one of four tennis courts in the palace, and the Cockpit, which appears to have been used for kitchens at some stage, since modern excavation of a rubbish pit nearby produced over 1,000 vessels deposited there about 1530.

STAPLE INN ABSORBED BY GRAY'S INN

Staple Inn, the Inn of Chancery whose c.1580 hall still survives behind the Tudor row of houses and shops fronting Holborn, was this year absorbed by Gray's Inn.

REFORMATION GATHERS PACE

The want of a male heir, the temporary disadvantage of a Spanish connection, and his fancy for Anne Boleyn were leading Henry VIII to disentangle himself from his marriage to Catherine of Aragon. The complicated negotiations to persuade the pope to annul his marriage on the ground that it was invalid at the time, she being the widow of his brother, are part of national history and mark the beginning of many aspects of the Reformation in this country. Most particularly, the suppression of the monasteries which followed and the dispersal of their lands and wealth brought numerous changes in land ownership in and around London, where most manors were held either by the Crown or by an ecclesiastical body. The forced change of ownership put land in private hands whenever market forces made it desirable to expand and develop, whereas the natural inertia of institutions such as monasteries would have delayed or significantly altered the nature of such changes. (This was to be echoed in more recent years, when the old landed estates – heirs to this reformation – were themselves targeted by property speculators.)

In May a legatine court opened in the great hall of the Black Friars to hear evidence from both king and queen as to the validity of their marriage.

1531

ST JAMES'S HOSPITAL ACQUIRED

The suppression of the monasteries from this year onward included hospitals or almshouses attached to them. The poor and sick could then no longer rely on organized charity for shelter or welfare, and in 1531 the king's acquisition of St James's Hospital for lepers, on the site of today's St James's Palace, threw on to the streets a group of people it was in the interest of London to have settled.

This particular surrender of property was the result of the king intimidating the ground landlord, Eton College, which was a royal foundation. In exchange the college was compelled to receive less attractive lands in Kent. The surrender was not relevant to the king's suppression of collegiate bodies but was part of his plan to adorn his newly acquired Whitehall Palace with a park, for the hospital had not only a building but also about 185 acres of fields, stretching from today's Whitehall to Hay Hill, north of Piccadilly. In the course of time some of these fields, together with others prised from the abbot of Westminster, became St James's Park.

CONVENT OF ST CLARE, ALDGATE, SUPPRESSED

The first ecclesiastical body in London suppressed as part of the king's break from Rome appears to have been the convent of St Clare, later called Holy Trinity Minories. It was not, as it happened, an unpopular move, since the prior was an ill-regarded ex-officio alderman of London, and the convent enjoyed privileges exempting it from the jurisdiction of the City and the bishop.

POISON FOR THE BISHOP

The town house of the bishop of Rochester in Lambeth (later to be the home of the bishop of Carlisle) was called La Place; it is marked today by Carlisle Lane and Hercules Road. In 1531 a household cook, Richard Rose, attempted to kill Rochester by poisoning his soup, but the bishop, feeling unwell, did not have any. Unfortunately, others did, and two or three died (accounts vary). Rose, according to Stow, was boiled alive at Smithfield.

REGIONAL SEWER COMMISSIONERS APPOINTED

An Act this year (superseded only in 1848) provided for the appointment of eight regional boards to inspect and govern the provision of sewers in the City and liberties. The boards compelled local residents to serve on juries which carried out the actual inspections.

FREE SCHOOL IN RATCLIFF

It is appropriate that the first school in the dockside community of Ratcliff should have been founded at the instigation of a mariner's son – Nicholas Gibson, a prosperous City grocer. This school, located by The Highway and Schoolhouse Lane, at first had almshouses attached; it was later administered by the Coopers' Company, and in more recent years was removed to Upminster.

1532

TRANSFORMATION IN WHITEHALL

The rebuilding of York Place, Wolsey's palace in Whitehall, began the moment the king laid hands on it in 1530. Work spread over a number of years, but a description of the features is clearer in one summary. The 'Agas' map of c.1560 (shown here) includes the Whitehall area. Charing Cross, where today a statue of Charles I stands, is at the northern end. South of that is a fence across Whitehall, and immediately beneath, to the right, is a two-storey gateway leading to court buildings. This stood opposite today's Horse Guards and north of the Banqueting House, which had not yet been built. Then, still going south, is the famous Holbein Gate, straddling the road, and very soon after that the King Street Gate, just above today's Downing Street. King Street then led down to a smaller gate which opened into the

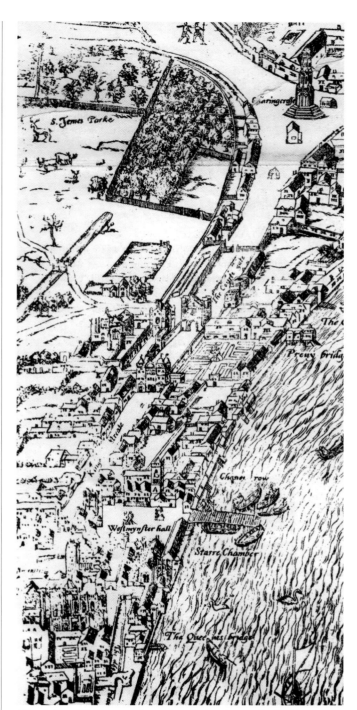

Whitehall and Westminster depicted on the 'Agas' map of c.1560.

Westminster Abbey precinct. Before this, on the right, is another gateway to the east, this time leading to New Palace Yard, Westminster Hall and the king's former home, the Palace of Westminster.

As important as the road were the entrances from the river, and it is likely that these too were rebuilt in this period. From north to south are Whitehall Stairs (above the words 'The Courte' on the river) and Privy Stairs (marked 'Privy Bridge'); Westminster Stairs, on the site of today's bridge, are shown above the 'Starre Chamber'. Steps reminiscent of these, running down to the foreshore of the Thames, still exist in Wapping High Street.

On the right, between the Holbein and King Street gates, is shown the Privy Garden; to its north is the Privy Gallery, and above that are various court buildings, such as the council chamber, the great hall built by Wolsey in 1528, kitchens and a chapel. To the left of these gates the buildings are mainly given over to tennis courts and a cockpit, and above the Holbein Gate may be seen that other object of the king's recreational obsessions, a tilt-yard. It will be seen from this that the roadway went between parts of the palace grounds; it was in fact a public right of way, just as was a path from the Whitehall Stairs, through the court buildings, into Whitehall.

The Holbein Gate was a spectacular affair, although nothing to do with the painter Holbein it seems. The great artist was in England in 1527–8, before Whitehall Palace was contemplated, and did not arrive back until 1532, by which time the gate was virtually complete. It is assumed that he may have added to its decoration, since he was later employed to embellish palace buildings, but there is no evidence. The building itself remained a London landmark until its demolition in 1759. Three storeys high, of chequered stone and flint tessellated in two colours, with plaques of Roman emperors on the front, it had a central arch for traffic and two side arches for pedestrians. The width of the main arch is not certain, but was probably between 12 and 13 ft.

The King Street gate, an architectural hybrid, was also finished in 1532; it disappeared in 1723. The Cockpit, a castellated building with a pointed roof and a weathervane in the shape of a lion, was prominent to the west. Tennis was not the only game played in the other buildings – in 1584 badminton is implied from a description of a game where they play 'at featherballs', and in 1603 the word 'shuttlecocke' appears.

St Andrew Undershaft Rebuilt

Though much altered and restored, the present St Andrew Undershaft, Leadenhall Street, is substantially that which was rebuilt this year at the expense of Stephen Gennings, Merchant Taylor and mayor of London.

It is a significant building in London history, not only because it was one of the few inner-London churches to escape the Great Fire. It was built immediately before the Reformation, and could be said to be the last church in London to be built for Catholic worship.

1533

The Birth of Elizabeth

Anne Boleyn had been installed at Greenwich Palace since 1528, to the distress of Queen Catherine. On 25 January, the king secretly married his mistress, even though he had yet to obtain an annulment of his previous marriage. This was not announced until Anne was some months pregnant, and in May the City was obliged to stage a pageant and procession appropriately magnificent for her coronation. A contemporary witness described the procession thus:

Then came the Queene in a white litter of white clothe of gold, not covered or vailled, which was led by two palfries clad in white damaske downe to the ground, head and tail, led by her footmen. She had on a kirtle of white cloth of tissue, and a mantle of the same furred with armyns, her haire hanging downe, but on her head shee had a coife with a circlet about it full of rich stones; over her was borne a canapie of clothe of golde with foure gilte stares and foure sil-verbelles; for bearing of the which capies were appoynted sixteene knights.

Their daughter, Elizabeth, was born at Greenwich on 7 September.

1534

The Holy Maid in London

The king's arbitrary banishment of Catherine and his subsequent marriage to Anne Boleyn caused much resentment. It was necessary to oblige the citizens of London to acknowledge Elizabeth as heir to the throne instead of Mary, who was now declared illegitimate. The scandal attracted in particular the opposition of a woman called Elizabeth Barton, who was mentally disturbed and affected by religious mania. Superstition had transformed her into a prophet, and a manipulative prior had persuaded her that she was in direct communication with the Virgin Mary; soon a miracle was contrived for her to perform.

Her fame and influence grew at the time of the king's divorce. She inveighed against it, and by 1532 she was the champion of Catherine and the Catholic Church in the country. She was wooed by churchmen, from monks to bishops, and she even personally importuned the king on the matter of his proposed divorce. The king did not die, as she prophesied, within six months of his marriage to Anne, but she nevertheless incited enough alarm to warrant a full-scale interrogation by Cranmer in 1533. At the end of November a scaffold was erected at Paul's Cross at which 'the Holy Maid' and some clerical supporters were compelled to confess that their views were mistaken, and by March it was politic that she should be executed.

Elizabeth was executed at Tyburn on 20 April; her head was fixed on London Bridge. Henry Gold, rector of the church of St Mary Aldermary, shared her fate.

King's Stables Burn Down

North of Charing Cross, on the site now occupied by the National Gallery, stood the palace stables, called the Royal Mews. These burnt down this year, with the loss of many horses; the stables were not fully rebuilt until 1559. Probably the first king to keep the mews was Edward I, and it appears that they were used for the housing of falcons. John Stow in his *Survey of London* (1598) states that the stables were in fact in Bloomsbury:

the king having faire stabling at Lomsbery (a Manor in the farthest west part of Oldborne) the same was fiered and burnt, with many great horses, and a great store of Hay. After which time, the forenamed house called the Mewse by Charing Crosse was new builded, and prepared for stabling of the King's horses, in the raigne of Edward the sixt and Queene Mary.

There is, however, no evidence for the king having stables in Bloomsbury – where they would, in any case, be at an inconvenient distance from Whitehall. But Edward Hall's *Chronicle*, published in 1548, says, 'The xvj day [of August 1534] was burned the kynges stable at Charing crosse other wise called the Mewse, wherein as brent many great horses and great store of haye.'

1535

A Question of Supremacy

In 1534 all clergy had been obliged to take the Oath of Supremacy, which recognized the king, and not the pope, as head of the country's church. Sir Thomas More, once the king's adviser, was an early casualty and so was John Fisher, bishop of Rochester. They were both beheaded on Tower Hill: Fisher on 22 June and More on 6 July. Legend has it that the latter, at the foot of the scaffold, begged his captor, 'I pray you, Master Lieutenant, see me safe up, and for my coming down let me shift for myself.'

The prior of Charterhouse, John Houghton, and some of his brethren were executed at Tyburn on 4 May for refusing to take the Oath. Houghton's head was placed on London Bridge, and one limb across the gateway into Charterhouse.

1536

THE FALL OF ANNE BOLEYN

After the birth of her daughter, the future queen Elizabeth, the fall of Anne Boleyn was rapid. Her lack of favour with the king was evident to many when at a tournament held at Greenwich Palace on 1 May he left early, and pointedly without her. Charges and rumours of adultery, incest and milder passions were in the air. Events moved quickly. The next day the queen was escorted to the Tower. Several men were arraigned for being her lovers, and on 15 May, before 26 peers, she and her brother were found guilty of high treason. She declared her innocence until the last.

Alleged lovers were hanged or beheaded on Tower Hill on 17 May and buried in the churchyard of St Peter ad Vincula. On the 19th, at noon, Anne was beheaded by the public executioner of Calais, and she too was buried in St Peter's.

The day afterwards, at Hampton Court, the king married Jane Seymour, a member of the households of the two previous queens, and described as intelligent but as 'of middle stature and no great beauty'. By the end of May she was in London, and on 22 December she rode with the king in state through the City; in January the following year she is recorded as having ridden on horseback across the frozen Thames.

SUPPRESSION OF THE SMALLER MONASTERIES

All monasteries with an income below £200 per annum were suppressed and given to the king. In London these included Kilburn Priory, in Kilburn High Road, Elsing Spital for blind people, and Greenwich Monastery, attached to the king's own palace. The establishment at Kilburn, recalled today by street names in the area, was a small one, holding about 45 acres of land and few possessions, according to the inventory of the time. The king exchanged the land with the Order of the Knights of St John at Clerkenwell for their manor of Paris Garden in Southwark, which he promptly presented to his new queen. As for the hospital for the blind at Cripplegate, its chapel was given to the local parish of St Alfege, London Wall, for use as its parish church. The prior, who had already acknowledged the king's supremacy in Church matters, was made the king's chaplain, but the fate of the inmates and arrangements for the subsequent care of blind people are not known.

THE REDUCTION OF WESTMINSTER ABBEY

The suppression of Westminster Abbey did not officially take place until 1540, but it had started long before. In 1533 a new abbot, totally subservient to Thomas Cromwell and the king, had been appointed, and gradually the wealth of the foundation was stripped for royal nominees or for the king himself.

In 1536 the king acquired the London manors of Ebury, Hyde, Todington and Neyte and the land of today's Covent Garden, and in exchange the abbey received some land in Berkshire. At this time Covent Garden was the convent garden of the abbey, consisting of about 40 acres stretching from today's Aldwych to Bedfordbury, north of Maiden Lane. It belonged to the convent by the end of the 12th century, and we know that the orchard yielded apples, pears, nuts, plums and cherries; attached were two smaller pieces of land which form today's Long Acre.

NEW BURIAL GROUND IN SOUTHWARK

The church of St Margaret, Borough High Street, stood in the middle of the road by the beginning of the 12th century; its site is readily seen today at the division of the High Street before it reaches Southwark Street. In 1536 the churchwardens obtained an act to buy an acre for a new churchyard, the old one being 'in the mydell of the kynges high way' and so full that recently they had been compelled to bury 'ffower deade boddyes … in one Sepulchre' to the 'Right perillous daungyer and pestyferous infeccon of the ayre'.

Very soon the church had ceased to operate, for at the Reformation St Mary Overie became the parish church of the area and St Margaret's and its land were sold. In 1676 the building, by then a court house, was burnt down.

1537

A BIRTH AT HAMPTON COURT

With two daughters from two previous marriages, the king was delighted by the birth of a son, the future Edward VI, at Hampton Court on 12 October. Sumptuous celebrations were organized in London, but the queen died 12 days afterwards.

BEGINNINGS OF THE HONOURABLE ARTILLERY COMPANY

The Honourable Artillery Company resides today in castellated premises in City Road. It is the descendant of an incorporation made by the king this year, and claims to be the oldest military body in the country. The king actually granted a charter to a company of archers, called the Fraternity of St George, which enabled the members to practise archery in the City and suburbs with longbows and crossbows, and also to use handguns.

TORTURE OF CHARTERHOUSE MONKS

Ten monks at Charterhouse who had refused to sign the Oath of Supremacy were imprisoned at Newgate, where they were chained and fettered upright for days. Nine died of starvation and another was sent to the Tower, where he was executed three years later.

1538

THE LARGER MONASTERIES SUPPRESSED

The Reformation claimed some larger prizes in London this year. The following establishments were dissolved and their lands and possessions were acquired by the Crown: Bermondsey Abbey on 1 January; Black Friars on 12 November (after which the church was given to the parishioners of the nearby St Anne's, Blackfriars); Charterhouse on 15 November (its site was later taken by the famous Charterhouse School); the convent of St Clare, Aldgate (after which the building became the church of Holy Trinity Minories); Grey Friars in Newgate Street (its church became Christ Church, and the rest of the site was later used for the General Post Office); White Friars, south of Fleet Street (the great hall later became the Whitefriars Playhouse); the priory of St Helen's, Bishopsgate: (the church was used by local parishioners, and the rest of the property was given to a relative of Thomas Cromwell); St Mary Spital, Bishopsgate; St Mary, Merton, on 13 April; Austin Friars, Old Broad Street, on 12 November (part of the church became that of Dutch people living in London; when, soon after, the new owner of the church proposed to demolish the beautiful steeple on the grounds that it was unsafe, the mayor tried to resist this and committed the owner to Newgate for obstructing his officers); St Martin's le Grand (its buildings were demolished); and Stratford Langthorne Abbey.

NONSUCH PALACE BUILT
Having acquired the priory of St Mary, Merton, the king held the village and church of Cuddington, near Cheam. Here, flush with new revenue, he began building Nonsuch Palace – requiring the demolition of the village and church in the process. The name indicated Henry's plan to have a unique building. It consisted of two storeys around two courtyards, decorated in Renaissance style by Italian craftsmen; the south front had two towers topped by cupolas.

INTRODUCTION OF PARISH REGISTERS
On 5 September Thomas Cromwell introduced a scheme whereby each parish would keep a register of births, deaths and marriages, which was to be held in a 'sure coffer' with two locks, the parson having custody of one key. The entries were generally made on loose sheets of paper, but 60 years later it was ordered that these entries be copied into bound books: thus registers from that time (16 of which survive in the City of London) are copies. Records of this nature are extant in two London parishes from 1536, when Cromwell issued an earlier instruction.

1539

MORE DISSOLUTIONS
Almost all the rest of the London monastic institutions were suppressed this year. They were St Bartholomew's Priory and Hospital (the church became parochial and the hospital was revived); Barking Abbey on 14 November; Holywell Priory at 186 Shoreditch High Street; St Mary Overie, Southwark; St Mary Graces on the site of the Royal Mint; Syon Abbey (which later became the home of the dukes of Northumberland); St Giles's Hospital for Lepers off today's Charing Cross Road (its church became the parish church of St Giles-in-the-Fields); Richmond (Shene) Monastery; and St Mary's Nunnery, Clerkenwell (the church became a parish church).

MARYLEBONE PARK FORMED
Not content with the delights of his new St James's Park and the hunting facilities around Nonsuch Palace, the king this year acquired parts of the manors of Tyburn and Rugmere, from which he formed Marylebone Park – in the 19th century this became Regent's Park.

The area concerned was, and still is, of circular shape, but it had no relation to manorial or parish borders then existing. In the manor of Tyburn it left a part (now called Barrow Hill) stranded and unenclosed. Rugmere, quite a small manor mostly belonging to St Pancras parish, was cut in two, with part (now called Chalk Farm) remaining outside the new park.

1540

SUPPRESSION OF WESTMINSTER ABBEY
Despite the collaboration of the abbot with the king, Westminster Abbey was suppressed anyway. On 16 January the abbot and 24 monks signed a deed of surrender and the king's agents ransacked the building, melting down gold ornaments and offerings, even reburying Edward the Confessor in a secret place. The surviving financial accounts indicate that the outgoing abbot had been guilty of diverting abbey funds to relatives and himself.

It is not clear what happened to the abbey immediately after its dissolution – or even if it functioned as a church at all. But from 17 December it became briefly a cathedral, with its own see and bishop. The first bishop was appointed, and the former abbot became dean.

THE END OF THE ORDER OF ST JOHN
The Order of the Knights of St John, descendant of the organization which accompanied the crusades, and which had inherited the lands and possessions of the more militant Knights Templar, was suppressed this year in England. Its priory at St John's Gate, Clerkenwell, was used by the king for storing his 'tents and toils for hunting and for the war'.

TWO MARRIAGES FOR THE KING
After the death of Jane Seymour in October 1537, the king took as his fourth wife Anne of Cleves, daughter of the most fervent Protestant ruler in Germany. It was an unsatisfactory match, arranged before either of the two parties had met, and the king was mightily disappointed not only by her looks but by her inability to speak English. He could find no way out of the contract, however, and she was welcomed by London dignitaries in a tent of gold at Blackheath, and from there the couple rode to Greenwich, where they were married on Twelfth Night this year. On 4 February came the customary procession by river to Westminster.

Londoners, who had been spared the expense of the coronation of Jane Seymour because of her premature death, were now excused paying for a similar ceremony for her successor. Within months the marriage was politically an embarrassment, as Henry's policy was now to appease the Catholic part of Europe. By July, Parliament obliged him by declaring the marriage annulled, partly on the grounds of non-consummation. In the meantime, Thomas Cromwell, the architect of the match and the old anti-Catholic policy, was in the Tower.

Cromwell had come far in the royal service. His own father had been a blacksmith and fuller in Putney, where he also kept a brewhouse and inn. Thomas's career earned him many enemies, and when his execution for treason became politically desirable he had few friends in high places. He was refused a proper trial, and the king took no notice of his plea for mercy. On 28 July he was beheaded at Tower Hill.

The king was swiftly remarried – on 28 July he secretly married Catherine Howard, proclaiming the marriage publicly at Hampton Court on 8 August.

BUILDING OF THE CHAPEL ROYAL

The marital affairs of the king proceeded at such a brisk pace that evidence of two of his marriages is found in one building begun during his brief marriage to Anne Boleyn and completed in the year which saw the end of his even briefer alliance with Anne of Cleves. The Chapel Royal at St James's Palace, on the other side of his park from Whitehall, was built during this period, and the ceiling, which survives (though repainted from time to time), was designed by Holbein. Two heraldic devices in the ceiling bear reference to those two queens, and there are also initials of the king and of Anne of Cleves.

MORE BURNINGS AT SMITHFIELD

Henry would as soon burn those who were heretical Protestants as hang those opposed to his supremacy of the Church. On 30 July six victims were drawn from the Tower to Smithfield on hurdles. Three of them were Protestants: the rector of All Hallows, Honey Lane, the vicar of Stepney, and a preacher from Oxford. They had had no trial, and their offences were judged too great to be recited. They were brought to the stake without charge against them, and, as a chronicler remarks, 'great pitee it was, that suche learned menne should so bee cast a waie, without examination, neither knowing what was laied to their charge, nor never called to answere'. The three Catholic priests, one of whom had been chaplain to Catharine of Aragon, were hanged on gallows before St Bartholomew's church.

1541

DEMOLITION OF BARKING ABBEY

The once influential abbey at Barking, founded by St Erkenwald, bishop of London in the 7th century, and lived in by William the Conqueror when he first came to England, was demolished unceremoniously this year. Only the curfew tower (which also served as a gateway to the parish church) and a wall were spared; otherwise the stone was carted away to repair Greenwich Palace.

1542

THE REBUILDING OF ST MARTIN-IN-THE-FIELDS

One of the disadvantages for the king in having his new palace of Whitehall straddle a public highway was that the public could go through it. The traffic included corpses from the northern part of the parish on their way to burial at the parish church of St Margaret in today's Parliament Square, and in those days of endemic plague these were considered to pose an undesirable risk. In 1535 the king was at pains to rectify this. He wrote to the vicar of St Martin-in-the-Fields, then just a chapel under the control of St Margaret's, suggesting that the parish boundaries be redrawn so that St Martin's became a parish church with its own churchyard. But this meant that the tiny building had to accommodate all the parishioners from along the Strand as far as St Clement Danes and any in the mainly rural areas now known as Covent Garden, Soho and Hanover Square.

This resulted in the rebuilding of St Martin-in-the-Fields from 1542, though it remained a small building (45 ft by 25 ft), and this ensured a short life – it was demolished in 1607 because the neighbouring population had grown so much.

EXECUTION OF CATHERINE HOWARD

The downfall of Thomas Cromwell in 1540 had been engineered by the Catholic Norfolk family, which had promptly flaunted the promiscuous Catherine Howard in front of the king until he married her. But Norfolk's enemies and the progressive Protestants at court were not slow to reveal her infidelities to a vexed king, and she too, like Anne Boleyn before her, was executed at Tower Hill, on 13 February this year.

MERCERS' SCHOOL ESTABLISHED

The Mercers' Company this year founded a free grammar school, which was in effect a continuation of a school which since at least 1447 had functioned in association with the hospital of St Thomas Acon. The new school, in Old Jewry, opened at Michaelmas, and was for 25 boys.

1543

THE LAST MARRIAGE

Undaunted, the king married for a sixth time, at Hampton Court on 12 July. Catherine Parr, who had had two husbands herself, was a studious, serious and sensible woman. She persuaded the king to soften punishments for alleged heretical offences, and she reinstated Mary and Elizabeth as legitimate heirs to the throne.

After the marriage the king presented her with Chelsea Manor House, on the site of today's 19–26 Cheyne Walk, which he had built after his acquisition of the manor in 1536. It was a large house in 5 acres. On the ground floor were three halls, five parlours, three kitchens and nine other rooms; on the first floor were three drawing rooms and seventeen chambers. The queen retired here after the king's death in 1547.

CHINGFORD STANDING BUILT

Chingford manor (acquired from St Paul's at the Reformation) and Epping Forest were favourite royal hunting areas. This year the king had built a three-storey building called the Great Standing, which survives today under the name of Queen Elizabeth's Hunting Lodge. On a promontory, its function was to provide a viewing platform for the hunt, and at that time it had no walls.

PAVING IN THE CITY

An Act this year empowered the paving of various streets in the City, including Chiswell Street, Whitecross Street, Grub Street and Water Lane, and, outside the wall, Shoreditch, Goswell Street, the Strand and Petty France in Westminster. The paving was to include a channel in the middle of the road, and was to be done at the expense of the residents.

1544

REFOUNDING OF ST BARTHOLOMEW'S HOSPITAL

The hospital of St Bartholomew had continued to function on a reduced scale after the suppression of the monastery. It was seen as a necessary institution, and on 23 June the king re-established it as a new foundation providing 'comfort to prisoners, shelter to the poor, visitation to the sick, food to the hungry, drink to the thirsty, clothes to the naked, and sepulture to the dead'.

WAPPING EMBANKED

The foreshore from the Tower to Limehouse was frequently flooded by high tides. This year work began on a rather unsuccessful embankment, and by 1600 the stretch was described as a 'continual street of filthy straight passage'.

FOOD FOR THE SOLDIERS

The king, emboldened by his new title of King of England, France and Ireland, embarked on an ill-considered offensive against France. The City was dragooned into providing provisions for his forces, and 'five wey' of cheese was bought from St James's Fair and sent by water to Kingston and then on to Guildford to the soldiers stationed there. The bakers of Stratford were contracted for two cartloads of bread.

The king also wanted money for the venture, of course. One alderman, Richard Read, declined to pay his share and was compelled by the king to serve as a foot soldier in Scotland, where he was taken prisoner; he was eventually to pay a large sum to secure his release.

1545

A BAN ON HUNTING

A royal proclamation this year forbade all pursuit of game in Westminster, Islington, Highgate, Hornsey and elsewhere in the suburbs of London.

1546

THE CITY TAKES OVER ST BARTHOLOMEW'S

As we have seen (1544), the hospital of St Bartholomew's had continued functioning after the dissolution of the old priory, but it required a surer financial basis. On 27 December the City of London was empowered to take control, and the old master and chaplain were replaced by a board consisting of City nominees.

When regulations were published by the governors in 1552, they included a direction to the surgeons that they were 'to the uttermost of their knowledge to help cure the diseases of the poor without favouring those with good friends; they are not to admit the incurables, so as to keep out those who are curable'.

THE BURNING OF ANNE ASKEW

Anne Askew, a young woman highly educated in theology, had been examined in 1545 at Saddlers' Hall in London and then before the mayor of London and Bishop Bonner, for Protestant heresy. At this stage she could, without much compromise, have saved her own life, but her behaviour became increasingly uncooperative with the authorities; she was singularly uncowed by the status of those interviewing her, and was able to retaliate with her own interpretation of the Scriptures in any argument. On 18 June 1546 she was interrogated at the Guildhall, and within a few days was racked in the Tower. On 16 July, carried in a chair because she was so weak, she was taken to the stake at Smithfield. Even at this stage she was assured of the king's pardon if she recanted. She refused, and the fire was lit.

The burning of Anne Askew and others for heresy, at Smithfield in 1546. A gallery has been erected for important witnesses.

1547

A NEW KING

Henry VIII died at 'hys most pryncely howse at Westminster, comenly called Yorkeplace or Whytehall' on 28 January. There his corpse remained until 14 February, when it was moved to Syon House, Isleworth, and from there, accompanied by a host of attendants including ten aldermen of the City dressed in black, to Windsor. An unpleasant episode is believed to have taken place at Syon House, where the coffin burst open in the night and dogs were discovered licking up remains in the morning.

The new king, Edward VI, was nine years old. Although his father had sought to appoint a regency council which would have no predominating party, it was inevitable that the king's uncle, Edward Seymour, first earl of Hertford, would take power. In a sequence of events that must have seemed familiar to Londoners, Hertford was made Protector and duke of Somerset, and set about the persecution of his enemies.

The coronation on 20 February was preceded by a procession on the 19th which had the traditional pomp of London: conduits flowing with wine; dignitaries in scarlet gowns. One unusual feature was a Spaniard who descended on a rope, stretched from the battlements of St Paul's steeple and fastened to an anchor near the gate of the Deanery, 'lying on the rope with his head forward, casting his arms and legs abroad, running on his breast on the rope from the battlements to the ground, as if it had been an arrow out of a bow'.

CATHOLIC IMAGES REMOVED

Two measures in the sustained Protestant purge had their effect on London this year. One was the abolition of chantries in churches – this deprived large numbers of clergy of income. The second was the removal of images, both statues and stained glass, from churches. The mayor was instructed that 'Stories made in glasse wyndows' relative to Thomas à Becket were to be altered at as little expense as possible.

Images and pictures to which no offerings and no prayers were made might remain for 'garnisshement' of the churches. If any 'storye in glasse' of the pope existed the mayor might paint out the papal tiara and alter the story. Each alderman was ordered to discreetly visit each parish church to assess what needed to be done. Churches were stripped of ornament, walls were whitewashed, and images were removed – especially roods with the image of the Virgin. In St Paul's during this work the rood fell down and killed a workman – a sign, many said, of the Lord's displeasure.

SYON HOUSE TO SOMERSET

The new owner of Syon House was the Protector, the duke of Somerset. This year he began the reconstruction of the house to substantially the shape of the one we see today.

BETHLEHEM HOSPITAL TO CITY

The hospital of St Mary Bethlehem, on the site of today's Liverpool Street station, had in theory been dissolved, but it was regranted this year to the City of London. It was the only hospital of the period known to have specialized in the care of lunatics.

1548

HOUSE OF COMMONS TAKES OVER ST STEPHEN'S CHAPEL

The royal palace had now moved up Whitehall, leaving the buildings of the Palace of Westminster – or at least those left standing after the fire of 1512 – to the use of civil servants. The House of Commons usually met in the chapter house of the abbey, but this year St Stephen's Chapel, the chapel of the old palace, was secularized for its use. This old building, roughly on the site of the present chamber, measured 90 ft by 30, and had an octagonal tower at each corner. It was lit by five windows on each side, and its walls were buttressed beneath each window. On the whole it was a plain building inside – at least it was once it had been stripped of its Catholic decoration – and only in Wren's time were galleries added at the sides for spectators.

The altar was replaced by a table behind the Speaker, and the choir stalls were used by members. This arrangement continued when the Houses of Parliament were rebuilt after the massive fire of 1834, so that the chamber continues, in effect, to be a converted church.

1549

DEMOLITION IN THE STRAND

The Protector, the duke of Somerset, began to build himself a palace on the Strand. A number of buildings were demolished to make way for it. They included the church of St Mary le Strand (which did not then, as it does today, stand in the middle of the highway, but was on the south side of it) and the London residences of the bishops of Chester, Worcester, Lichfield and Coventry, and Llandaff. Also demolished was the Inn of Chancery called Strand Inn. The church was not rebuilt until the 18th century on its present site.

Searching for stone for his Somerset House, the duke obtained some from the old buildings of the priory of St John at Clerkenwell and he attempted, unsuccessfully, the demolition of St Margaret's,

Westminster. He was more successful at St Paul's, where the charnel house was taken down for its stone; the bones were, according to legend, carried in 1,000 cartloads to be buried in Bunhill Fields, Finsbury. Unfortunately for the legend, the name Bunhill, which is almost certainly a corruption of Bone Hill, was in use before this event.

Somerset House, with gardens stretching down to the Thames, was said to be the first Renaissance palace in the country; it was designed by either John of Padua or Sir John Thynne. It is doubtful if Somerset ever lived in the building, since, in those unpredictable times, he was in the Tower the same year, and again in 1551, and was beheaded for high treason in 1552. The building itself was demolished in the 18th century, when the present Somerset House was built.

LONDON AGAINST SOMERSET

The Privy Council and the City joined forces to depose the Protector, the duke of Somerset. A contingent of men mustered in Moorfields as a preliminary on 11 October, but there is no evidence that they actually marched to Windsor, where the duke had retreated together with the young king and the armoury pillaged from Hampton Court. Emboldened by this, the lords felt able to go to Windsor to see the king, and to demand that Somerset be given up. The duke was brought 'riding through Oldborne' on the 14 October to the Tower; he remained there until the following February, when he was banished to Richmond Palace.

ST BARTHOLOMEW'S TAKES OVER LEPER HOSPITALS

At the Reformation there were ten leper, or lazar, hospitals in the London area. St James's went out of existence when its building was transformed into St James's Palace; St Giles's was taken by a parish church. Of the rest, six – at Hammersmith, Highgate, Mile End, Knightsbridge, Kingsland and Southwark – were made over to the administration of the newly refounded St Bartholomew's Hospital.

The leper hospital in Southwark, administered by St Bartholomew's.

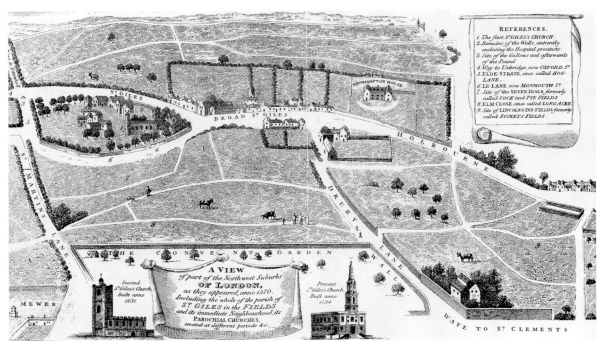

REFERENCES.
1. The first St GILES's CHURCH.
2. Remains of the Walls, anciently enclosing the Hospital precincts.
3. Site of the Gallows and afterwards of the Pound.
4. Way to Uxbridge, now OXFORD St LANE.
5. ELDE STRATE, since called HOG-LANE.
6. LE-LANE, now MONMOUTH St.
7. Site of the SEVEN DIALS, formerly called COCK and PYE FIELDS.
8. ELM CLOSE since called LONGACRE.
9. Site of LINCOLNS INN FIELDS formerly called FICKETS-FIELDS.

A projected map of St Giles-in-the-Fields in 1570. The church, utilizing the old leper-hospital buildings, is on the left.

JOHN DAY, PRINTER

John Day, a prominent printer, this year moved his press from 'the signe of the Resurrection' near Holborn Conduit to above Aldersgate. Much of his output was religious – he was himself an enthusiastic Protestant, and he printed a Bible in his new premises this year, dedicated to the young king. He was one of the earliest music printers in the country, and was a renowned typographer, cutting his own fonts.

1550

PROTESTANT ACCOMMODATION

The political and ecclesiastical policy of the realm was demonstrated this year with the granting of the old Austin Friars church to the Dutch Protestants and St Anthony's Hospital to French Protestant refugees.

After the Reformation the old Austin Friars building had been used for storing wine, corn and coal, and on the site of the conventual buildings Sir William Paulet, afterwards marquess of Winchester, built Winchester House. But on 29 June this year, as the king recorded in his diary, the church was granted to the 'Germans' (meaning Flemings), who numbered between 600 and 800 in London.

St Anthony's, in Threadneedle Street, was not dissolved at the Reformation, because it was united to the collegiate church of Windsor, but in 1550 it was let to French refugees, who were put to flight again three years later when Mary came to the throne. They returned during Elizabeth's reign. Rebuilt after the Great Fire, the French church was demolished in 1840 to permit road widening.

HENRY MACHYN'S DIARY

One of the most interesting accounts of early London life appears in the diary, beginning in 1550, of a funeral-trappings supplier called Henry Machyn. He lived near Queenhithe, was a devout Catholic and welcomed the restoration of the old religion when Mary came to the throne. He recorded, and possibly died from, the plague which hit London in 1563.

At first his account (which has been published by the Camden Society) is related only to his business, but gradually he intersperses his narrative with London events, from the committal of Bishop Gardiner to the Tower, to the Lord Mayor's Show.

BUYING UP SOUTHWARK

Southwark was, in theory, mostly under the jurisdiction of the City, but there were enough anomalies to make it difficult to administer. To remedy this, on 29 March the City purchased from the Crown the royal rights which still existed in Southwark, with the exception of Southwark Place, an estate formerly occupied by the duke of Suffolk in which a mint had been founded. Henceforth the area was, for the City, Bridge Ward Without, but the residents seem not to have exercised their citizenship of the City, nor to have ever elected aldermen to represent them. Instead, the Court of Aldermen elected representatives for them.

BELSIZE TO WESTMINSTER

The manor of Belsize (meaning 'beautifully situated') on the southern slopes of Hampstead was granted this year to Westminster Cathedral, as it was now called. The manor was promptly relet to a royal official, at a rent of £19 2s 10d and ten cartloads each of hay and oats.

EARLIEST MAP OF LONDON

The earliest surviving map of London is that of the engraver Frans Hogenberg, from a drawing by George Hoefnagel. It was not published until 1572, but it appears to be based on a survey made about 1550.

In the west the gateways recently built across Whitehall are complete; the road leads down to the old Palace of Westminster and the abbey. North of Charing Cross a road (today's St Martin's Lane) leads up to St Giles's church, which really was in the fields at this time. Buildings front the Strand with the 'convent garden' behind them, all the way to the Aldwych and Fleet Street. The City wall is clearly seen, at times with a moat before it – the Tower is surrounded by water. St Paul's still has its enormous spire (lost in 1561), and the shape of Smithfield is clearly shown.

The extent of development on the south of the river is also shown. A line of buildings, assumed to be mostly taverns and brothels, stretches from Southwark almost to Lambeth Palace and includes two arenas for bull- and bear-baiting. Paris (a corruption of 'Parish') Garden was owned briefly by Jane Seymour, but at the time of the map had probably begun its career as an entertainment place.

1551

THE REFOUNDING OF ST THOMAS'S HOSPITAL
The one hospital in Southwark, which had lain derelict since the Dissolution, was refounded by Edward VI. The effect of its closure was revealed in the official state record:

In view of the sick and infirm poor men lying begging in the public streets and places of London and its suburbs to the infection and annoyance of the King's subjects using these street and places: Grant to the mayor ... the house and site of the late hospital of Thomas Becket in Southwarke, of late called the hospitall of Saynt Thomas in Suthwarke ... with the church, steeple, churchyard etc.

It will also be seen from this that under the Protestant regime the dedication to Becket had been dropped: in future its saint was St Thomas the Apostle.

The hospital was also to act as a poorhouse for Southwark. A census compiled by the City authorities found that in the City as a whole, and including their part of Southwark, the following needed some provision for their welfare or detention: fatherless children 300; sore and sick persons 200; poor men overburdened with children 350; aged persons 400; decayed householders 650; idle vagabonds 200.

The Steelyard in Upper Thames Street, home of the Hanseatic merchants. In 1551 the yard was seized by Edward VI and the merchants' privileges revoked.

SWEATING SICKNESS
Henry Machyn (see 1550) records in his diary (no doubt with some anticipation that an ill wind would do him some good), that a 'swet' began in London on 6 July, which carried off many people, both nobles and commoners. The king retired to Hampton Court.

STEELYARD TAKEN
The premises and privileges of the Hanseatic merchants at the Steelyard in Upper Thames Street had been under threat since Henry VII. This year the Steelyard was seized by Edward VI and its privileges were revoked. Both were restored under Mary, taken away again under Elizabeth, and restored again under James I.

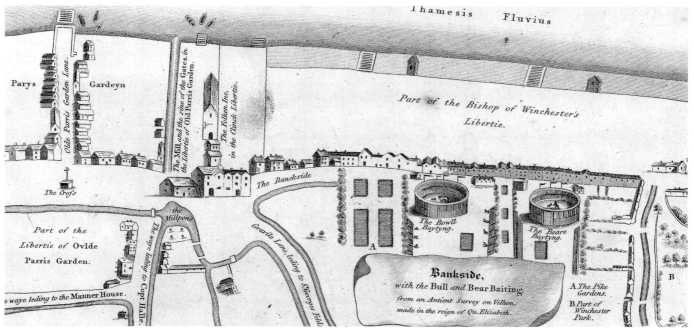

A projected plan of Bankside in the later 16th century, depicting bull-baiting and bear-baiting arenas.

1552

THE BEDFORDS TAKE COVENT GARDEN

A significant land transaction took place this year when the Covent Garden estate, recently appropriated by the Crown, was granted on 28 May to John Russell, earl of Bedford, lord privy seal, to hold to him and his lawful male heirs for ever.

It was the Bedfords who, over the years, developed Covent Garden, including the church, the first proper square in London and, of course, the fruit and vegetable market. It remained in the family's hands until modern times.

CHRIST'S HOSPITAL FOUNDED

Christ's Hospital (the word 'hospital' was quite often used to denote a school or almshouse) opened in November this year; it was granted a charter by Edward VI in 1553 and was housed in the old buildings of the Grey Friars, in Newgate Street. The school was intended for 380 poor and orphaned children – it is now, of course, a public school charging considerable fees. The first record of a girl being admitted is in 1554.

The distinctive uniform of long blue coats and yellow stockings was adopted soon after foundation – the school was known as the Blue Coat School. Two other customs were associated with the scholars: they were used as mutes at funerals, and they also attended an annual service for the lord mayor and went to tea with him at the Mansion House afterwards.

SOMERSET EXECUTED

The fall of the Protector, Edward Seymour, duke of Somerset, was final this year. He was beheaded on Tower Hill between 8 and 9 a.m. on 22 January among tumultuous scenes. He made a dignified speech justifying the ecclesiastical reforms he had made, urging that they be continued. He had been, in effect, the first Protestant ruler of England.

ST JAMES'S STREET FORMED

The manor of St James, which Henry VIII had obliged Eton College to cede to him, contained the land on which today's St James's Street lies. A Crown lease of 1552 states that some of the lands attached to the old hospital had been laid out in roads, and it is more than likely that these included St James's Street.

A TUMBRIL FOR EDGWARE

The inhabitants of Edgware were reported for having neither a cucking-stool nor a tumbril. The former was a device for dipping people, usually women, into a river as a punishment; the latter was a two-wheeled cart used to parade adulterers and fornicators around the village.

1553

BRIDEWELL TO THE CITY

The dissolution of the monasteries had left the poor, the crippled and the sick without established charities. Although there was in this period a spurt in the foundation of almshouses, these buildings were usually restricted to members or dependants of livery companies. The City, to its credit, had already recognized that this left a very large number of people uncared for and had taken over the running of the hospitals of

Bridewell Palace, near Blackfriars, in 1666.

St Bartholomew, St Thomas and Bethlehem, all three of which were rather more than just medical centres. The foundation of Christ's Hospital, a school for poor children, recorded in 1552, stemmed from the same public concern for the less fortunate.

One group of people who roamed the streets – described by one historian as 'the tramp, the rogue, and the dissolute woman' – also needed housing, or rather detention and productive work. The inspiration behind a plan to use Bridewell Palace, virtually abandoned by Edward VI, for a workhouse and prison was that of Bishop Ridley and the City authorities. An application to the king in 1552 was granted by him on 12 June 1553.

The lands and rents of the Savoy Hospital in the Strand, founded by Henry VII, were granted to Bridewell, and powers were given to the authorities to search alehouses, skittle-alleys, cockpits, dancing saloons, gambling dens and the like and convey ruffians and masterless men to detention in the new building.

THE CITY AND THE SUCCESSION

Henry VIII's will had named his daughter Mary as heir to the throne should Edward VI die without issue. This posed a dilemma for zealous Protestants, since Mary was a Catholic and reform would be discouraged. The duke of Northumberland, the most powerful man in the kingdom after the toppling of Somerset, persuaded the ailing Edward VI to make a will which named as his successor Lady Jane Grey, granddaughter of the youngest sister of Henry VIII; he took the further precaution of marrying her to his own son. Senior officers of the Crown and City dignitaries felt obliged to witness the will and uphold its legal veracity.

Lady Jane was brought down to the Tower from Richmond Palace on 10 July, four days after the death of the king, and that same evening she was proclaimed queen at the Cheapside Cross. That she was a Protestant was not enough, however, and the choice was received unenthusiastically; elsewhere in the country the Northumberland ploy was unacceptable, and on 19 July Mary was declared queen at the same Cheapside Cross.

Northumberland, failing in an attempt to pose as a supporter of Mary, was sent to the Tower on 25 July. Mary and her sister, Elizabeth, arrived in London on 3 August, greeted by the City dignitaries at Aldgate. Lady Jane, her husband, the aged Cranmer (who had been a signatory to Edward's will), and others were brought to trial at the Guildhall for treason.

The attitude of Londoners appears to have been that, although they were prepared to draw back from the energetic reforms Somerset had put in motion and, indeed, to go back to the Church ritual and tenets held during the reign of Henry VIII, they were against the restoration of the pope's supremacy. This was evidenced on 13 August, when a riot occurred at Paul's Cross led by John Day, rector of St Ethelburga, Bishopsgate, who was later punished by being pinned by his ears in a pillory.

But in December every London church was ordered to obtain a staff-cross and a cope to go on procession, and a few days later the English service and communion were abolished and Latin was reintroduced with holy bread and water. The first church to resume Catholic worship was that of St Nicholas Cole Abbey, where the Latin mass was celebrated on 23 August.

Perhaps symbolically, the flagship of Henry VIII, *Harry Grace-à-Dieu*, was destroyed by fire at Woolwich this year.

PORTMAN ESTATE ESTABLISHED
A year after development of the Covent Garden estate had its beginnings in the estate's acquisition by the Bedford family, Sir William Portman, soon to be lord chief justice, bought 270 acres in St Marylebone. This area was developed 200 years later, and the street names reflect Portman's family estates in Dorset, such as Blandford, Bryanston and Crawford.

BILLS OF MORTALITY ESTABLISHED
The bills of mortality, made up each week and analysed yearly by the Company of Parish Clerks, are one of the guides to the population of London in the later 16th century. A few survive from 1527–8 and from 1553, when there was issued a definite ordinance instructing parish clerks to make themselves responsible for returns of deaths. The cause of death, unless it was plague, was not recorded.

1554

THE WYATT REBELLION
The ostensible cause of the so-called Wyatt Rebellion this year was the resolve of Mary to marry Philip, heir to the king of Spain. Forces under Sir Thomas Wyatt assembled in Kent, and there were risings in Devon and Norfolk. On 1 February Wyatt appeared in Southwark. Prevented from using London Bridge, he crossed the river at Kingston, circled the City, and attempted to break in at Ludgate; but after a short struggle he was taken at Temple Bar.

His execution, at Tower Hill on 11 April, was inevitable. His failure was also fatal to Lady Jane Grey, who, though just an instrument of a man's ambition, was executed at the same place on 12 February.

The wedding between Mary and Philip took place on 25 July, a few days after their first meeting.

ELIZABETH RELEASED
The Wyatt Rebellion was fraught with danger for Elizabeth, Mary's sister. But Wyatt refused to implicate her in any plot to overthrow the new queen, and on 19 May she was released from the Tower, where she had been under arrest and in fear of her life, only to be removed to Woodstock. However, two London legends grew up about the day of her release. One is that she came out of the Tower and sat down for dinner at the London Tavern, Mark Lane; it was her first meal in

freedom, and in her honour the tavern was later renamed the Queen's Head. The second is that the future queen went immediately on her release to All Hallows Staining, also in Mark Lane, and gave thanks for her good fortune. One version of the story is that she gave the parish clerk a gratuity which he promptly spent on a dinner for his friends – an annual custom kept up long after his and her deaths – and another is that she presented the church with new bell ropes, as the bells had been music to her ears while she was in the Tower.

1555

THE BLOODIEST OF YEARS
London was used to public executions of the most barbaric nature. Drawing, quartering, boiling, roasting and burning were all part of public spectacle. In a spate of heretic-burning this year the queen had a zealous accomplice in Edward Bonner, bishop of London. In his palace at Fulham or even in Fulham church, he interrogated and tortured supposed Protestants. In a petulant letter to the archbishop of Canterbury he complained of having these prisoners at Fulham and asked if they could be burnt at Hammersmith.

On 25 January 1555 the Catholic church was formally restored. One of the first victims of conscience thereafter was John Rogers, former vicar of St Sepulchre's and father of eleven children, who was burnt at Smithfield on 4 February. John Foxe, whose *Book of Martyrs* was to commemorate the unfortunate Protestants, related of Rogers that, once the fire 'had taken hold both upon his legs and shoulders he, as one feeling no smart, washed his hands in the flame as though it had been in cold water. And after lifting up his hands unto heaven, not removing the same until such times as the devouring fire had consumed them, most mildly this happy martyr yielded up his spirit.' Two other parsons, those of St Bride's, Fleet Street, and All Hallows, Bread Street, perished in the same way.

On New Year's Day 30 Protestants were found holding a secret conventicle in St Mary-le-Bow churchyard. On 29 January seven people, including a woman, were burnt at Smithfield.

In Westminster one William Flower entered the church of St Margaret and physically assaulted the vicar, who was conducting a service in the Catholic tradition. Flower was arrested and burnt in the churchyard there, having had his hand cut off first.

A NEW HIGHWAY ACT
An important Act governing the upkeep of highways was passed this year. It instituted the practice of statute labour, by which parishioners, according to their affluence, were to provide labour, tools, carts and horses annually for the repair of their local roads. They worked under the direction of a new parish official, a surveyor of highways.

OVERSEERS OF THE WATER
Not only was there reform on the roads. The City this year began the custom of electing eight watermen to oversee the river Thames between Greenwich and Windsor and prevent abuses.

This measure was the result of an Act which sought to regulate the watermen on the Thames. The Act related that many accidents occurred on the river through the ignorance and incompetence of watermen, that boys who might be serving in the navy were instead working on the river and indulging in such pastimes as gambling, and that many boats were badly constructed. In future, watermen could

Tudor London

City of London

Mercers

Grocers

Drapers

Fishmongers

Goldsmiths

Merchant Taylors

Skinners

Haberdashers

Salters

Ironmongers

River Fleet

St Paul's Wharf

TUDOR CITY OF LONDON

The reconstruction above shows the growth of London by the 16th century. The street patterns have been outlined for clarity, although the actual buildings were more densely packed and smaller than in the illustration.

MAJOR SITES
1 Middle Temple
2 Holborn
3 Bridewell Palace
4 Fleet Street
5 Gray's Inn
6 Ludgate
7 Baynard's Castle
8 The Swan
9 Newgate
10 St John Clerkenwell
11 St Paul's

12 St Bartholomew's Hospital
13 The Rose
14 The Globe
15 Queenhithe
16 Aldersgate
17 Cripplegate
18 Guildhall
19 Royal Exchange
20 Austin Friars
21 Custom House
22 Bishopsgate
23 Holy Trinity

London Bridge

Billingsgate

Tower of London

qualify only after rowing the Thames for two years, and no boat was to take passengers unless its waterman held a licence from the overseers.

One of the principal objects of the new Act was to create a pool of competent sailors for impressment in the navy – anyone who resisted was to be subject to imprisonment and banishment from the Thames.

COLLEGE OF ARMS MOVES

This year the College of Arms moved to Derby House, a mansion overlooking the Thames between Knightrider Street and Upper Thames Street. Nowadays its successor, built after the Great Fire, faces Queen Victoria Street.

1556

WESTMINSTER ABBEY RESTORED

At what had become Westminster Cathedral, change was inevitable under the new regime. Nine of the prebendaries had already fled abroad in fear for their lives, and the other three had acquiesced to the new regime – in the records against their names is written the word 'Turncoats'. On 27 September the chapter was dissolved, and a month later the Benedictine monks returned to the abbey. It was to prove a short-lived triumph.

BELLMEN INTRODUCED

An Act of Parliament this year required the appointment of bellmen to patrol London streets and to ring at stated hours a handbell and cry out, 'Take care of your fire and candle, be charitable to the poor, and pray for the dead.'

EASTBURY HOUSE BUILT

This year Clement Sysley acquired an estate in Barking and began to build Eastbury House, a fine house which still survives and is now a local museum. A date of 1572 is on some brickwork, but it is thought that the house was built over a long period, from the time of the purchase of the estate until 1578.

Built in the shape of an H, the house is of red brick with black diapering. The great hall has since been subdivided, but some of the original fireplaces remain.

REBUILDING OF GRAY'S INN HALL

The great hall of Gray's Inn was rebuilt in 1556–60 and, although it was severely damaged in the last war, still stands. The remarkable screen, said to be made out of the wood of a captured Spanish Armada galleon, had been removed in time, but is now back in place, and the hammerbeam roof has been restored.

1557

FIRST PLAYS AT INNS

Before the first London theatre was built, plays were performed in the courtyards of inns. Inns had two advantages for the players: an audience was certain, and the courtyard (surrounded as it quite often was on all sides by galleried walls) was a perfect acting area. The first clear record of plays performed at inns occurs this year, at the Saracen's Head in Islington and the Boar's Head in Aldgate.

THE ISLINGTON MARTYRS

The Saracen's Head at Islington was in the news for another reason this year: John Rough and others were apprehended holding an illegal Protestant meeting here. Rough was burnt at Smithfield, and four others at Islington in the same fire. In 1558 'in a back close' in Islington 40 men and women were taken for the same reason. Most of them were arraigned before the lord chief justice, Sir Roger Cholmeley (who later founded Highgate School), and 13 were eventually burnt.

CHARTER FOR THE STATIONERS

The meaning of the word 'stationer' has undergone some changes. It was first applied to the writers and illustrators of books, particularly those for the Church. Then, after the invention of printing, it referred to bookbinders and booksellers. The last phase found stationers selling paper goods. However, the first charter of the Stationers this year incorporated them as printers, and until 1911 the company was responsible for registering most books published.

1558

ENFIELD GRAMMAR SCHOOL REFOUNDED

On 25 May Enfield Grammar School was properly refounded. The trustees were to employ a schoolmaster to 'teach, within the town of Enfield the children of the poor inhabitants of the parish, to know and read their alphabet letters, to read Latin and English, to understand grammar, and to write their Latin according to the use and trade of grammar schools'.

A NEW QUEEN

Mary died of dropsy on 17 November, 'wondering why all that she had done, as she believed on God's behalf, had been followed by failure on every side'. Her sister, Elizabeth, whose life so far had been perilous, was welcomed by a population surfeited by public death. The new queen, now 25, was at Hatfield House when news of Mary's death was received. On 19 November she was met at Highgate by the mayor and aldermen and by all the bishops, whom, with the exception of Bonner, she received well. Sir Richard Baker, himself a resident of Highgate, records that she was staying at Charterhouse, now a private residence, on the 23rd, and a few days later removed to the Tower.

1559

REARRANGING THE CUSTOMS

The Custom House in Lower Thames Street was rebuilt this year after a fire had destroyed the previous building. The opportunity was taken to reinforce the regulation that all imported cargo should be reported to the officials here, and a decree this year stated, once again, what were the 'legal' quays for trading. By the reign of Charles II there were 20 of them, between London Bridge and the Tower, within sight of the Custom House.

WESTWOOD RESERVED FOR SHIPBUILDING

The continued concern of the Tudor monarchs for their navy is underlined this year when on 28 October the trees of Westwood Common, in Sydenham, were reserved for the purposes of shipbuilding.

1560

SCHOOLS FLOURISH

The movement to establish grammar schools, already begun in the reign of Edward VI, continued apace during the time of Elizabeth. A number of these developed from schools previously attached to cathedrals or abbeys, many of them temporarily suppressed. One of the most important in this category was Westminster School, refounded this year, which had been previously attached to the monastery of St Peter, Westminster Abbey. It had been continued at the Reformation, and in 1560 the queen encouraged its refoundation, with a headmaster and deputy. There were 40 free scholars ('Queen's Scholars'), together with fee-paying pupils known as 'town boys', who were kept separate. It was described as a 'publique schoole for Grammar, Rethoricke, Poetrie, and for the Latin and Greek languages', and it occupied the monastic buildings, as it still does.

Two noted traditions have evolved in the school. One is that at any coronation the pupils are the first to acclaim the new sovereign with cries of 'Vivat Rex'. A second is the custom of producing a play in Latin each Christmas.

1561

LIGHTNING HITS ST PAUL'S

During a violent thunderstorm in June, lightning struck the steeple of St Paul's Cathedral and set it ablaze. The timber framework caught alight, and the lead covering flowed like lava from the roof. A contemporary witness relates that 'a long and a spear-pointed flames of fier runne through the toppe of the Broache of Shaft of Paules steple'. The steeple, whose loss was put down to the influence of popery, was never replaced. The nave roof, which had also been seriously damaged, was repaired promptly, aided by gifts of money and timber from the queen.

Another church to suffer, nearby, was St Martin's Ludgate: 'Between one and two of the clocke at afternoone, was seene a marueilous great fyrie lightning … at which instante the corner of a turret of ye steple of Saint Martin's Churche within Ludgate was torne and diuers great stones casten down.'

THREE NEW SCHOOLS

Kingston Grammar School was founded this year, a descendant of the chapel school of St Mary Magdalene. St Olave's Grammar School in Southwark received its royal patent on 25 July.

While these two schools were representative of a concern to provide education for the poor, Merchant Taylors' School, founded this year in Suffolk Lane, was typical of a new breed of schools run by City livery companies.

DISTURBING LENT

It became the law that abstinence from flesh meat was to occur not just on Fridays, but on Wednesdays too. The queen declared that this was not for religious reasons but to encourage the fishing industry. Anyone eating meat on the proscribed days was given six hours in the pillory and ten days in prison, though dispensation was given to the sick if necessary. A butcher of Eastcheap this year was fined £20 for killing three oxen during Lent, and two years later two women who

refused their fish were set in the stocks all night at St Katharine's by the Tower. Inspectors were sent round to eating houses to see if meat was on their tables.

THE AGAS VIEW OF LONDON

A bird's-eye view of London, called for convenience the 'Agas' map, was compiled about this time. It has usually been attributed to Ralph Agas, a Suffolk land surveyor, who died in 1621. The map, which remained unpublished for 100 years, was cut on wood and measures just over 6 ft wide and 2 ft deep. Only two copies of the original exist: one in the Guildhall Library, the other at Magdalen College, Oxford – a gift from Pepys.

1562

PLAGUE IN LONDON

It is stated by Stow that plague killed about 20,000 people in the 108 parishes and liberties of London this year. Dr John Jones, a contemporary writer, related that 'The most corrupte and pestering is S. Poulkars parish, by reason of many fruterers, pore people and stinking lanes as Turnagain lane, Secolayne, and other such places, there dyed most in London, and were soonest infected and longest continued.' He was here referring to St Sepulchre's parish, which, significantly, ran along the eastern bank of the pestilential Fleet river as far up as Smithfield. With 1,000 people dying each week, the queen withdrew to Windsor and, so it is said, erected gallows in the market place on which to hang any other Londoners who followed.

The authorities issued a number of orders. Bonfires were to be lit in the streets three times a week, blue crosses were to be put on houses which contained the disease, and all dogs found in the streets were to be destroyed. The terrible plight of Londoners was compounded by a great shortage of money and food.

1563

NEW CHURCH FOR STOKE NEWINGTON

The small village of Stoke Newington replaced its medieval church with a new building this year, though some features of the earlier church were utilized. The parish was unusual in that when the population expanded dramatically in the 19th century it built a new church on another site and left the 1563 building standing – it is still there today. It contains a monument to the wife of Thomas Sutton, founder of Charterhouse School.

1564

RECORDS OF THE THAMES

Henry Chamberlain in his *History of London* (1770) relates some striking detail of the Thames for this year. On 26 January 'the river Thames was so agitated, that the tide recoiled twice, five hours before its time and the same on the twenty-seventh; and likewise once the day after'. On 21 December the Thames was frozen over so 'as to admit all sorts of carriages and diversions on it'.

1565

HIGHGATE SCHOOL FOUNDED

Sir Roger Cholmeley obtained permission to found a 'Free School' in Highgate village in April 1565, a few months before he died. Already the largest landowner in the area, to provide a site for a school and chapel he had acquired from the bishop of London a piece of land at the very top of Highgate Hill on which previously had stood a hermit's chapel. The school's rules were framed in 1571, which is probably the year it opened, and a headmaster was appointed of 'good, sober and honest conversation, and no light person, who shall teach and instruct young children as well in their ABC and other English books, and to write, and also in their grammar as they shall grow ripe thereto'. Forty boys, paying fourpence each, from Highgate, Holloway, Kentish Town, Hornsey and Finchley, were to be admitted. At 7 a.m. the boys were at prayer; lessons followed until 11 a.m. and then from 1 p.m. until 6 p.m. This establishment developed into Highgate School, which is still on the same site, next to the remnants of the old chapel burial ground.

1566

FOUNDATION OF THE ROYAL EXCHANGE

London merchants had no recognized building in which to transact business. It was common to use the inside of St Paul's or its church-yard, and also livery company halls, but there was no central bourse as there was in some Continental cities. Stow tells us that it was the custom for merchants to do their deals in Lombard Street, the centre of commerce, but, as he says, 'these meetings were unpleasant and troublesome, by reason of walking and talking in an open narrow streete; being there constrained either to endure all extremities of weather, viz., heat and colde, snow and raine, or else to shelter them-selves in shoppes'.

Leadenhall Market had been suggested as a place for such trading, but the merchants, it seems, conservatively refused to desert Lombard Street. Sir Richard Gresham, mayor in 1538, therefore proposed the erection of a bourse for the merchants on the site of those shops in Lombard Street which already played host to them. The land belonged to a fellow alderman who, eventually, was persuaded to sell the site to the City. Nothing came of this plan, however, and it was left to Gresham's son, Sir Thomas, to revive it. It has been suggested that his interest was spurred by the death of his only son in 1563, and a desire to leave an alternative mark on posterity.

A new site was chosen – that of the present building, at the junction of Cornhill and Threadneedle Street – which required the demolition of 38 houses. The building was designed by an architect called Hendryck van Paesschen from Antwerp, and it was in the style of the bourse of that city. Stone, slate, panelling and iron were all imported from Antwerp, and the timber came from Gresham's estate in Suffolk. To the disgust of London craftsmen, many of the workers on the site were foreign, and a special guard was employed to make sure they suffered no abuse. Gresham, who paid for the building, laid the first stone on 7 June.

THE QUEEN AT HENDON

To the delight of future local historians, Queen Elizabeth is recorded as dining at various houses around the outskirts of London during her reign, giving rise to the number of places in which visitors are assured that she slept. She certainly stayed at Hendon Place, the manor house of Sir Edward Herbert, a cousin of Sir Philip Sidney. He entertained the queen there on 8 July, when she was on her way to Shenley, and again in August 1571 and July 1576.

1567

A CENSUS OF FOREIGNERS

A census of foreigners in the City was held this year. It was found that there were 40 Scots, 428 Frenchmen, 45 Spaniards and Portuguese, 140 Italians, 2,030 Dutch, 44 Burgundians, 2 Danes and 1 Liegois.

1568

BARKING MARKET HOUSE REBUILT

The market at Barking had been owned by the Crown since the sup-pression of Barking Abbey, its previous owner. This year the queen paid for the erection of a new building, and the local inhabitants con-tributed £100 towards the levelling of the site and the construction of 16 shops or stalls. The building was located at the end of East Street, near the Curfew Tower entrance to the church and abbey.

ALTERATIONS AT HAMPTON COURT

The queen put in hand some additions to Hampton Court. A three-storey building was built south-east of Wolsey's house; it bears her initials and the date 1568.

A FÊTE AT BERMONDSEY

A fascinating painting by Joris Hoefnagel survives at Hatfield House. Mixed together in the picture are people of all classes. Nobles look on while the younger people dance; musicians and an improvised kitchen are in the background, and a long table awaits diners. In the distance are the Thames and the Tower of London, though other features such as hills appear to be fanciful. It is fair to assume that it was a painting commissioned to celebrate a particular event, but it has not been pos-sible to identify this. It may be the visit of the queen to the home of the earl of Sussex, on the site of Bermondsey Abbey, but the absence of a central portrayal of a royal party belies this. Alternatively it may just be a local celebration attended by the earl and his wife, or a wedding feast.

1569

THE DRAWING OF THE FIRST LOTTERY

Drawing of the winning tickets of the first lottery in England began on 11 January at the west door of St Paul's churchyard and, as Stow relates, 'continued day and night till the sixth of May'.

To explain this extraordinary business it is necessary to go back to 1567, when the State, needing money badly, gave permission to Peter Grimaldi (State fund-raising through lotteries was an Italian idea) and George Gilpin to launch a scheme. A publicity broadsheet of the time referred to a 'very rich Lottery General, without any blanks, containing a great number of good prizes, as well of ready money as of plate'. It was intended to raise the vast sum of £200,000, and therefore £100,000 of the anticipated proceeds were set aside for prize money. First prize was £5,000 (in cash, plate and furnishings), second prize £3,500, and so on down to 9,418 prizes of 14 shillings in cash. In addition, those who bought tickets were given freedom from arrest unless it were for felonies, murder, piracy or treason. Tickets were priced at ten shillings, so only the affluent could buy them.

The closing date for purchase was 1 May 1568, but, due to the poor response, this was extended, and interest was paid on money invested after June 1568 and before the date of the draw. Considerable pressure was put on corporations and livery companies to buy batches of tickets, but even so only about a twelfth of the hoped-for income was obtained and it was announced that the total prize money would now be £9,000.

The method of finding the winners was incredibly complicated. Each ten-shilling ticket holder had his name put 12 times into the draw. In one pile were 400,000 counterfoils naming purchasers, and in another were 29,505 winning tickets with a value scaled down by one-twelfth, and also 370,495 blanks. The draw then began, matching one counterfoil against whatever came out of the other pile.

Derisory prizes were received because of the scaling down. The mayor won ⅛d, as did towns such as Bexley and Cambridge.

1570

MIDDLE TEMPLE HALL BUILT

One of the most notable Tudor buildings which survives in London is the hall of Middle Temple. Opened about this year, it has the finest double hammerbeam roof in England, and a magnificent screen, both made of oak. Three tables now adorn the hall, two of which are almost contemporary with the building. One is the Benchers' Table, made of three planks of over 29 ft, from the same tree in Windsor Forest, given by Elizabeth I; a second table, actually called the Cupboard, is made from the timbers of Sir Francis Drake's ship the *Golden Hind*. The building was badly damaged during the last war, but it has been sympathetically restored – Queen Elizabeth, who quite often dined here, would find the place familiar.

A HOUSE ON BETHNAL GREEN

A remnant of the Bethnal Green today is a green space called Bethnal Green Gardens, by the Underground station. Here, in 1570, an eccentric house called Kirby Castle was built. An owner about 100 years later was Sir William Ryder, master of Trinity House (Trinity Green is nearby), whom Pepys visited. The diarist recorded:

Sir W. Batten, Sir J. Minnes, my lady Batten, and I by coach to Bednal Green, to Sir W. Rider's to dinner, where a fine place, good lady mother and her daughter,

Mrs Middleton, a fine woman. A noble dinner, and a fine merry walk with the ladies along after dinner in the garden: the greatest quantity of strawberries I ever saw, and good.

AN END TO COMMUNAL CHIMNEYS

The City ordered that all houses in alleys were to have their own chimneys, privies and gutters and were not to share communal ones.

1571

OPENING OF THE ROYAL EXCHANGE

On 23 January the queen dined with Sir Thomas Gresham at his house in Bishopsgate and then proceeded to officially open and name the Royal Exchange, which he had paid to have built.

In fact the building had been used since 1568, while it was still being constructed. John Norden, a contemporary writer, described it as 'quadrate, with walks round the mayne building supported with pillars of marble, over which walkes is a place for the sale of all kinde of wares, richly stored with varietie of all sorts'. There were walks above as well as below, the upper part of the building being divided into no less than 100 small shops or 'pawns', from the rents of which Gresham proposed in part to reimburse himself. Stow records that these were substantially empty up to the time of the queen's visit, when an effort was made to dress up for the occasion by the simple and modern technique of persuading merchants to take additional space by offering lower rents for the empty units. Merchandise was stored in the vaults, but these were found to be too dark to be useful.

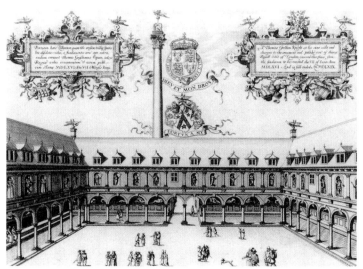

The first Royal Exchange, built by Sir Thomas Gresham, depicted c. 1569.

CANALIZING THE LEA

An Act of Parliament, sponsored by the City, was passed to build a canal from Hoddesdon to the Clerkenwell area, where it would connect with the Fleet river. At least two advantages would accrue: a considerable addition to London's water supply, and barge transport of agricultural produce direct into the City, thereby undercutting the cost of bringing this in by cart. It was a major undertaking, and one which was probably beyond the technical expertise of the time. It was also very expensive, and the canal stood no chance of being built once Parliament, bowing to the lobbying of grain dealers and the like, had refused to allow tolls to be charged. In the light of this the City appears then to have changed its plan to a less expensive project whereby water from the river Lea near Tottenham would be diverted into a canal through Shoreditch and then to Moorgate, where a market would be built.

Neither scheme came to anything, and it was left to Sir Hugh Myddelton in the next century to solve London's water problem.

1500s

NEW PARISH SCHOOL FOR ST MARTIN'S

According to the churchwardens' accounts, the parish of St Martin-in-the-Fields built a new parish school by the churchyard about this year. Ben Jonson, the playwright, received his early education here before going on to Westminster School.

1572

THE FIRST BANQUETING HOUSE

The original building on the site of today's Banqueting House in Whitehall was a temporary structure erected this year. The accounts of the Revels Office record its construction in time to entertain the duc de Montmorencie, constable of France, and his delegation to the English court:

The Banketting Howse made at White Hall (then for the entertaynment of the seide duke) did drawe the Charges ensving for the Covering thereof with Canvasse; The decking thereof with Birche & Ivie: And the ffretting, and garnishing thereof, with flowers, & Compartments, with pendentes & armes paynted & gilded for the purpose. The ffloore therof being strewed with Roze leaves pickt & sweetned with Sweete waters &c.

It cost about £225 to finish.

HARROW SCHOOL FOUNDED

Though an earlier school existed in Harrow, the public school we know today dates back to a charter obtained by John Lyon, yeoman, in 1572 (though the school prefers to use the old-style date of 1571). Fortunately for the school, the master was permitted to take in fee-paying boys from outside the area, and by 1720, while there were 40 'free' boys (as with Highgate School, see 1565), there were also 104 paying 'foreigners'. It seems likely that the school functioned in the buildings of the earlier school, but by 1615 a new schoolroom was completed which, known as the Fourth Form Room, still exists. Famous subsequent pupils include Byron, Trollope, Sheridan, Peel and Winston Churchill.

WALLINGFORD HOUSE BUILT

On the site of today's Admiralty in Whitehall, Sir Francis Knollys, just appointed treasurer to the royal household, began to build what became known as Wallingford House. The site, on the west side of Whitehall, north of the tilt-yard, was previously used as a timber yard.

1573

ATTEMPTED MURDER IN THE STRAND

Stow records that the famous naval commander Sir John Hawkins, out riding in the Strand with his friend Sir William Wynter on 11 October, was attacked and nearly murdered in error. The assailant was Peter Burchett, a lawyer of the Middle Temple, who in a fit of 'fanatical fury' stabbed him under the impression that he was the queen's favourite courtier, Sir Christopher Hatton. Hawkins was dangerously wounded, and the queen sent her own surgeon to attend him. Her first inclination was to have Burchett hanged immediately without trial, but he was eventually legally executed in the Strand at the

location of the attack. Previously his right hand had been cut off and nailed above the scaffold.

QUEEN ELIZABETH GRAMMAR SCHOOL FOUNDED

On 24 March a charter was granted for the foundation of the Free Grammar School of Queen Elizabeth at Chipping Barnet. Later historians such as Daniel Lysons relate that the queen gave the parish a house and garden for a free school at which nine pupils could be educated without fee and all other children at five shillings a quarter, but there is nothing of this in the charter. More likely it was begun at the instigation of the rector of the united parishes of East Barnet and Chipping Barnet, Edward Underne.

1574

A BAN ON PLAYS

The performance of plays at inns was increasing in popularity, despite the growing puritanism of the age. The City instituted censorship of plays which it considered encouraged riot, sedition and lewdness. No innkeeper could allow any play on his premises which had not been first perused by the lord mayor and the Court of Aldermen, and in return for a licence the innkeeper had to give certain sums to hospitals in the City.

About this time also the City closed upwards of 200 alehouses in the City area, on the ground that there were too many. Westminster and Tower Hamlets followed suit.

DROWNED AT DOWGATE

Stow records that during a storm this year

a lad of eighteen years old, minding to have leapt over the channel near unto the said conduit [near Dowgate], was taken with the stream and carried from thence towards the Thames with such a violence, that no man with staves or otherwise could stay him, till he came against a cart wheel that stood in the said water-gate, before which time he was drowned and stark dead.

COLFE'S SCHOOL FOUNDED

A charter was obtained to found a free grammar school at Lewisham, based on a bequest of £100 by a former vicar of Lewisham, the Revd John Glynn. It was not a great success and it was refounded in the next century by the Revd Abraham Colfe, whose grammar school bearing his name survives today.

1575

THE QUEEN AT THE BEAR GARDENS

Baiting animals was the most popular sport in London. In the 'Agas' map of London, of about this period, two arenas may be seen in Southwark: one for bears, the other for bulls. Baiting was popular with all classes – this year the queen took the Spanish ambassador to Southwark to see it. Official approval by the queen led the mayor to prohibit performances of plays on days on which bear-baiting was due; he complained that 'in divers places the players do use to recite their plays to the great hurt and destruction of the game of bear-baiting and such like pastimes which are maintained for her Majesty's pleasure'.

There were baiting pits near Whitehall, at Islington and, more notoriously and slightly later, at Hockley-in-the-Hole in Clerkenwell. This latter place, one of the most insalubrious in London, derived its name from its location in the deep valley of the Fleet river – a site easily recognized today at the junction of Back Hill and Warner Street, behind the present offices of the *Guardian* newspaper.

Bulls and bears were fastened to a stake by a 15-ft chain. The dog, attended by its owner, was held in front of the chained animal by the ears until it was wild with fury, and was then let go. Quite often the bull or bear was decorated with a rosette between its eyes, and it was regarded as a great victory if the dog could emerge from the fray with that in its teeth.

A population which could enjoy and savour the niceties of public executions was also one which did not blanch at the considerable cruelties of these sports. On occasions human beings would take part, whipping a blindfold bear.

1576

LONDON'S FIRST THEATRES OPENED
On 13 April James Burbage, who lived in Holywell Street, Shoreditch, leased a piece of ground on which he built London's first playhouse. It was called simply the Theatre, and its site was that of today's 86–90 Curtain Road. Made of timber, it was probably circular or polygonal in shape. At the end of the theatre's 21-year lease, the building was dismantled and moved to Bankside, where it was resurrected as the Globe.

Because of the prevailing puritanical view of theatrical performances, companies of players sought the protection of noble patrons. Burbage was adopted by the powerful earl of Leicester and was granted a royal patent to perform. It is likely that works by Marlowe and many of Shakespeare's plays were performed here during the Theatre's brief life.

Burbage's theatre opened in the autumn. A few months later, probably early in 1577, the Curtain Theatre began in the same road, south of today's Holywell Lane; it is thought to have been built by one Henry Lanman. Superficially it would seem that Curtain Road derives its name from its theatrical past, but in fact there were no curtains in Elizabethan theatres. The theatre and road instead were named from a cluster of buildings which probably supplanted a fortification wall (curtain wall) here.

The Curtain managed to survive until 1627, but was gradually eclipsed by the fame of the theatres in Southwark.

OSTERLEY PARK BUILT
The mansion called Osterley Park was built about 1576 by Sir Thomas Gresham, founder of the Royal Exchange. The queen came to dine here this year, an occasion made more memorable by the presence of local inhabitants tearing up fences in protest against Gresham's enclosure of land. Later residents of the house included the attorney-general Sir Edward Coke, the Roundhead general Sir William Waller, and the property developer and pioneer of fire insurance Nicholas Barbon.

The house is now substantially an 18th-century building, but some of the earlier structure survives.

A TUMBRIL FOR STOKE NEWINGTON
The lord of the manor was required, in line with current legislation (see 1552), to provide a tumbril on which to transport 'scolds' – overtalkative or critical women – to the ditch to be immersed in water.

ROMAN FINDS IN SPITALFIELDS
Stow describes the uncovering of Roman remains in the Spitalfields area this year, when the field called Spittle Field was broken up for clay to make brick. In the digging, earthen pots and burnt bones were found. In each pot were ashes and some copper money, with the inscription of a Roman emperor such as Claudius, Vespasian or Nero.

1577

FIRST BLACKFRIARS THEATRE OPENED
Since the 13th century, children of cathedral schools and of royal chapels had been performing plays, most (but not all) of them religious. The first 'indoor' theatres (as opposed to buildings such as the Theatre or the Globe, which were open to the elements) were used by these companies of children. In 1577 the frater of the old Blackfriars Monastery was taken by the Children of the Chapel Royal, Windsor, under the direction of Richard or Nicholas Farrant. The premises consisted of 'six upper chambers, loft lodgings or rooms lying together within the precincts'; here, in 1585, the queen saw the first performance of *Alexander and Campaspe*, a play by the minor 16th-century playwright John Lyly.

HATTON HOUSE ON THE ELY LANDS
In 1575 Queen Elizabeth obliged the bishop of Ely to let the great garden and orchard to the west of Ely Palace in Holborn to Sir Christopher Hatton, her favourite of the time; the bishop retained the right to walk in his own garden and to gather 20 bushels of roses each year. Two years later, in 1577, Hatton obtained a more secure lease of the land and on it built a mansion called Hatton House. This effectively cut off access to the bishop's Ely House in the north and took up most of the frontage on to Holborn.

About 80 years later the house was taken down and the street of Hatton Garden was erected.

SWANS ON THE THAMES
Evidence for the relative purity of the Thames at this period, despite the sewage of the Fleet and Tyburn draining into it, is given by the contemporary chronicler Raphael Holinshed, who records that in the river 'fat and sweet salmons [are] dailie taken' and 'the water ittselfe is very cleare' with 'infinit number of swans daile to be seene'.

NONESUCH HOUSE ON LONDON BRIDGE
One of the most extraordinary buildings ever built in London was begun this year – on London Bridge. The old drawbridge gate had been in decay for some years and it was demolished in 1577. On 28 August the first stone was laid for the foundations of Nonesuch House, which, above foundation level, was made entirely of wood and held together by pre-formed pegs: it is reputed that not a single nail was used in its construction. This remarkable building, the frame of which had been made in Holland, took two years to build and was described by Stow, a contemporary witness, as 'a beautifull and chargeable peece of worke'. Although the building overhung the pier upon which it was built, it was still standing when the houses on the bridge were demolished in 1757.

The architectural style was a mixture of medieval and Renaissance. At each corner was a tower with a cupola and weather-vane. Numerous windows crowded the lower two floors; many

1500s

The remarkable Nonesuch House, which was constructed on London Bridge.

exterior panels were richly carved and adorned with armorial bearings. Nonesuch House was demolished *c.* 1757.

LAMB'S CONDUIT BUILT

A conduit already existed running south from today's Guilford Street to a standard at Holborn (see 1498). The system, which seems to have utilized a tributary of the Fleet river, was rebuilt this year by William Lamb(e) – Lamb's Conduit Street and The Lamb pub nearby still commemorate him, as does a plaque in the street denoting the position of the conduit head. A commentator in 1707 said that the water flowed for 2,000 yards in lead pipes to the conduit in Snow Hill, on which was a statue of the benefactor.

1578

ALMSHOUSES IN LONDON

It had become common for wealthy men to leave money in their wills enabling their own livery company to construct and maintain almshouses. Typical of these were those founded this year in Monkwell Street by the Salters' Company, using a bequest of Sir Ambrose Nicholas. These augmented the almshouses built over a century earlier by the same company, from money bequeathed by Thomas Beaumond. The Merchant Taylors built almshouses at Tower Hill in 1593; the Dyers founded theirs in 1545 in White Cock Alley on the basis of a bequest by Sir Robert Tyrwhilt; the Girdlers' almshouses were built *c.*1612 in Old Street, in memory of George Palyn.

1579

FOUNDATION OF GRESHAM COLLEGE

The death of Sir Thomas Gresham, the immensely rich London merchant, this year effectively led to the foundation of Gresham College. In his will he had provided that upon the death of his widow (she died in 1596) their house in Bishopsgate should be used for a college in which lectures were to be given free. The rents of the Royal Exchange were vested in the Corporation of London and the Mercers' Company

to be used to pay the salaries of lecturers, who were to talk about divinity, astronomy, geometry, music, law, medicine and rhetoric. The professors were to be unmarried and chaste, and were each provided with apartments.

The building survived the Great Fire (though the rents from the Royal Exchange did not), but was demolished in 1768. Gresham College was built in 1843 and rebuilt in 1913 in Gresham Street, where the lecture programme is now part of the City University.

1580

EARTHQUAKE IN LONDON

On 6 April an earthquake struck London and the South-East. Unsurprisingly, at a time when the pope was trying to dislodge Elizabeth as queen, the occurrence was judged by Catholics and Protestants alike to have religious significance, and broadsheets galore appeared on the streets. The actor Richard Tarleton recorded that two men sitting on a cannon at Tower Hill were thrown off, that a number of chimneys collapsed, that the animals of the City roared, and that stall-owners at the Royal Exchange shut up their businesses for the day.

Thomas Grey, an apprentice cobbler, was killed by masonry falling from Christ's Hospital, Newgate Street – the only known fatality of an earthquake in London.

SPRING GARDENS LEVELLED

The Crown lands at Whitehall included a plot at the top of the road where it joins today's Mall. This was called Spring Gardens (a street name today recalls it); it is shown on the 'Agas' map of 1561 as mostly covered with trees. In 1580 work began on the levelling and planting of this land to make an ornamental garden, and by 1603, when James I came to the throne, it contained archery butts, a bathing pond, a pheasant yard and a bowling green; orange and other fruit trees are recorded here. A traveller noted in 1598 that there was 'a jet d'eau, with a sun-dial, at which, while strangers are looking, a quantity of water forced by a wheel, which the gardener turns at a distance through a number of little pipes, plentifully sprinkles those that are standing round'.

A BAN ON BUILDING

A royal proclamation this year (which was incorporated into a law in 1592) prohibited the erection of buildings on new foundations within 3 miles of the City. It also banned the subdivision of existing houses into new lodgings.

A DANGEROUS STRATFORD BRIDGE

The lord mayor was informed that the bridge at Stratford-atte-Bowe had been decayed and dangerous, 'by reason of great inundations', and several people had drowned while crossing it. The Crown had had it repaired and exacted a toll for two years, but had found that this bore heavily on the victuallers and charcoal burners who used it. The mayor was invited to ask the City to contribute to its repair, since much of the traffic consisted of carts carrying produce to the City.

A NEW HALL FOR STAPLE INN

Behind the surviving Tudor houses and shopfronts in Holborn lies the hall of Staple Inn, built *c.* 1580 by Richard Champion, principal of this Inn of Chancery; it was followed about five years later by the houses on the Holborn frontage which have inspired so many photographs. The hall has an impressive hammerbeam roof and a fine screen, but much of the rest was heavily restored in 1886 and again after bomb damage in the last war.

1581

A WATERWORKS AT LONDON BRIDGE
In 1580 Peter Morice, a Dutchman in the employ of Sir Christopher Hatton, had dramatically demonstrated to the City authorities that he could pump water from the Thames into residences in the City. He did this by directing a stream of water from the river over the steeple of St Magnus in Lower Thames Street. He was granted a lease of 500 years to utilize the most northern arch of London Bridge for his works, at a rent of ten shillings a year; he used the rapid flow of the water through the arch to turn a wheel which drove a pump.

Supplies seem to have begun by 1581, and in 1582 a second arch was taken over. Stow records that it supplied Thames Street, New Fish Street and Gracechurch Street, and as far as Leadenhall.

DRAKE KNIGHTED ON THE GOLDEN HIND
Francis Drake had arrived back in Deptford on his ship the *Golden Hind* after a spectacular circumnavigation of the globe (the first by an English ship) and some piracy on the way. On 4 April the queen dined on board and knighted him for his achievement. Such was the crush to see the event that a bridge on which many people were crowded collapsed into the water, but without loss of life. The ship itself was retained at Deptford 'as a memorial of national honour and imperial enterprise', and the cabin was transformed into a banqueting place. Eventually, long after the deaths of both navigator and queen, the ship fell to bits and parts were used for a table in the Middle Temple and for a chair which is kept in the Bodleian Library.

PLAGUE IN LONDON
The queen left London as plague raged in the City and suburbs. The authorities limited the number of burials in St Paul's churchyard, as overcrowding meant the graves were now very shallow. Public performances of plays were banned, killing of cattle in or near the City was prohibited, and the settlement of 'strangers' in the vicinity was discouraged. Parish clerks were ordered to shut up houses infected by the disease, and each parish was to employ two 'discreet matrons' to inspect and confirm reports of plague deaths.

This last measure is probably the origin of a parish officer called a 'searcher', which lasted until the 19th century. Almost invariably the two searchers in an area were women, who probably obtained not only a fee from the parish, but also another for dressing the corpses for burial as well; in a number of cases they were also local midwives. Their function originally was to notify the authorities of plague deaths, but they are found in later centuries as being responsible for the confirmation to the sexton of any deaths brought to their notice.

NEW BANQUETING HOUSE BUILT
The temporary Banqueting House in Whitehall (see 1572) was replaced this year with another structure. Again it was erected for a political purpose – this time the visit of the representatives of the last of Elizabeth's foreign suitors, the duc d'Alençon. Stow records that the building was begun on 26 March and was finished in three weeks.

It was made a long square, with 332-ft sides, had 292 glass windows, and consisted largely of decorated canvas fixed to upright poles. This temporary building survived until 1606, when it was described as old, rotten and 'sleight-builded'.

The festivities extended across the road, where jousting tournaments took place on the tilt-yard, the site now occupied by Horse Guards.

CAMPION EXECUTED AT TYBURN
Thomas Campion, a Jesuit priest who had arrived secretly in the country to give encouragement to Catholics, was taken prisoner in July, together with seven laymen. They were brought to the City to face the howling London mob and were lodged at the Tower, where at first Campion was placed in the narrow dungeon called, with good reason, Little Ease. At his trial he was offered his life by the queen, who had respect for him, but he refused to accept the terms required. He was returned to prison and torture, and was eventually tried for sedition on 14 November at Westminster Hall. Despite the weakness of the evidence against him, the jury were prevailed upon to find him guilty and his end was then inevitable. On 1 December he and others were hanged, drawn and quartered at Tyburn.

1582

A GLUT OF BOOKSHOPS
The religious ferment of the era inspired many books and pamphlets. It is thought that as many as 175 booksellers were in London at this time, of whom 22 were printers. Their principal place was St Paul's churchyard, but there were also printing presses in the churchyards of St Bride's, St Dunstan, Fleet Street, St Peter upon Cornhill and St Mildred, Poultry, to name but some.

CORNHILL STANDARD ERECTED
One of the outlets for the water which travelled from the London Bridge waterworks (see 1581) was a new standard at Cornhill, a feature which until quite modern years was used as a fixed spot from which distances from London were calculated. Its four faces looked towards Cornhill, Leadenhall Street, Bishopsgate and Gracechurch Street. It was demolished in 1674.

A view of Cornhill and the Cornhill standard, which stood at the intersection of Gracechurch Street, Cornhill and Bishopsgate.

1583

COLLAPSE AT THE BEAR GARDEN

Stow relates that on 13 January scaffolds crowded with people watching bear-baiting on the Bankside collapsed. Eight persons were killed and many others were hurt – 'a friendly warning', he cautioned, 'to such as more delight themselves in the crueltie of beasts, than in the workes of mercy'. This disaster was at Paris Garden, to the west of Southwark and outside the jurisdiction of the City authorities, who tetchily complained to Sir Francis Walsingham, the queen's chief official at the time, that there was no point in the City prohibiting bear-baiting in Southwark in an effort to prevent the spread of plague if it was allowed 'in the places adjoining': Paris Garden was held by the Crown. To make matters worse, the spectacle was on the Sabbath.

ARCHERY AT SMITHFIELD

A grand archery contest, lasting two days, took place in September at Smithfield. The 3,000 participants were led by mock nobles, such as the duke of Shoreditch and the marquis of Clerkenwell. On the evening of the second day the victors were led off the field mounted on horses and attended by 200 persons, each bearing a lighted torch.

RALEGH MOVES INTO DURHAM HOUSE

Today, Durham House Street covers the site of the former house of the bishop of Durham, held intermittently by the see from the 13th to the 17th century. Residents included Cardinal Wolsey, bishop of Durham and of York, Anne Boleyn and Cranmer. John Norden described it during the reign of Elizabeth as 'stately and high, supported with lofty marble pillars', and said that it was 300 years old.

One of its most illustrious residents was Sir Walter Ralegh, who received tenancy from the queen in 1583 and lived here until his fall from grace 20 years later. In fact James I took it away from him in 1603, and gave it back to the bishop of Durham, whereupon Ralegh said that this was harsh dealing on a tenant who had spent £2,000 on it out of his own purse. Both Ralegh and Drake are credited with bringing back potato and tobacco plants from the New World; these plants are recorded as growing in Ralegh's garden in the Strand in 1596.

THE WHITECHAPEL BELL FOUNDRY MOVES

Some uncertainty exists about the beginning of this foundry – it was possibly begun in 1570 by Robert Mot, though there is some evidence that it existed at least a century earlier. It became the most prestigious bell foundry in the country, and in 1583 and 1598 Mot recast two bells for Westminster Abbey; his successors have cast or recast or replaced the remainder of the abbey's bells. In 1662 the foundry supplied six bells for Samuel Pepys's church, St Olave, Hart Street. In 1583 Mot moved the foundry from Aldgate to the north side of Whitechapel High Street. It relocated nearby in 1738, to 32–34 Whitechapel Road, where it took over the Artichoke inn, and there the firm remains today.

1584

MUSTER IN GREENWICH PARK

The queen's policy of avoiding war had swollen her coffers, but now, with conflict looming, she needed a potential army. Men were drilled and taught at places like Mile End and St George's Fields, and in May there was a grand muster of some 4,000 men before the queen at Greenwich.

NEW ALMSHOUSES IN SOUTHWARK

New almshouses were founded this year by Thomas Cure, saddler to the queen, in the unfortunately named Deadman's Place, Southwark. Sixteen poor people were to be housed and given 20 pence a week.

1585

WESTMINSTER BECOMES A MUNICIPALITY

Westminster was now an anomaly. Home of government, law and the court, it was, as a parish, unable to manage itself properly. In contrast, the City had had autonomy from early times (albeit diminished or increased now and then by the Crown) as well as a substantial body of privileges and a wealth of administrative experience. Elsewhere in the kingdom, many towns had corporate status. Westminster, armed only with the limited powers of open vestries, had difficulty coping with the problems and advantages of a burgeoning population. To remedy this, ordinances issued on 29 May granted Westminster its own laws and constitution; it was, at last, a municipality.

Despite all the royal proclamations inhibiting development, Westminster's population would expand dramatically in the next 50 years. John Norden's map of 1593, before Covent Garden and Leicester Fields were built on, shows the concentration of houses along the Strand and going north-west up today's Tothill Street.

THIEVES' KITCHEN AT BILLINGSGATE

A training school for young male thieves was discovered in a house at Billingsgate. A purse and a pocket were hung up, each guarded by a bell which would sound if the attempt to rifle them of their coins was too clumsy. A boy judged to be good at picking a pocket was called a 'foyster'; one good at purses was a 'nypper'.

1586

LUDGATE REBUILT

Ludgate, opposite St Martin's church in Ludgate Hill, was rebuilt. This time it was embellished with statues of the queen and of the mythical King Lud and his two sons. These effigies were removed on the gate's demolition in 1760 and eventually found their way to the church of St Dunstan in the West, Fleet Street, where they can be seen today.

DRAKE DINES AT THE MIDDLE TEMPLE

Sir Francis Drake, back in triumph from an expedition of aggression and plunder at the expense of the Spanish in the New World, was fêted at the Middle Temple on 4 August. Drake was not a hero to everyone. Stow records that there was a clamour against him 'terming him the master thief of the unknown world'.

BABINGTON EXECUTED

A Catholic plot led by Anthony Babington to rescue Mary, Queen of Scots, and to murder Elizabeth, was discovered; there was evidence in plenty that Mary had connived in the scheme. Babington was taken in August, and in September he and his conspirators were found guilty. On 20 September Babington and six others were drawn on hurdles from Tower Hill 'through the cittie of London, unto a fielde at the upper end of Holborne, hard by the high way side to S. Giles, where was erected a scaffolde convenient for the execution'. This is thought by some authorities to be the site of Lincoln's Inn Fields. In view of the nature of the crime, the executions were particularly barbaric: the leaders were taken down from the gallows while still alive and were disembowelled before being quartered.

Later that year the Commons proclaimed Mary, Queen of Scots, guilty of treason and urged that she too should be executed.

BEDFORD HOUSE BUILT

The Bedford family, which had acquired the Covent Garden estate in 1552, had a mansion on the south side of the Strand, a development of the old house of the bishop of Carlisle. It was, however, on a restricted site, without space for the expansion thought proper for a family now so wealthy. A new mansion was built this year on the north side of the Strand; its buildings and gardens occupied the land running south of today's Covent Garden Piazza down to the Strand.

It appears to have been of two storeys, irregular in plan, towards the Southampton Street end of the site, and with a courtyard by the Strand and stables to its east; in 1673 (by which time the house had grown) the earl was taxed for 60 hearths. Substantial gardens faced the Piazza, guarded by a high wall.

1587

ROSE THEATRE BUILT

The building of the first Bankside theatre, the Rose, was begun this year – its remains were found almost exactly 400 years later, in 1989, by the side of Southwark Bridge, backing on to Rose Alley. It appears to have been an irregular polygon in shape, based on a circle, and to have been three storeys high, with galleries on each floor. The walls were constructed of lath and plaster around a timber frame on a stone foundation (some of which survives); the roof was thatched. Its instigator was Philip Henslowe, father-in-law of the actor Edward Alleyn.

At the Rose were staged most of the Marlowe plays and the first performances of *Titus Andronicus* and at least part of *Henry VI* by Shakespeare.

SOUTHALL MANOR HOUSE BUILT

The timber-framed manor house of Southall (in South Road) was built this year by Richard Awsiter, a London merchant. Apart from the addition of a new wing in the 18th century, it survives virtually unchanged and is now the office of the local chamber of commerce.

THE FUNERAL OF SIR PHILIP SIDNEY

The poet, soldier and statesman Sir Philip Sidney had died in October 1586 after being wounded in battle in Holland. His family found it difficult to find the costs of a public funeral befitting a hero, and it was not until 16 February 1587 that the ceremony took place. Seven hundred mourners, including the lord mayor, escorted the body from a house in the Minories, Aldgate, where it had lain for three months, to St Paul's. The procession was headed by 32 poor men and Sidney's former regiment of horse.

1588

ARMADA THANKSGIVING

After weeks of rumours, official news of the destruction of the Spanish Armada was finally given to Londoners on 20 August, in a sermon preached at Paul's Cross. A celebratory thanksgiving service was held at St Paul's on 24 November, to which the queen came in state.

BAKEWELL HALL REBUILT

The only wool market permitted in London was in Bakewell Hall, a building to the south of the Guildhall, owned by the City. It was rebuilt this year.

1589

DEVELOPMENT IN HOLBORN

Baldwin's Rents (now Baldwin's Gardens) off Holborn were built this year, an investment of Richard Baldwin, one of the queen's gardeners. This area deteriorated during the 17th century and became, for reasons unknown, a place of sanctuary for debtors and a hiding place for criminals; the sanctuary, of which the composer Henry Purcell once took advantage, was abolished in 1697.

DISPUTE ON BARNES COMMON

A dispute arose between residents of Barnes and Putney over the use of Barnes Common, the outcome of which was that the men of Barnes prevented those of Putney using it.

1591

FIRST SHAKESPEARE PLAYS IN LONDON

Scholastic debate still continues as to the order, let alone the authorship, of Shakespeare's plays. None was published before 1597, and none with his name on the title-page was printed until the year after. However, scholars are agreed that the first of his plays performed was *Love's Labour's Lost*, in the first Blackfriars Playhouse this year. The following year, on 3 March 1592, *Henry VI Part I* was performed at the Rose Theatre, and by the end of that year it appears that the other two parts of that trilogy had been seen.

1592

WESTMINSTER TEARS UP CITY FENCES

The City's water supply from the Paddington and Tyburn springs ran through a field west of today's Regent Street – Conduit Street now recalls this. This year 40 residents of both St Martin-in-the-Fields and St Margaret's, Westminster, went to the fields and tore up fences which the City had erected enclosing their conduit.

AFTERMATH OF A FIRE

In the days before fire insurance, the loss of property in a blaze could be a disaster. A letter from the lord mayor to the lord treasurer this year reveals one way in which citizens might rally round to help some-one in such distress. The mayor, while sympathetic about the plight of one Peter Clemens, was unwilling to organize a collection for him on the grounds, first, that he was a stranger and, second, that he was a tallow chandler, whose trade was prohibited in the City for the very reason so amply demonstrated by the fire in his house.

1593

JOHN NORDEN'S LONDON

In this year John Norden was given a letter notifying the lieutenants of each county that he was authorized and appointed by the queen 'to travil through England and Wales to make more perfect descriptions, charts and maps'. He published this year the first part of his *Speculum Britanniae*, which dealt with Middlesex. This volume included two maps, one of the City and one of Westminster, measuring 8 ft by 6 ft and 9½ ft by 6 ft respectively. Norden, who lived in Fulham, was the first to design a complete series of county histories, but the project got no further than the volume mentioned and one on Hertfordshire. Other volumes, which he left in manuscript form, were published after his death.

Norden also published an odd double view of London about this time, showing two stretches of the river one above the other. The main interest in this map is the depiction of the large houses along the Strand, with their gardens down to the foreshore.

WILLIAM CAMDEN HEADMASTER OF WESTMINSTER

The historian William Camden (1551–1623) was this year appointed headmaster of Westminster School. Camden was born in Old Bailey, son of a painter/stainer, and went to Christ's Hospital for his early schooling. After his university days he began collecting material for his famous work on the ancient history of England, *Britannia*, while earning his living as a master at Westminster School from 1575. The book appeared in 1586 and established his reputation as an antiquary — he was already a member of a group of scholars who had founded a society from which the present Society of Antiquaries can claim some descent.

Ben Jonson was a pupil of Camden, and dedicated his 1601 play *Every Man in his Humour* to him.

Indirectly, Camden's name has been remembered in Camden Town. When he retired he lived in Chislehurst at a house subsequently called Camden Place. In the late 18th century this was the residence of the lord chief justice Charles Pratt, who, when ennobled, chose the title 'marquess of Camden'. When he developed his land in the parish of St Pancras from 1791 the area took his name.

MARLOWE DIES IN TAVERN BRAWL

The poet and playwright Christopher Marlowe was under a cloud at the time of his death. His atheist views had attracted influential dis-pleasure, and on 18 May the Privy Council issued a warrant for his apprehension at the house of Thomas Walsingham in Chislehurst, Kent. Marlowe escaped arrest, only to meet his death in a drunken brawl a few days later in a tavern in Deptford. Several versions exist of his untimely death (he was only 29), but the burial register for St Nicholas, Deptford, records, '1 June 1593. Christopher Marlowe, slain by ffrancis Archer.' Marlowe, who made no secret of his atheism, died, according to one version, with an oath on his lips.

A supposed portrait of Christopher Marlowe, the poet and playwright, who died in a tavern brawl in 1593, at the age of 29.

IRISH IMMIGRANTS

In this period we first hear of large-scale Irish immigration into London, and of the hostility the immigrants encountered. They were to be found in the poorer areas of London such as Wapping and espe-cially in St Giles-in-the-Fields, though their more affluent countrymen studied at the Inns of Court, and indeed were to be found in close contact with the royal household.

The main problem with them was, of course, that they were Catholic, and it was thought that any attack from Spain would come via Ireland. In 1593 the queen, alarmed at the prospect of assassina-tion, ordered

that no manner of person born in the realm of Ireland except he were a house-holder, known in some town where he lived in obedience to her Majestie's laws; or were a menial servant with some nobleman, gentleman or other honest householder; or did reside and were in Commons in any House of Court or Chancery; or a student in the laws or a student in any of the Universities ... should without Delay repair unto the Realm of Ireland, to the places of their natural Habitation, etc. upon pain of Imprisonment and Punishment as vagabonds.

1594

PLAGUE AND PLAYS

A persistent enemy of the London theatres was the endemic plague — severe enough at times to cause an exodus from the City and a suppression of playhouses, and from February 1593 in fact closing theatres for nearly a year. Another main foe of theatre managers was religious disapproval, but this was to exercise its full effect only after the works of Shakespeare, Marlowe and Jonson had been performed in this marvellous period for English dramatic writing.

We know that *Titus Andronicus* was produced in January this year, and on 25 August *The Merchant of Venice* appeared at the Rose. It has been suggested that the character of Shylock derived from the sensational trial this year of Roderigo Lopez, the queen's Jewish physician. Lopez, a Portuguese, had a flourishing practice in London. He was the first house physician of St Bartholomew's Hospital in 1568, was sought after at court, and was shown many favours by the queen, including the grant of a monopoly to import aniseed. However, the country was in an xenophobic mood, with constant alarms of plots to kill the queen. One plot, of Spanish origin, seemed to implicate Lopez; although the evidence was very slight, a confession from a friend, extracted under torture, sealed the physician's fate. On 7 June he was taken on a hurdle to Tyburn and hanged.

Theatres were not the only venues for the production of plays. This year the first performance of *The Comedy of Errors* took place in the hall of Gray's Inn on 28 December, before a crowded audience of benchers and students. Guests from the Inner Temple, who were dissatisfied with the seats given them, created a disturbance and left during the performance.

1595

SWAN THEATRE BUILT

The Swan Theatre was built either this year or the next in the liberty of Paris Garden, outside the jurisdiction of the City, on the west side of today's Hopton Street – a 1746 map shows part of Hopton Street called 'Bare Lane', a reminder of the bear pit here.

The Swan is unusual in that it is the only Elizabethan theatre of which we have a visual record of its interior. It was drawn by a Dutchman visiting London, and is accompanied by a description of London theatres:

There are four theatres in London of notable beauty, which bear diverse names according to their diverse signs. In them a different play is presented daily to the people. The two finest of these are situated in the south-west beyond the Thames, and, from the sign suspended before them, are named the Rose and the Swan ... Of all the theatres, however, the largest and most distinguished is that of which the sign is a swan ... since it has seating accommodation for 3,000 persons, and is built of a mass of flint stones ... and supported by wooden columns painted in such excellent imitation of marble that it might deceive even the most knowing.

In 1597 a play produced at the Swan was considered so seditious that all the playhouses were closed as a punishment, and for the remainder of Elizabeth's reign only two theatrical companies were sanctioned. In 1602 (q.v.) there was a riot there.

SOUTHWELL EXECUTED

In 1584 it had been enacted that any native-born subject who had become a Catholic priest since the first year of Elizabeth's succession was guilty of treason and punishable by death. Robert Southwell, Jesuit and poet, who had been ordained in the same year, sought

martyrdom by coming to the country in 1586. He was eventually arrested at a house in Harrow in 1592, but it was not until 1595 that he was taken to Newgate prison and put in the ominously named 'Limbo' cell. He was unrepentant to the last, and achieved his martyrdom at Tyburn in the unpleasant way usual for the time.

1596

SECOND BLACKFRIARS PLAYHOUSE OPENED

James Burbage, owner of the Theatre in Shoreditch, took a lease on several parts of the old Blackfriars Monastery and converted the first floor into an indoor playhouse, probably utilizing the great hall. His intention appears to have been for his company, The King's Men, to perform here and attract the City trade that would otherwise have crossed the Thames, but for some reason this did not happen. Instead the building was leased to one Henry Evans, who formed a new children's company; this, complained Shakespeare, was an 'aery of children, little eyases, that cry out on the top of questions; and are most tyranically clapp'd for't; these are now the fashion, and so berattle the common Stages (so they call them) that many wearing rapiers, are afraid of goose-quills, and dare scarce come thither'.

The playhouse tried some innovations, including the use of a variety of coloured stage lighting, simulated ghostly effects, and the use of music to entertain before the performance and to act as scene breaks.

1597

NEW CHURCH AT BLACKFRIARS

Stow records that the parish church of St Anne, situated within the precinct of the old Blackfriars Monastery, was demolished in the 1538 dissolution and replaced with a temporary building by the new lay owner. According to Stow, this structure collapsed in 1597 and was rebuilt, this time in Ireland Yard, and allocated a new churchyard. St Anne's would have been familiar to those (including Shakespeare) who worked at the Blackfriars Playhouse. Its registers include the christening of a daughter to the painter Sir Anthony Van Dyck, who lived locally. John Bill, the king's printer, who built the first Kenwood House in Highgate, directed in his will that he be buried there.

St Anne's was destroyed in the Great Fire and was not replaced, but its churchyard, used until 1849, survives as a public garden. The church is recalled by the street name 'Church Entry'.

ACCIDENTAL DEATH IN WHITEHALL

At the opening of the parliamentary sessions, 'divers people, pressing betwixt Whitehall and the Colledge Church, to have seene her Majestie' were crushed to death.

THE CONVERSION OF THE BOAR'S HEAD

Theatres were now banned in the City – a prohibition which resulted in the growth of new auditoriums on Bankside and the greater use of inns for performances. One of the latter was the Boar's Head in Whitechapel, just outside Aldgate. Conversion began in 1597 and was still going on in 1599. The project was beset with legal wrangles, had to overcome a prohibition on acting in inns, and failed, even in such a prime position on the north bank, to be particularly profitable.

1598

STOW'S HISTORY OF LONDON

The first edition of John Stow's *The Survey of London*, a topographical history of the city, was published this year. Its main value lies in its exhaustive account of London in the Elizabethan era, but some of its historical material has to be taken on trust in the absence of any other documentation. The book has been through a number of editions since, most notably John Strype's edition of 1720 and C. L. Kingsford's annotated editions of 1908 and 1927.

Stow himself was born *c.* 1525, son of a tallow chandler in the parish of St Michael, Cornhill, a church which his father supplied with candles. Stow did not follow the same trade. Instead he became a tailor in a house near the well at Aldgate (over which the famous Aldgate pump was later placed).

His first publication was an edition of Chaucer's works, but from the 1560s his time was increasingly spent collecting old manuscripts and documents relating to the history of England and, in particular, to London. This was not the quiet pursuit it seems, for the collection inevitably included papers that could be construed as supportive of the state of things before the Reformation, and Stow endured several visits from the authorities.

His enthusiasm for his interest and neglect for his own welfare led to poverty. However, an application to James I for a pension in the closing years of his life resulted only in a licence to solicit alms from other people. The letters patent described him as 'a very aged and worthy member of our city of London, who had for forty-five years to his great charge and with neglect of his ordinary means of maintenance, for the general good as well of posterity as of the present age, compiled and published divers necessary books and chronicles'. Stow's efforts to collect money by erecting basins in the streets were, it seems, not very successful.

He died on 5 April 1605, and was buried in St Andrew's Undershaft church, where each year a commemorative service under the auspices of the London and Middlesex Archaeological Society is held. An effigy of Stow, holding a quill pen which is changed each year, is prominent in the church.

THE THEATRE DEMOLISHED

James Burbage, the owner of the Theatre in Shoreditch, the first purpose-built theatre in London, had died in 1597, and his sons Cuthbert and Richard (the actor) inherited the building. On 28 December they dismantled it and transported the materials across the river to a site which they had leased immediately south of today's Park Street on Bankside. There, next year, the famous Globe Theatre was to open.

THE BEN JONSON DUEL

Ben Jonson, the dramatist, fought a duel with Gabriel Spencer, an actor, at Hoxton (near the Theatre and the Curtain in Shoreditch) in September. Spencer died from a sword thrust, and Jonson was obliged to plea 'benefit of clergy' (mitigation of a death sentence by virtue of being able to write and to read the Bible). He was branded on the thumb and imprisoned, and forfeited his goods.

Legend has it that the duel was fought in a field behind a pub called The Pimlico in Hoxton Street. The Pimlico, noted for its brown ale and cakes and custard, had a variety of customers, depicted in a poem of 1609 called ''Tis a Mad World at Hogsdon' which lists villains who could scarce raise fivepence to provide bail for themselves but who came here and spent eightpence, lawyers who here pleaded not for their clients but for ale and cakes, and doctors, proctors, clerks and attorneys.

SHAKESPEARE IN WHITEHALL

Love's Labour's Lost, 'newly corrected and augmented by W. Shakespeare', was presented to the queen at Whitehall Palace on 'St Stephen's night' this year. It was followed on New Year's Day 1599 by the newly written *The Merry Wives of Windsor*.

THE BANNING OF THE STEELYARD

Londoners retained their vehement hostility towards foreigners, and in particular foreign merchants. The Hanseatic merchants who had enjoyed, with intermittent breaks, considerable privileges at their headquarters called the Steelyard, in Upper Thames Street, were finally banished this year.

It was a popular move in an age in which Ralegh supported a bill to exclude aliens and even John Stow exuded prejudice against them. Others were wiser, including a secretary to the queen, Sir John Wolley, who recognized the value of 'entertaining strangers and giving liberty unto them' – a view upheld a hundred years later when so many Huguenots found shelter in London. 'Antwerp and Venice', he said, 'could never have been so rich and famous but by entertaining of strangers; and by that means had gained all the intercourse of the world.'

1599

THE BUILDING OF THE GLOBE

The most famous of the Southwark theatres, the Globe, was built this year by the Burbage brothers, using materials from their demolished theatre in Shoreditch (see 1598). They shared half the cost of the lease on Bankside, the other half being divided between Shakespeare and four others, all of whom were members of the Lord Chamberlain's company. The name of the theatre – perhaps the 'Wooden O' mentioned in *Henry V* – derived from its sign of Hercules carrying the world.

Plays performed in this building before it was burnt down in 1613 included *Romeo and Juliet*, *King Lear*, *Macbeth*, *Pericles*, *Othello* and *The Taming of the Shrew* by Shakespeare. Also performed were *Every Man out of his Humour* and *Volpone* by Jonson.

The Globe had no roof, excepting thatch whch protected the stage and galleries. In the pit, where the audience sat on cushions or stood, admission was 1d; in the gallery a seat cost 3d, and privileged customers could sit on a stool on the stage.

THE WHITGIFT BEQUEST

The name of the unattractive Whitgift Centre in Croydon today commemorates a set of almshouses for 28 men and women and a school established in 1596 by John Whitgift, archbishop of Canterbury, and completed on 29 September 1599. Inmates of the almshouses, whose dwellings were around a grassed quadrangle, were allowed to continue their trades if they wished, so long as they were not involved in alehouses and did not break any windows in the building by doing so.

The old school was not rebuilt until 1871, this successor itself being demolished in 1965 to make way for the modern development of shops and offices.

1600

EAST INDIA COMPANY FOUNDED

A charter was granted this year to the Company and Merchants of London trading with the East Indies, whose headquarters was Craven House, Lime Street. Trade in that part of the world was largely monopolized by the Dutch, who in 1599 tried to corner the price in pepper, raising it from 3s to 8s a pound. This so incensed London merchants that a meeting was held under the chairmanship of the lord mayor at Founders' Hall and it was determined to form an association to trade with the East Indies.

EXECUTION IN HOLLOWAY

The area at the junction of today's Holloway Road and Liverpool Road was once known as Ring Cross – the name (first recorded in 1494), which has obvious ancient connotations, is perpetuated in a housing estate to its west. Islington parish registers record the burial in 1600 of 'William Wynche, the first that was executed at Ring Crosse'. Later, Islington parish confirmed the area's unpleasant associations by putting a workhouse there.

DEVELOPMENTS IN TOTTENHAM

Most of the village of Tottenham was gathered around its green; the rest was agricultural, though some forest remained at Wood Green. Two prominent features in the village were built this year: one still survives, the other lasted until the 1920s.

At the top end of the green a wayside cross, probably replacing a medieval one, was erected. It was built of brick, but in 1809 it was stuccoed over and embellished in Gothic work.

The Sanchez Almshouses, founded in 1596, opened this year in the High Road. Their benefactor was a Spanish confectioner, Balthazar Sanchez of Jerez, who came to England in the entourage of Philip of Spain and decided, despite the blatantly anti-Spanish views of Londoners, to become a Protestant and stay. He became 'the first confectioner or comfit maker and grane master of all that professe the trade in this kingdom'. When the houses were demolished in the 1920s a store called Burgess's was built on their site.

A NEW THEATRE

This year theatrical performances were officially restricted to two venues: the Globe and the Fortune. It was a rule largely ignored, since the Swan, the Rose, the Curtain, the Blackfriars Playhouse and the Boar's Head remained open, and two years later the inevitable was accepted and the rules were relaxed.

The Fortune was a newcomer and, furthermore, on the north side of the river. Henslowe and Alleyn, its owners, recognized that their own theatre at Bankside, the Rose, was now a declining asset. It was in poor condition, it could not compete with the Globe (which had official sanction and the better company of players), and Londoners were somewhat reluctant (just like today) to go south of the river for their theatre, especially in the winter. The Fortune, in Golden Lane outside Cripplegate, was modelled on the Globe, and indeed was built by the same man. It became the only serious rival to the syndicate that controlled the Globe and the Blackfriars Playhouse, of which Shakespeare was a leading member.

The Fortune was often the scene of 'tumults and outrages' due to the 'divers cutt-purses and other lewde and ill-disposed persons' who frequented it.

THE CLIMBING HORSE

A horse called Morocco, owned by a Cheapside vintner, was led to the top of St Paul's – to the delight, as the playwright Thomas Dekker put it, of 'a number of asses who stood braying below'.

1601

THE ESSEX REBELLION IN LONDON

Robert Devereux, 2nd earl of Essex, formerly the queen's favourite, was by now in disgrace – not only, it is suggested, for returning without permission from an unsuccessful campaign to quell rebellion in Ireland, but for bursting into the queen's apartment at Nonsuch Palace on his arrival, at 10 a.m., before she had had time to don wig or rouge. In truth Essex had become too full of himself and disliked being treated as a subject. He was also facing bankruptcy after the queen refused to renew his income from the import duties on sweet wines.

A plot of sorts began to evolve at Essex House, where a number of discontented men gathered. The ostensible reason for the proposed capture of the queen's person was that her advisers intended to hand the throne to the Spanish infanta rather than the acknowledged heir, James VI of Scotland, on the queen's death. At least this accusation gave some legitimacy for what was an act of treason on the part of Essex and his friends.

At the beginning of February Essex was ordered to appear before the queen's council. At this he and his followers panicked and their plot, the mechanics of which were made up almost as they went along, was precipitated. On 5 February his friends paid the actors at the Globe 40 shillings to perform *Richard II* as a symbolic warning to the authorities. On 8 February the lord chief justice and others came to Essex House to investigate rumours of treason. Casting caution aside, Essex had them imprisoned there and, instead of attacking Whitehall, went to the City expecting to inspire popular support. To his dismay, he faced hostile forces organized by the mayor and retreated hastily to Queenhithe, from where he went back to his house on the Strand.

Here, he was arrested. The trial and his execution at the Tower were inevitable.

1602

DRAMATIC HAPPENINGS

A dramatic happening at the Swan on Bankside was contributed by the audience which had assembled to watch a performance of a spectacle entitled *England's Joy*. In fact the evening was a hoax, and the perpetrator, Richard Venner, had already absconded with the takings before this was realized. The audience 'revenged themselves upon the hangings, curtains, chairs and stools, walls and whatever came their way'.

More important was the first production at the Globe of Shakespeare's *Hamlet*. Richard Burbage is acknowledged to have been the first to take the title role, and he is thought to have been corpulent by then. It is suggested that the lines

KING: Our son shall win
QUEEN: He's fat and scant of breath

The actor Richard Burbage, from the original portrait in Dulwich College. He was responsible for creating most of Shakespeare's great tragic roles.

were written by Shakespeare to take account of his friend's unfit state.

Also recorded is a performance of *Othello* given by Burbage at Harefield Place, the country home of Sir Thomas Egerton, in front of the queen.

SALISBURY HOUSE BUILT

Sir Robert Cecil (later the first earl of Salisbury) became the latest court favourite to parade his affluence alongside the river. Following the example of Somerset, Essex and Wolsey, the foremost civil servant of the age built himself a house just east of today's Ivybridge Lane running down to the river from the Strand. (The Cecil family also owned land and a house on the opposite side of the Strand, on which Burleigh Street and Exeter Street were later formed.)

Cecil held a house-warming at his new house on 7 December, at which the queen was the principal guest. John Manningham in his contemporary diary noted that 'On Munday last the Queen dyned at Sir Robert Secil's newe house in the Strand. Shee was verry royally entertained, richely presented, and marvelous well contented; but at hir departure she strayned her foot. His hall was well furnished with choise weapons, which her Majestie took speciall notice of.'

1603

DEATH OF THE QUEEN

Elizabeth I died at Richmond Palace on 24 March, having reigned over 44 years. On the 26th her corpse was carried, lit by torches, by river to Whitehall. The barge in which it was carried was covered with black, and in it rode privy councillors and ladies-in-waiting. The funeral at Westminster Abbey was not until 28 April. Her body, embalmed and enclosed in lead, was borne in an open chariot drawn

by four horses. It was thought by Stow that the grief displayed was unique and that there was no precedent 'for any people, time or state to make like lamentations for the death of their sovereign'.

THE STUART COMETH

The joining of the two Crowns, in the person of James I of England and James VI of Scotland, ended the long-standing intermittent hostility between England and Scotland for the time being. On 7 May James approached London from Theobalds, the country residence of Sir Robert Cecil, where he had rested. At Stamford Hill he was presented with the sword and keys of the City and met by knights and aldermen in scarlet gowns, and at Charterhouse he was entertained by songs from the children of Christ's Hospital. From there he went to Whitehall, and thence by water to the Tower.

There was, however, no immediate coronation. Plague gripped London – one of the worst outbreaks ever known – and the ceremony, held with diminished pomp and grandeur, was not until 25 July. The mayor and some aldermen were invited, but other leading citizens were not. Over 33,000 plague deaths were recorded that year. 'Never did the English nation behold so much black worn as there was at her [Elizabeth's] funeral,' wrote Thomas Dekker. The usual precautions were in place. Those in families with plague victims were contained in their houses, fairs and theatres were banned, dogs on the street were killed and those in contact with the sick, such as searchers, were required to walk holding a red rod in front of them.

A LATE EXECUTION

Though many prisoners in London's jails were set free to celebrate the new reign, one was not so fortunate. Valentine Thomas was brought to trial for the offence, five years earlier, of declaring that he had been sent by the king of the Scots (now James I of England) to murder Queen Elizabeth; he had been incarcerated in the Tower since that time. Now, condemned for treason, he was hanged and disembowelled by the Old Kent Road in Southwark.

1604

JOHN GERARD'S GARDEN IN THE STRAND

John Gerard's *Herball*, published in 1597, is the most famous of the early books on horticulture. As a surgeon, Gerard interested himself in the use of herbs in medicine, and in his garden at Holborn he grew many plants for this purpose: a list of those grown there, which he prepared in 1596, is the first known catalogue of any garden, private or public. He also superintended Lord Burghley's garden on the Strand, but his pet scheme was to create a physic garden. This came to fruition this year, when the king's consort, Anne of Denmark, granted him 2 acres in the gardens of Somerset House 'abutting on the south upon the bank or wall of the River Thames and on the north upon the back of tenements standing in the High Street called the Strand'. (Somerset House had been a gift to Anne from the king the previous year.)

DELAYED CELEBRATIONS

King James and the City were determined to have their coronation celebrations, albeit nearly a year late. On 15 March the royal family made a triumphal passage from the Tower to Westminster, accompanied by the appropriate dignitaries. Along the way (which had been gravelled for the occasion), seven great decorated gates had been erected. The first, near Aldgate, was painted with a London scene; the second, by Gracechurch Street, was built by Italians; the third represented the seventeen Dutch provinces; and so on. The sixth was above the conduit in Fleet Street, which, like those of Cheapside and Cornhill, ran with claret wine all day.

Six weeks later the king and queen were to be found watching a masque by Ben Jonson at Highgate. Their host was Sir William Cornwallis, whose mansion in South Grove was on the site of today's Old Hall. The house, as now, had magnificent views over London. Norden, describing it in 1593, wrote that 'Cornwalleys Esquire, hath a very faire house from which he may behold with great delight the staitlie citie of London, Westminster, Greenwich, the famous river Thamsye, and the country towards the south very farre.'

A Lion Baited

Stow records the rare sport of lion-baiting. The king decided to match mastiff dogs against one of the lions in the Tower. The theatre proprietor and master of the bear gardens Edward Alleyn brought three of the best dogs from Bankside to the Tower, where the king, the queen and Prince Henry secretly watched the contest.

[The first dog] straightaway flew to the face of the lion. But the lion shook him off, and grasped him fast by the neck, drawing the dog upstairs and downstairs. So another dog was put into the den, who likewise took the lion by the face, and he began to deal with him as with the former; but whilst he held them both under his paws they bit him by the belly, whereat the lion roared so extremely that the earth shook withal; and the next lion ramped and roared as if he would have made rescue. The third dog was then put in and likewise took the lion by the hip. The two first dogs are dead but the third is like to recover, concerning which the Prince hath commanded that he shall be sent to St. James' and there kept and made much of, saying that he that hath fought with the King of Beasts shall never after fight with any inferior creature.

The lions caused further interest in August, when a lioness gave birth to a cub. The king gave special orders for its well-being, but it died within days.

The Minstrels' Charter

A very large number of new charters were granted to City companies in the reign of James I. Musicians also were regulated, and in turn were jealous of their privileges – there had been demarcation disputes between the king's minstrels and the City minstrels for some time. This year a new charter was given to the latter.

1605

Gunpowder Plot Revealed

Early on the morning of 5 November 'a most horrible conspiracy of the Papists against the King and the whole realm was discovered, being no less than to destroy the Parliament House and all therein by gunpowder this day'.

The scheme had actually begun on 24 May the previous year, when Thomas Percy had hired a tenement adjoining the Parliament chambers so that the conspirators might tunnel through at cellar level – work which began in December. But in March 1605 they were lucky to obtain the lease of a cellar directly beneath the chamber of the House of Lords, and set about hiding barrels of gunpowder in wait for the appropriate time.

That time was 5 November, when Parliament and the king would be above. The plot came to grief because of a natural wish on the part of some of the conspirators to warn their Catholic friends not to attend that day; one of those warned, Lord Monteagle, was curious about the oblique message he received and inspired a secret

The Gunpowder Plot conspirators of 1605. The scheme was led by Robert Catesby, Robert Winter and John Wright.

investigation into what was happening. The sequel is well known. Guy Fawkes was caught in the cellar preparing his grisly deed, and the conspirators were taken where they had fled.

There is a persistent legend that Parliament Hill in Highgate obtained its name from being the vantage point of the conspirators to see the result of their plan, but of course they were either dead or in flight before Parliament met that day.

THE BEGINNINGS OF NORTHUMBERLAND HOUSE

One of the most magnificent large houses in London, which survived until the 19th century, was Northumberland House; this had a frontage on the Strand facing Trafalgar Square and extensive grounds down to the river. Its original form was a house built this year by Henry Howard, earl of Northampton, warden of the Cinque Ports.

The house, much admired by Londoners, was associated with tragedy. In 1619, according to the parish registers of St Martin-in-the-Fields, spectators lining the roof to watch the funeral of Anne of Denmark pushed off a coping stone, which killed a man beneath. A later owner, Elizabeth Percy, was married very young to a Cavendish who died before he was of age to cohabit with her; her second husband was murdered in a jealous fight in his coach in Pall Mall in 1682, and she then married the duke of Somerset. She was, in fact, married three times before she was 17.

LIONS IN THE MOAT

The lions at the Tower continued to fascinate the king. He had constructed a walk and breeding place for them outside by the moat. On 3 June he and friends came to see them feed. Two racks of mutton were thrown down to the beasts, and then two live cocks. Stow records:

After that the King caused a live lamb to be easily let down by a rope, but the lions stood in their place and only beheld the lamb. But the lamb rose up and went towards the lions, who very gently looked upon him and smelled on him without sign of any further hurt. Then the lamb was softly drawn up again in as good plight as he was set down. Then they caused these lions to be put into their dens, and another lion to be put forth and two lusty mastiffs at a by-door to be let unto him. These flew fiercely upon him, and perceiving the lion's neck to be defended with hair they sought only to bite him by the face. Then was a third dog let in, as fierce as either, a brended dog, that took the lion by the face and turned him upon his back; but the lion spoiled them all.

ROSE THEATRE CLOSES

The Rose Theatre, now decayed, and in any case forsaken by Henslowe and Alleyn for their new Fortune, was closed this year. It was probably demolished soon after – though not entirely, as we know, since some of its foundations were revealed in 1989.

A new theatre opened, again on the north bank. This was built within the rectangular courtyard of the Red Bull inn, St John Street, Clerkenwell. Its impresario was Aaron Holland, and it seems to have continued in operation long after the ban on theatres of 1641. The company which used it was the Queen Anne's Men, who after her death in 1619 renamed themselves the Company of Revels. French companies who performed there in the next decade shocked audiences by including women performers, and there were many occasions of public disorder. One description, which probably related to events there, recorded that 'the Benches, the tiles, the laths, the stones, Oranges, Apples, Nuts, flew about most liberally and ... there were mechanicks of all profession who fell everyone to his own trade, and dissolved a house in an instant, and made a ruine of a stately Fabrick'.

A BELL FOR THE CONDEMNED

A macabre charity was established this year by a Merchant Taylor called Robert Dowe. It provided that on the night before the execution of a Newgate prisoner a cleric from the nearby St Sepulchre church in Newgate Street should go to his cell and with a handbell give 'twelve solemn towles with double strokes' and then admonish the prisoner to prepare for his end. On the following morning the main bell of the church would be rung and a nosegay would be presented to the prisoner on his way to the place of execution.

There is today a blocked-up tunnel in the church which is thought to have led to the prison, and by this, in a case, is Robert Dowe's handbell.

THE BATTLE FOR WESTWOOD COMMON

Henry VIII had appropriated the manor of Lewisham, including its Westwood Common, from the monastery at Sheen (Richmond) in 1531, and in 1605 one Henry Newport, 'of ye boiling house', begged of King James the lease of the common. This immediately stirred up opposition. At the local courts, residents in their nineties were represented who claimed that the common (otherwise called Shenewood) had been used for common pasture and had never been enclosed. Legal battles continued for a good many years, until in 1614 a court found against the villagers. Ditches were dug round the land, cattle were removed from the pasture, and the villagers – 100 strong – set out to London to petition the king. Later court proceedings ended in victory for the commoners, although of course the land was taken for development eventually.

1606

WATER FROM HERTFORDSHIRE

The famous New River had its origins this year. A proposal to bring fresh water to London in a canal from Hertfordshire had been suggested first by a Captain Edmund Colthurst. He obtained letters patent to proceed, but the City, jealous of an individual intruding on what it thought was its preserve, obtained its own Act in 1606 and then did nothing. It was left to another individual – a goldsmith called Hugh Myddelton – to brave the expense and the engineering problems and take over the City's licence; he began work in February 1609 (see 1613).

EXECUTIONS AT WESTMINSTER

On 31 January some of the Gunpowder Plot conspirators, including Guy Fawkes, were drawn from the Tower to their execution outside the Parliament building at Westminster. Thomas Winter was the first to be brought to the scaffold. 'He went up the ladder with a very pale and dead colour and after a swing or two with the halter was drawn to the quartering block and there quickly despatched.' Rookwood and Keyes came next, and last Guy Fawkes, helped up the ladder as he was frail from torture. He repented his action, urged Catholics not to resort to such measures in the future, and went quietly to his death.

THE BEGINNINGS OF GREAT QUEEN STREET

Today's Great Queen Street, between Drury Lane and Kingsway, was formerly a royal track much used, it seems, by James I on his way to Theobalds, the mansion in Hertfordshire previously owned by Sir Robert Cecil, the earl of Salisbury, and which the king had exchanged for the rather more valuable Hatfield House. The track veered north to the end of today's Kingsway (which is a modern road), where stood two gates, one of which led into what is now Theobalds Road. The path ran through 'Oldwitch Close' and was described as 'a private way for the King and Councell to pass through'. By 1600 two houses existed on the close, but in 1607 a large slice of the land was leased out for development and the White Horse, at the junction of Great Queen Street and Drury Lane, was built; but generally the first development was on the north side of the road. Sometime between 1605 and 1609 the new inhabitants petitioned the queen 'to gyvve a name unto that place', and the name Queen Street was adopted; 'Great' was added about 1670.

A New Banqueting House

The 'temporary' Banqueting House in Whitehall was still being used for theatrical presentations, but, in comparison with the purpose-built theatres devised since its erection, was scarcely satisfactory. This year it was demolished and a third building, this time of a permanent nature, was begun.

Aldgate Replaced

The medieval Aldgate, the structure over which Chaucer had once lived, was this year demolished and work began on a new gate. The old one, as described by Stow, had one of its pair of gates missing and was much decayed. It is reported that many Roman coins were found beneath the old structure, two of which were reproduced in stone and placed on the new gate.

The new structure, completed in 1609, was decorated with 'a fair golden sphere with a vane on it', and figures of two Roman soldiers, each holding a stone ball, stood there as though denying entry to invaders. Below stood a figure of James I in gilt armour with a golden lion at his feet.

Voyage to Virginia

A momentous event occurred, probably without much public attention, on 19 December at Blackwall, to the east of London. There, three ships set sail to colonize part of the New World called Virginia, after Queen Elizabeth. When James came to the throne England had no colonies, but during the next 60 years the foundations of the Empire were to be laid – the work of nobles and artisans alike. But those who set out from Blackwall that day were to meet quite unexpected difficulties, and by the time that supplies from England reached them three years later their numbers were reduced from 143 to 38.

1607

Holland House Built

Sir Walter Cope advanced his career at speed in the reign of James I. Knighted in 1603, chamberlain of the Exchequer in 1609, keeper of

Hyde Park in 1613, lord of the Kensington manors, he nevertheless died in 1614 £27,000 in debt. In the meantime he had completed in 1607 a large house in Kensington called Cope Castle, which he left to his wife on condition that she did not remarry. When she did, it passed to his daughter, who herself wed the future earl of Holland. Holland House, thought to have been designed by John Thorpe, was to be one of the most fashionable houses of the 18th century. Fragments of the house survived the bombing of the last war, and its grounds are now Holland Park.

Royal Security

When the king and the prince of Wales dined at the hall of the Merchant Taylors on 7 June, security was strict – the result, no doubt, of the shock of the Gunpowder Plot. Extensive searches were made of the premises before the royal party's arrival. Ben Jonson presented an entertainment and Dr John Bull provided some music. Etiquette demanded that the prince dined separately from his father, but he was able to watch proceedings through a hole cut in the woodwork.

A north view of Holland House, built by Sir Walter Cope in 1607.

Moorfields Drained

Moorfields, to the north of the City, was marshy and crossed by many channels, some of them sewers. As a contemporary writer put it, 'This field, until the third year of King James, was a most noysome and offensive place, being a generall laystall [dungheap], a rotten morish ground whereof it first tooke the name. This fielde for many yeares was burrowed and crossed with deep stinking ditches and noysome common shewers, and was of former times held impossible to be reformed.' However, the draining of Wapping marsh showed that it could be reformed, and from this year the draining of Moorfields began; indeed, the City authorities went further and laid it out into walks for recreation.

1608

An Early Golf Club

In the 19th century the Royal Blackheath Golf Club began to claim that it was established in 1608. There is, however, no evidence for the attractive story that James I, occasionally staying at Greenwich, suggested that a club be formed on the slopes of Blackheath. There is circumstantial evidence of the club being formed in the 1740s, and it owns a silver club inscribed with the date of 1766.

Third Banqueting House Opened

The first permanent (but short-lived) Banqueting House in Whitehall opened this year with a performance of Ben Jonson's *Masque of Beauty*. A Venetian described the hall as *a large hall arranged like a theatre, with well secured boxes all around, the stage is placed at one end, and facing it at the other end, his majesty's chair under a large canopy, and near him stools for the foreign ambassadors ... While waiting for the King we took pleasure in admiring the decorations, in observing the beauty of the hall, with two orders of columns one on top of the other, their distance from the wall the full width of the passage, the upper gallery supported by Doric columns, and above these the Ionic, which hold up the roof of the hall. It is all of wood, including even the pillars, carved and gilded with great skill. From the roof hang garlands and angels in relief. There were two rows of lights, which were to be lit at the proper time.*

ARCHERY LEADS TO ALMSHOUSES

The traditional story of the founding of the Dame Alice Owen's Almshouses and School in Islington is that when she was young she narrowly escaped death from a stray arrow in fields near the town. This encouraged a vow that if she lived to be a lady she would erect on the site a building which would denote thanks for her deliverance. This long-broadcast story may be true, but there is not even an oblique reference to it in the letters patent granted this year. Daughter of a local landowner, she married three times, lastly to Thomas Owen, a justice of the common pleas and himself a philanthropist. He died in 1598, leaving her rich enough to carry out her pledge.

1609

THE NEW EXCHANGE OPENS

A combination of bourse and bazaar was opened by the king in the Strand on 11 April. It was on the site of the stables of Durham House, on the south side of the road, where now stand nos. 54–64, opposite Bedford Street. The venture, a speculation of the earl of Salisbury, had a difficult beginning. Merchants were unwilling to move their business out of the Royal Exchange to this new building outside the walls of the City, but the Great Fire of 1666, which destroyed the Royal Exchange, encouraged the use of this New Exchange.

We have a description of it in the reign of Charles II:

The building has a façade of stone, built after the Gothic style, which has lost its colour from age and become blackish. It contains two long and double galleries, one above the other, in which are distributed in several rows great numbers of very rich shops of drapers and mercers filled with goods of every kind, and with manufactures of the most beautiful description.

Facilities included a set of stocks for shoplifters, and, traditionally at least, one of the galleries was used for assignations between men and prostitutes.

ENCOURAGING SILKWORMS

The northern part of today's Buckingham Palace occupies the site of a garden in which James I this year encouraged the planting of mulberry trees, the staple diet of silkworms. This was an unsuccessful attempt to establish a native silk-producing industry. Pepys was a frequent visitor to the Mulberry Gardens, as was Dryden, who came here to eat mulberry tarts with his mistress.

CHELSEA COLLEGE FOUNDED

A theological college – a 'spiritual garrison' to refute papist doctrines – was founded this year in Chelsea, on the site subsequently used by the Royal Hospital. It was the brainchild of the dean of Exeter, and James I laid the foundation stone of what was intended to be a considerable building around two quadrangles. The scheme was not a success and only one side of one quadrangle was ever built.

PAPER BUILDINGS BUILT

Paper Buildings in the Temple were built this year; they were then named after Edward Heyward, their developer. The derivation of the present name, first recorded in 1669, is unknown, but it clearly has to do with their use for legal and clerical purposes. These original buildings were destroyed in the Great Fire.

1610

LAMBETH LIBRARY FOUNDED

What is claimed to be the oldest public library in England, that of Lambeth Palace, was founded this year by a bequest of Archbishop Bancroft of 'all the books in my study over the cloisters to my successor, and to the Archbishops of Canterbury successively for ever'. It is mostly, of course, a theological library, and its treasures include a copy of Henry VIII's attack on Luther, *Assertio Septem Sacramentorum*, which earned him the papal title of Defender of the Faith. It also contains the draft of a sermon intended to be delivered at the funeral of Mary, Queen of Scots.

HAM HOUSE BUILT

Ham House, Ham, was built by Sir Thomas Vavasour, knight marshal to James I – the loyal inscription 'Vivat Rex' is carved on the front door. The house, beautifully situated by the Thames, was in a typical Jacobean H shape, with a central doorway leading to the end of the hall, but it has been much altered since. By 1637 it had become the possession of William Murray, earl of Dysart, whose boyhood had been spent as the whipping-boy of the young Prince Charles – he received the punishments the prince was deemed to deserve. John Evelyn described a visit in 1678:

After dinner I walked to Ham, to see the House & Garden of the Duke of Laiderdaile, which is indeede inferiour to few of the best Villas in Italy itselfe, The House furnishd like a great Princes; The Parterrs, flo: Gardens, Orangeries, Groves, Avenues, Courts, Statues, Perspectives, fountaines, Aviaries, and all this at the banks of the sweetest river in the World, must needes be surprizing &c.

1611

FOUNDATION OF CHARTERHOUSE SCHOOL

In 1610, Thomas Sutton, a remarkably rich man, obtained an Act to inaugurate a combined hospital (almshouses) and school at Hallingbury, Essex, for 'poor people, men and children'. But at the last moment the site for his philanthropic project was switched to the old Charterhouse monastic buildings, which, since the Reformation, had been used for residential purposes. At the time of Sutton's purchase, the buildings were in the hands of Thomas Howard, earl of Suffolk, then much engaged in the construction of Audley End. Howard was also much in debt to Sutton, and the sale of Charterhouse went a long way to clearing his debts and helping him to proceed with Audley End.

Sutton took over the buildings on 9 May 1611. When the alms-people (known as 'brothers') moved in, they were billeted in the old monastic quarters, while the scholars were housed in an old indoor tennis court. Alterations, which included the erection of a writing school and hall, were completed in 1614. As with Highgate and Harrow schools, the number of 'free' scholars was fixed at 40, but the schoolmaster and usher were permitted to take a further 60 fee-paying pupils, who had to be 'dieted and lodged' elsewhere.

'PRINCE HENRY'S' ROOM BUILT

Number 17 Fleet Street is called by two other names: Prince Henry's Room and the Inner Temple Gatehouse. This seemingly Tudor building was built about this year, replacing an inn called the Prince's Arms, whose eastern part contained rooms extending over the gateway to the Temple, as they still do. The publican, John Bennett, was granted the right to rebuild it in June 1610. His application asked that the Inner Temple Gate 'be stopped up for a month or six weeks in order that it may be rebuilt, together with his house called the Prince's Arms, adjoining to and over the gate towards the street'. In return Bennett offered to raise the height of the gate to 11 ft and increase the width to 9 ft. In fact Bennett sold the premises to a William Blake as the rebuilding was about to begin.

The 'Prince Henry' connection is not clear. The premises do indeed have the initials P. H. and depictions of the prince of Wales's feathers, but the most likely reason for these is that the inn was, in a fit of loyalty (and being named the Prince's Arms already), dedicated to the heir to the throne, who had been made prince of Wales in 1610. It has been suggested that the house was at one time the office and council chamber of the Duchy of Cornwall, which is under the jurisdiction of any prince of Wales, but this possibility is remote.

The house escaped the Great Fire and survived various uses, including that of a waxworks.

PUNISHMENT OF A SCOLD

The usual punishment for a scold, a woman whose tongue was not to the liking of the parish fathers, was a ducking in a stream. This year, on 9 August, a more severe variation was played out when Maudlin Tichon of the parish of St Martin-in-the-Fields was towed across the Thames at the tail of a boat.

1612

THE BUILDINGS OF SIR BAPTIST HICKS

Two London buildings which became famous were erected this year by the same man, Sir Baptist Hicks. He derived his wealth from his mercer's shop at the sign of the White Bear in Cheapside, and continued with this business after being knighted early in the reign of James – an almost unheard of thing.

On 13 January this year what was officially a sessions house, but was always called Hicks's Hall, was opened in St John Street, Clerkenwell, in the middle of the wide part of that road at its junction with St John's Lane. It was the first purpose-built court house in Middlesex – previously the magistrates had used whatever halls were available, such as tavern rooms. The building was known well beyond the confines of London, since it was taken as a distance marker for scores of milestones in the suburbs of London. It was a plain brick building with a stone pediment, but it served its purpose until the

grander building (which survives) on Clerkenwell Green replaced it (see 1779).

In the same year Hicks either built or rebuilt a large house in Kensington which eventually gave its title to many street names. This, once he had been made a viscount, was called Campden House, after his estate in Gloucestershire. Legend has it that he won the land upon which it was built in a game of cards with Sir Walter Cope of Holland House. The house had 60 rooms and was of three storeys; it was flanked by two square turrets surmounted by cupolas, and the entrance was carved and enriched in the Jacobean fashion. Unfortunately, this beautiful house was lost in a fire in 1862.

FIRST BAPTIST CHURCH IN ENGLAND

The first General Baptist church in England was opened this year in White's Alley, Spitalfields, a place of mean houses which was hardly built up until the end of the 17th century. The Baptists originated with a church in Amsterdam, founded in 1609, and were led by Thomas Helwys. They moved to Crosby Place, Bishopsgate, in 1618.

THE BEGINNING OF PICCADILLY

The name 'Piccadilly' continues to tantalize scholars: its derivation is still far from certain. The preferred version is that the land to the north and north-west of today's Piccadilly Circus was owned from 1612 by a tailor called Robert Baker, whose fortune had come from the sale of 'pickadils', either a kind of stiff collar then in vogue or the hem of a skirt. His house, or perhaps shop, here was derisively called Piccadilly Hall. In a 1633 edition of his *Herball* John Gerard mentions that 'The little wilde Buglosse groweth upon the drie ditch bankes about Pickadilla.' A survey *c.* 1647 shows just a few houses at the junction of Piccadilly and Haymarket and a windmill slightly to the north (which gave Great Windmill Street its name). Piccadilly Hall itself was just slightly to the north of today's intersection of Shaftesbury Avenue and Great Windmill Street.

CHARLTON HOUSE BUILT

One of the finest Jacobean houses in the country is Charlton House, the old manor house of Charlton village, completed in 1612 as a 'nest for his old age' by Adam Newton, dean of Durham and tutor to Prince Henry. Later owners were the Maryon-Wilson family, one of whose members was notorious for his attempts to build on Hampstead Heath. The house, made of red brick with stone dressings and probably designed by John Thorpe, is an H shape. The hall was one of the first in England to be set at right angles to the entrance and no longer the main living apartment.

1613

THE NEW RIVER OPENS

The most important addition to London's water supplies was ceremonially opened on 29 September. Sixty neatly dressed labourers shouldered their digging tools and marched in procession round the pond, as their spokesman recited a lengthy piece of doggerel in honour of those who had brought about this miracle. The floodgates were then opened, and 'the streame ranne gallantly into the cisterne drummes and trumpets sounding in triumphall manner, and a brave peal of chambers [cannon] gave full issue'.

The New River was a canal approximately 10 ft wide and 4 ft deep

A late-17th-century view of New River Head at Clerkenwell, the distribution point of the New River Company.

which wound 39 miles from springs at Chadwell and Amwell, near Ware, to a reservoir called the New River Head off Amwell Street in Clerkenwell. Work had begun in 1609, and by September of that year 130 labourers were employed. The most serious hindrance to the scheme was not related to the mechanics of its construction, but was a banding together of landowners along its route to try to repeal the project's licence, and if Parliament had not been conveniently adjourned for four years, leaving the proprietors free to proceed, the scheme could well have ended in disaster. As it was, its main instigator, Hugh Myddelton, a London goldsmith, was almost bankrupted. The City, which stood to gain most from its success, declined to oblige him when asked for a contribution towards the cost, and it was James I who offered to pay half the previous and future costs in return for half the profits. With the king's money at stake there was of course no further question of difficulty from landowners, and the mayor of London was happy to be present at the opening.

More difficult than bringing the water to Clerkenwell was its distribution to London households. It was fed through pipes hollowed out of elm trunks which tapered into one another; this was the only technology available, but was scarcely satisfactory, because there was a great deal of water seepage and the operating life of a pipe was only about 4–5 years. Furthermore, the water could not be pressurized, because the pipes would burst apart; consequently only the ground floors of houses could be supplied.

It was some years before the scheme was a success. There was a popular belief that water from pipes was more contaminated than that from the London wells, and of course it wasn't free. The king became concerned about his investment, and informed the City authorities that all houses which could use the water from the New River should do so. It is not to be supposed, he said, that two Acts of Parliament and an Act of Common Council affecting the health and safety of the City should be passed to no other purpose than to injure those who undertook so useful a work on the part of the City. The following year brewers who wanted to erect a waterworks on the Thames at Dowgate were prevented from doing so and were instructed to use New River water instead. Only by 1622 was the venture in profit, and Charles I, in despair at ever making much out of the royal investment, sold his

holding in 1631; he was not to know that early in the 20th century just one share would be sold for £125,000.

GLOBE THEATRE BURNS DOWN

On 29 June the Globe Theatre on Bankside burnt down. Cannon fired during a performance of *Henry VIII* caught the roof thatch alight, and the theatre was destroyed. Everyone escaped unhurt through the two narrow doors, excepting one man whose breeches caught fire; these were put out with a bottle of ale.

1614

NEW THEATRES ON BANKSIDE

The temporary absence of the Globe probably persuaded the indefatigable Philip Henslowe and Edward Alleyn to establish yet another theatre in the vicinity, the Hope. This was situated next to the Paris Garden bear garden, and in fact replaced it by being both a theatre and a bearpit. Despite a presentation of Jonson's new play *Bartholomew Fair*, it was not a success and the rebuilt Globe re-established its superiority.

The new Globe, with a tiled rather than a thatched roof, opened by 30 June. It was the property of a consortium which included Shakespeare, Richard Burbage, John Heming and Henry Condell, and cost £1,400 to build. Shakespeare was also a man of property in Blackfriars: in March the previous year he had acquired a house 'abutting upon a streete leading doune to Pudle Wharfe'.

HOUSE OF COMMONS ADOPTS ST MARGARET'S

The long tradition of St Margaret's, Westminster, being the 'parish' church of the House of Commons began officially on 17 April this year, when the Commons, increasingly enamoured of Puritan ideas, eschewed the rather papist practices of the abbey and decamped corporately to the neighbouring church. The dean allowed the removal of the rails and the relocation of the communion table in the middle of the chancel.

THE EAST INDIA COMPANY AT BLACKWALL

This year the East India Company, growing fast since its formation in 1600, took a site of over 10 acres at Blackwall, east of the Isle of Dogs. This East Marsh, as it was often called, was virtually un-inhabited, but it had a number of advantages. First, there was deep water here and larger ships (which would not have got near the Port of London) were offloaded on to lighters at Blackwall and the goods transported to the legal quays beyond the Tower. Second, its original dockyard at Deptford was too far upriver for the company's liking. Third, being on the north bank of the Thames, the new depot was within easier reach of the company's office in the City. By 1618, 232 men were employed in the yard and difficulties occurred owing to the strong quality of the beer supplied to them, the time wasted in the barber-surgeon's shop, and the embezzling of wood and iron for fires and tools.

1615

LONG ACRE BEGUN

The next London district to be developed was north of St Martin-in-the-Fields. St Martin's Lane, an old track, was already being built on by this year, and Long Acre (actually a long strip containing 7 acres) was now laid out. The earl of Bedford, who owned the land as part of his Covent Garden estate, jointly developed the road with the Mercers' Company – that company's insignia, a saint of indeterminate sex, is on many buildings in the area. It was required that the street should be built 'substantiallie and stronglie and in a convenient decent and comelie forme, and three stories in height (yf not above) and the forepart or front thereof at the least of brick'. Unfortunately for Long Acre, it became dispersed among various landlords and was not built

with the uniform dignity of the rest of the Covent Garden estate. During the 17th century the street became the centre for the coach-building trade – a specialization which continued into the 20th century, when car dealers had taken over.

NEW PRISON IN CLERKENWELL

The school which now stands at the northern end of St James's Walk in Clerkenwell is on the site of two prisons, one of which was built this year and was called the New Prison. A fairly contemporary writer recorded that the Middlesex justices 'builded a House of correction neere unto the east-end of Clerkenwell Church, for the punishment and employment of sturdy Roagues and Vagabonds of the County of Middlesex, and for the furtherance of the said House, the City of London gave unto it five hundred pounds in money to make a stock for the Employment of their Poore'.

SMITHFIELD PAVED

This year 'the rude vast place' of Smithfield was transformed into 'a faire and comely order' by paving it over, building sewers and putting rails around the area. The cattle market must indeed have been an unpleasant place before: churned up into a muddy quagmire for most of the year, awash with animal sewage and remains, and no doubt dangerous when an animal escaped.

1616

BUILDING OF THE QUEEN'S HOUSE

The royal palace at Greenwich, named Placentia when the Tudor dynasty united the York and Lancaster houses, was given by James I to his queen, Anne of Denmark. This year she commissioned Inigo Jones

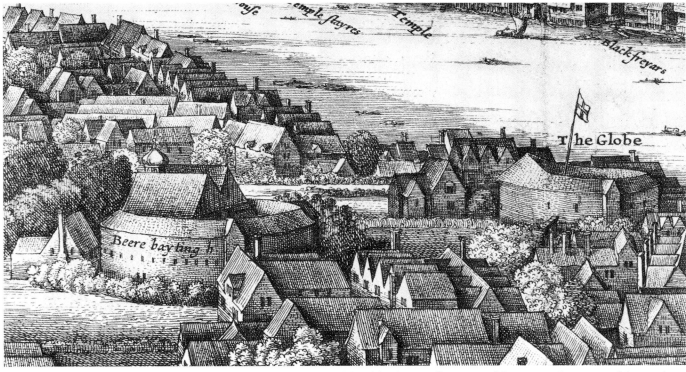

Wenceslaus Hollar's map of Bankside in 1647, depicting a bear-baiting pit and the Globe Theatre, reflecting two of the most popular pastimes of the period.

to build a new palace in two halves on either side of a public road, connected by a bridge. It was the first royal commission in the Palladian style, and is undoubtedly one of the most perfectly proportioned villas in England. The great hall is a 40-ft cube, and Jones followed this with the large double-cube Banqueting House in Whitehall. In keeping with the developing fashion of the time, this first great hall was an introduction to the house and not the chamber in which everyone lived; it set the scene, impressed the visitor, and encouraged a gradual introduction to the owner of the house.

COCKPIT INTO THEATRE

A cockpit had been built in Drury Lane in 1609. This year it was converted into a theatre by Christopher Beeston, and became, in effect, the first theatre to be opened in the Covent Garden area. It was situated in Cockpit Alley, which ran between Wild Street and Drury Lane – a site now covered by Peabody Buildings.

DULWICH COLLEGE CHAPEL CONSECRATED

Dulwich College, now a famous public school, was a surprising benefaction of Edward Alleyn, actor and stager of animal fights for royalty and the masses. He was a self-made man, and in 1605 he was rich enough to buy the manor of Dulwich for £5,000; he also bought the nearby Rycotes estate of 1,100 acres, stretching from Denmark Hill to Sydenham Hill.

In 1612 he moved to Dulwich and determined to set up the usual arrangement of an almshouse and school for poor children. The building contract for what was known as the 'College of God's Gift' was signed in 1613, and the chapel was consecrated three years later by the archbishop of Canterbury. The school was fairly moribund until the 1860s, when an energetic master transformed it from a poor-boys' school to one which was a desirable place for middle-class boys.

A NEW ENFIELD MARKET

A meat market existed in Enfield in Elizabethan times. It was held at the church gate before divine service on Sundays, which was probably of great convenience but irritated the new vicar appointed in 1579. The member of Parliament for the area, a strong Protestant, was called upon to help in the campaign to abolish this affront to the sabbath, but found that his dislike of the vicar and his curate (one Leonard Thickpenny) exceeded his religious fervour.

In 1616, however, the parish was granted an official Saturday market, with the appropriate court and market house. Its site was that of the Elizabethan meat market, in the space between the church gate and the Vine public house. By 1648 the Vine had been demolished, the market was extended and railed, and permanent market stalls were built.

VISSCHER'S VIEW OF LONDON

A Dutchman, Nicholas John Visscher, this year published his famous view of London, although there is no firm evidence that he was ever in the city. In essence it shows the London of Shakespeare, which would not change very much before the Great Fire erased the jumble of houses and graceful spires for ever. The old St Paul's – larger than the present Wren building – dominates the city, the other church towers being clustered like so many attendants to a monarch.

The view reminds us just how reliant on and familiar with the Thames people were. Clearly depicted are the numerous stairs – public and private – which served as landing places by the river; the quickest way to go from the City to Westminster was to find a waterman to take

The Queen's House at Greenwich, built by Inigo Jones from 1616. It was the first royal residence to be commissioned in the Palladian style.

you there, though if you were east of London Bridge you would probably get off the boat and walk round the structure rather than take your chance when it shot the rapids between its piers.

While numerous churches on the north bank proclaim that London's citizens had their eyes on the next world, the view of the south bank, with its places of dubious entertainment, suggests that pleasures of the present were important too.

1617

THE APPRENTICES RIOT

A century after Evil May Day (see 1517), the London apprentices again went on a May Day rampage. The new Cockpit theatre off Drury Lane was one target, and on Shrove Tuesday the mob invaded it, 'cutting the players' apparel into pieces, and all their furniture and burnt their playbooks'. The apprentices were active in Wapping too, where they pulled down seven or eight houses and defaced five times as many, 'besides many other outrages, as beating the Sheriff from his horse with stones and doing much other hurt too long to write'.

A NEW CHURCH FOR WAPPING

The residents of Wapping, after the shock of the riot, were compensated by the consecration on 7 July of their new church of St John the Baptist. This small building on the banks of the Thames was a chapel of ease to St Mary Matfelon, Whitechapel; not until the end of the 17th century, when Wapping's population had increased, was the area made a parish in its own right and a new church built nearby.

The parishioners were mostly occupied in the docks or on ships. Inscribed on the gallery of the new church were the words 'This gallery was built with part of the Benevolence which was given for the Use of this Chapel, by the Marriners that went to the E. Indies, Anno 1616, under the command of Captain Martin Pring, in the Royal James ... '

The siting of the church here confirmed the shift of Wapping's settlement. In early times its population had been further inland, by the Ratcliff ('red cliff') Highway, because the riverside land to its south was too marshy to be of much use. But in the reign of Henry VIII a Dutchman called Vanderdelf had successfully drained

Wapping Marsh and a wall of earth was raised along the river to protect the reclaimed meadow land. Gradually Wapping in the Wose (the 'ooze') was built as a high street along the river bank, consisting of warehouses, workshops, mean houses and pubs. Its most famous feature was, as Stow described, the gibbet for hanging pirates: 'From this precinct of St Katharine to Wapping in the Wose, the usual place of execution for hanging of pirates and sea rovers, at the low-water mark, and there to remain, till three tides had overflowed them.'

ALDERSGATE REBUILT
The Aldersgate depicted by Stow was this year demolished and rebuilt. On one side of the new structure James I on horseback was featured in relief, with the prophets Jeremiah and Samuel in niches on either side of him; on the inner (City) side James was shown sitting in his chair of state. This served to remind people that the king had entered London through the old gate in 1603 to claim his throne, and was now firmly ensconced.

1618

WALKS ON LINCOLN'S INN FIELDS
Fields at this time stretched west from Lincoln's Inn and across today's Kingsway. What is now Lincoln's Inn Fields was originally the major part of two fields separated by a stream which ran to the Thames. At the Reformation this land went to the Crown, and it was still pasture by 1613, when Purse Field (the Kingsway side) was acquired by Sir Charles Cornwallis. He immediately applied for a building licence, which was hardly surprising since, with the City's population burgeoning, development outside the old boundary was needed. The Society of Lincoln's Inn, however, was not without influence, and when it objected the application was refused. Moreover, the Privy Council issued instructions to the local justices to ensure that no buildings were erected there to 'the greate pestring and annoyaunce of that Society'.

The local population, however, was perceptive enough to realize that development could not be indefinitely staved off without good reason. On the offensive instead, and with Moorfields as an example of what could be done, the gentlemen of the Inns of Court, Chancery and the four parishes adjoining the Fields petitioned the king this year 'that the feildes commonly called Lincolnes Inn Feildes … might for their generall Commoditie and health be converted into walkes after the same manner as Morefeildes are now made to the greate pleasure and benefite of that Citty'. The Privy Council agreed, and urged the petitioners to solicit subscriptions to carry out the work, which 'wil be a meanes to frustrate the covetous and greedy endeavors of such persons as daylie seeke to fill upp that small remaynder of Ayre in those partes with unnecessary and unproffittable Buildinges'.

A commission, of which Inigo Jones was a member, was appointed to draw up a scheme. It has often been suggested that Jones designed the buildings of Lincoln's Inn Fields; however, his brief was merely to lay out the walks, and there appears to be no evidence that any work of that nature took place either.

EXECUTION OF RALEGH
The death of Queen Elizabeth was a turning point in the career of Sir Walter Ralegh. She had protected him from such enemies as Sir Robert Cecil, but he was suspected of conspiring to prevent the succession of James I. After a trumped-up trial in 1603 he was condemned to death, but was then reprieved and spent 12 years in the Bloody Tower, during which he wrote his *History of the World*. On release, he set about an ill-fated expedition to Guiana, in which he sank his remaining wealth, but it was not a success, and his preying on Spanish possessions, which he had undertaken to forgo, brought the displeasure and discomfiture of the king.

The commissioners who examined him on his return came to the conclusion that it was impossible to know which of his statements to believe, if any. There was no need for a trial, since he was already under sentence of death from 1603. On 29 October 1618 in Old Palace Yard, on a 'cold hoar-frosty morning', he was beheaded and his remains, other than his head (which was embalmed and kept by his widow), were interred in St Margaret's church across the road.

PETITION FROM THE CHIMNEY SWEEPERS
The chimney sweepers of the City petitioned the king that there were over 200 of them unemployed and that an overseer should be appointed to enter houses and compel persons to have their chimney swept in the interest of safety. The City was opposed to such an appointment and felt the present arrangements were satisfactory.

VAGRANT CHILDREN FOR VIRGINIA
A scheme was begun to send vagrant children off the streets of London to Virginia, there to be industriously employed. The Virginia Company agreed to take 100 boys and girls between the ages of 8 and 16, to educate them, and to give each of them 50 acres of land at 24 or on marriage.

1619

BANQUETING HOUSE BURNS DOWN
The third Banqueting House in Whitehall burnt down on 12 January. A contemporary, writing to a friend, said:

I doubt not but you heard of the great mischance by fire at Whitehall ten days past, which burnt all the Banqueting-house, and was feared the whole house of Whitehall would also have been consumed; but that my Lord Chamberlain and his brother being present, whose industry, pains, and great providence, all the time, through the abundance of water brought and pulling down of some places, God be thanked! prevented any more hurt. The fire arising by the neglect and heedlessness of two men that were appointed to sweep the room, and having candles, firing some oily clothes of the devices of the masque, that fire inflaming suddenly about and to the roof, which the two men, not able to quench and fearing to be known that they did it, shut the doors, parting away without speaking thereof, till at last, perceived by others, when too late and irrecoverable. The two, since confessing the truth, are put to prison.

KING JAMES AT THE CHICKEN HOUSE
For reasons which are not known, the king and his favourite George Villiers, duke of Buckingham, visited and stayed the night at a large house, usually known as the Chicken House, in Hampstead High Street on 25 August. Commemorative glass portraits of the two men were later incorporated in the house, together with the inscription 'Icy dans cette chambre coucha nostre Roy Iacques, premier de nom. Le 25 Aoust 1619.' The owner of the house and the reason for the use of French are unknown.

TAPESTRY AT MORTLAKE

Prevailing fashion was away from the wood-panelled rooms of the Tudors and towards walls decorated with tapestries. Though they could be imported from the Continent, particularly from Gobelins, it was felt that their manufacture should be encouraged in this country. Sir Francis Crane, secretary to the prince of Wales, set up a tapestry works in two houses at Mortlake this year and brought over Flemish weavers. The four rooms on the ground floor were used for accommodation, and the first floor was converted to a large workroom, 82 ft long and 20 ft wide; above this were studios for artists.

The works were always financially precarious and needed a constant injection of royal money, but they survived until 1703.

1620

MORE ALMSHOUSES

Numerous almshouses were founded throughout this century. It was now commonplace for each City livery company to have its own, and these were joined by others built by rich men, such as those founded by Sir Noel de Caron in Lambeth in 1618 and those already noticed at Islington built by Dame Alice Owen. Edward Alleyn – actor, theatre proprietor, master of the bears on Bankside and founder of Dulwich College – was a generous benefactor. He endowed three sets of almshouses, one of which was in Bath Street (at that time called Pest House Lane) off the City Road. This year, on 13 July, he laid the first brick himself. The area was probably well known to him, since his own theatre, the Fortune, was nearby.

1621

APPRENTICES KEPT INSIDE

Riots by apprentices such as took place in 1617 may possibly have been threatened again, for in 1621 the Lords of the Council wrote to the mayor regarding the disorders committed in 'former years at Shrovetide by apprentices and other lewd and ill-affected persons. His Majesty,' they said, 'expected a real reformation of the licentious and rude customs formerly used at that season' and required that every man within the City's jurisdiction should keep in his servants and apprentices on the following Shrove Tuesday, and that troops should be ready to quell any disturbances.

THE FORTUNE BURNS DOWN

Edward Alleyn, in the middle of building his almshouses, must have wondered if his good works were being properly rewarded, because his nearby Fortune Theatre, in Golden Lane, was burnt down in two hours on the night of 9 December. The theatre had staged spectacular productions. In 1620 the presentation of *Dr Faustus* had included 'Shagg-hayr'd Deuills [which] runne roaring ouer the Stage with Squibs in their mouthes, while Drummers make Thunder in the Tyring-house, and the twelue-penny Hirelings make artificiall Lightning in the Heauens'.

EMBANKING DAGENHAM

Very high tides on the Thames were a constant worry. As can be seen from the Visscher view of 1616, London was not embanked and could easily be flooded. Inundations were commonplace – the Calendar of State Papers for 1621 notes that Westminster Hall was yet again swept by water.

Low-lying areas such as the south bank had no defences. But in Dagenham on the north bank, where the marshes were particularly subject to flooding, a positive step was taken with the appointment this year of a Dutch engineer, Cornelius Vermuyden, to stem a breach and to reorganize the defences of the area. His work at Dagenham was successful enough to land him the contract to drain Windsor Great Park, even though the commissioners who employed him complained that the works were ineffective and the inhabitants said that the water levels were as dangerous as ever. The 62 workmen engaged at Dagenham petitioned the government that their wages had been withheld. Vermuyden retorted that he had not been paid by the commissioners, and by 1623 they were reporting that the county of Essex was not happy with the work and refused to sanction payment.

1622

NEW BANQUETING HOUSE OPENED

The new Banqueting House in Whitehall – the building which survives today – was begun in June 1619 and completed on 31 March this year, though the ceilings by Rubens were not installed until 1635.

This plain, Palladian building, set among the red-brick Tudor architecture of Whitehall Palace, must have been a remarkable innovation. It is one of the landmarks of English architecture. Built in the shape of a double cube, measuring 110 ft long, 55 ft high and 55 ft wide, it is said to have been the first building in London to use Portland stone, and indeed the construction accounts include an amount of over £700 for the building of a pier on the Isle of Portland for the loading of stone for London. The opening event, *The Masque of Augurs*, was performed by Prince Charles and members of the court and staged by the building's architect, Inigo Jones. Once the painted ceiling by Rubens had been completed, masques were relegated to a nearby wooden building.

When the ceilings were being cleaned in 1832, the antiquarian John Thomas Smith, taking advantage of the scaffold to examine them, calculated that the children in the paintings were 9 ft high and the full-grown figures between 20 and 25 ft. The pictures, commissioned by Charles I, depict the apotheosis of James I, the union of the Crowns of Scotland and England, and quite clearly indicate that the king reigned by divine right. Adherence to this concept helped to bring about Charles's execution outside this very building in 1649.

TOO MANY COACHES

According to Stow, the first coach seen in London, in 1555, belonged to the earl of Rutland, and its manufacturer then made one for the queens Mary and Elizabeth. Certainly coaches were late into London – they were much more common on the Continent. When they did come, of course, they caused considerable congestion in the London streets and unemployment for the watermen. John Taylor, the 'water-poet', writing in 1622, bemoaned the poor circumstances of the men, already impoverished by the reduction of the navy. He wrote:

Carroaches, coaches, jades and Flanders mares
Do rob us of our shares, our wares, our fares;
Against the ground we stand and knock our heeles,
Whilst all our profit runs away on wheels.

1623

THE 'FATAL VESPERS' AT BLACKFRIARS

At a house in Blackfriars occupied by the French ambassador, a service was held in an upper room on 26 October. It is reported that 300 people were present and the floor, unable to take the weight, collapsed. Ninety-four people and the preacher died, and many were badly injured. The disaster was judged an act of God by Protestants, and a Protestant plot by Catholics.

LINCOLN'S INN CHAPEL BUILT

The present chapel of Lincoln's Inn was consecrated this year by the poet and clergyman John Donne. The building has, like so many of this period, been attributed to Inigo Jones, but more likely it was by John Clarke. Underneath was an undercroft intended for students 'to walk in and talk and confer their learnings'.

WESTMINSTER OPENS A PRISON

This year Westminster opened a house of correction by Tothill Fields, to the south of Horseferry Road. A Richard Betts, hempdresser, was appointed supervisor, living above the prison; he provided hemp and set the convicts to work on it. He was contracted to 'find and provide diett and lodging for all such prisoners as shal bee from time to time to him Comitted being above the age of 12 years by anie of H.M. Justices of the Peace'.

A CRASH OF STEEPLE

The parish church of St James, Clerkenwell, was the old choir of the former Benedictine nunnery. This year the steeple collapsed while it was being repaired, and with it fell the bells, 'their carriages and frames beating a great part of the roof down before them, the weight of all these together bearing to the ground two large pillars of the south aisle, a fair gallery over against the Pulpit, the Pulpit, all the Pews and whatsoever was under or near it'.

FORTUNE THEATRE REOPENS

The Fortune Theatre in Golden Lane was reopened. The previous building, burnt down in 1621, was square-shaped and made of lath and plaster, but the new building was round and built of brick and tile. But ill fortune dogged the theatre. The king died early in 1625 and mourning was obligatory, and then the plague returned to London.

1624

BAPTISTS IN LONDON

The Baptist sect was founded by John Smyth, a former clergyman of the Church of England in the reign of James I, who, from the safety of Amsterdam, declared the Baptists' two main principles: that baptism was for believers and not for infants, and that all new members were received into the church with a confession of faith. It was not until 1689 that Baptists were free to worship unhindered.

The first Baptist church appears to have been formed in 1612, close to the Artillery Ground by Moorfields, though other authorities suggest that it might have been at Newgate. The second church was opened in 1624 in Deptford. What is considered to be the first church of the Particular Baptists – a breakaway sect from the General Baptists – was opened on 12 September 1633 in Old Gravel Lane, Wapping. In 1909 the congregation moved to Walthamstow.

1625

THE PENULTIMATE GREAT PLAGUE

Just as the accession of James I was marred by a virulent plague in London, so was that of his son Charles. It was a miserable year for Londoners altogether. The Thames flooded even more than usual in March, when the highest tide ever known put Westminster Hall under 3 ft of water and presumably did considerable damage elsewhere. King James died on 25 March at Theobalds, thereby plunging court and London into mourning; he was buried at Westminster Abbey on 5 May.

The first signs of the plague were recognized in April, and the authorities implemented the required measures, with which they were by now wearily familiar. By the end of the year 35,417 plague deaths had been recorded, nearly half of them in August. During this Charles arrived from Hampton Court with his new bride, Henrietta Maria, on 13 June, and was welcomed by bonfires and incessant bell-ringing. But the celebrations were only a respite. Gripped by plague, London's trade shut up shop, markets were moved outside, and people were forbidden to go near any of the royal residences and were urged to stay within the capital and not take the infection outside. John Donne wrote, 'The citizens fled away as out of a house on fire'; they 'stuffed their pockets with their best ware and threw themselves into the highways, and were not received so much as into barns, and perished so, some of them with more money about them than would have bought the village where they died.' Castigated though they were, aldermen, clergymen, parish officials and other people of authority also fled.

By winter the plague was gone again.

CATHOLIC CHAPEL AT ST JAMES'S

In 1623 the proposed bride for Prince Charles had been the Spanish infanta. The match had fallen through, but during the lengthy (and unpopular) negotiations Inigo Jones had begun work on the construction of a Catholic chapel in St James's Palace for the use of the infanta and her household. By the time of its completion the bride had changed but the religion had not, and the Queen's Chapel, as it was called, was used by Henrietta Maria.

1626

BERKSHIRE HOUSE BUILT

Berkshire House was begun this year in today's Cleveland Row, opposite the western end of St James's Palace. It was built for Thomas Howard, earl of Berkshire, though his residence in it was brief. He retired abroad when the royalists were defeated in the Civil War, and by 1654 the Portuguese ambassador was living there; at that time the house was described as having 45 chimneys to sweep. In 1668 it was bought by Charles II for his mistress Barbara Villiers, later duchess of Cleveland, whose title was then given to the house.

A GATEWAY TO THE THAMES

Off the bottom of Villiers Street, by the side of Charing Cross station, is Watergate Walk, in which survives York Watergate. This reminds us, first, that the river was much wider than it is now and, second, that in this location stood York House. The street names here, which were adopted as a condition for the demolition of the house and the redevelopment of the site in the 1670s, denote a previous owner and his son, George Villiers, duke of Buckingham — even the word 'of' was at one time commemorated in the name of an alley. His widow retained the house after his murder in 1628.

The watergate, which led down to the river landing stage, was erected in 1626 and designed by Nicholas Stone. The Villiers coat of arms is on the river side.

PORTENTS AT THE CORONATION

The coronation of Charles I did not pass off without hitch or adverse comment. His Catholic queen declined to be part of the ceremony and did not even attend; there was no procession, which was galling to the spectacle-loving Londoners; the royal barge fouled the landing stage and ran aground at Parliament Stairs, so that the king had to come ashore in an undignified way in another boat. As a further portent of evil times ahead, a slight earthquake occurred in the London area on the day.

1627

LATYMER SCHOOL FOUNDED

Edward Latymer, a minor Crown official, provided in his will a school in 1624 'to clothe and educate eight poor boys between the ages of 7 and 13'. This began on 1 July 1627 in a building in Fulham churchyard, before moving to a purpose-built school in Hammersmith in 1648.

EXETER HOUSE DAMAGED BY FIRE

Opposite the Savoy in the Strand, a small estate was acquired by Sir William Cecil in the second half of the 16th century. He enlarged one of the houses on the property, and this became Cecil House, and then Burghley House on his elevation to the peerage, and then Exeter House when his elder son, Thomas, became earl of Exeter. Henrietta Maria lodged in this house in 1625 before her marriage to Prince Charles, and she returned here as a widow in 1660, to worship at a chapel specially set aside for her.

Norden described the house, which was extensively damaged by fire this year, as 'a verie fayre howse raysed with brickes, proportionablie adorned with four turrets placed at the four quarters of the howse; within it is curiouslye bewtified with rare devises, and especially the oratory, placed in an angle of the great chamber'. Another writer remarks that Cecil had 'fourscore persons in family, exclusive of those who attended him at court'. His expenses were £30 a week in his absence, and between £40 and £50 when he was present.

Exeter Street and Burleigh Street now recall the house's former existence.

BUILDING OFF ST MARTIN'S LANE

With the building up of St Martin's Lane and Long Acre, it was inevitable that the rest of the land between them and the wall around the Covent Garden estate should be filled in. By this year Bedfordbury, running parallel with St Martin's Lane, was built and a number of alleyways were constructed to link the two roads. Three of these alleys survive today, but only one, Goodwin's Court, retains its early secretiveness.

The area between the two streets later became one of much squalor. In the 19th century it was reported that some courts off Bedfordbury were less than 4 ft wide, and when raising one's elbows one could touch both sides. It was only in 1880 that the worst of the slums in this road were eradicated.

A CONTRIBUTORY INSURANCE

An early example of both employer and employees contributing to an insurance plan is provided by the East India Company's almshouses in Blackwall. These were opened this year with the aid of a bequest and a compulsory levy on wages of employees of the company 'for an hospital or almeshouse for maymed men or releif of orphans or widowes, whose parents dyed in the Companies Service'. A 'large and convenient bricke house with some three acres of ground thereunto belonging, lyeing in Blackwall' was bought.

1628

TWO HOUSES LOST IN TWO DAYS

Sir Edward Cecil, first Baron Putney and Viscount Wimbledon, had the extreme ill luck to lose two substantial houses in two days this year. The first was his country house at Wimbledon, which was largely destroyed by an accident with gunpowder. The following day his new house on the Strand, Wimbledon House, just east of today's Wellington Street, was destroyed by fire.

Ill fortune dogged Cecil. He was ennobled shortly before leading a particularly inept and disastrous naval expedition against the Spanish in 1625, in which, at a critical moment of attack, it was found that all his soldiers were completely drunk.

CHARTER FOR PLAYING-CARD MAKERS

One of the more obscure City livery companies is that for the Makers of Playing Cards. It received a charter this year, so that it might protect itself against the importation of foreign (and inferior) packs, with power to search anywhere for them in England and Wales.

1629

THE TABARD DEMOLISHED

Chaucer's meeting place for pilgrims in Borough High Street, Southwark, the Tabard inn, was demolished about this year. Oddly, the new brick inn built on its site was named the Talbot. The derivation of the original name is a sleeveless jacket, but that of its replacement is unknown. The site of the inn is today marked by Talbot Yard.

FORTY HALL BEGUN

The Cecil family owned much property during the reigns of Elizabeth and James I. They held Theobalds in Hertfordshire before exchanging it for James I's Hatfield; to finance the repair of Hatfield, the king gave Sir Robert Cecil 17 other manors, one of which, Worcesters, in Enfield, Cecil sold to Nicholas Rainton in 1616.

In 1629 Rainton began building Forty Hall on his estate here. Much of it survives (though damaged in a recent fire) as a local museum. Three storeys high and six bays wide, it is another of those houses attributed to Inigo Jones, but there is no evidence for his involvement.

Inigo Jones, creator of Covent Garden and the Queen's House.

SALISBURY COURT THEATRE OPENS

West of St Bride's church in Fleet Street stood the old house of the bishop of Salisbury. This year two actors opened the Salisbury Court Theatre in the barn belonging to the house. It was used by the leading companies of the time, and continued in operation, even when illegal, until its demolition in 1649.

1630

COCKPIT-IN-COURT OPENS

Despite, or perhaps in spite of, the growing puritanism, a new theatre was begun in Whitehall this year, for the pleasure of the king and his court. The building, designed by Inigo Jones, was octagonal within a square shell, and was on the site of the cockpit-cum-theatre erected by Henry VIII; its remains, if any, are now beneath the parade ground of the Horse Guards. The building accounts show that it was of two storeys, contained 20 Corinthian columns, and was decorated in the Palladian manner. The ceiling of calico was painted blue with silver stars.

NEW VILLAGE CHURCH FOR CHARLTON

Still surviving in Charlton is the church of St Luke, rebuilt about this year at the expense of Sir Adam Newton, the wealthy owner and builder of Charlton House opposite. The church contains a monument to his wife, who died this year, and also the remains of Spencer Perceval, prime minister, assassinated in 1812.

1631

THE BUILDING OF COVENT GARDEN

This year Covent Garden Piazza and its church of St Paul were begun – historically, one of the most important architectural developments in London. They were the consequence of the drive by the 4th Earl of Bedford to develop his agricultural estate, the genius of Inigo Jones, the architect for the scheme, and the encouragement of Charles I, who wished to have a capital of buildings which could rival those of cities on the Continent. The layout and uniformity of the development, and the use of classical styles, were startling innovations to Londoners, who were used to piecemeal developments and indigenous architecture.

Two features particularly distinguished Jones's piazza. One was the church; the other, which has not survived, was the arcaded houses on two sides of the piazza. The first buildings completed (those to each side of the church) would have given curious Londoners no clue to the nature of the finished scheme. They stood as single, unremarkable four-storey premises. But then were built on the north and east sides of the piazza the houses set over public arcades in the Italian manner, so that in good weather and bad the piazza and arcades were places of social intercourse.

There were provided 22 'houses and buildings fitt for the habitacons of Gentlemen and men of ability', in two terraces each cut in two by wide intersecting roads; the principal view of the square was that approached from Russell Street, where, with the church immediately in sight, the northern terrace and the piazza would gradually emerge. The houses were five storeys above ground, the top three extending over the arcade, and at arcade level there were hall and mezzanine floors. The best rooms were at the front of the first floor, which extended over the arcade. There were also substantial basements and cellars projecting considerably beyond the house line.

Oddly, there was no adornment, such as a fountain or statue, in the square at first. The earl of Bedford had promised to provide

St Paul, Covent Garden. Originally, the main exit was to be from the east door on to the piazza, but Jones had to locate it at the west end of the church.

'a beautiful Structure' in the centre, but he never did, and there was only a single tree and later a solitary column. The coming of the market precluded any later addition.

St Paul, Covent Garden, was one of the earliest churches built for Protestant worship and the first on a new site. The 4th Earl of Bedford, imaginative entrepreneur though he was, was also reputed to have been mean. Horace Walpole, writing in 1765, published a well-known anecdote about the church's early days. 'When the Earl of Bedford sent for Jones, he told him he wanted a chapel for the parishioners of Coventgarden, but added he "wou'd not go to any considerable expense; in short," said he, "I wou'd not have it much better than a barn." "Well then," replied Jones, "you shall have the handsomest barn in England."' Four simple Tuscan columns, an emphasized pediment and exposed roof eaves make it unique in London. Nowadays, with the market building in front of it, it cannot command the square as it once did – then, too, the piazza level was lower, and there were steps up to the level of the portico columns. Jones originally had the main door of the church on the piazza, but theological convention of the time required the altar at the east end, obliging Jones to keep a sham entrance on the square and to put his door at the west.

The church is a rectangular building, 100 ft by 50 ft, and the interior – not much of which survived a disastrous fire of 1795 – is without division. From its nearness to the theatres it became the 'actors' church', and many actors are buried or commemorated in it or its burial ground.

Other roads were laid out this year. Henrietta Street was begun, though none of its original houses remains. Its early residents tended to be tradesmen, with a sprinkling of titled people; in 1633 the occupiers included shoemakers and four victuallers. Maiden Lane, which occupies the site of an ancient track from Drury Lane, was started, and Bedford Street had residents by 1633 and so presumably was also laid out in 1631. The south side of the piazza was not at first developed, because the wall of the garden at Bedford House was there; neither was there, until the 19th century, a market building of any substance.

NEW CHURCH FOR ST GILES-IN-THE-FIELDS

The bishop of London, William Laud, consecrated the new church of St Giles-in-the-Fields on 23 January. The previous structure had originally been the chapel of the St Giles leper hospital, put entirely to parochial use at the Dissolution, when it was in a very decayed state. In contrast to the simplicity of St Paul, Covent Garden, the new St Giles was not a complete break with the past, since we find that the Puritans later washed 'the twelve apostles off the organ loft'. This new building lasted 100 years.

A CHAPEL OF EASE FOR HAMMERSMITH

Churchgoers in Hammersmith had to make a long trek to All Saints, Fulham, to worship. On 7 June this year a chapel of ease was consecrated on the site of today's St Paul's, to make this unnecessary for most Sundays of the year.

1632

A NEW CHURCH IN GREAT STANMORE

A new church dedicated to St John the Evangelist was built in Great Stanmore this year at the expense of the immensely rich merchant Sir John Wolstenholme, a member of both the East India Company and the Virginia Company. The building – one of the first brick churches in the country – was declared unsafe in 1845 and the roof was removed. Local opposition prevented its demolition, and the present parish church was erected nearby, leaving Wolstenholme's building an ivy-clad ruin.

UNRULY DEVELOPMENT

The City petitioned the king complaining about the 'multitude of newly erected tenements in Westminster, Strand, Covent Garden, Holborn, St Giles's, Wapping, Ratcliff, Limehouse, Southwark … which had brought great numbers of people from other parts, especially of the poorer sort, and was a great cause of beggars and other loose persons swarming about the City'. The price of food had gone up as a result, there was a great deal more sewage flowing into the Thames, and in the event of plague the City was now so hemmed in by buildings that it would be dangerous for the citizens.

1633

DISASTROUS FIRE ON LONDON BRIDGE

On the night of 11 February, when the Thames was nearly frozen over, a maidservant in a house at the northern extremity of the bridge placed a tub full of hot coal ashes beneath some stairs before going to bed. The house caught fire. The occupants escaped, but the blaze continued on its way across the bridge and, despite the nearness of water, could not be checked. A contemporary Bible-thumper, Nehemiah Wallington, wrote about it in dramatic terms, but he also recorded an interesting list of those who had lost their premises in the blaze. They included numerous grocers, hatters, drapers, glovers and mercers.

A commission set up this year to investigate the rebuilding of those houses destroyed also investigated 'whether it be fit to build the houses again, or to demolish the rest'. The king himself was against the new buildings and did his best to prevent them, and work only proceeded in 1647–8 when he was in no position to prevent it.

RESTORING ST PAUL'S

A commission had also been set up, in the reign of James I, to consider the restoration of St Paul's Cathedral. The building had lost its spire in 1561, had been patched up, but was otherwise in a bad state of repair. Inigo Jones was the most important member of this commission, as dominant in London's architectural history of this period as Wren was to be after him.

Bishop Earle, writing in 1628, complained at the use of the church at that time. The nave, which he describes as 'Paul's Walk', was 'an heape of stones and men, with a vast confusion of languages, and were the steeple not sanctified, nothing liker Babell. The noyse of it is like that of bees, an humming buzze mixed with walking tongues, and feet.' More in the same vein confirms that the church was an important place for traders to do business, for thieves to get pickings, for merchants to get news, and for those who just wanted to have shelter. William Laud, the bishop of London, invited the City to contribute to the church's restoration; one merchant, Sir Paul Pindar, gave £10,000.

Work began this year but did not get very far and was halted in 1634 by the outbreak of the Civil War.

CASTING KING CHARLES

The equestrian statue of Charles I at the top of Whitehall is nowadays the scene of an occasional bizarre ceremony in which modern admirers

Sir Paul Pindar gave handsomely to the restoration of St Paul's Cathedral. His house in Bishopsgate reflected the rise of the wealthy merchant class.

dress in royalist costume to pay homage to his memory. The statue, cast in bronze in 1633, has had a complex history. The sculptor was a Huguenot, Hubert le Sueur, who lived in both Drury Lane and Bartholomew Close. The work was commissioned at a cost of £600 by the lord high treasurer, Lord Weston, who owed much to the king, and was intended for his garden at Roehampton. It is not clear that it ever was set up there, and after the death of Weston it was proposed that it be erected in Covent Garden Piazza instead. This would have been an appropriate site, but national events were in motion that made it impolitic, and after the execution of the king it was unthinkable.

The Commonwealth in 1650 ordered the destruction of statues of the king, but le Sueur's work escaped. It had been concealed in the crypt of St Paul, Covent Garden, and it was not until 1655 that it was found and sold for its brass value to John Rivett, a brazier, who lived near Holborn Conduit. Rivett, although he later sold many articles as souvenirs which were supposedly made from the statue, hid it to wait for happier times. It is not known if Rivett (possibly a Huguenot himself) did this out of friendship for le Sueur and as an expression of royalist sympathy, or if he had seized the chance to make a great deal of money by selling people false souvenirs and then even more by producing the statue later. At any rate, he got the best of both worlds.

Subsequently the statue was set up on the site of the Eleanor Cross, destroyed by the Puritans, at the top of Whitehall.

A Whipping Post at Bridewell

The old palace of Bridewell was now used as a prison and workhouse by City parishes. This year a whipping post for the parishes of St Bride and St Dunstan was erected here in a room to which the public were admitted. A writer describing the room in 1662 was 'almost afrighted at the dismalness of the place'. Its four walls were 'laid all over from top to bottom in black', and 'there stood in the middle of it a great whipping-post, which was all the furniture it had'. A gallery for spectators was installed in 1677, and the whipping post was raised in 1682 'for the better witnessing the correction'.

1634

Getting about London

'Hackney' coaches had been established in London in about 1605, to the detriment of the streets and the dismay of the watermen. John Taylor's lament of the damage done to his colleagues' welfare (see 1622) could not undo the invention. This year saw two developments which worsened the watermen's lot.

Operating from a base near the Strand maypole, one John Bailey introduced a highly successful system of an established place where coaches could be hired at a set rate – in other words, a taxi service. A contemporary writer said that Bailey had

erected according to his ability some four hackney coaches, put his men and appointed them to stand at the Maypole in the Strand, giving them instructions at what rate to carry men into several parts of the town, where all day they may be had. Other hackney men seeing this way they flocked to the same place and performed their journeys at the same rate, so that sometimes there is twenty of them together which disperse up and down, so that they and others are to be had everwhere as watermen are to be had at the waterside. Everyone is much pleased with it.

Everyone, that is, but the authorities, who disliked the congestion, the damage to the primitive road surfaces and the nuisance to pedestrians, since there were no raised pavements. In the following year the use of coaches was restricted to journeys of at least 3 miles, but it is doubtful if this regulation had much effect.

Even more competition for the watermen (and for the coaches) emerged this year in the form of sedan chairs. In September Sir Sanders Duncombe was granted the sole right for 14 years to provide 'covered chairs' for hire and prevent the unnecessary use of coaches. Sedan chairs were, of course, ideal for short trips, but they were also used extensively for long journeys – the wife of the French ambassador went from Edinburgh to London in 1603 in an early version. And once the duke of Buckingham had made them fashionable their numbers increased.

1635

General Post Office Established

The use of the royal mail carriers for public post and, historically, the jurisdiction over the mail by the sovereign began this year. A proclamation was issued 'for settling the letter office of England and Scotland', in which it was enacted that there shall be 'a running post or two, to run night and day, between Edinburgh and Scotland and the City of London, to go thither and come back in six days'. But it was an Act of 1656 which really established the Post Office.

Leicester House Built

Robert Sidney, 2nd earl of Leicester, this year completed a large mansion on the site of today's 7–15 Leicester Square, its rear grounds stretching back to Lisle Street; from him the square derived its name. The form of the house is not known for certain – there are contradictory illustrations – but it was sizeable, despite Leicester's dismissive description of it as a 'little House; which was not built for a Levie, but only for a privat Family'. At that time the front aspect was open, the

1600s

land sloping down to Whitehall. But the house was on common land, and a condition of his licence to build was that Leicester should enclose his property with brick walls and the ground in front was to be 'turned into Walkes and planted with trees alonge the walkes, and fitt spaces left for the Inhabitantes to drye their Clothes there as they were wont'. From this provision the gardens of Leicester Square can be said to descend, though it was necessary in the 19th century to mount a campaign to save them as an open space.

In the event, Leicester hardly lived there. He was posted to Paris in 1636, where he remained for five years, and in 1640 the house was briefly sublet to Sir Thomas Wentworth, 1st earl of Strafford, who was ill at the time and had to be carried around the grounds in a sedan chair. Strafford, however, was so unpopular a figure that the house had to be guarded against rioters, and Leicester was relieved when his tenant moved out the same year. Back in England, Leicester generally lived at Penshurst, and the house was let in 1662 to the queen of Bohemia – as will be seen later, it was a residence quite often occupied by members of the royal family in the 18th century. John Evelyn dined here in 1672. They were entertained by a fire-eater 'who before us devour *Brimston* on glowing coales, chewing and swallowing them downe'.

An Academy in Bedford Street

One of the first buildings to be occupied in the newly laid-out Bedford Street, Covent Garden, was the Musaeum Minervae, an academy opposite the churchyard gates. It was a short-lived enterprise, directed by the poet and courtier Sir Francis Kynaston, in which noblemen and young gentlemen were educated 'in armes and artes and all generous qualities'. It was stressed in Kynaston's appeal for financial support that it would be best to teach young men these skills in this country rather than send them abroad or import foreign teachers. But he was very anxious about failure – and indeed appears to have been of a nervous disposition altogether, for an acquaintance noted that Kynaston was cupbearer to the king but trembled so much that he had to resign the office.

The curriculum emphasized the martial arts, but other subjects studied included mathematics, philosophy, medicine, music, astronomy, languages and geometry. In February 1636 a masque was performed here for an audience which included the king's three children. But by 1637 the Musaeum appears to have gone – a collapse, it is thought, which was the result of overambition on Kynaston's part coupled with a lack of financial endowment.

Death of 'Old Parr'

The death occurred this year of Thomas Parr, who, in those days before registration of births, was said to have been born about 1483. Legend and John Taylor, the 'water-poet', assert that Parr married for the first time at the age of 80 and had two children, both of whom died in infancy. In 1588, then about 105 years old, he was obliged to do penance in a white sheet in his local village for having fathered an illegitimate child, and when he was 122 he married again.

In 1635 he was 'discovered' by Thomas Howard, 2nd earl of Arundel, a keen curiosity-seeker, who carted him off to London in a litter to see the king. Parr told Charles I that he remembered the monasteries and had lived under ten kings and queens; furthermore, he said, quite wisely, that it was safest to be of the religion of the king or queen of the day. He was exhibited at the Queen's Head in the Strand, but did not long survive his notoriety. He died at Arundel's house, and William Harvey, the discoverer of the circulatory system, did an autopsy at which he declared Parr's organs to be in singularly good condition.

Parr was buried in Westminster Abbey. He left no children, but a good many public houses are still named after him.

Lambeth Flooded

William Laud, now archbishop of Canterbury, recorded in his diary on 15 November 'At afternoon the greatest Tide that hath been seen. It came within my gates, walks, cloysters, and stables at Lambeth.'

1636

Lock Hospitals

Leper hospitals had been established around London in medieval times (see 1117, 1280, 1473 and 1475). An alternative name for them was 'lock hospitals', possibly derived from the French word 'loques', the term for the rags used for dressing leper sores. The leper hospital in today's Tabard Street, Southwark, was from early times known as the Lock Hospital. Most of the leper hospitals were eventually managed by St Bartholomew's Hospital and, as the disease died out, the buildings were used to house other contagious patients, and especially to treat venereal disease.

The two central-London establishments, those of St Giles and St James, had been closed at the Reformation; Highgate closed in 1653, Mile End in 1589, and Knightsbridge some time after 1708. But other buildings were still being maintained. The Tabard Street hospital, for example, acquired a new chapel this year – the building was being used for the care of incurables and for male patients with venereal disease, while the old leper hospital at Kingsland, in Hackney, received female patients. Both of these buildings were closed in 1760 as being too expensive to run, but by that time a hospital had been established which specialized in venereal disease (see 1746).

1637

The Creation of Richmond Park

Charles I created, about this year, what is now called Richmond Park. It was a major enterprise, which involved the compulsory acquisition of local commons. This land, divided between the (royal) manors of Richmond, Petersham and Ham, the town of Kingston and the manor of Wimbledon (which included Mortlake, Roehampton and Putney), also contained pockets in private ownership, all of which had to be bought up. By April 1635, although only 5 acres had so far been secured, the king had set about the work of enclosuring the entire area with a high brick wall, and by 1637 most of the private landowners had been induced to come to terms by generous compensation.

More Developments in Covent Garden

More roads were completed in Covent Garden. The most stylish, King Street, was let to a mixture of titled people, members of Parliament and tradesmen. Strype, in 1720, noted that it was 'well inhabited and resorted unto by gentry for lodgings'. Today, none of the earliest houses survives, and not many of the second generation either. Chandos Place, named after the earl of Bedford's father-in-law, was completed. Bow Street did not then open up to Long Acre, nor did it extend to the Strand until 1835 – the way out was via Russell Street. It is thought that the street's name derives from its curved line.

1638

THE PROCESSION OF MARIE DE' MEDICI

At a time when the king was faced with hostility in both England and Scotland for his Catholic sympathies, not to mention his general disregard of Parliament, it was undiplomatic to parade his Catholic mother-in-law, Marie de' Medici, through London this year. However, the occasion has left us with one of the most celebrated views of Cheapside as it was shortly before the Great Fire swept it away. The artist was standing on the south side of Cheapside, roughly on the present intersection with New Change. In the centre of the road to the right is the famous Cheapside Cross, and beyond that the Cheapside Standard (see 1395). The former, decorated with statues of the pope, the Virgin and Child and the Apostles, fell to the Puritans; the latter was destroyed in the Great Fire.

A NEW PLACE FOR MASQUES

It was possibly in an attempt to impress Marie de' Medici that a timber building was erected this year, next to the Banqueting House in Whitehall, for the staging of masques. This was made necessary anyway because after the installation of the Rubens ceiling in the Banqueting House it was agreed that the use of too many candles for theatrical productions was harmful to the paintings. The first production in this new theatre was William Davenant's *Britannia Triumphans*.

The king was still confident enough of his future to inaugurate plans this year for the rebuilding of Whitehall Palace. These – probably by Inigo Jones, but drawn up by his pupil John Webb – show a palace consisting of a series of courts extending to a riverside panorama. Webb was even summoned by the king as late as 1646, when Charles was in captivity, to discuss details.

THE DEVELOPMENT OF LINCOLN'S INN FIELDS

The man responsible for building around the walks of Lincoln's Inn Fields was William Newton, who by 1638 had purchased the land. He pointed out to Charles I that the king received very little rent for the land as it now stood, and asked for permission to build 32 houses – a proposition that he must have known would interest a king short of cash. Though the Society of Lincoln's Inn protested, using the same arguments as before (see 1618), this time it failed and Newton began building straight away. By 1641 the southern side had mostly been erected, together with houses in the Great Queen Street area.

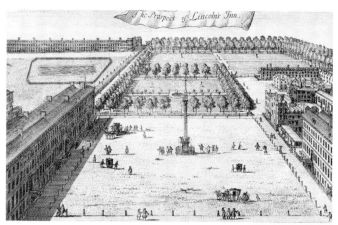

A 1755 view of Lincoln's Inn Fields. Development had begun in 1638 when William Newton was granted permission from Charles I to build 32 houses.

The dispute between Newton and the Society of Lincoln's Inn dragged on for several years. In 1645 the society alleged to a Protestant House of Commons that in his pursuit of 'private lucre' Newton was letting houses to popish sympathizers and that local people were deprived by the building works of the use of the fields. A compromise between Newton and the Society in 1657, virtually ordered by the Commonwealth administration, led to the creation of the open space that we now have.

CROMWELL HOUSE, HIGHGATE, BUILT

One of the outstanding houses of this period left in London is what is now known as Cromwell House, on Highgate Hill. It was built about this year by Sir Richard Sprignell on the site of an older property. Its name does not appear to be contemporary – it is first recorded in 1809. There have been a number of additions since 1638, notably the extension over the carriage arch, and the cupola, but it is still much as it was, including a magnificently carved wooden staircase.

The house was later the home of one of the first Jewish families allowed to settle in the country during the Commonwealth, and when Alvaro Mendes da Costa bought the freehold in 1675 he was the first Jew to own property in London since the Middle Ages. A private synagogue was installed, remains of which were revealed in recent restoration work.

1600s

Cheapside in 1638 welcoming the arrival of Marie de' Medici. The illustration shows houses destroyed by the Great Fire, and the Cheapside Cross and Standard.

TROUBLE IN PICCADILLY

Mary Baker, widow of Robert Baker, who had built 'Piccadilly Hall' (see 1612), had in recent years developed the site she held. She appears frequently in her dealings with authority in this period. In 1636 she and neighbours infected by plague had been shut up in their houses and a guard had been put outside them for four weeks. In 1638 the Court of Star Chamber imposed upon her the enormous fine of £1,000 'for continuing buildings unlawfully erected to the annoyance and putrefaction' of the springs of water which flowed through her ground and supplied the Palace of Whitehall. The court also ordered her to 'pull downe her house [the hall], and Stables in Pickadilla for that the same was conceaved to bee a Nuisance to the Water'.

Mrs Baker did not take such a disaster lying down. She petitioned the Privy Council to be allowed to convey the 'freshe and servicable' waters to Whitehall by a different route in a brick culvert, at her own expense. By June the following year much still remained to be done, but by November Inigo Jones, the king's surveyor-general, was able to report that the work had been done successfully. Demolition of the houses was respited, and Mrs Baker's request for a return of the £1,000 fine was received, but the records reveal no decision in the matter.

RICHARD BUSBY OF WESTMINSTER SCHOOL

The most famous of the celebrated headmasters of Westminster School was Richard Busby; he was appointed in 1638 and died in office in 1695, revered and feared in equal measure.

He took over the school at a difficult time. The previous incumbent, Lambert Osbaldeston, had fallen foul of Archbishop Laud, who had ordered his dismissal, the loss of his prebendaryship at the abbey, a fine of £5,000 and a punishment of being nailed by his ears in a pillory. Osbaldeston got wind of what was in store and disappeared, it was thought to France, but possibly only to a garret in Drury Lane, from where he emerged in 1641 when it was safe to do so.

School records throw light on the battles of the age. In 1641 muskets and powder were bought for use against Puritans, and indeed the following year the scholars resisted a mob which wished to tear down ornaments in the school which did not conform to the new religious fashion. By the 1650s aristocratic pupils were joining those from minor country seats. They must have rued their parents' ambitions for them, as they were absorbed into the routine of rising at six, seven hours in the schoolroom, plus other mind-improving activities afterwards. One mother, a countess, who viewed the school where her son was a pupil in 1690, recorded that 'In the great cold Scoul he sitts the whole day over with out a hatt or cap; and all the windows broke and yet thanks be to God he taks very wel with it tho he never seeth a fir but in my hous.'

The school had a high academic reputation. But Busby was notoriously free with his cane, and probably no boy escaped its punishment. The frequency and ferocity of caning were well known, and a character called Sneer, in Thomas Shadwell's *Virtuoso* (1676), declared that he came to the brothel to be flogged because 'I was so us'd to't at Westminster School, I cou'd never leave it off since'.

PEST HOUSES IN WESTMINSTER

Near to Westminster School – possibly indeed on the space in Vincent Square the scholars now use for sport – were pest houses built in 1638 by Westminster parish for plague sufferers. They were merely wooden sheds with doors crossed with oak. So many victims were interned that the premises were enlarged in 1642, when the churchwardens were instructed to build 'tenne roomes in Tuthill ffeilds for Pesthouses neere the Shedde now there with Garrettes over'. In course of time, this site became a burial place for plague victims and also for Scottish prisoners taken at the Battle of Worcester, many of whom died here of wounds or privations. Vincent Square is now on the site.

SWAKELEYS BUILT

The mansion called Swakeleys, in Ickenham, was completed this year. It was built, on the site of an older house, for Sir Edmund Wright, lord mayor of London, in red brick with stone and plaster dressings, in an H shape. It has been remarked that the unknown architect 'was aware of the new ideas that Inigo Jones had brought back from Italy to the English court, but was not quite sure of how he should use them, so he did his best'.

Pepys was a visitor here to Sir Robert Vyner, another lord mayor, in 1665. He records in his diary:

He [Vyner] took us up and down with great respect, and showed us all his house and grounds; and it is a place not very moderne in the garden or house, but the most uniforme in all that ever I saw; and some things to excess ... The window-cases, door-cases, and chimneys of all the house are marble. He showed me a black boy that he had, that died of consumption, and being dead, he caused him to be dried in an oven, and lies there entire in a box.

1639

RIOT AT MARSHALSEA

The Marshalsea prison stood off Borough High Street, south of Axe and Bottle Court. It was of medieval origin and had a formidable reputation for its ill treatment of prisoners. The keeper in 1381, when it was attacked by Wat Tyler's followers, was described as a 'tormentor without pity', and in 1504 a riot and breakout occurred in protest against the conditions. The prison's original purpose was to house those who had offended against the king's authority – Bishop Bonner was imprisoned here twice 'in the most vile dungeon', and during the second spell, in 1569, he died. By Victorian times, when it was demolished, it was primarily used for debtors, including the father of Charles Dickens.

In 1639 there was another riot, in which warders were attacked. It was alleged that conditions were so bad there that 23 women were confined to one room, without the space to lie down.

1640

STEPS TO WAR

Parliament had not met for 11 years, and the king's efforts to raise money and to suppress a rebellion in Scotland had been met with open hostility in London. A new assembly, known to history as the Short Parliament, was opened on 13 April and dissolved on 5 May without the king obtaining the financial help he wanted. The City had been approached for a loan of £100,000, but showed no willingness to find it. On 7 May the mayor and aldermen were told that the king's demand was now £200,000, and if that were not forthcoming then £300,000 would be needed. On 10 May the City replied that it was not prepared to help in the matter, nor to supply a list of the wealthier men in the wards. The king's adviser, Strafford, urged that a few aldermen be hanged; instead, four were imprisoned.

Lambeth Palace in 1647. It was this building that the mob was incited to destroy, in 1640, as revenge against Archbishop Laud. Laud had already fled.

The City was already in ferment. A notice had been posted at the Royal Exchange on 9 May which incited the London apprentices to demolish Archbishop Laud's palace at Lambeth. On the 11th, as Laud recorded in a letter, his 'house was beset at midnight, with 500 people that came thither with a drumme beatinge before them. I had some little notice of it about 2 hours before, and went to White Hall leaving mye house as well ordered as I could with such armes and men as I could gett readye. And I thanke God, bye his goodness, kept all safe.'

On 9 June the mayor and sheriffs were summoned to attend the king's council to relate why the tax called ship money had not been collected. The mayor replied that he had sent his officers to collect it, but few or none would pay. The king insisted that a new attempt be made, but the sheriffs declined to help the mayor in the task.

The political momentum increased thereafter. The Long Parliament was convened in November and Strafford was immediately impeached, as was Laud in December. The Civil War was beginning.

LINDSEY HOUSE COMPLETED
The only original house in Lincoln's Inn Fields which survives was completed this year. Lindsey House, now nos. 59–60, was built by Sir David Cunningham as a speculation and very soon afterwards was sold for £4,000 to Henry Murray, one of the grooms of the king's bedchamber. The 4th Earl of Lindsey was here early in the 18th century. Although there is no conclusive evidence, it is thought that this house was designed by Inigo Jones.

1641

THE BEGINNINGS OF THE ELEPHANT AND CASTLE
The origins of the famous public house called the Elephant and Castle at its island site in south London derive from this year, when John Flaxman, a blacksmith, was granted a site for a workshop. It was a good place for his business, situated at the junction of roads to Lambeth, Kennington and Camberwell, and 100 years later it had been transformed into a tavern known by every coach driver (and later still by every tram crew) for whom it was a terminus.

The fanciful explanation of its name is that it is a corruption of that of the infanta de Castille, who was at one time proposed as a wife for Charles I, until a connection of the English Crown with that of Spain became ever more unpopular and impolitic. But the tavern seems not to have been in existence before the middle of the 18th century, and it is most unlikely that it would have been named, so long after a non-event, after a non-person. There are, moreover, several pubs called the Elephant and Castle in London – one nearby at Vauxhall, for example.

The most likely explanation is an association with the Cutlers' Company, whose insignia features an elephant with a castle; or else it is the depiction of a chess piece, frequently carved as an elephant with a castle on its back.

THE EXECUTION OF STRAFFORD
The trial of the king's most able and unpopular minister, Lord Strafford, began in Westminster Hall on 22 March. He had many enemies, both personal and political, but the chief complaint about him as recorded by the Commons was that he was attempting to alter the constitution from that of a limited monarchy to that of an absolute monarchy. The king told both houses that he could not in conscience condemn Strafford of high treason and suggested that misdemeanour be substituted as a charge. An armed mob, led by a Puritan divine called Burgess, gathered at Westminster demanding the impeachment of the prisoner, and the Commons (which suspected that the king was planning to subjugate its authority altogether) needed a decisive execution. Revelation that the king was planning to free Strafford from the Tower in an armed coup hastened the peer's death.

Popular pressure obliged the king to accede to the execution of 'Tom the Tyrant', and it was estimated that a crowd of 200,000 went to see the deed done. Strafford went to his death on Tower Hill with great dignity on 12 May, passing a window where the imprisoned Laud could see him go by; the archbishop raised his hands in blessing and then fainted.

INIGO JONES IN TROUBLE
The church of St Gregory by Paul's was a small church actually adjoining the cathedral at the south-west end – it was used extensively for services while St Paul's was being repaired. However, it was

inconveniently in the way of the new portico that Inigo Jones intended to erect at the west door, and he began to demolish the little church. This so infuriated its small band of parishioners that he was made to put the stones back again.

Eventually St Gregory's (named after Pope Gregory the Great) was destroyed in the Great Fire and not replaced.

1642

THE CIVIL WAR BEGINS

By the end of 1641 antagonism between king and Commons was near to armed conflict. It was important for Charles to have the City in his pocket, and he went so far as to grant honours to those of his supporters who, at that time, ruled London. But in the elections for Common Council held in October that year the Puritan faction won the day, leaving the mayor and the Court of Aldermen to side with the king and the Lords. A move by the king to instal 'a debauched ruffian' as lieutenant of the Tower in place of the popular Sir William Balfour was a pre-emptive but much disliked gambit. On 26 December the new mayor informed the king that unless the new lieutenant was removed he could not answer for the peace of the City; the king acquiesced. Meanwhile, clashes took place on 27 December between London apprentices and the army at Westminster. The officers drew their swords and drove the close-cropped apprentices, or 'roundheads' as they were disparagingly called, back up Whitehall.

High drama was to come when Parliament assembled on 3 January. Charles ordered the arrest of five leading members of the Commons for treason; on the 4th, having taken a coach along Whitehall, surrounded by loyal redcoats and preceded by rumour, the king appeared at the Commons himself and demanded that the five be given up, though, as he realized himself on looking round, they were not there. The next day the king went to the City, where he suspected the mem-

bers were in hiding, and demanded of the Common Council that they should be found. Turmoil then ensued as the two factions in the council shouted their loyalty to either Parliament or king. Once the king had left, the City put in hand defences against the army, each alderman being in charge of a section of trained bands.

On 10 January Charles unwisely left London, leaving the missing members to emerge and arrive at Westminster in triumph by river from the City. On the streets of London and Westminster, Parliament reigned, though the Tower still remained loyal to the king.

Sir Richard Gurney, the pro-royalist mayor, was impeached by the Commons, sentenced to prison, and discharged from his office. On orders from Parliament, the City elected a new mayor – this time a Puritan – though it was found impossible to retrieve from Gurney the insignia of office. On 22 August Charles set up his standard at Nottingham and the Civil War began in earnest.

By the time of the inconclusive Battle of Edgehill in October the royalist cause was in better shape. Outside the hothouse of London, provincial people were less inclined to care about the dignity of Parliament, if they cared at all. At Edgehill the forces were even and so were the rewards, and in the short hiatus which followed Charles set up his headquarters at Oxford, there to threaten the key area, the Thames valley. A minor engagement then took place in Brentford, commemorated today by a neglected plaque; the king held Kingston bridge for five days in November, and then Parliament assembled 20,000 men at Turnham Green, but the king declined to fight.

THE FORTIFICATION OF LONDON

The City, of course, was protected by its wall, though London, and with it the area supporting Parliament, was by then substantially larger than the old Roman square mile. Both sides knew that success would require the possession of London, and as soon as hostilities began the fortification of the area started. In October the Committee for Militia, responsible for the organization of the war, ordered the building of trenches and ramparts near the main roads out of London, such as

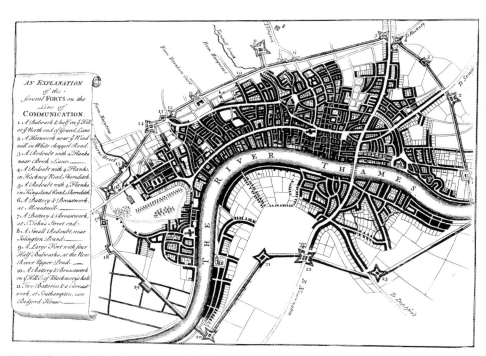

The plan for fortifying London against royalist forces. This quickly constructed system was never tested in battle.

those at Islington, St Pancras and Mile End. The Venetian ambassador wrote home and described the frantic activity:

They do not cease to provide with energy for the defence of London. There is no street, however little frequented, that is not barricaded with heavy chains, and every post is guarded by numerous squadrons. At the approaches to London they are putting up trenches and small forts of earthworks at which a great number of people are at work, including the women and little children.

The immediate defences were consolidated in 1643, when the Common Council introduced a more comprehensive scheme, which today may be traced from its description. It consisted of 18 miles of trenches, connecting 24 forts and redoubts. We read of defences at Whitechapel windmills, redoubts between them and Shoreditch, a battery and breastwork at Islington windmill and a redoubt at the nearby pound, two batteries and breastwork at Southampton House (by itself in fields in Bloomsbury), and other works at St Giles, at Goring's House (the site of Buckingham Palace), at Hyde Park and at Tothill Fields. This line of defences on the northern bank was complemented by another on the south, running through Vauxhall, St George's Fields and Southwark all the way to a place called Redriff Port opposite Wapping.

Building these fortifications was work that engaged Londoners' enthusiasm. In May 1643, for example, 'the whole company of gentlemen Vintners went out with their wives, servants and wine porters. On Thursday the Shoemakers of London took 4,000 and all the inhabitants of St Clement Danes. On Friday at least 9,000 men, women and children of St Giles-in-the-Fields, Queen Street and other parts there about.' Those belonging to Parliament and the Inns of Court were mustered in Covent Garden Piazza at seven one morning with 'spades, shovels, pickaxes and other necessaries', and fishwives marched from Billingsgate through Cheapside to Crabtree Fields to help – described as 'the goddess Bellona leading them in a martial way'.

THEATRES SUPPRESSED

Parliament this year closed the London playhouses, on the ground that 'public sports do not well agree with public calamities, nor public stage plays with the seasons of humiliation'. So for some years the genius of Shakespeare, Marlowe and Jonson went unstaged, grouped together with bearpits, bishops and maypoles as bad influences. An ordinance of 1647 was even more severe – issued, no doubt, because the 1642 proclamation had been disobeyed by some. Magistrates were empowered to enter houses where performances took place, and to order the destruction of stages and seats. Theatre, like unofficial religious views, went underground, to return only with Charles II.

BROADWAY CHAPEL BUILT

What was then called Tothill Fields Chapel or New Chapel was completed this year on the north side of today's Victoria Street, opposite Strutton Ground. The open space at that site now is the last vestige of its burial ground, which stretched up to Caxton Street. Victoria Street did not exist then, and Strutton Ground continued up to Broadway. To the south of the chapel was an artillery ground, which later was taken by a brewery.

A PRISON AT WINCHESTER HOUSE

The bishop of Winchester's London palace stood on the ground now occupied by Stoney Street and the eastern part of Clink Street, in Southwark. It had a great hall about 80 ft long, a long river frontage

and substantial parkland. The last bishop to use it appears to have been Lancelot Andrewes, who died in office in 1626, although part of the building was by then let out in tenements. In 1642, with the suppression of the episcopacy, the House of Lords agreed that it should be converted into a temporary prison – notable royalists were the first inhabitants – and a man with the extraordinary name of Joseph Zin Zan took part of the building for a riding school the following year.

To the west of the house a prison already existed, owned by the bishop of Winchester. This jail, the Clink, has become synonymous with prisons of ill repute (and is even exploited today in a commercial exhibition at the site), but it was a small jail of no particular significance. Its main function was to hold people for offences in the local brothels, bearpits, theatres and taverns.

1643

DEMOLITION OF THE CROSSES

Parliament set about the systematic removal of idolatry in churches and the streets. Three of the more famous crosses in London were this year demolished. One was Paul's Cross, at the eastern end of St Paul's churchyard, a venue for sermons and political speeches – an early form of Speakers' Corner. Spital Cross in Bishopsgate was also removed, although after the Restoration 'Spital' sermons were resumed, but in St Bride's, Fleet Street. Cheapside Cross, whose last form we saw in 1638, was taken down: 'The 2 of May, 1643, the Crosse in Cheapside was pulled downe, a troope of horse and two companies of foote wayted to garde it, and at the fall of the tope crosse dromes beat, trumpets blew, and multitudes of capes wayre throwne in the ayre, and a great shoute of people with joy.'

A FRACAS AT ST MARY'S

At St Mary-at-Lambeth a parliamentarian soldier was rebuked from the pulpit for sitting there with his hat on. A fight developed in which the soldiers present were ejected from the church by the local watermen, at the expense of the life of one waterman.

THE CAMPDEN CHARITY ESTABLISHED

The widow of Sir Baptist Hicks, builder of the first Middlesex Sessions House and later created Viscount Campden, left in her will this year a sum of money to be devoted to the poor of Hampstead. This charity, which then derived an income from land in Childs Hill, still survives, joined together with the Wells Trust, formed at the end of the 17th century to exploit the lands and spa water around today's Well Walk, Hampstead.

1644

THE END OF THE GLOBE

The most celebrated theatre in London, the Globe in Southwark, was demolished by its owner, Sir Matthew Brand, on 15 April, and houses were built on its site.

LILLY'S ALMANAC

William Lilly, astrologer, first published his celebrated almanac this year. A man of leisure since marrying the widow of his former employer, Lilly, son of a Nottinghamshire farmer, first became interested in astrology in 1632, when he was introduced to an astrologer called Evans, who lived in Gunpowder Alley. The credulity of the time ensured that Lilly should still be successful despite failed predictions, a recycling of other men's work and a general lack of originality in his own. For example, in the troubled year of 1644 he foresaw 'a troubled and divided court, an afflicted kingdom, a city neere a plague, and Ireland falling into discontent'. It required no astrologer to tell the nation that. He had, however, to tread carefully, since his predictions were acceptable only if they appealed to the ruling party of the time; a parliamentarian supporter during the Civil War, he found himself in trouble at the Restoration.

GRAND HOUSES IN ALDERSGATE

Aldersgate Street was, for London, a wide street – and still is. A writer in 1657 recorded:

This street resembleth an Italian street more than any other in London, by reason of the spaciousness and uniformity of buildings, and straightness thereof, with the convenient distance of the houses; on both sides whereof there are divers fair ones, as Peter House, the palace now and mansion of the most noble Marquess of Dorchester. Then is there the Earl of Thanet's house with the Moon and Sun tavern.

Dorchester, ennobled by Charles I for his opposition to Parliament, prudently used his original title of earl of Kingston during the Commonwealth, and spent much of his time at another very large house he owned at the top of Highgate West Hill, where he devoted himself to academic studies. (This was roughly on the site of today's mansion called Witanhurst.) In the meantime his Aldersgate residence was used as a prison – the royalist poet Richard Lovelace was held there in 1648.

Thanet House was built in 1644 by Inigo Jones for the earl of Thanet, on a site now covered by Ironmongers' Hall and the Museum of London. By 1734 it was a tavern, and from 1750 until 1771 it was occupied by the London Lying-in Hospital.

STRAND MAYPOLE DEMOLISHED

The coach drivers who used the Strand maypole as a hiring place found themselves without a marker this year when the Puritans ordered the maypole's demolition as being redolent of the old religion or pagan. It was not replaced until the Restoration.

1645

EXECUTION OF ARCHBISHOP LAUD

The archbishop of Canterbury, William Laud, appointed in 1633, had been one of the king's most consistent supporters, and with the Civil War raging it was perhaps inevitable that Parliament should demand his life. He was conservative in his religious beliefs, and unwilling to acknowledge Christian belief in England beyond the official episcopal Church of England. He had no sympathy with people who wished to interpret the Gospels for themselves. He responded to any opposition severely where he could. Just as importantly, his management of ecclesiastical affairs led many people to suspect that he intended a reunion with the Catholic Church. He insisted on a strict arrangement in churches, including the positioning of the communion table at the

east end (which led to the rearrangement of the new church of St Paul, Covent Garden – see 1631).

His position became weaker as the king's own situation became dangerous, and in December 1640 Parliament impeached him, and the following year imprisoned him in the Tower. It was not until 1644 that he was actually brought to trial, and by then Parliament was in no mood to give him a fair one. In 1645 he was sentenced to death, although the Commons reluctantly agreed that he should be beheaded rather than suffer the usual barbaric punishment for treason. He was executed on Tower Hill on 10 January.

1646

COVENT GARDEN A SEPARATE PARISH

Some time elapsed between finishing building work and the consecration of the new church of St Paul, Covent Garden. It was the hope of the earl of Bedford, and the wish of the Privy Council, that it should have its own parish, but national events prevented the necessary legislation. The Act was passed in January this year, but, in the prevailing circumstances, it could not receive the royal assent. It was not until the very end of 1660, at the Restoration, that Covent Garden was officially made a parish.

1647

APPRENTICE POWER

The physical clout of the London apprentices was not to be underestimated. They had played a significant part in the flight of the king from his capital, and they continued to flex their muscles in the face of Parliament. They also, as Parliament found, formed a pool of able recruits to its army.

Under the Puritan regime the holidays usually celebrated by the apprentices and on which it was customary for them to get drunk and riot, such as Shrove Tuesday, were abolished. In 1647 the apprentices petitioned Parliament to replace their former holidays with others, otherwise they would be tempted to use the Sabbath. In April they marched from Covent Garden to Westminster to urge their case, and in June they threatened a mass meeting. Parliament caved in and granted them the second Tuesday of each month.

Their actions were not restricted to such self-interest. One faction of the apprentices was hostile to the Presbyterian attempt in the Commons to cut Parliament's own army down to size; another urged that the king be protected, that the army be paid fully and then disbanded, but that Parliament's rights be upheld.

On 21 July a gathering of apprentices, watermen and others took place at Skinners' Hall and pledged to procure the king's restoration on the terms he had already proposed: the abandonment of the episcopacy for three years and of the militia for ten. The last demand incensed the army, and on 24 July Parliament denounced the apprentices in a declaration. In a few days the army, having gathered at Hounslow, marched on London and took control.

CHARING CROSS DEMOLISHED

The largest and most beautiful of the Eleanor crosses, Charing Cross, standing at the top of Whitehall, was this year demolished by the

Puritans – its stone was used for paving. After the Restoration, the site was used for the execution of eight regicides, who were made to face the Banqueting House where Charles I had been executed, and here the statue of the king was later erected (see 1633).

SALISBURY COURT THEATRE RAIDED

Despite regulations forbidding theatrical performances, some plays did see the light of day, as evidenced by the fact that soldiers broke into a production of Beaumont and Fletcher's *A King and No King* at the Salisbury Court Theatre, off Fleet Street, this year.

1648

THE BATTLE OF SURBITON

In May 1646 Charles I had been taken prisoner by the Scots, who handed him over to the parliamentarian forces; then in 1647 he was captured by elements in the army who were alarmed that he might conclude a deal with Parliament and was imprisoned at Hampton Court. Though the king had lost the war, he now spent his time dividing the victors in the hope of winning the peace.

The army was full of men who were disaffected either because they were unpaid or because they felt betrayed, and their depredations of the countryside enraged Parliament's supporters. On 9 April a large demonstration took place in London urging the restoration of the king and the country's laws; this was broken up in the Strand, but on 4 May a petition from the people of Essex asked for the same things. On 16 May the gentry and farmers of Surrey also converged on London with a petition, and they were permitted by the City to take it to Westminster. The presentation, however, was marred by an argument with soldiers guarding the House of Commons, and a riot ensued in which eight petitioners and one soldier were killed.

Feeling against the army, and Parliament its supporter, ran high everywhere in the country, and this incident made things worse. Henry Rich, earl of Holland, was the king's choice to take advantage of the mood of the country and foment a London uprising. Rich, however, was inept, and the government was well aware of his plans – especially of his bid to capitalize on the Surrey discontent. On the night of 4 July about 100 royalists left London on horseback and joined with others at Kingston. Here, on the 5th, a force of about 500 assembled, but this was swiftly scuttled by a vastly inferior force of the army. Rich led his men around the southern outskirts of London, with seemingly little plan, enduring various skirmishes in the areas of Reigate, Ewell and Dorking. The matter came to a proper battle on Surbiton Common, where Rich was decidedly routed.

The revolt was a debacle, and London did not rise. It was probably the king's last chance.

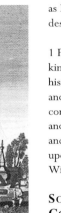

St Pancras church, which continued to attract Roman Catholics after the Reformation.

1649

EXECUTION AT THE BANQUETING HOUSE

Before daybreak on the morning of 30 January the king – now at St James's Palace – rose, dressed warmly, and took his last communion in the Chapel Royal. Later, accompanied by parliamentarian forces and with a few friends, he walked across St James's Park, entered Whitehall through the Holbein Gate, and then went to the Privy Gallery. His execution was to be at two in the afternoon, and it was to be in full view of a large crowd, on a scaffold reached from one of the windows of the Banqueting House in Whitehall (there is some uncertainty as to which window).

From all accounts he went to his death bravely. His words to the crowd were confused, but he firmly laid his head on the block and spread his arms when ready. The executioner, heavily disguised and still unidentified, severed his head with one blow and held it up to view with the words 'Behold, the head of a traitor.' A spectator recalled 'such a universal grone among the thousands of people who were in sight of it, as it were with one consent, as I never heard before and desire I may not hear again'.

The *Perfect Diurnall* on 1 February recorded that 'The king's head is sowed on, and his corps removed to St James and embalmed, a committee to consider of the time, manner and place of his funeral, by his ancestors but not yet agreed upon.' Later he was buried at Windsor.

SOME LONDON CONSEQUENCES

The execution was carried out in the name of God, but it was not popular. In the City the mayor declined to proclaim the abolition of the monarchy and the House of Lords. For this he was deposed, fined £2,000, and imprisoned in the Tower. It was difficult at this time to find leading citizens prepared to take office, as many preferred to pay a fine and be excused.

Soldiers roamed the City 'plundering and roystering', and rarely a day went by without trouble. In April there was mutiny. A contemporary writer on 26 April recorded:

This night at the Bull in Bishopsgate there has an alarming mutiny broken out in a troop of Whalley's regiment there. Whalley's men are not allotted for Ireland: but they refuse to quit London as they are ordered: they want this and that first: they seize their colours from the Cornet who is lodged at the Bull there. The General and the Lieutenant-General have to hasten thither; quell them; pack them forth on their march; seizing fifteen of them first to be tried by Court-Martial. Tried by instant Court-Marshal, five of them are found guilty, doomed to die, but pardoned; and one of them, Trooper Lockyer, is doomed and not pardoned. Trooper Lockyer is shot in St Paul's Churchyard on the morrow.

Outside London unrest was reported. At St Pancras, in whose churchyard burials still using the liturgy of the Catholic faith were known to take place, a rebellious service was held in June, as reported by a news-sheet:

On Saturday last there was in Pankridge churchyard a great congregation met, and a parson with them that did read the booke of common Prayer all the parts thereof (according to that rubrick) appointed for the day, and prayed for the late Queen of England and her children thus: That God would blesse the Queen, wife to the late King of England, Charles the first, her dread Lord and Soveraigne husband, and to restore the royall issue to their just rights, or wordes to that purpose.

Most playhouses had already closed, but in March the zealots destroyed the Salisbury Court Theatre, off Fleet Street. This was not reopened until 1660 (q.v.).

The property of the Crown and some of that of the bishops was taken by the Commonwealth and gradually sold. Manors and houses were quite often purchased by supporters of the parliamentarian cause, such as Sir John Wollaston, who bought the manor of Hornsey in 1647, even before the king was dead. Hornsey included one side of Highgate, a village where the Civil War highlighted the division in the country – or at least division among the upper classes. Wollaston's neighbours in the village included Colonel Ralph Harrison (related to General Thomas Harrison, who was bold enough to offer to execute the king himself), Sir James Harrington (one of those judges who signed the death warrant), John Ireton (brother of the leading Model Army general Henry Ireton) and Sir Richard Sprignell (connected by marriage to the regicide Sir Michael Livesey). But nearby there were John Bill, the king's printer at Kenwood (who was twice fined for supporting the royalist cause), the earl of Lauderdale (who was to come to prominence at the Restoration) and the marquess of Dorchester (who wisely buried his head in his books).

In Richmond, the vast new park which the king had created was given to the City of London as a reward for its loyalty to Parliament; it was returned to the Crown at the Restoration.

1650

GUNPOWDER EXPLOSION AT ALL HALLOWS

On 4 January, at seven in the evening, 27 barrels of gunpowder, stored by a ship's chandler by the wall of All Hallows Barking by the Tower, exploded with devastating force. Fifty houses, including the busy Rose tavern, were destroyed; at least 67 people were killed (because of the force of the explosion, the precise number was difficult to ascertain).

A pamphlet entitled *Death's Master-Peece or A True Relation of that great and sudden Fire in Tower Street, London; which came by the fireing of Gunpowder* says that there were 43 buried who could be identified, and 24 who could not. In his 1720 edition of Stow, John Strype records that the next morning a baby girl was found alive in her cradle on the leads of the church.

QUARTERING SOLDIERS

There were a number of large empty houses in London, many of them the residences of royalists, prudently abroad or in their country seats remaining neutral for the time being, or else with the royalist forces still threatening the new regime. The Interregnum Order Book for 30 November this year orders 'That the house of the Lord Thanett in Aldersgate Street [see 1644], and likewise the house in Pickadilly, bee

both made use of for the quartering of 200 souldiers in each, for which houses a reasonable rent is to be paid, and especially care is to be taken that noe spoil bee done to the said houses by the souldiers.'

1651

HAY'S WHARF BEGINS

This year Alexander Hay took over the lease of a brewhouse from the City, on the south bank of the river, between London Bridge and Tower Bridge. Within five years he appears to have been using his premises as a warehouse, specializing in providing storage for elm-tree trunks used for water pipes by water companies, particularly the New River. From this developed one of the largest warehouse wharfs in London, which in the 19th century pioneered cold-storage facilities. The interesting 1931 version, designed by H. S. Goodhart-Rendel, has in recent times been redeveloped into an attractive office complex.

WAR PRECAUTIONS

It was as well to remind Londoners that they were on the side of Parliament in the Civil War. An effective way was to review the available local troops, and on 25 August this year the Speaker of the House of Commons reviewed 14,000 of the trained bands of the City and Westminster on Tothill Fields.

DEPTFORD FLOODED

The Thames flooded Deptford on New Year's Day when, at 2 p.m., during a violent storm, the water forced down embankments and entered the shipping yards, setting afloat great tree trunks stored for shipbuilding and 'baulks of timber that twenty horses could scarcely move'. In half an hour there was 7 ft of water in the lower part of town, and soon it was 10 ft deep. Those residents who hadn't fled to higher ground were rescued from rooftops and upper windows, but about four o'clock the waters began to abate, leaving immense damage behind them, including 200 cattle dead in the meadows.

1652

THE FIRST COFFEE HOUSE

It is ironic that in the rather joyless days of the Commonwealth the coffee house, the most convivial of places for at least the next 100 years, began in London this year. Two stories exist about the original establishment, but both agree that it was in St Michael's Alley, off Cornhill.

One story is that a Mr Edwards, a Smyrna merchant, brought home with him a servant called Pasqua Rosee who, each morning, made him and his friends coffee. So popular was it that Edwards was compelled to establish his servant in a coffee house so as to retrieve his own privacy. Coffee was advertised as 'a very good help to digestion, quickens the spirits, and is good against sore eyes'. However, John Aubrey in his *Anecdotes* recalls that the first coffee house in St Michael's Alley was set up by a man called Bowman, coachman to a Turkey merchant.

The coffee habit caught on and, as a commentator wryly remarked much later, 'From the days of Charles II to the days of George II, more coffee was bought and brewed by the Londoner than by any citizen in the world. There is no evidence to show that he ever learned or wished to learn the knack of making it, or knew that there was one.'

ANOTHER DOWNPOUR
John Evelyn recorded in his diary that in June

There fell this 25t day (after a drowth of neere 4 monethes) so violent a Tempest of haile, raine, wind, Thunder & lightning, as no man alive had seene the like in this age: The haile being in some places 4 & 5 Inches about, brake all the glasse about Lond: especially at Deptford, & more at Greenewich, where Sir Tho: Stafford, Vice-Chamberlaine to the Queene, affirm'd some had the shape of Crownes: others the order of the Gartyr about them; but these were fancies: it was certainly a very prodigious Storme.

CHURCHES CLOSE ON CHRISTMAS DAY
John Evelyn also recorded this year that, by order of the government, churches were closed on Christmas Day this year.

PROMOTION FOR A NURSE
Originally there were four sisters at St Bartholomew's Hospital, their designation as such deriving from their religious vows. After the Reformation sisters did not belong to religious orders but were in effect cleaners and laundresses who also looked after the patients. They were illiterate, had no medical skill, and were badly paid. It was not until the middle of the 17th century that women named as nurses came on to the staff to help the sisters, and it was only in 1652 that Margaret Whitaker became the first nurse to be promoted to sister, after five years spent at the hospital.

However, the governors never appointed a sister as matron; this post was usually taken by a competent housewife.

REFOUNDING OF COLFE'S SCHOOL
The Revd Abraham Colfe was vicar of Lewisham for 50 years. He endeared himself to his parishioners by his strident defence of the 500-acre Sydenham Common.

But he is remembered now by a grammar school named after him, the successor to a free school established in 1574 (q.v.), and which he refounded on 10 June 1652. To the new school was attached a free library, and there was a reading school near the church where elementary education was given, so that brighter boys could then graduate to the Colfe School. The school is now at Lee Green.

HYDE PARK SOLD
At first the royal parks were thrown open to the public, but in 1652 the government sold Hyde Park in three lots. In April 1653, when he 'went to take the aire in *Hide-Park*', John Evelyn reported that 'every Coach was made pay a shill: & horse 6d. by the sordid fellow who had purchas'd it of the State, as they were cald'.

CLEANING THE FLEET
An order was issued this year to scour the Fleet river. It complained that the river was impassable to boats because of encroachments, the keeping of hogs nearby, the dumping of offal and other garbage, and the number of 'houses of office' (lavatories) built over it.

1653

HIGHGATE LEPER HOSPITAL CLOSED
About this year the long-established leper hospital on Highgate Hill was closed. In 1650 it had been sold to 'Ralph Harrison of London

Esq.' for £130. It consisted of a timber building with a tiled roof, a hall, a kitchen, three rooms on the ground floor and five above, with an orchard and a garden. By this time, with leprosy rarely seen it was, most likely, simply an isolation hospital for infectious diseases. Coincidentally, 200 years later the site was chosen for a smallpox hospital, and its old grounds are now covered by the Whittington Hospital complex.

1654

THE BEGINNINGS OF COVENT GARDEN MARKET
The first known reference to the market which grew up in the piazza of Covent Garden occurs this year, when Thomas Cotton was described as living 'about the new market in Covent Garden'. As early pictures show, the market was merely a group of traders, using tables and carts, railed off on the south side of the square by the wall of Bedford House. Whether the Bedford Estate intended a serious market at this point is unknown, but by 1670 it had caught on sufficiently for a royal charter to be sought and obtained.

A market may be thought an odd facility to encourage in such a prestigious scheme, but it was by then a trend to make each new development self-sufficient – stables and markets were common appendages around the new squares of London, to the dismay of the City, which thought it had the monopoly of markets within 7 miles of the City wall.

A CHAPEL IN POPLAR
The East India Company this year built a chapel in Poplar. It was modelled on the Broadway Chapel in Westminster (see 1642), and in many ways it retains its original form. The chapel and the burial ground attached were not at first consecrated, and even by 1685 nothing had been done about this. The bishop of London confided to its minister with 'great emotion … that the grief of it disturbed his rest in the night', thereby becoming an early example of an influential man piously but ineffectively declaiming on an East End matter. To be fair, the Civil War had made it difficult to carry out the usual arrangements, and proposals afterwards to divide the great parish of Stepney so that Poplar could be autonomous had not persuaded the East India Company, which, having built the chapel at the expense of a local family, refused to release it as a parish church or provide it with a permanent endowment. As a result the chapel fabric deteriorated.

Poplar remained a hamlet of Stepney until 1817, and it was to be another 50 years before the chapel was officially made into a church called St Matthias.

CROMWELL IN THE CITY
Oliver Cromwell had been proclaimed Lord Protector on 16 December 1653. On 8 February the following year he was entertained by the City authorities at Grocers' Hall, after he had been met by the mayor and aldermen, who had ridden out on horseback.

1655

SAMUEL PEPYS MARRIES
In the church of St Margaret, Westminster, on 10 October the 22-year-old Samuel Pepys was married to the 15-year-old Elizabeth St Michel, daughter of an impoverished French Protestant father and an Anglo-

Irish mother. It was not to be a compatible marriage, and this may perhaps have led to the secret keeping of his famous diary in the short-hand of the time.

Pepys was then living at Whitehall Palace, in a small room in a turret by the great gateway. Here he was a clerk in the Exchequer, employed by George Downing (after whom Downing Street is named), and was also an assistant to his cousin Edward Mountagu. Four years later Pepys moved to Axe Yard, off Whitehall, and there resolved to keep a diary. He began in the lively style which has made him famous:

Blessed be God, at the end of the last year I was in very good health, without any sense of my old pain but upon taking of cold. I lived in Axe Yard, having my wife and servant Jane, and no more in family then us three. My wife, after the absence of her terms for seven weeks, gave me hopes of her being with child, but on the last day of the year she hath them again.

1656

JEWS READMITTED TO LONDON

Jews had been expelled from the country in 1290 – to the gratification of many Londoners, who resented their business ability. They were officially readmitted in 1656, but in reality a number of them, Marranos from Portugal and Spain who were outwardly converted to Catholicism, had been arriving as refugees much earlier, and by 1650 there were 60 or 70 of them in London.

The most important of these crypto-Jews was Antonio Fernandez Carajal, who had been living in London since before 1635. A ship-owner and dealer in bullion, he was also a contractor and information-gatherer for the Commonwealth. But he remained a covert Jew, and even when a delegation arrived in England in 1654 to petition Cromwell to readmit Jews into the country he continued his life as a Catholic and did not become involved at that stage.

The time was right for readmission. The use of the Old Testament and the study of Hebrew texts obligatory in the new religious regime made the authorities more sympathetic to the Jews, and Cromwell also saw possibilities in their trading opportunities. In 1656, when readmittance had been agreed, permission was sought to use the house of Moses Athias in Creechurch Lane as a synagogue, and for the acquisition of an orchard in Mile End for use as a burial ground. Mrs de Brito, widow of one of the signatories to the petition sent to the Lord Protector, was the first to be buried there, and the bell of St Katharine Cree church was tolled at her funeral and the church pall was lent by the Christians for her Jewish burial.

CLARE MARKET BEGINS

About this year the earl of Clare, John Holles, one of the country's richest men, created what was called the New Market, south of his house in Lincoln's Inn Fields. It was built on ground then known as Clement's Inn Fields (after the Inn of Chancery), and his grant restricted it to trading on Tuesdays, Thursdays and Saturdays. Referring to it in 1657, James Howell in his *Londinopolis* said, 'There is towards Drury Lane, a new market called Clare Market; then is there a street and palace of the same names, built by the Earl of Clare, who lives there, in a princely manner, having a house, a street and a market both for flesh and fish, all bearing his name.' A member of Parliament drily commented that Lord Clare was 'one of those who had forsworn the building of churches; that he had built a house for the flesh [the butcher's section of the market] but that he doubted he would hardly do as David did, build a house for the spirit'.

MOVING ST GILES'S POUND

Each parish outside the City had at least one pound – a pen in which stray animals were kept and from which they could be retrieved in return for a fee paid to the pinder. The pound for St Giles-in-the-Fields was a well-known landmark, situated as it was in the middle of St Giles High Street where now Endell Street joins it. This year it was transferred to an even more frequented junction, that of Tottenham Court Road and Oxford Street, where previously there had been a gallows.

Its place in St Giles High Street was taken by almshouses, on land donated by the son of Shakespeare's patron, the earl of Southampton. There were five houses, each of two rooms, for widows. They were, like the pound, in an inconvenient place even for the traffic of the time, and in 1783 they were moved to what is now Macklin Street; their rebuilt successors are the last remaining almshouses in central London.

CHAPEL AT SHADWELL OPENS

Evidence of development along the eastern waterfront is provided this year by the consecration of St Paul's, in the High Street at Shadwell, as a chapel of ease to St Dunstan's, Stepney. It adorned a new village created by property speculator Thomas Neale; a contemporary print shows it to be of red brick with stone quoins, its square tower and parapet decorated with globe ornaments. Perhaps the illustration flattered it, for just before its demolition, *c.* 1817, a writer described it as 'a most disgraceful building of brick totally unworthy of description'.

1657

PROSECUTION FOR SELLING COFFEE

At first the authorities regarded coffee houses as a nuisance; later Charles II referred to them as 'seminaries of sedition', but for some even the smell of coffee was too much. This year James Farr, barber, and keeper of the Rainbow coffee house by Inner Temple Gate, was arraigned by St Dunstan in the West parish for 'making and selling a sort of liquor called coffee, as a great nuisance and prejudice of the neighbourhood'. An appreciation of the smell of roasting coffee had obviously not yet been acquired. He was prosecuted for his 'evil smells and for keeping of ffier for the most part night and day, whereby his chimney and chamber hath been set on fire, to the great danger and affrightment of his neighbours'.

Two competitors to coffee were introduced into London about this time. It is thought that tea was first sold here this year and chocolate the year after.

THE BEGINNINGS OF SOUTHAMPTON HOUSE

This year the earl of Southampton planned a new mansion on his Bloomsbury estate, located on the north side of what is today Bloomsbury Square, with agricultural views stretching all the way to the northern heights of London. The architect is unknown, although the inevitable attributions to Inigo Jones have been made; if it was by him, then the plans would have had to be drawn up before 1652, the year of his death.

A view of Westminster by Wenceslaus Hollar in 1647. From left to right are the 'Parliament House', Westminster Hall and Westminster Abbey.

1658

DEATH OF CROMWELL

Oliver Cromwell, Lord Protector, died at Whitehall on 3 September, the anniversary of his great triumphs at Dunbar and Worcester. His body was embalmed and removed to Somerset House, where his effigy, dressed in robes of state, was exhibited for several days. Because of the complexity of the arrangements, the funeral at Westminster Abbey did not take place until 23 November, when, Evelyn records, his effigy (his remains had been privately interred at the abbey several weeks before) was

carried from Somerset-house in a velvet bed of state drawn by six horses houss'd with the same: The Pall held-up by his new Lords: Oliver lying in Effigie in royal robes, & Crown'd with a Crown, scepter, & Mund, like a King: The Pendants, & Guidons were carried by the Officers of the Army, The Imperial banners, Atchievments &c by the Heraulds in their Coates, a rich caparizon'd Horse all embroidred over with gold: a Knight of honour arm'd Cap a pè & after all his Guards, Souldiers & innumerable Mourners: In this equipage they proceeded to Westminster … it was the joyfullest funerall that ever I saw, for there was none that Cried, but dogs, which the souldiers hooted away with a barbarous noise; drinking & taking Tabacco in the street as they went …

The funeral is reported to have cost the enormous sum of £60,000. As on the death of a sovereign, the mayor and City officers, and 80 other persons, were allowed 9 yards of mourning cloth for the occasion.

WHALE KILLED IN THAMES

John Evelyn recalls in his diary that a whale 58 ft long appeared in the Thames between Deptford and Greenwich and 'drew an infinite Concourse to see it, by water, coach, on foote from Lond, & all parts'. It was 'killed with the harping yrons & struck in the head, out of which spouted blood & water, by two tunnells like Smoake from a chimny: & after an horrid grone it ran quite on shore & died'.

BUILDING IN PICCADILLY

About this year building began on the south side of what is now Piccadilly, at the Haymarket end. At that time 'Piccadilly' denoted only the houses in the area around Piccadilly Hall (see 1612), and for many years this new main road going west out of London was called Portugal Street, after Charles II's wife, Queen Catherine of Braganza. (Pall Mall was originally called Catherine Street for the same reason.)

On the other side of the road, Air Street appeared in the rate books for the first time, and was thought to be the most westerly street in London at that time. This short street was named after Thomas Ayres, a local brewer and landowner.

1659

FIRST CHEQUE ISSUED AT A LONDON BANK

The first piece of paper regarded as a cheque was drawn on Messrs Clayton & Morris, bankers of Cornhill, to the sum of £10. It was drawn by Nicholas Vanacker on 22 April this year. In 1976 it was sold at Sotheby's for £1,300.

THE BEGINNING OF STREATHAM SPA

In 1659, according to one report, people weeding in dry weather slaked their thirst from a mineral spring near Streatham Common. The water was claimed to be purgative, good for eyes and worms, but with a 'mawkish taste'. Streatham became a popular spa, though it did not develop as a commercial enterprise. At the beginning of the 19th century it was reported that the water was sent in large quantities to the London hospitals.

1660

A NEW KING

The Restoration, and immediately events in London become more numerous. Innovations occur, buildings are opened, societies are formed, social life returns, as though some floodgates have opened. Whatever the political or religious opinions of people, the departure of the rigorous Cromwell and his joyless supporters, and the arrival of a good-natured and high-living king, seems to have released vitality and energy.

Charles II entered London on 29 May, recorded Evelyn,

with a Triumph of above 20000 horse & foote, brandishing their swords and shouting with unexpressable joy: The wayes straw'd with flowers, the bells ring-ing, the streets hung with Tapissry, fountaines running with wine: The Mayor, aldermen, all the Companies in their liver[ie]s, Chaines of Gold, banners; Lords

Thomas Killigrew, one of two men permitted to stage plays in London, after the Restoration.

& nobles, Cloth of Silver, gold & velvett every body clad in, the windos & balconies all set with Ladys, Trumpets, Music & [myriads] of people flocking the streets & was as far as Rochester, so they were 7 houres in passing the Citty, even from 2 in the afternoone 'til nine at night …

Pepys was also there, and had indeed been on the boat which brought the king to Dover. He preens himself that the duke of York remembered his surname, and finds himself for a time in charge of the king's dog, 'which shit in the boat, which made us laugh and me think that a King and all that belong to him are but just as others are'.

THE REVENGE

Prominent parliamentarians who had not made their escape were now brought to trial. A number of regicides, particularly those who had signed the death warrant of Charles I, appeared at the Old Bailey from 9 October before a court of 34 commissioners. They were hanged and barbarously quartered at Charing Cross soon after, within sight of the Banqueting House where the king had been beheaded.

Pepys reports, 'I went out to Charing Cross to see Maj.-Gen. Harrison hanged drawn, and quartered – which was done there – he looking as cheerfully as any man could do in that condition. He was presently cut down and his head and his heart shown to the people, at which there was great shouts of joy.'

THE RESTORATION OF THEATRES

The Restoration brought both revival and restriction to theatres. On 21 August Thomas Killigrew and Sir William Davenant obtained patents to erect two theatres in London, to raise two new companies, and to have sole regulation of them. For Killigrew this was a reward for service to the king during his exile; he had also married one of the queen's ladies.

Both entrepreneurs chose to develop new theatres on indoor tennis courts, which had been found suitable venues in France in preceding years. Killigrew was first to open, on 3 January 1661 at Gibbons's former tennis court in Vere Street off Clare market (now erased by today's Aldwych), where he presented the King's Players. Pepys was present and records in his diary that actresses performed there. Davenant bided his time and took a short lease on the rebuilt theatre in Salisbury Court, off Fleet Street, where he presented his Duke of York's Players, until his own conversion of Lisle's tennis court in Portugal Street, Lincoln's Inn Fields. This opened late in June 1661. Davenant had been wise to wait, for in his conversion of the building he was able to incorporate facilities to use scenery. Killigrew had to compete, and in 1663 he abandoned his Vere Street premises and opened a new theatre, which could take scenery, in a former riding stable which became the first of the many buildings of the Theatre Royal Drury Lane.

ROYAL SOCIETY CONSTITUTED

What became the Royal Society for the Advancement of Natural Science began during the Interregnum when a group of scholars interested in natural philosophy met from 1648 at Wadham College, Oxford, in the rooms of Dr Wilkins. In 1659 they were able to meet in Gresham College, London, and in 1669 they were formally constituted as a society, to which in 1662 Charles II granted a charter.

HACKNEY CABS RESTRICTED

A proclamation on 18 October forbade hackney-cab drivers to ply for hire; they were in future to remain in their yards and wait for a fare to come to them. It was probably ineffectual (since more stringent regulations followed), and Pepys records on the very first day of the new arrangements that he picked a cab up in the street after dining out.

FLOODING AT THE ISLE OF DOGS

The most serious breach of the river defences in the Isle of Dogs occurred on 20 March this year. It was reported that it would cost £12,000 to repair, paid for by a tax of 40 shillings on every acre of ground owned in the vicinity. Pepys relates that, when journeying to see a ship, 'in our way we saw the great breach which the late high water had made, to the loss of many 1000£ to the people about Limehouse'.

The Royal Society's headquarters in Crane Court, where they moved in 1710.

1661

PALL MALL LAID OUT

Pall Mall is named after a form of croquet – the road was laid out this year covering the site of the 'alley' on which it was played. The game was a French import, originating in Italy, and its name, though from the French *palle-maille*, derives from the Italian *palla* (ball) and *maglio* (mallet).

The game seems to have been introduced into Scotland by Mary, Queen of Scots, and into England by her son, James I. In the reign of Charles II the alley on which it was played was just north of the old road from the top of Whitehall to St James's Palace, and with the advent of coaches the dust thrown up by the wheels made the site unpleasant. It was decided in 1661, therefore, to redirect the road on to the site of the alley, a long strip between two rows of elms, and to build a new alley nearby to the south. The new road was officially known as Catherine Street, to commemorate Catherine of Braganza, but informally became Pall Mall and the new alley The Mall.

VAUXHALL GARDENS OPENED

It did not take Londoners long to start enjoying themselves again. The New Spring Garden at Vauxhall was opened this year. Evelyn notes in his diary on 2 July, 'I went to see, the new Spring-Garden at *Lambeth*, a pretty contriv'd plantation.' There seems to have been an Old Spring Garden nearby, but it was this new one which made Vauxhall famous. The pleasure-loving Pepys, needless to say, also went there – but, unusually, later than the dourer Evelyn. In May 1662 he notes:

Thence home and with my wife and the two maids and the boy took the boat, and to Fox-hall – where I had not been a great while – to the Old Spring garden. And there walked long, and the wenches gathered pinks. Here we staid, and seeing that we could not have anything to eate but very dear, and with long stay, we went forth again without any notice taken of us, and so we might have done if we had had anything. Thence to the new one, where I never was before, which much exceeds the other; and here we also walked, and the boy crept through the hedge and gathered abundance of roses, and after a long walk, passed out of doors as we did in the other place.

Pepys is here using one of the many spellings for the place which in the reign of King John was a manor held by Falkes de Breaute: hence Falkes Hall. It is thought that the name has also somehow travelled east to become the Russian word for railway station, '*voksal*'.

The attractions of the place included ornamental gardens – romantically lit at night by thousands of lights – music, dancing, food and, it seems from the accounts of people like Pepys, unattached women.

Part of the site today, just across Vauxhall Bridge, is now covered by a rather desperate municipal open space.

SOME EXHUMATIONS

The remains of parliamentary leaders Oliver Cromwell, Henry Ireton and John Bradshaw were exhumed so that they could be hanged. The grisly process began on 29 January, when their coffins were transported to the Red Lion Inn in Holborn, and thence next day by sledge to Tyburn. There, still in the shrouds, the bodies were hung till dusk; the heads were then cut off, and the remains buried in a 'deepe pitt' below the gallows. Pepys seems to have missed this, but he was of course at the coronation, perched in scaffolding at the north end of the abbey. He was there at 4.30 a.m. and the king did not arrive until 11.

THE FIFTH MONARCHY MEN

The rout of Puritanism was not quite over. Republicanism still lurked, though most who had professed it had been given an amnesty, unless they had been regicides. A fanatical fringe still existed, such as a sect known as the Fifth Monarchy Men, whose aim was to usher in an eternal age of saints to follow the previous fallen monarchies of Assyria, Persia, Greece and Rome. The reality was a small group of militant republicans that met in Swan Alley, off Coleman Street, under the leadership of Thomas Venner, a retired local cooper.

On 6 January this year, worked into a frenzy by Venner, they sallied forth in an insurrection which, given the small number of them, assumed surprisingly large proportions. They killed a man in St Paul's churchyard who declared his loyalty to the king, eluded the trained bands called out to quell them, went in and out of City gates, killed a citizen who tried to prevent their escape, and made their way to the comparative safety of St John's Wood. From there they were driven to Hornsey, and then they set up a camp at Kenwood, in Highgate.

In a few days, still bolstered by frenzied vows, the 50 or so men attacked the City again. This time they were caught and Venner was hanged, drawn and quartered in Coleman Street on the 19th.

SHELTON'S SCHOOL

William Shelton is now commemorated in a small street in the Seven Dials area. In 1661 he bought up some houses in nearby Parker Street and here founded a school for 50 poor boys. This lasted until 1763, when it closed for lack of funds, but was revived again in 1815.

A NEW MAYPOLE IN THE STRAND

Maypoles, including the famous one at the east end of the Strand, had been taken down by the Puritans. A pamphlet issued in 1661 entitled *The Cities Loyalty Display'd* describes its successor:

This Tree was a most choice and remarkable Piece, 'twas made below [London] Bridg, and brought up in two parts to Scotland Yard, near the King's Palace, and from thence it was conveyed, April the 14th, to the Strand to be erected. It was brought with a Streamer flourishing before it, Drums beating all the way, and other sorts of Musick; it was supposed to be so long, that Landsmen [carpenters] could not possibly raise it. Prince James, the Duke of York, Lord High Admirall of England, commanded twelve Seamen off a Boord, to come and officiate the business, whereupon they came and brought their Cables, Pullies, and other tacklins, with six great Anchors ... The Maypole then being joynted together, and hoopt about with bands of Iron, the Crown and Vane with the King's Armes richly gilded, was placed on the head of it, a large top like a Belcony was about the middle of it.

It stood until 1713.

1662

FLIGHT OF THE PRIESTS

In the years immediately after the Restoration the 'Clarendon Code' established the new religious rules, and from these we have inherited not only the clear division between Established Church and Dissent but the class division of their adherents. Generally speaking, those who were Nonconformists were lower class, trade and businessmen, and when the 1661 Corporation Act restricted membership of municipal bodies to those who accepted the rites of the Church of England the seeds were sown of social disunity. The Code excluded from public life not only the extreme sects, but also the Presbyterians, who on the whole disliked the concept of absolute monarchy. One of its consequences, more visible in retrospect than at the time, was that those Puritan families who sought to keep their social status by unheroically embracing the Church of England were to be supporters of the Whigs in any dispute with the royal faction.

When the Act of Uniformity of 1662 required a clergyman's 'unfeigned consent and assent' to everything in the Prayer Book, this resulted in a mass eviction of priests who then set up dissenting chapels which appealed to the new middle class of merchants and businessmen and to the lower classes. Three years later the Five Mile Act (1665) made it impossible for the outgoing clergymen to preach within 5 miles of the City, and so we find from this time London ringed by nonconformist chapels in places like Highgate, Hampstead, Chelsea and Fulham. The same Act also applied to schoolmasters, and this probably encouraged the many private schools in similar villages outside the City.

AN ARREST IN HAMPSTEAD HIGH STREET

In late June 1660 a force of soldiers, no doubt hot and sweaty in the summer heat, had marched up the hill to Hampstead and there arrested Sir Harry Vane at his house in the High Street (it is marked today by Vane Close). Vane had been indecisive during the Civil War, supporting first one side and then the other, and when the restored House of Commons considered the matter in June that year not one vote opposed his exclusion from the general pardon. The House of Lords in fact singled him out as being liable to trial. The king for his part was happy to see Vane's life saved, but a later, and less merciful, Parliament accused him of high treason in 1662. Vane, being unrepentant, did not help his own case, and was condemned to death.

His execution took place on Tower Hill on 14 June this year. He conducted himself boldly and, as one commentator described, as 'rather a looker-on than the person concerned in the execution'. 'In all things [he] appeared the most resolved man that ever died in that manner' was the verdict of Pepys, and four days later the diarist noted that people everywhere talked of Vane's courage.

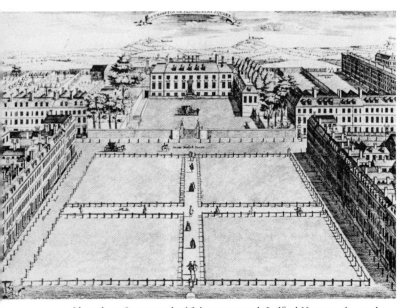

Bloomsbury Square in the 18th century, with Bedford House to the north.

A TAX ON HACKNEY CABS

By now there were 400 hackney cabs in London, and this year the owners were ordered to pay £5 for each cab towards the cost of cleaning and paving the streets of London and Westminster.

The Act which included this tax also ordered the widening of certain streets, such as that by the Stocks Market, Ludgate Hill and Cheapside by St Paul's churchyard, and the paving of St James's Street, Petty France and other streets more likely to be used by the court.

A NEW MARKET IN BLOOMSBURY

The 1st earl of Southampton had been licensed as early as 1640 to build a mansion on his Bloomsbury estate, but this had been delayed by the Civil War and Southampton House was not completed until soon after the Restoration (see 1657). In 1661 he obtained another licence, to build on the land between this house (on the north side of today's Bloomsbury Square) and High Holborn, occupied at that time by orchards and market gardens. From this development Bloomsbury Square evolved, as well as the streets to its west. Following the trend of the time, Southampton wanted to include a market, so as to make the venture self-supporting from the tolls, as well to provide a convenience to the residents. The City's stranglehold on markets had already been broken at Covent Garden, at the Haymarket and at Clare Market, and his licence was easily obtained in 1662.

The site of the market may today still be discerned around Barter Street, south of Bloomsbury Way. In 1666, when its frequency was increased to four days a week, it was a fish and meat market, and it was by then sufficiently established for at least two of the traders to issue their own trade tokens because of the shortage of coinage.

While this was going on, the earl's scheme for a square of houses in front of his own was beginning. The earliest building leases were issued this year.

1663

FIRST THEATRE ROYAL DRURY LANE

The first Theatre Royal on its present site was opened on 7 May by Thomas Killigrew. The first production, Beaumont and Fletcher's *The Humourous Lieutenant*, cost £1,500 to stage. Pepys was there with his wife on the second night:

The house is made with extraordinary good convenience, and yet hath some faults, as the narrowness of the passages in and out of the pit, and the distance from the stage to the boxes, which I am confident cannot hear; but for all other things is well; only, above all, the musique being below, and most of it sounding under the very stage, there is no hearing of the bases at all, not very well of the trebles, which sure must be mended.

1664

ST JAMES'S MARKET OPENS

The earl of St Albans, later the developer of the streets between Piccadilly and Pall Mall, opened St James's Market on 27 September. It was held for three days and sold all sorts of provisions, but the actual market house was not complete until early in 1666. It lay off the south of Jermyn Street, between Babmaes Street and Lower

Regent Street. Here also, from 1665, the St James's Fair, previously held outside St James's Palace, was transferred. Theoretically, this ran for 15 days each year, but there is no evidence that after being transferred it functioned at all.

A NEW GREENWICH PALACE

The old Tudor palace at Greenwich had been used as a biscuit-making factory during the Commonwealth and was in a bad state. The king decided not to attempt its restoration but instead to erect a new building by John Webb, in the current architectural style. The foundation stone for this palace was laid this year. The plan was for three linking wings around a square, open at one end to the river, in a line with the Queen's House. Unfortunately only one wing, now called the King Charles Block, was even partially completed.

ELTHAM LODGE BUILT

A similar story was to be told about Eltham Palace. John Evelyn recorded in his diary in 1656 'both Palace & Chapell in miserable ruines, the noble woods & Park destroied'. After the Restoration Sir John Shaw, a banker of great influence with the king, leased the manor, despaired of the ruins of the palace (and fortunately left them alone, for the palace was restored as much as possible in the 1930s), and commissioned Hugh May to build him another house nearby, called Eltham Lodge. This building, seven bays wide and one of the most important surviving houses of the period, is now the headquarters of the Royal Blackheath Golf Club.

1665

THE YEAR OF THE PLAGUE

It is not known how many died in the Great Plague, nor where it began. As an epidemic, it was first rife in St Giles-in-the-Fields, but there were casualties elsewhere before that. As to reliable numbers, these will never be had. The bills of mortality were still showing numbers of cases similar to those of 'non-plague' years while the government was issuing special instructions to deal with an epidemic. Partly, this under-recording was a reaction to the usual precautions, which included the incarceration of any family touched by the disease. The women searchers, medically untrained anyway, could be bribed to give a different cause of death – a practice encouraged by the parish clerks, who did not want the reputation of plague in their parish. Halfway through the epidemic the parish clerk of St Olave, Hart Street, admitted to his parishioner Pepys that nine had died from plague that week, but he had recorded only six. To quarantine the healthy with the sick was a horror for the healthy, but there were not enough pesthouses for the sick to die in.

The signs of the disease were readily known: high fever and delirium, nut-like swellings in the groin and other parts (hard at first but then soft and evil-smelling) and black haemorrhages beneath the skin.

There had been an extremely hard winter, during which the Thames had frozen, and Londoners were familiar enough with such epidemics to know that cold weather killed whatever caused the disease. But that familiarity was partly the cause of downfall – so usual was plague in this century, so helpless did the population feel in its face, so sure were they that it was God's punishment, that a few plague cases here and there were an inevitable part of London life.

But this was far worse than usual. Having gained a grip on the

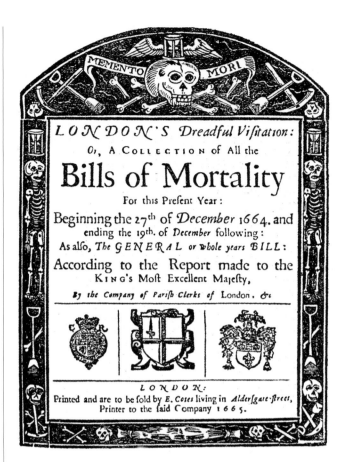

The bills of mortality compiled by the parish clerks reveal the growth of plague deaths. Above is the title page of all of those collected for 1665.

slums outside the City walls, the disease then picked off the inner parishes. By 13 June the official figures were 112 plague deaths, but six weeks later those in St Giles-in-the-Fields alone amounted to 323. At the peak there were some 7,165 recorded victims in a week. One remedy that the harassed St Giles officials tried was 'fuming' – burning brimstone, saltpetre and amber in houses. It worked not because it killed the plague, as was thought, but because the black rats which carried the infectious fleas did not like the smell. Others took up smoking, and even children were obliged to inhale. In the belief that they carried the disease, cats and dogs were exterminated.

People fled the capital, taking the infection with them. Businesses and government were bereft of people. The scholars of Westminster School moved to Chiswick. There were no sessions at the Old Bailey, and the prisoners exchanged the possibility of judicial death for one by plague in Newgate jail. By July the court had decamped to Hampton Court and Syon House – the safety of the king was more than usually important at this time, for he had no heir other than his brother James, in whom there was little confidence. More shamefully, the Royal College of Physicians was left empty, and as a consequence its entire treasure, worth then £1,000, was stolen from its secret hiding place.

Various estimates of the number of deaths have been made. Walter Bell, who wrote the most comprehensive book on the subject, thought between 80,000 and 100,000, and he thought also that the total population of the area involved was originally under 500,000.

It has been suggested that the Great Fire the following year killed the plague once and for all – it destroyed not only the unhealthy infrastructure of sewers and water supply, but the rotten houses as well. It is correct to say that there was never another epidemic, but the truth is less simple. The epidemic began in an area (St Giles-in-the-Fields) later untouched by the Great Fire and, indeed, badly affected many locations outside the conflagration. But the epidemic did not come back to those places either. There were some deaths in succeeding years, but the disease seems to have just petered out, the last case being notified in Rotherhithe in 1679.

BUILDING ON PICCADILLY

Piccadilly was alive with construction work. The largest mansion, Clarendon House (see 1666), was still being built, but on either side of it two other important houses were emerging.

Sir John Denham, poet and, in his own eyes, architect too, began a new house this year on the north of Piccadilly; in later years this was to be developed into Burlington House and then the Royal Academy. Some of the original structure survives, but not much. Sir John, however, suffered from bouts of madness, including a belief that he was the Holy Ghost, and did not complete the house, and two years later he sold the unfinished building to Richard Boyle, 1st earl of Burlington, for £3,300. Boyle continued with the construction under difficult circumstances – after the Great Fire, labour and materials were hard and expensive to come by – and he did not live in it until 1668, by which time he had spent another £5,000. Pepys went there in September that year and managed to set his wig on fire with a candle.

Further west on Piccadilly, Berkeley House was also being built, by the 1st Lord Berkeley of Stratton, a prominent royalist and husband of a wealthy East India Company heiress. The house, designed by Hugh May, who had just completed Eltham Lodge (see 1664), was located on the site of today's Berkeley Street and Stratton Street, and replaced Hay Hill Farm. It was a larger building than Denham's, and its grounds were more extensive, including what is today Berkeley Square. It consisted of a central building and two forward wings, connected by curved Palladian colonnades. Evelyn thought it 'truely … very well built' but pointed out that it was an inconvenient and ill-planned house. About twenty years later, when Berkeley's widow was thinking of allowing the gardens to be developed for streets, Evelyn had changed his mind, for he records that he 'could not but deplore that sweete place (by farr the most pleasant & noble Gardens Courts and Accommodations, statly porticos &c any where about the Towne) should so much of it [be] streitned & turn'd into Tennements'.

ST JAMES'S SQUARE BEGUN

South of Piccadilly even grander schemes were afoot. Henry Jermyn, earl of St Albans, was this year granted the freehold of land he leased there and was able to begin the building of St James's Square. This development was not popular with the City, which feared that its own water supply would be affected by diversion to the new houses, but in seeking his licence St Albans pointed out to the king 'ye beauty of this great Towne and ye convenience of your Court are defective in point of houses fitt for ye dwellings of Noble men and other Persons of quality'. Building work seems to have begun before the freehold was granted, and the first names were in the rate books by 1667. The houses were destined for just the people described to the king. Possibly designed by Sir John Denham, the large residences were of red brick with stone dressings and the square became immediately the most fashionable in London. Some were portioned off to prominent builders such as Nicholas Barbon (the creator of Red Lion Square in Holborn) and Richard Frith (of Frith Street in Soho).

1666

A RAVENOUS FIRE

On Sunday 2 September, very early in the morning, a fire gained hold in the bakery of Thomas Faryner in Pudding Lane, near the Thames. There was nothing particularly unusual about it, nothing that might threaten the destruction of virtually all the City of London. But there were circumstances which contrived that disaster.

Faryner and his family, waking upstairs, detected smoke at about two in the morning, a time of the night when most were asleep and not prepared to stir themselves. It was also the day of the week when no help could be got from Billingsgate workers. The primitive aids to hand were used to dampen, beat and extinguish, but plans to restrict the path of this dragon were missing.

Faryner's house burnt slowly, but once the fire had crossed the road and reached the Star Inn's yard of combustibles a rapid advance began. Flames jumped easily down to the Thames, and there devoured the unprotected wharves, shacks, warehouses and sheds of flammable pitch, tar, timber, hemp, hay, hops and brandies. Here was food for fire indeed, and the consumption of these premises along the Thames meant that a water supply large enough to fight the fire was cut off. Not only was the Thames out of reach, but the fire destroyed the waterworks at London Bridge, where equipment there could have raised a supply that might have been effective.

Thomas Vyner, a dramatic witness, reported, 'But now the fire gets mastery and burns dreadfully; and God with his great bellows blows upon it!' Here he is emphasizing the strong westerly wind that was blowing.

Samuel Pepys, whose diary covered momentous years of London's history.

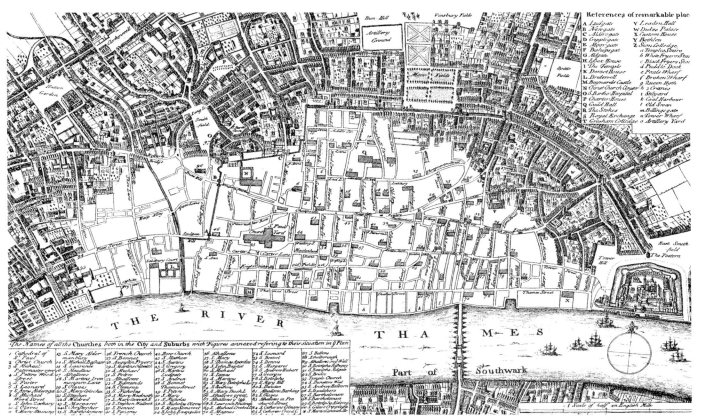

A plan showing the extent of the Great Fire. It jumped the wall to the west as far as the Temple, but did not consume the north-eastern part of the City.

The inability of London to organize itself in the first crucial six hours was probably the main factor in the fire becoming so large, so uncontrollable, so fierce. Soon, short of withdrawing some distance and taking the time to demolish a swathe of buildings in the face of the opposition of their owners, so as to block the fire's path, there was little that could be done to impede it. Even then, sparks on the wind might have jumped the man-made divide.

If the behaviour of Pepys is typical of that of other officials in those first dark hours, lit first by flames and then by dawn, then it is no wonder that the fire travelled. His servants, up late, noticed the fire quite early and roused him.

Jane called us up, about 3 in the morning, to tell us of a great fire they saw in the City. So I rose, and slipped on my nightgown and went to her window, and thought it to be on the back side of Mark Lane at the farthest, but being unused to such fires as followed, I thought it far enough off, and so went to bed and to sleep.

The lord mayor had arrived at 3 a.m.; displeased at being fetched out of his bed, he quickly returned to it. The fire was not unusual at that stage, and the thought of all the merchandise around the wharves did not stir his imagination.

Two churches went early – St Margaret's on Fish Street Hill, and St Magnus by London Bridge. On the bridge itself some of the houses went, but the structure survived. If the fire here found little of interest it did, however, manage to block the route from which help might come from south of the river. The wind, blowing strongly, pushed the flames to Fishmongers' Hall, the first of the livery-company halls to be consumed.

If we are to believe his diary, it seems to have been Pepys who gave the bad news to the court at Whitehall: 'I did give them an account which dismayed them all; and word was carried in to the King. So I was called for and did tell the King and Duke of York what I saw, and that unless his Majesty did command houses to be pulled down, nothing could stop the fire.' Pepys received authority to command such demolition, but when he got back to the blaze he found the lord mayor in Cannon Street 'like a man spent, with a scarf about his neck. To the King's message, he cried like a fainting woman: "Lord, what can I do? I am spent! People will not obey me. I have been pulling down houses. But the fire overtakes us faster than we can do it."'

Evening came with the fire gaining ground and London facing a night awake. The fire was

more visible and dreadful; instead of the black curtains of the night which used to be spread over the City, now the curtains are yellow … Now hope begins to sink, and a general consternation seizes upon the spirits of the people; little sleep is taken in London this night: the amazement which the eye and ear doth effect upon the spirit, doth either dry up or drive away the vapour which used to bind up the senses … Some are on their knees in the night, pouring out their tears before the lord, interceding for poor London in the day of its calamity, but alas … London's sins were too great and God's anger against the City was too hot, so easily and presently to be quenched.

John Evelyn retrieved his nest egg of treasure, ready to carry it away. All over London people gathered possessions, calculated the need to evacuate, made tentative and exorbitantly expensive arrangements for transport, and felt at last that an awful disaster could not be prevented.

1600s

On the next day the fire was strong enough to fight the wind as it went northward and eastward up Gracechurch Street and Fenchurch Street. The flames were in a great arc, 'a dreadful bow it was, such as mine eyes never before had seen; a bow which had God's arrow in it with a flaming point'. Into Cornhill the fire went; no building could withstand it. Around the galleries of the Royal Exchange, such a fertile territory, the flames licked. 'Rattle, Rattle, Rattle was the noise which the fire struck upon the ear round about, as if there had been a thousand iron chariots beating upon the stones.'

More pertinently, the fire went westward along the Thames, dividing Londoners from water. By the end of the second day it was at Blackfriars. There was now not much water available from other sources, for it had been a long and hot summer and the wells were low.

The houses of the rich were now being burnt, those around Cornhill, Cheapside and Lombard Street, while their occupants were probably on carts leaving the City, or on boats that congested the Thames. Everywhere there was flight, for it was now obvious that the fire was too large to be fought. By the end of the day the scaffolding around St Paul's, put there for work on the building's restoration, was alight. During the night the fire also went backwards, against the wind and towards the Tower. John Evelyn lamented:

God grant mine eyes may never behold the like, who now saw above ten thousand houses all in one flame, the noise & crakling & thunder of the impetuous flames, the shreeking of Women & children, the hurry of people, the fall of towers, houses & churches was like an hideous storme, & the air all about so hot & inflam'd that at last one was not able to approch it, so as they were force'd [to] stand still, and let the flames consume on which they did for neere two whole mile[s] in length and one in bredth.

The fire did not restrict itself within the City walls. To the west it jumped across the Fleet and continued towards the Strand and died out around the Temple and Fetter Lane, to the relief of those in Whitehall who imagined it roaring along the Strand to reach them. In this surge to the west much of St Paul's was taken, its hot lead running down the building into the streets, stones flying off 'like grenades'. The Newgate and Fleet prisons were consumed. Pepys was more worried about the eastern side of the fire, which was dangerously near his own office and parish church, and here he used his influence to create an effective firebreak. Houses were blown up to save the Tower.

And then, on the fourth day, the wind dropped and the fire was controlled around its perimeter. It did not end at Pye Corner, as the legend says: it went on from there. It did not end anywhere in particular, and by the fifth day there were still odd pockets, smouldering and occasionally leaping into life. Evelyn viewed the remains of St Paul's on the Friday:

Thus lay in ashes that most venerab[l]e Church, one of the [ancientest] Pieces of early Piety in the Christian World, beside neere 100 more; The lead, yronwork, bells, plate &c mealted; the exquisitely wrought Mercers Chapell, the Sumptuous Exchange, the august fabricque of Christ church, all the rest of the Companies Halls, sumptuous buildings, Arches, Enteries, all in dust. The fountaines dried up & ruind, whilst the very waters remained boiling.

It has been estimated that the fire consumed 13,200 houses, St Paul's Cathedral, 87 parish churches, 6 consecrated chapels, the Guildhall, the Royal Exchange, the Custom House, 52 company halls, various markets and prisons, 3 gates and 4 stone bridges. As to lives lost, remarkably few were recorded.

CLARENDON HOUSE FINISHED

Edward Hyde, earl of Clarendon, the lord chancellor, had been rewarded well for his help in restoring the king to his throne. He had been granted 30 acres of land north of Piccadilly, and on this he intended a mansion to match his importance. Its location is the site of today's Albemarle Street, directly opposite St James's Street, symbolically facing St James's Palace down the hill. Sir Roger Pratt was engaged as architect (he had just completed Coleshill in Warwickshire), and work began in 1664 on one of the most prominent, and short-lived, mansions in London's history. In the end it cost £50,000 and the labour of 300 men, and it was virtually complete as the City was reduced to ashes.

Pepys tells us in February 1665, 'Rode into the beginnings of my Lord Chancellor's new house, near St James's, which common people have already called Dunkirke House, from their opinion of his having a good bribe for the selling of that towne.' By January of 1666 Pepys is admiring 'the finest pile I ever did see in my life', and in February he is at the top of the house to see 'the noblest prospect that ever I saw in my life, Greenwich being nothing to it; and in everything, it is a beautiful house, and most strongly built in every respect'.

Evelyn is rather more critical at times: 'a goodly pile to see too, but had many defects as to the Architecture, though placed most gracefully'.

1667

BUILDING ON THE ASHES

The hand of a malevolent god must have been imagined by many who had experienced the Plague and the Fire. And, even while the recovery was being devised, still more ill fortune came, as the Dutch blockaded the Thames, captured and sank English ships, and sent the Navy Office, where Pepys was a senior offical, into depression. Evelyn summed up the latest agony: 'this alarme was so greate, as put both Country and Citty into a pan[i]que; feare & consternation, such as I hope I shall never see more: for every body were flying, none [knew] why or whither'. Every able-bodied man was ordered to enlist, and the king reviewed the City Militia on Tower Hill.

The Rebuilding Act which emerged this year ruled that houses on small streets should all be two-storey, those fronting streets of note or overlooking the Thames were to be three-storey, and merchants' mansions and those of the 'greatest bigness' were to be no more than four storeys. The medieval practice of jettying upper storeys was prohibited.

To raise money for the rebuilding, the City was granted a tax on coal. Of the £738,000 raised in this way, about half was used on new public works, such as the Guildhall, prisons and the Fleet Canal, £265,000 on parish churches, and the remaining £88,000 on the rebuilding of St Paul's.

By March of this year the new road pattern, which was not too different from the previous one, was marked out and site-holders were obliged to clear their land of burnt debris. Progress was slow, with individual buildings rather than terraces being completed. The foundation stone of the new Royal Exchange was laid, but it would be a long time before the commercial life of London revived. By the end of this year only 150 new premises were complete, though in the next five years 8,000 were built.

STORMING OF CLARENDON HOUSE

The lord chancellor, the earl of Clarendon, was accused of several things by the populace, in addition to being despised for his wealth in the midst of so much distress. First, that he had purposely contrived the match of the king to a barren queen; second, that he had taken money for the sale of Dunkirk back to the French in order to finance a Portuguese struggle with Spain, and to fund the establishment of the port of Tangier; and, third, that he was in league with the Dutch, who even now were blocking the Thames.

In June this resentment spilled over as the mob attacked the most obvious sign of his ascendancy – his new house in Piccadilly. Windows were broken, trees were cut down, a gibbet was set up outside, and upon his gates were painted the words 'Three sights to be seen, Dunkirke, Tangier and a barren Queene.' By December Evelyn found him disconsolately sitting in a 'Gowt wheel chayre' in the garden, and next morning he was gone. In August next year he lost the Great Seal, and by November he was impeached, with the support of the king, for high treason.

Clarendon, who died in 1674, admitted in his autobiography that the building of this ambitious house did him more harm than his deeds. Appropriately, it survived him by fewer than ten years.

Hedges & Butler Established

It is thought that the wine merchant Hedges & Butler originates in the establishment this year by Edmund Harris of a business in Hungerford Street, near the Strand (a site now covered by Charing Cross station). A William Hedges took over the business in 1733, but in an 1817 directory a 'William Hedge' here is described as a wax and tallow chandler.

New Fire Regulations

The City of London announced new regulations for fighting fires this year. The City was divided into four, and each quarter was provided with 800 leather buckets, 50 ladders (of which 10 were to be 42 feet long), 24 pickaxes and 40 shovels. Each of the 12 principal City livery companies was obliged to provide an engine, 30 buckets, 2 water squirts and 3 ladders. The smaller companies were also to make as much provision as they could. As for households, each was to have a fire bucket and was obliged to quench ashes at night and put them in a safe place.

1668

Rebuilding News

Among the many who desired the quick rebuilding of London it is odd to find the inmates of the notorious Fleet prison, but this year they petitioned from their temporary accommodation at Croome House in Lambeth for the speedy rebuilding of their old home. Their new abode, they complained, was too far for visitors to travel to see them. But the new building and the regulation of it were to be as appalling as before, and in 1691 Moses Pitt in his *The Cry of the Oppressed* was to detail its misery and squalor.

Most likely the first new buildings were taverns, to feed the building workers. The Boar's Head, in Eastcheap, is known to have been built this year, and Ye Olde Watling in Watling Street cherishes its tradition that it was built by Wren this year and that he designed St Paul's in an upper room. A contemporary writer, Samuel Rolle, was pessimistic:

Is London a village that I see, the houses in it stand so scatteringly? The major part of houses built upon the ruins let out to alehouse keepers and victuallers to entertain the workmen employed about the City … A goodly uniformity there is

in so much of it as is built together, but ruins and confusion round it … Few expect to trade within the walls (so far as the ruins do extend) till the City be built again.

Three livery-company halls appear to have been finished. The Butchers' Company relocated from Bartholomew Close to Pudding Lane, the seat of the Great Fire; the Haberdashers rebuilt on their traditional site in Staining Lane, and the Salters' Company erected its hall in St Swithin's Lane.

Riot in Clerkenwell

The Great Fire had not destroyed the tendency of City apprentices to riot on Shrove Tuesday. On 24 March this year, Pepys records:

To Whitehall, where great talk of the tumult at the other end of the town about Moorefields among the prentices, taking the liberty of these holidays to pull down bawdy-houses. And Lord, to see the apprehensions which this did give to all people at Court, that presently order was given for all the soldiers, horse and foot, to be in armes. And we heard a Justice of Peace this morning say to the King that he had been endeavouring to suppress this tumult, but could not; and that imprisoning some in the new prison at Clerkenwell, the rest did come and break open the prison and release them.

1669

New Royal Exchange Opens

The new Royal Exchange, essential to the recovery of London's commerce, was opened on 28 September. The king was expected at the ceremony but failed to appear; however, the lord mayor came and, walking twice around the building, congratulated the merchants on their new Exchange. It was similar to the first building, with two storeys containing 200 shops around a central courtyard open to the skies. The main entrance, beneath a tower, sported a gilded grasshopper – the emblem of the Exchange's founder, Sir Thomas Gresham – and in the courtyard stood an absurd statue of the king dressed in Roman costume. The new building was not a success, and in 1701 it was reported that many of the shops stood empty.

Fracas at the Temple

In March this year a near riot occurred at the Temple over a ceremonial dispute. The City claimed to include the Temple in its jurisdiction, which many of the legal students declared was wrong. The mayor, going to dine at the Inner Temple, had the City's sword-bearer carry his sword, tip up, demonstrating the mayor's right to be there and to bear arms. Pepys relates how the students rebelled and obliged their guest to go to another chamber.

Fire in the Strand

The house in the Strand belonging to Lady Hungerford burnt down in April. Pepys records it:

A great fire happened in Durham Yard last night, burning the house of one Lady Hungerford, who was to come to town to it this night; and so the house is burned, new furnished, by carelessness of the girl sent to take off a candle from a bunch of candles, which she did by burning it off, and left the rest, as is supposed, on fire. The King and court were here, it seems, and stopped the fire by blowing up of the next house.

London 1666

River Fleet

St Paul's Wharf

LONDON 1666. THE GREAT FIRE

The Great Fire, which started on Sunday 2 September 1666 in a bakehouse in Pudding Lane, near London Bridge, virtually destroyed the whole city. A strong easterly wind fanned the flames, which spread across the City, over the walls and across the River Fleet.

This reconstruction shows the state of the fire five days after it had started. Over 13,000 houses, 85 churches, and 52 livery company halls were destroyed or gutted.

MAIN SITES DESTROYED OR BADLY DAMAGED

1 Temple
2 Bridewell Palace
3 Baynard's Castle
4 College of Arms
5 St Paul's
6 Exchequer office
7 Christ Church cloisters
8 Queenhithe fire break

9 Sion College
10 Guildhall
11 Bakewell Hall
12 Stocks Market
13 Royal Exchange
14 Leadenhall
15 Thomas Faryner's bakehouse in Pudding Lane.
   The fire started here in the early morning of 2 September 1666.

The Great Fire

London Bridge

Tower of London

REVELS IN ST JAMES'S SQUARE

Henry Jermyn, earl of St Albans, lent his house in St James's Square to Cosmo III of Tuscany, here on a state visit this year. The Grand Duke was delighted and supplied a display of fireworks in the square and a free distribution of wine and beer to the spectators.

HAPPENINGS IN SPITALFIELDS

Immigration and the exodus of people caused by the Great Fire increased the population of the parishes outside the walls. In particular the poorer classes favoured Spitalfields, where they joined those already living in crowded circumstances, many in houses destined for a good-class tenant. Daniel Defoe, born *c*. 1661, recalled that the area was all fields when he was a boy, but all town within his lifetime: 'the lanes were deep, dirty and unfrequented, the part now called Spittlefields-market, was a field of grass with cows feeding on it … Brick Lane, which is now a long well-paved street, was a deep dirty road, frequented chiefly by carts fetching bricks that way into Whitechapel from brick-kilns in those fields'. In 1669 the parishioners opened a 'Town Hall' in which to hold meetings.

More lastingly, the Black Eagle Brewery in Brick Lane was founded. Its works grew haphazardly, taking in adjacent buildings, including a Huguenot chapel. By the 18th century the brewery was owned by Joseph Truman, whose son, Benjamin, made it famous.

Slightly to the east, in Houndsditch, a man called Zachary Crofton began this year a school for 40 boys and 30 girls. This was refounded in 1710 by Alderman Sir John Cass, and its descendant survives today.

GARRAWAY'S COFFEE HOUSE REOPENS

Thomas Garraway's coffee house, reopened in Exchange Alley this year, was a well-known haunt of merchants, particularly those selling furs. It was also celebrated for its sherry, ale and punch, and for its tea. Its owner is sometimes credited with being the first to sell tea in England; it was then a very expensive drink (at one time, according to one pamphlet, it was selling at £10 per pound weight).

SHADWELL WATERWORKS FORMED

The developing area of Wapping and Stepney needed fresh water. The problem was solved by one of the smart developers of the day, Thomas Neale, who was later to create Seven Dials near Covent Garden. By 1669 he was a major developer in Shadwell; he also built the church, to give it respectability. He had a lease on land reclaimed from the river at Shadwell, now quite valuable because of the increase in London maritime trade. By the church he erected a four-horsepower engine which raised water from the Thames and circulated it via pipes to the neighbouring hamlets. When Daniel Lysons described it in the 1790s it was supplying nearly 8,000 houses with water, though by then this must have been heavily polluted.

1670

THE FLEET CANAL

Powers were obtained this year to construct the Fleet Canal – in effect a widening and deepening of the last 700 yards of the disgusting Fleet river, between Holborn Bridge and Blackfriars. The new channel was 50 ft wide, lined on each side by wharves. Wren designed a new Holborn Bridge, but the heroic work of its construction was the responsibility of Thomas Fitch. The river continually silted up as it was being deepened, rubbish and sewerage were still pouring into it, and the work was of course immensely unpleasant – when the workmen were press-ganged to fight the Dutch this was possibly a better fate.

The effort was unappreciated anyway. It was asked why there was such a large expenditure just 'to bring up a few Chaldrons of Coles to two or three Pedling Fewel-Marchants', and the point was made that the cellar warehouses were so damp as to be of use only to 'frogs, toads and other vermin'. The criticism was harsh, but it had some justification. In none of the first three years of use did the revenue exceed £60, and after its management was farmed out the canal went to ruin. By 1733 the City authorities were willing to accept the inevitable: the canal was arched over and the central strip became the site of Fleet Market.

A GRANT OF COVENT GARDEN MARKET

With the City in such disarray, the use of Covent Garden Piazza as a market must have increased. We do not know a great deal about everyday trading in the aftermath of the Fire, but we must assume that much of it was lost to the suburbs – not the least because the customers had moved out for the time being. The problem for the 5th earl of Bedford was that he derived no income from the groups of pedlars in his piazza. His application for a grant to regulate a market on every day except Sundays and Christmas Day for the buying and selling of fruit, flowers, roots and herbs was granted on 12 May, but it was worded so loosely that it was possible to challenge the Bedfords' right to levy a toll at all.

The grant also had another sting in its tail. It set out exactly the area of the market: 420 ft eastward from the church and 316 ft northward from the wall of Bedford House. This was fine in the earlier days of the market, because it allowed it to grow to fill the entire area of the piazza – apart from Smithfield, much the largest London market. But by the 19th century the area was not commodious enough; the traders took up premises in the streets around and, although their ground landlord was still the Bedford Estate, in theory they were free of market tolls.

THE END OF CLAUDE DUVAL

The life of the highwayman Claude Duval has been more embroidered than recorded. He was born in Normandy of poor parents, but at the age of 14 he came to England in the service of the duke of Richmond. It was not long before he was a prominent highwayman, admired for his gallantry to women, which has caused a romantic frisson in many writers. However, he was caught while drunk at the Hole in the Wall tavern in Covent Garden. Arraigned in January 1670, he was found guilty on several counts of highway robbery.

By that time, like Jack Sheppard after him, his reputation was enormous. Sympathetic crowds attended his execution at Tyburn on 21 January, his body was cut down and laid in state in a pub in St Giles, and he was buried in the centre aisle of St Paul's, Covent Garden, with the inscription:

Here lies Du Vall: Reder, if male thou art,
Look to thy purse; if female, to thy heart.'

THE HALLS REBUILT

The livery companies were among the first to re-establish themselves in the still ruined City. Halls for the Coopers, Cordwainers, Painter-Stainers, Pewterers, Saddlers, Skinners, Stationers, Turners and Wax Chandlers were completed this year.

DEVELOPMENTS IN CHELSEA

One of the more important houses in Chelsea was completed this year. Lindsey House, today's 96–100 Cheyne Walk, was the creation of Robert, 3rd earl of Lindsey. The previous house had been the principal farmhouse on Sir Thomas More's Chelsea estate and had been occupied by the physician to James I and Charles I, Sir Theodore Mayerene. One of the most illustrious of subsequent residents was Count Zinzendorf, who began a Moravian community here; others, in different parts of the property, were the great civil engineer Marc Brunel and the painter James Whistler.

Around the corner, the nave and tower of the Old Chelsea Church were rebuilt this year.

1671

BACK TO THE GUILDHALL

The Guildhall was rebuilt sufficiently by this year for a banquet to be held there. The exterior walls had survived the Fire, and these were extended 20 ft higher, including a row of windows above the level of the old cornice. A flat roof, attributed to Wren, was installed.

BUILDING A BRIDGE AT FULHAM

Only London Bridge crossed the Thames in inner London, and, to preserve its toll revenue, the City Corporation ensured that it had no rival. A proposal in the House of Commons to build a bridge between

Dorset Garden Theatre, south of Fleet Street, built by Wren in 1671.

Fulham and Putney this year was met with opposition by the City and the ferrymen. One of the members of Parliament for the City stated that the water at Putney was shallow at ebb and if a bridge were built there not even the common wherries would be able to pass the river at low water. It was a wild and silly scheme, he proclaimed. Sir William Thompson was concerned that a new bridge at Fulham would extend the boundaries of London away from its walls and gates, and even prophesied that 'when the walls of London shall no longer be visible and Ludgate is demolished, England itself shall be as nothing'. The bill was lost by 67 votes to 54.

WILL'S COFFEE HOUSE OPENS

One of the most famous coffee houses opened its doors this year at 1 Bow Street, Covent Garden. The proprietor was William Urwin, from whom the place took its name, but its fame rested on the frequency with which Dryden was to be seen there, in a reserved position by the fire, or by the window, depending on the season, holding loquacious court.

MORE REBUILDING

Buildings completed in the City this year included the Custom House in Lower Thames Street, the Fleet prison, and halls for the Blacksmiths, Cutlers, Fishmongers, Innholders, Merchant Taylors, Parish Clerks and Vintners.

A NEW DORSET GARDEN THEATRE

Wren found time to build a theatre this year. The Dorset Garden Theatre (also known as the Duke's Theatre, because its usual performers were of the Duke's Company) was built for Sir William Davenant (see 1660), who had transferred here from his theatre in Lincoln's Inn Fields. The new building was situated facing the Thames, south of Fleet Street and east of the old Salisbury Court Theatre. It was built on the gardens of Dorset House, with stairs down to the river so that the audience might arrive by water. The first production, on 9 November, was Dryden's *Sir Martin Mar-All*, which sold out for three days.

By all accounts it was a sumptuous proscenium-arch theatre, complete with musicians' gallery, but its fashionable life was short. When the Duke's Company merged with the King's Players in 1682 they used the new Theatre Royal Drury Lane most of the time, and Dorset Garden had to make do with second-rate shows or divertissements such as wrestling. The site was later used by a timber yard, and in modern times was the playground of the City of London School.

THE DISCOVERY OF GRINLING GIBBONS

The discovery and promotion of the genius of the woodcarver Grinling Gibbons is to the credit of the diarist John Evelyn. Evelyn wrote in his diary on 18 January this year:

I this day first acquainted his Majestie with that incomparable young man, Gibson [sic], whom I had lately found in an Obscure place, & that by meere accident, as I was walking neere a poore solitary thatched house in a field in our Parish neere Says-Court [Deptford]: I found him shut in, but looking into the Window, I perceiv'd him carving that large Cartoone, or Crucifix of Tintorets, a Copy of which I had also my selfe brought from Venice, where the original Painting remaines: I asked if I might come in, he opned the doore civily to me, & I saw him about such a work as for the curiosity of handling, drawing, & studious exactnesse, I never in my life had seene before in all my travells: I asked why he worked in such an obscure & lonesome place; he told me, it was that he might apply himselfe to his profession without interruption; & wondred

Diarist John Evelyn, who fostered the career of woodcarver Grinling Gibbons.

not a little how I came to find him out ... Of this Young Artist, together with my manner of finding him out, I acquainted the King, and beged of his Majestie that he would give me leave to bring him & his Worke to White-hall, for that I would adventure my reputation with his Majestie that he had never seene any thing approch it, & that he would be exceedingly pleased, & employ him.

1672

A REBUILT NEWGATE PRISON

Newgate prison was rebuilt this year, but the building was hardly an improvement on the older structure. According to a publication of 1724, written by a 'B. L.' of Twickenham, prisoners in Newgate were kept in irons as soon as they were incarcerated, for whatever offence, and it was customary to house newcomers in the awful condemned hold in fetters until they had paid the warden the sum of 2s 6d. This room, far from being underground, was according to the anonymous author of *The History of the Press Yard* (c. 1715) between the top and bottom of the arch under Newgate, 'from whence there dart in some glimmerings of light, though very imperfect, by which you may know that you are in a dark, opaque, wild room'. The floor and walls were made of stone, and an open sewer ran through the middle. Food was thrown through a hatch at the top; candles for light had to be paid for.

The wardenship of this appalling place was evidently profitable, for it was sold in 1696 for £3,500.

Whole families, and sometimes their pets, lived with the prisoners in the jail. For those who were able to pay to be released from the most unpleasant rooms, or from irons, life was convivial, with drink, gambling and sexual favours freely available.

THEATRE ROYAL BURNS DOWN

The Theatre Royal Drury Lane burnt down in January. Pepys had twice complained that, seated in the pit, he had been affected by rain coming in the roof, and no doubt it would have had to be rebuilt anyway. Its absence briefly left the Dorset Garden Theatre as the principal playhouse in London.

THE FIRST WREN CHURCH

The first completed Wren church appears to have been St Michael, Cornhill, which was finished this year, though the tower, which survived the Fire, was only renovated and was not replaced until 1722, when Wren was 90 and the work was probably done by Hawksmoor. Much of Wren's work was disguised by an enthusiastic renovation by Sir George Gilbert Scott in 1858–60, but the original organ, installed in 1684, is still there.

A GAZEBO IN CROOM'S HILL

In Croom's Hill, Greenwich, halfway up, there is a gazebo which was built this year for Sir William Hooker, lord mayor of London, whom Pepys described as 'a plain, ordinary, silly man ... but rich'. The building, which is attached to the oldest house in the road, The Grange, is marked by a plaque, and was designed by the physicist and astronomer Robert Hooke.

1673

THE NEW TEMPLE BAR

Hardly a building in London has appeared in so many prints as the Temple Bar, completed by Wren in March this year. In effect, this structure at the western end of Fleet Street was the 'new' west gate to London. Originally Ludgate, halfway along Ludgate Hill, had served that purpose, but when, in medieval times, the jurisdiction of the City was extended to its present boundary, just beyond the Temple, a bar had been built to regulate entry to the City. It was first mentioned c. 1191, and was then merely a chain and some posts, but by 1353 it was a timber gate.

It acquired a ceremonial significance. Placed as it was on the principal road from the City to Westminster, it was particularly decorated for coronation processions, which went from the Tower to Westminster Abbey, and on state occasions even today the monarch coming from Westminster is met at this spot to be admitted to the City's domain.

The old gate survived the Great Fire, but it was thought better to replace it anyway. Wren's design, classical but rather French, included four statues – of James I and his queen, and kings Charles I and Charles II. It was made of Portland stone, with a main gateway and a postern on each side for pedestrians. On top were three iron spikes, so that the heads of executed felons – usually those of men convicted of treason – might be exhibited there.

This structure, long a bottleneck, was dismantled in the 19th century (see 1877) and now stands, considerably dilapidated, in the grounds of Theobald's Park, Enfield.

FULHAM POTTERY ESTABLISHED

John Dwight, an Oxford man who had 'discovered the mystery of the stone or cologne wares hitherto made only in Germany', set up a pottery in Fulham High Street about this year to exploit his invention.

There are two pieces of Dwight's pottery in the Victoria & Albert Museum, one a half-length effigy of his little daughter, who died in 1673, and the other a full-length figure of a female child, possibly the same girl. Dwight also had six sons; four of them died very young and, of the two remaining, one entered the church and would have nothing to do with the business and the other was disinherited for bad behaviour.

Fulham Pottery still survives, albeit in Battersea.

NAVY OFFICE BURNT DOWN

During the Great Fire, Pepys, who was clerk of the Navy Office, had used his influence to save the building from the flames by having near-by buildings destroyed to break their path. Unfortunately he had discontinued his diary by this year, and we do not know the circumstances of a local fire which burnt down the Navy Office in 1673.

REBUILDING ST PAUL'S CATHEDRAL

After the Great Fire, St Paul's Cathedral was patched up and services continued there despite Wren's advice that it should be replaced by a new building. This year the government agreed to the demolition of the old cathedral and Wren was commissioned to build anew. He had been designing a new St Paul's since 1670, and had suggested that a dome be placed over the crossing, but it was not until 1675 that his plans for a new cathedral were accepted, and even then there was much interference.

Temple Bar, where the City and Westminster meet, was designed by Wren and completed in 1673.

At first Wren used gunpowder to bring down the remains of the old building, but this so terrified a number of people that he had to resort to battering rams.

A NEW SCHOOL

The curriculum of most schools was very narrow – grammar, Latin, theology and not much else. Samuel Pepys played a part this year in establishing the Royal Mathematical School at Christ's Hospital. His interest was to train boys for service at sea, and the royal charter, obtained on 19 August, stipulated that 40 boys were 'to be maintained and taught the Art of Arithmatique and Navigacon', entry being restricted to those boys already shown to be adept at 'comon Arithmatique as farr as the Rule of Three'. Books, globes and maps were provided, and at the age of 16 the boys were apprenticed to a ship's captain.

Two years later, when the first boys had passed their examination at Trinity House, the demand for them in the Royal Navy had diminished and they were apprenticed to merchant-navy ships. The early history of the school was unpromising, complicated by the ill management of Christ's Hospital, but the RMS still functions at today's school in Horsham.

BEGINNINGS OF THE PHYSIC GARDEN

This year the Society of Apothecaries obtained on lease on 4 acres of Chelsea Reach as a site on which to build a barge house to shelter its processional barge – that site its now sandwiched between Royal Hospital Road, the Chelsea Embankment and Swan Walk. At that time the embankment did not exist and the river lapped up to the site of the Physic Garden, which the society seems to have begun there by about the following year.

Botanic gardens were not a new idea – Chelsea's was predated by Oxford's, and by those in London formed by John Gerard (in Holborn) and by the Tradescants (father and son) at Lambeth. However, with the acumen of the society behind it, the garden at Chelsea became the finest of its kind in the world.

1674

A NEW THEATRE ROYAL

The second Theatre Royal Drury Lane was opened on 26 March, this time designed by Wren for £4,000. Dryden described the building as 'plain-built' and 'a bare convenience only'. Plain it may have been, but the merged theatre companies of the King's and Duke's players preferred it as their home to the Dorset Garden Theatre (see 1671).

MURDER REVEALED

Demolition work was proceeding by the White Tower at the Tower of London this year. Ten feet beneath a staircase workmen discovered a wooden chest which contained the skeletons of two children, and it was declared that these must be the bones of the two princes, allegedly murdered on the instructions of Richard III. They were reinterred in Westminster Abbey. When in 1933 the bones were examined, experts agreed that the age and period of the skeletons matched the hypothesis.

STREETS IN THE MAKING

Development continued in two separate areas. In Covent Garden, Burleigh Street and Exeter Street had been partly built in 1673, and

The Theatre Royal Drury Lane, built by Wren, but shown here after the embellishments of the Adam brothers in 1775, when owned by David Garrick.

Catherine Street was now extended into the Strand to give better access to the piazza. On the earl of St Alban's St James's estate, Charles II Street, Ryder Street and King Street were taking shape.

JOHN MILTON'S FUNERAL

The poet John Milton died on 8 November when 'gout struck in'. Though he lived near Bunhill Fields and was himself a prominent Dissenter, he was not buried there. Instead he was interred, with the rites of the Church of England, in his father's grave at St Giles without Cripplegate – the location is not now known. 'All his learned and great friends in London, not without concourse of the vulgar, accompanied his body to the Church.' In 1790 an attempt was made at a squalid disinterment to locate his remains, but with no success.

A NEW DEVELOPER

The Great Fire had stimulated, but not begun, the residential move westward from the City. Nobility had already decamped to the Strand and Westminster, but until the earl of St Albans began his estate south of Piccadilly on St James's Fields there were, as he perceptively told the king, few fit houses for that class of resident. Briefly, Covent Garden and Lincoln's Inn Fields promised much, but the greater exclusivity of Bloomsbury Square and St James's Square fed a new appetite.

This year Nicholas Barbon bought up Essex House, a mansion on the south of the Strand opposite St Clement Danes church, on the site of the bishop of Exeter's inn. We have already come across Barbon

sharing with the earl of St Albans the financial risk of St James's Square (see 1665), but he was now to launch into major developments in his own right. He may fairly be called London's first commercial property developer.

He was the son of a famously eccentric member of Parliament known as 'Praise God' Barbon or Barebones, who has the distinction of having a parliament named after him. The son, qualified as a surgeon, turned to far different matters. He was, for example, the founder of fire insurance and a pioneer in land banks. In development, Barbon aimed at a clientele different from that of St Albans. Barbon's houses which lined such roads as Essex Street were for the gentry and the middle class, not for nobility. Furthermore, he did not exclude services such as coffee houses and public houses. He was also fortunate in being able to dispose of some of his land to the adjacent Temple, where in 1675 he was helping to build New Court, and when in 1688 a serious fire damaged buildings there he was back again rebuilding chambers. His first scheme of any size involved the demolition of York House at the western end of the Strand *c.* 1672 and the erection of roads such as Villiers Street and Buckingham Street.

Barbon, like many developers since, lived precariously on credit, always gambling on the success of a scheme, paying off old debts with money newly borrowed. Some of his houses were jerry-built, and often those who lent him money had to wait much longer than agreed before they got it back. But he served his purpose at a decisive time in London's building history. He showed that money could be made from professional exploitation. He also wrote an intelligent pamphlet called *An Apology for the Builder*, in which he defended the great increase of houses in London, urging that there should be considerably more.

A NEAR DISASTER

The market house of the earl of St Albans's St James's Market (see 1664) was occasionally let out for uses other than trade. In 1674 the Presbyterian preacher Richard Baxter held a number of meetings in the upstairs rooms; he was particularly anxious to bring his message to this area of London, where he was convinced that many of the residents 'live like Americans, and have heard no Sermon of many years'. During one meeting, when the room was very crowded, a great crack was heard, and then another, which 'set them all on running and crying out at the windows for Ladders'. Baxter's wife, however, kept her nerve, grabbed hold of a passing carpenter, and had him put a prop beneath the beam concerned. When the beam was later examined, it was found that only a thin section of it was then unbroken and the prop had undoubtedly averted a catastrophe.

1675

BEGINNING ST PAUL'S

The royal warrant authorizing Wren to be architect for the new St Paul's Cathedral and the start of work was issued on 14 May, and the first stone was laid by the master mason Thomas Strong on 21 June. It was to be over 22 years before divine service was performed in the new building.

Wren's original plan was considered too modest. He then produced a second, in the shape of a Greek cross, with nave, chancel and transepts of equal length; the great dome was central, and beneath it were eight smaller domed areas to serve as choir, chapels, vestibule etc. Everything opened into everything else, so that, unlike the compartmental Gothic churches, the whole place was a unified auditorium. To demonstrate what he had in mind, he had made (for £600) the magnificent model usually found today in the crypt of the building.

But, although many liked the design, the ecclesiastical authorities had strong reservations. They wanted a church in which the congregation was still concentrated on the preacher. Wren's subsequent hybrid design was the one that obtained the royal warrant this year, but fortunately the wording allowed him 'liberty in the prosecution of his work to make some variations rather ornamental than essential, as from time to time he should see proper'. It was a fortunate clause, inserted some think with the royal version of a knowing wink, because it enabled Wren to transgress its terms and virtually go back to his Greek-cross design.

Work began on the *whole* cathedral; Wren did not limit himself to building part by part as the money became available (it still had to be raised from coal duties), for he was shrewd enough to know that otherwise the work could be delayed or economies made once enough of the building was available for worship.

AN OBSERVATORY AT GREENWICH

Wren's energy and versatility were boundless. Not only was he about to begin the largest building in the country, not only was he engaged on 50 other churches, not only had he already built two theatres and the Temple Bar, but he was also to be found south of the river designing Flamsteed House, home of the first Greenwich Observatory. The foundation stone was laid on 10 August.

John Flamsteed, still not yet 30, had been born near Derby, the son of a maltster. Usually without much money, always troubled by rheumatics, he was virtually self-taught in most things, and his concentration on astronomy was hardly a way of making a living. But he was deservedly fortunate in his patrons, and in 1674 he took a degree at Cambridge with the intention of taking holy orders and settling near Derby. That year, in London, he supplied a table of the tides and a barometer of his own design to the king, who, when it became essential to study the stars anew so as to find a way of calculating longitude, chose him as the first royal 'astronomical observator'. Wren, a fellow astronomer, concocted the observatory of bricks from Tilbury fort, and 'wood, iron and lead from a gatehouse demolished in the Tower'.

WORSHIP AT ST BRIDE'S

In December the first service was held in one of Wren's most beautiful churches, St Bride's in Fleet Street. The spire, described as a 'madrigal in stone', followed in 1703, and it is said that William Rich, a pastrycook who worked in Ludgate Hill, had the happy idea of fashioning his wedding cakes in the shape of the new steeple.

BEGINNING OF GOLDEN SQUARE

Despite being so close to Piccadilly Circus, Golden Square is unfamiliar to many. (Even in 1708 Edward Hatton spoke of it as 'being not exactly in anybody's way'.) Though a licence to build had been obtained in 1673, disputes between the landowners delayed matters and building work probably began about this year, and even then was very slow. The site was called Gelding Close (a field for geldings), and 'Golden Square' appears to be a corruption of this.

It was intended to be a good-class area. The scheme, approved by Wren in his role of surveyor-general, was to have houses of brick and stone, there were to be 'substantial pavements' and 'sufficient sewers', and 'noysome and offensive trades' were banned. The houses on the western side had uninterrupted views at that time to Hyde Park.

By the beginning of the next century the square had a sprinkling of nobility, such as the king's sometime mistress Barbara Villiers, duchess of Cleveland, but in the 18th century it was much occupied by artists, such as Angelica Kauffmann, and in more modern times by woollen and clothing manufacturers and entertainment businesses.

THREAT TO COFFEE HOUSES

By this time coffee houses had become an 'important political institution ... and the chief organs through which the public opinion of the metropolis vented itself'. It was no wonder that a government proclamation ordered their closure as they were 'a seat of scandal'. However, so much stock of coffee and tea was still in hand that the government relented and then abandoned its plan.

One celebrated house was founded this year: the Amsterdam Coffee House, behind the Royal Exchange. It was a place favoured by the Hudson's Bay Company, which used it for hiring seamen.

A NEW WATERWORKS

Ralph Bucknall and Ralph Wayne obtained a licence to erect a waterworks at the end of today's Villiers Street. This became the York Buildings Waterworks Company, named after the development on the site of York House. Water was pumped from the Thames to supply the Strand area.

1676

SOUTHWARK ON FIRE

Fire touched London again. Those who ten years earlier had lined the southern banks of the Thames and gazed at the City burning were now themselves victims. The blaze began in the early hours of 26 May in the cellar of an oil shop in Borough High Street. It was spotted by letter carriers, but before the door could be broken down the oil had exploded and the fire expanded. It is thought that about 500 premises were destroyed, including the George and Talbot (Tabard) inns, the White Hart, St Margaret's church and the meal market. The old courthouse and jail were blown up to provide a firebreak before St Mary Overie, but this blast resulted in the death of several people. The church was saved and so too was St Thomas's hospital.

A NEW BETHLEHEM

The hospital of St Mary Bethlehem, the principal hospital for mentally ill patients, was moved this year to a new site in Moorfields. The old building was fairly decayed and inadequate. It had been described in 1632 as having 'twenty-one rooms wherein the poor distracted people lie, and above the stairs eight rooms more for servants and the poor to lie in, and a long waste room now being contrived and in work, to make eight more rooms for poor people to lodge where they lacked room before'.

Robert Hooke was the architect of the new asylum, which cost £17,000 and was completed in July this year. It was located on London Wall, on a site now occupied by Finsbury Circus.

SHOPS IN THE STRAND

Exeter Change was built on the site of Exeter House in the Strand, immediately to the east of Burleigh Street. A long, classical building, it was essentially a shopping mall with workshops above. John Strype described it in 1720 as having *two walks below stairs and as many above with shops on each side for seam-stresses, milliners, hosiers, etc., the builders judging that it would come into great request, but it received a check in its infancy, I suppose by those of the New Exchange, so that, instead of growing in better esteem, it became worse and worse, in so much as the first walk near the street can hardly meet with tenants, those backwards lying useless, and those above converted to other uses.*

In fact the premises above were made into a funeral parlour in which bodies were laid out for visitors – in 1732 John Gay, composer of *The Beggar's Opera*, was displayed here before his burial at Westminster Abbey.

NEW CHURCHES IN THE CITY

Rebuilt churches in the City, all by Wren, were now commonplace. This year St Mary Aldermanbury, St Mildred (Poultry), St Olave Old Jewry, St Stephen Coleman, St Magnus the Martyr (the first to be destroyed in the Great Fire), and St Christopher le Stocks were all finished. In 1674 St Dionis Backchurch was completed, as was St George (Botolph Lane). Some churches, such as St Benet Fink and St Michael (Wood Street), were in use by 1673 before they were finished.

Wren was also involved with a new church – St James Piccadilly. The foundation stone was laid on 3 April.

INTRODUCTION OF CALICO PRINTING

The first calico-printer in England was established in West Ham this year. This industry was to continue on the banks of the river Lea and its tributaries for the next 200 years.

1677

THE MONUMENT COMPLETED

The Great Fire at last got its memorial. An Act of Parliament had ordered 'That a Column or Pillar of Brase or Stone be erected on or as neere unto the place where the said Fire soe unhappily began as conveniently may be, in perpetual Remembrance'. Inevitably the Monument, in Fish Street Hill, was to be Wren's responsibility, but it was probably his friend Robert Hooke who did much of the design.

On the north panel the inscription relates that the column (still the largest stone column in the world) is 202 ft high – the distance from its base to the house in Pudding Lane where the Fire began. (Some five years later the inscription was amended to blame papists for the fire; they had already, in the distrustful atmosphere of the day, been accused of beginning the Southwark fire of 1676.) The pillar is hollow and contains a black marble staircase of 345 steps to the exterior balcony.

A NEW MAP OF LONDON

The first map of London after the Fire was published this year. It was compiled by a former dancing master, John Ogilby (1600–1676), whose career was cut short when he badly injured a leg during a court masque. He went on to teach dancing and become a soldier in Ireland, but he arrived back in London in 1641 quite destitute. He was an industrious man, for he then went to Cambridge and learned Latin and Greek, and was soon launched on a new career of writing and publishing. He was living at Whitefriars when the Great Fire devoured his stock.

The City appointed him to survey disputed areas of the City, but it was not until he was nearly 70 that, with the assistance of William

The Monument to the Great Fire, designed by Wren, in Fish Street Hill.

Morgan, he began work on one of the greatest cartographic treasures we have. His map, on 20 sheets, is to the scale of 100 ft to the inch, and it was measured out by the use of a 'waywiser', in effect a wheel pushed along that measured the distance travelled. Ogilby's map remained the most accurate depiction of London until the Ordnance Survey in the 1850s.

St Paul's is shown laid out in its eventual shape; the Fleet Canal is prominent, with lighters moored in its lower reaches; the Monument is marked as 'The Pillar where ye Fire began 1666'; many spaces (or at least churchyards) show where churches formerly stood. North of Cheapside, Honey Lane Market is a new foundation: it is a meat market with about 100 stalls. From the Guildhall a new road goes straight to the Thames (now King Street and Queen Street). More prominent is the arrangement at the riverside; here the fire debris was used to create a new embankment – the New Quay as it was called – which for the time being created a uniform landing space (preserving behind it quite a lot of the old medieval wall).

FIRST LONDON DIRECTORY

In October a *Directory of London Merchants* was issued by Roger L'Estrange. This is thought to have been the first London directory.

A GREEK CHURCH IN SOHO

Some Greek Christians fled to London to escape the renewed ascendancy of the Ottoman Turks. In 1674 three of them wrote to the Privy Council seeking a site outside the City on which to erect a church, and this project was eventually carried through by Joseph Georgirenes, a priest, in 1677. The church was situated in what was then Hog Lane, on a site now occupied by St Martin's School of Art in Charing Cross Road.

In 1681 it was realized that the wrong area of London had been chosen (the potential congregation consisted mainly of Greek seamen or merchants, who were in the East End or the City), and it was decided to dispose of the building and start again somewhere else. Georgirenes then found himself caught in the 17th-century equivalent of small print that he had either not looked at or not understood. He did not, in fact, own the church as he thought, and he was obliged to sell his interest at a reduced price to the parish. However, there is a lasting reminder of his church in the name of Greek Street, which runs behind the site of the church.

BEGINNINGS OF A LONDON FORTUNE

The marriage took place on 10 October at St Clement Danes between Sir Thomas Grosvenor and the 12-year-old Mary Davies. He was a scion of an old family originally settled in Cheshire, she the daughter of a scrivener, Alexander Davies, who owned 100 acres of what is now Mayfair and 400 acres of what is now Belgravia and Pimlico, which were then little better than marshland. Davies himself had inherited these properties from an immensely rich uncle, Hugh Audley. At this stage Grosvenor had the larger income, but she, of course, had the greater potential.

1678

ARUNDEL HOUSE DEMOLISHED

Another nobleman's house in the Strand was demolished. Possibly inspired by the example of Nicholas Barbon's development to the east, on the grounds of Essex House, the earl of Arundel demolished his own house and on it constructed Arundel Street, Howard Street, Norfolk Street and Surrey Street. The site had previously been that of the inn of the bishop of Bath and Wells, set back and hardly visible from the roadway, and with gardens down to the Thames. During the minority rule of Edward VI, this property had been grasped by Lord Thomas Seymour, the brother of the Protector, Somerset. Seymour was later beheaded, and the house was bought by the earl of Arundel for just over £40.

It was from the top of Arundel House that Wenceslaus Hollar, brought to England by the earl of Arundel in 1636, drew his famous perspective of London.

As to the early Arundel Street, John Gay described it for us in his *Trivia*:

Behold that narrow street which steep descends,
Whose buildings to the slimy shore extends;
Here Arundel's fam'd structure rear'd its frame,
The street alone retains the empty name.

PLEASURES NORTH AND SOUTH

Two pleasure gardens, of the kind becoming common in London, began this year. One was Mother Huff's, off the Spaniard's Road in Hampstead – principally a tea garden, but also licensed to sell alcohol. A larger establishment was Cuper's Gardens in Lambeth, its site today taken by the National Theatre and the southern approach to Waterloo Bridge. The demolition of Arundel House prompted the earl's gardener, Boydell Cuper, to take this land on the other side of the river and decorate it with many of the busts and statues in the old mansion. John Aubrey, writing at about this time, said that 'the conveniency of its arbours, walks and several remains of Greek and Roman antiquities, have made this place much frequented'.

But the speciality of the house was fireworks. A mid-18th-century writer recorded that Cuper's Gardens

had been once famous for this summer entertainment; but then his fireworks were so well understood, and conducted with so superior an understanding, that they never made their appearance to the company till they had been well cooled, by being drawn through a long canal of water, with the same kind of refinement that the Eastern people smoke their tobacco through the same medium.

THE MURDER OF EDMUND GODFREY

Sir Edmund Berry Godfrey, magistrate of Westminster, was murdered on 12 October; his body was found on the 17th on the south side of Primrose Hill. The crime was a famous one, since in the anti-papist atmosphere of the day it was alleged that the murderer was a Catholic. Godfrey had been killed by his own sword, but he had not been robbed. The inquest tended to show that he had been suffocated first and then stabbed, and that his body had been brought to Primrose Hill.

Popular agitation was fomented by Titus Oates and his followers, and eventually a silversmith called Prance, a Catholic, was found who could be tortured to confess; he retracted his story later, and then repeated it again. As a result three Catholics – Green, Berry and Hill – were arrested, the first two of whom were hanged. For a time Primrose Hill, which had previously been known as Greenberry Hill, was again known by its old name, due to the coincidence of the names of the accused. In 1682 Prance again withdrew his story, was fined £100, and was whipped from Newgate to Tyburn, where he stood in the pillory. The truth remains elusive to this day.

EXECUTION AT KENNINGTON

As a 'warning to bad wives', Sarah Elston was burnt at the stake at Kennington Common this year for the murder of her husband. At her execution 'she was dressed in white, with a vast multitude of people attending her, and after very solemn prayers offered on the said occasion, the fire was kindled, and giving two or three lamentable shrieks, she was deprived both of voice and life, and so burnt to ashes'.

A NEW COLLEGE OF ARMS

The records of the College of Arms were saved in the Fire, but the building was not. The present building, finished this year, was designed by Maurice Emmett as four sides around a quadrangle – one side of which has since been lost to Queen Victoria Street. The wrought-iron gates, though old, were not installed until 1956.

1679

FIRE AT THE MIDDLE TEMPLE

A lawyer called Narcissus Luttrell recorded in his diary for 26 January a large fire at the Temple:

1600s

about 11 at night, broke out a fire in the chamber of one Mr Thornbury, in Pump court, in the Middle Temple. It burnt very furiously, and consumed, in the Middle Temple, Pump court, Elm Tree court, Vine court, Middle Temple lane, and part of Brick court. It burnt down also, in the Inner Temple, the cloysters, and greatest part of Hare court; the library was blown up. The Thames being frozen, there was great scarcity of water; it being so bitter a frost, the water hung in isecles at the e'ves of the houses. The engines plaid away many barrells of beer to stop the fire; but the cheif way of stopping the fire was the blowing up houses.

One of the most serious losses was the library of the scholar Elias Ashmole, whose chamber was near where the fire began. He lost the collection of 33 years, 9,000 coins and a large repository of seals, charters and other antiquities. Fortunately, his collection of manuscripts, which formed the basis of the Ashmolean Museum, was in his house at Lambeth.

DRYDEN ATTACKED IN COVENT GARDEN
An attack on the poet John Dryden is today commemorated on the ceiling of an alleyway next to the Lamb and Flag public house in Rose Street, Covent Garden. The incident happened late at night on 18 December, when Dryden was returning from Will's Coffee House in Bow Street to his lodgings in Long Acre; as today, Rose Street was a dark and secluded place. It is thought that the assault (by three men) was paid for by the earl of Rochester, who believed that Dryden had satirized him in a recent publication. However, a painted plaque in the narrow passageway next to the Lamb and Flag suggests that the instigator of the attack was the duchess of Portsmouth. The culprits were never caught, despite the offer of a £50 reward. The poet Samuel Butler died of consumption in his lodgings in the same alley in 1680.

THE FIRST TURKISH BATH
A bagnio was opened in December in a court off Newgate Street. According to John Aubrey, this first Turkish bath in London was opened by Turkish merchants. Edward Hatton's *New View of London*, published in 1708, records, 'Here is one very spacious room with a cupola roof, besides others lesser; the walls are neatly set with Dutch tile. The charge of the house for sweating, rubbing, shaving, cupping, and bathing, is 4 shillings each person. There are nine servants who attend.' Women had special days twice a week.

The building was demolished in 1876 for extension of the General Post Office.

DEMONSTRATION IN THE CITY
Anti-Catholic feeling was rife in the City. Quite unsubstantiated accusations of papist plots were commonplace, and broadsides spread their lies. With the king's health poor and the prospect of the Catholic duke of York mounting the throne, there was something akin to religious panic. A fire which had on 9 May destroyed much of the New Prison, Clerkenwell, was blamed on papists.

NEW CHURCHES
St Edmund the King in Lombard Street was finished in 1679. It was in this church that Joseph Addison married the countess of Warwick in 1716.

St Stephen Walbrook was also completed, though it too had been in use for several years. In this building Wren tried out some of his ideas for St Paul's, and it remains one of his most admired parish churches; the parishioners gave him a hogshead of claret as a mark of their gratitude, and Lady Wren 20 guineas in a silken purse. The steeple was not

begun until 1713. Dr Nathaniel Hodges, a doctor who had stayed in London during the Plague and had treated many of the victims, is commemorated in a memorial in the middle of the north wall. He put his own preservation down to a regular glass of sack.

1680

MORE NEW CHURCHES
A church which survived the Fire, St Clement Danes, was this year demolished. Unfortunately its fabric had been found to be unsafe, and all but the tower, rebuilt in 1670, was taken down. Wren – inevitably – designed the new building, keeping but altering the old tower; the building was completed in 1682. The spire which adorns the Strand today was added *c.* 1719 by James Gibbs. This was to be one of the favourite churches of Dr Johnson.

Though already in use for several years, the new St Mary-le-Bow was completed this year. In excavating for the new building a Roman pavement was found, and it is on this that Wren rested the foundations of the tower which protrudes into Cheapside. Classical orders from Tuscan to Corinthian go up the tower to the dragon weathervane at the top, and the famous Bow Bells were installed (which came crashing down in the Blitz in 1940).

Across the river, St Mary Magdalen, Bermondsey, next to the site of the old monastery, was rebuilt this year.

FIRE AT GRAY'S INN
A year after a serious fire in the Temple, in February a fire burnt 50 or 60 chambers in Gray's Inn.

FIRST FIRE-INSURANCE COMPANY
Fire, as we have seen from the devastation of the Great Fire and the Southwark fire, was, like plague, a familiar force to be reckoned with in London. In 1680 the first fire-insurance company was formed, working from premises behind the Royal Exchange; the brainchild of the developer Nicholas Barbon, this company was by 1705 known as the Phenix Office. Though the first such company, it was not the most successful, for it did business only until 1713, just as more durable companies, such as the Hand-in-Hand, the Sun and, a few years later, the Westminster, were getting into their stride.

Initially insurance was only for buildings, but it was later extended to contents. However, it was some years before the fire brigades formed by insurance companies were obliged to rescue occupants. Firemen were usually specially recruited watermen.

DEVELOPMENTS IN SOHO
Soho Square was begun about this time, and 14 houses were in the rate books by 1683. It was originally known as Frith Square, after Richard Frith its developer, then King Square, by which time a statue of Charles II was in the middle of the square, and from the 1740s Soho Square. ('Soho' is an old hunting call, and the name is presumed to have been derived from that.)

Frith Street first appears in the rate books this year, though its development took ten years. Many of its first residents were minor aristocracy, who gradually gave way to an artistic clientele. Greek Street appears the same year, taking its name from the Greek church behind it (see 1677). The Pillar of Hercules pub can, with not too much assumption, be traced back to 1709.

CONCERT ROOMS OFF THE STRAND

Some professional musicians about this year began a concert rooms in York Buildings in Villiers Street, off the Strand. The rooms were occasionally used for auctions, and became known as the Vendu.

1681

THE BEGINNINGS OF THE ROYAL HOSPITAL, CHELSEA

Evelyn's diary for 14 September touches on the beginnings of this famous institution. 'Din'd with Sir *Step: Fox* [of the Royal Society, but also the paymaster general]: Who proposed to me the purchasing of *Chelsey Coll*; which his Majestie had sometime given to our *Society*, & would now purchase it of us againe, to build an Hospital for Souldiers there.' The Chelsea College was a theological teaching institution (see 1609) which had never proceeded very far and had been abandoned.

In this project the king was following the example of the Hôtel des Invalides in Paris. Fox provided much of the money himself, Evelyn organized the venture, and Wren designed it.

HORTICULTURAL HAPPENINGS

The most celebrated garden nurseries in the London area have been at Brompton, Fulham, Hackney and Highgate: that at Brompton Park, between today's Kensington Road and Cromwell Road, covered about 100 acres. It was founded this year by George London, with gardener Henry Wise as his partner. Thomas Bowack described it in 1705:

The riverside front of the Royal Hospital Chelsea, designed by Wren.

And in this parish is that spot of Ground call'd Brompton-Park, so much Fam'd all over the Kingdom, for a Nursery of Plants, and fine Greens of all sorts, which supply most of the Nobility and Gentlemen in England. This Nursery was rais'd by Mr London and Mr Wise, and now 'tis brought to its greatest Perfection, and kept in extraordinary Order, in which a great number of Men are constantly Employ'd. The stock seems almost Incredible, for if we believe some who affirm that the several Plants in it were valued at but 1d a piece, they would amount to above £40,000.

Evelyn later described here the 'store of elms, limes, platans, Constantinople chestnuts, and black cherry trees'.

The site of these gardens is today taken up by Queen's Gate and roads off, and the Natural History and Victoria & Albert museums.

A WAVE OF HUGUENOTS

The persecution of French Protestants (Huguenots) did not begin with the revocation of the protective legislation, the Edict of Nantes, in 1685 – their flight to England had begun much earlier. Part of the Savoy Palace (which in the late 1620s had been used as a hospital for soldiers injured in the expedition to La Rochelle to help the Huguenots) was by this time used as a French church. This year

Charles II was petitioned by the leaders of this church to help the immigration of those Huguenots fleeing from France, to which the king agreed. In August 322 of these 'distressed poor Protestants who fled from Popish cruelty in France' arrived in London to find a City still gripped by anti-Catholic fever. Evidence of their number in London at this time includes their leasing of the Greek church in Soho in 1682.

1682

THREE NEW LONDON MARKETS

John Balch, an entrepreneur who obtained a licence this year to establish Spitalfields Market, was particularly lucky – within three years the influx of Huguenot refugees into the area was to ensure its success. It did not, in fact, open until 1684.

Hungerford Market, on the site of Charing Cross station, was opened in 1682. It was built by Sir Edward Hungerford, and possibly designed by Wren, on the site of Hungerford's old house, which had been mostly destroyed by fire in 1669 and was now too ruinous to restore. The market, vying with Covent Garden (which at that time had no market building), had several advantages over its neighbour. First, it had access to the Thames and the market gardens of Pimlico; Hungerford built a new set of stairs down to the river.

Second, it had an elegant market building, with a colonnade on the west for shops, and rooms above. And, third, it was adjacent to the major developments south of the Strand. It was not a failure but not a great success (and, indeed, was rebuilt in 1833 by Charles Fowler, the architect of Covent Garden Market). Its main drawback as trade increased was its restricted site – Covent Garden had the whole square for its business and, because the Bedfords owned the land around, could expand into the side streets.

Hungerford Market and its tolls were made over in 1685 to Sir Christopher Wren himself and to Sir Stephen Fox, his friend the paymaster general, and the market was later bought by Henry Wise, partner in the Brompton nurseries (see 1681).

A smaller market was also licensed this year on the grounds of Brooke House, Holborn, where the sheriff proclaimed it open in October.

A BAGNIO IN LONG ACRE

The Duke's Bagnio was opened in Long Acre this year, on the south side, by Conduit Court. In this Turkish bath was 'a large hall where the porter stands to receive the money. Hence we pass through an entry into another room, where hangs a pair of scales to weigh such as, out of curiosity, would know how much they lose in weight while they are in the Bagnio'. The bagnio was a 'stately edifice, of an oval figure, in length 45 feet and in breadth 35'. On 'Women's Days there are all imaginable conveniences of privacy, and not a man to be seen, but all the servants are of the female sex'.

THE BUILDING OF DOWNING STREET

A house stood on the site of No. 10 before Downing Street was built. It was occupied in 1605 by Thomas Knyvet, magistrate, who, with an armed guard, was to surprise and arrest Guy Fawkes in the cellars of the Houses of Parliament that November. Knyvet had acquired the property, which was or had been the Axe Brewery, from the Crown in 1581. The next owner was his niece, Elizabeth Hampden, mother of John Hampden, one of the five members of Parliament whom Charles I attempted to arrest in the chamber of the House of Commons in 1642, and aunt of Oliver Cromwell: after the Restoration the late Protector's exhumed head was displayed on the roof of Westminster Hall within a short distance of the ageing Mrs Hampden.

Her property was acquired in 1654, subject to a lease to Mrs Hampden, by George Downing, but he was unable to start building on much of the land because the Hampden family relentlessly held on to the title. Downing was not able to proceed with his full scheme for the erection of the street until 1682. This famous street is named after one of the less attractive characters in English history. Even the restrained *Dictionary of National Biography* remarks that his military and political career was stained by 'servility, treachery and avarice'. Pepys was rude about him, and so was his own mother.

FLOODS IN LONDON

There was a severe storm on 25 April, which flooded St James's Park and inundated areas close to the river; the vestry minutes for Brentford report that it was possible to row a boat up the main street.

1683

MR SADLER'S WELL

A Thomas Sadler, surveyor of highways, had workmen dig gravel in his own garden this year. They found the remains of an old well which the astute Sadler found to be 'medicinal' and immediately proceeded to exploit, with Tunbridge and Epsom as his examples. A wooden music hall was opened on 3 June, staging occasional events; it was not until 1765 that a more permanent structure was built there.

ANOTHER TURKISH BATH

The craze for Turkish baths was catching on. In the south-east corner of Covent Garden Piazza a new one opened called a 'hummums' (from the Turkish *hammam*). The Hummums not only offered the usual 'sweating and bathing' but overnight lodgings as well.

NEW ALMSHOUSES FOR ST MARTIN'S

The parish of St Martin-in-the-Fields opened new almshouses about this year in what is now Charing Cross Road. They surrounded the old Greek church (see 1677) on three sides, and eventually were to house 60 old women. The successors to these houses still stand in Camden Town, off Bayham Street, where new buildings were erected in 1818.

A BLACKHEATH FAIR

A fair on Blackheath began this year. The ever-travelling John Evelyn was there to see it:

went to Black-heath, to see the new faire, being the first, procured by the L: Dartmoth, this being the first day, pretended for the sale of Cattell; but I think in truth to inrich the new tavern at the bowling-greene, erected by Snape, his Majesties farrier, a man full of projects: There appeared nothing but an innumerable assemblie of drinking people from Lond, Pedlers &c: & I suppose it too neere Lond; to be of any greate use for the Country.

EXECUTION IN HOLBORN

In July, William, Lord Russell, condemned to death for his part in the Rye House Plot against the monarchy, was brought from Newgate in his own coach with a guard of watchmen and trained bands, to fields west of Lincoln's Inn. The scaffold was lined with black and the crowd was numerous. 'Ketch the executioner severed his head from his body at three strokes, very barbarously.'

CLARENDON HOUSE SOLD

The immense mansion on Piccadilly of the disgraced earl of Clarendon was sold again this year. It had been bought by the duke of Albemarle in 1675 for £25,000 (at best, half of what the house had cost to build), but the spendthrift lord was unable to hold on to the property and in 1683 sold it on again, making a reported £10,000 profit. Among the syndicate of 'rich bankers & Mechanics', as Evelyn called them, who bought the house and grounds was Sir Thomas Bond; other members were Henry Jermyn, later created Baron Dover, and Margaret Stafford, a Northamptonshire lady.

At first a square was planned, apeing the successful St James's Square, but instead streets were built, whose names commemorate the participants. Bond Street stretched only as far as Burlington Gardens, which was the limit of the Clarendon estate, and was not extended to Oxford Street until the 1720s, when the City of London estate of Conduit Fields was developed.

1684

FROST FAIR ON THE THAMES

From the beginning of December 1683 until 5 February this year the weather was so cold that the Thames froze hard enough for a small town to be erected on it. John Evelyn described it on 24 January:

The frost still continuing more & more severe, the Thames before London was planted with bothes in formal streetes, as in a Citty, or Continual faire, all sorts of Trades & shops furnished, & full of Commodities, even to a Printing presse, where the People & ladys tooke a fansy to have their names Printed … on the Thames: This humour tooke so universaly, that 'twas estimated the Printer gained five pounds a day for printing a line onely, at six-pence a Name, besides what he gott by Ballads &c: Coaches now plied from Westminster to the Temple, & from severall other staires too & froo, as in the streetes; also on sleds, sliding with skeetes; There was likewise Bull-baiting, Horse & Coach races, Pupet-plays & interludes, Cookes & Tipling, & lewder places …

A NEW CHURCH IN PICCADILLY

St James Piccadilly was consecrated on 13 July, although the building, designed by Wren, was still far from finished; the church was given its own parish in the same year. The vestrymen were still discussing the steeple and spire two years later, when Wren's design was rejected in favour of that of a local carpenter. But when the tower and spire were constructed the spire was found to be so unsafe, and likely to cause

A view of the fair on the Thames during the severe winter of 1683–4, taken by the riverside stairs near the Temple.

disaster once lead had been laid on top and the bells installed, that it was taken down and put into storage. One can only wonder at Wren's forbearance, for the architect – at the height of his powers, and with so many buildings to his credit – was then asked by the vestry to come back, check on the building of the tower and, in 1700, complete the work; it is still not certain whose design the existing spire is.

Wren was particularly pleased with this church, built as it was without the restrictions on space that he usually encountered. He was confident that all 2,000 people attending it could hear the preacher – in sharp contrast to pre-Reformation buildings, where, as he commented, 'it is enough if they hear the Murmer of the Mass, and see the elevation of the Host'.

Other Wren churches completed or open this year or the last were All Hallows the Great in Upper Thames Street, St Antholin in Watling Street – a remarkable building needlessly demolished in the 1870s – St Augustine in the same road, St Mildred, Bread Street, and St Martin, Ludgate Hill.

TROUBLE IN RED LION SQUARE

The developer Nicholas Barbon turned his attention this year to Holborn, where the Red Lion Fields presented him with a new development opportunity. But it also brought violence. The fields were to the rear of the Red Lion public house in Holborn and were extensively used for recreation, particularly by law students at Gray's Inn. Barbon began laying out the site in June, but on the 10th a battle using bricks and other building materials took place between 100 lawyers and the workmen; some of the participants were injured.

The development was of good quality, and among the early tenants were many lawyers from Gray's Inn itself. Barbon was also developing Bedford Row nearby – nos. 42–43 are surviving houses from his scheme.

A NEW SPA AT ISLINGTON

The success of Sadler's Wells prompted the opening of another 'spa' this year, just to the south of it. It was grandly called Islington Spa (although it was in Clerkenwell) or the Threepenny Academy (a name deriving from its admission fee), or, even more grandly, New Tunbridge Wells. An advertisement in the 1690s announced that the waters were free to poor people 'bringing a Certificate under the hand of any known Physician'.

POWIS HOUSE BURNS DOWN

Powis House, one of the principal houses in Lincoln's Inn Fields, burnt down on 26 October; the family escaped but lost all their possessions. Powis rebuilt it to a larger scale, employing the Dutch architect William Winde, but work was still unfinished when, in 1688, the marquis went into exile with James II. In December that year the house was lucky to escape damage when an anti-Catholic mob destroyed a nearby Catholic chapel. In 1705 the house came into the possession of the duke of Newcastle, after whom it was subsequently called. It still survives as nos. 66–67 Lincoln's Inn Fields.

A PUBLIC LIBRARY IN WESTMINSTER

John Evelyn relates in his diary in February that he had been approached by Dr Tenison, vicar of St Martin-in-the-Fields, for advice on the foundation and erection of a public library in the parish. Tenison said that 'there were 30 or 40 Young Men in *Orders* in his Parish, either, Governors to young Gent: or Chaplains to Noble-men, who being reprov'd by him upon occasion, for frequenting Taverns or Coffé-houses, told him, they would study & employ their time better, if they had books'. Christopher Wren was brought in to design the building, which, with its 4,000 books, was open to all Westminster parishioners. (The collection included an early Chaucer manuscript.) The building, located at the southern end of today's Charing Cross Road, was demolished in 1861 to make way for an extension to the National Gallery.

1685

MORE HUGUENOTS

Those French Protestants who had not already left France were this year presented with a religious dilemma. With the revocation of the

Edict of Nantes, which tolerated their own worship, they had either to flee or to abjure their faith. Most of those who took flight went to the Low Countries or to England. In London they settled particularly in Spitalfields, where weaving was a speciality, in Clerkenwell, which became the area for jewellery, clocks and instruments, and in Soho. There were already established Huguenot communities in all three places.

The Huguenots, like many immigrants after them, were resourceful in forming a structure of support for those of their members who were experiencing hard times. Soon there was a Spitalfields soup kitchen, a French hospital was founded in Old Street, Clerkenwell, and a Huguenot Masonic lodge helped those in need in Soho, where they already had a church – they had other churches in Threadneedle Street and the Savoy. By 1700 there were 28 of their churches in the area now comprising Greater London.

This 'Quiet Conquest', as it has been called, was probably not entirely welcome to Londoners, for the incomers represented considerable trade competition, as the quality of their goods, particularly their silk, was usually better than the home manufacture. One may see opposition to them shrouded in a 'planning appeal' when the parishioners of St Martin Orgar protested at the proposal by Huguenots to renovate what was left of the old church (it was badly damaged in the Fire, and the congregation had abandoned it for St Clement, Eastcheap). One of their reasons to oppose was that the renewal of a church here would 'create a perpetual settlement for Foreigners in the Heart of the City to the prejudice of our own merchants and Traders'.

A CATHOLIC KING

Charles II died at Whitehall on 6 February and was buried in Westminster Abbey. He had no legitimate heir, and his brother, James, duke of York, succeeded to the throne. The coronation was held on 23 April; since the new king was a Catholic, the ceremony was one of tempered Protestant ritual, but at least the music was composed by Purcell and Dr Blow, the king's organist. The new queen had a crown estimated to have cost £300,000, and the king's crown which his brother had worn was too large for James and at times it sat precariously on his head; this was taken as an omen of things to come.

TITUS OATES TAKEN

The last years of Charles II's reign had been dominated by anti-Catholic propaganda, sermons, broadsheets and riots. In particular, the future James II had been vilified, and most frequently by one Titus Oates, a demagogue and persistent perjurer. He warned of a 'popish plot' – allegedly a scheme to replace Charles II by his brother, the Catholic duke of York. The extravagance of the slanders caught the imagination of the mob, the fantasy became the fact, and for a time Oates was the most lauded man in London. When a justice of the peace, Sir Edmund Godfrey, was found murdered on Primrose Hill (see 1678) it served only to confirm the existence of a plot and to inflame the already explosive atmosphere. Even Parliament was swept along, announcing its belief that a conspiracy existed. At the height of his power, Oates could apparently accuse anyone and with perjured evidence condemn him to death. Over 30 men were executed during the mania.

Credulity waned eventually, and in 1685 Oates was imprisoned himself. Found guilty of perjury, he was fined and sentenced to stand in the pillory annually at certain places and times, to be whipped from Aldgate to Newgate and from Newgate to Tyburn, and to be imprisoned for the rest of his life.

He remained intransigently opposed to James II during his imprisonment. He also fathered a child on a bedmaker in the prison. He was released in 1689 after the flight of James II.

INTRODUCTION OF THE GREENHOUSE

Evelyn records this year in his diary possibly the first greenhouse in England. Visiting John Watts, keeper of the Physic Garden at Chelsea, he noted 'what was very ingenious the subterranean heate, conveyed by a stove under the Conserveatory, which was all Vaulted with brick; so as he leaves the doores & windowes open in the hardest frosts, secluding onely the snow &c'.

DEVELOPMENT IN KENSINGTON

London's expansion leapt this year to Kensington, where, south of the High Street, Kensington Square was laid out and mostly erected by Thomas Young, a local builder, after whom an adjoining street is

The duke of Monmouth was executed for treason on Tower Hill in 1685, by a hangman renowned for his inefficiency (see 1686).

named. It was a daring gamble among the fields, but Young was lucky because within a few years the court of William and Mary moved to nearby Kensington Palace and demand for houses in his square ensured its success.

CARLISLE HOUSE BUILT

The principal residence in Soho Square was Carlisle House, on the site of today's St Patrick's church. Its first occupant, this year, was Edward Howard, 2nd earl of Carlisle, whose family retained it until 1753.

1686

A CHURCH IN SOHO

Evidence of the growing population of Soho was the consecration of St Anne's, in Wardour Street, on 21 March. Oddly, it is not known if the architect was Wren or William Talman – or both. At that stage the church was without its spire.

The body of this building was destroyed in the last war and only the tower (itself a rebuilding of 1803) survives.

THE HANGMEN DEPOSED

The public hangman at this period was Jack Ketch, a name applied willy-nilly to executioners since. On two prominent occasions – the execution of William, Lord Russell, in 1683 and of the duke of Monmouth in 1685 – he performed his task with notorious inefficiency. In January 1686 he offended the City sheriffs and was imprisoned himself in the Marshalsea. His place was taken by one Pascha Rose, a butcher, but he was himself hanged in June and Ketch took up the position once more.

MONTAGU HOUSE DESTROYED

Great Russell Street had been laid out in about 1670. One of the first mansions here, near Southampton House, was Montagu House, finished about 1678 for Ralph Montagu, who 'obtained both an earldom and a dukedom from different monarchs, and married in succession two of the richest widows of his day'. In 1673 his wife was a niece of the earl of Southampton, and it was therefore possible to build his own mansion near Southampton House, which stood at the northern side of Southampton (later Bloomsbury) Square, and to share the view of extensive fields stretching north to the hills of Highgate and Hampstead. Unfortunately, no illustrations exist of the house that Robert Hooke built for him – it was destroyed by fire in January this year. Narcissus Luttrell recorded the event in his diary: 'About 12 at night, began a dreadful fire in Montague house, which in a short time consumed the greatest part of that stately fabrick; the losse is computed to be above £60,000 to the lord Mountague and the earl of Devonshire, who had taken the house for some time.' By March rebuilding had begun of a house later to be used for the British Museum.

About the same time, to the west of Montagu House, Thanet House was completed – its site today is taken by nos. 100–102 Great Russell Street. There is a tradition that the house was built by Wren, but no evidence for this appears in the Bedford estate records.

A MARKET FOR SOHO

There is still evidence of Soho's first market. Newport Court and Newport Place, off the Charing Cross Road, today almost entirely taken up by Chinatown shops, were once part of Newport Market, established this year for all merchandise except live cattle. In 1720 John Strype described it as 'a good Market-house, with Shambels for Butchers in the Midst, with Shops round about it: But at present is not so well served with Provisions as in Time it may be by the Resort of Country People to it with their Necessaries, Clare Market much eclipsing it'. In 1693 a Huguenot congregation hired a room over the market house for their worship.

With so many butchers and slaughterhouses the market gradually became a slum, and in the 19th century it was one of the more notorious areas that particularly concerned Gladstone in his campaign to rescue prostitutes.

1687

ZOAR CHAPEL AND SCHOOL BUILT

On a site between today's Southwark Street and the new Tate Gallery stood Zoar Chapel (Zoar was the city that Lot turned to for refuge after fleeing Sodom), sometimes known as Bunyan's Meeting House. Possibly John Bunyan did preach here, but he died the following year and so his association with the building would have been very short. It was one of the earliest Baptist chapels, and also served as the first Nonconformist school of which we have records. Interior and exterior views published early in the 19th century show it to have been probably a converted barn.

BRIDGEWATER HOUSE ABLAZE

A nobleman's house still in the City was that of the duke of Bridgewater. It stood to the east of Aldersgate, where Bridgewater Square, part of the Barbican development, now stands. In April 1687 a serious fire here resulted in the death of two of the duke's sons and their tutor.

1688

FLIGHT OF THE KING

It was a difficult time to establish religious tolerance in London, where huge numbers of Huguenot immigrants testified to Catholic bigotry in France. And if James II hoped to enlist the support of Dissenters by including them in a toleration policy which was primarily aimed at helping his fellow Catholics, then he was misguided, because the ruse was immediately apparent. But he proceeded with his policy, and probably the issuing of a second Declaration of Indulgence became the decisive moment of his reign. Bishops meeting at Lambeth declared that they would not have it proclaimed in churches, and throughout the country the declaration generally remained unread. In June seven bishops were committed to the Tower – taken there by water, with the banks lined with sympathetic crowds. The acquittal of the bishops at the King's Bench at the end of June was a famous popular victory; bonfires were lit, guns were fired, and bells were rung. The enthusiasm of the people affected the army, drawn up on Hounslow Heath.

In the meantime the birth of a prince in June worsened the crisis, for a dynasty of Catholic rulers now seemed certain. On the day of the release of the bishops a letter was sent to William of Orange, inviting him to accept the crown of England. On 5 November William landed in Torbay, and by easy stages then marched on London. James tried to rally the City behind him, but failed.

On 11 November anti-Catholic mobs broke into St John's, Clerkenwell, where rumour had it that instruments for torturing Protestants were stored. On 12 December the king accepted the reality of his plight and left London. That evening the mob 'gott together, and went to the popish chapel in Lincolns Inn Fields, and perfectly gutted the same, pulling down all the wainscot, pictures, books, &c: and part of the house, and burnt them, and then proceeded to Wild house, the Spanish ambassadors, and did the same, and continued in a great body, several thousands, all night'. A contemporary newspaper described the apprentices in full voice, wrecking and plundering any house remotely connected with the exiled king.

James escaped, but his notorious agent, Judge Jeffreys, did not. Jeffreys, famous for his presidency of the Bloody Assize of 1685, in which 300 victims were hanged and 1,000 sent as slaves to West India, had also been instrumental in committing the bishops to the Tower. He went into hiding in Wapping, disguised as a sailor, but on 12 December he ventured out to a public house for a drink and was recognized by a scrivener who had appeared before him in court. Rescued from the mob by trained bands, Jeffreys was taken before the lord mayor and then to the Tower. He escaped execution: he died in the Tower a few months later, aged 40, seemingly of a number of disorders including the effect of alcohol.

THE SARDINIAN CHAPEL
The Roman Catholic chapel at Lincoln's Inn Fields which had been demolished by the mob was that opened only on 2 February this year by a Franciscan monk, Father Cross. By 1700 the house which had contained the chapel had been taken by the Portuguese ambassador, happy to have a private Catholic place of worship on the premises, and by c. 1723 it had become the Sardinian Embassy. The Sardinian Chapel was for many years one of the few Catholic places of worship in London; Sardinia Street today is a reminder of its existence.

LIGHTING THE STREETS
The building of the better-class streets around St James's Square prompted an improvement in street lighting. From November this year St James's churchyard was lit by the 'Lights as are used in Jermine Streete', oil lamps supplied by the 'Copartnership of the New Invention of Lights'. The square itself had similar lights.

EDWARD LLOYD'S COFFEE HOUSE
The first record we have of Edward Lloyd's Coffee House, from which the insurance organization developed, is an advertisement in February this year offering a reward for a robbery. Information was to be taken to 'Edward Loyd's Coffee House in Tower Street', described as 'a spacious street, well built and inhabited by able tradesmen'. Undoubtedly, so close to the docks and Wapping, Lloyd's most usual clientele must have been mariners.

1689

A NEW ROYAL PALACE
This year was to be an important one for both Kensington and Whitehall. The asthmatic William III disliked the dampness of Whitehall Palace, and his queen, Mary, bemoaned the views of either wall or water, and so they declined to live there. Instead, they bought Nottingham House in Kensington – no doubt causing confusion among their court, who had nowhere to live in the immediate vicinity other than the newly built Kensington Square. The court partly functioned still from St James's Palace, and so the development of the area around there, together with such streets to the north of Piccadilly as Albemarle Street and Dover Street, within moderately easy reach of Kensington, hastened the shift of wealthier residents ever westward. Nine years later the fire which destroyed Whitehall erased the royal connection there altogether, and the growth of government offices filled its place.

Nottingham House had been built about 1605 for Sir George Coppin; the architect was probably John Thorpe. In 1689 the owner was the 2nd earl of Nottingham, who sold it to the king for 18,000 guineas. Work, supervised by Wren, began on its refurbishment as Kensington Palace. The Jacobean frame received some galleries, a portico and a clock tower, but this country house never achieved the grandeur thought necessary for a palace. Both William and Mary died here.

FIRST ADMISSIONS AT THE ROYAL HOSPITAL
A scheme devised in the reign of Charles II began on 28 March when the first admissions were made to the Royal Hospital, Chelsea; the foundation stone had been laid in February 1682.

The king's intention had been to establish a home for wounded soldiers – a scheme made more urgent since the recent establishment of a standing army – and Wren's design provided three courtyards surrounded by colonnades in which the old soldiers could exercise. Architects such as Robert Adam and Sir John Soane have added other buildings since. There is a great hall in which the pensioners still eat communally, and Wren's provision of shallow steps on the staircases is probably still welcomed.

1690

MORE CHURCHES
Wren's industry did not seem to flag. Twenty-four years after the Fire, churches were still being rebuilt by him. This year (or perhaps earlier – there are different accounts) he finished a church which had escaped the Fire altogether: that of St Andrew, Holborn, his largest parish church. It was a dilapidated building and, apart from the 15th-century tower, had to be demolished.

St Margaret, Lothbury, was also finished. Today that church has a number of items, such as the pulpit and reredos, from other, now demolished, Wren churches. St Michael, Crooked Lane, had been used since 1689, and St Anne and St Agnes, Gresham Street, now a Lutheran church, had been finished in 1687. St Margaret Pattens in Rood Lane was also completed in 1687, except for its pointed lead spire. Inside, an hourglass behind the pulpit can time the sermons, and here are some of the few remaining canopied pews left in London – one of them carved 'CW 1686', which may be Wren's own or, less romantically, may just be the churchwarden's.

YORK WATERWORKS DESTROYED
The York Buildings Waterworks at the end of Villiers Street was destroyed this year by fire. Next year, after a new Act of Parliament had been obtained, a pointed water tower, a familiar object in mid-18th-century prints of the Adelphi, was erected.

ANOTHER WESTMINSTER FLOOD

No sooner had the king left Whitehall than there was a severe flood in Westminster. Once again, water flowed into Westminster Hall and did much damage, 'spoiling much goods and merchantdizes' – a record which indicates that the hall was being used as a trading place.

HABERDASHERS' ASKE'S SCHOOL ESTABLISHED

One of the best-known City livery schools is that founded this year by Robert Aske, silk merchant, who endowed almshouses and a school to be administered by his own livery company, the Haberdashers. In 1692 they occupied a building, designed by Robert Hooke, in Pitfield Street, Hoxton; its splendid 1823 replacement still survives and is used still for education. Here the school, which originally had almshouses on part of the site, remained until the boys' school moved to Hampstead and the girls' to Acton c.1898.

A HOUSE IN ILFORD

Valentine's Park in Ilford takes its name from the mansion built there in 1690 for the son-in-law of Archbishop Tillotson. It had fine carving by Grinling Gibbons and it developed splendid gardens, including a magnificent vine which is said to have been the 'parent' of that at Hampton Court.

1691

FIRES AT THE PALACES

Evelyn and Luttrell both recorded a serious fire at Whitehall Palace in April. The strait-laced Evelyn described

a suddaine & terrible Fire burnt downe all the buildings over the stone Gallery at W-hall, to the waterside, begining at the Appartments of the late Dut[c]hesse of Portsmouth (which had ben pulled down & rebuilt to please her no lesse than 3 times), & Consuming other Lodgings of such lewd Creatures, who debauched K Char: 2d & others, & were his destr[u]ction.

Soon the inevitable Wren was on the scene, building a new terrace walk which was complete by 1693.

But fire pursued the king to Kensington, where in November the southern side of his courtyard was destroyed; the queen suspected treason. In the rebuilding, Wren's assistant Nicholas Hawksmoor was the architect. Evelyn recorded a visit he made there in 1696: 'The House is very noble, tho not great; the Gallerys furnished with all the best Pictures of all the Houses, of Titian, Raphel, Corregio, Holben, Julio Romano, Bassan, V: Dyke, Tintoret, & others, with a world of Porcelain; a pretty private Library; the Gardens about it very delicious.'

BATTLE IN ALSATIA

The area of the old White Friars' monastery south of Fleet Street had deteriorated throughout this century. It was now a recognized haunt of criminals, because it had a right of sanctuary, and had acquired the nickname 'Alsatia' from an allegedly lawless area in France. When, after the Great Fire, the last vestiges of grandeur had gone, slums were erected. But of course this was next to the Temple, and in 1691 the benchers of the Inner Temple ordered that the gate which connected the two precincts be bricked up. The Alsatians attacked the workmen doing the work, and killed one of them; when the sheriff arrived to restore order, they knocked him down and stole part of his chain of office. It needed Foot Guards to suppress the disorder.

A CHAPEL ON WHEELS

At the Hounslow army camp James II had constructed a chapel on wheels for his own use, and there it remained after the king had fled. Dr Tenison begged it of William III and re-erected it in Conduit Street (near today's Regent Street) for a temporary place of worship – Evelyn, needless to say, was on hand in July to hear the first sermon preached. A permanent building replaced it in 1716.

LLOYD'S COFFEE HOUSE MOVES

Edward Lloyd this year moved his coffee house from near the Tower to the corner of Lombard Street and Abchurch Lane – a good site, indicating a profitable business at the old location. The following year an advertisement for the sale of the goods on three ships says that inventories may be obtained at Lloyd's.

Lloyd had the wit to see that his business could be built up by establishing a clearing house of shipping information there; he organized a network of correspondents around the world, and in 1696 began the publication of a short-lived *Lloyd's News*. His coffee house became the haunt not only of those who made their living in shipping but of those who were in the burgeoning business of marine insurance – they too needed the intelligence which Lloyd's agents and customers provided.

1692

COUTTS' BANK ESTABLISHED

Coutts' Bank has its origins in the establishment of a business this year by John Campbell, a goldsmith, at the sign of the Three Crowns in the Strand – an emblem still used today. His son-in-law inherited the bank in 1716, the year that it had its first connection with royalty, when the future George II bought some gold plate; it was not until 1755 that James Coutts, son of an Edinburgh banker, married into the Campbell family and was made a partner.

SLAUGHTER'S COFFEE HOUSE

One of the more famous coffee houses, Slaughter's, in St Martin's Lane, was established this year by Thomas Slaughter. It became well known for its card games, gambling and chess. The mathematician Abraham de Moivre used to supplement his income by advising players on probability here. Its head waiter in the mid 18th century was renowned for taking sips of a customer's drink on the way to serving it at table and then apologizing for spilling some on the way.

A CEMETERY FOR OLD SOLDIERS

The first interment of an inmate of the Royal Hospital, Chelsea, took place this year in the hospital's burial ground. It was of Simon Cox, an old soldier who had served during the reigns of four monarchs. Several centenarians are buried here as, unexpectedly, are two women who were soldiers. Christiana Davis (d. 1739) joined the army, disguised as a man, to search for her husband. She was imprisoned by the French, and fought at Blenheim and Ramillies; her sex was discovered only when she was wounded. In 1712 she was given a pension by Queen Anne. Hannah Snell joined the army for the same reason, but fared less fortunately. She suffered a punishment of 500 lashes and died insane in 1792.

1693

THE FIRST CHOCOLATE HOUSE

The longest-established men's club in London derives from this year, when chocolate still vied with coffee as a popular beverage. White's Chocolate House began on the east side of St James's Street, on or very near the present site of Boodle's clubhouse. By 1698 it was at no. 69, on the other side of the road, where later the establishment was run by White's assistant, John Arthur.

White's became the most fashionable establishment in town, renowned for its gambling and its company, but when it became a club is uncertain. The first set of rules is dated 1736, and there is no reason to believe that the transition from public chocolate house to private club had been formally made before that. From 1755 the club has been on the east side of the road, at nos. 37–38.

BULL-BAITING SUPPRESSED IN CLAPHAM

According to the minutes of the Clapham Vestry, bull-baiting was banned in the parish this year.

FENTON HOUSE BUILT

The oldest surviving mansion in Hampstead is Fenton House, in Hampstead Grove, built in 1693. Early in the 18th century it was called Ostend (East End) House and was owned by the silk merchant Joshua Gee, whose initials are incorporated in its magnificent wrought-iron gates. Philip Fenton, a Riga merchant, bought the house in 1793.

1694

BANK OF ENGLAND FOUNDED

A national bank was the suggestion of a Scottish merchant called William Paterson. With others in 1691 he proposed to the government the foundation of a Bank of England with a perpetual income, from which it would be possible for the government and Crown to borrow. Though almost certainly the inspiration behind the scheme, Paterson parted company from the bank a year after its foundation in 1694. (His other main interests were the harnessing of the waters on Hampstead Heath to form a water supply for the City, and the establishment of a Scottish colony on the Darien isthmus, Panama, to control trade between the East and the West.)

The bank was granted the 'Rates and Duties upon the tunnage of ships and Vessels, and upon Beer, Ale and other liquors', to be paid as interest to those voluntarily advancing subscriptions to the total sum of £1,200,000. This money was immediately borrowed to finance the pro-Dutch supporters in the war against France.

The bank first rented space in Mercers' Hall for a few months, and then, until 1734, in Grocers' Hall, after which it removed to new premises built on the present site. The first governor was a Huguenot, Sir John Houblon.

A DUEL IN BLOOMSBURY

Duelling, as a way of settling arguments and slights, was to be an 18th-century obsession. Luttrell records this year one of the many duels which took place in the fields behind Southampton House in Bloomsbury:

A duel was yesterday fought between one Mr Lawes [John Law] and Mr Wilson [Beau Wilson] in Bloomsbury Square; the latter was killed upon the spot and the other is sent to Newgate. 'Tis that Mr Wilson who for some years past hath made a great figure, living at the rate of £4000 per annum, without any visible estate; and the several gentlemen who kept him company, and endeavured to find out his way of living could never effect it.

Lawes was eventually convicted of murder, but in October 1695 he tried to escape from prison by 'filing down 4 bars, but was discovered'. He later obtained his liberty.

AN OBELISK IN SEVEN DIALS

John Evelyn, as ever among the first to see anything new in London, records in his diary of 5 October, 'I went … to see the building begining neare St. Giles's, where seven streetes make a starr from a Doric Pillar plac'd in the middle of [a] Circular Area.' On the summit of the pillar were dials, each facing a street. Although the area was called Seven Dials, the obelisk had in fact only six faces. This is probably because an original plan of the development of streets, dated 1691, shows only six streets radiating; no doubt the column was made first to adorn the development and the seventh street was an afterthought.

The obelisk, removed in 1733, now stands in Weybridge with a coronet on its summit, and the hexagonal block of stone on which the dials were placed was used as a horse block. The pillar in Seven Dials today is a replica, unveiled in 1989, and likewise has six dials.

This area, intended by its developer, Thomas Neale, to be a fashionable location between Covent Garden and Soho, deteriorated into one of the worst slums in London.

AN ELITE QUARTER

One of the most luxurious developments in the St James's area is St James's Place, where the best houses overlook Green Park. Begun in 1685, it was completed *c*.1694. It has been occupied by rich and famous people ever since. The writer, Joseph Addison, lived here until he married Lady Warwick. John Wilkes lodged here, as did Francis Burdett, Edward Gibbon and Warren Hastings. The most notable residence is Spencer House, designed by John Vardy, identified in the 19th century as the home of the immensely rich poet, Samuel Rogers.

BARN ELMS REBUILT

The mansion called Barn Elms in Rocks Lane by Barnes Common had been occupied by Sir Francis Walsingham in the reign of Elizabeth. It was rebuilt this year by Thomas Cartwright, but its most famous occupiers were members of the Hoare banking family in the 18th century, Jacob Tonson, publisher and secretary of the Kit Kat Club, who usually resided in a cottage adjoining from 1703, and William Cobbett, who rented the farm in 1828–30. Unfortunately, this attractive house, which had previously been taken by the Ranelagh Club, was demolished following a fire in 1954. Only the ornamental pond and the ice house remain.

1695

NEW ALMSHOUSES

One of the finest buildings in Blackheath is Morden College, a group of almshouses, reputedly the work of Wren, and the benefaction of Sir John Morden, a wealthy merchant. The foundation is associated with a doubtful legend that three ships laden with Morden's merchandise went missing but reappeared ten years later to save him from penury, whereupon he vowed to establish an almshouse for poor merchants of the Turkey Company. By the beginning of the 20th century there were 40 residents and up to a 100 out-pensioners in receipt of annual grants.

Each of the dwellings arranged around the quadrangle consists of a sitting room and bedroom, and the occupants each have a half-share of a bathroom and kitchen. Daniel Defoe noted that it was the intention that the inmates should live as gentlemen, but the income was insufficient to achieve this.

The master mason was Edward Strong, one of Wren's usual builders, and Morden sat on a committee with the great architect, so it is not unlikely that Wren supplied the design. The chapel contains some carvings attributed to Grinling Gibbons.

The Corporation of Trinity House built almshouses in Mile End Road the same year, on land given by Captain Henry Mudd, citizen of Ratcliff. The chapel has since been truncated, and the houses (attributed to Wren) were damaged in the last war, but they still stand with their gable ends ornamented with model ships. Originally, and until the last war, the inmates were always retired seamen. A plaque outside records, 'This Almes House wherein 28 decay'd Masters & Comanders of Ships, or ye widows of such are maintain'd was built by ye corp. of Trinity House Ano. 1695. The ground was given by Capt Heny Mudd of Ratcliff and Elder Brother, whose Widow did also Contribute.'

A COFFEE HOUSE IN CHELSEA

'Don Saltero's', a coffee house, was established in Lawrence Street, Chelsea, this year. The proprietor was John Salter, an Irish barber, who for some time had been a household servant of the physician and collector Sir Hans Sloane. The coffee house moved twice, and its famous days were in Cheyne Walk, where it was established from 1718 (q.v.).

LINCOLN'S INN THEATRE REOPENS

The first Lincoln's Inn Fields Theatre, or Duke's Theatre as it was often called in its early days, had been converted from an indoor tennis court in 1660 (q.v.). Its heyday, after the Restoration, was cut short when Davenant's company moved in 1671 to the new and prestigious Dorset Garden Theatre. It is thought that at Lincoln's Inn Fields the building reverted to use for tennis, but on 30 April 1695 it was reopened for plays. The four proprietors included the actor Thomas Betterton and the playwright William Congreve, whose *Love for Love* was the first production – a splendid occasion attended by William III.

GUNPOWDER AT WOOLWICH

In the 16th century the area called Woolwich Warren, close to the Naval Dockyard, was used for storing military supplies. In 1671 the Crown bought the adjoining estate, which included a house called Tower Place that became the residence of the lieutenant general of ordnance. In 1695 the Royal Laboratory for the manufacture of gunpowder and fireworks moved there.

HAPPENINGS IN THE STRAND

There had been a rapid change in the nature of the buildings south of the Strand. This once aristocratic area backing on to the Thames was being developed with streets. This year Salisbury House, built by Sir Robert Cecil in 1602, was finally demolished, and its site was covered by Cecil Street and Salisbury Street (now the line of Ivybridge Lane and Adam Street) and by a half-hearted and unsuccessful shopping area which earned the name of 'Whore's Nest'.

To the east the demolition of Worcester House in 1683 had resulted in that area being redeveloped with some poor-class buildings – one street on the site, now the line of Carting Lane, was called Dirty Lane, a steep and narrow passage down to the Thames, with timber yards adjacent. Both these developments bear testimony to the exit of the wealthy to new developments further west and north, until the Adam brothers gambled by building the Adelphi scheme in the area in the 18th century. However, part of the site of Worcester House was taken by Beaufort Buildings, which must have had some grander pretensions since a fire reported this year destroyed here the house of John Knight, treasurer of the Custom House.

BAN ON CABS IN HYDE PARK

A newspaper called *The Postboy* reported that on 7 June 'several persons of quality having been affronted at the Ring in Hyde Park, by some of the persons that rode in Hackney-Coaches in Masks, and complaint thereof being made to the Lord Justices, an order is made that no Hackney-Coaches be permitted to go into the said Park, and that none presume to appear there in masks'. This ban on cabs in Hyde Park lasted until the 1920s.

1696

THE ORIGINS OF BERKELEY SQUARE

This year Lord Berkeley of Stratton sold Berkeley House on Piccadilly to the duke of Devonshire. At the same time he agreed to protect the northern aspect of the house as far as the extent of his own land could allow; in effect this prohibited building on the Berkeley land north of the house to the width of the garden of Berkeley House. When Berkeley Square was built in the 1730s and 1740s this open space became the gardens of the square, and the residents of Berkeley House enjoyed its view until the grounds of the house itself were developed.

WELLS AT RICHMOND

A chalybeate spring had been discovered at Richmond in the 1670s, but it was not until 1696 that a leaseholder developed the area with a pump room, an assembly room and gaming rooms. Daily concerts and weekly balls became a regular feature. The wells were situated in the grounds of what is now Cardigan House on Richmond Hill.

FORMATION OF THE HAND-IN-HAND

Another fire-insurance company was formed this year, at a meeting held at Tom's Coffee House in St Martin's Lane on 12 November. By the following month an office had been opened in the Royal Coffee House, Buckingham Gate, and was later to be found at Angel Court, off Snow Hill. The company was originally named the Contributors for Insuring House, Chambers or Rooms from Loss by Fire, by Amicable Contributions, but was later known more conveniently as the Hand-in-Hand Company.

TROUBLE AT THE SAVOY

A tailor trying to collect a debt from a client who had taken refuge in the precincts of the Savoy in the Strand was tarred and feathered and tied to the Strand maypole. This was in retribution for breaching the traditional right of sanctuary of the area – a right abolished by an angry Parliament the following year.

DANISH CHURCH OPENED

Rebuilding London increased demand for timber from Denmark and Norway. One result was that a church was built this year for the many Scandinavian sailors concentrated around Ratcliff. It was designed by the sculptor Caius Gabriel Cibber, who had settled in London during the Commonwealth. His work decorated Chatsworth, St Paul's, Hampton Court and Trinity College Library, Cambridge.

The church was paid for by King Christian V, and was later maintained by contributions from Copenhagen and levies from Danish exports to England. St Paul's School now occupies the site.

1697

OPENING OF ST PAUL'S CATHEDRAL

The great day arrived. On 2 December the first service was held in Wren's new cathedral, although the final stone was not laid until 1710. Even by 1697 Parliament was impatient enough at progress to halve Wren's salary. The rate of progress was in part the result of Wren's deliberate policy of proceeding with the whole building in stages, rather than completing it part by part.

The service was held to celebrate the Peace of Ryswick. Though William III did not attend, it was a grand affair, with the bishop of London officiating. A special anthem by Dr John Blow was played.

NEW WELLS

The number of spas and wells was still growing. Lambeth Wells, on the site of today's Lambeth Walk, was opened about this year and offered not only medicinal water, at 1d per quart, but regular concerts. An advertisement this year announced, 'In the great Room at Lambeth Wells (every Wednesday for the ensuing Season) will be performed a Consort of vocal and instrumental Musick, consisting of about thirty instruments and voices ... ', but Lambeth Wells seems not to have been a successful venture.

The Cold Bath in Clerkenwell was discovered by one Walter Baynes this year. It was situated in the middle of what is now Cold Bath Square, near Mount Pleasant Post Office. Baynes, advertising the bath in 1698, claimed that the water was of 'the nature of St Magnus's in the north, and St Winifred's in Wales, and famed for the curing of the most nerval disorders'. The hours for bathing were from five in the morning to one in the afternoon, and the charge was half a crown to persons who were so ill that they had to use the 'chair' – a contraption in which the customer was lowered into the bath – and two shillings to those who could manage this themselves.

SANCTUARY WITHDRAWN

As noted for 1696, the right of sanctuary in the Savoy precinct was withdrawn by Act of Parliament this year. Included in the same measure was Brooke Street in Holborn and the notorious Alsatia area, south of Fleet Street. Two weeks' grace was given before the Act became effective. Macaulay, later describing its effect in Alsatia, says that 'when, on the prescribed day, the Sheriff's officers ventured to cross the boundary, they found those streets where, a few weeks before a cry of "A writ!" would have drawn together a thousand raging bullies and vixens, as quiet as the cloisters of a cathedral'.

1698

WHITEHALL DESTROYED

Whitehall Palace was destroyed by fire on 4 January. According to Luttrell:

Part of Whitehall Palace c. 1645. All the main buildings of the palace by the river were destroyed in the fire of 1698.

The fire at Whitehal began the 4th instant about 5 in the afternoon, and continued till about 7 the next morning; it is said to begin by the carelessnesse of a servant putting charcoal ashes into a closet; the lord Portland and the earl of Essex's lodgings were saved, but the kings, queens, earl of Montagues, lord chancellors and archbishops lodgings, the treasury and council chambers, and the long gallery leading to the gatehouse, were all burnt: the banquetting house is standing; and in the afternoon his majestie took a view of the ruins, and seem'd much concerned, and said, if God would give him leave, he would rebuild it much finer than before.

Evelyn, more economically, records, 'White-hall utterly burnt to the ground; nothing but the walls & ruines left.'

Another account neatly lays the blame on the unpopular Dutch (reminiscent of the Catholics being held responsible for the Great Fire):

a Dutch woman, who belonged to Colonel Stanley's lodgings which were near and joining to the Earl of Portland's house in Whitehall, having a sudden occasion to dry some linen in an upper room, for expedition sake lighted a good quantity of charcoal and carelessly left the linen hanging round about it, which took fire in her absence, to such a degree that it not only consumed the linen, but had seized the hangings, wainscots, beds, and whatnot, and flamed and smoked in such a violent manner, that it put all the inhabitants thereabouts into consternation … in an instant (as it were) the merciless and devouring flames got such an advantage, that, notwithstanding the great endeavours used by the water-engines, numerous assistance, and blowing up houses to the number of about twenty, it still increased with great fury and violence all night, till about eight of the clock next morning, at which time it was extinguished after it had burnt down and consumed about one hundred and fifty houses, most of which were lodgings and habitations of the chief of the nobility.

King William, however, did not attempt to rebuild the palace – he had already abandoned it except for ceremonial occasions, and the court now divided its activities between St James's Palace (which is still the official residence of the Crown) and Kensington Palace. Whitehall, to most intents and purposes, was abandoned by the royal family, although the surviving Banqueting House was fitted up as a chapel royal and a new organ was installed, the old one being 'packt up in Boxes there, in order to be sent to Barbadoes'.

PETER THE GREAT AT DEPTFORD

The tsar of all the Russias, Peter the Great, this year lived for four months at John Evelyn's house, Sayes Court, at Deptford, and there was able to study at close quarters the business of shipbuilding at Deptford Dockyard. He proved a prestigious but unsatisfactory tenant, as Evelyn was to complain, and there was damage caused during numerous drinking bouts. The tsar also amused himself by riding in a wheelbarrow through the holly hedges that the fastidious gardener Evelyn had planted. The Crown allowed Evelyn £150 compensation for damage done by the 'right nasty' Russian court.

THE WELLS AT HAMPSTEAD

On 20 December the infant lord of the manor of Hampstead, Baptist, earl of Gainsborough, granted to certain residents 6 acres of land containing a chalybeate spring, to be used for the relief of the poor. The 6 acres, now a most desirable part of Hampstead to the west of East Heath Road, were then mostly a boggy swamp and, apart from the medicinal well, held little promise of much income for the needy. However, the waters and the aspect from that part of Hampstead helped to develop the village – the 'New End' was built on part of the heath.

This drawing, by John Thomas Smith, entitled 'Part of the old Palace of Whitehall by the Water' was published by the artist in 1804.

The spring itself was in Well Road, but the bathhouse was built south of it in Well Walk, where a Long Room and bowling green, now covered by Gainsborough Gardens, provided for social occasions and recreation.

SCHOMBERG HOUSE BUILT

Schomberg House at 80–82 Pall Mall was a reconstruction of an older house this year for the 3rd duke of Schomberg, whose father had been second in command to William III at the time of the Glorious Revolution. In 1769 the house, too large to sell as one entity, was divided into three, and in 1850 the easternmost house was demolished. All that now survives is the façade of nos. 80 and 81; in 1956 the actual body of the houses behind was reconstructed and a copy of the original façade of the eastern house was reinstated to match that which still remained.

Famous tenants of parts of the house have included the painters Richard Cosway and Thomas Gainsborough, but the most notorious was the quack doctor James Graham, who in 1779 established here a 'Temple of Health and Hymen' where patients might conceive on his 'grand celestial bed', which was supported by 40 pillars of brilliant glass and was covered by a dome lined with mirrors; in addition, clients were cosseted between coloured sheets and entertained by music. Graham had gone by 1784, and was later confined in a lunatic asylum.

1600s

Blue Coat School, founded by worshippers at Broadway Chapel (see 1698).

SPCK FOUNDED

The Society for Promoting Christian Knowledge was founded in the vestry room of St Mary-le-Bow, Cheapside, this year. Its founder was Thomas Bray, a parson, and its functions included the distribution of Bibles and religious tracts and the fostering of Christianity in the colonies.

A CLUTCH OF CHARITY SCHOOLS

A number of 'charity schools' were founded in this period and were especially encouraged by the SPCK (see above). It was usual for each child to receive a gift of a distinctive uniform – hence the various 'Bluecoats', 'Greencoats' etc. to be found in London. Usually the schools were the responsibility of a vestry or a charity, although the Grey Coat Hospital (School) in Greycoat Place was formed in 1698 by eight local shopkeepers appalled at the many parish children begging in the streets of Westminster. On the occasion of the opening of this school, the eight governors assembled to see the clothes tried on and to supervise a barber they had hired to cut the children's hair. Already in the area was the Blue Coat School, founded in 1688 by worshippers at the Broadway Chapel. Some Greencoat and Bluecoat schools still survive, or else their buildings remain with statues of charity scholars set in niches outside.

The SPCK formed the first girls' charity school, in Carnaby Street. Other charity schools were founded in the parishes of St James, Clerkenwell, St Andrew, Holborn, St Martin-in-the-Fields and St Paul, Shadwell.

After only 12 years of effort by the SPCK there were 80 such schools in London alone. Addison wrote in 1713, 'I have always looked upon the institution of Charity Schools, which of late has so universally prevailed throughout the whole nation, as the glory of the age we live in.'

Boys typically wore a single-breasted collarless coat long enough to cover the knee, with flapped pockets, metal buttons from top to bottom, and, until the 19th century, breeches. The hat was quite often a tam o'shanter cap. The uniform of the girls was more inclined to follow fashion. It consisted of an overgown, cut and open at the front beneath the waist to reveal an undergown; both of these were ankle length, and later on an apron was added. Both boys and girls also wore a white collar.

COCOA TREE ESTABLISHED

The Cocoa Tree Chocolate House was established in Pall Mall this year, on the site of the present RAC clubhouse, and was later to settle at 64 St James's Street, where it eventually became a private club. When it ceased to exist in 1932, it was, with White's, the only club which could trace its history back to the coffee and chocolate houses of the late 17th century.

By the reign of George III it was a venue of Tories. Edward Gibbon records in his journal in 1762 how he

dined at the Cocoa-tree with Holt … We went thence to the play … and when it was over, returned to the Cocoa-tree. That respectable body, of which I have the honor to be a member, affords every evening a sight truly English. Twenty or thirty, perhaps, of the first men in the Kingdom, in point of fashion and fortune, supping at little tables covered with a napkin, in the middle of a Coffee-room, upon a bit of cold meat, or a Sandwich, and drinking a glass of punch.

WESTMINSTER CLOCK TOWER DEMOLISHED

The Clock Tower in New Palace Yard, Westminster, built by Henry Yevele in 1365, was this year taken down, and its distinctive pyramidal roof was no more. Its 4-ton bell, known as 'Edward of Westminster', was transferred to St Paul's Cathedral.

1699

A CHARTER FOR BILLINGSGATE

The ancient market of Billingsgate this year received a charter which permitted it to sell fish for six days a week and mackerel on Sundays. Most likely this charter confirmed a long-established trading practice and was secured to protect the market's interests. The charter was not obtained without an exchange, however. William III insisted that special concessions be allowed to Dutch boats importing live eels. It was said that these boats would have lost their concession if one had not always been tied up at the port, and therefore one did not cast off until another had taken its place.

Today, Billingsgate is associated primarily with fish, but it also dealt in other commodities, notably coal. In medieval times it traded in corn, salt and malt and its prosperity grew as boats became larger and unable to get beneath London Bridge to disembark at Queenhithe.

The illustration on page 60 suggests that it had a building, though as far as we know no proper market building was constructed until 1850. A proclamation of 1559, which declares that Billingsgate was 'an open space for the landing and bringing in of any fish, corn, salt stores, victuals and fruit' appears to confirm that no market hall existed, but certainly there were plenty of wooden sheds on the quay.

1700

TOM'S COFFEE HOUSE

One of the best-known coffee houses in London was Tom's Coffee House at 17 Russell Street. It was founded between 1698 and 1703 by Captain Thomas West, who, deranged by gout, jumped to his death from a second-floor window in 1722. Writing that same year, a traveller recorded, 'After the Play the best company generally go to Tom's and Will's Coffee Houses near adjoining, where there is playing at Picket, and the best of conversation till midnight. Here you will see blue and green ribbons and Stars sitting familiarly, and talking with the same freedom as if they had left their quality and degrees of distance at home.'

HOWLAND GREAT DOCK CONSTRUCTED

A major enterprise was completed this year in Rotherhithe. The Howland Great Wet Dock derived its name from a Streatham family, a daughter of which had married the 15-year-old marquess of Tavistock, son of Lord William Russell. The price to be paid for marrying into the aristocracy was that the Howland land should pass into the hands of the Russells, who immediately obtained parliamentary approval to construct over 10 acres the largest dock in London. The owners claimed that 120 ships could be moored there safely, and in 1703, when a storm damaged much shipping on the Thames, they boasted that only one vessel in the shelter of Howland Dock had been harmed. The ships were protected from the immediate effects of a fast tide by a lock at the entrance to the dock. Another feature boasted was freedom from danger of fire, since facilities for cooking were provided on shore and fires were forbidden on board.

The dock was not a great success, and in the 1760s it was adapted for the whaling trade. It was eventually part of the Surrey Dock complex, and is now a Water Recreation Centre off Redriff Road.

A PAROCHIAL SCHOOL IN CLERKENWELL

Clerkenwell Parochial School still flourishes in Amwell Street, but it began in 1700 in Aylesbury Street, to the east of Clerkenwell Green. Originally there were two schools here: one for 60 boys and the other for 40 girls.

The school was under the auspices of the pious SPCK, whose views on any deviation from a simple curriculum were noted in 1711:

John Honeycott, the master of the Charity School at Clerkenwell, had yesterday, with the children of the above school, publicly acted the play called Timon of Athens, and by tickets signed by himself had invited several people to it. And Mr. Skeete, laying before the society an original ticket, together with an account of several observations made by a friend of his, who was present at the said entertainment, both which being read, it was agreed that the acting of the said play by the master and children of the Charity School is a great reproach to the design of charity schools, and that it is highly worthy the design of the society to bear testimony against it as scandalous, and of pernicious consequence to the charity schools in general.

A 'PYRAMID' IN HOG LANE

The Huguenots opened a chapel this year in Hog Lane (now West Street, off Charing Cross Road), which they called La Pyramide de la Tremblade. As a plaque on the building now tells us, it was famous for its connection with John Wesley, who took a lease on the building in 1743 and lived in a house next door.

1701

A NEW SYNAGOGUE IN BEVIS MARKS

After the Jews had been permitted by Cromwell to return to England, the principal synagogue had been in Creechurch Lane. This year the new Spanish and Portuguese Synagogue in Bevis Marks was opened.

CAPTAIN KIDD HANGED

The pirate William Kidd was hanged at Execution Dock, Wapping, on 23 May. This dock was located opposite today's Brewhouse Lane, where it joins Wapping High Street; the custom, as Stow described it, was for victims to be hung at the low-water mark and left there till three tides had flowed over them. Kidd's effects, worth about £6,500, were forfeited to the Crown and then given to the Royal Hospital, Chelsea.

Kidd had been hired by the government to catch pirates off the Massachusetts coast, but in 1698 and 1699 complaints were received that he had actually become a pirate himself. Taken in Boston in 1699, he was shipped to London in 1700 and given an inadequate trial at the Old Bailey.

Tom's Coffee House in Russell Street, founded by Captain Thomas West. It was one of the most popular in the heyday of coffee houses.

MORE BUILDINGS AT HAMPTON COURT

Wren's buildings at Hampton Court were proceeding. The apartments around Fountain Court were ready for William III to occupy in 1699, and Wilderness House, built for the king's master gardener, was finished. In this latter house the landscape gardener Lancelot 'Capability' Brown lived, and it was he who introduced the Great Vine from a cutting off a plant in Valentine's House in Ilford; the girth of the stem is now at least 7 ft. Between the gardens and the river Wren added a Banqueting House this year; this is a single storey high and includes carvings by Grinling Gibbons and a room painted by Antonio Verrio.

LONDON BRIDGE WATERWORKS SOLD

The waterworks established beneath the northern arches of London Bridge had remained in the Morice family since their inception in 1580. This year they were sold to Richard Soames, a London goldsmith, who obtained a confirmation from the City for the remainder of Morice's 500-year lease at 20s per annum.

The waterwheels were 19 ft long and 3 ft in diameter, and they were arranged so that, by means of a windlass, one man could raise or lower them to the appropriate level as the tide rose or fell. Roughly 2,000 gallons of water could be raised per minute.

The clatter of the wheels and the turmoil of water at high tide through the narrow arches of the bridge were very noisy. Ned Ward in his book *The London Spy*, published about this date, records, 'We now turn'd down to the Thames-side, where the frightful roaring of the Bridge Water-falls so astonish'd my Eyes, and terrified my Ears, that, like Roger in his Mill, or the inhabitants near the Cataracts of the Nile, I could hear no Voice softer than a Speaking Trumpet, or the audible Organ of a Scolding Fish-Woman.'

1702

A NEW QUEEN

William III died in March after an illness which followed a fall from his horse at Hampton Court, though his health, like his sense of humour, had never been strong. He was buried without pomp in Westminster Abbey, generally unlamented by the nation.

The king died without issue, either legitimate or natural, and his successor was his sister-in-law Anne, Anglican daughter of James II and his first wife, Anne Hyde. Of the eight children born of that marriage only two, Mary (wife of William III) and Anne, survived. By the express command of Charles II, these two children of his brother, then duke of York, had been brought up in the Anglican Church in order to provide an avenue of Protestant succession.

Anne had been married to George, prince of Denmark, in 1683. She had 17 children, each giving hope for an uncomplicated Protestant succession, but only one survived infancy and he died at the age of 11. Meanwhile, the exiled Catholic faction threatened in the form of James, son of James II, who became the 'Old Pretender' to the throne. Towards the end of William's reign, with Anne unlikely to produce an heir, an Act of Settlement was passed which, on Anne's death, would allow George, Elector of Hanover, to succeed to the throne.

Reporting Anne's coronation on 23 April 1702, Narcissus Luttrell noted that

Her majestie was carried in an open chair of state by 4 yeomen of the guard under the royal canopy, supported by 4 dukes, and carried by the barons of the

Cinque ports; and being seated on a throne in the abby, the lords and commons present, the bishop of Rochester read the service for the day, and the archbishop of York preach't; after which the archbishop of Canterbury gave her the coronation oath, crowned and invested her as usual with the sword of state, spurrs, &c.; then returned to Westminster hall, about 6 at night, where her majestie dined.

THE FIRST DAILY NEWSPAPER

The *Daily Courant*, the first daily newspaper, was published in March, bearing the imprint 'Sold by E. Mallet next door to the King's Arms at Fleet Bridge'. It published nothing but news, 'supposing other people to have sense enough to make reflections for themselves'. The first nine editions were printed on one side of a sheet only, but soon it expanded to four and even six pages. This pioneer survived until 1735. A plaque in Ludgate Hill records its publication.

THE FIRST PANTOMIME

It is claimed that the first pantomime was produced this year at the Drury Lane Theatre. It was entitled *The Tavern Bilkers,* and was the work of a Mr Weaver, a dancing master. It was not a success and lingered only for five nights, but in 1716 Weaver tried again with a more successful production, at Lincoln's Inn Fields Theatre, called *Loves of Mars and Venus.* Other authorities claim that *The Tavern Bilkers* was a ballet.

NEW GATEWAY FOR BART'S HOSPITAL

The present gateway to St Bartholomew's Hospital was built this year by Edward Strong. It includes a statue by Francis Bird of Henry VIII, who had refounded the hospital; this was restored by Philip Hardwick in 1834.

1703

A HURRICANE IN LONDON

On 26 November at about 11 at night a hurricane struck London – the most severe in memory. Henry Chamberlain in his *History of London* (1770) said that

houses were entirely stripped of their covering, and the brick walls and stacks of chimnies fell with such impetuosity, that many people were killed, and others dreadfully mangled in the ruins. It destroyed a great number of spires and turrets, and upon churches and other public buildings sheets of lead were rolled up like scrolls, and blown from their places to the distance of many feet. The damage at sea far exceeded that at land; for, in that dreadful night, twelve men of war were lost, with above eighteen hundred men on board; besides the loss of a great number of merchant ships computed at ten times the value. All the ships in the river Thames were drove from London-bridge to Limehouse, except four, which were so damaged by beating against each other, as to be entirely unfit for any future service.

When Wren was told that after the wind every steeple in London had been touched, he is said to have replied, 'Not St Dunstan's, I am sure.' In fact the tower of St Dunstan in the East, in Idol Lane, was safe and survived even the destruction of the rest of the church in the last war.

BURGH HOUSE, HAMPSTEAD, BUILT

Burgh House, built this year in New End Square, Hampstead, is indicative of the development of Hampstead at this period when the nearby wells were drawing fashionable society from London. It was later the house in which the spa physician William Gibbons lived – his initials are still entwined within the gates to the mansion, the name of which is derived from a 19th-century resident, the Revd Allatson Burgh. The house is now a community centre and local-history museum.

A SCHOOL IN MARYLEBONE

The old manor house in Marylebone High Street was this year converted into a school that prepared boys for entry into Westminster School. It was run by a Dennis de La Place, thought to be a Huguenot, and high in its list of subjects was the teaching of French. The dramatist George Colman the Younger, who was a pupil here c. 1770, recorded that it still gave the teaching of French pride of place in its curriculum. There were, he said, two resident French masters, one of whom helped to teach Latin. Four non-resident masters – teaching writing, arithmetic, dancing and fencing – came in on days fixed for these subjects.

The building, roughly where Devonshire Street now joins, was demolished in 1791.

1704

BOYS' CHARITY SCHOOL IN PICCADILLY

The St James's parish watch house stood at the eastern end of the churchyard, fronting Piccadilly. In 1704 an extra floor was built on top to serve as a schoolroom for poor boys, and a pew in the north gallery of the church was allocated for their use. According to Edward Hatton, writing in 1708, the school had 50 boys, 'who have Cloaths and Learning at the Charge of well-disposed Subscribers'.

1705

THE FIRST HER MAJESTY'S THEATRE

The present Her Majesty's Theatre in the Haymarket is the third on the site. It began this year as the Queen's Theatre (and was alternatively called the Italian Opera House), designed by Sir John Vanbrugh. It opened on 9 April with a performance of an opera by Giacomo Greber called *The Loves of Ergasto,* produced by William Congreve, who had a financial interest in the venture. The theatre was evidently also a financial investment for Vanbrugh, for he informed Jacob Tonson, the publisher, two years earlier that he had bought the ground for £2,000, but had designed the theatre in such a way that he would be reimbursed by the ground left over. The site it covered was known as Phoenix Stable Yard – a prophetic name, since the theatre burnt down twice and was rebuilt each time.

This first building was not, however, a success. Congreve left the next year and Vanbrugh the year after, both the poorer. Colley Cibber criticized the architecture severely: 'For what could their vast columns, their gilded cornices, their immoderate high roofs avail when scarce one word in them could be distinctly heard in it?'

BEDFORD HOUSE DEMOLISHED

Demolition began this year of Bedford House, on the north side of the Strand and one of the few remaining aristocratic houses on that street; its grounds are now taken by Southampton Street and Tavistock Street.

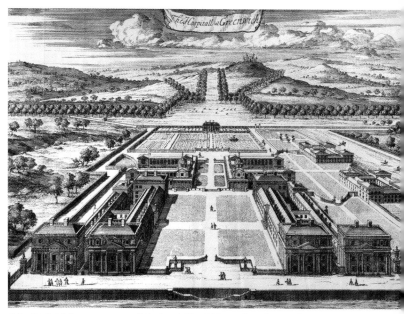

John Kip's 18th-century view of the Royal Naval Hospital at Greenwich. It was intended to provide the same facilities as Chelsea's Royal Military Hospital.

The house fronted the Strand with a timber-framed range, two storeys high; through an arched opening was a courtyard that led through a central passage to a great hall. The number of rooms is not known, but in 1673 the earl was taxed for 60 hearths.

FIRST ADMISSIONS AT THE ROYAL NAVAL HOSPITAL

The Royal Naval Hospital at Greenwich had its origins in the wish of Queen Mary in 1694 to build a hospital for wounded sailors similar to the military hospital at Chelsea. Wren, offering his services free, wanted to demolish virtually everything on the site already, which would have included the beautiful Queen's House by Inigo Jones and all the Tudor buildings. The queen, however, vehemently opposed that proposal and in addition stipulated that her house was to retain its view over the Thames in any new scheme, and, furthermore, that the King's Building, erected during the reign of Charles II as part of an abortive plan to build a new palace, was to remain.

Wren's compromise was to use the Queen's House as the axis for his buildings; architecturally it was unsatisfying, as, looking at the scheme from the river, his two new buildings draw the eye towards what should be a larger, more dominant centrepiece, and the Queen's House, perfect though it is, is of the wrong scale.

The King William block to the west was completed by 1705 and the first pensioners were admitted. The buildings were until recently occupied by the Royal Naval College, which moved there in 1873, but now house the University of Greenwich.

QUEEN ANNE'S GATE BUILT

The road which is now Queen Anne's Gate was originally two streets separated from each other by a wall which contained a statue of Queen Anne. The western street, built in 1705, was called, misleadingly, Queen Square, although it was a T shape; the eastern, built a few years earlier, was Park Street. The houses in these two streets are without doubt some of the most graceful in London, with beautifully carved doorcases. The location of the wall which divided the two streets may be noted today in the kink in the line of the road.

Buckingham House, built for the 1st duke of Buckingham and Normandy in 1702–5, described by John Macky as 'one of the great beauties of London'.

BUCKINGHAM HOUSE COMPLETED

A house was completed this year for John Sheffield, the duke of Buckingham. It was designed by a Dutchman, William Winde or Wynne, and was built partly on the mulberry garden planted by James I. Buckingham Palace now stands on its site.

1706

THE BEGINNINGS OF QUEEN SQUARE

Another Queen Square (see 1705) was soon to take shape – in Bloomsbury. Here, by this year, a proprietary chapel called Ormond Street Chapel or St George's had already been completed and plans were afoot to build a square which ranged on three sides only, leaving the northern aspect clear for the views of Hampstead and Highgate. The church still survives, though much altered in the 19th century, but none of the original houses, complete by 1720, remains. The square was very fashionable for a time – the musicologist and composer Dr Burney was one of its residents – but its reputation had declined by the end of the century.

THE BEGINNINGS OF TWINING'S

This year Thomas Twining acquired the Tom's Coffee House in Devereux Court, off the Strand. Here he sold tea as well as coffee, and, though expensive, it was popular enough for him to establish himself as a tea dealer in 1717 at 216 Strand, where the company remains today. The business made Twining rich enough to own a large house at Twickenham, and to have his portrait painted by Hogarth.

REBUILDING AT ST THOMAS'S HOSPITAL

During this period substantial improvements were taking place at the ancient St Thomas's Hospital in Borough High Street. Not only was rebuilding going on, but in 1703 Dr Richard Mead was appointed

physician to the hospital – he was to become the most eminent doctor in the reigns of Anne and the first two Georges.

An indication of the prevailing administration of the hospital may be gained from the set of rules adopted in 1699. They included the following: the sisters were to see that no card play nor dicing took place in the house; the sisters were to clean the wards by six a.m.; every tenth bed was to be left empty to air, and not more than one patient was to be put into each bed; the porters were not to suffer the poor to go out except upon necessary occasions, and if they returned late or drunk they were to be expelled.

1707

A NEW SOCIETY OF ANTIQUARIES

With some justification the Society of Antiquaries can trace its ancestry to the 16th century, but the present institution truly derives from a reconstitution of the body in 1707, when men with antiquarian interests began to meet at the Bear Tavern in the Strand. Meetings were held at various taverns until 1753, when the society had its own premises in Chancery Lane.

A FLY EPIDEMIC

About the middle of August there was an epidemic of flies in London so prodigious that, as Henry Chamberlain related in 1770, 'many of the streets were so covered with them, that the people's feet made as full an impression on them as upon thick snow'.

DAGENHAM FLOODED

The worst known flooding of Dagenham took place on 17 December, when 1,000 acres were covered. It appears that the inundation was caused first by neglect of a sluice designed to prevent such happenings and second by an inefficient replacement. The flooding caused large amounts of soil to be swept into the Thames and, despite huge works, it reoccurred at any wind-driven high tide. The problem was to continue for at least seven years, and by 1713 the soil which had been swept into the river formed a shelf which reached halfway to the opposite bank and was a mile long – a considerable hazard to navigation.

KENSINGTON CHARITY SCHOOL

Until its demolition *c.* 1878, one of the best-known buildings in Kensington was the charity school on the north side of the High Street. It had a high tower with a pediment, looking rather like a modern neo-classical building. It was built by Hawksmoor in 1711–12 for a school which had been founded in 1707. This building was sadly lost when it was replaced by Kensington Town Hall – itself in modern times the subject of a shabby demolition by the council before conservationists knew what was happening.

1708

CHEYNE ROW BUILT

Ten houses in Cheyne Row, Chelsea, now numbered 16 to 34, were built this year on a bowling green leased from Lord Cheyne, lord of the manor. At no. 24 Thomas Carlyle lived for much of his life. An interesting example of how the perception of various parts of London has changed is Frederick Harrison's record of a visit he paid to Carlyle in 1872: he wrote, 'I was struck with humiliation when I went to see the Old Prophet of Chelsea. He seems to live in a very dismal corner of this foul city. When I thought of the poor, soured, wild old genius, coiling himself up in his own virtue in that alley, where one might expect to find one's washerwoman … '

ATTEMPT TO BAN THE MAY FAIR
Present-day Mayfair derives its name from an annual fair held between Curzon Street and Piccadilly, west of today's Shepherd Market. An advertisement of 1700 states, 'In Brookfield Market, at the east corner of Hyde Park is a Fair to be kept for a space of 16 days, beginning the 1st May. Three days for cattle and leather, with the entertainments as Bartholomew Fair.' In 1705 the land was bought by Edward Shepherd, architect, who let off part of it for the market and fair, and gradually developed what is today's Shepherd Market.

The fair itself was the usual rumbustious sort of thing which scandalized the puritanically minded. There were numerous sideshows and puppets. Its most famous personality was a gingerbread seller called Tiddy Dol, whose name is today commemorated by a local restaurant. He was tall, handsome and dressed like a person of rank, with a white and gold-lace suit of clothes, a laced ruffled shirt, a laced hat with a feather, and white silk stockings. He was also to be seen at lord mayor's processions and at execution days at Tyburn.

In 1708 it was decided to prohibit the fair as it was thought to be too disreputable, but it was still in full swing at least 20 years later. By 1746 it had moved slightly eastward and was concentrated around Shepherd Market.

WHITECHAPEL MARKET ESTABLISHED
A hay market previously at Ratcliff, Wapping, was this year moved to Whitechapel, to a market place outside the church, in the roadway by today's Whitechapel Gallery. Whitechapel was on an important east–west route – Commercial Road did not exist, nor did Commercial Street, and most travellers from eastern parts of England came through Whitechapel and Aldgate. The market dealt in garden and farm produce, brewing ingredients, and animals killed in the local abattoirs. There were numerous inns: Rocque's map of 1746 shows many yards off the High Street named after them. Other names of courtyards denote local industries: Sugar Baker's Court, Brick Lane, Brewhouse Yard, Trype Yard etc.

1709

NEW RESERVOIR FOR THE NEW RIVER
The New River Company this year constructed a reservoir in what is now Claremont Square, fronting the Pentonville Road. A six-sailed windmill was erected by George Sorocold at the New River Head to its south to pump up water to the reservoir. This was assisted from 1720 by a contraption driven by four horses. The reservoir not only acted as an emergency supply for outlets to the south but also could supply by gravity new districts to the north and north-west. Remains of the old windmill still survive.

BEAR ATTACK
The proprietor of the notorious bearpit at Hockley-in-the-Hole (today's junction of Warner Street and Back Hill in Clerkenwell) was attacked by one of his own bears and 'almost devoured before his friends were aware of his danger'. The tragedy brought even greater crowds to the place, which was then managed by the victim's widow. Bears were quite valuable and were usually allowed to survive whatever torments were presented them, but an advertisement for the place in 1716 proclaims:

At the request of several persons of quality, on Monday, the 11th of this instant June, is one of the largest and most mischievours bears that ever was seen in England to be baited to death, with other variety of bull and bear baiting, as also a wild bull to be turned loose in the game-place with fireworks all over him. To begin exactly at three o'clock in the afternoon, because the sport continues long.

THE TATLER FOUNDED
The first edition of an innovatory journal, the *Tatler*, was published on 12 April this year, edited by Richard Steele. It appeared two or three times a week; the first four numbers were free, but after that an edition cost a penny. The paper developed, with the aid of Addison, from a hotchpotch of gossip and news to a journal of social comment, but it did not last long – it ceased publication after 271 issues in 1711. It is thought that Steele, who had a government post, was in danger of losing this because of the parodies of prominent people contained in his paper.

BUILDING REGULATIONS
Building Regulation Acts of 1707 and 1709 were to have a significant effect on London's architecture. The Act of 1707 prohibited overhanging wooden eave cornices, so that in future walls went straight up to a roof parapet. In 1709 it was required that all windows be recessed 4 inches into the wall, so that flames climbing up the outside of the wall should not immediately reach the wooden window frames.

THE BEGINNING OF MARLBOROUGH HOUSE
On 24 June the foundation stone of Marlborough House was laid in Pall Mall. Designed by Wren, the house originally consisted of two floors only – a third was added by the third duke. Sarah, duchess of Marlborough, was high in the queen's estimation but detested by many – a hostility revealed in the way that Sir Robert Walpole later ensured that three of the entrances to her new house were blocked. First he persuaded the king that her right to an exit into the park was to be taken away. Next he bought up for his own family two houses in Pall Mall which the duchess had intended to buy and demolish so that she would have a grand driveway into Pall Mall; the duchess was reduced to driving out through what was known as the Friary, a congested and narrow passage which also contained a sedan-chair stand. Even her later plan to buy four more houses on Pall Mall to the west of the two originally intended was thwarted by Walpole. On Walpole's fall from power in 1741 she eventually acquired the lease of the four houses and got her grand, though rather off-centre, exit to Pall Mall. But she died soon afterwards.

DORSET GARDEN THEATRE DEMOLISHED
The magnificent theatre built by Wren on the banks of the Thames, south of Fleet Street, after the Great Fire was this year demolished. Theatrical activity was now concentrated around Drury Lane, and when the principal acting company left in 1682 the Dorset Garden or, as it was often called, the Duke's Theatre was left with trifling fare and an unfashionable audience.

1710

THE SACHEVERELL RIOTS

Riots broke out in London this year in support of a High Church Tory, the Revd Henry Sacheverell, whose sermons had offended the government. In November 1709 he had preached a vituperative sermon at St Paul's in which he warned that the Church was in danger from its tendency to tolerate Nonconformists; it was thought by the House of Commons that the sermon contained 'malicious, scandalous, and seditious libels' reflecting on the queen, the government, the Glorious Revolution and the succession of the house of Hanover.

In 1710 proceedings for trial began, but the country as a whole was behind Sacheverell and it is said at least 40,000 copies of his sermon were printed. In microcosm it became a trial of strength between Tories, who were obliged by popular opinion to champion Sacheverell, and the Whig government. The latter determined, unwisely as it happened, to have a showcase trial at Westminster Hall.

On 27 February Sacheverell's trial began and the coach carrying him from the Temple to Westminster was followed by six others and a multitude of people. On the 28th riots occurred in the capital; Nonconformist buildings such as the Carter Lane Meeting House were damaged, and houses of prominent Whigs were attacked.

The Lords found Sacheverell guilty but gave him the lightest possible sentence – he was to abstain from preaching for three years and have his sermon burnt publicly by the public hangman. The verdict was thought to be a triumph for the Tories and the High Church, and there were many celebrations all over London.

The architect Sir Christopher Wren, from the portrait by Godfrey Kneller. He was responsible for rebuilding up to 30 churches after the Great Fire.

Mrs Salmon's Waxworks in the late 18th century.

ST PAUL'S CATHEDRAL COMPLETED

The final stone was placed on St Paul's Cathedral – by Wren's son, who placed it on the summit of the lantern. His father, now aged 78, was present during the ceremony that followed. The new cathedral – which, despite its size, was smaller than its predecessor – had cost about £850,000, most of which was derived from a tax on sea coal.

1711

FIFTY NEW CHURCHES

An Act was passed on 28 May for the building of 50 new Anglican churches in the London area, to cope with the vast increase of population. Now that St Paul's Cathedral was finished they would be built with money received from coal duties.

The Act was not just a matter of providing more space for worship, but a confirmation that the Tories and the Anglican Church were now firmly back in government – a return to be commemorated in fine buildings 'of stone and other proper Materials with Towers or Steeples to each of them'.

It is doubtful if anyone computed just how many churches were required. In the event, between 1711 and 1730 only 12 were built, although they are among London's finest. They include Hawksmoor's Christ Church at Spitalfields, St Anne at Limehouse, St George in the East, St George, Bloomsbury, and St Mary Woolnoth; James Gibbs's St Mary le Strand; Thomas Archer's St Paul at Deptford; Henry Flitcroft's St Giles-in-the-Fields and John James's St George Hanover Square.

LONDON'S FIRST WAXWORKS

The first waxworks in London was that of a Mrs Salmon, who was originally at the Golden Ball, St Martin's le Grand, and then, in 1711, moved to the north side of Fleet Street near Chancery Lane. Her exhibits included the execution of Charles I and a tableau of 'Margaret,

Countess of Heningbergh, Lying on a Bed of State, with her Three
hundred and Sixty-Five Children, all born at one Birth'.

A DUEL IN TOTHILL FIELDS

An odd duel took place in Tothill Fields, Westminster, this year, when
Richard Thornhill and Sir Cholmondeley Dearing fired at each other
with their pistols touching each other. Dearing was killed and Thornhill
was charged with his murder, but lightly punished by being burnt on
the hand. The matter did not end there, however, as the incensed
friends of Dearing waylaid Thornhill and murdered him.

FIRST LONDON TURNPIKE ROAD

The first road in the country to be put in the care of a turnpike trust
was part of the Great North Road in the Cambridge and
Huntingdonshire region, in 1663. It was not until 1711 that the first
stretch of road in the London area was turnpiked. This was part of the
present Edgware Road, from Kilburn as far as Sparrow's Herne in
Hertfordshire. In the same year the road leading from Highgate gatehouse to Barnet was also under the care of trustees.

1712

BUTTON'S COFFEE HOUSE ESTABLISHED

Button's Coffee House, on the south side of Russell Street, became a
famous place, but its life was a short one – and presumably unsuccessful, as Daniel Button, its proprietor, died in penury in 1731.

It drew the fashionable world from Tom's Coffee House, and it
became the headquarters of Addison, who set up here a postbox in the
shape of a metallic lion's head for the receipt of news and contributions
for the *Spectator*.

QUEEN ANNE STATUE AT ST PAUL'S

The absurd statue of Queen Anne, surrounded by four figures representing her dominions, was erected outside St Paul's Cathedral. (One
of the dominions was France, where Britain still had a foothold.) The
statue was by Francis Bird, but it lost sceptre, orb and arms in vandalis-
tic attacks in 1743 and 1749. The damaged work remained until 1884,
when it was taken down, to be replaced in 1886 with a copy.

DUEL IN HYDE PARK

A duel took place in Hyde Park between the duke of Hamilton and
Lord Mohun. They fought with swords, Colonel Hamilton acting as
second to the duke and General Macartney for the lord. Mohun was
killed on the spot. The duke was severely wounded and as his second
helped him up he died. It was related by Colonel Hamilton on oath
that Macartney had stabbed the duke surreptitiously when he,
Hamilton, had been assisting the duke, and a reward of £800 was
offered for Macartney's apprehension. Macartney escaped abroad, but
was later convicted of manslaughter.

1713

TWO NEW BURIAL GROUNDS

The new chapel in Queen Square (see 1706) and the new church of
St George, Bloomsbury, had no adjacent burial grounds. The com-

*One of the busiest turnpikes in London was that at Islington, by the junction
of the High Street with Liverpool Road. This print, by Pugin, is dated 1819.*

missioners for building the proposed 50 new churches in London purchased 3 acres in the parish of St Pancras off Gray's Inn Road on 8 July,
allocating a part to each of the new churches. Collectively now called
St George's Gardens, they lie south of Regent Square.

Burials here included a number of those hanged for their part in the
Jacobite rebellion, Zachary Macaulay, father of the historian, and Nancy
Dawson, hornpipe dancer.

POWIS HOUSE BURNS DOWN

Like its namesake in Lincoln's Inn Fields (see 1684), Powis House in
Great Ormond Street was burnt down in January. It was rented at the
time by the French ambassador, and either arson or carelessness by
French servants was suspected.

The house stood just past Queen Square on the north side of the
road, with grounds stretching to open fields and with unobstructed
views of the northern heights. With a strong resemblance to the new
Buckingham House, it was built late in the reign of William III for
William Herbert, 2nd marquis of Powis.

TWICKENHAM CHURCH COLLAPSES

The nave of the medieval church of St Mary the Virgin, Twickenham,
collapsed from neglect on 9 April; no one was hurt. At the time, one of
the churchwardens was the painter Sir Godfrey Kneller, and it was he
who supervised the church's replacement. John James, later to be the
architect of St George Hanover Square, was engaged to build the new
church while retaining the medieval tower. The building was consecrated in 1715 and still stands, though much altered in Victorian times.

This was not James's first building in Twickenham – in 1710 he had
been responsible for the rebuilding of Twickenham Manor House, which
was then called Orleans House. Unfortunately the James part of the
house has since been demolished, and only the splendid Octagon Room
added by James Gibbs 20 years later survives. Orleans House is now an
art museum of the London Borough of Richmond-upon-Thames.

The building of a new church was timely, as the village of
Twickenham was about to enter a fashionable period. Alexander Pope,
its most famous resident, is commemorated by a plaque in the church.

1714

DISASTER AT THE CORONATION

There was thick fog on the Thames when George I, the first of the Hanovers to be king of the United Kingdom, came to claim his throne. He arrived at Greenwich on 18 September, and the next day a succession of court luminaries went to pay homage there.

The coronation was held at Westminster Abbey on 20 October. It was marred by an accident at Palace Yard when the scaffolding holding spectators collapsed, and several people were killed.

A CHURCH AT KEW

Up to this year the people of Kew either attended church at Richmond or went by ferry across the river to Brentford. But in 1710 local residents obtained some land from Queen Anne on Kew Green and raised a subscription to build a chapel, dedicated to St Anne, there. It was consecrated on 12 May this year.

Kew, like Richmond, has been very much influenced by the residence of various members of the royal family. Henry VII's daughter had lived there briefly, as had James I's daughter, Elizabeth; but the close and continuous royal association began in 1728, when Queen Caroline rented Kew Farm and what was called the Dutch House, and three years later Frederick, prince of Wales, acquired the lease of Kew Park.

PAROCHIAL SCHOOLS AT HACKNEY

Two small schools for poor children had existed at Hackney since the 17th century, but in 1714 they were merged into one charity school and located in Urswick House in the parish churchyard. There were 30 boy pupils and 20 girls.

1715

THE JACOBITE REBELLION

The Hanoverian succession did not go unopposed. An influential faction wished to continue the Stuart line, in the person of the exiled James, son of James II. However, he had insisted on remaining a Catholic, and there was therefore little public resistance to the installation of George I. But in 1715, while there was still a chance of enlisting popular support, the Stuart faction contrived a rebellion.

Jacobite supporters rioted in London on 28 May, George I's birthday, and on the following day, the anniversary of the restoration of Charles II, there were bonfires in the streets and a portrait of William III was burnt at Smithfield. A mob gathered in Snow Hill and drank loyal toasts to the late James II, stripping any passers-by who refused to join in. On 20 July Parliament was told of an invasion plan by the Pretender. As a precaution, General Cadogan marched the Life Guards, the Horse Grenadiers and other battalions into Hyde Park and put them under canvas.

The Pretender eventually landed on Christmas Day near Aberdeen, where he began his campaign on the assumption that the Scots would provide support. During 1716 the rebellion was put down, resulting in an orgy of executions at Tyburn.

A MUSEUM IN THE MAKING

What is now the Geffrye Museum in Kingsland Road, Shoreditch, began life as the Ironmongers' Almshouses this year. They were founded by Sir Robert Geffrye, lord mayor of London, who had made his fortune from ironmongery. In his will, made in 1703, he left the Ironmongers' Company what Strype describes as 'a great sum of money amounting as it is thought, to near ten thousand pounds, to build so many almshouses as the said monies will purchase, for the maintaining of so many poor, and allowing them gowns, of fifteen shillings a piece, yearly'.

A SCHOOL FOR NAVIGATION

This year a school specializing in the teaching of navigation and mathematics was established. It derived from an endowment of Joseph Neale, a barrister of Gray's Inn, which in 1705 provided money for charity schools in the neighbourhood. In 1715 the Court of Chancery directed that some of the endowment should be invested so that 'an able master, skilful in such part of mathematics as was requisite to instruct youth in the art of navigation to fit them for sea service, either in men-of-war or in merchantment' could be employed. Boys were chosen from local parishes, and a schoolroom, originally in the parish of St Bride, Fleet Street, was taken; quite soon the school was moved to Hatton Garden. From 1715 to 1735, 105 boys were bound out to serve on ships.

NEW ROTHERHITHE CHURCH COMPLETED

The medieval church of St Mary, Rotherhithe had been crumbling for years and was finally demolished in 1710. The parishioners thought, not without some justification, that they could obtain money from the fund set up under Queen Anne in 1711 to build 50 new churches. Their petition to the commissioners was quite blunt in describing the parishioners generally as being 'chiefly seamen and watermen who venture their lives in fetching those coals from Newcastle which pay for the Rebuilding of the Churches in London'. Their pertinacity was rewarded by a refusal of funds.

However, the church was rebuilt very handsomely, in red brick and stone quoins, by an unknown architect – complete with three-decker pulpit, high family pews, and rows of benches for the poorer people. The tower, designed by Launcelot Dowbiggin, who also built the tower that adorns St Mary, Islington, was added in 1839. St Mary, Rotherhithe, still stands, but for much of its existence it has been hemmed in by warehouses. The buildings included a watch house so that guard against body-snatchers could be kept on the graveyard.

Christopher Jones, captain of the *Mayflower*, had been buried in the churchyard in 1622 – almost all the crew of that ship came from the locality. There is a plaque in the church to Prince Lee Boo, son of the king of the Pelew Islands in the Pacific; his father had befriended the crew of an East India ship, and as a return of his favours they brought his son home to England to see civilization. Unfortunately he died of smallpox within a year.

ALLEN & HANBURY'S FOUNDED

This year the lease of 2 Plough Court, Lombard Street, was taken by Silvanus Bean, apothecary, son of a Welsh Quaker, on the completion of his seven years' apprenticeship. It was this building which was to be the starting point of the well-known pharmacists Allen & Hanbury: a William Allen joined the firm as a clerk in 1792, to be followed later by his nephew, Daniel Bell Hanbury.

A NOTABLE HOUSE IN FULHAM

About this year two cottages in North End, Fulham, were demolished and a double-fronted villa, later called The Grange, was built in their place. During its existence – it was pulled down in 1957 – it had two famous residents. One was the novelist Samuel Richardson, who was there from 1738, and the other was the pre-Raphaelite artist Edward Burne-Jones. It was at this house that Richardson wrote his most famous novels, *Pamela*, *Clarissa* and *Sir Charles Grandison*. A housing estate is now on the site.

1716

THE LIBRARY OF DR WILLIAMS

When the noted Presbyterian minister Dr Daniel Williams died this year, part of his property was bequeathed for 2,000 years to 23 trustees for various purposes, including the education of children and the distribution of 'bibles, catechisms and good practical books ... to the poor'. Williams also left his large theological library to the trustees, with sufficient funds to eventually find a 'fit edifice' to house it for others to study. It was some years before his will could be effected, and so the library remained in his old house at Hoxton until about 1729, when it moved to Red Cross Street, Cripplegate. The library, much enlarged since, is now housed at 14 Gordon Square, Bloomsbury.

LIGHTING UP WESTMINSTER

An Act was passed compelling Westminster householders to 'furnish a light before their doors from 6 to 11 p.m. except on evenings between the seventh night each new moon and the third after it reached its full'.

LEOPARD BAITING IN SOHO

To the rear of Soho Square this year was 'At the desire of several persons of quality a leopard 12 feet in length to be baited to death, and gentlemen who chuse to risk their dogs are allowed to assist. The leopard on view at the Boarded House, Marylebone Fields.' This was a period of exotic beasts and barbaric sports. In Hockley-in-the-Hole the following year an African tiger was to be worried by six bull and bear dogs.

A FRENCH HOSPITAL FOUNDED

A hospital for Huguenots in London was made possible this year by a bequest by M. de Gastigny, master of the buckhounds to William III. A piece of land in what was then Pest House Row and is now Bath Street, off Old Street, was purchased; it stood opposite today's Peerless Street. Due to financial problems, the hospital was obliged to sell off much of the land surrounding the building and so became hemmed in, but in 1865 it moved to an extraordinary new building in Victoria Park, Hackney. The descendant of this institution in Pest House Row is now in Rochester as flatlets for the elderly.

1717

ST MARY LE STRAND FINISHED

The church of St Mary le Strand, on its new site in the middle of the road, was completed in September this year, but not consecrated until 1 January 1724. It was the first of the 'Fifty Churches' to be finished, and was subject to change halfway through the building work. According to James Gibbs, the architect, his design at first made provision for a small campanile or turret, but when the church was 20 ft above the ground the commissioners decided that it required a steeple.

This view of the buildings south of the Strand in 1700 shows the maypole towering above the area. It stood outside the new church of St Mary le Strand.

It was impossible for him to spread the church east to west to accommodate it, and therefore the building was extended north and south. What was originally planned as a square steeple finished up an oblong.

St Mary's had originally stood to the south, but was demolished to make way for Somerset House in 1544.

Outside the church stood the Strand maypole. This year it was taken down and the 100-ft pole was taken to the seat of the earl of Sidney at Wanstead, on the instructions of the scientist Sir Isaac Newton, and there was used as a base for a telescope.

WESTMINSTER FIRE OFFICE FOUNDED

A good number of fire-insurance offices had been founded since the Great Fire of London. One of the better-known ones was the Westminster, founded this year. It was a breakaway business from the Hand-in-Hand Company, which was founded at Tom's Coffee House in St Martin's Lane in 1696 (q.v.). In 1699 the company established a permanent office in St Martin's Lane, but a number of the partners wanted to move the office to the City, where a great deal of business was done, and decided to establish their own company. Again, it was at Tom's Coffee House, but in May 1751 it moved to Bedford Street, Covent Garden, and in 1808 to King Street, where its name and coat of arms may still be seen on no. 27.

REBUILDING THE ROLLS HOUSE

The old House for Converted Jews in Chancery Lane, which had been used for storing the rolls and records of the Court of Chancery since the reign of Edward III, was demolished this year and a new building

Now called Thomas Archer House, no. 43 King Street was built in 1717 on the site of an old arcaded house of Covent Garden Piazza.

was begun. The house was also the residence of the Master of the Rolls. The architect for the new building was Colen Campbell, who was to have a brief period of fashion in London. He was at this time also building the Palladian masterpiece Wanstead House (see 1720), and in 1717 he was also commissioned to build Pembroke House between Whitehall and the Thames. Pembroke House, with its recessed portico at first-floor level, has been described as the first completely Palladian villa in English architecture.

DEMOLITION IN THE PIAZZA
The first of the arcaded houses in Covent Garden Piazza to be demolished was replaced this year by the only house that now survives from that early fashionable period. This is now the magnificent 43 King Street, a Palladian mansion designed by Thomas Archer for the earl of Orford, and rescued from the depredations of the fruit and vegetable market when the latter moved out in the 1970s. The front elevation of the new house was brought forward to align with the rest of King Street, and thus the piazza arcade was brought to a halt at the eastern end of Orford's house; though the present adjacent arcaded buildings are relatively new, that full-stop feature still exists, the arcade ending at a side entrance of no. 43.

A MATHEMATICAL SOCIETY IN SPITALFIELDS
We have seen (in 1715) how a school to teach boys mathematics and navigation was set up. This relationship between mathematics and the instruments of navigation is further illustrated by the foundation this year, by John Middleton, a retired sailor, of the Spitalfields Mathematical Society in Monmouth Street, Spitalfields. Many members were Huguenots involved in the manufacture of optical and navigational instruments – such as the Dollonds, who founded the firm of Dollond & Aitchison.

Information and equipment was lent between members, so as to increase the general level of experience among them. As surety for the loan of instruments (air pumps, reflecting telescopes, reflecting microscopes, electrical machines, surveying instruments etc.), with instruction books, the borrower had to give a note of hand for their value. The

members met on Saturday evenings; each was to employ himself in some mathematical exercises or forfeit one penny, and if he refused to answer a mathematical question asked by another member he was forfeited twopence.

This admirable society survived until 1845.

LAYING OUT THE CAVENDISH ESTATE
By 1717 Edward Harley, 2nd earl of Oxford, who was married to Lady Henrietta Cavendish Holles, was ready to start the development of his estate north of Oxford Street. Cavendish Square was laid out this year, and the central garden was enclosed with a low wall surmounted by wooden railings. In the original plan the entire north side of the square was reserved for the mansion of the duke of Chandos, to be designed by John Price, but only the wings, which later marked the corners of Chandos Street and Harley Street, were built. The wing on the Harley Street side still survives.

A general scheme for the other streets around was also published, but work on the whole project ground to a halt in 1720 on the collapse of the South Sea Company's stocks. But even by 1754, on the Sutton Nicholls map, the square was in some isolation, and a contemporary observer remarks that 'we shall see the folly of attempting great things before we are sure we can accomplish little ones. Here it is the modern plague of building was first stayed; and I think the rude, unfinished figure of this project should deter others from a like infatuation.'

1718

HANOVER SQUARE BEGUN
It was the ill luck of the earl of Oxford that his development of today's Cavendish Square (see 1717) coincided with the laying out of Hanover Square to the south. The latter was a huge success and encouraged the spread of building westward to Park Lane, thereby glutting the market and causing considerable delay to the completion of the Cavendish estate.

Hanover Square was the centrepiece of the estate of the 1st earl of Scarborough, Richard Lumley, a firm supporter of the Hanoverian succession to the throne – hence the name of the square. His land was bounded roughly by Oxford Street, Regent Street and the backs of houses in Bond Street and Conduit Street. This first of the three Mayfair squares was further enhanced by the building of St George's church (see 1724), which became the most fashionable church in London.

The first house to be built in the square was on the south corner of Tenterden Street; belonging to Sir James Dashwood, this was in the rate books by 1719.

WELSH CHARITY SCHOOL FOUNDED
This year 'a few benevolent Welsh gentlemen' opened a subscription for the purpose of 'setting up and supporting a school in or near London, for instructing, clothing, and putting forth apprentices poor children, descended of Welsh parents, born in or near London'. The first schoolhouse, for 12 children, was in Hatton Garden, but in 1737 (q.v.) the school moved to Clerkenwell Green.

A COFFEE HOUSE IN CHEYNE WALK
This year the well-known Chelsea coffee house Don Saltero's (see 1695) moved to its final home at 18 Cheyne Walk. The house was known for its rum and its fiddle music, and also for a museum of miscellania. The *Weekly Journal* in 1723 noted that

Monsters of all sorts here are seen;
Strange things in nature as they grew so;
Some relicks of the Sheba queen,
And fragments of the fam'd Bob Crusoe.

A contemporary catalogue listed 'a wooden shoe that was put under the Speaker's chair in the reign of King James II, a Staffordshire almanack in use when the Danes were in England, a starved cat found between the walls of Westminster Abbey when repairing etc.' It was all sold up in 1799.

THE HANGMAN HANGED

The public hangman, John Price, was found guilty of the murder of Elizabeth White, wife of a watchman in Moorfields. He was hanged at Bunhill Fields and gibbetted at Holloway Road for several years, roughly at the junction with today's Liverpool Road.

1719

FIRST RICHMOND THEATRE

It is recorded that the first play staged in Richmond outside the palace was in 1714, when the Earl of Southampton's Company used a barn on Richmond Hill. In 1719 the comedian William Pinkethman opened a new theatre in a building converted from an 'ass house' – one used to house donkeys which were hired out. This early theatre died with Pinkethman in 1725.

LANESBOROUGH HOUSE BUILT

About this year a large house was built for James Lane, 2nd Viscount Lanesborough, at the entrance to the village of Knightsbridge. Over the door he inscribed: ''Tis my delight thus to be Both in the town and country.' The building, consisting of an almost square central block and two wings, was of red bricks; there were three floors and a basement. It was not to be a private mansion for long, for in 1733 it was converted into what became St George's Hospital. The Lanesborough Hotel is now on the same site.

WEAVERS RIOT

Large numbers of Huguenots took part in a demonstration by 4,000 Spitalfields weavers in the City this year. Women wearing India calicoes and linens were attacked and doused with ink, aqua fortis and other liquids. Troops were called out to quell the disturbance.

TURNPIKE PROGRESS

A number of roads had been turnpiked since the first in the London area in 1711. Similar arrangements had been made for Shoreditch to Enfield (1713), Tyburn to Uxbridge (1714), Kensington to Staines and Colnbrook (1716), Kent Street, Southwark, to East Greenwich and Lewisham (1717), and Westminster Ferry to New Cross in 1719.

1720

THE GROWTH OF MAYFAIR

Building work was progressing steadily over the fields of the old Davies and now Grosvenor estate – today's Mayfair. Davies Street itself was developed from 1720, but only two buildings of note were erected, one of which survives. This is Bourdon House at no. 2, which is now partly of the 1720s and partly of the Edwardian era, and was first occupied in 1725 by a Captain William Bourdon.

Grosvenor Street was also begun this year and finished by about 1729. In 1735 it was described as 'a spacious well built Street, inhabited chiefly by People of Distinction'. Twenty of those first houses, though much altered, still survive.

Mount Street, supposedly named from an earthwork erected at the time of the Civil War, was begun too, but this does not seem to be a street that the Grosvenors had earmarked for 'people of distinction', because the frontages were smaller and within five years a workhouse had been established in the road. Much of the northern side was devoted to trade. None of the original buildings survived the 1890s rebuilding in terracotta.

South Audley Street was probably begun about the same time. The northern end of the road had a different character (as it still does), with trade and smaller premises built, whereas the southern end had larger properties, some of which remain.

CIGARS AND SNUFF IN THE HAYMARKET

Until 1981 the tobacconists and snuff suppliers Fribourg & Treyer were at 34 Haymarket – their distinctive building remains, but is now a gift shop. The old business was begun in 1720 by Mr Fribourg at what was then the Sign of the Rasp and Crown further south on the same side of the Haymarket, next to the Haymarket Theatre. By the end of the century the business was joined by Martha Treyer.

DEVELOPMENTS IN HAMPSTEAD

The most stylish street in Hampstead, Church Row, was built about this date. Most of the elegant houses survive, although Gardnor Mansions, itself an attractive enough Edwardian block, has since intruded on the road's symmetry. Nowadays it would seem logical that such a fashionable avenue should lead up to the parish church, but it should be remembered that when it was built the Heath Street end of the road (away from the church) finished in an area of alleys and hovels – one of the few areas of Hampstead ever to contain slums.

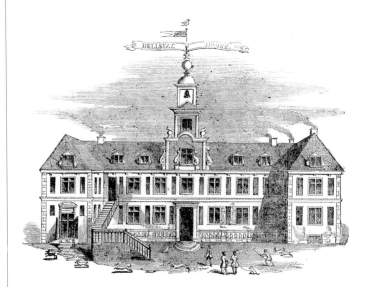

Belsize House, Hampstead, c.1721, in its heyday as a pleasure resort.

Down the hill from Church Row, Belsize House had a new tenant, a man called Howell, who styled himself 'His Excellency the Welsh Ambassador'. The house and grounds had since 1704 been a pleasure ground of the sort that Ranelagh and Vauxhall were to emulate, but Howell extended the range of attractions to include duck-shooting, footman-racing, and a plenitude of private arbours for romantic meetings. The place was renowned enough to warrant a visit from the prince and princess of Wales in 1721, and sometimes between 300 and 400 coaches would arrive on a day.

Hampstead Brewery was founded this year – the entrance may be discovered today next to the King of Bohemia pub in the High Street in what is now Old Brewery Mews. At this time the owner of the brewery seems to have had a private pipe leading from the Hampstead Wells spring off Well Walk, though as the spring water had a strong chalybeate taste it seems unlikely that it would have been used for making beer.

WANSTEAD HOUSE COMPLETED
One of the most spectacular Palladian residences in the London area was Wanstead House, completed for Richard Child, Earl Tylney, this year. The family had made a great deal of money from a bank founded in the 17th century and were able to construct what was described as 'one of the most elegant houses in England, both for the building and the gardens'. The principal rooms on the ground floor were mostly about 25 ft square, and the ballroom was 75 ft long and 27 ft wide. The house was designed by Colen Campbell.

Unfortunately Wanstead House was hardly used by its owner, who lived mainly in Italy. After a succession of tenants it was taken down in 1822 and its contents were auctioned over a period of 32 days.

FIRST PATIENTS AT WESTMINSTER HOSPITAL
The beginning of Westminster Hospital had been a meeting in 1715 – at the instigation of Henry Hoare, of Hoare's Bank – at the St Dunstan's Coffee House, Fleet Street, to discuss a proposal for 'Relieving the Sick and Needy and other Distressed Persons'. In 1720 a house was rented in Petty France to serve as the first hospital in the country entirely supported by voluntary contributions.

HAYMARKET THEATRE OPENS
The Haymarket Theatre, whose early-19th-century successor still stands, was begun this year by John Potter, a carpenter, who seems merely to have provided an auditorium over the backyard of a house just north of the existing building. It was known as the Little Theatre in the Hay-market, and indeed it was small, being not much wider than one house, with part of the frontage let to Mr Fribourg, the snuffman (see above).

On 15 December this year Potter advertised, 'At the New Theatre in Haymarket, between Suffolk Street and James Street, which is now completely finished, will be acted French Comedies, as soon as the actors arrive from Paris, who are daily expected.' A fortnight later the curtain rose on a production of *La Fille à la Mode: ou le Badeaut de Paris*.

1721

LONDON MOVING WEST
A sure sign that London was extending westward was the relocation of the Piccadilly turnpike away from the end of Berkeley Street down to Hyde Park Corner.

In this year New Bond Street appears in the rate books for the first time, as a continuation of Old Bond Street to Oxford Street, across the Conduit Field estate of the Corporation of London. It was a venture funded by the earl of Oxford. The land was then an open field, and Oxford Street itself had buildings on the south side but was largely a highway described as a 'deep hollow road full of sloughs, with here and there a ragged house, the lurking place of cut-throats'.

Maddox Street was also built this year, and indeed building work was progressing all over the area. An impressionable diarist in *Applebee's Journal* in 1725 described the scene:

I went towards Hyde Park, being told of a fine avenue made to the east side of the park, fine gates and a large vista or opening from the new square called Hanover Square … In the tour I passed an amazing scene of new foundations not of houses only, but I might say of new cities, new towns, new squares and fine buildings, the like of which no city, no town, no place in the world, can shew, nor is it possible to judge where or when they will make an end, or stop building.

New Bond Street was largely residential when built, but it contained some good-class shops to catch the affluent residents settling in the area.

LAST SERVICE AT ST MARTIN'S
The medieval church of St Martin-in-the-Fields had been substantially enlarged in 1607 to cope with the growth of Westminster. By 1721 it was hopelessly inadequate again. This had been recognized by the parishioners much earlier, for they had petitioned the commissioners for permission (and funds) to rebuild the church as one of the 50 new churches in London. In 1717 the parishioners obtained their own Act of Parliament, but had to shoulder the expense themselves.

This year the last service was held in the old church and demolition began.

1722

KEEP TO THE LEFT
What appears to be the origin of the UK driving on the left-hand side of the road is a regulation governing London Bridge this year, made by the Corporation of London. The bridge was a particularly congested stretch of road, and there seems to have been no recognized order of travelling on it previously. It was ordered that all 'Carts, Coaches, and other Carriages, coming out of Southwark into this City, do keep all along on the West Side of the said Bridge [i.e. to the left]; and all Carts, and Coaches, and other Carriages, going out of this City, do keep on the East Side of the said Bridge'. It is most likely that this rule spread to streets leading from the bridge and, without further legislation, became the custom on London's roads.

Why on the left? Several suggestions have been made. The one most likely is that coachmen carrying horsewhips in their right hands were less likely to accidentally strike pedestrians if they were on the left-hand side of the road. This seems plausible, but it has to be asked why the drivers on the Continent did not see the wisdom of this.

SLOANE CONVEYS THE PHYSIC GARDEN
The Physic Garden established by the Society of Apothecaries on the banks of the Thames at Chelsea (see 1673) was now a flourishing

concern and justly renowned. In 1722, a year after buying the manor of Chelsea, Sir Hans Sloane, physician and collector, presented the freehold of the garden to the society, provided it supplied the Royal Society with 50 'specimens of distinct plants, well dried and preserved, which grew in their garden the same year, with their names or reputed names; and those presented in each year to be specifically different from every former year, until the number of two thousand shall have been delivered'. Failing this the garden was to be reclaimed and held in trust either for the Royal Society or for the College of Physicians.

A New Street in Twickenham

With a new parish church in Twickenham built by a celebrated architect (see 1713) and an influx of wealthy people settling in the picturesque area, new buildings of quality were required. This year the elegant Montpelier Row was built. This terrace, in which the poets Tennyson and de la Mare later lived, still survives.

A New Kind of Beer

This year a London brewer called Harwood sold for the first time a beer which he called 'Entire' or 'Entire Butt' but which was generally called 'Porter', since it was drunk mostly by porters and labourers. It was a cheap, dark-brown bitter brewed from charred or browned malt.

Billingsgate in the 19th century shows demure female customers and formidable fishwives.

Another Large House in Cavendish Square

Though the projected house for the duke of Chandos on the north side of Cavendish Square (see 1717) did not materialize, Harcourt House on the west side, a splendid mansion designed by Thomas Archer, did. Begun this year, it was originally built for Robert Benson, Baron Bingley, and was later acquired by the Harcourt family – the 3rd earl lost a 99-year lease on the house to the duke of Portland at a game of cards in 1825.

Horace Walpole liked the house and remarked that 'it has a grand air and a kind of Louis XIV old-fashioned quality that pleases me'. It was demolished in 1906.

A Barking Workhouse

The parish of Barking in Essex opened its first workhouse, being merely the conversion of four tenements in North Street. These were replaced by a new building in 1788.

Vanbrugh's House in Blackheath

Between 1719 and 1722 the dramatist and architect Sir John Vanbrugh built himself a new house on Blackheath. It was the first example in this country of deliberately 'medievalizing' a building: the house, which still stands, has towers, turrets and castellations, and it is said it was modelled on the Bastille, where Vanbrugh had once been imprisoned. It has now been converted into flats.

1723

Three New Churches

Two new churches were consecrated this year, and one other was finished but, because of a shortage of funds, not consecrated until 1729. Of the first two, St George the Martyr, Queen Square, was the former Ormond Street Chapel (see 1706); in 1721 it was transferred to the Commissioners for Building New Churches and made into a parish church, but it was not until September 1723 that it was consecrated.

The church of St John, Clerkenwell, also consecrated this year, had had a mixed career. It began as the priory church of the Knights Hospitaller, but after the Dissolution most of the priory was taken down and the church was left to decay. It was then briefly a playhouse, a private chapel of Lord Burghley and a Presbyterian meeting house, till in 1721 it was bought by one Simon Michel, who restored it. In 1723, by then called the Aylesbury chapel of ease, it was made over to the Church Commissioners, allocated a parish, and consecrated on 27 December.

St George in the East, by Hawksmoor, was completed about this year. Its majestic tower and part of its original walls still overlook The Highway in Wapping, but, because of war damage, not much else is left. There was always something rather fantastical and mysterious about this building – not least being the four prominent doors on each side of the church leading down to the charnel house beneath.

King Street Gate Demolished

Across Whitehall at this time two gates stood: the very decorative Holbein Gate just by today's Horse Guards, and the King Street Gate just above Downing Street. South of this the highway split into two as it went down to Westminster Abbey: on the west into King Street and on the east into Parliament Street. Now there is one wide highway.

King Street Gate had two openings for pedestrian traffic and one centre opening for vehicles, and it was probably the narrowness of the latter which caused the gate to be demolished this year.

A Women's Boxing Match

A notice issued this year advertised:

I, Martha Jones of Billingsgate, fish-woman, who have fought the best fighting women that ever came to that place, and hearing the fame that is spread about the Town of this noble City Championess, of her beating the Newgate Basket-woman, think myself as brave and stout as any, therefore invite her to fight me on the stage for ten pounds.

It is alleged that during the contest the women were obliged to carry coins in their fists to prevent them pulling each other's hair.

London 1720

St Marylebone

Pasture
Grounds

Paris Garden

Bank

Tothill Fields

GEORGIAN LONDON

*This reconstruction is based on an
updated Survey of London by John
Stow, produced by John Strype in 1720.
It shows the growth of London beyond
the confines of the old City walls.*

*The development of the area between
Westminster and the City redefined the
nature of the capital.*

1 Buckingham House (later Palace)
2 Hyde Park
3 Hanover Square
4 Westminster Abbey
5 St James's Park
6 Pall Mall
7 Piccadilly
8 Houses of Parliament
9 Lambeth Palace
10 Haymarket

Haberdashers'
Aske's School

Bethnal Green

Hackney

London
Bridge

Billingsgate

Wapping

Rotherhithe

11 Whitehall	21 Fleet Street	31 St Mary Magdalen, Bermondsey	41 Execution Dock
12 Bloomsbury	22 Baynard's Castle	32 Moorfields	42 Hangman's Acre
13 Drury Lane	23 Smithfield	33 Holy Trinity Priory	43 Bell Wharfe
14 Covent Garden	24 St Paul's	34 Tower of London	44 Ratcliff Docks
15 Savoy	25 St Bartholomew's Hospital	35 Spitalfields	
16 Tom's Coffee House, Russell Street	26 Charterhouse	36 Whitechapel	
17 Somerset House	27 Southwark	37 Savory Dock	
18 Lincoln's Inn Fields	28 Royal Exchange	38 Goodman's Fields	
19 Gray's Inn	29 London Bridge Waterworks	39 Garden Grounds	
20 Temple	30 Artillery ground	40 Wapping Stairs	

TWO LEONI HOUSES

What began in 1721 as a mansion for the earl of Darnley in Burlington Gardens was completed this year as Queensberry House for the duke of Queensberry. It was another Palladian villa, this time by the Venetian architect Giacomo Leoni. He used the device, later imitated many times in England, of imposing pilasters on the front elevation from first- to second-floor level, thereby emphasizing that the principal rooms of the house were on the upper floors. A protégé of the 3rd duke of Queensberry, John Gay, the composer of *The Beggar's Opera*, died here in 1732. The house was later renamed Uxbridge House and is now used by the Royal Bank of Scotland.

In Chelsea, Leoni finished what is now Argyll House at the junction of King's Road and Oakley Street. His client was John Perrin. The building was described as a 'little country house' with rooms 'suitable to a private Family'.

SIR CHRISTOPHER WREN BURIED

Wren, the architect of the reborn London, died in February, aged 90, and was buried in the crypt of his greatest building, St Paul's Cathedral. His epitaph, in Latin, reads 'If you seek my memorial, look around you.'

A WATERWORKS IN CHELSEA

This year the Chelsea Waterworks Company was incorporated, with powers to supply the City of Westminster and adjacent areas. The water was taken from the Thames at Chelsea (by today's Churchill Gardens Estate) and was conveyed by high tide into a system of small canals as far as north of the site of Victoria station, where much of it was retained when the water level receded again. In 1725 two reservoirs were constructed in Green Park and another one was added in Hyde Park.

The first economically successful pumping engine was constructed by this company, roughly on the site of the Grosvenor Hotel at Victoria.

1724

A NEW CHURCH IN HANOVER SQUARE

What became the most fashionable church in London, St George Hanover Square, was consecrated on 23 March. The architect was John James, who, despite having a privileged and prestigious position as one of the surveyors for the building of the 50 new churches in London, did not, apart from his earlier church in Twickenham, build another. St Alfege in Greenwich is sometimes attributed to him, but this was more likely by Hawksmoor.

St George Hanover Square has a massive portico jutting out into the road, of similar style to the slightly later St George, Bloomsbury, and St Martin-in-the-Fields. It was originally intended to plant a statue of George I on top of the pediment, but this plan fortunately had to be abandoned.

PINDAR OF WAKEFIELD DESTROYED

A public house called the Pindar of Wakefield, in the Gray's Inn Road, was destroyed by a hurricane this year; the landlord's two daughters were buried in the ruins. The pub, at the King's Cross end of the road, has been rebuilt twice since on the opposite side of the highway, and is now called The Water Rat.

MAIDS OF HONOUR ROW BUILT

When Frederick, prince of Wales, acquired the duke of Ormonde's house in the Old Deer Park, Richmond, it was found that there was insufficient room for the ladies-in-waiting attached to Princess Caroline. Some houses on Richmond Green were therefore demolished and a terrace of four houses, each three storeys with basement, was built to house the ladies.

The houses were not used by the ladies for long; a few years later one of them was occupied by John James Heidegger, manager of the King's Theatre, Haymarket, who was described as the 'ugliest man in the world'.

JACK SHEPPARD HANGED

The most famous execution for many years took place on 16 November at Tyburn. Jack Sheppard, highwayman, aged 23, was hanged in front of an assembly said to be 200,000 strong.

The attendance figure was probably an exaggeration, but there is no doubting the interest of the public. Sheppard, whose exploits while escaping prison were more famous than his crimes, was popular with a London mob delighted to see the authorities bemused.

Sheppard was born in Spitalfields in 1702, the son of a carpenter. By the age of 19 he was an habitual criminal, quite often in league with his woman friend 'Edgeworth Bess'. It was Sheppard's older brother, Tom, who was persuaded to inform on him, and in February 1724 Jack Sheppard was arrested and incarcerated in the St Giles roundhouse. From here he escaped on the first night.

Imprisoned again, at Clerkenwell, he escaped once more and found himself a celebrity. Then Jonathan Wild, the fence and police informer, had him taken, and at the Old Bailey in August Sheppard was sentenced to death. From the condemned cell Sheppard escaped again — a remarkable feat for someone in fetters — and was at large for ten days before his own bravado led to his recapture. Back in Newgate he was chained to the floor with double irons, and here he held court to hundreds of visitors who paid good money to his jailers to see him. He was then transferred to a room called the Castle, quite the strongest of those in Newgate, and on 15 October he escaped yet again when most of the keepers were attending court. This was his most remarkable escapade, requiring ingenuity, strength and bravery. Free once more, he got drunk, bragged about his exploit, and was promptly rearrested. From then on he was watched day and night and there was no repetition. In his final days he was painted by both Thornhill and Hogarth, and the keepers again became rich from his visitors.

A RESERVOIR IN MARYLEBONE

Lord Harley was having difficulty in developing his estate north of Oxford Street, of which Cavendish Square was the principal feature. Apart from the competition he faced from the building boom south of Oxford Street, between Hanover Square and Park Lane, he also had the problem of water supplies. Though he had a great plan of streets, he did not have a water source capable of serving the proposed houses. He began negotiations with the York Buildings Waterworks, whose rather unhealthy source of supply was the Thames by the Strand. About this year he persuaded the company to pump water up to his Marylebone estate, but the next problem was that there was hardly any pressure at the end of the pipeline to supply the houses. To get over this, Harley bought back the gardens behind the proposed Chandos mansion on the north side of Cavendish Square and there had a reservoir constructed — this space is now occupied by Mansfield Street and Queen Anne Street.

LONGMAN'S ESTABLISHED

Thomas Longman, then aged 25, this year bought out John Taylor, the first publisher of *Robinson Crusoe*, and set up business at the sign of the Ship and Black Swan in Paternoster Row. In his early days as a publisher he took a one-sixth share in the new *Cyclopædia* by Ephraim Chambers, which was to be very profitable, and he was one of the six booksellers who entered into an agreement with Dr Johnson for the production of his famous dictionary.

On Longman's death in 1755 his nephew, also Thomas, became head of the firm. Thomas's son, Thomas Norton Longman, was to be its most famous proprietor, at the forefront of 19th-century developments in English literature.

THE OXFORD CHAPEL OPENS

Oxford Chapel, now St Peter's in Vere Street, was completed this year. It was designed by James Gibbs, who used a model of the chapel as a basis for his proposed new church of St Martin-in-the-Fields when submitting plans to the Church Commissioners in 1721.

1725

GROSVENOR SQUARE BEGUN

The major feature of the Grosvenor Mayfair estate was, and is, Grosvenor Square, begun this year and completed all but for a few houses by 1729. Apart from Lincoln's Inn Fields, it is the largest square in London. When first built, the houses were usually three storeys above ground plus a dormer floor, and, although the houses were large, this modest height emphasized the generous space given to the central gardens. Sutton Nicholls's 1731 engraving of the square, looking north, shows the gardens formally laid out in a circle, complete with iron railings and ornamental gates, with the Grosvenor Estate being laid out around, and Hampstead and Highgate in the distance as a backdrop.

As was the custom, the Grosvenors let out the plots to numerous speculators and developers and tried, with only partial success, to achieve a symmetry of design. An early commentator, James Ralp, writing in 1734, said that the square was 'meant to be fine, but has miscarried very unfortunately in the execution. There is no harmony or agreement in the parts which compose it.'

Lack of harmony or not, the square attracted the rich and the famous from the start, and is still one of the best business addresses in London. Only two houses from this earliest period survive, nos. 9 and 38. Number 9 was the home in 1785 of John Adams, the first 'minister plenipotentiary' from the United States, and he had for his neighbours not only the foreign secretary, Lord Carmarthen, but the former prime minister Lord North. From this relatively humble beginning, the expense of which was partly borne by the Adams family, the United States Embassy developed, and it now occupies the western end of the square. This international character of the square is also reflected in no. 38, which is now the Indonesian Embassy.

GUY'S HOSPITAL OPENED

In 1721 Thomas Guy, a governor of St Thomas's Hospital, applied to his fellow governors for a lease of some of the hospital ground on which to erect a new hospital for incurables. He instructed his trustees, before his death in December 1724, that the building was to be for the reception of 400 poor persons, 'labouring under any distempers, infirmities, or disorders, thought capable of relief by physick or surgery; but who, by reason of the small hopes there may be of their cure, or the length of time which for that purpose may be required … are, or may be adjudged or called Incurable, and as such not proper Objects to be received into or continued in the present Hospital of Saint Thomas'.

The location of the hospital is, confusingly to the uninformed, in St Thomas's Street, which is a reminder of the time when St Thomas's was across the road from Guy's new establishment.

Thomas Guy, a wealthy bookseller and publisher, had been born in Southwark; his father was a coal merchant or carpenter. After his apprenticeship to a bookseller, Guy set up business in 1668 at the corner of Cornhill and Lombard Street. His fortune was at first based on the importation from Holland of Bibles in the English language, which undercut those printed by the university printers who had the monopoly in this country, but later he was himself a university printer. He became a governor and a frequent benefactor of St Thomas's Hospital in 1704, but it was not until the 1720s, when he sold out his South Sea Company stock at a high profit before the crash came, that he was rich enough to consider founding his own institution.

Unfortunately, though Guy lived to see his hospital nearly complete, he died in 1724 before it opened. The first patients were admitted on 6 January 1725.

JONATHAN WILD HANGED

Nothing quite so epitomizes the lawlessness of London at this period than the career of Jonathan Wild, which came to an abrupt end at Tyburn this year.

Wild was a police informer and is said to have sent 60 criminals to the gallows, but he was himself a criminal and a fence, who organized gangs of thieves. He provided the model for Peachum in John Gay's *The Beggar's Opera*.

When Wild, a buckle-maker by trade, first came to London he got into debt and finished in Wood Street compter, where the company of criminals persuaded him to change his career. He opened a brothel in association with a woman friend, and later took a public house in Cripplegate. He then evolved a scheme in which he commissioned thieves to steal from people whom Wild knew would pay good money to retrieve their goods. Wild was both the fence and the 'honest' returner of stolen goods. He managed a large number of thieves, and his reputation for doing so was widely known, but he kept out of custody himself by throwing the authorities a criminal every now and then. Indeed, though he paid good money to many criminals for the goods they stole, he portrayed himself in public broadsheets as a 'thief-taker'.

Wild was eventually convicted of receiving a reward for restoring stolen property and was sentenced to death. After an attempt the night before to commit suicide by taking laudanum, he was hanged to general delight at Tyburn on 24 May. He was buried in St Pancras churchyard the following day, but his body was stolen for the anatomists and was later exhibited at the Royal College of Surgeons.

CANONS COMPLETED

The duke of Chandos had become immensely wealthy as Marlborough's paymaster general earlier in the century. He directed his resources into the building of two large houses, but during the work much of his fortune was lost in the South Sea crash. Swift commented that all that the duke had 'got by fraud is lost by stocks'. Consequently, the large house he had hoped to build on the north side of Cavendish Square (see 1717) was hardly proceeded with, and Canons, the mansion at Stanmore, was finished only with great difficulty. Oddly, for such an important mansion, the architect is not known for sure – though it seems that James Gibbs, William Talman, Edward Shepherd and John Price were involved.

The house was run without regard to expense. Defoe asserts that, including the family, there were 120 people in residence, and that a choir entertained family and guests at dinner each day. However, when the duke died in 1744, his debts obliged his son to sell off the house piecemeal and what had cost perhaps £600,000 to build realized about £11,000. A gate and ironwork went to Hampstead parish church, the staircase went to Chesterfield House initially, the organ to a church in Hampshire, and it is said the portico went to the ill-fated Wanstead House.

FAIRLOP FAIR BEGINS

The great fair on Fairlop Heath began about this year at the instigation of a ship's blockmaker, Daniel Day, who owned some land in Hainault. It is said that his first intention was to provide some recreation for his own workpeople and that the event just grew. The fair was held around the famous Fairlop Oak, a tree which measured 36 ft in girth at 3 ft above the ground. The *Literary Chronicle* of 1823 relates that each year Day's 30 or 40 workmen went to the fair in a boat, like an Indian canoe, shaped from one piece of timber and adorned with flags and musicians; this was covered with an awning, mounted on a carriage and drawn by six horses.

FIRE ON THE BRIDGE

On 8 September a fire broke out at a brushmaker's house near the Southwark end of London Bridge. It spread to the bridge, destroyed all the houses on the first two arches, but was defeated by the stone gateway guarding the rest of the structure. The gateway was so badly damaged that in 1727 it was replaced by a new one wide enough for two coaches to pass each other.

1726

CONDITIONS IN THE FLEET

A parliamentary committee investigated this year the conditions in the Fleet prison. Its inquiries revealed gross extortion and corruption by the warden and his deputy. The warden refused to surrender the bodies of any deceased prisoners until his demands were met; he pleaded that many prisoners owed him money, and that it was only right that he should try to retrieve it from relatives. The committee reported on the case of one Jacob Solas, a Portuguese, who had been kept in irons in a room above the common sewer, adjoining the refuse heap. When at last a friend paid five guineas he was released from this hole, in which he had spent two months, 'but though his chains were taken off, his terror still remained, and the unhappy man was prevailed upon by that terror not only to labour gratis for the [deputy], but to swear also at random all that he hath required of him'. The warden and his deputy were both charged with murdering some of their prisoners, but were acquitted.

It is doubtful if the committee's findings would have shocked the hardened Londoners. A considerable number of them went to see Katherine Hayes burnt alive at Tyburn on 3 November for the murder of her husband.

ST MARTIN-IN-THE-FIELDS CONSECRATED

James Gibbs's masterpiece, the new church of St Martin-in-the-Fields, was consecrated on 20 October by the bishop of London; the steeple was rung in during the following year. George I was appointed a churchwarden – the only time a king has held such a post – but he provided an organ for the west gallery rather than perform his parochial chores.

The *London Spy* was quick to assess the social distinction of the congregation: 'The inhabitants are now supplied with a decent tabernacle, which can produce as handsome a show of white hands, diamond rings, pretty snuff boxes, and gilt prayer books as any cathedral whatever. Here the fair penitents pray in their patches, sue for pardon in their paint, and see their heaven in man.'

There is today an imposing view of the great portico of the church from Trafalgar Square, but when it was built the square did not exist and the church was hemmed in with buildings on all sides. The burial ground was across the road, on the site of the National Portrait Gallery.

NEW WORKHOUSES

A good many workhouses were opened in this period. Islington's first establishment was a house taken this year at Stroud Green, to be replaced about five years later by a larger establishment in Holloway Road. This year too the new parish of St George Hanover Square was, surprisingly, allowed to erect a workhouse roughly on the site of

The entrance to Fleet prison, 1691. Many of its prisoners were debtors, hence the plaintive call for money to secure their freedom.

today's 103 Mount Street; it consisted of workrooms and schools, with living space for between 150 and 200 people. In 1725 the parishes of Twickenham, West Ham and St Giles-in-the-Fields had also taken houses or constructed buildings for the same purpose.

A ROW OVER A PEW
Stephen Ram, a banker, who had bought the Homerton estate, this year fell out with the vicar and churchwardens of Hackney over what he regarded as his exclusive use of pew no. 13 in the parish church. In a fit of pique he went off and built his own chapel at the north-west end of Homerton High Street. This building continued as a proprietary chapel until 1933, when it was demolished and the remains of those in its burial ground were transferred to Chingford Mount Cemetery.

1727

ST MARY WOOLNOTH OPENED
Nicholas Hawksmoor's finest church, St Mary Woolnoth, was consecrated on 2 April. The medieval building had been patched together by Wren after the Great Fire, but by 1716, when Hawksmoor began his reconstruction work, the church needed to be completely rebuilt. The interior has an interesting arrangement of cubes and Corinthian columns.

The church has survived two serious threats. One was the creation of King William Street, which, in the event, opened up views of the church instead of bringing about its demolition. Another was the application by the City & South London Tube Railway to demolish it in 1897; the company was refused permission and had to construct its Bank station beneath it instead, having first removed any bones buried beneath the church to Ilford Cemetery. Happily, too, the church survived the last war intact.

NEWTON BURIED AT WESTMINSTER ABBEY
Sir Isaac Newton, the scientist, was buried in Westminster Abbey on 28 March; his body had lain in state in the Jerusalem Chamber beforehand. His funeral was attended by Voltaire.

1728

FIRST NIGHT OF THE BEGGAR'S OPERA
John Gay's magical creation *The Beggar's Opera* opened on 29 January at John Rich's Lincoln's Inn Fields Theatre. In 18th-century terms it was a huge success, having a run of 60 performances.

Though popular with the public, it met with the disapproval of magistrates, who considered that it celebrated crime. Which it did, of course. But the significance of Gay's piece lay in its breaking away from the Italianate opera with which the London audiences had been entertained for some years. It was about London, and was about very low life indeed, with characters that were loosely based on folk heroes and villains

The production of *The Beggar's Opera* had been a gamble, and many had predicted its failure. In the event it took London and the rest of the country by storm. In the words of a witticism of the time, it made 'Rich gay, and Gay rich'.

The church of St John in Smith Square, designed by Thomas Archer, was built in 1728. Due to costs, four small cupolas were substituted for pinnacles.

AN ACADEMY IN FULHAM
This year Lewis Vaslet, a French schoolmaster, bought a house in Fulham then divided into two dwellings in what became Burlington Road. He established there a school, which was continued by another Frenchman whose star pupil, at least as far as prestige and income were concerned, was the son of the earl of Northampton. The school was later taken by Dr Robert Roy, who had run a large and successful school in Old Burlington Street off Piccadilly, and from this time the school in Fulham was called the Burlington House Academy. It was to be one of the better-known private schools until the mid 19th century.

THE ROUND POND CONSTRUCTED
Kensington Gardens were once the private gardens of the royal palace of Kensington, the former Nottingham House (see 1689). In 1690 John Evelyn had noted that there was a 'straite new way through the park' to the palace, and part of this survives today as Rotten Row. The grounds were extensively laid out by the queen (a keen gardener), and about 1726 George I allowed respectably dressed people in on Saturdays if the court was elsewhere. The Round Pond was completed in 1728; it was used as a reservoir by the Chelsea Waterworks Company.

A 'FOOTSTOOL' IN SMITH SQUARE
One of the more extraordinary churches in London is St John's, Smith Square, now a public hall often used for concerts. This baroque building was designed by Thomas Archer. His original design had four towers surmounted by pinnacles, but cupolas replaced the pinnacles as a cost-cutting measure. The church does rather give the impression of an object lying on its back with four feet in the air, which probably led to the oft-repeated and, most likely, apocryphal story that when Archer asked Queen Anne, who was enthusiastically involved in the 1711 Act to build 50 new churches in London (of which St John's was one), how she would like the church to look she replied by kicking over her footstool and pointing at its shape. Consecration took place on 20 June this year, and the church was open for worship on 10 November.

A SWEDISH CHURCH IN WAPPING
One of the small squares of London swept away in rebuilding after the Second World War was Princes Square, just north of The Highway and

1700s

east of Wellclose Square. This year a Lutheran church, plain but pretty, was built there to cater for the many Swedish sailors who were temporarily at Wapping, but it was also later used by the general Swedish community in London.

The remains of the Swedish mystic Emanuel Swedenborg were interred here in 1772, beneath the communion table. Nearby Swedenborg Gardens is a reminder of this.

1729

TWO COUNTRY RETREATS

Two of London's most beautiful Palladian villas were completed this year – Marble Hill, in Twickenham, and Chiswick House.

Marble Hill was built for Henrietta Howard, countess of Suffolk – the long-standing, long-suffering and rather deaf mistress of George II. The site was bought for her by Lord Ilay, who lived at Whitton nearby, and the house was designed by Roger Morris in cooperation with Lord Herbert, a talented amateur architect. Inside, a great mahogany staircase leads to the Great Room on the first floor, which is modelled on Inigo Jones's Single Cube Room at Wilton.

As the countess detached herself discreetly from court life, so she developed her social life here in this house. John Gay was a frequent visitor, as also was Alexander Pope, a neighbour, who helped plan her gardens. Horace Walpole became a firm friend when he moved to Twickenham in 1747.

Pope and Gay were also frequent visitors at Chiswick House, the home of Richard Boyle, 3rd earl of Burlington. As with Marble Hill, the hand of a talented 'amateur' architect was at work here in the person of the owner himself. An older house already stood adjacent, which served for the mechanics of life, but Burlington saw his new creation as one to hold his library and art collection, and in which to entertain his friends. The latter included William Kent, who was responsible for much of the decoration of the house.

A BRIDGE AT FULHAM

A bridge was constructed this year across the Thames from Fulham to Putney. It was then called Fulham Bridge – only with its 19th-century replacement did it become, instead, Putney Bridge.

Putney (Fulham) Bridge, depicted c.1760, was built in 1729.

Earlier plans to span the Thames at this point had met with opposition (see 1671), as had plans to build a bridge at Westminster. Legend has it that the Fulham Bridge scheme received much-needed impetus only when the then prime minister, Robert Walpole, was left stranded on one shore one evening while the ferrymen caroused on the other.

Five designs were considered by a committee which first met in 1726. None of the constructions was expected (or required) to last more than 50 years. One was based on a succession of moored boats, and the other four were all made of wood. The design chosen was that of Sir Joseph Acworth, and work began on 25 March this year; the bridge was completed and opened on 29 November. Four tollmen were employed, on wages of 10s a week, and each was provided with a coat, a hat and a staff.

CHRIST CHURCH, SPITALFIELDS, OPENED

The brooding Christ Church, designed by Nicholas Hawksmoor, still stands among dereliction in Spitalfields, now facing an empty market and soon to be engulfed by developers' cranes and lorries.

When it was opened in 1729, many of its congregation were Huguenots. At that time, too, much of Spitalfields was being built in great style. Christ Church has seen successive waves of immigrants in the locality, and its regular Anglican worshippers disappeared many years ago; in 1958 it was declared unsafe and closed for worship. One of the '50 New Churches', it was, ironically, repaired after 1965, using money received from the sale of another of those famous churches, St John's, Smith Square (see 1728). The building is now closed, but is being extensively restored with the help of money from the National Lottery.

The most prominent feature is the huge portico, supported by four Tuscan pillars. Inside the church, for all its classicism, there is a honeycomb of almost random staircases and passageways leading to the organ loft and belfry.

A THEATRE IN STEPNEY

The Goodman's Fields Theatre was opened on 31 October by Thomas Odell, a dramatist, in a shop in Leman Street. It was a short-lived venture: a sermon was preached against the enterprise at nearby St Botolph, Aldgate, and Odell withdrew and sold up to his leading actor, Henry Giffard. In 1732 Giffard opened a new theatre in the locality, designed by Edward Shepherd; this too ran into trouble when Giffard proposed to produce a play which the government did not like. Apparently, Giffard and his players removed to Lincoln's Inn Theatre in 1735, but were back in Goodman's Fields by 1741, when the young David Garrick made his first appearance on a London stage – in a pantomime.

Goodman's Fields themselves made up a large open space which is nowadays bounded by Leman Street, Alie Street, Mansell Street and Prescot Street.

WIFE-SELLING IN THE CITY

It was reported that 'Last Wednesday one Everet, of Fleet Lane sold his wife to one Griffin of Long Lane for a 3 shilling bowl of punch; who, we hear, hath since complained of having a bad bargain.'

SHOOTING IN CHURCH

A deranged Frenchman, M. Compagnotte, who lived in Seven Dials, entered St Martin-in-the-Fields church in September and shot at the preacher. The preacher was unharmed, but a member of the congregation was wounded.

1730

THE MAKING OF THE SERPENTINE

Work began in September on the construction of the Serpentine lake in Hyde Park. The shape is not particularly serpent-like today, but in its early days the Westbourne river, of which it is a part, probably meandered more; by degrees its shape has since been tidied up. Six ponds in Hyde Park seem to have been made into the one lake. This required a great deal of excavation both in the existing ponds and in the land between them. There were also a good many substantial trees to destroy or move. It is recorded that 20 large elms were moved to other sites, the weight of each tree requiring the efforts of 60 men and 18 horses.

A CHURCH FOR LIMEHOUSE

The area of Limehouse derived its name from the lime kilns there – Rocque's map of 1746 shows a Lime Kiln Dock and Yard. Nearby is Ropemakers Field, an indication of another trade. But the most important asset from Tudor times onwards was its useful position on the river. From the 18th century it was a place for shipbuilding, and the population grew steadily.

The new church of St Anne, consecrated in September 1730, was built to cater for the expansion. It was set well away from the town's centre, with hardly a house near it, and with a large churchyard, part of which was taken when Commercial Road was constructed.

St Anne's was another of Hawksmoor's East End churches. It was finished in 1724 but for local-political reasons among the clerics was not consecrated for six years, and then there was insufficient money to pay a preacher a stipend. Once again, as in Christ Church, Spitalfields, although the building is of a simple shape, inside there are tortuous corkscrew staircases. The tower is particularly prominent, with, it is said, the highest church clock in London.

A NEW CHURCH BY THOMAS ARCHER

Archer's odd church in Smith Square (see 1728) was followed in 1730 by one of his best buildings – St Paul, Deptford High Street. The tower is circular, harmonizing with the impressive semicircular portico.

1731

THE SPREAD OF WORKHOUSES

The number of workhouses in London was increasing rapidly. In many cases a vestry would take an old house, usually in bad shape, and convert it to such use. Typical of these was the St Pancras workhouse, begun in St Pancras Way this year in a building which was never adequate for the job and seems to have been in very bad condition from the beginning. Arrangements for supplying the occupants were put in hand in the usual way: 'Mr. Broadhead Doe serve The house with Small beer att six shillings Per Barrell … Mr. Brown Serve The Said house with Beef and Muttons att one shilling Six pence per Stone & Mrs. King of Highgate & Mr. Tow Baker of Kentish Town Furnish Second Bread at the usual & Customary Prices each third month by turns.'

At Hampstead a workhouse had been opened in 1729 in a house in Frognal on the site of the later Mount Vernon Consumption Hospital. Before that the inmates had been housed in several cottages in 'nastiness as well as in poverty'. But the new place was hardly much better. By 1734 it was noted that hop sacks were hung against the lath and

Gin Lane *by William Hogarth, depicting the evils of cheap drink and poverty. The church of St George, Bloomsbury, may be seen in the distance.*

plaster where the rain beat through 'like a sive', so that bed and linen had to be dried. Special attention was paid to the children, 'which makes them appear quite other creatures than they were under the care of their own parents who fancied [that] slovenliness recommended them to the pity of those that relieved them'.

A NEW HAWKSMOOR CHURCH

The consecration on 28 January of Hawksmoor's St George's church, Bloomsbury Way, allowed the demolition of St Giles-in-the Fields so that it might be rebuilt by Henry Flitcroft. Lying between the two buildings was the infamous St Giles rookery, and it was now the turn – albeit a brief one – of the residents to the west of the parish to brave the slums in order to get to church.

Both new churches survive. St George's is on a very restricted site and, since road widening, hard against the main road. The cost of building it went way over budget – about £31,000, against an estimate of about £10,000. Its portico has six large Corinthian columns, two rows deep, but the most unusual feature is the stepped pyramid on top of the tower, resembling the tomb of Mausolos (from whom we derive the word 'mausoleum'), king of Caria; this itself is topped by a statue of George I donated by a local brewer. This tower is the one featured in Hogarth's famous print *Gin Lane*. The novelist Anthony Trollope was baptized in the church in 1815.

In January 1731 a burial ground for the new parish of St George, Bloomsbury, was also consecrated. This is now part of St George's Gardens, south of Regent Square, Bloomsbury.

BEGINNING OF THE GENTLEMAN'S MAGAZINE

In January publication began of the *Gentleman's Magazine*, which was to become one of the most famous and enduring journals – it survived until 1907. The magazine (it was the first to use such a term) was

1700s

An orchestra and singer entertaining a seemingly uninterested audience at Vauxhall Gardens. Illustration by Thomas Rowlandson.

founded by a printer, Edward Cave, whose printing presses were in the gatehouse of the old hospital of St John of Jerusalem in Clerkenwell. Cave was both a printer and a journalist. Since about 1725 he had compiled 'country news' for a London journal, and soon supplied London news to country papers – good experience for a journal which was to convey gossip and news from and to all parts of the country.

The intention with his new venture in 1731 was to form a collection or 'magazine' of 'the essays and intelligence which appeared in the two hundred half sheets which the London press then threw off monthly' – a digest, in fact, of other people's news. Though largely written by Cave himself, and later with much material from Samuel Johnson, it was ostensibly edited by 'Sylvanus Urban Esq.'. What made the journal unusual was its scarcely veiled reports of parliamentary proceedings, then prohibited from publication. Cave got round the law by thinly disguising the names of the speakers, or by placing the debates within the 'senate of Great Lilliput'. The magazine was a great success, and Johnson reports that its sale was about 10,000 by 1739 – in those days a considerable circulation.

FIRE AT THE COTTON LIBRARY

The antiquarian Sir Robert Cotton (1571–1631) had built up a vast and coveted library of ancient documents and deeds – a source used by historians and state legislators alike. However, towards the end of his life, his collection was impounded by the State on suspicion that it contained material harmful to the Crown. The loss to Cotton was so grievous that when he died it was suggested that it was his exclusion from his library which had been the chief cause of his ill health. The family later regained control of the library, which in 1700 was given to the nation. In 1730 the Cotton collection was newly housed in Ashburnham House in Little Dean's Yard, Westminster, but on 23 October 1731 a fire broke out in the house and destroyed or damaged 114 of the 958 volumes.

A POLITICAL DUEL

On 25 January a duel took place in Green Park between William Pulteney MP, leader of the Opposition, and Lord Hervey, a staunch supporter of the prime minister, Sir Robert Walpole. The two duellists had previously been good friends, but political events had placed them on different sides of the chamber and in an increasingly bitter exchange of pamphlets and satires they became enemies. The climax came when Pulteney accused Hervey of being a homosexual – a claim which could not go unanswered. The duel was inconclusive: both men were slightly injured, but their seconds prevented greater bloodshed.

GROSVENOR CHAPEL BUILT

Work began in 1730 on the erection of a proprietary chapel in South Audley Street at the direction of the landowner Sir Richard Grosvenor; its purpose was to serve the residents of the newly developing Grosvenor estate. It was built by Benjamin Timbrell, who quite possibly also designed it, in a rather New England style. Finished in 1731, it has survived many vicissitudes, alterations and plans for its replacement.

1732

A NEW VAUXHALL GARDENS

Although still noted in a London guide published in 1726 as one of the London sights, there is no doubt that the New Spring Gardens at Vauxhall had become of ill repute since their heyday in the Restoration period. In 1728 Jonathan Tyers obtained a 30-year lease of the premises, and on 7 June 1732, after considerable expenditure, they reopened as the Vauxhall Gardens with a *ridotto al fresco*. The 400-odd guests arrived between 9 and 11 in the evening bedecked with masks and domino gowns, and did not leave until the early hours of the morning. They included the prince of Wales, who arrived by barge from Kew. The royal patronage set the seal on Tyer's venture, and Vauxhall Gardens were one of the most fashionable places in London for many years.

THE FIRST COVENT GARDEN THEATRE

The first Covent Garden Theatre opened in Bow Street this year. The owner of this most luxurious playhouse was the successful theatrical entrepreneur and pantomimist John Rich. The construction of the building was not without incident, since the roof collapsed at one stage, killing a workman. The first production, on 7 December, was Congreve's *The Way of the World*. As is apparent from early advertisements, the best seats were actually on the stage.

1733

THE ROYAL MEWS BUILT

The most fashionable architect of the period was William Kent. About this year he completed a mews block on the present site of the National Gallery (Trafalgar Square did not then exist), to house the king's horses. Kent was to go on to design the Treasury and the Horse Guards in Whitehall.

FLEET RIVER COVERED OVER

The canal which had been constructed out of the southern reaches of the river Fleet (see 1670) had been a financial failure, though it had contributed greatly to a cleaning-up of a notorious London health hazard. In 1733 the City authorities bowed to the inevitable and arched over the canal between today's Holborn Viaduct and Fleet Street, and the wharves on either side became thoroughfares. A long market was

The Royal Mews on the present site of the National Gallery, Trafalgar Square. The buildings were designed by William Kent to house the king's horses.

in 1737 erected over the covered river – this route is marked today by Farringdon Street.

St George's Hospital Founded

The success of Westminster Hospital had led to it outgrowing two houses in the first 12 years. It was decided in 1733 to move again, this time to Castle Lane in Westminster, then a road with fields on both sides of it. This proposal did not meet with the approval of all the trustees of the hospital and, while the majority were happy to go to Castle Lane, a minority signed a lease to acquire Lanesborough House at Hyde Park Corner (see 1719). Heated letters and statements from both sides were published in the press, but in the end both sets of premises were taken and in Lanesborough House an entirely new hospital – St George's – was founded. A pamphlet published at the time claimed that those who favoured using Lanesborough House included all the physicians and surgeons of Westminster Hospital, who would, in the meantime, still attend at the older establishment if required until replacements could be found.

Rocque's map of 1746 shows the new hospital to be almost the only building in the area, with, as the same pamphlet claimed, 'the benefit of country air'.

The trustees were unsuccessful in their claim to part of the funds of the Westminster Hospital, but they were supported in their aims by fashionable and court personalities. An unpaid secretary was appointed, as was an apothecary, and two nurses were engaged, each paid £6 a year with board and lodging, together with a cook at £7 a year. A clock was purchased for £4 and a sedan chair for £3.

White's Club Destroyed by Fire

White's Club at 69 St James's Street was destroyed by fire on 28 April. A print by Hogarth in his *Rake's Progress* series shows the gamblers in disarray as smoke penetrates the gaming room. A contemporary account notes that the fire began in the early hours of the morning and that the owner's 'Wife leap'd out of Window a pair of Stairs upon a Feather-Bed without much Hurt'. The king and the prince of Wales 'were present on Foot for above an Hour … and encouraged the Fireman and People at the engines to work'.

Unfortunately most of the property, including the early records, was consumed in the blaze.

St Luke, Old Street, Consecrated

One of the saddest sights in Old Street is the dilapidated church of St Luke. It now stands without its roof – doomed to be a protected ruin for many years to come. It was consecrated on 16 October 1733, and, although formerly attributed to the architect George Dance the Elder, who was a churchwarden here, John James is more usually now given the credit for its design, with strong help from Hawksmoor. Dance was actually buried in the churchyard, which is today a public garden, as were also the Caslon typefounders, father and son. The church has an interesting obelisk spire.

Bishopsgate Rebuilt

The old Bishopsgate, by then decayed, was taken down in 1731. It was rebuilt this year, but collapsed before it was finished and was then rebuilt again. The nuisance of the City gates was already recognized – a contemporary noted that the new Bishopsgate was 'a gret incumbrance' – and it was to be less than 30 years before all of them were taken down.

1734

The New St Giles-in-the-Fields

The spire of the church of St Giles-in-the-Fields is now dwarfed by Centre Point, but when it was erected in 1734 it was a notable landmark at an important road junction. The building was designed by Henry Flitcroft, though he seems to have been much influenced by the style of Gibbs's St Martin-in-the Fields, which had recently been completed. (Flitcroft Street nearby is one of the few streets in London commemorating an architect.) A contemporary writer notes that the new building was 'one of the most simple and elegant of the modern structures: it is rais'd at very little expence, has very few ornaments, and little beside the propriety of its parts, and the harmony of the

The new church of St Giles-in-the-Fields, designed by Henry Flitcroft and opened in 1734. It is now hidden by Centre Point.

whole, to excite attention, and challenge applause: yet it pleases, and justly too'.

The churchyard continued to have a close connection with the Tyburn gallows. Convicts on their way from Newgate to Tyburn were offered a 'St Giles Bowl' as they passed the church, and a number of them were later buried in the churchyard.

NEW BANK OF ENGLAND BUILDING

The Bank of England, since its foundation in 1694, had used livery-company halls for its headquarters. This year its first building, designed by George Sampson, in Threadneedle Street, was opened on 5 June.

STATUE OF THOMAS GUY ERECTED

The brass statue of Thomas Guy which now stands in the new quad-rangle of Guy's Hospital was unveiled on 11 February. The design of the statue is by Peter Scheemakers, and depicts Guy in the livery of the Stationers' Company.

1735

AN OMINOUS BEGINNING

The year began ominously. A fire which began at the Queen's Head near St Katharine by the Tower also consumed 40 houses in the neigh-bourhood. On the same day a violent storm uprooted trees across London, including 36 large trees in St James's Park. Much damage was done to houses and shipping on the Thames.

THE BEGINNINGS OF NO. 10

The London *Daily Post* of 23 September recorded that Sir Robert Walpole, 'with his Lady and Family, [had] removed from their House in St James's Square, to his new House adjoining to the Treasury in St James's Park'. Here began the custom of the prime minister residing at 10 Downing Street.

The eastern part of No. 10 (which was then numbered 5) was acquired by the Crown in 1732. George II offered it to Walpole, who accepted it in the name of his office, which was First Lord of the Treasury. Walpole certainly didn't need another house (although he was heavily in debt from the expense of his many properties, his lifestyle and numerous mistresses), but this was probably a shrewd way of having a large house fixed up at the expense of the State rather than an altruistic gesture – he had the property extensively renovated and decorated by William Kent before he took up an occasional residence there.

Although in effect Walpole was head of the government, the term 'prime minister' was not an acceptable one at the time, since it was felt quite strongly that the constitution, such as it was, did not allow for a leading minister. The first mention of such a post does not officially occur until 1917. The title 'First Lord of the Treasury' is still recorded above the brass letterbox on the famous front door.

The property itself was quite substantial, but Downing Street itself was not a particularly good address. It was near to the Commons and, because of this, was partly taken up by lodging houses for members of Parliament. But the street was also quite near to the brothels and gaming houses of quite poor parts of Westminster.

A GOLDSMITH'S IN THE HAYMARKET

The origins of Garrard's, the famous goldsmith's and jewellers, date to 1735, when George Wickes, goldsmith, opened a shop at the corner of Haymarket and Panton Street. In 1792 the business was joined by Robert Garrard, who eventually took a controlling interest as well as altering the name to his own. The company became the 'Crown jew-ellers' in 1843, and have been in Regent Street since 1952.

THE CASLON TYPEFOUNDRY

The most famous of the Caslon typefoundries was established this year in Chiswell Street. William Caslon (1692–1766) had previously had a business at Helmet Row and Ironmonger Row, but it was in Chiswell Street that his business flourished, under the management of his son, also William.

A NEW CHURCH IN EALING BEGUN

The medieval church of St Mary, Ealing, had collapsed in 1729, although it had not been used since 1725, so bad was its condition. In the meantime worship had taken place in a 'slight timber tabernacle'. The parish found it difficult to raise the necessary funds for rebuilding and, although the first stone was laid in 1735, it was not until 1740 that the new church was open – and as long as 1789 before the accounts for rebuilding were wound up.

1736

A DEATH AT NEWGATE

John Bernardi, who had been sent to Newgate prison for political offences in 1689, died there this year after 47 years. During his incar-ceration his wife bore him ten children in the prison precincts.

REBUILDING OF THE TREASURY

The Treasury had been housed since 1698 in the old cockpit on the west side of Whitehall: the roof had been removed and the building raised by two storeys. But in 1736 the building was replaced by today's Treasury, designed by William Kent, who was at work on most of the government buildings of the day.

A CHURCH BUILT, A CHURCH DEMOLISHED

The rebuilt church of St George the Martyr in Borough High Street was opened this year. Designed by John Price, it commanded, as it still does, a busy road junction. Charles Dickens, who lived in nearby Lant Street as a boy when his father was in Marshalsea prison, has Little Dorrit sheltering in St George's vestry while a waif. The parish work-house was Dickens's model for the establishment in *Oliver Twist*. Nahum Tate, who wrote the carol 'While Shepherds Watch'd their Flocks by Night', is buried in the churchyard.

To the east of London, the old church of St Leonard, Shoreditch, was declared unsafe and demolished.

1737

A MARKET OVER THE RIVER

Work began on clearing the Stocks Market to allow the building of the Mansion House. The market was moved to present-day Farringdon Street, on the elongated stretch created when the Fleet river canal had been roofed over (see 1733), and stretched northward from Ludgate Circus. Opened on 30 September and designed by George Dean, the

Fleet Market, as it was called, consisted of two lines of shops one storey high, with a covered walk between them lit by skylights. Rocque's map of 1746 shows this potentially broad thoroughfare reached by narrow alleys.

A New Welsh Charity School

The Marx Memorial Library on Clerkenwell Green is today housed in a charming house built in 1737 for the Welsh Charity School. This institution had been formed in 1718 (q.v.), but the house in Clerkenwell was its first purpose-built school.

Devonshire House Rebuilt

Devonshire House – the old Berkeley House, which stood facing Piccadilly between Stratton Street and Berkeley Street – had been destroyed by fire in 1733. The commission to rebuild it went to the ubiquitous William Kent, who designed a restrained house of eleven bays; Samuel Ware described it as having 'a continued range of eleven rooms equally well calculated for state, as domestic use, uninterrupted by passage or staircase'. In front was a high stone wall, hiding and protecting the house from the street – a feature unpopular with the public.

Not far away Kent was also finishing a library, for Queen Caroline, in St James's Palace.

Landmarks Demolished

The New Exchange in the Strand, which had opened with great promise in 1609, had now so passed its heyday that it was this year demolished; 54–64 Strand now occupy its site.

In what is now Stratford Place, off Oxford Street, the so-called Banqueting House of the City of London, used when the City fathers inspected their water supply installation here (see 1236), was taken down.

Censorship of Plays Introduced

Productions under the auspices of Henry Fielding at the Haymarket Theatre this year incurred the wrath of the government. These parodies brought about the passing of the Licensing Act: from June 1737 no part of any play or performance could be played for box-office money without the sanction or licence of the lord chamberlain; all other plays not already licensed had to receive the same licence. The short-term effect was that the Haymarket Theatre closed and reopened only in 1747, when the proprietor evaded the law by charging only for the refreshments. The long-term effect was to introduce theatrical censorship, which was abolished only in 1968. A beneficial side effect of this absurd legislation was that the British Library is now custodian of most of the playscripts that the lord chamberlain had to read.

1738

Building of Westminster Bridge Begun

The need for a new bridge across the Thames in London had been apparent for some time, but firm proposals had been smothered in the Restoration period. The interests of the City and the watermen prevailed each time the matter arose, and the project made little headway. Necessity finally won, however. An Act for constructing a bridge was obtained in 1736, and then, to the consternation of many, a Swiss, rather than an Englishman, was chosen as the designer – though in fact Charles Labalye was a naturalized Englishman.

The first pile was driven on 13 September this year, and the first stone was laid by the earl of Pembroke on 29 January 1739. It would take 12 years to build.

The First Star and Garter

One of the most famous views in London is that from the Star and Garter Home at the top of Richmond Hill: it looks out over a majestic sweep of the Thames and across Twickenham. A successful Richmond publican, John Christopher, established the first Star and Garter public house this year on what was then part of Petersham Common. It developed over the years into a very large inn and then hotel as transport facilities from London improved.

The Star and Garter was not the only tavern in the vicinity – not far away the Roebuck on Richmond Hill (which still survives) had been trading since the 1720s.

Royal Society of Musicians Founded

The Royal Society of Musicians, a charity to help musicians or their families, was founded this year in London. Those involved in its establishment included Dr Thomas Arne, for ever identified as the composer of 'Rule, Britannia', Johann Christoph Pepusch, who wrote the music of The Beggar's Opera, and Handel. The last named was a generous benefactor to the new society, and the first English performance of Messiah was given for its benefit.

In its earlier years the society met in taverns, but in 1807 it secured premises in Panton Street. It is now in Stratford Place.

1739

The Start of the Foundling Hospital

Thomas Coram (1668–1751), a former sea captain, devoted his retirement years to establishing a home for the foundlings so blatantly and frequently left on the squalid streets of London. Addison had proposed such an institution in 1713, but it was Coram who was persistent enough to see it through – especially by appealing to society women for funds. He was 70 when, at a gathering at Somerset House on 20 November, the Foundling Hospital was incorporated by royal charter in the presence of 6 dukes, 11 earls, numerous peers, and well-known citizens such as Hogarth and the physician Richard Mead.

The official title of the institution was The Hospital for the Maintenance and Education of Exposed and Deserted Young Children, which summed up the social problem without linguistic economy. A petition by Coram to the king during his efforts to establish the hospital mentions the 'frequent Murders committed on poor Miserable Infant Children at their Birth by their Cruel Parents to hide their Shame and … the Inhumane Custom of exposing Newborn Children to Perish in the Streets or the putting out of such unhappy Foundlings to wicked and barborous Nurses who undertaking to bring them up for a small and trifling Sum of Money do often suffer them to Starve for want of due Sustenance'.

The First Midwifery School

The practice of midwifery was a haphazard one. Assistance at birth had traditionally been given by other women, most of them untrained except by experience, but in the last 100 years their role had increasingly been taken, at least in cities, by men with some medical training (though usually not in midwifery), who called themselves men-midwives. While practitioners in France, male or female, could gain proper experience from lying-in hospitals such as the Hôtel-Dieu, in England there was no such establishment.

In London, the first lying-in establishment at which midwives could be trained was in the infirmary of the St James's parish work-house, opened this year by a distinguished man-midwife, Sir Richard Manningham. As he explained in his advertisement for the enterprise, 'due Knowledge' of the practice of midwifery could not easily be obtained without going abroad, which for most pupils, especially women, was out of the question, with the result that they were not as fully qualified for their business as they should have been. His venture was successful, and within eight years a lying-in ward was established at the Middlesex Hospital.

DIGGING HIS OWN GRAVE
In the churchyard of St Mary, Kingston upon Thames, this year the sexton was digging a grave, assisted by his son and daughter, when the adjoining chapel collapsed. The sexton and another man were killed and were subsequently buried in the churchyard. His daughter took over the duties of sexton.

GREAT FROST ON THE THAMES
One of the Great Frosts took place on the Thames. It lasted from 25 December until 17 February 1740. As usual, stalls offering food, drink and novelties were set up, and a press was erected on the ice on which souvenirs were printed – Hogarth patronized this on 16 February and had the printer put his dog's name, Trump, on the card, rather than his own. Not all was fun. The weather brought to a standstill the building of Westminster Bridge, of course, and allowed foolhardy people to climb up the incomplete piers. More seriously, it put out of work many people – especially those in the construction industry – and, because shipping could not get up the Thames, raised the prices of food and coals.

1740

THE BOW STREET COURT ESTABLISHED
The most famous magistrates' court in England, that in Bow Street, was established this year. A Middlesex Justice of the Peace, Colonel Thomas De Veil, acquired the lease of 4 Bow Street. Judging from a contemporary illustration in which 'night walkers' are appearing before the magistrate, the courtroom was in his front parlour.

Though this was soon to be the pre-eminent and best regulated court in London, its most notable days were during the magistracy of the Fielding brothers (1749–c.1776).

LONDON HOSPITAL FOUNDED
On 3 November an infirmary opened in a house in Featherstone Street near the Bunhill Fields burial ground; this institution was to grow into the London Hospital. The intention was to treat the sick poor amongst 'merchant seamen and the manufacturing classes' in the East End of London. When the hospital opened there was one shilling in the bank account.

A SUBSCRIPTION LIBRARY
The first subscription library appears to have been established in Dunfermline, Scotland, in 1711. There are two claims for the first in

London, both for about 1740. One is for a bookseller called Wright, who set up a circulating library at 132 The Strand. The other is for the Revd Samuel Fancourt, who had an establishment in Crane Court, off Fleet Street.

BEAUFORT HOUSE DEMOLISHED
Beaufort House in Chelsea, Sir Thomas More's old house, was demolished by its new owner, Sir Hans Sloane. The house stood halfway up today's Beaufort Street, with grounds stretching down to the Thames. It was in this house, which Erasmus described as 'a modest yet commodious mansion', that More was living when taken for the interrogation that led to his execution, and it was here that the artist Holbein stayed and painted the More family and their servants on one canvas. Unfortunately, this picture was lost in a fire in the 17th century, but an early copy survives and is displayed in Chelsea Town Hall.

The main gate to the house, designed by Inigo Jones, was given by Sloane to the earl of Burlington, to place in his garden at Chiswick House.

A HANGING GONE WRONG
William Dewell, hanged for the rape of a woman in a barn at Acton on 29 November, was found to be still alive when his body was delivered at Surgeons' Hall for dissection. He was returned to Newgate prison, and the following year was transported.

EXPERIMENT IN INOCULATION
The prevention and treatment of smallpox was in its infancy – Edward Jenner was not to publish his proposals for vaccination until 1796. In 1740 a Dr Poole rented a house in Essex Road, Islington, for the treatment of smallpox patients. Local residents were outraged, because the virulence of the disease was well known. Patients were abused and insulted when they left the hospital, so that it was found necessary to go out only after dusk. Dr Poole's establishment was to lead, in 1753, to the building of a larger hospital at Cold Bath Fields.

A COACH IN THE PROCESSION
This is the first year in which the lord mayor travelled in a coach, pulled by six horses, for his procession to Westminster.

A lively scene at the Bow Street Magistrates' Office, drawn by Pugin and Rowlandson c. 1809. A prisoner is being led away to the right.

1741

First Admission at the Foundling Hospital

The governors of the newly established Foundling Hospital (see 1739) were originally offered the lease of Montagu House in Great Russell Street, later to be the home of the British Museum. It was estimated that this building would take over 600 women and nearly 1,700 children, but the governors wished to begin more modestly. They took instead a house in Hatton Garden, for which Hogarth designed a shield to go above the door. On 25 March 1741 the hospital admitted its first child, and in the course of the first year 136 children were received, of which 56 died.

Nurses there were forbidden to leave the building without permission, and they were ordered to keep the children neat and clean and not to give them any alcohol as an opiate. Wet-nurses were to be examined as to their general health before being employed.

Garrick's Debut

David Garrick, who became London's most famous actor, made a modest debut at Goodman's Fields Theatre, Ayliffe Street, in March in a pantomime. But his debut as a serious actor was in the same theatre on 19 October, in the title role of *Richard III*. Here he was described as 'a gentleman who never appeared on any stage'. He was an immediate success, and fashionable London flocked to see him. Walpole was not impressed, but Pope thought him marvellous, and the general public never tired of him.

Two Public Hangings

Two hangings drew the curious of London more than usually this year. The notorious pickpocket Jenny Diver (real name Mary Young) was hanged at Tyburn in March. She went to the gallows in a 'mourning coach veiled and strongly guarded, there being a design formed to rescue her … Her concern was so sensibly expressed when she took leave of her little child a few days before her execution that it drew tears into the eyes of the turnkey.'

James Hall, footman to John Penny of Clement's Inn, was hanged for the murder of his master. It was sometimes the custom to hang murderers near the scene of their crime, and so Hall was hanged in Catherine Street, Covent Garden.

The Strong Man of Islington

The landlord of an Islington pub, Thomas Topham, performed feats of strength. On 28 May he lifted three hogsheads of water (1,831 pounds) as a tribute to the national hero Admiral Vernon, who was in the audience together with several thousand spectators. He is also reported to have cracked a coconut by banging it against his head, to have broken a sturdy broomstick by thwacking it against his arm, to have heaved his horse over a turnpike gate, and to have rolled up a pewter dish as though it were paper.

A Notorious Chapel

About this year a Revd Alexander Keith opened the grandly named St George's Chapel in Curzon Street, on the site of the present cinema. He scandalized the clergy by his readiness to perform marriages without too many questions. In 1741 there were two ceremonies, but in 1742 there were 723, and by 1743 as many as 117 in one month. This activity was brought to an end by the passing of the Marriage Act of 1754, which required the publication of banns.

David Garrick in the character of Tancred — a painting by Thomas Worlidge.

1742

Ranelagh Gardens Opened

Between the Royal Hospital, Chelsea, and today's Chelsea Bridge Road stood the mansion and gardens of Lord Ranelagh, purchased by two partners in 1741 and developed by them and a syndicate of businessmen into the world-famed Ranelagh Gardens. They planned a pleasure garden to outshine the established Vauxhall, and to this end William Jones, architect to the East India Company, was commissioned to build an amphitheatre, later called the Rotunda, as its main attraction. This was a circular building, approximately 150 ft in diameter (about the same as the British Museum Reading Room), its roof held up by an octagonal arrangement of carved pillars between which an orchestra was accommodated. Later this space was occupied by a large open fire and the orchestra was moved to one side of the hall. An arcade ran right around the building between the four entrances, and two tiers of 52 boxes ran around the walls inside. The lower tier was at ground level, and it was the custom to promenade around the arena talking to those in the boxes.

Ranelagh opened on 5 April. Horace Walpole, a frequent customer, wrote in April:

I have been breakfasting this morning at Ranelagh Garden: they have built an immense amphitheatre, with balconies full of little ale-houses; it is in rivalry to Vauxhall and costs about twelve thousand pounds. The building is not finished, but they get great sums by people going to see it and breakfasting in the house: there were yesterday no less than three hundred and eighty persons, at eighteen pence a-piece.

The building was officially opened the following month by the prince of Wales.

In Smollett's *Humphrey Clinker*, the niece describes Ranelagh as an 'enchanted palace of a genius, adorned with the most exquisite performances of painting, carving, and gilding, enlightened with a thousand golden lamps, that emulate the noon-day sun; crowded with the great, the rich, the gay, the happy, and the fair; glittering with cloth of gold, and silver lace, embroidery, and precious stones'.

The admission charge was half a crown, which included the 'regale' of tea, coffee, bread and butter. On special firework nights the price was 3s or more, and masquerades cost anything from half a guinea.

The essential difference between Ranelagh and Vauxhall was that many of the attractions of the former were under cover and could be used most of the year, whereas Vauxhall was a place for the summer months only.

STORMING OF THE ROUNDHOUSE

Horace Walpole was also at hand to describe a rather different event which occurred at the St Martin-in-the-Fields lock-up, called the St Martin's roundhouse, which stood opposite the church on the present site of the National Portrait Gallery:

There has lately been the most horrible scene of murder imaginable; a party of drunken constables took it into their heads to put the laws in execution against disorderly persons, and so took up every woman they met, until they had collected five or six and twenty, all of whom they thrust into St Martin's Round House, where they kept them all night with doors and windows closed. The poor creatures, who could neither stir nor breathe, screamed as long as they had any breath left, begging at least for water, one poor creature said she was worth eighteen pence and would gladly give it for a draft of water, but in vain! So well did they keep them there that in the morning four were found stifled to death, two died soon after, and a dozen more are in a shocking way. In short it is horrid to think that the poor creatures suffered; several of them were beggars, who from having no lodging were necessarily found in the street, and others honest labouring women. One of the dead was a poor washerwoman, big with child, who was returning home late from washing. One of the constables is taken, and others absconded, but I question if any of them will suffer death.

The enraged populace tore down the building, and the chief constable was arrested and tried at Bow Street for murder. Sentenced to death initially, he was eventually transported to America, where he worked as a slave in the tobacco fields.

WHITBREAD'S ESTABLISHED

The brewer Samuel Whitbread began business this year in Whitecross Street in the City, in partnership with two brothers, Godfrey and Thomas Shewell. He moved to his famous brewery in Chiswell Street in 1750.

NEW CHURCHES

The rebuilding of London's churches continued apace. A new parish church for St Marylebone was opened in February on the site of the previous church at the northern end of Marylebone High Street. Evidently it was designed by one of the churchwardens, Mr Lane, who also put up the money. In return he received the pew rents and burial fees.

A new Christ Church in Blackfriars Road had been completed in 1741 – sadly, it was destroyed in the last war. Another church damaged in the last war but still standing, together with the parish stocks and whipping post in the churchyard, is St Leonard, Shoreditch, reopened on 23 August 1740. The architect was George Dance the Elder; his spire is reminiscent of Wren's St Mary-le-Bow.

An indication of the growing population to London's east was the replacement of the parish church of Bethnal Green. An old chapel on Bethnal Green was demolished and a new church, St Matthew's, designed by George Dance the Elder, was erected not only for Bethnal Green but also for the influx of people from nearby Spitalfields. The structure, begun soon after 1740, though much altered, still stands.

1743

THE PEERLESS POOL

A pond formed from a natural spring in the area now covered by Baldwin Street, off Old Street, and called the Perilous Pond, because of its danger to bathers, was this year converted into a swimming pond by one William Kemp. He renamed it the Peerless Pool, and as a side attraction added a fish pond and a bowling green. The writer William Hone in 1826 noted that the swimming pond was still there: 'On a summer evening it is amusing to survey the conduct of the bathers; some boldly dive, others timorous stand and then descend step by step, unwilling and slow; choice swimmers attract attention by divings and somersets, and the whole sheet of water sometimes rings with merriment.' Peerless Street is a reminder of this old attraction.

A BOXING THEATRE IN OXFORD STREET

John Broughton established a boxing amphitheatre near Hanway Street, off Oxford Street, this year. On 10 March he announced his first programme in the *Daily Advertiser*. It contained two novel features. He put eight champions on the stage and, instead of pairing them, invited the audience to do so. The second feature was a 'battle royal' in which one boxer took on the seven others single-handed in the ring.

Broughton, formerly a Thames waterman, is generally considered to be the father of English pugilism. He did sufficiently well out of it to leave £7,000 when he died, and at his funeral in 1789 all the pall bearers were pugilists.

A WESLEY CHURCH IN THE WEST END

On 29 May, John Wesley opened a chapel in West Street off the Charing Cross Road, formerly a Huguenot chapel (see 1700), and this

The pugilist Broughton sparring with James Figg.

remained the headquarters of Methodist work in the West End of London until 1798. The rent was £18 per annum.

1744

THE BEGINNINGS OF SOTHEBY'S

The auction house of Sotheby's began about this year with the establishment of a bookselling business by one Samuel Baker. By 1753 he was in York Street in Covent Garden, a stretch of road now covered by Wellington Street, and here he established the first saleroom dealing in books, manuscripts and prints. In 1776 this business was taken over by his nephew, John Sotheby, in partnership with George Leigh.

BOW PORCELAIN ESTABLISHED

Thomas Frye, a mezzotint engraver, and a glass merchant named Edward Heylyn established a porcelain business in Bow, east London, this year, having discovered a new process for making it. Initially he took an old glass-blowing factory, but later a new building was erected on the Stratford side of the river Lea.

The business was at its peak in the 1750s. The 'New Canton' ware, as it was called, was used for statuettes, tableware, bowls and vases; it was described as 'peasant porcelain'. W. B. Honey, in his *Pottery and Porcelain*, notes:

It can hardly have supplied an actual peasant market, but its qualities were such as appealed to an uneducated sense of beauty rather than to taste. An entirely unacademic love of bright colours, an ability to compose them regardless of the rules, and a probably unintended simplification of its sophisticated models — these are amongst the characteristics of peasant art found also in Bow porcelain.

1745

MIDDLESEX HOSPITAL FOUNDED

The Middlesex Infirmary, later the Middlesex Hospital, was begun this year when two small houses, 8–10 Windmill Street, were rented from a Mr Goodge in which to open an institution 'for the sick and lame of Soho'. Fifteen beds were provided, and there were an additional three to cope with accidents or confinements. Thus, in the 25 years since 1720, five of the great London hospitals had been established on the initiative of private citizens.

THE FOUNDLING HOSPITAL EXPANDS

Even before the Foundling Hospital opened its Hatton Garden doors in 1741, the governors had been looking for a more suitable site for what they hoped would be a substantial enterprise. In October 1740 they had been advised that the earl of Salisbury was prepared to sell them 56 acres near Lamb's Conduit Street, and terms were agreed for this large site.

The little-known architect Theodore Jacobsen was appointed to design the new buildings, and the foundation stone was laid on 16 September 1742. The first wing of the new premises was opened for admissions in October 1745.

The main problem for the hospital was the number of applicants for admission. There were unruly scenes when women fought to be

A view of the Foundling Hospital, published in 1751. The grand buildings have now gone, but a lodge and colonnade still survive.

first at the door on admission days. A system was devised in which different-coloured balls were placed in a box; if a woman drew out a white ball she was allowed in with her child. By 1747 the number of admissions was 100 yearly, and four years later over 800 children had been admitted, of whom over 300 died.

The coloured-ball system, hard though it was on the mothers, was replaced by a more extraordinary one in 1756, when a basket was hung at the gate of the hospital in Guilford Street, in which a child was put by the mother after she had rung a bell to give notice to the porter.

GREAT HOUSES IN BERKELEY SQUARE

About this time nos. 42–46 Berkeley Square were built. Number 44 — described by Nikolaus Pevsner as 'the finest terrace house in London' — was built for Lady Isabella Finch by William Kent. Its staircase was described by Horace Walpole as 'as beautiful a piece of scenery and, considering the space, of art, as can be imagined.' This house is now the Clermont Club. Number 45, built as a pair with no. 46, probably by Henry Flitcroft, was later the home of Sir Robert Clive, and where he committed suicide.

THE JACOBITE REBELLION

Another Jacobite Rebellion began in earnest when the Stuart pretender to the throne landed in the western Highlands of Scotland and on 19 August set up his standard at Glenfinnan. In September he was in Edinburgh, and defeated the English forces in his first battle with them. Alarm and panic began to set in, especially among those whose fortunes were tied to the Hanoverian succession to the throne. There was a run on the Bank of England, stopped only when London merchants stepped in to support it. London was put into a state of alert, and a camp was established at Finchley — Hogarth's famous print of the guards marching to Finchley immortalizes this.

By 4 December the rebels had entered Derby, and two days later, on 'Black Friday', the news of their advance reached London. There was immediate mobilization in London of trained bands, constables and some liverymen. But the advance on London did not take place. The rebels withdrew, seeing that their task was hopeless, and their aspirations were ruthlessly obliterated on the field of Culloden in April 1746.

Some of the Jacobite soldiers were tried in London in 1746. Sentenced at the courthouse of St Margaret, Southwark, on 30 July, they were conveyed on hurdles from Southwark jail to Kennington Common, where they were beheaded and disembowelled.

BARBERS AND SURGEONS SEPARATE
The union of barbers and surgeons in one livery company was dissolved this year. The Barbers retained the hall in Monkwell Street, and the Surgeons took temporary accommodation at Stationers' Hall until 1751, when they moved to their own premises in Old Bailey.

1746

A NEW MAP OF LONDON
John Rocque's famous map of London was completed this year, enabling Londoners to assess at a glance just how their city had grown. The map itself was a massive achievement – being 13 ft wide and 6½ ft deep, on 24 sheets drawn at a scale of 26 inches to the mile. The plan was based on trigonometrical calculations backed up by the simple method of walking every street with a wheeled gadget measuring the distance. It took Rocque nine years to complete it.

Compared with the great Ogilby & Morgan map of 1677, there are now a good number of new developments in grid formation spread around large squares, the neatness of their arrangements broken only by the need for mews for stabling. The scheme around St James's Square seems small compared with the growing Mayfair estate surrounding Grosvenor Square – a development contained on the west by 'Tiburn Lane' (Park Lane) and 'Hide Park'. To the north of Oxford Street the slow development around Cavendish Square had not got much further north than the square itself. There are tentacles northward in Bloomsbury, but here development was restricted for the time being by the endeavours of the dukes of Montagu and Bedford to keep the northern aspect from their mansions in Great Russell Street clear of impediment. This was to change in the next half-century, with the impetus for development provided by the 'New Road' from the City to Paddington. Another stretch of land soon to fall to bricks and mortar was that around the Foundling Hospital, shown on Rocque's map (together with the two burial grounds to the north) as a building isolated in the fields which it possessed.

But, despite the spread of building, the villages around London – even as near as Islington, St Marylebone and Kensington – still appear in pleasantly rural surroundings, the object of many an afternoon's country walk, the location of many tea gardens.

Not a great deal is known about Rocque himself. His family, which came to London from France c. 1735, was possibly of Huguenot extraction. John became a land surveyor and his brother, Bartholomew, a market gardener in Fulham. Rocque moved from Soho to the western end of Piccadilly, which is where he was to be found when he published his great achievement. In 1750 he was in Whitehall, and it was here that a disastrous fire destroyed his entire stock of prints and maps.

LOCK HOSPITAL BEGINS
The Lock Hospital, begun in Grosvenor Place this year, was for the treatment of venereal diseases – more specifically, it was stated, for 'females suffering from disorders contracted by a vicious course of life'. This was not the whole story, though, because many of the patients were children, victims of a popular fallacy of the time that venereal disease could be got rid of by passing it on to a child. The

main hospital was eventually located on the Harrow Road, but a branch for outpatients was first opened in Soho, where the governors emphasized that 'every precaution was taken to prevent the charity becoming an encouragement to vice'.

1747

THE BEGINNINGS OF STRAWBERRY HILL
The extraordinary villa Strawberry Hill, in Twickenham, has its origins this year. Horace Walpole bought this old house, then called Chopped Straw Hall, in 1747 and within a year began to transform it. He described it in 1748 as 'a little plaything of a house, the prettiest bauble you ever did see', and spent the next 30 years changing it to a Gothic castle, including numerous features copied from famous buildings. The building is now a Roman Catholic training college.

EXECUTION OF A JACOBITE
Lord Lovat, a Jacobite, had been taken prisoner after the Battle of Culloden in 1746. Conveyed by gradual stages to London – he was portrayed by Hogarth on the way – he was lodged in the Tower and tried for high treason, with inevitable consequences. An extraordinary crowd gathered at Tower Hill for his execution on 9 April – so immense that a temporary viewing gallery by the Ship ale house collapsed, resulting in the immediate deaths of up to ten people, including the carpenter of the scaffold, who was selling beer beneath.

It is said that Lovat was the last person to be executed in this country by beheading. His head was not exposed, and he was buried in the chapel of St Peter ad Vincula by the Tower.

A NEW CORN EXCHANGE
A new Corn Exchange, in which corn was sold by sample, seems to have begun functioning this year in Mark Lane. The building consisted at this time of stalls set around a courtyard which was open to the sky.

HAMPSTEAD CHURCH REBUILT
Hampstead vestry, conscious that the parish church was now inadequate both for the population and for the class of visitors that stayed nearby to take the waters of the wells, decided in 1744 to build a new parish church. A local resident, Henry Flitcroft, architect of the much praised St Giles-in-the-Fields, was invited to a vestry meeting that year and asked to submit a plan which would be considered against any other plan put forward by another architect. Flitcroft declined to avail himself of the offer – no doubt feeling that his fame and local residence were sufficient qualifications to obviate the need for others to be invited – and so the vestry went ahead with its competition without him.

The little known John Saunderson was the architect chosen – he was also a local resident. The church tower he built was soon found to be unsafe and in need of further work, but his church, St John's, still survives, albeit rather altered. It is now regarded as a highly attractive building, beautifully framed by the elegance of Church Row.

BOXING GLOVES AND TIGER BAITING
John Broughton, himself a former champion pugilist (see 1743) and owner of the amphitheatre near Hanway Street which staged boxing matches, began this year a boxing academy in the Haymarket. In the *Daily Advertiser* he announced that

Mr. Broughton proposes, with proper assistance, to open an academy at his house in the Haymarket, for the instruction of those who are willing to be initiated in the mystery of boxing, where the whole theory and practice of that truly British art, with all the various stops, blows, cross-buttocks, etc., incident to combatants, will be fully taught and explained and that persons of quality and distinction may not be debarred from entering into a course of those lectures, they will be given the utmost tenderness, for which reason mufflers are provided, that will effectually secure them from the inconveniency of black eyes, broken jaws and bloody noses.

This is probably the first reference to the use of boxing gloves.

Broughton diversified in another way this year. The same newspaper advertised 'there will be a large he Tyger baited on Wednesday next at Mr. Broughton's amphitheatre in Oxford Road, being the first that ever was baited in England. He is the largest that ever was seen here, being eight feet in length.'

A STATUE IN LEICESTER SQUARE

The unveiling of an equestrian statue of George I in Leicester Square this year had more significance than some kind of tribute to a rather unpopular king. The statue, modelled by C. Burchard, had been made *c.* 1720 and erected in the lavish gardens of Canons in Stanmore. When the estate was sold off, the 2nd duke of Chandos gave or sold the statue to Frederick, prince of Wales, who lived in Leicester House in the square. The prince was on bad terms with his father, George II, who in turn had had difficult relations with his own father – the subject of the statue. Horace Walpole suggests that the prince had the work erected in front of his house to annoy his father.

The statue had an ignominious end. When James Wyld's Great Globe was constructed in the square in 1851 the statue was taken down and buried in the ground; it was retrieved in bad condition in 1861, subsequently vandalized, and, once the rider had been stolen, sold for scrap. By that time the horse, left with only two legs, had been whitewashed and painted with black spots.

1748

FIRE IN CORNHILL

It must have seemed to the citizens of London on 25 March that history was about to repeat itself. In the early hours of the morning a fire began in the house of a peruke maker in Exchange Alley, off Cornhill, which, despite the best efforts of fire engines, continued blazing. By noon over 100 houses were destroyed and there were three deaths. Property destroyed included the house that the poet Thomas Gray was born in, as well as several well-known coffee houses

1749

A YEAR OF RIOTS AND PEACE

In the year in which the Peace of Aix-la-Chapelle was celebrated there were some serious riots in London. As will be seen in the following years, London was becoming more anarchic and volatile, causing the authorities much concern.

Causes of disturbance could be quite trivial. On 29 August at a racecourse at Tothill Fields a race was cancelled. This led to spectators

burning the starting gate, booth and benches. A hoax perpetrated at the Haymarket Theatre also ended in violence. It was advertised that a man would squeeze himself into a quart bottle, sing a song inside it, and allow the audience to handle the bottle. Needless to say there was a large and expectant crowd to see this impossible task, including the duke of Cumberland. After waiting an hour, the audience was told that the exhibition would not take place as it had been found impossible in London to find a bottle of exactly a quart size. The almost inevitable response was a theatre with its seats and decorations ruined. On 1 July some sailors who had been robbed at a brothel in the Strand returned with numerous friends from Wapping, broke open the house, turned the women on to the streets, ripped up the furnishings, and made a bonfire of the fittings. A troop of Guards from the Tower was necessary to quell the disturbance. None of the sailors was arrested, but an innocent bystander, himself rather the worse for drink, was tried and sentenced to be hanged at Tyburn. Though he had offers to rescue him from the gallows, he declined them, saying he was resigned to his fate.

Violent spectacle was always provided at Tyburn, but a different treat for the morbidly curious Londoners was the execution of two soldiers. The *Penny London Post* of 18 August describes how the men, both found guilty of desertion, were seen off:

Both men were kept in the Savoy Prison, marched up Birdcage Walk, unbraced with drums beating, up Constitution Hill to the fatal stone [on the north side of Hyde Park]. They pray'd for fifteen minutes in the hope of a reprieve, but none came. Caps were put over their eyes, a firing team of six and a reserve of six more men did the execution.

The Peace of Aix-la-Chapelle – a treaty signed by Britain, Holland and Austria on one side, and France and Spain on the other – was celebrated by a spectacular firework display in Green Park on 27 April. A large wooden pavilion, painted to resemble stone, was erected. The entertainment consisted of a 'grand concert of war like instruments', a royal salute of 101 brass cannon, 11 separate rocket displays, air balloons, and over 32,000 fireworks. Added attractions included the accidental burning of the pavilion and the first performance of Handel's *Music for the Royal Fireworks*. This had been rehearsed at Vauxhall in front of 12,000 people a week earlier.

THE FOUNDING OF A WINE MERCHANT

Perhaps the peace celebrations influenced the founding of a new wine merchant's in London. George Johnson and a young Italian, Giacomo Justerini, opened up shop at 2 Pall Mall. The business was sold in 1831 to a George Brooks, who renamed the firm Justerini & Brooks.

FIELDING TAKES OVER

Henry Fielding, the novelist, moved into the Bow Street magistrates' court, having been appointed a Justice of the Peace in December 1748. This post was obtained through the patronage of the duke of Bedford. It was Fielding who established a voluntary force of thief-takers which became known as the Bow Street Runners.

CHESTERFIELD HOUSE BUILT

One of the most notable houses built in this period was that for Philip Stanhope, 4th earl of Chesterfield. In what is now Great Stanhope Street, the young architect Isaac Ware constructed a fine Palladian, but rococo, building. The columns and grand staircase were taken from Canons in Stanmore, and the furnishings were bought from around Europe. At a time when rich noblemen were vying to display

1700s

not only their wealth but their taste for culture, Chesterfield House was the leading house in London.

Long after Chesterfield's departure the *Quarterly Review* was able to describe the house much as it had been during his lifetime:

On the mantelpieces and cabinets stand busts of old orators, interspersed with voluptuous vases and bronzes, antique or Italian, and airy statuettes in marble or alabaster, of nude or seminude Opera nymphs. We shall never recall that princely room without fancying Chesterfield receiving in it a visit of his only child's mother – while probably some new favourite was sheltered in the dim mysterious little boudoir within – which still remains also in its original blue damask and fretted goldwork.

1750

WESTMINSTER BRIDGE OPENED
At midnight on 17 November the long-awaited Westminster Bridge was opened for foot passengers and horses, to the sound of drums, cannons and trumpets. Many went beneath it in boats, sending blasts up to the arches with instruments such as French horns just to enjoy the echo. So many people milled about on the bridge on the 18th that the jealous watermen made one last killing in taking people home across the river, as the crowd on the bridge was too dense for them to cross otherwise.

Designed by a Swiss, Charles Labelye, the bridge was built on 14 arches and had a central span of 76 ft. Along the parapet were alcoves which provided shelter for legitimate activities – and quite often illegitimate ones too, to the extent that the bridge authority employed 12 watchmen at night to keep order.

The watermen, who opined that the bridge would be 'pernicious to Navigation, detrimental to Trade and likely to ruin thousands of families', had to live with this change of circumstances, and perhaps use their compensation money to begin a new trade. More of a prob-

lem was the warren of medieval alleys and courts in Old Palace Yard: picturesque and historic though they were (and, of course, insanitary), they were swept away. At the same time Whitehall was widened and Parliament Street was constructed to connect with the bridge – during the 19th century it became the widest street in central London.

The building of the bridge had not been without incident. The work was constantly sabotaged by watermen; the Thames froze in 1739–40 but those piers already erected survived this test, and the whole structure was untouched after two mild earthquakes in February and March 1750.

The official opening was celebrated at the Bear inn at the northern end – a large new public house of the 'hotel' style, forerunner of a new vogue in the building of inns.

Wordsworth's famous sonnet of 1803, 'Composed upon Westminster Bridge', seems to have been written from the top of a coach, since a 7-ft-high parapet wall obscured the view of the City immortalized by the poet.

EARTHQUAKE PANIC IN LONDON
Earthquakes caused much consternation in London. A slight tremor was felt on 8 February, and caused minor damage. When a further, slightly more positive, tremor was felt on the same day in March, apprehension grew. What would happen on 8 April? was the question people asked. The bishop of London was of the opinion that the earthquakes expressed the wrath of God at the depravity of Londoners, and no doubt watermen were hopeful that they were a sign of disapproval of the bridge. The *Gentleman's Magazine* thought the tremors were caused by 'subterranean waters cutting new courses' and 'the inflammable breath of iron pyrites and substantial sulphur causing thunder and lightning when they explode in the air'. A lowly preacher of the sort always thrown up on such occasions, a shoemaker from Carnaby Market, was able to convince many that, via an angel, he had had a direct message from God that the dissolution of the world would happen, and a mad guardsman had to be incarcerated after stirring up the populace with wild prophecies.

Westminster Bridge, depicted by Pugin and Rowlandson c. 1809, with the Houses of Parliament to the left in their old form, before destruction by fire in 1834.

Whatever was coming, Londoners didn't like it, and the gullible, superstitious and easily led fled the city – although, if the shoemaker's message was correct, retreating to places like Slough was not an answer. On the night before 8 April thousands slept on the open slopes of Highgate, Hampstead and Islington. Nothing happened, but it took months for the fear and apprehension to disappear.

WATER HOUSE BUILT
The handsome Water House in Forest Road, Walthamstow, was built about this year. The writer, craftsman and artist William Morris lived here from 1848 to 1856, and the building is now the William Morris Gallery and the grounds attached are Lloyd Park (see 1898). The name of the house derives from the moat which once surrounded it.

INFECTION AT THE OLD BAILEY
Conditions at Newgate prison were notoriously bad. A book of 1719 referred to the gaol as a 'place of calamity' and a 'habitation of misery'; it was fetid, oppressive, overcrowded, corrupt and diseased. The authorities received their reward for inaction this year when, at the sessions house at the Old Bailey nearby, over 50 of the dignitaries and officers present died of a rapidly infectious jail fever emanating from Newgate. As is woefully common in England, this dramatic happening did not bring action, in the shape of a new prison, for a long time, but it did give rise to an arcane tradition: the posies which the judges now carry on certain days in May and September are reminders of an old device which it was hoped would ward off infection.

NEW BUSINESSES
Several famous London businesses were established this year. John Dollond, a Huguenot, opened an optical workshop in Spitalfields. His son, Peter, opened an optician's shop in the Strand in the 1850s, an enterprise which developed into the opticians Dollond & Aitchison.

Thomas and James Harrison began a printing company in Warwick Lane in the City. The firm, with a royal warrant, later specialized in the production of stamps and banknotes.

Wiggins Teape, the papermakers, began in the City this year as Hathaway & Edwards.

The Parker Art Gallery, London's oldest print-sellers, began at 2 Albemarle Street. It is now in Pimlico Road.

BEAR-BAITING
A large Norway bear was baited in a booth at Tottenham Court on 27 December. Two large dogs were billed as its tormentors.

EXECUTION OF A HIGHWAYMAN
The London crowd was enlivened by the execution of a well-known highwayman, John MacLean, who usually passed himself off as an Irish squire with lodgings in St James's. Displaying good taste to the last, he was hanged wearing a silk waistcoat with lace trimmings and yellow Moroccan slippers.

MORAVIANS SETTLE IN CHELSEA
A Protestant sect, refounded in Bohemia in 1722 by Count Zinzendorf, established itself in England by buying Lindsey House, the duke of Ancaster's old mansion in Chelsea, now numbered 98–100 Cheyne Walk. The Moravians also took a long lease of some of the Sloane estate, and opened a burial ground off Millman Street which, according to their custom, was neatly divided into areas for married and for unmarried people.

Bear-baiting – a gruesome scene depicted by H. Alken.

1751

NEW ROADS SOUTH OF THE RIVER
An Act this year was instrumental in making the Elephant and Castle area a pivotal one in south London. It allowed the extension of the newly formed Westminster Bridge Road across the swampy St George's Fields, the formation of its extension, Borough Road, to Borough High Street, and the creation of New Kent Road to link Elephant and Castle to the Old Kent Road.

TROUBLE IN RICHMOND PARK
Richmond Park had been enclosed by Charles I (see 1637), but it had always been available for the use of local residents. It was often used by the royal family for hunting, and so many people came to watch that in 1735 the onlookers were considered 'not only troublesome but very dangerous'. In future, residents were informed, admission could be had only by a ticket previously applied for. Further restrictions followed. Those residents with keys to the gates in the wall found that the locks had been changed, and George II's daughter, Princess Amelia, who had become ranger of the Park, imposed more rules. Matters came to a head on 16 May 1751, when parishioners perambulating the bounds found that the ladders usually placed to enable them to cross the wall and so continue along the boundary through the park were not there. What happened then is not clear, although it seems that the parishioners found some way to circumvent the restriction, possibly by breaking down the wall. The imperious Amelia thenceforth banned future access to the park to anyone but her guests.

This resulted in a long-running legal battle. Once obsequious petitions to the princess had failed, John Lewis, a local brewer, managed at the assizes in 1758 to obtain the right of pedestrian access.

1752

CARPETS AND TAPESTRIES IN FULHAM
By this year a factory for the manufacture of carpets and tapestries had been established at what is now 49–55 Fulham High Street. Its

proprietor was Peter Parisot, whose background and venture attracted a great deal of partisan comment. He was variously described as a commercial adventurer, a spendthrift or a disguised Capuchin priest.

Thomas Faulkner, the 19th-century historian, said that here 'both the work of the Gobelins and the art of dyeing scarlet and black, as practised at Chaillot and Sedan, were carried on'. Parisot recruited workers from Chaillot and took on labour at Fulham to learn the arts of 'drawing, weaving, dyeing and other branches of the work'. He spoke of setting up an academy of drawing and painting, in the hope of attracting government assistance; he stressed that he offered 'employment to both sexes to the weakly as well as the robust' and that he afforded 'help to many families of the better sort who are burdened with numerous offspring'. He reassured the government that 'No apprentices or young persons … will be received but such as are natural born subjects of His Majesty and they will be educated in the Protestant religion.'

Despite this appearance of being a local benefactor loyal to the Protestant cause, Parisot was actually an anti-Jesuit priest called Father Norbett, who had sought refuge in Britain to work as a Catholic missionary.

The factory was short-lived: Parisot sold up in 1756.

FUNERAL OF THE HANGMAN
In May, 'the corpse of John Thrift, the late executioner, was brought in a hearse, without any coach to St Paul's, Covent Garden, when it was attended by a great concourse of people who seemed so displeased with his being buried there that the attendants of the funeral, among whom was Tallis, the present hangman, were afraid that the body would be turned out of the coffin, which was therefore first carried into the church. However, about eight o'clock they got him interred.'

A STRONG WIND OVER LONDON
On 15 March a very strong gale hit London. Two ships at Vauxhall were lifted out of the Thames and deposited on the shore, many chimneys were thrown down, roofs were blown off, and a painted window at Westminster Abbey was destroyed. At the King's Bench prison 160 ft of wall collapsed.

MURDER AT NEWGATE PRISON
Horace Walpole in a letter to a friend records a murder at Newgate prison this year: 'It is shocking to think what a shambles this country is grown! Seventeen were executed this morning, after having murdered the Turnkey on Friday night, and almost forced open Newgate.'

1753

MANSION HOUSE FINISHED
The first official residence of the lord mayor of London, the Mansion House, was this year completed on the site of the old Stocks Market. Initially there was an architectural competition for the building, in which a number of notable architects took part, but in the end the design was that of George Dance the Elder, clerk of the City works.

THE MESSIAH AT THE FOUNDLING
The composer Handel was a generous benefactor to Coram's Foundling Hospital. When he died in 1759 he bequeathed 'a faire copy of the score and all parts of my oratorio called *The Messiah*' to the

The building for the Royal Society of Arts was designed by Robert Adam in 1774, as part of the Adelphi scheme. The Society still occupies the building.

Hospital. From 1750 he supervised performances of this work for the benefit of the Foundling; in 1750 an enormous crush of people at the Foundling Chapel came to see a performance at the inauguration of the new organ, and more money was raised from concerts in successive years.

1754

ROYAL SOCIETY OF ARTS BEGINS
The Royal Society of Arts was established this year as the Society for the Encouragement of Arts, Manufactures and Commerce, meeting first above a circulating library in Crane Court. After several changes of address it settled in 1774 in its present imposing building in John Adam Street, which was specially built for it by the Adam brothers in their Adelphi scheme.

A NEW CHURCH IN ISLINGTON
The old church of St Mary, in Upper Street, Islington, had been demolished in 1751. The architect of the new structure, consecrated on 26 May, was Launcelot Dowbiggin, a master joiner, who is buried in the crypt. Pevsner thought that Dowbiggin's 'somewhat rustic floridity … resulted in a steeple of characteristic outline and robust detail'. Unfortunately the steeple is all that remains after the church was wrecked by a bomb on 9 September 1940 during the Second World War, but, lit up at night, it is an attractive local landmark.

A Bridge at Hampton Court

The first bridge across the Thames at Hampton Court was built this year. Designed by Samuel Stevens and Benjamin Ludgator, it was made of wood, had seven spans, and, despite its rather frail chinoiserie appearance, was meant to be a road bridge. It was short-lived, being demolished in 1778.

1755

A New Middlesex Hospital

The Middlesex Infirmary had outgrown its premises in Windmill Street. The lying-in section, established in 1747 with five beds, was partly the cause of the move to new premises this year. Dr Sandys, the man-midwife at the hospital, had secretly contrived to take over the entire infirmary for maternity cases. The board of governors discovered the plan and sacked several of the staff involved. The number of maternity beds was increased, but still the controversy remained and the need for a large lying-in section persisted.

With this in mind, it was decided to build a new and much larger hospital. In 1754 a site was acquired from a Mr Berners, and in 1755 the foundation stone of a new building was laid in the fields west of Tottenham Court Road. David Garrick gave two benefit performances in aid of the development fund, Dr Arne offered an oratorio, and the proprietors of Ranelagh Gardens also contributed. Sixty-four patients were admitted into the new building in 1757, although the operating theatre seems to have been forgotten, since it wasn't added until four years later.

A Landmark Book in Gough Square

Dr Samuel Johnson had moved into 17 Gough Square, off Fleet Street, in 1749. It was here, in the upper storey of the house, that the preparation of his famous *Dictionary* took place – a labour that consumed much of his prodigious energy until 1755, when it was published in two volumes. He had embarked upon the task to earn money, and had little love of the research required; but the amount he raised – about £1,575 – was not sufficient. The work took about eight years instead of the three expected, he employed at times six secretaries, and Samuel Richardson had to rescue him from a sponging house to which Johnson was sentenced for a debt of £5.

Before Johnson's publication the most useful English dictionary had been the *Universal English Etymological Dictionary*, published in the 1720s by Nathan Bailey, and before that there were barely adequate glossaries of words. But Johnson's book was more ambitious. It sought to be more comprehensive and exact, and to include quotations which threw light on word derivations. The task was daunting – hard enough to see through in good circumstances, let alone with the shadow of poverty always upon him.

Johnson's lack of money led eventually to the most famous letter declining financial aid in literary history. Johnson had originally sought the patronage of the 4th earl of Chesterfield, and had received some encouragement, though no material assistance. When, with publication in sight, the earl seemed to renew his support, a proud Johnson declined it. He wrote:

Seven years, My Lord, have now passed since I waited in your outward Rooms or was repulsed from your Door, during which time I have been pushing on my work through difficulties of which it is useless to complain … The notice which you have been pleased to take of my Labours, had it been early, had been kind; but it has been delayed till I am indifferent and cannot enjoy it, till I am solitary and cannot impart it, till I am known and do not want it.

I hope it is no very cynical asperity not to confess obligation where no benefit has been received, or to be unwilling that the Public should consider me as owing that to a Patron, which Providence has enabled me to do for myself.

Borough Market Moved

For centuries a market had been held in the middle of Borough High Street, with consequential chaos in such a narrow thoroughfare. This year the City of London abolished it, and the churchwardens of St Saviour's, Southwark, obtained permission to hold a new market on some open ground to the south-west of the church.

The Cogers Society

The heyday of the formation of men's clubs was approaching. White's Club, already well established, moved to larger premises at 37–38 St James's Street this year. But at the White Bear in Bride Lane a different kind of club was formed, basically a political debating society, called the Honourable Society of Cogers (a title derived from the Latin *cogito*, 'I think'). It was founded by David Mason; members were not obliged to speak, but they were required to drink. John Wilkes was its president in its second year.

The Society moved in 1856 to Shoe Lane, where Dickens is said to have been a member. Its membership declined at a similar rate to its changes of venue, but was reported as still meeting in 1951.

An Affray at the Theatre Royal

An unremarkable offering called *The Chinese Festival*, presented by David Garrick at the Theatre Royal in November, provoked a serious riot. The cause was not the quality of performance but patriotism. Garrick's Swiss troupe of dancers had been billed as French, to give them more appeal. However, during preparation for the show, war with France broke out and Garrick was too obstinate to renounce his subterfuge. There was pandemonium and riot on the first night, when George II came to see the show, and for the next six nights there were similar scenes. Benches were smashed, the candelabra were pulled down, and the mob attacked Garrick's house at 27 Southampton Street, where all the front windows were broken. The production cost Garrick a loss of over £4,000.

The new Middlesex Hospital in Mortimer Street, opened in 1757. To help raise funds for its development, David Garrick gave two benefit performances.

1756

A LONDON BYPASS

Work began this year on the construction of 'The New Road' — that route now described as Marylebone, Euston and Pentonville roads. It went almost entirely through open fields, and was considered then to be right out of London. Not only was it to have a significant effect on the streets of inner London at that time, but in the nineteenth century it was taken as the line beyond which no railway from the north or west could terminate.

The primary purpose of the road was to prevent the traffic of cattle from agricultural lands around London through central London to Smithfield. It was also hopefully suggested that soldiers could be moved from one side of London to another along it in an emergency.

There were, of course, objections to the scheme from aristocratic landowners nearby — in particular, the duke of Bedford, in Bloomsbury, claimed that the dust raised by the traffic would be detrimental. Fortunately others realized the economic potential of the road, which would give access to new developments north of Oxford Street and would make the fields on either side capable of producing more than cattle fodder — they would, initially, earn their masters substantial sums by being made into bricks.

The roadway was 40 ft wide, and building was forbidden within 50 ft of each side. Shops and commercial premises now sit on the long gardens which once fronted the new bypass.

WHITEFIELD BUILDS A CHAPEL

John Wesley is now the man chiefly associated with the Methodists, but at this period George Whitefield rivalled him in public estimation. He was sufficiently popular for his followers to build him in 1741 a wooden 'tabernacle' near to Wesley's Chapel in City Road. Having returned in 1748 from a long preaching trip to America, where he had purchased both a plantation and slaves, he was appointed chaplain to the Countess Huntingdon. With this aristocratic backing he was able to build a tabernacle on the west side of Tottenham Court Road — a square brick building of 70 ft dimensions. The building was opened on 7 November 1756. It was enlarged by an octagonal extension on the east side in 1759–60.

MARINE SOCIETY FOUNDED

The philanthropist Jonas Hanway is remembered now for his popularization of the umbrella and by a minute street off Oxford Street. But he was famous in his day for his good works. He was a governor of the Foundling Hospital and an inveterate social reformer, interested in the parochial care of infants, the plight of repentant prostitutes, and the working conditions of chimney-sweep boys.

His most enduring philanthropic act, however, was the foundation of the Marine Society, to aid recruitment to the Royal Navy and do away with the need to press-gang men. It first met on 25 June this year at the King's Arms tavern in Cornhill. The society concentrated on the funding and equipping of boys — there was a large pool of unemployed labour, but there was to be no coercion. It still exists to 'encourage boys to consider making their careers in the Merchant Navy upon which the prosperity of the nation so largely depends'.

LOCAL GUARDS

The records of the quarter sessions of this period show that life was becoming increasingly dangerous in and out of towns. Highway

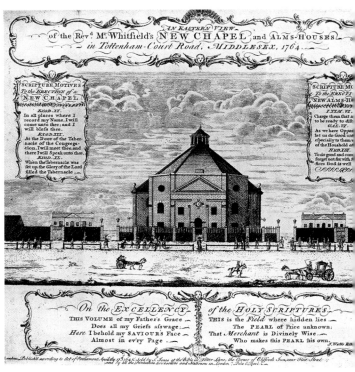

George Whitefield's second tabernacle in Tottenham Court Road. This view of 1764, shows the octagonal addition of 1759.

robbery, stripped of its romanticism, was a menace, and robbery by the less glamorous footpads was still more common.

Local communities formed guards to combat this. The inhabitants of Kentish Town, for example, paid voluntary subscriptions in 1756 to mount a guard or patrol to protect foot passengers to and from places, especially during the winter. By 1753 Blackheath, one of the more notoriously dangerous places, had a fund to offer rewards for the conviction of highwaymen and footpads. The extent of the problem may be imagined by the report in 1759 of a highwayman who robbed three coaches on Blackheath in one day.

1757

CHANGES AT LONDON BRIDGE

The construction of Westminster Bridge had inevitably pointed up the disadvantages of the picturesque but patched-up medieval London Bridge. Overhanging houses still lined the sides, and the carriageway was very congested. There was no popular sentiment to keep the old bridge, but the cost of completely rebuilding it was more than the City wanted to afford. Instead it was suggested that the houses be removed and the roadway be widened to 33 ft, with footways of 6 ft on each side. Despite all visible evidence to the contrary, the City's adviser, George Dance the Elder, was of the opinion that the main structure was sound and with the usual maintenance would last for many years.

It was decided to proceed with Dance's scheme, and a temporary oak bridge was constructed, running alongside the old structure, so that work could begin. This was opened in October, though work began on the demolition of the houses in the February before.

CONSTRUCTION OF THE LORD MAYOR'S COACH

The present Lord Mayor's Coach, which most of the time today gleams magnificently in the Museum of London, was completed this year. It was designed by Sir Robert Taylor and built by Joseph Berry. Each alderman was required to contribute £60 towards the total cost of £1,065. The paintings on the panels are attributed to Giovanni Battista Cipriani.

1758

FIRE ON THE TEMPORARY LONDON BRIDGE

Between 10.00 and 11.00 on the night of 11 April it was discovered that the temporary wooden London Bridge (see 1757) was ablaze; it was very badly damaged. Not only was that part of London left without a way of crossing the river on foot now that the old bridge was being rebuilt, but the debris in the river made it unsafe for a time for ships to come near. Despite rewards offered, no culprit for this disaster was ever discovered.

About 500 men were employed day and night to rebuild the temporary structure. Within a week foot passengers could get across, and by October carriages were permitted.

LOOKING AFTER THE ORPHANS

The Orphan Working School was founded on 10 May by 14 men meeting at the George inn, Ironmonger Lane. In the early days the intention was less to educate the children than to teach them to work. The inmates were taught shoemaking, garden-net making etc., and their employment went on for eight hours a day. Several years elapsed before anything but reading and religion was taught. The institution began in some houses in Hoxton, but moved in 1773 to a street off the City Road, where it stayed until 1847, when a large building on Haverstock Hill, Kentish Town, was erected.

LOOKING AFTER THE PROSTITUTES

The Magdalen Hospital for 'the relief and reformation of penitent prostitutes' began this year in a house in Prescot Street; its founders included the ubiquitous Jonas Hanway (see 1756) and the blind magistrate

Sir John Fielding. When Horace Walpole went there 'The Magdalens sung a hymn in parts, you cannot imagine how well', and the unfortunate Dr Dodd, who was later hanged for forgery (see 1777), gave a sermon.

A spacious building for this institution was later erected on St George's Fields on a site now occupied by the Peabody Estate in Blackfriars Road.

HOOVES THROUGH ISLINGTON

Islington was the gateway for much of the cattle traffic on its way to Smithfield – in Islington High Street today the depth of the roadway from the pavement is probably the result of many years of pounding as drovers manoeuvred their herds down to St John Street. It was estimated (presumably from turnpike figures) that 30,952 oxen and 200,180 sheep went through in 1757 and 28,602 oxen and 267,567 sheep in 1758.

1759

BRITISH MUSEUM OPEN TO THE PUBLIC

When Sir Hans Sloane died in 1753, he directed in his will that the immense collection of books, manuscripts, coins and botanical specimens at his Chelsea home should be offered to the government for a bargain price of £20,000. If this were not accepted, then the collection would be broken up and sold privately. An unusually sympathetic House of Commons agreed to buy on the advice of a committee that recommended the collection be 'kept intire, and maintained for the Use and Benefit of the Publick'.

At the same time as Sloane's collection was bought, the Harleian manuscripts, amassed by the 1st and 2nd earls of Oxford, became

Montagu House, from the garden, bought by the nation to house the British Museum. It opened to the public in a small way in 1759. To the right are the main hall and staircase, illustrated by Pugin and Rowlandson in 1808.

available, and the government was persuaded to buy these too, for £10,000. (Unfortunately the 2nd earl's collection of 50,000 books, 400,000 pamphlets and 41,000 prints was sold elsewhere by his family, which had been left short of money because of the collecting obsession of the two earls.)

But where to put this vast amount of material? The nation already owned (since 1700) Sir Robert Cotton's collection – which included thousands of manuscripts, cartularies and coins as well as copies of the Lindisfarne Gospels and the Magna Carta – but, since purchase, this had deteriorated in damp and poor conditions, virtually inaccessible to scholars. The commissioners investigated two buildings – Buckingham House (which later became Buckingham Palace) and Montagu House in Great Russell Street. The latter was chosen, and this simple decision probably determined the eventual character of the neighbourhoods of those two houses.

The first Montagu House had been built for the 1st duke of Montagu in 1675, but was destroyed by fire 11 years later. Montagu next hired a French architect, Puget, whose new building was in the style of a French *hôtel*. It was this house, together with its 7½ acres, that the government bought to house its collections, which were later augmented by George III's library of 65,000 volumes.

The museum first opened to the public on 15 January 1759, when only eight readers turned up. It was open for three hours a day to general visitors of whom the principal librarian approved and who had written in advance stating the day and time of their visit. These rules applied until 1808, and only in 1879 was general access allowed.

THE SPAS OF KING'S CROSS

The area that is now King's Cross was once famous for its medicinal springs and wells. St Pancras Wells, now covered by railway arches in Pancras Road, was probably the first to be exploited. By 1730 a trader in the City was offering to deliver 'Pancras and Bristol waters at 6s a dozen'. The sceptical were invited to view the 'Five Stones, together with one considerably larger than either, all voided almost instantly by drinking of the Pancras mineral waters'.

The Bagnigge Wells were opened in 1759. This establishment was very near the Fleet river, west of the King's Cross Road, and attached to a large residence called Bagnigge House. It became the best-known of the local spas. Discovery of the qualities of the water stemmed from the observation of the owner of the ground in 1757 that the more he watered his garden using the well's water, the less it thrived. A local doctor found that the water was chalybeate – quite an attraction in the eighteenth century: it was the equivalent of finding oil on one's estate.

Water cost 3d a gallon, although a season ticket at half a guinea was available. There was a pump room in the shape of a temple, and other attractions included skittles, a bowling green and a fountain. The banqueting hall of the old house, measuring 78 ft by 28 ft, had been turned into the Long Room, in which there were promenades, concerts and assemblies. In the grounds the aquatic nature of the place was emphasized by the use of a water organ.

North of this was St Chad's Well, entered between what are now nos. 364 and 366 Gray's Inn Road. The name was a dedication to St Caeadda, first bishop of Lichfield and patron saint of healing springs. The water here was strongly impregnated with sulphates of soda and Epsom salts, and also cost 3d a gallon; the headmaster of a school in Kentish Town used to march his boys down to it once a week, on the supposition that drinking it was cheaper than doctors' bills. St Chad's Place now covers the gardens, but the pump room survived until the construction of the Metropolitan Railway in 1860.

A BRIDGE AT KEW

The first bridge across the Thames at Kew was built this year. It was the project of Robert Tunstall, proprietor of the local ferry. Designed by John Barnard, the bridge had 11 arches – four of stone and seven of timber – the central arch having a span of 50 ft.

THE BEGINNINGS OF THE ROYAL ACADEMY

The Society of Dilettanti had proposed in 1749 that an academy for artists be founded, but nothing had come of the suggestion. On 5 November 1759 a proposal was made at a meeting of artists at the Foundling Hospital that an annual exhibition be held 'in order to encourage Artists whose Abilities and Attainments may justly raise them to Distinction and that their several Abilitys may be brought to Public View'. A committee formed after this included Joshua Reynolds, Francis Hayman, Richard Wilson and William Chambers, and a first exhibition was held at the Society of Arts, in the Strand. But it was to be another nine years before what became the Royal Academy, and its annual exhibition, became established.

A NEW BUILDING FOR THE LONDON HOSPITAL

The London Hospital, occupying some houses in Featherstone Street (see 1740), soon outgrew its modest beginnings. A move to Prescot Street was a slight improvement, but it was evident that a large, purpose-built hospital was needed. The governors paid the City Corporation £2,000 for the Mount Field on what was then the rural Whitechapel Road, just east of Mile End Green. The hospital was partially opened in 1757, but not finished until 1759.

THE MODERNIZATION OF WHITEHALL

The opening of Westminster Bridge and the consequent extra traffic along Whitehall meant, inevitably, that the colourful Holbein Gate had to be taken down. It had already survived many calls for its demolition – Sir John Vanbrugh in 1714 had pleaded against 'destroying one of the greatest Curiositys there is in London'. Unfortunately the planned re-erection of the gate in Windsor Park did not take place.

1760

A NEW KING PROCLAIMED

George II died on 25 October, and on the following day his grandson was proclaimed George III before Savile House, his home in Leicester Square. The assembly there included the great officers of the state as well as dignitaries from the City of London. As was customary, the proclamation was repeated at Charing Cross, at Temple Bar, at Cheapside and at the Royal Exchange.

THE GATES COME DOWN

The City at last took steps to abolish the anachronism of the London gates, which now served only to cause annoyance. The structures of Cripplegate, Ludgate and Bishopsgate were either sold or demolished this year.

EXECUTION OF A LORD

The treat for London ghouls this year was the execution of the 4th Earl Ferrers. An unstable man, he deliberately shot his steward in January this year, when vexed at a matter of estate business. He was tried by his peers in Westminster Hall in April, but his plea of

A particularly vindictive caricature of Mrs Cornelys, published in 1776.

temporary insanity was not accepted and he was unanimously sentenced to death. His execution on 5 May drew one of the largest ever crowds to Tyburn. He was dressed in a light suit of clothes, embroidered in silver, and was driven there in his own landau, drawn by six horses. His body was duly dissected at Surgeons' Hall and was then privately buried beneath the belfry of St Pancras church, from where, in 1782, his remains were disinterred and removed to Leicestershire. Ferrers was the last nobleman to be executed as a criminal in this country.

ENTERTAINMENT AT CARLISLE HOUSE

The most fashionable assembly rooms in London began this year in the house of Mrs Cornelys. She resided at Carlisle House on the east side of Soho Square (the site of today's St Patrick's church), which had originally been the house of the 2nd earl of Carlisle, built in 1685.

Theresa Cornelys was a Viennese actress and opera singer, and at times a courtesan: Casanova claimed paternity of one of her children. She had arrived for the second time in England in the company of an obscure but reasonably well-off musician, who had the idea of setting her up as hostess of an elegant assembly rooms in which dances and masquerades were the order of the night. So successful was the venture that she had to extend the premises. But, although the rooms continued to be popular, she was always hard pressed for money.

Her success lasted, somewhat perilously, for nearly a decade.

Eventually the twin attractions of Almack's Assembly Rooms (see 1764) and the nearby Pantheon in Oxford Street (see 1772) were to force her to close.

A MANSION ON PICCADILLY

One of the last surviving mansions on today's Piccadilly is that at no. 94, until recently occupied by the Naval and Military Club and popularly called the 'In and Out' Club, from the words on the gateposts. Designed by Matthew Brettingham, its first occupant, in 1760, was Lord Egremont, who set a new fashion for living in the western section of Piccadilly. A later resident was Lord Palmerston.

NEW BUSINESSES

The famous Hamleys toyshop originated this year, when William Hamley opened the 'Noah's Ark' at 231 High Holborn.

In Homerton, Lewis Berger began making paints, utilizing an artesian well he rented.

Two brothers from Milan, Paul and Dominic Colnaghi, established in London their art-dealing business.

THE COCK LANE GHOST

The credulous of London were attracted to a house in Cock Lane, near Newgate Street, this year, to a series of fraudulent seances conducted by Richard Parsons, the parish clerk of St Sepulchre without Newgate. The affair had begun in 1759, when Parsons had let out rooms in the house to a William Kent and a Miss Frances. The latter subsequently died, apparently of smallpox. Evidently some dispute then arose between Kent and Parsons, for in 1760 Parsons announced that his daughter, Elizabeth, was hearing in the house knockings from beneath her bed which a 'medium' had interpreted as the ghost of Miss Frances telling the world that she had been poisoned with arsenic by Kent.

Crowds flocked to the seances, and caused sufficient disorder for the City Corporation to set up a committee of inquiry (on which Dr Johnson sat). The committee thought that the whole thing was a fraud, and threatened Parsons and his daughter with imprisonment unless the seances stopped.

1761

OPENING OF THE CITY ROAD

The New Road having been built from Paddington to Islington (see 1756), its extension, the City Road, was constructed by one Charles Dingley from the Angel down to Finsbury Square. It was opened on 29 June this year.

THREE MORE GATES DEMOLISHED

Aldersgate, Moorgate and Aldgate were all demolished this year. Ebenezer Mussell, a resident of Bethnal Green, bought Aldgate and rebuilt it as an additional wing to his own house.

MUTINY AT THE SAVOY

Part of the old Savoy Palace building in the Strand was used as a military prison, in particular for any deserters due to be shot in Hyde Park. In 1761 over 200 prisoners here mutinied and a considerable battle developed. The *Universal Register* noted that 'An unconcerned spectator looking down from the roof was unfortunately taken for one of the rioters, shot and killed on the spot.'

BEAR AT THE BRIDGE FOOT DEMOLISHED

A celebrated tavern was the Bear at the Southwark end of Old London Bridge. It was probably built c. 1319 by the inaptly named Thomas Drynkwatre. Pepys went there in 1665 when he was 'full of wind and out of order', and he also records how 'the mistress of the Beare tavern, at the bridge-foot, did lately fling herself into the Thames, and drowned herself'. In 1761, as part of the demolition of houses on the bridge, the Bear itself was swept away.

1762

SOUTHWARK FAIR ABOLISHED

One of the more unruly sights of London was the annual summer fair in the Borough High Street. Conveniently, it followed on from Bartholomew Fair, and so the traders could pack up their stalls and goods at Smithfield, cross the river, and lay them out in Southwark.

One feature of Southwark was the acrobats. Each year a Mr Cadman, for example, would walk across a rope slung across the street from St George's church tower to the Mint opposite, until he met his death on some daring escapade across the Severn at Shrewsbury. John Evelyn described how he 'saw 'Monkyes and Apes daunce, & do other feates of activity on the high-rope' and how they 'turned heales over head, with a bucket of Eggs in it, without breaking any'.

Fortunately, Hogarth was on hand in 1733 to record his famous picture of events there, because in 1762 the City authorities abolished the fair, although in 1763 constables had to be called out to remove some stalls which had been set up in the usual place.

HANGING SIGNS BANNED

Contemporary prints of London streets show a forest of hanging signs depicting trades and professions. Without street numbering, and indeed without proper street naming, a sign was a necessity and had the extra advantage of being intelligible to the illiterate. There were, however, disadvantages. Such a vast number cut out daylight, and because of their size and frequency they could cancel out each other's usefulness; furthermore, they could be dangerous if not securely fixed.

It was enacted this year that hanging signs in the City and Westminster should be removed and be fixed instead to the face of the building – forerunners of the modern shop fascia. This followed similar legislation in Paris in 1761. Further regulations followed as other parishes were empowered to take such action.

Public houses seem to have disregarded the legislation altogether, and traditional signs such as the barber's pole and the pawnbroker's three balls continued.

A NEW SET OF BOW BELLS

The peal of bells installed in the church of St Mary-le-Bow at its rebuilding after the Great Fire were noted as being particularly fine. Strype, writing in 1720, says that 'for the number and melody of the bells, Bow, since the fire, surpasseth former times'. In 1762, however, a new peal of ten bells was installed, and was rung for the first time on 4 June, the King's birthday. They became the most famous of the church bells of London.

BUCKINGHAM HOUSE TO THE ROYAL FAMILY

Buckingham House in St James's Park, with its extensive grounds, was bought for £28,000 this year by George III for a residence of the dowager queens, who had previously lived in Somerset House. The title was transferred to Queen Charlotte in 1775 in exchange for her interest in Somerset House, which was needed for the Royal Academy.

The Duke of Buckingham put on paper a long description of his house. The entrance hall was 'Paved with square white stones mixed with dark coloured marble, the walls of it covered with a set of pictures done in the school of Raphael. On the ground floor at the back was a suite of four large rooms, 'including a bed chamber, 34 ft by 27 ft, within it a large closet, that opened into a greenhouse' in which the duke slept occasionally on warmer nights.

The house eventually became Buckingham Palace.

THREE NEW CLUBS

Three well-known men's clubs had their origins this year. The *Survey of London* (vol. 29) records that William Almack began a dining club in Pall Mall in January. In 1764 (q.v.) one of his managers, Edward Boodle, set up his own establishment next door at no. 50, and also two of his partners, Brooks and Ellis, ran a club called Almack's in Almack's tavern at no. 49, which in 1778 moved to St James's Street and became Brooks's Club. Almack himself opened the Almack's Assembly Rooms in King Street in 1764 (q.v.).

1763

THE JOHN WILKES AFFAIR

This year began the political upheaval caused by the activities of John Wilkes. It was to result in constitutional argument and riots in the streets.

Wilkes had been born in 1727 into a family made wealthy by a distillery in Clerkenwell. He married well (at least in financial terms, though emotionally the marriage was over very quickly), but in his thirties he was still pursuing such childish activities as the satanic rites devised by Sir Francis Dashwood. Wilkes bought his way into Parliament in 1757 (it cost him £11,000) and served as a supporter of Pitt until Bute became prime minister in 1762. From then on Wilkes was a frequent and vociferous critic of the government, using pamphlets and his own periodical, the *North Briton*, to deride and lampoon his ex-colleagues and the king at the same time. Matters came to a head in 1763 with edition no. 45 of the *North Briton*, when it was thought that his criticism of the king's speech from the throne was libellous. On 30 April Wilkes was arrested in London and committed to the Tower; his house was ransacked for incriminating material. On 6 May he was freed by Lord Chief Justice Pratt, to popular acclaim.

This, however, was not the end of the matter. Political tempers were running high, and the government was far from popular with Londoners. In November Wilkes was accused by Parliament of printing an obscene and impious libel, and on the same day the king ordered that no. 45 of the *North Briton* should be burnt by the public hangman as a seditious libel. The issue had become one of freedom of speech, and the burning of the paper outside the Royal Exchange provoked a riot in which the sheriff inside his coach was attacked by the mob. Pieces of the 'libel' were rescued from the flames and set up in triumph at Temple Bar that night. A jackboot, a derisory symbol of the prime minister, was set on fire there. (One of Islington's eccentric residents, the scholar Alexander Cruden, was so enraged by Wilkes's behaviour that he went around the area erasing the number 45 wherever he could find it.)

James Boswell (1740–95) – a portrait published in 1808.

Dr Samuel Johnson (1709–84), after the portrait by Sir Joshua Reynolds.

This was not the only excitement, for also in November Wilkes had been challenged to a duel in Hyde Park by the MP for Camelford, Samuel Martin; Wilkes was wounded in the stomach by a bullet.

More drama was to unfold the following year.

SERIOUS FLOODING OF THE THAMES
On the Surrey side of the Thames, houses by the river were flooded with 4 or 5 ft of water, and residents in Tooley Street were stranded in the upper rooms. Westminster Hall was once again flooded, to a depth of 4 ft.

RIOTS AT COVENT GARDEN
David Garrick, who had already faced mob hostility (see 1755), was this year at its sharp end again. Garrick had stipulated that a production of his at Covent Garden Theatre should remain at full price no matter what time in the performance someone paid to attend. This was contrary to usual practice, whereby it was possible to pay half-price after the third act. One Kirkpatrick appointed himself head of a set of young men about town to protest against this new restriction and caused riots at the theatre on 23 and 24 January.

DEATH IN THE RIVER FLEET
In January the *Annual Register* recorded that 'A man was found in Fleet Ditch standing upright and frozen to death. He had, it seems, unfortunately mistaken his way in the night, and slipped into the mud; and being in liquor could not disentangle himself.'

SILKWEAVERS RIOT
The *Annual Register* noted that 'Several thousand journeymen weavers assembled in Spitalfields, and in a riotous and violent manner broke open the house of one of the masters, destroyed his looms, and cut a great quantity of rich silk to pieces, after which they placed his effigy in a cart with a halter about his neck, an executioner on one side and a coffin on the other; they then drove it through several streets, hanged it on a gibbet, and burnt it to ashes; which having proved a sufficient vent for their fury, they dispersed of themselves without further mischief.'

RIOT AFTER A HANGING
Cornelius Saunders was hanged for stealing £50 from the house of a Mrs White in Spitalfields. His body was carried and laid before her door. A great crowd of people assembled and proceed to ransack the house in revenge for the execution, removing the furniture into the street and burning it.

A FAMOUS MEETING
One of the most famous meetings, equivalent to that between Livingstone and Stanley, occurred this year, when the eminent Dr Johnson met the timorous James Boswell. It took place at the bookshop of Tom Davies at 8 Russell Street, Covent Garden. Boswell describes it thus:

Mr. Thomas Davies, the actor, who then kept a bookseller's shop in Russel-street, Covent-garden, told me that Johnson was very much his friend, and came frequently to his house, where he more than once invited me to meet him; but by some unlucky accident or other he was prevented from coming to us …

At last, on Monday the 16th of May, when I was sitting in Mr. Davies's back-parlour, after having drunk tea with him and Mrs. Davies, Johnson unexpectedly came into the shop; and Mr. Davies having perceived him through the glass-door in the room in which we were sitting, advancing towards us, — he announced his awful approach to me, somewhat in the manner of an actor in the part of Horatio, when he addresses Hamlet on the appearance of his father's ghost, 'Look, my lord, it comes!'

Davies, knowing Johnson's aversion to Scotsmen, mischievously told Johnson that Boswell was Scots, and Boswell in some embarrassment said, 'I do indeed come from Scotland, but I cannot help it.' 'That, Sir,' replied Johnson, 'I find, is what a very great many of your countrymen cannot help.'

1764

HOUSE NUMBERING BEGINS
About this time the numbering of houses began – coinciding with the gradual removal of hanging signs. One historian claims that it was first introduced in New Burlington Street, followed by Lincoln's Inn Fields. However, another historian says that in 1763 the residents of New Burlington Street actually began the use of brass plates on their doors with their names and titles engraved on them; this fashion was followed by most of the streets in the area.

More tidying up occurred in 1765, when the City was obliged to affix name tablets to the corners of each street, lane or square, though it was six years or so before this legislation was effective.

MOZART IN LONDON
The eight-year-old Mozart arrived in London, together with his parents and sister, on 23 April, when they stayed for the night at the White Bear, Piccadilly. They moved the next day to lodge with a barber in Cecil Court, off St Martin's Lane, where they remained until August, after which the family moved to Ebury Street, where, it is reputed, the young composer wrote his first two symphonies. Leopold, his father, unwell at the time, wrote to a friend that they were on the edge of London and that he had been carried there in a sedan chair, 'in order to get more appetite and fresh strength from the good air'. They left at the end of September and moved to 20 Frith Street, where they stayed until 24 July 1765. The *Public Advertiser* for 11 March 1765 states that 'For the Benefit of Master Mozart, of eight Years [he was actually nine], there will be performed at the End of this Month, or the Beginning of April next, a Concert of Vocal and Instrumental Music. Tickets at Half a Guinea Each … '

THE WILKES AFFAIR CONTINUED
John Wilkes was expelled from the House of Commons in January for republishing the offending edition of the *North Briton*. In February, in his absence, he was found guilty of libel and subsequently outlawed. By now Wilkes had fled to France, where for some time he lived with a courtesan.

BROOKS'S AND BOODLE'S CLUBS FOUNDED
The club now called Brooks's had its origins in Almack's club (see 1762), but in 1764 it was a separate enterprise called Almack's in Almack's Tavern. Only from 1771 were the rates paid by 'Brooks and Ellis', although evidently still in partnership with Almack. When the club moved to St James's Street in 1778, however, it became known as Brooks's Club. There were 27 founder members, and originally the rules barred members of other clubs, except White's. Its main attraction was the gambling for high stakes. Horace Walpole commented that 'the gaming at Almack's which has taken the *pas* of White's, is worthy the decline of our Empire, or Commonwealth … The young men of the age lose five, ten, fifteen thousand pounds in an evening there.' Charles James Fox, an inveterate gambler, was elected a member in 1765, when he was only 16; he lost money heavily, and at one time borrowed from the waiters.

Edward Boodle, apparently an early manager of Almack's dining club of 1762, set up his own club next door, at 50 Pall Mall, in 1764, possibly in partnership with Almack. Boodle's Club moved to its present club house at 28 St James Street in 1783. Its members have included the duke of Wellington, Beau Brummell and Edward Gibbon.

1765

SADLER'S WELLS REBUILT
A Thomas Rosoman had bought the declining asset of the Sadler's Wells music house in 1746, and in 1765 he rebuilt it in a more substantial form, capable of being used as a proper theatre. The seats had ledges at the back of them for the audience to rest their glasses and bottles; a 1773 advertisement quoted the prices of 3s for a box and 1s 6d for the pit, which included a 'pint of Port, Mountain, Lisbon, or Punch'. The new building was opened on 8 April.

WEAVERS ON THE MARCH AGAIN
The agitation of the Spitalfields weavers reached new heights, with numerous demonstrations and processions in the West End. The most serious occurrence was the attack on the house of the duke of Bedford in Bloomsbury Square in retaliation for his opposition to a bill laying additional customs duties on imported silks. St James's Palace also received a deputation. A procession heralded by a black flag went to the palace to emphasize the distress of the weavers and their families, brought low by the cheapness of imports. However, the king had already gone to Richmond, and some of the deputation followed him there.

In May a three-pronged march from Spitalfields met at Westminster, with the marchers stopping carriages and making their point to anyone they could. Generally the demonstration was peaceful, but more damage was done at Bedford House, and a silk merchant in Ludgate Hill had his windows broken.

THE GREAT CORNHILL FIRE
A fire in 1748 had already consumed the western end of Cornhill, but this year another fire broke out, in the house of a peruke maker, it seems, and this was to be even more serious. It began on the morning of 7 November in Bishopsgate, just north of the corner with Cornhill and Leadenhall Street. It was eventually to leap across the road, where it destroyed all the property backing on to Merchant Taylors' Hall and part of the hall itself, and then across Leadenhall Street. At one time all the four corners of the crossing were on fire. A notable casualty was the church of St Martin Outwich, whose interior was destroyed, along with 51 houses.

NEW BUSINESSES
The old-established company of Price's Candles in Battersea can trace its origins to the establishment this year of the firm of James Wheble, candle manufacturer, in Kensington High Street, on the site of Barker's store.

A FRUSTRATED CROWD
A French visitor, M. Grossley, recorded an outbreak of violence in Seven Dials this year:

Happening to go one evening from the part of the Town where I lived, to the Museum, I passed by the Seven Dials. The place was crowded with people waiting to see a poor wretch stand in the pillory, whose punishment was deferred to another day. The mob, provoked at this disappointment, vented their rage upon all that passed their way, whether afoot or in coaches and threw at them dirt, rotten eggs, dead dogs, ordure, which they had provided to pelt the unhappy wretch according to custom.

1766

FOUNDATION OF CHRISTIE'S
About this year the auctioneer James Christie established his business in Great Castle Street; his first known catalogue was issued in December 1766 for a sale at an auction room in Pall Mall. He was not to be in Great Castle Street long, for in June 1767 he took premises in Pall Mall itself, at an unidentified address, and in 1768 he moved again, to new premises on the site of the Royal Automobile Club.

A FIGHT IN BUNHILL FIELDS
In May the *Annual Register* noted that 'A severe battle was fought between a lamplighter and a baker in Bunhill Fields which lasted one hour and five minutes, when the latter was obliged to yield to his antagonist with the loss of an eye and four guineas; the sum agreed to be paid the conqueror.'

NEW CHAPELS
Proprietary chapels of some importance were built in this period. Percy Chapel in Charlotte Street was built for one William Franks and opened in January this year. The first incumbent, the Revd Anthony Matthew, entertained the young John Flaxman as well as William Blake at his house in Rathbone Place. The new chapel served the growing population on each side of Tottenham Court Road, but was to achieve its main popularity with the building of nearby Fitzroy Square later in the century. The building stood on the site of nos. 15–17.

The impetus for private chapels was the lack of parish church accommodation over and above the parish church itself. This was the case in St Pancras, where for most of the time the old St Pancras church in the south of the parish was closed, leaving parishioners the long trek to Kentish Town to worship. It was not surprising that parishioners used the Foundling Chapel or Percy Chapel instead.

A similar problem obtained in St Marylebone, where the duke of Portland was exploiting the same situation: with the population grown to some 70,000, the one parish church and the odd chapel were nowhere near sufficient to cope. Portland was eventually to build three chapels, each bringing in pew rents. These were the Portland Chapel in Great Portland Street (built in 1766), the Welbeck Chapel in Westmoreland Street (1774) and the Brunswick Chapel in Upper Berkeley Street (1795). There were other private chapels in Baker, Quebec, Chapel and Margaret streets.

THE WILKES AFFAIR CONTINUED
With Wilkes still banished abroad, a bookseller, John Williams, was convicted of republishing the infamous edition no. 45 of the *North*

This illustration, by Pugin and Rowlandson (c. 1809), shows James Christie's auction house in Pall Mall, on the site of today's RAC clubhouse.

Briton (see 1763). He was fined £100, jailed for six months, and sentenced to stand in the pillory at Old Palace Yard. However, it is reported that 10,000 supporters of Wilkes surrounded him in the pillory, and so no punishment was ever carried out there.

THE WEAVERS CELEBRATE
This year a bill was passed which prohibited the importing of French-made silks. On their way home from celebrating in Westminster, the Spitalfields weavers halted at the Mansion House, their bands playing 'God Save the King'; at home most of the houses were illuminated for the evening, and there were bonfires and fireworks in the streets.

However, throughout the country there was severe distress due to a harvest failure and a dearth of bread; the export of corn was prohibited. In June, 400 haymakers had assembled at the Royal Exchange petitioning for help as heavy rains had put them out of work. Severe frost lasted from mid-December through to January, which only increased the misery, as meal boats could not get near the London docks for ice, and numerous fund-raising efforts were made to alleviate hunger.

SPENCER HOUSE COMPLETE
This handsome house at 27 St James's Place, overlooking Green Park, had a violent beginning. John Vardy had been commissioned to build the house, but his client, Henry Bromley, 1st Baron Montfort, in financial difficulties, shot himself minutes after signing his will and with his lawyer still leaving the house. Ownership of the site came into the hands of Earl Spencer, and building at last began in about 1756. It seems likely that it was complete by 1766.

1767

POPULAR EXECUTIONS
At a time when midwives were trying to resist the gradual takeover of their traditional work by men, their cause was not helped by the

celebrated conviction for murder of Elizabeth Brownrigg, a midwife who lived in Fleur de Lis Court off Fleet Street. She had been appointed midwife to the local workhouse and there had three apprentices, all of whom she treated inhumanely. One was found dying at Brownrigg's house, resulting in a murder charge. Brownrigg was hanged to popular acclaim at Tyburn on 14 September, and her skeleton was exposed at Surgeons' Hall in the Old Bailey so 'that the heinousness of her cruelty might make the more lasting impression on the minds of the spectators'.

In January a crowd estimated at 80,000 (though these estimates should not be taken too literally), many of whom were women, gathered to watch the execution at Moorfields of a man found guilty of causing the death of his wife by ill-treatment. The crowd had to be restrained from lynching the man.

INTRODUCTION OF THE PIANOFORTE

The first public notice indicating the introduction of the piano into England is on a playbill for Covent Garden Theatre dated 16 May 1767; as a solo instrument the piano appears to have made its debut the following year, with J. C. Bach as the pianist. Its invention is usually attributed to Cristofori of Florence earlier in the century, and it was the first keyboard instrument on which the strings were struck by hammers, so giving a greater range of tone than plucking.

DR HUNTER'S ANATOMY THEATRE

The dissection of corpses was fraught with taboos and religious considerations. It was widely thought that the dismemberment of criminals at the gallows after hanging would preclude them from ever resting in peace; the logical extension was that those criminals whose cadavers were increasingly used by surgeons for the study of anatomy met the same fate. Until the passing of an Act in 1752, only six bodies of criminals were available to anatomists each year, but, with the growing skills of surgeons, and their need to practise, this number was clearly insufficient. The Act, which provided bodies of all executed murderers to the surgeons, seems to have had in mind the greater punishment of the criminal rather than the benefit to scientific knowledge, and dissection was described as a 'further Terror and peculiar Mark of Infamy'.

The leading anatomist of the age was Dr William Hunter, who this year opened his School of Anatomy at 16 Great Windmill Street, in a building designed for him by Robert Mylne; the first lecture took place in October. In theory this school breached the monopoly in dissection which was held by the Royal College of Surgeons, and the lack of 'official' corpses must have been a problem for Hunter. This shortage is highlighted by a report this year of body-snatching, which was by no means a new offence, but was to grow in frequency throughout the rest of the century. It was recorded that 'The Burying-Ground in Oxford Road [Bayswater Road], belonging to the Parish of St George's, Hanover Square, having been lately robbed of several dead bodies, a Watch was placed there, attended by a large mastiff dog, notwithstanding which on Sunday last some villains found means to steal out another dead body and carried off the very dog.'

1768

UNREST IN THE CAPITAL

The Spitalfields weavers had only been briefly appeased. There was much tension in their quarter of London and in Saffron Hill over the continued introduction of machine looms, which, of course, reduced

The Adelphi provided not only residences, but a wharf on the Thames from which goods were transported beneath the houses directly to the Strand.

the amount of labour needed. A similar dispute was fomenting further east, in Limehouse, where the sawyers burnt down Dingley's sawmill for the same reason. In May sailors in the Port of London struck for more wages, and there were also stoppages among glass grinders and journeymen tailors. An effigy of the prime minister, Lord Bute, was burnt in the streets of the City.

THE WILKES AFFAIR CONTINUED

John Wilkes returned from his exile in France and announced his intention to stand as member of Parliament for the City in the forthcoming election. On 23 March he was placed last of seven in the poll, despite support on the streets. He also stood for election for the county of Middlesex, and when the poll was declared at Brentford on the 28th he was elected. His supporters accompanied him in triumph to London, creating havoc on the way. At the Mansion House every window was broken, and the cry 'Wilkes and Liberty' resounded throughout London.

To restore himself to full citizen's rights, Wilkes went through the process of surrendering himself to the law, which, in his absence abroad, had outlawed him. He was formally arrested, committed to jail, rescued on his journey there by his supporters, but gave them the slip and continued to the King's Bench prison. On 10 May a vast assembly of his supporters gathered at St George's Fields, ostensibly to escort him to the opening of Parliament that day, but blood was shed when troops were called in to quell the crowd.

On 18 June the lord chief justice overturned the outlawry conviction but sent Wilkes to prison for 22 months, fined him £1,000, and required recognizances for good behaviour. Wilkes appealed against this sentence and continued to wage a campaign on his own behalf from prison.

BEGINNINGS OF THE ADELPHI

Only remnants now survive south of the Strand of the magnificent development called the Adelphi; this had its origins this year in the sale of the site by the duke of St Albans to the Adam brothers, James, Robert, John and William (the Greek 'adelphoi' means 'brothers').

Previously, Durham House and its grounds had occupied the land.

The river was embanked as part of the scheme, infuriating the City of London, which claimed ownership of the Thames foreshore. The Adam brothers erected a series of arched vaults along the river, partly to support the development behind and above them, partly to counter the slope of the site towards the river, and partly to allow access of merchandise (particularly coal) direct into the Strand. Parts of those vaults may still be seen from near York Buildings.

The centrepiece, overlooking the river, was a twin row of 11 grand houses back to back, Royal Adelphi Terrace, with two large single houses on either side. This spectacular group was demolished in the 1930s. The finest house surviving is that at 8 John Adam Street, occupied since 1774 by the Royal Society of Arts. Number 7 Adam Street, the former offices of *The Lancet*, is also representative of the quality of houses which existed. Elsewhere in the development was work by Giovanni Battista Cipriani and Angelica Kauffmann.

ROYAL ACADEMY ESTABLISHED

The Royal Academy of Arts was founded this year, with Sir Joshua Reynolds as its first president and the architect Sir William Chambers as its treasurer. Other founding members included Gainsborough, Richard Wilson and Benjamin West. There were two aspects to the project: a school and a regular exhibition of members' work. Some apartments at Somerset House were made available for the school — early students included Turner and Constable — and exhibitions were held in a house at Pall Mall. When Somerset House was rebuilt in the 1770s the Academy was given its own set of rooms fronting the Strand, and it was possible here to hold much larger exhibitions than previously.

JOHN MURRAY FOUNDED

The publisher's John Murray was founded this year, when John Murray, having retired from the navy, bought the publishing and bookselling business of William Sandby at the Sign of the Ship, 32 Fleet Street, commenting that 'many blockheads in the Trade are making fortunes, and did we not succeed as well as they, I think it must be imputed only to ourselves'.

Held at Somerset House, the Royal Academy's summer exhibition was one of Georgian London's highlights.

Blackfriars Bridge being built in 1766. Officially known as William Pitt Bridge, it was designed in nine elliptical arches by Robert Mylne.

1769

BLACKFRIARS BRIDGE OPENED

The construction of Blackfriars Bridge was preceded by the making of Farringdon Street and New Bridge Street along the squalid and hazardous valley of the Fleet river as it went down to the Thames. On the south side of the bridge, Blackfriars Road (then called Great Surrey Street) was laid out to Newington Butts, and this encouraged considerable development in what were then open fields, especially to the east.

The first pile of the bridge had been driven in 1760; pedestrians were allowed across the structure in 1766, and horses in 1768. The bridge, consisting of nine arches, was officially opened at midnight on 18 November this year. It was designed by Robert Mylne at a cost of £230,000.

THE WILKES AFFAIR CONTINUED

John Wilkes was this year elected as an alderman for the ward of Farringdon Without in the City, but his eligibility was questioned by the Court of Aldermen, which declined to send him notification of his election. At the end of 1768 Wilkes had petitioned Parliament about his grievances, but in February 1769 he was expelled the House of Commons for claiming that the loss of life at St George's Fields the previous year had amounted to a massacre.

A further parliamentary election was held for Middlesex, and Wilkes once again won with a large majority. But his opponent was declared elected — a decision which provoked unrest in Westminster and the City, where Wilkes's supporters were numerous and dangerously excited. Six hundred merchants of the City marched to St James's to support the government in its expulsion of Wilkes, only to be pelted with mud by the crowds.

WEAVERS EXECUTED

The weavers once again rioted in Spitalfields. In July many people were injured and about 150 looms were damaged. Two of the ringleaders were tried and condemned to death; their procession led from the

1700s

prison at Newgate through to Bethnal Green, where they were executed. A crowd attacked the men building the gallows.

A BREWERY IN FULHAM

The Swan Brewery was founded in Walham Green this year by Oliver Stocken on the site of a manor house; the White Swan pub is now on the site. The business flourished, and its product was considered 'better than any fourpenny ale to be obtained in Fulham'.

THE GREAT VINE PLANTED

The famous Great Vine, still remaining at Hampton Court, was planted by Lancelot 'Capability' Brown this year.

THE KING'S OBSERVATORY

George III inherited Richmond Lodge in 1760 upon the death of his grandfather. As part of his grandiose plans to build a new palace here, the king bought all the houses of 'West Sheen' and demolished them to improve his views. In addition he had an observatory built in 1769, so that he could watch the transit of Venus across the sun in June.

A NEW LLOYD'S COFFEE HOUSE

A parting of the ways occurred among the merchants, underwriters, shipowners and speculators who made up the insurance business centred at Lloyd's Coffee House on the corner of Abchurch Lane and Lombard Street. This was signalled by an advertisement in the *Public Advertiser* on 20 March this year:

To the Merchants in general, Owners … of Ships, Insurance Brokers etc., etc. Thomas Fielding, Waiter from Lloyd's Coffee House begs acquaint them that his House in Pope's Head Alley, Lombard Street is now genteely fitted up and will open for the reception of Gentlemen, Merchants, etc. Tomorrow the 21st instant by the name of New Lloyd's Coffee House, where he hopes to receive their favours.

It is apparent that the patrons of the new house were the more progressive and professional men in the trade, and their ambition to be more than just a collection of people meeting for business in a public coffee house resulted in a new association (see 1771).

1770

THE WILKES AFFAIR CONTINUED

John Wilkes was this year released from the King's Bench prison and in April he was admitted as an alderman in the City of London. His fortunes had now turned. Though he had entered the King's Bench virtually ruined, on release he was the most celebrated man in London, with his effigy on thousands of souvenirs and broadsheets.

THE CITY CONFRONTS THE KING

The City Corporation and the king were at odds over a recent Middlesex parliamentary election which, the City claimed, had been subject to government skulduggery. The lord mayor, the immensely rich William Beckford, a supporter of Wilkes, presented an address at St James's Palace, drawing the attention of the king to the matter. The king replied with a reproof. Two months later Beckford, in the name of the City, presented a remonstrance, this time in person to the king, who once again dismissed it curtly. Beckford on impulse ventured to reply to this – an unheard-of piece of lese-majesty, leaving a red-faced

George III stunned at the impudence. Beckford, at one time threatened with imprisonment for his action, died the same year. The short speech of his which so upset the king was engraved around the base of the statue erected to him in the Guildhall in 1772.

NEW AIDS TO HEALTH

Two maternity hospitals of some importance had been established in recent years. The General Lying-in Hospital at Lambeth had opened its doors in April 1767, and in 1770 the foundation stone of the City Lying-in Hospital was laid at the corner of City Road and Old Street.

An important development in the improvement of health of the poorer classes was the beginning of the Free Dispensary movement. A typical dispensary was formed from the subscriptions of wealthier people and was funded to give medical attention and medicine to poor people who could obtain a letter of recommendation from one of the subscribers. The first establishment of this kind was founded in Red Lion Square in 1769, and in 1770 the General Dispensary in Bartholomew Close was opened.

SPECTATORS BANNED FROM BEDLAM

The principal lunatic asylum in London, the Bethlehem Royal Hospital, had long been a tourist attraction. Visitors were permitted to amuse themselves watching the antics of the inmates at 1d a time, from which the Hospital derived about £400 a year. However, the antics and behaviour of the visitors often made the inmates more unsettled, like animals provoked at a zoo. From this year the admission of such voyeurs was prohibited.

DEATH OF A POOR POET

The death, mentioned above, of William Beckford, lord mayor of London, had a bearing on one of the more famous suicides in literary history. A 17-year-old poet, Thomas Chatterton, had just obtained the promise of a personal interview with Beckford, whose patronage he sought. Because of Beckford's death the meeting did not take place, and Chatterton – unstable and in abject poverty – 'was perfectly frantic and out of his mind, and said he was ruined'. He had gradually been losing heart since coming to London from Bristol in April; he probably earned only about £12 in May and June. Rejection and poverty had a disastrous effect on him. Though literally starving, he declined all offers of food from friends, and when he changed his lodgings from Shoreditch to Brooke Street, Holborn, in June this neglect of his own welfare continued.

On 24 August his landlady, Mrs Angel, knowing that Chatterton had not eaten for three days, begged him to dine with her, but proudly he refused. He did not appear the next day, and when his door was broken down he was found dead with a nearly empty phial of arsenic in his hand. At the inquest, held at the Three Crows on 27 August, Mrs Angel, a sackmaker, said that Chatterton had lodged with her for eight or ten weeks in a room beneath the garret. He made, she said, one stale loaf last a week.

Chatterton was buried in the grounds of the Shoe Lane workhouse on 28 August. In the burial register he is listed as 'William Chatterton', and another hand has added the word 'poet'.

A SPA IN BERMONDSEY

The unpromising terrain of Bermondsey was enlivened by a spa this year, when a budding artist, Thomas Keyse, developed the potential of a chalybeate spring and added the attraction of his own pictures. Music and fireworks were featured, and on one occasion 4 acres of ground were given over to a pyrotechnic version of the Siege of Gibraltar. The spa closed a few years after the death of Keyse in 1800, and the only reminder now is Spa Road.

CONSTRUCTION OF THE LEA CUT

The river Lea, the old boundary between Middlesex and Essex, joined the Thames at Poplar, on the bend of the river where the East India Docks were sited. This was a disadvantage for traders using the barges coming down from Hertfordshire, because it was too far east of London docks and, what is more, entailed a long trip around the Isle of Dogs to the Pool of London. This year the Lea Cut was opened across open fields, from Bromley down to Limehouse on the west side of the Isle of Dogs.

1771

A NEW LLOYD'S COFFEE HOUSE

Following the schism among the insurers and shipping merchants in 1769 (q.v.), an announcement appeared on 13 December this year, with the backing of 79 men: 'We, the underwriters do agree to pay our several subscriptions into the Bank of England in the Names of a Committee to be chosen by ballot for the building of a New Lloyd's Coffee House.' In each putting in £100 the underwriters were establishing their own independent association, without the patronage of coffee-house owners. A list of subscribers from 1771 until 1800 shows a collection of shipowners, merchants, underwriters, bankers and brokers. In the early days their leading figure (who had also led the secession from the old premises in 1769) was one Martin van Mierop, a Dutchman.

It was, however, to be a few years before they were to move away from the clubbable atmosphere of a coffee house to do their business.

THE WILKES AFFAIR CONTINUED

In the continuing hostility between the City and the government and king, John Wilkes played a major part. One dispute, already mentioned, was the permission granted by the Commons to the Adam brothers to embank the Thames near the Adelphi site, which the City claimed infringed its jurisdiction over the Thames foreshore. A new row erupted over the printing and publication in the City of reports of the debates in the House of Commons, which Wilkes had instigated. Two printers were ordered to appear before the bar of the House, but they disregarded the order. Other printers were similarly summoned, but all of them sought and obtained the protection of the lord mayor, and the City arrested the messenger from the Commons who had come to detain the printers.

On two occasions immense crowds escorted a very sick lord mayor to make statements in the Commons. The second time Parliament had him put in the Tower. Wilkes himself was summoned three times to the bar of the House, but refused unless he was confirmed as MP for Middlesex. The lord mayor was released from the Tower on 8 May to a rapturous reception. There were processions through the City and at night the streets were illuminated.

Later in the year Wilkes was elected as a sheriff in the City, and, although he was to be taken up and supported by 'Junius' of the *Gentleman's Magazine*, his relations with prominent dignitaries and other friends were to deteriorate. More importantly, a new lord mayor was elected in November who was no friend of Wilkes.

AN OBELISK AT ST GEORGE'S CIRCUS

The new junction of roads at the southern end of Blackfriars Road, called St George's Circus, was this year graced by the erection of an obelisk to mark the opposition of the lord mayor, Brass Crosby, to the House of Commons in the matter of the printing of parliamentary debates.

THE HOLOPHUSIKON IN LEICESTER SQUARE

This year Leicester House in Leicester Square, once a royal home, was taken by Sir Ashton Lever, who filled 16 rooms of it with a bizarre collection of fossils, shells and stuffed animals which he called the Holophusikon. The collection was open to the public each day at the extraordinary price of 5s 3d per person.

Lever was decidedly eccentric if not quite mad. Fanny Burney records that in 1782, when she visited the house, Lever and two young men were each

dressed in a green jacket, a round hat, with green feathers, a bundle of arrows under one arm, and a bow in the other, and thus accoutred as a forester, he pranced about; while the younger fools, who were in the same garb, kept running to and fro in the garden, carefully continuing to shoot at some mark, just as any of the company appeared at any of the windows.

The collection was disposed of in 1786, and by 1789 was at the Rotunda in the Blackfriars Road. It was unsuccessful there as well.

THE BEGINNINGS OF GIEVES & HAWKES

The tailor's Gieves & Hawkes, at 1 Savile Row, began this year when Hawkes set himself up as a military tailor – he was later to fit out the duke of Wellington. The Gieves part of the business was a naval tailor, founded in 1785 in Portsmouth by Melchizedeck Meredith, and which later moved to Old Bond Street.

1772

THE PANTHEON OPENS

One of the most celebrated assembly rooms in London opened this year. The Pantheon was in Oxford Street, on the present site of the eastern branch of Marks & Spencer (which is called the Pantheon still). Its aim was to act as a 'winter garden', to be an indoor version of the lavish pleasure gardens such as Ranelagh now so popular in London.

The main room, designed by James Wyatt, was a very large rotunda modelled on that of St Sophia, Constantinople; grouped around this were 14 other rooms. Over 1,500 people were present when it was opened on 27 January, and immediately it became *the* venue for dances and masquerades. Horace Walpole thought it 'the most beautiful edifice in England', and Edward Gibbon said that it was the wonder of the British Empire. He relates in a letter that in 1774 Boodle's club held a masquerade there which cost 2,000 guineas – 'a sum that might have fertilized a province'.

RIVAL ATTRACTION IN TOTTENHAM STREET

What in modern times became the Scala Theatre began this year as concert rooms, a venture under the management of Francis Pasquali. It was to go through a large number of alterations and names during its existence.

1700s

THE FIRST LYCEUM

The Lyceum Theatre originated this year in a building designed to hold exhibitions for the Incorporated Society of Artists. It was designed by James Paine.

PRESSING ABOLISHED AT NEWGATE

Newgate prison, which was slowly being rebuilt, still had the facility of a press room. In here prisoners who stayed mute and refused to plead were tortured by the simple process of chaining them flat on the floor and gradually laying heavy weights on them. This practice was abolished this year and the press room was scrapped in the rebuilding.

ELY PALACE SOLD

Ely Palace in Holborn had been regained in the 17th century by the bishops of Ely for their town house, but it seems to have been used for a number of different purposes since then, including a temporary prison. In 1761 it was described as standing on open ground, with 'before it a spacious court and behind it a garden of considerable extent; but it is so ill kept that it scarcely deserves the name. The buildings are very old and consist of a large hall, several spacious rooms and a good chapel.' Within a few years the bishops were trying to sell the building, and a scheme was mooted to move the Fleet prison there. Four hundred parishioners of St Andrew, Holborn, petitioned against the scheme and won.

In 1772 the bishop managed to sell the estate to the Crown, and at the same time his new town house was built at 37 Dover Street to a design of Sir Robert Taylor. The new house still stands, but what remained of the old palace at Holborn was swiftly demolished. A property speculator, Charles Cole, pulled down everything except the chapel (now St Etheldreda's) and constructed a cul-de-sac, Ely Place, which is one of the most unexpected and charming of London enclaves.

1773

STOCK EXCHANGE ESTABLISHED

Stock brokers and jobbers had had a bad reputation. Defining a jobber in his *Dictionary*, Dr Johnson had written, 'a low wretch who makes money by buying and selling shares of stock'. In 1697 an Act, limited to ten years, restricted the numbers of brokers and jobbers and instigated a licence system which was to be managed by the City. Brokers paid a fee, entered into a £500 bond, and had to keep a register of deals. Further regulation was thought desirable after the chaos of the South Sea crash in 1720; two years later about 150 brokers set up an organization which exclusively rented Jonathan's Coffee House, but this was a shortlived scheme. In 1773 brokers established the Stock Exchange at New Jonathan's Coffee House in Threadneedle Street, but this time put up their own sign. Though its facilities were open to all, brokers were regulated by a committee.

A MENAGERIE IN THE STRAND

Apart from the small collection of animals at the Tower of London, the first public menagerie in London appears to be that established, in a small way, at Exeter Change, an odd arcade which was in the Strand, about where Burleigh Street is today, and which at first-floor level extended well over the footpath. It was a shopping development which was struggling for survival and was now used for miscellaneous purposes. In the auction room here in 1772 the body of Lord Baltimore

The interior of the first Lyceum. The building was originally a place for concerts and exhibitions for the Incorporated Society of Artists.

was laid in state, but he was so unpopular that as soon as it was removed the mob broke in and plundered the room. About 1773, and possibly before, a menagerie existed here, taking up the ground floor of the arcade. It was eventually managed by Edward Cross, and the Cross Menagerie was to be the best-known zoo before the establishment of London Zoo, moving to larger premises in 1829.

SEVEN DIALS PILLAR REMOVED

In July this year the pillar at Seven Dials (see 1694) was taken down in the mistaken belief that a considerable sum of money lay beneath. The pillar was taken to Sayes Court, Addlestone, for re-erection, but this never happened. It lay neglected until bought by the parishioners of Weybridge in 1820 to commemorate the local residence of Frederica, duchess of York.

PENTONVILLE BEGUN

Inevitably the New Road from Paddington to the City inspired building development on this new perimeter to north London. One of the first planned estates was that of Pentonville, east of today's King's Cross, which was on land owned by Henry Penton, MP for Winchester. Though commanding an excellent view over London, this new suburb, like Somers Town soon after it, was not a success, despite an early population of 'gentlemen and affluent tradesmen'.

1774

THE WILKES AFFAIR CONTINUED

Wilkes had already stood for the mayoralty of the City in 1772; he had won most votes, but had been rejected by the Court of Aldermen. However, this year he was again top of the poll, and no way could be found to oppose him. As always, Wilkes inspired enormous enthusiasm among the populace. In the struggle to be one of those drawing his coach through the streets of London, one man was killed; at the inquest, the culprit was adjudged to be the wheel which ran over him and, still governed by the ancient law of deodand, the jury judged the actual wheel guilty of the death and instructed that the City be fined 40s – the value of the wheel.

The same year a new general election took place and Wilkes once more stood for Middlesex, where he had been repeatedly deprived of his seat by the exertions of Court and Commons. Again Wilkes was overwhelmingly voted in, and this time he was allowed to take his seat.

NEW FIRE ENGINES

An Act of 1774 instructed all parishes within the area of the bills of mortality, plus St Pancras, St Marylebone and Chelsea, each to buy two fire engines, a leather pipe, three or more ladders and some lamps. The St Pancras vestry recorded the purchase of two large fire engines and one small one together with buckets, hose and materials. The expense of this and the rewards already given to persons attending fires amounted to nearly £200, and as the Poor Rate was insufficient to pay for this a special rate of fourpence in the pound was levied.

The possession of fire engines did not, however, guarantee much action anywhere in London. There were no full-time firefighting forces, and in the event of a blaze it was necessary to get the engine out of its shed, find the foreman, round up labour, and connect a water supply. The magistrate Sir John Fielding emphasized the last requirement:

And who is there that ever attended a fire in this metropolis on its first onset, that did not find cause to lament the want of water? Confusion, the common consequence of this alarming affliction, renders those nearly interested incapable of assisting themselves. The panic spreads, the fire plug is not to be found, the turncock is not at home or perhaps drunk, the fire rages, the fireman stands gnawing his fingers, with his engine ready to play, and the general cry is for water.

A NEW BUILDING ACT FOR LONDON

The Act which made provision for more firefighting equipment also consolidated the various Building Acts and added new requirements. It had already been enacted (in 1707) that the front elevation should extend above roof level to a parapet wall, and (in 1709) that window frames were to be recessed at least 4 inches from the external wall face. The Act of 1774 divided houses into four 'rates' and laid down building specifications for all of them. This Act, and the fact that most development at this time was on large estates subject to the conditions laid down by estate developers, ensured that the architecture of this period is one of uniformity and restraint.

FULHAM FLOODED

One of the highest tides ever known flooded the whole of Fulham town on 12 March.

A NEW HOTEL IN COVENT GARDEN

The Palladian house which is today numbered 43 King Street, Covent Garden, was this year converted into the Grand Hotel. It was intended for a wealthy clientele, with a top price of 15s a night for a suite of two rooms. Bedrooms were added at the rear of the building, and a door was made from the arcaded walk of the piazza. That door, though now blocked up, may still be seen at the end of the modern arcade which joins the house's flank wall.

FREEING OF A SLAVE

A young woman appeared before City magistrate John Wilkes. During questioning, it appeared that her husband, a black slave, had been in England for 14 years and had worked without wages all that time. Wilkes discharged the man from his slavery, and proceedings were set in hand to extract money from his master in lieu of wages for the period.

1775

THE BEGINNINGS OF BEDFORD SQUARE

Though agreements for the first houses in Bedford Square were not signed until 1776, it is likely that building was begun in 1775. It was the most substantial development since the creation of the Adelphi, which had left the Adam brothers virtually bankrupt and reduced to disposing of the houses there by lottery. Though conditions had been difficult for developers in the preceding five years, important and good-class houses were still being built in Berners Street and Grafton Street, and even in Finsbury Square; we have already seen that small developments such as Ely Place were under way, and its West End counterpart, Stratford Place, was also taking shape. And now, after much hesitation, part of the Bedford estate was released for development – there was no better place for an extension to London than in the lower reaches of Bloomsbury.

It was to be the most perfect of the London squares of the period. In fact the original plan of the old 4th duke of Bedford was for a 'Bedford Circus', but he died in 1771 and by the time his executors signed the first leases the more traditional square was back in favour. No conclusive evidence of the architect responsible for the houses' design is available. The name most consistently suggested is that of the estate's surveyor, Thomas Leverton, but a recent book, *Bedford Square*, by Andrew Byrne (1990), concludes that it is certain only that he designed the exterior of one of the houses.

Each side of the square is treated as one unit, the centre of each being adorned by a pediment astride Corinthian pilasters. An interesting feature is the doorways, which made extensive use of the new Coade artificial stone.

CONCERT ROOMS IN HANOVER SQUARE

A concert hall and ballroom were this year opened on the east side of Hanover Square by Sir John Gallini, formerly a manager of Italian opera. An early attraction was Johann Christian Bach, as we learn from a letter to the earl of Malmesbury in February:

Your father and Gertrude attended Bach's concert, Wednesday. It was the opening of his new room, which by all accounts is by much the most elegant room in town; it is larger than that at Almack's … 'Tis a great stroke of Bach's to enter-tain the town so very elegantly. Nevertheless Lord Hillsborough, Sir James Porter, and some others [who live nearby], have entered into a subscription to prosecute Bach for a nuisance, and I was told the Jury had found a bill against him.

THEATRICAL DEBUTS

Two important theatrical debuts occurred this year. Sarah Siddons, then aged 20, made her first appearance on a London stage when appearing as Portia in *The Merchant of Venice* at Drury Lane Theatre.

The first performance of *The Rivals* by Sheridan was at Covent Garden Theatre on 17 January. It failed on its first night and was withdrawn; after revision it was performed again at the end of January and has since been a consistent favourite.

LONDON AND THE AMERICAN COLONIES

George III and his advisers were pursuing a policy of disastrous taxation and restrictions in the American colonies. The City of London was opposed to the government's actions, thus perpetuating the long-running battle between the City and the Crown. A bill was introduced into Parliament to restrict the colonists' trade to Britain and to other

British colonies, which the Common Council claimed was unjust, cruel, partial and oppressive. When a further bill was passed restricting the trading activities of the Southern colonies the City presented a remonstrance to the king, who replied that he was astonished that the City should so encourage the disobedience of the colonies. The City was strongly opposed to armed force being used against the Americans, and the imposition of laws in the colonies without the colonists' consent. On 11 October a petition signed by 1,171 gentlemen and merchants of the City in favour of the Americans was presented to the king, but a few days later he was also sent a petition signed by 941 men in support of the government's actions.

THE UNBURIED WIFE

A Mr Van Butchell advertised in the *St James's Chronicle* in October that anyone who wished to see the embalmed body of his wife should make an appointment. The body was kept in his sitting room, and remained there until the widower remarried and his new wife, anxious to be rid of her predecessor, had the corpse removed to Surgeons' Hall. Here it remained until it was destroyed in the bombing of 1941.

1776

THE FIRST FREEMASONS' HALL

Great Queen Street today is dominated by buildings erected by Freemasons. The original Freemasons' Hall, opened on 23 May this year, was built on part of the site of today's Connaught Rooms to a design by Thomas Sandby. This was still standing in 1914, when it was described as having an interior like a Roman Doric temple, its walls enriched by pilasters.

A FIREPROOF HOUSE ON PUTNEY HEATH

The inventor and statesman David Hartley the Younger this year built a house on Putney Heath which he claimed was fireproof. To underline its qualities, he invited royalty and other notables to sit in the upstairs part of the house while he set light to the downstairs. He was also a well-known opponent of the war with America, so it is even more surprising that royalty was persuaded to try the experiment. Everyone emerged unscathed.

GARRICK'S LAST APPEARANCE

The popular actor David Garrick, who had arrived in London in 1737 with Dr Johnson, both of them then unknown, this year made his last appearance on the London stage. On 10 June he played the part of Don Felix in a play called *The Wonder, a Woman Keeps a Secret*, at the Theatre Royal Drury Lane. It was a gala night, attended by many admirers, and the receipts went to charity.

DANGERS ON THE ROAD

The records of the Middlesex and City of London Sessions indicate how much the offence of highway robbery had grown during this century. With poverty and privation rife and the lack of even a rudimentary police force in the area, this was hardly surprising. The *Annual Register* in 1772 had commented that 'villainy is now arrived to such a height in London, that no man is safe in his own house' – a fact taken to heart by, for example, the parishes of Hampstead, Camberwell and Stoke Newington, all of whom obtained Lighting & Watching Acts in this period. In 1776 the lord mayor of London in his chaise and four,

and within sight of his full retinue of attendants, was robbed near Turnham Green by a single highwayman.

A TRAGEDY IN FULHAM

Quite a few instances are recorded of people, thought to be dead, being found alive just as they were about to be buried. A less fortunate occurrence is recorded at Fulham this year:

The body of a coachman found without any of the common signs of life … in a stable at Fulham to which he went a few days before in a seeming state of good health to put up his horses, was buried at that place. But when the funeral was over, a person insisting that during the performance of the service he heard a rumbling and struggling in the coffin, the earth was removed, and the coffin taken out of the grave; when, on opening it there appeared evident proofs that the unhappy man, though then absolutely dead, had come to himself as his body was very much bruised in several places some of which were still bleeding, and there appeared besides a quantity of blood in the coffin.

A REPOSITORY FOR HORSES

One of the best-known places in which to buy a horse and carriage in London was Aldridge's Horse Bazaar, or Horse and Carriage Repository, in Upper St Martin's Lane. This stood on the west side, a site now taken by Orion House. Long Acre nearby was full of places in which to buy carriages, and it briefly became a street of car showrooms in the early days of motorized transport.

The first Aldridge was at this address in 1776. The first building was demolished in 1843, when the road was widened, and its attractive Grecian successor was lost *c.* 1955. An 1895 description of Aldridge's business says that it was a

well-known mart for nearly all kinds of horses, except racers. It is, however, specially famous for the sale of middle-class and tradesmen's horses. As soon as the West End season is over, the London job-master sells off his superfluous stock, and this market is the recognized medium for getting rid of the horses for which he has no further, or, at any rate, no immediate use. Many horses sold at this period are purchased by seaside men, whose harvest is about to commence.

1777

RICHMOND BRIDGE COMPLETED

The owner of the ferry at Richmond had proposed building a timber bridge across the Thames in 1760, but it was not until 1774 that a start was made on a stone structure designed by James Paine and Kenton Couse. Pedestrians were able to cross it in 1776, but vehicles had to wait until January this year.

It was financed by two issues of tontine shares – a system by which the total dividend was divided among the surviving shareholders until the last one died. Until that time, in 1859, the toll levied for the use of the bridge was the same as for the old ferry. The old bridge survives still, although in 1937 it was carefully widened by demolishing the upstream side, increasing the width of the carriageway and the arches beneath, and then replacing the old side of the bridge.

LAST LONDON GATE GOES

Newgate, the last of the old London gates, was this year demolished. During excavation in 1874/5, traces of the old Roman gate were found, which indicated that it was 31 ft wide.

The Vale of Health, Hampstead, in 1796, a view by T. Stowers. Until 1777, when it was drained, the area was a marshy swamp.

THE DODD FORGERY

London was gripped this year by the extraordinary trial of the preacher William Dodd for forgery. A popular writer of pious material, Dodd had once been tutor to Philip Stanhope, nephew to Lord Chesterfield. As his fortunes improved, he took a house in Southampton Row and another in Ealing to receive pupils from good families, and with money received from an inheritance and a lottery ticket he built the Charlotte Chapel in Pimlico. His reputation ran high in the fashionable classes, but his fall from grace came quickly. In 1774 he tried to bribe his way into the lucrative living of St George Hanover Square, and other scandals about him did the rounds. He was seriously in debt, sold the chapel, 'descended so low as to become the editor of a newspaper', and in February 1777 he committed the fraud that was to be his undoing. By forging the signature of the earl of Chesterfield he was able to borrow £4,200, but the offence was quickly discovered.

At first the authorities, having reclaimed most of the money and receiving assurances as to the balance, did not want to proceed, but the lord mayor insisted that they should. Dodd's trial attracted immense public interest. Dr Johnson pleaded for his life, a petition signed by 23,000 people asked for clemency, but the king declined. Dodd was hanged on 27 June at Tyburn, having made the traditional procession from Newgate.

BODY-SNATCHING IN BLOOMSBURY

It was revealed that many bodies, used for dissection, had been stolen from the burial ground of St George's, Bloomsbury, just north of the Foundling Hospital, with the connivance of the gravedigger and his assistant. These two were sentenced to six months' imprisonment and a public whipping from Holborn to St Giles's, a distance of half a mile, though the last part of this sentence was remitted because the authorities feared that the public would lynch the two on the way.

DRAINING A HAMPSTEAD MARSH

It is a popular misconception that the attractive enclave on Hampstead Heath called the Vale of Health derived its name from its use during the plague years as a healthy refuge. Like many legends, this one dies hard however many times it is proved to be wrong.

The area was, until 1777, a decidedly unhealthy marsh called Hatches Bottom. In this year the Hampstead Water Company, which supplied rather unsatisfactory water to London from the ponds on Hampstead Heath, created a fresh pond or reservoir here, and at the same time drained the area around. The first buildings – cottages for the parish poor, an indication of the lowly status of the place – appeared in 1779. The first reference to the name 'Vale of Health' is not until 1801, and it was no doubt either an ironic name, like that of the many Paradise Passages in slum areas of London, or else a title invented to rid the place of its reputation and attract house buyers.

ENCLOSURES

The enclosure of common lands was gathering pace as estate owners realized their potential for building development. It was not always possible for the local population to prevent this disposal of their grazing rights. In Enfield, for example, Enfield Chase, which had been used by the poorer cottagers for timber, pasture and pannage, was enclosed this year – to the acute distress of those who relied on this local facility. There were to be many celebrated disputes in future years over similar actions.

An enclosure of a different kind took place in Islington, where the unenclosed green had become a common dung heap and an eyesore. It contained also the parish lock-up and the fire-engine house. This year the lord of the manor granted the green to the parish, and it was enclosed with posts and rails to prevent nuisances.

NEW DEVELOPMENTS

Besides the building of Bedford Square (see 1775), some other important developments were taking place. Manchester Square was begun in 1776, framing Hertford House, the present home of the Wallace Collection. Originally it was planned to have a church in the centre of the square.

At 20 Portman Square, Robert Adam completed Home House in 1776 for the countess of Home. One of the most splendid of London houses, its rooms are rich with delicate stucco and inlaid woodwork, with paintings by Kauffmann and Zucchi, and the house is lit by a magnificent circular staircase hall reaching from ground level to the dome at the top. The countess, who was in her seventies when she acquired her new house, was renowned for her eccentric personality

James Lackington opened his bookshop in Finsbury Square in 1778. By the time of this view by Thomas Shepherd (1827), Lackington had long sold up.

and foul language, and was 'known amongst all the Irish chairmen and riff-raff of the metropolis by the name, style and title of Queen of Hell'. Until recently the house was used by the Courtauld Institute – the gift of Samuel Courtauld, a former owner.

A really speculative development was Finsbury Square, begun by George Dance the Younger in 1777 but not completed until 1791. Fanny Burney summed up the developer's gamble. She 'wondered that some very beautiful new buildings should be erected in Moorfields, in so shocking a situation as between Bedlam and St Luke's Hospital', and said *she* could not live there. But Samuel Johnson defended the development, and in 1778 James Lackington opened his renowned bookshop here; this was grand enough, it was boasted, to contain a central circular counter and leave room for a coach and four to drive round it.

In Chelsea, under the direction of the architect Henry Holland, work began on Hans Town. This development was to stretch from Knightsbridge to Sloane Square, and it was built well before Belgravia was conceived. The land had formerly been the property of Sir Hans Sloane, but the scheme was pursued by the 2nd Earl Cadogan, who had married a daughter of Sloane. Sloane Street was the core of the development – the houses on the east at this time having uninterrupted views towards St James's Park and Buckingham House.

THE SCHOOL FOR SCANDAL DEBUT

Sheridan, who had managed the Theatre Royal Drury Lane since 1776, this year produced his most popular play here. On 8 May *The School for Scandal* opened, but it was a near-run thing as it was very nearly suppressed by the lord chamberlain and only the intervention of Sheridan's patron, Lord Hertford, prevented this.

1778

WORKHOUSES FOR THE MASSES

The burgeoning population of London, and in particular the massive flow of people looking for work in the capital, put intolerable strains on the old ways of administering parishes. The conventional solution of what to do with the poor was to put them in workhouses, and about this period parishes were rebuilding or replacing their old buildings because they were now found to be inadequate. St Pancras took over the Mother Black Cap, on the site of today's Camden Town underground station, and converted it for poor use. In the parish of St Paul, Covent Garden, the old house in Exeter Street was overcrowded and no space could be found elsewhere, so in 1778 a site was taken in Cleveland Street, part of St Pancras, and a building, which included schools and cost £7,000, was erected. Like so many workhouse buildings, this became a hospital later on when the Middlesex took it over.

In Barnes the parish spent £1,000 on a similar venture, but for a much smaller population, and in Kensington the parish erected a house at Kensington Gate. Islington, in 1777, spent £3,000 on a 'commodious house' in what is today the western end of Barnsbury Street, which does not appear to have affected the quality of the later housing development in the vicinity.

PORTLAND PLACE BUILT

One of the effects of the construction of the New Road (see 1756) was the development of the Portland estate to its south. About this year Robert and John Adam designed Portland Place, a grand avenue of unusual width for London. Permission to lay it out in this way was

dependent on it being wider than Lord Foley's house at the southern end, so that he might still enjoy his view of the northern heights. The Langham Hotel is today on the site of Foley House.

TAX EVASION AT THE PRISON

Customs officials raided the Fleet prison this year and secured 2,491 lb of tea, 1,874 lb of coffee and 1,020 lb of chocolate, which had been smuggled into the building free of tax.

NEW BUSINESSES

Three well-known companies had their origins about this year. Booth's Gin Distillery was trading at the corner of Turnmill Street and Clerkenwell Road by this date. At 44 Wigmore Street, Flint & Clark opened their drapery shop; this business was later to be called Clark & Debenham, and later still Debenham & Freebody. The builder's Trollope & Colls was established this year too.

WESLEY CHAPEL OPENED

The Wesley Chapel on City Road was opened on 1 November, next to the house in which John Wesley lived and in front of the grave in which he was later to be buried. Robert Southey, in his *Life of Wesley*, records that at the ceremony of laying the foundation stone, in 1777, 'Great multitudes assembled. so that Wesley could not, without much difficulty, get through the press to lay the first stone.'

APSLEY HOUSE BUILT

Apsley House at Hyde Park Corner was completed this year for the lord chancellor, Henry Bathurst. It was designed by Robert Adam. Its association with the duke of Wellington began in 1808, when the lease was taken by his older brother, the Marquess Wellesley; Wellington lived here from 1816, and acquired its freehold in 1820. The Wellington family gave the house and its contents to the nation in 1947; it is now the Wellington Museum.

1779

A LARGE CHILD AT ENFIELD

Londoners delighted in freaks of nature, though often deceived. They were probably hoodwinked in the case, reported in a history of Enfield (1812), of a child born in the locality in 1779. It was claimed that at nine months he was 18 inches around the thigh, and his weight was guessed at 9 stone; his height was 3 ft 2 inches, and he had eight teeth. He was exhibited in London when 11 months old, by which time he had grown another inch. The child died in May 1780, aged 15 months.

MURDER BY A CLERGYMAN

The most celebrated crime of the year was the murder of Martha Ray, the mistress of John, 4th earl of Sandwich, by the Revd James Hackman. The clergyman had proposed to her without success, and on the evening of 7 April he shot her as she was leaving Covent Garden Theatre. He later failed in an attempt to kill himself, and was hanged at Tyburn on 19 April. In the mourning coach carrying the prisoner from Newgate was James Boswell, who quite enjoyed executions.

THE FUNERAL OF GARRICK

The actor David Garrick was given a remarkable funeral after his death in January. From his house at the Adelphi a procession went

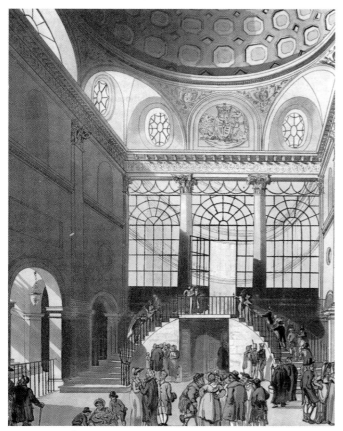

The interior of the Middlesex Sessions House on Clerkenwell Green, a view by Pugin and Rowlandson. The building is now occupied by the Freemasons.

through crowded streets to Westminster Abbey, where he was buried. The string of carriages extended from the Strand to the abbey, and the bishop of Rochester received the cortège. Pallbearers included Lord Camden and the duke of Devonshire; among the mourners were famous politicians such as Burke and Fox. Dr Johnson, Garrick's old tutor and friend, declared at the service, 'I am disappointed by that stroke of death which has eclipsed the gaiety of nations, and impoverished the public stock of harmless pleasure.'

A New Sessions House at Clerkenwell

The handsome building now occupied by the Freemasons which stands on Clerkenwell Green was begun this year. It was then the new Middlesex Sessions House, replacing Hicks's Hall in St John Street, which had been demolished in 1778. The architect was John Rogers, who, according to Pevsner, may have cribbed the design from the antiquarian John Carter.

1780

The Gordon Riots

Violence engulfed London this year. Ostensibly the so-called Gordon Riots were anti-Catholic and provoked by the passing of the Roman Catholic Relief Act in 1778, which restored some rights to Catholics, including that of land ownership. The Court of Common Council in the City was also opposed to such legislation and pressed for its repeal.

Leader of the anti-Catholic campaign was Lord George Gordon, a fanatic, who on 2 June headed a procession of thousands of blue-cockaded supporters through the streets of London to present a petition aimed at repeal. The mob, which no doubt included criminals and other disaffected people as well as anti-Catholics, was unable to obtain entry to Parliament. It therefore dispersed and attacked Catholic buildings such as the chapels attached to the Sardinian and Bavarian embassies, where the interiors were destroyed. On the 4th a crowd gathered at Moorfields and proceeded to a Catholic chapel in Ropemakers Alley, where they gutted the building; next day they returned and wrecked the schoolhouse and the houses of the priests nearby. The same day they destroyed the house of Sir George Savile, who had been responsible for the 1778 legislation. On the 6th the Bow Street magistrates' court was attacked. Another group went to Newgate prison and released prisoners, including those who had been committed there for rioting. The new prison, which had almost been finished, was destroyed by fire, and 300 prisoners escaped in the confusion.

The next target was the pro-Catholic Lord Mansfield, whose house in Bloomsbury Square was gutted and his furniture and books destroyed – soldiers were present but held their fire. Others set out with the intention of destroying Mansfield's other house in London, Kenwood House in Highgate, but there, under the influence of drink, they were apprehended. The house of Lord Justice Cox in Red Lion Square was also wrecked.

On the 7th the King's Bench, the Fleet and the Clink prisons were thrown open, as were the City compters and the Surrey Bridewell. The Clink was in fact burnt down and was never rebuilt. Fury even extended to the toll-house on Blackfriars Bridge; this was destroyed, ostensibly in protest against the tolls. The church of St Christopher le Stocks was garrisoned to guard the Bank of England, but generally the authorities were either powerless or thought it best not to intervene. Buildings were plundered without hindrance, many people got drunk, and some even died, insensible from alcohol, when a distillery in Holborn was set on fire. Shopkeepers, whatever their private feelings, shut up shop and plastered their shutters with anti-Catholic slogans.

It was not until the 9th that a warrant for the arrest of Lord George Gordon was issued. He surrendered quietly, but with the support of thousands of rioters.

As was usual in such matters, he escaped a capital conviction but others did not. Of 85 people tried at the Old Bailey, 35 were executed. The *Annual Register* calculated that over 450 people had been killed or wounded during the riots. It had been, as Dr Johnson said, 'a time of terror'.

First Sunday Newspaper

In an eventful year, the first Sunday newspaper in England was published. It was called the *British Gazette and Sunday Monitor*, and its proprietor was an E. Johnson, a London printer. In later years it was to become the mouthpiece of the religious sect which revered Joanna Southcott (see 1815).

Invention of the Toothbrush

At 64 Whitechapel High Street, William Addis set up business as a 'stationer and rag-merchant'. He invented the first toothbrush, made of bone and horsehair, which he sold through his contacts in the bookselling trade. Thus Addis became not only wealthy from his invention, but a great benefactor to a populace which suffered the scourge of tooth decay caused by the increased consumption of sugar. From this fortunate occurrence the company now called Addis is derived.

1781

NEW BUSINESSES

This year Robert Barclay bought the Anchor Brewery in Southwark, owned by Dr Johnson's close friend Hester Thrale after the death of her husband. Johnson, indeed, was one of the executors who handled the sale when Thrale died this year. When Johnson was asked what he thought the value of the business was, he replied, 'We are not here to sell a parcel of boilers and vats, but the potentiality of growing rich beyond the dreams of avarice.' The brewery had its origins in a brewhouse first noted in 1634. It was substantially enlarged by Edmund Halsey in the earlier part of the 18th century, and upon his death in 1728 it passed to his nephew, Ralph Thrale. The grounds of the brewery included the site of the Globe Theatre and the parish workhouse.

John Debrett, publisher, took over the business this year of John Almond, opposite Burlington House in Piccadilly. He seems to have inherited a publication related to the peerage, but it was not until 1802 that *Debrett's Peerage of England* was published.

The jeweller's and silversmith's Asprey & Co., in New Bond Street, originated with the calico and silk printing business set up by William Asprey in Mitcham about this year.

CHURCH DEMOLITION

The church of St Christopher le Stocks in Threadneedle Street was demolished to allow for the enlargement of the Bank of England. The old churchyard still exists within the walls of the bank, and it was because of this inbuilt security that special permission was given in 1798 for the burial here of Jenkins, a bank clerk, who was 6 ft 7 inches tall and whose corpse was much sought after by anatomists.

1782

SURREY THEATRE OPENED

The Bankside theatres had long gone, their attraction diminished by the thriving Covent Garden Theatre and Theatre Royal. But theatre, of an equestrian kind, returned to Southwark this year with the opening in November of the Surrey Theatre at 124 Blackfriars Road. It was opened as the Royal Circus and Equestrian Philharmonic Academy, but it was an unsuccessful and short-lived venture.

THE FIRST SHOPFRONT

The first recorded proper shopfront in London appears to have been that of a draper called Gedge, whose double-fronted shop, opened this year on the north side of Leicester Square, allowed passers-by to see the merchandise properly.

ESTABLISHMENT OF THE PHOENIX ASSURANCE COMPANY

Early in 1953, staff of the Phoenix Assurance Company found a locked wooden box in the vaults inscribed with the words 'Sugar Refiners Committee'. In this they found papers relating to sugar refiners of the 18th century onwards. It was no accident that the box should be with the Phoenix, because this insurance company had been established in 1782 by a group of refiners dissatisfied with the premiums charged by other insurance companies.

DEATH FROM LAUGHTER

A Mrs Fitzherbert began laughing during a production of *The Beggar's Opera* at the Theatre Royal. She was unable to stop, and gradually the whole audience became infected and joined in. She had to be removed from the theatre, still laughing, and she was unable to stop herself during the next day and a half; at the end of which she died.

1783

THE CARLTON HOUSE EXTRAVAGANZA

The conversion of the old Carlton House to be a short-lived residence of the prince of Wales, later George IV, was attended by controversy. The extravagance of the project and the endless calls for more money did not endear the future monarch to either Parliament or the people, much less to his own father. Work began on the house this year.

The original house, which stood at the southern end of today's Waterloo Place, overlooking Pall Mall on one side and St James's Park on the other, had been owned by Lord Carleton at the beginning of the 18th century, and was sold to the father of George III in 1732. George III made it over to his son, the prince of Wales, provided that he met its expenses. Although the gardens, which stretched westward on the land now occupied by Carlton Gardens, had been landscaped by William Kent and were much admired, the house itself was, as royal houses go, unremarkable. The future prince regent decided that he would transform it into a house for a future king. Under the guidance of the architect Henry Holland, who was commissioned in 1783, houses nearby were bought and demolished so that new wings could be added; a Corinthian portico was added (its columns are now in front of the National Gallery), and many rooms were decorated in fashionable chinoiserie.

A NEW NEWGATE PRISON

The new Newgate prison designed by George Dance the Younger had been nearly complete when it was burnt down by the Gordon Rioters in 1780. The walls were left, but little else. About 1783 this elegant, but soon to be squalid, building was completed much as it was before the riots.

The authorities took the opportunity to switch the traditional place of execution from Tyburn to the outside of the new prison. (At first the road junction at what is now Camden Town underground station had been considered, but it was thought to be too far from the jail.) For years the procession from Newgate to Tyburn had been the scene of civil disturbance and unrest, and it was thought that difficult situations could be handled better if the executions were just outside the prison walls. The last person to be hanged at Tyburn was John Austin, on 7 November. The first execution at Newgate under the new arrangements was on 9 December.

SURREY CHAPEL OPENED

Another new attraction in the Blackfriars Road (see 1782) was the Surrey Chapel, the creation of an itinerant, sometimes eccentric but well-known preacher, the Revd Rowland Hill. Attached to the chapel were 13 Sunday schools, which catered for 3,000 children. Hill was an evangelist, quite often at variance with the Established Church, and he was also a proponent of vaccination, which also made him unpopular with the general public at times. The chapel, opened on 8 June, was at the junction with Union Road.

A GIANT FOR THE SURGEONS

The fear of the bank clerk Jenkins (see 1781) that his unnaturally large corpse would find its way to the anatomists was fully justified. This year Charles Byrne, a 22-year-old Irishman, reputed to be 8 ft 4 inches tall when he died, had requested that his body should be taken out to sea and dropped in deep water to avoid being taken for the surgeons. A crew took out his body but evidently did not do as Byrne had wished, for the skeleton was in the Royal College of Surgeons until recent times.

FIRST BALLOON ASCENT IN ENGLAND

On 25 November the first balloon ascent, unmanned, was made from the Artillery Ground, Finsbury, launched by Count Zambecarri. The balloon landed 48 miles away at Petworth.

1784

A FOLLY AT SHOOTERS HILL

Severndroog Castle, the extraordinary folly at Shooters Hill, was built this year by the widow of Sir William James to commemorate his exploits against the Morattoe pirates, including the capture of the fortress of Severndroog on the coast of Malabar in 1755. Sir William had died in 1783 of apoplexy at the wedding festivities of his daughter.

FUNERAL OF DR JOHNSON

Dr Samuel Johnson died at his house in Bolt Court on 13 December and was buried in Poets' Corner, Westminster Abbey, near to the grave of his friend and pupil David Garrick, on the 20th.

FIRST MANNED BALLOON ASCENT

An attempt at a manned ascent in a balloon was made from the fields of what is now Belgravia in August. The aeronaut, a Frenchman called Dr Moret, did not get off the ground, as his balloon caught fire, but he disappeared with the takings from an expectant audience. The successful 'first' was that of an Italian diplomat, Vincenzo Lunardi, on 15 September. His red-and-white-striped balloon, filled with hydrogen, took off from the grounds of the Honourable Artillery Company in City Road. He landed at North Mimms, and then flew on to Ware, his name assured in the record books as the first man to fly in England. It was estimated that 100,000 people, including the prince of Wales, saw the launch.

1785

FOUNDATION OF THE TIMES

Numerous newspapers were founded in this period. On 1 January a new daily paper appeared called the *Daily Universal Register*; three years later it became *The Times*. Its proprietor, John Walter, claimed that the newspaper 'will be of no party, weakened as the country is by a long and expensive war, and rent by intestine divisions, nothing but the union of all parties can save it from destruction'. Competition was fierce, as Walter was also to admit. 'To bring out a New Paper at the present day, when so many others are already established and confirmed in the public opinion, is certainly an arduous undertaking.' The new paper consisted of four pages, over half of them taken by

The first (unmanned) balloon ascent from the Artillery Ground in 1783.

advertisements, and was printed by James Fleming in Printing House Square; its cover price was twopence-halfpenny.

LAMBETH WATERWORKS COMPANY FOUNDED

By the end of the 17th century a number of small undertakings supplied Southwark with water. William Paterson, who had founded the Hampstead Water Company, had acquired the right to supply the Borough area in 1693, and later this interest was bought up by the London Bridge Waterworks.

This year the Lambeth Waterworks Company was established, drawing its supplies from a site near today's Royal Festival Hall — it was not until 1847 that its intake was shifted upstream to Thames Ditton. Its territory was primarily Lambeth and adjacent parishes, but it was prohibited from supplying Southwark and the St George's Fields area.

STATIONERY OFFICE ESTABLISHED

The Stationery Office was established this year to supply the government with stationery, books and other forms of printing. Its original premises were in Buckingham Gate.

1786

SOMERS TOWN BEGUN

With Pentonville still being built, the next substantial development along the New Road was Somers Town, in the area of today's St Pancras

1700s

station. The land was owned by Sir Charles Cocks, who inherited the title of Lord Somers in 1784 and entered into building leases in the next few years. The principal developer was Jacob Leroux who laid out a grid of streets around the centrepiece of Clarendon Square, but his grand scheme was ruined by the outbreak of war with France in 1793. Inferior development then took place, much of which housed the growing number of French people fleeing from the Revolution.

FREEMASONS' TAVERN BUILT

A second building for Freemasons was built this year in Great Queen Street, next door to the original Freemasons' Hall. This was the Freemasons' Tavern, used for meetings and dinners. It was designed by William Tyler.

ALBION MILLS OPENED

The huge Albion Flour Mills were this year opened at the south-east end of Blackfriars Bridge. Designed by Samuel Wyatt, with the aid of the young John Rennie as engineer, the mills with their steam-powered engines became a tourist attraction. According to a contemporary observer, the two engines had the power of 150 horses. They drove 20 pairs of millstones, each 4 ft 6 inches in diameter, 12 of which were usually worked together, each pair grinding 10 bushels of wheat per hour, by day and night if necessary.

1787

VOYAGE TO AUSTRALIA

Transportation of convicts to the American colonies had been halted by the American War of Independence in 1776. Since then prisons had become crowded and prison hulks in the Thames had become a scandal. This year, in March, nine ships set out from London for New South Wales, bearing the first convicts transported to Australia. The original destination was Botany Bay, but eventually the prisoners were offloaded at Port Jackson, where Sydney now stands.

CRICKETING HISTORY

Two far-reaching events occurred in the small world of cricket this year. Thomas Lord, who seems to have earned his living by selling wine, leased from the duke of Portman land which is now covered by Dorset Square. He fenced it off and made it available to his friends who played cricket at the White Conduit Fields in Islington. The first recorded match on Lord's Cricket Ground was on 31 May this year, between Middlesex and Essex players for a wager of 100 guineas a side. At this time there were three stumps rather than the two previously used, there was one long bail, wides could be bowled without penalty, and leg byes were unheard of.

The Marylebone Cricket Club, the MCC, consisted of players from the White Conduit venue. The earliest minute book of the club records that it was founded in 1787, and in 1837 it celebrated its golden jubilee, so the establishment of the club in Marylebone must have happened when Lord offered them a ground. However, the club's first official match on the new turf was not until the following June, when they played against friends still belonging to the White Conduit Club.

KELMSCOTT HOUSE BUILT

What is now Kelmscott House, at 26 Upper Mall, Hammersmith, was built about this year. Its most famous resident has been William Morris,

who renamed it after his Oxfordshire house, Kelmscott Manor, and added many of its attractive features. An earlier resident was Sir Francis Ronalds, who invented the electric telegraph there in 1816.

A CHALLENGE TO THE PLAY MONOPOLY

The monopoly of Covent Garden Theatre and the Theatre Royal to present plays was challenged this year when the Royalty Theatre opened off Wellclose Square, near the Tower of London. No doubt the proprietor had hoped that the dedication to the monarch might help to overcome any objections to the infringement of his rivals' patent. *As You Like It* was the first production, and it was planned to carry on presenting proper plays. However, the lord chamberlain prevented this, and the management was reduced to pantomime and other trivia. The theatre was destroyed by fire in 1826.

1788

SUICIDE OFF THE MONUMENT

The first reported suicide by jumping from the top of the Monument appears to have been that of John Cradock, a baker, in July. In 1810 two more jumped – a diamond merchant and another baker. In fact bakers seem to have had a distinctly unfortunate association with the Monument, since, apart from the suicides already mentioned, the Great Fire of London which it commemorates actually began in a nearby bakehouse.

THE LAST BURNING

Jeremiah Grace and Margaret Sullivan, convicted of colouring copper coins to resemble silver, were both sentenced to be hanged at Newgate. The man was executed first. Then the woman was brought out, dressed in black, 'attended by a priest of the Roman persuasion. As soon as she came to the stake, she was placed on a stool, which after some time was taken from under her, and after being strangled, the faggots were placed around her, and being set fire to, she was consumed to ashes.' This was the last occasion that hanging was supplemented by burning.

CHURCH DEMOLITIONS

The church of St Peter-le-Poer in Old Broad Street, which had for long been a hindrance to traffic in the street, was this year taken down and rebuilt further back in its own churchyard.

The church of St James, Clerkenwell, which had been patched up in the 17th century after the steeple had fallen, was this year demolished and rebuilding began on 16 December; a medallion was struck to show both the old and the projected building. The new church was consecrated on 10 July 1792.

LINNEAN SOCIETY FOUNDED

The Linnean Society, now housed in Burlington House, was founded this year by James Edward Smith, a medical student and botanist. He had bought the extensive library and collection of the Swedish botanist Carl Linnaeus, who had died in 1778. It was decided that this valuable collection, housed in Smith's apartment in Paradise Row, Chelsea, should form the basis of a society specializing in the natural sciences, and so the Linnean Society was begun. The first meeting took place on 8 April in Smith's new house in Great Marlborough Street; there were soon 36 fellows, 16 associates and 50 overseas members.

1789

ENTERTAINMENTS ON THE THAMES

At the beginning of the year the Thames was frozen from Putney to Rotherhithe. At Shadwell on 9 January an ox was roasted whole on the ice, and on the same day, at Rotherhithe, a bear was baited.

SHAKESPEARE GALLERY OPENED

Number 52 Pall Mall was in 1788 taken by Alderman John Boydell, a wealthy City print-seller, and here he began the construction of a new art gallery. His intention was to commission all the best-known artists of the day to illustrate scenes from the works of Shakespeare. From these original works Boydell would make prints for sale. Painters such as Fuseli, West, Kauffmann, Romney and Opie were commissioned, and George Dance the Younger was appointed architect for the gallery.

The gallery did not open until June 1789, and Boydell spent about £100,000 on the venture only to be deprived of much of his overseas custom by the new war with France. Facing bankruptcy, he was obliged to obtain an Act of Parliament to sell the thousands of paintings and prints left on his hands by lottery. Just before he died, in 1804, 22,000 tickets had been sold.

ITALIAN OPERA HOUSE BURNS DOWN

Sir John Vanbrugh's Italian Opera House, or King's Theatre, in the Haymarket, burnt down on 17 June. It had been built on the site of a public house called the Phoenix, which was particularly apt since the replacement – what became Her Majesty's Theatre – was destroyed by fire in 1867.

SECOND KEW BRIDGE OPENED

In September, George III led a 'great concourse of carriages' across the new Kew Bridge. This stone bridge, replacing the old timber structure, was designed by James Paine, who had also designed the new Richmond Bridge.

DULWICH TOLL-GATE

The only toll-gate now to survive in London – much to the surprise of unfamiliar motorists – is that across College Road in Dulwich. It was set up this year by John Morgan, who had made up the road in 1787 to provide access to land he leased from the Dulwich College. The college took over responsibility for the road in 1809, and was allowed to continue the toll.

1790

BRUNSWICK DOCK OPENED

As a private speculation, in 1789 a Mr Perry began constructing a wet dock at Blackwall, for use by the East India Company. When it opened this year, it covered 8 acres, with two separate parts for large and small ships; facilities existed for masting and fitting out vessels, and there were cranes on the quayside for shifting guns and heavy stores, and also warehouses for blubber and whalebone. Though often called Perry's Dock, he had officially called it Brunswick Dock in honour of George III. An 1803 painting by William Daniell shows the dock packed with vessels and in the middle the Mast House with a crane on top – a well-known landmark in the area.

COVENT GARDEN OBELISK REMOVED

The Covent Garden Piazza once had an obelisk in the middle – it may be seen on old prints. Made of stone, it consisted of a Corinthian pillar supporting a stone on which three sundials were mounted. It was removed this year.

1791

THE BEGINNINGS OF CAMDEN TOWN

About this year the 1st earl of Camden, Charles Pratt, let out some plots of land on the eastern side of what is now Camden High Street, and in the same year an isolated collection of dwellings in the London countryside was dignified by the name of Camden Town. Until then the area had no designation, being referred to as part of Kentish Town. Not much existed before this development. Two inns, the Mother Red Cap and the Mother Black Cap, stood by the site of today's underground station, the latter then serving as a workhouse. On the west side of the road some rather mean premises faced the main street.

It was not a successful scheme. Plots and houses went slowly; speculators made little money, if any. No church was built – always an indication that things had not gone as planned.

VETERINARY COLLEGE FOUNDED

In the fields of Camden Town a group of gentlemen leased some acres from Lord Camden this year, intent on founding the first veterinary college in England. The first such college in Europe had

Tuition at the Veterinary College in 1795.

1700s

been established at Lyons in 1762, but no veterinary science was pursued in England, despite the country's heavy reliance on horses, and the care of animals was left to farriers.

The Royal Veterinary College, as it later became, was established at a general meeting on 8 April. A Monsieur Saint-Bel, from the Lyons establishment, was appointed the first principal. James Burton built the first premises, but it was not until 1 January 1793 that the first horse was brought here for treatment; by that time there were 14 pupils.

THE OBSERVER APPEARS

The first edition of the Sunday newspaper the *Observer* appeared on 4 December. Its founder was W. S. Bourne, and in that first (free) edition he proclaimed its commitment to reporting news and 'the Fine Arts, emanations of Science, the Tragic and the Comic Muse, the National Policies, Fashion and fashionable Follies'. His first investment was only £100, which was soon exhausted, and he had to turn to his brother, William H. Bourne, for financial assistance.

JOHN WESLEY BURIED

John Wesley was buried behind the chapel he had founded in City Road in March. His biographer, Robert Southey, records:

At the desire of many of his friends, his body was carried into the Chapel on the day preceding the interment, and there lay in a kind of state becoming the person, dressed in his clerical habit, with gown, cassock, and band; the old clerical cap on his head, a Bible in one hand, and a white handkerchief in the other.

A DISASTROUS FIRE

The vast Albion Flour Mills, erected at great cost in 1786 (q.v.), were destroyed by fire in March. Horace Walpole recorded the event in a letter to friends:

The Albion Mills are burnt down. I asked where they were; supposing they were powder mills in the country, that had blown up. I had literally never seen or heard of the spacious lofty building at the end of Blackfriars Bridge. At first it was supposed maliciously burnt, and it is certain the mob stood and enjoyed the conflagration as of a monopoly. The building had cost £100,000 and the loss in corn and flour is calculated at £140,000. I do not answer for the truth of the sums; but it is certain that the Palace Yard and part of St James's Park were covered with half-burnt grains.

A NEW THEATRE IN THE HAYMARKET

The King's (or His Majesty's) Theatre in the Haymarket, built on the site of its burnt-out predecessor (see 1789), was opened on 26 March; it was the largest in England. Because of the monopoly on plays enjoyed by the Theatre Royal Drury Lane and Covent Garden Theatre, it presented only opera, except in 1791–4, when the Drury Lane company performed here while their own theatre was being rebuilt. This concentration on opera explains the name of the nearby Royal Opera Arcade.

SERIOUS FLOODING OF THE THAMES

On 9 February the Thames rose 'to an amazing height'. The *Annual Register* recorded that

The water was considerably higher than it has been for the last twenty years past. New Palace Yard and Westminster Hall were overflowed, and the lawyers were actually conveyed to and from the courts in boats. The water rose through the sewers and overflowed the privy gardens, great part of Scotland Yard, and some parts of St James's Park. The damage done in the warehouses on the wharfs

on both sides the river is immense; they were overflowed almost without exception, as was also the Custom House Quay, Tower Wharf, Bankside, Queenhithe, great part of Tooley Street, Wapping High Street, Thames Street, etc., and all the adjoining cellars filled … The water was so deep in several streets that boats were used to remove the inhabitants. In New Palace Yard the scuttle for boats was so violent that several gentlemen of the long robe were thrown into the water; and Westminster Hall not being in the list of regulated fares, the fees insisted on by the watermen were universally complained of as exorbitant.

VARIOUS LOSSES

Some well-known buildings disappeared this year. Carlisle House in Soho Square, once the most fashionable assembly rooms in London, was demolished.

Another house which had seen much grander days was Leicester House, on the north side of Leicester Square. This had once been the residence of the current prince of Wales, but had ended its days as the home of a museum of miscellaneous artefacts. The house was demolished, and the eastern part of Lisle Street now runs across its site.

Richmond House in Whitehall, fronting the river, was destroyed by fire on 21 December. This house, designed by the earl of Burlington, had been used by the duke of Richmond to exhibit his collection of antiques and for the education of suitable connoisseurs.

1792

PANTHEON DESTROYED BY FIRE

The assembly rooms in Oxford Street called the Pantheon, erected at enormous expense in 1772, were destroyed by fire on 14 January. It was a night of severe frost, and the crowds gazed in astonishment at the destroyed building, which was described as a 'phenomenon of vast clusters of icicles, twelve and fifteen feet in length' hanging down. Some rumours alleged that the fire had been intentionally started by people with an interest in the new King's Theatre in the Haymarket, but in truth the Pantheon was now down at heel by this time, and if the fire was deliberately started it would have been more in the interest of its own proprietors, if they were properly insured.

W. H. SMITH FOUNDED

The newsagent's and bookseller's W. H. Smith was founded this year by Henry Walton Smith, just before he died. He bought a 'newswalk business' (a paper round) based on some premises in Little Grosvenor Street, Mayfair, and after his death his widow managed it until 1816. At the beginning the business probably brought in about £1 12s 0d a week clear profit – approximately the wage of a skilled workman. At this time there were about 80 daily papers in London, together with nine in the evening; Sunday papers included the *Observer*.

A SCHOOL FOR THE DEAF AND DUMB

In Fort Street, Bermondsey, construction began this year of a school for deaf and dumb children. It was the first such institution in England. The first teacher held the post for 37 years, and during his time over 1,000 pupils 'were thus able to read articulately, and to write and cipher'.

EGALITARIAN RUMBLINGS

One of the most influential of the early reform movements was the London Corresponding Society, which was founded by Thomas Hardy, a shoemaker, in the Bell Tavern, Exeter Street, off the Strand. The first meeting was in January, and Hardy described how the founder members

had finished their daily labour, and met there by appointment. After having had their bread and cheese and porter for supper, as usual, and their pipes afterwards, with some conversation on the hardness of the times and the dearness of all the necessaries of life, which they, in common with their fellow citizens, felt to their sorrow, the business for which they met was brought forward – Parliamentary Reform.

At its height the society had about 5,000 members drawn from the skilled artisan class and tradesmen, and was sufficiently influential for Edmund Burke to describe it as the 'mother of mischief'. Generally, its aims were annual elections, universal suffrage, lower taxation and prices, and the abolition of party politics.

In September the revolutionary massacres in Paris brought many refugees to London. Equally the revolutionary fervour which had culminated in the killings found sympathizers amongst those who sought reform in England. Measures were taken everywhere against seditious meetings.

NEW CHURCHES

New churches for the growing population of London were to be built almost every year from now on. In 1791 a new church, St Mary's, was built on Paddington Green to succeed a building which was now in bad condition and inadequate. The new church, designed by John Plaw in Greek style, was consecrated on 27 April 1791. In the churchyard, which is now overwhelmed by Westway, lie the artist Benjamin Haydon and the actress Sarah Siddons.

In the same year that Camden Town was being developed – 1791 – the parish of St James Piccadilly opened a chapel to the south, on Hampstead Road, which not only served a new burial ground but was used by local residents. Once again the vestrymen of St Pancras, who had declined to expand their own church accommodation, were scooped by outsiders. The chapel of St James was designed by Thomas Hardwick. It stood just south of the later Temperance Hospital – its burial ground, now public gardens, contains Lord George Gordon, catalyst of the 1780 riots, James Christie, founder of the auction house (d. 1803), and the painter George Morland (d. 1806).

The new St James, Clerkenwell, was consecrated on 10 July 1792. Designed by James Carr, it is brick-built with stone quoins and dressings; the spire, which can be seen tantalizingly through various road openings, was rebuilt in the 19th century.

More unusually, a Roman Catholic church was opened in central London. This was St Patrick, Soho Square, intended for the neighbourhood of St Giles, which was 'inhabited principally by the poorest and least informed of the Irish who resort to this Country'. The old two-storeyed assembly rooms behind Carlisle House were purchased and the chapel was consecrated on 29 September this year. The present church replaced it in 1893.

1793

THE FIRST PANORAMA

An unusual building was opened at the junction of Leicester Place and Leicester Square this year. An Irish artist, Robert Barker, had perfected a method of painting epic or topographical scenes on the inside of the walls of a circular gallery; the perspective was so adjusted that it was correct when viewed from the centre of the building. A 90-ft rotunda, containing three rooms (the predecessors of Screens One, Two and Three), opened in Leicester Place. Barker's panorama of London, drawn from the roof of the Albion Flour Mills before they burnt down, had already been exhibited the year before to much acclaim.

The building opened with a view of the fleet at Spithead, and Barker continued with battle scenes from the Napoleonic wars. The business was not, surprisingly, short-lived. Managed eventually by Barker's pupil John Burford, and then his son Robert, the ever-changing exhibition continued into the 1860s, when the building was converted into a Catholic church.

THE POLYGON BUILT

Another unusual London building was begun this year. This was the Polygon, in the centre of today's Clarendon Square, in Somers Town. Developed by Jacob Leroux, and built by Job Hoare, a carpenter, it consisted of 32 houses, each with four storeys and garrets, with the front elevation of each pair of houses forming one of the sides of the whole development. Thus the building's external shape had sixteen angles.

It was here that William Godwin and his wife Mary Wollstonecraft lived, shortly after the buildings were finished; their daughter, Mary, the future author of *Frankenstein*, was born here in 1797, but Mary Wollstonecraft died soon afterwards as a result of the birth.

BONHAM'S FOUNDED

The fine-art auctioneer's Bonham's was founded this year in Leicester Square by William Charles Bonham and George Jones.

1794

SMALLPOX HOSPITAL REBUILT

Despite public opposition, the treatment of smallpox patients had been progressing at a hospital at Cold Bath Fields in Clerkenwell since the late 1740s. In 1791, with the hospital badly needing repair but with the lease running out, it was decided to erect a new hospital on a piece of land in the parish of St Pancras, in which the charity already

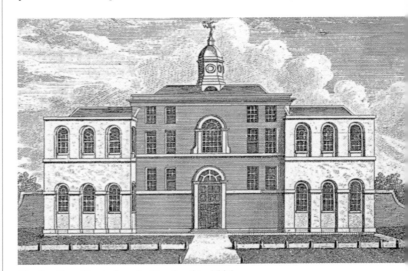

The Smallpox Hospital on the New Road in 1794.

had a building where inoculation was carried out. This was the site of today's King's Cross station. The first stone was laid in 1793, and in July 1794 the first patients were admitted to a handsome building then in open fields conveniently on the New Road to the City.

RATCLIFF DESTROYED BY FIRE

The hamlet of Ratcliff in Wapping, which consisted of mainly wooden shacks built by the river, was destroyed in July. Estimates vary, but between 450 and 730 houses were lost. A fire began when a builder's pitch kettle overturned. Spreading through a wood store, it reached barges. A warehouse containing saltpetre stocks belonging to the East India Company caught alight, and then, a contemporary writer says, 'the wind whirled destruction into the narrow streets, and houses perished by hundreds'. Thousands took shelter in Stepney church, and later they lived in tents in the fields.

TRAGEDY AT THE HAYMARKET

On 3 February the *Annual Register* noted that

This evening a melancholy accident happened at the Haymarket Theatre … It was occasioned in the following manner: in the crowd [to get in] one of the deceased was thrown down; the people kept pushing forward; others were thrown down over him, and all were trampled on by the crowd who pressed over their bodies into the house. The pit lies lower than the threshold of the door leading into it; those therefore who go in must go down steps. Here it was that the mischief happened; for the people who were unfortunate sufferers, either not knowing anything of the steps or being hurried on by the pressure of the crowd behind, fell down; while those who followed immediately were, by the same irresistible impulse, hurried over them. The scene that ensued may be easier conceived than described; the shouts and screams of the dying and the maimed were truly shocking …

Fifteen people died, one of whom was the Somerset Herald at the College of Arms. A tablet noting his death in the tragedy is in the church of St Benet Paul's Wharf.

ASTLEY'S DESTROYED BY FIRE

In a year of alarming incidents, Astley's arena for equestrian events was destroyed by fire. It was the first of the three Astley buildings to go up in flames.

THIRD THEATRE ROYAL OPENS

The third Theatre Royal Drury Lane, designed by Henry Holland, was opened on 12 March.

UNREST IN THE CITY

France had declared war on England on 1 February 1793. This was bad enough for authorities who feared there might be an invasion, but the revolutionary fervour sweeping Paris and France was seen to be a threat in London too. The City rushed through plans to form a volunteer unit, but in the end, instead of London being defended by six regiments of trained bands, of nominally 9,000 hastily trained men, a Militia Bill was passed which meant that London was supervised by two trained and professional regiments with powers to conscript. Recruiting offices were set up, and it was at one of these that an incident set off unrest. At an office near Charing Cross a young man who had been taken for enlistment was found dead in the street, killed by a fall from the garret of the office, with his hands tied behind his back. A mob gathered to tear the house down, and a few days later assembled

with the same intention outside an office in Shoe Lane. In the next few days there were attacks on other offices around London.

SCHWEPPE'S ESTABLISHED

A Swiss, Jacob Schweppe, established a soda-water manufactury in London this year. Soda water was then a medicinal drink, and an excise duty was charged on it.

A NEW PRISON IN CLERKENWELL

Mount Pleasant Sorting Office, at the junction of Rosebery Avenue and Farringdon Road, is on the former site of the Cold Bath Fields prison, or, as it was officially called, the Clerkenwell House of Correction. It was for short-term prisoners, and its treatment of them centred around work as a punishment. The ground itself was a mixture of marsh, dung and rubbish deposited over the years; nevertheless, piles were driven into it and building was begun this year.

Like Pentonville jail later, it was a prison designed by prison reformers, but the end product was to be disillusioning.

Men, women, and boys were indiscriminately herded together in this chief county prison, without employment or wholesome control; while smoking, gaming, singing, and every species of brutalizing conversation, tended to the unlimited advancement of crime and pollution. Meanwhile the Governor of that day walked about, bearing in his hand a knotted rope, and ever and anon he would seize some unlikely wight by the collar or arm and rope's-end him severely.

Other commentators remark on the amount of work prisoners had to do. 'All had to work for ten hours daily. For the first month or so they worked in solitude; afterwards they laboured twenty or thirty together, but were not allowed to speak to each other. The ordinary employment was oakum picking, but skilled hands are employed in matmaking, shoemaking, carpentry and joinery.' The great treadmill, which was long a prominent feature in the establishment, was destroyed by fire, but other wheels were subsequently erected.

1795

SOUP KITCHENS ESTABLISHED

It was a Scotsman who began the movement to set up soup kitchens to provide for London's poor and wretched. Patrick Colquhoun, whose efforts to improve the prosperity of Scotland had met with much acclaim, was appointed a magistrate soon after he moved to London in 1789. In 1794 he published a pamphlet indicating ways in which the industrious poor might be helped after the recent severe weather, and in 1795, when there was much political discontent, inspired not only by the revolutionary fervour spilling over from France, but also by the high price of food, he helped to found a soup kitchen at Spitalfields – the first of many.

Colquhoun was an innovative man. He was mainly responsible for the formation of the Thames police (see 1798), and he also suggested the formation of a sort of London police force and an elementary rate equalization scheme, so that the east-London parishes were partly subsidized by those in the western areas without such chronic social problems.

DISCONTENT

There was famine in London. The efforts of people like Colquhoun were aimed at keeping law and order as well as feeding those badly in need. The City voted two sums of £1,000 to the poor, and hypocritically discussed whether to cancel all City dinners and contribute what would have been spent to the same good cause but in the end shied away from such a self-denying ordinance.

There was a strong movement in London for peace with France. This was demonstrated in October, when a crowd estimated at 200,000 assembled to watch the king pass to open Parliament. He was hooted and hissed as he went by, and a marble or bullet broke the window of his carriage. Two weeks later the reformist London Corresponding Society held a well-attended meeting on Copenhagen Fields in Islington to protest against the government.

WAXWORKS IN FLEET STREET

The best-established waxworks in London was that of Mrs Salmon, whose exhibition had first been at the Golden Ball, by St Martin's le Grand, and had then moved in 1711 to the north side of Fleet Street, near Chancery Lane. Much of her display consisted of historical tableaux, such as the execution of Charles I and other dramatic happenings.

This year the waxworks moved to 17 Fleet Street, to premises now called Prince Henry's Room, where Inner Temple Lane begins.

FIRE GUTS ST PAUL, COVENT GARDEN

St Paul, Covent Garden, had been extensively renovated and reopened in 1789 – after work was carried out by Thomas Hardwick. But on 17 September builders having their midday break left a fire unguarded and virtually the whole of the interior of the church was gutted. It was rebuilt over the next few years, utilizing the old walls and closely following the designs of its original architect, Inigo Jones.

TRINITY HOUSE BUILT

A new headquarters was built for Trinity House, the authority which governs the provision of lighthouses and pilots in England and Wales. Designed by Samuel Wyatt, the building in Trinity Square, Tower Hill, was completed this year.

1796

HOUSES COLLAPSE IN CLARE MARKET

In Houghton Street, where now is the London School of Economics, two houses collapsed on 7 June and buried 15 people. The *Annual Register* told how

At noon 13 were got out and conveyed to the parish workhouse in Portugal Street. Of these three had been dug out, shockingly mangled, without the least symptoms of life: two children, apparently dead, were restored to life by means prescribed by the Humane Society in cases of suffocation; the rest received some of them slight and others severe contusions. The landlord of one of the houses it is reported, received notice of the insecurity of his house two days ago, but did not apprize the lodgers of their danger for fear of losing them.

SANS SOUCI THEATRE OPENS

The song-writer and dramatist Charles Dibdin opened the Sans Souci Theatre this year at the corner of Leicester Place and Leicester Square, transferring it from an address in the Strand; it opened on 8 October. In his autobiography, Dibdin mentions that the site had houses on either side of it and all he needed to do was build a wall at front and back. As for the interior, the dimensions of his new home were exactly

St Paul, Covent Garden, gutted by fire in 1795, is on the left in this print.

those of his building in the Strand, and so he was able to furnish his new theatre economically.

The productions here consisted of songs – particularly those of Dibdin himself – readings and recitations of poems.

1797

HATCHARD'S FOUNDED

John Hatchard, bookseller, began his business in Piccadilly this year. As good bookshops tended to then, it had something of the nature of a club in which customers could sit, drink coffee and read newspapers as well as browse.

Hatchard had served his apprenticeship at a shop in Great College Street, Westminster, and then worked in another in a road later to be part of Charing Cross Road. He recorded that 'I quitted the service of Mr Thomas Payne 30th of June, 1797, and commenced business for myself at No. 173 Piccadilly, where, thank God, things went on very well, till, my friends desiring me to take a larger shop, I then did so, I think June 1801, at No. 190 in the same street.' These premises, now renumbered 187, are occupied still by the company's successor.

SOUP SOCIETY FORMED

The Spitalfields Soup Society was formed this year to provide soup to unemployed weavers. One of the founder members of the committee was William Allen, chemist, whose company Allen & Hanbury was later to be famous. Soup was sold at 1d a quart, and 3,000 quarts were sold daily.

FIRST MEETING OF THE COLLEGE OF SURGEONS AT LINCOLN'S INN FIELDS

The College of Surgeons this year bought 41 Lincoln's Inn Fields for a headquarters. The college (which received a royal charter in 1800) rebuilt the premises in 1806–13 and again in 1835 (except for the portico). The Surgeons had been merged with the Barbers' Company in 1540 into the Barber Surgeons' Company, having a monopoly of surgery. They were separated from the Barbers in 1745.

A RESERVOIR IN HAMPSTEAD ROAD

The New River Company was finding difficulty in supplying, from Islington, the growing population in the Tottenham Court Road area. To help matters, about this year it constructed a large reservoir just to the north of Euston Road and to the east of Hampstead Road – the site of today's Tolmers Square.

1798

TIME OF WAR
The war with France dragged on, and invasion was threatened. In the City it was ordered that each ward should form an association 'for learning the use of arms, or to act as constables in sudden emergency'. Similar measures were put in place in the suburbs, where numerous volunteer units were established. In Clerkenwell, for example, the Clerkenwell Association was composed of 'respectable tradesmen and honest workmen'. The cavalry troop (about 50 in number) wore red coats ornamented with gold lace; the infantry (about 900 strong) wore red coats with blue epaulettes. Tower Hamlets had two regiments of militia, and nearby there were the Loyal Hackney Volunteers. The Blackheath Yeomanry was formed this year, and in Lewisham four corps formed the Lewisham Volunteers.

RIVER POLICE ESTABLISHED
Patrick Colquhoun (see 1795) and John Harriott were responsible this year for establishing the River Police, in an attempt to prevent the widespread pilfering that went on in London's docks. It was the first properly organized police force in the country, and was then mostly funded by the West India Company, which had much to gain from a reduction of theft in its docks. The Port of London at that time was chaotic – as many as 1,700 ships might be tied up there at any one time, their cargoes exposed to pilfering until unloading could proceed, which could be weeks.

NEW CHURCHES
In Hackney, the parish church of St Augustine was in a bad state of repair and in any case was inadequate for the growing population. A parish church, dedicated to St John and designed by James Spiller on a nearby site, was finished about this year; it could accommodate about 4,000 people. The old church was taken down to provide building materials – except for the tower, which still survives.

The medieval church of St Martin Outwich in Threadneedle Street had escaped the Great Fire, but had been damaged in another fire in 1765. It needed rebuilding, but, as the *Gentleman's Magazine* queried, for whom? There were, it noted, only 20 houses in the parish, and funds would have to come from elsewhere. The new building, by Samuel Pepys Cockerell, was consecrated on 26 November and was paid for by the Merchant Taylors' Company, in whose gift was the living.

AN ECCENTRIC IN KENTISH TOWN
An eccentric in Kentish Town died at the age of 84 from a chill caught by going into his wine cellar, rather than trusting a servant to do so. The *Annual Register* noted that

So great was his antipathy to the married state, that he discarded his brother, the only relative he had, for not continuing like himself in a state of celibacy. On his effects being examined, it appeared that he had £25,000 in the different tontines, £11,000 in four per cents, and £2,000 in landed property; 173 pairs of breeches, and a numerous collection of other articles of wearing apparel were found in a room which had not been opened for 14 years; 180 wigs were found in the coach-house'.

River Police headquarters in Wapping High Street c. 1900. This first police force was formed in 1798 to prevent theft and fraud in the Pool of London.

1799

A NEW MAP OF LONDON
Richard Horwood completed this year his vast map of London. Covering 32 sheets, it was the largest and most comprehensive yet undertaken, at a scale of 26 inches to the mile. Not only did it include the numbering of houses, where that existed, but for the first time south London was shown in detail.

Horwood, who had premises in Mare Street, Hackney, issued a prospectus for his map about 1790; the first sheets, covering the more fashionable parts of town, appeared in 1792. By the time of the last sections in 1799 it was (and remains, with the exception of the Ordnance Survey) the largest map ever produced in this country. Predictably, it did not make Horwood rich. Indeed the City and other interested parties were mean in their treatment of his labours – in contrast to the City of Liverpool, who straight away offered assistance and a monetary guarantee when he applied to map Liverpool as well.

Horwood died, aged 45, in 1801; he is buried in Toxteth, Liverpool.

ROYAL INSTITUTION FOUNDED
The Royal Institution for 'diffusing the knowledge and facilitating the general introduction of useful mechanical inventions and improvements' was founded on 9 March this year at the house of Joseph Banks.

1800

AN ATTEMPT ON THE KING'S LIFE

On the evening of 15 May, when George III had just entered his box at the Theatre Royal Drury Lane, a deranged man named Hadfield fired a pistol shot at him. The gun was deflected by a bystander and the bullet hit the upper part of the king's box instead.

A SCHOOL FOR POOR BLIND CHILDREN

Society was beginning to sort out specific needs, and this century was to see a large number of charities directed to particular groups of people. The School for Indigent Blind – for 'the moral, mental and industrial training of poor blind children of both sexes over ten years of age' – is a typical example. It was begun in a room at the Dog and Duck tavern at St George's Fields near today's Elephant and Castle this year. There were 15 pupils at first, but soon the school took over the whole building and later outgrew that as well.

BREAD RIOTS IN LONDON

The price of bread had dramatically risen over the past five years. By July 1800 wheat cost almost three times as much as in early 1799 and there were bread riots in many parts of the country. In London, soup kitchens helped to stem the rising tide of dissatisfaction, but this year serious rioting took place. In September the demonstrators ignored the Riot Act and broke the windows of corn dealers, cheesemongers and other food retailers; the Clerkenwell House of Correction, a symbolic Bastille, was stormed. A royal proclamation urged the reduction of consumption of flour in each household and that each person be restricted to one loaf a week.

THE CORNHILL PUMP ERECTED

During building works, an old well had been rediscovered outside the Royal Exchange. With contributions from the Bank of England and other traders in the neighbourhood, a handsome pump was erected this year over the well. It was decorated with emblematic figures, among which was the plan of a House of Correction which had previously stood near the pump.

COLLAPSE AT DAGENHAM

By 1770 it was known that the tower of St Peter and St Paul, the parish church of Dagenham, was unsafe. The foundations were crumbling, causing the tower to lean against the rest of the building. Faced with an estimate of at least £1,175 to rebuild it, the parishioners raised only £68 from voluntary contributions. On Advent Sunday 1800 the tower collapsed upon the nave with a great crash, destroying the south-west porch, the roof, and the singing gallery, font and pews. No lives were lost, as the congregation were waiting in the churchyard for the vicar, who was late for the service.

FIRST POST OFFICE DIRECTORY OF LONDON

London street directories had gradually been improving since their first appearance in the 17th century. Some concentrated on trade, others on 'court', depending on where the compilers thought they might best get subscriptions. The most adequate directory at the beginning of the 19th century was that of Henry Kent, printer of Finch Lane, Cornhill, who in 1734 published *The Directory*, based on information compiled by James Brown. In 1800 was issued the *Post Office Directory*. When compared with what was already on sale it is a disappointment. It was issued under the patronage of the postmaster general, but contained little that was new or in any way an improvement on what had already been compiled without the help of Post Office information. It was not until 1840, when the directory was published by Frederic Kelly, that there was much improvement in this semi-official publication, which by then had been entirely outstripped by the directories published by Pigot and Robson.

KING JOHN'S CASTLE BLOWN DOWN

There were several buildings in London known as King John's Castle or Palace. None of them was a castle or palace, and it is odd that such an unpopular king should have had so many buildings named after him. This year King John's Castle at Old Ford, near Bow, was blown down. Great claims were made for this particular building in the *Annual Register*, which reported the incident: 'here he [John] plotted the death of Prince Arthur; here he entertained the Brabancon chiefs, and here he usually slept, after having signed Magna Charta'.

1801

A CANAL IN LONDON

In July 1792, at the beginning of the second period of 'canal mania', banker William Praed (after whom Praed Street in Paddington is named) was appointed chairman of a company which proposed a canal to connect Birmingham with the Thames. Previously barges from the Midlands had used the Oxford Canal, transferring goods to road transport for the journey from Oxford to London. The new scheme involved cutting a canal from Braunston, near Daventry, on the existing Oxford Canal, to run 93 miles to the Thames at Brentford.

The route of the Grand Junction Canal between Uxbridge and Brentford was completed and opened in 1794. However, the outlet to the Thames was not without its problems. Brentford Lock was the final lock when the canal opened; south of that boats had to navigate the tidal Brent Creek, because local millers frustrated the use of the creek water to build another lock (later the Thames Lock) which would have enabled the boats to go on their way.

While construction work was in progress it was realized that 'a great public advantage could be derived if a cut was made from a part

Warehouses at the early Grand Junction Canal basin at Paddington, 1801. The smartly dressed people are possibly taking canal-boat trips.

of the Grand Junction Canal near Bull Bridge in the Parish of Southall … to Paddington'. This cut to what became Paddington Basin, where wharves and warehouses were built, was opened in 1801.

THE START OF A SCHOOL SYSTEM

A young man of reduced circumstances was responsible this year for beginning a system of teaching large numbers of children that was to be a prominent feature of English education for many years. Joseph Lancaster (1778–1838) had a missionary zeal when young; he persuaded his father to let him teach poor children to read at his home in Southwark. In 1801 he took a large room in Borough Road and inscribed over it, 'All who will may send their children and have them educated freely, and those who do not wish to have education for nothing may pay for it if they please.' This bold invitation seems to have taken no account of Lancaster's ability to pay for teachers, and the number of pupils obliged him to develop a 'monitorial' system whereby older pupils taught younger ones.

The education provided was of the most rudimentary, generally consisting of reading texts from the Bible. Pupils who misbehaved or were bad learners were disgraced rather than beaten – a change from the usual school regimes.

Always overambitious, Lancaster got heavily into debt. Friends rescued him in 1808, and in the same year founded the Royal Lancasterian Society to further his educational methods; in 1810 this became the British and Foreign School Society.

AN EXTRAORDINARY MILL IN BATTERSEA

A Captain Stephen Hooper this year built a 'Horizontal Air Mill' in Battersea. This most extraordinary structure, used for grinding linseed, was 140 ft high. David Hughson, in his *Circuit of London*, said that:

the outer part consists of ninety-six shutters, eight feet high and nine inches broad, which, by the pulling of a rope, open and shut in the manner of a Venetian blind. Inside, the main shaft of the mill is the centre of a large circle formed by the sails, which consist of ninety-six double planks, placed perpendicularly. The wind rushing through the openings of these shutters acts with great power upon the sails, and, when it blows fresh, turns the mill with prodigious rapidity.

However, the mill was not economical, and did not survive very long.

1802

WEST INDIA DOCKS OPENED

The Port of London was progressively more congested. Not only were there more ships trading there, but they were larger. Weeks might pass before a ship, lying midstream, could be offloaded. To ease this absurd situation – mainly caused by the City's reluctance to lose its monopoly over the London port and the watermen's fear of unemployment – the first part of the West India Docks on the Isle of Dogs was opened this year. It was designed by William Jessop, who had been responsible for much of the work on the new Grand Junction Canal. It was said in 1801 that 24 million bricks were made or being made in the Isle of Dogs for the new scheme, and that the local brickmakers had threatened to halt the project if bricks were imported from elsewhere.

The dock's features, which included the secluded protection of ships in a wet dock, were copied in subsequent years in a rapid

programme of dock development. This resulted in a significant change in the Port of London, whereby docking operations were located further and further east, using enclosed docks instead of loading and unloading in the stream as had been done for centuries.

William Daniell's magnificent view of the new docks is a reminder of the desolation of this part of London at the time. The docks built by the West India Dock Company, and the canal immediately to the south of them, built in 1805 by the City of London, allowed access to the Thames at both east and west: in effect, the Isle of Dogs, which was a peninsula, was made into an island.

The proprietors of the docks were able to obtain a 21-year monopoly for all trade from the West Indies except in tobacco, which continued to go to the king's tobacco warehouse further upriver. The scheme actually had two docks: the more northerly for imports and the lower for exports. At the ends of each there was a basin and a lock connected to the river. Generally the seagoing ships used the eastern basins and the lighters, which carried the cargo on into London, used those on the western side, thereby saving the 3 mile trek around the Isle of Dogs.

The public opening was on 22 August, when, in the presence of the prime minister, Henry Addington, a ship named the *Henry Addington* was the first to enter the new complex.

The new docks were not universally welcomed – they threatened the livelihood of those who plundered the ships in the more open docks on the river. It was reported by the management of the West India Company that:

considering the dread with which the Works at the Isle of Dogs are regarded by those numerous Classes at present engaged in a System of Plunderage upon the River and the threats which have from good Authority been communicated to the Directors of attempts to destroy by Fire or otherwise the Works wherever in a state of forwardness it is expedient to apply to the Chancellor of the Exchequer requesting that a Military Guard may be appointed as soon as possible to patrol by Night the environs of the Works already in a sufficient forwardness to be Combustible.

NEW STOCK EXCHANGE BUILDING

The Stock Exchange which had been established in 1773 in a building in Threadneedle Street was now inadequate, and in any case there were disagreements among the management committee. In 1802 new premises were opened in Capel Court, on the site of an old boxing saloon. Here the brokers congregated in a large room built by James Peacock, while on the gallery around it there were desks for clerks.

A magnificent view of the new West India Docks, drawn by William Daniell in 1802. Today, Canary Wharf occupies much of the site.

Albany, converted into apartments by Henry Holland in 1802–3.

CONVERSION OF ALBANY

Hidden between Piccadilly and Burlington Gardens is a set of chambers located in Albany House and its old gardens. The house itself was built by Sir William Chambers in 1771–4 for the first Lord Melbourne. The development of these apartments – some of the most sought-after in London – was the work of a young builder, Alexander Copland, who bought the mansion in 1802. With Thomas Coutts, the banker, providing the finance, he employed Henry Holland as his architect to convert the house with chambers, a common dining room and baths, and to build in the garden two rows of additional chambers in the manner of a college or Inn of Court. The first apartments, or 'sets' as they are called, appear to have been sold in 1803.

It was not permitted to carry on a trade or profession there. So obviously were the chambers intended only for male occupants that no rules were framed to prohibit wives or women tenants. The first woman ratepayer is noted in 1883.

MADAME TUSSAUD'S OPENS IN LONDON

Madame Tussaud's Waxworks, which had been established in Paris in 1780, were first shown in London at the Lyceum, Wellington Street, this year. They consisted of 35 figures inherited from her uncle. She then toured the display around the country and did not settle in London again until 1833, when she exhibited at the former Horse Bazaar in Gray's Inn Road, before going on to Baker Street in 1835.

SPORTING SPECTACULARS

On 21 September a Monsieur Garnerin ascended in a balloon from Vauxhall Gardens and descended from a great height by parachute.

At London Fields, Hackney, on 24 September a cricket match was held with the very substantial stake of 500 guineas going to the winning side. Eleven gentlemen of Clapton beat 11 gentlemen of London Fields by an innings and 49 runs.

1803

THE FIRST PUBLIC RAILWAY

The first public railway in the world, albeit with trucks drawn by horses and mules, was constructed this year from Frying Pan Creek on the Thames at Wandsworth through Merton, Mitcham and Waddon to Pitlake Meadows, Croydon. Each horse was able to pull ten wagons, and a toll was charged to those who were transporting goods by this method. The line opened on 26 July.

COMMERCIAL ROAD BUILT

Commercial Road was made this year, primarily at the expense of the East India Dock Company, from Whitechapel to Limehouse. A further extension, called East India Dock Road, later led down to the docks.

A NEW SMOCK MILL

The Upminster Smock Mill in St Mary's Lane still survives. It was built about this year by James Noakes, and a steam engine was installed in 1811.

RANELAGH CLOSES

Ranelagh Gardens, once the fashionable resort of Londoners, closed on 8 July this year. Demolition of the famous Rotunda began in September 1805, and the grounds in time became part of the Royal Hospital, Chelsea.

1804

DEVELOPMENTS IN BLOOMSBURY

Bloomsbury Square was originally built as two rows of houses on east and west; the southern development came later, and the north side was occupied by Bedford (formerly Southampton) House. This large mansion, with extensive grounds and views to the north, was demolished sometime after 1800 and on its gardens Russell Square was finished by about 1804. In Richard Horwood's map of 1799 the rear of Bedford House marks the northern extent of development of London, before it leaps to the properties being built along the New Road. Edward Dayes's view of the square in 1787, in which cattle are being driven along the south side to Bloomsbury Market, shows Bedford House in the centre.

In an age when Beau Brummell was horrified to be noticed by Sheridan as far east as Charing Cross, development of Bloomsbury began in earnest. Russell Square, one of the largest squares in London, was built by James Burton and landscaped by Humphry Repton. Some idea of it may be gained from the surviving houses on the west side. The square's nearness to the Inns of Court attracted the better-off lawyers.

This abandonment of the Bedford mansion and its gardens to bricks and mortar released substantial land for development: Woburn, Tavistock and Torrington squares followed. Simultaneously, the Foundling Estate exploited its ample fields with the building of Mecklenburgh and Brunswick squares and Handel and Coram streets.

NEW SOCIETIES

The next 50 years were to see the foundation of numerous learned and artistic societies, many of which still survive. Typical is what is now the Royal Horticultural Society, formed in a room above Hatchard's bookshop in Piccadilly on 7 March this year, by a group of gardeners and botanists at a meeting convened by a son of Josiah Wedgwood.

The (Royal) Society of Painters in Water Colours began at a meeting in the Stratford Coffee House, Oxford Street, on 30 November. There were 16 members, each contributing £2. Future members included de Wint, Cotman, Palmer and Sargent.

On 7 March the British and Foreign Bible Society was formed 'for the circulation of the Scriptures in the principal living languages'.

SMALL ARMS AT ENFIELD

With the war with France continuing, the government began a small-arms factory at Enfield by the River Lea, an isolated site at which gunpowder had been made in the mid 17th century. It was at the Royal Small Arms factory that the 'Enfield' rifle was later developed.

AN EGYPTIAN INFECTION

The war with France led also to the establishment of the Royal Infirmary for Diseases of the Eye, in Cork Street. Soldiers on the Nile campaign were contracting 'Egyptian ophthalmi', a virulent mix of purulent ophthalmia and trachoma. Little was known of effective treatment, and it was thought advisable to set up a specialist hospital to study the disease more intensively.

CONDITIONS AT THE TOWER MENAGERIE

At the Tower menagerie, Sir Richard Phillips reported in his *Modern London*, published this year, the wild beasts

are kept in a yard on the right hand, at the west entrance. A figure of a lion is over the door, and there is a bell at the side to call the keeper. The visitor pays one shilling here, for which the keeper shows him all the wild beasts, explaining their several histories. The principal of these, at present in the Tower, consist of lions, tigers, leopards, panthers, the laughing hyena, the Spanish wolf, the ant-bear, and some mountain cats and racoons. Among them there are, or latterly were, three royal hunting tigers, which are said to have belonged to a pack of the same kind kept by Tippo Sahib, with which he hunted beasts of prey ... The dens are very commodious; they are about 12 feet in their whole height, being divided into an upper and lower apartment; in the former the animals live in the day, and in the latter sleep at night.

1805

THE LONDON DOCKS OPEN

The London Docks in Wapping, on the slight bend of the river east of the Tower, were opened on 31 January. They were designed by Daniel Alexander and John Rennie.

The City, jealous of its trade privileges in the Pool of London, had opposed this dock scheme as well, although this did not prevent the lord mayor from becoming a director of the company which constructed it. Perhaps he was attracted by the company's 21-year monopoly of all vessels laden with tobacco, rice, wine and brandy, except those which came from the East and West Indies. Prominent features of the scheme were the Tobacco Dock, which still survives, and the enormous vaults for wine storage.

THE BEGINNINGS OF MOORFIELDS HOSPITAL

Moorfields Hospital has its origins this year in a meeting, convened by John Cunningham Saunders, on 4 January, to found the Dispensary for the Relief of the Poor Afflicted with Diseases of the Eye and Ear. Blindness was prevalent in the capital, much of it caused by infection from soldiers returning from the Nile campaign (see 1804); inevitably, it was the poorer classes who took the brunt of the contamination, and itinerant quacks selling useless remedies preyed on those afflicted. The dispensary, housed at 40 Charterhouse Square, was swamped by

patients and soon had to concentrate on diseases of the eye only, changing its name to the London Infirmary for Curing Diseases of the Eye.

NEW GUILDHALL AT WESTMINSTER

This year a new guildhall, or sessions house, for Middlesex was built on the site of the Westminster Abbey Sanctuary. It was a graceful, octagonal building with a classical, Ionic-columned front, designed by Samuel Pepys Cockerell.

SPORTING HIGHLIGHTS

The first cricket match between Eton and Harrow schools took place at Lords this year. Lord Byron was in the losing Harrow eleven; he used a runner, because of his club foot, and scored seven and two.

Tom Cribb, former bellhanger, porter and sailor – who was to become one of the most famous English pugilists – had his first public fight, against George Maddox at Wood Green on 7 January. He was proclaimed the victor after 76 rounds and received much praise for his coolness of temper despite unfair treatment in the bout.

A MUTED CELEBRATION

The Battle of Trafalgar had taken place on 21 October. The British victory was celebrated in an illuminated London on 6 November (it had taken 16 days for news of the battle to arrive), but, as Washington Irving noted, with the hero, Lord Nelson, dead, celebrations were repressed even 'among the lowest of the mob'.

TWO NEW BURIAL GROUNDS

A growing problem in London was the burial of the dead. With the population growing and mortality so high – particularly among children – the old parish burial grounds were grossly overcrowded. London was late in its provision of proper cemeteries, and in the meantime the inner London parishes resorted to purchasing land outside their boundaries for extra-mural grounds. St Giles-in-the-Fields parish purchased a few acres next to the burial ground of St Pancras church in Pancras Road, and in June 1803 this was consecrated. None too soon, it seems, for in 1793 Thomas Pennant in his *Some Account of London* had remarked that:

I have, in the churchyard of St Giles, seen with horror a great square pit with many rows of coffins piled one upon the other, all exposed to sight and smell; some of the piles were incomplete, expecting the mortality of the night. I turned away disgusted at the view, and scandalized at the want of police which so little regards the health of the living as to permit so many foetid corpses, tacked between some slight boards, dispensing their dangerous effluvia over the capital.

The condition of the churchyard of St Martin-in-the-Fields was hardly much better. On 12 September 1805 that parish opened a new burial ground, called the Camden Town Cemetery, in Pratt Street, also in the parish of St Pancras.

1806

THE FUNERAL OF NELSON

Lord Nelson, who had died in the Battle of Trafalgar, was buried at St Paul's Cathedral on 9 January. From the 5th to the 8th his body had lain in state at Greenwich, in the Painted Hall, where it is estimated about 60,000 viewed it. On the 8th it was taken across the river to the

Admiralty, in Whitehall, in a procession of 18 barges that was hampered by a severe hailstorm. On the following day the cortège was met by the lord mayor and aldermen at Temple Bar and from there escorted to the cathedral, where he was buried directly beneath the dome.

A NEW WATER COMPANY

The West Middlesex Water Works Company was incorporated this year to supply principally Hammersmith, Kensington and Fulham on the north side of the Thames and Battersea, Wandsworth and Barnes on the south (although it never did supply water south of the river). The company constructed its works at Hammersmith to the south of King Street, and in 1809 it built a reservoir on Campden Hill.

EAST INDIA DOCKS OPENED

Docks mania continued in London's East End. On 4 August the East India Docks were opened at Blackwall, east of the Isle of Dogs.

The docks – one for imports, one for exports – were built by the East India Company specifically for its own trade, and were designed by John Rennie and Ralph Walker.

SOME NEW THEATRES

The Sans Pareil Theatre (which became the Adelphi in 1819) opened in the Strand on 27 November. Designed by Samuel Beazley, it was built by John Scott, a colour-maker, who had acquired a large fortune by the invention of 'True Blue', a washing colour. His intention was to provide a theatre for the talents of his daughter, and it was she who opened the theatre with *Miss Scott's Entertainment*, a collection of songs, recitations and imitations, rounded off by fireworks. Surprisingly, Miss Scott prospered and appeared in successive melodramas, and was still starring by 1829, long after the theatre had passed out of her father's hands.

Further along the Strand in Wych Street (now demolished for the Aldwych) stood the Olympic Theatre, opened on 18 September this year for the circus proprietor Philip Astley. George Frederick Cooke, in his *Journal*, records in December:

To dinner at the Wheatsheaf Coffee House. Thence to the Olympic Pavilion; a new wooden building erected … by the celebrated Philip Astley; it is circular; the roof with a small dome is composed of sheets of tin and is supported by pillars … The stage is on a level with the area for horsemanship, and the orchestra rather strangely disposed upstairs on the left of the stage.

It is said that the theatre was constructed with the timbers of a French man-of-war. Needless to say, it burnt down (in 1849), as did most of Astley's theatres.

The Surrey Theatre, at 124 Blackfriars Road, had burnt down in 1805 without insurance cover. A new theatre was built on the site, designed by Rudolf Cabanel Jr, which opened on Easter Monday this year.

THE ARGYLL ROOMS

In Little Argyll Street, near today's Oxford Circus station, the Argyll Music Rooms were established about this year. They became very fashionable indeed, especially when they were remodelled by Nash when Regent Street was built. The Philharmonic Society gave concerts here from 1813 until the rooms were burnt down in 1830. The store Dickins & Jones is now on the site.

EXHIBITION OF A FAT MAN

This year the most corpulent man known in England, Daniel Lambert, was exhibited in Piccadilly. Lambert began putting on excessive weight

when he was about 21, and by the time he was 23 he weighed 32 stone. He decided in 1806 to turn this inconvenience into prosperity. After constructing for himself a special carriage, he was exhibited at 53 Piccadilly. 'When sitting,' said one account, 'he appears to be a stupendous mass of flesh, for his thighs are so covered by his belly that nothing but his knees are to be seen, while the flesh of his legs, which resemble pillows, projects in such a manner as to nearly bury his feet.'

Lambert returned to London in 1807, again for display. When he died, in 1809, at the age of 39, his coffin, which contained 112 superficial feet of elm, was built upon two axle-trees and four wheels, upon which his body was rolled down an incline to the burial ground at Stamford Baron. At death he weighed nearly 53 stone (739 lb).

1807

LONDON BY GASLIGHT

On 4 June, Frederick Winsor demonstrated gas lighting in Pall Mall to mark the birthday of the prince of Wales. This was the first public demonstration of gas in this country. Winsor, whose business was at 93–95 Pall Mall, was of German origin, and had scant knowledge of either chemistry or construction, but he convinced the authorities of his expertise and managed to have the necessary equipment made.

The demonstration lights were strung along the garden wall between Carlton House and St James's Park, and were fed by an iron pipe from the 'two close carbonizing iron furnaces' in Winsor's Pall Mall premises. The *Monthly Magazine* reported that 'The light produced by these gas lamps was clear, bright, and colourless, and from the success of this considerable experiment, in point of the number of lights, the distance and length of pipe, hopes may now be entertained, that this long-talked of mode of lighting our streets may at length be realized.'

The parish authorities, however, were less than convinced, and Winsor was unable to proceed without a great deal of supervision. At the end of that year 13 lamp-posts, each with three gas jets, were erected on the south side of Pall Mall, connected to the Winsor premises, and later more lamps were installed near Cockspur Street. For several years there were demonstrations only, but in 1812 Winsor was instrumental in the incorporation of the Gas Light and Coke Company, which was to be the premier supplier of gas in the London area in the years to come.

MILL HILL SCHOOL FOUNDED

Mill Hill School was founded this year for the sons of Nonconformists, in Ridgeway House, Mill Hill. The house was the former home of the botanist Peter Collinson. The present schoolhouse was built in 1825–7 to a design by William Tite, architect of the Royal Exchange.

TWO DISASTERS

A false fire alarm at Sadler's Wells Theatre on 7 September caused a stampede for the exits in which at least 18 people were killed.

At the execution of two prisoners, Haggerty and Holloway, at Newgate, a cart collapsed under the weight of spectators and up to 30 people died in the crush.

ABOLITION OF THE CITY HUNT

It was stated in a legal case in 1875 that the City of London had abolished the office of Common Hunt in 1807, had broken up the establishment of hounds that it kept, and had not hunted in Epping Forest since.

The London Female Penitentiary, which moved to Pentonville Road in 1807, shown here in an appeal brochure.

GRAND SURREY CANAL BASIN OPENS

The Grand Surrey Canal began with a meeting in 1800 at which a scheme, designed by Ralph Dodd, was approved; it was to link the Thames at Rotherhithe to Deptford, Peckham, Camberwell, Walworth, Vauxhall, Clapham and Streatham, and then continue all the way to Epsom before eventually linking up with Portsmouth and Southampton. In the event it got no further than the Camberwell Road.

When work began in 1802 it was decided that the Thames outlet at Rotherhithe should in fact be yet another grand dock, of 3 acres, and a considerable amount of the company's money was diverted to this purpose. By 1805 funds were almost exhausted and the project was nearly moribund. The dock basin now became the prime object, in the hope that it would provide revenue to complete the canal, and was opened on 13 March 1807, when a large assembly waited for the river to rise to the level of the water in the basin; the gates were then thrown open and the first ship moved in. The first stretch of the canal, to connect with the Croydon Canal (see 1809), was opened the same year.

The canal is now filled in, after closure in October 1970 and its basin at Camberwell is now a park.

A HOME FOR PENITENT PROSTITUTES

The London Female Penitentiary, founded in Blackfriars Road this year, moved the same year to a house in Pentonville Road, where it settled. The object of the charity, as a 19th-century writer put it, was 'to afford an asylum to females, who, having deviated from the path of virtue, are desirous of being restored by religious instruction and the formation of moral and industrious habits, to a reputable condition in society'. The women were taught domestic service.

WATERWORKS IN THE EAST

The East London Waterworks Company was established this year and in 1808 purchased the interests of the Shadwell and West Ham companies as well. The company opened its works at Old Ford, Bow, in 1809, consisting of two reservoirs, driven by two engines. At first it was restricted to the tidal waters of the Lea, but by 1829 the company had obtained permission to take water further up at Lea Bridge.

1808

A RAILWAY LINE IN EUSTON SQUARE

Richard Trevithick, generally regarded as the 'father of the railway engine', this year exhibited a steam-driven engine on a circular track in what is now Euston Square. Spectators were offered rides at a shilling a time, until after some weeks a rail broke and an engine overturned. The experiment was not a success in furthering his invention, but it was the first instance of a locomotive drawing passengers.

COVENT GARDEN THEATRE DESTROYED

The first Covent Garden Theatre went the way of so many other theatres, and was destroyed by fire on 20 August.

A STATUE OF WILLIAM III

An equestrian statue of William III, resplendent in Roman robes, which now stands in St James's Square, was unveiled this year. It had been a long time coming. It had been reported in 1697 that 'the kings statue in brasse is ordered to be sett up in St James's square, with several devices and mottoes trampling down popery, breaking the chains of bondage, slavery, etc.'. Nothing happened, but the project was occasionally revived in the 18th century – although at times William was superseded by George I in proposals. In 1724, however, in the will of Samuel Travers, a bequest was made which provided funds for the making of the statue to William, but it was not until 1794 that John Bacon was commissioned to begin the work. Matters dragged on so long that it was finished by Bacon's son, and, although the inscription notes that it was erected in 1807, it was not, unsurprisingly given the history of the project, unveiled until 1808.

Though the statue is almost entirely inaccurate in its depiction of William's features, it does include the molehill which tripped his horse in Richmond Park in 1701; William died from the fall. It will be seen that the horse is cast so that it is lurching over.

Richard Trevithick demonstrated his railway line and engine in what became Euston Square in 1808.

TOTTENHAM COURT FAIR ABOLISHED

The Tottenham Court Fair was held near the junction of today's Euston Road and Hampstead Road. It was a popular venue for a day out for young people from the City and Westminster, and inevitably it attracted the criticism of those who disliked the lower classes enjoying themselves. A writer in the 17th century observed that

… here you (perhaps) expect some lusty sport,
Such as rude custom doth beget in hay,
When straggling numbers court that jovial day …

The magistrates in 1727 prohibited the performance of plays and 'interludes' in the fields here, as well as the keeping of gaming tables. By that time a fair existed which, a newspaper declared, 'not only tends to the encouragement of vice and immorality, but even to sedition and disloyalty'. But that sort of comment was made about every fair in London, and it is difficult to know to what extent Tottenham Court Fair was more rumbustious than any other. Nevertheless, the authorities, aided by the trustees who built the New Road, had the fair suppressed in 1808.

Possibly the land was wanted for development, because this year a nearby building called King John's Palace (see also 1800) was demolished. This ramshackle structure stood on the north side of Euston Road, just to the east of Hampstead Road.

1809

THEATRICAL COMINGS AND GOINGS

The new Covent Garden Theatre, under the management of John Philip Kemble, opened on 18 September; it was designed by Robert Smirke and modelled on the Temple of Minerva in Athens. Its early days were marked by riots at the seat prices, which had been raised to pay for the new building.

Around the corner, the third Theatre Royal Drury Lane had been destroyed by fire on 24 February. The fire was a disastrous one for the owners, since they had not yet finished paying for the building and it was also underinsured. The blaze could be seen from the House of Commons, where it was moved that the House be adjourned; Sheridan, a member of Parliament and part owner of the theatre, urged the House that 'whatever might be the extent of the present calamity, he hoped it would not interfere with the public business of the country'. He is said later to have watched the flames from a nearby house and to have remarked that 'surely a gentleman may warm his hands at his own fireside'. Speaker Abbot mentions in his diary that residents of Fulham were able to see the time by their watches from the light of the fire.

Around another corner, the Lyceum Theatre opened as an opera house in Wellington Street. Building work had begun in 1795, but was completed only this year.

A POLITICAL DUEL

A bitter political dispute between George Canning and Lord Castlereagh over the conduct of the war, and in particular Castlereagh's part in it, led to a duel between the two men on Putney Heath on 21 September. Neither party fired in the air, but both missed with their first shot; at the second shot Canning was injured in the thigh, but he was able to walk away.

FLOODING AT BATTLE BRIDGE

The area around Battle Bridge (today's King's Cross) was always subject to flooding, especially from the Fleet river. But it was in any case a low-lying area, and in January 1809, when a thick snow thawed, the whole of Somers Town, Battle Bridge and the lower parts of Pentonville were inundated. In the centre of the highway the water was 3 ft deep, and the lower rooms of the houses around were filled.

THE END OF REAL TENNIS AT WHITEHALL

Henry VIII had installed tennis courts at Whitehall, Hampton Court, St James's Palace and Greenwich. The game (which is now called real tennis) was originally played without the use of rackets, the players using their bare hands instead. During the Stuart period the duke of York had a special tutor in the sport, and Charles II had a new court built at Whitehall, modelled on that at Hampton Court (which survives). During the Georgian period real tennis lost favour to tennis played on grass, and in 1809 the court at Whitehall was demolished.

THE CROYDON CANAL OPENS

The Croydon to Deptford Canal was a hopeless failure. Fully opened on 22 October this year, it had closed by 1836 – the victim of its own limitations and the coming of the London & Croydon Railway, which purchased its route. The difficulty for anyone using the canal was that there were 25 locks to negotiate within quite a short distance, so as to overcome the slope of Forest Hill.

1810

A NEW ROYAL MINT

The Royal Mint had long outgrown its space within the Tower of London. A new building for its operations was this year opened on Little Tower Hill, designed by James Johnson and Sir Robert Smirke. Here it was possible to install steam-powered machines which produced better coins.

NEW BUSINESSES

Several famous London businesses were established in this period. John Harris Heal, who had come to London in 1805 to work in a feather-dressing firm in Leicester Square, this year set up business on his own at 33 Rathbone Place. By 1818 he had moved to Tottenham Court Road. It was his son, John Harris Heal Jr, who first built premises on the present Heal's site nearby, from which he sold mattresses, upholstery and furniture.

The printer, Waterlow & Son, which was later to specialize in printing bank notes, was established this year, as were the wine and spirit dealers Matthew Clark & Son and Sun Life Assurance.

AN EARLY DOCK STRIKE

The Times reported an early strike in London Docks:

Yesterday [6 July] the workmen employed at the London Docks struck for an increase of wages. They demanded an advance of from 18s to a guinea per week. The number employed amounts to about 1,000 and such as were backward in approving the conduct adopted by the ringleaders were roughly treated. Constables were called in, and we are happy to say the malcontents did not betray any spirit of outrage other than that of persisting in the demand for an increase of wages.

The strike was broken by the 12th, with no increase in wages agreed to by the employers.

NEW DOCK ROADS

Two important roads connecting the new Commercial Road (see 1803) and the new docks were completed this year. These were East India Dock Road and West India Dock Road.

1811

FREEZING OF THE THAMES

The Thames was nearly frozen over – only a narrow channel of clear water remained in the centre. Two men walked on the ice from Battersea Bridge to Hungerford Stairs on 7 January.

THE RATCLIFF MURDERS

Two sensational and particularly grisly murders took place in The Highway, Ratcliff, this year. On 7 December a maid returned to find that her master, Mr Marr, a lace-seller, and a shop boy had been murdered in a blood-spattered room above the shop, and above that his wife and child were also dead. A chisel and a maul had been used for the killings.

Several days later a Mr Williamson, publican, his wife and a maid were found with their throats cut in a nearby pub.

The two killings caused panic in the neighbourhood. Extra watchmen were drafted in, a reward was offered by the government, and 40 false arrests were made. John Williams, a lodger in a local public house, was eventually charged, but committed suicide before his trial. His body was later carried on a platform past the houses of the victims and was thrown, with a stake through the heart, into a pit dug at a crossroads. This appears to have been the last occasion in London when the full procedure of burying suicides at crossroads was performed. In 1823, when a man was buried at a crossroads in Pimlico, a report said, 'The disgusting part of the ceremony of throwing lime over the body and driving a stake through it was dispensed with.' The custom had been abolished by Act of Parliament that year.

A lampooning sketch by Rowlandson of a women's cricket match at Hackney, in 1811.

BOOK SOCIETIES

A common method among the middle classes of distributing books among themselves at an economic cost was the formation of a book society in a locality. Each member made an annual contribution, and books were bought and transferred around the membership. Typical of these societies were the Uxbridge Book Society, formed this year, and the Highgate Book Society, which was established in 1822 and lasted for a hundred years. The Highgate group included the vicar, Dr Gillman, who was to obtain fame by his careful and prolonged care of the poet Coleridge, and Captain Peter Heywood, who had inadvertently taken part in the mutiny on HMS *Bounty*.

TWO MUSIC PUBLISHERS

Two of our principal music publishers were this year established in London. Vincent Novello began his business at 240 Oxford Street; as from 1847 he also printed music from his premises in Dean Street. In Bond Street, Chappell & Co., now part of Warner Chappell, began trading.

A WOMEN'S CRICKET MATCH

A match between two teams of women from Hampshire and Surrey took place on the unlikely venue of Newington Green this year. The match had been made by two noblemen of the respective counties for 500 guineas each. A typically lampooning sketch by Rowlandson shows only two stumps and one bail in use at each end, but there does seem to have been a hospitality tent.

1812

THE MAKING OF REGENT'S PARK

In 1809, Sir John Fordyce, surveyor-general of His Majesty's Land Revenue, had written that:

distance is best computed by time; and if means could be found to lessen the time of going from Marybone to the Houses of Parliament, the value of the ground for building would be thereby proportionately increased. The best and probably upon the whole, the most advantageous way of doing that, would be by opening a great street from Charing Cross towards a central part of Marylebone Park.

In this perceptive statement is the germ of both Regent Street and Regent's Park. Fordyce had realized that the development of the Crown's Marylebone Park lands was hampered by their distance from Westminster, and made more difficult by the mean and complicated street layout between them.

Fordyce died the same year, but fortunately the direction of these affairs came into the hands of the architect John Nash, working under the patronage of the prince regent. The project caught the imagination of the prince, and allowed Nash not only a magnificent architectural opportunity, but a financial opening.

Nash turned his back on a logical extension of the grid of streets which already existed south of the New (Marylebone) Road and planned instead for the park an open space surrounded by terraces and dotted with over 50 villas; a lake to the south-west would be adjacent to a double circus of houses. There would be an ornamental and elongated basin to supply water to the houses, and beside this there would be a small royal palace. To the north were barracks, and the proposed canal from Paddington Basin would sweep around the north and east. Nash also planned a service area to the east, on the other side of the canal, which would include three markets. The whole could be reached by a triumphal arcaded highway leading from Carlton House in the south, cutting through the slums south of Oxford Street, and then, in the last stage, taking advantage of the grand Portland Place, where his masterly design of All Souls, Langham Place, led the eye harmoniously from one road to the other.

Very little of this Nash plan of 1811 was built. There were fewer terraces, far fewer villas, and the double circus near the centre of the park was scrapped altogether. The barracks were moved to the east, near to the market area, and the canal had a different route. More to the point from the Crown Estate's point of view, the scheme never yielded the income promised by Nash. But even in its amended form it was a plan of magnificence and imagination.

In 1812 the Commissioners for Parks and Forests presented their first report, which revealed that work on the main drive and the plantations was nearly complete.

A TUNNEL COLLAPSE AT HIGHGATE

Going north from London was a hazardous journey in winter. There was no adequate break through the northern heights which did not involve a steep incline, and people and animals alike had to climb the hills of the Hampstead and Highgate area. In wet conditions, Highgate Hill, which met the Great North Road at the gatehouse in Highgate village, was particularly difficult for horses pulling carriages and carts, and sometimes impossible. Even under the turnpike trusts, road surfaces were still poor.

A number of proposals had been made to overcome this difficulty. For example, in 1808 an engineer had proposed a tunnel beneath Highgate – a scheme well beyond the technology of the age. But the same man, Robert Vaizey, then proposed the construction of an extension of the northern end of Holloway Road. This would involve tunnelling beneath the ridge carrying Hornsey Lane and out again to the flatter lands towards Finchley.

Those in Highgate village, particularly the innkeepers, who made their living out of travellers were not at all enthusiastic. Neither were residents of some of the most prestigious houses on Highgate Hill, who stood to lose some of their back gardens because of the plan.

However, an Act of Parliament in 1810 allowed the proposal. Vaizey's plan consisted of a tunnel, 200 yards long, with an arched roof; from this original construction we get the name of Archway Road. About 130 yards were completed when, in the early hours of 13 April 1812, the tunnel collapsed. The *Sun* newspaper reported it thus: 'Between four and five o'clock yesterday morning, the Highgate Tunnel fell in with a tremendous crash, and the labour of several months was, in a few moments, converted into a heap of ruins. Some of the workmen, who were coming to resume their daily labour, describe the noise that preceded it like that of distant thunder.' No one was injured, and the innkeepers of Highgate were delighted – for the time being.

AN EGYPTIAN FASHION

The Nile campaign had made fashionable an interest in things Egyptian. The most notable architectural result of this period was the exotic Egyptian Hall at 170–71 Piccadilly. It was built to hold the museum of curiosities belonging to William Bullock, a naturalist and antiquarian. The architect was Peter Frederick Robinson. The façade of the building, decorated in hieroglyphics, was framed by two large Coade-stone figures of Isis and Osiris.

The Egyptian Hall in Piccadilly, originally a museum of curiosities.

Bullock claimed that his collection had 15,000 items, of which the most famous, in 1815, was Napoleon's supposedly bulletproof field carriage, captured at the Battle of Waterloo. The contents of the museum were dispersed in 1819, and the hall was let out for miscellaneous entertainments thereafter.

FLOODING AT WESTMINSTER

Speaker Abbot records in his diary for 21 October this year:

About half-past 2, returning to Palace Yard, I saw the tide rushing in. It soon rose to the door of Westminster Hall; flowed into it; and three or four boats full of men went into the Hall. The tide still continued to rise for three-quarters of an hour. It filled my Court Yard, and the horses were up to their bellies in water in the stable.

THE BEGINNINGS OF CLARIDGE'S

In 1812 Lord William Beauclerk of 41 Brook Street took a lease of premises at no. 51 in the same street – a house sited approximately in the middle of the present Claridge's Hotel. He let this one house out to a James Mivart for use as a hotel. Over the next few years Mivart acquired other properties adjacent, so that eventually he leased nos. 51–57 Brook Street and 48 Davies Street to the rear. By 1827 the *Morning Post* had cause to remark that Mivart's was the 'fashionable rendez-vouz for the high Corps Diplomatique'. It was not until about 1853 that William Claridge and his wife became connected with Mivart's, and by 1854 the whole complex of interconnected houses had become 'Claridge's late Mivart's'.

THE PRIME MINISTER ASSASSINATED

On 11 May in the lobby of the House of Commons, the prime minister, Spencer Perceval, was assassinated by a man called John Bellingham. One pistol shot was sufficient. The assassin, clearly of deranged mind (he had a grudge against the government and Perceval over an obscure matter to do with Russian law), was found guilty and hanged at Newgate a week later.

SWAN & EDGAR FORMED

The triangular shop at Piccadilly Circus now occupied by Tower Records was once the famous department store of Swan & Edgar. It had begun as the partnership of William Edgar, a haberdasher, and George Swan, a draper, about whom we know very little and who died in 1821. In 1812 the two friends moved their separate businesses out of the City and took a lease on what was then 20 Piccadilly, before Regent Street had been constructed. After Piccadilly Circus was formed the shop was resited there, to flourish and expand as most drapers did in the Victorian era. The premises were rebuilt with the reconstruction of Regent Street after 1910.

NEW THEATRE ROYAL OPENED
The fourth (and present) Theatre Royal Drury Lane was opened on 10 October. It was a crowded evening. As well as an address by Lord Byron, there were performances of *Hamlet* and of a musical farce called *The Devil to Pay*. Designed by Benjamin Wyatt, the new building seated over 3,000 people. The present portico was added in 1820, and the colonnade in 1831.

AN EARLY ADVERTISING AGENCY
The oldest advertising agency still in existence today in England is undoubtedly Charles Barker. This company was formed in 1812 as Lawson & Barker – Lawson was the printer of *The Times*, and had a financial interest in the paper. The agency's office was at 12 Birchin Lane, and Barker was able to describe it as 'a branch of *The Times* where various articles are written'. Originally the business seems to have been a press agency, but soon Barker was placing advertising on behalf of clients.

1813

ARCHWAY ROAD OPENED
When the tunnel beneath Hornsey Lane collapsed in 1812 (q.v.), the promoters of the new road north to avoid the hills of Highgate had to reassess their scheme entirely. It was decided to make a cutting through the hill and then restore Hornsey Lane along a high arched bridge, for which John Nash was brought in as designer.

The Archway bridge in 1820. The road was cut through a ridge of high ground so as to provide a less arduous route to the north from London.

Twice as much money was required for this new plan, but the road opened in 1813 – a remarkably quick recovery from the debacle of the year before. The road was private, and could raise a toll even on pedestrians, unlike the turnpike trusts, which were in effect public roads under private management.

The main arch of the bridge was about 36 ft high and surmounted by three semicircular arches which carried Hornsey Lane. The carriageway beneath the main arch was only 16 ft wide, and there was a narrow footway on either side. But the road itself was ill-made at first, and quite a lot of custom was lost not just because of the toll, but because of the bad condition of the road surface.

MORE GAS LIGHTING
On 15 April the oil and candles at the Haymarket Theatre were replaced by gas lighting. On 31 December Westminster Bridge was lit by gas.

THE GREAT FOG
A great fog covered London from 27 December until 3 January the following year. The *Sun* newspaper of the day reported on 1 January:

The fog still continues. It was more dense and oppressive last night than at any time since its commencement on Monday last. Very few persons ventured out except on pressing business; and no sound was heard out of doors but the voices of the watchman or the noise of some solitary carriage cautiously feeling its way through the gloom. It extends as far as the Downs, a distance of 70 miles, but how far in other directions has not been ascertained.

THE BEGINNINGS OF HARVEY NICHOLS
The fashionable shop of Harvey Nichols began in 1813 when Benjamin Harvey opened a linen-draper's at Lowndes Terrace, at the top of Sloane Street – which was then the eastern end of the rural village of Brompton. When Harvey died in 1850 his daughter, who inherited the business, took into partnership a Colonel Nichols, the silk-buyer.

PHILHARMONIC SOCIETY FORMED
A group of professional musicians, including Muzio Clementi, this year formed the Philharmonic Society, one of the first permanent orchestras. Its first concert was given at the Argyll Rooms, Little Argyll Street, on 8 March. It was this society which commissioned Beethoven to write his 9th Symphony.

BROCKWELL HALL BUILT
Brockwell Hall, the handsome classical building that now ornaments Brockwell Park, was completed this year; the architect was D. R. Roper. This country house, built for John Blades, a glass-manufacturer, was bought by the local authority in 1891.

1814

A CELEBRATION OF PEACE
Napoleon abdicated this year, bringing to an end the war which had consumed Europe for so many years. The lord mayor waited upon the French king, who was staying at Grillon's Hotel in Albemarle Street, and there were many evenings of celebration. These included a Great Fair in Hyde Park, with sideshows and stalls, freak acts and sword-swallowers. The Battle of Trafalgar was re-enacted on the lake, with

guns blazing and 'French' ships sinking. When the allied sovereigns visited London this year a Chinese bridge was erected over the canal in St James's Park, but unfortunately it was destroyed a few years later.

A CHURCH IN ST JOHN'S WOOD

The handsome St John's Wood church has its origins in a prolonged and complicated series of events in which the interests of various noble landowners, the aspirations of the vestry, the French war and the pending development of Regent's Park were all factors.

The erection of a much-needed chapel of ease to St Marylebone church, to cater for the residents of the St John's Wood area, was delayed because of the war with the French. However, a new burial ground was wanted even more urgently and could not be postponed so easily. The duke of Portland promised 6½ acres of land near Primrose Hill, provided that an approach road was constructed across what was then Marylebone Park, but the Crown Estate was not prepared to jeopardize development of the park by agreeing to this, and in the event, when Nash designed Regent's Park, no such road was provided.

Having spent fruitless years trying to buy land in Lisson Grove for a burial ground, the vestry turned further north and bought, about 1806, 5 acres from a Mr Eyre and 1 acre from the duke of Portland – the site of the present St John's Wood church and churchyard.

The church was not proceeded with until 1812. The vestry, un-comfortably aware of how much income was going to the proprietary chapels elsewhere in the parish, wanted to proceed with a church-building programme based on a church rate. The duke of Portland, however, declined to give up his patronage of St Marylebone churches, and the vestry was anxious not to spend public money if it did not have control over the new buildings. The matter was resolved when Portland died in 1809; his son was happy not only to relinquish his patronage but to make over the already existing chapels.

Work on the construction of St John's Wood chapel, using part of the still-unused burial-ground site, began in 1812. The architect was Thomas Hardwick. The great and the good who attended the consecration service on 24 May 1814 assembled first at Mr Lord's cricket ground nearby (Lord was prominent in St Marylebone affairs) and, in a procession which included charity-school children, walked to the ceremony.

THE FROZEN THAMES

With the great fog still present (see 1813) came the great freeze. The frost began on 23 December 1813 and lasted well into February. On 30 January hundreds of people assembled at Blackfriars Bridge and London Bridge to see people crossing the frozen Thames. In some parts the ice was several feet thick, while in others it was dangerous to venture. One man, attempting to cross near Blackfriars with some lead in his hand, sank between two masses of ice and drowned. Opposite Queenhithe about 30 booths were erected to sell beer, gingerbread etc. Skittles were played, and booksellers sold broadsheets on the ice, some of them printed on presses there.

A CLIMBING PONY

A pony, the property of a fishmonger on Fish Street Hill, was in November led by a lad to the gallery at the top of the Monument and down again, without slipping once.

EXPLOSION AT MEUX'S BREWERY

Meux's Horseshoe Brewery occupied the site of today's Dominion Theatre in Tottenham Court Road. On 17 October, large vats there, containing 3,555 barrels of beer, burst. Eight people drowned.

The Dulwich Picture Gallery is the oldest public gallery in the country. Mostly, its quality comes from 371 pictures bequeathed by Sir Francis Bourgeois in 1811. John Soane built the interesting gallery building.

A CONSUMPTION HOSPITAL

In Brushfield Street, Spitalfields, this year the Infirmary for Asthma, Consumption and other Diseases of the Lungs was established. This became, in time, the Brompton Chest Hospital.

FIRST MATCH AT THE NEW LORD'S

Thomas Lord had had to move his cricket ground twice. Beginning on the site of Dorset Square (see 1787), he had moved to North Bank in St John's Wood; but because of the construction of the Regent's Canal he moved yet again – this time to the ground's present home. On 7 May 1814 Lord informed readers of the *Morning Post* that his 'New Ground is completely ready for Playing on'. In the first match there, on 22 June, the Marylebone Cricket Club beat Hertfordshire by an innings and 27 runs.

DULWICH PICTURE GALLERY OPENS

Dulwich Picture Gallery, the oldest public art gallery in England, was opened this year. It had its origins in a collection of portraits owned by Edward Alleyn, founder of Dulwich College (see 1616), and a bequest in 1811 of 371 pictures, the collection of Sir Francis Bourgeois RA. The college engaged Sir John Soane, then at the height of his powers, to design a gallery. Unusually, this includes a mausoleum which contains the remains of Bourgeois, Soane and M. and Mme Desenfans, who were instrumental in the building of the gallery. In 1815 Soane built a smaller version of this mausoleum in St Pancras churchyard, as a tomb for his wife. Originally the gallery was flanked by almshouses, but these have since been converted to further gallery space.

1815

BURIAL OF A FANATIC

One of the first to be buried in the St John's Wood churchyard, on 1 January this year, was the religious fanatic Joanna Southcott. Born in 1750, she had become progressively zealous, claiming to be the recipient of divine commands. In her forties she began writing doggerel

Joanna Southcott, a religious fantasist who attracted many more.

prophecies much admired by the credulous; that they hardly ever came true did not deter her, and she resorted to sealing them in a box which was to be opened only later, when the events had come about.

By the early 1800s she was attracting converts to her brand of religion – quite respectable some of them, including some clerics. In May 1802 she moved to Paddington and set about obtaining 144,000 adherents who would be certificated by her. In the spring of 1805, one William Tozer opened a chapel for her in Southwark.

In 1813 she claimed that she was soon to become the mother of a spiritual child called Shiloh. In 1814 she shut herself away for the birth; she was examined by several doctors, who testified that she was showing the appropriate signs of pregnancy, and there was enormous excitement among her followers. A crib costing £200 was made in Aldersgate Street, and £100 was spent on feeding spoons. On 19 November Joanna told her doctor that she was dying and that he should open her body four days after her death. Her body was kept warm after she died, but an autopsy revealed no reason for her pains or her death. She was certainly not pregnant.

Southcott had directed that her tantalizing box should be opened in the presence of 24 bishops. Although sect followers have urged that it be opened since her death, it remained in the custody of a Yorkshire family called Javett, until it was eventually presented to Annie Stitt, head of the Southcottian Society, who in 1966 gave it to the British Museum for safety. It is claimed in a recent article by Val Lewis in the *Guardian* that the box was later opened by museum officials, who put some of its papers in the library and stored the rest of the contents in the basement, where they have since been lost track of. Modern Southcottians, it seems, believe that Shiloh is now occupying the body of Prince William.

CONNAUGHT HOTEL ESTABLISHED

Francis Grillon this year set up a hotel called the Prince of Saxe-Coburg, at the junction of Mount Street and Carlos Place. By 1820, it occupied three houses and was very soon, just like Claridge's nearby,

a fashionable hotel. Later called the Coburg, its name was changed again, during the First World War, to the Connaught.

A NEW BEDLAM

The Imperial War Museum, Lambeth Road, now occupies the central block of the old Royal Bethlehem Hospital, commonly known as Bedlam, the principal London lunatic asylum in the 19th century. This building, designed originally by James Lewis with later additions by Philip Hardwick and Sidney Smirke, was opened this year for the reception of 198 patients. By the time the hospital moved to Addington, in Surrey, after the First World War, there were over 400 inmates.

UNITED SERVICE CLUB FOUNDED

The United Service Club was founded this year in temporary premises in Albemarle Street, moving in 1819 to a new clubhouse at the corner of Charles II Street and Regent Street. This second building, specially erected for the club, was the first clubhouse built in London, but it was soon too small. The club moved again in 1828, to a rather more splendid building designed for it at the corner of Pall Mall and Waterloo Place.

1816

A NEW CANAL

The opening of the Grand Junction Canal basin at Paddington in 1801 had changed that rural area into a trading depot. Goods coming from the manufacturing industries of the Midlands could reach the outskirts of London in bulk. What was now wanted was a direct route to the London dockside, and it was this which inspired the creation of the Regent's Canal, to run from the Paddington Basin down to Limehouse. A scheme projected by Thomas Homer was approved by Parliament at a time when Nash was happy to have an ornamental canal going through his new Regent's Park, and in 1811 the venture was given the blessing and the name of the prince regent – which was not always an advantage, though on the whole it augured well in this case.

Unfortunately for the canal company, there were hard times ahead. Homer embezzled money and skipped the country; the innovatory

The Bethlehem Hospital, known as Bedlam, provided treatment for the insane. Its new building of 1815 is now used by the Imperial War Museum.

locks installed at Camden Town did not work properly and had to be replaced with conventional ones; a litigious landowner near St Pancras seriously hampered progress; and in the end there wasn't time to recoup the costs of the canal (far more than anticipated) before the advent of railways began to siphon off business.

The first stretch of the canal, from Paddington to Camden Lock, was opened on the prince regent's birthday, 12 August, this year.

A PRISON ON THE THAMES

The Tate Gallery now occupies much of the site of the infamous Millbank Penitentiary, an experimental prison which took in its first prisoners in June this year. The living conditions may well have been an improvement on those in jails such as the Fleet and Newgate, but the regime was much harsher. Ironically, as with Pentonville prison, which opened in 1842, the harshness of the prisoners' treatment stemmed from philanthropic motives.

In his work *The Panopticon or Inspection House*, the social reformer Jeremy Bentham had proposed the building of a prison in which the inmates were kept perpetually under supervision and in solitude; if they were encouraged to love labour, they could be improved as people, he claimed. To that end a large dose of religion was also eventually added. Bentham was sufficiently influential to obtain the contract to build the prison in partnership with the government.

However, Bentham ran out of funds, and the government took up his scheme, modified it, and built the largest prison in the country. An octagonal wall enclosed massive buildings in the shape of a six-point star; in the centre was an observation tower from which it was possible to oversee each block. There were 1,000 cells for single prisoners, none of whom was allowed to communicate or share with other inmates. Silence was observed at any communal activity, such as chapel. That the prison represented a vast change from the old-style buildings, and that the inmates were cowed into silence, must have impressed the philanthropic people who sat on its administrative committee.

The prison housed men, women and at times children. A scandal erupted when it was discovered that three small girls – two aged ten, and one seven and a half – had been in solitary confinement for a year and faced two more of it. Many of those imprisoned here awaited transportation to Australia, their journey to an even worse fate beginning at a pier opposite.

A CATHOLIC CHURCH IN HAMPSTEAD

One of the delights of present-day Frognal, in Hampstead, is the little Catholic church of St Mary, in Holly Place. Refugees from France had formed a congregation in temporary premises in Hampstead before the end of the 18th century, and a permanent priest, the Abbé Morel, was assigned to it. By 1814 the congregation was large enough (despite the return to France of many of the refugees) to appeal for funds to build a new church. The new chapel of St Mary was opened in August 1816; the architect is unknown.

NEW HOSPITALS

The Westminster Ophthalmic Hospital was opened this year in what is now William IV Street, off the Strand. It was primarily intended for the treatment of poor people with eye diseases. In more recent years the hospital was in High Holborn, as the West End branch of Moorfields Eye Hospital.

The Royal Infirmary for Diseases of the Ear was founded this year. By 1831 it was in premises in Dean Street, where in 1904 a new hospital was constructed. The Royal Ear Hospital, as it was later called, is

known to be the oldest hospital with this specialization in Europe.

What became the Royal Waterloo Hospital for Women and Children was established this year in St Andrew's Hill, in the City, as the Universal Dispensary for Sick and Indigent Children. It moved to Lambeth in 1823.

THE NEW VAUXHALL BRIDGE

The idea of the Vauxhall Bridge Company was not just to span the Thames but to build Vauxhall Bridge Road so as to connect the Hyde Park area with the southern side of the Thames. It was an optimistic investment, because traffic was fairly light and there was little residential property on either side of the bridge.

Originally a stone bridge by John Rennie was planned, but, suddenly, even when construction had begun, the company opted for a cast-iron bridge (the first such over the Thames) mainly designed by James Walker. Progress was slow, due to lack of funds, but it was opened on 4 June this year.

1817

DIVIDING THE WATER SPOILS

Since 1810 Parliament had encouraged free competition between the various water companies, in the hope that customers would obtain a better supply and a cheaper rate. But the hurly-burly of competition was found to be uneconomic, and there was insufficient return to the water companies either to make a profit or to invest in improvements. It was, in any case, absurd for different companies' pipes to be laid beneath the same stretch of pavement or road.

Between 1815 and 1817, to the dismay of vestries, the water companies serving London north of the Thames came to mutual agreements, parcelling out areas for monopoly supply. They then raised their charges. In 1821 a select committee claimed that the supply of water was not subject to the operation of the usual laws of supply and demand and that unlimited competition would only result in the ruin of some of the companies.

A FREE SCHOOL FOR JEWS

A meeting held at the Talmud Torah of the Great Synagogue in the City in 1814 had agreed to found a free school for Jews of German descent; the pupils were to be taught by the Lancaster monitorial system. The school opened this year in Bell Street, Spitalfields. Its descendant is the Jewish Free School in Camden Road.

A NEW THAMES BRIDGE

Hard on the completion of Vauxhall Bridge, Waterloo Bridge was opened this year on 18 June. It was inevitable that any significant structure or street would this year be named after Waterloo, but at the time of the foundation stone, in 1811, the projected name was Strand Bridge. John Rennie was the designer of this, the best-looking bridge across the Thames since the old London Bridge. The Italian sculptor Antonio Canova described it as 'the noblest bridge in the world … alone worth coming to London to see'. But even this epithet, and much opposition, did not save it from destruction in 1936.

A NEW CHURCH IN ST MARYLEBONE

After many years of indecision, a new parish church was opened in St Marylebone on the Marylebone Road; it is the building we see today near the junction with Marylebone High Street. Consecration day was 4 February. This was too early in the year for a marquee for guests at Mr Lord's cricket ground (see 1814), and a suggestion that they should be entertained in the 'Decent Women's Eating Hall at the Workhouse' was thought to be inappropriate. Instead, a small party was arranged in the vestry room of the new church, where light refreshments augmented by fowl, ham, port, madeira and beer met the occasion.

The architect was Thomas Hardwick, who had also designed St John's Wood chapel.

A NEW WINDMILL AT WIMBLEDON

A museum is now housed in the Wimbledon windmill, the only surviving hollow-post mill in England. It was built by Charles March of Roehampton in 1817. The machinery, housed beneath the superstructure, was worked by a drive taken down from the sails through the hollow post. The mill was closed about 1865 and converted into a residence, but it has since been restored to a semblance of its old form.

1818

THE FIRST ARCADE

Between 1816 and 1818 John Nash and G. S. Repton remodelled the auditorium of His Majesty's Theatre (also known at times as the Italian Opera House), in the Haymarket, and added a Doric colonnade on three sides of the outside. To the rear they constructed the Royal Opera Arcade, which runs between Charles II Street and Pall Mall. The earliest shopping arcade in London, and the only part remaining of the Nash scheme, this consists of 18 small shops on one side, each with a basement, a small mezzanine and a Regency bowed window.

ST JAMES'S MARKET DEMOLISHED

The creation of Regent Street involved the disruption of old street patterns. Some roads disappeared completely; others, such as Charles II Street, off Lower Regent Street, were cut in half as Nash bulldozed his grand avenue north from Carlton House. One casualty this year was St James's Market, which lay between Haymarket and St James's Square, precisely on the route of the new road. The market had in any case had its day and was a distinctly insalubrious feature in an expensive area. A vicar writing in 1856 remembered the market and the streets adjoining as 'very properly avoided by all persons who respected their characters or their garments, and were consequently only known to a "select few", whose avocations obliged, or whose peculiar tastes induced them to penetrate the labyrinth of burrows which extended to Jermyn Street'.

A new and much smaller provisions market was constructed to the west of Haymarket and just south of Jermyn Street, but it had closed by the First World War. The site is now occupied by a cinema, and the only reminders of its past are the odd arrangement of narrow roads here and a street name.

A NEW THEATRE ON THE SOUTH BANK

The Royal Coburg Theatre opened at the junction of Waterloo Road and the street market The New Cut. Its architect was Rudolph Cabanel, who had earlier built the Surrey Theatre. The local clientele was unsophisticated and boisterous, and the usual fare presented was melodrama. The opening night consisted of a harlequinade and a melodramatic

The Royal Coburg Theatre when it opened in 1818. As the Old Vic, this establishment was to play a crucial role in English theatre in the 20th century.

spectacle entitled *Trial by Battle, or Heaven Defend the Right*. The name of the theatre was to honour the unlikely patronage of His Serene Highness the Prince of Saxe-Coburg. A handbill advertising the first night proclaimed that:

The Nobility, Gentry and the Public are respectfully informed that the [Royal Coburg], which has been erected ... will open on Whit Monday, the 11th May 1818, under the immediate patronage of His Royal Highness of Saxe-Coburg, with entirely new entertainments now preparing on a scale of magnitude and great expense. The audience part of the theatre will be lighted by a superb Central Lustre, while others of a most costly description will shed a beautiful and brilliant light over the whole house.

On 26 July a clown called Usher drove a carriage pulled by four tom-cats along the Waterloo Road to the theatre as a publicity stunt. It was an inauspicious beginning for a theatre which, under its later name of the Old Vic, was to be one of the most important in theatre history.

FLOODING AT BATTLE BRIDGE

The area of Battle Bridge (King's Cross) was again flooded this year (see 1809) and there was a great loss of property when, after torrential rain, the Fleet river rose several feet and inundated every house around the area. No lives were lost, but a poor woman with her newborn child was nearly drowned. At about four in the morning the flood increased and swept away or covered some 30–40,000 bricks which had been made in the area.

HELPING BEGGARS

Even the most illustrious parts of London had pockets of poverty, as we have seen above apropos St James's Market. The concentration in the capital of large numbers of beggars, criminals and prostitutes was to be a favourite cause of social reformers for years to come. The Society for the Suppression of Mendicity was one of a number of organizations which began this year to tackle specific problems in a practical way. The needy were given tickets by the society, and could often obtain food and work when they presented them to members of the public.

THE BEGINNINGS OF CHARING CROSS HOSPITAL

A young man of independent means, Benjamin Golding, following the example of Thomas Guy in the previous century, this year opened the West London Infirmary, in Suffolk Street, behind the Haymarket. It was from the start a teaching hospital, and its patients were of the poorest — most of them living in the desperately poor hinterland between Haymarket and Covent Garden. In 1827 this establishment became the Charing Cross Hospital.

1819

FORMATION OF PICCADILLY CIRCUS

The most enduring result of the construction of Regent Street was the formation of Piccadilly Circus. It was originally a crossroads with the buildings at the corners set back in a semicircular shape, thus forming a 'circus'. This arrangement was destroyed in the 1880s when a new road, Shaftesbury Avenue, was inserted into the north-east corner, and the London Pavilion theatre encroached on the old circular area.

BURLINGTON ARCADE BUILT

The Burlington Arcade was opened this year across the gardens of Burlington House, to a design by Samuel Ware. The format chosen, with shops either side of a central avenue, was to provide an exemplar for arcades throughout the country. In its planning stage the architect described it as a 'Piazza for all Hardware, Wearing Apparel and Articles not offensive in appearance nor smell', but in 1817 the *Gentleman's Magazine* reported that it was to be for 'the sale of jewellery and other fancy articles' and intended 'for the gratification of the publick, and to give employment to industrious females'. More likely, as was stated at the time, the prime intention was to insert a buffer between the grounds of Burlington House and the backs of the houses in Old Bond Street.

The character of the shops has hardly changed. By 1828 there was a predominance of hosiers, linen-drapers, milliners, shoemakers and jewellers, but Henry Mayhew observed that several of the bonnet shops used the upper storey (provided for living space) for prostitution.

Burlington Arcade off Piccadilly, the model for many later arcades. The shops included milliners, shoemakers and jewellers.

Beadles enforced the rules of the arcade, but presumably turned a blind eye to upstairs activities. It was forbidden, as it still is, to whistle, sing or play a musical instrument in the arcade, or to carry a bulky package or an open umbrella. Nor may anyone run or push a pram.

CHANGES AT ISLINGTON

The Angel inn at Islington was a place well known to cattle dealers. At Islington, the last stop before Smithfield, there were numerous cattle lairs, and the Angel was the principal place to stay in the vicinity. This year the old inn, which possessed a double-galleried courtyard, was demolished and replaced by a new public house.

Nearby, the handsome Claremont Chapel in Pentonville Road was opened on 1 October. This building, which still survives and is occupied by the Crafts Council, was for local Congregationalists.

Across the road two important estates were being developed: that of the Lloyd Baker family, on the west side of Amwell Street, sloping down to King's Cross Road, and that of the New River Company, on unused land around its river head.

JOHNSON'S HOUSE BURNS DOWN

Dr Johnson had lived at 8 Bolt Court, off Fleet Street, from 1776 until his death in 1784. On 26 June this year the house, which had survived a fire in 1807, was entirely consumed by another blaze.

VILLAS IN REGENT'S PARK

One of the earliest villas erected in the new Regent's Park was The Holme, a mansion until recently long occupied by Bedford College. It was designed by the 18-year-old Decimus Burton (no doubt with the help of his father, James, who was the client) and, to our eyes now, it is a graceful ornament to the park. However, the Commissioners of Woods and Forests of the time, responsible for the park's development, thought it was ugly, and Nash, who had no liking for James Burton, concurred. In a letter to Nash, the Commissioners referred to his adverse comments on the house and agreed that it should never have been built, before going on to lay the blame on Nash himself for allowing it to happen.

1820

REGENT'S CANAL FULLY OPENED

The toast drunk at the opening of the Regent's Canal down to Limehouse, on 1 August, was 'Prosperity to the Regent's Canal'. Unfortunately, the enterprise had not many years to recoup its outlay, for the age of railways was around the corner.

The making of the canal as far as Camden Town had been almost without incident. After that there were problems. A Mr Agar was a litigious thorn in the canal company's side as it sought to cut the route through his St Pancras lands; then, when the canal got just east of what is now Caledonian Road, a very long tunnel had to be cut beneath the Barnsbury Ridge. During the excavations for this the remains of a crocodile were found. The canal then went to the City Road Basin, where numerous wharves and warehouses were built, and then on to near the West India Docks at Limehouse.

A PRISON AT BRIXTON

In 1820 the Surrey House of Correction was opened on Brixton Hill, then an agricultural district. The individual cells were small — only

1800s

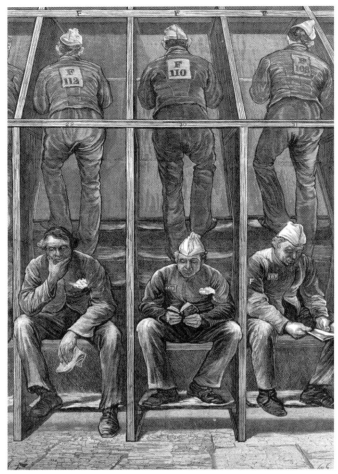

The treadmill was first introduced into what is now Brixton prison in 1820. It is here seen at the Clerkenwell House of Correction in 1874.

about 8 ft square and 6 ft high – ventilation was poor throughout, and the prison was soon overcrowded, with many of the larger cells containing three men.

It was the first English prison to use the treadmill, a large drum with slatted steps on which a line of men would continually tread, thereby turning a shaft connected to a millhouse. The buildings were later used for Brixton Prison.

BAKEWELL HALL DEMOLISHED
The old City woollen cloth market, Bakewell Hall, at the corner of Basinghall Street and Gresham Street, was demolished this year, and a courthouse was erected on its site.

FAIRLOP OAK BLOWN DOWN
The remains of the famous Fairlop Oak in Hainault Forest were blown down this year. As measured by a Swedish naturalist, at 4 ft above the ground it was 30 ft in girth, and its branches spread 116 ft. Around it took place the annual Fairlop Fair – an event which helped to shorten the tree's life, because visitors would use the inside of the trunk to light fires for cooking. The tree caught fire in 1805 and, although it was put out by the next day, the trunk was considerably weakened. It needed only the high winds in February this year to finish the job. Some of its timber was used the following year to build the pulpit in St Pancras New Church on Euston Road.

1821

A LAVISH CORONATION
The coronation of George IV was both lavish and unpopular. The extravagance of its presentation was in keeping with his previous lifestyle, and its unpopularity was a result not only of his persistent overspending, but of his treatment of Queen Caroline, who was reduced to appearing afterwards at Westminster Hall in the hope that she would be admitted to the festivities. She wasn't.

On 19 July the king walked in costumed procession from Westminster Hall to the abbey, led by the king's herb-woman and her attendants, who, as tradition required, strewed the way with herbs and flowers to ward off plague. It was a hot day, and most of the principal performers were weighed down with robes and ornamentation. The ceremony lasted five hours, and the king – in his late fifties – was often seen to be pale and near collapse. But he survived with dignity (and sal volatile), and then sat down with his guests at the last coronation banquet held at Westminster Hall.

THE SPREAD OF GAS
The Gas Light and Coke Company (GLCC) had begun selling gas in 1813; the City Gas Company was incorporated in 1817 and reached a boundary agreement with the GLCC in 1820. However, this cosy arrangement was threatened by the Imperial Gas Company (1821) – its later gasholders still dominate the King's Cross skyline. The incorporation had been got through Parliament with the aid of judicious bribes, and the management was corrupt. But it had a good potential territory, having been allocated (after agreement with the GLCC) the northern arc of London outside the City and Westminster.

The same year the first gas company in Essex was established – the Whitechapel Gas Light and Coke Company. Its prime task was to light the turnpike road from the City to Essex.

On the west of London the year saw the beginning of the Brentford Gas Light Company, which was empowered to supply a large territory from Richmond to Kensington.

NEW CHURCHES
It had lately been a relatively quiet time for church building, although numerous chapels had been established, such as the Gower Street Chapel, opened in 1820 by a breakaway congregation of the William Huntingdon Chapel in Gray's Inn Road. In Stamford Street, south London, a Unitarian chapel was begun in 1821 and had to be substantially enlarged later in the century; all that now remains of this once flourishing and handsome concern is the freestanding Doric portico overlooking the street.

A new St Paul, Shadwell, was consecrated on 5 April. It was designed by John Walters, who died this year.

THE NEW HAYMARKET THEATRE
One consequence of the building of Regent Street (the lower stretch from Carlton House to Piccadilly was opened this year) was that the Haymarket Theatre was rebuilt – this time further south, so that its frontage would face the vista along Charles II Street from St James's Square. Although the Corinthian-pillared exterior which we see today was much admired, the interior was not popular and was twice remodelled in later years. The new theatre, designed by Nash, opened on 4 July with a production of *The Rivals*, but its predecessor continued to stand for nearly a century, converted into shops and restaurant.

WEST END FAIR SUPPRESSED

One of the liveliest fairs around London was that which took place on three days in July on West End Green, west of the village of Hampstead. But, like many fairs, if the pillars of local society are to be believed, it became too boisterous and unmanageable. In 1819, according to a local clergyman, some 200 'London roughs' assembled at the fair and 'assaulted the men and the women with brutal violence, cutting their clothes from their backs'. Constables were brought in to subdue a riot. A magistrate testified that when he was a boy the fair consisted of five toy and gingerbread booths and a single show, but, since a cowkeeper near the green had let out a field for more sideshows and stalls, the fair had mushroomed. It was finally suppressed in 1821.

1822

THE ERECHTHEUM ON EUSTON ROAD

One of the most noticed churches in London is St Pancras New Church on Euston Road, a Greek Revival building owing much to the Erechtheum and the Tower of Winds in Athens, with prominent caryatides of terracotta very similar to Coade stone. It was designed by William and Henry William Inwood (father and son), who were responsible for several other churches in the neighbourhood.

The church, consecrated on 7 May, was much criticized for its 'pagan' architecture at a time when Gothic was coming into fashion. The St Pancras vestry wasn't happy either because of its cost – it was the most expensive church of its time. But, as the first Greek Revival church in the country, it represents an architectural milestone. It was built at a time when Londoners were admiring the recently arrived Elgin Marbles.

A ROTUNDA IN WOOLWICH

The Rotunda in Green Hill, Woolwich, which now houses the Museum of Artillery, began as an ornamental tent in St James's Park, erected as part of the peace celebrations of 1814; the designer was John Nash. It was re-erected at Woolwich between 1819 and 1822.

PENANCE IN BETHNAL GREEN

A young woman was obliged to do penance in Bethnal Green churchyard in May, for calling her sister-in-law by a bad name. The woman, dressed in a white dress, confessed to the local population and asked forgiveness of God and them.

A NAKED ACHILLES

In the aftermath of Waterloo, Wellington was the nation's hero, and on 9 July a vast statue of Achilles was unveiled in his honour on the south-east corner of Hyde Park. However, its naked form shocked the Ladies of England, an organization which had suggested a statue in the first place, and a fig-leaf was added to the sculptor Richard Westmacott's design.

SUNDAY TIMES FOUNDED

On 20 October the *Sunday Times* first appeared, although it was the same paper which its proprietor, over a year earlier, had cheekily called the *New Observer*, and then the *Independent Observer*, in the hope of poaching sales from the *Observer*. It was published at 4 Salisbury Court and printed at 76 Fleet Street.

1823

THE LONDON MECHANICS

A significant meeting occurred on 2 December at the Crown and Anchor tavern, in the Strand, when the London Mechanics' Institution was founded. The educationalist Dr George Birkbeck was one of the promoters. The purpose of the institution was to provide evening education for those 'mechanics' who wished to better themselves. Later it became known as the Birkbeck Literary and Scientific Institution, and later still Birkbeck College. By 1850, 650 mechanics' institutions existed.

This pioneering institution, which had 1,300 pupils in its opening year, met first in Dr Lindsay's Chapel in Monkwell Street, in the City.

DANCING ON THE DEAD

Enon Chapel in Clements Lane, Clare Market, was established this year with vaults beneath for burials; a grave could be had here for 12s. A writer in 1839 described it thus:

Vast numbers of bodies have been placed here ... soon after interments were made, a peculiarly long narrow black fly was observed to crawl out of many of the coffins; this insect, a product of the putrefaction of the bodies, was observed on the following season to be succeeded by another, which had the appearance of a common bug with wings. The children attending the Sunday School, held in this chapel in which these insects were seen to be crawling and flying, in vast numbers, during the summer months, called them 'body bugs'.

There was nothing between the floorboards of the chapel and the coffins. By 1844 this highly obnoxious place was being hired out for dances, so that people could 'dance on the dead'.

THE DIORAMA OPENS

On 6 October a new panoramic entertainment called the Diorama was opened in Park Square East, Regent's Park. It had taken only four months to build, but had cost £10,000. It was the project of Louis Jacques Daguerre, a French scene-painter and inventor of 'daguerreotype', a process of photography on to metal. The exterior of the building was by Nash, and the interior by Augustus Welby Pugin.

The entertainment consisted of large scenes viewed in two circular darkened rooms, each with a revolving floor, with the paintings lit from windows behind and from skylights, so that some kind of reality was achieved. It was immensely popular – on Easter Monday in 1824 the receipts were £200.

A PROPRIETARY CHAPEL

The last surviving proprietary chapel in London is that of St John, Downshire Hill, Hampstead, a handsome classical building in an equally handsome street. Opened on 26 October 1823, it was the venture of a cleric, a builder and a land speculator; the architect is unknown, but it was probably William Woods, the builder. Most likely it was intended to be a chapel of ease to St John's Hampstead as development took place around the Pond Street area, but as funds were offered privately by the clergyman it became a proprietary chapel.

THE LANCET FOUNDED

The *Lancet* was first published this year, from Bolt Court off Fleet Street, to publicize new advances in medicine and to investigate what the proprietor, Thomas Wakley, thought was corruption in making medical appointments to public bodies.

1800s

Wakley's medical career had been temporarily halted by an unprovoked and murderous attack by several men in 1820; his house at the top end of Regent Street was burnt to the ground at the same time. It was conjectured that the gang consisted of remnants of the Cato Street conspiracy (which had aimed this year to murder the prime minister and his government and set up a new administration), and that they were revenging themselves on the man who they thought was the masked surgeon who had decapitated those executed for treason in the affair. However, the fire-insurance company refused to pay compensation on the house, alleging that Wakley himself had set fire to it. By 1821, when a court had pronounced in his favour, his medical practice had virtually disappeared.

The *Lancet* was unpopular among the medical establishment. Wakley sought to publish any lectures that practitioners had given, and to report the details of operations – the sort of knowledge that physicians and surgeons wished to keep to themselves – and his campaigns against malpractice in appointments and in surgical operations brought him the fierce opposition of leading medical men of the day.

ROYAL ASIATIC SOCIETY FORMED
The Royal Asiatic Society was formed at a meeting at the Thatched House tavern in St James's Street this year. It has an extensive and valuable library of manuscripts and books.

1824

A NEW LONDON BRIDGE
London Bridge, devoid of its picturesque houses, was now to many eyes an irregular, probably unstable, construction. But, though there were proposals to replace it, there were also doubts expressed as to the effect on the tides of the river if the narrow and numerous arches of the old bridge were succeeded by the wider and fewer arches of a new bridge. It was calculated that at high tide the width of free waterway would increase from 524 ft to 690 ft, and at low tide from 231 ft to the same 690 ft. Take away the barrier of the old bridge and what would happen? In a London that was periodically flooded at high tides, such uncertainties were grounds for much caution. And, with the increased volition of the water, would the river carve more deeply into its bed and so undermine shoreline wharves and buildings?

The hard winter of 1813–14 did much damage to the old structure, and fresh proposals were made to replace it. In 1823 John Rennie was awarded the contract to produce a design, and on 15 March 1824 the first pile was driven into the water, about 100 ft west of the old bridge.

THE BEGINNINGS OF THE NATIONAL GALLERY
The idea of a National Gallery had been around for some years, although it was not entirely popular. Constable thought that it would be 'the end of art in poor old England'.

Early in 1823 Sir George Beaumont offered his valuable collection of pictures to the nation, provided that a suitable building was found for them. This offer was put to Parliament, and at the same time it was remarked that in 1824 another collection, that of Sir Julius Angerstein, would be coming on to the market. Despite political difficulties, the government agreed to accept Beaumont's offer and to find the money to buy Angerstein's collection – 38 pictures for £57,000. On 10 May 1824 the Angerstein collection was put on display to the public in its late owner's house in Pall Mall – in effect, the first National Gallery exhibition.

A WAVE OF NEW CHURCHES
The quickly expanding London was about to see a dramatic increase in the number of churches built, and this key year marks the transition from classical to Gothic Revival buildings. Camden Town, for example, which had been built without a church, was graced by one by the Inwoods (see 1822) – Camden Chapel, now called All Saints, in Camden Street. It was consecrated on 15 July. All Souls, Langham Place, was finished by John Nash and was consecrated on 25 November.

South of the river, several important churches were opened. St John, Waterloo Road, designed by Francis Bedford, was consecrated on 3 November. Bedford was also the architect of the delightful church of Holy Trinity in the little-known gem called Trinity Church Square in the hinterland of Blackfriars Road; this was opened on 16 December. Another architect about to be heavily involved in London churches was D. R. Roper, who designed St Mark, Kennington, which opened on 30 June.

All the above were classical churches, but the first Gothic Revival church in England – St Luke, Sydney Street, Chelsea – complete with flying buttresses, was consecrated on 18 October. It was the work of James Savage, but the spire he planned was never built. Charles Dickens was married here to Catherine Hogarth in 1836.

CAMPAIGN FOR NEW CEMETERIES
An expanding population required larger burial grounds. In London, fragmented into small parishes, with no overall body to follow the example of Paris in providing a municipal cemetery, the problem was dealt with inadequately. There was also insufficient supervision of private burial grounds, some of which had become unspeakably fetid. George Carden, a barrister, concerned himself with this situation, and in the *Penny Magazine* this year he suggested that public cemeteries should be built. It was to take the cholera epidemic of 1832 to produce action.

TWO NEW CLUBS
The Athenaeum Club was founded this year by John Wilson Croker, who convened a meeting on 16 February to establish 'a Club for scientific and literary men and Artists'. A temporary home was found in

The Athenaeum Club in Waterloo Place. The clubhouse, shown here early in the 20th century, was designed by Decimus Burton and opened in 1830.

Waterloo Place, and permanent premises were planned straight away. Croker, a politician and writer, is credited with coining the political description of 'Conservative'.

The Oriental Club was founded by officers of the East India Company, who were ineligible for membership of the London military clubs. By 1891, when the club had fine headquarters in Hanover Square, it was described as 'composed of noblemen and gentlemen who have travelled or resided in Asia, at St Helena, in Egypt, at the Cape of Good Hope, the Mauritius, or at Constantinople'. The club now occupies a spectacular building in Stratford Place.

A Famous Forger

Buried in Bunhill Fields is Henry Fauntleroy, banker, who this year was executed for a sensational and enormous forgery, involving, so the more lurid newspapers said, about £250,000, which he had spent on gambling and women.

Fauntleroy had entered his father's own bank, Marsh, Sibbald & Co., of Berners Street, as a clerk in 1800, and became a partner in 1807. He soon became the manager, but on 14 September 1824 a notice appeared informing the public that the bank was suspending payments in consequence of 'the very unexpected situation in which we find ourselves placed by the extraordinary conduct of our partner, Mr. Fauntleroy'.

On 2 November Fauntleroy was sentenced to death for forgery and, although many attempts were made to commute the penalty, the law proceeded almost without hesitation. He was executed at Newgate before an estimated 100,000 persons.

Protection for Animals

Attempts to prohibit cockfighting and bull-baiting in 1822 were indicative of a new perception of animals. In 1824 the Society for the Prevention of Cruelty to Animals was founded by the Revd Arthur Broome, and it was to be the focal point for future activities in this sphere. The inaugural meeting was at Slaughter's Coffee House in St Martin's Lane (now marked by an RSPCA plaque), and those present included an Irish MP who in 1822 had sponsored an Act to protect horses and cattle.

The early concerns of the society were draught horses, the conditions and methods used in slaughterhouses, and the abolition of cockfighting and bull-baiting. It initially attracted little public support.

1825

Tunnelling beneath the Thames

Construction began in January of the first completed tunnel beneath the Thames. The financial motive for this was that a road connection between the two banks east of the Port of London was badly needed. A bridge was out of the question, as it would impede the increasingly larger ships that clogged the river.

A tunnel had already been proposed in 1798 by the ubiquitous Ralph Dodd, an engineer with experience of canals and bridges (see 1807). He proposed a tunnel between Tilbury and Gravesend, at an estimated cost of £16,000; this, he said, with an eye to government approval (and using one of the arguments favouring the construction of the New Road in 1756), would be very advantageous for the movement of troops. Surprisingly, Dodd's scheme received serious governmental support, and in 1799 an Act to make the tunnel was passed.

But after expenditure of about £17,000 without result, other than some useless shafts, the scheme was abandoned.

In 1802 Robert Vaizey, a Cornish mining engineer (whose 1812 scheme for a tunnel to allow the formation of the Archway Road was to end disastrously), proposed a tunnel between Limehouse and Rotherhithe, strategically placed to serve the docks. It was to be passable for horses, cattle and carriages. This tunnel also ran into very early difficulties, and the company directors called in another opinionated Cornishman, Richard Trevithick, to take over, with Vaizey as his deputy – an arrangement which lasted but a few months. But progress was made until 1808. Then, in January, when Trevithick himself was in the tunnel watching excavations, 1,000 ft from the entrance, there was a quick inrush of quicksand followed by Thames water. Running back for their lives, the men were swept along by a flood which reached up to their shoulders. They escaped to tell the tale, but from then on the scheme was effectively dead.

It was not until the appearance of Marc Isambard Brunel that another attempt was made. Brunel had patented a tunnelling machine called the Great Shield, an iron cylinder which could be propelled forward and housed workers using a cutting edge, followed by miners lining the tunnel behind it. The Thames Tunnel Company was formed in 1824 to construct a tunnel from Wapping to Rotherhithe, three-quarters of a mile upstream from the route chosen by Vaizey.

Work began in 1825, when Brunel laid the first brick of the shaft on the Rotherhithe side and his teenage son, Isambard, laid the second. The tunnel – the first to carry public traffic beneath a river – took 18 years to build. It is now used for the London Underground link between Wapping and Rotherhithe.

A New Road to Tottenham

Construction began this year on a road from Camden Town to Tottenham – along the present line of Camden Road and Seven Sisters Road. The road went through fields mostly, but it helped encourage the development of Camden Town, and where it crossed Holloway Road became the obvious place for a major shopping centre later in the century.

A Soane Church

An unexpected treat in today's Walworth, in Liverpool Grove, is Sir John Soane's first church, St Peter, consecrated in February this year. It is a fine classical building with an Ionic portico and a tower topped by a cupola. Unfortunately the church was badly hit in the last war.

St Katharine's Moves

To the consternation of the existing dock companies, yet another new dock was proposed – St Katharine's Dock, by the Tower of London. But the promoters of this scheme had more than just trade opponents, for their plan involved the destruction of not only a medieval almshouse and school, but an entire community. St Katharine's foundation, dating from 1148, had remained under the patronage of the queen of the day; in 1825 there was no queen and George IV was its owner. Its precinct had become a large community of about 1,250 houses, all threatened by the scheme.

The opposition and protests of the precinct's residents failed because there were vested interests against them – and in any case the foundation was prepared to go quietly, as well it might because it was paid a good sum to do so. No compensation was paid to the residents.

The last service in the foundation's chapel was held on 30 October. It was a moving affair. The *Gentleman's Magazine* reported on the 'expression of just feelings of indignation against the ruthless

1800s

A watercolour of the Grosvenor Canal, which originally ran from the Thames up to the site of Victoria station.

destroyers of the ill-fated building'. The institution was then rehoused comfortably in new premises in Regent's Park, in an incongruous Gothic Revival set of buildings designed by Ambrose Poynter.

GROSVENOR CANAL OPENED
The Grosvenor Canal, a project of the Grosvenor estate, was opened on 5 March. It ran from just east of the present-day Chelsea Bridge, where the remnants of a dock still survive, up to the area now covered by Victoria station. To a large extent the canal was an adaptation of the works and cuts of the old Chelsea Waterworks Company, whose pumping station had been on the Thames here.

By 1899 the canal, truncated by the extension of Victoria station, was only 550 yards long and was almost exclusively used by Westminster refuse barges.

NEW HOME FOR THE PHYSICIANS
The building to the west of Trafalgar Square now occupied by the insurance company Sun Life of Canada was built as the new head-quarters of the Royal College of Physicians. Designed by Sir Robert Smirke, it was opened on 25 June.

CLAPHAM PARK BEGUN
In 1825 Thomas Cubitt leased about 220 acres of farm land in Clapham, together with a mansion which Cubitt himself took, and there planned the Clapham Park estate. Wide, tree-lined roads were laid out and then, in the manner of the time, the plots were let out to individual developers. Progress was slow, but the quality was good – large mansions in spacious grounds. Many of these were demolished by the end of the 1930s, and almost all the rest went after the last war, to be replaced by municipal housing.

1826

BEGINNING OF LONDON ZOO
A meeting of the founders of the Zoological Society of London was held on 26 February. One of the society's principal spirits was the colonial administrator Sir Thomas Stamford Raffles, an enthusiastic

botanist and zoologist, whose own collection of papers and specimens had been lost at sea. A general meeting was held on 29 April, and a charter was obtained in 1829.

The nature of that original foundation has had repercussions in modern times. The purpose of the society was research; to that end, fellows could study animals in the comparative freedom of the site that was leased in Regent's Park, and could examine the specimens in the short-lived museum and use the library provided. The admission of the public was a secondary and later facility, which brought in money to finance the research functions. The reduced number of admissions of recent years and the escalating costs of providing a public zoo have therefore threatened the existence of the research programme.

The society had originally wanted the area within the Inner Circle later taken by the Botanic Society, but had to be content with 5 acres within the Outer Circle on the less fashionable Camden Town side, and another 6 acres between the Outer Circle and the canal.

Raffles died this year, before the society had proceeded very far. The vicar of Hendon, who derived much of his income from slave plantations, declined to officiate at Raffles's funeral, because the latter was an associate with his neighbour William Wilberforce in the campaign to abolish slavery. Nor would the vicar sanction a memorial in his church.

DESTRUCTION OF AN ELEPHANT
The hazards of keeping wild animals in restricted spaces were empha-sized by a well-publicized incident in the Strand very soon after that first meeting of the zoo founders. Edward Cross had a menagerie at the old Exeter Change, containing lions, tigers, monkeys, a hippopota-mus and an elephant called Chunee, which weighed 5 tons. *The Times* reported on 2 March that:

This enormous animal [the elephant], which for many years past has been the pride and boast of the well known menagerie at Exeter Change, was yesterday afternoon destroyed by order of the proprietor in consequence of its having exhibited strong symptoms of madness. The work of death was accomplished by repeated discharges of musketry, the noise of which, together with the agonized

Exeter Change in the Strand, housing a billiard room and Cross's Menagerie. Engraving by Thomas Shepherd.

groans of the poor beast, being distinctly heard in the Strand, caused such immense crowds to assemble, that it was found necessary to close the avenues leading to the shops at the lower part of the building ... Two parties of the Bow Street Patrol ... were also stationed ... This [animal] had been an inmate of the menagerie for 17 years. The effect of its unavoidable seclusion had displayed itself in strong symptoms of irritability during a certain season from the first, and these symptoms had been observed to become stronger each succeeding year.

THAMES BREAKS THROUGH INTO TUNNEL

In January the river broke into the newly cut Thames Tunnel. By then the tunnel had advanced only 14 ft and the matter was soon dealt with, but it was the first of many calamities in the construction of this massive venture. A first casualty was a ganger who fell down the shaft while drunk. More ominous were the patches of firedamp which occurred particularly at high tides; these would ignite and make the cutting shields very hot. Men were constantly ill with fever and diarrhoea. By March this year the tunnel was already halfway beneath the river, but the senior engineer collapsed from overwork and the conditions inside; Brunel's relatively inexperienced young son, Isambard, took over.

BRIDGE ACROSS THE SERPENTINE

This year the bridge across the Serpentine between Kensington Gardens and Hyde Park was completed. It was designed by John and George Rennie.

LAST STOCKS DEMOLISHED

What were thought to be the last stocks left in inner London, those in Portugal Street, belonging to St Clement Danes parish, were removed on 4 August.

SHOT TOWER BUILT

The round shot tower near Waterloo, which was still a feature when surrounded by the 1951 Festival of Britain, was built this year for Thomas Maltby & Co. Molten lead droplets fell 120 ft within it, cooling to lead shot.

NEW THOROUGHFARES

This year Parliament consented to a new turnpike road – the Finchley Road – to lead from St John's Wood chapel to Finchley. The promoter of the road was Henry Eyre, whose St John's Wood estate needed a principal road through it to increase its development potential. The main opponents were the residents of Hampstead, and in particular the lord of the manor, Sir Thomas Maryon Wilson, who was later to be the villain of a much more important parliamentary struggle over his plans to build on Hampstead Heath (see 1829). Though construction of the road began in the next few years, it took considerably longer before it got past Swiss Cottage.

Construction began of Caledonian Road through Islington, although at first it was called Chalk Road.

Most development, however, was taking place in the previously marshy area owned by the Grosvenor estate south-east of Knightsbridge. First it had to be drained – a task which had already begun under the guidance of the entrepreneur and builder Thomas Cubitt. Over the next few years he built Belgravia, a stuccoed, up-market scheme of roads around the centrepieces of Belgrave, Eaton, Chester and Lowndes squares; in the 1830s he added the more modest development of Pimlico down to the Thames.

CARLTON HOUSE DEMOLISHED

Carlton House, at the bottom of today's Waterloo Place, the former palace of the prince regent, on which so much money had been spent since 1783, was this year demolished. The grand avenue called Regent Street, constructed to lead in some magnificence from Regent's Park to the prince's residence, now came to an abrupt end at a sheer drop down to The Mall. The portico of the house was saved and used for the National Gallery in Trafalgar Square.

A NEW MARKET

Farringdon Market, for the sale of fruit, vegetables, meat and fish, was opened on 20 November. It was situated between Farringdon Street and Shoe Lane, and was demolished later in the 19th century to make new approach roads to Holborn Viaduct. Designed by the City's architect, William Montague, it was a well-ventilated, lofty structure, with buildings on three sides containing 79 shops, with space for more stands.

1827

LONDON'S FIRST SUSPENSION BRIDGE

Hammersmith Bridge, London's first suspension bridge, was opened on 6 October. Designed by William Tierney Clarke, it had a central span of 422 ft, and also included a mid-river steamboat pier so that services could operate whatever the state of the tide.

MARBLE ARCH ERECTED

The Marble Arch, which was unveiled this year, was designed by John Nash to stand outside the revamped Buckingham Palace. Based, it seems, on the Arch of Constantine in Rome, with reliefs by Richard Westmacott and Edward Baily, it had also been planned to have an equestrian statue of George IV on top, by Francis Chantrey, but this was eventually placed in Trafalgar Square instead. The arch was moved to its present site on the north-east side of Hyde Park in 1851.

CROCKFORD'S OPENED

Crockford's, the gambling club, was founded this year at nos. 50–53, St James's Street, in a building designed by Benjamin Wyatt. William Crockford, son of a fishmonger in the Strand, entered the same trade himself at a shop near Temple Bar. He managed to amass a considerable fortune by gambling, or the supervision of gambling, and was able to build his first clubhouse this year in extravagant style. It was immediately the rage in London, attracting aristocratic clients who were prepared to wage huge sums. At one stage Crockford was said to be worth £1,200,000, but after a number of unsuccessful speculations he died in 1844 worth about £350,000.

1828

A UNIVERSITY FOR LONDON

A self-styled London University, owned by a limited-liability company, opened University College in Gower Street in October. It eschewed religious affiliations – a factor which incurred the wrath of the educational and religious establishments and provoked the founding, also this year, of King's College, London, which sought most positively to include the Church of England's influence in its curriculum.

1800s

University College, Gower Street, an engraving by Thomas Shepherd dedicated by the artist to the exertions of Henry Brougham and Thomas Campbell.

The radical founders of University College owed much to the Scots poet Thomas Campbell, who had argued powerfully for a London university in a letter to *The Times* in 1825, but the enterprise was largely the work of Henry Brougham, the Scots politician. A site at the top end of Gower Street was bought in 1825, but it was not until 1828 that the magnificent buildings of University College, designed by William Wilkins (who was later to design the National Gallery), were in use. Pugin, absorbed in Gothic Revival, thought that Wilkins's design was pagan and 'in character with the intentions and principles of the institution'.

In the same year the University Dispensary was opened in Gower Street as part of the medical faculty of the university. It was another six years before a fully fledged hospital, University College Hospital, was available.

ST KATHARINE'S DOCK OPENED

St Katharine's Dock, just east of the Tower of London, was opened on 25 October. This enterprise, which had dispossessed so many people of their homes, was founded to exploit the situation in which the docks to the east, the East India, West India and London Docks, were in the next few years about to lose their monopolies on certain sections of trade granted to them as compensation for their initial capital investment. Unfortunately for the shrewd promoters, they had ignored the possibility of large steam-driven ships requiring deeper draughts than the dock they were building could provide.

Thomas Telford had been employed to design the docks within what was obviously a constricted space – he did not have the freedom of the virgin sites to the east of him. It was a massive construction. Bargeloads of excavated soil were taken upriver to form a base for Cubitt's Belgravia; up to 2,500 men were employed in a project which involved the use of iron railways and steam engines.

Telford packed the various functions of a 19th-century dock into a small space. Transit sheds were done away with; instead cranes, driven by treadmills, reached out from the warehouses straight over the ships. The warehouses themselves formed the walls of the docks and provided the necessary security.

NEW CHURCHES

The pace of church building was increasing. Most new churches were still classical, but a growing number were Gothic Revival. St Peter's,

opened on 27 June 1827 in Eaton Square to attract the nobility to Cubitt's new estate, was a Greek Revival design by Henry Hakewill. Two churches were built in Regent Square, south of the Euston Road. One, St Peter's, was designed by the Inwoods, who had built St Pancras New Church, in classical style; this was consecrated on 8 May 1826. (The Inwoods then dexterously turned their hands to a Gothic church in Eversholt Street, where they built St Mary's; though it was consecrated on 11 May 1826, construction was not completed until the following year.) The other church in Regent Square was the National Scotch Church, under the ministry of the famed Revd Edward Irving, which was designed by Sir William Tite in Gothic style and opened on 11 May 1827 at a consecration service attended by Sir Robert Peel and Samuel Coleridge.

St Mark's, North Audley Street, was opened on 25 April 1828. It was designed by J. Gandy Deering in a 'Corinthian' Greek style. In growing Islington, three churches were added. St John's, in the fields of upper Holloway Road, was consecrated on 2 July 1828; its architect was the young Charles Barry, and this was his first building in Gothic style. Barry was extremely busy in 1828. In the same year he built Holy Trinity, Cloudesley Square – a generous provision on an estate which was hardly yet built; its style is taken from that of King's College, Cambridge. He also built St Paul's at the junction of Essex Road and Ball's Pond Road.

On a more prominent site was Holy Trinity, Marylebone Road, designed by Sir John Soane and designed to catch both the populations south of that road and those moving into the terraces of Regent's Park. This was consecrated on 31 May.

A NEW CLUBHOUSE

At the junction of Pall Mall and Waterloo Place the new clubhouse of the United Service Club was opened on 18 November. Designed by John Nash, it included, as a gift from George IV, the central staircase from Carlton House. This building is now occupied by the Institute of Directors.

THE ROYAL CALEDONIAN ASYLUM

Caledonian Road, in Islington, derives its name from the Royal Caledonian Asylum, a home for the support and education of children of Scottish servicemen killed or wounded in action and of poor Scots living in London. Its original premises were in Hatton Garden, but this year it moved to a substantial building just north of today's Pentonville Prison, designed in Greek Revival style by George Tappen. The children were obliged to wear tartan dress.

A NEW GUILDHALL LIBRARY

This year the City opened, for the benefit of members of the Corporation, a new library, the predecessor of the one now in Aldermanbury. It was intended to create 'a library of all matters relating to this City, the Borough of Southwark and the County of Middlesex'. There were 1,700 books in all.

DISASTER AT THE ROYAL BRUNSWICK

The Royal Brunswick Theatre, off Wellclose Square, opened on 25 February with a gala performance in front of 3,000 people. Three days later, at a rehearsal, the entire roof fell in, bringing down the front façade of the building; 12 people were killed. The manager, who was watching the rehearsal at the time, had noticed a shaking chandelier just before the incident, and survived to tell the tale by leaping into a box, pulling a small girl after him.

THE BEGINNINGS OF THE ROYAL FREE

William Marsden, a compassionate surgeon who was unable to procure the admission of a poor woman into a hospital because she did not possess any letter of introduction from a patron, this year set up a dispensary-cum-hospital 'to receive all Destitute Sick and Diseased Persons, to whatever Nation they may belong, who may choose to present themselves as Out-Patients, and as great a number of In-Patients as the state of the Charity will permit'. Needless to say, he encountered opposition from the medical authorities for being so open-handed, but the institution's worth was recognized during the great cholera epidemic of 1832, when it alone received cholera patients.

1829

THE METROPOLITAN POLICE FOUNDED

Sir Robert Peel, home secretary since 1822, had been considering reform of the methods used to police London. Soon after his appointment, uniformed patrols, nicknamed 'Peelers', appeared on the streets of central London; however, this was very far from an organized system of crime deterrence and detection. To all intents and purposes, whatever central control there was still emanated from the magistrates' office in Bow Street, but in 1824 the horse patrol's need for new accommodation led to a historic move – premises were found for the patrol at 8 Cannon Row, almost on the site of New Scotland Yard.

It was not until Wellington became prime minister in 1828 that Peel found himself with sufficient support to proceed with a radical plan for a metropolitan force whose remit would extend from as far as Highgate in the north to Camberwell in the south. In April 1829 Peel introduced, with guarded words, his new scheme, and by July it had received the royal assent. Organization was swift, and premises for the new force were found at 4 Whitehall Place in Scotland Yard, part of the old Whitehall Palace area.

The metropolitan area was divided into 17 police divisions, each with 165 men. A uniform of dark blue, with top hat, was introduced, but the only weapon was a truncheon, augmented by a rattle to attract help.

Though short of uniforms at that stage, a 'dress parade' of those policemen recruited so far was held in the grounds of the Foundling Hospital on 26 September. The 1,000-odd men were read their terms, conditions and obligations and were sworn in. On Tuesday 29 September, from the still unfinished station house in Scotland Yard, the first metropolitan policeman went out on duty.

THE BATTLE FOR HAMPSTEAD HEATH BEGINS

The opening shot was fired this year in what became a famous battle to save Hampstead Heath. Sir Thomas Maryon Wilson, who lived in some style at Charlton House in south London, was also manorial lord of Hampstead. There he possessed two estates: the larger, of 356 acres, either side of the new Finchley Road and the other, of 60 acres, wedged between Hampstead Heath and the earl of Mansfield's Kenwood estate in St Pancras. As for the heath itself, Wilson had manorial jurisdiction, but his right to build on it was more questionable. The difficulty for Wilson was that his father's will had prohibited building on these estates, and this could be overturned only by an Act of Parliament or else by consent of Wilson's own heir on reaching the age of 21. As Wilson was unmarried (and remained so), an Act was necessary. His application, which principally concerned the two estates, over which he had undoubted title, was perfectly normal, and were it not for a minor clause it would have been passed without demur.

But Wilson asked also for powers to grant building leases for any parcels of land from the heath that he enclosed. It was this part of his application that began a cause célèbre and brought into sharp focus the diminution of London's commons. The ire of those copyholders who had grazing rights on the heath was aroused, and the matter also caught the attention of newspapers concerned about the loss of recreational ground for Londoners. The *Morning Herald* summed up the working man's viewpoint:

A group of Peelers in their original tall hats. To the right is a policeman in the helmet which was introduced in the 1860s, the probable date of this photograph.

1800s

Sir Charles Burrell [a supporter of Wilson's bill in Parliament], who can retire to his estate in Sussex for recreation, may think it unnecessary that the Heath should be preserved as 'a place of recreation for the tradesmen of the metropolis, their wives, children and friends' but if he were confined to a sedentary trade for six days out of the seven, in sooty London, he would probably argue differently. The comforts of the lower classes are too much neglected by the Aristocracy of the country, and we do hope that this attempt to deprive 'tradesmen' of the pleasures of fresh air, will be defeated.

The battle was to last 42 years. At the end of it Wilson was dead, his plans still unsuccessful, his name detested, and Hampstead's heath intact and even expanded. But if Wilson hadn't been greedy in the first place matters would have ended entirely differently and the heath as we know it today would not have been formed.

MR SHILLIBEER'S BUS

A Mr George Shillibeer, in business as a coach-builder and livery-stable keeper in Bury Street, Bloomsbury, introduced to the streets of London on 4 July an omnibus, drawn by three horses. Its design was copied from a vehicle he had seen in Paris. The route chosen for his service was from Paddington to Bank along the New Road; the fare for the whole journey was 1s 6d for those inside the bus, and 1s for those sitting outside on top.

The vehicle was a long, high-sprung, box-like structure with a flat roof and a door at the rear end, approached by three steps. It could hold 20 passengers inside, in two facing rows. The *Morning Post* of 7 July described it as 'a handsome machine, in the shape of a van, with windows on each side and one at the end'.

Shillibeer's choice of route had a reason: it was illegal for stage coaches to take up or set down passengers in central London, other than at recognized places, and the same prohibition would probably have extended to the omnibus. On Shillibeer's route – today's Marylebone, Euston, Pentonville and City roads – this restriction did not apply and, as another newspaper pointed out, 'there is no delay in taking up and setting down; no calling at booking offices'.

George Shillibeer's omnibus was introduced in 1829 from Paddington to the Bank. Within years there were numerous bus companies, and eventually the authorities permitted them into central London – to the fury of cabmen.

The Colosseum in Regent's Park, a rotunda for the display of panoramas. After its initial success, it lost its novelty and was demolished in 1875.

A STAG IN PADDINGTON CHURCH

A young boy, John Pocock, recorded in his diary on 20 February:

A beautiful stag, hunted by His Majesty's hounds and about 60 riders of distinction, passed our school room windows. He made off for Kilbourn and was turned close by our house; the whole neighbourhood presented a very lively appearance from the number of huntsmen in their scarlet coats. The stag set off in the direction of Paddington and, coming to the Grand Junction Canal, swam across towards the Church. It so happened the door was open and he bounded in and was caught inside the Church! The poor creature who was a victim to this inhuman 'sport' must have given chase at least 35 miles, as he was started at Hounslow and had made a long circuitous route.

A NEW GENERAL POST OFFICE

A new General Post Office, designed by Sir Robert Smirke, was built on the site of the old St Martin's le Grand monastery this year.

REBUILDING ST GEORGE'S HOSPITAL

St George's Hospital had long outgrown the old Lanesborough House at today's Hyde Park Corner. This year a new building, designed by William Wilkins, was opened. Much of it has been converted into today's Lanesborough Hotel.

COLOSSEUM OPENS

At Cambridge Gate in Regent's Park a large rotunda was this year opened to display a panoramic view of London, painted by E. T. Parris from 2,000 sketches by the brave Thomas Horner, who had made them while secured in a cage on the dome of St Paul's Cathedral. Decimus Burton designed the building, a 16-sided affair with a Doric portico. The Colosseum was finished by 1827, but by then Parris was still painting (he had 40,000 square feet to cover) and Horner and his chief financial backer had skipped the country, leaving a trail of debts behind them.

The exhibition finally opened on 10 January 1829. It was divided over two galleries on different levels, and spectators could also climb to the roof of the building to see the City in reality.

1830

A MARKET HALL FOR COVENT GARDEN

By the end of the 19th century the market in Covent Garden Piazza had become the largest in England for the sale of fruit, vegetables and flowers. By usage and tradition the various specialities were sold in different parts of the square, and in the centre there were even people selling birds, crockery or old iron. London was surrounded by market gardens. The growers loaded up their carts at sunset the night before and in the small hours of the morning made their way to Covent Garden market to catch the dealers at five o'clock. The crops were then dispersed by the dealers to shops around London, using ill-paid Irish women who quite often carried the loads on their heads. Under flickering oil or gas lamps the scene in Covent Garden must have been an extraordinary one.

Apart from the need to put up proper buildings for this expanding trade, the duke of Bedford, who owned the market, was anxious to regulate more precisely the tolls he could extract. To this end he acquired an Act in 1828 enabling him to demolish whatever buildings existed in the piazza and to build a new market hall.

The architect chosen, Charles Fowler, was already at work on plans to rebuild Hungerford Market in the Strand. His original building for Covent Garden opened in 1830 and was substantially what we see today, but without the iron and glass roof, which was installed in the 1870s.

However much better the market place was, there was no improvement in its access. There were still bars across Southampton Street, Burleigh Street and Maiden Lane, to prevent traffic coming in from the Strand. King Street led out to St Martin's Lane, but only through the very narrow New Row, and Bedford Street's exit to the Strand was, and still is, also restricted. Only from Russell Street and James Street could anything like adequate access be obtained.

COPING WITH FIRES

In 1828 the Fire Escape Society had been formed to encourage the provision of better firefighting and escape equipment. It solicited donations from the public and vestries to limited effect. The society's work in rescuing occupants was important because the insurance-company brigades were obliged only to rescue property, with occupants, in theory, as a secondary bonus. Such devices as 'escape conductors' were placed in streets, and could be wheeled to houses on fire to rescue occupants from upper storeys.

A new development was the invention in 1829 of the steam fire engine, by John Braithwaite. This was a horse-drawn vehicle on which was mounted a 10-horsepower steam-driven pump. This new engine's debut was a spectacular one – at the fire which destroyed the Argyll Concert Rooms off Oxford Street on 5 February. There the manually operated engines summoned to the scene froze up in the low temperatures, but the steam fire engine continued to function for five hours, until the fire was put out. (It was, indeed, a very cold winter: 22 degrees below freezing had been registered on Hampstead Heath towards the end of January.) The drawbacks of the new machine were that it was too slow getting up steam, was cumbersome to use, and needed more water than the street hydrants could supply.

NEW BUSINESSES

Some well-known businesses began this year. They included James Smith, maker of sticks and umbrellas, whose highly decorative premises in New Oxford Street are still a delight to residents and tourists.

Samuel French Ltd, the publisher and seller of playscripts, has its origins in a shop set up in 1830 by the 20-year-old Thomas Lacy in Wellington Street, selling acting editions of plays. With the lifting of the monopoly of Covent Garden Theatre and the Theatre Royal in the production of plays, there were soon more theatres than good playscripts to go round, and Lacy swapped new items with Samuel French, who had set up a similar business in America. French settled in London in 1872, buying out Lacy.

Chapman & Hall, the first publisher of Charles Dickens, was established this year by Edward Chapman and William Hall.

Edmund Crosse and Thomas Blackwell came to London in 1830 and were apprenticed to West & Wyatt, purveyors of 'condiments, relishes and other forms of chandlery' in premises on the present site of the Shaftesbury Theatre. These two young men later bought out their employers and so began the famous firm of Crosse & Blackwell, which moved to Soho Square in 1834.

KING'S ROAD GOES PUBLIC

The King's Road, Chelsea – or at least the part from Sloane Square to Old Church Street – was until this year a private road belonging to the king, his route to Hampton Court or Kew. In 1830 it was assigned to the care of the various parishes for its upkeep.

NEW SCHOOLS

University College School was opened this year in Gower Street, to act as a feeder of suitable scholars to the newly established University College. It had 80 boys in its first term, but so popular was it among dissenting and non-religious parents that a year later it had a roll call of 249. The school now occupies buildings in Hampstead.

LAST MAN IN THE PILLORY

Peter Bossey, convicted of perjury at the Old Bailey, stood in the pillory there as a punishment. He was the last man in London to do so.

1831

LONDON BRIDGE OPENS

The new London Bridge was opened on 1 August; William IV and Queen Adelaide came by state barge from Somerset House, as part of a river pageant, to perform the ceremony. The bridge had taken seven years to build. It was two and a half times broader than its medieval predecessor, the carcase of which still stood slightly to the east, awaiting its demolition. In 1832, when workmen were demolishing the undercroft of the chapel on the old bridge, the bones of Peter of Colechurch, the bridge's architect, were discovered. They appear to have been thrown away, probably into the Thames.

The new bridge, built by Sir John Rennie to his father's designs, was re-erected at Lake Havasu City, Arizona, when the present structure was built in 1967–72.

A NEW ASYLUM

In the village of Northwood, part of rural Hanwell, the Middlesex County Asylum was opened this year, set in a very large estate of 55 acres. It was a result of the passing of the 1808 County Asylums Act, which enabled magistrates to raise a county rate to provide proper care for mentally ill patients. At first the buildings accommodated only 300 people in long, low brick blocks arranged on three sides of a

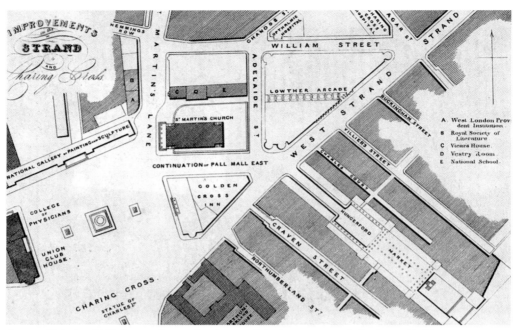

A map published in 1831 showing the actual and proposed developments around what became Trafalgar Square.

square with octagonal towers at the two open ends and in the middle of the third side; a large gatehouse fronted Uxbridge Road. Eight years later there were nearly 800 inmates crowded into the same buildings.

The patients constituted a small town. Under the humane supervision of Dr William Ellis, they worked at agriculture, kept livestock, and even made their own gas supply.

A RIVAL UNIVERSITY

The founding of the 'godless' London University in 1828 had inspired the swift establishment of an alternative but firmly Church of England university. On 8 October this year, on the Strand, King's College was opened at a ceremony attended by the duke of Wellington, archbishops and 30 bishops.

The building, designed by Sir Robert Smirke, was in effect another wing of Somerset House. It consisted of two parts. One was a junior school for middle-class boys, the other was for older boys about to begin their careers.

A SPA AT NORWOOD

The day of the spa was not yet over. In Norwood, a medicinal spring was this year exploited by landholder John Davidson. He employed Decimus Burton to convert what had been Bewlys Coppice into a health resort and place of entertainment with a maze, a library, a camera obscura and an orchestra. The water was pronounced by Michael Faraday as 'one of the purest and strongest of the saline spas in the country', and was enjoyed by people as famous as Mrs Fitzherbert. But the Royal Beulah Spa, as it was called, did not last long. By the 1840s it was in decline, and it was eclipsed in attraction by Crystal Palace in 1854. Burton's lodge still survives.

A NEW ARCADE

The head office of Coutts & Co., the bankers, at 440 Strand, occupies the site of Lowther Arcade, which was opened this year. The promoters aimed for a fashionable clientele, but by the second half of the century the arcade was the most popular place in London for toyshops.

Its construction was part of a general rebuilding of the area. The King's (Royal) Mews had only recently been demolished and its site was to be used for the National Gallery; Trafalgar Square was in the offing. Here, at the west end of the Strand, there were numerous insanitary alleys and courts leading up to Chandos Street. The whole lot was taken down and Adelaide Street and King William (now William IV) Street were built, forming a triangle which the arcade crossed.

In 1832, when the Reform Bill was passed, a grand ball was held in the gas-lit arcade, at which 700 persons danced to a late hour. Lowther Arcade was demolished in 1902 for the rebuilding of Coutts.

A CALUMNY REMOVED

In the later part of the 17th century, when the mood of London had been very anti-Catholic, the lord mayor ordered a new inscription to be made at the base of the Monument which repeated the lie that the Great Fire of London had been the work of Catholic arsonists. The words included 'The burning of this protestant City was begun and carried on by the treachery and malice of the Popish faction, in order to the effecting their horrid plot for the extirpating the protestant religion and to introduce Popery and heresey.' In the wake of new legislation aimed at restoring greater civil rights to Catholics, this inscription was removed on 26 January.

CHANGES IN GREENWICH

A Greenwich Hospital Improvements Act was obtained this year which resulted in the replanning of central Greenwich. This produced Nelson Road, College Approach, King William Walk and a new market.

GARRICK CLUB FOUNDED

The Garrick Club 'for the general patronage of the drama; for the purpose of combining a club on economical principles with the advantages of a Literary Society; for the formation of a Theatrical Library and Works on Costume', was founded this year at 35 King Street, Covent Garden. This apparently 'arty' venture did, however, include 1 duke, 5 marquesses, 6 earls and 12 barons.

PAGANINI'S LONDON DEBUT

The violinist Niccolò Paganini was mobbed on the streets of London on his first visit this year, when he performed at the King's Theatre on 3 June. According to the *Sunday Times*:

He entered from the side to the right of the audience, and advanced with an unsteady step. He acknowledged the plaudits which welcomed him, with an air of extreme humility and gratitude, which was as often repeated as the tributes of admiration were multiplied in the course of the evening.

EXETER HALL OPENED

At 372 The Strand, now occupied by the Strand Palace Hotel, the Exeter Hall was opened on 29 March this year. It provided space for very large meetings – religious, scientific and political – and as such was an important venue in the more tumultuous years of the 19th century. The Anti-Slavery World Convention was held here in 1840, Shaftesbury's Ragged School Union began here in 1844, but there were also concerts in which the large organ was used.

1832

CHOLERA SWEEPS LONDON

In a year in which an event of national importance, the Reform Bill, was finally resolved, London was devastated by a virulent epidemic of cholera. The disease had first appeared in the docks at Rotherhithe, Limehouse and Southwark. It was highly infectious, killing within hours, after a painful period of vomiting and dehydration.

The disease appeared at a critical time in the progress of the Anatomy Act through Parliament. This highly contentious piece of legislation was designed to provide more subjects for surgeons and anatomy schools by allowing dissection of the bodies of paupers whose relatives were too poor to pay for their funerals. Previously the demand of anatomy schools had been partially met by the legal use of the bodies of hanged murderers. The other clear intention of the promoters was to ensure such a sufficiency of legal corpses as to destroy the livelihood of body-snatchers, whose actions still scandalized the country.

The Zoological Gardens near the Elephant and Castle provided Edward Cross with the opportunity to move his animals from the Strand menagerie.

A UTOPIAN BUSINESS IN THE GRAY'S INN ROAD

In September, Robert Owen, who had eight years previously begun a London Co-operative Society, opened an Equitable Labour Exchange in the former premises of the North London Horse Repository in Gray's Inn Road. The purpose of this enterprise was to 'promote the exchange of all commodities by giving equal values of labour' – it was a way by which the artisan and poorer classes were able to obtain better value for their input. It was a short-lived home for the venture, which moved to Charlotte Street the following year.

A ZOO IN SURREY

Edward Cross's menagerie in Exeter Change in the Strand (see 1826) had been overcrowded, and in any case the Change was needed for redevelopment. He moved his collection this year to a site in today's Penton Place, between Kennington Park Road and Walworth Road, having helped found the all-embracing Surrey Literary, Scientific and Zoological Institution and, as part of the deal, sold it the animals for display. It became a public zoo, which the Regent's Park zoo was not, and was for a time a success, but it closed for lack of support in 1855.

THE EARLY CREMORNE GARDENS

About this year the grounds of Cremorne House, south-west of today's World's End in Chelsea, were turned into a sporting complex. The original house here, Chelsea Farm, built by the earl of Huntingdon (married to the appallingly pious countess of Huntingdon), overlooked the river. From 1778 it was enlarged by Thomas Dawson (later created Baron Cremorne). It was bought in 1831 by one Charles Random de Berenger, self-styled Baron de Beaufain or Baron de Berenger. The 'Baron' turned the grounds into a 'stadium' for 'various skilful and manly exercises', including swimming, rowing, shooting, fencing, archery, riding etc. (Stadium Street and Cremorne Road now indicate its location.)

The stadium does not seem to have been profitable, and it was reopened in 1845 as Cremorne Gardens, the latest of the London pleasure gardens, with outside and inside entertainments.

A LEATHER MARKET IN BERMONDSEY

The tanning industry, particularly unpopular because of the obnoxious odours it emitted, had long been concentrated in Bermondsey, a marshy and relatively unpopulated part of south London, where the flow of the Thames was made use of for cleaning and the oak bark plentiful in the neighbourhood was used for tanning. So awful was the smell that during the Great Plague of 1665 many people came here in the belief that the odour killed the infection.

Although the tanners of Bermondsey received a charter from Queen Anne, it was not until this year that a proper market was built, at the junction of Weston Street and Leathermarket Street.

CARLTON CLUB FOUNDED

The defeat of the Tories in 1831 brought about a reassessment of both policy and organization. That year a house in Charles II Street was used for a headquarters, but proved too small; it was agreed that a political club should be founded. At a meeting at the Thatched House tavern in St James's Street on 10 March this year, at which the marquis of Salisbury took the chair, a committee was appointed to look out for a clubhouse. It was not until 1836 that a permanent home was built by Sir Robert Smirke in Pall Mall, in which the social aspect was mixed with the straightforward running of the Conservative Party in the House of Commons. The club moved in 1940 to St James's Street.

THE BEGINNINGS OF TUFNELL PARK

Tufnell Park, in the north of Islington, had its origins this year in an Act enabling the trustees of the will of William Tufnell Esq., lord of the manor of Barnsbury, to grant building leases on his estate.

1833

A FIRE BRIGADE FOR LONDON

The haphazard arrangements for dealing with fires in London were improved this year when, on 1 January, the London Fire Engine Establishment came into being. Previously, responsibility for firefighting had been piecemeal. Individual insurance companies had brigades whose remit was to deal with fires on property insured by them; parishes had limited facilities and sometimes fatally slow mechanisms for gathering the necessary workforce together; the Lighting and Watching Act of 1830 enabled parishes to provide a proper fire service, and some, like Hackney and St Marylebone, did form brigades of part-time men; sometimes private fire brigades existed, such as the one at Hanwell Asylum.

The London Fire Engine Establishment was formed by the insurance companies, who pooled their resources to create one professional brigade under the leadership of James Braidwood, formerly head of the Edinburgh Fire Brigade, the first municipal brigade in the country. Inner London was divided into four districts for brigade purposes, each under a foreman with three engineers.

LONDON'S FIRST CEMETERY

Kensal Green Cemetery in Harrow Road was consecrated on 24 January this year, and the first interment took place a week later; 39 acres were set aside for Anglicans and the remaining land for Dissenters. It was the culmination of a long campaign to avoid the use of London's fetid burial grounds. George Carden, a barrister, had urged reform of burials since the 1820s; having helped to establish the General Cemetery Company, he persuaded businessmen to purchase about 54 acres of land (unfortunately, of heavy clay) and, with the cholera epidemic raging in 1832, Parliament was easily persuaded to grant the company the necessary powers to open a cemetery.

There was much discussion on whether the architecture of the cemetery should be classical or Gothic; the argument was so contentious that Carden, a pro-Gothic director, was voted off the board of the company. The classical buildings which we see today are thought to be the work of John Griffith, and were completed four years after the cemetery was opened. Laid out with triumphal arch, catacombs and grassed walks, Kensal Green became a model for other cemeteries to come. It was a world removed from the disgusting, overcrowded London churchyards and parish burial grounds that people were used to. The relocation of death into a respectable environment was probably as responsible as any other factor for the growing commercialization of the burial process and the morbid interest that attached itself to funerals in the rest of the 19th century.

Kensal Green was an enormous success. By 1842, 6,000 burials had taken place, and the monuments vied for attention in their expense, ornateness or peculiarity.

HUNGERFORD MARKET REOPENS

Hungerford Market, on the present site of Charing Cross station, was rebuilt this year to the designs of Charles Fowler, architect of Covent Garden Market; the new building was opened on 3 July. The old market, principally for provisions, had been declining for some years and was taken over by a private company. The new building revived trade for a while, and the Hungerford Suspension Bridge, opened in 1845, helped bring customers from across the river, but the market was never much of a success. It was demolished in 1860 to make way for the railway.

A SUBSCRIPTION LIBRARY IN HAMPSTEAD

At a time when there were no municipal libraries, it was common to find local subscription libraries in middle-class areas. That at Hampstead is one of the best-documented. It began with a meeting on 1 March this year, and its first premises were in Flask Walk. The original subscribers included the writers Lucy Aikin, Joanna Baillie and Samuel Rogers, and the artist John Constable. (Constable, incidentally, gave a talk on the history of landscape painting at Hampstead Assembly Rooms this year.) The publishers John Murray and Thomas Longman, both local residents, each gave 150 books, as did the populist publisher Charles Knight.

WIFE-SELLING IN LONDON

In the neighbourhood of Portman Market, in July, a husband sold his wife to the highest bidder. *The Times* recorded how

At the appointed time the husband, accompanied by his wife, entered the crowded arena, the latter having been led to the spot in the usual manner, with a halter round her neck. The business then commenced amid the hissings and hootings of the populace, who showered stones and other missiles on the parties. The first bidding was 4s., and the next 4s. 6d., after which an interval elapsed, amidst the call of 'Going, going' from the auctioneer. At last a dustman stepped forward, and exclaimed 'I wool give five bob' (5s.). The woman was 'Knocked down' for the sum, and the dustman carried her off, nothing loth, amidst the hisses of the crowd.

RIOT AT CLERKENWELL

At a meeting at Cold Bath Fields, Clerkenwell, convened on 13 May by the National Union of Working Classes, a policeman was killed when armed forces were brought in to suppress the gathering.

PETER ROBINSON ESTABLISHED

Peter Robinson, a Yorkshire linen-draper who had just served his apprenticeship, set up business this year at 103 Oxford Street, a site which was later covered by a large clothes shop bearing his name at Oxford Circus. Robinson's shop had a dressmaking department, and later on, in Victorian times, when death was so ritualized, he opened other premises dealing only with mourning clothes and accoutrements.

1834

PARLIAMENT DESTROYED BY FIRE

On 16 October a 'Dreadful Conflagration' destroyed the Houses of Parliament. The accident was caused by the burning of a large amount of wooden Exchequer tallies in the stoves of the House of Lords; the excessive heat set fire to the chimney flues, and the blaze spread to the Lords' chamber, the Painted Chamber and St Stephen's Chapel (the House of Commons). The London Fire Engine Establishment was called in at 7 p.m. to fight a fire which had been discovered an hour earlier. At 8 p.m. the roof of the House of Commons fell in, and efforts were then concentrated on saving Westminster Hall.

Sir John Cam Hobhouse MP, who witnessed the fire, recorded that:

The whole building in front of Old Palace Yard was in flames and the fire was gaining ground. I assisted in breaking open the entrance to Bennett's cloakroom and then, with several others, rushed upstairs to the Libraries above, next to Bellamy's Eating Rooms. There I directed the men with me to bring down the books from the Libraries, and sent for cabriolets and coaches to carry them over the way to St Margaret's Church. Shortly afterwards a large body of troops marched down and more fire engines came. The soldiers worked admirably; so did the police. I ordered liquor for them and the firemen, who now worked very earnestly and did great service.

Twelve engines and 64 firemen fought the blaze throughout the night, hampered by the low tide of the river. Westminster Hall was saved, but little else of the medieval group of buildings was left.

SUPPORT FOR THE TOLPUDDLE MARTYRS
This year, six farm labourers in the village of Tolpuddle, Dorset, were transported to Australia for the offence of combining in a trade union. The authorities were increasingly unhappy at the militancy of the lower classes, and in particular the formation of unions.

The Tolpuddle Martyrs became a cause célèbre. On 21 April a large meeting took place on Copenhagen Fields, Islington, to protest at the savagery of the sentence on the Dorset men, and to sign a statement to the home secretary to that effect. About 30,000 marched to Downing Street from Islington after the meeting. (Following nationwide protests, the Tolpuddle men were pardoned after two years.)

AN INSTITUTE FOR ARCHITECTS
The (Royal) Institute of British Architects began at a meeting this year; its first premises were at 43 King Street, Covent Garden.

NEW HOSPITALS
As part of the rebuilding of the streets between the Strand and Chandos Street, the Charing Cross Hospital was built to the designs of Decimus Burton. This hospital was a development of the West London Infirmary (see 1818).

Patients were first admitted this year to the new Westminster Hospital in Broad Sanctuary, opposite the west door of the abbey. The architects were William and Henry Inwood, here using an Elizabethan Gothic style, a departure from the Greek Revival style they used for their churches.

The North London Hospital (later renamed University College Hospital) was opened this year in Gower Street, opposite the quadrangle of University College, in buildings designed by Alfred Ainger. It was the first hospital that was a product of a medical school, rather than the other way around. There were beds for only 130 patients, and it was built for less than £7,600 – much more cheaply than University College itself. All 'architectural decorations,' it was stated, 'have for the sake of economy been studiously excluded'.

HANSOM CAB PATENTED
In December, Joseph Aloysius Hansom, architect of Birmingham Town Hall, took out a patent on a 'Safety Cab'. His original cab was an ungainly affair, with a wooden body slung low on 7 ft 6 inch wheels, the driver perched on top and doors at the front. A John Chapman modified this in 1836, and it was his design, rather than Hansom's,

which became the standard London cab of the 19th century, although, such is the whim of fame, it was Hansom's name which became attached to it. Hansom was later the first editor of the *Builder* magazine.

A MONUMENT IN WATERLOO PLACE
Once Carlton House had been demolished and Waterloo Place constructed as the tail-end of Regent Street, something had to be done about finishing off the grand avenue and coping with the sharp drop down to The Mall. In 1832 steps were constructed down to The Mall, and in 1834 Benjamin Wyatt's Duke of York Column, with a statue by Richard Westmacott, was unveiled to provide a suitably significant terminus to the road.

The duke of York in question was the famous one of the nursery rhyme, who marched his troops up and down hill. He died heavily in debt, and his creditors were scandalized at the expenditure on this monument in Waterloo Place. It was claimed jocularly that, perched on this column, he was out of the reach of creditors, and that the lightning conductor on top was useful for the spiking of bills.

A NEW LYCEUM
The portico of the present Lyceum Theatre in Wellington Street belongs to the theatre which was opened in July this year, built to the design of Samuel Beazley. It was the fifth Lyceum, but on a slightly different site from the previous buildings. In 1812 Beazley had also built the fourth Lyceum, which had burnt down in 1830.

The new theatre still operated within the laws governing the monopoly of theatrical productions, and could stage only light entertainments and opera until 1843.

1835

ST JAMES'S THEATRE OPENS
The St James's Theatre in King Street was opened on 14 December this year. Its owner was a tenor singer, John Braham, and the architect was Samuel Beazley, who only the year before had finished the Lyceum. The first night consisted of three pieces: a burletta and two farces.

THE BEGINNINGS OF HARROD'S
Henry Charles Harrod began his business as a wholesale grocer and tea-dealer in Cable Street, Stepney, this year. He moved to Eastcheap in 1849, and acquired premises on the Brompton site four years later. Expansion occurred during the management of his son, Charles Digby Harrod, in the 1860s.

NEW LIVERY HALLS
Two substantial, and in many ways magnificent, new livery halls were now in the City of London. The Fishmongers' Company had taken advantage of the construction of the new London Bridge, which took the site of the Fishmongers' post-Fire building, to erect a large new hall, designed by Henry Roberts with the young George Gilbert Scott as his assistant. It is an 11-bay building facing London Bridge, with Ionic columns supporting a five-bay pediment. This was opened in 1834.

The new Goldsmiths' Company Hall in Foster Lane, which was opened on 15 July 1835, was the work of Philip Hardwick. The hall itself is still lit by candle chandeliers which were shown at the Great Exhibition of 1851.

1836

THE RAILWAY REACHES LONDON

On 8 February the first railway train ran in London, between temporary stations at Spa Road, Bermondsey, and Deptford. Its owner, the London & Greenwich Railway, was able to run trains to a makeshift and primitive terminus at London Bridge on 14 December. On 24 December 1838 the first trains ran across the Ravensbourne river down to Greenwich. The line had been relatively cheap to construct. Mostly it ran through agricultural land or market gardens, and it was in any case raised on arches to take up the least land.

A RIVAL CATTLE MARKET

The inconvenience of having a live cattle market (and numerous slaughterhouses) at Smithfield, so close to the City and so far into the centre of town, had been acknowledged and commented on for some time. The City of London was not anxious to do anything about it, partly to avoid expense and partly because it feared it would lose its monopoly if the market was moved to a site outside the City's jurisdiction.

This tardiness led to a private venture of one John Perkins, who, armed with an Act of Parliament, opened the Islington Cattle Market off Essex Road this year. It was set up in the teeth of opposition from the City and those whose interests were tied to Smithfield, but some newspapers were pleased. One remarked that 'The citizens will be deprived of the wholesome excitement occasioned by the sight of half-strangled oxen dying of thirst, the bellowing of bullocks, and yelling of drovers; the salubrious smells arising from the city cellar-hole slaughter-dens; and many other delights which the said citizens have hitherto enjoyed in full swing.'

Perkins hoped to cream off the trade that came through Islington on its way to Smithfield, but, despite the relatively lavish provision of pens and the handsome and hygienic buildings, his hopes were unrealized. The Islington market was used instead to house cattle on their way to Smithfield, and Perkins made a loss of £100,000.

A STATUE AT BATTLE BRIDGE

It is odd that one of the best-known place names in London comes from a very short-lived monument. 'King's Cross' was the popular name for an absurd statue placed at the junction of roads called, in 1836, Battle Bridge. The story of this statue began in 1830, when a local landholder approached the St Pancras vestry with the suggestion for a statue of St George to be placed before the Small Pox Hospital; St George's Cross was the proposed name. It was to have an illuminated clock on two sides and space for fire ladders, and the lower part was to serve as a police station. The aim was to enhance the reputation of an otherwise sleazy part of outer London, as the landholder wanted to develop streets nearby.

As it happened, George IV died that year, and the promoters changed their proposal to a statue of that king rather than of the saint – although the late king was hardly likely to elicit more donations.

The statue, designed by Stephen Geary, an architect later to be credited with the building of the first gin palace as well as some of the work at Highgate Cemetery, took five years to complete. The police station was there by 1831, the illuminated clocks never appeared, and the much-ridiculed form of George IV did not crown the edifice until 1835 or 1836. The whole thing was taken down in 1845, but the name of King's Cross stuck and, once it had been appended to the railway station, that of Battle Bridge died out.

A UNIVERSITY FOR LONDON

The government founded the University of London this year for the purpose of 'ascertaining by means of examination the persons who have acquired proficiency in Literature, Science and Art'. The university was in effect an examining body enabled to grant degrees to scholars of University College, King's College and any other college of sufficient status. It retained this role until a reconstitution in 1900, when it became a federal organization, to which the constituent parts belonged, but more directly concerned with teaching and research.

REFORM CLUB FOUNDED

In response to the success of the Tory Carlton Club, the radicals in Parliament founded the Reform Club. The first committee meeting of the new association was held at 104 Pall Mall on 5 May this year.

STEAMING TO EPPING

The *Sunday Monitor* recorded how in October this year a man called Walter Hancock, accompanied by a party of gentlemen interested in scientific inventions, set off in his steam vehicle *The Automaton* from the City Road towards Epping. On arriving at Woodford, which he reached at a speed of 10 miles per hour, he stopped the carriage in front of the Horse and Groom, where the landlord procured a fresh supply of water. 'Mr Hancock then ascended Buckhurst Hill at the speed of 7½ miles an hour and entered Epping amidst the loud cheers of some thousands who were collected in the town, it being market day, and created much astonishment among many of the country folk who had never seen such a vehicle before, and could not imagine how it was moved without horses.'

Hancock's attempt to popularize steam omnibuses was not, however, a success: they were generally too slow and too expensive.

STIRRINGS OF DEMOCRACY

The Reform Act of 1832 hardly met the expectations of the country's wage-earners. It has been calculated that it enfranchised only another half a million of the well-to-do commercial classes, leaving the rest of the country still without a vote.

It was hardly surprising that working-class movements were to increase in number and influence – and the pardoning of the Tolpuddle Martyrs this year gave reformers a tremendous fillip. In 1836 William Lovett founded the London Working Men's Association to campaign for universal suffrage. Lovett was secretary, and its membership included the philanthropist and reformer Francis Place. It was probably Place who set out the six points of the famous 'People's Charter' – manhood suffrage, secret ballots, payment of members of Parliament, annually elected parliaments, abolition of property qualification for members of Parliament, and equal electoral districts. The 'Chartists' were now a force in the land.

1837

A NEW QUEEN

The Victorian age was nearly cut short in its first year. On 10 July *The Times* reported that

On Thursday evening, as Her Majesty and the Duchess of Kent, with their attendants, were proceeding from Highgate to Kentish Town, in descending the hill, the carriage, not having a drag chain, proceeded at a very rapid pace, and the

The Fox and Crown on Highgate West Hill, displaying the coat of arms which was the landlord's reward for coming to the assistance of Queen Victoria.

horses became restive and plunged violently, and great anxiety prevailed for the safety of the Royal party. Fortunately, however, Mr. Turner, landlord of The Fox, rendered the most prompt assistance by affixing a chain to the wheel of the carriage. Her Majesty, who alighted at Mr. Turner's house for a short time, while the preparations were being completed, was pleased to notice Mrs. Turner and her children in the kindest manner, thanked Mr. Turner for his prompt attention, and, seeing the ostler liberally remunerated for his trouble, took her departure for Kensington Place, highly gratified at her providential escape.

Mr Turner's inn, now no longer there, was the Fox and Crown on the west side of the steepest part of Highgate West Hill. He was granted a royal warrant for his troubles, and the magnificently decorated coat of arms which accompanied it is now housed in the Highgate Literary and Scientific Institution.

TRAINS INTO EUSTON

On 20 July the London & Birmingham Railway opened its line from a temporary station at Euston Square to Boxmoor in Hertfordshire; the full service to Birmingham did not begin until September the following year. The original plan had been for a terminus at Chalk Farm, where the Regent's Canal barred the way, but by 1835 it became obvious that a terminus nearer to London's centre was essential. The canal had to be crossed either under or over, and the latter method was chosen. This resulted in a steepish incline up from Euston, beyond the capabilities of the early engines. Robert Stephenson's answer was to build at Chalk Farm a stationary engine which could haul up trains up from Euston on an endless cable at 20 miles per hour; going the other way, the trains went down by gravity.

There was much opposition to the line. Farmers complained that it was impossible to let land contaminated by railways, and alleged that trains turned the sheep's wool black. Even though the carriages and engines were remarkably small, and the service from London to Birmingham in 1837 consisted of only three trains a day, the coming of the railway did have a significant effect on land development in the Chalk Farm and Camden Town areas.

The line's construction provided two tourist attractions. One was the spectacular tunnel of about 1,200 yards which ran beneath the

Eton College estate near Primrose Hill; the other was the pair of high chimneys at Chalk Farm which took away the furnace smoke of the engine which powered the hauling cable.

A CEMETERY AT NORWOOD

The success of Kensal Green Cemetery (see 1833) was bound to encourage imitations, and in any case there was enormous potential in a London growing, it seemed, without limitation.

The South Metropolitan Cemetery Company this year opened West Norwood Cemetery. Unlike Kensal Green, Norwood was built in Gothic style, identifying itself with the prevailing mood in architecture and tombstone decoration. The massive iron gates, designed by Sir William Tite, were a foretaste of the buildings to come inside; sadly, the cemetery's two chapels were damaged in the last war and needlessly demolished instead of being restored. Tite's monument to the banker J. W. Gilbart is almost a Gothic building in its own right.

DEATH IN A PARACHUTE

Above Kennington Common on 25 July, Robert Cocking stepped out of a hot-air balloon piloted by Charles Green, and descended to earth strapped in a parachute. Unfortunately, the parachute collapsed and Cocking was killed.

A SCHOOL OF DESIGN

A lukewarm government, hectored by the artist Benjamin Haydon about the need to improve textile design, decided this year to commit funds to establish a School of Design. As branches of this establishment were formed over the years throughout the country, art education preceded by some time a national education system. The school, whose descendant is the Royal College of Art, was allowed room at Somerset House in space left by the Royal Academy, which was moving to share space in the new National Gallery in Trafalgar Square.

Fees were fixed at 4s a month, payable in advance — a considerable sum for the artisans and apprentices the school hoped to attract. There were fewer than a score of pupils by the end of the year. Haydon —

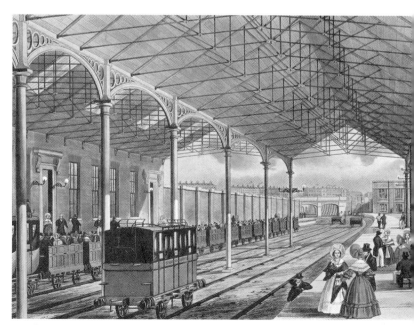

The first Euston station in 1837. The carriages were minute and were hauled up to Chalk Farm by cable.

always difficult and opinionated – complained loudly that there were only nine boys there drawing paltry patterns and that the 'Beautiful School of Design' was costing £1,500 a year to keep the mechanics as ignorant as before.

A RACECOURSE AT LADBROKE GROVE

St John's church, Ladbroke Grove, is on part of the site of the Hippodrome, a racecourse opened this year on 3 June. A newspaper forecast that it would form 'the greatest addition to the recreations of London which has been made during the last hundred years', but despite this optimism it was closed in four years. The enterprise was the brainchild of John Whyte, who leased the land from James Weller Ladbroke. Customers could watch the complete race from the top of the hillock on which the church now stands, and the venture should have been successful. But it was unpopular with local residents: it blocked an ancient footpath and brought 'undesirables' into the area. To add to Whyte's troubles, he had to change the shape of the course, and constantly had to deal with waterlogging.

NEW BUSINESSES

Daniel Neal in Portman Square, famed until recent years as a clothing shop for children, was established as a shoemaker's this year, specializing in children's shoes.

Marshall & Snelgrove, a large clothier's in Oxford Street until modern times, began this year when a James Marshall and a Mr Wilson opened a shop at 11 Vere Street; John Snelgrove came into the firm in 1848. By 1859 Marshall was sufficiently affluent to buy a house and 1,000 acres in Mill Hill.

James Watney of Wandsworth bought the Stag Brewery near Victoria Station; the brewery had been founded c. 1640.

The Lion Brewery, a landmark overlooking the Thames, was established east of the site of the former County Hall. It was sturdily built in classical style by Francis Edwards, and was surmounted by a prominent red-painted Coade-stone lion, believed in popular legend to contain the formula for the manufacture of that artificial material. The brewery was demolished in the late 1940s, but the lion reappeared to fascinate children at the Festival of Britain, was then erected at Waterloo Station, and now stands guard over Westminster Bridge.

1838

NATIONAL GALLERY OPENS

Since its foundation in 1828, the National Gallery's paintings had been displayed in the former house of Julius Angerstein. On 9 April 1838 the National Gallery building in Trafalgar Square, designed by William Wilkins, using the columns of the old Carlton House for his portico, was opened. It was less deep than it is now, and was soon overcrowded, as the government had intended that the Royal Academy should share the building; the western five rooms were given over to the national collection, and the eastern set of rooms were let to the Academy. This was a sure recipe for professional friction, and the relationship between the two organizations continued stormy until the removal of the Academy to Burlington House in 1869.

A GARDEN IN A PARK

The (Royal) Botanic Society, founded this year, opened a comprehensive garden on 18 acres of the inner circle in Regent's Park. It was much needed, for at that time only two major gardens existed: that of the Apothecaries' Company at Chelsea, which restricted itself to medicinal plants, and the Royal Botanic Gardens at Kew, which were then closed to the public. The annual flower shows here became social events of the year.

STATIONS WEST, SOUTH AND NORTH

The first stretch of the Great Western Railway, to connect London with Bristol, was opened on 4 June this year between Paddington and Maidenhead. The original London terminus was a wooden structure off Bishops Bridge Road, now part of the goods yard. In 1839 there were only 14 daily departures.

At Nine Elms, Vauxhall, a terminus was built for the new London & Southampton Railway (later the London & South Western); on 21 May, when the line opened, trains went to Woking only. Eight special trains were put on to take people to Epsom for the Derby in June, and about 5,000 passengers turned up. The flower section of the New Covent Garden market now stands on the site of the station.

Work had begun on building a prestige station at Euston for the London & Birmingham Railway. This year a massive Doric arch was erected in front of where the station would be, described by the directors of the company, rather modestly, as an architectural embellishment intended to become part of a 'Grand Avenue for travelling between the Metropolis and the midland and northern parts of the Kingdom'. It was designed by Philip Hardwick and erected by Cubitt's. This famous London landmark was scandalously demolished in 1962.

SERIOUS FIRES

On 10 January the second Royal Exchange was destroyed by fire. The weather was so bitterly cold that water froze and there was little that the fire engines could do.

Paper Buildings in the Temple were burnt down on 6 March, due to a candle overturning in Justice Maule's rooms.

1839

HAPPENINGS IN HIGHGATE

A third major London cemetery was opened on 20 May, on the slopes of Highgate. Built and landscaped on the grounds of Ashurst House, to

Highgate Cemetery in 1859, with St Michael's church as a backdrop.

The Westminster Literary and Scientific Institution in Great Smith Street was one of many formed in the 1840s for disseminating useful knowledge.

the west of Swain's Lane, it was to rival Kensal Green in its beauty and to surpass it in its social status. It was the property of the London Cemetery Company, which was also to open Nunhead Cemetery in 1840. Both of these burial grounds were designed by James Bunning, later the architect for the City of London and of the magnificent Coal Exchange in Lower Thames Street. At Highgate he built Gothic catacombs and a romantic layout of avenues, all viewed against the backdrop of the Gothic church of St Michael's, designed by Lewis Vulliamy and built on the site of Ashurst House itself.

At first the residents of Highgate did not welcome this 'great garden of sleep', but once the beauty of its flowers, shrubs and trees was realized many applied for visitors' keys so that they could walk there whenever they pleased.

In the village of Highgate itself, a meeting took place at the Gatehouse Tavern on 16 January 'For the purpose of forming an Institution designed to excite and cultivate an intelligent interest in the objects of Literature and Science'. In effect, this was another literary and scientific institution – one of many such middle-class organizations around the country and in London which ran in tandem with mechanics' institutions and working men's clubs. The difference is that the Highgate institution still survives – one of the few in the whole country – with its own library and lecture hall overlooking Pond Square in the centre of the village.

MORE RAILWAY LINES

The London & Croydon Railway was formally opened on 1 June, from Corbett's Lane Junction to the present West Croydon. The company had hoped to use the London Bridge station of the London & Greenwich line, but because that was inadequate it was obliged to build its own station on the north side of the nearby terminus.

The Eastern Counties Railway, later to be the nucleus of the Great Eastern Railway, opened a line between temporary stations at Mile End and Romford on 20 June; the intended route was London to Norwich, and a terminus at Bishopsgate was opened the following year.

SCOTCH HOUSE BEGINS

The Scotch House in Knightsbridge began with two Glasgow brothers called Gardiner, who in 1839 opened a shop in Aldgate selling tweeds and tartans. The shop moved to its present site in about 1900.

CHELSEA BUN HOUSE SOLD

The Chelsea Bun House, a one-storey building with a colonnade projecting over the pavement in Pimlico Road, was famed in the 18th century for the product noted in its name – even George II and George III were customers. There was also a lucrative itinerant trade around the streets, where the buns were sold still warm. Swift noted in his *Journal to Stella* (1713), 'As I walked into the City, I was stopped with clusters of boys and wenches buzzing about the cake shops like fairs. There had the fools let out their shops two yards forward into the streets, all spread with great cakes frothed with sugar and stuck with streamers of tinsel.'

The building and its contents were sold on 18 April this year, and were subsequently cleared away.

1840

A TRIO OF NEW CEMETERIES

Three substantial cemeteries were opened this year. Abney Park, in Stoke Newington, was for Nonconformists, and made necessary as Bunhill Fields had been closed for further burials. The grounds were those of Abney House, home of the Dissenter Sir Thomas Abney and the residence for many years of Dr Isaac Watts, the hymn writer, who was himself buried at Bunhill. The cemetery was opened on 20 May; a Gothic chapel was built on the site of the house, and the lodges were in Egyptian style. The architect for both was William Hosking. General William Booth, founder of the Salvation Army, is buried here, as are the philanthropist Samuel Morley, the fire chief James Braidwood, and the writers Anna Barbauld and Talbot Baines Reed.

Brompton Cemetery, in Old Brompton Road, was the work of Benjamin Baud, with Isaac Finnemore and J. C. Loudon as consultants on landscaping. However, workmanship was poor, faults developed, and Baud was dismissed and sued. It was a popular burial ground, especially with the military. Those interred here include Sir Henry Cole, moving force behind the Great Exhibition, the writer George Borrow, the steamship owner Sir Samuel Cunard, the editor of the *Builder* George Godwin, and suffragette Emmeline Pankhurst.

The London Cemetery Company, armed with powers to open cemeteries to the north, south and east of London, followed up its Highgate success with a cemetery at Nunhead. James Bunning laid out the ground, which, like Highgate, is on a hilltop. Thomas Tilling, pioneer of horse-drawn buses, is buried here.

MORE THEATRES

A Miss Fanny Kelly, an actress at the end of her career, established a school for acting at her house at 73 Dean Street, with a theatre attached. In 1834 she obtained a licence to produce public readings – the lord chamberlain, responsible for licences, was a friend of hers. Her theatre, designed by Samuel Beazley, was ready by 1837, but it was not opened until 25 May 1840. *The Times* liked it, and a number of the seats were taken up by members of the aristocracy. However, within a week the theatre closed, officially because the scenery machinery was faulty, but most likely because audiences were poor.

The theatre, known by various names but most often as the Royalty, reopened a year later but was only spasmodically used until the 1860s. Royalty House now stands on its site.

The Princess's Theatre at 73 Oxford Street, opened on 30 September, was an adaptation of a short-lived shopping mall called the

Queen's Bazaar. It was originally used for concerts, then came some years of miscellaneous productions, and from 1850 Charles Kean was in command, offering some of the best drama in London.

A RAILWAY THROUGH THE DOCKS
The London & Blackwall Railway, mostly built on viaducts through Poplar and Wapping, was opened on 6 July. It was a key line for those using steamers which docked at the Brunswick Dock at Blackwall, but it also served the dockland community. Nowadays the old route has been used for construction of the Docklands Light Railway.

Originally, the line went only as far as the Minories at Aldgate, but in 1841 it was extended to Fenchurch Street.

1841

DISASTER AT THE TOWER
On the night of 30 October a fire began in the Bowyer Tower in the Tower of London. The fire proved too large for the nine hand-operated engine pumps, and there was in any case only enough water to keep one engine going. Much confusion reigned as the Bowyer Tower was consumed by flames. As the newly founded *Punch* magazine pointed out:

In the first place, by way of ensuring the safety of the property, precautions were taken to shut out everyone from the building; and as military rule knows no exceptions, the orders given were executed to the letter by preventing the ingress of the firemen with their countermand. This of course took time, leaving the fire to devour at its leisure the enormous meal that fate had prepared for it.

With the Bowyer Tower irretrievably lost, efforts were made to save the Grand Storehouse, home of a great collection of old and new weapons. Many of the contents were dragged outside, but the building itself was destroyed, to the consternation of the thousands lining Tower Hill.

There was, needless to say, gunpowder within the Tower complex of buildings. This had to be removed as the fire threatened other parts. The crown jewels and regalia were almost lost because the only key was with the lord chamberlain; a forced entry was made, and the bravery of one policeman saved almost everything.

Eventually, the fire burnt itself out, but the loss of items was heavy.

FIELD LANE SCHOOL BEGINS
One of the best known of the London 'ragged' schools was that in Field Lane, a street in one of the worst of London's slum areas, around Saffron Hill. On 7 November, Andrew Provan, the newly appointed London City missionary, opened a Sunday school here for 45 boys and girls of various ages, all of whom were too dirty and poor to be admitted into a conventional charity school.

Essentially, this was a missionary school, in which the prime purpose was to teach the pupils the Bible, but it was taken up by the ever-reforming 7th earl of Shaftesbury and the pious Angela Burdett-Coutts, and was to make a substantial and prolonged contribution to the education of the poor in the area.

SPECIALITY IN DEATH
The opening of new, attractive and hygienic cemeteries persuaded the Victorians to take death more seriously. This year appeared the

ultimate in specialist stores: one devoted to the clothes and knick-knacks associated with funerals and mourning. At 247–249 Oxford Street, Jay's Mourning Warehouse was opened this year to great success, and there were a good many competitors before the decade was out. Peter Robinson had a similar establishment, popularly called Black Peter Robinson's, which occupied four houses in Oxford Street. Such shops were not a central-London phenomenon: others existed on the outskirts. Camden Town, for example, had one by Inverness Market, which was a branch of the principal draper's.

THE APPEARANCE OF PUNCH
On 17 July, under the joint editorship of Mark Lemon, Henry Mayhew and Stirling Coyne, appeared the first edition of *Punch*. The staff thought that the proposed name was stupid, and the artist G. F. Watts saw a gentleman toss the first copy aside and heard him declare, 'One of these ephemeral things they bring out; won't last a fortnight!'

THE BEGINNING OF MAPLE'S
One of the best-known furniture shops in London was Maple's in Tottenham Court Road. The business began in 1841, when John Maple and James Cook, brothers-in-law who had married sisters called Blundell, bought the Tottenham Cloth Hall at 145 Tottenham Court Road and set up shop as wholesale drapers, carpet factors, cabinetmakers and furnishing warehousemen. They expanded into bedding, and later, under John Maple's sole ownership, into the retail sale of furniture.

NEW CLUBHOUSE FOR THE REFORM CLUB
The Reform Club's new clubhouse in Pall Mall was opened on 1 March. Designed by Charles Barry, after a selection process which included most of the foremost architects of the day, the interior of the classical building was finished to a high standard – it cost twice as much as the Athenaeum building to complete and, indeed, twice as much as Barry's estimate. One novel feature was that the kitchens, overseen by the famous chef Alexis Soyer, were fuelled by gas.

KEW GARDENS FOR THE NATION
On 1 April Sir William Hooker, professor of botany at Glasgow, became the first director of the Royal Botanic Gardens at Kew, and at the same time the gardens became a public facility. Initially Hooker's domain consisted of 9 acres, being those of Princess Augusta's botanic garden, but 46 acres were soon added, which allowed him space to erect the great Palm House and to create new walks and vistas.

HOUSING FOR THE MASSES
The first experiment in building housing for the respectable working classes was launched this year with the formation of the Metropolitan Association for Improving the Dwellings of the Industrious Classes. Its objects were 'The purchase and construction of dwelling-houses, to be let to the poorer classes of persons, so as to remove the evils arising from the construction and arrangement of such dwellings, more especially in densely-populated districts.'

The association was the brainchild of the sanitary reformer Dr Thomas Southwood Smith, Lord Robert Grosvenor, Charles Gatliff and others. It was the first example of what became known as 'five-per-cent philanthropy' – a description of the aim of most of such societies, which was to build for poorer people but, at the same time, to get 5 per cent back each year on the investment. It took five years before the association's first building was erected (see 1847).

BOOKS FOR THE ÉLITE AND THE MASSES

Thomas Carlyle was the prime mover in the establishment this year of the London Library, now in St James's Square. On 3 May he and a crowd of literary figures borrowed books at the library's first address, 49 Pall Mall. In the same year, Horace Marshall & Son opened a book-stall at Fenchurch Street station. W. H. Smith opened their first book-stall in 1848 when the company came to an exclusive agreement with the London & North Western Railway to provide station bookstalls.

1842

A NEW PRISON IN ISLINGTON

In the same year that the squalid Fleet and Marshalsea prisons were abolished by Parliament, the misleadingly named Pentonville prison (it is a mile away from Pentonville) was opened on 21 December. It was known as the Model Prison, designed to usher in a new age of containing men in jail, although many of them were destined for transportation to Australia, where conditions were far from model. The home secretary, Sir James Graham, wrote in 1841, 'I propose … that no prisoner shall be admitted into Pentonville without the knowledge that it is the portal to the penal colony, and without the certainty that he bids adieu to his connections in England, and that he must henceforth look forward to a life of labour in another hemisphere.' The earthly life of Pentonville became a preparation for afterlife in the southern hemisphere, for the prisoner's freedom of movement and opportunity in Australia depended on his behaviour in Pentonville.

In this building, built prominently and proudly on the new Caledonian Road to a design by Charles Barry and Major J. Jebb, prisoners were to suffer what was probably the worst regime of all – total isolation. Outside their cells, at chapel or elsewhere, prisoners wore masks to prevent communication or recognition; inside their cells the prisoners were alone and were obliged to be silent. Some even exercised alone in small areas attached to their cells, like animals in quarantine. This treatment could last for 18 months and, unsurprisingly, many went insane.

It was an irony that this mistreatment of people should be based on the ideals of prison reformer John Howard. Although he was opposed to full-time solitary confinement, he did nevertheless believe that 'Solitude and silence are favourable to reflection; and may possibly lead to repentance.' In the prevailing mood of religious bigotry, keeping prisoners in isolation seemed an appropriate measure.

ILLUSTRATED LONDON NEWS FOUNDED

The *Illustrated London News* first appeared on 14 May, published in Crane Court, off Fleet Street. It was the first magazine to exploit the new advances in engraving and printing techniques, and was to be outstandingly successful until the advent of half-tones in newspapers diminished its appeal.

It was begun by Herbert Ingram, a printer, bookseller and newsagent at Nottingham. The first edition had a print run of 20,000 copies and contained some 20 illustrations. By 1851 the circulation had risen to 130,000.

PRIMROSE HILL MADE PUBLIC

Primrose Hill was part of the Chalcots estate owned by Eton College. The formation of Regent's Park now made the Chalk Farm area more promising for development, and it was the college's intention to build on Primrose Hill; but there was a popular move, which the government acceded to, to keep the hill open and perhaps connect it in some way with the park. In 1838 the Commissioner of Woods and Forests approached the college asking to buy Primrose Hill and a further 50 acres to be 'dedicated to the use and recreation of the Public'. The land was exchanged with some Crown property in Eton.

THE QUEEN GOES BY TRAIN

Queen Victoria's first train ride – one that gave still greater impetus to the railway-building mania – was on 13 June, when she travelled from Windsor to Paddington.

CONTENTS SOLD AT STRAWBERRY HILL

In the second half of the 18th century Horace Walpole had transformed a modest villa at Twickenham into a fantasy house called Strawberry Hill. Gothic architectural models from around Europe were pressed into service, and to assist him in his endeavour he formed a 'Committee of Taste', consisting of men familiar with Gothic architecture and design. Battlements were added outside, Tudor chimneys adorned the roof, and, inside, chimney pieces, woodwork and bookcases were constructed to Walpole's fancy.

This year the contents went up for sale. They consisted of vast quantities of china, bric-à-brac, glass and furniture, and it took the auctioneer 24 days to sell them all.

RAILWAY CLEARING HOUSE ESTABLISHED

The Railway Clearing House was established on the same principles as the Clearing House which handled debits and credits between banks. The business would increase enormously over the years, when there was a great deal of shared use of railway track and stations between the numerous railway companies, and what began as a business with 20 clerks was at its peak employing 2,000 in very large premises in Eversholt Street – buildings which still survive behind Euston Station.

The Clearing House had other functions. Because representatives of the various companies were part of its administration, it was possible to convene meetings of interested parties to discuss standardization in such matters as rolling stock and accounting procedures.

A CIRCULATING LIBRARY

The most famous of the circulating, or subscription, libraries in London was Mudie's, founded in Red Lion Square this year and moving to purpose-built premises in New Oxford Street in 1860. So popular was the library, and so immense its purchasing power, that it could make or break a book. Its vast trade in London, nationwide and in the colonies meant that publishers could afford to launch two- or three-decker novels, knowing that their production costs were assured from a Mudie order. It is claimed that the library ordered 2,500 copies of the last two volumes of Macaulay's *History of England*. The business thrived until the gradual development of the public library service.

1843

NELSON'S COLUMN COMPLETED

The project to build a memorial to Lord Nelson in Trafalgar Square was a prolonged one. A committee to erect a memorial was formed in 1838, long after the hero's death in 1805, and much of the money came from the public. After two rather botched competitions the design was awarded to William Railton, whose Corinthian column was modelled on that in the Temple of Mars the Avenger in Rome. Edward Baily was commissioned to sculpt the actual figure of Nelson, which, designed to be seen from a distance and from well below, is a crude and distorted item close up.

The column was erected in 1842, and in November this year the statue was raised – in two parts, inch by inch, using an engine perched on scaffolding at the top of the column. At the base of the column are bas-reliefs depicting Nelson's victories at Cape St Vincent, the Nile, Copenhagen and Trafalgar, which were put in place in 1852. The famous lions, designed by Sir Edwin Landseer and cast by Baron Marochetti, were not unveiled until 1867.

THAMES TUNNEL OPENED

The Thames Tunnel begun by Marc Isambard Brunel in 1825 – what *The Times* called 'the great bore' – was at last opened to foot traffic on 25 March. The first tunnel completed beneath the Thames, it was 1,300 ft long and 35 ft wide, and connected Wapping with Rotherhithe.

The tunnel was constructed at a great price in men's lives, in the health of Brunel himself, and in actual money. But despite all the gimmicks to popularize it, such as banquets in the tunnel, it was not a financial success. By 1865 it had been sold to the East London Railway, and is now part of the London Underground system.

It could not have been a pleasant experience to walk through it. Though 50,000 people did on the first two days, the description by Nathaniel Hawthorne in 1855 indicates why it had a limited appeal. It consisted, he said, of:

an arched corridor of apparently interminable length, gloomily lighted with jets of gas at regular intervals … There are people who spend their lives there, seldom or never, I presume, seeing any daylight, except perhaps a little in the morning. All along the extent of this corridor, in little alcoves, there are stalls of shops, kept principally by women, who, as you approach, are seen through the dusk offering for sale … multifarious trumpery … So far as any present use is concerned, the tunnel is an entire failure.

THE LAST DUEL

What is claimed to have been the last formal duel in England, to settle matters of honour between military men, took place near the isolated Brecknock Arms on the Camden Road on 1 July this year. At five o'clock that morning, farm workers nearby were talking to the local police constable when they noticed two carriages approaching. A short time later there was the sound of a shot, and soon afterwards one carriage, containing two men, reappeared and drove rapidly in the direction of London. It was found that a man had been shot and was lying in a field tended by two friends.

The two protagonists were brothers-in-law; Lieutenant Colonel Fawcett and Lieutenant Munro had married two sisters. The dispute arose over a remark that Fawcett had made about Munro's management of his affairs while he, Fawcett, had been away on army service in China. Munro took it amiss and issued the challenge which was to end in Fawcett's death, several days after the duel, in the public house to which he had been carried.

The affair provoked the press to great indignation. *The Times* commented, 'Duelling has become generally ridiculous – when not ridiculous, hateful, and requires but a blow from authority to become the crime of a past age.' The *Pictorial Times* noted that men of a lower class would be charged with murder in such circumstances.

It was not until 1847 that Munro was brought to trial, and by then tempers had cooled and the press had other causes. He was found guilty of murder, but with a strong recommendation of mercy; he spent a year in prison before release.

ADVANCES FOR WOMEN

The first general hospital for women was founded in April in Red Lion Square, largely through the efforts of Dr Protheroe Smith. It was later described as 'the first Institution established in this or any other country exclusively for the treatment of those maladies which neither rank, wealth, nor character can avert from the female sex'. In March 1852 the hospital moved to larger premises at 30 Soho Square.

The previous year the government had established a 'Female School of Art' at Somerset House, to accompany the School of Design which was already there.

The Governesses' Benevolent Institution was established in 1843 to 'raise the character of Governesses as a class, and thus to improve the tone of Female Education; to assist the Governesses in making provision for their old age; and to assist in distress and age those Governesses whose exertions for their parents, or families, have prevented such a provision'. The institution's large building erected in 1849 in Prince of Wales Road, Kentish Town, is still there, until recently being used for a school.

NEWS OF THE WORLD PUBLISHED

The *News of the World* was first published in London on 1 October. In a singular advertisement for it, the proprietor promised:

We must positively and distinctly state that upon no account shall any alteration ever be made in the price of the News of the World. We intend and are resolved that it shall be sold for threepence only. We distinctly pledge ourselves to this. We enter into an inviolable compact with the public never to charge for the News of the World more than its present price.

A STRIKING BUSINESS

This year began a partnership between William Bryant and Francis May as provision merchants at 133–134 Tooley Street and at 5 Philpot Lane. May had previously been a tea-dealer and grocer in Bishopsgate, and Bryant and an earlier partner were the inventors of 'Improvements in the Manufacture of Liquid and Paste Blacking by the introduction of India Rubber, Oil and other articles and things'.

Bryant and May's launch into commercial fame took place when, in 1850, a Swedish matchmaker visited London looking for new outlets. He met May, who, after examining the product, ordered a few cases; after a year or two the partners were ordering large quantities. As part of the agreement, Bryant and May sold the Swede's uncut wax taper used in the manufacture of 'vestas' – matches made with a waxed taper. By 1851, when the business of selling matches here was lucrative, Bryant and May were virtually the sole agents in this country for the Swedish product, and in 1855 they paid the Swede £100 for the patent of the first safety match.

CUBITT TOWN BEGUN

About this year the building firm of Cubitt's leased a large area of the south-eastern part of the Isle of Dogs, with about a mile of waterfront, and created a small industrial town. Adjoining the rows of small houses were cement factories, potteries, timber wharves and sawmills. The southern tip of the island, facing Greenwich, was left empty, in the vain hope of eventually attracting better-class residents.

1844

GILBERT SCOTT IN LONDON

George Gilbert Scott's first commission to build a church in London was for St Mary, Hanwell, in 1842. It was not a work he was afterwards proud of, more accustomed as he was at the time to churning out workhouses. But in 1844, in association with William Moffatt, he completed the building of St Giles, Camberwell, a church which replaced a medieval building destroyed in a fire in 1841. Scott lavished great care on St Giles, which established him in the forefront of the Gothic revival. He recorded that 'the pains I took over this church were only equalled by the terror with which I attended the meetings of the committee'.

A NEW ROYAL EXCHANGE

The present Royal Exchange building was designed by Sir William Tite. A larger site than that occupied by the building destroyed in 1838 was made possible by the demolition of St Bartholomew-by-the-Exchange (which also necessitated the removal of the ashes of the Bible translator Miles Coverdale to St Magnus the Martyr). The Royal Exchange Assurance occupied the west end, the London Assurance was on the south, Lloyd's was on the north, and its Subscribers' Room on the east, these sides at that time surrounding an open courtyard.

The building was opened by Queen Victoria on 28 October, although business did not begin until 1 January 1845. It was a full state occasion, with the monarch arriving at Temple Bar for a ceremonial welcome to the City.

BATHS FOR THE POOR

'Baths and Wash-houses for the Working Classes' originated this year in London with the founding of the Association for Promoting Cleanliness among the Poor, which opened a bathhouse and laundry in East Smithfield. It cost a penny to bathe and wash, and a farthing to do ironing. The association also gave whitewash and lent pails and brushes

Tom Thumb, just over 2 ft tall, did well out of a public appetite for the unusual.

The Irish in the St Giles rookery, outside a cheap lodging house.

to those willing to cleanse their homes. This successful experiment helped in the passing of an Act to encourage the establishment of baths and wash-houses two years later.

TOM THUMB IN LONDON

The dwarf Tom Thumb – 14 years old, 25 inches high and weighing only 15 lb – appeared in London this year under the promotion of Phineas T. Barnum. Fashionable society was among the stream of visitors to the Egyptian Hall in Piccadilly, and the duke of Wellington and Sir Robert Peel competed for the privilege of talking to Thumb in private. He went out to the Rothschild mansion and returned with a 'well-filled purse', and made appearance money of about ten guineas for each party he attended. During his four-month stay, from 20 March, he was received three times at Buckingham Palace.

YMCA FOUNDED

The Young Men's Christian Association was founded at a meeting held above a drapery shop at 72 St Paul's Churchyard on 6 June 1844. It was formed at a high tide of evangelical revival, and participants included Anglican and Dissenting churchgoers. The YMCA's principal enthusiast was a draper, George Williams, who earned £40 a year from his business when he first came to London in 1841, but left £250,000 in his will when he died in 1905.

1845

A NEW STREET THROUGH THE SLUMS

New Oxford Street, a continuation of Oxford Street to connect with Holborn, was opened for carriages on 10 June. It was cut across a maze of streets which included the St Giles rookery, and it made

St Giles High Street into the byway it remains today. All that was left of the slums in the area consisted of 95 houses in two streets called Church Lane and Carrier Street, wherein no less than 2,850 people were crammed.

At this time Charing Cross Road did not exist, although some semblance of the route (in a mixture of widths) did. Another improvement made this year was the extension of Cranbourn Street eastward from its Leicester Square end, to join Long Acre.

A PARK FOR EAST LONDON
After a persistent campaign, an open space of 244 acres for East Londoners was provided this year by the government sale of property of the late and bankrupt duke of York. It was called Victoria Park. (In 1840 some 30,000 residents had petitioned the queen for a royal park in the area.) The original plan, by James Pennethorne, allowed for luxury housing to be incorporated in much the same way as his mentor, John Nash, had wanted numerous villas in Regent's Park, but the housing market was slow and such housing as was eventually built was on the perimeter of the park.

Some 700 fruit trees – thought to encourage 'disorder' – were removed and replaced by evergreens and deciduous trees.

MODEL DWELLINGS
In Pakenham Street, near King's Cross, the Society for Improving the Condition of the Labouring Classes opened this year a group of 14 family dwellings, together with lodging for 'thirty aged females', ranged around a courtyard. They were designed by Henry Roberts, who was later to design Prince Albert's Model Dwelling House (see 1851), but the *Builder* was none too happy with them, complaining that the narrowness of the space between the houses and the meagre backyards created a 'hot-bed of infection'.

DEVELOPMENTS AT LINCOLN'S INN
A new hall and library were opened at Lincoln's Inn this year, designed by Philip Hardwick and P. C. Hardwick. In the hall is a large mural by G. F. Watts depicting 33 persons famous in the history of lawgiving.

GERMAN HOSPITAL ESTABLISHED
A hospital for 'poor natives of Germany and of German-speaking countries' was established in Dalston this year. Patients tended to come from the indigenous community, however, and it is not clear why

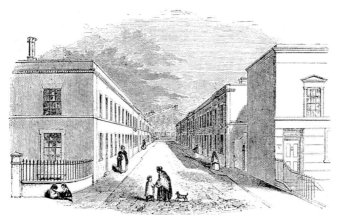

Model dwellings erected in 1845 in Pakenham Street, near King's Cross Road, by the Society for Improving the Condition of the Labouring Classes.

Dalston was chosen for this institution. The poorest German communities were those involved in sugar-refining at the docks and in sugar-baking at Whitechapel – jobs that even the poorest Irish declined. James Greenwood described a sugar-bakery: 'The floor was black, and all corrugated and hard, like a public thoroughfare after a shower and then a frost. The roof was black, and pendant from the great supporting posts and bulks of timber were sooty, glistening icicles and exudings like those of the gumtree.' Workers, stripped to the waist in the heat, their bare chests becoming encrusted with the melted sugar, laboured 12 hours a day.

A new German Hospital, designed by Professor T. L. Donaldson, was opened in 1864. The building is now part of the Hackney group of hospitals.

A SUSPENSION BRIDGE OVER THE THAMES
The Hungerford Suspension Bridge, from Lambeth to Charing Cross, was opened on 18 April; it was designed by Isambard Kingdom Brunel and was built to encourage trade at the new Hungerford Market. Its life was short, however, for in 1861 it was replaced by the Charing Cross Railway Bridge.

A FLAG OVER HAMPSTEAD
The flagstaff by Whitestone Pond, Hampstead, high over London, is on the site of one of the line of beacons constructed to communicate a warning of the approach of the Spanish Armada. 'High on bleak Hampstead's swarthy moor, they started for the north,' wrote Macaulay. The first flagpole was erected in 1845 by the lord of the manor, and his own flag was flown from this when the manorial court was in session nearby.

1846

ENDELL STREET LAID OUT
Hard on the construction of New Oxford Street, a new north–south road, Endell Street, was laid out through some of the more squalid parts of the Covent Garden and St Giles area. In effect, this was a rebuilding and widening of an existing route, but it enabled the authorities to push the slum-dwellers into other areas, since no effort was made to rehouse them. Endell Street, as will be seen, became a street of 'good works' – a baths, a church, a National School and a hospital.

BROMPTON CONSUMPTION HOSPITAL OPENED
The Brompton Hospital in Fulham Road was opened this year as a consumption hospital at a time when patients suffering from tuberculosis were routinely turned away from hospitals. The Brompton had been founded in 1841 by Philip Rose, moved by the plight of an employee who could not get treatment. Charles Dickens wrote of the charity in 1843, when it was still in temporary accommodation, 'If this charity had not existed, the doors of no sick house within London's wide bounds would have been open to these poor persons. Before this hospital was founded they would have suffered, lingered, pined and died in their poor homes without a hand stretched out to help them in their slow decay.'

PRESSURE FOR REFORM
The problems of London were visible to all those who would want to see them. The dreadful conditions of the poorer classes, the inadequate

sewage system, the lack of clean drinking water, the appalling over-crowding, the drunkenness, the state of the roads – all of these denoted a city that must either reform or explode.

There were, however, innumerable societies devoted to helping the deprived. They manned soup kitchens, built model dwellings, opened orphanages, pressed for prison reforms, and fought the scourge of prostitution. They could be quite small societies with a very specific aim, such as the King Edward Independent School and Refuge for Destitute Girls, founded in Spitalfields this year; or they could take on really large tasks such as that confronted by the ragged-schools movement. The Baths and Washhouses Act was making its way through Parliament this year in the vain hope that the labouring classes would be able to keep themselves clean and germ-free if they bathed more frequently. Not far from the legislators, in a district called Devil's Acre, south-west of Westminster Abbey, there were houses in which each room was let out to at least one family, and with no running water. Improvement schemes such as New Oxford Street and, soon, Victoria Street were mere window-dressing, because the occupants of the slums merely moved elsewhere and created new ghettos.

1847

THE FIRST FLATS IN LONDON

The first purpose-built flats in London appear to have been those constructed by the Metropolitan Association for Improving the Dwellings of the Industrious Classes opposite St Pancras Old Church in Pancras Road. They were five storeys high, and housed 110 families. Though the exterior was not liked, *The Times* noted that the rooms 'are so airy, so cheerful and so clean, an Oxford student might find himself at home in any one of the bedrooms and parlours'. Each flat had its own water supply, which served a WC and scullery; there was a refuse chute and a cooking range. To the rear of the buildings was a communal laundry and drying ground.

In the same year some model lodging houses which housed 104 single men at the price of 4d a day were erected in Dyott Street.

HOUSE OF LORDS OPENED

The rebuilding of the Houses of Parliament was proceeding. On 15 April the new House of Lords was opened.

ROUND HOUSE BUILT

The building of the Round House at Chalk Farm was begun this year. It was an ingenious construction, designed by R. B. Dockray, in which to service the engines of the London & North Western Railway, the successors of the London & Birmingham Railway. The engines entered through the west on to a large turntable, which would then revolve so that the engine could be sent to one of 23 inspection bays around the perimeter of the building. Beneath these bays there were interconnecting pits so that men could work beneath the engines, and beneath these a whole warren of tunnels connected the building with other parts of the Camden Goods Yard in which men and horses moved about without crossing the numerous sidings.

The Round House outlived its purpose very quickly. With the further development of steam power, engines became too large for either the turntable or the bays and other facilities became available anyway. It is extraordinary that the building, without its original function, has survived. It was used as a warehouse well into the age of conservation.

The Cricket steamboat is sunk in the Thames in 1847, with great loss of life.

EXPLOSION OF THE CRICKET

On 27 August a steamboat called *The Cricket*, running between the City and the West End, was on the point of leaving the Adelphi pier with 150 passengers on board when a violent explosion occurred. Some people were thrown into the air, others jumped over the side in panic; about 30 people died.

In the ensuing investigation it was acknowledged that the growing competition between the steamboat companies had led to a price war which had affected safety standards. It was also recognized that, while buses and cabs were licensed, steamboats were not, leaving the owners free to do as they liked in pursuit of trade.

A HOUSE OF DETENTION IN CLERKENWELL

A House of Detention north of Clerkenwell Green was opened this year. It contained 324 cells in which, as at Pentonville, prisoners were kept in isolation. Nearly all the prisoners were awaiting trial.

1848

REFORMING THE SEWERAGE SYSTEM

A Royal Commission appointed in 1847 to inquire into the sanitary condition of London reported that there were eight separate commissions of sewers in the metropolitan area, each with its own almost unlimited powers, its own staff and its own regulations. The Royal Commission also found that outbreaks of diseases such as cholera occurred in those areas where the water supply and the sewage system were the worst, and where sewers emptied direct into rivers.

The commission recommended that cesspools should be drained into sewers and that sewers should be covered over and should work by having water poured through them – which begged the question of where the water would come from. Its main proposal was that the eight authorities should be replaced by one and that the whole management should be more professional and standardized. It also considered that the management of sewers should be that which also looked after water supplies.

Twelve commissioners were appointed plus five ex-officio representatives from the City to manage the sewage system of London. The problem was that the commissioners had no powers to remove the London sewage to a more remote place, and therefore much of

1800s

The Chartist campaign petitioned for parliamentary reform. The great demonstration of 1848 included a mass meeting on Kennington Common.

the waste went into the Thames between Battersea and Vauxhall. The Thames itself was eventually to make this point when it stank so badly that even the House of Commons could not ignore it.

Nor were things much better in the streets. The increase in horse traffic had brought its own smells to add to those caused by pigsties, cow yards and chicken coops. The General Board of Health noted in 1850 that 'strangers coming from the country frequently describe the streets as smelling of dung like a stable yard'.

DEMONSTRATIONS WORRY THE AUTHORITIES

The police were called in to suppress two demonstrations in London this year. The first was on 6 March, when a gathering in Trafalgar Square, protesting against income tax, was dispersed by 500 police.

On 10 April, Chartists led by Feargus O'Connor held a great demonstration on Kennington Common and then marched to the House of Commons with a monster petition asking for parliamentary reform; along the route other contingents joined in. About 170,000 special constables were said to have been enrolled to keep order on the day. The Thames bridges were strongly guarded, detachments of soldiers were posted at key points, and heavy field ordnance was made ready at the Tower. No significant disorder occurred.

DEMOLITION OF THE QUADRANT

Nash's handsome Regent Street culminated at Piccadilly Circus in a curved group of buildings called the Quadrant, fronted by an arcade with a colonnade of cast-iron pillars. It was intended that the roof of the arcade should be a promenade for residents above, but this did not prove popular. Also, those shops contained within the arcade had to endure diminished daylight, and inevitably this kind of shelter attracted the very bystanders that the shopkeepers did not want. So in 1848 it was decided to demolish the colonnade, and the 270 pillars were auctioned off to a railway company.

FIRST RAILWAY BRIDGE ACROSS THE THAMES

The first railway bridge across the Thames was opened this year at Richmond; it carried the London & South Western line from Richmond to Windsor. The bridge, designed by Joseph Locke, had

three 100-ft spans made of cast-iron ribs. It is now made of steel, but the original appearance has been retained.

THE BEGINNINGS OF SIMPSON'S IN THE STRAND

In October, John Simpson notified the public that he was opening a 'Restauratum' adjoining the Divan in the Strand. The culinary arrangements, he said, would be 'carried out under the suggestions and plans of Mr. Soyer of the Reform Club'. This was the beginning of Simpson's Restaurant, using premises which had been in 1818 a room for chess, and which had been extended to a 'Grand Cigar Divan' – in effect a smoking room with refreshments.

Simpson specialized in roasts, and popularized a novel way of serving them. Richard Dana, in his book *Two Years Before the Mast*, described dining here in 1856:

Dined at six o'clock at Simpson's, Strand, where I had a piece of a joint of roast mutton. The joint is kept hot, and under cover is rolled to your table on a small stand upon castors, the cover taken off, and with the nicest skill and care, a hot slice is cut for you, with your due portion of fat, and the cutting is so done that the juice of the meat runs into, and lies in the hollow of the meat, and not into the dish, and thence is served by a spoon.

The Simpson premises were demolished in the widening of the Strand in 1903 and incorporated in the new Savoy Hotel buildings.

WATERLOO STATION OPENS

The London & South Western Railway, whose terminus had previously been at Nine Elms, opened Waterloo station on 11 July; the extension of its line may be seen on the brick viaduct which travels east from the present Vauxhall mayhem of roads. It was not a terminus to be proud of, being for almost the rest of the century merely a collection of miscellaneous wooden sheds and platforms that bemused the uninitiated. Other companies, such as the South Eastern Railway, used the station, and there was even a special daily service, called the 'funeral express', to take coffins and mourners down to Brookwood Cemetery near Woking.

CHOPIN IN BELGRAVIA

Frédéric Chopin gave his first public recital in England at 99 Eaton Place, Belgravia, on 23 June. He noted, 'I had a select audience of 150 at one guinea, as I did not want to crowd the rooms. All the tickets were sold the day beforehand.' But the impresario Willert Beale recalled, 'In a drawing-room he was to all a delight to hear, but in a larger space, before a more numerous audience, it gave more pain than pleasure. His appearance was so attenuated and his touch so enfeebled by long suffering.'

THE PRE-RAPHAELITES

The art movement called the Pre-Raphaelite Brotherhood began this year when William Holman Hunt wrote to Dante Gabriel Rossetti to ask if he might share his studio at 7 Cleveland Street. The formal beginning of the Brotherhood was signified the following year, when the initial mark P.R.B. was adopted.

QUEEN'S COLLEGE ESTABLISHED

Queen's College, the first school in the country for the higher education of women, was established this year in Harley Street. Originally the male tutors came from King's College, and the students were therefore supplied with a chaperone.

1849

AN IRON MASTERPIECE

The Coal Exchange on Lower Thames Street, so needlessly destroyed in the 1960s, was opened this year. It had a remarkable circular central hall, four storeys high, ringed by cast-iron galleries, and above these was a cast-iron-and-glass dome. The wooden floor was inlaid in the shape of a mariner's compass; motifs in the ironwork derived from the coal industry, and encaustic tiles painted by Frederick Sang added to the overall decoration. This masterpiece of Victorian construction was designed by the City's own architect, James Bunning.

On 30 October the building was opened by the prince consort, who had arrived by state barge – possibly the last occasion when this form of transport was used for state occasions.

GREAT HALL AT EUSTON OPENED

Another monumental building of the period, also destroyed in the destructive 1960s, was the Great Hall at Euston station, completed this year. The famous Doric arch was already in position in front of the station (see 1838). Behind this, as the main entrance to the station, Philip Hardwick designed a large building containing the Great Hall – measuring 125 ft by 61 ft – at the northern end of which a beautifully proportioned double curved staircase led to a vestibule floor from which offices issued. The ceiling of the hall was deeply coffered, and the whole was decorated by paintings, granite and marble.

THE FIRST BATHS AND WASHHOUSES

The first baths and wash-houses erected by a municipal authority in London appear to be those of St Martin-in-the-Fields, in Orange Street, which were opened on 8 March. They were followed in

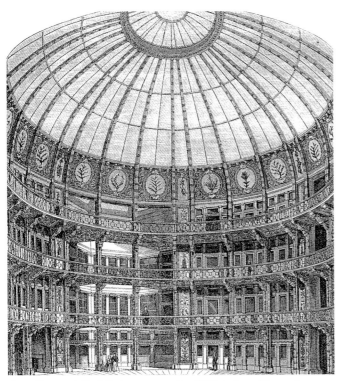

James Bunning's Coal Exchange, opened in 1849 in Lower Thames Street, was a masterpiece of iron and glass.

January 1850 by those erected by St Marylebone in the Marylebone Road, opposite Lisson Grove.

CATHOLIC CHURCHES

The Catholic Emancipation Act of 1829 enabled Catholics to build churches without hindrance, but nearly 20 years later, on 4 July 1848, it had been necessary to keep the dedication of St George's Roman Catholic Cathedral, near St George's in the Fields, a low-key affair. Hostility from the neighbourhood was expected, and there was no point in provoking it with ostentatious display. Similarly, ten years later, in 1858, when the Order of Passionists was inspecting some property in Highgate with a view to establishing a home there, its representatives disguised their priestly status to avoid early opposition to their scheme. Even so, the building of Catholic churches was now proceeding apace. The cathedral had been the work of Augustus Welby Pugin, who had ruined his health by overwork on the thousands of detailed designs for the new Houses of Parliament. He himself was a Roman Catholic convert, and he was the first man to be married at the cathedral.

The principal architect of Catholic churches of this period was J. J. Scoles. His first church in London was St Mary in Grove End Road, St John's Wood, in 1834, and he was later (1843) to design the striking St John the Evangelist in Duncan Terrace, Islington, and also the first Brompton Oratory (1851), whose library, some claim, was one of the loveliest rooms in London. In 1849 he completed the Church of the Immaculate Conception in Farm Street, a Jesuit church; the design is Gothic and derived from the west front of Beauvais Cathedral. Pugin designed the high altar and the candelabra.

DEATHS AT MR DREWETT'S

Another cholera epidemic swept London – 13,000 deaths from the disease were registered. The worst single tragedy occurred at a hostel in Tooting run by a Mr Drewett, which was used by parishes for boarding out workhouse children. Here, 112 children died in one week. The St Pancras vestry had in January taken the decision to send children there to avoid the cholera epidemic in its own area.

POPULATING THE COLONIES

The Female Emigrants' Home was established by Mrs Sidney Herbert in Hatton Garden this year. Its aims were to improve the prospects of many single and destitute women in this country, and at the same time provide them with a chance of a husband in Australia. The first boat-load of women left in 1850.

1850

GETTING TOUGH ON WATER

The water that most Londoners drank was thoroughly unhealthy. Although Dr John Snow had proved in Soho, during the 1849 cholera epidemic, that it was the water supply which spread the disease, it was still the general belief that cholera was spread as an infection in the air.

This year the General Board of Health presented a report, compiled by Edwin Chadwick, which recommended that the water companies should look elsewhere for their supplies (most water came unfiltered from the Thames), that water supply should in any case be taken into public control, and that a body should be set up to run both water and sewage systems for London.

EDUCATION FOR GIRLS

At 46 Camden Street, Camden Town, Miss Frances Buss on 4 April established the North London Collegiate School for Ladies. It was an important milestone in education for girls, for the school's pupils were daughters of professional people who, caught by a combination of class inhibitions and lack of income, were doomed to an education inferior to that of many girls from much poorer families. They came from middle-class homes unable to afford governesses and select academies, but were too far up the social scale to be seen in the charity schools. Miss Buss, who had herself been an early pupil at Queen's College in Harley Street, realized that there were numerous girls in this position.

HEALTH MATTERS

A meeting took place near Portman Square on 2 April to establish the London Dispensary Society, to increase the number of dispensaries for the poor.

In Streatham Street, near the British Museum, the Society for Improving the Condition of the Labouring Classes opened some Model Houses for Families, designed by Henry Roberts. These houses, built as a block of 54 flats (they still survive as Parnell House), were designed around a courtyard. Access to each flat was from a balcony – a device which enabled the Society to successfully plead exemption from the Window Tax.

Meanwhile, the Small Pox Hospital, on the present site of King's Cross station, was moved north to Highgate Hill, roughly to where the medieval Highgate leper hospital had been. Vaccination was made compulsory in 1853; but although its incidence was to diminish greatly, smallpox remained common – St Pancras borough, for example, in which the hospital had stood, recorded 147 cases in 1901. Part of the old Small Pox Hospital still survives within Whittington Hospital.

THE GREAT NORTHERN RAILWAY OPENS

The Great Northern Railway opened its line from a temporary station in York Way (then called Maiden Lane) to Peterborough on 7 August. This route, intended to run as far as York, incorporated the famous Copenhagen Tunnel, 594 yards long, just north of the station.

The line was built by Sir William Cubitt and his son Joseph. Unlike the London & Birmingham (see 1837), they decided to take the railway beneath the Regent's Canal, but this resulted in an incline difficult for trains even up to the time of electrification. The passenger terminus was a simple affair near the canal and the extensive goods yard.

THE SAVINGS OF THE NEEDY

The widely held view that the poor were victims of their own improvidence was dealt a blow this year when an experimental Penny Savings Bank was established in Commercial Street. It opened on 20 January, and it was reported in September that the number of depositors had grown to 7,853, the number of deposits to over 49,000, and the value of them to £2,017.

STAG HUNT IN EUSTON ROAD

The proximity of countryside is underlined by a report of a stag being chased and cornered at Mabledon Place off Euston Road this year. The hunt had begun in Hendon.

ST MARTIN'S HALL OPENS

A large assembly hall, called St Martin's Hall, was opened on 11 February at 89–91 Long Acre. It was the project of John Hullah, who directed singing classes and oratorios here, and it was the venue for the early public readings given by Charles Dickens.

BEGINNING OF THE BOLTONS

Numerous churches were in the making in all parts of London, but from now on there is room for only the more interesting buildings to be mentioned.

George Godwin, editor of the *Builder*, began construction this year of the development called The Boltons, in Kensington. In it he placed the fine church of St Mary, West Brompton, consecrated on 22 October. Consisting of expensive semi-detached villas, The Boltons – the name came from a local landholder – was laid out as two crescents facing each other across the central garden containing the church.

PROGRESS ON THE NORTH LONDON LINE

In 1846 Parliament had assented to a railway, 8 miles long, from the goods station of the London & North Western at Camden Town to the West India Docks at Blackwall. This shadowed the route of the Regent's Canal and imitated its purpose: to transport the goods of the manufacturing towns of the Midlands and North down to the lower Thames. The project – clumsily called the East and West India Docks & Birmingham Junction Railway, mercifully altered to the North London Railway in 1853 – was for goods traffic; passengers were not contemplated at first, but in time were of such importance to the line that a new terminus at Broad Street was built.

The first stretch of the line, from Islington to Bow, was opened on 26 September; at Bow a junction was formed with the London & Blackwall Railway, which effectively took the project down to the docks. The section from Islington to Camden Town was opened on 7 December.

1851

THE GREAT EXHIBITION

It was Prince Albert who suggested, at a meeting of the Royal Society of Arts in 1849, that there should be an exhibition to show the world that Machinery, Science and Taste could be combined; this ideal of industry and art joined together was one dear to his heart. Two years later the Great Exhibition was opened, on 1 May. When it closed, after 140 days, over 6 million people had paid to visit it.

The new railways and omnibus companies did particularly well out of it. The *Daily News* complained of 'the increasing exactions and insolent conduct of the omnibus people'. On wet days 'they absolutely run riot, refusing passengers for less than a shilling fare, and those which are appointed to run to long distances, such as Kennington and Islington, actually declining passengers for those distances at any price, in order that they may make short journeys to Charing Cross for which they insist on the full fare'. One person not affected by omnibus conductors was a Mary Callinack, aged 85, who walked all the way from Cornwall to see the exhibition, carrying her belongings on her head. She was received by the lord mayor on 23 September, by which time she had 5½d left – he gave her a sovereign for the return journey.

Three men were mainly responsible for the huge success of the exhibition: Prince Albert, by his diligence and enthusiasm and of course his patronage; Henry Cole, the civil servant in charge, by his organizing ability; and Joseph Paxton, by his design of the Crystal

Palace, a building which captured the imagination of Europe. Paxton had been designing glass structures for 20 years, mainly in the landscaped gardens of the aristocracy, and the Crystal Palace was a direct descendant of his lily house at Chatsworth.

Construction of the palace began in August 1850, when the ground in Hyde Park was levelled and concrete foundations were laid, together with 34 miles of iron pipes running through base plates to take the hollow iron columns that supported the building. Scaffolding was not used, but work went at a prodigious pace. Paxton himself noted that three columns and two girders were being erected in only 16 minutes; 18,000 panes could be fixed in a week. Many of the components came already made; others were cut to size on site, steam power being used for many of the operations. There were over 1,000 columns and 2,000 trellis girders; the building was 1,848 ft long and 408 ft wide, and its central transept rose to 108 ft.

Half a million people assembled for the opening ceremony; 1,000 carriages passed through the park gates, together with 2,500 other cabs and vehicles; some 30,000 gathered in the palace among the exhibits and the various trees. Admission cost £1 on the second and third days, then it went down to 5s and by degrees further downward until the final days.

Some 100,000 objects from all over the world were on display, each illustrated in the three-volume catalogue. Machines were the great attraction, even to the queen, who went there several times, proud of her husband's part in this unqualified success. It was, of course, an age of startling change and invention, and the influence of the exhibition in persuading people at large that they lived at a significant and exciting time cannot be underestimated. Generally speaking the British half of the hall was dominated by machinery and inventions; the half used by the rest of the world was mostly devoted to items derived more from art than from technology. This, more than anything else, summed up the British lead in industrial development.

The Times reported the closing ceremony on 11 October:

As soon as the National Anthem had closed there arose such cheers as Englishmen alone know how to give. These were continued for several minutes, and when the last of them had died away there passed over the entire building, and with an effect truly sublime, a tremendous rolling sound, like that of thunder, caused by thousands of feet stamping their loyalty upon the boarded floors.

THE GREAT GLOBE

In Leicester Square there was another attraction for the London visitor. Despite opposition from residents, James Wyld, a distinguished geographer and former MP, opened his Great Globe on 2 June. Work had begun on the building, designed by H. R. Abraham, in March. It consisted of a central rotunda 85 ft in diameter, around which were placed four quadrant-shaped galleries. Coming from the entrance, visitors found themselves in an enormous gaslit globe, 60 ft high and 40 ft in diameter on a framework of curved wooden ribs, on the inside of which was painted a representation of the earth's surface. A staircase could be used to get nearer the top of the globe.

A MUSEUM OF GEOLOGY

In Jermyn Street, on the site of today's Waterstone's bookshop, a Museum of Practical Geology was opened on 12 May. The brainchild of Henry de la Bêche, it had been first established in Craig's Court, off Whitehall, in 1837, but had outgrown the premises. The museum, in a new building funded by the government and designed by James Pennethorne, was opened by the prince consort and contained exhibi-

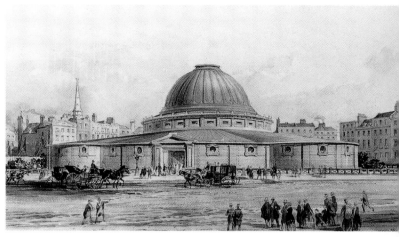

James Wyld's Great Globe, in Leicester Square, was opened in 1851 to cash in on the number of visitors in London that year for the Great Exhibition.

tion rooms, a library, a lecture hall and laboratories. Its collection was transferred to the South Kensington Museum in 1934 when the old building was demolished.

THE CONSTRUCTION OF VICTORIA STREET

Victoria Street, cut across slum property to provide better access from Belgravia to Westminster, was opened on 6 August, but it was not completed until the 1880s.

A MULTITUDE OF BUS WORKERS

At a meeting called to discuss the working conditions of omnibus workers, it was stated that there were in London 3,000 omnibuses, each with ten related horses, 6,000 drivers or conductors, 3,000 horsekeepers and 2,000 odd-jobmen. Each omnibus carried 300 people a day.

FIRST AND LAST APPEARANCES

Beethoven's opera *Fidelio* was performed (in Italian) at Her Majesty's Theatre in the Haymarket this year, its première in England.

An American woman, Mrs Bloomer, gave a lecture in London in which she advocated that women should wear a garment then known as 'pantaloons'. Cartoonists and gossips had a field day, and the word 'bloomers' was invented.

On 30 December the artist J. M. W. Turner was buried, at his own request, in St Paul's Cathedral, attended by numerous artists and dignitaries.

On 26 February, William Macready, the famous actor, took the last of his many farewells to the stage, appearing as Macbeth at the Theatre Royal Drury Lane. Later, a public dinner on 1 March was attended by Bulwer-Lytton, Dickens and Thackeray.

WINDOW TAX ABOLISHED

A tax on windows had first been imposed in 1696, to recoup the cost of reminting the coinage. By 1825 those houses with fewer than eight windows were exempt, but there was a tax on more windows than that. Inevitably this had an effect on the architecture of the period, or else it resulted in the blocking of windows so as to reduce liability. Opposition had been frequent since the tax began, and had grown in recent years. This year there were protest meetings at Islington and Westminster, and finally the tax was abolished.

LONDON RAILWAYS

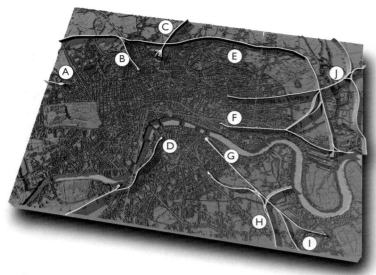

A Great Western
B London & North Western
C Great Northern
D London & South Western
E East & West India Docks &
   Birmingham Junction Railway
F London & Blackwall Extension
G London & Greenwich Railway
H Croydon Railway
I   North Kent Line
J Great Eastern

LONDON ROADS

London 1851

The Great Exhibition building

VICTORIAN LONDON

*The reconstruction above shows
the growth of London at the time
of the Great Exhibition and the
Crystal Palace.*

*All the routes of industry have been
established, as rail and roads supersede
the canals as the prime carriers of
passengers and material, and the
docklands grow.*

The Great Exhibition

PLACES OF INTERNMENT

What became the largest lunatic asylum in Europe was opened in the small village of Friern Barnet in July. Colney Hatch, as it was called, was a self-contained village, eventually employing a staff of about 300 to look after over 2,000 patients. Within its grounds were a farm and smallholding, a water supply, and even a burial ground. The architect of the main building was S. W. Daukes.

MORE MODEL HOMES

Prince Albert included housing for the poor among his many interests. On a site in Hyde Park adjoining the Crystal Palace was erected this year a block housing four model dwellings. Each was equipped with three bedrooms, a lavatory, a scullery, a coal bin, a dust shaft and a meat safe. They were designed by Henry Roberts under the auspices of the Society for the Improvement of the Condition of the Labouring Classes. When the Great Exhibition closed the houses were re-erected in Kennington Park, and they are still there today, used by the park superintendent.

The society also completed Thanksgiving Buildings in Portpool Lane, a development which included accommodation for single women.

THE TREATMENT OF CANCER

The surgeon William Marsden had already founded what became the Royal Free Hospital in 1828. In 1851 he opened a small house in Cannon Row, Westminster, for the treatment of patients with cancer – the first institution in the world for the specific study of cancer. Despite Marsden's fine reputation, his new creation did not enjoy universal support. Queen Victoria at first declined to donate money, on the grounds that the hospital dealt with 'a single malady'.

The Free Cancer Hospital moved to Brompton in 1859, and is now the Royal Marsden Hospital in Fulham Road.

1852

A NEW BILLINGSGATE

The hotchpotch of sheds which made up the old Billingsgate Market was swept away and a handsome new market hall for fish trading was partially opened on 4 August. In the process, much of the old Billingsgate dock was filled in to provide more space. The main trade at the dock was fish and coal, though the latter commodity, which came by sea from the coalfields of Durham, was soon virtually to disappear as its transportation was switched to the Great Northern Railway. (James Bunning's famous Coal Exchange was strategically sited across the road.)

The new Billingsgate, also designed by Bunning, had an Italianate tower connected by single storeys to two buildings containing offices. Behind this façade was the market hall, with an atmosphere, one journalist remarked, of 'unstudied, honest usefulness'.

The new market was meant to solve the problem of the increasing fish trade for many years to come. But it was built at precisely the wrong time, for no account was or could have been taken of the immense changes in food distribution that were to be made by the railways in the next decade. As the percentage of fish brought in via the Thames declined, that brought in by rail increased, necessitating an expensive and time-consuming transfer of the product from rail depots to Billingsgate, so that it could be sold on to the retail trade.

Construction of a tunnel on the Great Northern Railway line near King's Cross. The station opened in 1852.

Billingsgate was distant from any rail link, and so the whole of the area around the market became congested with carts.

A NEW CITY PRISON

James Bunning was also the architect of the new City House of Correction, opened on 5 October in the fields of Holloway. It was built on 10 acres of land that the City had purchased some years before, to be used as a burial ground in case of a cholera epidemic.

The gateway design of the building owed much to Warwick Castle, and the rest was a castellated fantasy – all of which was thought inappropriate in modern years when Holloway Prison was rebuilt, though the old foundation stone with the grim inscription MAY GOD PRESERVE THE CITY OF LONDON AND MAKE THIS PLACE A TERROR TO EVIL DOERS has been preserved.

The original accommodation was for 283 men, 60 women and 61 juveniles. The 'silent' system was enforced, though not so rigidly as at nearby Pentonville, and education and vocational activities were provided. The building was absorbed into the state system in 1877, and became a women-only prison in 1902.

THE NEW HOUSE OF COMMONS

The new House of Commons chamber was used for the first time on 3 February, six months before the death of Pugin, who was responsible for its ornamentation and furnishing. The authorities had at first demanded that Charles Barry, the architect, provide a large, square chamber, but it was realized that this was not practical or desirable, since on many occasions there were few members present. Instead an elongated shape, reminiscent of the previous chapel which housed the Commons, was built. This was small enough to look reasonably occupied on thin days, but was, of course, insufficient on crowded ones.

KING'S CROSS STATION OPENED

King's Cross station, designed by Lewis Cubitt, was opened on 14 October; it was then the largest station in the country. The name derived from the short-lived monument to George IV which had been erected at the crossroads here (see 1836). For the first ten years the station had only two platforms – arrivals and departures – the space between them being used for sidings. The façade, with its clock tower, two lunettes and six archways, is considered elegant today, but it was a no-frills design then. At that time, too, it could be seen in its entirety, without the mess of miscellaneous sheds that were later put in front or the inappropriate modern extension we have today.

THE DUKE IS BURIED

The duke of Wellington was buried with pomp and ceremony unparalleled for someone not of the royal family. He was, rightly or wrongly, the hero of his age, and if the common man had derived such political rights as he had only in the teeth of Wellington's opposition, then he was generous or curious enough to pay his respects at the old man's funeral.

Wellington's body lay in state at Walmer, where he had died, and was then brought to London, to the Royal Hospital, Chelsea, on 10 November. The queue to see his body there sometimes stretched as far as Ebury Gardens and entailed a wait of over five hours; on the 13th, several lost their own lives in the crush of people. The procession to St Paul's Cathedral on the 18th, with a specially made and decorated coach as its centrepiece, was watched by an estimated 1½ million people.

FIRST PERFORMANCES

In March the New Philharmonic Society gave its first concert, at the Exeter Hall in the Strand; Hector Berlioz was the conductor.

The première of a stage version of the immensely popular book *Uncle Tom's Cabin* was given at the Olympic Theatre.

METROPOLITAN IMPROVEMENTS

The Metropolitan Burial Act, passed this year, permitted local authorities to open cemeteries if it could be proved that existing burial grounds were insufficient or dangerous to health.

The Metropolis Water Act ordered water companies to cover reservoirs within 5 miles of St Paul's, to filter all water through sand beds, and to take water from the Thames only above Teddington. The results were soon apparent. In Lambeth, for example, where the local water company was obliged to obtain its intake much further upriver, the number of deaths in the local population declined from 130 per thousand to 37 per thousand.

It was estimated that a million and a half people watched the funeral of the duke of Wellington in 1852 – the largest number since Nelson's funeral.

The Crystal Palace was re-erected at Sydenham and was open in 1854, bringing prosperity to a previously little-known suburb of London.

A NEW PUBLIC LAVATORY

The first modern public lavatory was erected this year by the Society of Arts at 95 Fleet Street; for men only, it was known discreetly as a 'Public Waiting Room'.

KENNINGTON COMMON OPENED AS A PARK

An Act was passed this year to allow Kennington Common – scene of executions, parliamentary elections and demonstrations – to be opened as a public park.

RE-ERECTION AND DEMOLITION

Re-erection of the Crystal Palace on Sydenham Hill was begun this year. When it opened, on 10 June 1854, the palace became a popular place for entertainment and recreation.

Balmes House in Hackney, built in 1540, was this year demolished. The house was rich in carvings, armorial glass and panelling. The Balmes Estate, which included substantial gardens, was covered in the 1850s by the De Beauvoir Estate.

1853

A RAILWAY TO KEW

The prosaically named North & South Western Junction Railway was opened on 15 February between Willesden (where it connected with the London & North Western) and Kew (where it joined the London & South Western). This stretch was later to be incorporated in the North London Railway.

A CLEANER LONDON

In a year in which a dense fog shut railways and shops in November, several more steps were taken to improve the hygienic lot of poorer Londoners. The parish of St Giles opened baths and wash-houses at the northern end of Endell Street (a site now taken by the Oasis Baths). Baths were also opened in Marshall Street, Westminster.

The General Society for the Improvement of Dwellings of the Working Classes, which had been formed in 1852, opened some model dwellings in Broadwick Street, one of the slummier areas of Soho.

1800s

The area of Grosvenor Hill and Bourdon Street was virtually the only area of poverty on the Grosvenor Mayfair estate. In a court case in 1858 it was discovered that an owner of one property in this small hinterland let it out to 'fifty or sixty persons'. In 1853 the estate built St George's Buildings here, the first of several blocks of artisans' dwellings; at the same time baths and wash-houses were erected behind Davies Street.

STREET NAMES IN ISLINGTON

It was reported that the Islington vestry was to enforce the painting of street name panels within its boundaries – which the *Illustrated London News* thought would be a 'great accommodation to strangers if generally adopted throughout the metropolis'.

SEWING MACHINE IN LONDON

The sewing machine, an American invention, was displayed in London for the first time this year at a shop in Lawrence Lane, Cheapside. On 26 August it was demonstrated to Queen Victoria at Messrs Nicoll's shop in Regent Street.

1854

THE FIRST MUNICIPAL CEMETERY

The first municipally owned cemetery in London was that of St Pancras and Islington. Matters had become urgent, for in 1853 the St Pancras vestry had been instructed by the government not to inter any more bodies in its old burial ground from a year hence. That same year the vestry bought the 88-acre Horse Shoe Farm at Finchley, at a cost of £17,500, and it was estimated that providing two chapels and laying out the grounds would add £7,500 to the expense. Part of the ground was then sold on to Islington vestry for its use. The two cemeteries were opened on 25 July. People interred here include Henry Croft, the first Pearly King, and Ford Madox Brown, the Pre-Raphaelite painter.

The example was followed in 1855 by St Marylebone and Paddington, each of which formed a cemetery outside its own boundaries.

EDUCATIONAL VENTURES

At a time when few working men were literate and only one child in five received much education, the Working Men's College was established in a house in Red Lion Square by Frederick Denison Maurice, aided by John Ruskin, Dante Gabriel Rossetti and Thomas Hughes.

A free lending library was opened in Marylebone Road on 9 January. By July 1856 it had 1,000 volumes (there had been over 5,700 issues by then), and there was also a reading room with other books available.

The Royal Panopticon of Science and Art in Leicester Square was opened in March, on the site of today's Odeon. Its proprietor was Edward Marmaduke Clarke, an Irishman who had formed the first mechanics' institution in Ireland. His Panopticon was for the exhibition of scientific advances and for promoting discoveries in arts and manufactures. The Moorish building consisted of a central rotunda described by its owner as 'the most splendid room ever appropriated to scientific and artistic purposes'; it was 97 ft in diameter, with a ring of columns supporting galleries above. However, despite early promise, the Panopticon was not a financial success and it closed in 1856.

The Working Men's College, formed with the support of Ruskin and Rossetti, moved to its second home (above) in Great Ormond Street in 1857.

The St Martin's School of Art – one of the oldest in the country – was established in Shelton Street, off Long Acre, this year, under the auspices of the parish. It became independent in 1859, and from 1894 was aided by the London County Council.

NEW HOTELS

The age of railway hotels began in earnest this year. Two relatively small hotels had been built on either side of the Doric arch at Euston station in 1839, but this form of hotel began properly in London in 1854 with the construction of the Great Northern Hotel next to King's Cross station. At that time there were run-down houses where St Pancras station now stands across the road, and so Lewis Cubitt, the architect, had his hotel overlook the station itself. In many respects the exterior of the building is a large London terrace, of the sort that Cubitt was used to building. Inside, it was one of the first hotels to provide en-suite facilities with sitting rooms.

The new Paddington station and its adjacent Great Western Hotel were opened the same year. The former, replacing the earlier temporary terminus at Bishop's Bridge Road, was designed by Isambard Kingdom Brunel and Matthew Digby Wyatt. The hotel, opened on 9 June, was the work of Philip Charles Hardwick, who designed it in French Second Empire fashion with pavilion roofs – a style to reappear in the Grosvenor Hotel of the 1860s. The hotel's most illustrious feature was its beautifully embellished coffee room – lost, unfortunately, in some ruthless renovations in the 1930s.

A RAILWAY TO TILBURY

From just outside Forest Gate a new railway was opened on 13 April to Tilbury, via Barking. It reached its final destination, Southend, in 1856.

CUBITT'S ON FIRE

The extensive Pimlico premises of the builder Thomas Cubitt were burnt down on 17 August. Though insured for £10,000, the loss was about £30,000. Thirty thousand people watched the blaze. Cubitt himself died the following year, leaving behind him one of the longest wills ever recorded. It ran to nearly 35,000 words, covering 30 skins of parchment; the estate amounted to £1 million.

1855

LONDON REORGANIZED

The reorganization of metropolitan London was long overdue. Disparate entities made up the area. The City, of commercial wealth and with privileges that extended its influence well beyond its boundaries, was fast losing its residents; Westminster was uneasily divided between central government and rapid residential development; Southwark, under the control of the City, had few of the advantages that other City wards obtained and was a poor and powerless relation; each of the numerous parishes around, which bore the brunt of the influx of settlers from the provinces and those who moved for comfort out of the City, had different and mostly ineffective powers, and some, like St Pancras, had hardly any authority at all. In addition there were numerous miscellaneous bodies – mostly unelected – which looked after various aspects of London life, such as street lighting, water and gas supplies, the maintenance of pavements, and the care of the poor.

The local-authority units varied greatly in size. They could be as small as the liberty that governed a small area around the Old Artillery Ground near Bishopsgate, in which the population was under 1,500, or they could be as large as St Pancras, which stretched from Highgate almost to Oxford Street, had at least 170,000 residents, but was without even its own parliamentary representation. Sir Benjamin Hall, moving a bill in Parliament in 1855 to bring some order into the situation, gave St Pancras as one of his examples. There were in the parish, he said, 16 paving boards which functioned beyond the reach of the vestry's authority; in other parts of the parish there was no paving because there was no board and the vestry lacked the powers to do the work. He cited the case of the Strand area, where the 11 miles of streets were controlled by seven paving boards and where between 1 The Strand and Temple Bar the road was divided between those seven.

The vestries which governed parishes differed greatly. Some were open vestries, where any male ratepayer could come and vote, so that meetings could be of an immense size and of a disorderly nature. Others were select vestries, put in place by an Act of Parliament, which perpetuated themselves by filling any vacancies without recourse to public opinion. In some the main business of the vestry, the relief of the poor, was hived off to a separate body. To add to the confusion, there were wide differences in the qualifications for holding vestry office.

Crucial problems affected the whole metropolis, not the least of which were those of water supply and sewage disposal. Cholera and typhus epidemics since 1832 had added impetus to a movement to get to grips with London government. The water supply was in the hands of numerous companies whose motive was profit, and the sewage system was under the control of seven commissions which had a total of 1,065 members. In no other city in the country was government so fragmented and expensive.

The main reason for this situation was the anomalous relationship between the City Corporation and its neighbours. As London had grown, the City had not wanted to extend its boundaries to become in effect a metropolitan body; but at the same time it had resisted the establishment of any other authority which sought to bring order into the chaos, fearing a dilution of its own powers. The City was a powerful lobby, capable of persuading a lazy House of Commons to delay or compromise. Even when the Metropolitan Police Force had been formed, the government was frightened to include the City within its remit and allowed the Corporation to retain the arrangements it already had.

Edwin Chadwick had tried to centralize the control of water and sewage – a scheme which found many opponents and was, for various reasons, a failure. Sir Benjamin Hall, the promoter of the Metropolitan Management Act of 1855, was one of those opponents, but even he realized that some central control was necessary, hand in hand with radical rearrangement of local government. He resisted the idea of creating one giant municipal authority, such as those that would govern Liverpool, Manchester and Birmingham, and opted instead for upgrading the powers of the vestries and the creation of the Metropolitan Board of Works (MBW), whose prime function was to create a new sewage-disposal system for greater London.

The MBW consisted of 45 members who were elected by vestries and district boards; the City, as its price for not opposing the bill that established it, had three members.

Two other powers were specifically given to the board. One was the naming and renaming of streets and the numbering of houses: this was intended to rid London of duplicate street names in the same area – there were, for example, three Charlotte streets within half a mile of each other around Tottenham Court Road. The other power was that of general street improvements where circumstances demanded. As time went on the board assumed other responsibilities because no other body existed which could absorb them; these included the protection of threatened open spaces and the overall supervision of the development of tramways and underground railways.

A NEW CATTLE MARKET

The difficulty, let alone undesirability, of herding thousands of cattle into Smithfield Market virtually every day, and slaughtering many of them in the vicinity, had long been apparent. The City, from a combination of inertia and unwillingness to move the market outside its own boundaries, had dragged its feet in finding an alternative site. Some railway statistics of 1855 indicate the scale of the congestion at Smithfield: during the year the L&NWR, the GNR and the Eastern Counties Railway between them transported into London 630,000 sheep and 166,000 oxen.

Thirty acres of land in Islington attached to Copenhagen House were purchased by the City, and a new Metropolitan Cattle Market was designed and laid out by James Bunning. A clock tower dominated the scene, with at its base the twelve-sided Bank Buildings, housing banks which dealt with the traders. On the periphery of the animal pens were eight slaughterhouses, two blocks of model dwellings and four public houses. Only the clock tower (now surrounded by particularly unappealing blocks of flats) and the impressive outer railings now survive, together with three of the public houses.

The old Smithfield premises became a meat and poultry market, and the opportunity of this upheaval was taken to suppress once and for all the old Bartholomew Fair, which seems to have last been held in the autumn of 1854.

LAMAS FORMED

The London and Middlesex Archaeological Society was established on 30 July at 6 Southampton Street, Covent Garden, and a general inaugural meeting was held at Crosby Hall on 14 December. Oddly, London had been slow to join the fashion for archaeological societies, which had gathered pace since 1840.

The society still exists as the principal vehicle for the discussion and publication of new archaeological discoveries in London and Middlesex.

PRISONS CLOSED

With the opening of the House of Correction at Holloway, the City was able to close three of its smaller prisons – the Giltspur Street Compter, the Bridewell in New Bridge Street and the Borough Compter.

A RIOTOUS LONDON

The government, inefficiently conducting a war in the Crimea, also faced unrest at home. These were particularly hard times for the poorer classes. In February there were bread riots all over London, and in October there was a mass protest in Hyde Park. In March dockers rioted outside Whitechapel workhouse – they had no work and they wanted food. In June and July there were demonstrations against the Sunday Trading Bill then going through Parliament. The bill sought to prohibit trading on Sunday – the very day, of course, on which the poorer classes had time to shop. Karl Marx, who was present at one of these demonstrations, thought that the English revolution had begun.

LONDON'S FIRST PILLAR BOX

The introduction of the penny postage in 1840 had enormously increased the business of the Post Office, but it was not until 1855 that the simple idea of the pillar box was implemented in London – previously people had to take letters to receiving offices, or else there were itinerant collectors, who also delivered. The first London pillar box was on the corner of Farringdon Street and Fleet Street; there were ten collections a day, beginning at 9 a.m. and finishing at 10 p.m. Delivery was promised within the London area in about 1½ hours, and within three hours in a 12-mile radius.

It is frequently claimed that the pillar box was the idea of the novelist Anthony Trollope, who worked at the Post Office in a decidedly unharmonious relationship with Rowland Hill.

THE VICTORIA DOCK

The coming of steam ships brought about the decline of the inner London docks. Even with modifications to dock entrances and depths, the larger vessels then being built would have difficulty in offloading near London Pool. It was this situation which led to the opening this year of the Victoria Dock, between Blackwall and Galleons Reach. Later it would be joined by the Albert and George V docks, to make up together the largest enclosed dock in the world.

The Victoria Dock was cheap to build. The land was agricultural and, being over 8 ft below high-water level, was unsuited for building; it was therefore inexpensive to buy and required little excavation before construction.

WAGNER IN LONDON

Richard Wagner conducted eight concerts of the Philharmonic Society in London this year. They included excerpts from *Lohengrin*. He noted in his diary that 'It was here that I came to understand the true spirit of English musical culture, which is bound up with the spirit of English Protestantism … Everybody holds a Handel piano score in the same way as one holds a prayer book in church.'

1856

BIG BEN INSTALLED

The Houses of Parliament clock, with the bell of Big Ben, was first tested on 13 November in Palace Yard. The name was originally given only to the bell, though it soon came to denote the whole tower and everything in it. The origin of the sobriquet has not been established.

There was much argument about the design of the clock. A competition, to be assessed by the astronomer royal, Professor George Airy, was insisted on, and the commissioners in charge of the rebuilding chose the firm of E. J. Dent to manufacture the timepiece, with Edmund Denison designing it. It was on Airy's insistence that a fine accuracy for such a large clock was specified; it had to be correct to within one second a day, and its time was checked by telegraph with the Royal Observatory at Greenwich twice a day. A key feature of the Denison design was that the hands were unaffected by wind pressure on the pendulum.

The giant bell was cast at a foundry at Stockton-on-Tees, from where it was transported by rail, ship and road. Denison had specified a metal mix which the foundry declined to endorse – and the foundry was proved right, for in 1857 it was found that the bell was cracked.

NEW CEMETERIES

The City of London this year established its own burial ground, the second largest in London, in Aldersbrook Road in Ilford. There were 88 overfull churchyards in the City of London, and it was the intention of the Corporation that all new City burials should take place in this new ground; furthermore, as the churchyards were cleared and made into public gardens, or when churches were demolished and crypts emptied, disinterred remains were also transferred to Ilford.

Other new cemeteries formed this year included those for Camberwell, Greenwich, Tottenham and Woolwich.

A REFUGE IN FULHAM

The grounds of Burlington House Academy, at the junction of Rigault Road and Burlington Road, in Fulham, were bought by the govern-

The Refuge for Female Convicts at Fulham in 1856.

ment and used for the erection of the Fulham Refuge, a reformatory for women. It was surrounded by a high wall with a fortress-like gateway surmounted by spikes. The women were given industrial and laundry work, and usually spent two or three years there. After a while the refuge was converted into a normal two-sex prison.

THEATRICAL MATTERS
Ellen Terry made her first performance on the London stage, aged nine, at the Princess's Theatre, Oxford Street, on 28 April; she was in Shakespeare's *The Winter's Tale*. The queen, Prince Albert and Lewis Carroll were in the audience.

Robert Smirke's Covent Garden Theatre was again destroyed by fire, on 5 March, following a masked ball.

Nearby, at Evans' Hotel, the Palladian house which is now 43 King Street, Covent Garden, a music hall was constructed at the rear by the proprietor, Paddy Green.

The Surrey Music Hall was opened on 15 July on the site of the Surrey Zoological Gardens, near Kennington Park. Designed by Horace Jones, it had capacity for about 10,000 people. Built with pagodas and minarets, it was an odd sight in this part of London. On 19 October the same year, seven people were crushed to death in a panic at a sermon given here by the evangelist Charles Spurgeon.

A CASTELLATED PUMPING STATION
One of the most engaging buildings in Stoke Newington is the pumping station constructed by the New River Company this year in Green Lanes. It was designed by Chadwell Mylne in the style of a Scottish castle, with turrets and towers.

ROYAL NORTHERN HOSPITAL FOUNDED
The Royal Northern Hospital began in 1856, when Sherard Statham established at his own expense what was then called the Great Northern Hospital in York Way, just north of King's Cross station. The poor could receive free in- or out-patient treatment there, and nearly 12,000 patients were received in the first six months; by the following year there were 20 medical staff, including dentists. The hospital was later to be found in the Caledonian Road, on the site of the present swimming baths, before it was rebuilt in the Holloway Road in the 1890s.

1857

OPENING OF THE SOUTH KENSINGTON MUSEUM
A Museum of Manufactures had been opened in Marlborough House in 1852 – an enterprise spawned by the Great Exhibition, in which the relationship between art and manufacture had been a prominent theme. Together with the School of Design at Somerset House, it moved this year to Brompton, to a large building called the South Kensington Museum, made of corrugated iron, cast iron and glass, and usually known as the 'Brompton Boiler'. It was opened on 22 June by the queen, and its first director was Sir Henry Cole, the organizer behind the 1851 exhibition, whose intention was to assemble a collection of fine and applied art with the practical aim of instructing artisans. In time this enterprise became the Victoria & Albert Museum.

THE NEW READING ROOM
The British Museum as built by Sir Robert Smirke had an open courtyard at its heart. It was this space which Smirke's younger brother,

Sydney Smirke, utilized in constructing the famed circular Reading Room, covered by what was then the largest dome in the world other than that of the Pantheon in Rome. The Reading Room and its annexes opened in May, containing 25 miles of shelving to take 1.3 million books; it had an elaborate ventilation and heating system (which extended even to the desks), double glazing and soundproofing.

THE WORKHOUSE CHILDREN
Most central-London vestries were having problems in the education and welfare of children housed in workhouses. It was common to separate children from their parents, and certainly from the criminal influences they might encounter. Private workhouse schools such as Mr Drewett's in Tooting, which had succumbed to a cholera epidemic (see 1849), now had a bad reputation and could not be used without public opposition.

This year the City of London, together with the East London and St Saviour Workhouse Unions, opened the Central London District School in 190 acres at Hanwell. Often there were over 1,000 pupils, whose time was spent between formal lessons and learning trades; many of the boys were trained for the army. Unused land was farmed to provide fresh food for the pupils. The school, whose most famous pupil was Charlie Chaplin, was finally closed in 1933.

THE FIRST REDUCTION IN THE POSTAL SERVICE
A postal system which had ten collections a day and same-day delivery in the metropolis had its first reduction in service this year. Previously postmasters had been permitted *not* to postmark envelopes known to contain valentine cards – a delightful participation in the secretive game of that time of year. However, the Post Office stipulated this year that in future the envelopes must be postmarked.

OPPOSITION TO TOLL-GATES
There were still many toll-gates across roads and bridges – a source of general irritation and inconvenience. This year a meeting was held under the auspices of the Toll Reform Association, with Herbert Ingram (proprietor of the *Illustrated London News*) in the chair, calling for the abolition of toll-gates.

BUILDING DEVELOPMENTS
Grove House, in Kensington Gore, was demolished this year to make way for the new Albert Hall.

The final stretch of Commercial Street, a road cut from Shoreditch High Street to Whitechapel, was opened for foot passengers on 8 September. This, together with the construction of Commercial Road and the creation of a large junction with Whitechapel Road, virtually destroyed the old Whitechapel village.

The new Dorchester House in Park Lane was nearing completion. It was the property of a Gloucestershire squire, R. S. Holford, who had made a fortune out of water shares, and it was built on the site of the town house of the earls of Dorchester. Holford chose Lewis Vulliamy as the architect for this vast and impressive pile that had two façades: one on to Hyde Park and the other facing south. The centre of the house was taken up by a large staircase hall modelled on one in the Palazzo Braschi in Rome; the decoration was mainly in the hands of Alfred Stevens, who, having delayed its completion till long after the Holford family had moved in, inconveniently died before finishing his commission.

A handsome building in Covent Garden emerged this year at 27–28 King Street, the headquarters of the Westminster Fire Office.

1800s

No. 27 dated from about 1760, and no. 28 was built this year, but the two houses were modelled as one, with fine ironwork at ground- and first-floor levels. A very large cartouche of arms, displaying the prince of Wales's feathers, which replaced one of the windows, was erected and still survives.

1858

LONDON IN DISTRICTS
As from 1 January the inner London area was divided into postal districts.

A TURKISH BATH IN JERMYN STREET
Until 1976 there was a noted Turkish Bath at 91–92 Jermyn Street. This was originally opened in 1858 by the Metropolitan Baths Company, under the management of 'Mr. Mahomed and his wife'; it was rebuilt as the Savoy Turkish Bath in a spectacular building designed by G. Somers Clarke in 1862.

ST JAMES'S HALL OPENS
The Piccadilly Hotel in Piccadilly now covers the site of the St James's Concert Hall, opened in March this year. Designed by Owen Jones, it consisted of one large concert room on the ground floor, with two smaller halls above. Dvořák, Greig and Tchaikovsky all performed here.

GREAT EASTERN LAUNCHED
Brunel's steamship *Great Eastern* (then called *The Leviathan*) was finally launched at the sixth attempt on 31 January at the Scott Russell ship-yard, Millwall. It was a unique vessel. No larger ship was built any-where for 40 years – 700 ft long, it was made of iron, and it was the first ship to be powered by steam, paddle wheels and sail.

The first attempted launch had taken place back in November 1857; because of her vast size, the ship was edged broadside on to the river, but during this careful manoeuvre one of the dockers was

An orderly dinner time in the female wing of St Pancras workhouse early in the 20th century. Talking was not permitted.

Destitute boys were taught trades at the Boys' Home which moved to a building in Regent's Park Road, shown above, in 1865.

killed and everyone, including the tug operators on the river, panicked.

The purpose of the *Great Eastern* was to take passengers non-stop around the Cape to India and Australia, but it was put instead on the transatlantic run, burning up more fuel than was economic, and was later to be found being used for cable-laying in the Atlantic and as a floating amusement hall at Liverpool. It was broken up in 1888.

THEATRICAL HAPPENINGS
At the Royal Victoria Theatre (the Old Vic) in Waterloo Road, a panic ensued from a false fire alarm. In the mayhem, about 15 people were crushed to death.

The present Covent Garden Theatre (the Royal Opera House) was opened on 15 May; it was allegedly built in eight months, to the accom-paniment of heavy wagers as to its being ready on time. The classical building, with its raised Corinthian portico, was designed by E. M. Barry, who was also to design the iron-and-glass Floral Hall next door.

PLACES OF REFUGE
The Home for the Maintenance by Their Own Labour of Destitute Boys not Convicted of Crime was founded at 44 Euston Road this year. There were so many destitute young boys on the streets of London – sweeping crossings, selling from trays, performing music – that there was no shortage of subjects for this philanthropic venture. At the home, the boys' day began at 5.45 a.m. and was divided between drill, cleaning, schoolwork, parades, prayers, meals and industry. The home, which was to house 150 boys, later moved to Regent's Park Road.

The Nightly Refuge for the Homeless Poor opened in Edgware Road on 1 June. It was built in memory of Lord Dudley Coutts, who had founded a similar refuge in Marylebone Road.

The Workhouse Visiting Society was formed by Louisa Twining 'to promote the moral and spiritual improvement of workhouse inmates'. At first she offered the hapless inmates only Bible readings and sympa-thy, but, seeing the awful conditions in which the poor were kept, later supplemented her conversation with furnishings and other comforts.

A FIREWORKS DISASTER
A fireworks factory in Westminster Bridge Road, owned by a Mme Coton, caught fire; the rockets from this fire set ablaze another firework

factory opposite. In the incident at least four were killed, including Mme Coton herself, and 300 were injured.

BIG BEN CRACKED AGAIN

The large bell of Big Ben had been recast at George Mears's foundry in Whitechapel in 1858 (see also 1856). Placed on a flat cart, it was drawn by 16 horses through the streets to Westminster, and its raising up to the top of St Stephen's Tower and its installation in October this year inside the clock was a matter of intense public interest. Denison, the clock's designer, once again had disregarded professional advice and used a heavier clapper than was recommended by the bell's maker, and the bell was found to be slightly cracked again. However, the bell and the clock came into operation at the end of May 1859; until the installation of automatic winding gear in 1913, it used to take two men 32 hours to wind the clock up.

1859

A PLACE FOR FACES

The National Portrait Gallery was opened to the public on 15 January at 29 Great George Street; the collection then consisted of only 56 paintings, and viewing was by appointment on Wednesdays and Saturdays. The gallery had been proposed by the 5th earl of Stanhope, who suggested a 'Gallery of the Portraits of the most Eminent Persons in British History'.

A DELUGE OF FOUNTAINS

The Metropolitan Free Drinking Fountain Association (later known as the Metropolitan Drinking Fountain and Cattle Trough Association) was founded at Willis's Rooms on 12 April. It had three concerns: the supply of good water to the poorer classes, the furtherance of the temperance movement, and the plight of thirsty animals on their way to markets.

Development was rapid. What is claimed to be the first public drinking fountain in London, paid for by the Quaker Samuel Gurney, was opened by St Sepulchre's church in Newgate Street with much pomp on 21 April. However, Hampstead has a prior claim in London, for it was on 16 April that a new wall fountain was opened on the corner of Heath Street and Holly Hill. Other fountains unveiled this year were at the top of Endell Street, in Marylebone Road, in Horseferry Road and at Oxford Circus.

AN UNUSUAL CHURCH IN MARGARET STREET

The most notable church built this year was All Saints, in Margaret Street. It was the work of William Butterfield, and was built to conform to the ideas of ritualistic worship propounded by the Oxford Movement and the Cambridge Camden Society. At a time when dozens of Kentish ragstone churches were appearing all over London, Butterfield chose to make his of brick, and it remains one of the most striking churches in London, inside and out.

Margaret Street was then a slum area, and the creation of a church with rituals unfamiliar to the unwashed classes was something of an evangelistic experiment.

All Saints was opened in the same year that the first of several riots occurred at St George in the East, where the rector and his curate were harassed during their High Church services by supporters of Low Church practices. Organized disruption – including pelting the

priests and playing musical instruments, as well as catcalls – took place, and once the matter had been publicized others joined the fun. The trouble continued into 1860, and ceased only when the rector was persuaded to retire.

THE LAST NIGHT OF VAUXHALL

Entertainment fashions were changing, as were the locations found acceptable. Vauxhall Gardens, once the high spot of many evenings, had been in decline since 1841, when many of its assets were disposed of. But it had kept going with galas, masquerades, promenade concerts and carnivals, and gaslights had replaced the old oil lanterns. When its licence was renewed in 1853 it was with the condition that fireworks should not be let off after 11 at night and that the gardens should close by 3 in the morning.

The last night at Vauxhall – marked by a concert and a firework display which displayed the words 'Farewell for Ever' – was on 25 July.

FIRST SIGHT OF A GORILLA

London had its first sight of a gorilla this year – albeit a dead one – at the British Museum. The species was first known of in 1847.

WESTMINSTER PALACE HOTEL OPENS

The Westminster Palace Hotel in Victoria Street was opened this year, although building work was still in progress. Designed by W. & A. Moseley in French Renaissance style, the Westminster was the first new major hotel unconnected with a railway company, and the first to have lifts. Unfortunately, it included only 13 bathrooms.

1860

VICTORIA STATION OPENS

The first part of Victoria station – that used by the London, Brighton & South Coast Railway – was opened on 1 October. The company's old terminus south of the river at Battersea, misleadingly called Pimlico, was closed and absorbed into a goods yard there. The extension of the line entailed the construction of the Victoria Railway Bridge across the Thames.

THE BEGINNINGS OF BATTERSEA DOGS' HOME

At a meeting held at the headquarters of the Royal Society for the Prevention of Cruelty to Animals this year, the founding of a Home for Lost and Starving Dogs was formally approved. Its location was in what was then Hollingsworth Street, off Liverpool Road, Holloway – a site which is coincidentally, but aptly, now an urban farm. Within ten years there could be 200 dogs at a time housed there, which did not endear it to the neighbours, and in 1871 the home was moved to Battersea, where it has remained since.

A COMPANION TO THE OPERA HOUSE

The Floral Hall was opened on 7 March with a celebratory ball, next door to the new Covent Garden Theatre. Although in an entirely different architectural style from the theatre, making use of the new freedoms given by glass and iron, both buildings were by the same architect, E. M. Barry.

The hall was a speculative attempt by the proprietor of the theatre, Frederick Gye, to cash in on the adjacent flower and vegetable market, but it was not a success and was bought up by the duke of Bedford in

The Dogs' Home, Battersea, originated in a Home for Lost and Starving Dogs in Holloway. It moved to its present home in 1871.

1887 and converted into a foreign-fruit market. In later years the hall housed props for the opera house, and it is now an integral part of the new opera-house complex.

BUSINESS MATTERS
Moses Moses opened a tailor's shop at 25 Bedford Street, Covent Garden, this year, and in 1881 another just around the corner. This business eventually was to take over the whole corner site and be world-famous as Moss Bros.

Emily Faithfull, a leader of the Society for Promoting the Employment of Women, established this year the Victoria Press, so that women might be introduced into employment in the printing industry. The press was in Great Coram Street, where she planned to have female compositors. The following year she opened another factory, at 82a Farringdon Street, where ten girls were taken on as apprentices in a plant which had a steam printing press. It was thought that compositing was suitable work for women as it required 'a quick eye, a ready hand, and steady application'.

In Soho Square this year Arthur Sanderson founded a company selling wall coverings, fabrics and paints.

In Bermondsey, 1,000 workers in the leather trade were unemployed this year.

The first edition of the *Evening Standard* was published on 11 June. The literary *Cornhill Magazine* also first appeared this year, with William Thackeray as editor.

A NEW ORBITAL RAILWAY
The Hampstead Junction Railway was opened on 2 January. It ran from the North London Railway at Kentish Town to the North & South Western Junction Railway at Willesden.

VICTORIA SPORTING CLUB FOUNDED
The Victoria Sporting Club, which became a power in the world of horse racing, was this year formed by a group of Blackfriars bookmakers.

Professionals and other heavy gamblers went to the club's premises to hear the latest call-over of odds, and so successful was the enterprise that a clubhouse was built in Wellington Street, Covent Garden, in 1864.

A NEW HOUSE IN BEXLEYHEATH
The young architect Philip Webb this year completed the Red House in Bexleyheath for his client and friend William Morris. Dante Gabriel Rossetti described it as 'More a poem than a house'; certainly it remains one of the milestones of English architecture – a sophisticated version of medieval ideas, but heralding aspects of modern architecture. The most striking features of the house were the tall chimneys, the deep-pitched roofs and the extensive use of red brick.

1861

THE FIRST TRAMS
Work had already begun on the construction of the first underground railway, the Metropolitan Line, in London, but this year the beginnings of a new form of transport were seen as well. Tramways, or street railways, as they were often called, were introduced from America by the aptly named G. F. Train. He had experimented in Birkenhead, and at last obtained permission to lay a trial length of track on several routes in London. The first one, about a mile long, ran along the Bayswater Road between Marble Arch and Notting Hill; this was opened on 23 March. The second, opened on 15 April, ran down Victoria Street, and the third, on 15 August, from Westminster Bridge to the Horns public house, Kennington Park. The cars, drawn by two horses, could accommodate 20 people sitting inside and 12 strap-hanging.

Mr Train did not, however, obtain permission to continue his experiment – there were too many objections. Apart from complaints about the noise, the main problem was that the flange of the rails, which retained (but only just) the wheels of the car, was above the surface of the road and therefore a hazard to other traffic. When, ten years later, tramway licences were given away almost frenetically, the rails were sunk into the road. Train's other mistake was to lay his experimental lines along fashionable roads, where the complaining residents were influential.

In 1860 the Finchley Road station of the Hampstead Junction Railway was isolated, as development was held up by the dispute over Hampstead Heath.

THREE NEW HOTELS

Three important new hotels were opened this year. The London Bridge Terminus Hotel was a lavish affair, with 250 bedrooms, but it failed to attract custom, being on the wrong side of London. Closed at the end of the century, it was demolished after damage in the last war.

The Grosvenor Hotel is, happily, still with us. James Thomas Knowles Sr designed it in a Renaissance hybrid of French, Florentine and other styles; in the spandrels of the arches there are portrait busts of famous Victorians. It had a hydraulic lift (or 'rising-room').

The Buckingham Palace Hotel at Buckingham Gate, much used by members of the aristocracy and county families up in London for the season, was designed in Venetian style by James Murray. It is now used as offices.

METROPOLITAN TABERNACLE OPENS

Charles Haddon Spurgeon, a young Calvinist, was the most popular preacher since John Wesley and George Whitefield in the previous century. When he was 27, the Metropolitan Tabernacle at Newington Causeway, near the Elephant and Castle, was built for him — it accommodated 6,000 people, which, judging from attendances to hear his sermons elsewhere in London, was the right size. In 1864 a single sermon by Spurgeon on the subject of baptismal regeneration sold 300,000 copies. The Tabernacle, designed by W. W. Pocock, was partially opened on 31 March.

THEATRICAL AFFAIRS

The Surrey Music Hall, opened only in 1856, burnt down on 11 June.

The Bedford Music Hall in Camden High Street this year developed from the Bedford Tavern behind it. It was quite a small affair, and was rebuilt at the end of the century.

In Piccadilly Circus a 'sing-song' saloon was replaced by a music hall called the London Pavilion. This building was later rebuilt as a theatre whose façade still overlooks the circus.

Another music hall was the Oxford Theatre, opened on 26 March at 26–32 Oxford Street, on the site of the Boar and Castle. A year later Arthur Munby visited it:

The great gay glaring hall & balconies were crammed in every part; there was barely standing room in the crowd, which was chiefly made up of men; business men, clerks, & others, of no very refined aspect …

Socially speaking, the audience were a good deal higher than those I have seen in similar Halls at Islington & elsewhere. One result of this was, that the women present were whores, instead of respectable wives & sweethearts. Therefore another result was, that there was nothing wholesome or genial in the folks' enjoyment: they drank their grog staring gloomily or lewdly grimacing; and the worthless dread of your neighbour which halfeducated respectability creates kept them silent and selfish. At Islington, for instance, the whole audience, men and women, joined heartily in the chorus of wellknown songs, to the amusement of the singer: here, on the other hand, the popular favourite 'Sam Collins' did all he could to persuade the people to sing the chorus of his ditty, and yet scarcely a voice responded.

The Oxford was well known, but its buildings were short-lived — by 1893 the fourth theatre on the site was being opened.

DISASTERS

On 22 June a fire in a warehouse in Tooley Street, near Guy's Hospital, developed into the largest blaze since that of 1666. Hemp had apparently caught fire in the warehouse, and the blaze spread to warehouses nearby in which combustibles such as tallow, cotton, sugar and salt-petre were stored. The London Fire Engine Establishment brigade turned up in great numbers, even using engines floating on the Thames, but to little avail. It was two days before the blaze was brought under control. During the fire the much-esteemed superintendent of the brigade, James Braidwood, was killed, buried under a collapsed wall — he was later given a public funeral at Abney Park Cemetery at which the procession was over a mile long.

The deficiencies revealed by this fire led to pressure to reform London's fire brigade. The fire had cost £2 million in insurance claims, and in 1862 the insurance companies, who managed the fire brigade, notified the home secretary that they were no longer in a position to supply a free fire-fighting brigade without public support. Four years later the Metropolitan Fire Brigade took over.

On 2 September, at Gospel Oak, near Kentish Town, two trains collided due to a signalman's error. Four or five carriages, complete with passengers, fell from a viaduct on to the road beneath; 16 people were killed and 321 injured.

HORTICULTURALISTS TO KENSINGTON

Prince Albert was instrumental this year in providing the Royal Horticultural Society with a new home on grounds in South Kensington. Ornamental gardens with Italianate arcaded walks were laid out, conservatories were erected, and the whole was opened to the public on 5 June. The gardens were not an economic success, however, and in 1882 the society decided to give them up; the Imperial Institute and Imperial Institute Road were built on the site.

TIGHTROPE WALKERS IN LONDON

In the same year that Blondin was amazing everyone with displays at the Crystal Palace, Londoners were regaled by the sight of a 'Female Blondin'. *The Times* reported:

Considerable excitement prevailed yesterday in the vicinity of Cremorne Gardens on account of the announcement that a lady calling herself the 'Female Blondin' was about to cross the river on a tightrope extending from the gardens to a wharf at Battersea. Through some deficiency in the guide-ropes, as they are called, the feat was not completely accomplished, and when the lady, who had started from Battersea, had performed about four fifths of her perilous journey, she was compelled to sit down, and ultimately descended into a boat. The courage displayed under these trying circumstances created almost a greater amount of admiration than would have been produced had the artist walked all the way.

1862

THE AGRICULTURAL HALL

The Smithfield Club, which had organized livestock shows at its premises in Baker Street since 1798, needed a larger venue. It opened this year the first part of the Agricultural Hall at Islington, on the site of some old cattle lairs. The building, which has survived many vicissitudes and is now an exhibition centre, is a splendid construction of iron, glass and brick by Frederick Peck. It was used for a variety of purposes, such as concerts, exhibitions, meetings, circuses, cycle races and marathons. It was actually opened on 24 June with a dog show, and was to be the usual venue of Cruft's Dog Show; the first Smithfield Show held here was on 6 December.

1800s

NEW BRIDGES

The first Lambeth Bridge was opened on 10 November, on the route of the old horse ferry. It was a suspension bridge, designed by Peter William Barlow. But it was built on the cheap, and by 1905 all vehicles crossing it were obliged to go at walking pace and by 1910 vehicles were prohibited altogether. A replacement was finished in 1932.

Earlier in the year, on 24 May, the new Westminster Bridge, designed by Thomas Page, had been fully and formally opened. The ceremony took place at four in the morning, to mark the day and hour at which the queen had been born.

DEMOLITIONS

Familiar buildings disappeared this year. Lyon's Inn, a former Inn of Chancery belonging to the Inner Temple, was demolished this year. It stood on the later site of Australia House at the Aldwych.

Hungerford Market, built stylishly at Charing Cross as a retail market, was taken down so that Charing Cross station could be erected.

Campden House in Kensington, which had been a home of Baptist Hicks (see 1612), was destroyed by fire on 23 March. It was rebuilt in the same style, but demolished in 1900.

PEABODY LARGESSE

The American millionaire George Peabody this year donated £150,000 to the welfare of the poor of London, and the Peabody Trust was established to use the money. On 10 July Peabody was made a freeman of the City of London.

His relationship with London had begun in 1837, when he arrived to negotiate a loan to save the state of Maryland from bankruptcy. He established an American bank in Old Broad Street, and continued to prosper. It was when he retired that he decided to donate much of his fortune to the welfare of London's poor. In a letter to *The Times* he stated that the purpose of his fund was 'to ameliorate the condition of the poor and needy of this great metropolis and to promote their comfort and happiness'. The beneficiaries of his generosity had to be Londoners by residence or birth, poor, and of good moral character. By 1882 the Peabody Trust owned 3,500 dwellings.

EXODUS TO NEW ZEALAND

Many poor were anxious to leave. On 29 March, 800 Nonconformists emigrated to Albertland in New Zealand, taking ship from London Docks. The government of New Zealand paid their passages and promised 40 acres of free land to each on arrival.

AN INTERNATIONAL EXHIBITION

It had been intended to follow the Great Exhibition of 1851 with another ten years later, but the Franco-Austrian War enforced a delay until 1 May 1862. The International Exhibition, in a glass and iron structure designed by Captain Fowke of the Royal Engineers, was located in the grounds of the Royal Horticultural Society in South Kensington. The nation once again flocked to see inventions and arts, and the attendance figure was even greater than in 1851. Part of the exhibition hall was later used in the construction of Alexandra Palace.

MUSIC HALL IN ISLINGTON

Collins's Music Hall (named after Sam Collins, an early licensee) was opened on Islington Green this year. Variety artists who later appeared here included George Robey, Fred Karno, Marie Lloyd, Harry Lauder and Albert Chevalier. Part of the building now houses a Waterstone's bookshop.

The Metropolitan Line was constructed beneath the main roads from Paddington to Farringdon. The view here is east of King's Cross station.

1863

TRAINS IN TUNNELS

The Metropolitan Line, from Paddington to Farringdon, was opened to the public on 10 January. Thirty thousand people travelled on the little steam trains to celebrate this, the most important innovation in London travelling habits, and thereafter over 25,000 used it each day. Though underground, the railway was not a 'tube' as were later ones; it was constructed by the cut-and-cover method, which caused much dislocation in London. The line was not without its dangers. One locomotive exploded, there was worry about smoke in the tunnels (the remaining large grids at road level remind us of the ventilation system), and gaslighting in the carriages was rather primitive.

The railway to some extent was an extension of the Great Western, and had therefore broad-gauge rails, the GWR being the only large company to persist with them. But within a year the GWR had opted out of the scheme and the Metropolitan Railway swiftly converted the track to narrow-gauge track. There were three grades of carriages – first (6d), second (4d) and third (3d). Extensions soon followed. By 1864 the line reached down to Hammersmith, and in 1865 Moorgate (and therefore the lucrative City trade) was reached.

MORE TRAINS IN TUNNELS

In July 1861 an experimental railway had been demonstrated on a piece of land at Battersea. This was the Pneumatic Despatch Railway, a scheme whereby packages could be moved about in tunnels beneath London in vehicles propelled by pneumatic suction. The demonstration and trials were a success, even to the extent of transporting people in the cylinders, the quarter-mile distance being covered in less than a minute.

The promoters of the scheme therefore proposed to put it to profitable use. They built a line from Euston Station to the District Sorting Office at the northern end of Eversholt Street, a length of 600 yards. *The Times* optimistically hoped in February that 'between the pneumatic despatch and the subterranean railways, the days ought to be fast approaching when the ponderous goods vans which now fly between station and station shall disappear for ever from the streets of London'.

On the first day of operation, 20 February, the first mail train arrived at Euston at 9.45 a.m. and 35 mailbags were placed in the pneumatic cars two minutes later. In one minute they were in the sorting office; five months later the Post Office discontinued the use of street vans to convey mail between these two points.

Excavations were then begun in September to construct a line from Euston to St Martin's le Grand sorting office, a much more ambitious project, but it was 1865 before the line had got as far as Holborn, where a central motive station was established. The journey took seven minutes. More delays then ensued, and it was not until 1869 that St Martin's le Grand was reached. Despite all the effort, it is doubtful if very much mail was transported in this way from Euston to Newgate Street, and the line was abandoned by 1880.

TWO FAMOUS STORES

Two famous stores were established this year. One was that of William Whiteley, remarkable then not so much for its building or merchandise, but for its location in the comparatively rural area of Westbourne Grove, nicknamed 'Bankruptcy Avenue' for the number of businesses which had failed there. Once his shop had grown, Whiteley styled himself as 'The Universal Provider', which did not endear him to specialist shops nearby. The store was severely damaged by fire several times, possibly from arson, and, as we shall see (in 1907), Whiteley himself suffered a violent death.

The Lillywhite business began at 31 Haymarket, selling items devoted to cricket – John Lillywhite had been encouraged by customer response when he exhibited at the Great Exhibition the year previously. It was the first known shop specializing in sports goods, and its opening coincided with a new intense interest in sports such as croquet, tennis, golf and archery; soon skating and cycling were to become fashionable too.

A section of the Pneumatic Despatch Railway, crossing the route of the Metropolitan Line in Euston Road.

In the Pneumatic Despatch Railway, mailbags shuttled between Euston and a sorting office at Camden Town or the St Martin's le Grand main post office.

A RETREAT IN KENTISH TOWN

A house and grounds west of Highgate Road were this year turned into an old-fashioned pleasure gardens called Weston's Retreat. Charles Weston, also proprietor of Weston's Music Hall in Holborn, claimed that the 7 acres were lit by 100,000 gas jets – almost certainly a grand exaggeration. The project failed both because the day of pleasure gardens was over and because the site was out of the way for Londoners. Weston went bankrupt in 1868, and his land was bought by the Midland Railway for marshalling yards.

AN ITALIAN CHURCH

It had been intended in 1852, when a site was obtained in Clerkenwell Road, to build an international Roman Catholic cathedral centred on the Italian population of this area. This did not materialize, but in 1863 a church designed by J. M. Bryson, resembling a Roman basilica and dedicated to St Peter, was opened. Garibaldi visited this church on his triumphant visit to London in 1864, and Caruso and Gigli later sang on its steps.

ARTS CLUB FOUNDED

The Arts Club was founded this year at the instigation of Arthur Lewis, Ellen Terry's brother-in-law. It met first at 17 Hanover Square, beneath ceilings painted by Angelica Kauffmann, and early members included Dickens, Whistler, Gerald du Maurier, Rossetti and Swinburne. The club moved to its present address at 40 Dover Street in 1896.

1864

THE FIRST PEABODY BUILDINGS

The first dwellings erected by the Peabody Trust for the 'artisan and labouring poor of London' were opened in Commercial Street, Whitechapel, on 29 February. They were designed by H. A. Darbishire in a dreary style which firmly announced that the residents were in receipt of charity and which was, unfortunately, perpetuated around London. Darbishire could do better – witness his Holly Village in Highgate (see 1865) and the drinking fountain in Victoria Park, Hackney, both wonderful Gothic fantasies. In both the latter projects

The first Peabody buildings were built in Commercial Street, Spitalfields, and came to typify artisan housing.

he was being paid by Angela Burdett-Coutts, who also employed him to build the artisans' dwellings of Columbia Square, which had some style. But it is evident that the Peabody Trust was putting up housing of minimal standards – it was cramped, ugly and disliked by the tenants. The homes in Commercial Street did not have plaster on the walls, and there was a fireplace only in the living room.

NEW STATIONS

The London, Chatham & Dover Railway came comparatively late into London. In 1862 it took half of Victoria station for its West End terminus, and then pursued its aims in the City. It was eventually responsible for the awful bridge (removed in recent years) across Ludgate Hill which was allowed to impede the view of St Paul's Cathedral. On 21 December 1864 the company opened a temporary station south of Ludgate Hill, and in 1866 connected with the Metropolitan Railway at Farringdon.

Charing Cross station was opened by the South Eastern Railway on 11 January, partly on the site of the old Hungerford Market; the train shed was designed by John Hawkshaw. The SER line had had London Bridge Station as its terminus, but the necessity of competing for West End traffic impelled it to cut a line at rooftop level through the uncomplaining slums of south London, crossing the Thames by the new Hungerford Railway Bridge. Later on the SER was to extend to the City by crossing the Thames and opening Cannon Street station.

POLITICAL STIRRINGS

Trade-union activity had been increasing in recent years. There had been a long strike at Trollope's and at other builders in 1859, which had as its aim a nine-hour day, instead of ten. The London Trades Council, a body to coordinate the efforts of trade unions, was established in 1860, and there had been several demonstrations in London relating to foreign affairs, such as the Union cause in America and the freeing of slaves there. More significant was the Trades Council affiliated to the First International, which Karl Marx helped to convene on 25 September at the rebuilt St Martin's Hall, Long Acre. Here there were delegations from many European working-class organizations in countries where the imbalance between capital and labour was plain to see. The Trades Council was an enthusiastic supporter of the Italian freedom fighter Garibaldi when he visited London this year – it was estimated that 50,000 received him in London.

MIDDLESEX CRICKET CLUB FORMED

Teams purporting to represent Middlesex at cricket had existed since the 18th century – they played at the White Conduit Fields in Islington in the early days of the sport. But the Middlesex County Cricket Club, established at a ground at the Princes Club, Knightsbridge, was not officially formed until 2 February 1864. It moved to Lord's Cricket Ground in the 1877 season.

EASING TRAFFIC

This year most toll-bars in north London were removed. Also, what is thought to be the first traffic island was erected in St James's Street, at the expense of Colonel Pierpoint, to enable him to get to his club more safely. The following year the City bought Southwark Bridge and abolished its tolls.

STORE BEGINNINGS

John Lewis opened this year a small drapery shop at what was then 132 Oxford Street; he had previously been working as an assistant at Peter Robinson's. As the business prospered (and it did so without advertising) he bought up neighbouring properties.

The Civil Service Stores, once a familiar sight on the Strand, began in 1864 when a group of Post Office clerks bought a chest of tea for distribution among themselves. This bulk-buying experiment led them the following year to form the Post Office Supply Association. Membership was then extended to others in the Civil Service. The name was changed to the Civil Service Supply Association, and from premises in Victoria Street the association moved to a purpose-built store in the Strand in 1877.

STAR AND GARTER BUILT

The old Star and Garter inn, at the top of Richmond Hill, with glorious views over the bend of the Thames, was this year superseded by a French-chateau-style hotel designed by E. M. Barry. This caused much controversy and many letters to *The Times*. Barry also added a large banqueting hall on the northern side, to entice the new, mobile carriage trade, but this was lost in a dramatic fire in 1870. The whole was swept away in the early 1920s, when the present home for ex-servicemen was built.

NEW CLUBS

The Garrick Club (see 1831) moved along King Street in Covent Garden to the newly built Garrick Street. Its new clubhouse, designed by Frederick Marrable, was opened on 13 July. It contains an enviable collection of theatrical books and portraits.

As the waiting list to join the Carlton Club was so long, a Junior Carlton Club was established on 15 June, and on 1 July temporary quarters were taken at 14 Regent Street. The club's premises in Pall Mall were completed in 1869, to a design by David Brandon.

The Naval and Military Club was founded this year. By 1865 it had taken over Cambridge House at 94 Piccadilly, the former home of Lord Palmerston. The club was, until its recent move from this building, often called the 'In and Out Club', from the words on its two entrances into Piccadilly.

SOUTHWARK STREET OPENED

Southwark Street, linking London Bridge Station with Blackfriars Bridge, was formally opened on 1 January. The street, the first to be formed by the Metropolitan Board of Works, had the unusual feature of a subway beneath to carry utilities.

1865

RAIL EXTENSION TO THE CITY

The North London Railway, primarily built to carry freight, found that it had a profitable passenger business as well. The drawback for the company was that it had no terminus in the City, and to remedy this it constructed a costly branch from Dalston down to Broad Street, which displaced thousands in a thickly populated area and was environmentally destructive because most of the line was at rooftop level. The terminus building, the handsome Broad Street station, designed by William Baker, was formally opened on 31 October this year and by the end of the century was the third busiest London station. It was demolished in recent years to make way for the Broadgate development.

A NEW CHARING CROSS

The South Eastern Railway embellished its new station at Charing Cross with a hotel and a monument. The Charing Cross Hotel, designed by the busy E. M. Barry and opened on 15 May, was one of the first buildings to make extensive use of white-glazed terracotta as a cladding material. The *Illustrated London News* pointed out that the 'rising room [lift] is fitted with seats if visitors are indisposed to use the staircases'. The dining room was one of the most sumptuous in London. The old roof line was reminiscent of the Louvre in Paris, but has since been replaced by a double row of rooms.

In front of the hotel the railway company paid for a fanciful reincarnation of the old Eleanor Cross, first erected in the reign of Edward I (see 1290), which had been demolished during the Commonwealth. This also was designed by Barry.

A MISSION TO SAVE

William Booth, a former pawnbroker and an itinerant Methodist preacher, began, with his wife, the overwhelmingly pious Catherine, a Christian mission in Whitechapel this year. In 1878 this was to become the Salvation Army. Theirs was an urgent task, for they were convinced that eternal punishment was the fate of all those who had not been converted to Christianity before their deaths; but they were also concerned with the appalling poverty of the people of the East End.

Booth was immensely popular with a large section of the population. Bigoted he certainly was – even to the extent of considering

cricket an evil – and he was without much theological knowledge, but his transparent, almost childlike, sincerity and commitment appealed both to the poor, who were his congregation, and to the rich, who were happy to pay someone else to do the government's work.

THE LANGHAM HOTEL

The Langham Hotel was opened on 10 June. It was an enormous project – the building was half as large again as the Grosvenor at Victoria, and could accommodate 500 guests. Floor plans reveal such facilities as an Ambassador's Audience Room, a library, a Ladies' Coffee Room, and several capacious saloons for balls and dinners; the staff eating area alone could seat 260. The ovens could hold between 1,000 and 2,000 plates, and a small tramway was installed in the kitchen to ease the transportation of items. Two thousand visitors, including the prince of Wales, inspected the new attraction when it opened on 10 June. The building, which has recently been converted back to hotel use, is of a Florentine style designed by J. Giles and James Murray.

A GARDEN VILLAGE

One of the delights of Highgate is Holly Village, tucked away at the foot of Swain's Lane. It is a group of Gothic-style cottages, designed in an extremely ornate manner by H. A. Darbishire, and erected in 1865 at the expense of the immensely rich Angela Burdett-Coutts. It is often claimed (as on a modern plaque at the gateway) that they were built by the baroness for workers on her nearby estate or at Coutts' Bank, but this is untrue. None of the earliest known tenants worked for her, and in any case the rateable value of the houses would have been too much for the poorly paid workers that legend has in mind for residents. The *Illustrated Times* noted this year that the dwellings were 'suitable residences for clerks, commercial travellers and so on, the class of persons for whom they have been designed'.

KING'S CROSS DEVELOPMENTS

The Improved Industrial Dwellings Company was another organization erecting dwellings for poor artisans. It erected Cobden Buildings and Stanley Buildings near King's Cross in 1863 and 1865. A novel feature here was the use of balconies for access on each floor to four dwellings; each storey was reached by an open spiral staircase, so that, as the *Daily Telegraph* observed, 'the building was not unlike a theatre, or place of amusement; in ascending the staircase, one makes a series of public appearances'. The idea was also used by Horace Jones, the City architect, in designing Corporation Buildings this year in Farringdon Road – these stood on the site of the awful building now occupied by the *Guardian* newspaper.

In Pancras Road, the German Gymnastic Society opened a gymnasium on 28 January. This building, now subdivided inside, still survives.

The three large gasholders at the junction of Pancras Road and Goods Way were erected in 1864–5 by the Imperial Gas Company, although the ornamental ironwork so beloved of conservationists came later. A reminder of the dangers of gasholders was given this year at Nine Elms, when a million cubic feet of gas exploded and 11 workmen were killed.

A PUGILIST BURIED

The best-attended funeral this year was that of the pugilist Tom Sayers, at Highgate Cemetery; he was a popular hero, having gone 37 rounds against the American champion, Heenan, in 1860 in a drawn match. Costermongers, dog fanciers, fighters and thieves were part of the procession of 10,000 which went from Camden Town; fights occurred at

Holly Village, built by Baroness Burdett-Coutts, is now a desirable address.

the cemetery when many were refused entrance. Seated in a place of honour during the procession was Sayers's dog, whose effigy is now on the tomb.

SAVING THE COMMONS

The campaign to save commons in London and elsewhere was consolidated this year by the formation of the Commons Preservation Society. It was founded by George Shaw-Lefevre, at the time heavily involved in the fight to save Hampstead Heath, with the support of John Stuart Mill, Thomas Hughes and Leslie Stephen among others.

DEATH OF A DEBTOR

George Middleton Ball died in his eighties on 2 September at the Debtors Prison, Whitecross Street. He had been incarcerated for debt for 22 years.

1866

BLACK FRIDAY

The City was shaken by the biggest financial scandal since the South Sea stock collapse of the 18th century. The respected Overend Gurney bank and discount house collapsed on 11 May, causing a run on all the other banks as confidence in the system evaporated.

METROPOLITAN FIRE BRIGADE BEGINS

The Metropolitan Fire Brigade, under the auspices of the Metropolitan Board of Works, came formally into existence on 1 January. The area covered by the new force and the services provided were much enlarged from those of the old London Fire Engine Establishment. It had not only responsibility for saving lives, but also the duty of instigating a programme for the provision of fire escapes. The new brigade took over the buildings and equipment of the previous establishment, and at the same time the old parish fire brigades were disbanded.

The new brigade's first day was not a happy one. Fire occurred at St Katharine's Dock, where property to the value of £200,000 was lost. At the end of the year the brigade dealt with a fire which destroyed the northern part of the Crystal Palace at Sydenham.

The insurance companies, having relinquished their role in fire-fighting, formed the London Salvage Corps, whose function was to retrieve as much property as possible from fires. Though working in cooperation with the Fire Brigade, the corps is still a separate body.

1867

ST GEORGE'S HALL OPENS

St George's Hall was opened in Langham Place on 22 April. Designed by John Taylor Jr, it was designed for concerts given by the New Philharmonic Society, but within a few years it was given over to miscellaneous entertainments. The main use of the building as a concert hall came when the BBC used it from 1934 until it was bombed in 1941.

THEATRE NEWS

Her Majesty's Theatre in the Haymarket was burnt down on 6 December; it was thought that the fire was caused by a stove overheating.

There was panic in Lombard Street on Black Friday, 11 May 1866, when the Overend Gurney bank collapsed, in turn affecting many other banks.

A circus called the Royal Amphitheatre was opened at 85 High Holborn on 25 May. This later became the Holborn Empire.

The second East London Theatre, in the Whitechapel Road, was opened this year. It was burnt down only 12 years later and was rebuilt as The Wonderland, a theatre for Yiddish plays. Another short-lived venture was the rebuilt Shoreditch Olympia, reopened this year after a destructive fire in 1866, but gone by 1876.

The Broadway Theatre in New Cross, opened on 27 December, was one of the first of many theatres built by W. G. R. Sprague.

TWO STRIKES

Journeymen tailors went on strike from April to October as a protest against hours and conditions. The strike ended without concessions from the employers.

The London cabmen went on strike in November, after the government imposed a requirement that they should carry a lamp after dark. A compromise solution was achieved.

A FENIAN ATTACK

On 13 December three supporters of the Fenian cause in Ireland wheeled a beer cask covered with white cloth, but filled with explosives, to the pavement outside the Clerkenwell House of Detention, off Clerkenwell Green. Having detonated it, they ran off. The subsequent explosion made a large hole in the wall of the prison but also demolished houses across the road, where six people were killed immediately and 11 died of their injuries later. The object of the attack was to rescue two Fenian prisoners.

The action caused a sensation. *The Times* said that 'we could not have believed that there lived among us men capable of planning such a deed'. Nine men were arrested, one of whom, Michael Barrett, was the last person to be publicly hanged in England, in 1868.

DEMOLITION OF LANDMARKS

Demolition began in August of the rather squalid group of houses called Middle Row, which stood just west of Staple Inn, in the centre of the road called Holborn.

On Haverstock Hill a white house called Steele's Cottage was taken down to make way for streets. It was formerly a country home of Sir Richard Steele: irksomely far for his creditors to pursue him, but near enough to a coterie of Hampstead life that he enjoyed.

Last services were held at St Mary Somerset in Upper Thames Street and at St Benet, Gracechurch Street, both Wren churches considered superfluous. They were demolished.

Doctors' Commons in St Benet's Hill by St Paul's churchyard, formerly a college of law, but later used by lawyers specializing in ecclesiastical, matrimonial, admiralty and probate law, was sold up and demolished in 1867. It had been described by Dickens as a 'cosey, dosey, old-fashioned, time-forgotten, sleepy-headed little family party'.

PLAQUES IN LONDON

It was William Ewart MP, founder of the country's public library system, who proposed in 1863 that plaques be affixed to commemorate the residences of famous people in London. They were designed to give pleasure to 'travellers up and down in omnibuses' as well as to give instruction. The first scheme (the plaques were generally dark brown in colour) was administered by the Royal Society of Arts, and the first plaque was erected at 24 Holles Street, to the memory of Lord Byron.

DISASTER IN REGENT'S PARK

On 15 January 40 people lost their lives when ice on the Regent's Park lake gave way; at one time about 200 people were struggling in the freezing water.

FOUNDATION OF THE HURLINGHAM CLUB

The first activity at the Hurlingham Club, founded this year, was pigeon shooting, accompanied by heavy gambling. Polo was introduced from India in 1874, and gradually the club attained a social status and wealth that enabled it to double its grounds. The club was based on Hurlingham House, a mansion built in 1760 for Dr William Cadogan, an expert on gout and children's diseases. The house, with the two wings added later, still stands resplendent on the banks of the Thames.

1868

A RAILWAY TO ST PANCRAS

The Midland Railway, a major transporter of coal and beer, had extended itself to London in 1858, but only by using the lines and facilities of the Great Northern south of Hitchin. This was an unsatisfactory arrangement for both companies, especially after the boom in traffic at the King's Cross goods yard. It was inevitable that the Midland would have to make its own arrangements somewhere between Euston and King's Cross, and in 1863 a line was sanctioned from Bedford, which the Midland already served, and St Pancras.

By this time the area north of Euston Road was built up. In particular there was a shanty area called Agar Town, one of the worst slums in London, just east and north of old St Pancras churchyard. The Midland was cut through this dreadful place, and thousands of residents were given usually about a week to find new abodes; to the scandal of the locality, a second, underground, line displaced much of the graveyard by the old church.

It was decided to bridge the Regent's Canal, but, as this would result in a steep incline to the terminus at Euston Road, St Pancras station was raised to a high level. This ingenious solution left beneath the station a vast warehouse in which could be stored the thousands of beer barrels carried from Burton: as W. H. Barlow, the designer of the

station, remarked, 'in point of fact, the length of a beer barrel became the unit of measure, upon which all the arrangements of this floor were based'. Above this he perceived that the passenger and train floor could itself now act as an intermediate tie for the struts holding up a single-span roof. It was a daring concept, which had not been attempted before and, though three larger single-span roofs have since been constructed, none is as high as that of St Pancras.

This masterly station was opened on 1 October, while work on the Midland Grand Hotel was proceeding in front.

EXTENSIONS ON THE UNDERGROUND

Significant work was completed on the underground railway system this year. The Metropolitan Railway, which had reached Hammersmith in 1864, in October 1868 was extended south to South Kensington – in effect forming the western arm of what is now the Circle Line. In 1864 a new company, related but independent, the Metropolitan District Railway, had been incorporated with powers to build a line from South Kensington to Tower Hill; here it was to link up with the Metropolitan Railway and thereby complete an underground railway circle north of the river. The District Line (as it was soon called) opened stations from South Kensington to Westminster on Christmas Eve this year.

In April 1868 another branch of the Metropolitan Line led off from Baker Street to Swiss Cottage, with two intermediate stops (now closed) called St John's Wood Road and Marlborough Road.

EXECUTIONS, PUBLIC AND PRIVATE

The last public execution before the gates of Newgate prison was that, on 26 May, of Michael Barrett, Fenian, convicted for his part in the attack on the Clerkenwell House of Detention (see 1867). The first private execution there was on 8 September, when Alexander Mackay was hanged for the murder of his mistress.

DEVELOPMENTS BY THE RIVER

The construction of embankments along the side of the Thames had been proceeding for several years. This year the Victoria Embankment was opened for foot passengers from Westminster to the Temple, and also a stretch from Lambeth Bridge to the Houses of Parliament. This coincided with the laying out of Parliament Square. On the south side of the river the Albert Embankment was opened between Lambeth Bridge and Westminster Bridge.

By squeezing the Thames into a narrower channel within embankment walls, the work changed entirely the river shoreline. The embankments themselves were built on land reclaimed from the river, and beneath them public utilities were inserted, particularly new sewers, and in the case of the northern bank the underground railway as well. Indeed the main advantage to London of this scheme, devised by Joseph Bazalgette, was that at last the sewage system of London was reformed – it was a significant factor in the gradually improving health of the capital.

The project was dogged by complicated land disputes, occasional scandals, bankruptcies and vested interests. The Metropolitan Board of Works also wished to build a continuation road to the Mansion House – today's Queen Victoria Street – a proposal which aroused the opposition of the City.

BUILDINGS OF DISTINCTION

Several distinguished buildings, which still survive, were completed this year. One was the Hop and Malt Exchange in Southwark Street,

The spectacular Abbey Mills Pumping Station in Abbey Lane, Stratford.

designed by R. H. Moore. Another was the Abbey Mills Pumping Station in West Ham, designed by Joseph Bazalgette and E. Cooper. The utilitarian purpose of pumping sewage is disguised in a building rather Russian in appearance, inside which a vast iron galleried hall contains the engines.

The new Smithfield Market was opened on 24 November. Designed by the City architect, Horace Jones, its construction entailed the excavation of a deep basement in which a train station was located – this was on the line that now connects Ludgate Hill to Farringdon. Twenty enormous girders, each 240 ft long, spanned this subterranean floor, to hold the weight of the market floor above.

In Tufnell Park the circular church of St George was opened; it was designed by George Truefitt. The building, one of the first to install an electric organ, has been used since 1970 for 'theatre-in-the-round' performances.

A vinegar warehouse at 33–35 Eastcheap was completed by Robert Lewis Roumieu this year. It is in a distorted-Gothic style which Pevsner described as 'utterly undisciplined and crazy'. This extraordinary building has somehow survived into a City of bland office blocks.

Another fanciful building is a house called The Logs, at 12–13 East Heath Road, Hampstead. It was built this year by J. S. Nightingale for a civil engineer called Edward Gotto, though the variety of styles used – ranging from Italianate to Gothic, and featuring turrets and gargoyles – could indicate that Gotto may himself have had a hand in it.

THE FIRST TRAFFIC LIGHTS

The *Express* newspaper reported on 8 December that the regulation of street traffic was 'now to receive an important auxiliary':

In the middle of the road, between Bridge-street and Great George-street, Westminster, Messrs. Saxby and Farmer, the well-known railway signalling engineers, have erected a column 20 feet high, with a spacious gas-lamp near the top, the design of which is the application of the semaphore signal to the public streets at points where foot passengers have hitherto depended for their protection on the arm and gesticulations of a policeman – often a very inadequate defence against accident. The lamp will usually present to view a green light, which will serve to foot passengers by way of caution, and at the same time remind drivers of vehicles and equestrians that they ought at this point to slacken their speed. The effect of substituting the red light for the green one and of raising the arms of the semaphore – a simultaneous operation – will be to arrest the traffic on each side.

Most likely the site for this experiment was chosen for the protection of members of Parliament.

A CO-OPERATIVE AT WOOLWICH

The Co-operative movement was slow to take root in London. It derived from the ideas of Robert Owen at the turn of the century, and the establishment of the first proper co-op in Rochdale in 1844. The London Association for the Promotion of Co-operation was formed in 1863, and the Royal Arsenal Supply Association – an organization centred on Woolwich Arsenal – began in 1868. The association (soon to become the Royal Arsenal Co-operative Society, one of the most successful in London) had its first premises in Powis Street, Woolwich.

HORSE RACING AT HORNSEY

A large leisure park was being created in Hornsey, near Muswell Hill. The Alexandra Park Company had acquired the hill itself and then 220 acres of Tottenham Wood Farm in order to form a north-London version of the Crystal Palace complex at Sydenham. Construction began, but then the company went bankrupt and the half-finished building remained derelict for several years. In the meantime a racecourse was opened on the lower slopes – the first race was held in 1868. The course was never one of high status, but jockeys such as Steve Donoghue, Fred Archer and Gordon Richards later won races here. The Jockey Club withdrew the course's licence in 1970.

A CATHOLIC CENTRE

A Catholic church for the French community in Soho was constructed within the circular shell of the old Burford Panorama in Leicester Place, off Leicester Square, this year; it was officially opened on 10 June. Unfortunately, this interesting building was lost in the last war, though it has been replaced by a decorative modern *beaux arts* building.

1869

HOLBORN VIADUCT OPENED

So much was happening in London at this period: gigantic and innovative projects appeared one after another in a rush to transform the city.

Holborn Viaduct was opened on 6 November. It carried the main road from the City to Holborn, replacing an old arrangement whereby a traveller negotiated the steep inclines of the former valley of the Fleet river and crossed by Holborn Bridge. The viaduct was designed by William Heywood, the City surveyor, and was embellished with statues representing commerce, agriculture, science and art. The scheme also involved the construction of Holborn Circus.

On the same day the queen opened the new Blackfriars Bridge, 100 years after the first one was built. This time the designer was Joseph Cubitt.

PARKS FOR THE PEOPLE

Finsbury Park is a considerable distance from the parish of Finsbury; this came about because, when it was decided to form some open space for the people of that greenless area, Hornsey Wood, consisting of 115 acres, was the nearest that could be found. The park was opened on 7 August.

Another misnomer, and for a similar reason, is Southwark Park, also opened this year. It is located in Rotherhithe, and is separated from Southwark by the whole of Bermondsey.

A RAILWAY UNDER THE THAMES

The East London Railway was opened in December from New Cross to Wapping, the first railway beneath the Thames. The intention was to link the Great Eastern with lines south of the river. The company used the old Thames Tunnel that the Brunels had so laboriously made; nowadays this railway, including the tunnel, is part of the Underground system.

THE BEGINNING OF SAINSBURY'S

The 24-year-old John James Sainsbury opened his first shop this year, at 173 Drury Lane, soon after he married the daughter of a Somers Town dairyman. They sold milk, eggs, butter and cheese, lived above the shop, and were no different from thousands of similar one-family businesses around London. Sainsbury, however, was thrifty, innovative and more attentive to customers than most, and his wife, despite bearing numerous children, was a strong force in the business. By 1876 the couple had opened another shop, in Queen's Crescent, a street market in Kentish Town.

TWO WORKS BY TEULON

Samuel Sanders Teulon is a lesser-known, but much admired, architect. This year, two of his works were completed. One was St

Columbia Market in Bethnal Green, built by Baroness Burdett-Coutts. It was a white elephant from the beginning, disliked by traders and public alike.

Stephen's church on Haverstock Hill, opened on 31 December; this impressive building has now been dangerously empty for a number of years. The other was the Buxton Drinking Fountain, which today is by the river in the gardens to the south of the Houses of Parliament, but when first unveiled, on 7 April, was in Great George Street.

DOCKYARDS CLOSED

Links with the 16th century were cut this year when both Deptford and Woolwich Dockyards were closed, as dock work and shipbuilding went inexorably east up the river.

COLUMBIA MARKET OPENS

Angela Burdett-Coutts's grandest piece of philanthropy was about £200,000 spent on the erection of Columbia Market in Bethnal Green; it was also the most disastrous. Opened on 28 April, to the designs of the inevitable H. A. Darbishire, the building was a flop almost immediately. It had the atmosphere more of a church than of a market, with admonitory engravings around the walls, bells that rang hymn tunes, and Gothic windows. Miss Burdett-Coutts's religious inhibitions ensured that the market was not allowed to trade on Sundays. This was clearly a mistake in a largely Jewish area; furthermore, Sundays were the only days when non-Jewish working-class people could do serious shopping.

The ownership of the market was shuttled round for the next few years as idea after idea was tried. But in the end this fantasy building, now replaced by some extremely uninspiring local-authority housing, was demolished.

Darbishire also built the Columbia Square dwellings around it. In these he contrived deliberate draughts, on Miss Burdett-Coutts's instructions, so that the tenants should not live unhygienically.

ROYAL ACADEMY MOVES TO BURLINGTON HOUSE

A hundred years after its first exhibition in rooms in Pall Mall, the Royal Academy moved into the rebuilt Burlington House; the move ended about 30 uneasy years sharing the National Gallery's building in Trafalgar Square.

AN ARCHITECTURAL MUSEUM

Oddly, there is now no architectural museum in London to replace that which opened on 21 July in Tufton Street, Westminster. The

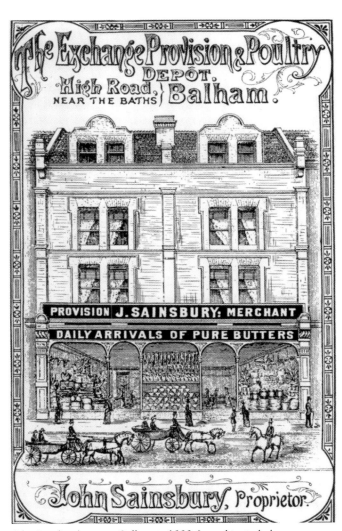

John Sainsbury's store in Balham in 1888. It was his ninth shop.

building, designed by George Somers Clarke and Ewan Christian, was then the headquarters of the Architectural Association. When it closed, in the 1930s, the collection was given to the V & A.

ALL ENGLAND CLUB FOUNDED

The Wimbledon tennis championships derive from the establishment this year of the All England Croquet Club. As the popularity of tennis increased, it became the All England Croquet and Lawn Tennis Club, and in 1882 the sports were reversed in the title to indicate their relative importance. That is still the official name for the club which owns the famous lawns.

THEATRICAL DISPLAYS

The lord chancellor sent a circular to managers of all the theatres, complaining of 'the impropriety of the costume of the ladies in the pantomimes, burlesques, etc., which are now being performed in some of the metropolitan theatres' which has meant that 'many who have hitherto frequented the theatres … now profess themselves unwilling to permit the ladies of their families to sanction by their presence such questionable exhibitions'.

1870

THE TRAMWAYS ARRIVE

The first tramways, as we have seen (1861), did not meet the approval of the authorities. It was not until 1868 that Parliament authorized the laying of tramways in Liverpool, and by 1870 the pressure to do the same in London could not be withstood. The first line was opened on 2 May between Brixton and Kennington; a week later a stretch was opened between Whitechapel and Bow; by December, Blackheath and New Cross were also linked.

TOWER SUBWAY OPENED

The expense and fate of Brunel's Thames Tunnel had been a deterrent to tunnel building beneath the Thames since. However, a man called Peter Barlow, responsible for much of the work of the Metropolitan Line, was behind a project for a new tunnel between the Tower of London and Tooley Street. To the astonishment of everyone, a young engineer, James Greathead, proposed to build it for £16,000, compared to the £614,000 expenditure of the Brunels. To do this he used his own new cutting-shield invention, much smaller and more efficient than previously known, and the whole project was finished in under a year. At first passengers were conveyed through the tunnel in cable cars, but this was not successful and eventually it became a foot-passenger tunnel only, financially viable until Tower Bridge opened.

DR BARNARDO'S FIRST HOME

Dr Thomas John Barnardo, diverted from his intention to do mission work in China, and alarmed by the number of destitute young boys in London, this year opened his first home, in a small house in Stepney Causeway. In 1873 he converted the Edinburgh Castle gin palace in Limehouse into a coffee house, and in 1876 he opened a girls' village home at Barkingside.

NEW BUSINESSES

William Jones, who had been a draper's apprentice since 1867, opened a drapery with his brother, John, in Peartree Terrace,

Holloway Road this year. Jones Brothers became the largest department store in the area, drawing custom from miles around which used new tramway systems at a time when Holloway Road was a prime, and reasonably fashionable, shopping street in north London. The shop was closed in 1991.

Another shopping area to rival the West End was Kensington High Street. The road here had been widened, and at the same time new emporiums had been built. Joseph Toms and Charles Derry had joined forces in 1862, and in 1870 John Barker had two small drapery stores.

A GASWORKS AT BECKTON

A gasworks east of London on the Thames, which produced the largest gas supply for London, was built at this period. It was owned by the Gas Light and Coke Company, which fortunately had rejected sites at Millbank and Victoria. The company built a housing estate for workers around the works and named it Beckton, after the company chairman, Simon Beck.

A UNIVERSITY IN THE WEST END

The government-funded University of London, founded in 1836 mainly as an examining body chartered to award degrees to students at University College and King's College, had its first offices in Somerset House. Several more temporary offices followed until in May 1870 Queen Victoria was present when a new building in Burlington Gardens, backing on to the Royal Academy, was opened. The architect was James Pennethorne. It has an ostentatiously decorative front adorned by no less than 22 statues representing learned figures of the past. From 1970 the building was known as the Museum of Mankind and housed the British Museum's ethnographic collection, but this has since been transferred to the museum's main site and the building does not now have a public use.

Dr Thomas Barnardo, founder of the world-famous children's society.

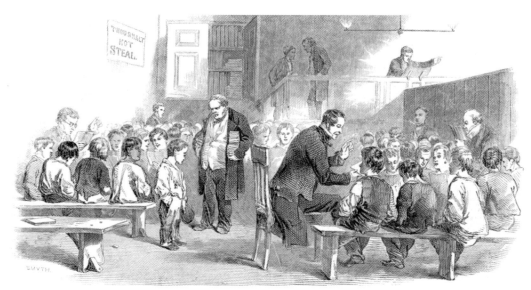

Ragged schools, such as this one in Lambeth, were made superfluous by the introduction of Board schools in 1870.

LONDON SCHOOL BOARD FORMED

William Forster's Elementary Education Act this year divided England into districts for educational purposes; elementary schools, administered by local boards, were to be built in places where school provision from other sources was insufficient. Board schools were thus at first complementary to (but eventually competitive with) the charity, British, National and grammar schools. The London School Board was first elected on 29 November, and held its first meeting on 15 December.

LORD MAYOR ALONG THE EMBANKMENT

The Victoria Embankment was officially opened in July, and on 9 November the Lord Mayor's Show was held for the first time along it.

A RISING ARCHITECT

Two houses completed about this year typified the work of Philip Webb, a leading architect of the Queen Anne revival. At 1 Palace Green, Kensington, he designed for George Howard, the 9th Earl of Carlisle and amateur artist of the Pre-Raphaelite circle, a house which affronted the Commissioners of Woods and Forests, who had jurisdiction over what buildings went up on Crown land. The Commissioners' own architect, Sir James Pennethorne, said that the house would be 'far inferior to anyone of the Estate – it would look most commonplace – and in my opinion be perfectly hideous'. He did not like the materials that were proposed: 'So far as I understand the drawings there would scarcely be any stone visible in the fronts of the house, the whole of the surfaces would be masses of red brickwork without relief from stone or from any important strings or cornices.' Webb was forced to concede some stone dressings, but otherwise there were few changes.

In the same year Webb completed 19 Lincoln's Inn Fields for a firm of solicitors.

FARES FOR THE CHOOSY

From 1 January perfect free trade was instituted in the city's cabs; each vehicle was allowed to adopt its own tariff of fares, provided the rates were legibly painted on the door panels. The London General Omnibus Company was reported to be obtaining more comfortable omnibuses and revising its tariffs on the different routes, to meet the threat of competition.

1871

HAMPSTEAD HEATH SAVED

It had taken 42 years to save Hampstead Heath (see 1829). The gentry and professionals of Hampstead had outmanoeuvred the stubborn and blundering lord of the manor, Sir Thomas Maryon Wilson, so that his numerous bills to Parliament applying for building powers on his Hampstead estates had become a laughing stock. In 1829 he had unwisely included a clause to build on enclosed parcels of the heath, instead of restricting his application to the two estates over which he had undisputed title. As soon as a year later, when he did the sensible thing and deleted the heath clause from his bill, the public and politicians were in such full cry that he was henceforth treated differently from any other landholder anxious to capitalize on his outer London fields. But Parliament also did the sensible thing and considered what would happen to the heath if he were permitted to develop his East Heath estate: the East Heath itself would be sandwiched between Wilson's proposed development and the built-up Hampstead village and would, as a place of recreation, be therefore much reduced – especially once access roads to the development had been cut through.

And so for nearly 40 years the parties took part in a war which revolved around applications to Parliament. The outcome was a growing public awareness of the need to preserve open space in London, a more sceptical view of the Englishman's right to call his castle his own, and the formation of the Commons Preservation Society. A Hampstead Heath was saved which was extended to include Wilson's East Heath estate and create a solid wedge of land which made it easier to ensure that other open tracts adjacent, such as Parliament Hill, Golders Hill and Kenwood, could be added.

The Hampstead Heath Act, by which the Metropolitan Board of Works acquired the land for the use of the public, was passed in 1871. The Act provided that the Board should 'for ever keep the Heath open, unenclosed and unbuilt upon' and should 'preserve, as far as may be, the natural aspect and state of the Heath'.

In the same year Wandsworth, Wimbledon and Putney Commons were also purchased by the MBW, and Shepherd's Bush Green came into public ownership.

1800s

NEW ROADS

Queen Victoria Street was opened from the Mansion House to the Victoria Embankment on 4 November.

Farringdon Street, from Fleet Street to the new Holborn Viaduct, was opened on 20 November.

The construction of Chelsea Embankment was begun on 5 August. It was to reclaim nearly 10 acres from the Thames foreshore.

The MBW proposed to build what became the Charing Cross Road. Half the cost of making it would be paid by the promoters of the proposed underground railway from Charing Cross to Euston.

THE UNDERGROUND EXPANDS

The underground railway system was still being extended. The District Line was taken eastward to Blackfriars in 1870, and to the Mansion House on 3 July 1871; westward it went to Earls Court in 1871, and northward from there to South Kensington in the same year.

ROYAL ALBERT HALL OPENS

Sir Henry Cole, the administrator behind the Great Exhibition and, since then, the chief influence in the development of the 'museums' area of South Kensington, was not a man to let in other professionals easily. He was a civil servant, and suspicious of people over whom he had little control. It was probably for this reason that the International Exhibition of 1862, and the first museum building at South Kensington, were designed by Captain Francis Fowke of the Royal Engineers, rather than an independent architect, though there was nothing wrong or inefficient in the manner in which Fowke performed. Such inhibitions still persisted in the matter of the Royal Albert Hall when the architect of the day, George Gilbert Scott, who had already been engaged to build the Albert Memorial opposite, was edged aside and Fowke was employed to prepare drawings for a hall of unspecified use which would commemorate the late prince consort. Fowke died in 1865, and Cole passed the commission on to Fowke's colleague, Henry Young Darracott Scott, who was an engineer rather than an architect.

The interior of the hall is largely from Fowke and the exterior and the roof from Scott, the latter construction being a triumph of engineering.

The Royal Albert Hall of Arts and Sciences was opened by the queen on 29 March at a ceremony which included an orchestral concert involving 500 players and 1,200 choristers.

ANIMALS IN BATTERSEA

One Thomas Brown left money to the University of London in 1852 for founding 'an Institution for investigating, studying, and … .endeavouring to cure maladies, distempers, and injuries, of any Quadrupeds or Birds useful to man'. It was not until 1871 that the university opened the Brown Institution in Wandsworth Road, Battersea, where the diseases of animals were studied. The building was bombed in the last war.

In the same year, on 3 June, the dogs' home founded in Holloway in 1860 reopened in Battersea, where it acquired its world-famous name and reputation.

EPIDEMICS IN LONDON

In an epidemic of diarrhoea in London, 300 died in three weeks, the majority of them children. Milk that had 'turned' was blamed.

The Metropolitan Asylums Board, charged with hospital provision in London, heard that during the smallpox epidemic this year there were 129 patients at Stockwell, 301 at Homerton and 455 at Hampstead. The old workhouse at Islington was taken over for convalescence.

NUMBERING HOUSES

The registrar-general urged local authorities to name all streets properly and to number all houses. New streets were to be named with one word and then the word for street or road, and numbering should have odds and evens on either side of the road, and should begin at the end of the road nearest St Paul's Cathedral. The registrar observed that there were some 30,000 streets in London, the longest being one mile in length, and that the highest street number was 929.

A NEW ST THOMAS'S

The site of St Thomas's Hospital had been acquired by the Charing Cross Railway Company for its London Bridge station. The hospital found temporary refuge in the Surrey Zoological Gardens, where the giraffe house became a cholera ward, the music hall was divided into three levels to hold 200 beds, and the pavilion became a laboratory. Armed with compensation money, St Thomas's was able to invest in a new building, designed by Henry Currey, in Lambeth Palace Road, opposite the Houses of Parliament; it was opened on 21 June this year.

A CIRCUS IN ARGYLL STREET

The site of today's London Palladium was acquired by Frederick Hengler, who opened in 1871 here his 'Grand Cirque'. It was a successful venture, and he was able to completely rebuild his arena in 1884. But it was a one-man business, and when he died in 1887 the attraction soon met hard times.

MORE TUNNELS BENEATH LONDON

Beneath London today are the tunnels of the now defunct London Hydraulic Power Company, founded in 1871. The network of pipes contained in them stretched from the East End to Earls Court and from Pentonville to Southwark, crossing the Thames on five bridges. By using water pumped at a pressure of 400 pounds per square inch through the pipes, a hydraulic capacity was obtained which powered lifts, cranes, hoists and other items of machinery. So powerful was the pressure that a safety officer of the company had to be present at any public procession in case one of the pipes burst. An early customer was the Midland Railway's Grand Hotel at St Pancras station. Hydraulic power was used to power the hotel lifts (see 1873) – the pipes may still be seen in the building.

A MILITARY CO-OP

Following the example of the Post Office clerks who had begun the Civil Service Supply Association, some officers this year, having experimented with the bulk buying of wine, began the Army & Navy stores in Victoria Street. For a membership of 5s officers could shop here and use the reading room and restaurant. The business became in time the principal supplier to military personnel abroad – the arrival of its catalogue and its merchandise was eagerly awaited in climes both hot and cold.

TEMPERANCE IN THE WARDS

As Dr Barnardo was opening a coffee house in Limehouse in an attempt to break the dependence of the working-classes on drink, the London (later National) Temperance Hospital was being opened in Gower Street. This was not, as the name is frequently thought to indicate, a hospital for teetotallers, but one in which the use of alcohol was eliminated as far as possible in the treatment of patients. It opened to much derision. One newspaper went so far as to say that if the experiment failed the doctors should be tried for manslaughter, and others were quick to point out, when the hospital moved ten years later to Hampstead Road, that it was conveniently close to a burial ground.

TWO NEW BRIDGES

The Albert Bridge, designed by R. M. Ordish, was opened on 23 August. A month later, on 26 September, the first Wandsworth Bridge, a lattice-girder structure designed by J. H. Tolme, was opened. Kew Bridge was made free of toll this year, following the examples of Kingston, Walton and Staines in 1870.

FIRST BOARD SCHOOL

The first, temporary, school erected by the London School Board opened on 12 July, in Old Castle Street, Whitechapel. At first the school was boycotted by many local – mainly Jewish – residents, because it was seen as a Christian proselytizing institution, but after the appointment of a Jewish headmaster it became popular. Permanent schools were opened by the board from 1873.

1872

NEW MUSEUMS

The Bethnal Green Museum, at this time administered by the local authority, was opened on 24 June. The iron structure (known as the Brompton Boiler) had previously provided temporary museum accommodation at South Kensington; it was here encased in brick, to a design by James Wild. Major-General Scott, whom we have already encountered above building the Royal Albert Hall, was overall architect. The museum began with a showing of the Wallace Collection, which remained there until Hertford House in Manchester Square was ready to accommodate it.

The Guildhall Library and Museum was opened on 5 November. The architect of this Gothic building was Horace Jones.

CHARTERHOUSE MOVES OUT

Some City schools were to move out to greenfield sites during the next 50 years. One of the first was Charterhouse, which had been ensconced in the old priory buildings at Charterhouse Square since 1614. This year it moved to Godalming, but its buildings were then taken over by the Merchant Taylors' School.

THE BEGINNINGS OF SPEAKERS' CORNER

The Crown Commissioners of Works this year had a granite pillar and an iron stand erected on the north-east side of Hyde Park where it was lawful to hold public meetings. This instituted formally what is now known as Speakers' Corner, but it probably confirmed a practice that already existed.

PAYMENT BY NON-RESULTS

The board of guardians of St George Hanover Square resolved that the Local Government Board discontinue the practice 'opposed to common prudence, common sense and common humanity' of handing over insane paupers to the parish medical officer on the understanding that he would be paid if he failed to restore them, but not be paid if he succeeded.

SPORTING FIRSTS

On 29 June officers of the 9th Lancers in the garrison at Woolwich played one of the first games in this country of 'hockey on horseback' against the Royal Horse Guards, on Woolwich Common. It is thought that polo was imported from India.

The first Football Association Cup Final was played at the Oval Cricket Ground on 16 March. The Wanderers beat the Royal Engineers 1–0.

HIGHS AND LOWS FOR MISS COUTTS

Angela Burdett-Coutts was this year granted the freedom of the City of London in recognition of her philanthropic work. However, her main gift to London, Columbia Market, continued to fare badly. Having failed as a consumers' market, it had been reopened in 1870 as a fish market, again a failure, and this year she gave the building to the City of London to use as it thought fit.

A more successful new market was the new Flower Market erected this year by the Bedford estate in Covent Garden Piazza. Its success undermined the viability of the privately-owned Floral Hall (see 1860). This building now houses the London Transport Museum.

1873

THE FIRST ALEXANDRA PALACE

The first Alexandra Palace was opened on 24 May, and burnt down 16 days later – the result of an accident by a builder. On the same day a rail link from Highgate station was inaugurated. Huge crowds travelled to the palace – 60,000 were there on Whit Monday. The fire was a disaster both for the company which owned the building and for that which had built the railway line.

MIDLAND GRAND HOTEL OPENS

The Midland Grand Hotel at St Pancras station was formally opened on 5 May, although it was not until spring 1876 that George Gilbert Scott's masterpiece was finished. It is frequently said that Scott merely rehashed his unsuccessful competition design for the new Foreign Office, but this is not true. The project went well over budget and time – it took eight years to complete – but in the end the Midland got what it wanted: the most prestigious of the railway hotels in London. It cost in all about £437,000. It has a magnificent staircase, a giant coffee room that has been ruined by British Rail, and a Ladies' Smoking Room – all much admired. Because much of the budget was taken up by the exterior – one of the landmarks of London – there was nothing very special about the architecture of the rooms. There were no en-suite bathrooms, and all bedroom heating was by coal fire – deficiencies which were to be the hotel's undoing as new hotels in the West End ousted the Midland Grand in location, facilities and labour costs.

OLD INNS DEMOLISHED

While travellers found comfort in new hotels – complete with lifts, reading rooms and bathrooms – the places they used to frequent were demolished. The Talbot, which used to be the Tabard, in Southwark, was sold this year and was demolished two years later. The Four Swans, a galleried inn in Bishopsgate, was taken down this year, as was La Belle Sauvage, in Ludgate Hill, a famous coaching inn dating back to the 15th century.

NEW BUSINESSES

The White Bear inn in Piccadilly Circus, another noted coaching inn, had been demolished in 1870. Its site was used for the construction of the Criterion Restaurant, a prestigious building designed by Thomas Verity, with two floors of dining rooms complete with buffet and smoking room. This was opened on 17 November, and was so successful that in 1878 the premises were extended with the acquisition of two more properties. In the basement was built the Criterion Theatre, one of the first theatres to be built entirely underground, a feature that worried the Metropolitan Board of Works so much in 1883 that much reconstruction had to be done before its licence was renewed. The theatre, which first opened on 21 March 1874, is a small one, well suited to intimate plays – its best-known modern success was Samuel Beckett's *Waiting for Godot* in 1955.

Thomas Ponting had begun a drapery store off Westbourne Grove in 1863. Two of his brothers established a milliner's shop in Kensington High Street in 1873 – a business which was to become a large department store well known in London until its demolition in 1971.

1874

DEMOLISHING CHURCHES

It had been determined to reduce the number of churches in the City of London – there was simply not a large enough population to support their upkeep. This year two of the non-Wren churches were demolished. St Martin Outwich, in Threadneedle Street, was the work of Samuel Pepys Cockerell in 1796. St James, Dukes Place, Aldgate, a 17th-century building, was in a state of decay and described in the *Builder* as being 'very dilapidated and dirty and quite unworthy of description'. St Antholin in Watling Street, which was a Wren church, was sold for £45,000 and the proceeds were spent on the new church of St Antholin in Nunhead Lane, Peckham. More promisingly, the church of St Etheldreda, the old chapel of Ely Palace, was sold to the Roman Catholics – the first in London to return to its pre-Reformation style of worship. This beautiful building was reopened on 23 June 1876.

EXPLOSION ON THE CANAL

Early on the morning of 2 October a steam-tug left the City Road basin of the Regent's Canal, pulling barges laden with grain, sugar, petroleum, and 5 tons of gunpowder destined for Nottingham. As the convoy got to Macclesfield Bridge (opposite today's Avenue Road) the consignment of gunpowder exploded with a noise heard all over London. Animals in the zoo were found huddled together in fear, and a detachment of soldiers arrived from Albany Street barracks ready for a Fenian outrage. Part of the tug's keel was projected 300 yards, and was found embedded in a house. The three-man crew of the tug carrying the powder were killed.

LIVERPOOL STREET STATION OPENED

The various lines which made up the newly constituted Great Eastern Railway had a terminus at the Shoreditch end of Bishopsgate. This was both inconvenient and inadequate, and on 2 February the company opened a new station in Liverpool Street. It was refused permission to build a high building, and so the station, designed by Edward Wilson, is dug deep into the ground on the site of the old Bethlehem Hospital.

Northumberland House at Charing Cross, surmounted by the Percy family lion, was demolished in 1874. Northumberland Avenue now crosses its site.

LEICESTER SQUARE SAVED

The gardens of Leicester Square had been purchased in 1872 with the intention of building on them. It required the philanthropy of the flamboyant member of Parliament for Kidderminster, 'Baron' Albert Grant, to retrieve the situation. He bought the gardens himself, laid them out, and handed them over to the MBW in 1874. Grant – formerly Albert Gottheimer, a merchant who had made a great deal of money and bought his way into society (and was thought by many to have been the model for Augustus Melmotte, the swindling financier in Trollope's *The Way We Live Now*) – went into bankruptcy in 1879.

A SPORTING FIRST

The first baseball match in London occurred on 3 August at Lord's Cricket Ground. Two American teams demonstrated the sport in front of 4,000 spectators.

DISASTER IN MOTCOMB STREET

The Pantechnicon in Motcomb Street, Belgravia, was an enormous warehouse used for storing furniture – of particular usefulness to British people serving for periods in the colonies, or county families who put their best effects into safe storage at the end of the London season. But, like many Victorian institutions, it was not just a functional building – it had a small shopping arcade and a reading room for customers. It was supposed to be fireproof, but this year it was virtually destroyed on 13 February by a blaze which could not be fought properly because the water supply was inadequate.

A FLOATING SWIMMING BATH

The ingenuity of the Victorians knew no bounds. The Floating Swimming Bath Company announced this year the completion of a bath which would be moored by Hungerford Bridge, filled with filtered water from the Thames. In February 1875 the contraption was towed to its mooring there and the company proudly proclaimed that it would accommodate 'hundreds' in a bath that measured 125 ft by 25 ft.

NONCONFORMISTS IN THE CITY

The Church of England might be reducing the number of its churches in the City, but this year the City Temple was built on Holborn Viaduct to replace a previous chapel in Poultry. Built to the designs of Lockwood and Mawson, it was opened on 19 May.

LONDON SCHOOL OF MEDICINE FOR WOMEN FOUNDED

Sophia Jex-Blake had been obliged to study medicine in Boston, Massachusetts, because no British university would admit her. She was not allowed to take a degree here, and in her legal fight to be permitted to take a doctorate in Edinburgh she placed herself at the head of the movement for women to qualify in medicine. In 1874 she opened the London School of Medicine for Women, in Hunter Street, near King's Cross, but clinical experience was not available until 1877, when the Royal Free opened its doors to women students.

THE CREMATION SOCIETY FORMED

The queen's surgeon, Sir Henry Thompson, founded the Cremation Society this year in London; supporters included Millais, Trollope, Voysey and Tenniel. In 1875 a lecture given at the London Institution on the advantages of cremation was given by the aptly-named Armytage Bakewell.

DEMOLITION OF NORTHUMBERLAND HOUSE BEGINS

Northumberland House, standing between Charing Cross station and Trafalgar Square, was the last of the old aristocratic mansions along the Strand, apart from Somerset House. Its gardens, now disturbed by clanking, smoking trains, stretched down to the Thames, and its day had come. This year the Percy family lion surmounting the pediment was taken down and re-erected at Syon House, and demolition of this grand house began so that Northumberland Avenue could be constructed.

1875

A NEW OPERA HOUSE

Work began in September on the construction of a National Opera House, the idea of the impresario J. H. Mapleson. Designed by Francis Fowler, it was modelled on La Scala in Milan, and was intended to contain an auditorium larger than that of Covent Garden. The 2-acre site was on the Embankment near Westminster Bridge, but due to lack of capital the project did not get beyond the stage of laying foundations, some of which are visible in the basements of Norman Shaw's New Scotland Yard, built in its place at the end of the decade.

A CRAZE FOR SKATING

A craze for ice skating began this year. Two skating rinks were opened: the Belgrave in Ebury Street, which appears to have been the first in London, on 3 June, and the Lillie Bridge Skating Rink in Fulham, at the end of the same month.

CHUBB'S IN ST JAMES'S STREET

Chubb's, the locksmiths, moved into their famous premises at 68 St James's Street about this year. The business had originated with Charles Chubb, a ship's ironmonger in Portsea, in about 1804, but he seems to have gone early into the locksmith trade, because he held royal warrants by 1823. By then his factory was in Wolverhampton, where lockmaking was concentrated, and in 1820 he had a shop in St Paul's Churchyard, London.

THE FIRST GILBERT AND SULLIVAN

Richard D'Oyly Carte presented the first opera by Gilbert and Sullivan on 25 March. Carte, born in 1844, had set himself up as a concert promoter in Craig's Court, Charing Cross, in 1870. Arthur Gilbert and William Sullivan's *Trial by Jury* was staged at the Royalty Theatre in Dean Street, and was such a success that Carte formed a syndicate to present more of their work in the years to come. By 1881 profits were running at £60,000 a year and Carte was able to invest in building his own theatre, the Savoy.

A NEW ALEXANDRA PALACE

A new Alexandra Palace was constructed on the ruins of the old – it is substantially the same building that we see today, although that too was badly damaged by fire in 1980.

LIBERTY'S OPENED

The famous shop Liberty's was opened at 218a Regent Street on 15 May. Arthur Lasenby Liberty, born in Chesham in 1843, above his father's drapery shop, was himself an apprentice draper in Baker Street. His first job, in 1862, was at a renowned Shawl and Cloak Emporium in Regent Street, where royal warrants were profuse on the walls. In that same year he became fascinated by the Japanese work displayed at the International Exhibition; some of the objects were bought by his own employers to form the basis of an Oriental Warehouse in which Liberty himself worked. It was in this situation that he met and talked to the many artists interesting themselves in the newly discovered Oriental china, fabrics and drawings. Liberty built the Oriental side of the business up to a level of profit at which he could reasonably expect a partnership, but this was refused and he then began his own business with a staff of three. Fifty years later the company employed 1,000 people.

BEDFORD PARK BEGUN

A start was made on constructing London's first garden suburb, Bedford Park, at Turnham Green, a carefully irregular arrangement of Queen Anne-style houses constituting a respectable revolt against Victorian architectural excess. It was associated, as was Liberty's business, above, with the growing 'artiness' of London society and the more openly stated 'aesthete' views which were to reach their peak at the time of Beardsley and Wilde.

Bedford Park was the creation of a speculator called Jonathan Carr, who, by marriage, had inherited Bedford House and its grounds soon after the railway had opened at Turnham Green. But the style of Bedford Park was chiefly that of Norman Shaw, the architect of many of the houses. (He was also this year building his own unusual house in Ellerdale Road, Hampstead.)

On a different social scale, the Queen's Park Estate in Kensal Green was being developed by the Artisans, Labourers and General Dwellings Company, with small incongruously Gothic houses in roads laid out and named, like Washington DC, from A Street to P Street.

SHELTERS FOR CABMEN

Around London still survive a few of the 64 huts built to provide cabmen with temporary shelter and food, and to ensure that what they drank was not alcoholic. The temperance organization which built these cosy and much missed buildings opened its first one on 6 February in Acacia Road, St John's Wood.

The temperance movement was also to be found behind the establishment this year of the People's Café Company. Its first café opened in Whitecross Street on 16 April.

MARKET NEWS

The future of Columbia Market was still unsettled. After a year, in 1874, the City had given the building back to Angela Burdett-Coutts, because it could find no use for it. In December 1875 it was opened as a market 'for the poorer classes', under the auspices of the Great Eastern, Great Northern and Midland railway companies.

In November the new Metropolitan Poultry Market was opened at Smithfield, in a building designed by Horace Jones.

1876

UNVEILING ALBERT

The final part of the Albert Memorial, the figure of Prince Albert himself, was unveiled on 8 March, three years after the memorial itself had been finished. This delay had been occasioned by the death of John Foley, its sculptor. Albert is not holding a Bible, as many think, but a catalogue of the 1851 Great Exhibition.

The overall work is by George Gilbert Scott. By this time Gothic Revival was under attack, and the memorial attracted considerable criticism from the new breed of architects and art lovers.

MORE SKATING

Ice skating caught on seriously. New rinks opened included the Grand Central in High Holborn, one at Oxford Circus (now the site of the Salvation Army Hall), the Glaciarium at the Old Clock House in the King's Road, Chelsea, the Victoria Rink in Cambridge Heath Road, which boasted 30,000 square feet of ice, and the Clapham Rink in Clapham Road.

FISHES, LIONS AND GREYHOUNDS

The Royal Aquarium was opened in Storey's Gate, Westminster, on 22 January. It was not just a collection of fish tanks: the palatial building included a music-hall-cum-theatre, a good deal of palm-court foliage and statuary, a reading room, an art gallery, a skating rink, a restaurant and an orchestra. It was not a success, and was demolished in 1906 to make way for the Methodist Central Hall.

Anthony Salvin's new lion house at London Zoo was opened to much acclaim this year. This building is nowadays considered very cramped for the animals, but at the time of building it was a considerable improvement on what the poor beasts had had before. A magazine commenting on the proposed new building observed:

Lions at play, free as their own jungles at home; tigers crouching, springing, gambolling, with as little restraint as on the hot plains of their native India – such is the dream of everyone interested in Zoology. We are all tired of the dismal menagerie cages. The cramped walk, the weary restless movement of the head … the bored look, the artificial habits … Thousands upon thousands will be gratified to learn that a method of displaying lions and tigers, in what may be called by comparison, a state of nature, is seriously contemplated at last.

By the Welsh Harp reservoir a mechanical hare for greyhound racing was exhibited. The invention of a Mr Geary, 'It so closely resembles the running of a living animal as to be eagerly pursued by greyhounds.'

NEW PLACES OF LEARNING

The Grocers' Company opened a Middle-Class School at Hackney Downs on 27 September. It was to serve 'that class who desire to educate their children up to the age of 14 or thereabouts'.

The South Hampstead High School for Girls, which still thrives in Maresfield Gardens, was begun on 27 March in Winchester Road, Hampstead, as the St John's Wood High School.

The National Training School for Music was founded this year for the 'cultivation of the highest musical talent in the country, in whatever station of society it may be found'; its first principal was Sir Arthur Sullivan. The building, which lies behind the Royal Albert Hall, was designed in Tudor style by yet another Royal Engineer (see 1871), Lieutenant H. H. Cole. It was built free of charge by the property developer C. J. Freake, and was described by Sir Hubert Parry as 'about the worst building ever constructed for any purpose'. It is now used by the Royal College of Organists.

THE FIRST TELEPHONE CALL

An event of far-reaching significance took place in a room at Brown's Hotel on 10 March this year, when Alexander Graham Bell made the first telephone call on his primitive invention. The message consisted of one line: 'Mr Watson, come here; I want you.' On 14 July the following year the first public demonstration of the telephone was held at the Queen's Theatre.

A FEMINIST BREAKTHROUGH

The first woman to hold elected office in local government was a Miss Merington, who was elected to the Kensington Guardians of the Poor this year.

1877

A NEW BILLINGSGATE

A new Billingsgate Fish Market, designed by Horace Jones, was opened on 20 July. Once again the City Corporation had decided to retain the traditional site, despite the fact that most fish came in by rail and then had to be transported through the narrow and congested streets to Billingsgate by the Thames.

The new building was built of yellow brick in a vaguely French style. Two large market halls were included, each decorated with attractive ironwork. Below ground, deep vaults were used for storage in ice until refrigeration was introduced.

FAREWELL TO TEMPLE BAR

The demolition of Temple Bar, the barrier which separated the City from Westminster, was begun on 10 December, though work continued for at least another year. This Wren building had been decayed and isolated for some time. Premises nearby had been cleared to make way for the new law courts, and the structure, a hindrance to traffic, was not worth spending money on. Oddly, the building has survived, albeit in a much deteriorated state. It lay in a thousand pieces in a yard off Farringdon Street for ten years, and was then re-erected by Sir Henry Meux, the brewer, in the grounds of his house Theobalds Park, where it stands today. The house later came into public ownership, but the old Temple Bar did not, and, though there have been many proposals for its re-erection in the City, notably in the St Paul's Churchyard area, the City Corporation has not yet felt able to fund such an expensive transfer.

NEW STORES

What is thought to be the first purpose-built department store in the country was Bon Marché in the unlikely location of Brixton Road. It was opened in April this year by James Smith, a printer and proprietor of the magazine the *Sportsman*, who had won a great deal of money in a betting coup. The *Builder* described it as a 'novelty in market accommodation in the metropolis, embracing the sale of almost every imaginable article in food, furniture and dress, under one management, the whole of the employees residing on the premises'. The staff dining room could hold 300 at one sitting. In fact, from the *Builder*'s description, the store appears to have been more of a shopping mall than a department store in the usual sense of the word.

Bon Marché did not flourish and Smith committed suicide. The old store building may still be seen in Brixton Road.

The Civil Service Supply Association built a new store in the Strand this year, a rather brooding terracotta affair on to which was later added a 1930s frontage. Almost all of it was destroyed in a dramatic fire in 1982.

Peter Jones, a draper, had begun business in Hackney nearly 20 years before. In 1877 he acquired 4–6 King's Road, Chelsea, and gradually, in the usual way of drapers of the period, he acquired shops adjacent, so that by the time of his death in 1905 he had most of the block that the present store absorbs. John Lewis of Oxford Street then bought the business.

SUGAR BARONS

Henry Tate, whose sugar business had begun in Liverpool, this year established a refining factory in Silvertown in the East End. Another sugar refiner, Abram Lyle of Greenock, established a similar business at Silvertown in 1881 – his fortune was to be made with Golden Syrup. The two companies merged to form Tate & Lyle in 1921.

FIRST MEN'S TENNIS CHAMPIONSHIP

The first men's tennis championship took place under the auspices of the All England Croquet and Lawn Tennis Club at Wimbledon. It was a leisurely affair, including a two-day break while the potential audience went off to attend the Eton–Harrow cricket match at Lord's. A player called Spencer Gore won the first final with a heavy reliance on volleys.

PROTECTING OLD BUILDINGS

The Society for the Protection of Ancient Buildings was established this year, its first offices being at 26 Queen Square, in the house of its founder, William Morris. Its first committee included Thomas Carlyle, Leslie Stephen, Holman Hunt and Edward Burne-Jones. The concern of the members was to prevent not merely the demolition of old buildings, but also the sort of Gothic restoration that was then common, or else the scraping down of medieval walls to a pristine state.

THE LIMIT OF THE DISTRICT LINE

Construction of the District Line had gradually been going west. Hammersmith was reached in 1874, and in 1877 a large new length of line was opened to Richmond, which proved to be the terminus of that particular branch. In the east the Metropolitan Line was still incomplete – in 1877 there was still no track between Mansion House and Aldgate, which meant that the much desired circle was not complete, a source of great irritation to Londoners.

SERIOUS FLOODING

There was serious flooding of the Thames at the beginning of the year – Lambeth, Southwark and Wapping were badly affected, but so were areas to the west. 'The Thames has risen to such a height that the ground floor of Eel Pie Island Hotel, Twickenham, is under several feet of water, and the pigs and calf have to be kept in an upstairs bedroom and the fowls located in the drawing room,' the *Middlesex Chronicle* observed.

Temple Bar, one of London's most familiar landmarks, being demolished early in 1878.

GROSVENOR GALLERY OPENS

One of the best-known art dealerships, the Grosvenor Gallery, was founded this year by Sir Coutts Lindsay, an amateur artist. He decided to buy up some stabling and workshops in Grosvenor Mews and erect an art gallery; at the same time he purchased nos. 135–137 New Bond Street to provide a better access. On this property he built what became known as the Aeolian Hall, designed by William Thomas Sams, which consisted of an entrance hall with a library and club premises on either side, and two galleries on a north–south axis at the rear. The first exhibition was held on 1 May, when artists shown included Whistler, Millais, Holman Hunt, Alma Tadema, Burne-Jones and Walter Crane. On the opening day some 7,000 people paid 1s to be admitted.

1878

A NEEDLE ON THE EMBANKMENT

That an ancient Egyptian monument should be located on the Victoria Embankment is surprising. But the acquisition of Cleopatra's Needle, its transportation to England and its erection is an odd story altogether. The granite monolith was cut in the Aswan quarries about 1475 BC and

After its extraordinary journey from Alexandria, Cleopatra's Needle, as the English called it, was erected on the Victoria Embankment.

taken to Heliopolis, where it was carved with the names of gods and pharaohs; Cleopatra's name, with which the London population connected, was added later. During the Roman occupation of Egypt *c.* 23 BC the obelisk was moved to Alexandria, where it stood for centuries before it fell over. In 1820 the monument was offered as a gift by the Turkish viceroy of Egypt to the British, but it was not until the 1870s that serious consideration was given to actually taking delivery. A way was found to transport it in a metal cylinder, towed by a boat. It was a hazardous journey. In the Bay of Biscay a storm wrecked the towing ship and six seamen lost their lives; but the Needle was found, pulled in to Spain, and eventually taken to London.

A number of sites were considered for its display in London – by the Houses of Parliament or in front of the British Museum were but two. Eventually it was erected on 12 September this year, on a site on the Victoria Embankment.

STEAMBOAT COLLISION

On 3 September a disastrous collision occurred on the Thames. At about 7.40 p.m. the steamer *Princess Alice* was returning from Sheerness with about 800 passengers, when in a bend in the river near Woolwich she was rammed by a ship carrying ballast. The *Princess Alice* was virtually cut in half and sank in about 18 ft of water in about five minutes. Even her sister ship, running ten minutes behind her, was too late to offer much assistance. There were only 150 survivors. In November the official report stated that 'men whose lives were passed on the river were totally ignorant of its regulations'.

MORE CHURCH DEMOLITIONS

The programme of City church closures and demolitions continued. This year St Dionis Backchurch, a Wren building at the junction of Lime Street and Fenchurch Street, was taken down. This followed the demolition in 1876 of two other Wren churches: St Michael Queenhithe, in Upper Thames Street, and All Hallows, Bread Street.

CITY AND GUILDS FOUNDED

The City and Guilds of London Institute was founded this year to provide technical and scientific education.

THE BEGINNINGS OF GAMAGE'S

Almost all the large department stores of London began as draper's shops. Gamage's, in the unfashionable quarter of Holborn, was an exception. It began this year when Albert Walter Gamage, aged 21 and working as an assistant in a draper's in St Paul's Churchyard, took a watch for repair to a shop in Holborn. The watchmaker mentioned that he thought a hosier's would do well in the area. Using borrowed money, Gamage rented 128 Holborn and lived behind the shop. It was an unpromising business – so much so that Gamage's partner, who had lent him the money at the start, sold out to him in 1881 in despair at ever finding enough in the venture to support both of them.

Gamage's policy of selling everything cheaper than elsewhere gradually brought crowds to his shops, and also lawsuits from manufacturers. Bicycles were a speciality – there were 49 pages of them in his 900-page catalogue in 1911 – as was camping gear. In the 1880s he acquired shops along the block, and soon most of the stretch from Leather Lane to Hatton Garden was taken, a maze of buildings beloved of families and especially children, hunting for bargains. It is reputed that when Gamage died in 1930 his body lay in state in the motoring department, with staff as a guard of honour.

NEW ROADS

Clerkenwell Road was completed in April this year, an entirely new route linking Theobalds Road to Old Street. It cut ruthlessly across haphazard road patterns, and in so doing divided in two the old monastic precinct at St John's Gate.

The Maryon Wilson family, having cooperated in the acquisition of Hampstead Heath once Sir Thomas Maryon Wilson had died (see 1871), was permitted to develop on its land to the south of Hampstead village. But even then the open-space lobby did not give up. Octavia Hill mounted a public fund-raising campaign to save the woody slopes and almost succeeded in finding enough to buy the land, but in 1875 50 acres were sold to developers for £50,000. The axial road in what became a large concentration of red-brick, turn-of-the-century housing is Fitzjohn's Avenue, formed in 1878 and soon to be lined with the most sumptuous, and at times bizarre, buildings in Hampstead.

EPPING FOREST TO THE CITY

It is one of the quirks of London history that several large tracts of open space outside the borders of metropolitan London are in the care of the City. The Metropolitan Board of Works lacked powers to acquire land for recreation outside its own area, and in any case the vestries would have probably opposed it. Thus on several occasions when land frequently used by Londoners, such as Epping Forest in Essex and Highgate Wood in Middlesex, came on to the market it was only the City Corporation that had powers and resources to buy them. In the case of Epping the City already possessed some land within the forest and had instituted proceedings against the lord of the manor for encroachment and illegal enclosure. This resulted in 1878 in an Act of Parliament which handed over the 3,000 acres of remaining forest to the City, though it was not until 1882 that it was formally opened to the public. The City declined to have representatives of the MBW on the committee which looked after the forest from then on.

There were other victories for the open-space preservers. This year the Ecclesiastical Commissioners attempted to enclose part of Eel

Brook Common, only to be thwarted by local residents who tore up the fences. The common was later bought by the London County Council.

In 1877 Clapham Common was purchased by the MBW.

CARMEN IN LONDON

Her Majesty's Theatre had been reconstructed expensively in 1869 in the shell of the second building which had burnt down in 1867 (q.v.), but it remained empty for several years. It was actually reopened when the American evangelists Sankey and Moodey used it for 'revival meetings' in 1875, but opera was soon restored. On 22 June 1878 the first English performance of Bizet's *Carmen* was given here.

1879

THE MAN FOR THE PRU

Alfred Waterhouse was to leave his architectural mark on London from this year, when the first part of the Prudential office block in Holborn was completed. The offices of the company, which had pioneered life insurance, were extended at the turn of the century, and the 1879 part was replaced in the 1930s. When completed, this building was probably the last great Gothic Revival design in London, here using, as Waterhouse often did, a great deal of red brick and red terracotta. This is not to everyone's taste, but his use of materials was copied frequently in the late Victorian period.

Waterhouse made his reputation in the north of England, particularly in Manchester and Liverpool, and he was one of the architects invited to put forward proposals for the new law courts in the Strand; Waterhouse came second – it is thought that he received, in 1868, the commission to build the Natural History Museum in Kensington as compensation (see 1881).

INNOVATIONS

The use of electricity in public places was increasing. Electric light was introduced into Billingsgate Market and on Holborn Viaduct in 1878, though in the following year the City Commission of Sewers decided not to continue the experiment on the viaduct, as electricity proved 7.5 times as expensive as gaslighting. But in 1879 the Embankment

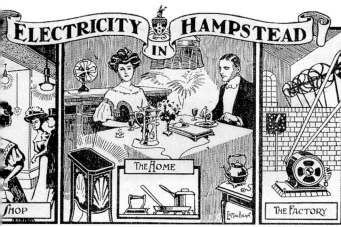

London vestries supplied electricity at first for public lighting, but later were anxious to supply other outlets, as this 1909 postcard shows.

was lit by electricity, and users of the reading room of the British Museum enjoyed its advantages.

The first telephone exchange in London was opened this year in Lombard Street.

And in Cranbrook Road, Ilford, Alfred Harman founded a company, named after the small town in which he had chosen to produce photographic materials. Ilford was preferred because of the clean air away from London.

CHANGES AT WORMWOOD SCRUBS

The open common unattractively called Wormholt (or Wormwood) Scrubs had formerly been purchased by the War Office as a possible firing-practice ground on the western boundary of London. In 1879 it was redundant, and was transferred free of charge to the Metropolitan Board of Works for recreational use, provided that it would be returned to military use when needed.

In the meantime work had begun at its edge on the building of Wormwood Scrubs prison, using convict labour. The scheme was to give convicts something to do and learn, provide cheap labour, and, of course, keep the construction wholly within the province of the prison commissioners; the local clay was used to make the 35 million bricks used in the building.

D. H. EVANS FOUNDED

The D. H. Evans department store began this year when Dan Harries Evans, son of a Llanelli farmer, moved from a draper's shop in Westminster Bridge Road to 320 Oxford Street. His wife was a dressmaker and, close to the fashionable area of Marylebone, trade prospered, with good-class lace as his speciality.

1880

THEATRE NEWS

The Old Vic (or the New Victoria Theatre, as it was then called) was very much in the doldrums. Up for sale in 1880, it was bought by the redoubtable social reformer Emma Cons, and was converted into the Royal Victoria Coffee and Music Hall. The acts had to be respectable, and there were also lectures and penny readings. From this rebirth developed Britain's National Theatre.

LONDON TOPOGRAPHICAL SOCIETY BEGINS

The London Topographical Society was begun at the suggestion of a Major-General J. Baillie, and was advanced by the energies of the London historian H. B. Wheatley. 'There is,' pointed out Baillie, 'an immense mass of unappropriated material which would naturally fall to it, such as plans and views of towns, parishes and estates, plans of railways, &c.' which might be reproduced.

The inaugural meeting of the society took place at the Mansion House on 28 October. It had many ambitions – the collecting of books on London, the unravelling of place names, the preparation of maps, and publication of plans, drawings and documents. The publication of essays on London topics and of maps and panoramas has continued unabated since then.

MORE RAILWAYS

The underground railway system was extending still, but almost entirely in the open air. The District Line veered north from Turnham

Green to reach Ealing Broadway in 1879; in 1880 it went south again, this time on the spur from Earls Court down to Putney. In these two years the Metropolitan stretched north from Swiss Cottage out into Betjeman's Metroland as far as Harrow-on-the-Hill.

A NEW ARCADE

The relatively unknown Royal Arcade, between Old Bond Street and Albemarle Street, was opened on 7 June. An earlier plan for a Royal Arcade had been mooted in 1862 – this was to have stretched from Regent Street to New Bond Street.

NEW VESTRY HALLS

The new London vestries, now assuming additional responsibilities as local government at last came of age in London, were building new vestry halls, some of which became town halls when borough status was achieved. Hampstead, for example, without room in the actual village for a substantial building, went south to Haverstock Hill for a site and erected a building there in 1878. Holborn built a hall at the corner of Gray's Inn Road and Clerkenwell Road in 1879, and in 1880 Bermondsey and Kensington proudly opened new buildings. The Kensington building was destroyed by stealth by the modern-day borough in June 1982.

THE ROYAL ALBERT DOCK

The reason for building the Victoria Dock – the increasing size of ships – was also that for its extension, called the Royal Albert Dock, which was opened on 24 June this year. The new dock measured 1¾ miles long – by far the largest London dock – and, like the Victoria Dock (see 1855), was cheap to build.

MUSIC AND DRAMA IN THE CITY

The Guildhall School of Music was opened on 27 September by the City Corporation this year, in warehouse premises in Aldermanbury.

FIRST TEST MATCH

The first Test Match between England and Australia took place on 6–8 September at the Oval. England won by five wickets.

TEMPLE BAR MONUMENT UNVEILED

The replacement for Temple Bar, a monument where the Strand and Fleet Street meet, was unveiled on 8 September. Designed by Horace Jones, it is not one of his best pieces of work. Its decoration includes figures of Queen Victoria and her son, the future Edward VII. The monument is at the boundary between City and Westminster and it is where the monarch, on an official visit to the City, is met by the lord mayor who, in an absurd ceremony, presents the City's sword of state as a mark of loyalty and is then handed it back. The mayor then carries the sword before the monarch wherever they go in the City.

1881

LEADENHALL MARKET OPENED

Contrasting with Richard Rogers's Lloyd's Building is Leadenhall Market (now splendidly restored) in Gracechurch Street. This new Leadenhall, making much use of iron and glass, was opened on 15 December, replacing a post-Fire building grouped around three courtyards. The market principally deals in poultry and game.

A NEW MUSEUM IN KENSINGTON

The Natural History Museum, designed by Alfred Waterhouse, was formally opened on 18 April. The building is in fact part of the British Museum, and was intended to contain the growing collection in Bloomsbury of zoological, botanical, mineral and geological specimens. This building, for many tourists the first intimation of 'London' on their journey from Heathrow (the second is Harrods), is in a Romanesque style derived from France and Germany. But it could have been substantially different. The competition to build it was won by Captain Fowke, who designed much of the Royal Albert Hall, but he died before the museum project had advanced. Waterhouse was engaged to carry out Fowke's design, but inevitably produced something entirely different.

THREE NEW THEATRES

Richard D'Oyly Carte had staged early and very successful Gilbert and Sullivan operas at the Opéra Comique in the Strand, but when his lease there ended, instead of renewing it or going to another theatre, he decided to build a theatre of his own. He bought the freehold of a piece of sloping land in the old precinct of Savoy on the other side of the Strand. On this he built the first Savoy Theatre, designed by C. J. Phipps, which opened on 10 October. It was the first theatre lit by electricity, with gas as a standby in case the supply failed. In a notice to the public, Carte said, 'The incandescent lamps consume no oxygen, and cause no perceptible heat. If the experiment of electric lighting succeeds, there can be no question of the enormous advantages to be gained in purity of air and coolness.' Another claim made for Carte and this theatre was that they invented the queue – people got tickets or entrance on a first come, first served basis in an orderly queue, instead of forming a general crush.

The Comedy Theatre in Panton Street opened five days later. Designed by Thomas Verity, architect of the Criterion, it was in an area of previously dubious reputation, but, as the *Daily Telegraph* remarked, 'recent improvements have now removed altogether the doubtful resorts of the roisterers of other days'. The same building still stands, though there has been drastic interior reconstruction.

Phipps was also the architect for the third version of the Princess's Theatre at 73 Oxford Street – its predecessor had been burnt down in 1880. The new theatre, opened on 6 November, was closed in 1902 and converted into shops, and then a Woolworth's was built on its site.

ADVANCE OF UTOPIA

The first meeting of the Kyrle Society was on 27 January. This society, born in an age of great innovation and improvement in a London that contained extreme poverty and squalor, set out 'to diffuse the love of beautiful things amongst the poor and preserve open spaces and the formation of choirs etc.'. Little is known of the society's success in the matter of choirs, but it had a significant hand in the introduction of many small public gardens in London.

The same striving for a Utopia in which even the poorest could have access to fine arts was exemplified by the exhibitions begun this year in Whitechapel by Canon Samuel Barnett, vicar of St Jude, Whitechapel; his work was to develop into the Whitechapel Art Gallery, and he was to be closely associated with his wife, Henrietta Barnett, in the building of Hampstead Garden Suburb.

KANGAROO STEAKS

It was reported that kangaroo meat was being sold in London eating houses from 16 September – it was part of a refrigerated consignment received recently from Australia. Tinned kangaroo meat had been sold in London seven years previously.

1882

LAW COURTS OPENED

The civil law courts were only just kept in their traditional Westminster home when the new Royal Courts of Justice were opened in the Strand on 4 December – they are the last building before the City of London boundary is met. Their design came about as a result of a typically botched competition. Most of the big architectural names entered – Scott, Barry, Waterhouse, Street, Brandon and Burges among them. The architect judges rated Barry first and Scott second, and the lawyer judges chose Scott first and Waterhouse second, with the result that the commission was offered to Street and Barry as joint architects – a fate which Barry soon escaped.

Street's designs were not particularly popular. People thought them too severe and ecclesiastical, and the newer breed of architects, eschewing Gothic Revival, had hardly a good word to say. Street is now identified with this building, although he was himself an early Arts and Crafts architect, with people like Philip Webb and Norman Shaw in his office.

Apart from the magnificent, but rather uninviting, great hall there are over 1,000 rooms and some 3½ miles of corridors.

EDUCATIONAL HAPPENINGS

The London School Board began evening schools this year. It was reported that there were 83 open (43 for men, 40 for women), and that 9,000 students had enrolled.

The National Library for the Blind, with 50 volumes in Braille, was founded this year in Fairfax Road, Hampstead. It moved to Tufton Street, Westminster, in 1916, and to Stockport in 1978.

Nearby, in Maresfield Gardens, Hampstead, Constance Maynard, who had been a scholar at Girton, founded Westfield College 'for the higher education of women on Christian principles'. The college acquired Kidderpore Hall near Finchley Road, Hampstead, former home of a wealthy East India merchant in 1890, and in 1902 it became part of the University of London. The college stayed there for a hundred years.

The City of London School opened new buildings on the Victoria Embankment on 12 December. The school had begun in 1837 in Milk Street.

Quintin Hogg, a noted philanthropist who had been active in many institutions that catered for the poor, needy and illiterate, on 24 September opened the Regent Street Polytechnic in premises already called the Polytechnic, which had previously contained 'a judicious, but unlucrative, mixture of instruction and amusement for the young'.

OFFBEAT THEATRES

Three theatres on the fringes of theatreland were opened this year. The Avenue Theatre, at the Embankment end of the newly formed Northumberland Avenue, was a short-lived affair as it was destroyed in 1905 (q.v.) – not by the usual fire, but by the collapse of part of Charing Cross station on to it. This theatre later became the Playhouse.

The Novelty Theatre in Great Queen Street, an interesting mix of classical and art-nouveau architecture, opened on 9 December. It was known under six other names before its final reincarnation as the Kingsway Theatre.

The Royal Strand Theatre, on the site of the later Aldwych Underground station, was rebuilt this year to the designs of C. J. Phipps. It presented mainly farces, but a musical play called *A Chinese Honeymoon* ran for over 1,000 performances – its most successful production.

More centrally, the Alhambra Theatre in Leicester Square (present site of the Odeon) was burnt down on 7 December.

At Her Majesty's Theatre, in the Haymarket, the first complete performance in England of Wagner's *Ring* cycle was given here this year.

THE JUMBO SAGA

The story of Jumbo, the elephant in London Zoo, aroused the ire and stirred the conscience of newspapers and public this year. Jumbo had been a star attraction in the zoo since 1865, but in 1882 a good offer for him was received from Barnum's Circus in the United States. The press recounted how Jumbo was to be separated from his lifelong mate for the economic benefit of the zoo, and when Jumbo repeatedly refused to be shipped out of his cage into a transporter the story assumed national proportions. The truth was more prosaic. Jumbo did not have a lifelong mate, but, more seriously, had in his old age become very temperamental and dangerous; the zoo authorities wanted to sell him to Barnum's because otherwise it was most likely that he would have to be put down. Eventually the elephant was persuaded to leave, and he ended his days in America.

SAVING BURIAL GROUNDS

What became the Metropolitan Public Gardens Association was founded this year, its main aim being to save the many burial grounds in London from building development and to convert them into small public gardens. The work of this association in the promotion of the Disused Burial Grounds Act of 1884, together with that of the Kyrle Society (see 1881), is evident in many gardens throughout London today. The Act prevented any further building on burial grounds.

THE GROWTH OF FOOTBALL CLUBS

Several Association Football clubs had been formed in recent years. Fulham FC was begun in 1879 by boys who attended the Sunday school at St Andrew's church in Greyhound Road; its first matches were as 'Fulham St Andrew's'. It was not until 1896 that the club acquired the derelict house called Craven Cottage. Leyton Orient was formed in 1881, and Tottenham Hotspur in 1882.

DEMOLITION AND BUILDING IN KENSINGTON

This year saw the end of a *folie de grandeur* called Kensington House in Kensington Road. It had been built by 'Baron' Albert Grant MP, who in 1874 had bought Leicester Square and presented it to the public. Grant's financial position was actually shaky, but this did not prevent the grand gesture. In the 1870s he commissioned James Knowles Jr to build him a Kensington mansion which required the demolition of the old Kensington House, Colby House and Jennings Rents, the displacement of 1,200 people, and the expenditure of about £300,000. In the event Grant went bankrupt and never lived in the sumptuous house, which was demolished in 1882, six years after completion.

Elsewhere in Kensington the remarkable Harrington Gardens was being laid out and built. This development, in Flemish-German style – a more ornate development of the 'Pont Street Dutch' houses of Norman Shaw – was by Ernest George and Harold Peto.

1800s

1883

BOMBINGS IN LONDON

On 15 March Fenians attempted to blow up government offices in Westminster. The Local Government Board's office in Charles Street was damaged, as also was that of *The Times*.

On 30 October a bomb planted by 'dynamiters' exploded on the Metropolitan Railway near Praed Street. Two third-class carriages were shattered and 62 people were injured.

POWER STATIONS BUILT

This year Edison built a small power station at 57 Holborn Viaduct, to supply the Old Bailey and the General Post Office.

The newly established Grosvenor Gallery in New Bond Street (see 1877) installed a generator to light its galleries by electricity. Very soon neighbours were asking to be connected to the supply, and the following year the gallery established a new company with a larger generator and went seriously into the supply of electricity. The Grosvenor Gallery Station, fully operational by 1885, supplied customers over a very large area by means of overhead cables radiating from a tower on the gallery rooftop; in 1886 the business employed the young Sebastian de Ferranti as chief engineer.

DISASTROUS FIRES

The collection of properties that made up Harrods was destroyed by fire in December. Mr Harrod wrote to his customers, 'I greatly regret to inform you that, in consequence of the above premises being burnt down, your order will be delayed in the execution a day or two.'

In Southall, a private lunatic asylum was burnt down. Six lives were lost, including that of the proprietor.

ROYAL COLLEGE OF MUSIC ESTABLISHED

The Royal College of Music was established this year to supersede the National Training School for Music in Kensington Gore. Its first director was George Grove, compiler of *The Dictionary of Music*. The college moved to its present address in Prince Consort Road in 1894.

WATER COLOURS IN PICCADILLY

On 27 April the Royal Society of Painters in Water Colours opened a new gallery in Piccadilly.

DR JAEGER'S CLOTHING

The 'Dr. Jaeger Woollen Sanitary Clothing' relied entirely on animal fibre and was for a time fashionable in London – the unlikely duo of Oscar Wilde and Bernard Shaw both advocated its use. A 'Jaeger' store was established this year in Fore Street, in the City, by an enthusiast, Lewis Tomalin, who found that it was a commercial success.

1884

COMPLETING THE CIRCLE

At last, on 6 October, the Metropolitan Railway extended its line from Tower Hill to Mansion House, so completing what became the Circle Line on the north bank of the Thames – a route which served most of the main-line stations but, of course, missed entirely the West End of London.

The new gallery of the Royal Society of Painters in Water Colours, Piccadilly.

TRAMS ON CABLES

The spread of tramways in London required fairly level terrain. In places like Highgate, where even the shortest journey involved a hill, the conventional tram was not an option. But a tramway system already existed in hilly San Francisco, and the inventor of that, Andrew Smith Hallidie, came back to this country to popularize his patent further. In 1881 the Steep Grade Tramway issued a prospectus to build a tramway from the Archway Tavern to Highgate village, using an endless cable sunk in the road. The trams were attached to the cable and were hauled up and down by the use of stationary engines. The first trams ran on 28 May this year, and a similar system was installed later on Brixton Hill.

FUNERAL OF A COSTERMONGER

Mary Robinson, self-styled 'Queen of the Costermongers', was buried at Finchley Cemetery on 14 January. She had amassed a fortune from lending money to other costermongers, but her normal activity was selling cats' meat. It was rumoured that when she died she had amassed £50,000. For the funeral, she had arranged that the coffin should be carried by four men wearing white smocks, followed by 24 women in violet dresses and white aprons and feathers.

LAVATORIES FOR LADIES

Attempts to persuade vestries to erect public lavatories for ladies had been strongly resisted, not because it wasn't recognized that ladies needed them but because it was thought somehow indiscreet of a lady to use a public facility of this kind. When in 1880 a Mr Alfred Watkyns of Paris proposed to the St Pancras vestry that his company erect a '*chalet de toilette et de necessité*' in Camden Town, complete with billboards and shoeblack outside, the local residents opposed the plan, saying that the chalet 'would have a tendency to diminish that innate sense of modesty so much admired in our countrywomen'. It was only in 1884 that the Ladies' Lavatory Company erected a convenience at Oxford Circus which appears to have been the first such in London.

A LINE THROUGH THE WORLD

An international conference this year agreed that the meridian of zero longitude should pass through Greenwich Observatory and that degrees of longitude should be calculated from it; a brass line, set into the ground, marks its place at the former Royal Observatory at Greenwich. Previously countries had used their own version of a zero meridian – some, for convenience, used that of Greenwich, where the principal astronomical research was carried on, but others used a point within their own country.

FABIANS FORMED

The socialist Fabian Society adopted its name at a meeting held at 17 Osnaburgh Street near Marylebone Road, the home of solicitor Edward Pease, on 4 January 1884. The name derived from the Roman general Fabius Cunctator, renowned for moving slowly but then with great decisiveness – a trait which appealed to the earnest and generally learned people who made up this gathering. The society was in effect a breakaway from a group, formed in 1883, called the Fellowship of the New Life, although some retained membership of both groups. Some members also belonged to the oddly named Hampstead Historic Society, also formed this year, to discuss left-wing politics. The young George Bernard Shaw joined the Fabians in May – looking, as another member remarked, like a fairly respectable plasterer, his cuffs trimmed with scissors, his black coat green with age, his boots shabby and cracked, and his tall hat worn back to front because the brim was broken.

MORE BOMBINGS IN LONDON

Fenians struck three more times in London. On 27 February a bomb exploded in Victoria station, injuring two people. On 30 May bombs were left at Scotland Yard and St James's Square, and on 13 December there was an attempt to blow up London Bridge.

WAXWORKS HAPPENINGS

Madame Tussaud's Waxworks moved this year from Baker Street to its present site on Marylebone Road. By this time, as Dickens had commented, it was more an institution than a sideshow, with topical updates of exhibits and the ever fascinating Chamber of Horrors. The new building contained a great white marble staircase which had been taken from the recently demolished Kensington House, home of Albert Grant (see 1882).

In Shoreditch, the East London Aquarium, which included a waxworks, burnt down on 4 June.

A NEW ST PAUL'S SCHOOL

Until its demolition in the late 1960s, the red-brick and terracotta pile of St Paul's School in Hammersmith was a notable landmark – more digestible from afar than close up, but still a striking building. Designed by Alfred Waterhouse, it was opened this year, the school having moved from its old site by St Paul's Churchyard.

In the same year Waterhouse completed his remarkable Congregational chapel at the corner of Lyndhurst Road and Rosslyn Hill, Hampstead, now converted into a recording studio.

NEW THEATRES

The Theatre Royal, Stratford East, was opened on 17 December with a play by Bulwer-Lytton about Richelieu; some of the audience had to be reproved from the stage for their behaviour. The building had been opened despite the opposition of the local vicar, who claimed that it 'would not tend to the moral elevation of the people of the neighbourhood'. Almost certainly he would not have liked the theatre, in its prime, under Joan Littlewood in the 1950s and '60s.

The Prince of Wales Theatre in Coventry Street was opened, with a comedy by W. S. Gilbert, as the Prince's Theatre on 18 January, together with a hotel and a restaurant; it was designed by C. J. Phipps. Generally speaking, farces and comedies of no great promise were staged here. The theatre was rebuilt in 1937.

A MAJOR CATHOLIC CHURCH

The Brompton Oratory, designed by Herbert Gribble, was completed this year. The Oratory of St Philip Neri was established in England in 1848 by the future Cardinal Newman and Frederick Faber. A temporary church, designed by J. J. Scoles, was established in Brompton in 1854, to be superseded by this, a building in the Italian style, unlike the Gothic which so dominated Anglican churches. The competition to build it was the usual fiasco: the chosen design was not that approved by the assessors – it was not even an entry, and the architect was an unknown. Until the construction of Westminster Cathedral in 1903 (q.v.), this building was the principal Roman Catholic church in London.

NEW ROADS

The Metropolitan Board of Works was in the process of building both Charing Cross Road and Shaftesbury Avenue. The architecture was to be mundane, not to say abysmal. Typical of a cheeseparing approach to these new highways was the construction of Sandringham Buildings in Charing Cross Road, erected this year on the board's behalf by the Improved Industrial Dwellings Company to rehouse those displaced by the schemes. The new blocks were to house 900 people, each tenement having no more than three rooms.

1885

RABIES IN THE CAPITAL

On 8 November the police ordered that all dogs within 6 miles of Charing Cross were to be muzzled and kept on a leash, owing to numerous cases of hydrophobia.

NEW GREENS TO THE PUBLIC

West End Green was this year acquired by Hampstead vestry for recreational use.

Highbury Fields, a larger space of 27 acres, was bought jointly by the MBW and Islington. On 20 October it was the scene of a march of the unemployed, who gathered outside the house of Joseph Chamberlain, president of the Board of Trade.

A UNITARIAN SCHOOL

The Misses Matilda and Emily Sharpe this year founded Channing School on Highgate Hill, a Unitarian school for girls, with the assistance of the prominent Unitarian the Revd Robert Spears. The boys of nearby Highgate School were always a threat in the minds of the two ladies, and only males under eight or over 80 were allowed at the girls' parties and functions; even male lecturers were chaperoned.

LONDON PAVILION OPENED

The London Pavilion, the façade of which survives in Piccadilly Circus, was opened as a music hall on 30 November. It was on the site of the old Black Horse coaching inn, which had a 'sing-song' saloon, later converted to a music hall in 1861.

A RIVAL TO BILLINGSGATE

The new market at Billingsgate was inadequate. Congestion resulted from delivery vehicles arriving from railways and departing to retailers, and on the river side the landing facilities were very poor indeed. Many boats could not moor beside the market; instead, cargo was carried across a rickety system of planks stretched across moored boats, and porters had to fetch and carry across it. A safer system was installed only in 1885, when a passing ship disturbed the arrangement and threw five porters into the river.

Meanwhile a rival scheme had been growing, the brainchild of the surveyor to the Limehouse Board of Works and of the principal fishing fleet operating from Barking. Their plan was for a new fish market downriver at Shadwell, where there was a rail link and three times the river frontage. The market, opened this year, was not a success: there was not enough trade to keep both markets economic, and many of the dealers were wary of disturbing trade traditions and arrangements by moving to Shadwell.

1886

ANARCHISTS IN LONDON

At a time when unemployment throughout the country was severe, socialists and anarchists were attracting greater support. This year the Club Autonomie was established at 32 Charlotte Street, from where it moved to Windmill Street in 1890. The International Anarchist Club at Stephen Mews (the Fitzrovia area was the centre of anarchist political activity) had been raided in 1885 as part of police investigations into bomb explosions at the House of Commons, the Tower and Westminster Hall. A hysterical mob followed the police and stripped the place bare. The club, which catered for European émigrés, particularly from Germany, was connected with the Socialist League, of which William Morris was a member.

Elsewhere in London the working class were at last questioning their lot and getting restless. On 8 February some 20,000 dockers and building workers marched to Trafalgar Square demanding work. Rioting and looting of West End shops took place.

OLYMPIA OPENED

A National Agricultural Hall had been opened two years previously in Hammersmith Road, but this year the name was changed to Olympia, and the building became a place for circuses and spectacles. It was not until the beginning of the 20th century that it was consistently used for exhibitions, though Bertram Mills's Circus continued to perform here until modern times.

HIGHGATE WOOD BOUGHT

Gravel Pit Wood, off the Archway Road, came on to the market in 1884. The site, so near Highgate station, was ready for development. A Hornsey vestryman led the cause to save the wood as open space: at that time the open spaces now associated with Highgate – Waterlow Park, Parliament Hill, Kenwood and Queen's Wood – were still private property. The Metropolitan Board of Works was debarred from purchasing it, and there was no suitable Middlesex authority in existence, and so the City of London was persuaded that, with the railway running down to the City, many of its citizens would find recreation in the wood. The Corporation formally took possession of Highgate Wood on 30 October 1886, and remains its custodian.

SOME NEW SISTERS

The group of seven elms on Page's Green, Tottenham, called the Seven Sisters and from which an area of London takes its name, had been decayed for some time. The trees were cut down this year and replaced by seven new trees, which were planted by the Misses Hibbert, the only known family of seven sisters in Tottenham.

NEW FOOTBALL CLUBS

Several of the famous football clubs of today were formed in this period. Woolwich Arsenal was established in 1886 south of the river; in 1885 Queen's Park Rangers and Millwall had been founded.

SHAFTESBURY AVENUE OPENED

Shaftesbury Avenue, connecting Piccadilly Circus to New Oxford Street, was officially opened in June. For reasons of economy it followed much the same route as the earlier smaller streets, and on the whole its architecture was undistinguished. Its fortunes were, however, to improve, as within the next 20 years six theatres were to be built in it.

A NEW BRIDGE AT PUTNEY

What was previously called the Fulham Bridge was replaced on 29 May by Putney Bridge, designed by Joseph Bazalgette. The new structure followed a different line from the old, with the result that the lower part of the Fulham High Street was bypassed and businesses, particularly the Eight Bells, were compensated for loss of trade. On the other hand the new line was better for Putney, for instead of the bridge ending directly in front of the parish church it was placed to the west of it.

A NEW STATUE OF QUEEN ANNE

The statue of Queen Anne which had been placed outside St Paul's Cathedral at its completion had been the butt of many remarks: it was by no means a great work of art, and much was made of the fact that the queen, renowned for her love of brandy, was facing towards a gin shop. Over the years the statue lost some of its parts from vandalism, and in 1884 it was removed altogether; what is left of it now stands in the gardens of a school in Holmhurst, Sussex. A bad copy took its place in 1886 – the one we see today. The surrounding figures represent her dominions, though the possessions indicated in North America and France had been lost by the time of this replica.

THE FIRST CRUFT'S DOG SHOW

The first exhibition organized by Charles Cruft took place at the Royal Aquarium, Westminster, this year: it was restricted to terriers only. Cruft had previously been an assistant to dog-food manufacturer James Spratt, whose dog-food logo many will remember. Cruft's Show was taken over by the Kennel Club after Cruft's death in 1938.

1887

A PEOPLE'S PALACE IN THE EAST END

A building more luxurious than the East End of London was used to was opened on 14 May in the Mile End Road. It had its origins in the Beaumont Trust, established by the 1841 will of John Barber Beaumont, a Unitarian; the Beaumont Philosophical Institution in Beaumont Square, Mile End, at one time existed 'for the mental and

The People's Palace in Mile End Road in 1887.

moral improvement of the inhabitants of the said Square, and the surrounding neighbourhood'. By the 1880s the trust had still not produced any scheme which would have satisfied the benefactor, the institution had closed its doors, and considerable income had accrued. One of the people who helped to devise the idea of a People's Palace was the London historian and writer Walter Besant. A novel of his, dealing with conditions to be found in the East End, included the building of a 'Palace of Delights'.

The plan for a People's Palace was launched at the Mansion House in 1884, when Thomas Huxley addressed the fund-raising gathering. The first part of the scheme, the Queen's Hall, was opened by Queen Victoria, who laid the foundation stone of the technical school at the same time. The hall, designed by Edward Robson, was palatial; it measured 130 ft by 75 ft, and was 60 ft high, with a stained-glass roof supported by buff and gold columns and a gallery supported by caryatids.

The enthusiasm for the palace did not last, however. The buildings remained largely unfinished, and the hall itself was burnt down in 1931. The technical college became part of Queen Mary College, which in turn became a college of the University of London.

BLOODY SUNDAY

In a year in which the London population celebrated the golden jubilee of Queen Victoria's reign with good humour, two died and at least 100 were injured on what became known as 'Bloody Sunday' on 13 November. The occasion was a large procession of left-wing and Irish demonstrators, mainly from south of the river, who marched to Westminster despite a prohibition on the event. Ostensibly the demonstration was to protest against the imprisonment of an Irish leader, William O'Brien MP, but it represented also the explosive exasperation of the underprivileged, unemployed and disaffected. Battles raged in front of Westminster Hall, across the nearby bridge and up Whitehall. The Life Guards were eventually brought in to dispel the rioters.

ENTERTAINMENT AT EARLS COURT

Amid the railway lines that crossed the Earls Court area an entertainment park was opened on 9 May by one J. R. Whitley. It opened with a Wild West show, featuring Buffalo Bill and Annie Oakley, but soon

there were permanent fairground features, such as the famous Big Wheel (see 1894). The ground was closed when the First World War began, and was replaced in the 1930s by an exhibition hall.

TWO DISASTERS

Yet another fire, on 6 August, consumed Whiteley's store in Queensway. This was the fifth and worst of a series of blazes thought by many to be caused by arson. This time the fire burnt for several days and four people died.

On 18 January, in a panic caused by a fire alarm, 17 people were trampled to death at the Hebrew Dramatic Club in Spitalfields.

NEW CLUB ROOMS

The cavernous and echoing National Liberal Club in Whitehall Place was completed this year. Alfred Waterhouse, the architect, made extensive use of tiles in the building – a feature which prompted a remark by Lord Birkenhead, who, though not a member, used the club for its lavatory: he affected to be surprised to learn that the building housed a club as well.

The Queen's Club, laid out on a former cricket ground, was opened this year in Palliser Road, near Hammersmith. The aim was to cater for athletics and tennis, and by 1900 there were over 30 grass tennis courts, surrounded by a running track, with indoor facilities for rackets, cricket and skating.

The Bloody Sunday march on Trafalgar Square in 1887 left two dead.

NEIGHBOURHOOD PARKS

Ravenscourt Park, Hammersmith, was opened on 20 November. The 32 acres and the mansion house, sadly destroyed in the last war, had been sold to the Metropolitan Board of Works by the Scott family.

Kilburn Park, another piece of land acquired by the City of London, was opened on 5 November.

CHARING CROSS ROAD OPENED

The formal opening of Charing Cross Road took place in February, the duke of Cambridge (after whom Cambridge Circus is named) performing the ceremony. The road was essentially a widening and adaptation of existing streets, and, like that of Shaftesbury Avenue (see 1886), its architecture was of a poor standard and has hardly improved since.

1888

TERROR IN THE EAST END

The efforts of social reformers to give the East End new heart and respectability were lastingly damaged this year by the Jack the Ripper murders. This appalling series of crimes began, it is thought, with the murder of prostitute Mary Nicholls, who was found with her throat cut in Durward Street on 31 August. A week later Annie Chapman was found disembowelled off Hanbury Street; then on the night of 30 September two women were found mutilated. The fifth and last victim was Mary Kelly, another prostitute. No one was ever convicted of these murders.

NEW THEATRES

The first theatre opened in Shaftesbury Avenue, on 20 October this year, was the Shaftesbury itself, but it was not the building using that name today at the northern end of the road. The original Shaftesbury stood on the south-east side of the road, between Gerrard Place and Little Newport Street, next to the fire station. It was destroyed in the last war.

Two Lyric theatres opened this year: one in Shaftesbury Avenue and the other in Hammersmith, though strictly speaking the latter was merely the Lyric Hall at this stage and was reconstructed as an opera house in 1890. The West End Lyric, which still survives, opened on 17 December; it was designed by the ubiquitous C. J. Phipps.

In Sloane Square a new building was opened on 24 September for the Royal Court Theatre, which had previously occupied a nearby chapel. Early in the 20th century the management specialized successfully in Shaw plays.

The Grand Theatre, Islington, arose at 40 Islington High Street on the ashes of the Philharmonic Theatre, burnt down on 29 December 1887. Frank Matcham was the architect of the new building, as he had been of the earlier one. Almost certainly Matcham achieved some sort of record when he was also the architect for this new theatre's successor in 1900, after yet another devastating fire.

THE MATCHGIRLS' STRIKE

One of the most celebrated and publicized strikes in Victorian times was that of the women who worked at the Bow match factory of Bryant & May. The strike aroused strong emotions and accusations, but it was unique in being a strike by women, and it was led by the self-publicist Annie Besant, with strong support from the Fabian Society. According to the contemporary *Annual Register*, the women were paid piecework; when this year they were asked to change the manufacturing process used, a girl refused since it would reduce the number of matches she could manufacture. She was dismissed, and in a gesture of solidarity 1,200 other women walked out. This was on 5 July.

But in fact the factory had been the focus of controversy earlier that year. The Fabian Society had made it the subject of one of its publications – *White Slavery in London* – which detailed conditions there and told shareholders in the company that, while they were receiving dividends of 20 per cent, the women workers were paid just 4s a week. This is denied in a modern history of the company, which says that the women were unreliable attenders at the factory but if they worked there full-time their potential wage was 11s 2d (56p). There were also allegations that the use of phosphorus induced cancer in the employees. It was known that the employers imposed fines for small things such as talking, going to the lavatory at unauthorized times, and dropping matches. A radical magazine called the *Link* then took up the fight. It was soon after this that the strike began.

The Times complained that the match girls had been egged on by 'Social Democrats' (the radicals, and especially Annie Besant). The strike ended after two weeks with the women receiving concessions. The system of fines which the management had imposed was abolished, no striker was penalized, and the women's trade union was recognized. The London Trades Council later issued a report to say that many of the charges levelled against the company were unfounded, and other journalists recorded that conditions in the factory were satisfactory.

A JOURNEY TO BRIGHTON

A stage coach called *Old Times* travelled to Brighton and back on 13 July in 7 hours 50 minutes, for a wager that the journey could not be done in less than eight hours. Horses were changed 16 times.

GRIEG IN LONDON

The composer Edvard Grieg paid his first visit to London this year, staying with a friend in Clapham. He conducted a work of his own on 3 May: 'When I showed myself at the orchestra doorway, the whole of the vast St James's Hall, completely full, broke into an uproar, so intense and so continuous (I think for over three minutes) that I didn't know what to do … ' The young Delius was in the audience.

1889

NEW GOVERNORS OF LONDON

The Metropolitan Board of Works had done great works in London, but throughout its brief existence both vestries and the press had accused it of profligacy and corruption. The board's principal drawbacks were a lack of powers and the fact that it was a clique and not a directly elected authority – generally its members were selected by the vestries.

Following the Local Government Act of 1888 London's government was reorganized again, but in a botched way characteristic of central government's attitude towards it. Firstly, London was established for the first time as a county – this entailed the absorption of areas from the surrounding historic counties of Middlesex, Kent, Essex and Surrey, which in turn were formed as county councils. But the City still remained an anomaly – while the London County Council had overall jurisdiction for the area, the City managed to retain many of its privileges and much of its autonomy. In practice, little was changed.

Few powers not already held by the MBW were added to those of the new LCC. The Act did not affect the status of the London School Board, the Metropolitan Asylums Board (which had overall charge of hospital provision), the Thames and Lea Conservancy Boards, the Poor Law guardians, and various boards administering burial grounds, libraries and baths. The numerous vestries and district boards were left largely untouched, thereby perpetuating the ineffectiveness of government at local level.

The new LCC consisted of two councillors elected for three years from each of the 60 parliamentary divisions in the new county, together with four elected by the City voters. In addition there were 20 aldermen elected for six-year terms by the councillors.

The creation of the LCC ushered in the era of party politics at local level. Candidates flaunting party labels such as 'Progressives' and 'Moderates' contended, and the result of the first election, on 17 January 1889, was a decisive victory for the Progressives – a mixture of Liberals, Socialists and Radicals. The Moderates were, in effect, the Conservative Party. The early LCC attracted 2 dukes and 38 other members of the peerage to its membership, together with several cabinet ministers. The council met for the first time on 21 March.

The net result was to impose on a largely unmodernized and inadequate local structure a county administration more suited to the shires.

THE GREAT DOCK STRIKE

The most notable dock strike of Victorian times occurred this year. Henry Mayhew had already spelt out the working conditions of the East End dockers to those who would care to read. The 'casual' system, whereby dockers were employed on a job-by-job basis, ensured that wages could be kept down, that competition between men would be fierce, and that there would be little dignity in the employment process. A docker worked long hours and for scandalously low rates of pay for on average five or six months a year. The 'call-on' process in which an employer chose his labour for the day was particularly degrading: the men were herded into a shed, and the foreman walked up and down as if at a cattle market. As Ben Tillett, leader of the strike, was to record:

The last remnants of strength [were] exerted in an effort to get work for an hour, a half hour, for a few pence. Such strugglings, shoutings, cursings, with a grinning brute selecting the chosen of the poor wretches ... [who were] men ravening for food [and who] fought like madmen for the ticket, a veritable talisman of life. As a brute would throw scraps to hungry wolves to delight in the exhibition of the savage struggle for existence, with beasts tearing each other to pieces, so these creatures would delight in the spectacle, which, while it imbruted the victims of such a tragedy, impeached and cursed society.

It was in the context of the successful strike of the Bryant & May matchgirls (see 1888) and another strike earlier in 1889 by gas workers that the dock strike started in mid-August. Ostensibly the dispute began over the offloading of one ship's cargo, but it was really the culmination of years of discontent. The strikers' leaders, who included Tillett and John Burns, demanded that in future no man should be taken on for less than four hours, or be paid less than 6d per hour, and that contract and piecework be abolished.

The strike was long-lasting, and there were many processions and meetings – notably a march of about 50,000 people through the City. In the end the arbitration of a committee of the great and good, including Cardinal Manning, helped to bring the strike to a close in September, with some concessions.

THE SAVOY HOTEL OPENS

The original part of today's Savoy Hotel, designed by T. E. Collcutt, was opened on 6 August – a development by Richard D'Oyly Carte alongside his flourishing Savoy Theatre. César Ritz was the first manager, and Auguste Escoffier the first chef. Other features were 80 private bathrooms, electricity throughout, and the facility for the guest to turn off the light after he or she was in bed.

MALE BROTHEL IN FITZROVIA

After a police raid in July, the country was scandalized by the revelation of a homosexual brothel operating in Cleveland Street. To add spice to the affair, a mixture of Post Office messenger boys and supposedly respectable members of the public were involved – the editor of the *North London Press* was jailed for implying that the moronic duke of Clarence was a customer, though good evidence of this was revealed later.

MORLEY COLLEGE OPENS

Morley College was born at the back of the Old Vic theatre. It was the work of the indefatigable Emma Cons, who owned the theatre, and it began with classes for impecunious local people. The college, which was formally established on 29 September, was named after Samuel Morley MP, textile manufacturer and benefactor of the Old Vic. The classes continued in the theatre building until 1924.

A NEW PARK IN HACKNEY

Clissold Park, Hackney, was opened on 24 July. The area consisted of the grounds of a large mansion occupied at one time by a member of the Hoare banking family and more lately by a Mr Crayshaw, who detested parsons. Unfortunately for him his daughter fell in love with the Revd Augustus Clissold, and thereafter much of the father's life was spent trying to sabotage the romance. On his death the couple married and the house was renamed Clissold Park.

THE WOOLWICH FERRY APPEARS

The Woolwich Free Ferry, a creation of the old MBW, began operation on 23 March. Three boats were bought, and compensation for loss of employment was paid to those watermen who still operated in the area. The ferry's old paddle steamers, beloved of children, were phased out in 1963.

WHITE HART INN GOES

The White Hart inn in Borough High Street was demolished in July. This splendid building, with a double set of galleries around a courtyard, was here by 1406 (the White Hart was the badge of Richard II).

A NEW END TO THE DISTRICT LINE

The District Line reached another of its several termini on 3 June, when the extension across the river from Putney Bridge was completed down to Wimbledon.

BUILDING WORK IN THE CHARING CROSS ROAD

Development in the new Charing Cross Road included new vestry offices for St Martin-in-the-Fields, and the erection of the Garrick Theatre. The latter was opened on 24 April with a Pinero play called *The Profligate*, which dared to suggest that women might reasonably expect their husbands to be as faithful as they themselves were obliged to be. The theatre, founded by the librettist W. S. Gilbert, was designed by Walter Emden.

1890

THE FIRST TUBE

Those sections of the Metropolitan and District lines which were in tunnels had been constructed by the cut-and-cover method. Roads were closed or severely restricted while the tunnel was excavated and lined, and then the road surface replaced. This brought severe disruption and inconvenience, and it was also expensive. The invention by James Greathead of a tunnelling machine to build the Tower Subway (see 1870) indicated that underground railways could be constructed more cheaply by tunnelling. Even before the Tower Subway was completed, Peter Barlow, its promoter, and Greathead had proposed a bill to build tunnels from Borough High Street to King William Street in the City, intended for omnibus traffic. In 1884 Greathead and others floated a company which proposed a cable-train system from King William Street to the Elephant and Castle, and work began in 1886. By this time electric traction had developed, and the tunnel was extended to Stockwell and built for electric trains. In 1890 the company changed its name to the City & South London Railway, and on 18 December this year a service between Stockwell and King William Street was initiated with a standard 2d fare. The London tube had arrived.

The King William Street station was very restricted and was closed in 1900; the line then went straight from London Bridge to the Bank. This first underground railway was later incorporated into the Northern Line.

POLICE IN THE NEWS

The location 'Scotland Yard' has followed the Metropolitan Police about. When the force was established in 1829, some premises were taken at Old Scotland Yard, and when in 1889 it moved to large buildings designed by Norman Shaw, near the Houses of Parliament, these were christened New Scotland Yard. Now that the police have moved to Broadway, the name New Scotland Yard has gone with them, and their old headquarters have been been renamed Norman Shaw Buildings.

In 1889 a police strike was threatened. There was discontent in the junior ranks over pay and pensions, and when in June a sergeant and constable in Borough were suspended for disobeying an order, colleagues refused to go on duty unless they were reinstated. Soon police were demonstrating outside Bow Street police station. An uneasy truce was arranged while Parliament hurriedly rushed through legislation to improve pensions, but dissidence still existed. This was crushed when the commissioner dismissed all those who still dared to voice discontent.

CYCLING TO BRIGHTON

A cyclist, F. W. Shortland, set out on 25 June at 7 a.m. on a 'geared' Facile bicycle from Piccadilly Circus. He reached Brighton at 10.40 a.m., rested for ten minutes, and was back in London at 2.19 p.m. – a total of 7 hours 19 minutes.

TRAGEDY AT FOREST GATE

A fire which broke out on New Year's Day at the Forest Gate Industrial School cost the lives of 26 children. They were buried in a mass ceremony on 6 January at West Ham Cemetery.

A HOSPITAL FOR WOMEN

The New Hospital for Women (founded as a dispensary in St Marylebone in 1866) transferred this year to a new building in Euston Road, designed by J. M. Brydon. The hospital had been founded by Elizabeth Garrett Anderson, one of the first women in England to qualify in medicine. Its unique feature was that it was staffed entirely by women, and its patients, either alarmed at the prejudices of male medical practice or simply embarrassed to be in its care, therefore felt more at ease. The hospital was later renamed after its founder.

HORNIMAN MUSEUM OPENS

The tea merchant Frederick Horniman amassed a large collection of curios on his world travels, and from 24 December these were displayed to the public in his own house in Forest Hill; Horniman also paid for the services of a curator, naturalist and librarian. In 1901, at a cost of nearly £40,000, he completed nearby what is now the Horniman Museum; it is splendidly designed in the art-nouveau style by C. Harrison Townsend.

A SOCIAL CENTRE IN GORDON SQUARE

Mary Ward, successful in writing novels under the name of Mrs Humphry Ward, this year established a social centre at University Hall, Gordon Square, in which people of different social status could mix, and in which simplified Christianity could be disseminated. The project attracted the attention of the wealthy philanthropist John Passmore Edwards, who provided a new building in Tavistock Place. The Mary Ward Centre is today in Queen Square, but the handsome building in Tavistock Place survives as part of the local social services department.

THE DEMISE OF PINDAR'S HOUSE

A spectacular merchant's house built by Sir Paul Pindar c. 1600 was demolished this year to make way for the extension of the Great Eastern Railway to Liverpool Street. It was a sad loss, but at least its value was realized at the time, because the carved-oak façade – or what was left of it – was moved to what became the Victoria & Albert Museum, where it may be seen today by the bookshop.

ROSEBERY AVENUE

Rosebery Avenue was one of the first new roads constructed by the new London County Council, of which Lord Rosebery was chairman. In its southern stretch, from Clerkenwell Road to Farringdon Road, it followed the dismal example of Charing Cross Road and Shaftesbury Avenue in having the barrack-like architecture of many 'artisans' dwellings'. Lord Rosebery officially opened the first part of the road on 21 July this year; he also headed the ceremony when the final stretch was opened in 1892.

1891

THE ORIGINS OF THE TATE

On 19 March the sugar magnate Sir Henry Tate offered to donate £80,000 towards the construction of a new national gallery of modern art, to be built in South Kensington. It was eventually built on Millbank (see 1897).

NEW BUSINESSES

James Fenwick, a successful dressmaker in Newcastle, this year opened a store in New Bond Street. Fenwick's 1907 catalogue, which claimed that all the goods were 'marked in plain figures at modern prices', had nightdresses for sale from 4s 11d.

William Morris began his famous Kelmscott Press in Upper Mall, Hammersmith, this year. It is doubtful if the enterprise ever made any money, since Morris was inclined to give the beautifully crafted limited editions away to friends.

Stanley Gibbons, the stamp dealer's, this year moved from Plymouth, where the business was founded in 1856, and set up its London company.

The Birmingham & Midland Bank, founded in Birmingham in 1836, was established in London this year when it acquired the Central Bank of London and a bank called Lacy, Hartland & Woodbridge. The purchase of the Central gave the Midland membership of the Bankers' Clearing House. After this the company was called the London and Midland Bank, which was eventually shortened to just the Midland. It is now the HSBC.

No Buses
Three thousand bus drivers and conductors working for the principal bus company, the London General Omnibus Company, went on strike during May. They settled for a 12-hour day.

Chelsea Arts Club Opened
The first Chelsea Arts Club originated in rooms at 181 King's Road rented from James Christie, the auctioneer; founder members included Whistler, Clausen, Steer, Sickert and Brangwyn. The club moved to its present premises in Old Church Street in 1902.

Rearrangement of the Charities
There were numerous charities in the City, some of them too small to be economic, others fallen into disuse but still gathering income. The City of London Parochial Charities Act 1883 consolidated the majority of these into larger units. A few parishes, such as St Botolph without Bishopsgate and St Giles without Cripplegate, were exempted and allowed to consolidate their own charities under the aegis of the City Parochial Foundation, set up in 1891. Out of this event grew the three institutes which still exist in the City – Bishopsgate, St Bride's and Cripplegate.

More Parks for the People
The Victorians tenaciously carved out parks from the growing London brick-field. An example of a park obtained by the generosity of an individual is Waterlow Park in Highgate, the unexpected gift in 1889 of Sir Sydney Waterlow, a former lord mayor. The grounds were his own personal estate, and included the 17th-century Lauderdale House. The park was formally opened by the LCC on 17 October.

Dulwich Park was the corporate gift of Dulwich College. Consisting of 72 acres, it had become public property on 26 June 1890.

In 1890 too, Vauxhall Park, on the site and grounds of a house called The Lawns, the home of Sir Henry Fawcett, was opened by Lambeth vestry on 7 July.

A small park also encloses Bruce Castle, in Tottenham, an Elizabethan manor house thought to be on the site of a castle owned by Robert the Bruce's father. In 1891 the house and grounds were acquired by the local authority, and the house now houses a museum and local-history collection.

Palace Theatre Opened
The Palace Theatre in Cambridge Circus was opened on 31 January as the Royal English Opera House, under the management of Richard D'Oyly Carte. Since restoration about ten years ago – finished in time for its 100th birthday – it is possible to appreciate even more the design of this building by T. E. Collcutt and G. H. Holloway. Unfortunately Carte's hope for a national opera house here failed, and by 1892 the building had became a music hall.

1892

Theatrical Landmarks
The first Oscar Wilde play performed in London, *Lady Windermere's Fan*, was presented at the St James's Theatre in King Street on 20 February. It was a brilliant and packed occasion, for word and anecdotes of it had gone before. Lily Langtry, Frank Harris, Henry James and Richard Le Gallienne were among the first-night audience and, except for James, contributed to the immense praise the play received. Wilde, sporting a green carnation and mauve gloves and holding a cigarette, gave a self-satisfied curtain speech which infuriated those unable to digest his mannerisms. The producer had offered Wilde £1,000 outright for the play, but the author had shrewdly opted for commission, and had made £7,000 on it within the year.

Later that year, on 9 December, the young George Bernard Shaw's first play, *Widowers' Houses*, was produced at the Royalty Theatre in Dean Street. There was little acclaim and much criticism – in fact, 'the fall of the curtain was attended with some disorder'. Shaw's next play, *The Philanderer*, in 1893, fared even worse.

The failure of Shaw's play was bad news for the management of the Royalty, which had not had a commercial success for some time and was now faced with additional competition from the newly opened Shaftesbury Theatre. But on 21 December, once Shaw's play had been unceremoniously abandoned, there was the first night here of a farce which was to become part of English theatrical tradition. Called *Charley's Aunt*, it played here for a month before transferring to the Globe (now Gielgud), where the auditorium was larger.

The first theatre to be built in St Martin's Lane was the Trafalgar Square Theatre (now the Duke of York's), which was opened on 10 September. The building was designed by Walter Emden.

Hostels for Men
A large number of single and homeless men were obliged to sleep rough or in scandalously overcrowded and unsafe lodging houses. These were not men who were alcoholics, drug addicts or social misfits, but for the most part artisans and casual workers who just needed somewhere to stay.

Their cause was taken up by the unlikely Lord Rowton, a wealthy establishment Tory and former secretary to Disraeli. His interest had begun in 1889, when he had been invited to become a trustee of the Guinness Trust Fund, set up by Lord Iveagh with £250,000, of which £200,000 was to be spent in London. Rowton formed the idea of building hostels for men which would have the feel of a club, containing lodging, catering and social contact, and he was prepared to sink £30,000 of his own money to support this innovation. The first Rowton House, accommodating 447 men, was opened in Bond Street, Vauxhall, on 31 December this year. Throughout its development Rowton had involved himself with the design in every particular. It was at his insistence that, unusually, each man had a cubicle to himself instead of being placed in dormitories; Rowton, in this way, sought to introduce some dignity and privacy into the life of a homeless man.

DISASTER AT HAMPSTEAD HEATH

Hampstead Heath Fair at holiday times attracted vast crowds from the poorer parts of London, a convenient ride away on the North London Railway. On Easter Monday this year there was a substantial downpour of rain and sleet during the afternoon, sending thousands running for Hampstead Heath station. As they pressed into the building, a bottleneck developed on the narrow stairway down to the platforms; many were trapped, struggling and screaming, and by the time the crowd could be dispersed two women and six young boys had been trampled to death.

1893

LIBRARY PROGRESS

London's local library service got off to a slow start. Vestries held regular referendums on library provision, and those people who were entitled to vote usually declined the opportunity to provide public libraries at the expense of the ratepayers. This was due partly to meanness, and partly to a reluctance to allow the lower classes facilities to better themselves. It was not until the philanthropic intervention of men like Sir Henry Tate and John Passmore Edwards, and later of Andrew Carnegie, that a momentum of library openings built up. This year public libraries were opened in Brixton, Great Smith Street and Shoreditch, while in Hampstead a poll of ratepayers decided to implement a programme of library provision.

DESTRUCTION IN BROMLEY

The destruction of what was called the Old Palace at Bromley-by-Bow became a cause célèbre among the growing band of conservationists. Behind the 18th-century front was a Jacobean building which was pulled down by the London School Board in order to build a new school. But the loss was not in vain. In the hope of preventing further losses through ignorance of what existed, the *Survey of London* publishing project was formed a few years later – volumes on different parts of London have been published ever since.

BUILDING WORK IN SOHO

Only a week separates the opening of the two churches in Soho Square. On 17 March, the Italianate St Patrick's Roman Catholic church, designed by John Kelly, was consecrated, just over 100 years after the first chapel was established there. The French Protestant church, a Flemish-Gothic building designed by Sir Aston Webb, was dedicated on 25 March. It can claim descent from the earliest congregation of Protestant refugees in London.

Just around the corner the food suppliers Crosse & Blackwell erected this year a large warehouse designed by Roumieu & Aitchison, which was later converted to the Astoria Cinema.

FIRST CONCERT AT THE QUEEN'S HALL

A building with a classical exterior and a Victorian interior in Langham Place became the principal concert hall in London. After a children's party in the afternoon, the first concert was given on 2 December, the principal works being by Mendelssohn, and the featured organist being the young Henry Wood. The Queen's Hall became eventually the home of the 'Proms', under the direction of Wood, until destruction in the last war. The site is now covered by the St George's Hotel.

EROS UNVEILED

The statue of Eros in Piccadilly Circus began as a monument to the philanthropist and social reformer the 7th earl of Shaftesbury. The young Alfred Gilbert was passed the commission, and he chose Eros – in Greek mythology the god of dispassionate as well as passionate love – to symbolize Shaftesbury's life.

The figure is made of aluminium – the first time this metal had been used in a large sculpture. The fountain is much reduced from the sculptor's original plan, because Gilbert later found himself paying for much of the work and materials after having neglected to obtain for himself a firm contract – the cost was to drive him into bankruptcy. The statue was unveiled on 29 June this year, mostly to acclaim, but to some criticism of the nudity of the figure.

THE IMPERIAL INSTITUTE

The Imperial Institute, founded after the Imperial Exhibition of 1886, was opened this year. This extravagant late-Victorian building was the work of T. E. Collcutt, whose Palace Theatre (see 1891) is the best example of his work today, since only the tower of the Institute survives now as part of Imperial College; the rest of this splendid building was destroyed by the University of London.

1894

TOWER BRIDGE OPENED

Tower Bridge, one of the modern symbols of London, was opened on 30 January by the prince of Wales. It was designed by the City architect, Sir Horace Jones, together with the engineer John Wolfe Barry, though Jones died within a year of the start of building. Barry remarked later that many people wanted the bridge to reflect the style of the Tower of London, and that Jones had originally designed towers in feudal style. The bridge took eight years to build, mainly because at least 160 ft of the navigable river had to be available during any stage of the construction.

THE FIRST LYONS' TEASHOP

Lyons' Teashops weren't the first in London – the Aerated Bread Company (ABC) whose main bakery was at Camden Town had begun them in 1880 – but it was the Lyons company which made them famous. The first of their teashops was permitted to open on 20 September this year at 213 Piccadilly, on condition that it should be run on the same lines as the ABC tearooms along the road. J. Lyons & Co. was established by the Salmon and Gluckstein families, who already ran a chain of tobacconists.

DIGGING FOR BOUDICCA

The tumulus near Parliament Hill has always excited interest. It is most probably a burial mound, but for whom? Popular legend said that Queen Boudicca was buried there, and it was with much interest that a professional excavation of the barrow took place this year. Hardly anything at all was found, except evidence that someone had already excavated it. But the conclusion was that it was probably the burial place of someone comparatively unimportant.

A BIG WHEEL AT EARLS COURT

The Big Wheel at Earls Court was erected this year. Based on the Ferris Wheel displayed at the Chicago Exhibition the year before, it

The eagerly awaited excavation of the tumulus on Parliament Hill was disappointing. No evidence of any burial was found.

was an impressive structure – larger than any other in the world, but not as high as the wheel built in London in 1999. It could contain 1,600 people at any one time, in 40 cars, took 20 minutes to revolve completely, and weighed 1,100 tons.

TWO INSTITUTES IN THE CITY
The Bishopsgate and the St Bride's Foundation Institutes were both opened this year, products of the consolidation of numerous City charities (see 1891).

The Bishopsgate Institute, opposite today's Broadgate development, was opened on 24 November. The building, designed by C. Harrison Townsend, architect of the Horniman Museum, had been constructed to include a large hall with seating accommodation for 500, lending and reference libraries, and, on the first floor, a reading room with newspaper stands and tables, with separate arrangements for men and women. The lending library was immensely popular, as none existed in the City or the surrounding areas: a man convicted in 1897 for stealing books from it was sentenced to three years' penal servitude.

The St Bride's Institute, in Bride Lane, near to the publishing world of Fleet Street, specialized in printing. Technical classes were given (later to be part of the London School of Printing), and a library devoted to the history of printing was developed, based largely on the collection of William Blades. The building was designed by R. C. Murray.

MR BOURNE AND MR HOLLINGSWORTH
The department store Bourne & Hollingsworth began, inevitably, as a draper's shop. Mr Bourne and Mr Hollingsworth, brothers-in-law, opened a drapery store in Westbourne Grove, but due to the competition, from Whiteley's in particular, they moved to the less fashionable eastern end of Oxford Street in 1902.

A CONSERVATOIRE IN HAMPSTEAD
The Hampstead Conservatoire of Music was founded this year, with Cecil Sharp, the folk-dance and music pioneer, as its principal. The Central School of Speech and Drama at Swiss Cottage now occupies its site.

1895

FIRST NIGHTS
The very first night of the Promenade Concerts was 10 August this year, when the 26-year-old Henry Wood conducted a programme of music at the Queen's Hall, Langham Place. The Proms remained here until the hall was destroyed in the last war and were then transferred to the Royal Albert Hall.

The most dramatic opening night was that of Wilde's *The Importance of Being Earnest*. The play opened on Valentine's Day at the St James's Theatre to a rapturous reception. Even the *New York Times* noted that 'Oscar Wilde may be said to have at last, and by a single stroke, put his enemies under his feet.' Its critic was either unaware of or ignored the enemy about to bring about Wilde's downfall. The marquess of Queensberry, father of Lord Alfred Douglas, Wilde's lover, had intended to mount a demonstration on the first night, publicizing Wilde's homosexuality. Queensberry was barred entrance, but four days later he left at Wilde's club a visiting card which merely contained the words 'To Oscar Wilde posing Somdomite [*sic*]'. The fateful events began from that moment. Wilde was persuaded to sue Queensberry for libel, and, having lost his case, was in turn tried and found guilty of homosexual acts, and sentenced to two years' hard labour. He died in exile in France five years later, still in disgrace and his supporters in disarray.

A CLOCK TOWER IN CROUCH END
A landmark in Crouch End Broadway is the red-brick and stone clock tower. This structure, built entirely from public subscription, was a monument to a local politician, Henry Reader Williams, who had been instrumental in the preservation of both Highgate Wood and Queen's Wood. The opening was on 22 June, on a very hot day, so that, according to the *Hornsey Journal*, 'Mr H. R. Williams was bathed in glory and the spectators in perspiration'.

NEW EDUCATIONAL CENTRES
The London School of Economics and Political Science was founded by the Fabian writer Sidney Webb, using a bequest of £10,000 from an eccentric Derby solicitor. The first prospectus of the school this year announced, 'While much attention will be given to the study of economic and political theory, the special aim of the School will be, from the first, the study and investigation of the concrete facts of industrial life and the actual working of economic and political institutions as they exist or have existed.' The school's first home in October this year was at 9 John Street, Adelphi; in 1902, by then a college of the University of London, it was large enough to warrant its own building in the old Clare Market area near the Aldwych.

The South Western Polytechnic in Manresa Road, Chelsea, was partly opened this year, in a building designed by J. M. Brydon. Here politics were prohibited. Its main strength was that it contained what became the Chelsea School of Art.

REMEMBERING CARLYLE
The writer and historian Thomas Carlyle lived at what is now 24 Cheyne Row, Chelsea, from 1834 until his death in 1881. In 1895 the house was acquired for the nation and turned into a Carlyle shrine – the desk on which he wrote *The French Revolution* is housed here. The house itself is very early 18th-century; Carlyle himself described it as 'a right old strong, roomy brick house, likely to see three races of

their modern fashionable fall before it comes down'. It was becoming too noisy for him even by 1881.

A NEW HOMEOPATHIC HOSPITAL

The London Homeopathic Hospital in Great Ormond Street was opened in July this year; it had been founded in 1850 by Frederick Quin, the first professional homeopathic doctor. The new building was designed by W. E. Pite.

FORMATION OF THE NATIONAL TRUST

The National Trust was formed this year in London, at a time when a flourish of rebuilding threatened old and distinguished buildings, and when shrewd landholders were enclosing footpaths and commons with a view to development. A leading campaigner against demolition and enclosure was Octavia Hill, eighth daughter of a corn merchant and banker, himself an enthusiastic social reformer. Her maternal grandfather was the celebrated sanitary reformer Dr Southwood Smith, and it was from him that the young Octavia absorbed her mission to improve the lot of other people. She ran housing schemes, and worked enthusiastically for the Charity Organization Society, the Kyrle Society (which her sister had founded) and the Commons Preservation Society. It was the work of the last named that led her, together with the solicitor Sir Robert Hunter and Canon H. D. Rawnsley, to found the National Trust for Places of Historic Interest or Natural Beauty.

A POLITICAL TIE

The elections for the London County Council this year resulted in 59 Progressives and 59 Moderates being elected. Since they had first been swept into power in 1889, the Progressives had steadily lost ground. But the zeal and 'revolutionary' ideas of the Progressives alarmed the national Conservative Party to such an extent that in 1894 it had formed the London Municipal Society to encourage support for the Moderate Party on the council.

1896

THE AGE OF THE CAR

Karl Benz is generally credited with unveiling the modern motor car when, in 1885, he drove his three-wheel vehicle round a cinder track in Mannheim at 10 miles per hour. Simultaneously, and only 60 miles away, Gottlieb Daimler was developing the first motorcycle. Though these two famous names were joined in a famous marque in 1926, the two men never met.

By 1896 there was a sufficient number of cars in Britain to warrant the passing of the first Highways Act relating to them. The Act was marked by a run of 54 cars from London to Brighton, and in the same year an exhibition of 'horseless carriages' was held at Crystal Palace – the first motor show.

In 1896, too, cyclists were permitted to use Hyde Park – a decision which helped Whiteley's to sell out their vast stock of bicycles on the first day.

THE AGE OF RADIO

Guglielmo Marconi, who had demonstrated a primitive radio to an uninterested Italian government in 1895, this year came to England to arouse interest in his invention. The Post Office was encouraging, and

on 27 July, from the roof of the General Post Office in Aldersgate Street, the first public transmission of wireless signals was made.

THE AGE OF THE POPULAR PRESS

Tabloid newspapers derive from the *Daily Mail*, founded by Alfred Harmsworth (Lord Northcliffe) this year. Compulsory elementary education (since 1870) had created a generation of literate readers curious about home and world events that were previously the preserve of their social superiors. Northcliffe, selling his paper at a halfpenny, sought to engage their appetite, made a particular bid to interest women, offered prizes in competitions, encouraged features, and promoted interest in motoring and flying. By 1900 the circulation of the *Mail* was 1 million, and new rivals were inevitable. The *Daily Express* was born in 1900 and the *Daily Mirror* in 1903.

A VAST HOTEL IN THE STRAND

There was a flurry of new hotel building and speculation at this time. On the Strand, the Hotel Cecil was completed; with approximately 1,000 rooms, it was almost the largest hotel in the world. It was the project of Jabez Balfour MP, who had already built the Hyde Park Hotel, but the Cecil was completed after Balfour's financial downfall and imprisonment for fraud – he received a sentence of 14 years' penal servitude. Shell-Mex House now occupies the site.

In the same year the Coburg (now the Connaught) Hotel in Carlos Place was rebuilt, much as it is now, to the designs of Lewis Isaacs and Henry Florence. Principal shareholder in this building was Sir Blundell Maple, whose furniture store in Tottenham Court Road, also rebuilt this year, supplied most of the furniture.

A NEW NATIONAL PORTRAIT GALLERY

The National Portrait Gallery, which had begun in 1859 with a small collection in Great George Street, had since 1869 been in a building at South Kensington. The present gallery by Trafalgar Square was opened on 4 April this year; it was built at the expense of a Mr William Alexander of Andover, to the design of Ewan Christian.

THE BIG WHEEL FRIGHT

The Big Wheel at Earls Court (see 1894) went wrong on 22 May, leaving 60 people high and dry. One report says that they were stranded for 15 hours, another 4½ hours; they each got £5 compensation.

MOVING PICTURES

At the Egyptian Hall in Piccadilly there was an exhibition of 'Animated Photographs' – the 'first and finest in London'. This appears to have been the first appearance of 'cinematography' in England.

THE MODERN BARCLAY'S BANK

Barclay's Bank in its modern form stems from a merger of some 20 private banks this year. About 200 years earlier, in 1694, a John Freame, goldsmith, had established a business in Lombard Street which, in the 18th century, a relative, James Barclay, was to join.

1897

THE OPENING OF THE TATE

It was a good period for contemporary art. The Camberwell School of Arts and Crafts and the Central School of Art and Design had been opened in 1896. This year the Tate Gallery, intended to house a growing collection of contemporary art, was opened on 16 August on Millbank. The building, together with a collection of 67 Victorian paintings, was the gift of the sugar magnate Sir Henry Tate, whose generosity had been only grudgingly accepted by the government. The architect for the building was Sidney J. R. Smith.

The Beginnings of Muswell Hill

Muswell Hill is still virtually all of a piece, an assembly of houses and shopping parades mostly built between 1897 and 1914. A few villas of an earlier period survive from a time when the area was agricultural. It has been suggested that development began in 1896, when the murder of an old and rich man here excited public attention to the extent that thousands of sightseers came to see the scene of the crime – an isolated house in what is now Tetherdown; the *Hornsey Journal* reported that some 15,000 to 20,000 people went to view the house on one Sunday in February. Once on the peak of Muswell Hill, the suggestion goes, with magnificent views around them, the voyeurs all wanted to live there. However, Alexandra Palace had already familiarized thousands of people with the area.

The most significant step to development was the purchase this year of a house called The Limes, by the Broadway roundabout, previously owned by the circulating-library proprietor Charles Edward Mudie, and an estate on the other side of the Broadway, so that it was possible to develop in grid system much of the area from 1897. The purchaser and developer of the estates was James Edmondson.

A County Hall Turned down

The London County Council had outgrown the old offices of the Metropolitan Board of Works in Spring Gardens and needed a new building. However, the government was still pursuing its policy of trying to contain the council's expenditure, and an application to buy land at Trafalgar Square was turned down.

More Theatres

Music hall was now the most popular form of mass entertainment in London, and new, large and usually ornate theatres were being built in most areas. Typical was the Grand Theatre, in Fulham, opened on 23 August, which was built on a triangular site to a design by the noted theatre architect W. G. R. Sprague. The interior was in the style of Louis XIV, the columned vestibule had a domed ceiling, and on top of the building was a huge statue of the Muses.

In Camden Town, the Bedford Palace of Varieties was inadequate for the growing audiences and the new Bedford Theatre was opened on 6 February, in a splendid building designed by Bertie Crewe. It was to become one of the most successful of London music halls, in which appeared Marie Lloyd and George Robey.

Rather larger was the Metropolitan Theatre in Edgware Road. This new music hall, replacing another, was opened this year, with a capacity of nearly 2,000. The architect was Frank Matcham – he and Sprague vied in building theatres at this time.

Collins's Music Hall, on Islington Green, was begun by Samuel Collins Vagg, a former chimneysweep; he had taken over a music room attached to a pub here, but died young after he had turned it into an extremely successful music hall. A successor rebuilt it, dispensing with the public house, in 1897. The Alexandra Theatre in Stoke Newington Road opened on 27 December; another Matcham building, this was intended for drama but within a few years had succumbed to music hall.

The fourth (and present) Her Majesty's Theatre was built on the site of the previous building as a development by Herbert Beerbohm Tree, to a design by C. J. Phipps; it opened on 28 April.

A Theatrical Murder

One of the most popular actors of the day, William Terriss, was stabbed to death by a deranged actor outside the Adelphi Theatre, where Terriss was appearing, on 16 December. His funeral, on 21 December at Brompton, attracted a large crowd of sympathizers.

A Magazine for Country Folk

The magazine *Country Life* first appeared on 8 January this year, published in Southampton Street, Covent Garden. Its creator was Edward Hudson, owner of a printing company, Hudson & Kearns in Southwark, who was hoping, in collaboration with the publisher George Newnes, to create work for his presses. Hudson was also an early patron of the young Edwin Lutyens, who was given the commission for the *Country Life* offices in Tavistock Street, Covent Garden, built in 1906.

More Demolitions

The 19th-century version of Furnival's Inn in Holborn, which had long ceased to have legal connections, was demolished this year to make way for an extension to the Prudential Assurance building. Charles Dickens had lived there in the 1830s while working as a reporter for the *Morning Chronicle*. Nearby, what was probably the last galleried inn in London north of the river, the Old Bell in High Holborn, was taken down; its history could be traced back to 1384. The church of St Michael Bassishaw, in Basinghall Street, a Wren building, was found to be unsafe this year and was demolished.

One church which escaped demolition was Nicholas Hawksmoor's St Mary Woolnoth. The City & South London tube railway wanted to take it down and use the site for a station; when permission was refused, the company formed its station (Bank) beneath it, underpinned the church, and removed any bones from the crypt to the City of London cemetery at Ilford.

A Polytechnic in Holloway

The Northern Polytechnic in Holloway Road had first admitted students in 1896, but it was not until 15 July 1897 that the great hall was formally opened by the lord mayor of London. This City connection stemmed from the substantial donations to the foundation of the polytechnic by the London Parochial Charities and the Clothworkers' Company. The architect was Charles Bell. The building is now part of the University of North London.

Another Tunnel beneath the Thames

The Blackwall Tunnel, between Poplar and Greenwich, had been one of the last projects of the old Metropolitan Board of Works, though it was not entirely popular. So keen was the board to see the new project committed that it announced that it would award the contract to construct the tunnel at its last meeting on 22 March 1889, despite the opposition of the newly elected members of the London County Council. The latter were so outraged that they persuaded the government to dissolve the board on 21 March.

The original MBW plan was for two tunnels: one for vehicles, the other for pedestrians. The LCC changed this to a single (now northbound) tunnel to encompass both, just over a mile in length. The tunnel, designed by Sir Alexander Binnie, was opened on 22 May this year. The southbound tunnel was constructed 1960–67.

ROYAL AUTOMOBILE CLUB FOUNDED

What is now the Royal Automobile Club was founded this year to give 'encouragement for the motoring movement and the motor and allied industries in the British Empire', but it was not until 1915 that the club took possession of its famous clubhouse in Pall Mall. It has recently abandoned its mutual status and is owned by a public company.

1898

WATERLOO & CITY LINE CONSTRUCTED

The Waterloo & City Railway, an underground line between Waterloo and the Bank, was opened on 8 August as an extension of the south-west suburban railway system. This line – nicknamed 'The Drain' for reasons which are apparent when travelling on it, is now part of the Underground system.

FIRST ESCALATOR IN LONDON

The first 'moving staircase' in London was installed at the rebuilt Harrods store. At first an attendant stood at the top of the escalator, equipped with sal volatile to revive the nervous.

A DISASTROUS LAUNCH

The Thames Ironworks Company launched its largest ever battleship in June this year, but the occasion ended in disaster. It is thought that about 100,000 people were present to see the duchess of York launch HMS *Albion*, many seated on special stands erected for the occasion. A rush of people, mainly women and children, to obtain a better view-point overpowered police stationed to prevent it. Very soon after, as the ship was launched, a wave was set up which demolished the small bridge upon which the people were standing, sending a countless number into the water to be trapped in the mud or the current or beneath beams of wood. The river police were soon at the scene, pick-ing up many, and other spectators joined in the rescue operation, but by nine that night 35 bodies had been recovered.

A PLENITUDE OF PARKS

More parks were opened to the public. Golders Hill in north London was a particularly good coup for the conservationists. The house and mansion, once the estate of a prosperous merchant who had had a role in the financing of the New Road in the 1750s, came on the market in 1897. Fortunately, the estate failed to reach its reserve price and it was put up for sale again in June 1898, by which time a public cam-paign had been mounted to save it as an addition to Hampstead Heath. There was little time to raise the money, and in the end £35,000 was guaranteed by several affluent local people. When the bidding went beyond that figure, Thomas Barratt, a Hampstead worthy who was also chairman of Pear's Soap, continued bidding on his own account and bought the estate for £38,000. The necessary money was raised by the public soon after, and the park officially opened in December.

The Water House in Walthamstow, together with the surrounding grounds, was presented by the family of a publisher, Edward Lloyd, to Walthamstow this year. The house is now the William Morris Gallery (Morris had lived there), and the grounds have become Lloyd Park.

Other parks formed were those at Barking in 1898 and Deptford on 7 June 1897, and Fortune Green in Hampstead was preserved as a public open space on 21 October 1897.

THE NEW CLARIDGE'S

The present Claridge's Hotel replaced the accumulation of individual, knocked-through houses acquired over the years. Demolition of these began in 1894, and the new 260-room building, designed by C. W. Stephens, was formally opened in December 1898. The Savoy Group had by then become the owners.

1899

THE LONDON BOROUGHS FORMED

In the year in which Charles Booth's massive *Life and Labour of the People in London* revealed just how badly London's government had failed its millions, the new London boroughs were formed under the London Government Act. Twenty-eight new authorities were estab-lished, superseding a large number of ineffective vestries, district boards and liberties. The new bodies took office in 1900.

The opportunity of the rearrangement was taken to tidy up some historical anomalies. One example was an area near Muswell Hill granted in medieval times to the nunnery of St Mary, Clerkenwell, and which until 1900 was administered by Clerkenwell vestry; this area was now included in Hornsey.

A NEW STATION ON THE MARYLEBONE ROAD

The Great Central Railway came late to London, and Marylebone station, designed by H. W. Braddock and opened for passengers on 15 March this year, was the last main-line station built in the metro-polis. From 1 July, people arriving there could stay at the new Hotel Great Central. The line, opposed by local residents, was never a success, and the station has been threatened with demolition several times since.

THE LAST FLEET FROM BARKING

For centuries, the principal fishing centre near London had been Barking in Essex, which in its day was the home of hundreds of fishing vessels large and small. As late as 1885 (q.v.) the main fishing company there had attempted to revive its dominance by helping to found the unsuccessful Shadwell Fish Market as a rival to Billingsgate. But trade was inexorably moving eastward beyond the Essex town; an efficient railway system could move fish almost as quickly from Durham and Grimsby as from Barking, and there was no longer the need for a Thameside base. The last fishing fleet, a small one, set out from Barking in April this year.

REBUILDING THE ANGEL

The Angel at Islington has long been a place name without a building. The old inn of that name at the southern end of Islington High Street, focus in pre-Georgian times of two roads leading to the City – St John Street and Goswell Road – had been a double-galleried inn in which plays were produced. The original building was pulled down in 1819, and its successors were replaced in 1899 by the present structure, in pale terracotta, which also served as a hotel. This building, plus cupola, became a Lyons' Corner House in 1921.

A NEW MOORFIELDS

The present Moorfields Eye Hospital in City Road was opened on 4 September this year in a building designed by Keith Young. What was the Royal London Ophthalmic Hospital (it wasn't officially called Moorfields until 1956) was by then the premier eye hospital in the world.

1900

MORE TUBE LINES

The underground railway from Stockwell to King William Street, opened in 1890 by the City & South London Railway, was the first 'tube' line – that is, one constructed by tunnelling and not by the cut-and-cover method employed by the Metropolitan and District lines. It was also the first electric railway – the other lines still used steam engines.

In 1900 the City & South London closed its inadequate terminus at King William Street and built a stretch of track via London Bridge station up to a new Bank station and then on to Moorgate; simultaneously the line was extended from Stockwell to Clapham Common to catch commuters in that fast-growing suburb. This all opened on 25 February, but on 30 July came the first underground line through the centre of London – one which carried not only commuters, but shoppers to Oxford Street and Bond Street. This, the Central Line, ran originally from Shepherds Bush to the Bank. With its white-tiled stations and its flat-rate twopenny fare, it was the first of the modern tube railways. It also made money, which the other lines did not.

SOUNDS OF WAR

Patriotism overcame doubts about Britain's colonial role in South Africa when Mafeking was relieved this year. Ecstatic celebrations occurred in London on 18 May when news came through. In Hampstead the news was relayed to the fire station in Heath Street and thence by word of mouth to the rest of the village. It was reported, such was the lack of traffic, that in Hampstead the noise of celebrations in neighbouring Highgate could be heard.

But the war continued, as did production at Eley's Cartridge Factory in Gray's Inn Road. On 10 September the premises were wrecked by a large explosion; three people were killed and many injured. The incident sparked off yet another debate on why such dangerous manufactures were allowed in built-up areas.

A NEW POLITICAL FORCE

The birth of the Labour Party on 27 February excited little attention in the press, preoccupied as it was by events in the Transvaal. On this date a meeting was held at the Congregational Memorial Hall in Farringdon Street, with delegates from 65 trade unions and three socialist societies, to implement a resolution passed at the Trades Union Congress the previous September. That resolution was not exactly the stuff of revolution – it merely proposed an alliance between trade unionists, socialists and cooperative societies to devise ways to increase the 'number of Labour members in the next Parliament'.

The wording was carefully low-key because its promoters, Keir Hardie and Ramsay MacDonald, were aware that anything more positive might fail; in the event it scraped through with a small majority, opposed by some trade unions which felt that disaster might ensue if they were deflected from their legitimate preoccupations with the interests of their members.

WALLACE COLLECTION OPENED

The Wallace Collection had derived from purchases made by the 1st marquess of Hertford, but it was Sir Richard Wallace, a son born out of wedlock to the eccentric 4th marquess, who was responsible for its maturity when he acted as his father's agent. Most of the works were kept in Paris, where the 4th marquess lived, but some were at Hertford House in Manchester Square, the London town house of the Hertford family. After Wallace inherited the collection, he moved from Paris to London in 1871 and a temporary home was needed for the pictures while Hertford House was converted to take them; many were therefore displayed to the public for four years in the Bethnal Green Museum. The items taken there included 736 pictures, 446 pieces of furniture, and hundreds of other objects.

Wallace died in 1890, leaving his property to his wife, and when she died in 1897 the collection went to the nation on condition that a home was provided for it. The government was obliged to buy the freehold of Hertford House as the most obvious solution, and it was opened as a public gallery on 22 June this year by the prince of Wales.

NEW STORES

The John Barnes department store was opened in Finchley Road, Hampstead, this year, shortly after its founder had been drowned in a shipwreck. Like Bon Marché in Brixton and Whiteley's in Westbourne Grove, the new store set out to capture new middle-class incomers, for in Hampstead there were new red-brick developments of substantial houses on both sides of the Finchley Road. The John Barnes store was owned by a consortium which included Barnes, who was also a director of John Barker's store in Kensington, and Edwin Jones of Bon Marché, who took over its management on Barnes's death this year. The building had accommodation for 400 assistants, who ate in three sex-segregated dining rooms.

Austin Reed, aged 27, opened a gents' outfitters in Fenchurch Street on 2 July. He was the eldest son of a hosier and hatter, but had taken the unusual step of leaving his father's firm to study business methods in the United States. When he returned to England he borrowed money from his father for his first shop, which was run on the retailing principles he had learned. By 1908 he had three shops in the City and in 1911 a branch in Regent Street, though the famous shop there now was not built until 1926.

A NEW SORTING OFFICE

The General Post Office was outgrowing St Martin's le Grand. This year it opened a new sorting office on the former site of the Clerkenwell House of Correction, on a road sardonically called Mount Pleasant.

NEW THEATRES

The London Hippodrome in Charing Cross Road was opened on 15 January as a circus and variety theatre, the project of Edward Moss, founder of the Moss Empire group. A man particularly interested in spectacular productions, in his new theatre Moss made extensive use of water stored in a large tank on the roof; one evening the actor Lupino Lane nearly lost his life when a huge torrent of water swept on to the stage. The theatre has been a nightclub since 1958.

On the corner of Camden High Street and Crowndale Road, the Camden Theatre was opened on 21 December by Ellen Terry, who, as a girl, had lived just down the road. The building, designed by W. G. R. Sprague, was considered the best theatre in the suburbs – with accommodation for nearly 2,500 people, it was certainly one of the largest. This building, too, has become a nightclub in recent years, after a long spell as an auditorium for BBC shows.

A MUSEUM OF EAST LONDON

One of the great philanthropists of this period was John Passmore Edwards (1823–1911). The son of a carpenter, he had augmented a rudimentary education by studying at night and digesting the *Penny Magazine*. In 1850 he used his £50 savings to begin a weekly magazine, which he produced and printed in his room in Paternoster Row. He went bankrupt, but by 1862 had recovered sufficiently to buy up an ailing paper called *Building News*, which he returned to profit. His journalistic and social-reforming life increased enormously from this time – he supported causes ranging from temperance to repeal of the Corn Laws – and his later years were spent in endowing numerous hospitals and libraries. The Passmore Edwards Museum in Stratford, specializing in the history of East London, was opened this year in a building provided by him.

A New Hotel

The Russell Hotel, a fantastic mixture of château and terracotta, designed by Charles Fitzroy Doll, was opened this year. Fortunately it still survives, but its neighbour of 1905, the Imperial (also by Doll), was taken down in 1966 and replaced by arguably the ugliest hotel building in London.

1901

An Age Seen out

Queen Victoria had reigned longer than most people had been alive – a span of so many years that memories of her early unpopularity and the tedium of the excessive period of mourning for Albert that she imposed on her court and herself had faded. When she died, on 22 January, a system of values and a way of doing things within her own sphere of influence was ended: John Galsworthy's Soames Forsyte did well to mark the significance of her funeral procession. The pace of change was underlined not only by her death but by the beginning of that artificial thing, a new century. The Boer War still raged; there was a quickening pace to invention; civil unrest and gross social inequality affected the poor and threatened the elite. The future, perhaps, could not be controlled. Britain, supervisor of trade and territories around the world for its own benefit for so long, and whose royal head seemingly pulled the strings of every monarch of any worth, was seen to be in decline and, as often happens in these circumstances, an era of great pleasure and indulgence was ushered in.

New Attractions

A building which typified the London of the next ten years was the Trocadero Restaurant in Shaftesbury Avenue. It was an expansion by J. Lyons & Co. of an old music hall; the restaurant was partly built by 1896, but in 1901 the famous Long Bar was opened, designed by Davis & Emanuel in a rich mixture of wood and mirrors to appeal to the clientele that used the nearby Café Royal.

Another dining institution that began this year was Schmidt's restaurant in Charlotte Street, renowned for its German cooking and the rudeness of its waiters.

A Recital Hall

The Wigmore Hall (originally the Bechstein Hall) was opened in June this year by Frederick Bechstein next to his piano showrooms in Wigmore Street. It was an indulgent investment, and one that was taken over, together with his other property, when the businesses of German nationals were closed down at the outbreak of war in 1914. It reopened as the Wigmore Hall in 1917.

Mansions Saved

The expansion of London threatened numerous mansions in their landscaped grounds. Cranbrook in Ilford had been lost the previous year, but in 1901 the London County Council intervened to buy Marble Hill House in Richmond Road, Twickenham. This Palladian villa, built for a mistress of George II, was up for sale at £40,000, having been empty since 1887.

In Willesden the council bought Dollis Hill House, one-time residence of Lord Aberdeen, and with the grounds around formed Gladstone Park. Gladstone and Mark Twain had stayed in the house.

A Garden Estate in Ealing

A product of the garden-city movement pioneered by Ebenezer Howard was Brentham Village Estate in Ealing. Howard was keen to develop building cooperatives that erected houses for themselves, and it was an Ealing cooperative in 1897 which decided to buy plots of land near Pitshanger Lane to build nine houses. Encouraged to do more, in 1901 they formed Ealing Tenants Ltd, a 'Co-Partnership in Housing', which gradually developed the Brentham estate not only with houses, but with communal facilities such as a hall, a school and allotments.

Last and First Tramways

At the beginning of this century all public road transport was horse-drawn. The London General Omnibus Company was reckoned to be the largest user of horse power in London – each bus required 11 horses to service it during its average 60 miles a day. Over 3,700 horse buses carried Londoners in 1901, and there were also horse trams – as a generalization, buses served the middle classes and the trams, with lower fares, the working classes.

This year the last stretch of line built for horse trams was opened on 22 August; it was in Agincourt Road, Hampstead, and merely provided a one-way track from the terminus at South End Green to rejoin the main route to Camden Town.

On 4 April, the first electric trams appeared on a track between Shepherds Bush, Chiswick and Kew, owned by London United Tramways. But the major expansion of electric tramways was pushed through by the London County Council, which by this time owned, but did not necessarily manage, most of the old horse tram routes.

Art for East Enders

The resources needed to ease living conditions in London's East End have defeated even the chequebooks of borough councils in modern times. At the turn of the century, when problems were considerably worse, most efforts to alleviate them came from individual charities, such as those of Peabody and Guinness in the field of housing, while others specialized in soup kitchens or temperance halls, and the Salvation Army and Dr Barnardo took in those beyond any other form of help. A notable social worker in this period was Samuel Barnett, who in 1873 was appointed vicar of St Jude, Whitechapel – a parish described by his bishop as 'the worst in the diocese, inhabited mainly by a criminal population'. He took up his post soon after his marriage to Henrietta Rowland, later to make her mark as the founder of Hampstead Garden Suburb. Barnett, despite ecclesiastical promotion, maintained his links with Whitechapel for the rest of his life. It was due to his early work in staging art exhibitions in his parish (see 1881) and the generosity of John Passmore Edwards that the Whitechapel Art Gallery was opened on 12 March this year. This is a splendid art-nouveau building designed by C. Harrison Townsend, who in the same year completed the Horniman Museum in Forest Hill.

1902

WATER GOES PUBLIC

As far back as 1876 the Metropolitan Board of Works had promoted a bill in Parliament to acquire the private water companies supplying the metropolitan area. But not only was the bill rejected, the board members were threatened with surcharge for the expense of promoting it. Numerous efforts by the London County Council to the same end were frustrated until in 1900 a Royal Commission concluded that a single authority should control water supplies in the London area; the LCC was ruled out since local authorities outside the then London area were involved. On 18 December 1902 the London Water Bill was passed, permitting the purchase of eight water companies by a Metropolitan Water Board that consisted of 69 members nominated by councils within the region concerned.

BOUDICCA ON THE BRIDGE

The dramatic statue of Queen Boudicca on Westminster Bridge has an odd history. Its genesis, in 1856, was the sculptor Thomas Thornycroft's ambition to depict the great events of English history. In this he was encouraged by Prince Albert, and work began on the modelling of Boudicca. After the prince's death, however, no commission materialized and the statue, though completed as far as modelling stage, was for many years left in separate bits in a Chiswick shed. The excavation of the tumulus on Parliament Hill (see 1894) aroused speculation that Boudicca's tomb might be uncovered there, and Thornycroft's family offered to donate the statue for erection at the site if the LCC paid for the work involved. The tumulus yielded no evidence of Boudicca (and little of anything else), and in any case academics were generally sceptical that it was the right place. So instead the bronze statue was unveiled on Westminster Bridge this year. The outraged queen and her violated daughters sum up the popular conception of them, but the accuracy of the rest leaves much to be desired.

BURNING THE DEAD

The first crematorium in London was opened this year at Golders Green. Before this the Cremation Society of England had laid on special trains from a depot in Westminster Bridge Road to Woking Cemetery, where the first British crematorium had been established in 1885; by the beginning of this century as many as 50 bodies a day were making the final journey by rail.

A NEW TUNNEL UNDER THE THAMES

A white-tiled tunnel beneath the Thames, from the Isle of Dogs to Greenwich, was opened this year. At each end of the tunnel are imposing domed shafts containing what are probably the most spacious lifts in London, and around each is a spiral staircase beloved of generations of children. The by-laws command that 'No persons may enter the tunnel in a state of intoxication ... No person shall spit on or upon the tunnel or its approaches, stairs, lift, passages, or other means of ingress or egress ... '

PRISON CHANGES

The last hanging at Newgate prison, shortly before it was closed, was on 6 May. At an auction of Newgate's contents, the bracket which supported the beam of the gallows sold for £1 15s and the apparatus itself was frugally moved to Pentonville for more service.

Brixton prison was rebuilt this year. It had begun life as the Surrey House of Correction, with sufficient ground nearby for extension 'should the increasing depravity of the Lower Orders subject the County to that burthensome obligation'. It became the first women-only prison, and in 1856 its staff of 65 included only 17 men, employed mostly on maintenance. In 1887 Brixton became briefly a military prison, but in 1902 it was reopened with additional buildings for civil prisoners. In the meantime Holloway prison, previously built by the City of London as a general house of correction, was turned into a women-only jail. One prisoner in Brixton was Bertrand Russell, who wrote his *Introduction to Mathematical Philosophy* here while imprisoned for a seditious article in 1918; the complex manuscript had to be vetted by a prison officer before it was allowed out.

1903

A PENNY BAZAAR IN BRIXTON

The first Marks & Spencer Penny Bazaar in London appears to have been that opened in a part of the Bon Marché store in Brixton this year; soon similar bazaars existed in Islington, Kilburn, Kingsland, Croydon and Tottenham. By 1910 the Brixton bazaar, with an annual take of £9,367, was the most profitable of them all. Michael Marks had begun trading in 1884 as a door-to-door hawker, had graduated to selling off a stall in Lancashire and Yorkshire markets, and in 1894 had taken Tom Spencer into partnership to keep the books. The message they put on their stalls was simple: 'Don't ask the price, it's a penny.' The merchandise — such as needles, buttons, handkerchiefs, cotton, soap etc. — was also straightforward. An innovation once Marks opened shops was that he enticed people in to browse around with no particular purchase in mind; there was no haggling, and everything was on display and clearly priced.

WESTMINSTER CATHEDRAL OPENED

The project to build a Roman Catholic cathedral in London began after the death of Cardinal Wiseman, in 1865, as a tribute to his work for the Catholic community. In 1867 his successor, Cardinal Manning, controversially appointed a relation, Henry Clutton, to design the building, but only by 1892 was there sufficient money to begin building, and even then Clutton's Gothic design was too expensive to attempt. Furthermore, Gothic was no longer seen as desirable. Cardinal Vaughan, Manning's successor, therefore appointed the most eminent Catholic architect of the day, John Francis Bentley, whose Byzantine-style cathedral more nearly reflects the early architecture of Catholic churches. Money was very short, and the interior was virtually undecorated when the building was opened in 1903, but the building was even then one of the most impressive in London, and has remained so. Its interior has since been handsomely decorated with marble and mosaic, as well as Eric Gill's bas-reliefs of *Fourteen Stations of the Cross*.

The first public service to be held there was a requiem mass for Vaughan, who had died just before completion of the building.

A BOOKSHOP IN PECKHAM

William and Gilbert Foyle this year began trading as booksellers at their home in Peckham. Their first catalogue was handwritten, and they had to ask customers to return it so that it could be used again. Very soon the Foyle brothers moved their business to London — first to the City, and then to Cecil Court and Charing Cross Road.

TRAGEDY AT COLNEY HATCH

Fire broke out at the Colney Hatch Lunatic Asylum in Friern Barnet on 27 January. Over 50 patients died in the blaze.

THE FIRST BLUE PLAQUE

The London County Council had taken over from the Royal Society of Arts responsibility for erecting commemorative plaques to notable former residents. The first of the LCC plaques – blue instead of the RSA's brown – was installed this year in Campden Hill, on a previous residence of Lord Macaulay.

MOVING THE GAIETY GIRLS

The first Gaiety Theatre was opened in the Strand in 1868; its stock in trade was burlesque and musical comedy and when, in 1893, *A Gaiety Girl* was produced it began a vogue of productions which included the talents of the Gaiety Girls. When the Strand was widened as part of the new Aldwych development the Gaiety Theatre was demolished and a new Gaiety was opened on 26 October this year at the corner of Aldwych and the Strand.

The Shepherds Bush Empire, designed by Frank Matcham, was opened on 17 August. At first a variety theatre, it has for many years been used by the nearby BBC for programme recording.

Matcham's rival W. G. R. Sprague this year completed the New (now Albery) Theatre in St Martin's Lane; it was opened on 12 March. Charles Wyndham had erected Wyndham's Theatre in 1899 in Charing Cross Road on a plot of land which extended to St Martin's Lane, and the New Theatre occupied what was left of that ground.

1904

JUBILEE MARKET OPENS

The duke of Bedford this year opened the Foreign Flower Market at the corner of Covent Garden Piazza and Southampton Street. This red-brick building of two storeys was later called the Jubilee Market, and was rebuilt in 1987.

EXTENDING THE HEATH

The residents of tranquil Hampstead were shocked to discover that the proposed Hampstead tube (part of today's Northern Line) was to have a station at North End, near the historic building called Wyldes Farm. A station here would, of course, spawn development: as Henrietta Barnett (see 1901) put it, 'It would result in the ruin of the sylvan restfulness of that portion of the most beautiful open space near London. The trains would also bring the builder, and it required no imagination to see the rows of ugly villas such as disfigure Willesden and most of the suburbs of London … '

At the instigation of Mrs Barnett, a Heath Extension Council was formed to buy land which would prevent the station being built. It began negotiations with the land's owners, Eton College, and obtained an option to purchase for £48,000. There was, however, a disappointing response from the LCC and local councils when asked for donations to the purchase fund, and it was only with some difficulty that the price was raised and the land added to Hampstead Heath. Soon afterwards Mrs Barnett herself bought up an adjacent 240 acres of land on which to build Hampstead Garden Suburb. Although no station was built at North End, the platforms were and remain today.

The London Fire Brigade was formed in 1904, when motorized engines were becoming more familiar. However, horse-drawn engines were more usual.

A NEW CONCERT ROOM

Hard on the success of the Bechstein (Wigmore) Hall, a new concert room was opened on 19 January in New Bond Street, where the premises of the old Grosvenor Art Gallery were converted by the Orchestrelle Company of New York, manufacturers of musical instruments – in particular the newly invented pianola. The building was done with some style under the charge of Walter Cave, secretary of the Art-Workers' Guild. This concert room, later called the Aeolian Hall, was taken over by the BBC in 1941 and was used by them until 1975.

FIRST PERFORMANCES

A disagreement between Henry Wood and members of his Queen's Hall Orchestra led to the formation of the breakaway London Symphony Orchestra this year. Its first concert, conducted by Hans Richter, was on 9 June at the Queen's Hall.

The Duke of York's Theatre in St Martin's Lane became the home of plays by J. M. Barrie. In 1902 *The Admirable Crichton* was produced; on a memorable opening night the scene-shifters went on strike after the second act and the cast had to shift for themselves until the end. The first performance of *Peter Pan* was on 27 December; this was Barrie's most successful play, and was revived annually until the First World War.

The Easter Parade of van horses in Regent's Park was first held on Easter Monday this year. The most numerous parade was in 1922, when 705 horses took part.

NEW THEATRES

The Coliseum in St Martin's Lane was conceived by Oswald Stoll as a vast variety theatre; it was designed by Frank Matcham and opened on 24 December. The building was novel in many ways: it was the largest theatre in London; it had a three-section revolving stage and also a revolving electrically lit advertising globe on the roof, where there was also a garden restaurant; there were lifts and a mobile royal lounge which could be electrically moved into a reception foyer while the royal guests remained stationary and without exertion; there were also telephones, a messenger service and a pillar box. The LCC objected to the revolving globe because it infringed advertising regulations, and Stoll instead installed intermittent lights inside it which simulated movement. This large enterprise was almost an immediate flop. The theatre closed in 1906, but reopened to better fortune the following year.

The Lyceum in Wellington Street has had an unstable career. It began, facing the Strand, in the 18th century as an exhibition and concert hall, and later had an indifferent reputation as a theatre, although Tussaud's waxworks were here early in the 19th century. The portico which still faces Wellington Street is the only part left of the 1834 version designed by Samuel Beazley; the LCC declared the building unsafe for public performances, and it was rebuilt behind the columns by Bertie Crewe and reopened on 31 December this year. The Lyceum's subsequent history was undistinguished and it became a dance hall after the last war; it is now back in use as a theatre.

The spectacular increase in the number of theatres in this period encouraged Herbert Beerbohm Tree to found what became the Royal Academy of Dramatic Art this year; its first premises were in the dome of Her Majesty's Theatre, but the same year it moved to a house in Gower Street which it still occupies.

CELEBRATING HORTICULTURE

To mark its centenary, on 22 July the Royal Horticultural Society opened an exhibition hall and headquarters in Vincent Square; these buildings, designed by E. J. Stebbs, superseded rooms in a house in Victoria Street and a hired drill hall. So popular was the new hall that the society flourished enormously and was obliged to open another hall nearby in Greycoat Street in 1928.

ADMINISTRATIVE CHANGES

The London School Board was abolished this year and its responsibilities were taken over by the London County Council.

The Metropolitan Fire Brigade became the London Fire Brigade, although it remained the responsibility of the LCC. It was a period of change in firefighting equipment. Though most engines were still horse-drawn, many stations were buying motorized vehicles. From 1905 turntable ladders were used, and breathing apparatus was being introduced.

Underlining the eastern sprawl of London, East Ham became a county borough. The previous year an impressive new town hall had been opened there on land which not long before had been a cabbage field. A local paper commented that Barking Road, where the town hall was located, was 'three years ago a horribly dreary thoroughfare, but now it is lighted up by electric arc lamps and the intermittent flash of the brilliantly lighted electric cars relieve the district of all gloom at night'. By then East Ham had a population of 100,000.

A NEW RAILWAY

The Great Northern & City Railway was opened on 14 February, connecting Finsbury Park and Moorgate, via Highbury, and linking at Finsbury Park with the Great Northern's main line to King's Cross, so giving it a branch to the City. From 1913 the line became an integral part of the London Underground system, but in 1976 it was reinstated as part of British Rail.

PICTURES IN EALING

The origin of Ealing Studios, noted for their comedy films in the 1940s, was the purchase in 1904 by William George Barker of a house near Ealing Green. Here he set up Barker Motion Photography Ltd, and by 1912 the studios, built in the garden of his house, were the largest in England. In 1929 they were bought by Associated Radio Pictures; by 1938 Michael Balcon was in charge, and it was during his reign that the 'Ealing comedies' were produced.

1905

A REBIRTH IN HOLBORN

On 18 October Aldwych and Kingsway were officially opened, essential elements of a late-19th-century scheme to reorganize London's traffic and obliterate some slum areas. Earlier street developments such as New Oxford Street, Shaftesbury Avenue and Charing Cross Road were cut through existing street patterns without ceremony and with the minimum of architectural distinction, but Kingsway and Aldwych were different: here the London County Council was creating a new commercial district to compete with that of its old rival, the City of London. The concept and the architecture were grand – even pompous – but slow to come to fruition. The W. H. Smith building at 7 Kingsway made an early appearance, as did Kodak House, but the take-up of sites was bedevilled by the First World War, and the last major block, Africa House, was not completed until 1922.

Kingsway crossed a very old street pattern. Great Queen Street, for example, was truncated, leaving an eastern vestige entering Lincoln's Inn Fields. Most of the narrow streets around Clare Market were taken down and, opposite Somerset House, destruction was complete when the Aldwych scheme was erected.

In Aldwych (from 'Aldwic', an early name for the area), the Strand Theatre opened on 22 May and the Aldwych Theatre on 23 December. The former was first called the Waldorf, as it was part of a development which included the hotel of that name; the two theatres were designed by W. G. R. Sprague as an identical pair on each side of the hotel. The Gaiety Theatre, as we have seen (1903), had already been

Wych Street, leading from the southern end of Drury Lane to St Clement Danes, was demolished to make way for the building of Kingsway and Aldwych.

The construction of Kingsway in 1905. This road of offices eventually ended the physical relationship between Covent Garden and Lincoln's Inn Fields.

located on the corner of the Aldwych, but other theatres were lost in the general demolition of the area – the Olympic in Wych Street, the Opéra Comique in the Strand and the Globe in Newcastle Street. The Waldorf Hotel, finished in 1908 and designed by A. G. R. Mackenzie, has an elegant palm court.

The Aldwych half-circle includes three large set-piece buildings – Australia House (1918), India House (1930) and Bush House. The latter was a grandiose but unsuccessful scheme. Designed by Harvey Corbett, it was planned by an American, Irving Bush, as a trade centre furnished with shops and display areas; it was not completed until 1935. The BBC has occupied most of it since 1940.

To the north, Southampton Row was also widened, and the distinctive arcade of shops Sicilian Avenue was built to a design by W. S. Wortley; it is paved with Sicilian marble.

BUILDING IN GOLDERS GREEN
Plans to build the Hampstead tube sent speculators scurrying to the fields of Golders Green. The first new house built, at the corner of Finchley Road and Hoop Lane, was finished this year, two years before the tube arrived.

DISASTER AT CHARING CROSS
Part of Charing Cross station collapsed on 5 December, crushing the Avenue (now Playhouse) Theatre in Northumberland Avenue beneath it and killing six people.

A NEW COLLEGE
The Working Men's College moved into purpose-built premises in Crowndale Road, Camden Town, this year, although the official opening was not until January 1906.

UNDERGROUND DEVELOPMENTS
Charles Tyson Yerkes, an American, obtained control of the District Line in 1901 and announced his intention to modernize and electrify it. His plans necessitated the building of a power station at Lots Road, Chelsea, and this was opened in 1905 when electrification was complete. Yerkes was an ambitious man. Not only did he also control the Baker Street & Waterloo (Bakerloo) Line – which had not yet opened – he was in the process of building the Hampstead tube (Northern Line), and hoped also to supply the power necessary for the Brompton & Piccadilly Circus (Piccadilly Line) Railway then being built. But in December, at the height of his extensive plans, Yerkes died.

DEMOLITIONS IN PICCADILLY
The last performance at St James's Hall, the concert room in Piccadilly, was on 11 February. The building was replaced by the Piccadilly Hotel, designed by Norman Shaw in his Imperial style. Construction was immensely expensive, and the de Keyser family, who built it and who had spent 50 years building up a large fortune, went bankrupt in ten years because of its expense.

The building of the hotel was part of a transformation of Regent Street begun about this year. Nash's elegant curved avenue, which had declined in commercial attraction, was rebuilt over a long period in a larger and much heavier style, mainly to the designs of Sir Reginald Blomfield.

Meanwhile, in Piccadilly, the famed Egyptian Hall was demolished. The buildings at nos. 170–73 took its place.

NEW FOOTBALL CLUBS
Three of the best-known London football clubs were formed this year – Chelsea, Crystal Palace and Charlton Athletic.

LOOKING AFTER MOTORISTS
The Automobile Association was formed this year at 18 Fleet Street, by a group of motorists seeking to alleviate what they thought were undue restrictions by the police.

1906

TRAINS AND TRAMS IN TUNNELS
The central-London network of tube railways assumed much of its present form this year. The Baker Street & Waterloo Railway (Bakerloo Line) opened between Baker Street and the Elephant and Castle on 10 March, connecting key shopping areas such as Piccadilly and Oxford Street, but also picking up south-London trade from the City & South London Railway at the Elephant. The Bakerloo was extended the following year to Edgware Road, and during the First World War was built to suburban Wembley.

The Great Northern, Piccadilly & Brompton Railway (Piccadilly Line) began on 15 December. It was the longest tube at the time, running from Finsbury Park, where it linked with the Great Northern, down to Hammersmith, via Piccadilly Circus, where it shared the station with the District Line. The stations on the Piccadilly Line and the later Northern Line, designed by Leslie Green, displayed a distinctive red-glazed tile outside and attractive Arts and Crafts features in the booking halls. Many of these stations survive, though the task of replacing damaged red tiles seems to have defeated the modern management and the ironwork has generally been left to deteriorate. To serve the new Aldwych development, a spur of the Piccadilly Line was built down to the Strand in 1907.

A further innovation was the single-deck tramcars which ran in a tunnel beneath Kingsway down to Aldwych. These came into service on 24 February. This tramline was extended in 1908 to the Embankment, where it could connect with south-London services. In 1930 the line was closed so that the tunnel could be deepened to take double-decker trams. The new service was inaugurated on 14 January 1931.

A Garden Estate in Muswell Hill

On the southern slopes of Muswell Hill, W. J. Collins, a land speculator, bought a piece of land in 1899 which contained three houses, one called Rookfield (previously the home of A. W. Gamage, of department-store fame) and another called Lalla Rookh (a former residence of the poet Tom Moore). Collins's two sons developed 15 of the 23 acres into a garden estate on the lines made popular by Ebenezer Howard in Letchworth. The houses, spread irregularly around the informal (and unadopted) roads, are Arts and Crafts. Work began on building about this year, but the estate was not completed until about 1922.

From Plants to Arms

A large tract of land at Twyford, near Acton, had been bought by the Royal Horticultural Society as a permanent showground and given the name of 'Park Royal'. The venture was not a success, however, and this year the society sold the land for £28,500. During the First World War it was used for the manufacture of munitions, and after that was developed into an industrial estate.

Dining at the Ritz

The Ritz Hotel, which opened in Piccadilly on 24 May, was the creation of César Ritz, whose hotel of the same name in Paris was known throughout Europe. Ritz began his working life as a waiter, but has received the ultimate accolade of having his name used as an adjective. Ritz had established the Carlton Hotel in the Haymarket (site of New Zealand House) as the most desirable hotel in London. The Ritz was opened after his retirement, but its general layout was planned by him, including the arcade reminiscent of Paris. Behind the stone fascia, the architects, Mewes & Davis, who had also built the Paris Ritz, produced here the first major steel-framed building in the country. An incessant worker, obsessive about detail, function and management, Ritz died at the age of 68 in 1918, mentally exhausted and confused.

The Poor Man's Carlton

Bruce House, a hostel in Kemble Street for men of no fixed abode, was opened by the London County Council this year. It was known derisively as the 'Poor Man's Carlton'.

Ada Lewis Hill, widow of the immensely rich Samuel Lewis, this year left not only £500,000 in personal bequests, but £350,000 in public endowments. £50,000 was to be spent on lodging houses for single women in London, and a further £50,000 went to the Governesses' Benevolent Institution. The Samuel Lewis Trust erected model dwellings in several parts of London; these were a considerable improvement on those erected by Peabody and Guinness, and blocks of them may be seen today in Liverpool Road, Islington.

Hainault Forest to the Public

Part of Hainault Forest was bought this year by the LCC. Once owned by the abbess of Barking, the land had been disafforested and turned into arable land since the mid 19th century. The purchase price for 551 acres of arable and 254 acres of remaining forest was £21,830.

1907

The Hampstead Tube Opened

Today's Northern Line is the marriage of two rail systems. One was the City & South London Railway (see 1890 and 1900), which in 1907 was extended to King's Cross and Euston, where it terminated. The other was the Charing Cross, Euston & Hampstead Railway (usually called then the Hampstead tube), opened from Charing Cross to Golders Green on 22 June this year, with a spur from Camden Town to what is now Archway station.

The construction of the terminus at Charing Cross, beneath the main-line station, had been made complicated by the refusal of the surface railway to allow excavation for the Underground booking hall to be made in the forecourt of the railway station, but, just when it seemed that the tube company would have to dig upwards to construct its lift shaft and booking hall, the tragic accident of 1905 (q.v.), in which part of the Charing Cross main-line station collapsed, closed the station and temporarily freed the forecourt for work at a crucial period.

In 1924 the Hampstead tube and the City & South London were linked at Euston, and in 1926 the Hampstead line was extended to Kennington, there to meet again the old C & SL.

The Northern Line at the time of its first construction in 1907. At the top are the untouched fields of Golders Green, the terminus of the line.

Camden Town station was important as the junction where trains went off to either Hampstead or Highgate. It was also the stop for London Zoo.

A SUBURB IN HAMPSTEAD

While the Underground system was reaching Hampstead and Golders Green, the first properties in Hampstead Garden Suburb were being built – the lord mayor opened the first set of houses on 2 October this year. The suburb was built, as we have seen in 1904, indirectly because of the tube and at the instigation of Henrietta Barnett. Her aim was that people of all walks of life would share the same environment, but this has been rarely achieved: the suburb, since its inception, has been almost entirely a middle-class preserve.

The layout was planned by Raymond Unwin and Barry Parker, and there are some fine individual buildings by Edwin Lutyens, including the notable St Jude church – named from Canon Barnett's church in Whitechapel. Deliberately, there are no shops, pubs or other temptations at all in the central area.

WHITELEY MURDERED

A violent event sent a frisson of excitement around London this year. This was the murder on 24 January of the flamboyant store owner William Whiteley. He was shot dead in his office by Horace Rayner, a man claiming to be his illegitimate son. Whiteley considered the man a blackmailer and was trying to summon a constable to eject him when he was killed. Rayner was at first sentenced to death at the sensational trial which followed, but the home secretary commuted the sentence to life imprisonment in view of extenuating circumstances.

OPENING A GRAVE

The cause to open the Druce grave at Highgate Cemetery was a bizarre affair. Thomas Charles Druce, a successful furniture dealer at the Baker Street Bazaar, had been buried at Highgate in 1864. In 1896 the widow of Druce's son claimed that Druce senior had really been the reclusive 5th duke of Portland, leading a double life. She claimed that Portland, having decided to rid himself of his more humdrum persona, contrived the 1864 burial, using a coffin filled with weights. The widow was, of course, interested in a share of the Portland inheritance on the death of the 5th duke. The claim was pursued relentlessly by her son, G. H. Druce, and at last, in 1907, with a large police guard at the cemetery gates keeping back an expectant crowd, an exhumation took place. The hopes of both the public and Druce were dashed when the coffin was found to contain human remains.

TWO GATHERINGS

A congress of exiled Russian Social Democrats was held in a chapel in Southgate Road, Hackney, in May. Those attending included Lenin, Stalin, Trotsky, Rosa Luxemburg and Maxim Gorky.

Quite a different sort of gathering occurred on 1 July, when the newly built Union Jack Club in Waterloo Road was opened by the king.

STUDENTS AGAINST ANIMAL RIGHTS

The case of the Brown Dog statue in Battersea excited considerable interest. In 1906 anti-vivisectionists erected in the Latchmere Recreation Ground in Battersea a fountain surmounted by the statue of a brown dog. The inscription was a provocative one – it stated that the dog had been done to death by the students of University College as part of their experiments. This led in 1907 to the statue being vandalized by medical students from various colleges after protest meetings had failed to have the inscription removed. The incident united London medical students, and the fountain was removed by Battersea Borough Council in 1910.

A NEW OLD BAILEY

The present Central Criminal Court at the Old Bailey, on the site of Newgate prison, was opened on 27 February. It was designed by Edward Mountford in a style which intimidates guilty and innocent alike.

A MERRY WIDOW IN LONDON

Musical comedy was at its most popular in London, perfectly complementing the ornate new breed of theatres. Two venues were famous in this field – the Gaiety in the Strand and Daly's Theatre by Leicester Square, both under the management of George Edwardes. In 1907, however, Edwardes was in bad financial straits and without a promising production to stage at Daly's. In desperation he took off the shelf a Viennese operetta which he had bought, but was not much moved by, and put it on with a scratch production on 8 June. The first night of *The Merry Widow* by the unknown Franz Lehár was a sensation, and soon the waltzes were the rage of London. The show ran until July 1909, and the king saw it four times.

EPSTEIN FIGURES

The British Medical Association opened its new headquarters at the junction of the Strand and Agar Street this year, in a distinctive building designed by Charles Holden at the beginning of the most productive part of his career. Noticeable on the outside are the remains of 18 nude figures carved by the young Jacob Epstein, which caused much philistine outrage. The building later became Rhodesia, then Zimbabwe, House.

MURDER IN CAMDEN TOWN

The murder of a prostitute, Emily Dimmock, this year became a famous case of the period. As with the Crippen murder in 1910, there was nothing particularly extraordinary about the crime, but its occurrence in what many people regarded as the demi-monde of Camden Town, the unpredictability of the jury's verdict, the performances of the legal adversaries, and the apparent respectability of the accused made it the sensation of the tabloids. Robert Wood was acquitted of the crime, and no one else was ever arrested for it.

1908

CELEBRATING FRANCE AND BRITAIN

A large and successful Franco-British exhibition was held this year near Shepherds Bush. Numerous white stuccoed buildings were erected on 140 acres near Wood Lane; these included a stadium in which the 4th Olympic Games were held. The area was nicknamed the White City, and so it has remained since. Much of it is now occupied by BBC Television.

POLITICAL WOMEN

An Act of 1907 permitted women to sit on borough and county councils. The first woman candidate stood for election to the LCC in Hampstead this year; she represented the Progressive Party, but failed to gain election. As compensation, the first woman mayor was appointed this year – Elizabeth Garrett Anderson in Aldeburgh, Suffolk.

A NEW TUNNEL

The Rotherhithe Tunnel, connecting Rotherhithe with Stepney, was opened on 12 June; it was designed by Sir Maurice Fitzmaurice.

THE FIRST BOY SCOUTS

The best substantiated claim to be the first troop of Boy Scouts in the country is that of the 1st Hampstead. The scoutmaster of the troop wrote in 1910 that

Shortly after the publication of the first part of the handbook [Scouting for Boys by Robert Baden-Powell] a boy called at my house and asked me to form a patrol of Boy Scouts. Assent was willingly given on condition that six other boys were recruited within a week. This was done and the patrol duly formed … Thus in January 1908 our troop came into being and as far as can be discovered it was the first troop to appear in the now well-known uniform.

1909

SELFRIDGES OPENED

The building of the Selfridges store in Oxford Street was a London spectacle. Not only did the construction of this giant steel-framed building provide wonders for the curious but its concept attracted both ridicule and excitement. Londoners were not used to vast retailing ventures – almost all the big London stores had grown gradually with a proprietor (usually a draper) adding shop after shop, knocking through walls to provide a bewildering muddle, and then at a convenient time, perhaps when some insurance money was available after a fire, rebuilding from scratch. But here was someone – an unknown and pushy American – beginning with a store that dwarfed in size every other store in town. As the Ionic columns, equalled in size only by those of the British Museum, were put in place, Londoners could hardly believe that it was a shop being built. The architect was Frank Atkinson.

Gordon Selfridge, born in either 1856 or 1858, had been a junior partner in Marshall Field in Chicago and then opened his own store there in 1902. But he decided to start afresh in London, and from a retailing point of view he arrived at the right time. There was a promising upturn in trade and, most importantly, the newly built tube lines, extending from middle-class suburbs into central London, all served Oxford Street.

When the time arrived to employ staff, queues stretched along Oxford Street for a place in one of the 130 departments envisaged; nearly 10,000 candidates were interviewed, and 1,200 were taken on.

The opening day of 15 March was semi-arctic. Occasional snow blizzards swept Oxford Street, but even so a considerable crowd had gathered by eight in the morning, an hour before opening. An army trumpeter blew a fanfare, Selfridge himself unfurled the house flag, and, simultaneously, drapes hiding each display window were drawn to reveal elaborate tableaux. The doors were opened and the crowd, complete with slush on their feet, converged on to the new Wilton carpet.

The whole day and succeeding weeks were a triumph for Selfridge – his gamble, for the time being, had paid off.

THE V & A OPENS

The Victoria & Albert Museum was opened by the king on 26 June. Its origin was in the Museum of Manufactures opened at Marlborough House in the aftermath of the Great Exhibition; five years later it moved to South Kensington (see 1857). The intention of the museum was to house items displaying the application of fine art to manufacture, but gradually the scope increased away from this narrow emphasis.

The new terracotta building was designed by Aston Webb.

REORGANIZATION IN THE DOCKS

A Royal Commission appointed in 1900 had considered the parlous position of the London docks. A surfeit of space existed now that shipping had moved east towards the mouth of the river, but the facilities were inadequate for that which still came in – the channel wasn't deep enough, the system of labour was outdated and demarcational, and the railway connections were poor – there were too many dock companies, and their charges were excessive.

The Commission recommended the formation of one authority and the abolition of the various dock companies, but it was not until 1909 that the Port of London Authority was set up to spearhead the modernization of the docks while also being responsible for the river itself from Teddington to the sea.

MORE STORE NEWS

Arding & Hobbs, the Clapham department store, was destroyed by fire on 20 December. Hatchard's bookshop in Piccadilly was reconstructed to the designs of Horace Cheston and J. Craddock Perkin. A rebuilt store was opened by Debenham & Freebody (telephone Mayfair 1).

1900s

HOGARTH'S HOUSE OPENED

From 1749 until 1764 William Hogarth had used his Chiswick house as a retreat from the seedier parts of the London he portrayed and enjoyed. This 'little box of a house' had fallen into decay until a Colonel Shipway bought it in 1902, restored it and refurnished it with Hogarth engravings, and in 1909 presented it to the Middlesex County Council as a museum.

AN OBSERVATORY IN HAMPSTEAD

An observatory was established in Hampstead this year, near Whitestone Pond – it still exists. It was the project of the Hampstead Astronomical and General Scientific Society, whose formation was inspired by the availability of a reflecting telescope and the enthusiasm of a local amateur astronomer. Of the 192 members in the first year, 49 were women.

MOVING A MANSION

The remains of Crosby Place in Bishopsgate (see 1466) were this year taken down and moved to the junction of the Embankment and Danvers Street in Chelsea. It was an appropriate site, because Sir Thomas More was once the owner (but probably not a resident) of the Bishopgate house, and the Chelsea site was part of the grounds of his Beaufort House. Crosby Place had also been the home of Sir Walter Ralegh, but in recent years it had been used for a restaurant. In 1908 the University and City Association of London had bought it, and in Chelsea it became the headquarters of the British Federation of University Women until recent years.

1910

THE CINEMA TAKES OVER

The age of the cinema in London effectively began this year with the construction of some of the earliest cinemas and, more ominously, the conversion of theatres. The Ritzy at Brixton (which still survives) was opened, as was the Electric Cinema in Portobello Road. The use of the word 'Electric' was common in the early cinema period; another cinema, called the Electric Pavilion, was built in Holloway Road the same year. In the West End the Windmill Theatre was built as a cinema called the Palais de Luxe, perhaps the first in central London; oddly, it eventually bucked the trend and was converted into a theatre in 1931. From about this year the Greenwich Theatre in London Road was used as a cinema, and, in the Strand, Terry's Theatre became a silver screen as well.

But theatres – riding high on variety and musical comedy – were still being opened. The Finsbury Park Empire, yet another Frank Matcham building, was opened by Oswald Stoll in September, and on Boxing Day (a popular date to launch a new theatre with pantomime) the Wimbledon Theatre began. The most important addition, however, was the London Palladium, rebuilt on the site of a circus and skating rink. It was the project of Walter Gibbons, who wanted to outdo variety rivals such as the Coliseum and the Hippodrome.

A FAMOUS MURDER IN ISLINGTON

The famous murder by Dr Hawley Harvey Crippen of his wife, music-hall artiste Belle Elmore, occurred on 1 February at 39 Hilldrop Crescent, Islington. The house itself has now disappeared and a block of flats is on the site.

Dr Crippen's house at 39 Hilldrop Crescent became a ghoulish attraction after his execution. This postcard depicts Sandy McNab, its new owner.

As murders go it was run-of-the-mill, but it caught the public's imagination. A straightforward love triangle which ended in death was given interest by the elements of mild-mannered, middle-aged paramour, a music-hall victim, and an arrest after the use of modern technology – a telegram sent at sea by the captain of the ship on which Crippen and his lover (disguised as a boy) were fleeing. The house was subsequently opened as a museum of Crippen mementos, but as this was regarded as in very bad taste it was converted instead into a lodging house for music-hall performers, which was hardly much better.

FIRST PERFORMANCES

The ballerina Anna Pavlova made her first London performance on 10 April at the Palace Theatre at Cambridge Circus. She scored an immediate success.

Just down the road, at the London Hippodrome, a Russian ballet company brought *Swan Lake* to London for the first time.

DISCOVERY OF A ROMAN BOAT

Excavation work on the foreshore of the south bank of the Thames for the foundations of County Hall in May revealed the remains of a Roman boat sunk deep in the mud. Made of oak, it measured about 38 ft long and 18 ft wide, and after retrieval it was taken to the London Museum.

POST-IMPRESSIONISTS IN LONDON

It was at the instigation of Roger Fry that an exhibition of 'modern foreign artists' was assembled in London. It was held at the Grafton Gallery, which did not expect much interest in it, but what Fry called the Post-Impressionists became the talk of artistic circles. Pictures by Matisse, Gauguin, Cézanne, Van Gogh, Seurat and Picasso were all on show for the first time. The press was suitably scandalized on behalf of its readers, the public flocked in – either curious or outraged – and Fry was accused of being a subverter of morals and art, and a blatant self-advertiser.

Philip Burne-Jones, the painter's son, castigated the director of the National Gallery for attending the exhibition. 'The deliberate lowering of standards,' he said, 'should not be encouraged by an official imprimatur.' Another critic pontificated that 'Mr Fry … must not be surprised if he is boycotted by decent society.' The apoplexy was not eased by the appearance of both Virginia and Vanessa Stephen dressed in Tahitian sarongs at the exhibition.

NEW MONUMENTS

The statue of the actor Henry Irving outside the National Portrait Gallery was unveiled on 5 December. It is the work of Thomas Brock.

The Admiralty Arch opening into the Mall was completed this year by Sir Aston Webb.

As a plaque notes on the monument, Paul's Cross in St Paul's Churchyard was re-erected this year under the will of H. C. Richards. Previously the old cross had been the venue for open-air proclamations and sermons.

1911

SIEGE IN SIDNEY STREET

Sidney Street, running between Whitechapel Road and Commercial Road, this year achieved a chance notoriety. In December 1910 a group of Russian-speaking anarchists (possibly Letts) had been disturbed robbing a jeweller's in Houndsditch. Three policemen were killed in attempting to arrest them, and there was intense public interest thereafter in their whereabouts. On 3 January 1911 the police surrounded 100 Sidney Street in the belief that they were inside. The besieging forces included 400 armed police and members of several

The Sidney Street Siege in east London in 1911. The marksmen on the ground are Scots Guards.

regiments of soldiers, with Winston Churchill, as home secretary, helping to supervise the affair. One policeman and fireman were killed in the five-hour operation, at the end of which the house was on fire and the two fugitives inside were dead.

MORE CINEMAS

The Radium Cinema in Drayton Gardens was opened this year as a conversion from a gymnasium – it later became known as the Paris Pullman. The Screen on the Green in Upper Street, Islington, has had numerous name changes; it began in 1911 when the Pesarasi Brothers opened the Picture Theatre there. In Charing Cross Road the Cinematograph Theatre was opened – after the Second World War this became one of the several 'news' cinemas that have now completely disappeared. In Finchley Road, Hampstead, the Frognal Bijou Picture Palace opened its doors.

MORE THEATRES

The Victoria Palace opened as a variety hall on 9 November, on the site of the Royal Standard Music Hall; it was built to the design of the almost inevitable Frank Matcham. Originally the building was surmounted by a statue of Anna Pavlova, whom the owner of the theatre had first presented in London, but Pavlova was so superstitious in these matters that she refused to look at the statue when she passed it.

In Portugal Street, near Lincoln's Inn Fields, the London Opera House was opened on 13 November. A misjudged venture of Oscar Hammerstein, this large French Renaissance-style building, designed by Bertie Crewe and seating over 2,400 people, was intended to challenge Covent Garden Theatre as the opera venue in London, but Hammerstein retired hurt and £43,000 poorer the following year. The theatre was open intermittently thereafter for a medley of productions until Oswald Stoll took it over in 1916 and changed its name to the Stoll Theatre; but even he was defeated, and the building was a cinema by 1917.

There was, in any case, theatrical competition nearby in the form of the New Middlesex Theatre of Varieties (later called the Winter Garden), which opened on 30 October. Again, Matcham was the architect and Oswald Stoll one of the partners in the enterprise.

Another building on the periphery of theatreland opened this year was the Prince's Theatre in Shaftesbury Avenue, which is now called the Shaftesbury. Designed by Bertie Crewe, it was intended as a house for melodrama.

This year saw the first performance in this country of Chekhov's *Cherry Orchard*, at the Aldwych Theatre.

CAMDEN TOWN PAINTERS

The Camden Town Group of painters stemmed from the Fitzroy Street Group. Common to both was Walter Sickert, who in 1905 returned to England after nearly seven years abroad and took lodgings in Mornington Crescent, Camden Town. Two years later a group of painters, including Sickert, Spencer Gore, Augustus John, Walter Russell, Harold Gilman and William Rothenstein, were making their reputations from studios in Fitzroy Street. A year after the Post-Impressionist exhibition had enraged London critics, some of the Fitzroy Street Group, anxious to distance themselves from the establishment view of the Post-Impressionists, began a new society called the Camden Town Group. This revolved around Sickert, Gore, Gilman, Charles Ginner and Robert Bevan, and later Jacob Epstein. In 1913 the Camden and Fitzroy Groups merged to form the London Group.

THE FIRST LONDON AERODROME

The first London aerodrome was established at Hendon this year, on the initiative of the aviation pioneer Claude Grahame-White. He had been taught to fly by Blériot, and by 1910 was Britain's best-known pilot.

A STONE VICTORIA

The sculptor Thomas Brock made numerous effigies of Queen Victoria, but his best-known one is that unveiled in front of Buckingham Palace on 16 May this year. Coincidentally it was he, as a young assistant to John Foley, who had finished the figure of her beloved Albert which is part of the Albert Memorial.

1912

A LONDON MUSEUM

Today's Museum of London comprises the old Guildhall Museum, founded in 1826, and the London Museum opened on 8 April 1912 at Kensington Palace. Intended as a museum of London's social life, the latter was here only briefly, moving to Lancaster House, which had been given to the nation by the 1st Lord Leverhulme, in 1914. Here it remained until 1946, when it moved back to Kensington Palace.

EXTENDING THE CENTRAL

With proposals in the air to merge under one management the Underground system and the omnibus companies, the Central Line was extended this year from Bank to Liverpool Street. Construction of tube railways had been otherwise quiet since the frantic activity of the first seven years of the century. The Bakerloo had been extended to Edgware Road in 1907, and from 1913 was to reach Metroland Pinner.

This first heyday of motorized public transport and cabs is reflected in the statistic that only 400 hansom cabs still plied in London, as opposed to well over 7,000 at their peak.

A SALVATIONIST'S FUNERAL

'General' William Booth, founder of the Salvation Army, was buried on 29 August in Abney Park Cemetery with full 'military' honours. Fifty-one Salvation Army brigades accompanied the coffin from the Embankment to the cemetery, and thousands of people lined the route.

DISCONTENT

A demonstration of a different kind was that of the suffragettes in central London on 1 March. Windows were broken, the police were out in force, and Emmeline Pankhurst and Mr and Mrs Pethick were arrested and sent to prison for nine months.

There was a major strike at London Docks, which lasted for ten weeks. It was a disaster for the unions. The management hardly budged from its ground, and men were reinstated in their jobs only grudgingly and had to work alongside others who had continued to work during the strike.

NEW RESTAURANTS

Bertorelli's Restaurant in Charlotte Street was established this year by four Italian brothers. It offered good cheap food, and the place was popular with the artistic community in Fitzrovia.

In the previous year the Ivy Restaurant had been opened in West Street. It has been traditionally patronized by the theatrical profession.

The famous Lyons' Corner House in the Strand was opened this year, complete with the celebrated waitresses called 'nippies'. It wasn't the first corner house – that had been in Coventry Street five years earlier.

A BUILDING FOR THE PEARL

Pearl Assurance opened its handsome building in High Holborn this year, just down the road from its rival, the Prudential; the architects were Moncton & Newman.

1913

WOMEN'S AFFAIRS

Women dominated the headlines. Among the happier items were the opening of the new Bedford College for Women buildings in Regent's Park on 4 July, and the appointment of the first woman magistrate – a Miss Emily Duncan, who was a West Ham Poor Law guardian.

Less happily the suffragettes had to resort to desperate measures to publicize their cause. On 20 February women set fire to the Kew Tea Pavilion. This caused annoyance, but it was hardly a major target. However, on 6 May – the day that the Suffrage Bill was lost in Parliament – an unexploded bomb was found in St Paul's Cathedral. On Derby Day Emily Davidson threw herself in front of the king's horse and was killed. Earlier in the year someone had attempted to burn down Lloyd George's country house, and Mrs Pankhurst was arrested and charged with incitement to commit a felony. She was sentenced at the Old Bailey to three years' imprisonment, and soon afterwards the home secretary introduced what was known as the Cat and Mouse Act, whereby those suffragettes who went on hunger strike in prison were released when their health was in danger and were then re-imprisoned for as many times as it took to complete the sentence.

In May suffragettes attempted to start a fire in the Royal Academy, and on 15 December there was a dynamite explosion at Holloway Prison where Emmeline Pankhurst and Lady Constance Lytton, another prominent suffragette, were kept.

HOME DECORATION

The Omega Workshops, one of the numerous manifestations of the Bloomsbury Group, were opened on 8 July at 33 Fitzroy Square. Largely the project of Roger Fry, Duncan Grant and Vanessa Bell, the aim was to apply Post-Impressionist ideas to articles of everyday use – furniture, fabrics, pottery and the like. A number of young artists worked there, including Wyndham Lewis until he had a row with Fry and went off to found the Vorticist movement. Artists were paid 7s 6d a day or 30s full time. They worked cooperatively on pieces – nothing was signed except with the Omega logo. Though the workshops, which were wound up in 1919, failed to sell to the large retailers, the pieces found a ready market with private buyers.

FLOWERS IN CHELSEA

On 4 May the annual exhibition of flowers by the Royal Horticultural Society was held for the first time in the grounds of the Royal Hospital, Chelsea. Previously the exhibition had taken place in the gardens of the Inner Temple, but the need for a larger space (and the society's poor relations with the Inner Temple) led to the move to Chelsea, where the nearness of Sloane Square Underground station was helpful. Visitors this year included Archduke Franz Ferdinand of Austria, whose assassination the following year precipitated the First World War.

COVENT GARDEN NEARLY SOLD

The state of the property market and increasing criticism of the way in which the duke of Bedford managed Covent Garden Market and the surrounding premises were instrumental in the duke's decision this year to sell his Covent Garden estate. He accepted an offer, variously reported at between £2 million and £2.75 million, from Mr Harry Mallaby-Deeley, Unionist MP for Harrow, a speculator who had recently been involved in the purchase of the Piccadilly Hotel from its bankrupt owners. Though the Covent Garden deal was the talk of the financial world, the duke was pained to discover that he had inadvertently also sold his ownership of boxes at Covent Garden Theatre and the Theatre Royal; Mallaby-Deeley refused to sell them back again.

Not much money changed hands now, since the purchase was to be made in easy stages. Mallaby-Deeley was interested in the development potential of the area, and realized that he had struck a good bargain – so much so that he was able to sell his option to purchase the estate for £250,000 to the pharmaceutical manufacturer Sir Joseph Beecham (father of the conductor) the following year. However, within a month war broke out and the deal between the duke and Beecham was suspended because of restrictions on the application of capital.

ENTERTAINMENT BEFORE THE STORM

The building of theatres and cinemas continued apace before war overtook the economy and people's spirits. The Ambassador's Theatre opened on 5 June, a small building seating only about 450, designed by W. G. R. Sprague as one of a pair of theatres, the other being the St Martin's, although the latter had to wait until 1916 for its opening.

Now that the Underground had reached Golders Green a large Hippodrome was opened there on 26 December. Designed by Bertie Crewe, it began as a variety hall but by 1923 was regularly used as a try-out theatre for productions intended for the West End. Also in Golders Green was the Ionic Theatre, actually a cinema. The building was opened by Anna Pavlova, a local resident, who in 1930 was to make her last public performance at the nearby Hippodrome.

The Rialto cinema, complete with restaurant beneath (which later became the Café de Paris nightclub), was opened this year in Coventry Street.

REFACING THE PALACE

The present, rather unappealing, east front of Buckingham Palace was completed this year by Sir Aston Webb. The basic mansion, designed by Nash originally, had a courtyard open at the east side between wings, but in the 19th century Edward Blore designed an uninspiring range of buildings which joined the two wings and created an east front. Webb was commissioned to give this range more presence, and once he had finished he was knighted in front of it.

A BOOKSHOP FOR POETS

A spectator at the official opening in January of the Poetry Bookshop in what is now Boswell Street, Holborn, was the poet Robert Frost, who, because it was so crowded, perched on the staircase to listen to the readings. The shop was owned by Harold Monro, a minor poet himself, and editor and founder (in 1912) of the *Poetry Review*. Both projects enjoyed more prestige than financial success.

CABBIES ON STRIKE

London's motorized cabmen went on a long strike against the price they were charged for petrol. The strike began on 1 January and ended on 19 March, when they agreed to pay 8d a gallon.

1914

EXPLOSIONS BEFORE THE WAR

The First World War did not begin until 4 August. Before that, in London, suffragettes engineered some remarkably violent incidents. On 1 March a bomb exploded at St John the Evangelist church, Westminster; on 10 March Mary Richardson badly damaged the Velázquez 'Rokeby Venus' at the National Gallery, and on 12 May a portrait of Wellington at the Royal Academy was defaced; on 5 April there was an explosion at St Martin-in-the-Fields, which was followed on 11 June by one at Westminster Abbey, and another three days later at St George Hanover Square. The Women's Enfranchisement Bill was rejected by the Lords on 4 May.

FIRST PERFORMANCES

On 11 April the first British performance of Bernard Shaw's *Pygmalion* took place at His Majesty's Theatre in the Haymarket.

On 9 April what was billed as the world's first full-length film was shown at the Holborn Empire. It was called *The World, the Flesh and the Devil* – a title which might explain its length.

Wagner's *Parsifal* was produced for the first time at Covent Garden on 2 February.

A FURNITURE MUSEUM

The Geffrye Museum of furniture in Kingsland Road was opened on 2 April at a time when the nearby Shoreditch area was the centre of furniture manufacture, although retail sales were concentrated in Tottenham Court Road. The museum was originally a set of 14 almshouses and chapel erected by the Ironmongers' Company in 1715; it was saved from demolition by the London County Council.

DR JOHNSON'S HOUSE SAVED

Dr Johnson had lived at 17 Gough Square from 1746 to 1759 while he compiled his famous *Dictionary*. In 1911, when demolition was threatened, Lord Harmsworth stepped in and bought the house so that it could be opened as a memorial to Johnson. The house opened this year, and in 1929 Harmsworth made the house over to trustees for the benefit of the public.

EXIT THE GERMAN BAND

Hardly a more poignant image exists of the beginning of the First World War in London than the recollection of a woman who, at the Earls Court Exhibition on 4 August, was enjoying an open-air band concert given by a German band, one of the many groups of foreign musicians that made a living in this country. Abruptly, during the concert, the music stopped and the bandmaster announced, 'Ladies and gentlemen, war has been declared.' The musicians silently filed off the bandstand.

1915

WAR OVER LONDON

The threat of aerial bombardment was both a novel and an unnerving one. London had little in the way of air defences; searchlights were used to pinpoint the hostile airships, aeroplanes attempted to bring them down if they could get high enough, and a primitive warning system was established using the services of policemen wearing placards and blowing whistles to sound the alert, and those of Boy Scouts sounding bugles from bicycles to give the all-clear.

The Zeppelins were thought to be a German trump card, but they were rather at the mercy of winds and were difficult to control and manoeuvre. Their first success in London was traumatic. About midnight on 31 May a Zeppelin strafed east London with about 90 incendiaries and explosive bombs, killing five and injuring 35. Practical moves to provide anti-aircraft defences were taken after raids on 7 and 8 September, when Zeppelins attacked south London with the loss of 16 lives, and east London, where another 16 were killed. The worst raid was that of 13 October, when over 40 people were killed. A priest, returning home to Gray's Inn Square, was given up for dead when a bomb exploded nearby. He had been buried in falling brickwork and knocked unconscious, but recovered sufficiently to get on the tube at Chancery Lane and to stay with his father at Hampstead for the rest of the night.

Only one gun was available to give battle that night, and that was located near Wormwood Scrubs. It was decided to carry it to the Artillery Ground, Moorfields, and the journey there took 20 minutes – which says a lot about the speed of the operation and the lack of traffic to hold it up.

The first bomb that fell on the City of London was one that exploded in Fenchurch Street on 8 September, the same day that a Zeppelin was chased all over London by British aeroplanes. Leyton was bombed in August, and Enfield and Epping in September.

Anti-German riots erupted in London in May after the sinking of the *Lusitania* by German torpedoes, and premises owned by traders with German-sounding names were attacked.

Meanwhile, Croydon and Northolt aerodromes were opened for military aircraft.

Kitchener's army consisted of regular soldiers and volunteers, and it was not until 1916 that conscription was introduced. In the meantime an enthusiastic recruitment campaign was held. It began with a grand assembly at the Guildhall on 14 September 1914, but heavy losses of men led to frequent appeals for replacements. Kitchener himself appeared at the Guildhall on 19 July 1915, as part of a new drive. But by the autumn of that year the nature of the war and its conduct was being judged anew, and hearty patriotism was now tempered by circumspection – numerous blinded soldiers returning home were a stark reminder of the trenches. Sir Arthur Pearson, the rich publisher who had himself become blind, founded what became St Dunstan's Hostel for the Blind, first in Bayswater Hill and then, in 1916, at a villa in Regent's Park.

1916

A QUIETER YEAR
Kitchener had predicted that the war would last three years – a forecast received with incredulity as being an overestimate. This year conscription was introduced, confirmation (if any were needed) that he was right to be pessimistic. Though bombing of London continued, it was reduced in both its extent and its effect. On 3 September an airship was shot down over Enfield and its crew were killed after a chase over north London and the Home Counties. The pilot who shot it down, William Robinson, was awarded a VC, but he himself was shot down in April 1917.

A LONG-RUNNING MUSICAL
Before *The Mousetrap* (see 1952) came along, the longest-running stage production in London was *Chu Chin Chow*, a 'musical tale of the East', presented by Oscar Ashe with music by Frederick Norton. It opened on 31 August this year at His Majesty's Theatre in the Haymarket, and closed in July 1921, after a run of 2,238 performances. It cost £5,300 to produce and netted £700,000.

1917

A YEAR OF CASUALTIES
As the Germans introduced Gotha aeroplanes to replace the unwieldy Zeppelins, bombing raids were stepped up. In June a random bomb hit an infant school in Poplar, killing 16 children. The main damage in London was during a raid by about 20 aeroplanes on 7 July. In this a bomb fell on Bartholomew Close, when five were killed; the Ironmongers' Hall in Fenchurch Street was destroyed; an attack was made on the Midland Railway goods yard at St Pancras, when one man was killed; nearby, the German Gymnasium in Pancras Road (before the war the headquarters of a German Gymnastic group but now used by defence volunteers) was hit and badly damaged. On 24 September a 50 kg bomb was dropped outside the Bedford Hotel in Southampton Row – 13 people were killed and 26 injured. In the last raid by a Zeppelin, Swan & Edgar's shop in Piccadilly Circus was hit. A big aeroplane raid took place on 6 December over Chelsea, Brixton, Battersea, Stepney, Whitechapel, Clerkenwell and Shoreditch.

AN EXPLOSION AT SILVERTOWN
In 1894 the firm of Brunner, Mond & Co. had opened a factory in Silvertown to produce caustic soda; at the outbreak of war the plant was adapted by the government for the manufacture of TNT, although the area around was densely populated. Just before seven on the evening of 19 January a vast explosion swept through the works and the locality. Seventy-three people died and 94 were seriously injured; 900 homes were damaged, and the sound of the explosion was heard 100 miles away. The local *Stratford Express* reported that 'The whole heavens were lit in awful splendour. A fiery glow seemed to have come over the dark and miserable January evening, and objects which a few minutes before had been blotted out in the intense darkness were silhouetted against the sky.'

The cause of the explosion was never established.

1918

ARMISTICE
The last bombing raid over London took place on 19 May; an armistice was signed on 11 November. In summary, there had been 12 airship attacks and 19 with aeroplanes on London, but the bombing had not been as destructive or effective as had been feared. In London there were 670 deaths and 1,962 wounded (the national total was 1,413 killed).

A positive result of the war, in which women had filled the jobs of men abroad, was that opposition to women's suffrage crumbled. In February legislation was passed enabling women over 30 to vote, and they did so at the next general election, on 2 December.

An incendiary bomb exploded at Odhams printing factory in Long Acre in November 1918. Thirty-five people were killed and nearly 100 injured.

COVENT GARDEN ESTATE SOLD

The sale by the duke of Bedford of his Covent Garden estate had been suspended at the outbreak of war (see 1913), but on 30 July the duke conveyed the estate – 231 properties and the market – to the Covent Garden Estate Company, of which the late Sir Joseph Beecham's sons, Thomas and Henry, were directors. The Beechams then proceeded to sell off properties, including the magistrates' court and the Theatre Royal, to recover the purchase price, but they retained the market buildings.

COMMUNIST CLUB CLOSED DOWN

The Communist Club, which had rooms at 107 Charlotte Street from 1902, was closed down as being subversive this year. Speakers at the club's meetings had included Marx, Engels, Keir Hardie, William Morris and Bernard Shaw.

1919

THE PROMISED LAND

The LCC this year began buying land – 3,000 acres at first – on a flat plain between Barking, Dagenham and Ilford. In this area the council planned Becontree, the largest garden estate of them all, with tidy arrangements of mainly red-brick houses, some carefully similar, some carefully different. In precisely calculated places shopping parades were planted, or an occasional pub (but not too many), or a clinic and a library. Nothing could be inserted into this plan later, and nothing

taken away, and what was first built was not the seeds of a town but the full realization. Sure of their statistics and observations of human behaviour, the council's planners moved thousands from the East End and elsewhere who were persuaded that Utopia was a front and back garden, an inside lavatory and a private kitchen. To many it was – people who had shared stoves on landings in old, unhygienic houses, or who had brought up children without easy access to hot water. But Becontree was dead in spirit from the moment of its planning, and remains so.

In 1920 the council agreed to the expenditure of £5 million for the erection of 20,000 houses.

DANCING IN HAMMERSMITH

The Hammersmith Palais – once billed as the most famous night spot in the world – was opened in Shepherds Bush Road this year.

1920

REMINDERS OF WAR

After wars come monuments. Numerous war memorials, carved with the names of young people lost in that most fruitless of wars, were built around London. Two monuments, both unveiled this year, were not to be forgotten. One was the Cenotaph in Whitehall, a simple pillar designed by Sir Edwin Lutyens, adorned only with the flags of the armed services and the merchant navy and its name, from the Greek for 'empty tomb'.

The statue of Edith Cavell in St Martin's Place had a mixed reception, some people not liking the modernistic design. Cavell, who had cared for both Allied and German troops under the auspices of the Red Cross in Holland, had been shot for aiding the escape and return of Allied soldiers to the battlefront. She herself thought the sentence a just one, but it caused outrage in this country. The words now on the statue – PATRIOTISM IS NOT ENOUGH I MUST HAVE NO HATRED OR BITTERNESS FOR ANYONE – were not in the sculptor's original model and were

After the First World War, the LCC began buying land at Barking and Dagenham on which to build its vast Becontree estate.

placed there at the insistence of a women's group. The artist was George Frampton.

The Imperial War Museum was established by Act of Parliament this year and opened on 10 June in temporary premises at Crystal Palace.

A THEATRE IN HAMPSTEAD
An old drill hall at Hollybush Vale in Hampstead was this year converted into the Everyman Theatre; the opening night was 15 September. The building still survives as the Everyman cinema. Despite its artistic successes, the theatre lasted only until 1933 – today it would have a subsidy.

The likes of Edith Evans, Mrs Patrick Campbell and Claude Rains performed here. The most famous production was the 1924 production of *The Vortex*, which its writer, Noël Coward, directed and starred in. The lord chancellor, whose duties included theatre censorship, objected to a reference in the play to two young ladies going away together, as it might be inferred that they were lesbians. Coward's reaction was 'If only I had thought of that myself!'

A LONDON AIRPORT
Briefly Hounslow Airport had served as London's civil airport, complete with customs offices, but on 29 March this year Croydon Airport replaced it, being not only on a main road, but nearer to the Continent. It was gradually extended, and remained London's airport until the Second World War, after which Heathrow superseded it. The old Croydon buildings mainly survive as part of the industrial estate which now covers the area, and the Aerodrome Hotel is still in business.

REVIVAL IN HAMMERSMITH
The new Palais de Dance was not the only attraction in Hammersmith. The Lyric Theatre had reached the low ebb of being known as the 'Blood and Flea Pit', but in 1918 Nigel Playfair had taken the place over and on 5 June 1920 he presented a famous revival of John Gay's *The Beggar's Opera*. It ran for 1,463 performances – an unheard-of run for a theatre outside the West End.

FOUNDATION OF THE TAVISTOCK CLINIC
The first outpatients' clinic dealing in psychotherapy was founded this year off Malet Street, near Tavistock Square; its pioneer, Dr H. Crichton-Miller, had acquired much experience of treating shell-shocked soldiers in the last war. The Tavistock Clinic is now housed in a modern building in Hampstead.

NEW HEADQUARTERS FOR WATER
The tradition of good architecture in the water business was maintained this year with the opening of a new headquarters for the Metropolitan Water Board in Rosebery Avenue, on the former site of the offices and works of the New River Company. The building, officially opened in May, was designed by Austen Hall. It is now converted into private apartments.

DEVONSHIRE HOUSE SOLD
Devonshire House, the 18th-century mansion in Piccadilly between Berkeley Street and Stratton Street designed by William Kent, was this year sold to a consortium of London and Liverpool financiers and the builder's Cubitt's; the price was reported as £1 million. A block of flats, showrooms and an Underground station took its place.

1921

BIRTH CONTROL IN THE OPEN
Sensibilities were outraged this year when Dr Marie Stopes and her husband, Humphrey Vernon-Roe, founded the Mothers' Clinic for Birth Control in Marlborough Road, off Holloway Road.

THE LAST DOCK
The last dock to be built in central London, the George V Dock, was a long-delayed extension of the Albert Dock. It was opened on 8 July, when a steam yacht, carrying the king, cut through a silk tape at the entrance. The dock was a substantial construction – large enough to take the *Mauretania* liner in 1939.

1922

THE OPENING OF COUNTY HALL
The new headquarters of the London County Council, County Hall, was formally and partly opened on 17 July. The man chosen to design this colossal and prestigious building was Ralph Knott, an almost unknown architect, aged 29, who had been an assistant in the office of Sir Aston Webb. Knott died young, before County Hall was complete, and, apart from a few houses, this vast building was his only commission.

BROADCASTING BEGINS
The first regular broadcast from the British Broadcasting Company (as it was then called) was made on 14 November this year, but it was not until March 1923 that the BBC moved its 2LO station to a decrepit building in Savoy Hill, where it developed broadcasting until May 1932, when there was a further move to Broadcasting House in Portland Place.

A PRIVATE HEARING
In 1919 the young composer William Walton had gone to live at the Sitwell family house at 2 Carlyle Square, Chelsea, and he stayed there intermittently until the early 1930s. It was at this house on 22 January

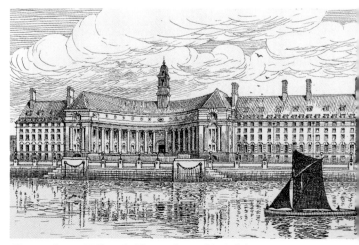

The new County Hall on the Thames, designed by Ralph Knott. It now contains an aquarium and is scheduled to be a hotel.

1922 that the first performance of *Façade* was given to an invited audience, with Edith Sitwell as reciter and Walton himself conducting.

An Elegant Bank
The most elegant high-street bank in London is that of Barclay's at 160 Piccadilly. It was originally built as a showroom for Wolseley Motors Ltd by William Curtis Green, but when that business went bankrupt in 1926 the same architect was brought in to convert the building into a bank, while retaining its unique Japanese and lacquered features.

A New Waterloo
The present Waterloo station was formally opened by Queen Mary on 21 March. It was long overdue, for the terminus had been a jumble of platforms and facilities. Work had begun on rebuilding in 1909, but completion was interrupted by the war.

New Building for the PLA
The Port of London Authority had commissioned a new headquarters on Trinity Square in 1913, when the London docks were still thriving. Sir Edwin Cooper designed a front entrance of Corinthian columns surmounted by a massive tower, but because of the war the building was not completed until this year.

1923

Wembley Stadium Opened
Wembley Stadium was built to house part of the 1924 British Empire Exhibition, but was opened on 28 May this year for the football cup final between Bolton and West Ham. It was nearly a disastrous debut, because the stadium, with a capacity of 120,000, was invaded by far more fans than it could take and thousands had to take refuge on the pitch. The stadium, with its famous twin towers, was designed by Sir John Simpson and Maxwell Ayrton, with Sir Owen Williams as engineer.

Astaire in London
The dancer Fred Astaire made his first appearance on the London stage this year in a musical offering called *Stop Flirting*, at the old Shaftesbury Theatre in Shaftesbury Avenue, now demolished. The evening began with some coldness and polite applause, but ended in encores and critics hailing Astaire and his sister, Adele, as 'dancers of genius'.

Last Service for the Deaf and Dumb
St Saviour's Church for the Deaf and Dumb had been opened at 419 Oxford Street in 1874, at the instigation of a charity that sought to provide employment and religious instruction for deaf and dumb people. The church, designed by Sir Arthur Blomfield, was unique inasmuch as the prime concern of the architect was to provide as much light and visibility as possible. The Grosvenor estate was anxious to regain the site for redevelopment and declined to renew the church's lease. The last service was on 31 December this year, and the church was relocated in Acton in a building designed by Sir Edward Maufe.

A New Couturier
The young Norman Hartnell, just out of university and the Footlights revue, set up a couture establishment in Bruton Street this year. It was the beginning of a successful society career.

1924

The British Empire Exhibition
The British Empire was at its most influential when this exhibition opened at Wembley on St George's Day this year. Fifty-six countries of the Empire took part, and the whole patriotic extravaganza was opened by the king. The exhibition was, however, without funds and was built on debt.

The event was largely the work of a former civil servant, Ulick Wintour. He dreamed of a permanent Imperial city in which all the countries involved had their own quarters, and he therefore bought 216 acres of nondescript land at Wembley which could now be reached by the Underground railway. At least £1 million was needed to advance the exhibition, and Wintour was lucky that the prince of Wales took up the project as one which could provide jobs for the many unemployed — at one time about 12,000 people were working on the construction. Many of the 'palaces', even the Indian Pavilion, were built in concrete. There were a 40-acre amusement park, a West African walled city, a model coal mine, and a railway running through the park. Almost at the last moment the building workers went on strike and the Labour government was obliged to overcome this with a police presence.

The opening ceremony — broadcast live by the BBC and held in miserable weather — went off as scheduled; Sir Edward Elgar conducted a 3,000-strong choir to celebrate the occasion. *The Times* trumpeted 'the wondrous reality of Britain's might and magnitude, her grandeur and her glory'.

A Road to Southend
Another part of outer London was being developed. The London–Southend road was opened by Prince Henry, precipitating a sprawl of factories through the marshlands of Barking and Dagenham.

A New Fortune
The Fortune Theatre in Russell Street is notable in at least three respects: it was the first theatre built in the West End after the war; with its vaguely medieval features, it was a break from the Matcham/Sprague grandiloquence of the Edwardian era; and it incorporates beneath it a passageway into the Crown Court Scottish church at the rear. The attractive theatre, designed by Ernest Schaufelberg, opened on 8 November with a play written by the owner, but its main successes have been since 1956.

Woolworth's in London
The bazaar shops of F. W. Woolworth came slowly to London. Frank Winfield Woolworth had established a chain of shops in America, and opened one in Liverpool in 1909, but by 1916 the only branches in London were in Edgware Road and Deptford High Street. By 1926, however, there were 19 of them, including a large store opened this year at 311 Oxford Street.

Dickens's House Bought
Charles Dickens lived at 48 Doughty Street from March 1837 until 10 December 1839. The family moved here a few days after his first wedding anniversary and the birth of his first child, when *Pickwick Papers* was the rage. Dickens, who paid a rent of £80 a year, employed a cook, a housemaid, a nurse and a manservant. His happiness in his new home was shattered on 7 May when his sister-in-law, Mary

Hogarth, for whom he had a decided passion, died in the house. *Pickwick* and *Oliver Twist*, both produced as serials, were continued here, and *Nicholas Nickleby* was begun.

The house was in danger of demolition in 1922, and the Dickens Fellowship hastily secured some kind of title to it while money was raised; in 1924 the purchase was completed. The house was opened to the public in 1925. It contains mementoes of Dickens and his family, portraits, and some of their furniture.

MORLEY COLLEGE MOVES
Morley College, founded by Emma Cons in the back rooms of the Old Vic theatre, had outgrown its premises. A new building (destroyed in the last war) was opened on 10 December in Westminster Bridge Road.

ST JOAN IN LONDON
The first performance of one of Shaw's finest plays, *St Joan*, was on 26 March at the New Theatre. Sybil Thorndike was in the title role.

1925

SAVING THINGS
Undoubtedly the most important prize of the conservationists this year was the acquisition of the fields south of Kenwood House in Highgate. In 1914 the Commons Preservation Society had learned that Lord Mansfield, the owner of the house and its grounds, intended to sell the whole estate for development; it amounted to about 200 acres, including two lakes and three of the Highgate Ponds. Mansfield agreed to postpone the sale to speculators if £550,000 could be found to purchase for the public. War then intervened, but afterwards the Kenwood Preservation Council, under the chairmanship of the soap magnate Sir Arthur Crosfield, took up the matter again. But public response was very poor. A new target was set – merely the purchase of the meadows and woodland south of Kenwood House – an admission that the house was beyond capture. These purchases were completed on 23 February this year and the land was merged with Parliament Hill Fields.

In the same year Edward Cecil Guinness, 1st earl of Iveagh, bought Kenwood House and its grounds and made clear his intention of donating them to the nation. This generous gift became real when Iveagh died in 1927.

Not far away, in Keats Grove, Hampstead, the house in which John Keats spent much of his last few years was opened as a museum this year. In fact in Keats's time the house was two houses – one being that in which his beloved Fanny Brawne had lodged. In 1839 the two properties were bought by Eliza Chester, a retired actress, and converted into one residence, but by 1920 there was threat of demolition, and only a spirited fund-raising campaign, in which Americans shamed the home country, saved it.

In south London, Charlton House, a magnificent Jacobean mansion previously owned by a family which also provided the lords of the manor of Hampstead, was acquired by Greenwich Council.

There had been two notable triumphs in the previous year. Swakeleys, a 17th-century mansion in Ickenham, had been saved by Humphrey Talbot from demolition and then sold on to the Foreign Office Sports Association; it is now converted to offices.

In Brentford the local council stepped in to acquire Boston Manor, a red-brick early-17th-century house, now open to the public.

A NEW FORTNUM'S
Fortnum & Mason was founded some time in the reign of George III, when Charles Fortnum, a court footman, began a grocery shop – he first appears in the rate books for Piccadilly in 1770. It seems likely that he continued at court, which he probably supplied, and, at the same time, worked in his shop until his retirement *c.* 1789. The shop in question was on part of the site of the present store. Mason does not appear in the title before 1817, by which time the business was described as 'grocers and tea dealers'; it is also likely that nearby Mason's Yard was connected with the business.

The shop was greatly expanded in the later part of the 19th century, when adjacent premises were swallowed up. The present building, designed by Wimperis, Simpson & Guthrie, was begun this year.

A NEW LIBERTY'S
The reputation of Liberty's store had increased greatly. Oriental furniture and china, fabrics from the famous Silver Studio, and the classic Liberty patterns of peacocks, peonies and pheasants gave the firm a unique retailing niche; and by now clothes were a sizeable part of the business – no shop was more in tune with the elegant fashions of the 1920s.

Having purchased nearby properties, Liberty's now owned an island site together with a limited frontage on Regent Street: this arrangement was preferred because the store was not happy with the rebuilding style of Regent Street – the scale was wrong for its business. So, tucked away outside the building restrictions imposed on Regent Street, Liberty's was rebuilt from about this year in a semi-Tudor style, as though a series of shops, to the design of Edwin and E. Stanley Hall. The layout bucked the trend – no clear-cut design here – in fact, the uninitiated shopper is as much confused as in the old Gamage's, where it seemed possible to discover a new room on each visit.

THE FOUNDLING SALE
The Foundling Hospital owned some lucrative acres in the centre of Bloomsbury – far more than it needed – and it was thought anyhow that the children would be healthier in the country. This year the hospital entered into a sale contract for the property with a Mr White, at a reported price of £1,650,000. He intended to transfer Covent

Kenwood House and its grounds were bequeathed to the nation by Earl Iveagh in 1927, including his collection of paintings.

Garden Market here and develop surrounding land with industrial premises. This was vehemently opposed by local residents, and the scheme fell through. When the property was once more advertised for sale, it was taken up by a voluntary committee, headed by Lord Rothermere, so that the open space could as far as possible be preserved for the use of children – the Harmsworth Memorial Playground is the result of this. The hospital then bought back a quarter of the site and built itself new headquarters here which today includes an art gallery.

BARRYMORE ON STAGE

The American actor John Barrymore decided to play Hamlet in London, but no English producer dared back an American in the title role. Barrymore therefore financed his own production, and with an all-English cast, including Fay Compton as Ophelia, he opened at the Haymarket Theatre on 19 February. James Agate of the *Sunday Times* declared his performance 'magnificent', and the scheduled six-week run was extended by nine weeks – Barrymore made a profit of £10,000.

While here, Barrymore was asked earnestly by a member of a women's organization devoted to the advancement of the arts if he thought that Hamlet had ever had sexual relations with Ophelia. He replied, 'Only in the Chicago production, madam.'

GOING WEST

The first stretch of the Great West Road (today's A4) was opened by the king this year – it began where the Chiswick flyover is now, and went to Brentford and Hounslow. The construction of the road opened up the area for industry, and some of the more famous industrial buildings such as the Gillette, Pyrene and Firestone factories were built as a result.

A NEW IRONMONGERS' HALL

The Ironmongers' Hall in Fenchurch Street was the only livery hall bombed in the First World War. This year the company erected a new building off Aldersgate Street, to an attractive neo-Tudor design by Sydney Tatchall – even handmade bricks were used. This hall escaped destruction in the Second World War while all around it was flattened, and it even survived the erection of the Barbican and the Museum of London, both of which isolate it from passing gaze.

1926

SELFRIDGE EXPANDS

Gordon Selfridge had made enough money from his new store in Oxford Street to expand. This year he took over Whiteley's in Westbourne Grove – a store renowned more for its sensational happenings and publicity stunts than for a secure balance sheet – and Jones Brothers in Holloway Road. The latter shop, begun as a draper's in a small way in 1870, now claimed, like Whiteley's, to be a 'Universal Provider'.

INVENTIONS

The 500,000th telephone was installed this year, and, to gain the most publicity, it was put in the Press Gallery at the House of Commons.

At 22 Frith Street on 26 January, John Logie Baird, a Scottish electrical engineer, demonstrated television to an informal assembly of

The interior of Aldridge's Horse Repository in Upper St Martin's Lane. Orion House now stands on the site.

members of the Royal Institution. In 1924 the impoverished Baird had transmitted an image a few feet in the attic which served as his residence in Hastings; two years later he moved into two attic rooms in Frith Street. The apparatus used in this first public demonstration of television is now in the Science Museum.

A NEW PARK IN ACTON

Gunnersbury Park, on the Ealing–Acton border, was on 21 May opened to the public under the joint administration of Ealing and Acton councils. It consisted of about 200 acres divided, since the early 19th century, into two parts, each with a house – one called Gunnersbury Park, owned by the Rothschild family since 1836, the other Gunnersbury House.

HORSES DISAPPEAR

There is no better evidence of the reduced number of horses in London than the last horse sale this year at Aldridge's Horse Repository in Upper St Martin's Lane. This well-known auction house had been the principal place for acquiring middle-class and tradesmen's horses since the mid 18th century, but car sales, begun in 1907, were now the profitable part of the business. When Aldridge's moved out to St Pancras in 1940 they also sold greyhounds.

Congestion caused by cars was making itself felt, and the first roundabout system was introduced this year, in Piccadilly Circus.

1927

MORE ENTERTAINMENT

Though this was mostly a period of large cinemas, three new theatres were opened. The Arts Theatre Club had been founded in 1925 'to create a social rendez-vous with all the amenities of a London club, and bring together in an artistic and congenial atmosphere those interested

1900s

The official opening of the rebuilt Regent Street in June 1927. George V and Queen Mary drive north along the flag-bedecked street.

in the theatre from both sides of the curtain'; more to the point, it could encourage the work of new writers and be free of the constraints of theatre censorship. The new building in Great Newport Street, designed by P. Morley Horder, was opened on 20 April this year with a revue by Herbert Farjeon.

On the first floor of 6 New Compton Street another theatre club, called Play-Room Six, began in January; when, two years later, it moved down to the ground floor it changed its name to the Players' Theatre. In 1934 the club moved to the old Evans' Music Hall at 43 King Street, Covent Garden, and then went out of business. Two years later another theatre club opened there, using the same name, but with a penchant for Victorian music hall. It was this theatre which kept the genre going into modern times in the building beneath Charing Cross railway station that had once been Gatti's Music Hall.

Grander, but far less durable, was the Carlton Theatre in Haymarket; this opened with a musical on 27 April, but was converted to a cinema two years later.

And it was cinemas which held the attention. The Plaza in Lower Regent Street had been opened in 1926; this year the Astoria, in the shell of the old Crosse & Blackwell building in Charing Cross Road, was opened. The last performance of drama took place in February at the Empire Theatre, Leicester Square, before demolition and the erection of a cinema.

A different kind of entertainment was begun in the windswept acres of White City – greyhound racing. This began here on 20 June, and the sport was also presented at Harringay Stadium later in the year.

REGENT STREET FINISHED

The reconstruction of Regent Street in its present, rather ponderous, form was completed this year. The king and queen drove up it to celebrate the occasion on 23 June.

A POST OFFICE TUNNEL

The Pneumatic Despatch Railway, which had promised so much in transporting mail between sorting offices (see 1863), had long since lain dormant, a victim of design faults which could not be remedied. In 1913 the Post Office decided to construct a new underground railway to carry mail between principal sorting offices and main-line stations. But war intervened, and it was not until 1927 that the system was completed. It is a miniature electric railway, without drivers, and is fully automated to receive mail from chutes.

LINDBERGH IN LONDON

An enormous crowd gathered at Croydon Airport on 29 May to welcome Charles Lindbergh, the first man to have flown solo across the Atlantic. By the time he arrived in Croydon, via Paris and Brussels, he had flown 3,610 miles in his small Ryan aeroplane. The *Daily Sketch* hired an air-force pilot and his DH50 to get pictures of Lindbergh in his cockpit as he came over England, but it was found that the wing of the Ryan obscured Lindbergh's face. By sign language the problem was conveyed to Lindbergh, and at treetop height near Croydon he leaned out of the cockpit window so that the other pilot could take photographs of him.

At Croydon numerous other craft circled around in those days of lax air control; spectators, estimated at 120,000, rushed on to the airfield, pushing aside the small posse of police, to drag Lindbergh from his cockpit, leaving many anxious pilots stranded above anxiously looking at their fuel gauges.

THE BEGINNINGS OF NATIONAL CAR PARKS

National Car Parks, a company now familiar all over London, began this year when a Colonel Frederick Lucas and his wife rented some land opposite White City in Wood Lane. There, wearing a peaked cap to make the venture look respectable, he operated a car park for those visiting the arena, but he hardly made money for years. He formed a company in 1931, and by 1947 had 650 employees.

1928

A NEW LCC STYLE

The London County Council had embarked on two massive housing schemes – Becontree and another called St Helier in the Sutton area, both neo-Georgian, monotonous and much influenced by garden-city ideals. In 1927/8 a quite different architectural style emerged from the LCC when the Ossulston Street Estate north of Euston Road, at Somers Town, was built. The scheme, reminiscent of Viennese municipal architecture, was an early example of local-authority high-rise. The architect, Topham Forest, included striking high arches into each of the polygonal courts, and balanced these with very strong horizontal balcony lines.

MAKING TOBACCO IN CAMDEN TOWN

The origins of the Carreras tobacco firm are not clear. An advertising leaflet published by the company in 1928 claims that it was established in 1788. One story is that it began with a Spanish maker of cigarettes in Soho who owned a black cat which sunned itself in his window – an animal subsequently commemorated in the most famous Carreras brand. The first known address of the company is Museum Street in 1851, and towards the end of the century its factory was at 238–240 City Road.

The *Evening Standard* in December 1946 reported on the death of a William Yapp, who left £4.5 million which derived from an early

investment in Carreras when it consisted of little more than a Knightsbridge tobacconist, where cigarettes were made by hand. Yapp bought a controlling interest in the firm and later met Bernhard Baron, who wanted to market a patent cigarette-making machine, and they went into business together. Baron also founded the Rothman cigarette company.

It was Baron who commissioned what became known as the Black Cat factory in Hampstead Road, on the site of gardens fronting Mornington Crescent. Completed in November 1928, it was built in Egyptian style, similar to Firestone House (see below), and its two large black stone cats outside had sufficiently endeared themselves to the public for protests to be made when, Carreras having departed, the building was blandly transformed into offices in the 1960s. In 1999, the new Taiwanese owners restored the building to its former exterior glory, and put the cats back.

BUILDINGS OF DISTINCTION

The Firestone factory building on the Great West Road at Hounslow was completed this year. Designed by Thomas Wallis, it was Egyptian in style, like a giant industrial mansion, and, lit up at night, it was a commanding sight. It was wantonly destroyed by the Trafalgar House Company in 1980, just before a listing was to be obtained.

The underground concourse of Piccadilly Circus station, designed by Charles Holden, was completed on 10 December. It was hailed as a masterpiece, but over the years it lost some of its features and received other unsuitable ones, so that by the time of its renovation in the 1980s it was in a bad state. Holden was also designing the head-quarters of London Transport in Broadway, which featured sculptures by Jacob Epstein, Henry Moore and Eric Gill.

The Ossulston Street Estate at Somers Town, designed by the LCC Architect's Department. It has strong Viennese influences.

The Carreras tobacco factory, Mornington Crescent, was built in an Egyptian mode then fashionable for some factories and cinemas.

Palladium House, at 1 Argyll Street, was built this year by Raymond Hood, an American architect, in a spectacular combination of black granite and floral motifs.

In Park Lane, the Grosvenor House Hotel was built to a design of Alfred Edwards, with a colonnaded west front by Lutyens. It was the only hotel in London to contain a swimming pool, and from 1929 a skating rink too.

SAVING MANSIONS

Chiswick House, the Palladian villa built and designed by its owner, Richard Boyle, 3rd earl of Burlington, was this year acquired by the Middlesex County Council for public use.

Valence House, the only old mansion of any importance left in Dagenham, was this year bought by the local council and is now a local-history centre and museum. It is basically a wood-framed house of the late 16th century with 18th-century additions.

GREYHOUNDS IN THE EAST

Greyhound stadiums were opened at both Clapton and West Ham this year, following the successful introduction of the sport at White City the year before.

AN AIRPORT AT CROYDON

These were stirring times in Croydon. After the Lindbergh landing on 2 May this year, the new airport buildings of 1927 were opened. A contemporary description of the terminal noted that:

A few shallow steps lead one into the spacious booking hall, where an arrival and departure indicator occupies the central space. The air line companies' public offices occupy the ground floor, while some of their private offices are situated on the floor above. One gets the immediate impression that civil aviation in England has been established on a sound basis, that it is a reality and not a toy played with by enthusiasts.

It was the first major civil airport in the world.

1900s

1929

FIRST PERFORMANCES

Yehudi Menuhin, aged 13, gave his first public violin performance, at the Royal Albert Hall, on 10 November.

In July, Noël Coward's *Bitter Sweet* opened at His Majesty's Theatre, Haymarket. It was an instant success, and ran for 697 performances.

The Russian School of Dancing was established by Marie Rambert in an old Congregational school, later called the Mercury Theatre, in Ladbroke Road.

Paul Robeson appeared in Jerome Kern's *Show Boat* in London, and introduced 'Ol' Man River' to British audiences. He was an immediate success, and was entertained by many distinguished artists. When he was invited to a party in his honour at the Savoy Hotel he was refused entry to the Savoy Grill because he was black.

END OF THE WORKHOUSES

A Local Government Act this year abolished workhouses, and the last meetings of the Poor Law guardians were held on 31 May. Thereafter, responsibility for the homeless poor passed to the London County Council.

MORE ENTERTAINMENT

Still more theatres were being built. Two had been opened in 1928 – the Piccadilly on 27 April, designed by Bertie Crewe, and the Embassy Theatre at Swiss Cottage. The Piccadilly was almost immediately taken over for 'talkies', but reverted to drama at the end of 1929. The Embassy was a conversion of the old Hampstead Conservatoire of Music, and was in 1957 converted for use by the Central School of Speech and Drama.

The Dominion Theatre, in Tottenham Court Road, opened on 3 October 1929, but was a cinema within three years.

In Catherine Street, the Duchess Theatre was opened on 25 November. The architect of this unusual mock-Tudor building was Ewan Barr, and inside there were sculptured bas-reliefs by Maurice Lambert. The first production, a First World War play, had the young Emlyn Williams in a minor role – six years later Williams starred here in his own play *Night Must Fall*.

Less glamorously, the Conway Hall in Red Lion Square was opened in September. This hall, the headquarters of the South Place Ethical Society, is used for talks and music – the chamber-music concerts, which are still held here regularly, began in 1887.

1930

A FLUSH OF THEATRES

Theatres are built by optimistic people when the affairs of the nation seem thriving, and in 1930 and 1931 they were still being opened. In 1930 no less than six theatres began, all of which survive today in some form or other.

The fourth Adelphi Theatre in the Strand opened on 3 December, with a musical show. It was designed, according to the *Architects' Journal*, with 'a complete absence of curves', by Ernest Schaufelberg. The Cambridge Theatre in Earlham Street opened on 4 September with a revue starring Beatrice Lillie; the building was by Wimperis, Simpson & Guthrie.

Nearby, in Charing Cross Road, the Phoenix Theatre opened the same month with a smash hit – Noël Coward's *Private Lives*; the original cast included the author, Laurence Olivier and Gertrude Lawrence. The architects were Sir Giles Gilbert Scott, Bertie Crewe and Cecil Masey.

At the junction of Old Compton Street and Greek Street the Prince Edward Theatre opened in April; six years later it became a cabaret restaurant called the London Casino. After the last war it was converted to take 'Cinerama' films, but since then has reverted to its original name and purpose as a theatre.

Yet another theatre opened in September – the Whitehall Theatre, on the site of the 17th-century Ye Olde Ship Tavern. It became famous after the last war for its 'Whitehall Farces'.

In December the Leicester Square Theatre opened – a venture which made the proprietor bankrupt, and within a year the building was sold for conversion to a cinema.

A NOTABLE CINEMA

In this period of cinema building, the most notable this year was the Astoria in Seven Sisters Road, Holloway. Designed by E. A. Stone (who had also been the architect for the Whitehall Theatre above), this striking building was opened by the Islington mayor with fanfares of trumpets from Life Guards. In the foyer there was a green and gold fountain with goldfish; a model Spanish village surrounded the 4,000-seat auditorium. The entertainment on the first day included a Ronald Colman film, a stage show and a large orchestra.

The building in more recent years became the Rainbow, a celebrated rock venue, and since then has been the headquarters of an evangelical religious organization.

A DISASTER FOR GAMAGE'S

The successful department store of A. W. Gamage in Holborn opened, in September, a new store at the western end of Oxford Street, on its south side. It was a financial disaster, and closed within eight months. Fortunately for the Holborn store, the new building – which cost over £1 million to build – was owned by a separate Gamage company, and it was this which was forced into liquidation. The store, much altered, is now occupied by C & A Modes.

A HOUSE ON TOP OF THE HILL

At the top of Hampstead Village, where East Heath Road joins Heath Street, stood a large house called Bellmoor which had remarkable views over London and the suburbs. It had been the home of Thomas J. Barratt, Hampstead local historian and manager of Pear's Soap, a product he had made popular by the use of the famous 'Bubbles' painting by Millais, and the launch of the *Pear's Cyclopaedia*. His old house was demolished this year and gave way to a block of flats of the same name; affixed to them is a plaque noting that they are 435½ ft above sea level and higher than the cross of St Paul's.

A MUSEUM IN WALTHAMSTOW

The Vestry House Museum in Walthamstow opened this year; it occupies an old workhouse built in 1729. The building had seen a number of uses – police station, armoury and institution – but now holds exhibits depicting the history of the locality.

A NEW MARKS & SPARKS

Marks & Spencer was now a mature organization. A recognizable architectural style had been adopted – many of the 1930s stores still survive – and customers found consistent interior layouts with excellent lighting and clear descriptive price tags. The decade was one of considerable expansion for the company, not least in central London. The first store in Oxford Street – the one next to Selfridges – was opened this year, and the 'Pantheon' store, on the eastern stretch of Oxford Street, was opened in 1938. This latter store takes its name from the Pantheon assembly rooms, which were originally on the site. In 1931 Marks & Spencer opened its headquarters in Baker Street.

A Folk Dance Home

In the 1920s there had been a resurgence of interest in traditional English dance and song, largely due to the enthusiasm and diligence of musician Cecil Sharp. He founded the English Folk Dance Society in 1911, and when he died in 1924 he left it his library. The Dance Society amalgamated with the Folk Song Society, and together as the English Folk Dance and Song Society they built neo-Georgian headquarters in Regent's Park Road, Camden Town, which were opened this year. The architect was H. M. Fletcher.

1931

Building at Hay's Wharf

In 1926 the church of St Olave, Tooley Street – little used and certainly dilapidated – was pulled down apart from its tower. In 1928 legislation was obtained to sell the site and the tower to Hay's Wharf for redevelopment. This provoked some protest, and for years afterwards members of Parliament who had voted for the necessary bill were reminded of their action by a local resident who sent them a postcard each anniversary printed with the words: 'In affectionate remembrance of St Olave's Churchyard and Tower, which "birthright" of Bermondsey 149 members of the House of Commons "sold" for "a mess of potage" on May 14th, 1928.'

On the site was completed this year a distinguished new block for Hay's Wharf by the architect H. Goodhart-Rendel – it is now a listed building. The style is quintessential 1930s, with glazed pottery reliefs on the river side designed by Frank Dobson.

The Courtauld Established

The Courtauld business was transformed in 1904 when the family silk-weaving firm bought the British rights to manufacture rayon yarn by the viscose process. It made Samuel Courtauld immensely rich. Fortunately he was a lifelong art patron; not only did he amass an important collection of paintings at his home at 20 Portman Square, but he gave the Tate Gallery £50,000 with which it bought pictures. In 1931 he provided funds for the endowment of the Courtauld Institute of Art, which was very soon established in his own magnificent house.

'A Wonder Building of Modern Commerce'

This year saw the completion of Unilever House at the junction of Victoria Embankment and New Bridge Street. It was 'designed to accommodate 4,000 workers under the most ideal conditions conceivable … What worker there could fail to be happy and efficient?' The architecture, by J. Lomax Simpson and Sir John Burnet, is Thirties Classical, eschewing the modernity displayed in the Hay's Wharf headquarters of the year before, or in the *Daily Express* building (see below) also completed in 1931.

Unilever was the creation of the soap magnate Lord Leverhulme,

The Daily Express *building in Fleet Street by Ellis & Clarke. Like most newspapers, the* Express *has now moved from Fleet Street.*

whose Sunlight Soap and margarine products were the mainstay of the business. The company had moved to this site by 1924, when it occupied the old De Keyser Hotel, but after a merger with a Dutch margarine company in 1929 a new building was necessary. Particular care was taken to reduce noise getting into the building; to this end the ground floor has a blind wall to the road and the upper storeys are stepped back so that a thick glass roof on the projecting ground floor can let in light but no sound.

Buildings for Newspapers

The mid-1920s to mid-1930s saw a concentration of new newspaper buildings on both sides of Fleet Street. Northcliffe House in Tudor Street, designed by Ellis & Clarke, was particularly notable, as was the stylish but rather old-fashioned *Daily Telegraph* building in Fleet Street, designed by Elcott & Sutcliffe with Thomas Tait in 1928. The most innovatory was the *Daily Express* offices and factory in Fleet Street, clad in black glass and chrome, and reputed to be the first curtain-wall building in London; this, too, was the work of Ellis & Clarke.

The First Tesco

Jack Cohen, born in the City of London in 1898, the fifth son of a Jewish tailor, decided after the First World War to go into grocery, and soon operated market stalls in various East End streets. His most popular commodity was tea, which he bought wholesale from T. E. Stockwell of Messrs Torring & Stockwell, and it was from the initials

TES and the first two letters of his own name that he contrived the brand name 'Tesco' for his tea. The first two Tesco shops were established in 1931 in Burnt Oak, and in Becontree where the same year the Ford Motor Works was built.

NEW THEATRES

With one exception (see 1936) the last new theatres to be built in London before war broke out opened this year. The Saville Theatre in Shaftesbury Avenue opened on 8 October with 'a play with tunes'. The building, now a cinema, was by T. P. Bennett, and has a striking exterior bas-relief frieze depicting drama through the ages, modelled by Gilbert Bayes.

A day earlier the Westminster Theatre in Palace Street had opened with a play produced by Tyrone Guthrie. Against the trend, this building was a conversion from a cinema – the old St James's Picture Theatre, which itself had once been a chapel.

Another cinema disappeared this year when the Windmill, in Great Windmill Street, became a theatre. In 1932 Vivian van Damm introduced 'Revuedeville', a new concept of non-stop variety which included near-nude but, by law, absolutely stationary girls. It was the only theatre to remain open throughout the war.

In Islington the fourth Sadler's Wells Theatre, given new life by Lilian Baylis, was opened on 6 January with a production of *Twelfth Night*. The building, designed by F. G. M. Chancellor, was received with reservation at the time, and it was never a popular auditorium.

On the other side of the ledger, the Queen's Hall at the People's Palace in Mile End Road burnt down, and the Princess's Theatre in Oxford Street (closed since 1902) was demolished to make way for a Woolworth's.

A NEW HOTEL

The present Dorchester Hotel was opened on 18 April. It was designed by William Curtis Green for Sir Robert McAlpine's company. It was the headquarters of General Eisenhower during the last war.

1932

A THEATRE IN REGENT'S PARK

Open-air theatre in Regent's Park was first presented in 1900, by Ben Greet's Woodland Theatre. In 1932 Sydney Carroll presented four matinees of *Twelfth Night* in the Botanic Gardens, and the following year the Open Air Theatre was formally established.

CLASSIC STATIONS

Some of the handsomest stations on the Underground are those of the extended Piccadilly Line opened this year. Simple, elegant buildings, designed by Charles Holden, brought a new image to the Underground system. Sudbury Town, opened in 1931, had been the first departure from the usual Underground style, but stations north of Finsbury Park, from where an extension was opened to Arnos Grove in 1932, are to this day some of the most striking. Typical is Arnos Grove itself, a circular building with pleasing brass lamps on the escalators and unfussy detailing in the booking hall.

A HOME FOR THE BBC

In 1927 the expanding British Broadcasting Company had become a corporation with public-service responsibilities. Savoy Hill (see 1922)

Broadcasting House in Langham Place. A number of young architects were involved in its design, and Eric Gill was commissioned to sculpt the figures.

was now too small, and a site for a new building was found at the southern end of Portland Place, where a block of flats had been proposed. It was a sensitive location. Not only was there an unbroken harmony of Georgian buildings on both sides of Portland Place, but Nash's church of All Souls had been delicately designed to lead the eye easily from Regent Street round the curve into that thoroughfare.

The BBC went to great effort to produce a building of its age. By 1929, well before the move, a group of young architects, including Raymond McGrath, Serge Chermayeff, Wells Coates and Edward Maufe, were working on studio layouts. The architect chosen for the building, Val Myers, had already been appointed to build the flats on the site before the BBC came along, and it is his building that we see now, with sculptures on the side by Eric Gill. Not everyone was happy with the design, and many are still not, though it fits more harmoniously now that so much of Portland Place has been changed.

GARDENS UPROOTED

The Royal Botanic Society's gardens within the Inner Circle in Regent's Park had not maintained their early success – the society was always short of money, and the gardens were not well kept. By 1932 they were described as deplorable if not dangerous, with the great conservatory beyond repair. The society was disbanded at the end of the lease in the Inner Circle, and the gardens were taken over this year by the Royal Parks Department. Though the old conservatory was demolished, what became the Queen Mary Rose Garden was planted; the new gardens were opened to the public on 30 April.

JEWISH MUSEUM OPENS
The Jewish Museum in Upper Woburn Place was opened this year, its archives and objects recording Anglo-Jewish history. It is now in Albert Street, Camden Town.

ARMSTRONG AT THE PALLADIUM
The first appearance of the jazz trumpeter Louis Armstrong at the Palladium was not an unqualified success. He was then 32 and at the peak of his career, but, though appreciated by the cognoscenti, his playing did not charm the ordinary British variety-goer: it was, for them, unsanitized jazz. But when he returned the following year he was a success – the song 'Stormy Weather' became popular, and Lord Beaverbrook gave a party for the band at which Armstrong met the prince of Wales.

A SHELL CLOCK
The large electric clock was fixed on the Shell-Mex building off the Strand. The hands are 12 ft and 9 ft long, and the dial is 25 ft square.

1933

MERGING TRANSPORT
The London Passenger Transport Board was established this year to take control of the numerous companies that ran buses, trams and railways in the London area and to plan the provision of transport in the capital. The board took over 61 bus companies, 17 tramways and five railway companies within nearly 2,000 square miles.

DEMOLITIONS
The last of the 17th-century arcaded houses in Covent Garden Piazza was this year taken down.

Park Lane was particularly vulnerable to change. Its views across Hyde Park on the other side of what was then a very much narrower road made it profitable to demolish the mansions of the rich and nouveau riche along it and replace them with apartment blocks and hotels. Dorchester House had been taken down in 1929; Aldford House, designed for the German financier Alfred Beit as recently as 1897, was demolished in 1931 and replaced with a block of the same name designed by Val Myers, the architect of Broadcasting House. Brook House, built for the banker Sir Dudley Coutts Marjoribanks by T. H. Wyatt in 1869, was taken down in 1933.

A CIVIC SHOWPIECE
Hornsey Council had been using cramped accommodation in an inconvenient Highgate road for some time, whereas the bulk of development in the borough was taking place much to the north, in Crouch End and Muswell Hill. Its new town hall, opened in November, was built in Crouch End Broadway by a young architect called Reginald Uren in a rather Scandinavian style, but is said to have been inspired by a town hall in Hilversum, Holland; it received the RIBA prize for the best building in London this year.

AUTOMATIC LIGHTS
The first automatic traffic lights in London were those installed in Trafalgar Square on 3 April. A further set was erected in Piccadilly Circus on 22 May.

CHANGES OF USE
The Royal Court Theatre in Sloane Square had been converted into a cinema in 1932. The more discerning theatregoer was further deprived this year when the Everyman Theatre in Hampstead, an avant-garde enterprise, was also converted for movies, but the cinema proved to be one of Hampstead's more enduring assets.

REMEMBERING MARX
To mark the fiftieth anniversary of the death of Karl Marx, a Marx Memorial Library was established this year in a pleasant building on Clerkenwell Green, once the home of the Welsh Charity School and, from 1892, of left-wing publishers such as Twentieth Century Press. From this house Lenin, who lodged not far away, had published 17 editions of a newspaper called *Iskra* in 1902–3. The first public lecture here was by Tom Mann, a leader of the 1889 dock strike and a friend of Eleanor Marx and Engels.

A NEW FREEMASONS' HALL
The present Freemasons' Hall in Great Queen Street was opened by the duke of Connaught this year. Designed by H. V. Ashley and F. W. Newman, it served also as a memorial to English Freemasons killed in the First World War.

1934

A POWER STATION AT BATTERSEA
The most forceful London building of the 1930s was the Battersea Power Station, commanding as it does an isolated position on the Thames – a daily sight for commuters on nearby railway lines. Much of it was completed this year by the London Power Company, a consortium of ten electricity-supply companies. It was not built without opposition. It was wondered why it had to be so near the centre of London when the power could be so easily transmitted from further afield, and it was also felt that smoke would damage not only buildings in the vicinity but also paintings at the Tate Gallery. At a late stage – no doubt to mollify local opinion – Sir Giles Gilbert Scott was appointed consultant architect, and the building is a blend of Scott's long experience in building churches and of the techniques of the Modern Movement style.

The building now stands derelict.

A NEW HOME FOR ARCHITECTS
Another 1930s building disturbed the Georgian harmony of Portland Place – this time the headquarters of the Royal Institute of British Architects. A competition for this prestige commission had been held in 1930, attracting 284 entrants. The winner was the relatively unknown Grey Wornum. He had numerous people to please – the entire and disparate architectural profession, the local estate owners, and the general public. The architect Clough Williams-Ellis, for example, described the result as 'a tedious mass of uninspired stodge', and others were alarmed by its Scandinavian influences. But it was generally liked, and it has worn well.

1900s

FLATS FOR THE AVANT-GARDE

Some flats in Lawn Road, Hampstead, completed this year, are still regarded as a landmark of the Modern Movement, some of whose artists were congregated around the Mall Studios off nearby Parkhill Road – people of the calibre of Henry Moore, Ben Nicholson, Barbara Hepworth, Paul Nash and Naum Gabo. Nearby was also a group of architects and designers, headed by Jack Pritchard and Wells Coates, who developed what in short was called the 'Isokon' idea, but which in full was known as the Isometric Unit Construction; it inspired not only fairly minimalist architecture but also the furniture to go in it – moulded plywood was freely used. The Isokon flats were in fact furnished apartments, leaving the occupants free to move in and out without the inconvenience that arises from house-moving. There were 32 flats in the Isokon scheme, mostly for single people, with their own restaurant.

Another architectural group, called the MARS Group, was also formed in the vicinity; its leading light was the architect Maxwell Fry, whose Sun House in Frognal Way, built in 1935, is still required viewing for students.

A POOL FOR PENGUINS

Modern architecture also came to the penguins at London Zoo this year, when the Penguin Pool – a synthesis of architecture and sculpture, designed by Berthold Lubetkin and Tecton – was completed. In the same year Pets' Corner was opened at the zoo.

DESTRUCTION OF WATERLOO BRIDGE

It is one of Herbert Morrison's more dubious claims to fame that, as leader of the London County Council, he was influential in the destruction of Waterloo Bridge this year – in fact he underlined his contribution by the rare ceremony of removing the first stone.

There was no disputing the fact that the old bridge, designed and built by John Rennie, senior and junior, was in a bad way. It wasn't wide enough for modern traffic, and some of the piers had sunk. There was also no disagreement that it was the most beautiful bridge surviving in London. The chairman of the LCC Finance Committee declared that

if ... the only function of the bridge is to be beautiful, or that if it is beautiful it can dispense with performing other functions, I have nothing more to say; but if you hold that the first function of Art is to add beauty to utility, and that utility must come first, and that a growing city with growing demands must perforce sometimes have to let things go ...

An alternative to demolition was devised. This involved widening the bridge, replacing some of the piers, and the erection of other bridges to cope with traffic, but the LCC would agree to this only if the government would contribute 75 per cent of the cost. The government would not, and the LCC, with some justification, decided to build a new Waterloo Bridge.

The Isokon flats in Lawn Road, Hampstead, designed by Jack Pritchard and Wells Coates.

EMPIRE POOL OPENS

One of the outstanding buildings of this period was the Empire Pool, Wembley. Designed by Sir Owen Williams, it has a 240-ft roof span supported on the outside by hanging concrete buttresses.

A COLLEGE FOR POLICEMEN

The quality of recruitment to the Metropolitan Police had hardly improved since the force was formed. While the standard of education and training of the force was low, it was a principle generally adhered to that appointments to many senior positions came from below; conversely, the highest positions of all were almost invariably filled by people from outside, with no police experience.

In the heat of the moment, a straightforward proposal for a police college at which the most talented officers could be given advanced training attracted considerable opposition. It was thought that the creation of an 'officer class' in such an organization would be the start of the establishment of a Fascist state. Despite such opposition, the Metropolitan Police College was established at Hendon this year.

LABOUR TAKE CONTROL

On 8 March the Labour Party took control of the London County Council for the first time; it was not to lose control until the LCC's abolition in 1965.

A COUTURIER'S SALON

The magnificent Bruton Street salon of the couturier Norman Hartnell was completed this year by the young architect Gerald Lacoste. At this time, before he became overwhelmed by royal commissions, Hartnell was the most important name in British fashion, designing very elegant clothes. He needed an outstanding salon, and Lacoste, who was making a name for himself with beautifully designed residences and penthouses, was a happy choice. Lacoste's salon still survives.

WESTERN AVENUE OPENED

A formal opening of Western Avenue was performed on 14 December. The road had been in the making for some years, and, like the Great West Road, was intended to take pressure off the old Uxbridge Road and to open up industrial heartlands to the west of London. One handsome adornment was the Hoover factory, completed about this year.

1935

PIONEER HEALTH CENTRES

The Peckham Health Centre – an attempt to pioneer community care – was established this year. For a modest subscription a whole family could be enrolled for curative and preventative care, but they were expected to attend for regular examinations so that meaningful data could be assembled. The husband and wife doctors who inspired the project, Scott Williamson and Innes Pearse, had large ideas. Their building, designed by Sir Owen Williams, contained a swimming pool, a gymnasium and a theatre. In effect, it was a community centre. However, it was closed during the war, and its revival in 1950 failed due to financial problems.

The Finsbury Health Centre, begun this year and completed in 1938, designed by Lubetkin and Tecton, had a different function, in that the disparate aspects of health care – maternity services, child welfare and dental health included – were gathered under one roof. Artistic slogans around the walls, urging the patients to get 'Fresh Air Night and Day' and so forth, were strongly reminiscent of the religious texts engraved on the walls of Columbia Market in the 19th century. The centre was to be the nucleus of what was called the 'Finsbury Plan', which was to cover education, housing and recreation.

FLATS IN HIGHGATE
These were busy times for the architectural practice of Berthold Lubetkin and his Tecton colleagues. Apart from the Finsbury Health Centre, this socialist practice of architects – renowned internationally for its housing schemes for the less well-off – was completing some flats in Highgate destined only for the affluent. These buildings, known as Highpoint One and Highpoint Two and completed in 1935 and 1938 respectively, were regarded then, and still are, as architectural landmarks. Le Corbusier was enthusiastic: the buildings, he said, contained 'the seed of the vertical city' and were 'an achievement of the first rank and a milestone that will be useful to everybody'.

Highpoint One is double-cruciform in plan, and it contained at the time 59 flats, a porter's flat and 16 servants' bedrooms, with a communal tearoom and a winter garden. The client was Zigismund Gestetner, of duplicating-machine fame, who had set out originally to build a hostel for his staff in Camden Town, but when this fell through he acquired this site in Highgate on which to build flats for the open market. Lubetkin persuaded him that he should make some of the apartments low-rent accommodation, so as to achieve a mix of people, but the idea was abandoned soon after the flats were built.

NEW MUSEUMS
The Geological Museum at South Kensington was opened on 3 July in a building designed by J. H. Markham. It derived from a Museum of Economic Geology, formerly housed in Craig's Court, off Whitehall, which was based on the first geological survey of the country, begun in 1835.

Eastbury House, an Elizabethan manor, was purchased by Barking Council this year for use as a museum. This was only briefly its function, as for a long time it served as a day nursery, but is now a cultural and local-history centre. It is remarkable that the house had survived for so long. By the 1830s it was very dilapidated and just before the First World War the Eastbury estate was built around it. The Society for the Protection of Ancient Buildings managed to save it and ensure that it went into the hands of the National Trust.

INTERCHANGING ROMEO
In October a production of Shakespeare's *Romeo and Juliet* began at the New Theatre which ran for a record 186 performances. The parts of Romeo and Mercutio were taken alternately by Laurence Olivier and John Gielgud, while Juliet was played by Peggy Ashcroft.

THE MIDLAND GRAND CLOSES
Gilbert Scott's masterpiece, the Midland Grand Hotel fronting St Pancras station, this year closed as a hotel. Its deficiencies had become increasingly obvious. It did not have en-suite bathrooms; it did not have central heating in the rooms – each had a coal fire; it was in a part of town which was depressed and dirty and so was unable to charge West End prices; and it needed a ratio of staff to guests which, as labour became more expensive, was uneconomic.

The building was then used as offices by the London Midland & Scottish Railway and, after nationalization of the railways after the last war, by the architects' department of the British Transport Commission.

1936

SENATE HOUSE COMPLETED
Senate House, the tallest building in the country at the time, was officially opened on 21 August. The Haldane Commission of 1913 had recommended that the University of London 'should have for its headquarters permanent buildings appropriate in design to its dignity and importance, adequate in extent and specially constructed for its purposes, situated conveniently for the work it has to do, bearing its name and under its own control'. This statement of intent served to encourage acrimony between various academic factions for many years to come, especially as Haldane himself, without consulting the university senate, solicited funds for a site in Bloomsbury. The recommendation presupposed a radical restructuring of the university, and in such an articulate and close world Haldane was beset by contention at every turn.

After the war the constituent parts of the university increased in size and the need for a new building became more pressing than ever. It was not until the late 1920s that the university resolved to build on the site that had been originally suggested in Bloomsbury, and in 1931 Charles Holden was appointed architect.

In the event he produced a controversial building. Pevsner thought that it was not as good as his smaller Underground stations, and generations of students who have used Senate House have reservations, especially about the the windswept, sometimes freezing cold and apparently pointless entrance floor.

THE BATTLE OF CABLE STREET
The rise of Fascism in Europe had reverberations in the East End of London, where anti-Jewish or anti-immigrant polemics found fertile ground. With high unemployment fuelling the causes of extremists, of both Left and Right, some kind of physical confrontation was perhaps inevitable. The Jews were the scapegoats for the Fascists, and the Fascists in their turn were the target of Communists, just as they were in the war in Spain then in progress.

On the morning of Sunday 4 October, Oswald Mosley led 3,000 Blackshirts into the East End from Royal Mint Street, protected by 7,000 police. At the junction of Cable Street and Leman Street barricades were erected by their opponents, and a large crowd assembled at Gardiner's Corner, Aldgate. After scuffles, the police decided that it was unsafe to allow the Fascists to proceed east and they went west instead, along the Embankment. The East End celebrated a famous victory.

POLITICAL THEATRE
It was a political year. The Mosley march and that of the unemployed from Jarrow to London heightened the tension in the capital.

1900s

Convictions were expressed in another way when Unity Theatre staged its first production. This theatre, which at the outset reflected Communist ideals, resulted from several initiatives. In 1929 Tom Thomas, a Communist Party member, revived the virtually moribund Workers' Theatre Movement, and from this developed several performing groups dedicated to agitprop rather than the production of the few vaguely left-wing plays that existed in repertoire. One group called the Red Players, mainly Jewish, made a wider name for themselves and early in 1936 they took up residence in a church hall in Britannia Street, off King's Cross Road. In February that year they changed their name to Unity Theatre, and on the 23rd Labour MP Dr Edith Summerskill officially opened its new auditorium. It was not until 25 November 1937 that Unity opened in its famous converted chapel to the rear of Goldington Crescent in Somers Town.

DEVELOPMENTS TO THE EAST

Two new buildings in the Barking and Dagenham area reflected the urbanization of that previously agricultural area. The South East Essex Technical College was established in Barking – one of a new breed of high schools for working-class pupils destined for commerce and industry. And in Dagenham a large civic centre, epitomizing new civic values and aspirations, was opened; the architect was E. Berry Webber.

MOVIE NEWS

What was possibly the first cinema in London specializing in newsreels was opened this year – the Monseigneur, in Charing Cross Road.

The Odeon chain was active. A large art-deco Odeon was opened in Muswell Hill (it still survives), and another at the northern end of Tottenham Court Road, on the site of the old Shoolbred furniture shop. Meanwhile the Alhambra, Leicester Square, was demolished to make way for another Odeon – one of the most original cinema fascias in London, designed largely by Thomas Braddock. The word 'Odeon' is derived from the name of the proprietor of the cinemas – Oscar Deutsch.

In this heyday of cinema building the seeds of competition were sown – this year the first high-definition public television service was begun by the BBC from Alexandra Palace.

NEW STORES

Una Dillon established a book shop in Store Street this year. She was later to collaborate with the University of London in opening a university bookshop in Gower Street.

Three stores were built this year of notable architectural quality. The main part of Simpson's, between Piccadilly and Jermyn Street, stands on the site of the Museum of Practical Geology, demolished after the opening of the Geological Museum at South Kensington. Designed by Joseph Emberton (who did much work for Austin Reed), this welded-steel building, now a Waterstone's bookshop, is still one of the most handsome in the road. Another landmark was completed in Kings Road, Chelsea. William Crabtree, the principal architect of the new Peter Jones store, had previously worked in Emberton's office; his building – steel-framed with curtain walling – was the first of its kind in the country.

In Finchley Road the department store of John Barnes was rebuilt by T. P. Bennett.

CRYSTAL PALACE DESTROYED

On 30 November a small fire in a lavatory in the central transept of the Crystal Palace at Sydenham developed into a conflagration which destroyed the entire building. By the time Penge Fire Brigade got there nothing could be done, as the dry wood floors burnt easily and the glass panes exploded. Thousands of people gathered on the slopes of the hill to watch a favourite building burn down. One by one the great iron sections collapsed, sending flames sometimes 300 feet into the air, and when the great transept fell the noise could be heard 5 miles away. The red glow of the fire, it was said, could be seen from Brighton.

Lloyd's paid out the full insured figure of £110,000 a week later.

IMPERIAL WAR MUSEUM MOVES

A former occupant of the Crystal Palace was the Imperial War Museum, which had opened there in 1920 before moving to the Imperial Institute in South Kensington. This year the museum was rehoused in the building which had formerly contained the Bethelem Royal Hospital (Bedlam) in Lambeth Road.

1937

HEADQUARTERS FOR THE FIRE BRIGADE

The Albert Embankment now has a depressing array of office blocks. Among them is the 1937 headquarters for the London Fire Brigade, a dreary building designed by E. P. Wheeler.

FLATS FOR THE MIDDLE CLASSES

One of the largest developments of apartments in Europe is Dolphin Square on Grosvenor Road, Westminster, by the Thames – some 1,250 flats covering 7½ acres, designed in red brick by Cecil Eve and Gordon Jeeves. Opened this year, the development includes a restaurant, shops and other facilities. It derives its name from a 'dolphin' pump which existed nearby for drawing water from the river.

PAINTING IN THE EUSTON ROAD

The Euston Road School of Painting was founded by a group of painters that included William Coldstream, Victor Pasmore and Claude Rogers, who all worked at the School of Drawing and Painting. This was in October 1937, when the school was at 12 Fitzroy Street, but in February 1938 it moved to larger premises in an old garage at 316 Euston Road.

A REBUILT EARLS COURT

On the site of an old entertainment ground, the Earls Court Exhibition Hall was completed this year to the design of C. Howard Crane. At the time it was the largest reinforced-concrete building in Europe.

A NATIONAL TRUST PUB

What was left of one of Southwark's galleried inns, the George, in Borough High Street, was handed over to the National Trust this year – the north and central wings had been demolished for railway development in 1889, and only the southern range survives. The building dates from after the 1676 Southwark fire.

CLOSURES AND DEMOLITIONS

Daly's Theatre in Leicester Square was closed on 25 September; the Warner Cinema was built on the site.

The Lion Brewery in Broadwick Street closed. The abysmal Trenchard House (demolished in the 1990s) replaced it.

Mudie's Circulating Library in New Oxford Street stopped trading was then held in abeyance until after the war. A new building for the Hospital for Sick Children in Great Ormond Street was completed, and London Zoo took delivery of its first panda. But the attention of Londoners was now to be on more sombre things.

1939

INTERRUPTED LIVES

At 11.15 a.m. on 3 September the prime minister, Neville Chamberlain, told the nation that it was at war with Germany. Within 20 minutes air-raid sirens sounded in London, and without panic people hurried to shelters for the first time in earnest. But it was a false alarm.

Farewells began. Evacuation of children started promptly, though far fewer left the capital than the government had anticipated. Conscription was stepped up, and London's stations were crammed with men, newly in uniform, saying tearful goodbyes in tearooms and on platforms. For once, the people left behind were themselves in danger, and worry would be two-sided.

THREE NEW BUILDINGS

Three significant buildings were completed this year, before the war effectively halted any construction work. The Imperial Airways terminal (later used by BOAC) was opened in Buckingham Palace Road; it was extended in the late 1950s, when an absurd piece of sculpture was added. In Savile Row a new police station was finished, handsomely designed by Sir John Burnet Tait & Partners. St Martin's School of Art, founded in 1854 by the parish of St Martin-in-the-Fields, was rehoused in Charing Cross Road in a building which also contained the Technical Institute for the Distributive trades; the architect was E. P. Wheeler.

1940

THE BLITZ BEGINS

The first bomb to fall on central London damaged premises in Fore Street, in the City, on 25 August, and in the same raid the church of St Giles without Cripplegate was mostly destroyed. It was the turn of the dock area on 7 September, when 400 planes brought terror to the neighbourhood and revealed the inadequacies of shelter provision there. A week later an angry group of East Enders, led by the Communist MP Phil Piratin, marched to the Savoy Hotel and demanded shelter there, to point up the difference in provision for rich and poor; the management of the hotel was not able legally to refuse them entry. The East End, which could expect to bear the brunt of bombing by virtue of its concentration of industry and shipping, had few Underground stations in which to take refuge. Places like Barking (even closer to the enemy, and with substantial targets such as Beckton Gas Works and a large power station) and Dagenham (with the Ford Motor Works) were reliant almost entirely on Anderson and Morrison shelters – structures which gambled on their not receiving a direct hit.

The use of Underground stations was not an automatic provision. London Transport discouraged their use as shelters – notices appeared which proclaimed 'During air-raids, passengers only admitted'. Public pressure prevailed eventually and 79 stations were used as shelters. The Aldwych spur (reserved for children) and the disused King William Street station on the old City & South London Railway were pressed

The London passenger terminal for Imperial Airways (later called BOAC) was completed in Buckingham Palace Road just as war began.

in July. Once the essential book supplier to thousands of homes, Mudie's was driven out of business by public libraries.

All Hallows, Lombard Street, with hardly a congregation remaining, was sold and the site was used for a headquarters for Barclays Bank.

The last edition of the *Morning Post* was published on 30 September; the paper was then merged with the *Daily Telegraph*.

Chesterfield House in Great Stanhope Street (see 1749) was taken down.

1938

LONDON IN LIMBO

The Second World War did not come without warning, and it is not surprising that London's normal activities were in limbo this year. Hardly a building of note was begun or finished, other than the Warner Cinema in Leicester Square and the Finsbury Health Centre (see 1935). Plans to demolish the Doric arch in front of Euston Station were in the air – to the dismay of the Georgian Group and the Society for the Protection of Ancient Buildings – and there were also fears that Savile Row might be demolished in favour of modern development. The London County Council introduced a 'Green Belt' policy, which

1900s

into service. A count taken late in September showed about 117,000 taking refuge in the tunnels despite the chronic lack of hygienic facilities.

The stations were only comparatively safe. Some of the worst disasters this year took place in their tunnels. On 17 September 17 people died when a bomb pierced Marble Arch station, and a month later a bomb exploded in a tunnel between King's Cross and Farringdon, killing 14. On 12 November Sloane Square station and the Royal Court Theatre were hit, causing many deaths and injuries. At Balham a bomb fractured a water main and 600 people were drowned, and on 11 January 1941 a bomb bounced down an escalator at Bank station and exploded on a platform, killing 117 people in horrendous circumstances.

Architecturally, the most substantial damage this year occurred on 29 December, when a major raid destroyed the company halls of the Haberdashers, Saddlers and Parish Clerks, virtually destroyed Christchurch, Newgate Street, and St Mary Aldermanbury, and damaged St Bride's, St Lawrence Jewry, St Andrew's by the Wardrobe, the Guildhall and its library, Goldsmiths' College and the church of St Anne & St Agnes. Austin Friars had been severely damaged on 15 October, the same night that a severe loss of life occurred at Morley College in Westminster. Seven people died when a bomb hit Broadcasting House, though the newsreader carried on reading in the best Reithian tradition, and a bomb hit the roof of nearby All Souls, Langham Place.

Other buildings destroyed this year included Holy Trinity Minories, most of St Anne, Soho, and St John, Wapping, St Alban's, Wood Street, St Paul's, Avenue Road, in St John's Wood, and the company halls of the Brewers, Coopers and Joiners; badly damaged were St Stephen, Coleman Street, St Augustine, Watling Street, the Britannia Theatre, Hoxton, the Holborn Empire, St James Piccadilly, the Middle Temple hall, the British Museum Newspaper Library at Colindale, and Cecil Sharp House in Camden Town.

1941

MAJOR RAIDS

Three major raids occurred over London. The first, on 11 January, involved 137 bombers; the second, on the night of 8 March, had 125 bombers; and the third, the most destructive in architectural terms, was on 10 May. On 8 March a direct hit on the underground Café de Paris, a dance hall with an interior modelled on the ballroom of the *Titanic*, beneath the Rialto cinema in Coventry Street, killed 34 people. On 17 April the original Shaftesbury Theatre in Shaftesbury Avenue was destroyed and old Chelsea church was badly damaged.

On 10 May the House of Commons chamber was gutted, though Westminster Hall, which had already escaped the 1834 fire at the Palace of Westminster, survived yet again. In the neighbourhood, the War Office, Westminster Abbey Deanery and Lambeth Palace were hit; in the City the Mansion House, Temple church, the Tower of London, Middle Temple Library, Inner Temple Hall, St Dunstan in the East, St Mary-le-Bow and St Nicholas Cole Abbey were all badly damaged.

Bombardment of the East End continued, and the area around St Paul's Cathedral was extensively flattened. The fact that the great cathedral emerged virtually unscathed had a talismanic effect on those Londoners who knew the situation, though press censorship restricted general knowledge.

A machine-gun post near the Houses of Parliament, disguised as a W. H. Smith bookstall: an anti-invasion measure.

Elsewhere the company halls of the Clothworkers, Cordwainers, Curriers, Cutlers and Salters were destroyed, as were the churches of St Mary Haggerston and St Swithin, Cannon Street. Badly damaged were the Old Bailey, the Royal Hospital, Chelsea, St Anne, Limehouse, St Andrew, Holborn, St John, Smith Square, St George's Hall in Langham Place, the Metropolitan Tabernacle at Kennington, St John, Clerkenwell, and the Corn Exchange in Mark Lane.

1942

A QUIETER TIME

Just as the government managed to complete a number of deep-level shelters, so the bombing raids eased off as the Royal Air Force and civil defences mastered the art of interception. The shelters were something of an afterthought, as was the use of Underground stations, and only the unexpectedly severe effects of bombing in 1940 persuaded the government into such a major undertaking.

The deep-level shelters were tunnels beneath Underground stations, and thus very deep indeed. Ten were planned: eight beneath the Northern Line and two beneath the Central Line. Those destined for Oval and St Paul's stations were not completed; Chancery Lane and Clapham were built but not brought into service; Stockwell and Goodge Street were used by American troops; the remaining four – at Belsize Park, Camden Town, Clapham South and Clapham North – were used by the public. Each consisted of twin 1,200-ft tunnels destined, once peace was restored, to be part of an express tube system; for the time being they had two levels containing sleeping accommodation, and at right angles there were smaller tunnels containing services. Surface evidence of these tunnels (now mostly used for storage) may be seen at Belsize Park, Goodge Street and Clapham.

Disused Underground stations were also pressed into service. Down Street (between Green Park and Hyde Park Corner, closed in

1932) was used by the Railways Executive Committee, and Brompton Road (by the Oratory, closed 1934) was an anti-aircraft command centre – it is still used by the Territorial Army.

During 1942 and 1943 there were fewer than 30 air raids on London. A notable casualty of one was the house at 30 Holford Square, Clerkenwell, in which Lenin had once lodged.

1943

LOOKING TO THE FUTURE

A number of people had already turned their attention to rebuilding London, though the end of the war was some way from prediction and realization. At the National Gallery an exhibition entitled 'Rebuilding Britain' was held.

The London County Council published the County of London Plan by J. H. Forshaw and Patrick Abercrombie, and a year later Abercrombie produced a Greater London Plan, crammed with statistics and proposals, most of them largely ignored in the post-war era. In particular his remedies for traffic congestion fell by the wayside. He visualized five concentric ring roads around London, connecting the radial roads: these would direct traffic on to express arterial motorways to other cities. The second-innermost ring was the one that, when proposed in the 1970s, aroused the most opposition, since it crossed areas which had by then risen in value and esteem; had it been built directly after the war, when almost everything was a potential sacrifice to replanning and few people cared about places like Camden Town and Clapham anyway, it would have been met with little protest. In central London itself Abercrombie had tunnels beneath Hyde Park to link Knightsbridge and Bayswater, and other tunnels linked key destinations. But he made the elementary error of proposing a tunnel beneath Buckingham Palace – a sufficiently outrageous piece of lese-majesty to scupper the whole tunnel scheme.

Two private architects, Kenneth Lindy and Winton Lewis, were bent on changing the City of London into a more monumental area. A processional way to the Guildhall was proposed, the Corporation would be housed in a skyscraper up to 500 ft tall, and St Paul's was to be surrounded by a vast ellipse of paved landscaping which, from the air, would make the cathedral seem to be placed within a Roman amphitheatre.

A reminder that all was not over occurred at Bethnal Green Station on 3 March, where in an air-raid panic 173 people were killed.

1944

PILOTLESS PERILS

The appearance of the V1 flying bomb came as a shock to Londoners, though not to those in the governmental know. Conventional mass bombing had been resumed in January – on 21 January 447 German aircraft were counted in the attack – but it was now ineffective, and in any case the Germans had dwindling resources to sustain such a campaign. But on 13 June the first flying bomb attack caused immediate consternation. The first V1 landed on agricultural land at Swanscombe, and the first to reach London hit Grove Road in Bow. Five days later a flying bomb hit the Guards Chapel at Wellington Barracks, where 119 people were killed and nearly as many seriously injured. About 100

bombs a day were launched from the northern coast of Europe, and these unpredictable projectiles, with their ominous whirr and their even more worrying silence as they descended to earth, were for many people the most frightening element of the war.

The missiles were of primitive technology and indiscriminate in their targets. Many were intercepted by brave pilots and shot down over unpopulated areas, but others got through to land on buildings which were certainly not strategic in any way, such as the London Library on 23 February, or Highbury Corner on 27 June, when five houses at the end of Compton Terrace were demolished with the loss of 24 lives. A row of houses in Whitfield Street was demolished, also in June, and the Brown Institution for animal health studies at Battersea was demolished and another flying bomb damaged Staple Inn.

On 29 June, Glenn Miller and his band arrived in London and spent the night in Sloane Square Underground station, sheltering from flying-bomb attacks. The band's headquarters was at Sloane Court, but two days later Miller managed to get the band moved to Bedford; during the following week Sloane Court was hit – 26 were killed and 78 were dug out of the ruins of the building. Miller was subsequently killed in an aeroplane crash in France in 1945.

Just as the RAF was getting to grips with the flying bombs the V2 rocket arrived. This was a 45-ft-long ballistic missile, travelling too fast to engage; the first one fell on Chiswick on 8 September. It is estimated that 518 V2s fell on London, resulting in the deaths of 2,724 people and serious injuries to about 6,000.

The last flying bombs and rockets fell on 25 March the following year; the last major casualty was Whitefields Tabernacle in Tottenham Court Road, destroyed by a rocket.

SAVING THE ROYAL OPERA HOUSE

With many distractions elsewhere, it was fortunate that the music publisher Leslie Arthur Boosey discovered that the Royal Opera House, Covent Garden, was about to be let to the Mecca company for a dance hall. Acting quickly, he secured the lease for his own firm, Boosey & Hawkes, and the building was saved for future operatic use; but it was a close-run thing. Mecca took over the Lyceum Theatre for a dance hall instead the following year.

1945

INTO THE TURMOIL OF PEACE

The war in Europe ended on 8 May, and London was soon awash with parades and street parties. They were joyous, tearful, intensely patriotic days, for ever fixed in an uncomplicated way in the memories of those who enjoyed them. There was relief, of course, and there was anticipation of the return, for better or for worse, of lovers and friends who would take up old relationships or else find them impossibly altered. There was a belief too – how could there not be? – that a new age had arrived: one that might perhaps be better.

1946

DIFFICULT TIMES

A Labour government, armed with a large majority and high hopes after the July 1945 general election, found itself enmeshed in intractable problems of labour and supply. There were numerous strikes in London alone – on the railways, in the docks, in hotels, in power stations, to name just some. There was a shortage of labour, productivity was poor, rationing still existed, and there were strict controls on spending, investment and the movement of capital. Some goods were in acutely short supply – a queue nearly three-quarters of a mile long tried to buy sheets on sale at Ponting's. While the press noted the large number of requisitioned buildings still used by civil servants, or else standing empty, hundreds of people left homeless by war and its aftermath were squatting in semi-derelict buildings such as the old Columbia Market in Bethnal Green and the Ivanhoe Hotel in Bloomsbury. Squatters also took over a gun-site in Gladstone Park and staked claims on other army sites in Blackheath and the East End. Requisitioned buildings rankled particularly: it was calculated that the government still held 8,000 Kensington houses and hotels, 904 St Marylebone residences, and even 193 houses, flats and garages in Hampstead.

By May it was estimated that about 4,500 prefabs had been built in London, and another 5,500 were under construction. Caledonian Market, which had been used for storing army vehicles, was derequisitioned, but its future use was uncertain – the City, which owned the site, had not yet decided if the market activities would be resumed, and Islington council wanted the site for housing. In the 1960s, it was the City which built charmless blocks on the market site, which Islington eventually took over. Smithfield was derequisitioned, and in a limited way the meat market was re-established.

A New Site for the Mirror
The *Daily Mirror* bought a site for new offices at Holborn Circus this year, for £200,000. Previously there had been a department store there called Thomas Wallis, which had been bombed during the war. Wallis reopened on Oxford Street during the war, and had the sense to remain there rather than return to Holborn.

LCC Plans
The London County Council proposed three major schemes this year. One was the comprehensive redevelopment of 49 acres at the Elephant and Castle area. About a third of the premises there were damaged or beyond repair, and the LCC wanted at the same time to deal with a long-recognized traffic bottleneck.

The LCC also proposed to take over the Hurlingham Club polo grounds in Fulham for housing and public open space. There was little the club could do to prevent this – the use of these attractive acres by the privileged few could hardly be sustained when so many homes were needed.

In Stepney it was calculated that about a quarter of the housing stock had been damaged during the war. The LCC proposed to purchase, in association with the borough councils, two-thirds of Stepney and one-third of Poplar. It was noted that in Stepney 60 per cent of families shared accommodation, and in Poplar 73 per cent.

It was also revealed that the government planned to move a million people out of London to new towns and selected existing towns.

Sale of the Smallest House
What was thought to be the smallest house in London, 10 Hyde Park Place, consisting of a doorway and two rooms, one above the other, was sold by Lockhart Mummery, a surgeon, to the Adorers of the Sacred Heart, Tyburn Convent, who owned the house next door. The greatest width in the house was 4 ft.

Extending Heathrow
On 31 May Heathrow superseded Croydon as the civil airport for London. There were ambitious plans for extension of the new airport, and within four years the villages of Sipson and Harlington, 1,200 houses, 4 schools, 12 pubs, 2 churches and 1 greyhound stadium were due to disappear.

The Air Ministry handed Fairlop Airport to the Ministry of Civil Aviation. It had originally been developed by the City of London before the war as a municipal airfield.

Greyhounds Galore
While soccer and cricket resumed full activity with some difficulty, as many men were still in the armed forces, greyhound racing boomed. Some stadiums became public companies, and what had previously been the province of a few enthusiasts became the passionate interest of thousands. Romford Stadium, for example, a venture begun by a sweet manufacturer, had been worth £54,000 after the war but, going public this year, was now valued at £500,000. A Hoxton bookmaker who had built Walthamstow Stadium on wasteland made a great deal of money when this too went public.

A Hanging at Wandsworth
Three hundred people gathered outside Wandsworth Prison on 3 January to mark the hanging of the Nazi propagandist William Joyce, 'Lord Haw-Haw' to millions.

Recovering Treasures
A few of London's treasures were reappearing from their wartime hideaways. Pictures in the National Gallery had been kept in a disused mineshaft in Wales, and items from the Tate and the London Museum had been partly stored in Piccadilly Underground station. The statue of Charles I, at the top of Whitehall, had been at Leighton Buzzard, and that of George III was reinstalled at Somerset House. However, Eros was still at Englefield Green, and General Gordon, previously in Trafalgar Square, was still at Mentmore (it was re-erected on Embankment Gardens only in 1953). The British Museum was partly open and in 1945 had been able to buy the famous Portland Vase, dating from c. AD 25, which had been on display in the museum since 1810.

1947

A Cold Winter of Discontent
Labour troubles and general misery continued – not helped by a very severe winter indeed: 17 degrees of frost were recorded in central London, and a thin layer of ice covered the Thames at Windsor. Inevitably there was a power crisis. With the fuel industries disorganized, understaffed and occasionally on strike, it was necessary to shut off fuel to most of London during 9–12 a.m. and 2–4 p.m. from February.

There were more strikes: on railways and buses, at Smithfield, at the docks and in the Post Office. Sir Stafford Cripps, president of the Board of Trade, announced the cancellation of the proposed World Fair to be held on the South Bank in 1951, as he did not think that men or resources could be spared to prepare for it.

On the Horizon
The press and politicians were much exercised this year with the proposal to build Bankside Power Station on the Thames opposite

St Paul's. The plan was strongly opposed by distinguished critics – whom Lewis Silkin, minister of town and country planning, described as 'a few highbrows' – and the architect, Sir Giles Gilbert Scott, was obliged not only to bring down the height of the proposed 300-ft chimneys, but to reduce them to one only. He described his building as one which would be built in 'silver and grey bricks, which will bring brightness to the City and Bankside'. Silkin, in stating his intention to let the plan proceed, said that the building 'would not be discordant with St Paul's. It will be a good neighbour. It will not overshadow the cathedral and will be a relevantly inconspicuous feature of the landscape.' The power station was not completed until 1963, and the building has now been converted to the Tate Gallery of Modern Art, which is due to open in 2000.

A New Sport
Greyhound stadiums, already doing well, found another money-spinner – speedway. For the next ten years this sport was enormously successful – more than 80,000 saw the championship races at Wembley this year, and the average crowd at Harringay Stadium was 28,000. Other London tracks were at New Cross, Wimbledon, West Ham, Park Royal, Charlton, Dagenham, Wandsworth, Clapton, Romford, Catford, Walthamstow, White City and Stamford Bridge.

Disturbances in Dalston
Several serious civil disturbances occurred in the area of Ridley Road market, Dalston, when neo-Fascists held gatherings in the largely Jewish area.

First of the Many
The first of the many post-war American musicals to open in London was *Oklahoma*, whose opening night was on 30 April at the Theatre Royal Drury Lane.

Traffic Jams
London was beset by traffic jams. In May it was announced that yellow lines, indicating parking restrictions, were to be introduced on some roads; these were painted on lamp-posts, and there were yellow arrows on pavements. Serious congestion was still a novelty, and when in June there was a traffic jam between Kings Cross and Euston it warranted a special item in the *Evening Standard*.

Nash Terraces in Disrepair
A report published this year strongly criticized the Crown Commissioners for their care of the Nash terraces in Regent's Park. The report said that there was no indication that the state of the buildings would be any better even if there had not been a war.

Extension on the Central Line
The Central Line, running between Liverpool Street and Ealing before the war, had been pushed eastward to Stratford in December 1946. In 1947 there was further expansion to Woodford, and a spur was begun to Hainault; simultaneously it was built westward to Greenford, and then up to West Ruislip in 1948.

A New Attraction at the Zoo
On Guy Fawkes' Day a gorilla, named Guy, was installed at London Zoo. He became one of the most popular attractions for many, but a sad sight for others, who found his apparently profound boredom in his small enclosure a depressing indictment of his human custodians.

1948

West Indians in London
The manpower shortage was the reason why workers from the Caribbean were invited to Britain this year. The first arrivals – nearly 500 of them – arrived on the *Empire Windrush* on 22 June, were housed in a Clapham shelter as a temporary measure, and were given a civic reception at the Brixton Astoria two days later.

The Olympics at Wembley
It was both a tonic and a gamble for London to host the 14th Olympic Games from 29 July. There were, of course, few countries in Europe that could have staged them – most were devastated or else consumed with political upheaval – and holding the games outside of Europe was impractical. London itself was poorly endowed with facilities, manpower, funds and venues, but it managed.

The gold-medal list was dominated by the United States, with countries like Holland and Sweden also doing well – the Soviet Union and Eastern Bloc countries were yet to achieve their domination of many events. The host country did badly.

Theatrical News
Mae West opened in *Diamond Lil* at the Prince of Wales Theatre on 24 January; it received poor notices.

Terence Rattigan's *The Browning Version* had its first performance at the Phoenix on 8 September, with Eric Portman in the lead, and was an immediate success.

The Unicorn Theatre for Children, a touring group, was begun this year; it did not move into its permanent home in Great Newport Street until 1967.

Disaster in Burnt Oak
An RAF Anson plane crashed on a block of half-completed flats in Burnt Oak on 9 February; the crew of two were killed.

Bacchus at Hampton
The Great Vine at Hampton Court, planted by Capability Brown 180 years previously, yielded 500 lb of black grapes this year; they were sold to the public at 6s a pound.

1949

Television in the Making
Development of the infant television service had been interrupted by the war, but even so it was evident that existing premises were inadequate for television's expansion – the various BBC enterprises were already on 44 sites in London, and space of the kind needed for television production was not available near Broadcasting House. In March the LCC agreed to buy the whole of the White City site and make 13 acres available to the BBC to build a Television Centre.

Theatrical Ups and Downs
The Tennessee Williams play *A Streetcar Named Desire* opened sensationally in London at the Aldwych Theatre on 11 October. It was produced by Laurence Olivier, with Vivien Leigh in the lead. People queued for 24 hours to get in.

Another American import, Arthur Miller's *Death of a Salesman*, was also a success, opening at the Phoenix on 28 July.

Ivor Novello's *King's Rhapsody* opened at the Palace Theatre on 15 September and ran for 839 performances.

There was a flop, however, for Bernard Shaw. His last play, called *Buoyant Billions*, written in shorthand at the age of 91, came off five weeks after opening on 10 October at the Prince's Theatre.

STORE REBUILDING
The John Lewis department store in Oxford Street had been badly damaged by a fire bomb in 1940, and much of the building was unusable. This year the company was permitted to put up a temporary building, but full-scale redevelopment of the island site was not of sufficient priority in the use of materials and labour.

REDUCING CHURCH NUMBERS
It was proposed that the number of diocesan churches in the City of London be reduced to 40, and that the sites of six churches should be sold. Stipends were fixed at £750 a year plus £250 expenses.

SAVING STATELY HOMES
Osterley Park was this year given to the National Trust by the 9th earl of Jersey. It had originally been built by Sir Thomas Gresham in the 16th century, but its form is predominantly the 18th-century adaptation by Robert Adam for the Child banking family.

The government had announced the previous year that Ham House was to be purchased from the Dysart family and administered by the Victoria & Albert Museum.

IT'S THAT MAN FOR THE LAST TIME
ITMA comedian Tommy Handley died in January. Large crowds gathered outside his home in Craven Road, Paddington, to see the cortège leave for its journey to Golders Green Crematorium.

LIGHTS ON AGAIN
From 18 March it was permitted to light shop windows after closing time and to use flashing advertisement signs.

HANGING ON TO POWER
The Labour government's unpopularity was reflected in the LCC elections this year, when Labour almost lost control. Conservatives and Labour obtained an equal number of seats, but by the vote of its majority of sitting aldermen Labour was able to elect enough aldermen and a chairman to ensure its majority for the next three years. It was to retain control until the council's abolition in 1965.

1950

THEATRES LOST
The Bedford Theatre in Camden Town closed and Gatti's Music Hall in Westminster Bridge Road was demolished. The Bedford was a sad loss – it was a famous variety theatre, but cinema and the prospect of television held out no hopes for its future. Repertory had been tried after the war, with stars such as Dirk Bogarde and Anne Crawford, but conventional drama could not be sustained in the Camden Town of that period. The building had a splendid interior, but its exterior was unexceptional.

A QUEUE AT THE ZOO
There were long queues at London Zoo to see Brumas, the baby bear born on the premises. The animal was to be the biggest draw until the arrival of the panda Chi-Chi in 1958.

OPPOSITION TO THE FESTIVAL
The politics surrounding the Festival of Britain – due to open in 1951 on the south bank of the Thames – had never been less than acrimonious. Many people, especially Conservative members of Parliament, thought that the government should not use scarce materials, manpower and money on such an extravaganza, and some Labour ministers also were notably reluctant to champion the project in case it was a disaster. It was pointed out that St Thomas's Hospital, not far from the site, was still a wreck after bombing in 1941, and still using an old coal cellar for an emergency operating theatre. The materials taken to build the festival complex could, it was suggested, have been used to rebuild the hospital. Conservative boroughs Chelsea and Kensington announced that they would not be taking part in festival events. In the event Herbert Morrison, the deputy prime minister, was given the task of seeing the festival through, and this he did with enthusiasm – and eventually with much success.

SCRAPPING THE TRAMS
The gradual replacement of trams by trolleybuses and buses, interrupted by the war, was resumed. As from October trams were abolished in Battersea, Camberwell, Lambeth, Southwark, Westminster, Holborn, Finsbury and Chelsea.

MEMBERS IN THEIR HABITAT
The king opened the reconstructed House of Commons chamber on 26 October.

OFFICES IN HOLBORN
One area transformed as from 1950 was the part of Holborn at the western end of Theobalds Road and High Holborn. Two truly awful office blocks, Ariel (later Adastral) House and Lacon House, were built for the government in Theobalds Road and in 1955 were joined by Mercury House. In High Holborn, State House had been built and was not made any more palatable by the placing of a Barbara Hepworth statue outside. At the same time the unsympathetically conceived one-way traffic system was installed, to complete the sterilization of this part of London.

1951

A TONIC TO THE NATION
The Festival of Britain, like its ancestor the Great Exhibition of 1851, was an unpredicted and immense success. The king, looking down at thousands gathered on Ludgate Hill, opened it on the steps of St Paul's on 3 May, and when it closed at the end of September nearly 8½ million visitors had paid to get in to the festival buildings, mainly on the South Bank.

The festival began as a suggestion of the Royal Society of Arts in 1943. The idea was followed up in 1945 by Gerald Barry, then editor of the *News Chronicle*, in an open letter to the president of the Board of Trade, Stafford Cripps. At first an international exhibition was proposed, but by 1947 it was obvious that resources could cope only with

The Dome of Discovery at the Festival of Britain, with the Skylon in the distance.

a national affair. As it happened, this reduction to a national celebration suited the circumstances of 1951, for by then years of stringent financial restraints and the onset of the Korean War had sapped the nation's morale. A jingoistic tonic was needed.

As has already been mentioned (1950), the festival was opposed by leading Conservatives, including a Churchill embittered by his 1945 election defeat, though the festival council did include Tories of the calibre of R. A. Butler, and establishment figures such as Sir Kenneth Clark, John Gielgud, Malcolm Sargent and A. P. Herbert. Opponents in the press included Sir Thomas Beecham, who described the festival as a 'monumental piece of imbecility', and Evelyn Waugh and Noël Coward, who both despised it. The proposal to open a funfair at Battersea Park as an integral part of the festival was also unpopular, especially among Sabbatarians.

Preparations began in 1947. Leading architects and artists of the day were brought in to evolve what is now recognized as a Festival of Britain style. The late Hugh Casson was director of architecture, and artists included Abram Games (who designed the famous logo), John Minton, Victor Pasmore, John Piper, Josef Herman, Ben Nicholson and Keith Vaughan. Henry Moore, Jacob Epstein, Eduardo Paolozzi and Barbara Hepworth supplied sculptures, and murals and mobiles were popular.

The main site chosen for the festival was a stretch of fairly derelict land on the south bank of the Thames, east of County Hall. What arose here was a concentration of 'modern' architecture – no neo-Georgian frills, but a style that broke with the past and used new building technology.

The Dome of Discovery, designed by Ralph Tubbs, was a circular, 365-ft-diameter building housing exhibits illustrating the British inventive genius. The Skylon, 296 ft high, designed by Powell & Moya with Frank Newby as engineer, was a slim, pointed pencil of a structure supported by cables; lit at night, it seemed to be suspended in space. The Regatta Restaurant was designed by Mischa Black. Londoners were particularly taken by the Bailey bridge slung across the Thames from Charing Cross. But above all there was the Royal Festival Hall – the first major British building in contemporary style. This 3,000-seat concert hall was designed by Robert Matthew, Leslie Martin and Peter Moro, and it has remained in both function and appearance the most successful of the arts venues that side of Waterloo Bridge. The archi-

tects made full use of the river setting. Early visitors, used to the narrow passageways, staircases and decor of older London concert halls and theatres, appreciated the physical and visual freedom that the hall provided. The building's main faults, to many, are its dry acoustics and its uneasy use of ornamentation, especially outside. Architects of the day stressed function in their design, eliminating the devices beloved of previous generations which broke up surfaces, but the hall's designers still had to visually temper the mass of the exterior, and in so doing they succumbed to irritating geometric patterns.

At Battersea Park the festival gardens were laid out by Osbert Lancaster and John Piper, and were to survive for a considerable number of years. The funfair was very popular – especially a ride called the Rotor, in which people were held by centrifugal force to the inside of a spinning drum.

Elsewhere in London there were events sponsored by local councils and organizations. One lasting manifestation has been the Regent's Canal boat trips.

A less publicized and much less frequented part of the festival were the Lansbury Estate buildings in Poplar. The purpose of including the Lansbury Estate in the festival was to show the directions in which new housing and community planning could go, but many found that the wide roads flanked by low-rise, unprepossessing houses – neither urban nor suburban – sent them back with relief to the relative vitality of grubby central-London terraces. It was all very worthy, but who would want to live there? The estate is now a rather sterile architectural curiosity, though it is better mannered than most that have been built around it since.

1952

THE KING IS DEAD

The death of George VI on 6 February ushered in what some romantically and optimistically called a new Elizabethan Age, whatever that may have meant to them. The king's body lay in state in Westminster Hall from 12 February until removed for his burial at Windsor on the 15th; 300,000 people filed past it.

London 1951

FESTIVAL OF BRITAIN

The Festival of Britain expressed a postwar vision of a society which was technologically and materially better off than ever before.

The South Bank exhibition offered a vision of that future in the various pavilions and in the 'Dome of Discovery'. The only building remaining today is the Royal Festival Hall.

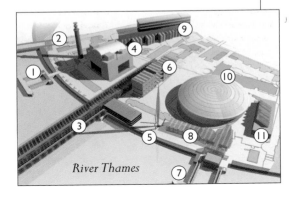

River Thames

THE SOUTH BANK SITE

1 Rodney Pier
2 Shot Tower
3 Hungerford Bridge
4 Royal Festival Hall
5 Skylon
6 People of Britain Pavilion
7 Nelson Pier
8 Sea & Ships Pavilion
9 Homes & Gardens Pavilion
10 Dome of Discovery
11 Power & Production Pavilion

Festival of Britain

DISASTER AT HARROW

On 8 October an express train from Perth to Euston hit a local train at Harrow and Wealdstone station and a Euston to Manchester train ploughed into the wreckage; 112 people were killed.

DISTINGUISHED HOUSES

Fenton House in Hampstead Grove was this year bequeathed to the National Trust by its former owner, Lady Binning. The gift included her furniture, porcelain and pictures. Since then the house has contained an important collection of musical instruments.

The Wellington Museum in Apsley House, Hyde Park Corner, was opened to the public this year. The house had been built by Robert Adam *c.* 1778 for Henry Bathurst, whose family names included Apsley. It was bought by Lord Wellesley, Wellington's elder brother, in 1805, and was sold to the duke in 1817. The house and its contents were given to the nation by the 7th duke in 1947. On display are paintings, furniture, trophies and other mementoes of war.

Holland House, hit by a bomb in the last war, had remained derelict since. This year the London County Council bought the remnants from the earl of Ilchester and restored what it could, but only parts of the ground floor and arcades could be saved.

FIRST PERFORMANCES

An ordinary detective story made into a play opened at the Ambassador's theatre on 25 November: *The Mousetrap*, by Agatha Christie. It is still with us. For some time now it has been able to benefit from its own longevity, but there seems to have been no particular literary or artistic reason for its beginning a long run in the first place – the reviews were not spectacular, though Richard Attenborough was in the lead, and, in the nature of things, a detective story with an ending that must be kept secret is an unlikely candidate for such a long run.

The famous Italian conductor Arturo Toscanini made his debut in London at the age of 85, with two concerts at the Royal Festival Hall.

THE LAST TRAM

The last tram ran in London on 5 July. Three months earlier, on 5 April, the last use had been made of the Kingsway Tram Tunnel beneath Aldwych (see 1906); the tunnel then remained unused until the authorities were persuaded to open it for motor traffic in 1964.

A SIGN OF THINGS TO COME

Office building was a matter of controversy. It was noted that, while private developers found it impossible to obtain the necessary permits to use scarce building materials, the government was happy to build accommodation for its growing force of bureaucrats.

Some small-scale schemes were allowed. One involved the demolition of Lord Rosebery's handsome house at 36–38 Berkeley Square; it was replaced by an office block for Lewis Berger & Co., designed by Howard Souster and Partners in a style and size that had nothing in common with the rest of the square.

1953

A SOMBRE DAY AT WANDSWORTH

Crowds gathered outside Wandsworth Prison on 28 January, many of them to protest at the execution early that morning of Derek Bentley. The case had engaged consciences. Armed with a pistol, small-time

The Kingsway Tram Tunnel was reconstructed in 1931 to take double-decker trams. It was closed in 1952, and later used for motor traffic.

crooks Bentley and Christopher Craig had gone on a burglary. When challenged by a policeman, Craig had shot him dead. The defence contended that Bentley had urged Craig to give the gun up, but the jury found them both guilty of murder, as they were bound to do. Craig, under age at the time of the offence, was jailed; Bentley was sentenced to death and, despite appeals, the home secretary declined to vary the punishment. In 1999 Bentley was given a posthumous pardon.

DISASTER ON THE CENTRAL LINE

A Central Line train to Epping crashed into a stationary train in a tunnel at Leyton on 8 April. The second coach of the Epping train telescoped into the roof of the tunnel, and 11 people died.

MURDERS IN NOTTING HILL

On 27 March the bodies of four women were found in a house at 10 Rillington Place, a cul-de-sac in Notting Hill now demolished. In all, six bodies were found there, and John Christie, a bespectacled 55-year-old haulage clerk who lived in the house, was unsure if he had murdered seven or eight altogether. He confessed to the murder in 1950 of another tenant in the house – Beryl Evans. She and her baby daughter had been found dead there, and her husband, Timothy Evans, had already been found guilty and hanged for the death of the baby, though proclaiming his innocence. Christie never did admit responsibility for the baby's death, but the authorities were obliged in the circumstances to give a free posthumous pardon to Evans.

MORE CAR PARKS

Car ownership in London had risen by a third since 1949. Indiscriminate parking had been discouraged since 1947 and this year plans were announced for the construction of nine underground car parks beneath Lincoln's Inn Fields and Grosvenor, Cavendish, Berkeley, Soho, St James's, Leicester, Finsbury and Portman squares. In addition, kerbside meters were to be introduced in some areas, where the charge for parking would be 6d per hour.

LAST PRIVATE HOUSE IN BERKELEY SQUARE

The last private house in Berkeley Square – no. 3 – was put up for sale. It consisted of six storeys, with 12 rooms. The owner, Mrs Maud Knott, who had lived there since 1919, was asking £27,000.

A MODERN CORONATION

The coronation of Elizabeth II on 2 June was the first to be televised. The street decorations, like those of the 1937 coronation, when Grey Wornum was chosen as designer, were devised by an architect – this time Hugh Casson, one of the organizers of the Festival of Britain. Stands to seat 100,000 people were constructed in the streets, and the police had to ensure that 7,700 people got into Westminster Abbey on time.

A HEALTH CENTRE

A health centre was built on the new LCC estate at Woodberry Down, north London – the first established since the National Health Service began in 1948. The building housed general practitioners, facilities for minor operations, a school health unit, a dental surgery, and sections for other specialties.

A STRATFORD REVIVAL

The declining Theatre Royal in Stratford, east London, was taken over in February by a new group called Theatre Workshop, whose artistic director, Joan Littlewood, had founded what was termed a 'British People's Theatre' in Westmorland in 1945. The intention at Stratford was to produce good theatre for a working-class community, but in the event it was well attended by middle-class audiences prepared to make the trek eastward. The company's heyday began in 1958 with *A Taste of Honey* and *The Hostage*; *Fings Ain't Wot They Used T'Be* was produced in 1959, and *Oh, What a Lovely War!* appeared in 1963.

SAMARITANS BEGIN

The Samaritans, an organization dedicated to counselling people contemplating suicide, were established this year at St Stephen Walbrook church by the Revd Chad Varah.

NEW ARCHITECTURE

The Time-Life building at the corner of Bond Street and Bruton Street was finished this year; it was designed by Michael Rosenauer, who was to go on to build the Westbury Hotel opposite. The Time-Life building, like Berger House in Berkeley Square (see 1952), created a considerable stir by its radical departure from the established street architecture of what was, after all, one of the most prestigious streets in London. The *Architect's Journal* critic thought it a dull building with a high finish.

Another intrusion in an established streetscape was the erection of the YMCA Indian Students' Union and Hostel in Fitzroy Square, the work of Ralph Tubbs. It was generally well regarded, but it does not sit easily in the Georgian square, especially with its balconies at an upper level instead of at the usual first floor.

SUCCESS BENEATH THE ARCHES

The most famous success of the Players' Theatre beneath Charing Cross arches opened in April. This was *The Boy Friend*, a musical by Sandy Wilson, which established both the theatre and the writer.

1954

A CITY LORD OF LIGHT

Archaeologists excavating a bomb-site near the bed of the Walbrook, to the rear of the Mansion House, found on 18 September a carved marble head depicting Mithras, lord of light. This excavation, under the direction of Professor W. F. Grimes, then proceeded to reveal other marble figures, including Minerva, goddess of learning, Serapis, Egyptian god of the harvest and the underworld, and Mercury. Bacchus appeared in October, together with Silenus and Pan.

What had been discovered was a Roman temple, a 3rd-century establishment which derived from the worship of Mithras introduced from Asia Minor in the 1st century. The building itself had been a rectangle measuring about 55 ft by 25 ft, aligned east–west.

Bucklersbury House now stands on the site – the temple remains were reconstructed in front of the office building, while the artefacts, including a superb silver incense box, are in the Museum of London.

A COMPREHENSIVE SCHOOL

The first comprehensive school designed by the LCC was opened in September at Kidbrooke, Blackheath. Designed by Slater, Uren & Pike, it was to accommodate 1,700 pupils.

A WALK ALONG THE NEW RIVER

The 17th-century London water supply called the New River still winds its way through Haringey to Islington, occasionally at surface level, but usually well hidden from the general public. On 29 May this year a surface stretch in Islington was revamped and opened as the New River Walk, an ornamental oasis much needed in this built-up area.

CHURCHES BACK TO LIFE

St James Piccadilly was rededicated to mark its restoration after war damage, St Stephen Walbrook was reopened after repairs, and St Anne & St Agnes in Gresham Street was taken over by Lutherans. But St Peter, in Great Windmill Street, Soho, was demolished, and St James's, the chapel attached to the St James's parish burial ground in the Hampstead Road, was closed prior to demolition.

A MUSEUM IN HENDON

Church Farm Museum, a 17th-century building in Hendon, was opened to the public; the rooms have been arranged as they would have been in the 18th or early 19th centuries.

1955

HOLBORN RESTAURANT DEMOLISHED

A sad loss this year was the extravagantly decorated Holborn Restaurant at 218 High Holborn. Not only had it a grand dining room, often used for large functions, but there were 14 other dining rooms and, near to Great Queen Street as it was, three Masonic temples. The building had been designed by Archer & Green in 1874 with further embellishments by T. E. Collcutt in 1896. Offices now occupy its site.

FAREWELL TO HORSES

Two famous horse auction rooms were demolished this year. The best-known, Tattersall's, was at Knightsbridge Green, on a site now taken by Bowater House. In 1766 Richard Tattersall (1724–95), groom to the 2nd duke of Kingston, took a long lease on premises at Hyde Park Corner to establish an auction room. Sustained by a reputation for integrity and a talent for spotting a good horse, his premises were used extensively by Jockey Club members as a venue for regulating odds and placing bets. His name is commemorated at most racecourses by a 'Tattersall' section. The business moved to Knightsbridge Green in 1865 and out to Newmarket in 1939, leaving his old auction rooms empty.

The former Aldridge's auction room in Upper St Martin's Lane (see 1926) was demolished this year to make way for Thorn House, an elegant Basil Spence tower block.

WESTBURY HOTEL

An American hotel, the Westbury, was opened by the American ambassador on 1 March at the junction of New Bond Street and Conduit Street. Designed by Michael Rosenauer, it had 219 bedrooms, but space for only 90 people in the dining room. There were no public rooms on the upper floors and so there was no grand staircase, but there were ice-making machines and there was air-conditioning.

INNOVATION AT THE ARTS

The Arts Theatre Club in Great Newport Street, free of the lord chancellor's censorship, was more innovative than many theatres. This year *Waiting for Godot*, by the unknown Samuel Beckett, was staged, and in 1956 Ionesco's *The Waltz of the Toreadors* was produced.

1956

OFFICES IN THE SKY

Office tower blocks were soon to be commonplace. Sentinel House in Southampton Row, by T. P. Bennett, was a depressing foretaste of how that area of Holborn was to emerge. The New Zealand government unveiled plans for an elegant tower block at the southern end of Haymarket, on the site of the old Carlton Hotel, and the London County Council announced plans for an 18-storey block of flats for its Brandon Estate in Kennington.

A very large development was secretly in the making at the corner of Euston Road and Hampstead Road, opposite Warren Street station. In 1952 a development company, Stock Conversion, owned by Joe Levy, had obtained planning permission to build a block of offices here, but four years later Levy discovered that the LCC proposed to take much of his site for road-widening. Rather than pay substantial compensation, the council made a deal with Levy. In return for a free gift of the land needed for road-widening, the developer received permission to develop the 13 acres stretching along the Euston Road, provided that he bought the freeholds of the old shops already there. The deal was kept secret, and Levy was able to purchase the freeholds at their old value. The result of this lucrative arrangement was the Euston Centre.

FIRST AND LAST PERFORMANCES

John Osborne's play *Look Back in Anger* opened at the Royal Court Theatre on 8 May; despite less than capacity audiences, it was a sensational debut, providing much copy for the tabloid press, and the words 'angry young man' became a familiar epithet for almost anyone opposed to the established way of doing things. (It was an era of serious young men wearing duffel-coats, and they were pursued with glee by the press.)

The Royal Court, under the management of the English Stage Company, led by George Devine, also produced this year Kurt Weill

and Bertolt Brecht's *The Threepenny Opera*, a modern version of John Gay's *The Beggar's Opera*.

In a rare thawing of diplomatic relations, Russia's Bolshoi Ballet appeared in London for the first time, at the Royal Opera House, on 3 October.

But two theatres went out of existence. The Kingsway in Great Queen Street, rarely a good investment, was demolished – Newton Street now covers its site. It had, however, staged the first modern-dress version of *Hamlet*, in 1925. The Embassy Theatre at Swiss Cottage was taken over by the Central School of Speech and Drama, which opened on 23 September 1957.

A CLEANER LONDON

The Clean Air Act was passed this year, signalling the end of the London fogs beloved of fiction writers. Discretionary powers were given to local authorities to set up smoke-free zones – a belated response to the disastrous year of 1952, when it was calculated that the polluted atmosphere had cost over 3,500 lives. From 1956 London's air improved, but in fact the use of coal had been diminishing rapidly. Domestic coal sales in London fell by 12.5 per cent between 1951 and 1952, and by the time the Act came into force sales were down by another 12 per cent, as Londoners switched to gas fires and central heating.

A NEW TERMINAL

The Queen's Building at Heathrow Airport was completed. Designed by Frederick Gibberd, it was certainly an improvement on the mess of buildings which already existed, but there was still no architectural or visual cohesion at Heathrow.

A CHURCH CONVERTED

Sir John Soane's Holy Trinity church, in Marylebone Road, facing Great Portland Street, was now without a congregation. The last vicar had left in 1951, and the building had been closed in 1955, providing an early example of a recurring problem to face the Church Commissioners – a fine building, but how to use it? This year the Society for Promoting Christian Knowledge moved in, having converted it for office use.

1957

THREE THEATRES LOST

Three theatre buildings were lost this year. The most important and most scandalous loss was the St James's Theatre in Jermyn Street. The main blame lay with the LCC, which in 1954 granted a land speculator permission to to demolish it. Many letters were written to the press, and Sir Winston Churchill offered to start a fund to buy the building; Vivien Leigh, with great courage, stood up during a debate in the House of Lords and called out, 'My Lords! I wish to protest against the St James's Theatre being demolished.' Equity organized marches of protest, and the matter was raised several times in Parliament. To no avail. On the final night, 29 July, a sombre John Gregson stepped forward and addressed the audience: 'In this historic, beautiful theatre, the scene of so many great successes, you share the awful distinction of being in at the death. The talk has now become a grim reality. It should never have been allowed to happen. I want you to make a resolution in your hearts that such a thing shall never happen again.' The theatre was replaced by mundane offices designed by Richard Seifert.

Gregson's admonition seemingly had effect. Since then hardly an important theatre building in central London has been lost, though several variety theatres in the immediate suburbs have gone. In fact, overall, London has gained theatres.

Theatres on the eastern fringe were in difficult straits. The area of Kingsway and Aldwych was now rather quiet at night, unable to shake off its commercial mien; the Kingsway Theatre in Great Queen Street had already gone in 1956, and was followed this year by the Stoll on the east side of Kingsway, but in this instance the LCC, chastened no doubt by the St James's fiasco, insisted that the office development which replaced the Stoll should include a theatre. This was an ill-judged decision, since it was perfectly evident that a theatre here would have a precarious existence, and the Royalty Theatre, which opened on the site in 1960, was swiftly converted to a cinema.

The Gaiety Theatre, at the west end of Aldwych, was also demolished and a building for Citibank was erected in its stead.

The Strand area was further bereft when the Tivoli cinema, on the south side of the road, was also taken down. A store for Peter Robinson was built in its place.

DEVELOPMENT AREAS
Large development schemes were already in hand in the Elephant and Castle, Brixton and Notting Hill. In September the City announced plans for rebuilding around St Giles without Cripplegate: this became the Barbican scheme. The public was not reassured about office blocks when State House in High Holborn was erected for the government; this depressing pile was by Trehearne & Norman, Preston & Partners. More encouraging architecture was found in Great Russell Street, where the Trades Union Congress had opened new headquarters. On a restricted site the architect, David du R. Aberdeen, included a training college, a conference hall and offices. Overlooking Highgate Ponds, the Soviet Trade Delegation – without the obligation to obtain local planning permission – erected 36 depressing flats designed by Eric Lyons.

THE BEGINNINGS OF CARNABY MARKET
Carnaby Street market achieved its worldwide fame in the 1960s, though it had been a local mixed market since at least the early 19th century. Its modern manifestation appears to have originated with the opening of a boutique this year by John Stephen, John Vince and Andreas Spyropoulus, selling clothes that attracted a young clientele starved of smart fashion.

The heyday of Carnaby Market was the 1960s and early 1970s. But, packed with young tourists, it went down-market and was superseded as a place for buying fashionable clothes by Kings Road, Chelsea and, later, by the Covent Garden area.

BRUNEL UNIVERSITY ESTABLISHED
The Brunel College of Advanced Technology was this year established at Acton, a railway town which had good cause to remember the engineer's name. After rapid development the college moved to Uxbridge in 1962, to a larger site, and became Brunel University.

TERRACES SAVED
The Crown Commissioners, having been strongly criticized for their custodianship of the Nash terraces in Regent's Park, announced in November that they were to begin a programme of restoration rather than demolition.

1958

TROUBLE IN NOTTING HILL
Clashes between black and white residents occurred in Notting Hill on 30 August. There were further incidents on the following four evenings, the trouble spreading as far east as the Edgware Road.

STARGAZING IN MARYLEBONE ROAD
The Planetarium, owned by Madame Tussaud's Waxworks, was opened this year in Marylebone Road, on a site where there had once been a cinema attached to the waxworks. The dome of the building, designed by George Watt, is 67 ft in diameter. The projector contains nearly 200 smaller projectors which can display about 9,000 stars; the auditorium is air-conditioned to remove specks of dust which could be picked up in the beams of light.

THE FIRST OF MANY
What appears to have been the first office block in London featuring a tower on top of a podium block was Fountain House in Fenchurch Street, completed this year; the architect was W. H. Rogers.

A MODEL ESTATE
Where once had stood villas in ample grounds, the LCC's housing estate in Roehampton was now mostly finished. Regarded highly, it was and still is almost compulsory viewing for architectural students. Great effort was made to retain a rural feeling – as much as one can when building tower blocks – and the estate was well landscaped. Claims were made that here was a 'rural city', but the individual buildings are too modest to have much hold on posterity and the whole scheme is too planned to have a city's vitality.

NEW CINEMAS
In 1951 the British Film Institute had established a cinema, called the Telekinema, on the South Bank, to demonstrate advances in cinematic technology. It continued as a cult cinema, showing only films of artistic merit, and a new building, now called the National Film Theatre, was opened this year; a second auditorium was added in 1970. It was designed by the LCC, the job architect being N. Engleback.

The Columbia Theatre – actually a cinema – was opened in Shaftesbury Avenue this year as part of a distinctive office block designed by Sir John Burnet Tait & Partners. It was the first commercial cinema to be built in London after the war, and, with only 750 seats, it marked a new departure in cinema building. Not only was it part of an office complex, to maximize the value of the site, but it recognized that audiences were getting smaller as television grew: the old, barn-like auditoriums were now uneconomic.

THE END OF COLLINS'S MUSIC HALL
Collins's Music Hall on Islington Green was badly damaged by fire on 13 September. Enough remained of the old place to inspire talk of rebuilding, but the day of music hall had gone; instead, the site was taken over by Anderson's, the timber merchant next door. Anderson's has now also gone, and its site has been redeveloped. The remnant of the music hall is now a Waterstone's bookshop.

CABARET IN CRANBOURN STREET
The London Hippodrome in Charing Cross Road had led a precarious existence from its early circus days of 1900; it had staged ballet,

operetta, variety, jazz, revue featuring George Robey and Sophie Tucker, musical comedies, straight plays and 'Folies Bergère' productions. After considerable reconstruction, on 11 September it was opened as the Talk of the Town, a dine and cabaret venue. It is now the Hippodrome nightclub.

RUNNING OUT OF TELEPHONE NAMES

The expanding telephone system was running out of prefix names. While businesses and residents enjoyed the coveted MAYfair code, and the undertakers in Barking boasted RIPpleway in their numbers, the Post Office had the problem of inventing new names that made linguistic and mechanical sense and were appropriate to the area covered. It became apparent that only all-figure numbers would solve the dilemma, and from this year the old letter codes were phased out, to much lamentation.

This ended the harmless pursuit of divining the origin or thinking behind some of the exchange names. BYRon was easy in Harrow, as it marked the fact that Lord Byron went to Harrow School, but others were not so easy. ACOrn for Acton referred to Oaktown, an early form of the place name, and KEAts at Enfield referred to the poet's early residence there. Others were obscure. So far as anyone knew, ELGar had no residence in Harlesden and DICkens none in Canonbury, and what was ATLas doing in Isleworth? It was also fairly unlikely that Lord RAGlan had much acquaintance with Leytonstone.

A PANDA AT THE ZOO

London Zoo's declining fortunes were revived this year by the arrival of a giant panda, Chi-Chi. Enormous crowds came to view her, and subsequent attempts to mate her with other hyphenated pandas, both at home and away, made front-page news.

TWO INSTITUTES IN WOBURN SQUARE

The Courtauld Gallery and the Warburg Institute were opened this year in new buildings in Woburn Square, designed by Charles Holden. The Courtauld's collection was basically that of the textile millionaire Samuel Courtauld (see 1931); it is now housed at Somerset House. The Warburg Institute – part of the University of London – specializes in the influence of the classical tradition in European culture.

COLUMBIA DEMOLISHED

Demolition of the Columbia Market (see 1869) began this year. At the end of the 1950s there were few meaningful uses for this splendid building, which nowadays would probably be kept until one came along. It is a pity that it was replaced by some extremely boring housing – it deserved a better reminder.

1959

WELCOME TO THE M1

A significant stretch of road was opened on 2 November. The first 55 miles of the M1, north of London, were finished, and for some weeks the motorway was used intensively by motorists determined to find out just how quickly they dared drive their vehicles.

Of more local concern to Londoners was the Cromwell Road extension, which opened this year. Previously, a traveller going west on the Cromwell Road would have got no further than Warwick Road, where the railway barred his route; he would then have had to go north to Kensington Road and turn west again. The new extension took a good proportion of westward traffic over the railway and straight to Hammersmith Broadway, utilizing the line of the narrow Talgarth Road.

The Cromwell Road extension inevitably brought congestion to Hammersmith Broadway, and plans were announced this year for a cantilevered flyover to be built there.

THEATRICAL BREAKTHROUGHS

Billed as the first new theatre in the City of London since the 17th century, the Mermaid opened in a converted Victorian warehouse on 28 May. (In fact the City of London Theatre had been built in Norton Folgate in 1835, and lasted until 1871, when it was destroyed by fire.) The Mermaid had begun in 1951 as a private venture in an old school hall in St John's Wood, belonging to actor Bernard Miles; here he brought back the shape and some of the atmosphere of an Elizabethan theatre. Miles persuaded the Corporation to bear its theatrical history in mind (the Mermaid is near the old Blackfriars Theatre and to property that Shakespeare owned) and let him have the building at Puddle Dock for a nominal rent and also to put up money for its transformation. The architects, Devereux & Elidir Davies, retained the original thick walls and cast-iron Doric columns and, in a restricted site, contrived a 500-seat theatre, a restaurant and a spacious foyer. The first production, Lock up Your Daughters, was an immense success.

A smaller, but in the end more significant, beginning was made in an old church hall in Hampstead. The Hampstead Theatre Club, under the direction of James Roose-Evans, began in the Moreland Hall, renewing the tradition established by the Everyman and then the Embassy Theatre. Three years later Hampstead Council provided a shell of a building at Swiss Cottage, on a large site destined then to be a grand Hampstead Civic Centre complex. A new, but still small, building has been occupied since, but the Club still awaits a more substantial theatre.

During the war the Queen's Theatre in Shaftesbury Avenue had been damaged by bombing, although much of the auditorium was unharmed. It was reopened in September this year, with a new façade and foyer designed by Bryan Westwood.

BARBICAN SCHEME UNVEILED

The City unveiled its plan for the redevelopment of the Barbican area, then a mixture of bomb-sites and damaged buildings. Pedestrians and vehicles were to be kept separate from each other in this new vision of city planning. There were to be over 2,000 dwellings, with rents ranging from £190 to £575 per annum, mostly in blocks of six storeys, but with three blocks of 37 storeys. The architects were Chamberlin, Powell & Bon.

MORE OFFICE BLOCKS

Several distinguished office blocks were completed this year. Thorn House, in Upper St Martin's Lane, designed by Basil Spence, was much admired, but that did not save it from postmodernist cladding in the 1990s and a change of name to Orion House.

A store for Peter Robinson, with offices above, was opened in the Strand. Designed by Denys Lasdun, it made innovatory use of bronze cladding on the outside.

Castrol House, another tower on a podium, was completed on Marylebone Road. The Royal Fine Arts Commission had originally wanted an elongated block to maintain the height line of nearby properties, but the authorities were persuaded that some higher buildings were needed in the road.

HELICOPTERS IN BATTERSEA
Westland Aircraft opened Battersea Heliport on 23 April – the first heliport in the country. It is situated on 1 acre between Battersea and Wandsworth bridges.

A SCHOOL IN HOLLAND PARK
An outstanding school building was opened this year – the Holland Park Comprehensive. It was designed by Leslie Martin on an 8-acre wooded site which included the grounds of three former mansions, one of which, Thorpe Lodge, was retained as a school library. The school, designed to accommodate 2,000 pupils, has remained a showcase ever since.

1960

RIOTS IN ST PANCRAS
The new Conservative administration in St Pancras had introduced a council rent scheme based on ability to pay. This provoked extraordinary scenes both in the council chamber and on the streets. In September mounted police were called to disperse demonstrators around the town hall, and the eviction of two rebel tenants led not only to violent scenes but to strikes by railway workers. The evictions were carried out early one morning under strong police guard, the bailiffs having to circumvent barricades. Strikers from the Shell Centre building site marched up to Kentish Town and there tried to reoccupy the flat of one of the tenants in Leighton Road; the following day 450 police fought about 2,000 demonstrators outside St Pancras station. The home secretary banned all processions in the borough other than on religious occasions.

TELEVISION CENTRE OPENED
The BBC Television Centre at White City was officially opened, though still incomplete. It consists of a large central drum of offices and an outer, but smaller, ring of studios. The architects were Norman & Dawbarn.

NEW AMERICAN EMBASSY
The 1960s saw many changes in Grosvenor Square. The first was the erection of the United States Embassy on the west side; this was officially opened on 24 September. It was rumoured at the time that the USA had paid the Grosvenor family over £1 million for a 999-year lease of the site. The architect for this unaggressive building, the winner of a limited competition, was Eero Saarinen.

THE SANDERSON BUILDING
The outstanding building of the year was the headquarters and showrooms of Sanderson's, the wallpaper and furnishings company, in Berners Street. Outside there was a handsome Japanese-style courtyard garden, and inside the building was spacious and light; the stairways, unlike those of other stores, were a delight to use, and there was a large stained-glass mural by John Piper and an interior window by Patrick Reyntiens. The new building was opened in the company's centenary year.

END OF A HOSTEL
The role of Rowton Houses (see 1892) in providing hostel accommodation for homeless men was in decline. It was a Victorian institution, well regarded in the past for providing inexpensive shelter with some degree of privacy, but by now its buildings were in need of expensive modernization. Rowton Houses was a company rather than a charity, and a decision was made to reduce its commitment to hostels and to raise money from the existing buildings or sites. One very large hostel, at Mount Pleasant, was this year closed and converted into a hotel. That building has now gone altogether and a particularly unlovely Holiday Inn is on the site.

THEATRICAL HAPPENINGS
The Winter Garden Theatre in Drury Lane was closed this year, but only after the developers were obliged to promise a new theatre in the office block that was to be built.

Nearby, an experimental drama venue was opened in Earlham Street, where the Donmar Theatre operated in a warehouse – an early use of Covent Garden market buildings for arts purposes.

To the east, the Royalty Theatre was opened on the site of the old Stoll Theatre (see 1957).

Two old variety theatres were demolished or closed. The Holborn Empire in High Holborn, devastated by bombing, was finally taken down and replaced by offices. Another Empire disappeared – that of Finsbury Park, also an old Stoll theatre, and of late run by Val Parnell.

NEW COMPANY HALLS
The rebuilding of City livery-company halls had not been a high priority after the war, but by 1958 building restrictions were more relaxed. That year the premises of the Mercers, Saddlers and Clothworkers were finished; in 1959 Merchant Taylors' Hall was rebuilt; in 1960 the Brewers, Butchers and Carpenters all reopened new halls; and in 1961 the Girdlers, Painter-Stainers and Pewterers were rehoused.

TRAFFIC WARDENS APPEAR
Though parking meters were first introduced into London in 1959, their attendant wardens did not appear until 19 September 1960, in Westminster.

ABOLISHING THE LONDON COUNTY COUNCIL
A warning shot was fired at the LCC in October when a Royal Commission on Local Government recommended the abolition of the London County Council and the creation of a Greater London Council whose area would contain 52 borough authorities.

A NEW LIBRARY IN HOLBORN
The first major public library built in London after the war was opened by Holborn borough in Theobalds Road this year. Designed by the borough architect, Sydney Cook, it specialized in law books and was very popular with students attached to Gray's Inn and Lincoln's Inn, who found their own libraries overcrowded.

1961

A YEAR OF SATIRE
Satire became the rage. In May, *Beyond the Fringe*, a revue by Peter Cook, Alan Bennett, Jonathan Miller and Dudley Moore, created a new audience almost overnight when it opened at the Fortune Theatre, where it ran for four years. The Establishment Club was opened in Greek Street; here, political satire was soon fashioned for a

1900s

television transfer. More enduringly, the magazine *Private Eye* was first published on 25 October, also from Greek Street; the very early, rather juvenile, editions give no indication of the publication it was to become.

A NEW SCOUT HEADQUARTERS
Baden-Powell House in Queen's Gate, a new headquarters and London hostel for Scouts, was opened in July. Designed by Ralph Tubbs, it includes accommodation for 95 Scouts and also a museum devoted to the life of the founder of the Scout movement; the exhibits include the manuscript of *Scouting for Boys*, his famous hat, watercolours, and memorabilia of the Boer War that brought him to fame.

HABERDASHERS' SCHOOL MOVES AGAIN
The successive moves of the Haberdashers' Aske's School neatly reflect the growth of London. It was founded in 1690 by an endowment of Robert Aske, silk merchant of London, in part of the premises of the Haberdashers' Company in Staining Lane. Two years later it was rehoused on a greenfield site in Hoxton, where its gradual success required a 19th-century expansion – the handsome school building of that period still survives in Pitfield Street, though it is now a local-authority college. By the end of the 19th century Hoxton was no longer a desirable location, and so the girl pupils went to a new building in the fields of Acton and the boys to a pleasantly suburban site in Westbere Road, Hampstead. By 1961 the school needed even more space to expand; Hampstead was vacated (it became the Hampstead Comprehensive School) and the boys went even further afield – to Elstree, where in 1974 they were joined by the girls.

HOTEL DEVELOPMENTS
The government provided strong financial incentives to build hotels in London, and large new ones came thick and fast in the 1960s. The Carlton Tower Hotel, designed by Michael Rosenauer, was opened in Cadogan Square this year; it provided 318 rooms in its 16 storeys. At Heathrow Airport, Russell Diplock & Associates were responsible for the circular Oriel Hotel.

RESTORING WREN
Two Wren churches reopened this year after war-damage repairs. Both were named from St Andrew, both lost much of their church-yards in the 19th century to road-building schemes, and both had been severely damaged in 1941. St Andrew, Holborn, had been left with just walls and tower; the interior, insensitively altered in the 19th century by S. S. Teulon, could not be rescued. The church was sympathetically rebuilt by Seely & Paget, and was reconsecrated in October.

St Andrew by the Wardrobe in Queen Victoria Street, built by Wren after the Great Fire, was burnt out in a fire-bomb attack in 1940. It, too, had suffered from Victorian embellishment, and when renovation was done by Marshall Sisson this was removed. As there is hardly a congregation in this part of London (and its parish now includes at least six old City parishes), at the same time the tower was converted to house the Redundant Churches Fund, and part of the north aisle was allocated to the British and Foreign Bible Society.

PUPPETS IN ISLINGTON
In the dimunitive Dagmar Passage in Islington, near the parish church, John Wright this year began the Little Angel Puppet Theatre in an old temperance hall.

REORGANIZING LONDON
A government White Paper in November concurred with the earlier recommendation of a Royal Commission that the London County Council be abolished and a Greater London Council be created. Within the area, new boroughs would be created, each with a population of at least 200,000, and the old county boroughs of Croydon, East Ham and West Ham would disappear. Except in the central area, the boroughs would be responsible for education.

1962

ALAS! POOR DORIC
Two important London buildings were destroyed this year with the connivance of the highest authorities. Paradoxically, 1962 may be seen as the year in which the conservation movement began to wield influence. The losses were of such magnitude that the articulate, but fragmented, opposition to the haphazard demolition of old buildings was obliged to combine forces if it was to prevent further disasters.

For the destruction of the Euston Arch, that giant and positive Doric entry to Euston station and the railway age, there is, looking at the sterile railway forecourt of today, seemingly no excuse. The structure could, many claim, have been retained in situ if the architects for the new station had used some imagination; failing that, money should have been found to relocate it nearby. To break it up seemed wanton then, and remains so. For the demolition of the Coal Exchange in Lower Thames Street there was, perhaps, a valid contemporary argument, but who now, looking at the arid north side of Lower Thames Street, transformed into one of the most unappealing highways in central London, could be sympathetic?

The matter of the arch arose in 1959, when the British Transport Commission, in proposing the rebuilding of Euston, signalled the demolition of the listed Grade II Great Hall of the old station (see 1849) and of the famous arch. The LCC allowed the case on the hall (an even greater loss), but said that the arch should be kept. The Royal Fine Art Commission intervened in the hope of bringing the parties together, but the BTC and the responsible ministry evaded the issue. The government declined to put up the money (£180,000) to dismantle and rebuild the arch, as did the BTC. Three major amenity organizations – the Society for the Protection of Ancient Buildings, the Georgian Society and the Victorian Society – went on a joint deputation to Harold Macmillan, the prime minister. To no avail.

But the British Transport Commission was to pay heavily for its crass disregard of public opinion. In 1966 it was outgunned by an influential conservation movement, now underpinned by public opinion, when it proposed to demolish both King's Cross and St Pancras stations; in more recent times it has had, against its will, to keep and restore Liverpool Street station in the Broadgate development, and its grandiose plans for the redevelopment of the King's Cross goods yard have been hampered at every turn by conservationists.

As part of the Euston development scheme, the Adelaide and Victoria hotels were demolished; these, the first railway hotels in the world, had stood on either side of the Doric arch in front of the station.

The cast-iron rotunda of the Coal Exchange was a remarkable building that needed another use. In 1958 the government proposed to list the building, but was told by the City of London of its intention to demolish it for road widening. The Victorian Society succeeded in

The majestic Doric arch at Euston station, needlessly demolished in 1962 after a famous conservation battle. Some of its stones weighed 13 tons.

delaying matters, but in January 1962 the ministry delivered a judgement which allowed demolition, preferring this to a scheme to include a pedestrian walkway under arcades within the structure of the exchange. When the matter was next discussed by the City Corporation, the chairman of the Streets Committee described the exchange as a dingy place devoid of any paintings or other objects of artistic beauty. The much-admired ironwork, he opined, would not be acceptable for use as public-lavatory railings. The City allowed the redevelopment to proceed, but gave the Victorian Society four weeks to raise £20,000, half the cost of shipping the rotunda, when demolished, to Melbourne, Australia, where it would be re-erected. Time was of the essence, the City insisted, and the building was hurriedly destroyed in November 1962 when the money was not forthcoming. The site was then left vacant for nearly ten years.

The City, like British Rail, also paid for its decision later, when conservationists won a long battle to save Billingsgate Market across the road and so reduced the amount of money the Corporation could obtain for the building.

GIANT ON THE SOUTH BANK

Whatever buildings might have come along to delight the eye on the South Bank, they would have had to compete with the backdrop of the Shell Building, which was opened in March. It is 26 storeys high, can house about 5,000 staff, and has endless corridors and a swimming pool. (When it was built, there was also a rifle range and a cinema.) It was the largest air-conditioned building in Europe and, from the South Bank's point of view, a dismal addition. The architect was Sir Howard Robertson.

AN UNDERGROUND CAR PARK

The Hyde Park underground car park was opened on 15 October; it could contain 1,100 cars in a single storey. An innovation was an automatic barrier which allowed entry only when a ticket, stamped with the time of entry, was taken. At the same time Park Lane was doubled in width – land having been taken from the fringes of Hyde Park – and made into a dual carriageway.

MORE DEMOLITIONS

Printing House Square, containing the offices of *The Times*, was demolished this year. Included was the house in which John Walter, the founder of the newspaper, had lived and which had remained a dwelling house related to the paper until 1910.

Londonderry House, at the junction of Hertford Street and Park Lane, was demolished, and in 1967 the Londonderry Hotel opened on its site.

RESTORING WOBURN WALK

Not everything was bad news on the conservation front. St Pancras Council this year received an award for its restoration of Woburn Walk, and another for its renovation of Goldington Crescent.

QUEEN'S GALLERY OPENS

A former conservatory at Buckingham Palace was this year converted into an art gallery to display some of the paintings in the queen's collection.

THEATRICAL LOSSES AND GAIN

The West London Theatre in Church Street, off Edgware Road, had been bombed in 1941; what was left of it was destroyed by fire in 1962.

The Marlborough Theatre, a Frank Matcham building in Holloway Road, used as a cinema by 1919, was demolished this year and its site taken for offices.

The Prince Charles Theatre, the first completely new theatre in the West End since the war, was built as part of an office block in Leicester Place and opened on 26 December with a Canadian revue, *Clap Hands*. It was not a financial success, and closed in 1965, reopening as the Prince Charles cinema in 1969.

ART CENTRE IN CROYDON

Croydon, which before the war had hardly changed from its old market-town days, had been systematically redeveloped since the late 1950s. A complex of skyscrapers, a shopping centre, civic offices and an arts centre replaced the old streets and the extensive bomb damage, and for those who still wanted to work in London the rail service made it a convenient dormitory town. In 1963 a plan was approved to redevelop the former Croydon Airport land for housing and light industry.

On 2 November this year the Fairfield Halls arts complex was opened by the queen. It included the Ashcroft Theatre, the Fairfield Hall itself – primarily a concert hall, but one which can be adapted for stage shows, boxing and films – and a gallery. The architects were Robert Atkinson & Partners.

1963

CHANGES AT THE OLD VIC

The Old Vic temporarily ended its illustrious independent career this year with a production of *Measure for Measure* and a valedictory speech by Sybil Thorndike. The National Theatre Company, which had been formally established in 1962, then took up a long residence here while awaiting construction of the National Theatre buildings on the South Bank. The company's first production at the Old Vic was *Hamlet*, produced by Laurence Olivier and starring Peter O'Toole.

1900s

A new theatre-cum-cabaret was added in the West End, where the newly built Mayfair Hotel included the Mayfair Theatre. But further west still the old Metropolitan Theatre in the Edgware Road was demolished to make way for the Westway flyover.

MUSIC IN BRENTFORD
The Musical Museum was opened in High Street, Brentford, this year. It was founded by Frank Holland, principally to show his collection of automatic pianos, but there is much more there, including pianos of all sorts, phonographs, organs, a self-playing Wurlitzer, and thousands of piano rolls. The museum is housed in the old church of St George, designed by Sir Arthur Blomfield.

DISTINCTIVE TOWERS
New Zealand House, at the southern end of Haymarket, was completed this year, to plaudits from the architectural profession and others besides. It had, in fact, been the first office block allowed to breach the old London height restrictions, but it had been so long in the making that other towers had appeared before it. The architects were Robert Matthew, Johnson-Marshall.

The tallest building in London, at 387 ft, was now the Vickers Tower on Millbank. The architects of this were Ronald Ward & Partners.

In Park Lane the Hilton Hotel was opened to a barrage of press publicity. The upper bar, overlooking London, and the Playboy Club were considerable attractions. There are four basement floors and 30 above, with 512 air-conditioned bedrooms. Lewis Solomon, Kaye & Partners were the architects.

DEVELOPMENTS PENDING
The London County Council opposed, but failed to stifle, the scheme designed by Basil Spence for the rebuilding of Knightsbridge Barracks. The earliest buildings for the Horse Guards had been erected at the end of the 18th century, with space for 600 men and 500 horses; these were replaced in 1880 by new accommodation designed by T. H. Wyatt. Opposition to the Spence scheme was not confined to the LCC: many were disquieted by the proposal for a 270-ft tower overlooking the park.

The Crown Commissioners, the Church Commissioners and the Army and Navy Store announced a scheme to redevelop an 8-acre site to the west of Victoria Street. An end benefit would be a vista of Westminster Cathedral from Victoria Street.

SPEEDING TO HEATHROW
Getting to Heathrow Airport was a tiresome trial when accompanied by heavy suitcases. There was no Underground extension to the airport, and there were only coaches from specific pick-up points, such as Victoria station. A small improvement was effected on 6 November, when British European Airways opened an air terminal in the Cromwell Road, designed by Sir John Burnet Tait & Partners; but in the matter of convenience it was still far inferior to the direct rail link from Victoria to the underused Gatwick airport, because the new terminal building was erected some distance from the nearest Underground station, and therefore required a laden walk to reach it.

HOUSES FOR THE BETTER-OFF
Since the war, the emphasis had been on building, as quickly as possible, local-authority housing. But a number of private housing schemes had been completed in the suburbs. That of Span Housing, adjoining

the Paragon at Blackheath, was notable inasmuch as the dwellings were open-plan and mostly designed for couples without children. Around a courtyard were grouped 23 flats and ten houses, with from one to three bedrooms and costing from £4,250 to the penthouse at £8,500.

FIRE AT HIGHGATE
Fire gutted the historic Lauderdale House on Highgate Hill this year, and considerable doubts were expressed as to whether the building was worth repairing.

1964

A NEW ROYAL COLLEGE
The most stylish new building of the year, opened on 5 November, was that for the Royal College of Physicians in Regent's Park. Designed by Denys Lasdun, it is a T shape with a half-sunken lecture theatre beside it; the style is decidedly modern, but harmonizes with the Nash Terraces. The materials and finish are of a high standard – the Censors' Room is lined with the same Spanish oak that once adorned the college's first building in Warwick Lane, and the library (which contains a near-contemporary manuscript of Chaucer's *Canterbury Tales*) is similar to that in the college's former home.

SERMON AT ST PAUL'S
Four thousand people gathered at St Paul's Cathedral on 6 December to hear the black American civil-rights leader the Revd Martin Luther King give a sermon entitled 'The Three Dimensions of a Complete Life'.

FAMOUS CLOCKS
Beneath the clock at Victoria station was a favourite real and fictional meeting place, but this year the clock – affectionately known as Little Ben – was taken down because of road widening. It reappeared again, thoroughly restored, in 1981 – a gift from a French oil company to mark the wedding of the prince of Wales.

The entertaining clock outside Fortnum & Mason in Piccadilly was added to the building this year. The mechanics feature at hourly intervals Mr Fortnum and Mr Mason, who acknowledge and bow to each other. The clock was designed by Berkeley Sutcliffe.

THE ARTS AT CHALK FARM
In 1960 the Trades Union Congress was persuaded by the playwright Arnold Wesker to pass an innocuous resolution, no. 42 on the agenda, 'to make proposals … to ensure a greater participation by the trade-union movement in all cultural activities'. It was what is known in political circles as a 'pious' resolution – one that could hardly be opposed, but it was assumed also that no one would bother to take it up seriously. But Arnold Wesker, fired with a vision of a centre in which artists of different disciplines would work with each other and in which the public could involve themselves in both a practical and a personal way, pursued it with great enthusiasm. The new centre, he hoped, would tour arts events to those parts of the country (working-class areas in particular) that were then badly served in such matters.

What Centre 42 (named from the resolution) needed was a suitable building, and when the Round House, the old engine shed at Chalk Farm, came on the market Louis Mintz, art patron and businessman, bought the 16-year lease and donated it to the cause. But the building needed a vast sum of money to convert it, even by degrees, and gradually Wesker's dream disappeared in financial realities. When Kenneth Tynan's salacious *Oh! Calcutta!* was staged in the hope that it would bring much-needed revenue (it did), Wesker left.

The subsequent history of the building and its occupants has been one of occasional bouts of optimism and triumph, but generally tempered by a frail hold on life. The building now hosts visiting companies.

PART CIVIC CENTRE

Ambitious plans for 'civic centre' complexes were not unusual in London at this time, but they needed rethinking in the wake of the pending merger of London boroughs within the Greater London area. One such plan was that of Hampstead Council – soon to be merged rather reluctantly into Camden – which envisaged a number of civic buildings on a large island site at Swiss Cottage. Only two of these buildings were built – the central library and the swimming pool, both by Basil Spence. These were opened this year, but the Hampstead Theatre Club, which had hoped for a purpose-built auditorium on the site, had to make do with a temporary building (which has since been replaced by another). In later years much of the rest of the site was taken by a decorous office block and a useful five-a-side football area, but as a cohesive landscape it is a failure.

REOPENING A TUNNEL

The old Kingsway Tram Tunnel, connecting Waterloo Bridge to Kingsway, had lain derelict since the last tram had used it in 1952. There had been frequent calls to reopen the route for car traffic, but the LCC had prevaricated, and it was not until this year that the southern section was opened for that purpose. The northern section, running up Kingsway and into Theobalds Road, is ostensibly used by an organization pledged to defend and warn London against flooding.

SPORTS CENTRE AT CRYSTAL PALACE

The National and Youth Sports Centre in Crystal Palace Park was opened on 13 July. It includes a stadium, a multi-sports hall, a swimming pool and a dry ski slope.

CASTELLATION ON THE HEATH

The famous pub Jack Straw's Castle, at the top of Hampstead Heath, had been bombed during the war. The old building was in fact a knocking together of several dwellings, and architecturally it was no great loss – though it had charm. On 23 March its replacement was unveiled, designed by Raymond Erith. Displaying a castellated and weatherboarded exterior, it is not a building for purists, but it has many admirers.

A SLOGAN SURRENDERED

The Windmill Theatre in Great Windmill Street, Soho, had proudly boasted for many years, 'We Never Closed', referring to the fact that its mildly titillating shows had continued throughout the war. However, it did close this year, on 31 October, for conversion into a cinema.

BUILDINGS IN ST JAMES'S

What were known as the Economist Buildings were virtually complete: one smaller building was on St James's Street, keeping Boodle's Club company; the rest, in a high-rise formation, were in its eastern

hinterland. The scheme, designed by Alison and Peter Smithson, was much admired for its sensitivity to its surroundings.

A CYLINDRICAL CAR PARK

It was determined this year to incorporate a car park beneath Bloomsbury Square, but there were restraints on its size owing to the trees above. This resulted eventually in a car park consisting of a cylinder 70 ft deep and 157 ft in diameter, which drivers had to navigate until they found a parking space.

1965

A LONDON FUNERAL

On 30 January the funeral of Sir Winston Churchill occupied central London. His body had lain in state at Westminster Hall, where some 320,000 people filed past it. On the day of the funeral the coffin was carried from the hall by Grenadier Guards, placed on a gun carriage, and taken to St Paul's, where the service was conducted by the archbishop of Canterbury and the bishop of London. The pallbearers included Earl Avon, Lord Mountbatten, Field Marshal Slim and Harold Macmillan. The coffin was then taken to Tower Pier, where it was conveyed by river to Waterloo and thence on to Bladon churchyard.

UNDER NEW MANAGEMENT

The Greater London Council took over from the London County Council this year. The population it governed was about the same as that inherited by the LCC when it was formed at the end of the 19th century, but in an area of 610 sq. miles against the LCC's 117 sq. miles. This shift of population to the suburbs may be illustrated by St Pancras borough, which in the 19th century had a population roughly the same as that of the newly created London Borough of Camden, of which St Pancras was just a part.

The responsibilities of the GLC included overall strategic planning of resources and transport; the maintenance of major roads; sewage; arts on a London-wide basis; historic houses and various museums, stately homes and open spaces; fire services; and, through the Inner London Education Authority, education within those inner-London boroughs previously administered by the LCC.

Old boroughs of London, Middlesex, Surrey, Kent, Essex and Hertfordshire were fashioned into 30 new authorities. In the rearrangement, the ancient anomaly of North Woolwich on the north side of the Thames being under the control of Woolwich borough on the south of the Thames was abolished, and the northern area became part of Newham. The anomaly of the City of London remained.

A THREAT TO MARYLEBONE

St Marylebone station, the last of the main-line stations to be built along the Euston/Marylebone Road axis, had always seemed superfluous. The station and the goods yard behind had become increasingly surplus to requirements, and this year British Rail announced that it was selling the goods yard and sidings in the Lisson Grove area to the GLC and Westminster for redevelopment. The station's days, it was assumed, were numbered.

AN ELEPHANT HOUSE

The delightful Elephant and Rhinoceros House at London Zoo was opened this year. Designed by Casson, Conder & Partners, its form is a strong reminder of elephants grouped in a circle. The Aviary was finished in July. Designed by Lord Snowdon and Cedric Price, the engineering was by Frank Newby, who had helped to build the Skylon at the Festival of Britain.

SHOPPING AT THE ELEPHANT

The large shopping centre at the Elephant and Castle was opened. Designed by Bossevin & Osmond, it had the misfortune to be on the London County Council's new road system, and consequently faced uninvitingly inwards away from the traffic. The centre was once a dreary concrete grey, but is now a violent pink.

THE POST OFFICE TOWER

The Post Office Tower, a telecommunications centre, was opened on 8 September in Cleveland Street. Then the highest building in London, it is 620 ft high (including the mast) and 35 ft in diameter, and at the time of its opening it had an observation floor and a revolving restaurant near the top. The chief architect was Eric Bedford.

1966

MOVING A CHURCH

St Mary Aldermanbury had been damaged in both world wars: a Zeppelin bomb hit it in the First, and a fire bomb in the Second burnt it out. The church remained a ruin after the last war and, with hardly a local congregation to sustain it, its future was bleak. But the president of Westminster College, Fulton, Missouri, conceived of the idea of moving a Wren church to the university canvas to commemorate Sir Winston Churchill and, in particular, his 'iron curtain' speech, delivered there. St Mary Aldermanbury was chosen.

Twelve columns and 7,000 numbered stones were shipped to the USA, together with others made from the same quarries that Wren had used nearly 300 years earlier. St Mary's was re-hallowed in Fulton in 1969.

HOTEL DEVELOPMENTS

The hotel-building fever still raged. In 1964 the Europa Hotel had opened in Grosvenor Square; in 1965 the Royal Garden Hotel, a Richard Seifert tower, spoilt the view from the Kensington Gardens it overlooked; and in 1966 the Cavendish Hotel in Jermyn Street, designed by Maurice Hanna, replaced the intimate old hotel on the site. In Russell Square the demolition of the grandiose Imperial Hotel (see 1900) was a severe loss, especially as it was superseded by a building so inappropriate to the square, and hardly becoming to anywhere else. Doll's other hotel nearby, the Russell, demonstrates the quality of what was needlessly demolished.

EXPANDING LIBRARIES

Hornsey opened its long-planned new central library at Crouch End just as it was being merged into Haringey in 1965. A new Barking central library was opened in 1966 to replace the old one which had been burnt down.

Public libraries were making a concerted comeback now that the novelty of television had receded. New services such as the lending of records and paintings, information bureaux and the erection of lighter, less fusty, library buildings were winning new customers. This could not be said of the Hampstead Subscription Library, a 19th-century

The Post Office (now Telecom) Tower heralded a new age of communications.

institution which had once counted John Constable as a member; it closed its doors on 2 April this year.

CARNIVAL IN NOTTING HILL

After the race riots of previous years, a more hopeful activity emerged in Notting Hill. It began as a local pageant and mild celebration, and grew year by year into the most flamboyant carnival in London, held on August Bank Holiday.

KEEPING A TRAFFIC HAZARD

For years the old toll-house which projected into the road opposite the Spaniards inn in Hampstead Lane had been regarded with either hostility or affection. Moves to have it demolished, led by Barnet Council but opposed by Camden across the road, were this year defeated by the Greater London Council which noted that 'part of its [the toll-house's] charm consists in the obstruction it causes, making it a reminder of the days of horse-drawn vehicles paying toll'.

THE SWISS IN LEICESTER SQUARE

The architect of the TUC's Congress House in Great Russell Street, David du R. Aberdeen, this year completed another interesting building – the Swiss Centre, in Coventry Street, by Leicester Square. Its podium contains three storeys of shops and showrooms, and on an upper storey there are cinemas.

A NEW UNIVERSITY

The Northampton Polytechnic in Finsbury, founded in 1896, formed this year the basis of City University, an institution substantially financed by the City of London. The main university buildings in Northampton Square are on the former site of the manor house of Clerkenwell. The polytechnic building, designed by the architect of the Old Bailey, E. W. Mountford, still stands, but the modern buildings were built between 1969 and 1970.

1967

SURROUNDING ST PAUL'S

St Paul's Cathedral, surrounded by the scars and craters of war, was both a potent symbol of resistance and endurance and the subject of protracted argument. What now should be built in its periphery? Most fundamentally, should the Saxon street pattern be restored or the opportunity be taken radically to alter this part of London? The discussion began while the bombs still fell, and it continues to this day now that the 1960s solution, planned by Lord Holford and completed in 1967, is to be taken down.

The challenge was unique in 1666, when Wren proposed a total landscaping of the area around the cathedral, so as to give it a more exposed and monumental environment. That chance was lost and in 1957 the main argument was related to the architecture which should once again hem in the building. Good-mannered buildings could disappear set against Wren's masterpiece, but anything more aggressive and self-assured could be condemned as intrusive. Some wanted neo-classical offices; others 'modern' architecture within a formal and monumental precinct.

The Holford Paternoster Square development, though it has three tower blocks on podiums linked by lower buildings, is not aggressive, but it found few friends and there was no rush to prevent its demolition so soon after it was built. Perhaps Holford was too long involved with the problem to present something satisfactory. As far back as 1947 it was his plan for the rejuvenation of the City that was the basis for redevelopment. He wanted traffic removed from St Paul's altogether by making Ludgate Hill pedestrian-only except on ceremonial occasions; his solution was to widen Carter Lane to provide an east–west route, sweeping away the crowded arrangement of streets between the cathedral and the river. But, as with Wren before him, the old street pattern survived virtually unchanged.

One building completed this year in the vicinity did, however, please most people. This was the St Paul's Choir School in New Change, designed by M. Powers.

MORE BUILDINGS ON THE SOUTH BANK

The Queen Elizabeth Hall and the Purcell Room were opened by the queen on 1 March, the former for small orchestral and chamber concerts, the latter for soloists and chamber music. Architecturally, the buildings are far removed from the style of the Royal Festival Hall,

whose function they complement. Designed by the Greater London Council Architects' Department under the direction of Sir Leslie Martin and Sir Hubert Bennett, they have to be seen in the context of the buildings that came afterwards – the Hayward Gallery and the National Theatre. Their shapes are uncompromisingly sculptural and, on a fine day from the river, of much interest. But the close reality is more frequently experienced. The walkways that have to be negotiated to get to the joint and unimpressive foyer of the two concert halls are unappetizing, sometimes treacherous, stained with water at the least, and of an uninviting texture. The overall impression within the building is of introspection, with no sense of occasion or joy, but the acoustics are thought good. Like Paternoster Square, the buildings on this stretch of the South Bank are, at the time of writing, under siege and with few defenders. A recent scheme envisages the retention of the buildings, but a wholesale improvement in the approaches to them.

A LAST APPEARANCE

In the rather more ornate auditorium of the Royal Albert Hall, on 16 September, the Promenade Concert audience rose to its feet to say goodbye to Sir Malcolm Sargent. He had conducted the Proms for many years, and was as much part of their emotional attraction as the knockabout jingoism of the Last Night celebrations. But by the end of 1966 Sargent was too ill to conduct. This night he was escorted to the rostrum by Colin Davis for what he and his audience knew would be his last address to them, and he managed better than many of his listeners to get through his words. He died three weeks later.

DEMOLITION BY THE ARCHWAY ROAD

One of the few charms of the Archway Road in Islington was the group of Whittington almshouses erected on a greenfield site in the 1820s. They were swept away this year, superseded by local-authority housing that turns its back on the world.

A NEW TOWN AT PLUMSTEAD

A start was made this year on the creation of Thamesmead, a new town on the marshes of Plumstead. The 1,300-acre development includes housing, 200 acres of parkland, a health centre and various shopping precincts and out-of-town large stores, as well as a yacht basin and two lakes.

A DOCK CLOSURE

The post-war years had been difficult ones in the London docks. Inadequate facilities for larger ships, poor labour relations and demarcation disputes, resistance to mechanization, primitive and undignified employment practices and political troublemaking had all combined to consolidate an already poor reputation. In the ten years from 1945 to 1955 there were 37 strikes, and business was for various reasons moving inexorably eastward.

The East India Docks had not been commercially viable for some years and were now suitable only for smaller loads. This year they were closed, the first of the chain of docks to go, and in 1968–9 both the London and St Katharine's docks, each operating at a loss, were also shut. The end of London as a port was to come quickly.

SCOTLAND YARD MOVES

Scotland Yard this year moved again (see 1890), when the Metropolitan Police relocated to a modern office block in Broadway, taking the old name with them. The new block was designed by Chapman Taylor.

1968

DISASTER IN THE EAST END

At six in the morning on 16 May, while most were still asleep, a gas explosion on the 18th floor of Ronan Point, a block of flats in Newham, blew out the walls of an apartment and caused a vertiginous and catastrophic collapse of one corner of the tower. People woke to find their homes open to the sky as the outer walls became disconnected and floors slid downward. Miraculously, only four people were killed and 11 injured.

The Ronan Point tragedy ended in the most dramatic way the era of tower-block homes. There were still many to be built, because the nature of the housing pipeline prevented an immediate cessation, but to all intents and purposes 'cities in the sky' were a thing of the past in London. Architecturally, the disaster had exposed a weakness in a particular type of tower-block construction that could be overcome, but the damage caused to the public's perception of high-rise housing was not likely to be remedied. The problems associated with tower blocks – their inconvenience for those with children, the vandalism, the broken lifts, the litter, the windswept spaces around them, the loneliness of many residents, none of these peculiar to Ronan Point – gave rise to public outrage at the incident.

EUSTON STATION OPENED

The queen opened the new Euston station on 14 October. A general criticism of the building was that it was as bland as an airport, with no sense of railway. It is, however, much easier to use than, say, King's Cross, where the congested concourse has long queues and motorized luggage trolleys competing for space.

A NEW TUBE LINE

The Victoria Line between Walthamstow and Highbury was opened without ceremony on 1 September; on 7 March the next year the queen was invited to insert sixpence into a ticket machine to obtain a fivepenny fare (the machine did not cooperate and another sixpence had to be found), before 'driving' a train between Green Park and Oxford Circus, thereby officially opening the line. It was the first railway to be built across London for over 60 years, and had a considerable effect on house prices in the new areas it served – in particular, Islington's terraces and houses, already being gentrified, were now convenient to travel from. An extension from Victoria to Brixton opened in 1971.

TWO NEW GALLERIES

The Hayward Gallery on the South Bank opened in July with a Matisse exhibition. The architecture (by the Greater London Council Architects' Department) was in much the same vein as for the Queen Elizabeth Hall and the Purcell Room.

The uncompromisingly modern architecture of the Hayward was in contrast to the new classical premises of the Institute of Contemporary Arts, in the Mall. Here, utilizing old stables, a new gallery and meeting place were provided this year. The institute had been established in Dover Street in 1947 by Roland Penrose and Herbert Read.

DEMOLITION IN HAMMERSMITH

St Paul's School, which had moved to an Alfred Waterhouse building in Hammersmith in 1884, moved further out to Barnes this year. The building left behind – a red-brick pile whose vivid colour seemed never to mature – was demolished.

LONDON TELEVISION

London Weekend Television opened this year; it was eventually to be housed in a specially built block on the site of some Bowater's warehouses on the South Bank, next to the National Theatre. Thames Television, founded a year earlier, had the weekday evening franchise for the capital, and operated from a new block in Euston Road.

LONDON BRIDGE TO AMERICA

Demolition of the old London Bridge, opened in 1831, had begun in November 1967 – but not haphazardly. The bridge had been sold to McCulloch Properties, an American company, for £1,025,000, and it was to be re-erected at Lake Havasu City, an artificial town by an artificial lake, founded in Arizona by one of the creators of Disneyland. Demolition was therefore a delicate operation, and it was not until July 1968 that the first shipload of bridge sections – officially certified by US Customs as a 'large antique' and declared duty-free – arrived at Long Beach, California.

1969

NUNHEAD CLOSES

The famous Victorian cemeteries of London, in which the quality of a monument once ensured that Death was not the great leveller it was supposed to be, were now casualties of fashion, economics and lack of space. And, as care of the cemeteries deteriorated, so did vandalism increase, with monuments smashed as mindlessly as telephone boxes.

Nunhead Cemetery, opened by the London Cemetery Company in 1840, was in a bad state by the mid-1950s, after a long history of financial problems. The first superintendent had defrauded the company of thousands of pounds, and the cemetery was not as 'fashionable' as Highgate, Norwood or Kensal Green; even between the wars it was hardly economic. The railings were taken for scrap during the war, and vandalism took control afterwards. Staff were difficult to afford, because the income from investment of the once-and-for-all fees of plotholders was insufficient to cope with inflation. In 1960 a property company proposed to take the cemetery on if it were allowed to build on part of the ground, but local opinion defeated this. Monuments and catacombs were destroyed or ransacked for lead, and there were stories of black-magic rituals in its grounds. This year the company closed Nunhead, and it was not until 1975 that the borough council bought it for £1 so as to restore it for public use as a burial ground, nature reserve and park.

MOTORWAYS PROPOSED

The GLC announced details of an 11-mile ringway motorway through south London, costing £158 million and requiring the demolition of 2,189 houses. This was soon to be followed by another proposal for an inner-London motorway connecting with the M1, cutting a swathe across politically articulate areas of Camden Town and Hampstead. Both schemes were defeated years later after opposition campaigns.

ON THE BARRICADES

Numerous squatters occupied a mansion at 144 Piccadilly in September and had to be evicted by police. The squat was in essence a political demonstration, comparing, in the 'never had it so good age', the existence of homelessness with the way in which property developers seemingly had carte blanche in the capital. The University of London also came in for a great deal of criticism for its destruction of most of the once elegant Woburn Square.

THEATRE HAPPENINGS

The Greenwich Hippodrome, long since closed, formed the basis for the construction of the Greenwich Theatre, which opened this year with a play, *Martin Luther King*, written by its director, Ewan Hooper.

In Camden Town, the last of the Bedford Theatre in the High Street was finally demolished. But near Lisson Grove the Inner London Education Authority opened the Cockpit Theatre, a theatre-in-the-round auditorium used extensively by students of dramatic techniques. The building was designed by Ed Mendelsohn.

The Prince Charles Theatre in Leicester Place was this year reopened as a cinema. In Panton Street the Cinecenta cinema was launched. It was an innovative building with four small cinemas in the basement of an office block, each one seating only about 150 people. The architects were Cassidy, Farrington & Dennys.

1970

SCHEMES IN THE OFFING

The government announced that it was to construct a new British Library in Bloomsbury, on a site opposite the British Museum. Most users of the library agreed that a new building was necessary, although the loss of the circular Reading Room was generally lamented, but there were many who felt that the destruction of a unique part of Bloomsbury to make way for it was an unnecessary sacrifice.

There had been enough close calls to convince the Greater London Council that a flood-control system for the Thames was urgently needed. The council this year revealed a plan to construct a movable barrier across the river between Woolwich and Blackwall.

The giant Aylesbury scheme in Southwark was nearing completion. Records were established: it was the largest single housing scheme by a London borough, providing 2,400 homes over 64 acres, and it contained the largest systems-built housing block in Europe.

It was proposed by Ealing Council to redevelop its central shopping area. This was one of six such schemes in the Greater London area, Lewisham being another.

An unusual housing and shopping scheme was planned for the Foundling Estate in Bloomsbury, where homes would be provided in stepped terraces, ziggurat fashion.

In the wake of the Ronan Point disaster, Hackney Council, with an ample supply of tower blocks, announced that in future it would restrict itself to two- or three-storey houses and flats. But Barking Council, however, announced that it would proceed with the building of three 12-storey blocks designed by the borough architect.

A GALLERY IN THE PARK

The old tea house in Hyde Park was this year opened as the Serpentine Gallery, devoted to contemporary artists.

MORE HOTELS

The rush to take advantage of a generous government scheme to offset the expense of building hotels gathered pace as the expiry date approached. This year three major hotels were opened in the West End: the Inn on the Park, a Canadian venture on the site of Gloucester House in Hamilton Place, designed by Michael Rosenauer; the London International Hotel in Cromwell Road, architect George Beech; and the Churchill Hotel in Portman Square, looking particularly to the American market, by Stone, Toms & Partners.

A NEW MUSEUM

The administrative headquarters of the University of London had been in Burlington Gardens, in an elegant classical building designed for the university by Sir James Pennethorne, resplendent with effigies of what were judged to be the great names in arts and sciences. After the university's removal to Senate House, its old building was taken by the Civil Service, but in 1970 the British Museum's Department of Ethnography, rather cramped in Bloomsbury, opened here the Museum of Mankind.

CHANGES AT HOLLOWAY

What to do with good-looking prison buildings is a problem for conservationists. Almost certainly the facilities inside an old prison will be grossly inadequate, and the structure of the place will usually preclude realistic conversion. Pentonville, for example, is a handsome building (at the front anyway), but it is no way to house people; Brixton will have few defenders when the time comes to demolish it. Holloway prison, modelled on Warwick Castle (see 1852), had long been inadequate, and a decision was taken this year to demolish the old building. A new prison has subsequently been built.

SMALL THEATRES

An American, Dan Crawford, this year revived the old London tradition of using part of a pub, in this case the King's Head in Upper Street, Islington, for theatre. The King's Head has had numerous successes, and is the longest-surviving enterprise of its kind.

In The Cut, off Waterloo Road, an old butcher's shop and a piece of wasteland were utilized to fashion a home for the Young Vic Theatre, opened by Dame Sybil Thorndike in August. The shop formed the entrance and refreshment area, and on the land a simple steel structure supported a modest in-the-round auditorium. The Young Vic was then part of the National Theatre at the Old Vic, but it became an independent organization in 1974. The building was intended to be temporary, but was still in use in 2000.

FORMATION OF POLYTECHNICS

In a rearrangement of further-education facilities, mergers of established institutions took place. The Polytechnic of the South Bank was formed out of four local colleges; the Polytechnic of North London was a merger in 1971 of the North Western Polytechnic in Kentish Town and the Northern Polytechnic in Holloway; the Polytechnic of Central London consisted of the Regent Street Polytechnic and the Holborn College of Law, Language and Commerce – its new, rather brutish, buildings in the Marylebone Road were opened in 1971 by Lord Hailsham, whose grandfather had founded the original Regent Street Polytechnic (see 1882); the Thames Polytechnic was formed in 1970 out of the old Woolwich Polytechnic.

WESTWAY OPENED

London's first motorway on stilts, Westway, was opened in July, cutting a formidable swath through Paddington and North Kensington. At its eastern end it dominates the old Paddington Green, where some of

St Mary's churchyard was taken. By way of compensation, money was given to restore the church, which, overshadowed though it is by such a noisy neighbour, is a delightful place inside.

1971

THE END OF QUEENHITHE
Queenhithe Dock, one of the oldest in London and the last in the City, was this year demolished and the site taken for hotel building. It had consisted of two wharves – Abbey Wharf, which belonged to the Fishmongers' Company, and Smith's Wharf, owned by the City Corporation itself. Outline planning permission was applied for in December 1970, and demolition began in February 1971 – the unusual speed no doubt related to the government bonus of £1,000 per room which could be obtained for hotel work begun before the end of March.

EXPLOSION AT THE POST OFFICE TOWER
On 31 October a bomb planted by the IRA exploded at the top of the Post Office Tower, severely damaging three floors of the building. A consequence was that the popular observation floor was in future closed to the public.

A NEW LIBRARY AND THEATRE
Princess Anne opened the Shaw Theatre and the St Pancras Library in Euston Road on 2 April. The building had an extended history. St Pancras Council had bought nearby premises in the 1930s for a branch library, but in the 1960s the council decided that Euston Road should be the site of a central library (St Pancras did not then possess one) and a municipal theatre. The existing site was not large enough, and the council, with the aid of developers, was able to acquire the present location. The library and theatre were built virtually free of cost to the council in exchange for permitting the developers to erect the office tower above. The architect of the complex was Elidir Davies, who had built the Mermaid Theatre.

The theatre (named after George Bernard Shaw, a former vestryman of St Pancras) was rarely a financial success and was a shortlived enterprise (see 1994).

DEVELOPMENT PLANS
A major development of Hay's Wharf on the south bank of the Thames was announced. It was planned that Southwark Cathedral should be visible from the north bank in the new scheme.

A NEW TUBE LINE
Work began on the construction of the Fleet Line (now the Jubilee Line). The first section would run from Baker Street to Trafalgar Square, and necessitated the reconstruction of Bond Street station beneath a protective roof in Oxford Street.

A THEATRE UPSTAIRS
The rehearsal room of the Royal Court Theatre was on 23 November opened as the Theatre Upstairs, a studio auditorium for experimental and innovative drama.

A NEW SKYSCRAPER
Centre Point, an office tower at the junction of Charing Cross Road and New Oxford Street, was to be as emblematic of the frenetic office

building of the 1970s as Canary Wharf and Docklands came to be of the excessive developments of the 1980s and early 1990s. The building's height was permitted by the Greater London Council in exchange for some land around it intended for a traffic scheme that did not materialize. Centre Point remained empty for years, and, to the scandal of those unused to the niceties of such things, made its owner richer as those years went by, because the value of the building increased as the office boom continued. The architect was Richard Seifert.

1972

FAREWELL TO FAMILIAR NAMES
Familiar stores, known to generations of Londoners and visitors, were finding it difficult to cope with new retailing trends. Large stores outside Oxford Street were the most affected. B. B. Evans, for example, a draper's-cum-department store in Kilburn High Road, closed in 1971 after 74 years' trading, and there were ominous rumours of closure for Jones Brothers in Holloway and John Barnes in Finchley Road, Hampstead. Bowman's, the celebrated furniture store in Camden Town, was already being run down.

Gamage's, the department store in Holborn, closed its doors in March, to make way for the redevelopment of the site. But it was not quite the end of Gamage's, for it made a brief reappearance in Oxford Street and an even sadder one in the remnant of the Bowman store in Camden Town.

Maple's, an old-established furniture emporium in Tottenham Court Road, was closed this year. The name was perpetuated in a new store built on the site, but this was a shadow of the former extensive version.

In 1970 the Ponting's department store in Kensington High Street had closed, and the building was demolished the following year.

REBUILDING A GIANT
Much secrecy surrounded a redevelopment of Queen Anne's Mansions, a vast and inappropriate block of mansion flats overlooking Queen Anne's Gate and St James's Park. (The building of the original 14-storey flats in 1879 by Henry Hankey and E. R. Robson was said to have resulted in a prohibition on buildings over 80 ft high in London. One commentator described them as having 'real ugliness unsurpassed by any other great building in all London'. Queen Victoria was not amused either.)

The Architect's Journal, which had offices in Queen Anne's Gate and therefore more than a passing interest in the matter, attempted to obtain descriptive plans. The buildings that eventually went up, designed by Fitzroy Robinson assisted by Basil Spence, and which dominate the area, were approved by the Royal Fine Art Commission.

A HIGHGATE BATTLE
An immense Highgate house called Witanhurst was the centre of a fierce local battle. There were development plans not only for the house itself, but also for its spacious grounds contiguous to the Kenwood fields. An application was made to build 121 flats in the grounds, but permission was given only for 63. This was far from the end of the matter, and the Witanhurst saga continued for another ten years.

COVENT GARDEN PLANS
The most important conservation issue, however, concerned a large chunk of the West End. What to do with the Covent Garden area

when, in the 1970s, the fruit and vegetable market moved out to Nine Elms had exercised planners and public since the late 1960s. The exodus would free not only the market buildings but also numerous premises in the surrounding streets taken up by market traders. A plan was published by a consortium formed by the two boroughs concerned, Camden and Westminster, and by the GLC, which proposed a radical transformation of the whole area. Essentially, the opportunity was available to rebuild almost completely an integral part of inner London. The plan would include a hotel and conference area; new roads would be constructed, and others, like Maiden Lane, would disappear altogether. In 1971 Lady Dartmouth of the GLC advocated the demolition of the market building and the transformation of the piazza with lawns, water features and cherry trees.

Opposition to the proposals was considerable; influential Londoners, having seen the Barbican, were now wary of comprehensive schemes, and the cause of conservation was in the ascendancy. The consortium also found, to its surprise, a dedicated and well-organized residents' association against them.

Meanwhile, a serious fire which had occurred at the empty Odhams' factory in Long Acre prematurely raised the question of the future nature of the surrounding area. The ruins of the factory were demolished this year, and the developers planned to erect a tower block of the same capacity as Centre Point, and by the same architect, Richard Seifert.

RAF MUSEUM OPENED

The RAF Museum was officially opened this year, although it had been established for some time; appropriately, it is located on the old Hendon Aerodrome, where one of the old hangars serves as the main hall. Its exhibits portray the history of the RAF and its predecessors and the history of aviation generally. On an adjacent site another museum, featuring the Battle of Britain, was opened in 1978.

FINAL SERVICE AT ST MARY'S

On 31 October the final service was held at St Mary-at-Lambeth, the church in the shadow of Lambeth Palace. This part of Lambeth was a place of office blocks and, as in the City, there was hardly a congregation to speak of. The building was taken over by the Tradescant Trust for conversion to a museum of gardening history in memory of two of the church's former parishioners, the Tradescants, father and son, from whom the plant tradescantia is named.

1973

COVENT GARDEN DECISION

In January the government approved in principle the Greater London Council's plan to redevelop the Covent Garden area, but at the same time listed a further 250 buildings there. It was a perplexing decision, since the listing of so many buildings effectively ruled out the sort of redevelopment the GLC had in mind: one can only conclude that a Conservative government found this the easiest way not to embarrass a Conservative GLC.

A NEW THEATRE

The New London Theatre in Drury Lane was opened in January on the site of the old Winter Garden. Designed by Paul Tvrtkovic, it is a highly adaptable building, suitable for theatre, exhibitions and confer-

A photograph of a timeless image of the old Covent Garden Market, taken in 1972, the year of its removal to Nine Elms.

ences — its flexibility has enabled it to stage the musical *Cats* very successfully. The interior design is by Michael Percival and Sean Kenny, and owes much to the *Totaltheater* ideas of Walter Gropius. The building ignores its neighbours, possibly anticipating their removal in the grand Covent Garden scheme; the architecture is cold and without charm.

AN ABUNDANCE OF HOTELS

A large number of new hotels made their appearance this year. These included the Gloucester Hotel, as different as could be from the stylish Harrington Gardens it overlooks; the Sheraton Park Hotel in Knightsbridge, a circular tower designed by the ubiquitous Richard Seifert; the Holiday Inn at Swiss Cottage; and the Tower Hotel by the Tower of London, which, though rather large at 826 rooms, was at least designed with some consideration for its ancient neighbour.

A RETURN TO HOLLOWAY

The industrialist Michael Sobell, who had grown up in Holloway in humble circumstances, donated this year a sports centre to this rundown area. The building, which cost over £2 million, was opened by the duke of Edinburgh on 21 November. The main arena seats 3,000, and there are numerous halls, rooms, rinks and courts for various sports. The building was designed by W. Laming of Richard Seifert & Partners.

FIRE IN TRINITY HOUSE SQUARE

The church of Holy Trinity, in the elegant and diminutive Trinity Church Square in the hinterland of Borough station, was gutted by fire on 2 October. With good acoustic qualities, it was destined to be converted into a rehearsal room for the London Symphony Orchestra and the London Philharmonic. The owners quite quickly threatened complete demolition of the building unless funds were found to restore it. In November the Henry Wood Memorial Trust announced plans to renovate the building at a cost of £450,000 so that it could be used for music as intended.

DEVELOPMENTS IN FULHAM

Charing Cross Hospital, still retaining its name, this year opened in a new building in Fulham Palace Road. It displaced the Fulham Hospital – to the initial indignation of local residents, who feared, as a local Labour Party spokesman warned, that there would be no guarantee that Fulham people would get priority in the new hospital. The new building, which at the outset had 900 beds and ten operating theatres, was designed by Ralph Tubbs.

Fulham Palace, the 'country' home of the bishop of London, had been an episcopal and expensive irrelevance for some time. Diocesan reorganization was needed, and it was the Revd Robert Stopford who decided this year that he would be the last bishop to reside there. This left, of course, a building of some antiquity to be cared for, and after some years of delay and controversy it is now open to the public under the aegis of the local council.

LOCAL RADIO

Governmental prohibition of commercial radio was loosened this year, and both Capital Radio and the London Broadcasting Company began transmitting.

A BRIEF ENCOUNTER

A great deal of money was spent in transforming the stylish Derry & Toms store in Kensington High Street into a fashion store called Biba, which opened this year. The timing was unfortunate. Biba had been founded in 1964 by Barbara Hulanicki and her husband, Stephen Fitzsimon, as a boutique in Kensington Church Street and was immensely successful there, riding high on the appetite for fashion in the 1960s. The reputation and goodwill did not, however, translate into volume sales in the new 'dream emporium' in the High Street, and, when recession struck, the end of Biba – at least in this store – was imminent. The shop closed in 1975.

A WOMAN REFUSED

In November and again the following January, Mrs Edwina Coven was elected as the first woman member of the Court of Aldermen of the City of London, but on both occasions her election was vetoed by the existing body. No reason was given publicly, but it was assumed the veto was because of her sex. Shortly before a third election Mrs Coven withdrew her candidature and the only other (male) contestant was therefore elected. Explaining her withdrawal, Mrs Coven said that if she were elected again she would no doubt be rejected again, and the Court could then appoint whom it wished. She hinted that she had been warned that her professional position in the City would be harmed if she persisted in her candidature.

In 1975 the Court of Aldermen did accept the aldermanic election of (Lady) Mary Donaldson, who then went on to become the first female lord mayor of London in 1983–4.

1974

THE IRA IN LONDON

London this year had its first extended experience of terrorist attacks by the IRA. On 5 January a bomb was placed at the Earls Court Boat Show, and 10,000 visitors had to be evacuated; the same day a bomb exploded at Madame Tussaud's. On 17 July a bomb killed a woman at the Tower of London. Three bombs exploded on 17 December in Chelsea, Soho and Tottenham Court Road, killing one person. Two days later five were injured in a blast at Selfridges, and on 21 December a bomb went off at Harrods but caused no casualties.

A COUNTY HALL ANNEXE

An annexe to County Hall was completed this year on a roundabout site facing Westminster Bridge, near the main building. The Greater London Council, like the London County Council before it, had always had difficulty in housing all its central staff in one complex. In 1968 a third of them were scattered in peripheral accommodation, but the council declined to accept consultants' advice that it should decentralize. Instead it was decided to build on the island site at the end of Westminster Bridge, and at first a 15-storey tower was proposed. In the face of opposition the project was whittled down to a more modest seven storeys, and the annexe was opened on 21 October this year. It is hexagonal in shape, and made use of supposedly solar-controlled bright orange blinds, but these did not function as intended.

COVENT GARDEN MOVES

After over 300 years the fruit and vegetable market at Covent Garden closed on 8 November and reopened at its new centre at Nine Elms, Battersea, three days later. The new site, consisting of 68 acres, was land formerly used as a goods yard by British Rail. The building, designed by Gollins, Melvin, Ward & Partners, cost £40 million.

THE BATTLE FOR TOLMERS SQUARE

A battle raging in 1974 over a proposed development off the Euston Road serves to illustrate the conflicts of interests brought about by the drive to build office blocks. The country was in recession, but there was still money to be made in property: provided that a site could be obtained cheaply, commercial rents could still bring handsome profits. Also, borough councils were finding that the only way they could build houses in what had become commercial areas was to be in league with developers. The councils got their housing, the developers their rents, the residents were removed from their Victorian houses, and the general public had to contend with huge office developments.

The development in this case centred around Tolmers Square, which lay behind Euston Road, to the east of Hampstead Road – a run-down enclave of houses with a cheap cinema, converted from an old mission hall, in its centre. The corner site by the main roads had obvious potential for office building, and generally speaking the premises there were also run-down. When the Euston Road underpass was constructed in the 1960s, inhibiting casual journeys from south of the road to the north, this northern area became further dilapidated.

Enter the same developers who had made a good profit on the construction of the Euston Centre across the road. Stock Conversion had quietly been buying up properties in the Tolmers Square area since 1962. By 1974 many of the houses it owned in the square were empty or squatted, and almost all were very run-down or boarded up. Indeed, in October 1973, one of the houses collapsed altogether. The scheme the developers proposed involved a large amount of office space, a hotel, shops, and 600 dwellings for the borough council to take over as housing. Camden Council was not happy with the situation, but it was not in a position either to buy the Stock Conversion interest or to obtain a compulsory purchase order to do so.

Meanwhile the local tenants' association had waged a noisy and well-publicized campaign to prevent demolition and, as the affair reached the national press, more and more militant squatters moved in to the square, daring Stock Conversion to evict them. (Squatters caused a furore in January this year by occupying the vacant Centre Point – see 1971.)

Eventually, in 1975, Camden bought out Stock Conversion's holding, thereby ensuring that the company made a good profit and the ratepayers had to pay an excessive amount for slum property simply because of its commercial development potential. In the end Tolmers Square was demolished and it was a classic case of everyone losing except those who could afford to do so.

PAINTING RECOVERED

A valuable painting by Vermeer, *The Guitar Player*, stolen from Kenwood House in Highgate, was found on 6 May, wrapped in paper in the churchyard of St Bartholomew-the-Great.

OVERLOOKING HAMPSTEAD HEATH

The Royal Free Hospital, an enterprise of modest beginnings in 1828, was now a conglomeration of local hospitals each with separate buildings. A new hospital building which enabled the various institutions to be housed in one complex was opened this year in Pond Street, Hampstead. It was designed by Watkins, Gray, Woodgate International, and its charmless bulk may be seen from almost anywhere on Hampstead Heath. The first patients were admitted on 14 October.

LISTING CINEMAS

The rapid disappearance of cinema buildings was causing concern. This year the government listed the Chinese-style Liberty cinema in Ealing (1929), the Astoria (then the Rainbow rock venue) at Finsbury Park, the Carlton (a Mecca bingo hall) in Islington, the Granada and Odeon in Woolwich, Odeons in Northfield and Shepherd's Bush, the Astoria (Odeon) in Brixton, the Plaza (Paramount) in Regent Street, and the Electric in Portobello Road.

A CHANGE OF SITE

After a sustained campaign by residents and Camden Council, the GLC was persuaded to oppose the siting of the new British Library in Bloomsbury. Camden suggested that the British Library should be built on surplus railway land at Somers Town.

WALKING THE CANAL

The Regent's Canal was no longer a commercial facility. With lack of use, interest and maintenance, the canal had become derelict in many places; furthermore, it was not possible for the public to use much of it. This year, as part of a larger scheme, 1¼ miles of the canal towpath were opened up by Camden Council for a walkway between Camden Town and York Way.

THEATRE IN A MORTUARY

The old New End Mortuary in Hampstead was this year converted and opened as a theatre. The enterprise has had a tenuous hold on life ever since.

1975

UNITY DESTROYED

Unity Theatre, in Goldington Crescent, Somers Town, was destroyed by fire in the early hours of 8 November. No one was hurt – not even the theatre cat – although the roof collapsed during the two hours it took the fire brigade to bring the blaze under control. The cause of the fire was never established. Arson was suspected, as was an electrical fault. Unity was under-insured, and appeals did not raise enough money to attempt rebuilding.

SIEGES IN LONDON

Two dramatic sieges took place in London this year. One concerned the Black Liberation Front, which held up seven members of the staff of the Spaghetti House, Knightsbridge, on 28 September after an attempt to seize the day's takings had gone wrong. The staff were taken hostage, and it was five days before the raiders surrendered, with no one harmed.

On 7 December four IRA gunmen took refuge in a flat in Balcombe Street, an address chosen at random and in haste, where they held an elderly couple hostage. The gunmen surrendered six days later, with the man and woman physically unharmed but psychologically in shock.

DISASTER AT MOORGATE

The worst accident on the London Underground took place on 28 February. A train destined to terminate at Moorgate station inexplicably overshot the platform and went at speed into a dead-end tunnel siding, where the carriages exploded into the walls and ceiling. Over 40 people were killed, and the task of rescuing the others was a harrowing and protracted one. The driver was killed in the crash, and the subsequent inquiry did not come to any clear conclusion as to why the crash had occurred.

MORE BOMBS

On 19 January an IRA bomb exploded at the Thames Water works in Woodford; 12 days later there were five blasts in central London. On 28 August the Prudential offices in Oxford Street were attacked, and the next day an army captain was killed while trying to defuse a bomb in Kensington Church Street. On 5 September a bomb exploding at the Hilton Hotel killed two people.

BRITISH LIBRARY DECISION

Hugh Jenkins, the new minister for the arts, announced in August that he accepted that the new British Library building should be in Somers Town and not in Bloomsbury.

SAVE ESTABLISHED

The ranks of conservation societies were this year joined by a new organization – SAVE. It was formed at the instigation of Marcus Binney, John Harris and Simon Jenkins. Binney, its chairman, well known as a writer for *Country Life*, announced that there were daily, up and down the country, six applications to demolish listed buildings. SAVE was to play a prominent part in several London causes.

1976

A MUSEUM OF LONDON

The Museum of London derived from two forerunners. One was the Guildhall Museum, established in 1826 to provide a 'suitable place for the reception of such antiquities relating to the City of London and the suburbs, as may be procured or presented to this Corporation';

the second was the London Museum, opened at Kensington Palace in 1912 – an attraction that had considerably more flair, partly because it dealt with the social history of London and not just with antiquities.

Relations between the two establishments were not always easy. The Guildhall had specific duties, whereas the London Museum had a wider remit which could impinge on the territory of the other. In 1927, when both museums were having difficulty finding accommodation, the archaeologist Mortimer Wheeler suggested their amalgamation, but it was not until after the Second World War that serious discussions to this end took place.

The site eventually chosen for the combined museum was on a corner of the Barbican scheme, utilizing also space above a roundabout. The architects, Powell & Moya, not only had a difficult site on which to build a museum and office block, but their buildings had to encompass Ironmongers' Hall, a listed building.

The museum was opened by the queen in December this year.

NATIONAL THEATRE OPENS
The National Theatre had also endured a long gestation. It had been suggested in 1848, but it was not until early in the 20th century that serious attempts were made to raise money for the project, with the Shakespeare Memorial National Theatre Committee coordinating endeavours. In 1944 the committee and the Old Vic were amalgamated, and in 1949 a bill to allocate £1 million to fund a scheme to build a National Theatre on the South Bank was passed. The foundation stone was laid in 1951, and in March 1976 the Lyttelton Theatre, the first auditorium completed, was inaugurated with a production of *Plunder*, by Ben Travers. The Olivier Theatre and the Cottesloe opened in the autumn.

Shakespeare was also alive and well in Tufnell Park, where the St George's Theatre, in an old circular church, began presentation of Shakespeare in the round – the opening night this year was both the Bard's birthday and St George's Day. The theatre was founded by George Murcell in 1970, after he had seen the possibilities for theatre-in-the-round in this unusual building.

COVENT GARDEN SAVED
In December the GLC accepted the inevitable and finally announced that it had dropped all plans for grandiose redevelopment in the Covent Garden area; instead, as the local residents' organization had suggested, it would press for rehabilitation.

A CHANGE OF POLICY
In January the GLC announced that it was ending its policy of encouraging the dispersal of population from the Greater London area to new towns and other areas. In the previous 15 years London's population had dropped from 8 million to just over 7 million, but half a million jobs had been lost. There was now, because of the vast area vacated by London's docks, a need for additional population.

A SHOPPING EXPERIENCE
On 2 March, Brent Cross Shopping Centre was opened at the junction of three trunk roads in north London. Spread over 82 acres, the covered and air-conditioned shopping area included two department stores and over 80 individual shops.

AN END OF BREWING
Beer was brewed for the last time this year at Whitbread's Brewery in Chiswell Street. Samuel Whitbread had acquired the King's Head

Brewery here in 1750, and by the time of his death it was the largest brewery in London.

NEW ROLE FOR WHITEFIELD'S
It was appropriate that Whitefield's Tabernacle in Tottenham Court Road, the last building of significance to be destroyed by bombing in the Second World War, should be rebuilt this year by the American Church in London. George Whitefield (1714–70) was as famous a Methodist preacher in his day as Wesley, and particularly well known in America, where he died.

BORN TO BE FREER
The Lion House at London Zoo, long thought to be inadequate and very inhibiting for the animals, was in June superseded when the queen opened the new Lion Terraces, to a fanfare composed for the occasion by William Walton. The terraces cover 2½ acres, and there are separate enclosures for seven species.

A NEW HOSTEL
The YMCA's building in Tottenham Court Road had been built in 1912 as a memorial to George Williams, founder of the association. By the 1960s the hostel was both inadequate and unsuitable for conversion, and so a new and much larger hostel was embarked upon. It was to become a nightmare for the association, and almost brought it to bankruptcy.

The original plan was for a club room in the basement, and above ground a third of the rooms would be hostel and two-thirds hotel, with the latter subsidizing facilities such as a swimming pool. What was budgeted to cost £6½ million eventually cost £15½ million. There were three principal reasons for this enormous difference. One was the rapid increase in inflation during the building period; the second was the extended length of the building period itself, mainly due to numerous strikes against the contractor employed; and, third, there were technical problems. The YMCA was rescued from its immediate financial quagmire only by reversing the ratio of hostel and hotel rooms and, by technically becoming a housing association, claiming a government grant for housing.

1977

ENLARGING THE NATURAL HISTORY MUSEUM
The architects Pinckheard & Partners had the difficult task of adding a modern extension to Waterhouse's superb and newly cleaned Natural History Museum in Cromwell Road. The new building, opened this year, reflected the perpendicular nature of the Waterhouse style but otherwise went much its own way, to general acclaim.

NEW CIVIC SCHEMES
On 4 May the new town hall for the borough of Kensington and Chelsea was opened. Begun in 1972, it cost over £13 million and was one of the last buildings designed by Sir Basil Spence before his death.

Newham's new civic offices, which opened this year, took an extraordinary ziggurat form, entirely at odds with surrounding architecture.

The Alfred Beck Centre was opened in September in Grange Road, Hayes, designed by Thurston Williams, the borough architect, in neo-vernacular style. There is an auditorium for music and a large adaptable foyer which may be used for anything from banquets to cabaret shows.

UNDERGROUND TO HEATHROW

The long-awaited Underground extension to Heathrow Airport was opened by the queen in December – London thus became the first city in the world to have a direct urban rail link with its principal airport. The station above ground is of modest appearance, since most travellers will never see it.

THEATRICAL HAPPENINGS

The Prince of Wales opened the Churchill Theatre in Bromley. The show *No Sex Please – We're British!* reached 2,548 performances, the longest run of any comedy production in this country. The experimental Open Space theatre, directed by Charles Marowitz, was evicted from its Tottenham Court Road home and opened in a converted post office in Euston Road. Plans to erect a theatre on Bankside modelled on the Elizabethan Globe Theatre were approved by the GLC; the project was that of the American actor and director Sam Wanamaker. It was to be over 20 years, and after his death, that Wanamaker's ambition was fulfilled.

It was announced by the GLC that Wilton's Music Hall in the East End was to be restored. It is the oldest music-hall building in London, and has a handsome interior. It was built in 1858 by John Wilton, as an extension to his public house, but from 1888 it was a Methodist mission hall and of late it had been a rag warehouse.

The first arts building completed in the Barbican complex was the Guildhall School of Music and Drama, which opened on 25 October. It has a large hall for orchestral rehearsal and performances, and there is a wide-stage theatre auditorium. The architects were those for the main Barbican scheme, Chamberlin, Powell & Bon.

A PALLADIAN HOUSE RESCUED

Before Covent Garden Market moved out to Nine Elms, one of the best buildings in King Street, no. 43, had been used as a market trader's warehouse. This Palladian house, designed by Thomas Archer in 1717, replaced one of the original piazza buildings. The market trader had taken down the original portico and pillars and the main staircase inside, and had constructed a lorry ramp through the building to a small warehouse behind. This year, Thomas Archer House was restored under the aegis of Fitzroy Robinson. The main staircase was not replaced, but the pillars were. Unfortunately, the only survivals of its grander days are the rooms on the first floor. Otherwise, it makes awkward office space.

PUBLIC RECORDS IN KEW

The Public Record Office in Chancery Lane had long been overcrowded, but the decision to rehouse a major part of the collection in a place as difficult to get to as Kew was an odd one. The new building, which was opened this year, houses a wide time-span of government records, from medieval to modern.

CONVERSION IN BOUNDS GREEN

A large warehouse in Bounds Green was this year transformed into the Middlesex Polytechnic (now the Middlesex University) by Rock Townsend. It is an exciting building to encounter – its expose-all architecture a refreshing change from the endless, featureless corridors of most new higher-education buildings, with their veneered, anonymous doors.

1978

JUBILEE WALKWAY COMPLETE

In July the duke of Gloucester opened the final section of a permanent London walkway to mark the silver jubilee (in 1977) of the queen's reign. It is a circuit, almost 9 miles long, taking in both sides of the Thames. From the Tower, it goes through Eastcheap, from where the Monument may be reached, up to the Mansion House and the Bank, down to St Paul's, along Fleet Street and Lincoln's Inn, through Covent Garden, Trafalgar Square and St James's Park (where there are fine views of Buckingham Palace and the buildings of Whitehall), past Westminster Abbey and Parliament, over Lambeth Bridge to Lambeth Palace, and then along the south bank of the river to the South Bank complex, past the former Bankside Power Station and the new Globe Theatre, and so on to London Bridge and then over Tower Bridge.

A NEW PARK IN EALING

A large new park was begun in Ealing along the valley of the river Brent. It takes in three existing parks: those of Perivale, Pitshanger and Brent Lodge. Other land, whether private or used for recreation, was to be landscaped as part of the whole scheme and footpaths were to be contrived, and at the southern end the Grand Union Canal was to be incorporated. The park runs in a large arc from Western Avenue down to the M4 motorway.

REBUILDING COUTTS'

Coutts' Bank has been in the Strand since its foundation by John Campbell in 1692; a Coutts first appeared as a partner in 1755. For most of its first 212 years the bank was at 59 The Strand, but in 1904 it moved to no. 440. Here the old Lowther Arcade, famed for its toyshops, was removed, and a building designed by McVicar Anderson was inserted, which butted without ceremony but quite successfully into a triangular block erected by Nash in 1826 as part of the rebuilding of the area.

Over the years Coutts & Co. obtained control of the whole block, and in 1959 applied for permission to demolish it entirely; it was unsuccessful in this, and instead the Nash buildings were listed but the Anderson bank was not. Coutts' architect, Frederick Gibberd, was reduced to gutting the buildings behind the façades and also the Anderson building, leaving Nash at the front and rear and his 'pepperpot' features at either end. Facing the Strand, Gibberd built the present entrance to the bank, which consists of a wall of glass fronting a vast marble atrium hall of the sort beloved of American bankers, an ornamental pool of water, a tree which revolves during the day to catch the sun evenly, and escalators. The directors of the bank, however, have retained neo-Regency for their own boardroom.

The new building was opened by the queen, one of the bank's customers, on 14 December.

CEMETERY SALES

Nunhead Cemetery, as we have seen (1969), had fallen to the combined forces of inflation and vandalism. Highgate Cemetery, founded by the same company as formed Nunhead, had similar problems, compounded by a lack of space which could be used to generate fresh income. In 1975 the western, and older, side of the cemetery was closed. It was later purchased by a reluctant Camden Council and then farmed out to a charitable trust to maintain it.

Abney Park Cemetery, the Nonconformist burial ground in Stoke

1900s

Newington, opened in 1840, was virtually full by the end of the century. Once again the bodies, as a clergyman aptly put it, 'for the most part sleep in freehold', and fresh income was so small that maintenance inevitably declined. Arsonists burnt out the lodge and the records, and the chapel was wrecked. In 1978 Hackney Council was persuaded to buy the cemetery and begin the long task of restoring it.

A MOSQUE IN REGENT'S PARK
In 1940, when relations between the British government and Arab countries reflected the need they had for each other, Neville Chamberlain gave his support to a scheme to erect a mosque in London. This bore fruit in 1944, when a piece of land on the western extremity of Regent's Park was handed over for that purpose, but the mosque itself was not completed until 1978. The architect was Sir Frederick Gibberd.

THE COVENT GARDEN SPORTS HALL
The deserted Jubilee Market in Covent Garden (see 1904) was this year converted into a sports hall with market stalls beneath. It was thought, however, that the building, unlike the other market buildings, would eventually be replaced. Uncertainty over its future encouraged an active campaign to save the building, led by the Covent Garden Residents' Association and the Jubilee Market Traders' Association.

1979

REPLANNING THE CIRCUS
Discussions about Piccadilly Circus had been going on fitfully, and with rancour, for some years. Various schemes were considered, including one which separated pedestrians and vehicles completely. Two sites held the key to any changes: the so-called Monico site, a triangular block at the corner of Glasshouse Street and Shaftesbury Avenue, and the London Pavilion site, where a listed building faced the circus. A new plan was announced this year which retained the shape of the circus but moved the statue of Eros to the southern side, out of the middle; the façade of the London Pavilion would be preserved, but all else behind it would be rebuilt, and the Monico site would be redeveloped as shops, flats and advertising features. On the south side the Criterion Restaurant and Theatre would be kept, along with Lillywhite's, but buildings to the east of that would be demolished and a new block designed by Dennis Lennon would take their place.

A NEW LLOYD'S
In 1978 Lloyd's, the insurance organization, announced the appointment of Richard Rogers to design a new building for its headquarters. This year Rogers produced preliminary plans. The Royal Fine Art Commission described the scheme as a 'most enlightened piece of architectural patronage', and thought any losses would be justified by 'what should be one of the most remarkable buildings of the decade'.

STORE TRANSFORMATION
The old Waring & Gillow store in Oxford Street was being transformed into offices by Richard Seifert. The 'Wrenaissance' building had been erected in 1905–6 by Frank Atkinson, who also designed Selfridges. The façade was kept, though considerably modified, and the rest was rebuilt.

DEATH AT THE HOUSE OF COMMONS
On 30 March, Airey Neave MP, chief government spokesman on Northern Ireland, was killed when an IRA bomb exploded beneath his car as he drove out of the House of Commons underground car park.

END OF A MATCH FACTORY
In August, Wilkinson Match, current owners of the old English safety-match firm Bryant & May, announced the closure of the large match factory at Fairfield, Bow. The building had been the scene of the famous 'matchgirls' strike' (see 1888), and at one time employed about 1,500 women, mostly poorly paid. At the time of its closure the factory was being used for the manufacture of book matches.

JUBILEE LINE OPENED
What had begun as the Fleet Line finished up as the Jubilee Line. The later name indicated not only that it rather belatedly marked the silver jubilee of the queen's reign, but also that the original plan to extend it along Fleet Street had been abandoned: it was to have gone to Fenchurch Street and then as far as Thamesmead.

The line was opened on 30 April. At that time it began at Charing Cross, utilizing the old Trafalgar Square station, and a new tunnel then took it to Green Park, Bond Street and Baker Street. Thereafter it took over the old Bakerloo Line to Stanmore.

REVIVING THE LYRIC
The Lyric Theatre, Hammersmith, began in 1888 as the Lyric Hall; it was reconstructed as an opera house in 1890, and again five years later by Frank Matcham. This year the queen was present when the theatre, which retained much of Matcham's auditorium, was reopened on 17 October with a production of Bernard Shaw's *You Never Can Tell*. The old Lyric had had some notable productions, such as the 1920s revival of *The Beggar's Opera* and the first plays of both Harold Pinter and John Mortimer in 1958.

RELOCATING TEMPLE BAR
The City Corporation proposed in May that Wren's Temple Bar, which had been quietly mouldering at Theobalds Park since the 1880s, should be re-erected near St Paul's Cathedral. The cost of this would be £600,000, and an appeal was to be launched. But nothing came of it.

1980

THE EVENING NEWS CLOSES
Before and after the last war London had three evening newspapers – the *Star*, the *Evening News* and the *Evening Standard*. The *Star* had long fallen by the wayside, and this year the *News* was absorbed into the *Standard*, although the name was retained for some years on the *Standard*'s masthead and the paper briefly returned years later as part of a 'spoiler' tactic when Robert Maxwell launched his *London Daily News*. The *Evening News* did not quite make its centenary – it closed, to all intents and purposes, on 31 October, 99 years and 3 months after the first edition, a victim of a decline in sales of evening newspapers as television satisfied the appetite for late news. It had also just failed to survive into the new era of newspaper production, when advanced technology and reduced staffing levels might have saved it, although when it was cynically revived to fight Maxwell's new title in new circumstances there was still not a sufficient readership to sustain it.

COVENT GARDEN AWAKES

The rebirth of Covent Garden has been one of the most remarkable happenings in London in modern times – not to everyone's liking, but still quite extraordinary. The centrepiece is Charles Fowler's market building, restored with exemplary attention to detail and reopened on 19 June this year as a shopping centre selling, for the most part, items that appeal to a transient clientele. But the buoyant atmosphere of the place has had a considerable effect on the commercial values of the properties around. Many of the handsome warehouses and showrooms have been renovated to a state which the original builders would have hardly recognized, to become restaurants, galleries, studios, shops and offices. The media industry, which could afford the rents and could get away with the unorthodox nature of the buildings, moved in, encouraging other service industries in its wake.

It was not what the residents' association had envisaged but, once the rents of the buildings had been freed from restraint, there was no holding the trend. Even the less expensive years of the late 1980s did not dent Covent Garden's attraction to those who could afford the price, but since then firms of substance have moved out to less frenetic environments.

On 28 March the London Transport Museum was opened in the Flower Market on the south-east side of the piazza. The collection was begun in a small way at the Chiswick works of the London General Omnibus Company in the 1920s; after the last war it became part of a British Transport Museum at a disused bus garage at Clapham, and then moved to Syon Park in 1973. Exhibits include buses, trams, trolleybuses, Underground trains, and furniture and paraphernalia associated with London's transport system.

GOODBYE PICCADILLY

Jackson's of Piccadilly, a famous vendor of exotic provisions, was closed this year. The shop claimed to have its roots in the 17th century; more certainly, by 1828 Richard Jackson, wax and tallow chandler, had taken over John Hatchard's old premises at 190 Piccadilly and within 20 years had moved to nos. 171–172, where the business expanded to include the things that Jackson's was eventually noted for – groceries, poultry and game, fruit, wine and tobacco goods.

Along the road to the east, the Royal Society of Painters in Water Colours moved out of the gallery and headquarters it had occupied since 1883 and went to a new gallery at Hopton Street, Bankside; this opened on 11 November with a Turner exhibition.

SIEGE IN PRINCES GATE

On 30 April, Iranian gunmen took over the Iranian Embassy at 27 Princes Gate, demanding autonomy for Khuzestan and the release of political prisoners in Iran. With television cameras watching, SAS men stormed the building on 5 May, killing five of the gunmen and releasing the 19 hostages.

FIRESTONE FACTORY DEMOLISHED

On a Saturday in August, Trafalgar House, the new owners of the Firestone factory on the Great West Road in Hounslow, demolished the central portion of the Egyptian-style building by the crude method of hitting it with a ball and chain. In many people's opinion it was a pre-emptive strike, for the Department of the Environment was about to list the factory. The central portion was, of course, the building's chief glory – the two wings were untouched for some time – and to erase that part of the building was to make the retention of the remainder pointless. The features which had so long delighted people

travelling that road were simply smashed, without any attempt to salvage them.

TWO NEW HOSPITALS

After years of delay, the rebuilding of St Thomas's Hospital was completed on its old site by the Thames opposite the Houses of Parliament; some of the earlier building was retained. St George's Hospital, meanwhile, had relocated from Hyde Park Corner to Tooting, where its new building was opened this year.

NEW UNIVERSITY BUILDINGS

New University of London buildings, including the School of Oriental and African Studies, were completed this year between Woburn Square and Bedford Row. They were designed in an uncompromising style by Denys Lasdun.

COIN STREET BATTLE BEGINS

The largely derelict area between Stamford Street and Upper Ground, loosely called Coin Street in development plans, was this year the subject of a new plan by property speculators, employing Richard Rogers as their architect. The scheme proposed a series of office towers across the site, with most of the housing along Stamford Street.

BILLINGSGATE IN DANGER

Moving the fish market from its ancient site at Billingsgate to Poplar (see 1982) was to cost the City Corporation at least £7 million. The Corporation was anxious to recoup its costs and, indeed, make a handsome profit on the site of the market building and the land to the west used for market purposes. Maximum profit could only be obtained if the market building was demolished. However, on the prompting of conservationist groups, Michael Heseltine, secretary of state for the environment, spotlisted Billingsgate and set in train a series of events which was to result in an immaculately restored building that has stood empty ever since.

SAVE (see 1975) played a major part in the saving of Billingsgate. It proposed this year a scheme, designed by Chrysalis Architects and Richard Rogers, in which the market might be converted into shopping and restaurant units – rare commodities in this part of London – and attract the thousands of tourists visiting the nearby Tower of London. The spare land to the west could be redeveloped for office building. A much broadcast forecast, beloved of journalists, was that the building would collapse once the years' build-up of permafrost in the Billingsgate basements melted – a popular image that was eventually disproved. But there was very big money at stake, and, at the City's insistence, the issue of demolition went to an official inquiry. The City lost, and eventually sold the building to a financial-services company, with permission to convert the interior.

The building was then taken on by the American bank Citicorp. This was an expansive time in the City: with the prospect of the so-called Big Bang, banks and financial-services corporations were vying for market share. Citicorp, one of the larger players in the anticipated financial revolution, wanted new premises to bring together its various parts; it also required a trading floor. What better than Billingsgate, a wonderful open space in a potentially prestigious building redolent, in more ways than one, of London's history?

A first-rate but expensive restoration and conversion of the building, undertaken by Richard Rogers & Partners, then took place, but by the time it had been completed the financial scene in the City was quite different. The Big Bang had been somewhat of a whimper, staff were being laid off in the preliminary stages of a London recession, and, in any case, modern technology had made trading floors superfluous – as had been shown in the new Stock Exchange building. Furthermore, Citicorp itself was not expanding as it had imagined, and in any case many of its staff thought the building unsuitable. With millions of pounds spent, the decision was made not to move into Billingsgate. The old market building is now the handsomest empty building in London.

FIRE IN MUSWELL HILL

For the second time in its history, Alexandra Palace at Muswell Hill was ablaze. On 10 July thousands gathered on the surrounding slopes from the afternoon and into the darkness of night, when the flames lit up their faces. So public was the blaze and so prominent the building that many were able to watch it at a considerable distance, from their own windows. Firemen lay precariously on outstretched ladders above the building as the heat sent bullets of expanding glass into the night.

The fire began in the organ loft in the Great Hall, where workmen had been renovating the instrument. Much of the palace was damaged, though the Great Hall, the skating rink and the rooms on the south front suffered the worst. Firemen, who arrived 25 minutes after the blaze was discovered, found that the water pressure was too weak for the extent of the fire. At its height 250 firemen and 35 fire appliances were there.

The borough council, which had ambitious plans for the building, was consoled by insurance compensation, but the work on restoration became tangled in controversy and overspending; as a result, rebuilding the palace left an enormous deficit.

1981

THE TALLEST BUILDING IN EUROPE

The NatWest Tower, built for the National Westminster Bank, was officially opened by the queen on 11 June. At 600 ft and 52 storeys, it was the highest building in Europe, and, on a fine day, eight counties could be seen from the top. The architect was Richard Seifert.

A WEDDING IN LONDON

London was at a standstill on 29 July when the prince of Wales married Lady Diana Spencer at St Paul's Cathedral. The day's events included a ceremonial drive in a glass coach from Westminster.

FIRST LONDON MARATHON

A procession of a different kind occurred on 29 March, when the first London Marathon was held. Some 6,700 runners, most of them competing in their first marathon, left Greenwich Park on their journey to Westminster. It is now an annual event.

MORE BOMBS

There were more IRA outrages. On 10 October a nail-filled bomb was detonated near Chelsea Barracks when a coachload of Irish Guards went by. Two were killed and 40 were injured.

On 17 October a Royal Marine was killed by a car bomb at Dulwich.

On 28 October a bomb exploded at a restaurant in Oxford Street, killing the man trying to defuse it. Another bomb was found at Debenham's, but was rendered harmless.

OLD NAMES COME AND GO

The Lyons' Corner House in the Strand was reopened in June, complete with the famous 'nippie' waitresses.

But two old stores closed prior to rebuilding. Whiteley's in Queensway and Debenham & Freebody's in Oxford Street were both to reopen as multi-unit stores.

Fribourg & Treyer, snuff suppliers and tobacconists of 34 Haymarket, closed this year leaving behind premises which remind us of the elegance of that road in the 18th century.

WOOD GREEN SHOPPING CITY OPENS

Traditional shopping centres were now under threat from out-of-town warehouse stores accessible only by car. Just as chain stores had pushed individual shops out of the high street, the likelihood now was that the same chain stores would move to air-conditioned malls that had car parks attached. This has concentrated the minds of many borough councils, and some have encouraged the wholesale rebuilding of inner shopping areas to keep high streets popular. This year Haringey completed its building of Wood Green Shopping City, opened on 13 May. Designed by Richard Sheppard, Robson & Partners, it contains a new central library, 200 dwellings, major stores and small traders.

ARTS IN THE BARBICAN

By far the largest addition to the arts facilities available in London has been the City of London's Barbican scheme. The Barbican Centre was used for the first time on 30 April this year, but the official opening by the queen did not occur until 3 March 1982.

This enormous complex was built by one firm of architects – Chamberlin, Powell & Bon – who had first drafted their plans in the 1950s, and unfortunately the architecture is very reminiscent of that period. Though blessed with good spaces and auditoria, the entrances to the various buildings are relatively insignificant within the shroud of residential buildings – difficult to find, unpleasant to travel to on a rainy night, and without presence.

The art gallery is one of the largest new spaces for visual art in London; there is a concert hall with a stage that can be extended to take a choir – this is the home of the London Symphony Orchestra; the theatre is the London base of the Royal Shakespeare Company, which moved here from the Aldwych Theatre; and there are three cinemas and a claustrophobic conference centre and exhibition hall.

1982

EXPLOSIONS IN THE PARKS

On 20 July the IRA caused explosions and carnage in both Hyde Park and Regent's Park. Mid-morning a bomb exploded as a group of Household Cavalry soldiers rode by. Two soldiers were killed, 23 were injured and seven horses were killed. Two hours later when the band of the Royal Green Jackets were playing at the bandstand in Regent's Park, another bomb, planted beneath the bandstand, wreaked havoc. Six soldiers were killed and 30 were injured.

THE BATTLE OF MANSION HOUSE SQUARE

The so-called Battle of Mansion House Square was to be both protracted and expensive. A developer, Peter Palumbo, had gradually acquired the freeholds of properties contained in a triangle bounded by Poultry, Bucklersbury and Cannon Street, very near to the Mansion

House. He had received preliminary approval for a 290-ft tower on the site as far back as 1969, when the City was inclined to favour the demolition of virtually the whole of its historic area, but he was not allowed to redevelop until he had obtained more of the site. By the time in the 1980s when he was ready to proceed with his plans, which contained a tower block by the architect Mies van der Rohe, the world had changed. The City, despite the predictable support of Lubetkin for the block and the unexpected encouragement of Sir John Summerson, was less happy about a tower block next to the Mansion House, and most Londoners were tired of box-like structures, whether designed by van der Rohe or anyone else. Architectural styles had moved on into the postmodernist era, in which decorative features, brickwork, and more imaginative shapes were the order of the day – a slab, however pure, was not needed in a City already replete with them.

The conservationists, however, wanted to keep the existing buildings (which included a Mappin & Webb shop) as a good example of Victorian architecture in this area. It was contended that these complemented rather than competed with the Mansion House, and that any comprehensive redevelopment of the triangle would be inappropriate.

At a public inquiry in 1984 Palumbo was refused planning permission for the Mies van der Rohe building, but was tacitly encouraged to try again with a new design (see 1988).

A New Billingsgate
Trading began at the new Billingsgate fish market at the West India Docks on 19 January; the old bell, brought from Lower Thames Street, was rung to commence business. The new buildings cover over 13 acres and contain space for about 70 merchants in the market hall. But, like Smithfield, the market has a difficult trading future. Increasingly fish goes direct from the ports to large supermarket packaging depots, and gradually the tonnage handled at Billingsgate has gone down – although the value has not deteriorated in the same ratio, because more exotic and expensive fish are being stocked, especially for restaurants.

More Stores Go
Swan & Edgar in Piccadilly Circus closed its doors this year. The well-known building, scene of many assignations, had been designed by Sir Reginald Blomfield in 1910–20, but was now, according to Debenham's, which owned it, too expensive to modernize. Most likely, too, it was not large enough to function as a department store – especially after the installation of the necessary escalators.

In the Strand the Civil Service Stores was burnt down in a spectacular fire and did not re-emerge when a new building was erected on the site: department stores were no longer economic in this part of London.

On the Finchley Road, John Barnes (part of the John Lewis Partnership) also went, blaming competition from Brent Cross. It was replaced by a supermarket owned by John Lewis and a Habitat store.

Another Pre-Emptive Strike
The borough of Kensington and Chelsea this year copied the strategy of those who had destroyed the Firestone building in Hounslow (see 1980) when over the night of 10–11 June it demolished the essential parts of the old Kensington Town Hall in the High Street before it could be listed. It was not a distinguished building, but it was certainly more interesting than its replacement of shops and offices. And the point was made that cynical destruction by a local authority charged with the responsibility of conservation could be carried out without prosecution.

Happenings in Covent Garden
A much-needed extension of the Royal Opera House, fronting on to James Street, was completed this year; it was designed in a convincing replica of the existing building's architectural style.

In Long Acre, the Odham's Walk scheme was built on the site of the Odham's factory demolished in 1972. Though with many interesting features, it is inward looking and therefore at odds with the nature of the Covent Garden area.

Temporary Buildings
Two interesting temporary structures were erected to the designs of Terry Farrell this year. One was also in Covent Garden, where, on a space to the rear of the opera house, Clifton Nurseries were housed in a decorative pavilion which made substantial use of a Teflon-coated glass-fibre fabric. In Alexandra Park, north London, the giant Alexandra Pavilion, made of PVC-coated polyester, was put up while the palace was being renovated after fire damage (see 1980); it was large enough to attract many of the events that would normally have been in the palace.

Thames Barrier Finished
Extensive flooding of the Thames estuary in 1953 had concentrated efforts to formulate new river defences for London. That flooding had covered 160,000 acres of farmland, affected 24,000 houses, put out of action railways and factories, and taken 300 lives. It had not reached as far as London, but the effects on the capital if it had were almost unthinkable. It was calculated that if the surge tide had been 6 ft higher – by no means unlikely – both banks of London would have been flooded by up to 10 ft, the central Underground system would have been inundated and out of action for months, drains would have flowed backwards, and thousands would have been drowned.

It had been observed for some time that the south-east of England was slowly sinking and that the sea was simultaneously rising, so that each century the sea, in relation to the land, was 0.8 m higher. For various reasons, this process was probably speeding up. It was thought that, given the right circumstances of strength of surge tide, gravitational pull, wind power and weather, London would be seriously in danger in the near future. The dire consequences of inaction required a solution rather more radical than raising river defences, which, through negligence or miscalculation, would most certainly be breached.

The Thames Barrier at Woolwich Reach – a series of gates across the Thames, which are usually open for shipping – was devised. There were immense technical problems and no comparable structures elsewhere as role models. Even while the barrier was being built, in 1978, two very high surge tides hit London, just failing to result in the scenario that had been feared; the tides were so high that the specification of the barrier was changed so as to cope with a greater height of water.

On 31 January 1982 the first full testing of the barrier gates took place. It was successful, and for the time being London was safe-guarded. The barrier was fully installed by 1984.

1983

A Bomb at Harrods
The IRA was responsible for a bomb which exploded outside Harrods, Knightsbridge, on 17 December – a Saturday, when the store was filled

with Christmas shoppers. Six people, including three policemen, were killed and 91 injured in the blast.

TV-AM BEGINS

The new morning television station, TV-am, began transmitting on 1 February. Early optimism was soon dampened, and a very public boardroom revolution forced out some of the station's founders. A distinctive building in Camden Town was built, designed by Terry Farrell. It is, without doubt, a media building – the architecture is jokey, brash, reminiscent of between-the-wars cinema design, but mixed with art deco and modern technology. At the rear, two blue and yellow fibre-glass egg-cups are dominant on the canal. TV-am has since lost its broadcasting franchise, and the building is now occupied by another media company.

MERMAID SOLD

In September the Mermaid Theatre in Puddle Dock was sold to Gomba Holdings (who already owned the Garrick and Duchess theatres), thereby breaking the City of London's connection with it. At the same time its founder, Sir Bernard Miles, was removed from involvement.

SCHEMES AFOOT

The plan by architects Ahrends, Burton & Koralek for an extension to the National Gallery was approved by Michael Heseltine, secretary of state for the environment. Selected originally by some of the trustees of the National Gallery after a competition, it also received the blessing of the Royal Fine Art Commission. But it was not to everyone's liking, and many of the trustees preferred instead the entry of the American architectural practice Skidmore, Owings & Merrill. The chosen scheme was eventually abandoned after adverse criticism by the prince of Wales in 1984 (see 1991).

A massive redevelopment of the Hay's Wharf dock was proposed by its Kuwaiti owner, the St Martin's Property Co. It involved the conversion of some of the buildings and the erection of an office and shop complex; it would also provide public access to the river.

NEW BUILDINGS IN SOUTH KENSINGTON

Important additions were being made to the Victoria & Albert Museum. In 1982 a gallery, sponsored by Terence Conran, was opened to display modern industrial design in a space taken from what was called the Boilerhouse Yard. A year later the Henry Cole Wing, named from the museum's first director, was opened. This conversion of the former Royal College of Science contained an impressive staircase, a large room on each floor, and a good deal of space above the ground-floor lecture room, which was used to build extra galleries.

Across the road the Ismaili Centre, designed by Casson, Conder & Partners for the use of London's Ismaili community, was opened on 17 March.

END OF A LANDMARK

The well-known Ebonite Tower in York Way, Islington, was spectacularly demolished by explosives in June. It had been built in 1870 for the calibration of water-testing devices: three water tanks at different heights in the tower provided regulated pressures against which the instruments were tested.

OLD VIC REOPENS

When the National Theatre moved out of the Old Vic there were serious doubts as to whether the old theatre at Waterloo could survive. But it was rescued by a Canadian chain-store owner, Ed Mirvish, who put a great deal of money and commitment into its renovation. The first production in the restored building, *Blondel*, opened on 8 November this year.

A LADY MAYOR

The City of London this year elected its first woman mayor – Lady Donaldson.

1984

DIORAMA SAVED

Plans to demolish the Diorama building in Park Square East (see 1823) were turned down in August by the Department of the Environment; the developer intended to build 54,000 sq. ft of offices. Nothing is left of the mechanics of the Diorama, but the building is good space for studios and was used by groups of visual and dramatic artists who hoped to raise the money to renovate it.

SIEGE IN ST JAMES'S SQUARE

On 17 April demonstrators outside the Libyan People's Bureau at 5 St James's Square were, without warning, fired on by gunmen inside the building. Policewoman Yvonne Fletcher, on duty outside, was killed in the hail of shots. Diplomatic immunity made it impossible for the police or anyone else to storm the building to arrest the persons concerned, and after ten days, during which the house and its adjacent buildings were sealed off, the occupants left of their own volition and were taken to Heathrow Airport. A memorial to the dead police-woman has since been erected nearby.

BOURNE & HOLLINGSWORTH CLOSES

The Bourne & Hollingsworth department store in Oxford Street (see 1894) closed this year and was later replaced by a multi-unit store.

1985

RIOTS IN LONDON

The unhappy relationship between black youths and the police escalated this year into some of the worst civil violence that London has known.

On 28 September Mrs Cherry Groce, a black woman living in Brixton, was accidentally shot when police raided her home in search of a suspected criminal. Riots of black youths took place; petrol bombs were thrown at police stations, local shops were smashed and looted, fires were started, and motorists passing through Brixton were dragged from their cars and beaten up. The atmosphere remained tense, and further riots occurred in Peckham on 1 October.

On 6 October a large police raid on the Broadwater Farm Estate in Tottenham, in a quest for drug dealers, resulted in riots and demonstrations by black youths. A police constable, Keith Blakelock, was set upon by a mob and hacked to death.

EXPLOSION ON PUTNEY HILL

On 10 January a gas explosion destroyed the centre portion of a block of flats on Putney Hill, killing eight people and injuring seven.

The former Islington Literary and Scientific Institution hall was converted in 1985 for the highly successful Almeida Theatre.

DEVELOPING DOCKLANDS

The London Docklands Development Corporation, armed with planning powers that avoided most local controls, announced in January a £1 billion scheme to build a new city on the derelict dock land.

A NEW ART GALLERY

The Saatchi Gallery was opened this year in a 1920s car-repair depot in St John's Wood. Behind this new venture was Charles Saatchi, an immensely rich partner of the Saatchi & Saatchi advertising company, and his wife, Doris. Both had a passion for contemporary art, and their collection – one of the largest in private hands – was opened to the public here in five gallery rooms designed by Max Gordon and John Mackenzie.

RENOVATING COMYN CHING

The Comyn Ching Triangle was not a secret oriental society but a group of properties in Covent Garden bordered by Monmouth Street and Shorts Gardens, containing some very old shops owned by the celebrated and long-established ironmonger's there called Comyn Ching. Though much of the property was renovated, new buildings by Terry Farrell were incorporated.

A NEW EALING CENTRE

The residents of Ealing had managed to defeat plans in the 1970s for the worst kind of shopping redevelopment in the centre of their town. The aborted scheme included a 17-storey office block, a shopping mall which would be locked at night, and a 10-storey block of flats for childless couples. What the residents got instead was a great improvement, architecturally and socially. Though some thought it was a product of an unholy alliance of modernist architects and commerce, others regarded it as a victory for the community. The new centre was officially opened by the queen on 7 March.

SMALL THEATRES

The Half Moon Theatre, which had functioned in rather derelict premises at Aldgate for some years, was this year installed in a new theatre in Mile End Road, designed by Florian Beigel. It was the first new playhouse in the East End for 100 years.

In Islington the premises of the old Islington Literary and Scientific Institution in Almeida Street, a handsome building designed by

Robert L. Roumieu, were converted this year into the Almeida Theatre.

A much larger auditorium became temporarily available when the Lyceum, Wellington Street, which had been a dance hall since the end of the last war, was used for a National Theatre production of *The Mysteries*. The success of this led to a concerted campaign to keep the Lyceum for theatre use.

1986

LONDON WITHOUT GOVERNMENT

On 31 March the Greater London Council ceased to exist, and for the first time since 1855 London was without overall administration. Though it was claimed by the government at the time that this tier of local government was expensive and unnecessary, this remarkable state of affairs seems to have come about because of a deep dislike by Mrs Thatcher, the prime minister, of the policies and public actions of the council, and in particular the council's leader, Ken Livingstone. At the same time other metropolitan counties were disbanded.

The numerous responsibilities of the GLC were handed out to borough councils or semi-autonomous bodies. Most of the GLC's staff were re-employed by the borough councils, and an organization called, unappetizingly, the London Residuary Body carried out the depressing work of clearing up the odds and ends left by the carnage.

One major problem not resolved was the administration of Hampstead Heath, where the options for the management body were Camden Council as the most appropriate local authority (although part of the heath is in Barnet), the City of London, English Heritage, or an independent trust. The City of London was eventually chosen, thereby extending its activities so that it should be seen to have another function beyond the City if the question of its own dissolution ever arose again. But it was an untidy solution in many respects, with English Heritage running Kenwood House and its immediate grounds (generally to much criticism) and the City running the heath around it (usually to grudging applause).

The Inner London Education Authority, which administered state education in the old LCC area, was permitted to function until 1991.

NEW BUILDING FOR LLOYD'S

Richard Rogers's new Lloyd's building (see 1979) was opened on 18 November. It is a building so different from its surroundings and the

The Lloyd's building by Richard Rogers was a landmark design.

traditions of the City, and so remarkable in its own terms, that it is likely to remain a landmark in architectural history.

Basically, it is a rectangle around a vast atrium. Twelve gallery floors lead up to cut-back upper floors; vertiginous lifts on the outside of the building and escalators running through the lower parts of the atrium provide stunning views. Services are either detached from the main building or cling to its exterior, leaving the interior virtually free of pipes and channels. Only on the 11th floor is there a concession to tradition, where the Adam Room, originally taken from Bowood House, an 18th-century house in Wiltshire, has been incorporated.

FIRE AT HAMPTON COURT
On 31 March fire swept the south wing of Hampton Court, causing damage estimated at several million pounds. Lady Gale, in whose apartment the fire started, from a candle, died in the blaze.

GO-AHEAD FOR THE GLOBE
The dream of American actor Sam Wanamaker of creating of a replica of the Elizabethan Globe Theatre at Bankside (see 1977) had for some time been opposed by Southwark Council, which regarded it as an elitist enterprise of no value to local residents. There had been protracted negotiations between the two parties, and in June Wanamaker was at last allowed to proceed with his project.

1987

REFURBISHING THE TUBE
London Transport had been renovating central-London Underground stations for some years. The decor which the earlier builders and managers of the system had installed was now chipped, quite often obliterated and badly maintained; visual cohesion had been lost in a plethora of signs and colours; the central stations looked and were as run-down as though there had been little maintenance or repair since they were opened; grimy booking halls were often a congested disgrace, and some stations, such as Tottenham Court Road, were squalid, awash with litter for much of the time, redolent of public lavatories, and hopelessly outdated for the simple task of issuing tickets; antiquated lifts and escalators made getting to platforms or surface an unpredictable experience.

Not everyone was happy with the refurbishment of the stations – many objected that the original decor, especially the old tilework, was covered up. But there were some notable gains, particularly the frieze of medieval workers at Charing Cross, designed by David Gentleman. The largest commission went to Eduardo Paolozzi, whose tile mosaics at Tottenham Court Road are intended to convey the nature of the numerous electrical-goods shops nearby. Many of the stations have been given a design identity by the use of a local topographical feature in tiles or mural form, ranging from extensive reminders of the National Gallery at Charing Cross to the simple use of the outline of the Caledonian Market clock tower at Caledonian Road. A determined attempt was made, particularly on the Central and Bakerloo lines, to hide the numerous rows of filthy cables and wires that ran along platform walls behind a duct cover which served also as a station name indicator. In 1983 work began on restoring the Metropolitan/Circle Line platforms at Baker Street to their Victorian state – brickwork was cleaned, ceramic tiles were renewed, and sodium lights were introduced to simulate daylight through the original lighting shafts.

DISASTER AT KING'S CROSS
The refurbishment of the Underground system carried on against the background of an appalling disaster at King's Cross, where poor management, staff neglect and lack of attention to safety procedures resulted in a fire in which, finally, 31 people lost their lives.

The blaze began in a small way on an escalator from the Piccadilly Line; the subsequent inquiry could not be sure of the cause but thought that a cigarette end, thrown on to the escalator, had ignited inflammable material trapped beneath the staircase through neglect of proper cleaning procedures. The fire, probably fanned by sudden air currents from below as trains came in to platforms, suddenly exploded above the stairway, igniting immediately the plastic panels overhead. With great ferocity it billowed up the staircase into the booking hall, to catch not only those fleeing the blazing escalator but those who had sought to escape by going up the nearby Victoria Line stairway; other victims were those already in the entrance hall. The intensity of the heat and smoke was devastating, and the injuries were horrendous.

A NEW USE FOR AN OLD HALL
The Royal Agricultural Hall in Islington had lain derelict since the Post Office had last used it as a sorting office in 1971. It seemed destined for demolition, but its site was such an integral part of plans to rebuild the triangle of land bounded by Islington High Street and Liverpool Road that, inevitably, nothing was done either to demolish or to maintain it. The hall therefore survived long enough for conservation to come into fashion, and it was decided to retain it. But for what? Several schemes surfaced, but the final result was a Business Design Centre, opened this year, the venture of Sam Morris. The old Upper Street frontage was taken down and a new Crystal Palace-type entrance was tacked on, but inside the building was restored.

CLORE GALLERY OPENED
The Turner Bequest of paintings and drawings was rehoused this year in a new gallery at the Tate, the gift of Charles Clore. The new postmodernist building, designed by James Stirling and Michael Wilford, was opened on 1 April.

It had been the artist's intention, when he died in 1851, that 100 of his best works should hang in the National Gallery, but eventually 290 oils and over 20,000 works on paper went to an ungrateful nation which for over 100 years declined to spend the appropriate amount of money to display properly the work of its most famous artist.

A NEW STAND AT LORD'S
The new Mound Stand at Lord's Cricket Ground was opened this year. Designed by Michael Hopkins, it is regarded as one of the most important London buildings of recent times.

A DOCKLANDS TOWER
An agreement to build an office development at Canary Wharf on the Isle of Dogs was signed on 17 July by Olympia & York, a Canadian property company. The development would cost £3 billion to build.

CONFRONTATION IN WAPPING
New technology in typesetting, reproduction and printing had for years made the arrangements for printing national newspapers in the Fleet Street area seem primitive and extremely costly. Within a few years the traditional use of this location by the newspaper industry was virtually erased in a series of moves, mainly to Docklands, to new

factories relatively remote from the centre of town. In the surrounding controversy, the printing unions were perceived as clinging to outdated practices and manning arrangements, the management as interested only in profitability.

This year the worst and most violent dispute in the industry occurred. Workers at Rupert Murdoch's News International newspapers, still being printed in the Fleet Street area, went on strike. Murdoch, who already had a new, but unused, factory at Wapping, ostensibly for the publication of a new title, switched the production of all his main titles – *The Times*, the *Sun*, the *Sunday Times* and the *News of the World* – to the Wapping factory, with the cooperation of the electricians' union, the EETPU. The first editions of these papers from the new plant were published at the end of January. There were violent scenes outside as former print workers sought to prevent workers getting in or out, or to prevent distribution of papers. So many police were called in to wage nightly battle that the printing plant became known as Fortress Wapping.

A Railway in Docklands

The most welcome addition to Docklands this year was the Docklands Light Railway, officially opened by the queen on 30 July but, owing to technical problems, not opened to passengers until 31 August.

In the 1970s London Transport had considered extending the Jubilee Line (then the Fleet Line) to the docks and then across the river to Thamesmead, but the high cost of tunnelling beneath the water table and the relatively few stations in the distance contemplated made it an uneconomic proposition, socially desirable though it might have been. Instead, in October 1982, the government agreed to fund, in collaboration with the GLC and the London Docklands Development Corporation, a light railway which would utilize much of the track of disused and underused railways of the 19th century – the London & Blackwall, built almost entirely on viaducts in 1840, was the core of the first section of 7½ miles from Tower Hill to Island Gardens and Stratford. Since then the railway has been extended to Bank station in the west, to Beckton in the east, and to Greenwich in the south.

The carriages are driverless, though with a 'train captain' to look at tickets and presumably deal with any emergency, and it is an exhilarating ride at the front of the train going at speed on the viaducts through the futuristic landscape of office blocks.

1988

A Flood of Postmodernism

The intervention of Prince Charles in several debates on architectural style served to attract public attention to arguments taking place within the architectural profession. Modernist architects – now the old guard – were opposed to postmodernists. Increasingly, the rather minimalist architecture of the modernists, as shown in South Bank buildings, office towers and slab housing estates, was losing favour. Postmodernists seemed to have no inhibitions about the shapes of their buildings, or the motifs or decorative features used: the atrium became a common feature; brick was used decoratively; windows pointed outward in V-shapes; dormers appeared without logic; classical pediments graced modern buildings; and kitsch decor appeared to have become respectable. To a layman, architectural rules seemed to be set aside.

The postmodernist style became identified with the political atmosphere of the day. It was an era of office building, particularly for the financial-services industry, at a time when the government was encouraging a rapid expansion of the City's scope and influence.

And when recession came, and those numerous offices remained empty, the style itself was a reminder of avaricious dreams gone awry.

Substantial postmodernist schemes were in progress at this time. Terry Farrell, one of the busiest of the architects concerned, was transforming Charing Cross station; the Broadgate development by several architects at Liverpool Street was impressively large even when half-finished; CZWG's remarkable Cascades building in Docklands was either liked immensely or detested, while its China Wharf scheme and its Clerkenwell house for the broadcaster Janet Street-Porter were usually admired. At London Wall a giant development by Terry Farrell was being constructed bridging the road; Robert Venturi was about to begin his Sainsbury Wing extension of the National Gallery (see 1991); Ray Moxley's Chelsea Harbour, an amalgam of architectural clichés from pagodas to Robert Adam, was due for completion in 1989; the office block by Ted Levy Benjamin & Partners at Swiss Cottage, finished in 1985, was regarded as an honest application of postmodernist ideas.

Even small housing schemes were affected by the new language – witness that by MacCormac Jamieson Prichard & Wright in Vining Street, Brixton, where classical shapes, emphasized entrance stairways, pedimented porches and oddly placed corner windows produced a variety of surfaces and planes far removed from the low-cost housing Brixton was used to. Some buildings were distinctly playful, such as the Storm Water Pumping Station on the Isle of Dogs, strongly reminiscent of an aeroplane, or Ian Pollard's Homebase store in Warwick Road, Kensington, with Egyptian figures and columns.

The curved corner was reinvented. The skill with which the Victorians and Edwardians had designed their corners so that the eye slid easily round to the next plane had been ignored by modernist architects obsessed with rectangles. Postmodernists devised the 'hinge' feature, usually a tall tube of glass and metal which visually connects the front and sides of a building and moves the eye easily from one to the other. This may be seen to great effect on Terry Farrell's Comyn Ching building or the Fitzpatrick Building in York Way, designed by Chassay Architects. Not a new discovery – just a modern form of an old device.

The third Lansdowne House at the southern end of Berkeley Square was completed this year. The first had been a Robert Adam building of 1768, mostly erased in the 1930s when a new Lansdowne House – designed by Wimperis, Simpson & Guthrie and containing flats and shops – had been built on its front garden, facing the square. The newest is purely an office block in postmodernist style, designed by Chapman Taylor. The obligatory atrium is in the centre, and the change of surface colour for the upper storeys serves to visually reduce the height to Mayfair levels.

Neoclassicism at Richmond

Quinlan Terry was pursuing his own brand of architecture at Richmond, where he designed river-front buildings – a development of shops, restaurants, offices and civic buildings – in a mixture of classical styles to merge with older buildings. It is a scheme generally popular with the public, but architectural opinion is divided. It is certainly a more welcome group of buildings than those proposed in previous plans for the site.

Alexandra Palace Restored

The attractive and wildly expensive restoration of Alexandra Palace, seriously damaged in a fire in 1980, was reopened to the public on

1900s

22 January. The Palm Court includes date palms brought from Alexandria, Egyptian-style obelisks and mock sphinxes.

DISASTER AT CLAPHAM

On 12 December a stationary commuter train, halted near Clapham Junction, was hit by an express train and another ploughed into the wreckage, the result of a signal-equipment failure. Thirty-four people were killed and 111 injured.

OLD THEATRES REOPEN

The Playhouse Theatre at the foot of Northumberland Avenue, long an auditorium used by the BBC, was this year reopened as a theatre. It was later bought by the novelist Jeffrey Archer.

In Kingsway, the Royalty Theatre, which had until recently been a cinema, was converted back to a theatre. Its name was later changed to the Peacock.

FAREWELL FLEET STREET

The departure of the newspaper industry from Fleet Street was remarkably abrupt and was virtually complete by this year. Taking advantage of modern technology and capacious factories on new sites in Docklands and elsewhere, and capitalizing while the going was good on the papers' old sites in and around Fleet Street, the migration took just a few years. Only the *Daily Mirror* remained on the fringes of Fleet Street, and that too has since left for Canary Wharf.

The Times had already migrated to Gray's Inn Road in 1972, where it continued until the dramatic switch to Wapping in 1987. The *Financial Times* moved its printing factory to a new building near the northern end of the Blackwall Tunnel.

DIGGING DEEP

The astonishing rate of office building had the odd side effect that archaeology was funded properly for the first time. In the City, in particular, building permission was given on the understanding that, if archaeological finds were expected, sufficient time had to be included for excavation, which was to be funded by the developer. The Museum of London considerably increased its archaeological unit to cope with the work.

In 1988 it was calculated that 60 separate archaeological excavations had taken place within the last year. In that year 30 people were at work beneath the arches of Cannon Street station looking for remains of a 13th-century trading post. At the Thames Exchange building site, by the north end of Southwark Bridge, another 20 were looking at medieval wharves. At Huggin Hill the remains of a 2nd-century Roman bathhouse were found.

The most significant find, however, was by Guildhall Yard in March, when archaeologists discovered the remains of the eastern exit or vomitorium of Roman London's elusive amphitheatre. It was thought that much of the surface of the amphitheatre was beneath Guildhall Yard itself, and that wooden seating, raised on banks, ran around it – possibly, St Lawrence Jewry is on one of those banks. The site of the amphitheatre here, and the significant position of the bowed roads of Aldermanbury and Basinghall Street, could indicate that there was continuous use of the site until medieval times, when the Guildhall was built.

NEW PLAN FOR MANSION HOUSE SQUARE

The developer Peter Palumbo, defeated in his ambition to place a Mies van der Rohe tower on a site near the Mansion House (see 1982),

returned to the fray with a proposal for a postmodernist building by James Stirling and Michael Wilford. Conservationists, of course, did not want the existing Victorian buildings disturbed at all, but, as Palumbo still had a valid planning option for the site, the subsequent inquiry focused on the merits of the new scheme rather than the desirability or otherwise of keeping what was already there.

An inquiry decision, later confirmed by the House of Lords, gave Mr Palumbo permission to proceed. The proposed office block has since been built.

1989

KING'S CROSS TUSSLE

Behind King's Cross Station exists a hinterland of derelict goods yard extending over 120 acres. Some of it is taken up with a cement processing plant, some parts for vehicle storage, but on the whole it is unused. It is the largest and possibly the most valuable potential redevelopment site in central London.

British Rail had high hopes of a substantial windfall when it invited proposals from well-known developers and architects for the exploitation of the site. Inevitably, offices were to be the feature which would pay for the scheme, though a few historic buildings and the Regent's Canal were to be safeguarded. On 2 June 1988 British Rail chose the London Regeneration Consortium (LRC), which was already developing Broadgate in the City, as its developer; the architect subsequently chosen was Norman Foster. The scheme proposed included a glazed building between St Pancras and King's Cross stations, a large oval park in the centre of the site, through which the canal would wend its way, relocation of the famous gasholders at Goods Way, and various arts facilities. However, there was a very heavy concentration of office blocks and apparently not very much lower-price housing. The Great Northern Hotel by King's Cross Station would have to be demolished, and question marks hung over some of the other buildings on the site of particular interest to architectural historians.

By 1989 another consideration presented itself. British Rail decided that it wanted to place its principal passenger terminal to the Channel Tunnel rail link at King's Cross or St Pancras – a scheme which would involve the compulsory purchase of about 17 acres of shops and houses, mainly in Islington. This plan was only slightly modified when the government proposed that Stratford, east London, should be the terminal, though it was prepared to entertain the idea of a rail link between Stratford and King's Cross. Opposition to the King's Cross scheme lamented the demolition of listed buildings, the very high concentration of offices, the bad effects that such a development would have on the roads of surrounding areas, where traffic congestion would be increased, and the apparent lack of homes and jobs for local people.

Subsequently an important component in the LRC went bankrupt in the recession in the early 1990s and the plan was abandoned.

THEATRICAL DISCOVERIES

Remarkably, the remains of two of London's first theatres were discovered in Southwark this year. The location of the Rose was well known – between Rose Alley and the approach to Southwark Bridge. What was not expected, as archaeologists went on the site before an office development, was the extent of the remains that would be found.

The Granary building, once an important element in the King's Cross goods yard. It is now a listed building.

Extraordinary scenes took place at the site. Thousands of sight-seers, consumed with curiosity and a sense of participating in a distant past, converged on the site only to find not the walls of a circular theatre they could identify with but the usual groups of miscellaneous and apparently meaningless stones in the ground typical of archaeological sites. Yet enthusiasm about the find continued undiminished. As it became apparent that the government was unwilling to schedule the building as an ancient monument and therefore pay compensation to the developer, matters became acrimonious. Heated open-air meetings were held at the site, and vigils were mounted to prevent workmen coming back and damaging the remains. The developers, however, were very cooperative, but during all this they themselves were bought by another company, casting both complication and doubt into the affair.

The campaign to preserve the remains as a significant part of the national heritage and have them publicly displayed gathered momentum. No one got quite what they wanted in the end. The design of the office block, Rose Court, was altered so as to provide a permanent display area in the basement, and the remains of the Rose were covered up with protective material awaiting more excavation once money was available.

In October remains of the more famous Globe Theatre were discovered, to the west of the Rose. Actually only 1 per cent of the building was found, and it was then, like the Rose, covered over with protective material. The situation here is quite different from that of the Rose. About 40 per cent of the Globe – probably including the stage – is beneath Southwark Bridge Road, 10 per cent on the eastern side had been destroyed in the 19th century, but about 30 per cent is likely to be found beneath the Grade II-listed Anchor Terrace, with about 20 per cent east of that beneath empty land. The question is, should Anchor Terrace, which many conservationists want to keep, be demolished so that a good portion of the Globe area can be excavated? Theatre historians would welcome excavation for the insights into Elizabethan theatre it might reveal.

WHITELEY'S REOPENED

The old Whiteley's store in Queensway was reopened on 10 May, after radical conversion. When the store closed in 1981 there seemed little prospect that the building could be economically retained, but in 1986 it was bought by a company called The Whiteley's Partnership, which embarked on an expensive transformation. It is now a multi-store

shop, with 37 units on the ground floor, 34 on the second, restaurants and food kiosks on the third, and financial services and special facilities on the fourth. In addition, there is an eight-screen cinema. Its old 'La Scala' staircase has been retained, as has much of the marble that Whiteley provided.

PLANS FOR A POWER STATION

Battersea Power Station, empty for some time, was a listed building waiting for a new use. In June 1988 Mrs Thatcher, the prime minister, fired a laser gun over the River Thames to signify the start of a development by John Broome, proprietor of the amusement park Alton Towers, in Staffordshire, which would transform the old building into a leisure centre. By 1989 the project was in deep trouble, and since then the building has sunk deeper into dereliction.

The plan, however, was adventurous. There were to be five floors of restaurants and entertainments in the cavernous interior. Ice rinks, holograms, air balloons and sharks were all part of the feast. Unfortunately, it was discovered that the building would be extremely expensive to convert. The foundations are poor, a great deal of asbestos had been used in the construction, and the brickwork is crumbling from the effects of over 50 years of sulphur fumes.

DISASTER ON THE THAMES

On 20 August, the Thames pleasure boat *Marchioness* was cruising in bright moonlight below Southwark Bridge. It was crowded with party-goers enjoying a disco. The boat was rammed at 1.50 a.m. by the dredger *Bowbelle*. The *Marchioness* broke up immediately and those in the lower part of the boat had no chance to survive. In all, 51 people drowned in the worst river accident of the 20th century. A public inquiry into the incident was at last ordered in March 2000.

PATERNOSTER SQUARE SOLD

The much criticized Paternoster Square development around St Paul's Cathedral was sold by its Venezuelan owners to two developers for £160 million.

1990

REMOVING AN EYESORE

A railway bridge across Ludgate Hill, which obscured the view of the west front of St Paul's, was taken down this year. The demolition, in which the workers faced television cameras and a man in a pinstriped suit and bowler preaching to them, was the result of railway works beneath Ludgate Hill, where a new station was constructed for a line which now connects railways on both sides of the Thames.

SPITALFIELDS THREATENED

The closure of Spitalfields Market was proposed for 1991, together with the development of it and its hinterland, so close to Broadgate, as offices. All sorts of questions were raised by this prospect. First, if the area was redeveloped for commercial use, thereby extending the City eastward, what would happen to the property built to contain the expected financial boom then standing empty in the City and in Docklands? There was already more office accommodation in the pipeline in London, and still more envisaged, including that on the King's Cross railway lands. Was it realistic to pursue a scheme in Spitalfields, the profitability of which was based on office rents?

1900s

Then there was the question of the residential neighbourhood and the nature of its population and architecture. Spitalfields had some of the oldest streets in London, containing beautiful terrace houses from the late 17th century onwards. Should not the opportunity be taken to utilize the Spitalfields Market site for housing, as part of a regeneration of the area? If so, the City of London, which owned the market site, was probably the wrong authority to handle it, since the residents who most needed housing came from Tower Hamlets.

The developers originally appointed MacCormac Jamieson & Prichard as architects, later to be joined by Fitzroy Robinson, and a scheme which drew support from many quarters was approved in 1987. But shortly afterwards the developers changed architects and appointed Swanke Hayden Connell, an American practice, which came up with a scheme that many disliked.

RESTORATION OF SUTTON HOUSE
The 17th-century Sutton House, in Hackney, was owned by the National Trust, but for long had been in a fairly derelict state. Restoration began this year. Part was to be let out as offices to provide income, and there were to be exhibition rooms and meeting rooms for local community groups.

HAPPENINGS IN THE STRAND
For once, Somerset House was converted to a suitable use when the Courtauld Gallery opened there on 11 June.

Along the road, in February fire destroyed the splendid 1929 interior of the Savoy Theatre. *Country Life* had that year described it thus:

Every part bears evidence of imagination ... the general effect is one of glowing sunshine. Only gold and silver leaf are employed on the walls, and all the lighting is indirect ... [and is] so arranged that it picks out in vivid gilding the clean lines of the decoration, thus livening up the otherwise prevailing flat treatment. The walls are lined with broad vertical flutes which, in fact, are ventilating shafts.

DEVELOPMENT IN DOCKLANDS
Despite predictions that more office space was not wanted in the foreseeable future, the development of Docklands continued apace. The largest scheme of all was Canary Wharf: 10 million sq. ft of offices, 24 buildings, numerous shops, and 50,000 office workers – a colossal undertaking on behalf of the Canadian property firm Olympia & York, with the central tower rising above any building in London. By the end of 1990 the main building had reached its peak, dwarfing the postmodernist offices around it. It had been built at an astonishing rate – the start date was the summer of 1987 – but not so speedy were plans to improve transport into the area. The whole Docklands complex had been allowed to proceed without adequate new roads and with a light railway from Tower Hill that was already stretched at peak times before most of the buildings were tenanted. The owners of Canary Wharf promised to help fund an Underground line to the area – a sad commentary on the government's unwillingness to finance public transport even to an area which it saw as exemplifying its entrepreneurial beliefs.

Meanwhile, lettings of those buildings which had been completed had fallen disastrously in volume. Bankruptcies loomed as the rent value of buildings depreciated in a climate of rising interest rates. The hoped-for continuation of this new city through the Royal Docks seemed a pipe dream; the City Airport, opened in November 1987, still awaited its potential clientele. Warehouses converted into apartments that would have sold readily in Chelsea were marked down in price, and those frontier people who had moved in found they had to go miles to find the shops they needed.

It was a sad, botched result – made worse by the substandard houses and facilities of the indigenous residents, many of them former dockers, which stood in awful and accusing contrast on the fringes.

1991

PLANS IN THE AIR
A number of significant architectural schemes were announced to the public. That involving Paternoster Square, the post-war shop and office development around St Paul's Cathedral, was the most important, since any new buildings would either set off or mar the cathedral itself. With modern architects and developers temporarily in thrall to the comments of the prince of Wales, a neoclassical scheme was revealed by a team of architects led by Terry Farrell for a conglomeration of British, American and Japanese developers called Paternoster Associates. An exhibition opened to the public in May was well attended, and it was asserted that three out of four people who voiced an opinion approved of what they saw. With some amendments, the scheme was proceeded with – beginning with demolition in the late 1990s.

Terry Farrell – whose work at Charing Cross station, especially its illuminated face to the Thames, was generally popular – was also involved in a scheme to tear down the Hayward Gallery and the Queen Elizabeth Hall on the South Bank and build anew. This was not proceeded with.

Other schemes announced were those thoroughly to modernize the Royal Albert Hall, and the redevelopment of 30 fairly derelict acres around Paddington station as a commercial centre. The health secretary, William Waldegrave, announced a plan to build a major new hospital near the junction of Gower Street and Euston Road which would replace University College Hospital, the Middlesex Hospital and Elizabeth Garrett Anderson Hospital. About 500 beds would be lost overall.

Meanwhile, plans to redevelop the goods yard behind King's Cross were thrown into disarray when on 9 October Malcolm Rifkind, the transport secretary, announced that the Channel Tunnel rail link would run to King's Cross via Stratford.

DERELICT BATTERSEA
Conservationists were also concerned about the fate of the old Battersea Power Station. Costs of the development scheme launched by John Broome (see 1989) had escalated, and by 1991, when conservationists were making their concern felt, the roof had been taken off, leaving the building even more exposed to the elements, and work had stopped. Nearly ten years later no progress had been made.

NEW WING AT THE NATIONAL
The argument about the architecture of the proposed extension to the National Gallery in Trafalgar Square had raged for much of the 1980s. The design agreed in 1983 by the trustees had been described by the prince of Wales as a 'carbuncle' on the face of a much-loved feature of London, and this had struck such a popular chord that the scheme had been abandoned. In its place the trustees eventually selected a design by American architect Robert Venturi, which was officially opened by

the queen on 9 July this year. The new wing was generally popular with the public, but Brian Sewell, art critic of the *Evening Standard*, noted that 'we have a building that will inspire neither awe nor affection; outside it is all clever clowning'. The extension houses the gallery's early-Renaissance paintings.

SPITALFIELDS MARKET CLOSES

The Spitalfields fruit and vegetable market in Commercial Street closed on 10 May and reopened on 13 May on Hackney Marshes. It had originated in 1682, and in 1920 it had been bought by the City Corporation, which built the present buildings in 1928.

As one market closed, another was in jeopardy. At Smithfield meat market, traders agreed that they wanted to leave the premises, despite the City's offer to spend over £50 million updating them. The traders felt that European hygiene regulations would make Smithfield unusable, even after conversion. Other sites being examined were at Hackney Marshes, Charlton, Beckton and Stratford.

IRA CAMPAIGN IN LONDON

The IRA bombing campaign in London was particularly severe this year. The most dramatic event was on 7 February, when a mortar-bomb attack was made on 10 Downing Street from a van parked on the other side of Whitehall, 200 yards away. No one was hurt, but a cabinet meeting had to be abandoned. Later in the month (the 18th), bombs left on two railway stations – Victoria and Paddington – exploded. One person was killed at Victoria and all trains into the capital were halted.

The campaign resumed on 1 December, when four stores in central London were damaged by firebombs; another firebomb exploded at Brent Cross on 14 December, and on 16 December a small bomb exploded at Clapham Junction.

SUMMERHOUSE BURNT DOWN

Dr Johnson's summerhouse, in the grounds of Kenwood House in Highgate since the 1960s, was destroyed on 1 March by vandals. The structure had originally been in the garden of Johnson's friends Henry and Hester Thrale at Streatham, and in it he had written his book *The Lives of the English Poets*.

NEW HALL AT CAMDEN LOCK

A new market hall for Camden Lock was opened, designed by John Dickinson. The Camden Lock market was by this year one of the most popular tourist attractions in London. A remarkable phenomenon, it had begun as a temporary affair while the lock area had been under threat by motorway proposals (see 1969), which were abandoned in 1976. Since then the number of stalls and visitors had increased enormously, and had encouraged the development of another market complex, the Stables, to its north.

1992

MORE BOMBS

The IRA bombing campaign in London again dominated headlines. Bombs exploded in Whitehall Place (10 January) and at London Bridge station (28 February), where 29 people were hurt. Two days later a bomb was defused at White Hart Lane station, Tottenham, before a League Cup semi-final game, and on 10 March a bomb

exploded on the track at Wandsworth Common station. On 10 April a devastating attack took place in the City, where three people were killed and 91 injured when a 100 lb bomb exploded – it destroyed the Baltic Exchange and blew the windows out of numerous office blocks, including the NatWest Tower. The next day a similar bomb went off at Staples Corner in north London. The campaign resumed in September with firebombs at the Imperial War Museum, Madame Tussaud's and the London Planetarium, and on 10 December ten people were injured by a bomb at Wood Green Shopping Centre.

CANARY WHARF IN TROUBLE

The recession caught up with the vast Canary Wharf scheme. At the end of April the Canadian developers Olympia & York asked the High Court to appoint administrators for the development, as losses of £1.2 billion were now expected. This was serious news for the builders of the Jubilee Line extension, for Olympia & York were due to contribute a large percentage of the line's building costs.

Also, in the City, the Mountleigh property group had collapsed, leaving a number of schemes uncompleted, and the Japanese Daiwa securities group scrapped plans for an £85 million office block on London Wall, to be designed by Richard Rogers. The financial news was further depressed by the announcement by Lloyd's insurance market that there were record losses on its 1989 trading account of £2.06 billion, which would mean that hundreds of Lloyd's 'names' would have to make the losses good from their personal resources.

ZOO TO CLOSE

The finances of London Zoo were also in the doldrums, so much so that the Zoological Society of London announced in June that the zoo was to close on 30 September. It was revealed that income from visitors no longer sustained the expense of managing a zoo and the more academic activities of the society. Critics noted that the management of the society had been poor, and that in any case there was now a greater awareness that the confinement of animals on a site as restricted as that at Regent's Park was bad for them.

BART'S TO CLOSE

The Tomlinson Committee, appointed by the government, had for some time been examining the provision of hospitals in London. On 23 October it issued a report which recommended the closure of, among others, St Bartholomew's Hospital in Smithfield, the oldest hospital in London, and its merger with the Royal London in the East End. A campaign to resist closure was begun immediately.

LONDON CANAL MUSEUM OPENS

The London Canal Museum opened in New Wharf Road, Islington, in premises once occupied by the firm of Carlo Gatti. Gatti's had founded a number of well-known restaurants in Victorian London, and was well known as an ice-cream supplier. Also, it imported ice from Norway to supply to London butchers and fishmongers. The ice was towed up the Regent's Canal from London Docks, and was stored in vast ice wells, particularly at New Wharf Road in the premises now taken by the museum. Here there were two circular wells 42 ft deep and 34 ft wide, with a capacity of more than 500 tons of ice.

FAREWELL TO THE FLOOR

Trading on the Stock Exchange floor ended on 31 January. The old hurly-burly of shouted bids and waving arms was now superseded by dealing on computer screens.

1993

CITY CHURCH DESTROYED

The smallest church in the City, the much-loved St Ethelburga-the-Virgin in Bishopsgate, was almost totally destroyed by an IRA bomb on 24 April. The church was mainly a 15th-century building (though with a 14th-century window), with an 18th-century bell turret topped by a weathervane dated 1671. Its tranquil garden, much used by City workers, was also destroyed. By the end of the 1990s it had been determined to rebuild as much as possible in the style of the old building, to contain a Peace Centre.

OPENING OF AN EMPTY TERMINAL

The handsome Channel Tunnel rail link building at Waterloo was opened on 17 May, but was unused for over a year because the rail link itself was not yet fully built and the trains were not yet available. The building was designed by Nicholas Grimshaw and has five platforms, each a quarter of a mile long. It is still not clear what the future of this building is, for at the time of writing (April 2000) no firm decision has been made as to whether the rail link will be built to St Pancras instead.

THE MOST EXPENSIVE ROAD

The mile-long Limehouse Link was opened on 17 May to complete the 7-mile Docklands Highway. The link cost £345 million, and the rest of the highway a further £400 million. The construction of what was the most expensive road in Britain was planned in more optimistic days, when it was estimated that about 114,000 people would be working in the regenerated Docklands by 1992; in fact there were still only about 65,000 working there at the end of 1999. In the recession, office rents were now very low and only a third of Canary Wharf, seriously in trouble, had been let.

RENOVATION AT MARYLEBONE

The old Great Central Hotel fronting Marylebone station was reopened in February, once again as a sumptuous hotel – the Regent (now called Landmark). The building had been requisitioned during the last war as a transit station, and was later converted into headquarters for British Rail. The possibility of closure of the underused station had constantly threatened the hotel building, but the demand for good-class hotels in London encouraged the Hazama Corporation, its new owners, to completely restore it.

HOUSES FOR THE VERY RICH

When Bedford College moved out of Regent's Park, the opportunity was taken to demolish the college's less distinguished buildings in the grounds of Hanover Lodge and to initiate a scheme that would probably have pleased the park's original architect, John Nash. By this year, three distinguished (if pastiche) villas, out of six planned, had been erected in the Outer Circle in different architectural styles, to the designs of Quinlan Terry. The Ionic villa sold for £8.25 million this year, the Veneto villa was for sale at £9 million, and the Gothick Villa was up for sale at £6.75 million.

FRIERN HOSPITAL CLOSES

Friern Hospital in Colney Hatch Lane, Friern Barnet, closed in March. It had been London's largest mental asylum. Opened in 1851 (q.v.), after the Second World War, it had contained 3,500 patients, in space designed for 1,000.

FAREWELL TO THE OLD DEN

Millwall Football Club played its last game at the Den in Cold Blow Lane on 8 May, against Bristol Rovers. The club had been formed in 1885 as Millwall Rovers, by employees of a jam and marmalade factory in West Ferry Road on the Isle of Dogs. It moved south across the river to the Den in 1910, when it was in the Southern League. Millwall joined the Football League in 1920, and in 1937 it attracted its largest crowd – 48,672, at a cup tie, the season the club reached the semi-final of the FA Cup for the third time. The club opened in the New Den, a few hundred yards from the old ground, on 4 August.

THE SHROUDED STATUE

There was much public criticism of the Albert Memorial's having been shrouded in scaffolding and plastic for some years. Indeed, the scaffolding had entered the *Guinness Book of Records* as being, at 165 ft, the tallest ever free-standing piece of scaffolding in the world. In 1989 experts had assessed that the memorial, opposite the Royal Albert Hall, would cost £10 million to restore, and three years later a 'bare essentials' package costing that amount was approved. Unfortunately the money for its restoration had since been taken by the chancellor and nothing had been done.

COUNTY HALL BOUGHT

County Hall, the old home of the London County Council and its successor the Greater London Council, which had lain empty since the GLC's abolition in 1986, was sold at advantageous terms to a Japanese company, Shirayama, in October. There had been a strong campaign to relocate the London School of Economics there, but this had been thought to be too expensive. The company planned to convert much of the building to private housing and a hotel, together with an aquarium, but much of this plan was unrealized by the end of the century.

HARD TIMES

The strain on financial resources was noticeable in many institutions. The closure of Dulwich Picture Gallery (the oldest public art gallery in the country) was averted only by a donation of £200,000 by the Clore Foundation. The Royal Holloway College in Egham, founded as a college of higher education for women by the philanthropist Thomas Holloway, was obliged to sell a painting by Turner to the Getty Museum in Los Angeles; it raised £11 million.

CHANGING THE ASTORIA

The growing taste for live music, rather than discos, encouraged the owners of the old Astoria cinema (designed by Frank Verity in 1927) to announce a plan to convert it to the 'biggest live music venue' in London. One floor was to accommodate 1,600 customers, and the basement a further 1,000. The plan was, however, at risk because of a proposal to extend Tottenham Court Road station.

A NEW HOSPITAL

The Chelsea and Westminster Hospital, in Fulham Road, was opened on 25 January for outpatients and was to be available for in-patients in April. There were to be 665 beds on floors surrounding a glass-roofed atrium which itself was the size of Wembley Stadium. The same Tomlinson Committee report which declared Bart's Hospital redundant (see 1992) suggested that this new hospital would make the fairly new Charing Cross Hospital near Hammersmith also redundant as a general hospital.

1994

THE LONGEST TUNNEL

Thames Water in March completed a new water ring main beneath London – the longest tunnel ever built in the UK. Costing £250 million, it links pumping stations at Regent's Park, Streatham, Surbiton, Ashford and Kew, and can deliver 285 million gallons a day. It includes the facility to switch water supplies from one part of London to the other.

THEATRICAL CHANGES

On 2 November the Globe Theatre in Shaftesbury Avenue was renamed the Gielgud Theatre, after the veteran actor Sir John Gielgud. This cleared the way for the reconstructed Globe on the South Bank to hold the name without any confusion.

The restoration of the Lyceum Theatre in Wellington Street, with a new seating capacity of 2,000, was announced by Apollo Leisure and the American theatre-owner James Nederlander.

The Shaw Theatre, built together with the St Pancras Library in 1971, closed at the end of August. The office block above it and the old library were to be sold off – they were reopened, reclad, as the Shaw Park Plaza Hotel, in 1999.

The troubled financial position of the Riverside Studios at Crisp Road, Hammersmith, was eased when the local council, which owned the premises, sold them to a charitable company to run the complex. The company needed £3 million for a complete renovation, but much had already been done to introduce new theatre and cinema spaces.

HOP ON A TRAIN TO PARIS

On 14 November the Eurostar passenger train service between London and Paris and Brussels, via the Channel Tunnel, was inaugurated.

THE TATE TO EXPAND

On 28 April the trustees of the Tate Gallery announced that it was to take up the Bankside Power Station and convert it into a museum of modern art. With money from the Millennium Lottery Fund, it was hoped to open the new gallery in the year 2000. The architects for the conversion, announced later, were the Swiss firm of Herzog & De Meuron.

REDUNDANT CHURCHES

The City Churches Commission announced plans to replace 22 City parishes by 4 large parishes. Twenty-four churches were to be made redundant and available for other than parochial work.

1995

REVAMPING THE OXO TOWER

The Oxo Tower and its hinterland at the southern end of Blackfriars Bridge had been empty and in jeopardy for some time. The whole stretch of land from the bridge westward to the National Theatre had been coveted for large developments, in particular a scheme designed by Richard Rogers. A local group, the Coin Street Community Builders, had strongly fought all proposals and had eventually been able to buy 13 acres of land from the Greater London Council on which to build community housing. The first homes and flats were completed in

1988, and in 1994 a further (more architecturally distinguished) development of houses and flats was finished. Most welcome, however, has been the conversion – completed this year – of the Oxo Tower itself into mixed use of housing and shops, workshops and cafés, with a restaurant on the top floor.

GARDEN RESTORATIONS

One of the largest garden-restoration projects in this country was completed in July. This was the reinstallation of William III's Privy Garden at Hampton Court Palace. Archaeologists were able to find the old paths laid down by Henry Wise, the original landscape gardener. Each side of the garden is bounded by raised walks, with two-thirds of the western walk covered by an 80-yard tunnel arbour.

In Hampstead, the magnificent Pergola Walk near Inverforth House, North End Way, was reopened by the City of London, its most recent guardian. The walk, erected in 1906 to the design of Thomas Mawson, had been deteriorating for years and was closed altogether after the hurricane of 1987. During the restoration, which cost £1.3 million, about half of the 400 stone columns and balustrades were replaced.

STUDIOS SAVED

In 1994 the derelict Shepperton Studios had been bought by a group led by film-makers Ridley and Tony Scott. At the same time Ealing Studios went into liquidation. These were bought on 1 June 1995 for conversion into a National Film and Television School.

LOTTERY MONEY FOR THE ROYAL OPERA HOUSE

To complaints that money was being thrown at an elite art form seen mainly by affluent people, it was announced that the Royal Opera House was to receive a lottery grant of £55 million to proceed with the redevelopment of its building.

1996

WANAMAKER'S DREAM

The Globe Theatre on the South Bank was opened on 21 August with a production of Shakespeare's *The Two Gentlemen of Verona*. Though the great and the good were there, the one man who had made it possible, the American actor and director Sam Wanamaker, had died earlier in the year.

Wanamaker had first determined to raise a replica Globe soon after the war, when he found that the 16th-century building which had been so important in the flowering of Shakespeare's career was marked only by a grimy plaque on the wall of a bottling plant. When he first conceived this idea, that part of the south bank was an isolated and culturally unpromising area for a theatre. But gradually the whole stretch of river here has accumulated 'heritage' attractions such as the London Dungeon and the Clink Prison Museum, and in 2000 it is to have the Tate Gallery in the old Bankside Power Station and a new footbridge from St Paul's as neighbours.

Wanamaker's idea has, of course, had many detractors – from those who believe such replica buildings are of little value, to those who think that he was building to the wrong plan anyway. In the 1980s he also had to take on Southwark Council, which opposed the plan as being elitist (although elitist people quite often complained that the project was designed to appeal only to simplistic tourists). In

The interior of the reconstructed Globe Theatre on the South Bank. It is, for the most part, open to the skies.

the end he was triumphant, and in 1986 he obtained a 125-year lease of the site for a nominal rent.

END OF A CEASEFIRE
An IRA ceasefire, negotiated patiently by the government 18 months before, was on 9 February dramatically broken by a large bomb explosion at South Quay, Canary Wharf. Two people were killed. Nine days later an IRA member was killed and others were injured when a bomb he was carrying exploded on a bus.

FAREWELL TO SADLER'S WELLS
A gathering at Sadler's Wells Theatre on 23 June said goodbye to the 1931 building in Rosebery Avenue – a possibly sad occasion, but relieved by the anticipation of replacing F. G. M. Chancellor's rather drab and inconvenient theatre with a brand new one provided mostly by lottery money. Work began on the new building in July.

A FIND ON THE FORESHORE
Archaeologists scouring the Thames foreshore discovered in July the remains of a Tudor jetty at the old palace of Greenwich. It was thought that it could have been used by Henry VIII, Elizabeth I and Samuel Pepys.

A SPIRAL AT THE V & A
The Victoria & Albert Museum announced that it was to build an extension designed by Daniel Libeskind. The anarchic form of the building attracted the opprobrium of local societies but the admiration of many people in the arts world.

1997

FUNERAL OF DIANA, PRINCESS OF WALES
A most extraordinary funeral procession and service took place in London after Diana, princess of Wales, had died in a car crash in

Paris on 31 August. Her death caused intensely emotive scenes, and between the announcement of her death and her funeral on 6 September the public surrounded the central-London royal palaces with numerous thousands of bouquets of flowers. The procession and service at Westminster Abbey brought London to a standstill as millions converged on the capital, and hundreds of thousands then lined the route of the cortège north via Swiss Cottage to the M1 and the burial place at the family home of Althorp. Even the motorway, including the southbound traffic lanes, was lined with people who continued the practice, begun in the central-London area, of throwing flowers at the hearse.

There were many attempts to analyse such widespread public mourning, taking into account her undoubted beauty, the tragic circumstances of her death, and the long-drawn-out failure of her 15-year marriage to Prince Charles leading to the eventual divorce in 1996. So many features of a legend were present. But, for all that, there was no doubting the genuine sorrow of those who came to pay their last respects.

FRICTION AT THE OPERA HOUSE
The troubles of the Royal Opera House were often in the news. The organization, facing a massive rebuilding programme, was in a perilous financial position, despite lottery money – day-to-day running costs were well beyond budget, and it was rumoured that London would end up with a wonderful new building which had no funds to pay performers to use it. On 13 May its chief executive, Genista McIntosh, resigned, claiming a stress-related illness which she later had to justify before a critical select committee of the House of Commons. The Opera House then appointed Mary Allen, secretary-general of the Arts Council, as its new chief executive – to much criticism for not following the usual recruitment procedures.

In November, Chris Smith, the secretary of state with responsibility for the arts, suggested that it might be a good idea for English National Opera, which operated from the Coliseum, to share the new Covent Garden building. A report, to be compiled by the theatre director Richard Eyre, was commissioned by the government, but the goading tactic by Smith was soon dropped. Lord Chadlington, chairman of the ROH, responded by announcing a privately resourced rescue fund. However, the Commons select committee on 3 December called for the resignation of the board of the ROH and its chief officer. Lord Chadlington resigned next day; Mary Allen proffered her resignation, but was persuaded to withdraw it.

BRITISH LIBRARY OPENS
The saga of the construction of the British Library on Euston Road had entertained or enraged newspapers and their readers for many years. The decision to build on the site was taken in 1975, and in 1982 the foundation stone was laid by the prince of Wales, who had previously aired his architectural views by likening the proposed building to 'an academy for secret police'. The architect who suffered this generalization from the prince was Colin St John Wilson.

The building went well over budget and well over time, and it was not until 24 November this year that the Humanities Reading Room was opened. The library – examined particularly closely because of its proximity to Scott's florid Midland Grand Hotel – has been the subject of both laudatory and critical comments for its architecture. Designed in the later 1970s, it is far more austere than the post-modernist developments of the 1980s and 1990s which we now accept as modern style. One commentator remarked that it 'offered no pomposity, no sentimentality and, above all, no crippling English nostalgia'.

At the heart of the building is the King's Library, contained in an eye-catching six-storey tower. Overall, the building houses 12 million books and millions of maps; it includes exhibition galleries, laboratories, lecture theatres, seminar rooms, a shop and restaurants. It has a complex book-retrieval system from the book stacks (which, when they kept collapsing after installation, were themselves the butt of many jokes in the press). Beneath the library there are four great basements, the depth of an 8-storey building.

The old and much-loved British Library Reading Room at the British Museum closed on 25 October. It was to be remodelled and enclosed by a courtyard to designs by Norman Foster.

NEW APARTMENTS

Throughout London, and particularly in Clerkenwell, Shoreditch and Finsbury, old offices and factories were being transformed into flats – generally called 'loft apartments' by estate agents, and usually typified by open-plan arrangements. These areas of London, which had been depopulated before and after the war, possessed many old and finely designed buildings that were now unsuitable for either commerce or manufacture but were attractive to the affluent young, unable to afford the amount of space they wanted in such established communities as Chelsea, Hampstead, Islington and Kensington.

Not all of these new dwellings were open-plan. This year the conversion of the old headquarters of the Metropolitan Water Board, in Rosebery Avenue, was begun. This was carved up into conventional dwellings, while retaining some of the best features of the building.

CONSTRUCTION OF THE DOME BEGINS

It was announced early this year that the government would support the erection of a Millennium Dome at Greenwich to mark the year 2000. The go-ahead for this costly project, funded by lottery money and corporate sponsorship, was confirmed by the new Labour government elected on 1 May.

Like the Festival of Britain in 1951, the project was dogged by criticism and pessimism – especially in view of its cost, which was thought by many to be excessive. Increasingly, there were difficult relationships between those managing and creating this enormous theme park, and there were persistent doubts that it could be ready in time and that the Jubilee Line extension would be in place to take visitors to the isolated location of the Dome in Greenwich.

1998

THINGS PRESERVED

Frank Dobson, the new health minister, announced on 3 February that St Bartholomew's Hospital would remain open, though its role would be modified.

It was announced on 25 January that St Pancras Chambers (the old Midland Grand Hotel) was to be converted into a new hotel and loft apartments. There would be 300 rooms, and the opening date was to be 2003. The project was, however, bedevilled by the indecision of London & Continental Railways as to whether the Channel Tunnel rail link was indeed to come into St Pancras. Many pessimists suggested that it would be economically viable only to construct a dedicated line into Waterloo.

Supporters of a project to restore and use Wilton's Music Hall, off Wellclose Square (see 1977), appealed for lottery money. Recently, performances of T. S. Eliot's *The Waste Land* were held there – the first theatrical presentation in the building since the 1880s.

THE RHINEBECK VIEW

A 9-ft-long panoramic bird's-eye view of London was bought by the Museum of London in June. Drawn in the first 20 years of the 19th century by an unknown artist, it was used as a lining for a barrel of guns that went to North America in the 1820s. It was discovered in 1940 on the death of its then owner, William Gray, in Rhinebeck, New York. It is a lively panorama which depicts spectators watching a fire at a building in Bermondsey, activity on board ships on the Thames, and a funeral procession.

OLD VIC SOLD

The Old Vic theatre, which had been rescued and restored by the Canadian Ed Mirvish in the 1980s, was sold on 2 July to the Old Vic Theatre Trust for £3.5 million.

'YES' VOTE

The government held a referendum on 7 May to determine Londoners' views on the creation of a new strategic authority for Greater London headed by a directly elected mayor. On a turnout of 34 per cent, the vote was 72 per cent in favour of the proposals.

MORE TROUBLE AT THE OPERA HOUSE

The Royal Opera House was rarely out of the headlines. On 15 January Sir Colin Southgate was appointed chairman in place of Lord Chadlington, but within a month the director of the opera company, Nicholas Payne, resigned to move to English National Opera. On 9 September it was announced that the ROH would shut down completely for 11 months in order to save money. Michael Kaiser, executive director of American Ballet Theatre, was appointed executive director on 16 September, but Bernard Haitink, long-standing music director, announced his resignation on 10 October, though he was subsequently persuaded to stay.

A NEW SADLER'S WELLS

The new Sadler's Wells Theatre opened on 12 October – but it was touch and go, as a safety certificate was obtained only on that day. The reopening was overshadowed by financial problems – the cancellation of performances there by the Royal Opera House meant that the theatre had no income for a large part of its first year. The new building was designed by RHWL Partnership and Nicholas Hare.

ALBERT UNVEILED

The results of the long restoration of the Albert Memorial were at last unveiled by the queen on 21 October. The structure was one of the most intricate built in the Victorian era, using a mix of stone, iron, enamel, lead, bronze, marble and gilt. One of the revelations to modern viewers was the 14-ft gilt statue of Albert (see 1876) – it had not been seen like that since 1914, when the gilding had been removed from the bronze. It seems an overwhelming use of gold now, and indeed, at its first unveiling, Albert's features could hardly be distinguished in the glow of the gilding. Restoration brought to life the intricacy of the memorial, though it is not now possible to view it close up without an appointment. The canopy is a mixture of enamels, stone and mosaics, and there are seven levels of statuary from the base

1900s

upwards. At the lower level four large statues depict Europe, America, Asia and Africa. Around the base of the memorial is a frieze of 169 life-size figures of famous artists, writers, architects and musicians.

SIMPSON'S CLOSES

Simpson's, the clothier's in Piccadilly, closed in December. The company had been founded in Stoke Newington in 1894, and its stylish Piccadilly building, designed by Joseph Emberton, had opened in 1936. The bookseller's Waterstone's was to be the next occupier, in 1999.

THE ZOO EXPANDS

The precarious financial position of London Zoo, which had at one time prompted a decision to close it (see 1992), had improved over the years thanks to a mixture of private and government money. In August a project for a conservation centre at the zoo was unveiled, to be funded by Millennium Lottery Fund money.

1999

A NEW THAMES BRIDGE

For some years, the availability of money from the National Lottery had encouraged building projects that would have been difficult to fund otherwise. The Millennium Dome was an example, as was the new Tate Gallery branch being built at Bankside Power Station. Another was a new Thames footbridge from St Paul's to this new outpost of the Tate. This imaginative structure, begun this year, was designed by the architect Norman Foster, the sculptor Sir Anthony Caro and the engineering firm Ove Arup. The bridge will feature sculptures, an aluminium deck and stainless-steel balustrades.

A NEW COUNTY HALL

Sir Norman Foster was involved in a number of major millennium projects. His design for new headquarters for the new London authority was accepted in preference to a rehabilitation of an insurance company's headquarters in Bloomsbury Square. The new County Hall will be on the Southwark side of the river, near London Bridge. Shaped like a giant eyeball, it will have an open-top roof terrace reached by two glass lifts that travel outside the building.

BUILDING THE GREAT COURT

Norman Foster's scheme for the use of the old British Library Reading Room and the surrounding courtyard in the British Museum was also proceeding this year — its funding topped up on 18 May by a gift of £20 million from the American billionaire Garry Weston. The Great Court will be enclosed with a glazed roof and will be entered from the ground level of the museum. There will be several floors, brought together by two grand staircases.

DISASTER AT PADDINGTON

On 5 October, to the west of Paddington station at Ladbroke Grove, a Thames Trains suburban train travelling west crashed into a First Great Western main-line train heading for the terminus. Diesel fuel caused the first few carriages of the main-line train to explode into a fireball, and many passengers were incinerated. Thirty-one people are known to have died, and well over 100 people were injured. The accident was caused by the suburban train going through a stop signal, though at the time of writing (April 2000) investigations are still in progress.

MORE BOMB HORRORS

Though almost inured to bombing incidents, London was shocked by three attacks in April which appeared to have nothing to do with Irish affairs. The first explosion was on 17 April, when 50 people were injured by a nail bomb in Brixton. It was thought that the target was the largely black clientele of Brixton Market. A week later another nail bomb injured six people in Brick Lane, where the population was mainly Bangladeshi or Sudanese. The most serious incident was at the Admiral Duncan, a pub renowned for its gay clientele, in Old Compton Street, Soho. A nail bomb placed by the door killed three people and seriously injured many more. A man was arrested on 2 May, and is due to stand trial in 2000.

JUBILEE LINE COMPLETED

The first part of the Jubilee Line extension was opened between Bermondsey and Canary Wharf on 20 September. Most of the rest of the line, connecting the West End of London to Stratford via Docklands, was quietly opened on 20 November, though Westminster station was still not completed. The project was running 18 months late — work had begun in 1993 — and at double its original budget.

There had been criticism about the speed of constructing the line, especially as it was to serve the Millennium Dome at Greenwich from 31 December, but there was unanimous praise for the new stations, which set a new standard for such buildings. North Greenwich, designed by Will Alsop, is cathedral-size — the largest underground station in Europe. Norman Foster's Canary Wharf station, which will be the busiest on the line, has a striking escalator hall. Southwark station (by MacCormac Jamieson & Prichard), possibly the most beautiful, contains a wall of 600 blue-glass triangles. Overall direction of the station project was in the hands of Roland Paoletti.

ROYAL OPERA HOUSE REOPENED

The controversy surrounding the administration of the Royal Opera House did not diminish during the year, but there was general approval of the rebuilding work, especially the conversion of the old Floral Hall next door. The new ROH was formally opened on 1 December with a gala performance attended by the queen, featuring the ballerina Darcey Bussell and the tenor Placido Domingo. Later, however, there were problems with the computerized stage equipment, which resulted in the cancellation of at least one early production and the interruption of others.

The rebuilding had been partly funded by the construction on the north-east side of the piazza of an arcade of shops which, though by no means a copy, were reminiscent of the original buildings of the 17th century.

ELTHAM PALACE REOPENED

The little-known Eltham Palace was reopened to the public after extensive restoration by the National Trust. One of its glories is the main hall of c.1479, which contains the third largest hammerbeam roof in the country. Henry VIII and Elizabeth I both preferred to stay at nearby Greenwich Palace, and the condition of Eltham deteriorated over the years. John Evelyn, who visited it in 1656, noted that 'both Palace & Chapell [were] in miserable ruines' after the decision of their owner, Nathaniel Rich, to pull them down. Later that century the building was left in ruins, a lodge was built in the grounds, and the great hall was used as a barn.

The building was rescued by Stephen Courtauld from 1931, when the hall was restored and a new and elegant house was built.

BRONZE AGE LONDON

It was appropriate that, in the last year of the millennium which had seen London founded after the arrival of the Romans in AD 43, a discovery was made which revealed that London had seen either the transit or the settlement of people very much earlier. In September, archaeologists discovered the remains of a wooden Thames bridge on the foreshore at Vauxhall, made of oak and supported by scissor-form struts. The remains are visible only at the lowest of tides, but what is left of the oak supports has been carbon-dated to between 1750 and 1285 BC.

In prehistoric times, and indeed when the Romans arrived, the Thames was much shallower (and wider) than it is today. The bridge may have led from the shore to a midstream island and then across to the Pimlico side, though nothing of the bridge has been found on the north bank.

THE LAWRENCE INQUIRY

In April 1993 a young black man, Stephen Lawrence, had been murdered by several white youths at a bus stop in Eltham. The investigation into his killing became increasingly criticized as being bungled, possibly corrupt and most probably half-hearted because the victim was black. It became a cause célèbre in which the dignified behaviour of the victim's parents contrasted strongly with the reluctance of the police authorities to admit deficiencies on their part. In the end, the conduct of the case became a watershed in the history of relations between the police and black residents.

An official inquiry into the handling of the police investigation, headed by William Macpherson, reported to the public on 24 February. It was heavily critical of police incompetence in the case, and accused the Metropolitan Police of having institutionalized racism in its ranks. Of the officers blamed in the report, all but one had retired on a full pension by the time of its publication, and on 13 July it was announced that the remaining officer was not to face serious disciplinary action.

THE RACE TO BE MAYOR

By the end of 1999, the preliminaries to the following year's election of the first mayor of Greater London had degenerated into farce. The Conservative Party's main candidates were the millionaire novelist Jeffrey Archer and Steven Norris, a former MP and transport minister. The party eventually chose Archer, despite his colourful and contentious history. But in November a former friend of Archer revealed that in 1987 he had been asked by the novelist to submit false evidence in a libel trial in which Archer had sued a newspaper and won substantial damages. Archer admitted the offence and withdrew as candidate for mayor. The Conservatives then persuaded Norris to stand again, but his selection was embarrassingly vetoed by an internal committee whose decision had then to be overruled by the party leadership.

The Labour Party was meanwhile having its own embarrassments. From the outset, the main contender to be the party's candidate was maverick left-wing MP Ken Livingstone, who had been leader of the Greater London Council when it had been abolished (see 1986). Opinion polls suggested that Livingstone was by far the most attractive candidate in the eyes of the public, but the Labour leadership did not want him because of his long history of intransigence in the face of party policy. Eventually the health minister, Frank Dobson, who also had considerable experience in London government, was persuaded to stand. The leadership endorsed Dobson, who was then chosen by the party on 20 February 2000. As a result, Livingstone decided to stand as an independent.

The London Eye, built to mark the millennium, overlooks the Palace of Westminster which was built on Thorney Island, where these annals began.

THE DOME, THE WHEEL AND THE FIREWORKS

The months leading up to New Year's Eve and the year 2000 were frenetic for those working on the two most public new projects in London – the Dome at Greenwich and the London Eye by the old County Hall, the largest Ferris wheel ever built.

The Dome's structure – a rather flat dome in fact, designed by the architectural firm of Sir Richard Rogers – was finished in time, but the task of filling it with entertaining or educational 'zones' was hurried. On the night there were two much publicized hitches – many of those invited to the Dome opening did not receive their invitations on time and arrived late and flustered for the occasion. The London Eye, though structurally complete, was precluded from operating because of a fault found in a capsule which, it was felt, might be common to all the capsules. Aside from these setbacks there was a massive and good natured party by the Thames. It was estimated that up to two million people made their way to the Embankment where a grand firework display said farewell and hello to old and new centuries and millennia.

While the Dome had a mixed critical reception, the London Eye, sponsored by British Airways, was immediately popular as from February 2000, when it functioned full time. Designed by David Marks and Julia Atfield, it provided wondrous statistics. It weighs 1600 tons, and stands 435ft high as the fourth tallest structure in London, with only the Telecom Tower, the NatWest building and Canary Wharf above it. Raising it from a horizontal position on pontoons on the Thames was in itself a tourist attraction, as it was winched inch-by-inch to an upright position so that its 32 capsules, each to carry 25 people, could be attached. It does not, except in rare circumstances, stop, but travels slowly enough for people to step on and off without problems.

The Dome, the Eye and the Millennium celebrations were each sited by the river, where much of the surge of recent development in London has taken place. With the industrial buildings of Docklands to the east and of Wandsworth, Fulham and Chelsea to the west now vacated or run down, it is possible to rehabilitate and repopulate the riverside and, just as importantly, make it accessible to the general public in a way that has not been possible since the 19th century. In this aspect, if no other, London is resuming its old familiarity with a river which made its foundation possible in AD43.

1900s

London 2000

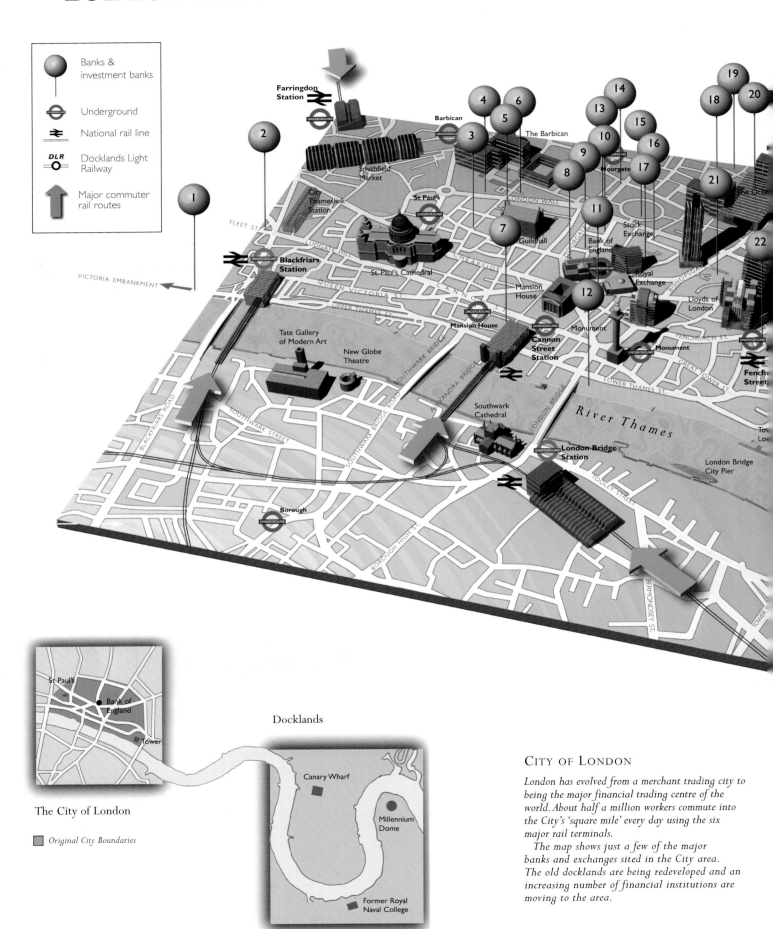

Legend:
- Banks & investment banks
- Underground
- National rail line
- DLR — Docklands Light Railway
- Major commuter rail routes

Map labels:

Farringdon Station
Barbican
The Barbican
Smithfield Market
City Thameslink Station
St Paul's
St Paul's Cathedral
Blackfriars Station
FLEET ST.
LUDGATE HILL
QUEEN VICTORIA ST.
UPPER THAMES ST.
VICTORIA EMBANKMENT
CHEAPSIDE
CANNON ST.
Guildhall
Mansion House
LONDON WALL
MOORGATE
Moorgate
Bank of England
Stock Exchange
Royal Exchange
BISHOPSGATE
Lloyds of London
The Ocean
Tate Gallery of Modern Art
New Globe Theatre
Monument
Cannon Street Station
Monument
FENCHURCH ST.
GREAT TOWER ST.
Fenchurch Street
LOWER THAMES ST.
SOUTHWARK BRIDGE
ALEXANDRA BRIDGE
Southwark Cathedral
LONDON BRIDGE
River Thames
London Bridge City Pier
London Bridge Station
BLACKFRIARS ROAD
SOUTHWARK BRIDGE ROAD
SOUTHWARK STREET
Borough
BOROUGH HIGH ST.
TOOLEY STREET
BERMONDSEY ST.
TOWER G...
London...

Inset map — The City of London

St Paul's
Bank of England
Tower

☐ Original City Boundaries

Inset map — Docklands

Canary Wharf
Millennium Dome
Former Royal Naval College

CITY OF LONDON

London has evolved from a merchant trading city to being the major financial trading centre of the world. About half a million workers commute into the City's 'square mile' every day using the six major rail terminals.

The map shows just a few of the major banks and exchanges sited in the City area. The old docklands are being redeveloped and an increasing number of financial institutions are moving to the area.

Financial City

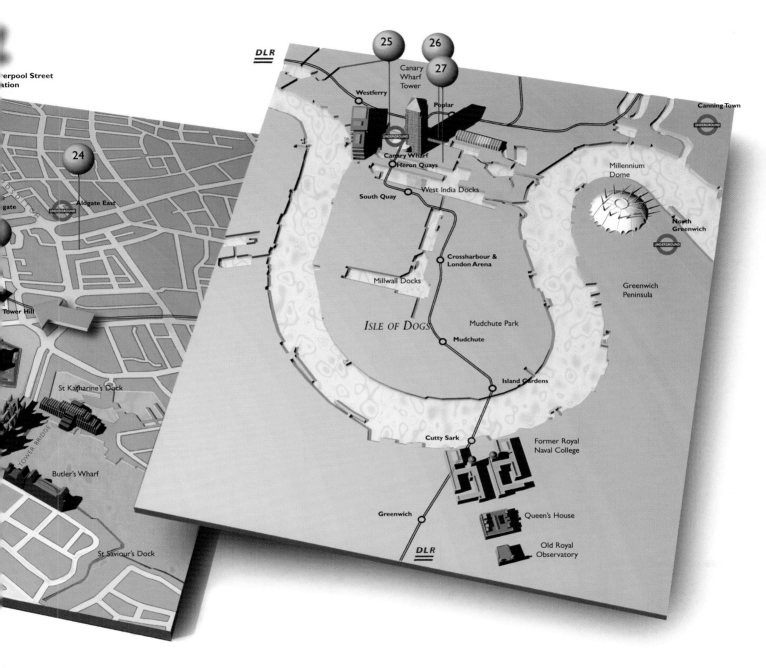

BANKS & INVESTMENT BANKS

THE CITY

1   JP Morgan, *Victoria Embankment*
2   Goldman Sachs, *Fleet Street*
3   Schroders, *Gresham Street*
4   Chase Manhattan, *London Wall*
5   Standard Chartered Bank, *Aldermanbury Square*
6   ING Barings, *London Wall*
7   NM Rothschild, *St Swithin's Lane*
8   National Westminster Bank, *Lothbury*
9   Arab Bank, *Moorgate*
10 Robert Fleming, *Copthall Avenue*

11 Lloyds TSB, *Lombard Street*
12 HSBC, *Lower Thames Street*
13 Lazard Brothers, *Moorfields*
14 Merrill Lynch, *Ropemaker Place*
15 Bank of Tokyo-Mitsubishi, *Finsbury Circus*
16 Commerzbank, *Austin Friars*
17 Deutsche Bank, *Great Winchester Street*
18 Lehman Brothers, *Broadgate*
19 Credit Lyonnais, *Appold Street*
20 UBS Warburg, *Liverpool Street*
21 ABN Amro, *Bishopsgate*
22 Dresdner Kleinwort Benson, *Fenchurch Street*

23 Société Générale, *Tower Hill*
24 Bank of America, *Alie Street*

DOCKLANDS

25 Credit Suisse First Boston, *Cabot Square*
26 Morgan Stanley Dean Witter, *Cabot Square*
27 Barclays Capital, *North Colonade, Canary Wharf*

Index

Italic numbers indicate an illustration.